SPANISH·ENGLISH
ENGLISH·SPANISH
DICTIONARY

DICCIONARIO
ESPAÑOL·INGLÉS
INGLÉS·ESPAÑOL

acabado, a [aka'βaðo, a] *a* finished, complete; (*agotado*) worn out; (*fig*) masterly // *nm* finish.

acabar [aka'βar] *vt* (*llevar a su fin*) to finish, complete; (*consumir*) to use up; (*rematar*) to finish off // *vi* to finish, end; ~**se** *vr* to finish, stop; (*terminarse*) to be over; (*agotarse*) to run out; ~ **con** to put an end to; ~ **de llegar** to have just arrived; ~ **por hacer** to end (up) by doing; **¡se acabó!** it's all over!; (*¡basta!*) that's enough!

acabóse [aka'βose] *nm*: **esto es el** ~ this is the last straw.

academia [aka'ðemja] *nf* academy; **académico, a** *a* academic.

acaecer [akae'θer] *vi* to happen, occur.

acalorado, a [akalo'raðo, a] *a* (*discusión*) heated.

acalorarse [akalo'rarse] *vr* (*fig*) to get heated.

acampar [akam'par] *vi* to camp.

acanalar [akana'lar] *vt* to groove; (*ondular*) to corrugate.

acantilado [akanti'laðo] *nm* cliff.

acaparar [akapa'rar] *vt* to monopolize; (*acumular*) to hoard.

acariciar [akari'θjar] *vt* to caress; (*esperanza*) to cherish.

acarrear [akarre'ar] *vt* to transport; (*fig*) to cause, result in.

acaso [a'kaso] *ad* perhaps, maybe // *nm* chance; (**por**) **si** ~ (just) in case.

acatamiento [akata'mjento] *nm* respect; (*de la ley*) observance.

acatar [aka'tar] *vt* to respect, obey.

acatarrarse [akata'rrarse] *vr* to catch a cold.

acaudalado, a [akauða'laðo, a] *a* well-off.

acaudillar [akauði'ʎar] *vt* to lead, command.

acceder [akθe'ðer] *vi* ~ **a** (*petición etc*) to agree to; (*tener acceso a*) to have access to; (*INFORM*) to access.

accesible [akθe'siβle] *a* accessible.

acceso [ak'θeso] *nm* access, entry; (*camino*) access, approach; (*MED*) attack, fit.

accesorio, a [akθe'sorjo, a] *a*, *nm* accessory.

accidentado, a [akθiðen'taðo, a] *a* uneven; (*montañoso*) hilly; (*azaroso*) eventful // *nm/f* accident victim.

accidental [akθiðen'tal] *a* accidental; **accidentarse** *vr* to have an accident.

accidente [akθi'ðente] *nm* accident.

acción [ak'θjon] *nf* action; (*acto*) action, act; (*COM*) share; (*JUR*) action, lawsuit; ~ **ordinaria/preferente** ordinary/preference share; **accionar** *vt* to work, operate; (*INFORM*) to drive.

accionista [akθjo'nista] *nm/f* shareholder, stockholder.

acebo [a'θeβo] *nm* holly; (*árbol*) holly tree.

acechanza [aθe'tʃanθa] *nf* = **acecho**.

acechar [aθe'tʃar] *vt* to spy on; (*aguardar*) to lie in wait for; **acecho** *nm*: **estar al acecho (de)** to lie in wait (for).

aceitar [aθei'tar] *vt* to oil, lubricate.

aceite [a'θeite] *nm* oil; (*de oliva*) olive oil; ~**ra** *nf* oilcan; **aceitoso, a** *a* oily.

aceituna [aθei'tuna] *nf* olive.

acelerador [aθelera'ðor] *nm* accelerator.

acelerar [aθele'rar] *vt* to accelerate.

acelga [a'θelɣa] *nf* chard, beet.

acento [a'θento] *nm* accent; (*acentuación*) stress.

acentuar [aθen'twar] *vt* to accent; to stress; (*fig*) to accentuate.

acepción [aθep'θjon] *nf* meaning.

aceptable [aθep'taβle] *a* acceptable.

aceptación [aθepta'θjon] *nf* acceptance; (*aprobación*) approval.

aceptar [aθep'tar] *vt* to accept; (*aprobar*) to approve.

acequia [a'θekja] *nf* irrigation ditch.

acera [a'θera] *nf* pavement (*Brit*), sidewalk (*US*).

hug.

abrazo [a'βraθo] *nm* embrace; hug; **un ~** (*en carta*) with best wishes.

abrebotellas [aβreβo'teʎas] *nm inv* bottle opener.

abrecartas [aβre'kartas] *nm inv* letter opener.

abrelatas [aβre'latas] *nm inv* tin (*Brit*) *o* can opener.

abreviar [aβre'βjar] *vt* to abbreviate; (*texto*) to abridge; (*plazo*) to reduce; **abreviatura** *nf* abbreviation.

abridor [aβri'ðor] *nm* bottle opener; (*de latas*) tin (*Brit*) *o* can opener.

abrigar [aβri'ɣar] *vt* (*proteger*) to shelter; (*suj: ropa*) to keep warm; (*fig*) to cherish.

abrigo [a'βriɣo] *nm* (*prenda*) coat, overcoat; (*lugar protegido*) shelter.

abril [a'βril] *nm* April.

abrillantar [aβriʎan'tar] *vt* to polish.

abrir [a'βrir] *vt* to open (up) // *vi* to open; **~se** *vr* to open (up); (*extenderse*) to open out; (*cielo*) to clear; **~se paso** to find *o* force a way through.

abrochar [aβro'tʃar] *vt* (*con botones*) to button (up); (*zapato, con broche*) to do up.

abrumar [aβru'mar] *vt* to overwhelm; (*sobrecargar*) to weigh down.

abrupto, a [a'βrupto, a] *a* abrupt; (*empinado*) steep.

absceso [aβs'θeso] *nm* abscess.

absentismo [aβsen'tismo] *nm* absenteeism.

absolución [aβsolu'θjon] *nf* (*REL*) absolution; (*JUR*) acquittal.

absoluto, a [aβso'luto, a] *a* absolute; **en ~** *ad* not at all.

absolver [aβsol'βer] *vt* to absolve; (*JUR*) to pardon; (: *acusado*) to acquit.

absorbente [aβsor'βente] *a* absorbent; (*interesante*) absorbing.

absorber [aβsor'βer] *vt* to absorb; (*embeber*) to soak up.

absorción [aβsor'θjon] *nf* absorption; (*COM*) takeover.

absorto, a [aβ'sorto, a] *pp de* **absorber** //

[aβ'sorto, a] *a* absorbed, engrossed.

abstemio, a [aβs'temjo, a] *a* teetotal.

abstención [aβsten'θjon] *nf* abstention.

abstenerse [aβste'nerse] *vr*: **~ (de)** to abstain *o* refrain (from).

abstinencia [aβsti'nenθja] *nf* abstinence; (*ayuno*) fasting.

abstracción [aβstrak'θjon] *nf* abstraction.

abstracto, a [aβs'trakto, a] *a* abstract.

abstraer [aβstra'er] *vt* to abstract; **~se** *vr* to be *o* become absorbed.

abstraído, a [aβstra'iðo, a] *a* absent-minded.

absuelto [aβ'swelto] *pp de* **absolver**.

absurdo, a [aβ'surðo, a] *a* absurd.

abuelo, a [a'βwelo, a] *nm/f* grandfather/mother; **~s** *nmpl* grandparents.

abulia [a'βulja] *nf* lethargy.

abultado, a [aβul'taðo, a] *a* bulky.

abultar [aβul'tar] *vt* to enlarge; (*aumentar*) to increase; (*fig*) to exaggerate // *vi* to be bulky.

abundancia [aβun'danθja] *nf*: **una ~ de** plenty of; **abundante** *a* abundant, plentiful; **abundar** *vi* to abound, be plentiful.

aburguesarse [aβurɣe'sarse] *vr* to become middle-class.

aburrido, a [aβu'rriðo, a] *a* (*hastiado*) bored; (*que aburre*) boring; **aburrimiento** *nm* boredom, tedium.

aburrir [aβu'rrir] *vt* to bore; **~se** *vr* to be bored, get bored.

abusar [aβu'sar] *vi* to go too far; **~ de** to abuse; **abuso** *nm* abuse.

abusivo, a [aβu'siβo, a] *a* (*precio*) exorbitant.

abyecto, a [aβ'jekto, a] *a* wretched, abject.

A.C. *abr* (= Año de Cristo) A.D.

a/c *abr* (= al cuidado de) c/o.

acá [a'ka] *ad* (*lugar*) here; **¿de cuándo ~?** since when?

~ro, a nm/f (AM) grocer.

abastecer [aβaste'θer] vt to supply; **abastecimiento** nm supply.

abasto [a'βasto] nm supply; (abundancia) abundance; **no dar** ~ **a** to be unable to cope with.

abatido, a [aβa'tiðo, a] a dejected, downcast.

abatimiento [aβati'mjento] nm (depresión) dejection, depression.

abatir [aβa'tir] vt (muro) to demolish; (pájaro) to shoot o bring down; (fig) to depress; ~**se** vr to get depressed; ~**se sobre** to swoop o pounce on.

abdicación [aβðika'θjon] nf abdication.

abdicar [aβði'kar] vi to abdicate.

abdomen [aβ'ðomen] nm abdomen.

abecedario [aβeθe'ðarjo] nm alphabet.

abedul [aβe'ðul] nm birch.

abeja [a'βexa] nf bee.

abejorro [aβe'xorro] nm bumblebee.

aberración [aβerra'θjon] nf aberration.

abertura [aβer'tura] nf = **apertura**.

abeto [a'βeto] nm fir.

abierto, a [a'βjerto, a] pp de **abrir** // a open; (AM) generous.

abigarrado, a [aβiɣa'rraðo, a] a multi-coloured.

abismal [aβis'mal] a (fig) vast, enormous.

abismar [aβis'mar] vt to humble, cast down; ~**se** vr to sink; ~**se en** (fig) to be plunged into.

abismo [a'βismo] nm abyss.

abjurar [aβxu'rar] vi: ~ **de** to abjure, forswear.

ablandar [aβlan'dar] vt to soften // vi, ~**se** vr to get softer.

abnegación [aβneɣa'θjon] nf self-denial.

abnegado, a [aβne'ɣaðo, a] a self-sacrificing.

abocado, a [aβo'kaðo, a] a: verse ~ **al desastre** to be heading for disaster.

abochornar [aβotʃor'nar] vt to embarrass; ~**se** vr to get flustered; (BOT) to wilt.

abofetear [aβofete'ar] vt to slap (in the face).

abogacía [aβoɣa'θia] nf legal profession; (ejercicio) practice of the law.

abogado, a [aβo'ɣaðo, a] nm/f lawyer; (notario) solicitor; (en tribunal) barrister (Brit), attorney (US); ~ **defensor** defence lawyer o attorney (US).

abogar [aβo'ɣar] vi: ~ **por** to plead for; (fig) to advocate.

abolengo [aβo'lengo] nm ancestry, lineage.

abolición [aβoli'θjon] nf abolition.

abolir [aβo'lir] vt to abolish; (cancelar) to cancel.

abolladura [aβoʎa'ðura] nf dent.

abollar [aβo'ʎar] vt to dent.

abominable [aβomi'naβle] a abominable.

abominación [aβomina'θjon] nf abomination.

abonado, a [aβo'naðo, a] a (deuda) paid(-up) // nm/f subscriber.

abonar [aβo'nar] vt (deuda) to settle; (terreno) to fertilize; (idea) to endorse; ~**se** vr to subscribe; **abono** nm payment; fertilizer; subscription.

abordar [aβor'ðar] vt (barco) to board; (asunto) to broach.

aborigen [aβo'rixen] nm/f aborigine.

aborrecer [aβorre'θer] vt to hate, loathe.

abortar [aβor'tar] vi (malparir) to have a miscarriage; (deliberadamente) to have an abortion; **aborto** nm miscarriage; abortion.

abotagado, a [aβota'ɣaðo, a] a swollen.

abotonar [aβoto'nar] vt to button (up), do up.

abovedado, a [aβoβe'ðaðo, a] a vaulted, domed.

abrasar [aβra'sar] vt to burn (up); (AGR) to dry up, parch.

abrasadera [aβrasa'ðera] nf bracket.

abrazar [aβra'θar] vt to embrace,

ESPAÑOL - INGLÉS
SPANISH - ENGLISH

A

PALABRA CLAVE
---

a [a] *prep* (*a* + *el* = *al*) **1** (*dirección*)
to; **fueron ~ Madrid/Grecia** they
went to Madrid/Greece; **me voy ~
casa** I'm going home
2 (*distancia*): **está ~ 15 km de
aquí** it's 15 kms from here
3 (*posición*): **estar ~ la mesa** to be
at table; **al lado de** next to, beside;
ver tb **puerta**
4 (*tiempo*): **~ las 10/~ medianoche**
at 10/midnight; **~ la mañana
siguiente** the following morning; **~
los pocos días** after a few days;
estamos ~ 9 de julio it's the ninth
of July; **~ los 24 años** at the age of
24; **al año/~ la semana** (*AM*) a
year/week later
5 (*manera*): **~ la francesa** the
French way; **~ caballo** on horse-
back; **~ oscuras** in the dark
6 (*medio, instrumento*): **~ lápiz** in
pencil; **~ mano** by hand; **cocina ~
gas** gas stove
7 (*razón*): **~ 30 ptas el kilo** at 30
pesetas a kilo; **~ más de 50 km/h**
at more than 50 kms per hour
8 (*dativo*): **se lo di** → **él** I gave it to
him; **vi al policía** I saw the policeman; **se lo compré** → **él** I bought it
from him
9 (*tras ciertos verbos*): **voy ~ verle**
I'm going to see him; **empezó ~
trabajar** he started working *o* to
work
10 (+ *infinitivo*): **al verle, le
reconocí inmediatamente** when I
saw him I recognized him at once; **el
camino ~ recorrer** the distance we
(*etc*) have to travel; **¡~ callar!**
keep quiet!; **¡~ comer!** let's eat!

abad, esa [a'βað, 'ðesa] *nm/f* abbot/

abbess; **~ía** *nf* abbey.

abajo [a'βaxo] *ad* (*situación*) (down)
below, underneath; (*en edificio*)
downstairs; (*dirección*) down, down-
wards; **~ de** *prep* below, under; **el
piso de ~** the downstairs flat; **la
parte de ~** the lower part; **¡~ el
gobierno!** down with the government!; **cuesta/río ~** downhill/
downstream; **de arriba ~** from top
to bottom; **el ~ firmante** the under-
signed; **más ~** lower *o* further down.

abalorios [aβa'lorjos] *nmpl* (*chuche-
rías*) trinkets.

abalanzarse [aβalan'θarse] *vr*: **~
sobre** *o* **contra** to throw o.s. at.

abanderado [aβande'raðo] *nm*
standard bearer.

abandonado, a [aβando'naðo, a] *a*
derelict; (*desatendido*) abandoned;
(*desierto*) deserted; (*descuidado*)
neglected.

abandonar [aβando'nar] *vt* to leave;
(*persona*) to abandon, desert; (*cosa*)
to abandon, leave behind;
(*descuidar*) to neglect; (*renunciar a*)
to give up; (*INFORM*) to quit; **~se**
vr: **~se a** to abandon o.s. to; **abandono** *nm* (*acto*) desertion,
abandonment; (*estado*) abandon,
neglect; (*renuncia*) withdrawal, retirement; **ganar por ~** to win by
default.

abanicar [aβani'kar] *vt* to fan;
abanico *nm* fan; (*NAUT*) derrick.

abaratar [aβara'tar] *vt* to lower the
price of // *vi*, **~se** *vr* to go *o* come
down in price.

abarcar [aβar'kar] *vt* to include, embrace; (*AM*) to monopolize.

abarrotado, a [aβarro'taðo, a] *a*
packed.

abarrote [aβa'rrote] *nm* packing; **~s**
nmpl (*AM*) groceries, provisions;

Consonantes

	Ejemplo inglés	Ejemplo español/explicación
d	men*d*ed	Como en con*d*e, an*d*ar
g	*g*o, *g*et, bi*g*	Como en *g*rande, *g*ol
dʒ	*g*in, *j*udge	Como en la *ll* andaluza y en *G*enerali-tat (catalán)
ŋ	si*ng*	Como en ví*n*culo
h	*h*ouse, *h*e	Como la *j*ota hispanoamericana
j	*y*oung, *y*es	Como en *y*a
k	*c*ome, mo*ck*	Como en *c*aña, Es*c*ocia
r	*r*ed, t*r*ead	Se pronuncia con la punta de la lengua hacia atrás y sin hacerla vibrar
s	*s*and, ye*s*	Como en ca*s*a, *s*esión
z	ro*s*e, *z*ebra	Como en de*s*de, mi*s*mo
ʃ	*sh*e, ma*ch*ine	Como en *ch*ambre (francés), ro*x*o (portugués)
tʃ	*ch*in, ri*ch*	Como en *ch*ocolate
v	*v*alley	Como en f, pero se retiran los dientes superiores vibrándolos contra el labio inferior
w	*w*ater, *wh*ich	Como en la *u* de h*u*evo, p*u*ede
ʒ	vi*si*on	Como en *j*ournal (francés)
θ	*th*ink, my*th*	Como en re*c*eta, *z*apato
ð	*th*is, *th*e	Como en la *d* de habla*d*o, ver*d*ad

b, p, f, m, n, l, t iguales que en español
El signo * indica que la r final escrita apenas se pronuncia en inglés británico cuando la palabra siguiente empieza con vocal. El signo ['] indica la sílaba acentuada.

PRONUNCIACIÓN INGLESA

Vocales y diptongos

	Ejemplo inglés	Ejemplo español/explicación
ɑː	father	Entre *a* de padre y *o* de noche
ʌ	but, come	*a* muy breve
æ	man, cat	Se mantienen los labios en la posición de *e* en pena y luego se pronuncia el sonido *a*
ə	father, ago	Sonido indistinto parecido a una *e* u *o* casi mudas
əː	bird, heard	Entre *e* abierta, y *o* cerrada, sonido alargado
ɛ	get, bed	como en perro
ɪ	it, big	Más breve que en *sí*
iː	tea, see	Como en *fíno*
ɔ	hot, wash	Como en torre
ɔː	saw, all	Como en por
u	put, book	Sonido breve, más cerrado que burro
uː	too, you	Sonido largo, como en uno
aɪ	fly, high	Como en fraile
au	how, house	Como en pausa
ɛə	there, bear	Casi como en vea, pero el sonido *a* se mezcla con el indistinto [ə]
eɪ	day, obey	*e* cerrada seguida por una *i* débil
ɪə	here, hear	Como en manía, mezclándose el sonido *a* con el indistinto [ə]
əu	go, note	[ə] seguido por una breve *u*
ɔɪ	boy, oil	Como en voy
uə	poor, sure	*u* bastante larga más el sonido indistinto [ə]

Vowels

a	[a]	p*a*ta	not as long as *a* in f*a*r. When followed by a consonant in the same syllable (i.e. in a closed syllable), as in am*a*nte, the *a* is short, as in b*a*t
e	[e]	m*e*	like *e* in th*e*y. In a closed syllable, as in g*e*nte, the *e* is short as in p*e*t
i	[i]	p*i*no	as in m*ea*n or mach*i*ne
o	[o]	l*o*	as in l*o*cal. In a closed syllable, as in c*o*ntrol, the *o* is short as in c*o*t
u	[u]	l*u*nes	as in r*u*le. It is silent after *q*, and in *gue, gui*, unless marked *güe, güi* e.g. antig*ü*edad

Diphthongs

ai, ay	[ai]	b*ai*le	as *i* in r*i*de
au	[au]	*au*to	as *ou* in sh*ou*t
ei, ey	[ei]	b*ue*y	as *ey* in gr*ey*
eu	[eu]	d*eu*da	both elements pronounced independently [e] + [u]
oi, oy	[oi]	h*oy*	as *oy* in t*oy*

Stress

The rules of stress in Spanish are as follows:
(a) when a word ends in a vowel or in *n* or *s*, the second last syllable is stressed: pat*a*ta, pat*a*tas, c*o*me, c*o*men
(b) when a word ends in a consonant other than *n* or *s*, the stress falls on the last syllable: par*e*d, habl*a*r
(c) when the rules set out in a and b are not applied, an acute accent appears over the stressed vowel: com*ú*n, geograf*í*a, ingl*é*s

In the phonetic transcription, the symbol ['] precedes the syllable on which the stress falls.

SPANISH PRONUNCIATION

Consonants

c	[k]	caja	c before a, o or u is pronounced as in cat
ce, ci	[θe, θi]	cero cielo	c before e or i is pronounced as in thin
ch	[tʃ]	chiste	ch is pronounced as ch in chair
d	[d, ð]	danés ciudad	at the beginning of a phrase or after l or n, d is pronounced as in English. In any other position it is pronounced like th in the
g	[g, ɣ]	gafas paga	g before a, o or u is pronounced as in gap, if at the beginning of a phrase or after n. In other positions the sound is softened
ge, gi	[xe, xi]	gente girar	g before e or i is pronounced similar to ch in Scottish loch
h		haber	h is always silent in Spanish
j	[x]	jugar	j is pronounced similar to ch in Scottish loch
ll	[ʎ]	talle	ll is pronounced like the lli in million
ñ	[ɲ]	niño	ñ is pronounced like the ni in onion
q	[k]	que	q is pronounced as k in king
r, rr	[r, rr]	quitar garra	r is always pronounced in Spanish, unlike the silent r in dancer. rr is trilled, like a Scottish r
s	[s]	quizás isla	s is usually pronounced as in pass, but before b, d, g, l, m or n it is pronounced as in rose
v	[b, ß]	vía dividir	v is pronounced something like b. At the beginning of a phrase or after m or n it is pronounced as b in boy. In any other position the sound is softened
z	[θ]	tenaz	z is pronounced as th in thin

b, f, k, l, m, n, p, t and x are pronounced as in English.

ABREVIATURAS

ABBREVIATIONS

tauromaquia	**TAUR**	bullfighting
también	**tb**	also
técnica, tecnología	**TEC(H)**	technical term, technology
telecomunicaciones	**TELEC, TEL**	telecommunications
televisión	**TV**	television
imprenta, tipografía	**TIP, TYP**	typography, printing
inglés norteamericano	**US**	American English
verbo	**vb**	verb
verbo intransitivo	**vi**	intransitive verb
verbo pronominal	**vr**	reflexive verb
verbo transitivo	**vt**	transitive verb
zoología, animales	**ZOOL**	zoology
marca registrada	®	registered trademark
indica un equivalente cultural	≈	introduces a cultural equivalent

ABREVIATURAS

ABBREVIATIONS

infinitivo	**inf**	infinitive
informática	**INFORM**	computers
invariable	**inv**	invariable
irregular	**irg**	irregular
lo jurídico	**JUR**	law
América Latina	**LAm**	Latin America
gramática, lingüística	**LING**	grammar, linguistics
masculino	**m**	masculine
matemáticas	**MAT(H)**	mathematics
medicina	**MED**	medical term, medicine
masculino/femenino	**m/f**	masculine/feminine
lo militar, ejército	**MIL**	military matters
música	**MUS**	music
sustantivo, nombre	**n**	noun
navegación, náutica	**NAUT**	sailing, navigation
sustantivo numérico	**num**	numeral noun
complemento	**obj**	(grammatical) object
	o.s.	oneself
peyorativo	**pey, pej**	derogatory, pejorative
fotografía	**PHOT**	photography
fisiología	**PHYSIOL**	physiology
plural	**pl**	plural
política	**POL**	politics
participio de pasado	**pp**	past participle
prefijo	**pref**	prefix
preposición	**prep**	preposition
pronombre	**pron**	pronoun
psicología, psiquiatría	**PSICO, PSYCH**	psychology, psychiatry
tiempo pasado	**pt**	past tense
sustantivo no empleado en el plural	**q**	collective (uncountable) noun, not used in plural
química	**QUIM**	chemistry
ferrocarril	**RAIL**	railways
religión, lo eclesiástico	**REL**	religion, church service
	sb	somebody
enseñanza, sistema escolar y universitario	**SCOL**	schooling, schools and universities
singular	**sg**	singular
España	**Sp**	Spain
	sth	something
sujeto	**su(b)j**	(grammatical) subject
subjuntivo	**subjun**	subjunctive
sufijo	**suff**	suffix

ABREVIATURAS

ABBREVIATIONS

adjetivo, locución adjetiva	**a**	adjective, adjectival phrase
abreviatura	**ab(b)r**	abbreviation
adverbio, locución adverbial	**ad**	adverb, adverbial phrase
administración, lengua administrativa	**ADMIN**	administration
agricultura	**AGR**	agriculture
América Latina	**AM**	Latin America
anatomía	**ANAT**	anatomy
arquitectura	**ARQ, ARCH**	architecture
astrología, astronomía	**ASTRO**	astrology, astronomy
el automóvil	**AUT(O)**	the motor car and motoring
aviación, viajes aéreos	**AVIAT**	flying, air travel
biología	**BIO(L)**	biology
botánica, flores	**BOT**	botany
inglés británico	**Brit**	British English
química	**CHEM**	chemistry
lengua familiar	**col**	colloquial usage
comercio, finanzas, banca	**COM(M)**	commerce, finance, banking
informática	**COMPUT**	computers
conjunción	**conj**	conjunction
construcción	**CONSTR**	building
compuesto	**cpd**	compound element
cocina	**CULIN**	cookery
economía	**ECON**	economics
electricidad, electrónica	**ELEC**	electricity, electronics
enseñanza, sistema escolar y universitario	**ESCOL**	schooling, schools and universities
España	**Esp**	Spain
especialmente	**esp**	especially
exclamación, interjección	**excl**	exclamation, interjection
femenino	**f**	feminine
lengua familiar	**fam**	colloquial usage
ferrocarril	**FERRO**	railways
uso figurado	**fig**	figurative use
fotografía	**FOTO**	photography
(verbo inglés) del cual la partícula es inseparable	**fus**	(phrasal verb) where the particle is inseparable
generalmente	**gen**	generally
geografía, geología	**GEO**	geography, geology
geometría	**GEOM**	geometry

INTRODUCCIÓN

Quien desee leer y entender el inglés encontrará en este diccionario un extenso léxico moderno que abarca una amplia gama de locuciones de uso corriente. Igualmente encontrará, en su debido orden alfabético, las abreviaturas, las siglas, los nombres geográficos más conocidos y, además, las principales formas de verbo irregulares, donde se le referirá a las respectivas formas de base, hallándose allí la traducción.

Quien aspire comunicarse y expresarse en lengua extranjera, hallará aquí una clara y detallada explicación de las palabras básicas, empleándose un sistema de indicadores que le remitirán a la traducción más apta y le señalarán su correcto uso.

INTRODUCTION

The user whose aim is to read and understand Spanish will find a comprehensive and up-to-date wordlist including numerous phrases in current use. He will also find listed alphabetically the main irregular forms with a cross-reference to the basic form where a translation is given, as well as some of the most common abbreviations, acronyms and geographical names.

The user who wishes to communicate and to express himself in the foreign language will find clear and detailed treatment of all the basic words, with numerous indicators pointing to the appropriate translation, and helping him to use it correctly.

first published in this edition 1982
revised edition 1989

© William Collins Sons & Co. Ltd. 1982, 1989

latest reprint 1992

ISBN 0 00 458544 5

---

contributors/con la colaboración de
Margaret Tejerizo, John Forry,
Carmen Billinghurst, Liam Kane, Pat Feehan,
Soledad Pérez-López, José Ramón Parrondo

editorial staff/redacción
Claire Evans, Jeremy Butterfield, Irene Lakhani

Ediciones Grijalbo, S.A.
Aragón 385, Barcelona 08013

ISBN 84-253-2111-5

Printed in Great Britain by
HarperCollins Manufacturing, Glasgow

COLLINS
GEM
DICTIONARY

SPANISH·ENGLISH
ENGLISH·SPANISH

ESPAÑOL·INGLÉS
INGLÉS·ESPAÑOL

Mike Gonzalez

HarperCollins*Publishers*

grijalbo

acerado, a [aθe'raðo, a] a steel; (*afilado*) sharp; (*fig*: *duro*) steely; (: *mordaz*) biting.

acerbo, a [a'θerβo, a] a bitter; (*fig*) harsh.

acerca [a'θerka]: ~ **de** *ad* about, concerning.

acercar [aθer'kar] *vt* to bring *o* move nearer; ~**se** *vr* to approach, come near.

acerico [aθe'riko] *nm* pincushion.

acero [a'θero] *nm* steel.

acérrimo, a [a'θerrimo, a] a (*partidario*) staunch; (*enemigo*) bitter.

acertado, a [aθer'taðo, a] a correct; (*apropiado*) apt; (*sensato*) sensible.

acertar [aθer'tar] *vt* (*blanco*) to hit; (*solución*) to get right; (*adivinar*) to guess // *vi* to get it right, be right; ~ **a** to manage to; ~ **con** to happen *o* hit on.

acertijo [aθer'tixo] *nm* riddle, puzzle.

acervo [a'θerβo] *nm* heap; ~ **común** undivided estate.

aciago, a [a'θjaɣo, a] a ill-fated, fateful.

acicalar [aθika'lar] *vt* to polish; (*persona*) to dress up; ~**se** *vr* to get dressed up.

acicate [aθi'kate] *nm* spur.

acidez [aθi'ðeθ] *nf* acidity.

ácido, a [a'θiðo, a] a sour, acid // *nm* acid.

acierto *etc* *vb* *ver* **acertar** // [a'θjerto] *nm* success; (*buen paso*) wise move; (*solución*) solution; (*habilidad*) skill, ability.

aclamación [aklama'θjon] *nf* acclamation; (*aplausos*) applause.

aclamar [akla'mar] *vt* to acclaim; (*aplaudir*) to applaud.

aclaración [aklara'θjon] *nf* clarification, explanation.

aclarar [akla'rar] *vt* to clarify, explain; (*ropa*) to rinse // *vi* to clear up; ~**se** *vr* (*explicarse*) to understand; ~**se la garganta** to clear one's throat.

aclaratorio, a [aklara'torjo, a] a explanatory.

aclimatación [aklimata'θjon] *nf* acclimatization; **aclimatar** *vt* to acclimatize; **aclimatarse** *vr* to become acclimatized.

acné [ak'ne] *nm* acne.

acobardar [akoβar'ðar] *vt* to intimidate.

acodarse [ako'ðarse] *vr*: ~ **en** to lean on.

acogedor, a [akoxe'ðor, a] a welcoming; (*hospitalario*) hospitable.

acoger [ako'xer] *vt* to welcome; (*abrigar*) to shelter; ~**se** *vr* to take refuge.

acogida [ako'xiða] *nf* reception; refuge.

acolchar [akol'tʃar] *vt* to pad; (*fig*) to cushion.

acometer [akome'ter] *vt* to attack; (*emprender*) to undertake; **acometida** *nf* attack, assault.

acomodado, a [akomo'ðaðo, a] a (*persona*) well-to-do.

acomodador, a [akomoða'ðor, a] *nm/f* usher(ette).

acomodar [akomo'ðar] *vt* to adjust; (*alojar*) to accommodate; ~**se** *vr* to conform; (*instalarse*) to install o.s.; (*adaptarse*): ~**se (a)** to adapt (to).

acomodaticio, a [akomoða'tiθjo, a] a (*pey*) accommodating, obliging; (*manejable*) pliable.

acompañar [akompa'ɲar] *vt* to accompany; (*documentos*) to enclose.

acondicionar [akondiθjo'nar] *vt* to arrange, prepare; (*pelo*) to condition.

acongojar [akoŋgo'xar] *vt* to distress, grieve.

aconsejar [akonse'xar] *vt* to advise, counsel; ~**se** *vr*: ~**se con** to consult.

acontecer [akonte'θer] *vi* to happen, occur; **acontecimiento** *nm* event.

acopio [a'kopjo] *nm* store, stock.

acoplamiento [akopla'mjento] *nm* coupling, joint; **acoplar** *vt* to fit; (*ELEC*) to connect; (*vagones*) to couple.

acorazado, a [akora'θaðo, a] a armour-plated, armoured //

battleship.

acordar [akor'ðar] *vt* (*resolver*) to agree, resolve; (*recordar*) to remind; ~se *vr* to agree; ~se (de algo) to remember sth; **acorde** *a* (*MUS*) harmonious; ~ **con** (*medidas etc*) in keeping with // *nm* chord.

acordeón [akorðe'on] *nm* accordion.

acordonado, a [akorðo'naðo, a] *a* (*calle*) cordoned-off.

acorralar [akorra'lar] *vt* to round up, corral.

acortar [akor'tar] *vt* to shorten; (*duración*) to cut short; (*cantidad*) to reduce; ~se *vr* to become shorter.

acosar [ako'sar] *vt* to pursue relentlessly; (*fig*) to hound, pester.

acostar [akos'tar] *vt* (*en cama*) to put to bed; (*en suelo*) to lay down; (*barco*) to bring alongside; ~se *vr* to go to bed; to lie down.

acostumbrado, a [akostum'braðo, a] *a* usual; ~ a used to.

acostumbrar [akostum'brar] *vt*: ~ **a uno a algo** to get sb used to sth // *vi*: ~ (a) **hacer** to be in the habit of doing; ~se *vr*: ~se a to get used to.

acotación [akota'θjon] *nf* marginal note; (*GEO*) elevation mark; (*de límite*) boundary mark; (*TEATRO*) stage direction.

ácrata ['akrata] *a, nm/f* anarchist.

acre ['akre] *a* (*sabor*) sharp, bitter; (*olor*) acrid; (*fig*) biting // *nm* acre.

acrecentar [akreθen'tar] *vt* to increase, augment.

acreditar [akreði'tar] *vt* (*garantizar*) to vouch for, guarantee; (*autorizar*) to authorize; (*dar prueba de*) to prove; (*COM: abonar*) to credit; (*embajador*) to accredit; ~se *vr* to become famous.

acreedor, a [akree'ðor, a] *a*: ~ **a** worthy of // *nm/f* creditor.

acribillar [akriβi'ʎar] *vt*: ~ **a balazos** to riddle with bullets.

acrimonia [akri'monja], **acritud** [akri'tuð] *nf* acrimony.

acróbata [a'kroβata] *nm/f* acrobat.

acta ['akta] *nf* certificate; (*de comisión*) minutes *pl*, record; ~ **de nacimiento/de matrimonio** birth/marriage certificate; ~ **notarial** affidavit.

actitud [akti'tuð] *nf* attitude; (*postura*) posture.

activar [akti'βar] *vt* to activate; (*acelerar*) to speed up.

actividad [aktiβi'ðað] *nf* activity.

activo, a [ak'tiβo, a] *a* active; (*vivo*) lively // *nm* (*COM*) assets *pl*.

acto ['akto] *nm* act, action; (*ceremonia*) ceremony; (*TEATRO*) act; **en el ~** immediately.

actor [ak'tor] *nm* actor; (*JUR*) plaintiff // *a*: **parte ~** a prosecution.

actriz [ak'triθ] *nf* actress.

actuación [aktwa'θjon] *nf* action; (*comportamiento*) conduct, behaviour; (*JUR*) proceedings *pl*; (*desempeño*) performance.

actual [ak'twal] *a* present-(day), current; ~**idad** *nf* present; ~**idades** *nfpl* news *sg*; **en la ~idad** at present; (*hoy día*) nowadays.

actualizar [aktwali'θar] *vt* to update, modernize.

actualmente [aktwal'mente] *ad* at present; (*hoy día*) nowadays.

actuar [ak'twar] *vi* (*obrar*) to work, operate; (*actor*) to act, perform // *vt* to work, operate; ~ **de** to act as.

actuario [ak'twarjo, a] *nm* clerk; (*COM*) actuary.

acuarela [akwa'rela] *nf* watercolour.

acuario [a'kwarjo] *nm* aquarium; **A~** Aquarius.

acuartelar [akwarte'lar] *vt* (*MIL*: *disciplinar*) to confine to barracks.

acuático, a [a'kwatiko, a] *a* aquatic.

acuciar [aku'θjar] *vt* to urge on.

acuclillarse [akukli'ʎarse] *vr* to crouch down.

acuchillar [akutʃi'ʎar] *vt* (*TEC*) to plane (down), smooth.

acudir [aku'ðir] *vi* (*asistir*) to attend; (*ir*) to go; ~ **a** (*fig*) to turn to; ~ **en ayuda de** to go to the aid of.

acuerdo *etc vb ver* **acordar** [a'kwerðo] *nm* agreement; **¡de ~!**

agreed!; **de ~ con** (*persona*) in agreement with; (*acción, documento*) in accordance with; **estar de ~** to be agreed, agree.

acumular [akumu'lar] *vt* to accumulate, collect.

acuñar [aku'ɲar] *vt* (*moneda*) to mint; (*frase*) to coin.

acuoso, a [a'kwoso, a] *a* watery.

acurrucarse [akurru'karse] *vr* to crouch; (*ovillarse*) to curl up.

acusación [akusa'θjon] *nf* accusation; **acusar** *vt* to accuse; (*revelar*) to reveal; (*denunciar*) to denounce.

acuse [a'kuse] *nm*: **~ de recibo** acknowledgement of receipt.

acústico, a [a'kustiko, a] *a* acoustic // *nf* (*de una sala etc*) acoustics *pl*.

achacar [atʃa'kar] *vt* to attribute.

achacoso, a [atʃa'koso, a] *a* sickly.

achantar [atʃan'tar] *vt* (*fam*) to scare, frighten; **~se** *vr* to back down.

achaque *etc vb ver* **achacar** // [a'tʃake] *nm* ailment.

achicar [atʃi'kar] *vt* to reduce; (*humillar*) to humiliate; (*NAUT*) to bale out.

achicoria [atʃi'korja] *nf* chicory.

achicharrar [atʃitʃa'rrar] *vt* to scorch; (*quemar*) to burn.

adagio [a'ðaxjo] *nm* adage; (*MUS*) adagio.

adaptación [aðapta'θjon] *nf* adaptation.

adaptador [aðapta'ðor] *nm* (*ELEC*) adapter.

adaptar [aðap'tar] *vt* to adapt; (*acomodar*) to fit.

adecuado, a [aðe'kwaðo, a] *a* (*apto*) suitable; (*oportuno*) appropriate.

adecuar [aðe'kwar] *vt* to adapt; to make suitable.

a. de J.C. *abr* (= *antes de Jesucristo*) B.C.

adelantado, a [aðelan'taðo, a] *a* advanced; (*reloj*) fast; **pagar por ~** to pay in advance.

adelantamiento [aðelanta'mjento]

nm advance, advancement; (*AUTO*) overtaking.

adelantar [aðelan'tar] *vt* to move forward; (*avanzar*) to advance; (*acelerar*) to speed up; (*AUTO*) to overtake // *vi*, **~se** *vr* to go forward, advance.

adelante [aðe'lante] *ad* forward(s), ahead // *excl* come in!; **de hoy en ~** from now on; **más ~** later on; (*más allá*) further on.

adelanto [aðe'lanto] *nm* advance; (*mejora*) improvement; (*progreso*) progress.

adelgazar [aðelɣa'θar] *vt* to thin (down) // *vi* to get thin; (*con régimen*) to slim down, lose weight.

ademán [aðe'man] *nm* gesture; **ademanes** *nmpl* manners; **en ~ de** as if to.

además [aðe'mas] *ad* besides; (*por otra parte*) moreover; (*también*) also; **~ de** besides, in addition to.

adentrarse [aðen'trarse] *vr*: **~ en** to go into, get inside; (*penetrar*) to penetrate (into).

adentro [a'ðentro] *ad* inside, in; **mar ~** out at sea; **tierra ~** inland.

adepto, a [a'ðepto, a] *nm/f* supporter.

aderezar [aðere'θar] *vt* (*ensalada*) to dress; (*comida*) to season; **aderezo** *nm* dressing; seasoning.

adeudar [aðeu'ðar] *vt* to owe; **~se** *vr* to run into debt.

adherirse [aðe'rirse] *vr*: **~ a** to adhere to; (*partido*) to join.

adhesión [aðe'sjon] *nf* adhesion; (*fig*) adherence.

adición [aði'θjon] *nf* addition.

adicionar [aðiθjo'nar] *vt* to add.

adicto, a [a'ðikto, a] *a*: **~ a** addicted to; (*dedicado*) devoted to // *nm/f* supporter, follower; (*toxicómano etc*) addict.

adiestrar [aðjes'trar] *vt* to train, teach; (*conducir*) to guide, lead; **~se** *vr* to practise; (*enseñarse*) to train o.s.

adinerado, a [aðine'raðo, a] *a*

wealthy.

adiós [a'ðjos] *excl* (*para despedirse*) goodbye!, cheerio!; (*al pasar*) hello!

aditivo [aði'tiβo] *nm* additive.

adivinanza [aðiβi'nanθa] *nf* riddle; **adivinar** *vt* to prophesy; (*conjeturar*) to guess; **adivino, a** *nm/f* fortune-teller.

adj *abr* (= *adjunto*) encl.

adjetivo [aðxe'tiβo] *nm* adjective.

adjudicación [aðxuðika'θjon] *nf* award; adjudication.

adjudicar [aðxuði'kar] *vt* to award; ~se *vr*: ~se algo to appropriate sth.

adjuntar [aðxun'tar] *vt* to attach, enclose; **adjunto, a** *a* attached, enclosed // *nm/f* assistant.

administración [aðministra'θjon] *nf* administration; (*dirección*) management; **administrador, a** *nm/f* administrator; manager(ess).

administrar [aðminis'trar] *vt* to administer; **administrativo, a** *a* administrative.

admirable [aðmi'raβle] *a* admirable.

admiración [aðmira'θjon] *nf* admiration; (*asombro*) wonder; (*LING*) exclamation mark.

admirar [aðmi'rar] *vt* to admire; (*extrañar*) to surprise; ~se *vr* to be surprised.

admisible [aðmi'siβle] *a* admissible.

admisión [aðmi'sjon] *nf* admission; (*reconocimiento*) acceptance.

admitir [aðmi'tir] *vt* to admit; (*aceptar*) to accept.

admonición [aðmoni'θjon] *nf* warning.

adobar [aðo'βar] *vt* (*CULIN*) to season.

adobe [a'ðoβe] *nm* adobe, sun-dried brick.

adoctrinar [aðoktri'nar] *vt*: ~ en to indoctrinate with.

adolecer [aðole'θer] *vi*: ~ de to suffer from.

adolescente [aðoles'θente] *nm/f* adolescent, teenager.

adonde [a'ðonde] *conj* (to) where.

adónde [a'ðonde] *ad* = **dónde**.

adopción [aðop'θjon] *nf* adoption.

adoptar [aðop'tar] *vt* to adopt.

adoptivo, a [aðop'tiβo, a] *a* (*padres*) adoptive; (*hijo*) adopted.

adoquín [aðo'kin] *nm* paving stone.

adorar [aðo'rar] *vt* to adore.

adormecer [aðorme'θer] *vt* to put to sleep; ~se *vr* to become sleepy; (*dormirse*) to fall asleep.

adornar [aðor'nar] *vt* to adorn.

adorno [a'ðorno] *nm* adornment; (*decoración*) decoration.

adosado, a [aðo'saðo, a] *a*: **casa adosada** semi-detached house.

adquiero *etc vb ver* **adquirir**.

adquirir [aðki'rir] *vt* to acquire, obtain.

adquisición [aðkisi'θjon] *nf* acquisition.

adrede [a'ðreðe] *ad* on purpose.

adscribir [aðskri'βir] *vt* to appoint.

adscrito *pp de* **adscribir**.

aduana [a'ðwana] *nf* customs *pl*.

aduanero, a [aðwa'nero, a] *a* customs *cpd* // *nm/f* customs officer.

aducir [aðu'θir] *vt* to adduce; (*dar como prueba*) to offer as proof.

adueñarse [aðwe'narse] *vr*: ~ de to take possession of.

adulación [aðula'θjon] *nf* flattery.

adular [aðu'lar] *vt* to flatter.

adulterar [aðulte'rar] *vt* to adulterate // *vi* to commit adultery.

adulterio [aðul'terjo] *nm* adultery.

adúltero, a [a'ðultero, a] *a* adulterous // *nm/f* adulterer/adulteress.

adulto, a [a'ðulto, a] *a*, *nm/f* adult.

adusto, a [a'ðusto, a] *a* stern; (*austero*) austere.

advenedizo, a [aðβene'ðiθo, a] *nm/f* upstart.

advenimiento [aðβeni'mjento] *nm* arrival; (*al trono*) accession.

adverbio [að'βerβjo] *nm* adverb.

adversario, a [aðβer'sarjo, a] *nm/f* adversary.

adversidad [aðβersi'ðað] *nf* adversity; (*contratiempo*) setback.

adverso, a [að'βerso, a] *a* adverse.

advertencia [aðβer'tenθja] *nf* warning; (*prefacio*) preface, foreword.

advertir [aðβer'tir] *vt* to notice; (*avisar*): ~ **a uno de** to warn sb about o of.

Adviento [að'βjento] *nm* Advent.

advierto *etc*, **advirtiendo** *etc vb ver* **advertir**.

adyacente [aðja'θente] *a* adjacent.

aéreo, a [a'ereo, a] *a* aerial.

aerobic [ac'roβik] *nm* aerobics *sg*.

aerodeslizador [aeroðesli'θor], **aerodeslizante** [aeroðesli'θante] *nm* hovercraft.

aeromozo, a [aero'moθo, a] *nm/f* (*AM*) air steward(ess).

aeronáutica [aero'nautika] *nf* aeronautics *sg*.

aeronave [aero'naβe] *nm* spaceship.

aeroplano [aero'plano] *nm* aeroplane.

aeropuerto [aero'pwerto] *nm* airport.

aerosol [aero'sol] *nm* aerosol.

afabilidad [afaβili'ðað] *nf* friendliness; **afable** *a* affable.

afamado, a [afa'maðo, a] *a* famous.

afán [a'fan] *nm* hard work; (*deseo*) desire.

afanar [afa'nar] *vt* to harass; (*fam*) to pinch; ~**se** *vr*: ~**se por hacer** to strive to do; **afanoso, a** *a* (*trabajo*) hard; (*trabajador*) industrious.

afear [afe'ar] *vt* to disfigure.

afección [afek'θjon] *nf* (*MED*) disease.

afectación [afekta'θjon] *nf* affectation; **afectado, a** *a* affected; **afectar** *vt* to affect.

afectísimo, a [afek'tisimo, a] *a* affectionate; ~ **suyo** yours truly.

afectivo, a [afek'tiβo, a] *a* (*problema etc*) emotionally.

afecto [a'fekto] *nm* affection; **tenerle** ~ **a uno** to be fond of sb.

afectuoso, a [afek'twoso, a] *a* affectionate.

afeitar [afei'tar] *vt* to shave; ~**se** *vr* to shave.

afeminado, a [afemi'naðo, a] *a* effeminate.

aferrado, a [afe'rraðo, a] *a* stubborn.

aferrar [afe'rrar] *vt* to grasp; (*barco*) to moor // *vi* to moor.

Afganistán [afvanis'tan] *nm* Afghanistan.

afianzamiento [afjanθa'mjento] *nm* strengthening; security; **afianzar** *vt* to strengthen; to secure; **afianzarse** *vr* to become established.

afición [afi'θjon] *nf* fondness, liking; **la** ~ **the fans** *pl*; **pinto por** ~ **I** paint as a hobby; **aficionado, a** *a* keen, enthusiastic; (*no profesional*) amateur; **ser** ~ **a algo** to be very keen on o fond of sth // *nm/f* enthusiast, fan; amateur.

aficionar [afiθjo'nar] *vt*: ~ **a uno a algo** to make sb like sth; ~**se** *vr*: ~**se a algo** to grow fond of sth.

afiche [a'fitʃe] *nm* (*AM*) poster.

afilado, a [afi'laðo, a] *a* sharp.

afilar [afi'lar] *vt* to sharpen.

afiliarse [afi'ljarse] *vr* to affiliate.

afín [a'fin] *a* (*parecido*) similar; (*conexo*) related.

afinar [afi'nar] *vt* (*TEC*) to refine; (*MUS*) to tune // *vi* to play/sing in tune.

afincarse [afin'karse] *vr* to settle.

afinidad [afini'ðað] *nf* affinity; (*parentesco*) relationship; **por** ~ by marriage.

afirmación [afirma'θjon] *nf* affirmation; **afirmar** *vt* to affirm, state; (*reforzar*) to strengthen; **afirmativo, a** *a* affirmative.

aflicción [aflik'θjon] *nf* affliction; (*dolor*) grief.

afligir [afli'xir] *vt* to afflict; (*apenar*) to distress; ~**se** *vr* to grieve.

aflojar [aflo'xar] *vt* to slacken; (*desatar*) to loosen, undo; (*relajar*) to relax // *vi* to drop; (*bajar*) to go down; ~**se** *vr* to relax.

aflorar [aflo'rar] *vi* to come to the surface, emerge.

afluente [aflu'ente] *a* flowing // *nm* tributary.

afluir [aflu'ir] *vi* to flow.

afmo, a abr (= afectísimo(a) suyo(a)) Yours.

afónico, a [a'foniko, a] a: **estar ~** to have a sore throat; to have lost one's voice.

aforo [a'foro] nm (de teatro etc) capacity.

afortunado, a [afortu'naðo, a] a fortunate, lucky.

afrancesado, a [afranθe'saðo, a] a francophile; (pey) Frenchified.

afrenta [a'frenta] nf affront, insult; (deshonra) dishonour, shame.

Africa ['afrika] nf Africa; **~ del Sur** South Africa; **africano, a** a, nm/f African.

afrontar [afron'tar] vt to confront; (poner cara a cara) to bring face to face.

afuera [a'fwera] ad out, outside; **~s** nfpl outskirts.

agachar [aɣa'tʃar] vt to bend, bow; **~se** vr to stoop, bend.

agalla [a'ɣaʎa] nf (ZOOL) gill; **~s** nfpl (MED) tonsillitis sg; (ANAT) tonsils; **tener ~s** (fam) to have guts.

agarradera [aɣarra'ðera] nf (AM), **agarradero** [aɣarra'ðero] nm handle; **~s** npl pull sg, influence sg.

agarrado, a [aɣa'rraðo, a] a mean, stingy.

agarrar [aɣa'rrar] vt to grasp, grab; (AM) to take, catch; (recoger) to pick up // vi (planta) to take root; **~se** vr to hold on (tightly).

agarrotar [aɣarro'tar] vt (lío) to tie tightly; (persona) to squeeze tightly; (reo) to garrotte; **~se** vr (motor) to seize up; (MED) to stiffen.

agasajar [aɣasa'xar] vt to treat well, fête.

agencia [a'xenθja] nf agency; **~ inmobiliaria** estate (Brit) o real estate (US) agent's (office); **~ matrimonial** marriage bureau; **~ de viajes** travel agency.

agenciarse [axen'θjarse] vr to obtain, procure.

agenda [a'xenda] nf diary.

agente [a'xente] nm agent; (de policía) policeman; **~ femenino** policewoman; **~ inmobiliario** estate agent (Brit), realtor (US); **~ de bolsa** stockbroker; **~ de seguros** insurance agent.

ágil ['axil] a agile, nimble; **agilidad** nf agility, nimbleness.

agitación [axita'θjon] nf (de mano etc) shaking, waving; (de líquido etc) stirring; (fig) agitation.

agitar [axi'tar] vt to wave, shake; (líquido) to stir; (fig) to stir up, excite; **~se** vr to get excited; (inquietarse) to get worried o upset.

aglomeración [aɣlomera'θjon] nf: **~ de tráfico/gente** traffic jam/mass of people.

aglomerar [aɣlome'rar] vt, **aglomerarse** vr to crowd together.

agnóstico, a [aɣ'nostiko, a] a, nm/f agnostic.

agobiar [aɣo'βjar] vt to weigh down; (oprimir) to oppress; (cargar) to burden.

agolparse [aɣol'parse] vr to crowd together.

agonía [aɣo'nia] nf death throes pl; (fig) agony, anguish.

agonizante [aɣoni'θante] a dying.

agonizar [aɣoni'θar] vi (tb: **estar agonizando**) to be dying.

agosto [a'ɣosto] nm August.

agotado, a [aɣo'taðo, a] a (persona) exhausted; (libros) out of print; (acabado) finished; (COM) sold out.

agotador, a [aɣota'ðor, a] a exhausting.

agotamiento [aɣota'mjento] nm exhaustion.

agotar [aɣo'tar] vt to exhaust; (consumir) to drain; (recursos) to use up, deplete; **~se** vr to be exhausted; (acabarse) to run out; (libro) to go out of print.

agraciado, a [aɣra'θjaðo, a] a (atractivo) attractive; (en sorteo etc) lucky.

agraciar [aɣra'θjar] vt (JUR) to pardon; (con premio) to reward.

agradable [aɣra'ðaßle] a pleasant, nice.

agradar [aɣra'ðar] vt: él me agrada I like him.

agradecer [aɣraðe'θer] vt to thank; (favor etc) to be grateful for; **agradecido, a** a grateful; ¡muy ~! thanks a lot!; **agradecimiento** nm thanks pl; gratitude.

agradezco etc vb ver **agradecer**.

agrado [a'ɣraðo] nm: ser de tu etc agrado to be to your etc liking.

agrandar [aɣran'dar] vt to enlarge; (fig) to exaggerate; ~se vr to get bigger.

agrario, a [a'ɣrarjo, a] a agrarian, land cpd; (política) agricultural, farming.

agravante [aɣra'ßante] a aggravating // nf: con la ~ de que ... with the further difficulty that ...

agravar [aɣra'ßar] vt (pesar sobre) to make heavier; (irritar) to aggravate; ~se vr to worsen, get worse.

agraviar [aɣra'ßjar] vt to offend; (ser injusto con) to wrong; ~se vr to take offence; **agravio** nm offence; wrong; (JUR) grievance.

agredir [aɣre'ðir] vt to attack.

agregado [aɣre'ɣaðo] nm aggregate; (persona) attaché.

agregar [aɣre'ɣar] vt to gather; (añadir) to add; (persona) to appoint.

agresión [aɣre'sjon] nf aggression.

agresivo, a [aɣre'sißo, a] a aggressive.

agriar [a'ɣrjar] vt (turn) sour; ~se vr to turn sour.

agrícola [a'ɣrikola] a farming cpd, agricultural.

agricultor, a [aɣrikul'tor, a] nm/f farmer.

agricultura [aɣrikul'tura] nf agriculture, farming.

agridulce [aɣri'ðulθe] a bittersweet; (CULIN) sweet and sour.

agrietarse [aɣrje'tarse] vr to crack; (piel) to chap.

agrimensor, a [aɣrimen'sor, a] nm/f surveyor.

agrio, a ['aɣrjo, a] a bitter.

agronomía [aɣrono'mia] nf agronomy, agriculture.

agropecuario, a [aɣrope'kwarjo, a] a farming cpd, agricultural.

agrupación [aɣrupa'θjon] nf group; (acto) grouping.

agrupar [aɣru'par] vt to group.

agua ['aɣwa] nf water; (NAUT) wake; (ARQ) slope of a roof; ~s nfpl (de piedra) water sg, sparkle sg; (MED) water sg, urine sg; (NAUT) waters; ~s **abajo/arriba** downstream/upstream; ~ **bendita/ destilada/potable** holy/distilled/ drinking water; ~ **caliente** hot water; ~ **corriente** running water; ~ **de colonia** eau de cologne; ~ **mineral (con/sin gas)** (fizzy/non-fizzy) mineral water; ~s **jurisdiccionales** territorial waters; ~s **mayores** excrement sg.

aguacate [aɣwa'kate] nm avocado pear.

aguacero [aɣwa'θero] nm (heavy) shower, downpour.

aguado, a [a'ɣwaðo, a] a watery, watered down // nf (AGR) watering place; (NAUT) water supply; (ARTE) watercolour.

aguafiestas [aɣwa'fjestas] nm/f inv spoilsport, killjoy.

aguafuerte [aɣwa'fwerte] nm o f etching.

aguamanil [aɣwama'nil] nm (jofaina) washbasin.

aguanieve [aɣwa'njeße] nf sleet.

aguantar [aɣwan'tar] vt to bear, put up with; (sostener) to hold up // vi to last; ~se vr to restrain o.s.; **aguante** nm (paciencia) patience; (resistencia) endurance.

aguar [a'ɣwar] vt to water down.

aguardar [aɣwar'ðar] vt to wait for.

aguardiente [aɣwar'ðjente] nm brandy, liquor.

aguarrás [aɣwa'rras] nm turpentine.

agudeza [aɣu'ðeθa] nf sharpness;

(ingenio) wit.

agudizar [ayuði'θar] *vt (crisis)* to make worse; ~**se** *vr* to get worse.

agudo, a [a'yuðo, a] *a* sharp; *(voz)* high-pitched, piercing; *(dolor, enfermedad)* acute.

agüero [a'ywero] *nm:* **buen/mal** ~ good/bad omen.

aguijar [axi'xar] *vt* to goad; *(incitar)* to urge on // *vi* to hurry along.

aguijón [axi'xon] *nm* sting; *(fig)* spur; **aguijonear** *vt* = **aguijar.**

águila [a'xila] *nf* eagle; *(fig)* genius.

aguileño, a [axi'leɲo, a] *a (nariz)* aquiline; *(rostro)* sharp-featured.

aguinaldo [axi'naldo] *nm* Christmas box.

aguja [a'xuxa] *nf* needle; *(de reloj)* hand; *(ARQ)* spire; *(TEC)* firing-pin; ~**s** *nfpl (ZOOL)* ribs; *(FERRO)* points.

agujerear [axuxere'ar] *vt* to make holes in.

agujero [axu'xero] *nm* hole.

agujetas [axu'xetas] *nfpl* stitch *sg;* *(rigidez)* stiffness *sg.*

aguzar [axu'θar] *vt* to sharpen; *(fig)* to incite.

ahí [a'i] *ad* there; **de** ~ **que** so that, with the result that; ~ **llega** here he comes; **por** ~ that way; *(allá)* over there; **200 o por** ~ 200 or so.

ahijado, a [ai'xaðo, a] *nm/f* godson/ daughter.

ahínco [a'inko] *nm* earnestness.

ahíto, a [a'ito, a] *a:* **estoy** ~ I'm full up.

ahogar [ao'xar] *vt* to drown; *(asfixiar)* to suffocate, smother; *(fuego)* to put out; ~**se** *vr (en el agua)* to drown; *(por asfixia)* to suffocate.

ahogo [a'oxo] *nm* breathlessness; *(fig)* financial difficulty.

ahondar [aon'dar] *vt* to deepen, make deeper; *(fig)* to study thoroughly // *vi:* ~ **en** to study thoroughly.

ahora [a'ora] *ad* now; *(hace poco)* a moment ago, just now; *(dentro de*

poco) in a moment; ~ **voy** I'm coming; ~ **mismo** right now; ~ **bien** now then; **por** ~ for the present.

ahorcar [aor'kar] *vt* to hang; ~**se** *vr* to hang o.s.

ahorita [ao'rita] *ad (fam)* right now.

ahorrar [ao'rrar] *vt (dinero)* to save; *(esfuerzos)* to save, avoid; **ahorro** *nm (acto)* saving; *(frugalidad)* thrift; **ahorros** *nmpl* savings.

ahuecar [awe'kar] *vt* to hollow (out); *(voz)* to deepen; ~**se** *vr* to give o.s. airs.

ahumar [au'mar] *vt* to smoke, cure; *(llenar de humo)* to fill with smoke // *vi* to smoke; ~**se** *vr* to fill with smoke.

ahuyentar [aujen'tar] *vt* to drive off, frighten off; *(fig)* to dispel.

airado, a [ai'raðo, a] *a* angry; **airar** *vt* to anger; **airarse** *vr* to get angry.

aire [a'ire] *nm* air; *(viento)* wind; *(corriente)* draught; *(MUS)* tune; ~**s** *nmpl:* **darse** ~**s** to give o.s. airs; **al** ~ **libre** in the open air; ~ **acondicionado** air conditioning; **airoso, a** *a* windy; draughty; *(fig)* graceful.

aislado, a [ais'laðo, a] *a* isolated; *(incomunicado)* cut-off; *(ELEC)* insulated.

aislar [ais'lar] *vt* to isolate; *(ELEC)* to insulate.

ajar [a'xar] *vt* to spoil; *(fig)* to abuse.

ajardinado, a [axarði'naðo, a] *a* landscaped.

ajedrez [axe'ðreθ] *nm* chess.

ajeno, a [a'xeno, a] *a (que pertenece a otro)* somebody else's; ~ **a** foreign to; ~ **de** free from, devoid of.

ajetreado, a [axetre'aðo, a] *a* busy.

ajetreo [axe'treo] *nm* bustle.

ají [a'xi] *nm* chili, red pepper; *(salsa)* chili sauce.

ajo ['axo] *nm* garlic.

ajorca [a'xorka] *nf* bracelet.

ajuar [a'xwar] *nm* household furnishings *pl; (de novia)* trousseau; *(de niño)* layette.

ajustado, a [axus'taðo, a] *a*

(*tornillo*) tight; (*cálculo*) right; (*ropa*) tight(-fitting); (*DEPORTE: resultado*) close.

ajustar [axus'tar] *vt* (*adaptar*) to adjust; (*encajar*) to fit; (*TEC*) to engage; (*IMPRENTA*) to make up; (*apretar*) to tighten; (*concertar*) to agree (on); (*reconciliar*) to reconcile; (*cuenta*) to settle // *vi* to fit.

ajuste [a'xuste] *nm* adjustment; (*COSTURA*) fitting; (*acuerdo*) compromise; (*de cuenta*) settlement.

al [al] = **a** + **el**, *ver* **a**.

ala ['ala] *nf* wing; (*de sombrero*) brim; (*futbolista*) winger.

alabanza [ala'βanθa] *nf* praise.

alabar [ala'βar] *vt* to praise.

alacena [ala'θena] *nf* cupboard (*Brit*), closet (*US*).

alacrán [ala'kran] *nm* scorpion.

alado, a [a'laðo, a] *a* winged.

alambique [alam'bike] *nm* still.

alambrada [alam'braða] *nf*, **alambrado** [alam'braðo] *nm* wire fence; (*red*) wire netting.

alambre [a'lambre] *nm* wire; **~ de púas** barbed wire; **alambrista** [alam'brista] *nm/f* tightrope walker.

alameda [ala'meða] *nf* (*plantío*) poplar grove; (*lugar de paseo*) avenue, boulevard.

álamo ['alamo] *nm* poplar; **~ temblón** aspen.

alano [a'lano] *nm* mastiff.

alarde [a'larðe] *nm* show, display; **hacer ~ de** to boast of.

alargador [alarγa'ðor] *nm* (*ELEC*) extension lead.

alargar [alar'γar] *vt* to lengthen, extend; (*paso*) to hasten; (*brazo*) to stretch out; (*cuerda*) to pay out; (*conversación*) to spin out; **~se** *vr* to get longer.

alarido [ala'riðo] *nm* shriek.

alarma [a'larma] *nf* alarm.

alarmante [alar'mante] *a* alarming.

alazán [ala'θan] *nm* sorrel.

alba ['alβa] *nf* dawn.

albacea [alβa'θea] *nm/f* executor/executrix.

albahaca [al'βaka] *nf* basil.

Albania [al'βanja] *nf* Albania.

albañal [alβa'nal] *nm* drain, sewer.

albañil [alβa'nil] *nm* bricklayer; (*cantero*) mason.

albarán [alβa'ran] *nm* (*COM*) delivery note, invoice.

albaricoque [alβari'koke] *nm* apricot.

albedrío [alβe'ðrio] *nm*: **libre ~** free will.

alberca [al'βerka] *nf* reservoir; (*AM*) swimming pool.

albergar [alβer'γar] *vt* to shelter.

albergue *etc vb ver* **albergar** // [al'βerγe] *nm* shelter, refuge; **~ de juventud** youth hostel.

albóndiga [al'βondiγa] *nf* meatball.

albor [al'βor] *nm* whiteness; (*amanecer*) dawn; **~ada** *nf* dawn; (*diana*) reveille; **~ear** *vi* to dawn.

albornoz [alβor'noθ] *nm* (*de los árabes*) burnous; (*para el baño*) bathrobe.

alborotar [alβoro'tar] *vi* to make a row // *vt* to agitate, stir up; **~se** *vr* to get excited; (*mar*) to get rough; **alboroto** *nm* row, uproar.

alborozar [alβoro'θar] *vt* to gladden; **~se** *vr* to rejoice.

alborozo [alβo'roθo] *nm* joy.

albricias [al'βriθjas] *nfpl*: **¡~!** good news!

álbum ['alβum] (*pl* **~s**, **~es**) *nm* album; **~ de recortes** scrapbook.

albumen [al'βumen] *nm* egg white, albumen.

alcachofa [alka'tʃofa] *nf* artichoke.

alcalde, esa [al'kalde, esa] *nm/f* mayor(ess).

alcaldía [alkal'dia] *nf* mayoralty; (*lugar*) mayor's office.

alcance *etc vb ver* **alcanzar** // [al'kanθe] *nm* reach; (*COM*) adverse balance.

alcancía [alkan'θia] *nf* money box.

alcantarilla [alkanta'riʎa] *nf* (*de aguas cloacales*) sewer; (*en la calle*) gutter.

alcanzar [alkan'θar] *vt* (*algo: con la*

mano, el pie) to reach; (*alguien: en el camino etc*) to catch up (with); (*autobus*) to catch; (*suj: bala*) to hit, strike // *vi* (*ser suficiente*) to be enough; ~ **a hacer** to manage to do.

alcaparra [alka'parra] *nf* caper.

alcatraz [alka'traθ] *nm* gannet.

alcayata [alka'jata] *nf* hook.

alcázar [al'kaθar] *nm* fortress; (*NAUT*) quarter-deck.

alcoba [al'koβa] *nf* bedroom.

alcohol [al'kol] *nm* alcohol; ~ **metílico** methylated spirits *pl* (*Brit*), wood alcohol (*US*); **alcohólico, a** *a, nm/f* alcoholic.

alcoholímetro [alko'limetro] *nm* Breathalyser ® (*Brit*), drunkometer (*US*).

alcoholismo [alko'lismo] *nm* alcoholism.

alcornoque [alkor'noke] *nm* cork tree; (*fam*) idiot.

aldaba [al'daβa] *nf* (door) knocker.

aldea [al'dea] *nf* village; ~**no, a** *a* village *cpd* // *nm/f* villager.

ale ['ale] *excl* come on!, let's go!

aleación [alea'θjon] *nf* alloy.

aleatorio, a [alea'torjo, a] *a* random.

aleccionar [alekθjo'nar] *vt* to instruct; (*adiestrar*) to train.

alegación [alexa'θjon] *nf* allegation; **alegar** *vt* to allege; (*JUR*) to plead // *vi* (*AM*) to argue.

alegato [ale'xato] *nm* (*JUR*) allegation; (*AM*) argument.

alegoría [alexo'ria] *nf* allegory.

alegrar [ale'xrar] *vt* (*causar alegría*) to cheer (up); (*fuego*) to poke; (*fiesta*) to liven up; ~**se** *vr* (*fam*) to get merry o tight; ~**se de** to be glad about.

alegre [a'levre] *a* happy, cheerful; (*fam*) merry, • tight; (*chiste*) risqué, blue; **alegría** *nf* happiness; merriment.

alejamiento [alexa'mjento] *nm* removal; (*distancia*) remoteness.

alejar [ale'xar] *vt* to remove; (*fig*) to estrange; ~**se** *vr* to move away.

alemán, ana [ale'man, ana] *a, nm/f* German // *nm* (*LING*) German.

Alemania [ale'manja] *nf*: ~ **Occidental/Oriental** West/East Germany.

alentador, a [alenta'ðor, a] *a* encouraging.

alentar [alen'tar] *vt* to encourage.

alergia [a'lerxja] *nf* allergy.

alero [a'lero] *nm* (*de tejado*) eaves *pl*; (*de carruaje*) mudguard.

alerta [a'lerta] *a, nm* alert.

aleta [a'leta] *nf* (*de pez*) fin; (*de ave*) wing; (*de foca, DEPORTE*) flipper; (*AUTO*) mudguard.

aletargar [aletar'xar] *vt* to make drowsy; (*entumecer*) to make numb; ~**se** *vr* to grow drowsy; to become numb.

aletear [alete'ar] *vi* to flutter.

alevín [ale'βin], **alevino** [ale'βino] *nm* fry, young fish.

alevosía [aleβo'sia] *nf* treachery.

alfabeto [alfa'βeto] *nm* alphabet.

alfalfa [al'falfa] *nf* alfalfa, lucerne.

alfarería [alfare'ria] *nf* pottery; (*tienda*) pottery shop; **alfarero, a** *nm/f* potter.

alféizar [al'feiθar] *nm* window-sill.

alférez [al'fereθ] *nm* (*MIL*) second lieutenant; (*NAUT*) ensign.

alfil [al'fil] *nm* (*AJEDREZ*) bishop.

alfiler [alfi'ler] *nm* pin; (*broche*) clip; (*pinza*) clothes peg.

alfiletero [alfile'tero] *nm* needlecase.

alfombra [al'fombra] *nf* carpet; (*más pequeña*) rug; **alfombrar** *vt* to carpet; **alfombrilla** *nf* rug, mat.

alforja [al'forxa] *nf* saddlebag.

alforza [al'forθa] *nf* pleat.

algas [algas] *nfpl* seaweed.

algarabía [alvara'βia] *nf* (*fam*) gibberish.

algarrobo [alva'rroβo] *nm* carob tree.

algazara [alva'θara] *nf* din, uproar.

álgebra ['alxeβra] *nf* algebra.

álgido, a ['alxiðo] *a* icy, chilly; (*momento etc*) crucial, decisive.

algo ['alvo] *pron* something; anything

// ad somewhat, rather; ¿~ más? anything else?; (en tienda) is that all?; por ~ será there must be some reason for it.

algodón [alɣo'ðon] nm cotton; (planta) cotton plant; ~ de azúcar candy floss (Brit), cotton candy (US); ~ hidrófilo cotton wool (Brit), absorbent cotton (US).

algodonero, a [alɣoðo'nero, a] a cotton cpd // nm/f cotton grower // nm cotton plant.

alguacil [alɣwa'θil] nm bailiff; (TAUR) mounted official.

alguien ['alɣjen] pron someone, somebody; (en frases interrogativas) anyone, anybody.

alguno, a, [al'ɣuno, a] a (delante de nm: algún) some; (después de n): no tiene talento alguno he has no talent, he doesn't have any talent // pron (alguien) someone, somebody; algún que otro libro some book or other; algún día iré I'll go one o some day; sin interés ~ without the slightest interest; ~ que otro an occasional one; ~s piensan some (people) think.

alhaja [a'laxa] nf jewel; (tesoro) precious object, treasure.

alhelí [ale'li] nm wallflower, stock.

aliado, a [a'ljaðo, a] a allied.

alianza [a'ljanθa] nf alliance; (anillo) wedding ring.

aliar [a'ljar] vt to ally; ~se vr to form an alliance.

alias ['aljas] ad alias.

alicates [ali'kates] nmpl pliers; ~ de uñas nail clippers.

aliciente [ali'θjente] nm incentive; (atracción) attraction.

alienación [aljena'θjon] nf alienation.

aliento [a'ljento] nm breath; (respiración) breathing; sin ~ breathless.

aligerar [alixe'rar] vt to lighten; (reducir) to shorten; (aliviar) to alleviate; (mitigar) to ease; (paso) to quicken.

alimaña [ali'maɲa] nf pest.

alimentación [alimenta'θjon] nf (comida) food; (acción) feeding; (tienda) grocer's (shop).

alimentador nm: alimentador de papel sheet-feeder; **alimentar** vt to feed; (nutrir) to nourish; alimentarse vr to feed.

alimenticio, a [alimen'tiθjo, a] a food cpd; (nutritivo) nourishing, nutritious.

alimento [ali'mento] nm food; (nutrición) nourishment; ~s nmpl (JUR) alimony sg.

alineación [alinea'θjon] nf alignment; (DEPORTE) line-up.

alinear [aline'ar] vt to align; ~se vr (DEPORTE) to line up; ~se en to fall in with.

aliñar [ali'ɲar] vt (CULIN) to season; **aliño** nm (CULIN) dressing.

alisar [ali'sar] vt to smooth.

aliso [a'liso] nm alder.

alistarse [alis'tarse] vr to enlist; (inscribirse) to enrol.

aliviar [ali'βjar] vt (carga) to lighten; (persona) to relieve; (dolor) to relieve, alleviate.

alivio [a'liβjo] nm alleviation, relief.

aljibe [al'xiβe] nm cistern.

alma ['alma] nf soul; (persona) person; (TEC) core.

almacén [alma'θen] nm (depósito) warehouse, store; (MIL) magazine; (AM) shop; (grandes) almacenes nmpl department store sg; **almacenaje** nm storage; **almacenaje secundaria** (INFORM) backing storage.

almacenar [almaθe'nar] vt to store, put in storage; (proveerse) to stock up with; **almacenero** nm warehouseman; (AM) shopkeeper.

almanaque [alma'nake] nm almanac.

almeja [al'mexa] nf clam.

almendra [al'mendra] nf almond; **almendro** nm almond tree.

almiar [al'mjar] nm haystack.

almíbar [al'miβar] nm syrup.

almidón [almi'ðon] nm starch.

almidonar *vt* to starch.

almirantazgo [almiran'taθɣo] *nm* admiralty.

almirante [almi'rante] *nm* admiral.

almirez [almi'reθ] *nm* mortar.

almizcle [al'miθkle] *nm* musk.

almohada [almo'aða] *nf* pillow; *(funda)* pillowcase; **almohadilla** *nf* cushion; *(TEC)* pad; *(AM)* pincushion.

almohadón [almoa'ðon] *nm* large pillow; bolster.

almorranas [almo'rranas] *nfpl* piles, haemorrhoids.

almorzar [almor'θar] *vt*: ~ **una tortilla** to have an omelette for lunch // *vi* to (have) lunch.

almuerzo *etc vb ver* **almorzar** // [al'mwerθo] *nm* lunch.

alocado, a [alo'kaðo, a] *a* crazy.

alojamiento [aloxa'mjento] *nm* lodging(s) *(pl)*; *(viviendas)* housing.

alojar [alo'xar] *vt* to lodge; ~se *vr* to lodge, stay.

alondra [a'londra] *nf* lark, skylark.

alpargata [alpar'ɣata] *nf* rope-soled sandal, espadrille.

Alpes ['alpes] *nmpl*: **los** ~ the Alps.

alpinismo [alpi'nismo] *nm* mountaineering, climbing; **alpinista** *nm/f* mountaineer, climber.

alpiste [al'piste] *nm* birdseed.

alquería [alke'ria] *nf* farmhouse.

alquilar [alki'lar] *vt (suj: propietario: inmuebles)* to let, rent (out); *(: coche)* to hire out; *(: TV)* to rent (out); *(suj: alquilador: inmuebles, TV)* to rent; *(: coche)* to hire; '**se alquila casa**' 'house to let *(Brit)* o to rent' *(US)*.

alquiler [alki'ler] *nm* renting; letting; hiring; *(arriendo)* rent; hire charge; ~ **de automóviles** car hire; **de** ~ for hire.

alquimia [al'kimja] *nf* alchemy.

alquitrán [alki'tran] *nm* tar.

alrededor [alreðe'ðor] *ad* around, about; ~**es** *nmpl* surroundings; ~ **de** *prep* around, about; **mirar a su** ~ to look (round) about one.

alta ['alta] *nf ver* **alto**.

altanería [altane'ria] *nf* haughtiness, arrogance; **altanero, a** *a* arrogant, haughty.

altar [al'tar] *nm* altar.

altavoz [alta'βoθ] *nm* loudspeaker; *(amplificador)* amplifier.

alteración [altera'θjon] *nf* alteration; *(alboroto)* disturbance.

alterar [alte'rar] *vt* to alter; to disturb; ~**se** *vr (persona)* to get upset.

altercado [alter'kaðo] *nm* argument.

alternar [alter'nar] *vt* to alternate // *vi*, ~**se** *vr* to alternate; *(turnar)* to take turns; ~ **con** to mix with; **alternativo, a** *a* alternative; *(alterno)* alternating // *nf* alternative; *(elección)* choice; **alterno, a** *a* alternate; *(ELEC)* alternating.

Alteza [al'teθa] *nf (tratamiento)* Highness.

altibajos [alti'βaxos] *nmpl* ups and downs.

altiplanicie [altipla'niθje] *nf*, **altiplano** [alti'plano] *nm* high plateau.

altisonante [altiso'nante] *a* high-flown, high-sounding.

altitud [alti'tuð] *nf* height; *(AVIAT, GEO)* altitude.

altivez [alti'βeθ] *nf* haughtiness, arrogance; **altivo, a** *a* haughty, arrogant.

alto, a ['alto, a] *a (persona)* tall; *(sonido)* high, sharp; *(noble)* high, lofty // *nm* halt; *(MUS)* alto; *(GEO)* hill; *(AM)* pile // *ad (de sitio)* high; *(de sonido)* loud, loudly // *nf (certificate of) discharge* // *excl* halt!; **la pared tiene 2 metros de** ~ the wall is 2 metres high; **en alta mar** on the high seas; **en voz alta** in a loud voice; **las altas horas de la noche** the small *o* wee hours; **en lo** ~ **de** at the top of; **pasar por** ~ to overlook; **dar de alta** to discharge.

altoparlante [altopar'lante] *nm (AM)* loudspeaker.

altura [al'tura] *nf* height; *(NAUT)* depth; *(GEO)* latitude; **la pared**

tiene 1.80 de ~ the wall is 1 metre 80cm high; **a estas ~s** at this stage; **a esta ~ del año** at this time of the year.

alubia [a'luβja] *nf* French bean, kidney bean.

alucinación [aluθina'θjon] *nf* hallucination; **alucinar** *vi* to hallucinate // *vt* to deceive; (*fascinar*) to fascinate.

alud [a'luð] *nm* avalanche; (*fig*) flood.

aludir [alu'ðir] *vi*: ~ **a** to allude to; **darse por aludido** to take the hint.

alumbrado [alum'braðo] *nm* lighting; **alumbramiento** *nm* lighting; (*MED*) childbirth, delivery.

alumbrar [alum'brar] *vt* to light (up) // *vi* (*MED*) to give birth.

aluminio [alu'minjo] *nm* aluminium (*Brit*), aluminum (*US*).

alumno, a [a'lumno, a] *nm/f* pupil, student.

alunizar [aluni'θar] *vi* to land on the moon.

alusión [alu'sjon] *nf* allusion.

alusivo, a [alu'siβo, a] *a* allusive.

aluvión [alu'βjon] *nm* alluvium; (*fig*) flood.

alverja [al'βerxa] *nf* (*AM*) pea.

alza ['alθa] *nf* rise; (*MIL*) sight.

alzada [al'θaða] *nf* (*de caballos*) height; (*JUR*) appeal.

alzamiento [alθa'mjento] *nm* (*aumento*) rise, increase; (*acción*) lifting, raising; (*mejor postura*) higher bid; (*rebelión*) rising; (*COM*) fraudulent bankruptcy.

alzar [al'θar] *vt* to lift (up); (*precio, muro*) to raise; (*cuello de abrigo*) to turn up; (*AGR*) to gather in; (*IMPRENTA*) to gather; **~se** *vr* to get up, rise; (*rebelarse*) to revolt; (*COM*) to go fraudulently bankrupt; (*JUR*) to appeal.

allá [a'ʎa] *ad* (*lugar*) there; (*por ahí*) over there; (*tiempo*) then; **~ abajo** down there; **más ~** further on; **más ~ de** beyond; **¡~ tú!** that's your problem!

allanamiento [aʎana'mjento] *nm*: ~ **de morada** burglary.

allanar [aʎa'nar] *vt* to flatten, level (out); (*igualar*) to smooth (out); (*fig*) to subdue; (*JUR*) to burgle, break into; **~se** *vr* to fall down; **~se a** to submit to, accept.

allegado, a [aʎe'ɣaðo, a] *a* near, close // *nm/f* relation.

allí [a'ʎi] *ad* there; **~ mismo** right there; **por ~** over there; (*por ese camino*) that way.

ama ['ama] *nf* lady of the house; (*dueña*) owner; (*institutriz*) governess; (*madre adoptiva*) foster mother; **~ de casa** housewife; **~ de cría** o **de leche** wet-nurse; **~ de llaves** housekeeper.

amabilidad [amaβili'ðað] *nf* kindness; (*simpatía*) niceness; **amable** *a* kind; nice; **es Vd muy ~** that's very kind of you.

amaestrado, a [amaes'traðo, a] *a* (*animal: en circo etc*) performing.

amaestrar [amaes'trar] *vt* to train.

amagar [ama'ɣar] *vt, vi* to threaten; (*DEPORTE, MIL*) to feint; **amago** *nm* threat; (*gesto*) threatening gesture; (*MED*) symptom.

amalgama [amal'ɣama] *nf* amalgam; **amalgamar** *vt* to amalgamate; (*combinar*) to combine, mix.

amamantar [amaman'tar] *vt* to suckle, nurse.

amanecer [amane'θer] *vi* to dawn // *nm* dawn; **el niño amaneció afiebrado** the child woke up with a fever.

amanerado, a [amane'raðo, a] *a* affected.

amansar [aman'sar] *vt* to tame; (*persona*) to subdue; **~se** *vr* (*persona*) to calm down.

amante [a'mante] *a*: **~ de** fond of // *nm/f* lover.

amapola [ama'pola] *nf* poppy.

amar [a'mar] *vt* to love.

amarar [ama'rar] *vi* (*avión*) to land (on the sea).

amargado, a [amar'ɣaðo, a] *a*

bitter.

amargar [amar'xar] *vt* to make bitter; *(fig)* to embitter; **~se** *vr* to become embittered.

amargo, a [a'marvo, a] *a* bitter; **amargura** *nf* bitterness.

amarillento, a [amari'ʎento, a] *a* yellowish; *(tez)* sallow; **amarillo, a** *a, nm* yellow.

amarrar [ama'rrar] *vt* to moor; *(sujetar)* to tie up.

amarras [a'marras] *nfpl:* **soltar ~** to set sail.

amartillar [amarti'ʎar] *vt (fusil)* to cock.

amasar [ama'sar] *vt (masa)* to knead; *(mezclar)* to mix, prepare; *(confeccionar)* to concoct; **amasijo** *nm* kneading; mixing; *(fig)* hotchpotch.

amateur ['amatur] *nm/f* amateur.

amatista [ama'tista] *nf* amethyst.

amazona [ama'θona] *nf* horse-woman; **A~s** *nm*: **el A~s** the Amazon.

ambages [am'baxes] *nmpl*: **sin ~** in plain language.

ámbar ['ambar] *nm* amber.

ambición [ambi'θjon] *nf* ambition; **ambicionar** *vt* to aspire to; **ambicioso, a** *a* ambitious.

ambidextro, a [ambi'ðekstro, a] *a* ambidextrous.

ambientación [ambjenta'θjon] *nf* *(CINE, TEATRO etc)* setting; *(RADIO)* sound effects.

ambiente [am'bjente] *nm* *(tb fig)* atmosphere; *(medio)* environment.

ambigüedad [ambixwe'ðað] *nf* ambiguity; **ambigüo, a** *a* ambiguous.

ámbito ['ambito] *nm* *(campo)* field; *(fig)* scope.

ambos, as ['ambos, as] *apl, pron pl* both.

ambulancia [ambu'lanθja] *nf* ambulance.

ambulante [ambu'lante] *a* travelling *cpd*, itinerant.

ambulatorio [ambula'torjo] *nm*

state health-service clinic.

ameba [a'meβa] *nf* amoeba.

amedrentar [ameðren'tar] *vt* to scare.

amén [a'men] *excl* amen; **~ de** besides.

amenaza [ame'naθa] *nf* threat.

amenazar [amena'θar] *vt* to threaten // *vi*: **~ con hacer** to threaten to do.

amenguar [amen'xwar] *vt* to diminish; *(fig)* to dishonour.

amenidad [ameni'ðað] *nf* pleasantness.

ameno, a [a'meno, a] *a* pleasant.

América [a'merika] *nf* America; **~ del Norte/del Sur** North/South America; **~ Central/Latina** Central/Latin America; **americano, a** *a, nm/f* American // *nf* coat, jacket.

amerizar [ameri'θar] *vi (avión)* to land (on the sea).

ametralladora [ametraʎa'ðora] *nf* machine gun.

amianto [a'mjanto] *nm* asbestos.

amigable [ami'vaβle] *a* friendly.

amígdala [a'miɣðala] *nf* tonsil; **amigdalitis** *nf* tonsillitis.

amigo, a [a'mivo, a] *a* friendly // *nm/f* friend; *(amante)* lover; **ser ~ de algo** to be fond of sth; **ser muy ~s** to be close friends.

amilanar [amila'nar] *vt* to scare; **~se** *vr* to get scared.

aminorar [amino'rar] *vt* to diminish; *(reducir)* to reduce; **~ la marcha** to slow down.

amistad [amis'tað] *nf* friendship; **~es** *nfpl* friends; **amistoso, a** *a* friendly.

amnesia [am'nesja] *nf* amnesia.

amnistía [amnis'tia] *nf* amnesty.

amo ['amo] *nm* owner; *(jefe)* boss.

amodorrarse [amoðo'rrarse] *vr* to get sleepy.

amolar [amo'lar] *vt (perseguir)* to annoy.

amoldar [amol'dar] *vt* to mould; *(adaptar)* to adapt.

amonestación [amonesta'θjon] *nf* warning; **amonestaciones** *nfpl* marriage banns.

amonestar [amones'tar] *vt* to warn; (*REL*) to publish the banns of.

amontonar [amonto'nar] *vt* to collect, pile up; ~**se** *vr* to crowd together; (*acumularse*) to pile up.

amor [a'mor] *nm* love; (*amante*) lover; **hacer el** ~ to make love.

amoratado, a [amora'taðo, a] *a* purple.

amordazar [amorða'θar] *vt* to muzzle; (*fig*) to gag.

amorfo, a [a'morfo, a] *a* amorphous, shapeless.

amorío [amo'rio] *nm* (*fam*) love affair.

amoroso, a [amo'roso, a] *a* affectionate, loving.

amortajar [amorta'xar] *vt* to shroud.

amortiguador [amortiɣwa'ðor] *nm* shock absorber; (*parachoques*) bumper; ~**es** *nmpl* (*AUTO*) suspension *sg*.

amortiguar [amorti'ɣwar] *vt* to deaden; (*ruido*) to muffle; (*color*) to soften.

amortización [amortiθa'θjon] *nf* (*de deuda*) repayment; (*de bono*) redemption.

amotinar [amoti'nar] *vt* to stir up, incite (to riot); ~**se** *vr* to mutiny.

amparar [ampa'rar] *vt* to protect; ~**se** *vr* to seek protection; (*de la lluvia etc*) to shelter; **amparo** *nm* help, protection; **al** ~ **de** under the protection of.

amperio [am'perjo] *nm* ampère, amp.

ampliación [amplja'θjon] *nf* enlargement; (*extensión*) extension; **ampliar** *vt* to enlarge; to extend.

amplificación [amplifika'θjon] *nf* enlargement; **amplificador** *nm* amplifier.

amplificar [amplifi'kar] *vt* to amplify.

amplio, a [am

'ampljo, a] *a* spacious; (*de falda etc*) full; (*extenso*) extensive; (*ancho*) wide; **amplitud** *nf* spaciousness; extent; (*fig*)

amplitude.

ampolla [am'poʎa] *nf* blister; (*MED*) ampoule.

ampuloso, a [ampu'loso, a] *a* bombastic, pompous.

amputar [ampu'tar] *vt* to cut off, amputate.

amueblar [amwe'βlar] *vt* to furnish.

amurallar [amura'ʎar] *vt* to wall up o in.

anacronismo [anakro'nismo] *nm* anachronism.

ánade [' anaðe] *nm* duck.

anadear [anaðe'ar] *vi* to waddle.

anales [a'nales] *nmpl* annals.

analfabetismo [analfaβe'tismo] *nm* illiteracy; **analfabeto, a** *a, nm/f* illiterate.

analgésico [anal'xesiko] *nm* painkiller, analgesic.

análisis [a'nalisis] *nm inv* analysis.

analista [ana'lista] *nm/f* (*gen*) analyst.

analizar [anali'θar] *vt* to analyse.

analogía [analo'xia] *nf* analogy.

analógico, a [ana'loxiko, a] *a* (*INFORM*) analog; (*reloj*) analogue (*Brit*), analog (*US*).

análogo, a [a'naloɣo, a] *a* analogous, similar (*a* to).

ananá(s) [ana'na(s)] *nm* pineapple.

anaquel [ana'kel] *nm* shelf.

anarquía [anar'kia] *nf* anarchy; **anarquismo** *nm* anarchism; **anarquista** *nm/f* anarchist.

anatomía [anato'mia] *nf* anatomy.

anca [' anka] *nf* rump, haunch; ~**s** *nfpl* (*fam*) behind *sg*.

anciano, a [an'θjano, a] *a* old, aged // *nm* old man/woman // *nm/f* elder.

ancla [' ankla] *nf* anchor; ~**dero** *nm* anchorage; **anclar** *vi* to (drop) anchor.

ancho, a [' antʃo, a] *a* wide; (*falda*) full; (*fig*) liberal // *nm* width; (*FERRO*) gauge; **ponerse** ~ to get conceited; **estar a sus anchas** to be at one's ease.

anchoa [an'tʃoa] *nf* anchovy.

anchura [an'tʃura] *nf* width; (*exten-*

sión) wideness.

andaderas [anda'ðeras] *nfpl* baby walker *sg*.

andadura [anda'ðura] *nf* gait; (*de caballo*) pace.

Andalucía [andalu'θia] *nf* Andalusia; **andaluz, a** *a, nm/f* Andalusian.

andamio [an'damjo], **andamiaje** [anda'mjaxe] *nm* scaffold(ing).

andar [an'dar] *vt* to go, cover, travel // *vi* to go, walk, travel; (*funcionar*) to go, work; (*estar*) to be // *nm* walk, gait, pace; ~se *vr* to go away; ~ a pie/a caballo/en bicicleta to go on foot/on horseback/by bicycle; ~ haciendo algo to be doing sth; ¡anda!, (*sorpresa*) go on!; anda por o en los 40 he's about 40.

andariego, a [anda'rjeɣo, a] *a* (*itinerante*) wandering.

andén [an'den] *nm* (*FERRO*) platform; (*NAUT*) quayside; (*AM: de la calle*) pavement (*Brit*), sidewalk (*US*).

Andes ['andes] *nmpl*: los ~ the Andes.

Andorra [an'dorra] *nf* Andorra.

andrajo [an'draxo] *nm* rag; ~so, a *a* ragged.

andurriales [andu'rrjales] *nmpl* wilds *npl*.

anduve, anduviera *etc vb ver* **andar**.

anécdota [a'nekðota] *nf* anecdote, story.

anegar [ane'ɣar] *vt* to flood; (*ahogar*) to drown; ~se *vr* to drown; (*hundirse*) to sink.

anejo, a [a'nexo, a] *a, nm* = anexo.

anemia [a'nemja] *nf* anaemia.

anestésico [anes'tesiko] *nm* anaesthetic.

anexar [anek'sar] *vt* to annex; (*documento*) to attach; **anexión** *nf*, **anexionamiento** *nm* annexation; **anexo, a** *a* attached // *nm* annexe.

anfibio, a [an'fiβjo, a] *a* amphibious // *nm* amphibian.

anfiteatro [anfite'atro] *nm* amphitheatre; (*TEATRO*) dress

circle.

anfitrión, ona [anfi'trjon, ona] *nm/f* host(ess).

ángel ['anxel] *nm* angel; ~ de la guarda guardian angel; tener ~ to be charming; **angélico, a, angelical** *a* angelic(al).

angina [an'xina] *nf* (*MED*) inflammation of the throat; ~ de pecho angina; tener ~s to have tonsillitis.

anglicano, a [angli'kano, a] *a, nm/f* Anglican.

angosto, a [an'gosto, a] *a* narrow.

anguila [an'gila] *nf* eel; ~s *nfpl* (*NAUT*) slipway *sg*.

angula [an'gula] *nf* elver, baby eel.

ángulo ['angulo] *nm* angle; (*esquina*) corner; (*curva*) bend.

angustia [an'gustja] *nf* anguish; **angustiar** *vt* to distress, grieve.

anhelante [ane'lante] *a* eager; (*deseoso*) longing.

anhelar [ane'lar] *vt* to be eager for; to long for, desire // *vi* to pant, gasp; **anhelo** *nm* eagerness; desire.

anidar [ani'ðar] *vi* to nest.

anillo [a'niʎo] *nm* ring; ~ de boda wedding ring.

ánima ['anima] *nf* soul; las ~s the Angelus (bell) *sg*.

animación [anima'θjon] *nf* liveliness; (*vitalidad*) life; (*actividad*) activity; bustle.

animado, a [ani'maðo, a] *a* lively; (*vivaz*) animated; **animador, a** *nm/f* (*TV*) host(ess), compère; (*DEPORTE*) cheerleader.

animadversión [animaðßer'sjon] *nf* ill-will, antagonism.

animal [ani'mal] *a* animal; (*fig*) stupid // *nm* animal; (*fig*) fool; (*bestia*) brute.

animar [ani'mar] *vt* (*BIO*) to animate, give life to; (*fig*) to liven up, brighten up, cheer up; (*estimular*) to stimulate; ~se *vr* to cheer up; to feel encouraged; (*decidirse*) to make up one's mind.

ánimo ['animo] *nm* (*alma*) soul; (*mente*) mind; (*valentía*) courage //

excl cheer up!

animoso, a [ani'moso, a] *a* brave; (*vivo*) lively.

aniquilar [aniki'lar] *vt* to annihilate, destroy.

anís [a'nis] *nm* aniseed; (*licor*) anisette.

aniversario [aniβer'sarjo] *nm* anniversary.

anoche [a'notʃe] *ad* last night; **antes de ~** the night before last.

anochecer [anotʃe'θer] *vi* to get dark // *nm* nightfall, dark; **al ~** at nightfall.

anodino, a [ano'ðino, a] *a* dull, anodyne.

anomalía [anoma'lia] *nf* anomaly.

anonimato [anoni'mato] *nm* anonymity.

anónimo, a [a'nonimo, a] *a* anonymous; (*COM*) limited // *nm* (*carta*) anonymous letter; (: *maliciosa*) poison-pen letter.

anormal [anor'mal] *a* abnormal.

anotación [anota'θjon] *nf* note; annotation.

anotar [ano'tar] *vt* to note down; (*comentar*) to annotate.

anquilosamiento [ankilosa'mjento] *nm* (*fig*) paralysis; stagnation.

ansia ['ansja] *nf* anxiety; (*añoranza*) yearning; **ansiar** *vt* to long for.

ansiedad [ansje'ðað] *nf* anxiety.

ansioso, a [an'sjoso, a] *a* anxious; (*anhelante*) eager; **~ de** *o* **por algo** greedy for sth.

antagónico, a [anta'ɣoniko, a] *a* antagonistic; (*opuesto*) contrasting; **antagonista** *nm/f* antagonist.

antaño [an'taɲo] *ad* long ago, formerly.

Antártico [an'tartiko] *nm*: **el ~** the Antarctic.

ante ['ante] *prep* before, in the presence of; (*encarado con*) faced with // *nm* (*piel*) suede; **~ todo** above all.

anteanoche [antea'notʃe] *ad* the night before last.

anteayer [antea'jer] *ad* the day before yesterday.

antebrazo [ante'βraðo] *nm* forearm.

antecedente [anteθe'ðente] *a* previous // *nm* antecedent; **~s** *nmpl* record *sg*; background *sg*.

anteceder [anteθe'ðer] *vt* to precede, go before.

antecesor, a [anteθe'sor, a] *nm/f* predecessor.

antedicho, a [ante'ðitʃo, a] *a* aforementioned.

antelación [antela'θjon] *nf*: **con ~** in advance.

antemano [ante'mano]: **de ~** *ad* beforehand, in advance.

antena [an'tena] *nf* antenna; (*de televisión etc*) aerial.

anteojo [ante'oxo] *nm* eyeglass; **~s** *nmpl* (*AM*) glasses, spectacles.

antepasados [antepa'saðos] *nmpl* ancestors.

antepecho [ante'petʃo] *nm* guardrail, parapet; (*repisa*) ledge, sill.

anteponer [antepo'ner] *vt* to place in front; (*fig*) to prefer.

anteproyecto [antepro'jekto] *nm* preliminary sketch; (*fig*) blueprint.

anterior [ante'rjor] *a* preceding, previous; **~idad** *nf*: **con ~idad a** prior to, before.

antes ['antes] *ad* (*con prioridad*) before // *prep*: **~ de** before // *conj*: **~ de ir/de que te vayas before going/before you go; ~ bien** (but) rather; **dos días ~** two days before *o* previously; **no quiso venir ~** she didn't want to come any earlier; **tomo el avión ~ que el barco** I take the plane rather than the boat; **~ que yo** before me; **lo ~ posible** as soon as possible; **cuanto ~ mejor** the sooner the better.

antesala [ante'sala] *nf* anteroom.

antiaéreo, a [antia'ereo, a] *a* anti-aircraft.

antibalas [anti'βalas] *a inv*: **chaleco ~** bullet-proof jacket.

antibiótico [anti'βjotiko] *nm* antibiotic.

anticiclón [antiθi'klon] *nm* anti-

anticyclone.

anticipación [antiθipa'θjon] *nf* anticipation; **con 10 minutos de** ~ 10 minutes early.

anticipado, a [antiθi'paðo, a] *a* (in) advance.

anticipar [antiθi'par] *vt* to anticipate; (*adelantar*) to bring forward; (*COM*) to advance; ~**se** *vr*: ~**se a su época** to be ahead of one's time.

anticipo [anti'θipo] *nm* (*COM*) advance.

anticonceptivo, a [antikonθep'tiβo, a] *a, nm* contraceptive.

anticongelante [antikonxe'lante] *nm* antifreeze.

anticuado, a [anti'kwaðo, a] *a* out-of-date, old-fashioned; (*desusado*) obsolete.

anticuario [anti'kwarjo] *nm* antique dealer.

anticuerpo [anti'kwerpo] *nm* (*MED*) antibody.

antídoto [an'tiðoto] *nm* antidote.

antiestético, a [anties'tetiko, a] *a* unsightly.

antifaz [anti'faθ] *nm* mask; (*velo*) veil.

antigualla [anti'ɣwaʎa] *nf* antique; (*reliquia*) relic.

antiguamente [antiɣwa'mente] *ad* formerly; (*hace mucho tiempo*) long ago.

antigüedad [antiɣwe'ðað] *nf* antiquity; (*artículo*) antique; (*rango*) seniority.

antiguo, a [an'tiɣwo, a] *a* old, ancient; (*que fue*) former.

antílope [an'tilope] *nm* antelope.

antillano, a [anti'ʎano, a] *a, nm/f* West Indian.

Antillas [an'tiʎas] *nfpl:* **las** ~ **the** West Indies.

antinatural [antinatu'ral] *a* unnatural.

antipatía [antipa'tia] *nf* antipathy, dislike; **antipático, a** *a* disagreeable, unpleasant.

antirrobo [anti'rroβo] *a inv* (*alarma etc*) anti-theft.

antisemita [antise'mita] *a* anti-Semitic // *nm/f* anti-Semite.

antiséptico, a [anti'septiko, a] *a* antiseptic // *nm* antiseptic.

antítesis [an'titesis] *nf inv* antithesis.

antojadizo, a [antoxa'ðiθo, a] *a* capricious.

antojarse [anto'xarse] *vr* (*desear*): **se me antoja comprarlo** I have a mind to buy it; (*pensar*): **se me antoja que** I have a feeling that.

antojo [an'toxo] *nm* caprice, whim; (*rosa*) birthmark; (*lunar*) mole.

antología [antolo'xia] *nf* anthology.

antorcha [an'tortʃa] *nf* torch.

antro [antro] *nm* cavern.

antropófago, a [antro'pofaɣo, a] *a, nm/f* cannibal.

antropología [antropolo'xia] *nf* anthropology.

anual [a'nwal] *a* annual; ~**idad** [anwali'ðað] *nf* annuity.

anuario [a'nwarjo] *nm* yearbook.

anudar [anu'ðar] *vt* to knot, tie; (*unir*) to join; ~**se** *vr* to get tied up.

anulación [anula'θjon] *nf* annulment; (*cancelación*) cancellation.

anular [anu'lar] *vt* (*contrato*) to annul, cancel; (*ley*) to revoke, repeal; (*suscripción*) to cancel // *nm* ring finger.

anunciación [anunθja'θjon] *nf* announcement; A~ (*REL*) Annunciation.

anunciante [anun'θjante] *nm/f* (*COM*) advertiser.

anunciar [anun'θjar] *vt* to announce; (*proclamar*) to proclaim; (*COM*) to advertise.

anuncio [a'nunθjo] *nm* announcement; (*señal*) sign; (*COM*) advertisement; (*cartel*) poster.

anzuelo [an'θwelo] *nm* hook; (*para pescar*) fish hook.

añadidura [aɲaði'ðura] *nf* addition, extra; **por** ~ besides, in addition.

añadir [aɲa'ðir] *vt* to add.

añejo, a [a'ɲexo, a] *a* old; (*vino*) mellow.

añicos [a'ɲikos] *nmpl:* **hacer** ~

smash, shatter.

añil [a'nil] *nm* (*BOT, color*) indigo.

año ['aɲo] *nm* year; **¡Feliz A-** **Nuevo!** Happy New Year!; **tener** 15 **~s** to be 15 (years old); **los ~s** 80 the eighties; **~s** *bisiesto/escolar* leap/school year; **el ~ que viene** next year.

añoranza [aɲo'ranθa] *nf* nostalgia; (*anhelo*) longing.

apabullar [apaβu'ʎar] *vt* (*tb fig*) to crush, squash.

apacentar [apaθen'tar] *vt* to pasture, graze.

apacible [apa'θiβle] *a* gentle, mild.

apaciguar [apaθi'xwar] *vt* to pacify, calm (down).

apadrinar [apaðri'nar] *vt* to sponsor, support; (*REL*) to be godfather to.

apagado, a [apa'xaðo, a] *a* (*volcán*) extinct; (*color*) dull; (*voz*) quiet; (*sonido*) muted, muffled; (*persona: apático*) listless; **estar ~** (*fuego, luz*) to be out; (*RADIO, TV etc*) to be off.

apagar [apa'xar] *vt* to put out; (*ELEC, RADIO, TV*) to turn off; (*sonido*) to silence, muffle; (*sed*) to quench.

apagón [apa'xon] *nm* blackout, power cut.

apalabrar [apala'βrar] *vt* to agree to; (*contratar*) to engage.

apalear [apale'ar] *vt* to beat, thrash; (*AGR*) to winnow.

apañar [apa'ɲar] *vt* to pick up; (*asir*) to take hold of, grasp; (*reparar*) to mend, patch up; **~se** *vr* to manage, get along.

aparador [apara'ðor] *nm* sideboard; (*escaparate*) shop window.

aparato [apa'rato] *nm* apparatus; (*máquina*) machine; (*doméstico*) appliance; (*boato*) ostentation; **~ de facsímil** facsimile (machine), fax; **~so, a** *a* showy, ostentatious.

aparcamiento [aparka'mjento] *nm* car park (*Brit*), parking lot (*US*).

aparcar [apar'kar] *vt, vi* to park.

aparear [apare'ar] *vt* (*objetos*) to

pair, match; (*animales*) to mate; **~se** *vr* to make a pair; to mate.

aparecer [apare'θer] *vi*, **aparecerse** *vr* to appear.

aparejado, a [apare'xaðo, a] *a* fit, suitable; **llevar** *o* **traer ~** to involve.

aparejo [apa'rexo] *nm* preparation; harness; rigging; (*de poleas*) block and tackle.

aparentar [aparen'tar] *vt* (*edad*) to look; (*fingir*): **~ tristeza** to pretend to be sad.

aparente [apa'rente] *a* apparent; (*adecuado*) suitable.

aparezco *etc vb ver* **aparecer**.

aparición [apari'θjon] *nf* appearance; (*de libro*) publication; (*espectro*) apparition.

apariencia [apa'rjenθja] *nf* (*outward*) appearance; **en ~** outwardly, seemingly.

apartado, a [apar'taðo, a] *a* separate; (*lejano*) remote // *nm* (*tipográfico*) paragraph; **~ (de correos)** post office box.

apartamento [aparta'mento] *nm* apartment, flat (*Brit*).

apartamiento [aparta'mjento] *nm* separation; (*aislamiento*) remoteness, isolation; (*AM*) apartment, flat (*Brit*).

apartar [apar'tar] *vt* to separate; (*quitar*) to remove; (*MINE-ROLOGÍA*) to extract; **~se** *vr* to separate, part; (*irse*) to move away; to keep away.

aparte [a'parte] *ad* (*separadamente*) separately; (*además*) besides // *nm* aside; (*tipográfico*) new paragraph.

apasionado, a [apasjo'naðo, a] *a* passionate; biassed, prejudiced.

apasionar [apasjo'nar] *vt* to excite; **le apasiona el fútbol** she's crazy about football; **~se** *vr* to get excited.

apatía [apa'tia] *nf* apathy.

apático, a [a'patiko, a] *a* apathetic.

apátrida [a'patriða] *a* stateless.

Apdo *abr* (= *Apartado de Correos*) PO Box.

apeadero [apea'ðero] nm halt, stop, stopping place.

apearse [ape'arse] vr (jinete) to dismount; (bajarse) to get down o out; (AUTO, FERRO) to get off o out.

apechugar [apetʃu'xar] vr: ~ con algo to face up to sth.

apedrear [apeðre'ar] vt to stone.

apegarse [ape'xarse] vr: ~se a to become attached to; **apego** nm attachment, devotion.

apelación [apela'θjon] nf appeal.

apelar [ape'lar] vi to appeal; ~ a (fig) to resort to.

apellidar [apeʎi'ðar] vt to call, name; ~se vr: se **apellida** Pérez her (sur)name's Pérez.

apellido [ape'ʎiðo] nm surname.

apenar [ape'nar] vt to grieve, trouble; (AM: avergonzar) to embarrass; ~se vr to grieve; (AM) to be embarrassed.

apenas [a'penas] ad scarcely, hardly // conj as soon as, no sooner.

apéndice [a'pendiθe] nm appendix; **apendicitis** nf appendicitis.

apercibirse [aperθi'βirse] vr: ~ de to notice.

aperitivo [aperi'tiβo] nm (bebida) aperitif; (comida) appetizer.

apero [a'pero] nm (AGR) implement; ~s nmpl farm equipment sg.

apertura [aper'tura] nf opening; (POL) liberalization.

apesadumbrar [apesaðum'brar] vt to grieve, sadden; ~se vr to distress o.s.

apestar [apes'tar] vt to infect // vi: ~ (a) to stink (of).

apetecer [apete'θer] vt: ¿te apetece una tortilla? do you fancy an omelette?; **apetecible** a desirable; (comida) appetizing.

apetito [ape'tito] nm appetite; ~so, a a appetizing; (fig) tempting.

apiadarse [apja'ðarse] vr: ~ de to take pity on.

ápice ['apiθe] nm apex; (fig) whit, iota.

apilar [api'lar] vt to pile o heap up;

~se vr to pile up.

apiñarse [api'narse] vr to crowd o press together.

apio ['apjo] nm celery.

apisonadora [apisona'ðora] nf (máquina) steamroller.

aplacar [apla'kar] vt to placate; ~se vr to calm down.

aplanar [apla'nar] vt to smooth, level; (allanar) to roll flat, flatten.

aplastar [aplas'tar] vt to squash (flat); (fig) to crush.

aplatanarse [aplata'narse] vr to get lethargic.

aplaudir [aplau'ðir] vt to applaud.

aplauso [a'plauso] nm applause; (fig) approval, acclaim.

aplazamiento [aplaθa'mjento] nm postponement.

aplazar [apla'θar] vt to postpone, defer.

aplicación [aplika'θjon] nf application; (esfuerzo) effort.

aplicado, a [apli'kaðo, a] a diligent, hard-working.

aplicar [apli'kar] vt (ejecutar) to apply; ~se vr to apply o.s.

aplique etc vb ver **aplicar** // [a'plike] nm wall light.

aplomo [a'plomo] nm aplomb, self-assurance.

apocado, a [apo'kaðo, a] a timid.

apocamiento [apoka'mjento] nm timidity; (depresión) depression.

apocarse [apo'karse] vr to feel small o humiliated.

apodar [apo'ðar] vt to nickname.

apoderado [apoðe'raðo] nm agent, representative.

apoderar [apoðe'rar] vt to authorize, empower; (JUR) to grant (a) power of attorney to; ~se vr: ~se de to take possession of.

apodo [a'poðo] nm nickname.

apogeo [apo'xeo] nm peak, summit.

apolillarse [apoli'ʎarse] vr to get moth-eaten.

apología [apolo'xia] nf eulogy; (defensa) defence.

apoltronarse [apoltro'narse] vr

get lazy.

apoplejía [apople'xia] *nf* apoplexy, stroke.

apoquinar [apoki'nar] *vt* (*fam*) to fork out, cough up.

aporrear [aporre'ar] *vt* to beat (up).

aportar [apor'tar] *vt* to contribute // *vi* to reach port; ~**se** *vr* (*AM*) to arrive, come.

aposentar [aposen'tar] *vt* to lodge, put up; **aposento** *nm* lodging; (*habitación*) room.

apósito [a'posito] *nm* (*MED*) dressing.

apostar [apos'tar] *vt* to bet, stake; (*tropas etc*) to station, post // *vi* to bet.

apostilla [apos'tiʎa] *nf* note, comment.

apóstol [a'postol] *nm* apostle.

apóstrofo [a'postrofo] *nm* apostrophe.

apostura [apos'tura] *nf* neatness; (*elegancia*) elegance.

apoyar [apo'jar] *vt* to lean, rest; (*fig*) to support, back; ~**se** *vr*: ~**se en** to lean on; **apoyo** *nm* (*gen*) support; backing, help.

apreciable [apre'θjaβle] *a* considerable; (*fig*) esteemed.

apreciación [apreθja'θjon] *nf* appreciation; (*COM*) valuation.

apreciar [apre'θjar] *vt* to evaluate, assess; (*COM*) to appreciate, value.

aprecio [a'preθjo] *nm* valuation, estimate; (*fig*) appreciation.

aprehender [apreen'der] *vt* to apprehend, detain; **aprehensión** *nf* detention, capture.

apremiante [apre'mjante] *a* urgent, pressing.

apremiar [apre'mjar] *vt* to compel, force // *vi* to be urgent, press; **apremio** *nm* urgency.

aprender [apren'der] *vt, vi* to learn.

aprendiz, a [apren'diθ, a] *nm/f* apprentice; (*principiante*) learner; ~**aje** *nm* apprenticeship.

aprensión [apren'sjon] *nm* apprehension, fear; **aprensivo, a** *a*

apprehensive.

apresar [apre'sar] *vt* to seize; (*capturar*) to capture.

aprestar [apres'tar] *vt* to prepare, get ready; (*TEC*) to prime, size; ~**se** *vr* to get ready.

apresurado, a [apresu'raðo, a] *a* hurried, hasty; **apresuramiento** *nm* hurry, haste.

apresurar [apresu'rar] *vt* to hurry, accelerate; ~**se** *vr* to hurry, make haste.

apretado, a [apre'taðo, a] *a* tight; (*escritura*) cramped.

apretar [apre'tar] *vt* to squeeze; (*TEC*) to tighten; (*presionar*) to press together, pack // *vi* to be too tight.

apretón [apre'ton] *nm* squeeze; ~ **de manos** handshake.

aprieto [a'prjeto] *nm* squeeze; (*dificultad*) difficulty, jam; **estar en un** ~ to be in a fix.

aprisa [a'prisa] *ad* quickly, hurriedly.

aprisionar [aprisjo'nar] *vt* to imprison.

aprobación [aproβa'θjon] *nf* approval.

aprobar [apro'βar] *vt* to approve (of); (*examen, materia*) to pass // *vi* to pass.

apropiación [apropja'θjon] *nf* appropriation.

apropiado, a [apro'pjaðo, a] *a* appropriate.

apropiarse [apro'pjarse] *vr*: ~ **de** to appropriate.

aprovechado, a [aproβe'tʃaðo, a] *a* industrious, hardworking; (*económico*) thrifty; (*pey*) unscrupulous; **aprovechamiento** *nm* use; exploitation.

aprovechar [aproβe'tʃar] *vt* to use; (*explotar*) to exploit; (*experiencia*) to profit from; (*oferta, oportunidad*) to take advantage of // *vi* to progress, improve; ~**se** *vr*: ~**se de** to make use of; to take advantage of; **¡que aproveche!** enjoy your meal!

aproximación [aproksima'θjon] *nf*

approximation; (de lotería) consolation prize; **aproximado, a** a approximate.

aproximar [aproksi'mar] vt to bring nearer; ~**se** vr to come near, approach.

apruebo etc vb ver **aprobar**.

aptitud [apti'tuð] nf aptitude.

apto, a ['apto, a] a suitable.

apuesto, a [a'pwesto, a] a neat, elegant // nf bet, wager.

apuntador [apunta'ðor] nm prompter.

apuntalar [apunta'lar] vt to prop up.

apuntar [apun'tar] vt (con arma) to aim at; (con dedo) to point at o to; (anotar) to note (down); (TEATRO) to prompt; ~**se** vr (DEPORTE: tanto, victoria) to score; (ESCOL) to enrol.

apunte [a'punte] nm note.

apuñalar [apuɲa'lar] vt to stab.

apurado, a [apu'raðo, a] a needy; (difícil) difficult; (peligroso) dangerous; (AM) hurried, rushed.

apurar [apu'rar] vt (agotar) to drain; (recursos) to use up; (molestar) to annoy; ~**se** vr (preocuparse) to worry; (darse prisa) to hurry.

apuro [a'puro] nm (aprieto) fix, jam; (escasez) want, hardship; (vergüenza) embarrassment; (AM) haste, urgency.

aquejado, a [ake'xaðo, a] a: ~ de (MED) afflicted by.

aquel, aquella, aquellos, as [a'kel, a'keʎa, a'keʎos, as] a that; (pl) those.

aquél, aquélla, aquéllos, as [a'kel, a'keʎa, a'keʎos, as] pron that (one); (pl) those (ones).

aquello [a'keʎo] pron that, that business.

aquí [a'ki] ad (lugar) here; (tiempo) now; ~ **arriba** up here; ~ **mismo** right here; ~ **yace** here lies; **de** ~ a **ocho días** a week from now.

aquietar [akje'tar] vt to quieten (down), calm (down).

ara ['ara] nf: **en** ~**s de** for the sake of.

árabe ['araβe] a, nm/f Arab // nm (LING) Arabic.

Arabia [a'raβja] nf: ~ **Saudí** o **Saudita** Saudi Arabia.

arado [a'raðo] nm plough.

Aragón [ara'γon] nm Aragon; **aragonés, esa** a, nm/f Aragonese.

arancel [aran'θel] nm tariff, duty; ~ **de aduanas** customs duty.

arandela [aran'dela] nf (TEC) washer.

araña [a'raɲa] nf (ZOOL) spider; (lámpara) chandelier.

arañar [ara'ɲar] vt to scratch.

arañazo [ara'ɲaθo] nm scratch.

arar [a'rar] vt to plough, till.

arbitraje [arβi'traxe] nm arbitration.

arbitrar [arβi'trar] vt to arbitrate in; (DEPORTE) to referee // vi to arbitrate.

arbitrariedad [arβitrarje'ðað] nf arbitrariness; (acto) arbitrary act; **arbitrario, a** a arbitrary.

arbitrio [ar'βitrjo] nm free will; (JUR) adjudication, decision.

árbitro ['arβitro] nm arbitrator; (DEPORTE) referee; (TENIS) umpire.

árbol ['arβol] nm (BOT) tree; (NAUT) mast; (TEC) axle, shaft; **arbolado, a** a wooded; (camino etc) tree-lined // nm woodland.

arboladura [arβola'ðura] nf rigging.

arbolar [arβo'lar] vt to hoist, raise.

arboleda [arβo'leða] nf grove, plantation.

arbusto [ar'βusto] nm bush, shrub.

arca ['arka] nf chest, box.

arcada [ar'kaða] nf arcade; (de puente) arch, span; ~**s** nfpl retching sg.

arcaico, a [ar'kaiko, a] a archaic.

arce [ar'θe] nm maple tree.

arcén [ar'θen] nm (de autopista) hard shoulder; (de carretera) verge.

arcilla [ar'θiʎa] nf clay.

arco ['arko] nm arch; (MAT) arc; (MIL, MUS) bow; ~ **iris** rainbow.

archipiélago [artʃi'pjelavo] nm

archipelago.

archivador [artʃiβaˈðor] nm filing cabinet.

archivar [artʃiˈβar] vt to file (away);
archivo nm file, archive(s) (pl).

arder [arˈðer] vi to burn; **estar que arde** (persona) to fume.

ardid [arˈðið] nm ploy, trick.

ardiente [arˈðjente] a burning, ardent.

ardilla [arˈðiʎa] nf squirrel.

ardor [arˈðor] nm (calor) heat; (fig) ardour; ~ **de estómago** heartburn.

arduo, a [ˈarðwo, a] a arduous.

área [ˈarea] nf area; (DEPORTE) penalty area.

arena [aˈrena] nf sand; (de una lucha) arena.

arenal [areˈnal] nm (arena movediza) quicksand.

arengar [arenˈgar] vt to harangue.

arenisca [areˈniska] nf sandstone; (cascajo) grit.

arenoso, a [areˈnoso, a] a sandy.

arenque [aˈrenke] nm herring.

arete [aˈrete] nm earring.

argamasa [arɣaˈmasa] nf mortar, plaster.

Argel [arˈxel] nm Algiers; ~**ia** nf Algeria; **argelino, a** a, nmf Algerian.

Argentina [arxenˈtina] nf: (la) A~ Argentina.

argentino, a [arxenˈtino, a] a Argentinian; (de plata) silvery // nmf Argentinian.

argolla [arˈɣoʎa] nf (large) ring.

argot [arˈɣo] (pl ~s) nm slang.

argucia [arˈɣuθja] nf subtlety, sophistry.

argüir [arˈɣwir] vt to deduce; (discutir) to argue; (indicar) to indicate, imply; (censurar) to reproach // vi to argue.

argumentación [arɣumentaˈθjon] nf (line of) argument.

argumentar [arɣumenˈtar] vt, vi to argue.

argumento [arɣuˈmento] nm argument; (razonamiento) reasoning; (de novela etc) plot; (CINE, TV) storyline.

aria [ˈarja] nf aria.

aridez [ariˈðeθ] nf aridity, dryness.

árido, a [ˈariðo, a] a arid, dry; ~**s** nmpl dry goods.

Aries [ˈarjes] nm Aries.

ariete [aˈrjete] nm battering ram.

ario, a [ˈarjo, a] a Aryan.

arisco, a [aˈrisko, a] a surly; (insociable) unsociable.

aristócrata [arisˈtokrata] nmf aristocrat.

aritmética [aritˈmetika] nf arithmetic.

arma [ˈarma] nf arm; ~**s** nfpl arms; ~ **blanca** blade, knife; (espada) sword; ~ **de fuego** firearm; ~**s cortas** small arms.

armadillo [armaˈðiʎo] nm armadillo.

armado, a [arˈmaðo, a] a armed; (TEC) reinforced // nf armada; (flota) fleet.

armadura [armaˈðura] nf (MIL) armour; (TEC) framework; (ZOOL) skeleton; (FÍSICA) armature.

armamento [armaˈmento] nm armament; (NAUT) fitting-out.

armar [arˈmar] vt (soldado) to arm; (máquina) to assemble; (navio) to fit out; ~**la, ~ un lío** to start a row, kick up a fuss.

armario [arˈmarjo] nm wardrobe.

armatoste [armaˈtoste] nm (mueble) monstrosity; (máquina) contraption.

armazón [armaˈθon] nf o m body, chassis; (de mueble etc) frame; (ARQ) skeleton.

armería [armeˈria] nf (museo) military museum; (tienda) gunsmith's.

armiño [arˈmiɲo] nm stoat; (piel) ermine.

armisticio [armisˈtiθjo] nm armistice.

armonía [armoˈnia] nf harmony.

armónica [arˈmonika] nf harmonica.

armonioso, a [armoˈnjoso, a] a harmonious.

armonizar [armoniˈθar] vt to

harmonize; (*diferencias*) to reconcile // *vi*: ~ **con** (*fig*) to be in keeping with; (*colores*) to tone in with, blend.

arnés [ar'nes] *nm* armour; **arneses** *nmpl* harness *sg*.

aro ['aro] *nm* ring; (*tejo*) quoit; (*AM*: *pendiente*) earring.

aroma [a'roma] *nm* aroma, scent.

aromático, a [aro'matiko, a] *a* aromatic.

arpa ['arpa] *nf* harp.

arpía [ar'pia] *nf* shrew.

arpillera [arpi'ʎera] *nf* sacking, sackcloth.

arpón [ar'pon] *nm* harpoon.

arquear [arke'ar] *vt* to arch, bend; ~**se** *vr* to arch, bend; **arqueo** *nm* (*gen*) arching; (*NAUT*) tonnage.

arqueología [arkeolo'xia] *nf* archaeology; **arqueólogo, a** *nm/f* archaeologist.

arquero [ar'kero] *nm* archer, bowman.

arquetipo [arke'tipo] *nm* archetype.

arquitecto [arki'tekto] *nm* architect; **arquitectura** *nf* architecture.

arrabal [arra'βal] *nm* suburb; (*AM*) slum; ~**es** *nmpl* outskirts.

arraigado, a [arrai'ɣaðo, a] *a* deep-rooted; (*fig*) established.

arraigar [arrai'ɣar] *vt* to establish // *vi*, ~**se** *vr* to take root; (*persona*) to settle.

arrancar [arran'kar] *vt* (*sacar*) to extract, pull out; (*arrebatar*) to snatch (away); (*INFORM*) to boot; (*fig*) to extract // *vi* (*AUTO*, *máquina*) to start; (*ponerse en marcha*) to get going; ~ **de** to stem from.

arranque *etc vb ver* **arrancar** // [a'rranke] *nm* sudden start; (*AUTO*) start; (*fig*) fit, outburst.

arras ['arras] *nfpl* pledge *sg*, security *sg*.

arrasar [arra'sar] *vt* (*aplanar*) to level, flatten; (*destruir*) to demolish.

arrastrado, a [arras'traðo, a] *a* poor, wretched; (*AM*) servile.

arrastrar [arras'trar] *vt* to drag (along); (*fig*) to drag down, degrade; (*suj: agua, viento*) to carry away // *vi* to drag, trail on the ground; ~**se** *vr* to crawl; (*fig*) to grovel; **llevar algo arrastrado** to drag sth along.

arrastre [a'rrastre] *nm* drag, dragging.

arrayán [arra'jan] *nm* myrtle.

arre ['arre] *excl* gee up!

arrear [arre'ar] *vt* to drive on, urge on // *vi* to hurry along.

arrebatado, a [arreβa'taðo, a] *a* rash, impetuous; (*repentino*) sudden, hasty.

arrebatar [arreβa'tar] *vt* to snatch (away), seize; (*fig*) to captivate; ~**se** *vr* to get carried away, get excited.

arrebato [arre'βato] *nm* fit of rage, fury; (*éxtasis*) rapture.

arreglado, a [arre'ɣlaðo, a] *a* (*ordenado*) neat, orderly; (*moderado*) moderate, reasonable.

arreglar [arre'ɣlar] *vt* (*poner orden*) to tidy up; (*algo roto*) to fix, repair; (*problema*) to solve; ~**se** *vr* to reach an understanding; **arreglárselas** (*fam*) to get by, manage.

arreglo [a'rreɣlo] *nm* settlement; (*orden*) order; (*acuerdo*) agreement; (*MUS*) arrangement, setting.

arremangar [arreman'ɡar] *vt* to roll up, turn up; ~**se** *vr* to roll up one's sleeves.

arremeter [arreme'ter] *vt* to attack, assault.

arrendador, a [arrenda'ðor, a] *nm/f* landlord/lady.

arrendamiento [arrenda'mjento] *nm* letting; (*alquilar*) hiring; (*contrato*) lease; (*alquiler*) rent; **arrendar** *vt* to let, lease; to rent; **arrendatario, a** *nm/f* tenant.

arreo [a'rreo] *nm* adornment; ~**s** *nmpl* harness *sg*, trappings.

arrepentimiento [arrepenti'mjento] *nm* regret, repentance.

arrepentirse [arrepen'tirse] *vr* to repent; ~ **de** to regret.

arrestar [arres'tar] *vt* to arrest; (*encarcelar*) to imprison; **arresto**

arrest; (*MIL*) detention; (*audacia*) boldness, daring; **arresto domiciliario** house arrest.

arriar [a'rrjar] *vt* (*velas*) to haul down; (*bandera*) to lower, strike; (*un cable*) to pay out.

PALABRA CLAVE

---

arriba [a'rriβa] ◆ **1** *ad* (*posición*) above; **desde ~ from above; ~ de todo** at the very top, right on top; **Juan está ~** Juan is upstairs; **lo ~ mencionado** the aforementioned

2 (*dirección*): **calle ~** up the street **3: de ~ abajo** from top to bottom; **mirar a uno de ~ abajo** to look sb up and down

4: para ~: de 5000 pesetas para ~ from 5000 pesetas up(wards)

◆ *a*: **de ~: el piso de ~** the upstairs flat (*Brit*) o apartment; **la parte de ~** the top o upper part

◆ *prep*: **~ de** (*AM*) above; **~ de 200 pesetas** more than 200 pesetas

◆ *excl*: **¡~! up!**; **¡manos ~!** hands up!; **¡~ España!** long live Spain!

arribar [arri'βar] *vi* to put into port; (*llegar*) to arrive.

arribista [arri'βista] *nm/f* parvenu(e), upstart.

arriendo *etc vb ver* **arrendar** // [a'rrjendo] *nm* = **arrendamiento**.

arriero [a'rrjero] *nm* muleteer.

arriesgado, a [arrjes'ɣaðo. a] *a* (*peligroso*) risky; (*audaz*) bold, daring.

arriesgar [arrjes'ɣar] *vt* to risk; (*poner en peligro*) to endanger; **~se** *vt* to take a risk.

arrimar [arri'mar] *vt* (*acercar*) to bring closer; (*poner de lado*) to set aside; **~se** *vt* to come close o closer; **~se a** to lean on.

arrinconar [arrinko'nar] *vt* (*colocar*) to put in a corner; (*enemigo*) to corner; (*fig*) to put on one side; (*abandonar*) to push aside.

arrobado, a [arro'βaðo. a] *a* entranced, enchanted.

arrodillarse [arroði'ʎarse] *vr* to kneel (down).

arrogancia [arro'ɣanθja] *nf* arrogance; **arrogante** *a* arrogant.

arrojar [arro'xar] *vt* to throw, hurl; (*humo*) to emit, give out; (*COM*) to yield, produce; **~se** *vr* to throw o hurl o.s.

arrojo [a'rroxo] *nm* daring.

arrollador, a [arroʎa'ðor. a] *a* crushing, overwhelming.

arrollar [arro'ʎar] *vt* (*AUTO etc*) to run over, knock down; (*DEPORTE*) to crush.

arropar [arro'par] *vt* to cover, wrap up; **~se** *vr* to wrap o.s. up.

arrostrar [arros'trar] *vt* to face (up to); **~se** *vr*: **~se con uno** to face up to sb.

arroyo [a'rrojo] *nm* stream; (*de la calle*) gutter.

arroz [a'rroθ] *nm* rice; **~ con leche** rice pudding.

arruga [a'rruɣa] *nf* fold; (*de cara*) wrinkle; (*de vestido*) crease.

arrugar [arru'ɣar] *vt* to fold; to wrinkle; to crease; **~se** *vr* to get creased.

arruinar [arrwi'nar] *vt* to ruin, wreck; **~se** *vr* to be ruined, go bankrupt.

arrullar [arru'ʎar] *vi* to coo // *vt* to lull to sleep.

arrumaco [arru'mako] *nm* (*caricia*) caress; (*halago*) piece of flattery.

arsenal [arse'nal] *nm* naval dockyard; (*MIL*) arsenal.

arsénico [ar'seniko] *nm* arsenic.

arte ['arte] *nm* (*gen m en sg y siempre f en pl*) art; (*maña*) skill, guile; **~s** *nfpl* arts.

artefacto [arte'fakto] *nm* appliance; (*ARQUEOLOGÍA*) artefact.

arteria [ar'terja] *nf* artery.

artesanía [artesa'nia] *nf* craftsmanship; (*artículos*) handicrafts *pl*; **artesano, a** *nm/f* artisan, craftsman/woman.

ártico, a ['artiko. a] *a* Arctic // *nm*: **el Á~** the Arctic.

articulación [artikula'θjon] nf articulation; (MED, TEC) joint; **articulado, a** a articulated; jointed.

articular [artiku'lar] vt to articulate; to join together.

artículo [ar'tikulo] nm article; (cosa) thing, article; ~s nmpl goods.

artífice [ar'tifiθe] nm/f artist, craftsman/woman; (fig) architect.

artificial [artifi'θjal] a artificial.

artificio [arti'fiθjo] nm art, skill; (artesanía) craftsmanship; (astucia) cunning.

artillería [artiʎe'ria] nf artillery.

artillero [arti'ʎero] nm artilleryman, gunner.

artimaña [arti'maɲa] nf trap, snare; (astucia) cunning.

artista [ar'tista] nm/f (pintor) artist, painter; (TEATRO) artist, artiste; **artístico, a** a artistic.

artritis [ar'tritis] nf arthritis.

arveja [ar'βexa] nf (AM) pea.

arzobispo [arθo'βispo] nm archbishop.

as [as] nm ace.

asa ['asa] nf handle; (fig) lever.

asado [a'saðo] nm roast (meat); (AM) barbecue.

asador [asa'ðor] nm spit.

asadura [asa'ðura] nf entrails pl, offal.

asalariado, a [asala'rjaðo, a] a paid, salaried // nm/f wage earner.

asaltador, a [asalta'ðor, a], **asaltante** [asal'tante] nm/f assailant.

asaltar [asal'tar] vt to attack, assault; (fig) to assail; **asalto** nm attack, assault; (DEPORTE) round.

asamblea [asam'blea] nf assembly, (reunión) meeting.

asar [a'sar] vt to roast.

asbesto [as'βesto] nm asbestos.

ascendencia [asθen'denθja] nf ancestry; (AM) ascendancy; **de ~ francesa** of French origin.

ascender [asθen'der] vi (subir) to ascend, rise; (ser promovido) to gain promotion // vt to promote; **~ a** to amount to; **ascendiente** nm in-

fluence // nm/f ancestor.

ascensión [asθen'sjon] nf ascent; **la A~** (REL) the Ascension.

ascenso [as'θenso] nm ascent; (promoción) promotion.

ascensor [asθen'sor] nm lift (Brit), elevator (US).

ascético, a [as'θetiko, a] a ascetic.

asco ['asko] nm: **¡qué ~!** how revolting o disgusting; **el ajo me da ~** I hate o loathe garlic; **estar hecho un ~** to be filthy.

ascua ['askwa] nf ember; **estar en ~s** to be on tenterhooks.

aseado, a [ase'aðo, a] a clean; (arreglado) tidy; (pulcro) smart.

asear [ase'ar] vt to clean, wash; to tidy (up).

asediar [ase'ðjar] vt (MIL) to besiege, lay siege to; (fig) to chase, pester; **asedio** nm siege; (COM) run.

asegurado, a [aseɣu'raðo, a] a insured; **asegurador, a** nm/f insurer.

asegurar [aseɣu'rar] vt (consolidar) to secure, fasten; (dar garantía de) to guarantee; (preservar) to safeguard; (afirmar, dar por cierto) to assure, affirm; (tranquilizar) to reassure; (tomar un seguro) to insure; **~se** vr to assure o.s., make sure.

asemejarse [aseme'xarse] vr to be alike; **~ a** to be like, resemble.

asentado, a [asen'taðo, a] a established, settled.

asentar [asen'tar] vt (sentar) to seat, sit down; (poner) to place, establish; (alisar) to level, smooth down o out; (anotar) to note down // vi to be suitable, suit.

asentir [asen'tir] vi to assent, agree; **~ con la cabeza** to nod (one's head).

aseo [a'seo] nm cleanliness; **~s** nmpl toilet sg (Brit), cloakroom sg (Brit), restroom sg (US).

aséptico, a [a'septiko, a] a germ-free, free from infection.

asequible [ase'kiβle] a (precio) reasonable; (meta) attainable;

(*persona*) approachable.

aserradero [aserra'ðero] *nm* sawmill; **aserrar** *vt* to saw.

aserrín [ase'rrin] *nm* sawdust.

asesinar [asesi'nar] *vt* to murder; (*POL*) to assassinate; **asesinato** *nm* murder; assassination.

asesino, a [ase'sino, a] *nm/f* murderer, killer; (*POL*) assassin.

asesor, a [ase'sor, a] *nm/f* adviser, consultant.

asesorar [aseso'rar] *vt* (*JUR*) to advise, give legal advice to; (*COM*) to act as consultant to; ~se *vr*: ~se **con** *o* **de** to take advice from, consult; **~ía** *nf* (*cargo*) consultancy; (*oficina*) consultant's office.

asestar [ases'tar] *vt* (*golpe*) to deal, strike; (*arma*) to aim; (*tiro*) to fire.

asfalto [as'falto] *nm* asphalt.

asfixia [as'fiksja] *nf* asphyxia, suffocation.

asfixiar [asfik'sjar] *vt* to asphyxiate, suffocate; **~se** *vr* to be asphyxiated, suffocate.

asgo *etc vb ver* **asir.**

así [a'si] *ad* (*de esta manera*) in this way, like this, thus; (*aunque*) although; (*tan pronto como*) as soon as; ~ **que** so; ~ **como** as well as; ~ **y todo** even so; **¿no es** ~? isn't it?, didn't you? *etc*; ~ **de grande** this big.

Asia ['asja] *nf* Asia; **asiático, a** *a*, *nm/f* Asian, Asiatic.

asidero [asi'ðero] *nm* handle.

asiduidad [asiðwi'ðað] *nf* assiduousness; **asiduo, a** *a* assiduous; (*frecuente*) frequent // *nm/f* regular (customer).

asiento [a'sjento] *nm* (*mueble*) seat, chair; (*de coche, en tribunal etc*) seat; (*localidad*) seat, place; (*fundamento*) site; ~ **delantero/trasero** front/back seat.

asignación [asiɣna'θjon] *nf* (*atribución*) assignment; (*reparto*) allocation; (*sueldo*) salary; ~ **(semanal)** pocket money.

asignar [asiɣ'nar] *vt* to assign, allocate.

asignatura [asiɣna'tura] *nf* subject; course.

asilado, a [asi'laðo, a] *nm/f* inmate; (*POL*) refugee.

asilo [a'silo] *nm* (*refugio*) asylum, refuge; (*establecimiento*) home, institution; ~ **político** political asylum.

asimilación [asimila'θjon] *nf* assimilation.

asimilar [asimi'lar] *vt* to assimilate.

asimismo [asi'mismo] *ad* in the same way, likewise.

asir [a'sir] *vt* to seize, grasp.

asistencia [asis'tenθja] *nf* audience; (*MED*) attendance; (*ayuda*) assistance; **asistente** *nm/f* assistant; **los ~s** those present.

asistido, a [asis'tiðo, a] *a*: ~ **por ordenador** computer-assisted.

asistir [asis'tir] *vt* to assist, help // *vi*: ~ **a** to attend, be present at.

asma ['asma] *nf* asthma.

asno ['asno] *nm* donkey; (*fig*) ass.

asociación [asoθja'θjon] *nf* association; (*COM*) partnership; **asociado, a** *a* associate // *nm/f* associate; (*COM*) partner.

asociar [aso'θjar] *vt* to associate.

asolar [aso'lar] *vt* to destroy.

asolear [asole'ar] *vt* to put in the sun; **~se** *vr* to sunbathe.

asomar [aso'mar] *vt* to show, stick out // *vi* to appear; **~se** *vr* to appear, show up; ~ **la cabeza por la ventana** to put one's head out of the window.

asombrar [asom'brar] *vt* to amaze, astonish; **~se** *vr* (*sorprenderse*) to be amazed; (*asustarse*) to get a fright; **asombro** *nm* amazement, astonishment; (*susto*) fright; **asombroso, a** *a* astonishing, amazing.

asomo [a'somo] *nm* hint, sign.

aspa ['aspa] *nf* (*cruz*) cross; (*de molino*) sail; **en** ~ X-shaped.

aspaviento [aspa'βjento] *nm* exaggerated display of feeling; (*fam*) fuss.

aspecto [as'pekto] *nm* (*apariencia*)

look, appearance; *(fig)* aspect.

aspereza [aspe'reθa] *nf* roughness; *(agrura)* sourness; *(de carácter)* surliness; **áspero, a** *a* rough; bitter, sour; harsh.

aspersión [asper'sjon] *nf* sprinkling.

aspiración [aspira'θjon] *nf* breath, inhalation; *(MUS)* short pause; **aspiraciones** *nfpl* aspirations.

aspiradora [aspira'ðora] *nf* vacuum cleaner, Hoover ®.

aspirante [aspi'rante] *nm/f* *(candidato)* candidate; *(DEPORTE)* contender.

aspirar [aspi'rar] *vt* to breathe in // *vi:* ~ a to aspire to.

aspirina [aspi'rina] *nf* aspirin.

asquear [aske'ar] *vt* to sicken // *vi* to be sickening; ~**se** *vr* to feel disgusted; **asqueroso, a** *a* disgusting, sickening.

asta ['asta] *nf* lance; *(arpón)* spear; *(mango)* shaft, handle; *(ZOOL)* horn; **a media** ~ at half mast.

astado, a [as'taðo, a] *a* a horned // *nm* bull.

asterisco [aste'risko] *nm* asterisk.

astilla [as'tiʎa] *nf* splinter; *(pedacito)* chip; ~**s** *nfpl* firewood *sg.*

astillero [asti'ʎero] *nm* shipyard.

astringente [astrin'xente] *a*, *nm* - astringent.

astro ['astro] *nm* star.

astrología [astrolo'xia] *nf* astrology; **astrólogo, a** *nm/f* astrologer.

astronauta [astro'nauta] *nm/f* astronaut.

astronave [astro'naβe] *nm* spaceship.

astronomía [astrono'mia] *nf* astronomy; **astrónomo, a** *nm/f* astronomer.

astucia [as'tuθja] *nf* astuteness; *(ardid)* clever trick; **astuto, a** *a* astute; *(taimado)* cunning.

asueto [a'sweto] *nm* holiday; *(tiempo libre)* time off *q.*

asumir [asu'mir] *vt* to assume.

asunción [asun'θjon] *nf* assumption; *(REL)* **A**~ Assumption.

asunto [a'sunto] *nm* *(tema)* matter, subject; *(negocio)* business.

asustar [asus'tar] *vt* to frighten; ~**se** *vr* to become frightened.

atacar [ata'kar] *vt* to attack.

atadura [ata'ðura] *nf* bond, tie.

atajo [a'taxo] *nm* short cut; *(DEPORTE)* tackle.

atañer [ata'ɲer] *vi:* ~ a to concern.

ataque *etc vb ver* **atacar** // [a'take] *nm* attack; ~ **cardíaco** heart attack.

atar [a'tar] *vt* to tie, tie up.

atardecer [atarðe'θer] *vi* to get dark // *nm* evening; *(crepúsculo)* dusk.

atareado, a [atare'aðo, a] *a* busy.

atascar [atas'kar] *vt* to clog up; *(obstruir)* to jam; *(fig)* to hinder; ~**se** *vr* to stall; *(cañería)* to get blocked up; **atasco** *nm* obstruction; *(AUTO)* traffic jam.

ataúd [ata'uð] *nm* coffin.

ataviar [ata'βjar] *vt* to deck, array; ~**se** *vr* to dress up.

atavío [ata'βio] *nm* attire, dress; ~**s** *nmpl* finery *sg.*

atemorizar [atemori'θar] *vt* to frighten, scare; ~**se** *vr* to get scared.

Atenas [a'tenas] *n* Athens.

atención [aten'θjon] *nf* attention; *(bondad)* kindness // *excl* (be) careful!, look out!

atender [aten'der] *vt* to attend to, look after // *vi* to pay attention.

atenerse [ate'nerse] *vr:* ~ a to abide by, adhere to.

atentado [aten'taðo] *nm* crime, illegal act; *(asalto)* assault; ~ **contra la vida de** uno attempt on sb's life.

atentamente [atenta'mente] *ad:* Le saluda ~ Yours faithfully.

atentar [aten'tar] *vi:* ~ a o contra to commit an outrage against.

atento, a [a'tento, a] *a* attentive, observant; *(cortés)* polite, thoughtful.

atenuante [ate'nwante] *a* attenuating, extenuating.

atenuar [ate'nwar] *vt* to attenuate; *(disminuir)* to lessen, minimize.

ateo, a [a'teo, a] *a* atheistic // *nm/f*

atheist.

aterciopelado, a [aterθjope'laðo, a] *a* velvety.

aterido, a [ate'riðo, a] *a*: ~ **de frío** frozen stiff.

aterrador, a [aterra'ðor, a] *a* frightening.

aterrar [ate'rrar] *vt* to frighten; to terrify; ~**se** *vr* to be frightened; to be terrified.

aterrizaje [aterri'θaxe] *nm* (*AVIAT*) landing.

aterrizar [aterri'θar] *vi* to land.

aterrorizar [aterrori'θar]   *vt*   to terrify.

atesorar [ateso'rar] *vt* to hoard, store up.

atestado, a [ates'taðo, a] *a* packed // *nm* (*JUR*) affidavit.

atestar [ates'tar] *vt* to pack, stuff; (*JUR*) to attest, testify to.

atestiguar [atesti'ɣwar] *vt* to testify to, bear witness to.

atiborrar [atiβo'rrar] *vt* to fill, stuff; ~**se** *vr* to stuff o.s.

ático ['atiko] *nm* attic; ~ **de lujo** penthouse (flat (*Brit*) o apartment).

atildar [atil'dar] *vt* to criticize; ~**se** *vr* to spruce o.s. up.

atinado, a [ati'naðo, a] *a* (*sensato*) wise; (*correcto*) right, correct.

atisbar [atis'βar] *vt* to spy on; (*echar una ojeada*) to peep at.

atizar [ati'θar] *vt* to poke; (*horno etc*) to stoke; (*fig*) to stir up, rouse.

atlántico, a [at'lantiko, a] *a* Atlantic // *nm*: **el (océano) A~** the Atlantic (Ocean).

atlas ['atlas] *nm* atlas.

atleta [at'leta] *nm* athlete; **atlético, a** *a* athletic; **atletismo** *nm* athletics *sg*.

atmósfera [at'mosfera] *nf* atmosphere.

atolondramiento   [atolondra-'mjento]   *nm*   bewilderment; (*insensatez*) silliness.

atollar [ato'ʎar] *vi*, **atollarse** *vr* to get stuck; (*fig*) to get into a jam.

atómico, a [a'tomiko, a] *a* atomic.

atomizador [atomiθa'ðor]   *nm* atomizer; (*de perfume*) spray.

átomo ['atomo] *nm* atom.

atónito, a [a'tonito, a] *a* astonished, amazed.

atontado, a [aton'taðo, a] *a* stunned; (*bobo*) silly, daft.

atontar [aton'tar] *vt* to stun; ~**se** *vr* to become confused.

atormentar [atormen'tar] *vt* to torture; (*molestar*) to torment; (*acosar*) to plague, harass.

atornillar [atorni'ʎar] *vt* to screw on o down.

atracador, a [atraka'ðor, a] *nm/f* robber.

atracar [atra'kar] *vt* (*NAUT*) to moor; (*robar*) to hold up, rob // *vi* to moor; ~**se** *vr*: ~**se (de)** to stuff o.s. (with).

atracción [atrak'θjon] *nf* attraction.

atraco [a'trako] *nm* holdup, robbery.

atractivo, a [atrak'tiβo, a] *a* attractive // *nm* attraction; (*belleza*) attractiveness.

atraer [atra'er] *vt* to attract.

atragantarse [atraɣan'tarse] *vr*: ~ (**con**) to choke (on); **se me ha atragantado el chico** I can't stand the boy.

atrancar [atran'kar] *vt* (*puerta*) to bar, bolt.

atrapar [atra'par] *vt* to trap; (*resfriado etc*) to catch.

atrás [a'tras] *ad* (*movimiento*) back(wards); (*lugar*) behind; (*tiempo*) previously; **ir hacia** ~ to go back(wards); **to go to the rear; estar** ~ to be behind o at the back.

atrasado, a [atra'saðo, a] *a* slow; (*pago*) overdue, late; (*país*) backward.

atrasar [atra'sar] *vi* to be slow; ~**se** *vr* to remain behind; (*tren*) to be o run late; **atraso** *nm* slowness; lateness, delay; (*de país*) backwardness; **atrasos** *nmpl* arrears.

atravesar [atraβe'sar] *vt* (*cruzar*) to cross (over); (*traspasar*) to pierce; to go through; (*poner al través*) lay o put across; **~se** vr to come in between; (*intervenir*) to interfere.

atravieso etc vb ver **atravesar**.

atrayente [atra'jente] a attractive.

atreverse [atre'βerse] vr to dare; (*insolentarse*) to be insolent; **atrevido**, a a daring; insolent; **atrevimiento** nm daring; insolence.

atribución [atriβu'θjon] nf: **atribuciones** (*POL*) powers; (*ADMIN*) responsibilities.

atribuir [atriβu'ir] vt to attribute; (*funciones*) to confer.

atribular [atriβu'lar] vt to afflict, distress.

atributo [atri'βuto] nm attribute.

atrocidad [atroθi'ðað] nf atrocity, outrage.

atropellar [atrope'ʎar] vt (*derribar*) to knock over o down; (*empujar*) to push (aside); (*AUTO*) to run over, run down; (*agraviar*) to insult; **~se** vr to act hastily; **atropello** nm (*AUTO*) accident; (*empujón*) push; (*agravio*) wrong; (*atrocidad*) outrage.

atroz [a'troθ] a atrocious, awful.

atto, a abr = **atento.**

atuendo [a'twendo] nm attire.

atún [a'tun] nm tuna.

aturdir [atur'ðir] vt to stun; (*de ruido*) to deafen; (*fig*) to dumbfound, bewilder.

atusar [atu'sar] vt to smooth (down).

audacia [au'ðaθja] nf boldness, audacity; **audaz** a bold, audacious.

audible [au'ðiβle] a audible.

audición [auði'θjon] nf hearing; (*TEATRO*) audition.

audiencia [au'ðjenθja] nf audience; **A~** (*JUR*) High Court.

auditor [auði'tor] nm (*JUR*) judge-advocate; (*COM*) auditor.

auditorio [auði'torjo] nm audience; (*sala*) auditorium.

auge ['auxe] nm boom; (*clímax*) climax.

augurar [auxu'rar] vt to predict; (*presagiar*) to portend.

augurio [au'xurjo] nm omen.

aula ['aula] nf classroom; (*en universidad etc*) lecture room.

aullar [au'ʎar] vi to howl, yell.

aullido [au'ʎiðo] nm howl, yell.

aumentar [aumen'tar] vt to increase; (*precios*) to put up; (*producción*) to step up; (*con microscopio, anteojos*) to magnify // vi, **~se** vr to increase, be on the increase; **aumento** nm increase; rise.

aun [a'un] ad even; **~ así** even so; **~ más** even o yet more.

aún [a'un] ad: **~ está aquí** he's still here; **~ no lo sabemos** we don't know yet; **¿no ha venido ~?** hasn't she come yet?

aunque [a'unke] conj though, although, even though.

¡aúpa [a'upa] excl come on!

aureola [aure'ola] nf halo.

auricular [auriku'lar] nm (*TEL*) earpiece, receiver; **~es** nmpl headphones.

aurora [au'rora] nf dawn.

auscultar [auskul'tar] vt (*MED*: *pecho*) to listen to, sound.

ausencia [au'senθja] nf absence.

ausentarse [ausen'tarse] vr to go away; (*por poco tiempo*) to go out.

ausente [au'sente] a absent.

auspicios [aus'piθjos] nmpl auspices; (*protección*) protection sg.

austeridad [austeri'ðað] nf austerity; **austero**, a a austere.

austral [aus'tral] a southern // nm monetary unit of Argentina.

Australia [aus'tralja] nf Australia; **australiano**, a a, nm/f Australian.

Austria ['austrja] nf Austria; **austríaco**, a a, nm/f Austrian.

autenticar [autenti'kar] vt to authenticate; **auténtico**, a a authentic.

auto ['auto] nm (*JUR*) edict, decree; (: *orden*) writ; (*AUTO*) car; **~s** nmpl (*JUR*) proceedings; (: *acta*) court record sg.

autoadhesivo [autoaðe'siβo] a self-adhesive; (*sobre*) self-sealing.

autobiografía [autoβjoɣra'fia] nf

autobiography.

autobús [auto'βus] nm bus.

autocar [auto'kar] nm coach (Brit), (passenger) bus (US).

autóctono, a [au'toktono, a] a native, indigenous.

autodefensa [autoðe'fensa] nf self-defence.

autodeterminación [autoðetermina'θjon] nf self-determination.

autoescuela [autoes'kwela] nf driving school.

autógrafo [au'tovrafo] nm autograph.

automación [automa'θjon] nf = **automatización.**

autómata [au'tomata] nm automaton.

automático, a [auto'matiko, a] a automatic // nm press stud.

automatización [automatiθa'θjon] nf automation.

automotor, triz [automo'tor, 'triθ] a self-propelled // nm diesel train.

automóvil [auto'moβil] nm (motor) car (Brit), automobile (US); **automovilismo** nm (actividad) motoring; (DEPORTE) (sports)car racing; **automovilista** nm/f motorist, driver; **automovilístico, a** a (industria) car cpd.

autonomía [autono'mia] nf autonomy; **autónomo, a**, (Esp POL) **autonómico, a** a autonomous.

autopista [auto'pista] nf motorway (Brit), freeway (US).

autopsia [au'topsja] nf autopsy, post-mortem.

autor, a [au'tor, a] nm/f author.

autoridad [autori'ðað] nf authority; **autoritario, a** a authoritarian.

autorización [autoriθa'θjon] nf authorization; **autorizado, a** a authorized; (aprobado) approved.

autorizar [autori'θar] vt to authorize; (aprobar) to approve.

autorretrato [autorre'trato] nm self-portrait.

autoservicio [autoser'βiθjo] nm (tienda) self-service shop (Brit) o store (US); (restaurante) self-service restaurant.

autostop [auto'stop] nm hitch-hiking; **hacer** ~ to hitch-hike; ~**ista** nm/f hitch-hiker.

autosuficiencia [autosufi'θjenθja] nf self-sufficiency.

autovía [auto'βia] nf ≈ A-road (Brit), state highway (US).

auxiliar [auksi'ljar] vt to help // nm/f assistant; **auxilio** nm assistance, help; **primeros auxilios** first aid sg.

Av abr (= Avenida) Av(e).

aval [a'βal] nm guarantee; (persona) guarantor.

avalancha [aβa'lantʃa] nf avalanche.

avance [a'βanθe] nm advance; (pago) advance payment; (CINE) trailer.

avanzar [aβan'θar] vt, vi to advance.

avaricia [aβa'riθja] nf avarice, greed; **avaricioso, a** a avaricious, greedy.

avaro, a [a'βaro, a] a miserly, mean // nm/f miser.

avasallar [aβasa'ʎar] vt to subdue, subjugate.

Avda abr (= Avenida) Av(e).

ave ['aβe] nf bird; ~ **de rapiña** bird of prey.

avecinarse [aβeθi'narse] vr (tormenta, fig) to be on the way.

avellana [aβe'ʎana] nf hazelnut; **avellano** nm hazel tree.

avemaría [aβema'ria] nm Hail Mary, Ave Maria.

avena [a'βena] nf oats pl.

avenida [aβe'niða] nf (calle) avenue.

avenir [aβe'nir] vt to reconcile; ~**se** vr to come to an agreement, reach a compromise.

aventajado, a [aβenta'xaðo, a] a outstanding.

aventajar [aβenta'xar] vt (sobrepasar) to surpass, outstrip.

aventar [aβen'tar] vt to fan, blow; (grano) to winnow.

aventura [aβen'tura] nf adventure; **aventurado, a** a risky; **aventurero, a** a adventurous.

avergonzar [aβerɣon'θar] vt to shame; (*desconcertar*) to embarrass; ~**se** vr to be ashamed; to be embarrassed.

avería [aβe'ria] nf (*TEC*) breakdown, fault.

averiado, a [aβe'rjaðo, a] a broken down; '~' 'out of order'.

averiguación [aβeriɣwa'θjon] nf investigation; (*descubrimiento*) ascertainment.

averiguar [aβeri'ɣwar] vt to investigate; (*descubrir*) to find out, ascertain.

aversión [aβer'sjon] nf aversion, dislike.

avestruz [aβes'truθ] nm ostrich.

aviación [aβja'θjon] nf aviation; (*fuerzas aéreas*) air force.

aviador, a [aβja'ðor, a] nm/f aviator, airman/woman.

aviar [a'βjar] vt to prepare; **estar aviado** (*fig*) to be in a mess.

avicultura [aβikul'tura] nf poultry farming.

avidez [aβi'ðeθ] nf avidity, eagerness; **ávido, a** a avid, eager.

avinagrado, a [aβina'ɣraðo, a] a sour, acid.

avinagrarse [aβina'ɣrarse] vr to go o turn sour.

avío [a'βio] nm preparation; ~**s** nmpl gear sg, kit sg.

avión [a'βjon] nm aeroplane; (*ave*) martin; ~ **de reacción** jet (plane).

avioneta [aβjo'neta] nf light aircraft.

avisar [aβi'sar] vt (*advertir*) to warn, notify; (*informar*) to tell; (*aconsejar*) to advise, counsel; **aviso** nm warning; (*noticia*) notice.

avispa [a'βispa] nf wasp.

avispado, a [aβis'paðo, a] a sharp, clever.

avispero [aβis'pero] nm wasp's nest.

avispón [aβis'pon] nm hornet.

avistar [aβis'tar] vt to sight, spot.

avituallar [aβitwa'ʎar] vt to supply with food.

avivar [aβi'βar] vt to strengthen, intensify; ~**se** vr to revive, acquire

new life.

axila [ak'sila] nf armpit.

axioma [ak'sjoma] nm axiom.

ay [ai] *excl* (*dolor*) ow!, ouch!; (*aflicción*) oh!, oh dear!; ¡~ **de mí!** poor me!

aya [ˈaja] nf governess; (*niñera*) nanny.

ayer [a'jer] ad, nm yesterday; **antes de** ~ the day before yesterday.

ayo [ˈajo] nm tutor.

ayote [a'jote] nm (*AM*) pumpkin.

ayuda [a'juða] nf help, assistance // nm page; **ayudante, a** nm/f assistant, helper; (*ESCOL*) assistant; (*MIL*) adjutant.

ayudar [aju'ðar] vt to help, assist.

ayunar [aju'nar] vi to fast; **ayunas** nfpl: **estar en ayunas** (*no haber comido*) to be fasting; (*ignorar*) to be in the dark; **ayuno** nm fasting.

ayuntamiento [ajunta'mjento] nm (*consejo*) town o city council; (*edificio*) town o city hall.

azabache [aθa'βatʃe] nm jet.

azada [a'θaða] nf hoe.

azafata [aθa'fata] nf air stewardess.

azafrán [aθa'fran] nm saffron.

azahar [aθa'ar] nm orange/lemon blossom.

azar [a'θar] nm (*casualidad*) chance, fate; (*desgracia*) misfortune, accident; **por** ~ by chance; **al** ~ at random.

azogue [a'θoɣe] nm mercury.

azoramiento [aθora'mjento] nm alarm; (*confusión*) confusion.

azorar [aθo'rar] vt to alarm; ~**se** vr to get alarmed.

Azores [a'θores] nmpl: **los** ~ the Azores.

azotar [aθo'tar] vt to whip, beat; (*pegar*) to spank; **azote** nm (*látigo*) whip; (*latigazo*) lash, stroke; (*en las nalgas*) spank; (*calamidad*) calamity.

azotea [aθo'tea] nf (*flat*) roof.

azteca [aθ'teka] a, nm/f Aztec.

azúcar [a'θukar] nm sugar; **azucarado, a** a sugary, sweet.

azucarero, a [aθuka'rero, a] *a* sugar *cpd* // *nm* sugar bowl.

azucena [aθu'θena] *nf* white lily.

azufre [a'θufre] *nm* sulphur.

azul [a'θul] *a*, *nm* blue.

azulejo [aθu'lexo] *nm* tile.

azuzar [aθu'θar] *vt* to incite, egg on.

B

B.A. *abr* (= *Buenos Aires*) B.A.

baba ['baβa] *nf* spittle, saliva; **babear** *vi* to drool, slaver.

babel [ba'βel] *nm o f* bedlam.

babero [ba'βero] *nm* bib.

babor [ba'βor] *nm* port (side).

baboso, a [ba'βoso, a] *a* (*AM fam*) silly.

babucha [ba'βutʃa] *nf* slipper.

baca ['baka] *nf* (*AUTO*) luggage *o* roof rack.

bacalao [baka'lao] *nm* cod(fish).

bacinica [baθi'nika] *nf*, **bacinilla** [baθi'niʎa] *nf* chamber pot.

bacteria [bak'terja] *nf* bacterium, germ.

báculo ['bakulo] *nm* stick, staff.

bache ['batʃe] *nm* pothole, rut; (*fig*) bad patch.

bachillerato [batʃiʎe'rato] *nm* (*ESCOL*) school-leaving examination (*Brit*), bachelor's degree (*US*), baccalaureate (*US*).

bagaje [ba'xaxe] *nm* baggage, luggage.

bagatela [baxa'tela] *nf* trinket, trifle.

Bahama [ba'ama]: **las (Islas)** ~ **s** the Bahamas.

bahía [ba'ia] *nf* bay.

bailar [bai'lar] *vt*, *vi* to dance; ~**in, ina** *nm/f* (*ballet*) dancer; **baile** *nm* dance; (*formal*) ball.

baja ['baxa] *nf ver* **bajo**.

bajada [ba'xaða] *nf* descent; (*camino*) slope; (*de aguas*) ebb.

bajamar [baxa'mar] *nf* low tide.

bajar [ba'xar] *vi* to go down, come down; (*temperatura, precios*) to drop, fall // *vt* (*cabeza*) to bow, bend;

(*escalera*) to go down, come down; (*precio, voz*) to lower; (*llevar abajo*) to take down; ~**se** *vr* to get out of; to get off; ~ **de** (*coche*) to get out of; (*autobus*) to get off.

bajeza [ba'xeθa] *nf* baseness *q*; (*una* ~) vile deed.

bajío [ba'xio] *nm* shoal, sandbank; (*AM*) lowlands *pl*.

bajo, a ['baxo, a] *a* (*mueble, numero, precio*) low; (*piso*) ground; (*de estatura*) small, short; (*color*) pale; (*sonido*) faint, soft, low; (*voz*: *en tono*) deep; (*metal*) base; (*humilde*) low, humble // *ad* (*hablar*) softly, quietly; (*volar*) low // *prep* under, below, underneath // *nm* (*MUS*) bass // *nf* drop, fall; (*MIL*) casualty; ~ **la lluvia** in the rain; **dar de baja** (*soldado*) to discharge; (*empleado*) to dismiss, sack.

bajón [ba'xon] *nm* fall, drop.

bala ['bala] *nf* bullet.

baladí [bala'ði] *a* trivial.

baladronada [balaðro'naða] *nf* (*dicho*) boast, brag; (*hecho*) piece of bravado.

balance [ba'lanθe] *nm* (*COM*) balance; (: *libro*) balance sheet; (: *cuenta general*) stocktaking.

balancear [balanθe'ar] *vt* to balance // *vi*, ~**se** *vr* to swing (to and fro); (*vacilar*) to hesitate; **balanceo** *nm* swinging.

balanza [ba'lanθa] *nf* scales *pl*, balance; ~ **comercial** balance of trade; ~ **de pagos** balance of payments; (*ASTROLOGÍA*) **B**~ Libra.

balar [ba'lar] *vi* to bleat.

balaustrada [balaus'traða] *nf* balustrade; (*pasamanos*) banisters *pl*.

balazo [ba'laθo] *nm* (*golpe*) shot; (*herida*) bullet wound.

balbucear [balβuθe'ar] *vi*, *vt* to stammer, stutter; **balbuceo** *nm* stammering, stuttering.

balbucir [balβu'θir] *vi*, *vt* to stammer, stutter.

balcón [bal'kon] *nm* balcony.

baldar [bal'dar] *vt* to cripple.

balde ['balde] *nm* bucket, pail; **de ~ ad** (for) free, for nothing; **en ~ ad** in vain.

baldío, a [bal'dio, a] *a* uncultivated; (*terreno*) waste // *nm* waste land.

baldosa [bal'dosa] *nf* (*azulejo*) floor tile; (*grande*) flagstone.

Baleares [bale'ares] *nfpl*: **las (Islas) ~** the Balearic Islands.

balido [ba'liðo] *nm* bleat, bleating.

balín [ba'lin] *nm* pellet; **balines** *nmpl* buckshot *sg*.

balística [ba'listika] *nf* ballistics *pl*.

baliza [ba'liθa] *nf* (*AVIAT*) beacon; (*NAUT*) buoy.

balneario, a [balne'arjo, a] *a*: **estación balnearia** (*bathing*) resort // *nm* spa, health resort.

balón [ba'lon] *nm* ball.

baloncesto [balon'θesto] *nm* basketball.

balonmano [balom'mano] *nm* handball.

balonvolea [balombo'lea] *nm* volleyball.

balsa ['balsa] *nf* raft; (*BOT*) balsa wood.

bálsamo ['balsamo] *nm* balsam, balm.

baluarte [ba'lwarte] *nm* bastion, bulwark.

ballena [ba'ʎena] *nf* whale.

ballesta [ba'ʎesta] *nf* crossbow; (*AUTO*) spring.

ballet [ba'le] *nm* ballet.

bambolear [bambole'ar] *vi*, **bambolearse** *vr* to swing, sway; (*silla*) to wobble; **bamboleo** *nm* swinging, swaying; wobbling.

bambú [bam'bu] *nm* bamboo.

banana [ba'nana] *nf* (*AM*) banana; **banano** *nm* (*AM*) banana tree.

banca ['banka] *nf* (*asiento*) bench; (*COM*) banking.

bancario, a [ban'karjo, a] *a* banking *cpd*, bank *cpd*.

bancarrota [banka'rrota] *nf* bankruptcy; **hacer ~** to go bankrupt.

banco ['banko] *nm* bench; (*ESCOL*) desk; (*COM*) bank; (*GEO*) stratum; **~ de crédito/de ahorros** credit/savings bank; **~ de arena** sandbank; **~ de hielo** iceberg.

banda ['banda] *nf* band; (*pandilla*) gang; (*NAUT*) side, edge; **la B~ Oriental** Uruguay; **~ sonora** soundtrack.

bandada [ban'daða] *nf* (*de pájaros*) flock; (*de peces*) shoal.

bandeja [ban'dexa] *nf* tray.

bandera [ban'dera] *nf* (*de tela*) flag; (*estandarte*) banner.

banderilla [bande'riʎa] *nf* banderilla.

banderín [bande'rin] *nm* pennant, small flag.

banderola [bande'rola] *nf* banderole; (*MIL*) pennant.

bandido [ban'diðo] *nm* bandit.

bando ['bando] *nm* (*edicto*) edict, proclamation; (*facción*) faction; **los ~** the banns.

bandolero [bando'lero] *nm* bandit, brigand.

banquero [ban'kero] *nm* banker.

banqueta [ban'keta] *nf* stool; (*AM: en la calle*) pavement (*Brit*), sidewalk (*US*).

banquete [ban'kete] *nm* banquet; (*para convidados*) formal dinner.

banquillo [ban'kiʎo] *nm* (*JUR*) dock, prisoner's bench; (*banco*) bench; (*para los pies*) footstool.

bañador [baɲa'ðor] *nm* swimming costume (*Brit*), bathing suit (*US*).

bañar [ba'ɲar] *vt* to bath, bathe; (*objeto*) to dip; (*de barniz*) to coat; **~se** *vr* (*en el mar*) to bathe, swim; (*en la bañera*) to bath, have a bath.

bañera [ba'ɲera] *nf* bath(tub).

bañero [ba'ɲero] *nm* lifeguard.

bañista [ba'ɲista] *nm/f* bather.

baño ['baɲo] *nm* (*en bañera*) bath; (*en río*) dip, swim; (*cuarto*) bathroom; (*bañera*) bath(tub); (*capa*) coating.

baptista [bap'tista] *nm/f* Baptist.

baqueta [ba'keta] *nf* (*MUS*) drumstick.

bar [bar] *nm* bar.

barahúnda [bara'unda] *nf* uproar, hubbub.

baraja [ba'raxa] *nf* pack (of cards).

barajar *vt* (*naipes*) to shuffle; (*fig*) to jumble up.

baranda [ba'randa], **barandilla** [baran'diʎa] *nf* rail, railing.

baratija [bara'tixa] *nf* trinket.

baratillo [bara'tiʎo] *nm* (*tienda*) junkshop; (*subasta*) bargain sale; (*conjunto de cosas*) secondhand goods *pl.*

barato, a [ba'rato, a] *a* cheap // *ad* cheap, cheaply.

baraúnda [bara'unda] *nf* = **barahúnda**.

barba ['barβa] *nf* (*mentón*) chin; (*pelo*) beard.

barbacoa [barβa'koa] *nf* (*parrilla*) barbecue; (*carne*) barbecued meat.

barbaridad [barβari'ðað] *nf* barbarity; (*acto*) barbarism; (*atrocidad*) outrage; **una** ~ (*fam*) loads *pl*; ¡**qué** ~! (*fam*) how awful!

barbarie [bar'βarje] *nf*, **barbarismo** [barβa'rismo] *nm* barbarism, savagery; (*crueldad*) barbarity.

bárbaro, a ['barβaro, a] *a* barbarous, cruel; (*grosero*) rough, uncouth // *nm/f* barbarian // *ad*: **lo pasamos** ~ (*fam*) we had a great time; ¡**qué** ~! (*fam*) how marvellous!; **un éxito** ~ (*fam*) a terrific success; **es un tipo** ~ (*fam*) he's a great bloke.

barbecho [bar'βetʃo] *nm* fallow land.

barbero [bar'βero] *nm* barber, hairdresser.

barbilampiño [barβilam'piɲo] *a* clean-shaven, smooth-faced; (*fig*) inexperienced.

barbilla [bar'βiʎa] *nf* chin, tip of the chin.

barbo ['barβo] *nm*: ~ **de mar** red mullet.

barbotar [barβo'tar], **barbotear** [barβote'ar] *vt, vi* to mutter, mumble.

barbudo, a [bar'βuðo, a] *a* bearded.

barca ['barka] *nf* (*small*) boat; ~ **pesquera** fishing boat; ~ **de pasaje** ferry; ~**za** *nf* barge; ~**za de desembarco** landing craft.

Barcelona [barθe'lona] *nf* Barcelona.

barcelonés, esa [barθelo'nes, esa] *a* of *o* from Barcelona.

barco ['barko] *nm* boat; (*buque*) ship; ~ **de carga** cargo boat.

baritono [ba'ritono] *nm* baritone.

barman ['barman] *nm* barman.

Barna. *abr* = **Barcelona.**

barniz [bar'niθ] *nm* varnish; (*en la loza*) glaze; (*fig*) veneer; ~**ar** *vt* to varnish; (*loza*) to glaze.

barómetro [ba'rometro] *nm* barometer.

barquero [bar'kero] *nm* boatman.

barquillo [bar'kiʎo] *nm* cone, cornet.

barra ['barra] *nf* bar, rod; (*de un café*) bar; (*de pan*) French loaf; (*palanca*) lever; ~ **de carmín** *o* **de labios** lipstick.

barraca [ba'rraka] *nf* hut, cabin.

barranca [ba'rranka] *nf* ravine, gully; **barranco** *nm* ravine; (*fig*) difficulty.

barrena [ba'rrena] *nf* drill; **barrenar** *vt* to drill (through), bore; **barreno** *nm* large drill.

barrer [ba'rrer] *vt* to sweep; (*quitar*) to sweep away.

barrera [ba'rrera] *nf* barrier.

barriada [ba'rrjaða] *nf* quarter, district.

barricada [barri'kaða] *nf* barricade.

barrido [ba'rriðo] *nm*, **barrida** [ba'rriða] *nf* sweep, sweeping.

barriga [ba'rriɣa] *nf* belly; (*panza*) paunch; **barrigón, ona**, **barrigudo, a** *a* potbellied.

barril [ba'rril] *nm* barrel, cask.

barrio ['barrjo] *nm* (*vecindad*) area, neighborhood (*US*); (*en las afueras*) suburb; ~ **chino** red-light district.

barro ['barro] *nm* (*lodo*) mud; (*objetos*) earthenware; (*MED*) pimple.

barroco, a [ba'rroko, a] *a, nm* baroque.

barrote [ba'rrote] *nm* (*de ventana*) bar.

barruntar [baruń'tar] *vt* (*conjeturar*) to guess; (*presentir*) to suspect; **barrunto** *nm* guess; suspicion.

bartola [bar'tola]: **a la ~** *ad*: **tirarse a la ~** to take it easy, be lazy.

bártulos ['bartulos] *nmpl* things, belongings.

barullo [ba'ruʎo] *nm* row, uproar.

basamento [basa'mento] *nm* base, plinth.

basar [ba'sar] *vt* to base; **~se** *vr*: **~se en** to be based on.

basca ['baska] *nf* nausea.

báscula ['baskula] *nf* (*platform*) scales *pl*.

base ['base] *nf* base; **a ~ de** on the basis of; (*mediante*) by means of; **~ de datos** (*INFORM*) database.

básico, a ['basiko, a] *a* basic.

basílica [ba'silika] *nf* basilica.

<u>PALABRA CLAVE</u>

bastante [bas'tante] ◆ *a* **1** (*suficiente*) enough; **~ dinero** enough o sufficient money; **~s libros** enough books

2 (*valor intensivo*): **~ gente** quite a lot of people; **tener ~ calor** to be rather hot

◆ *ad*: **~ bueno/malo** quite good/ rather bad; **~ rico** pretty rich; (**lo**) **~ inteligente (como) para hacer algo** clever enough o sufficiently clever to do sth.

---

bastar [bas'tar] *vi* to be enough o sufficient; **~se** *vr* to be self-sufficient; **~ para** to be enough to; **¡basta!** (that's) enough!

bastardilla [bastar'ðiʎa] *nf* italics *pl*.

bastardo, a [bas'tarðo, a] *a, nm/f* bastard.

bastidor [basti'ðor] *nm* frame; (*de coche*) chassis; (*TEATRO*) wing; **entre ~es** (*fig*) behind the scenes.

basto, a ['basto, a] *a* coarse, rough; **~s** *nmpl* (*NAIPES*) ≈ clubs.

bastón [bas'ton] *nm* stick, staff; (*para pasear*) walking stick.

basura [ba'sura] *nf* rubbish (*Brit*), garbage (*US*).

basurero [basu'rero] *nm* (*hombre*) dustman (*Brit*), garbage man (*US*); (*lugar*) dump; (*cubo*) (rubbish) bin (*Brit*), trash can (*US*).

bata ['bata] *nf* (*gen*) dressing gown; (*cubreropa*) smock, overall; (*MED, TEC etc*) lab(oratory) coat.

batalla [ba'taʎa] *nf* battle; **de ~** for everyday use.

batallar [bata'ʎar] *vi* to fight.

batallón [bata'ʎon] *nm* battalion.

batata [ba'tata] *nf* (*AM*) sweet potato.

bate ['bate] *nm* bat; **~ador** *nm* (*AM*) batter; batsman.

batería [bate'ria] *nf* battery; (*MUS*) drums *pl*; **~ de cocina** kitchen utensils *pl*.

batido, a [ba'tiðo, a] *a* (*camino*) beaten, well-trodden // *nm* (*CULIN*) batter; **~ (de leche)** milk shake.

batidora [bati'ðora] *nf* beater, mixer; **~ eléctrica** food mixer, blender.

batir [ba'tir] *vt* to beat, strike; (*vencer*) to beat, defeat; (*revolver*) to beat, mix; **~se** *vr* to fight; **~ palmas** to clap, applaud.

batuta [ba'tuta] *nf* baton; **llevar la ~** (*fig*) to be the boss, be in charge.

baúl [ba'ul] *nm* trunk; (*AUTO*) boot (*Brit*), trunk (*US*).

bautismo [bau'tismo] *nm* baptism, christening.

bautizar [bauti'θar] *vt* to baptize, christen; (*fam: diluir*) to water down; **bautizo** *nm* baptism, christening.

bayeta [ba'jeta] *nf* floorcloth.

bayo, a ['bajo, a] *a* bay // *nf* berry.

bayoneta [bajo'neta] *nf* bayonet.

baza ['baθa] *nf* trick; **meter ~** to butt in.

bazar [ba'θar] *nm* bazaar.

bazofia [ba'θofja] *nf* pigswill (*Brit*), hogwash (*US*); (*libro etc*) trash.

beato, a [be'ato, a] *a* blessed; (*piadoso*) pious.

bebé [be'ße] *nm* baby.

bebedero [beβe'ðero] nm (para animales) drinking trough.

bebedizo, a [beβe'ðiθo, a] a drinkable // nm potion.

bebedor, a [beβe'ðor, a] a hard-drinking.

beber [be'βer] vt, vi to drink.

bebida [be'βiða] nf drink.

beca ['beka] nf grant, scholarship.

befarse [be'farse] vr: ~ de algo to scoff at sth.

beldad [bel'dað] nf beauty.

Belén [be'len] nm Bethlehem; **b~** nm (de navidad) nativity scene, crib.

belga ['belɣa] a, nm/f Belgian.

Bélgica ['belxika] nf Belgium.

Belice [be'liθe] nm Belize.

bélico, a ['beliko, a] a (actitud) warlike; **belicoso, a** (guerrero) warlike; (agresivo) aggressive, bellicose.

beligerante [belive'rante] a belligerent.

bellaco, a [be'ʎako, a] a sly, cunning // nm villain, rogue; **bellaquería** nf (acción) dirty trick; (calidad) wickedness.

belleza [be'ʎeθa] nf beauty.

bello, a ['beʎo, a] a beautiful, lovely; Bellas Artes Fine Art.

bellota [be'ʎota] nf acorn.

bemol [be'mol] nm (MUS) flat; esto tiene ~es (fam) this is a tough one.

bencina [ben'θina] nf (AM: gasolina) petrol (Brit), gasoline (US).

bendecir [bende'θir] vt to bless.

bendición [bendi'θjon] nf blessing.

bendito, a [ben'dito, a] pp de **bendecir** // a (santo) holy; (afortunado) lucky; (feliz) happy; (sencillo) simple // nm/f simple soul.

benedictino, a [beneðik'tino, a] a, nm Benedictine.

beneficencia [benefi'θenθja] nf charity.

beneficiar [benefi'θjar] vt to benefit, be of benefit to; ~se vr to benefit, profit; ~io, a nm/f beneficiary.

beneficio [bene'fiθjo] nm (bien) benefit, advantage; (ganancia) profit, gain; ~so, a a beneficial.

benéfico, a [be'nefiko, a] a charitable.

beneplácito [bene'plaθito] nm approval, consent.

benevolencia [beneβo'lenθja] nf benevolence, kindness; **benévolo, a** a benevolent, kind.

benigno, a [be'niɣno, a] a kind; (suave) mild; (MED: tumor) benign, non-malignant.

beodo, a [be'oðo, a] a drunk.

berenjena [beren'xena] nf aubergine (Brit), eggplant (US).

Berlín [ber'lin] n Berlin; **berlinés, esa** a of o from Berlin // nm/f Berliner.

bermejo, a [ber'mexo, a] a red.

berrear [berre'ar] vi to bellow, low.

berrido [be'rriðo] nm bellow(ing).

berrinche [be'rrintʃe] nm (fam) temper, tantrum.

berro ['berro] nm watercress.

berza ['berθa] nf cabbage.

besamel [besa'mel] nf (CULIN) white sauce, bechamel sauce.

besar [be'sar] vt to kiss; (fig: tocar) to graze; ~se vr to kiss (one another); **beso** nm kiss.

bestia ['bestja] nf beast, animal; (fig) idiot; ~ de carga beast of burden.

bestial [bes'tjal] a bestial; (fam) terrific; ~idad nf bestiality; (fam) stupidity.

besugo [be'suɣo] nm sea bream; (fam) idiot.

besuquear [besuke'ar] vt to cover with kisses; ~se vr to kiss and cuddle.

betún [be'tun] nm shoe polish; (QUIMICA) bitumen.

biberón [biβe'ron] nm feeding bottle.

Biblia ['biβlja] nf Bible.

bibliografía [biβljoɣra'fia] nf bibliography.

biblioteca [biβljo'teka] nf library; (mueble) bookshelves pl; ~ de consulta reference library; ~rio, a nm/f librarian.

B.I.C. nf abr (= Brigada de Investigación Criminal) CID (Brit), FBI (US).

bicarbonato [bikar'βo'nato] *nm* bicarbonate.

bici ['biθi] *nf* (*fam*) bike.

bicicleta [biθi'kleta] *nf* bicycle, cycle.

bicho ['bitʃo] *nm* (*animal*) small animal; (*sabandija*) bug, insect; (*TAUR*) bull.

bidé [bi'ðe] *nm* bidet.

PALABRA CLAVE

bien [bjen] ◆ *nm* 1 (*bienestar*) good; **te lo digo por tu ~** I'm telling you for your own good; **el ~ y el mal** good and evil

2 (*posesión*): **~es goods; ~es de consumo** consumer goods; **~es inmuebles** o **raíces/~es muebles** real estate *sg*/personal property *sg*

◆ *ad* 1 (*de manera satisfactoria, correcta etc*) well; **trabaja/come ~** she works/eats well; **contestó ~** he answered correctly; **me siento ~** I feel fine; **no me siento ~** I don't feel very well; **se está ~ aquí** it's nice here

2 (*frases*): **hiciste ~ en llamarme** you were right to call me

3 (*valor intensivo*) very; **un cuarto ~ caliente** a nice warm room; **~ se ve que ...** it's quite clear that ...

4: **estar ~**: **estoy muy bien aquí** I feel very happy here; **está bien que vengan** it's alright for them to come; **¡está bien! lo haré** oh alright, I'll do it

5 (*de buena gana*): **yo ~ que iría pero ...** I'd gladly go but ...

◆ *excl*: **¡~! (*aprobación*) O.K.!; ¡muy ~!** well done!

◆ *a inv* (*matiz despectivo*): **niño ~** rich kid; **gente ~** posh people

◆ *conj* 1: **~ ... ~ ...** o **~ ... ~ ... en coche o en tren** either by car or by train

2: **no ~** (*esp AM*): **no ~ llegue te llamaré** as soon as I arrive I'll call you

3: **si ~** even though; *ver tb* **más**.

bienal [bje'nal] *a* biennial.

bienaventurado, a [bjenaβentu-'raðo, a] *a* (*feliz*) happy, fortunate.

bienestar [bjenes'tar] *nm* well-being, welfare.

bienhechor, a [bjene'tʃor, a] *a* beneficent // *nm/f* benefactor/ benefactress.

bienvenida [bjembe'niða] *nf* welcome; **dar la ~ a uno** to welcome sb.

bienvenido [bjembe'niðo] *excl* welcome!

bife ['bife] *nm* (*AM*) steak.

bifurcación [bifurka'θjon] *nf* fork.

bigamia [bi'xamja] *nf* bigamy; **bígamo, a** a bigamous // *nm/f* bigamist.

bigote [bi'xote] *nm* moustache; **bigotudo, a** *a* with a big moustache.

bikini [bi'kini] *nm* bikini; (*CULIN*) toasted ham and cheese sandwich.

bilingüe [bi'lingwe] *a* bilingual.

billar [bi'ʎar] *nm* billiards *sg*; (*lugar*) billiard hall; (*mini-casino*) amusement arcade.

billete [bi'ʎete] *nm* ticket; (*de banco*) banknote (*Brit*), bill (*US*); (*carta*) note; **~ sencillo, ~ de ida** solamente/de ida y vuelta single (*Brit*) o one-way (*US*) ticket/return (*Brit*) o round-trip (*US*) ticket; **~ de 20 libras** £20 note.

billetera [biʎe'tera] *nf*, **billetero** [biʎe'tero] *nm* wallet.

billón [bi'ʎon] *nm* billion.

bimensual [bimen'swal] *a* twice monthly.

bimotor [bimo'tor] *a* twin-engined // *nm* twin-engined plane.

binóculos [bi'nokulo] *nmpl* pince-nez.

biografía [bjoxra'fia] *nf* biography; **biógrafo, a** *nm/f* biographer.

biología [bjolo'xia] *nf* biology; **biológico, a** *a* biological; **biólogo, a** *a* nm/f biologist.

biombo ['bjombo] *nm* (folding) screen.

biopsia [bi'opsja] *nf* biopsy.

birlar [bir'lar] *vt* (*fam*) to pinch.

Birmania [bir'manja] *nf* Burma.

bis [bis] *excl* encore! // *ad:* **viven en el 27** ~ they live at 27a.

bisabuelo, a [bisa'βwelo, a] *nm/f* great-grandfather/mother.

bisagra [bi'saɣra] *nf* hinge.

bisbisar [bisβi'sar], **bisbisear** [bisβise'ar] *vt* to mutter, mumble.

bisiesto [bi'sjesto] *a:* **año** ~ leap year.

bisnieto, a [bis'njeto, a] *nm/f* great-grandson/daughter.

bisonte [bi'sonte] *nm* bison.

bistec [bis'tek], **bisté** [bis'te] *nm* steak.

bisturí [bistu'ri] *nm* scalpel.

bisutería [bisute'ria] *nf* imitation *o* costume jewellery.

bit [bit] *nm* (*INFORM*) bit.

bizcar [biθ'kar] *vi* to squint.

bizco, a [a ['biθko, a] *a* cross-eyed.

bizcocho [biθ'kotʃo] *nm* (*CULIN*) sponge cake.

bizquear [biθke'ar] *vi* to squint.

blanco, a ['blanko, a] *a* white // *nm/f* white man/woman, white // *nm* (*color*) white; (*en texto*) blank; (*MIL, fig*) target // *nf* (*MUS*) minim; **en** ~ blank; **noche en** ~ sleepless night; **estar sin** ~ to be broke.

blancura [blan'kura] *nf* whiteness.

blandir [blan'dir] *vt* to brandish.

blando, a ['blando, a] *a* soft; (*tierno*) tender, gentle; (*carácter*) mild; (*fam*) cowardly; **blandura** *nf* softness; tenderness; mildness.

blanquear [blanke'ar] *vt* to whiten; (*fachada*) to whitewash; (*paño*) to bleach // *vi* to turn white; **blanquecino, a** *a* whitish.

blasfemar [blasfe'mar] *vi* to blaspheme, curse; **blasfemia** *nf* blasphemy.

blasón [bla'son] *nm* coat of arms; (*fig*) honour; **blasonar** *vt* to emblazon // *vi* to boast, brag.

bledo ['bleðo] *nm:* **me importa un** ~ I couldn't care less.

blindado, a [blin'daðo, a] *a* (*MIL*) armour-plated; (*antibala*) bullet-proof; **coche** (*Esp*) *o* **carro** (*AM*) ~ armoured car.

blindaje [blin'daxe] *nm* armour, armour-plating.

bloc [blok] (*pl* ~**s**) *nm* writing pad.

bloque ['bloke] *nm* block; (*POL*) bloc; ~ **de cilindros** cylinder block.

bloquear [bloke'ar] *vt* to blockade; **bloqueo** *nm* blockade; (*COM*) freezing, blocking.

blusa ['blusa] *nf* blouse.

boato [bo'ato] *nm* show, ostentation.

bobada [bo'βaða], **bobería** [boβe'ria] *nf* foolish action; foolish statement; **decir bobadas** to talk nonsense.

bobina [bo'βina] *nf* (*TEC*) bobbin; (*FOTO*) spool; (*ELEC*) coil.

bobo, a ['boβo, a] *a* (*tonto*) daft, silly; (*cándido*) naive // *nm/f* fool, idiot // *nm* (*TEATRO*) clown, funny man.

boca ['boka] *nf* mouth; (*de crustáceo*) pincer; (*de cañón*) muzzle; (*entrada*) mouth, entrance; ~**s** *nfpl* (*de río*) mouth *sg*; ~ **abajo/arriba** face down/up; **a** ~**jarro** point-blank; **se me hace agua la** ~ my mouth is watering.

bocacalle [boka'kaʎe] *nf* (*entrance to a*) street; **la primera** ~ **the first** turning *o* street.

bocadillo [boka'ðiʎo] *nm* sandwich.

bocado [bo'kaðo] *nm* mouthful, bite; (*de caballo*) bridle; ~ **de Adán** Adam's apple.

bocanada [boka'naða] *nf* (*de vino*) mouthful, swallow; (*de aire*) gust, puff.

bocazas [bo'kaθas] *nm inv* (*fam*) bigmouth.

boceto [bo'θeto] *nm* sketch, outline.

bocina [bo'θina] *nf* (*AUTO*) horn, trumpet; (*AUTO*) horn; (*para hablar*) megaphone.

bocha ['botʃa] *nf* bowl; ~**s** *nfpl* bowls *sg*.

bochinche [bo'tʃintʃe] *nm* (*fam*) uproar.

bochorno [bo'tʃorno] *nm* (*vergüenza*) embarrassment;

(calor): **hace** ~ it's very muggy; **~so, a** a muggy; embarrassing.

boda ['boða] nf (tb: ~s) wedding, marriage; (fiesta) wedding reception; **~s de plata/de oro** silver/ golden wedding.

bodega [bo'ðeɣa] nf (de vino) (wine) cellar; (depósito) storeroom; (de barco) hold.

bodegón [boðe'ɣon] nm (ARTE) still life.

bofe ['bofe] nm (tb: ~s: de res) lights.

bofetada [bofe'taða] nf, **bofetón** [bofe'ton] nm slap (in the face).

boga ['boɣa] nf: **en** ~ (fig) in vogue.

bogar [bo'ɣar] vi (remar) to row; (navegar) to sail.

Bogotá [boɣo'ta] n Bogotá; **bogotano, a** a of o from Bogotá.

bohemio, a [bo'emjo, a] a, nm/f Bohemian.

boicot [boi'kot] (pl ~s) nm boycott; **~ear** vt to boycott; **~eo** nm boycott.

boina ['boina] nf beret.

bola ['bola] nf ball; (canica) marble; (NAIPES) (grand) slam; (betún) shoe polish; (mentira) tale, story; **~s** nfpl (AM) bolas sg; **~ de billar** billiard ball; **~ de nieve** snowball.

bolchevique [boltʃe'βike] a, nm/f Bolshevik.

boleadoras [bolea'ðoras] nfpl (AM) bolas sg.

bolera [bo'lera] nf skittle o bowling alley.

boleta [bo'leta] nf (AM: billete) ticket; (: permiso) pass, permit.

boletería [bolete'ria] nf (AM) ticket office.

boletín [bole'tin] nm bulletin; (periódico) journal, review; **~ escolar** (Esp) school report; **~ de noticias** news bulletin; **~ de pedido** application form; **~ de precios** price list; **~ de prensa** press release.

boleto [bo'leto] nm ticket.

boli ['boli] nm (fam) Biro ®, pen.

boliche [bo'litʃe] nm (bola) jack; (juego) bowls sg; (lugar) bowling alley.

bolígrafo [bo'liɣrafo] nm ball-point pen, Biro ®.

bolívar [bo'liβar] nm monetary unit of Venezuela.

Bolivia [bo'liβja] nf Bolivia; **boliviano, a** a, nm/f Bolivian.

bolo ['bolo] nm skittle; (píldora) (large) pill; **(juego de) ~s** nmpl skittles sg.

bolsa ['bolsa] nf (cartera) purse; (saco) bag; (AM) pocket; (ANAT) cavity, sac; (COM) stock exchange; (MINERÍA) pocket; **~ de agua caliente** hot water bottle; **~ de aire** air pocket; **~ de papel** paper bag; **~ de plástico** plastic bag.

bolsillo [bol'siʎo] nm pocket; (cartera) purse; **de ~** pocket(-size).

bolsista [bol'sista] nm/f stockbroker.

bolso ['bolso] nm (bolsa) bag; (de mujer) handbag.

bollo ['boʎo] nm (pan) roll; (bulto) bump, lump; (abolladura) dent.

bomba ['bomba] nf (MIL) bomb; (TEC) pump // a (fam): **noticia ~** bombshell // ad (fam): **pasarlo ~** to have a great time; **~ atómica/de humo/de retardo** atomic/smoke/time bomb; **~ de gasolina** petrol pump.

bombardear [bombarðe'ar] vt to bombard; (MIL) to bomb; **bombardeo** nm bombardment; bombing.

bombardero [bombar'ðero] nm bomber.

bombear [bombe'ar] vt (agua) to pump (out o up); (MIL) to bomb; **~se** vr to warp.

bombero [bom'bero] nm fireman.

bombilla [bom'biʎa] nf (Esp) (light) bulb.

bombín [bom'bin] nm bowler hat.

bombo ['bombo] nm (MUS) bass drum; (TEC) drum.

bombón [bom'bon] nm chocolate.

bonachón, ona [bona'tʃon, ona] a good-natured, easy-going.

bonaerense [bonae'rense] *a* of *o* from Buenos Aires.

bonanza [bo'nanθa] *nf* (*NAUT*) fair weather; (*fig*) bonanza; (*MINERÍA*) rich pocket *o* vein.

bondad [bon'daδ] *nf* goodness, kindness; **tenga la ~ de** (please) be good enough to; **~oso, a** *a* good, kind.

bonito, a [bo'nito, a] *a* pretty; (*agradable*) nice // *nm* (*atún*) tuna (fish).

bono ['bono] *nm* voucher; (*FINANZAS*) bond.

bonobús [bono'βus] *nm* (*Esp*) bus pass.

boquear [boke'ar] *vi* to gasp.

boquerón [boke'ron] *nm* (*pez*) (kind of) anchovy; (*agujero*) large hole.

boquete [bo'kete] *nm* gap, hole.

boquiabierto, a [bokia'βjerto, a] *a*: **quedar ~** to be amazed *o* flabbergasted.

boquilla [bo'kiʎa] *nf* (*para riego*) nozzle; (*para cigarro*) cigarette holder; (*MUS*) mouthpiece.

borbollar [borβo'ʎar], **borbollear** [borβoʎe'ar], **borbotar** [borβo'tar] *vi* to bubble.

borbotón [borβo'ton] *nm*: **salir a borbotones** to gush out.

bordado [bor'δaδo] *nm* embroidery.

bordar [bor'δar] *vt* to embroider.

borde ['borδe] *nm* edge, border; (*de camino etc*) side; (*en la costura*) hem; **al ~ de** (*fig*) on the verge *o* brink of; **ser ~** (*Esp: fam*) to be a pain (in the neck); **~ar** *vt* to border.

bordillo [bor'δiʎo] *nm* kerb (*Brit*), curb (*US*).

bordo [bor'δo] *nm* (*NAUT*) side; **a ~** on board.

borinqueño, a [borin'kenjo, a] *a*, *nm/f* Puerto Rican.

borra ['borra] *nf* (*pelusa*) fluff; (*sedimento*) sediment.

borrachera [borra'tʃera] *nf* (*ebriedad*) drunkenness; (*orgía*) spree, binge.

borracho, a [bo'rratʃo, a] *a* drunk //

nm/f (*que bebe mucho*) drunkard, drunk; (*temporalmente*) drunk, drunk man/woman.

borrador [borra'δor] *nm* (*escritura*) first draft, rough sketch; (*cuaderno*) scribbling pad; (*goma*) rubber (*Brit*), eraser.

borrajear [borraxe'ar] *vt*, *vi* to scribble.

borrar [bo'rrar] *vt* to erase, rub out.

borrasca [bo'rraska] *nf* storm.

borrico, a [bo'rriko, a] *nm/f* donkey/she-donkey; (*fig*) stupid man/woman.

borrón [bo'rron] *nm* (*mancha*) stain.

borroso, a [bo'rroso, a] *a* vague, unclear; (*escritura*) illegible.

bosque ['boske] *nm* wood; (*grande*) forest.

bosquejar [boske'xar] *vt* to sketch; **bosquejo** *nm* sketch.

bosta ['bosta] *nf* dung; (*abono*) manure.

bostezar [boste'θar] *vi* to yawn; **bostezo** *nm* yawn.

bota ['bota] *nf* (*calzado*) boot; (*saco*) leather wine bottle.

botánico, a [bo'taniko, a] *a* botanical // *nm/f* botanist // *nf* botany.

botar [bo'tar] *vt* to throw, hurl; (*NAUT*) to launch; (*fam*) to throw out // *vi* to bounce.

bote ['bote] *nm* (*salto*) bounce; (*golpe*) thrust; (*vasija*) tin, can; (*embarcación*) boat; **de ~ en ~** packed, jammed full; **~ salvavidas** lifeboat; **~ de la basura** (*AM*) dustbin (*Brit*), trashcan (*US*).

botella [bo'teʎa] *nf* bottle.

botica [bo'tika] *nf* chemist's (shop) (*Brit*), pharmacy; **~rio, a** *nm/f* chemist (*Brit*), pharmacist.

botijo [bo'tixo] *nm* (earthenware) jug.

botín [bo'tin] *nm* (*calzado*) half boot; (*polaina*) spat; (*MIL*) booty.

botiquín [boti'kin] *nm* (*armario*) medicine cabinet; (*portátil*) first-aid kit.

botón [bo'ton] *nm* button; (*BOT*)

bud; (de florete) tip; ~ **de oro** buttercup.

botones [bo'tones] nm inv bellboy (Brit), bellhop (US).

bóveda ['boβeða] nf (ARQ) vault.

boxeador [boksea'ðor] nm boxer.

boxeo [bok'seo] nm boxing.

boya ['boja] nf (NAUT) buoy; (flotador) float.

bozal [bo'θal] nm (de caballo) halter; (de perro) muzzle.

bracear [braθe'ar] vi (agitar los brazos) to wave one's arms.

bracero [bra'θero] nm labourer; (en el campo) farmhand.

bracete [bra'θete]: **de ~** ad arm in arm.

braga ['braxa] nf (cuerda) sling, rope; (de bebé) nappy (Brit), diaper (US); ~**s** nfpl (de mujer) panties, knickers (Brit).

bragueta [bra'xeta] nf fly, flies pl.

braille [breil] nm braille.

bramar [bra'mar] vi to bellow, roar; **bramido** nm bellow, roar.

brasa ['brasa] nf live o hot coal.

brasero [bra'sero] nm brazier.

Brasil [bra'sil] nm: (**el**) ~ Brazil; **brasileño, a** a, nm/f Brazilian.

bravata [bra'βata] nf boast.

braveza [bra'βeθa] nf (valor) bravery; (ferocidad) ferocity.

bravío, a [bra'βio, a] a wild; (feroz) fierce.

bravo, a ['braβo, a] a (valiente) brave; (bueno) fine, splendid; (feroz) ferocious; (salvaje) wild; (mar etc) rough, stormy // excl bravo!; **bravura** nf bravery; ferocity; (pey) boast.

braza ['braθa] nf fathom; **nadar a la ~** to swim (the) breast-stroke.

brazada [bra'θaða] nf stroke.

brazado [bra'θaðo] nm armful.

brazalete [braθa'lete] nm (pulsera) bracelet; (banda) armband.

brazo ['braθo] nm arm; (ZOOL) foreleg; (BOT) limb, branch; **luchar a ~ partido** to fight hand-to-hand; **del ~** to walk arm in arm.

brea ['brea] nf pitch, tar.

brebaje [bre'βaxe] nm potion.

brecha ['bretʃa] nf (hoyo, vacío) gap, opening; (MIL, fig) breach.

brega ['breɣa] nf (lucha) struggle; (trabajo) hard work.

breve ['breβe] a short, brief // nf (MUS) breve; ~**dad** nf brevity, shortness.

brezal [bre'θal] nm moor(land), heath; **brezo** nm heather.

bribón, ona [bri'βon, ona] a idle, lazy // nm/f (vagabundo) vagabond; (pícaro) rascal, rogue.

bricolaje [briko'laxe] nm do-it-yourself, DIY.

brida ['briða] nf bridle, rein; (TEC) clamp; **a toda ~** at top speed.

bridge [britʃ] nm bridge.

brigada [bri'ɣaða] nf (unidad) brigade; (trabajadores) squad, gang // nm = staff-sergeant, sergeant-major.

brillante [bri'ʎante] a brilliant // nm diamond.

brillar [bri'ʎar] vi (tb fig) to shine; (joyas) to sparkle.

brillo ['briʎo] nm shine; (brillantez) brilliance; (fig) splendour; **sacar ~ a** to polish.

brincar [brin'kar] vi to skip about, hop about, jump about; **está que brinca** he's hopping mad.

brinco ['brinko] nm jump, leap.

brindar [brin'dar] vi: ~ **a o por** to drink (a toast) to // vt to offer, present.

brindis ['brindis] nm toast; (TAUR) (ceremony of) dedication.

brío ['brio] nm spirit, dash; **brioso, a** a spirited, dashing.

brisa ['brisa] nf breeze.

británico, a [bri'taniko, a] a British // nm/f Briton, British person.

brocal [bro'kal] nm rim.

brocha ['brotʃa] nf (large) paint-brush; ~ **de afeitar** shaving brush.

broche ['brotʃe] nm brooch.

broma ['broma] nf joke; **en** ~ in fun, as a joke; **bromear** vi to joke.

bromista [bro'mista] *a* fond of joking // *nm/f* joker, wag.

bronca ['bronka] *nf* row; **echar una** ~ **a uno** to tick sb off.

bronce ['bronθe] *nm* bronze; ~**ado**, **a** *a* bronze; (*por el sol*) tanned // *nm* (*sun*)tan; (*TEC*) bronzing.

broncearse [bronθe'arse] *vr* to get a suntan.

bronco, a ['bronko, a] *a* (*manera*) rude, surly; (*voz*) harsh.

bronquitis [bron'kitis] *nf* bronchitis.

brotar [bro'tar] *vi* (*BOT*) to sprout; (*aguas*) to gush (forth); (*MED*) to break out.

brote ['brote] *nm* (*BOT*) shoot; (*MED, fig*) outbreak.

bruces ['bruθes]: **de** ~ *ad*: **caer** *o* **dar de** ~ to fall headlong, fall flat.

bruja ['bruxa] *nf* witch; **brujería** *nf* witchcraft.

brujo ['bruxo] *nm* wizard, magician.

brújula ['bruxula] *nf* compass.

bruma ['bruma] *nf* mist; **brumoso, a** *a* misty.

bruñido [bru'niðo] *nm* polish; **bruñir** *vt* to polish.

brusco, a ['brusko, a] *a* (*súbito*) sudden; (*áspero*) brusque.

Bruselas [bru'selas] *n* Brussels.

brutal [bru'tal] *a* brutal.

brutalidad [brutali'ðað] *nf* brutality.

bruto, a ['bruto, a] *a* (*idiota*) stupid; (*bestial*) brutish; (*peso*) gross; **en** ~ raw, unworked.

Bs.As. *abr* (= Buenos Aires) B.A.

bucal [bu'kal] *a* oral; **por vía** ~ orally.

bucear [buθe'ar] *vi* to dive // *vt* to explore; **buceo** *nm* diving; (*fig*) investigation.

bucle ['bukle] *nm* curl.

budismo [bu'ðismo] *nm* Buddhism.

buen [bwen] *am ver* **bueno**.

buenamente [bwena'mente] *ad* (*fácilmente*) easily; (*voluntariamente*) willingly.

buenaventura [bwenaßen'tura] *nf* (*suerte*) good luck; (*adivinación*) fortune.

PALABRA CLAVE

bueno, a ['bweno, a] ♦ *a* (*antes de nmsg*: **buen**) **1** (*excelente etc*) es un libro ~ *o* es un buen libro it's a good book; **hace** ~, **hace buen tiempo** the weather is *o* it is fine; **el** ~ **de Paco** good old Paco; **fue muy** ~ **conmigo** he was very nice *o* kind to me

2 (*apropiado*): **ser bueno/a para** to be good for; **creo que vamos por buen camino** I think we're on the right track

3 (*irónico*): **le di un buen rapapolvo** I gave him a good *o* real ticking off; **¡buen conductor estás hecho!** some *o* a fine driver you are!; **¡estaría** ~ **que** ...! a fine thing it would be if ...!

4 (*atractivo, sabroso*): **está bueno este bizcocho** this sponge is delicious; **Carmen está muy buena** Carmen is looking good

5 (*saludos*): **¡buen día!**, **¡buenos días!** good morning!; **¡buenas (tardes)!** (good) afternoon!; (*más tarde*) (good) evening!; **¡buenas noches!** good night!

6 (*otras locuciones*): **estar de buenas** to be in a good mood; **por las buenas o por las malas** by hook or by crook; **de buenas a primeras** all of a sudden

♦ *excl*: **¡**~**!** all right!; ~, **¿y qué?** well, so what?

Buenos Aires *nm* Buenos Aires.

buey [bwei] *nm* ox.

búfalo ['bufalo] *nm* buffalo.

bufanda [bu'fanda] *nf* scarf.

bufar [bu'far] *vi* to snort.

bufete [bu'fete] *nm* (*despacho de abogado*) lawyer's office.

buffer ['bufer] *nm* (*INFORM*) buffer.

bufón [bu'fon, ona] *nm* clown.

buhardilla [buar'ðiʎa] *nf* (*desván*) attic.

búho ['buo] *nm* owl; (*fig*) hermit, recluse.

buhonero [buo'nero] *nm* pedlar.

buitre ['bwitre] *nm* vulture.

bujía [bu'xia] *nf* (*vela*) candle; (*ELEC*) candle (power); (*AUTO*) spark plug.

bula ['bula] *nf* (*papal*) bull.

bulbo ['bulβo] *nm* bulb.

bulevar [bule'βar] *nm* boulevard.

Bulgaria [bul'yarja] *nf* Bulgaria; **búlgaro, a** *a, nm/f* Bulgarian.

bulto ['bulto] *nm* (*paquete*) package; (*fardo*) bundle; (*tamaño*) size, bulkiness; (*MED*) swelling, lump; (*silueta*) vague shape; (*estatua*) bust, statue.

bulla ['buʎa] *nf* (*ruido*) uproar; (*de gente*) crowd.

bullicio [bu'ʎiθjo] *nm* (*ruido*) uproar; (*movimiento*) bustle.

bullir [bu'ʎir] *vi* (*hervir*) to boil; (*burbujear*) to bubble; (*mover*) to move, stir.

buñuelo [bu'ɲwelo] *nm* ≈ doughnut (*Brit*), donut (*US*); (*fruta de sartén*) fritter.

BUP [bup] *nm abr* (*Esp* = *Bachillerato Unificado Polivalente*) *secondary education and leaving certificate for 14-17 age group*.

buque ['buke] *nm* ship, vessel.

burbuja [bur'βuxa] *nf* bubble; **burbujear** *vi* to bubble.

burdel [bur'ðel] *nm* brothel.

burdo, a ['burðo, a] *a* coarse, rough.

burgués, esa [bur'ɣes, esa] *a* middle-class, bourgeois; **burguesía** *nf* middle class, bourgeoisie.

burla ['burla] *nf* (*mofa*) gibe; (*broma*) joke; (*engaño*) trick.

burladero [burla'ðero] *nm* (bullfighter's) refuge.

burlador, a [burla'ðor, a] *a* mocking // *nm/f* (*bromista*) joker // *nm* (*libertino*) seducer.

burlar [bur'lar] *vt* (*engañar*) to deceive; (*seducir*) to seduce // *vi*, **~se** *vr* to joke; **~se de** to make fun of.

burlesco, a [bur'lesko, a] *a* burlesque.

burlón, ona [bur'lon, ona] *a* mocking.

burocracia [buro'kraθja] *nf* civil service; (*pey*) bureaucracy.

burócrata [bu'rokrata] *nm/f* civil servant; (*pey*) bureaucrat.

buromática [buro'matika] *nf* office automation.

burro, a ['burro] *nm/f* donkey/she-donkey; (*fig*) ass, idiot.

bursátil [bur'satil] *a* stock-exchange *cpd*.

bus [bus] *nm* bus.

busca ['buska] *nf* search, hunt // *nm* (*TEL*) bleeper; **en ~ de** in search of.

buscapleitos [buska'pleitos] *nm/f inv* troublemaker.

buscar [bus'kar] *vt* to look for, search for, seek // *vi* to look, search, seek; **se busca secretaria** secretary wanted.

buscón, ona [bus'kon, ona] *a* thieving // *nm* petty thief // *nf* whore.

busilis [bu'silis] *nm* (*fam*) snag.

busque *etc vb ver* **buscar**.

búsqueda [bus'keða] *nf* = **busca**.

busto ['busto] *nm* (*ANAT, ARTE*) bust.

butaca [bu'taka] *nf* armchair; (*de cine, teatro*) stall, seat.

butano [bu'tano] *nm* butane (gas).

buzo ['buθo] *nm* diver.

buzón [bu'θon] *nm* (*en puerta*) letter box; (*en la calle*) pillar box.

C

C. *abr* (= *centígrado*) C; (= *compañía*) Co.

c. *abr* (= *capítulo*) ch.

C/ *abr* (= *calle*) St.

c.a. *abr* (= *corriente alterna*) AC.

cabal [ka'βal] *a* (*exacto*) exact; (*correcto*) right, proper; (*acabado*) finished, complete; **~es** *nmpl*: **estar en sus ~es** to be in one's right mind.

cabalgadura [kaβalɣa'ðura] *nf* mount, horse.

cabalgar [kaβal'ɣar] *vt, vi* to ride.

cabalgata [kaβal'ɣata] *nf* procession.

caballa [ka'βaʎa] *nf* mackerel.

caballeresco, a [kaβaʎe'resko, a] *a* noble, chivalrous.

caballería [kaβaʎe'ria] *nf* mount; (*MIL*) cavalry.

caballeriza [kaβaʎe'riθa] *nf* stable; **caballerizo** *nm* groom, stableman.

caballero [kaβa'ʎero] *nm* (*hombre galante*) gentleman; (*de la orden de caballería*) knight; (*trato directo*) sir.

caballerosidad [kaβaʎerosi'ðað] *nf* chivalry.

caballete [kaβa'ʎete] *nm* (*ARTE*) easel; (*TEC*) trestle.

caballito [kaβa'ʎito] *nm* (*caballo pequeño*) small horse, pony; ~s *nmpl* (*en verbena*) roundabout *sg*, merry-go-round.

caballo [ka'βaʎo] *nm* horse; (*AJEDREZ*) knight; (*NAIPES*) queen; ~ **de vapor** *o* **de fuerza** horse-power.

cabaña [ka'βaɲa] *nf* (*casita*) hut, cabin.

cabaré, cabaret [kaβa're] (*pl* **cabarés, cabarets**) *nm* cabaret.

cabecear [kaβeθe'ar] *vt, vi* to nod.

cabecera [kaβe'θera] *nf* head; (*de distrito*) chief town; (*IMPRENTA*) headline.

cabecilla [kaβe'θiʎa] *nm/f* ringleader.

cabellera [kaβe'ʎera] *nf* (*head of*) hair; (*de cometa*) tail.

cabello [ka'βeʎo] *nm* (*tb:* ~s) hair *sg*.

caber [ka'βer] *vi* (*entrar*) to fit, go; **caben 3 más** there's room for 3 more.

cabestrillo [kaβes'triʎo] *nm* sling.

cabestro [ka'βestro] *nm* halter.

cabeza [ka'βeθa] *nf* head; (*POL*) chief, leader; ~**da** *nf* (*golpe*) butt; **dar** ~**das** to nod off.

cabida [ka'βiða] *nf* space.

cabildo [ka'βildo] *nm* (*de iglesia*) chapter; (*POL*) town council.

cabina [ka'βina] *nf* cabin; (*de camión*) cab; ~ **telefónica** telephone box (*Brit*) *o* booth.

cabizbajo, a [kaβiθ'βaxo, a] *a* crestfallen, dejected.

cable ['kaβle] *nm* cable.

cabo ['kaβo] *nm* (*de objeto*) end, extremity; (*MIL*) corporal; (*NAUT*) rope, cable; (*GEO*) cape; **al** ~ **de 3 días** after 3 days.

cabra ['kaβra] *nf* goat.

cabré *etc vb ver* **caber**.

cabrío, a [ka'βrio, a] *a* goatish; **macho** ~ (*he-*) goat, billy goat.

cabriola [ka'βrjola] *nf* caper.

cabritilla [kaβri'tiʎa] *nf* kid, kidskin.

cabrito [ka'βrito] *nm* kid.

cabrón [ka'βron] *nm* cuckold; (*fam!*) bastard (!).

cacahuete [kaka'wete] *nm* (*Esp*) peanut.

cacao [ka'kao] *nm* cocoa; (*BOT*) cacao.

cacarear [kakare'ar] *vi* (*persona*) to boast; (*gallina*) to crow.

cacería [kaθe'ria] *nf* hunt.

cacerola [kaθe'rola] *nf* pan, saucepan.

cacique [ka'θike] *nm* chief, local ruler; (*POL*) local party boss; **caciquismo** *nm* system of dominance by the local boss.

caco ['kako] *nm* pickpocket.

cacto ['kakto] *nm*, **cactus** ['kaktus] *nm inv* cactus.

cacharro [ka'tʃarro] *nm* earthenware pot; ~s *nmpl* pots and pans.

cachear [katʃe'ar] *vt* to search, frisk.

cachemir [katʃe'mir] *nm* cashmere.

cacheo [ka'tʃeo] *nm* searching, frisking.

cachete [ka'tʃete] *nm* (*ANAT*) cheek; (*bofetada*) slap (in the face).

cachimba [ka'tʃimba] *nf* pipe.

cachiporra [katʃi'porra] *nf* truncheon.

cachivache [katʃi'βatʃe] *nm* (*trasto*) piece of junk; ~s *nmpl* junk *sg*.

cacho ['katʃo, a] *nm* (*small*) bit; (*AM: cuerno*) horn.

cachondeo [katʃon'deo] *nm* (*fam*)

farce, joke.

cachondo, a [ka'tʃondo, a] a (ZOOL) on heat; (fam) randy, sexy; (gracioso) funny.

cachorro, a [ka'tʃorro, a] nm/f (perro) pup, puppy; (león) cub.

cada ['kaða] a inv each; (antes de número) every; ~ día each day, every day; ~ **dos días** every other day; ~ **uno/a** each one, every one; ~ **vez más** more and more; **uno de** ~ **diez** one out of every ten.

cadalso [ka'ðalso] nm scaffold.

cadáver [ka'ðaβer] nm (dead) body, corpse.

cadena [ka'ðena] nf chain; (TV) channel; **trabajo en** ~ assembly line work.

cadencia [ka'ðenθja] nf cadence, rhythm.

cadera [ka'ðera] nf hip.

cadete [ka'ðete] nm cadet.

caducar [kaðu'kar] vi to expire; **caduco, a** a expired; (persona) very old.

C.A.E. abr (= cóbrese al entregar) COD.

caer [ka'er] vi, **caerse** vr to fall (down); **me cae bien/mal** I get on well with him/I can't stand him; ~ **en la cuenta** to catch on; **su cumpleaños cae en viernes** her birthday falls on a Friday.

café [ka'fe] (pl ~**s**) nm (bebida, planta) coffee; (lugar) café // a (color) brown; ~ **con leche** white coffee; ~ **solo** black coffee; **cafetal** nm coffee plantation.

cafetería [kafete'ria] nf (gen) café.

cafetero, a [kafe'tero, a] a coffee cpd; **ser muy** ~ to be a coffee addict // nf coffee pot.

cagar [ka'var] vt (fam!) to shit (!); to bungle, mess up // vi to have a shit (!).

caída [ka'iða] nf fall; (declive) slope; (disminución) fall, drop.

caiga etc vb ver **caer**.

caimán [kai'man] nm alligator.

caja ['kaxa] nf box; (para reloj) case;

(de ascensor) shaft; (COM) cashbox; (donde se hacen los pagos) cashdesk; (: en supermercado) checkout; till; ~ **de ahorros** savings bank; ~ **de cambios** gearbox; ~ **fuerte**, ~ **de caudales** safe, strongbox.

cajero, a [ka'xero, a] nm/f cashier.

cajetilla [kaxe'tiʎa] nf (de cigarrillos) packet.

cajón [ka'xon] nm big box; (de mueble) drawer.

cal [kal] nf lime.

cala ['kala] nf (GEO) cove, inlet; (de barco) hold.

calabacín [kalaβa'θin] nm (BOT) baby marrow; (: más pequeño) courgette (Brit), zucchini (US).

calabacita [kalaβa'θita] nf (AM) courgette (Brit), zucchini (US).

calabaza [kala'βaθa] nf (BOT) pumpkin.

calabozo [kala'βoθo] nm (cárcel) prison; (celda) cell.

calado, a [ka'laðo, a] a (prenda) lace cpd // nm (NAUT) draught // nf (de cigarrillo) puff.

calamar [kala'mar] nm squid.

calambre [ka'lambre] nm (tb: ~**s**) cramp.

calamidad [kalami'ðað] nf calamity, disaster.

calamina [kala'mina] nf calamine.

calaña [ka'laɲa] nf model, pattern.

calar [ka'lar] vt to soak, drench; (penetrar) to pierce, penetrate; (comprender) to see through; (vela, red) to lower; ~**se** vr (AUTO) to stall; ~**se las gafas** to stick one's glasses on.

calavera [kala'βera] nf skull.

calcañal [kalka'nal], **calcañar** [kalka'nar], **calcaño** [kal'kaɲo] nm heel.

calcar [kal'kar] vt (reproducir) to trace; (imitar) to copy.

calceta [kal'θeta] nf (knee-length) stocking; **hacer** ~ to knit.

calcetín [kalθe'tin] nm sock.

calcinar [kalθi'nar] vt to burn, blacken.

calcio ['kalθjo] nm calcium.

calco ['kalko] nm tracing.

calcomanía [kalkoma'nia] nf transfer.

calculadora [kalkula'ðora] nf calculator.

calcular [kalku'lar] vt (MAT) to calculate, compute; ~ **que** ... to reckon that ...; **cálculo** nm calculation.

caldear [kalde'ar] vt to warm (up), heat (up).

caldera [kal'dera] nf boiler.

calderilla [kalde'riʎa] nf (moneda) small change.

caldero [kal'dero] nm small boiler.

caldo ['kaldo] nm stock; (consomé) consommé.

calefacción [kalefak'θjon] nf heating; ~ **central** central heating.

calendario [kalen'darjo] nm calendar.

calentador [kalenta'ðor] nm heater.

calentar [kalen'tar] vt to heat (up); ~**se** vr to heat up, warm up; (fig: discusión etc) to get heated.

calentura [kalen'tura] nf (MED) fever, (high) temperature.

calibrar [kali'ßrar] vt to gauge, measure; **calibre** nm (de cañón) calibre, bore; (diámetro) diameter; (fig) calibre.

calidad [kali'ðað] nf quality; **de ~** quality cpd; **en ~ de** in the capacity of, as.

cálido, a ['kaliðo, a] a hot; (fig) warm.

caliente etc vb ver **calentar** // [ka'ljente] a hot; (fig) fiery; (disputa) heated; (fam: cachondo) randy.

calificación [kalifika'θjon] nf qualification; (de alumno) grade, mark.

calificar [kalifi'kar] vt to qualify; (alumno) to grade, mark; ~ **de** to describe as.

calizo, a [ka'liθo, a] a lime cpd // nf limestone.

calma ['kalma] nf calm; (pachorra) slowness.

calmante [kal'mante] nm sedative, tranquillizer.

calmar [kal'mar] vt to calm, calm down // vi (tempestad) to abate; (mente etc) to become calm.

calmoso, a [kal'moso, a] a calm, quiet.

calor [ka'lor] nm heat; (~ agradable) warmth.

caloría [kalo'ria] nf calorie.

calorífero, a [kalo'rifero, a] a heat-producing, heat-giving // nm heating system.

calumnia [ka'lumnja] nf calumny, slander; **calumnioso, a** a slanderous.

caluroso, a [kalu'roso, a] a hot; (sin exceso) warm; (fig) enthusiastic.

calvario [kal'ßarjo] nm stations pl of the cross.

calvicie [kal'ßiθje] nf baldness.

calvo, a ['kalßo, a] a bald; (terreno) bare, barren; (tejido) threadbare // nf bald patch; (en bosque) clearing.

calza ['kalθa] nf wedge, chock.

calzado, a [kal'θaðo, a] a shod // nm footwear // nf roadway, highway.

calzador [kalθa'ðor] nm shoehorn.

calzar [kal'θar] vt (zapatos etc) to wear; (un mueble) to put a wedge under; ~**se** vr: ~**se los zapatos** to put on one's shoes; **¿qué (número) calza?** what size do you take?

calzón [kal'θon] nm (tb: **calzones** nmpl) shorts pl; (AM: de hombre) pants, (: de mujer) panties.

calzoncillos [kalθon'θiʎos] nmpl underpants.

callado, a [ka'ʎaðo, a] a quiet.

callar [ka'ʎar] vt (asunto delicado) to keep quiet about, say nothing about; (persona, opinión) to silence // vi, ~**se** vr to keep quiet, be silent; ¡**cállate!** be quiet!, shut up!

calle ['kaʎe] nf street; (DEPORTE) lane; ~ **arriba/abajo** up/down the street; ~ **de un solo sentido** one-way street.

calleja [ka'ʎexa] nf alley, narrow street; **callejear** vi to wander (about) the streets; **callejero, a** *a* street *cpd* // **ciudad** *nm* street map; **callejón** *nm* alley, passage; **callejón sin salida** cul-de-sac; **callejuela** *nf* side-street, alley.

callista [ka'ʎista] *nm/f* chiropodist.

callo ['kaʎo] *nm* callus; (*en el pie*) corn; **~s** *nmpl* (CULIN) tripe *sg*; **~so, a** *a* horny, rough.

cama ['kama] *nf* bed; (GEO) stratum; **~ individual/de matrimonio** single/double bed.

camada [ka'maða] *nf* litter; (*de personas*) gang, band.

camafeo [kama'feo] *nm* cameo.

cámara ['kamara] *nf* chamber; (*habitación*) room; (*sala*) hall; (CINE) cine camera; (*fotográfica*) camera; **~ de aire** inner tube.

camarada [kama'raða] *nm* comrade, companion.

camarera [kama'rera] *nf* (*en restaurante*) waitress; (*en casa, hotel*) maid.

camarero [kama'rero] *nm* waiter.

camarilla [kama'riʎa] *nf* (*clan*) clique; (POL) lobby.

camarín [kama'rin] *nm* dressing room.

camarón [kama'ron] *nm* shrimp.

camarote [kama'rote] *nm* cabin.

cambiable [kam'bjaßle] *a* (*variable*) changeable, variable; (*intercambiable*) interchangeable.

cambiante [kam'bjante] *a* variable.

cambiar [kam'bjar] *vt* to change; (*dinero*) to change // *vi* to change; **~se** *vr* (*mudarse*) to move; (*de ropa*) to change; **~ de idea** to change one's mind; **~ de ropa** to change (one's clothes).

cambiazo [kam'bjaθo] *nm*: **dar el ~ a uno** to swindle sb.

cambio ['kambjo] *nm* change; (*trueque*) exchange; (COM) rate of exchange; (*oficina*) bureau de change; (*dinero menudo*) small change; **en ~** on the other hand; (*en lugar de*) instead; **~ de divisas** foreign exchange; **~ de velocidades**

gear lever; **~ de vía** points *pl*.

cambista [kam'bista] *nm* (COM) exchange broker.

camelar [kame'lar] *vt* (*con mujer*) to flirt with; (*persuadir*) to cajole.

camello [ka'meʎo] *nm* camel; (*fam: traficante*) pusher.

camilla [ka'miʎa] *nf* (MED) stretcher.

caminante [kami'nante] *nm/f* traveller.

caminar [kami'nar] *vi* (*marchar*) to walk, go; (*viajar*) to travel, journey // *vt* (*recorrer*) to cover, travel.

caminata [kami'nata] *nf* long walk; (*por el campo*) hike.

camino [ka'mino] *nm* way, road; (*sendero*) track; **a medio ~** halfway (there); **en el ~** on the way, en route; **~ de** on the way to; **~ particular** private road.

camión [ka'mjon] *nm* lorry (Brit), truck (US); **camionero, a** *nm/f* lorry *o* truck driver.

camioneta [kamjo'neta] *nf* van, light truck.

camisa [ka'misa] *nf* shirt; (BOT) skin; **~ de dormir** nightdress; **~ de fuerza** straitjacket; **camisería** *nf* outfitter's (shop).

camiseta [kami'seta] *nf* (*prenda*) tee-shirt; (: *ropa interior*) vest; (*de deportista*) top.

camisón [kami'son] *nm* nightdress, nightgown.

camorra [ka'morra] *nf*: **armar** *o* **buscar ~** to look for trouble, kick up a fuss.

campamento [kampa'mento] *nm* camp.

campana [kam'pana] *nf* bell; **~da** *nf* peal; **~rio** *nm* belfry.

campanilla [kampa'niʎa] *nf* small bell.

campaña [kam'paɲa] *nf* (MIL, POL) campaign.

campechano, a [kampe'tʃano, a] *a* (*franco*) open.

campeón, ona [kampe'on, ona] *nm/f* champion; **campeonato** *nm* championship.

campesino, a [kampe'sino, a] *a* country *cpd*, rural; (*gente*) peasant *cpd* // *nm/f* countryman/woman; (*agricultor*) farmer.

campestre [kam'pestre] *a* country *cpd*, rural.

camping ['kampin] *nm* camping; (*lugar*) campsite; **ir de** *o* **hacer** ~ to go camping.

campiña [kam'piɲa] *nf* countryside.

campo ['kampo] *nm* (*fuera de la ciudad*) country, countryside; (*AGR, ELEC*) field; (*de fútbol*) pitch; (*de golf*) course; (*MIL*) camp.

camposanto [kampo'santo] *nm* cemetery.

camuflaje [kamu'flaxe] *nm* camouflage.

cana ['kana] *nf ver* **cano.**

Canadá [kana'ða] *nm* Canada; **canadiense** *a, nm/f* Canadian // *nf* fur-lined jacket.

canal [ka'nal] *nm* canal; (*GEO*) channel, strait; (*de televisión*) channel; (*de tejado*) gutter; ~ **de Panamá** Panama Canal; ~**izar** *vt* to channel.

canalón [kana'lon] *nm* (*conducto vertical*) drainpipe; (*del tejado*) gutter.

canalla [ka'naʎa] *nf* rabble, mob // *nm* swine.

canapé [kana'pe] (*pl* ~**s**) *nm* sofa, settee; (*CULIN*) canapé.

Canarias [ka'narjas] *nfpl*: **(las Islas)** ~ the Canary Islands, the Canaries.

canario, a [ka'narjo, a] *a, nm/f* (*native*) of the Canary Isles // *nm* (*ZOOL*) canary.

canasta [ka'nasta] *nf* (round) basket; **canastilla** [-'tiʎa] *nf* small basket; (*de niño*) layette.

canasto [ka'nasto] *nm* large basket.

cancela [kan'θela] *nf* gate.

cancelación [kanθela'θjon] *nf* cancellation.

cancelar [kanθe'lar] *vt* to cancel; (*una deuda*) to write off.

cáncer ['kanθer] *nm* (*MED*) cancer;

C~ (*ASTROLOGÍA*) Cancer.

canciller [kanθi'ʎer] *nm* chancellor.

canción [kan'θjon] *nf* song; ~ **de cuna** lullaby; **cancionero** *nm* song book.

cancha ['kantʃa] *nf* (*de baloncesto, tenis etc*) court; (*AM*: *de fútbol*) pitch.

candado [kan'daðo] *nm* padlock.

candela [kan'dela] *nf* candle.

candelero [kande'lero] *nm* (*para vela*) candlestick; (*de aceite*) oil lamp.

candente [kan'dente] *a* red-hot; (*fig*: *tema*) burning.

candidato, a [kandi'ðato, a] *nm/f* candidate.

candidez [kandi'ðeθ] *nf* (*sencillez*) simplicity; (*simpleza*) naïveté; **cándido, a** *a* simple; naive.

candil [kan'dil] *nm* oil lamp; ~**ejas** [-'lexas] *nfpl* (*TEATRO*) footlights.

candor [kan'dor] *nm* (*sinceridad*) frankness; (*inocencia*) innocence.

canela [ka'nela] *nf* cinnamon.

cangrejo [kan'grexo] *nm* crab.

canguro [kan'guro] *nm* kangaroo; **hacer de** ~ to babysit.

caníbal [ka'nißal] *a, nm/f* cannibal.

canica [ka'nika] *nf* marble.

canijo, a [ka'nixo, a] *a* frail, sickly.

canino, a [ka'nino, a] *a* canine // *nm* canine (tooth).

canjear [kanxe'ar] *vt* to exchange.

cano, a ['kano, a] *a* grey-haired, white-haired // *nf* white *o* grey hair; **tener canas** to be going grey.

canoa [ka'noa] *nf* canoe.

canon ['kanon] *nm* canon; (*pensión*) rent; (*COM*) tax.

canónigo [ka'noniɣo] *nm* canon.

canonizar [kanoni'θar] *vt* to canonize.

cansado, a [kan'saðo, a] *a* tired, weary; (*tedioso*) tedious, boring.

cansancio [kan'sanθjo] *nm* tiredness, fatigue.

cansar [kan'sar] *vt* (*fatigar*) to tire, tire out; (*aburrir*) to bore; (*fastidiar*) to bother; ~**se** *vr* to tire, get tired; (*aburrirse*) to get bored.

cantábrico, a [kan'taβriko, a] *a* Cantabrian; **mar C~** ≈ Bay of Biscay.

cantante [kan'tante] *a* singing // *nm/f* singer.

cantar [kan'tar] *vt* to sing // *vi* to sing; (*insecto*) to chirp; (*rechinar*) to squeak // *nm* (*acción*) singing; (*canción*) song; (*poema*) poem.

cántara [kantara] *nf* large pitcher.

cántaro [kantaro] *nm* pitcher, jug; **llover a ~s** to rain cats and dogs.

cante [kante] *nm*: ~ **jondo** flamenco singing.

cantera [kan'tera] *nf* quarry.

cantidad [kanti'ðað] *nf* quantity, amount.

cantilena [kanti'lena] *nf* = **cantinela**.

cantimplora [kantim'plora] *nf* (*frasco*) water bottle, canteen.

cantina [kan'tina] *nf* canteen; (*de estación*) buffet.

cantinela [kanti'nela] *nf* ballad, song.

canto [kanto] *nm* singing; (*canción*) song; (*borde*) edge, rim; (*de un cuchillo*) back; ~ **rodado** boulder.

cantor, a [kan'tor, a] *nm/f* singer.

canturrear [kanturre'ar] *vi* to sing softly.

canuto [ka'nuto] *nm* (*tubo*) small tube; (*fam*: *droga*) joint.

caña [kaɲa] *nf* (BOT: *tallo*) stem, stalk; (*carrizo*) reed; (*vaso*) tumbler; (*de cerveza*) glass of beer; (ANAT) shinbone; ~ **de azúcar** sugar cane; ~ **de pescar** fishing rod.

cañada [ka'naða] *nf* (*entre dos montañas*) gully, ravine; (*camino*) cattle track.

cáñamo [kaɲamo] *nm* hemp.

caño [kaɲo] *nm* (*tubo*) tube, pipe; (*de albañal*) sewer; (MUS) pipe; (*de fuente*) jet.

cañón [ka'ɲon] *nm* (MIL) cannon; (*de fusil*) barrel; (GEO) canyon, gorge.

cañonera [kaɲo'nera] *nf* (*tb*: **lancha** ~) gunboat.

caoba [ka'oβa] *nf* mahogany.

caos [kaos] *nm* chaos.

cap. *abr* (= *capítulo*) ch.

capa [kapa] *nf* cloak, cape; (GEO) layer, stratum; **so ~ de** under the pretext of.

capacidad [kapaθi'ðað] *nf* (*medida*) capacity; (*aptitud*) capacity, ability.

capacitación [kapaθita'θjon] *nf* training.

capar [ka'par] *vt* to castrate, geld.

caparazón [kapara'θon] *nm* shell.

capataz [kapa'taθ] *nm* foreman.

capaz [ka'paθ] *a* able, capable; (*amplio*) capacious, roomy.

capcioso, a [kapˈθjoso, a] *a* wily, deceitful.

capellán [kapeˈʎan] *nm* chaplain; (*sacerdote*) priest.

caperuza [kapeˈruθa] *nf* hood.

capilla [ka'piʎa] *nf* chapel.

capital [kapi'tal] *a* capital // *nm* (COM) capital // *nf* (*ciudad*) capital; ~ **social** share capital.

capitalismo [kapita'lismo] *nm* capitalism; **capitalista** *a, nm/f* capitalist.

capitalizar [kapitali'θar] *vt* to capitalize.

capitán [kapi'tan] *nm* captain.

capitanear [kapitane'ar] *vt* to captain.

capitolio [kapi'toljo] *nm* capitol.

capitulación [kapitula'θjon] *nf* (*rendición*) capitulation, surrender; (*acuerdo*) agreement, pact; **capitulaciones** (*matrimoniales*) *nfpl* marriage contract *sg*.

capitular [kapitu'lar] *vi* to come to terms, make an agreement.

capítulo [ka'pitulo] *nm* chapter.

capó [ka'po] *nm* (AUTO) bonnet.

capón [ka'pon] *nm* (*gallo*) capon.

caporal [kapo'ral] *nm* chief, leader.

capota [ka'pota] *nf* (*de mujer*) bonnet; (AUTO) hood (Brit), top (US).

capote [ka'pote] *nm* (*abrigo*: *de militar*) greatcoat; (: *de torero*) cloak.

Capricornio [kapri'kornjo] *nm* Capricorn.

capricho [ka'pritʃo] *nm* whim, caprice; **~so, a** *a* capricious.

cápsula ['kapsula] *nf* capsule.

captar [kap'tar] *vt* (*comprender*) to understand; (*RADIO*) to pick up; (*atención, apoyo*) to attract.

captura [kap'tura] *nf* capture; (*JUR*) arrest; **capturar** *vt* to capture; to arrest.

capucha [ka'putʃa] *nf* hood, cowl.

capullo [ka'puʎo] *nm* (*BOT*) bud; (*ZOOL*) cocoon; (*fam*) idiot.

caqui ['kaki] *nm* khaki.

cara ['kara] *nf* (*ANAT, de moneda*) face; (*aspecto*) appearance; (*de disco*) side; (*fig*) boldness; **~ a** *ad* facing; **de ~** opposite, facing; **dar la ~** to face the consequences; **¿~ o cruz?** heads or tails?; **¡qué ~ más dura!** what a nerve!

carabina [kara'ßina] *nf* carbine, rifle; (*persona*) chaperone.

Caracas [ka'rakas] *n* Caracas.

caracol [kara'kol] *nm* (*ZOOL*) snail; (*concha*) (sea) shell.

caracolear [karakole'ar] *vi* (*caballo*) to prance about.

carácter [ka'rakter] (*pl* caracteres) *nm* character; **tener buen/mal ~** to be good natured/bad tempered.

característico, a [karakte'ristiko, a] *a* characteristic // *nf* characteristic.

caracterizar [karakteri'θar] *vt* (*distinguir*) to characterize, typify; (*honrar*) to confer a distinction on.

caradura [kara'ðura] *nm/f*: **es un ~** he's got a nerve.

carajo [ka'raxo] *nm* (*fam!*): **¡~!** shit! (!).

caramba [ka'ramba] *excl* good gracious!

carámbano [ka'rambano] *nm* icicle.

caramelo [kara'melo] *nm* (*dulce*) sweet; (*azúcar fundida*) caramel.

carapacho [kara'patʃo] *nm* shell, carapace.

caraqueño, a [kara'keɲo, a] *a, nm/f*

of o from Caracas.

carátula [ka'ratula] *nf* (*careta, máscara*) mask; (*TEATRO*): **la ~** the stage.

caravana [kara'ßana] *nf* caravan; (*fig*) group; (*AUTO*) tailback.

carbón [kar'ßon] *nm* coal; **papel ~** carbon paper; **carboncillo** *nm* (*ARTE*) charcoal; **carbonero, a** *nm/f* coal merchant; **carbonilla** [-'niʎa] *nf* coal dust.

carbonizar [karßoni'θar] *vt* to carbonize; (*quemar*) to char.

carbono [kar'ßono] *nm* carbon.

carburador [karßura'ðor] *nm* carburettor.

carburante [karßu'rante] *nm* fuel.

carcajada [karka'xaða] *nf* (loud) laugh, guffaw.

cárcel [ˈkarθel] *nf* prison, jail; (*TEC*) clamp; **carcelero, a** *a* prison *cpd* // *nm/f* warder.

carcomer [karko'mer] *vt* to bore into, eat into; (*fig*) to undermine; **~se** *vr* to become worm-eaten; (*fig*) to decay; **carcomido, a** *a* worm-eaten; (*fig*) rotten.

cardenal [karðe'nal] *nm* (*REL*) cardinal; (*MED*) bruise.

cárdeno, a [ˈkarðeno, a] *a* purple; (*livido*) livid.

cardíaco, a [kar'ðiako, a] *a* cardiac, heart *cpd*.

cardinal [karði'nal] *a* cardinal.

cardo [ˈkarðo] *nm* thistle.

carear [kare'ar] *vt* to bring face to face; (*comparar*) to compare; **~se** *vr* to come face to face, meet.

carecer [kare'θer] *vi*: **~ de** to lack, be in need of.

carencia [ka'renθja] *nf* lack; (*escasez*) shortage; (*MED*) deficiency.

carente [ka'rente] *a*: **~ de** lacking in, devoid of.

carestía [kares'tia] *nf* (*escasez*) scarcity, shortage; (*COM*) high cost.

careta [ka'reta] *nf* mask.

carga ['karɣa] *nf* (*peso, ELEC*) load; (*de barco*) cargo, freight; (*MIL*) charge; (*obligación, responsabilidad*)

duty, obligation:
cargado, a [kar'xaðo, a] *a* loaded;
(*ELEC*) live; (*café, té*) strong;
(*cielo*) overcast.
cargamento [karxa'mento] *nm*
(*acción*) loading; (*mercancías*) load,
cargo.
cargar [kar'xar] *vt* (*barco, arma*) to
load; (*ELEC*) to charge; (*COM: algo
en cuenta*) to charge; (*UNIFORM*) to
load // *vi* (*MIL: enemigo*) to charge;
(*AUTO*) to load (up); (*inclinarse*) to
lean; ~ **con** to pick up, carry away;
(*peso, fig*) to shoulder, bear; ~**se** *vr*
(*fam: estropear*) to break; (: *matar*)
to bump off.
cargo ['karxo] *nm* (*puesto*) post,
office; (*responsabilidad*) duty, obligation; (*fig*) weight, burden; (*COM*)
charge; **hacerse ~ de** to take
charge of *o* responsibility for.
carguero [kar'xero] *nm* freighter,
cargo boat; (*avión*) freight plane.
Caribe [ka'riβe] *nm*: **el ~** the Caribbean; **del ~** Caribbean.
caribeño, a [kari'βeno, a] *a* Caribbean.
caricatura [karika'tura] *nf* car-
icature.
caricia [ka'riθja] *nf* caress.
caridad [kari'ðað] *nf* charity.
caries ['karjes] *nf inv* (*MED*) tooth
decay.
cariño [ka'rino] *nm* affection, love;
(*caricia*) caress; (*en carta*) love...;
~**so, a** *a* affectionate.
caritativo, a [karita'tiβo, a] *a* charitable.
cariz [ka'riθ] *nm*: **tener** *o* **tomar
buen/mal ~** to look good/bad.
carmesí [karme'si] *a, nm* crimson.
carmín [kar'min] *nm* lipstick.
carnal [kar'nal] *a* carnal; **primo ~**
first cousin.
carnaval [karna'βal] *nm* carnival.
carne ['karne] *nf* flesh; (*CULIN*)
meat; ~ **de cerdo/cordero/ternera/
vaca** pork/lamb/veal/beef.
carné [kar'ne] *nm*: ~ **de conducir**
driving licence (*Brit*), driver's

license (*US*); ~ **de identidad**
identity card.
carnero [kar'nero] *nm* sheep; ram;
(*carne*) mutton.
carnet [kar'ne(t)] *nm* = **carné.**
carnicería [karniθe'ria] *nf* butcher's
(shop); (*fig: matanza*) carnage,
slaughter.
carnicero, a [karni'θero, a] *a*
carnivorous // *nm/f* (*tb fig*) butcher;
(*carnívoro*) carnivore.
carnívoro, a [kar'niβoro, a] *a*
carnivorous.
carnoso, a [kar'noso, a] *a* beefy, fat.
caro, a ['karo, a] *a* dear; (*COM*)
dear, expensive // *ad* dear, dearly.
carpa ['karpa] *nf* (*pez*) carp; (*de
circo*) big top; (*AM: de camping*)
tent.
carpeta [kar'peta] *nf* folder, file.
carpintería [karpinte'ria] *nf* carpentry, joinery; **carpintero** *nm*
carpenter.
carraspera [karras'pera] *nf* hoarse-
ness.
carrera [ka'rrera] *nf* (*acción*)
run(ning); (*espacio recorrido*) run;
(*certamen*) race; (*trayecto*) course;
(*profesión*) career; (*ESCOL*) course.
carreta [ka'rreta] *nf* wagon, cart.
carrete [ka'rrete] *nm* reel, spool;
(*TEC*) coil.
carretera [karre'tera] *nf* (*main*)
road, highway; ~ **de
circunvalación** ring road; ~
nacional ≈ A road (*Brit*), state highway (*US*).
carretilla [karre'tiʎa] *nf* trolley;
(*AGR*) (wheel)barrow.
carril [ka'rril] *nm* furrow; (*de
autopista*) lane; (*FERRO*) rail.
carrillo [ka'rriʎo] *nm* (*ANAT*) cheek;
(*TEC*) pulley.
carrizo [ka'rriθo] *nm* reed.
carro ['karro] *nm* cart, wagon; (*MIL*)
tank; (*AM: coche*) car.
carrocería [karroθe'ria] *nf* bodywork,
coachwork.
carroña [ka'rrona] *nf* carrion *q.*
carrusel [karru'sel] *nm* merry-go-

round, roundabout.

carta [ˈkarta] *nf* letter; (*CULIN*) menu; (*naipe*) card; (*mapa*) map; (*JUR*) document; **~ de crédito** credit card; **~ certificada** registered letter; **~ marítima** chart; **~ verde** (*AUTO*) green card.

cartel [karˈtel] *nm* (*anuncio*) poster, placard; (*ESCOL*) wall chart; (*COM*) cartel; **~ era** *nf* hoarding, billboard; (*en periódico etc*) entertainments guide; **'en ~era'** 'showing'.

cartera [karˈtera] *nf* (*de bolsillo*) wallet; (*de colegial, cobrador*) satchel; (*de señora*) handbag; (*para documentos*) briefcase; (*COM*) portfolio; **ocupa la ~ de Agricultura** she is Minister of Agriculture.

carterista [karteˈrista] *nm/f* pickpocket.

cartero [karˈtero] *nm* postman.

cartilla [karˈtiʎa] *nf* primer, first reading book; **~ de ahorros** savings book.

cartón [karˈton] *nm* cardboard.

cartucho [karˈtutʃo] *nm* (*MIL*) cartridge.

casa [ˈkasa] *nf* house; (*hogar*) home; (*edificio*) building; (*COM*) firm, company; **~ consistorial** town hall; **~ de huéspedes** boarding house; **~ de socorro** first aid post.

casadero, a [kasaˈðero, a] *a* of marrying age.

casado, a [kaˈsaðo, a] *a* married // *nm/f* married man/woman.

casamiento [kasaˈmjento] *nm* marriage, wedding.

casar [kaˈsar] *vt* to marry; (*JUR*) to quash, annul; **~se** *vr* to marry, get married.

cascabel [kaskaˈβel] *nm* (small) bell.

cascada [kasˈkaða] *nf* waterfall.

cascanueces [kaskaˈnweθes] *nm inv* nutcrackers.

cascar [kasˈkar] *vt*, **cascarse** *vr* to crack, split, break (open).

cáscara [ˈkaskara] *nf* (*de huevo, fruta seca*) shell; (*de fruta*) skin; (*de*

casco [ˈkasko] *nm* (*de bombero, soldado*) helmet; (*NAUT: de barco*) hull; (*ZOOL: de caballo*) hoof; (*botella*) empty bottle; (*de ciudad*): **el ~ antiguo** the old part; **el ~ urbano** the town centre.

cascote [kasˈkote] *nm* rubble.

caserío [kaseˈrio] *nm* hamlet; (*casa*) country house.

casero, a [kaˈsero, a] *a* (*pan etc*) home-made // *nm/f* (*propietario*) landlord/lady; (*COM*) house agent; **ser muy ~** to be home-loving; **'comida casera'** 'home cooking'.

caseta [kaˈseta] *nf* hut; (*para bañista*) cubicle; (*de feria*) stall.

casete [kaˈsete] *nm o f* cassette.

casi [ˈkasi] *ad* almost, nearly; **~ nada** hardly anything; **~ nunca** hardly ever, almost never; **~ te caes** you almost fell.

casilla [kaˈsiʎa] *nf* (*casita*) hut, cabin; (*TEATRO*) box office; (*AJEDREZ*) square; (*para cartas*) pigeonhole.

casino [kaˈsino] *nm* club; (*de juego*) casino.

caso [ˈkaso] *nm* case; **en ~ de...** in case of...; **el ~ es que** the fact is that; **en ese ~** in that case; **hacer ~ a** to pay attention to; **hacer ~ omiso** to be irrelevant.

caspa [ˈkaspa] *nf* dandruff.

cassette [kaˈsete] *nm o f* = **casete**.

casta [ˈkasta] *nf* caste; (*raza*) breed; (*linaje*) lineage.

castaña [kasˈtaɲa] *nf* chestnut.

castañetear [kastaɲeteˈar] *vi* (*dientes*) to chatter.

castaño, a [kasˈtaɲo, a] *a* chestnut(-coloured), brown // *nm* chestnut tree.

castañuelas [kastaˈɲwelas] *nfpl* castanets.

castellano, a [kasteˈʎano, a] *a* Castilian // *nm* (*LING*) Castilian, Spanish.

castidad [kastiˈðað] *nf* chastity, purity.

castigar [kasti'ɣar] vt to punish; (DEPORTE) to penalize; (afligir) to afflict; **castigo** nm punishment; (DEPORTE) penalty.

Castilla [kas'tiʎa] nf Castille.

castillo [kas'tiʎo] nm castle.

castizo, a [kas'tiθo, a] a (LING) pure; (de buena casta) purebred, pedigree.

casto, a ['kasto, a] a chaste, pure.

castor [kas'tor] nm beaver.

castrar [kas'trar] vt to castrate.

casual [ka'swal] a chance, accidental; **~idad** nf chance, accident; (combinación de circunstancias) coincidence; **¡qué ~idad!** what a coincidence!

cataclismo [kata'klismo] nm cataclysm.

catador, a [kata'ðor, a] nm/f wine taster.

catalán, ana [kata'lan, ana] a, nm/f Catalan // nm (LING) Catalan.

catalizador [kataliθa'ðor] nm catalyst.

catálogo [ka'taloɣo] nm catalogue.

Cataluña [kata'luɲa] nf Catalonia.

catar [ka'tar] vt to taste, sample.

catarata [kata'rata] nf (GEO) waterfall; (MED) cataract.

catarro [ka'tarro] nm catarrh; (constipado) cold.

catástrofe [ka'tastrofe] nf catastrophe.

catedral [kate'ðral] nf cathedral.

catedrático, a [kate'ðratiko, a] nm/f professor.

categoría [kateɣo'ria] nf category; (rango) rank, standing; (calidad) quality; **de ~** (hotel) top-class.

categórico, a [kate'ɣoriko, a] a categorical.

catolicismo [katoli'θismo] nm Catholicism.

católico, a [ka'toliko, a] a, nm/f Catholic.

catorce [ka'torθe] num fourteen.

cauce ['kauθe] nm (de río) riverbed; (fig) channel.

caución [kau'θjon] nf bail;

caucionar vt (JUR) to bail, go bail for.

caucho ['kautʃo] nm rubber; (AM: llanta) tyre.

caudal [kau'ðal] nm (de río) volume, flow; (fortuna) wealth; (abundancia) abundance; **~oso, a** a (río) large; (persona) wealthy, rich.

caudillo [kau'ðiʎo] nm leader, chief.

causa ['kausa] nf cause; (razón) reason; (JUR) lawsuit, case; **a ~ de** because of.

causar [kau'sar] vt to cause.

cautela [kau'tela] nf caution, cautiousness; **cauteloso, a** a cautious, wary.

cautivar [kauti'ßar] vt to capture; (fig) to captivate.

cautiverio [kauti'ßerjo] nm, **cautividad** [kautißi'ðað] nf captivity.

cautivo, a [kau'tißo, a] a, nm/f captive.

cauto, a ['kauto, a] a cautious, careful.

cava ['kaßa] nm champagne-type wine.

cavar [ka'ßar] vt to dig.

caverna [ka'ßerna] nf cave, cavern.

cavidad [kaßi'ðað] nf cavity.

cavilar [kaßi'lar] vt to ponder.

cayado [ka'jaðo] nm (de pastor) crook; (de obispo) crozier.

cayendo etc vb ver **caer**.

caza ['kaθa] nf (acción: gen) hunting; (: con fusil) shooting; (una ~) hunt, chase; (animales) game // nm (AVIAT) fighter.

cazador, a [kaθa'ðor, a] nm/f hunter // nf jacket.

cazar [ka'θar] vt to hunt; (perseguir) to chase; (prender) to catch.

cazo ['kaθo] nm saucepan.

cazuela [ka'θwela] nf (vasija) pan; (guisado) casserole.

cebada [θe'ßaða] nf barley.

cebar [θe'ßar] vt (animal) to fatten (up); (anzuelo) to bait; (MIL, TEC) to prime.

cebo ['θeßo] nm (para animales) feed, food; (para peces, fig) bait; (de *arma*) charge.

cebolla [θe'βoʎa] *nf* onion; **cebollín** *nm* spring onion.

cebra [θeβra] *nf* zebra.

cecear [θeθe'ar] *vi* to lisp; **ceceo** *nm* lisp.

cedazo [θe'δaθo] *nm* sieve.

ceder [θe'δer] *vt* to hand over, give up, part with // *vi* (*renunciar*) to give in, yield; (*disminuir*) to diminish, decline; (*romperse*) to give way.

cedro ['θeδro] *nm* cedar.

cédula ['θeδula] *nf* certificate, document.

CEE *nf abr* (= *Comunidad Económica Europea*) EEC.

cegar [θe'xar] *vt* to blind; (*tubería etc*) to block up, stop up // *vi* to go blind; **~se** *vr*: **~** (**de**) to be blinded (by).

ceguera [θe'xera] *nf* blindness.

ceja ['θexa] *nf* eyebrow.

cejar [θe'xar] *vi* (*fig*) to back down.

celada [θe'laδa] *nf* ambush, trap.

celador, a [θela'δor, a] *nm/f* (*de edificio*) watchman; (*de museo etc*) attendant.

celda ['θelda] *nf* cell.

celebración [θeleβra'θjon] *nf* celebration.

celebrar [θele'βrar] *vt* to celebrate; (*alabar*) to praise // *vi* to be glad; **~se** *vr* to occur, take place.

célebre ['θelebre] *a* famous.

celebridad [θeleβri'δaδ] *nf* fame; (*persona*) celebrity.

celeste [θe'leste] *a* sky-blue; (*ASTRO*) celestial, heavenly.

celestial [θeles'tjal] *a* celestial, heavenly.

celibato [θeli'βato] *nm* celibacy.

célibe ['θeliβe] *a, nm/f* celibate.

celo ['θelo] *nm* zeal; (*REL*) fervour; (*ZOOL*): **en ~** on heat; **~s** *nmpl* jealousy *sg*.

celofán [θelo'fan] *nm* cellophane.

celoso, a [θe'loso, a] *a* (*envidioso*) jealous; (*trabajador*) zealous; (*desconfiado*) suspicious.

celta ['θelta] *a* Celtic // *nm/f* Celt.

célula ['θelula] *nf* cell.

celuloide [θelu'loiδe] *nm* celluloid.

cementerio [θemen'terjo] *nm* cemetery, graveyard.

cemento [θe'mento] *nm* cement; (*hormigón*) concrete; (*AM*: *cola*) glue.

cena ['θena] *nf* evening meal, dinner.

cenagal [θena'xal] *nm* bog, quagmire.

cenar [θe'nar] *vt* to have for dinner // *vi* to have dinner.

cenicero [θeni'θero] *nm* ashtray.

cenit [θe'nit] *nm* zenith.

ceniza [θe'niθa] *nf* ash, ashes *pl*.

censo ['θenso] *nm* census; **~ electoral** electoral roll.

censura [θen'sura] *nf* (*POL*) censorship; (*moral*) censure, criticism.

censurar [θensu'rar] *vt* (*idea*) to censure; (*cortar*: *película*) to censor.

centella [θen'teʎa] *nf* spark.

centellear [θenteʎe'ar] *vi* (*metal*) to gleam; (*estrella*) to twinkle; (*fig*) to sparkle; **centelleo** *nm* gleam(ing); twinkling; sparkling.

centenar [θente'nar] *nm* hundred.

centenario, a [θente'narjo, a] *a* centenary; hundred-year-old // *nm* centenary.

centésimo, a [θen'tesimo, a] *a* hundredth.

centígrado [θen'tixraδo] *a* centigrade.

centímetro [θen'timetro] *nm* centimetre (*Brit*), centimeter (*US*).

céntimo ['θentimo] *nm* cent.

centinela [θenti'nela] *nm* sentry, guard.

centollo [θen'toʎo] *nm* spider crab.

central [θen'tral] *a* central // *nf* head office; (*TEC*) plant; (*TEL*) exchange; **~ nuclear** nuclear power station.

centralización [θentraliθa'θjon] *nf* centralization.

centralizar [θentrali'θar] *vt* to centralize.

centrar [θen'trar] *vt* to centre.

céntrico, a ['θentriko, a] *a* central.

centrista [θen'trista] *a* centre *cpd*.

centro ['θentro] *nm* centre; ~ **comercial** shopping centre; ~ **juvenil** youth club.

centroamericano, a [θentroameri-'kano, a] *a, nm/f* Central American.

ceñir [θe'nir] *vt* (*rodear*) to encircle, surround; (*ajustar*) to fit (tightly); (*apretar*) to tighten.

ceño ['θeno] *nm* frown, scowl; **fruncir el ~** to frown, knit one's brow.

CEOE *nf abr* (*Esp* = Confederación Española de Organizaciones Empresariales*) ≈ CBI (*Brit*), employers' organization.

cepillar [θepi'ʎar] *vt* to brush; (*madera*) to plane (down).

cepillo [θe'piʎo] *nm* brush; (*para madera*) plane.

cera ['θera] *nf* wax.

cerámica [θe'ramika] *nf* ceramics *sg*, pottery.

cerca ['θerka] *nf* fence // *ad* near, nearby, close; ~**s** *nmpl* foreground *sg*; ~ **de** *prep* near, close to.

cercanía [θerka'nia] *nf* nearness, closeness; ~**s** *nfpl* outskirts, suburbs.

cercano, a [θer'kano, a] *a* close, near.

cercar [θer'kar] *vt* to fence in; (*rodear*) to surround.

cerciorar [θerθjo'rar] *vt* (*asegurar*) to assure; ~**se** *vr* (*descubrir*) to find out; (*asegurarse*) to make sure.

cerco ['θerko] *nm* (*AGR*) enclosure; (*AM*) fence; (*MIL*) siege.

cerdo ['θerðo] *nm* pig.

cereal [θere'al] *nm* cereal; ~**es** *nmpl* cereals, grain *sg*.

cerebro [θe'reβro] *nm* brain; (*fig*) brains *pl*.

ceremonia [θere'monja] *nf* ceremony; **ceremonial** *a, nm* ceremonial; **ceremonioso, a** *a* ceremonious; (*cumplido*) formal.

cereza [θe'reθa] *nf* cherry.

cerilla [θe'riʎa] *nf* (*fósforo*) match.

cernerse [θer'nerse] *vr* to hover.

cernidor [θerni'ðor] *nm* sieve.

cero ['θero] *nm* nothing, zero.

cerrado, a [θe'rraðo, a] *a* closed, shut; (*con llave*) locked; (*tiempo*) cloudy, overcast; (*curva*) sharp; (*acento*) thick, broad.

cerradura [θerra'ðura] *nf* (*acción*) closing; (*mecanismo*) lock.

cerrajero [θerra'xero] *nm* locksmith.

cerrar [θe'rrar] *vt* to close, shut; (*paso, carretera*) to close; (*grifo*) to turn off; (*cuenta, negocio*) to close // *vi* to close, shut; (*la noche*) to come down; ~**se** *vr* to close, shut; ~ **con llave** to lock; ~ **un trato** to strike a bargain.

cerro ['θerro] *nm* hill.

cerrojo [θe'rroxo] *nm* (*herramienta*) bolt; (*de puerta*) latch.

certamen [θer'tamen] *nm* competition, contest.

certero, a [θer'tero, a] *a* (*gen*) accurate.

certeza [θer'teθa], **certidumbre** [θerti'ðumbre] *nf* certainty.

certificado [θertifi'kaðo] *nm* certificate.

certificar [θertifi'kar] *vt* (*asegurar, atestar*) to certify.

cervatillo [θerβa'tiʎo] *nm* fawn.

cervecería [θerβeθe'ria] *nf* (*fábrica*) brewery; (*bar*) public house, pub.

cerveza [θer'βeθa] *nf* beer.

cesación [θesa'θjon] *nf* cessation, suspension.

cesante [θe'sante] *a* redundant.

cesantía [θesan'tia] *nf* unemployment.

cesar [θe'sar] *vi* to cease, stop // *vt* (*funcionario*) to remove from office.

cese ['θese] *nm* (*de trabajo*) dismissal; (*de pago*) suspension.

césped ['θespeð] *nm* grass, lawn.

cesta ['θesta] *nf* basket.

cesto ['θesto] *nm* (large) basket, hamper.

cetro ['θetro] *nm* sceptre.

cfr *abr* (= confróntese) cf.

ch... *ver bajo la letra* CH, *después de* C.

Cía *abr* (= compañía) Co.

cianuro [θja'nuro] *nm* cyanide.

cicatriz [θika'triθ] *nf* scar; **~ar** *vt* to heal; **~arse** *vr* to heal (up), form a scar.

ciclismo [θi'klismo] *nm* cycling.

ciclo ['θiklo] *nm* cycle.

ciclón [θi'klon] *nm* cyclone.

ciego, a ['θjeɣo, a] *a* blind // *nm/f* blind man/woman.

cielo ['θjelo] *nm* sky; (REL) heaven; **¡~s!** good heavens!

ciempiés [θjem'pjes] *nm inv* centipede.

cien [θjen] *num ver* **ciento.**

ciénaga [θi'enaɣa] *nf* marsh, swamp.

ciencia ['θjenθja] *nf* science; **~s** *nfpl* (ESCOL) science *sg*; **~-ficción** *nf* science fiction.

cieno ['θjeno] *nm* mud, mire.

científico, a [θjen'tifiko, a] *a* scientific // *nm/f* scientist.

ciento ['θjento], **cien** *num* hundred; **pagar al 10 por ~** to pay at 10 per cent.

cierne ['θjerne] *nm*: **en ~** in blossom.

cierre *etc vb ver* **cerrar** // ['θjerre] *nm* closing, shutting; (con llave) locking; **~ de cremallera** zip (fastener).

cierro *etc vb ver* **cerrar.**

cierto, a ['θjerto, a] *a* sure, certain; (un tal) a certain; (correcto) right, correct; **~ hombre** a certain man; **ciertas personas** certain *o* some people; **sí, es ~** yes, that's correct.

ciervo ['θjerβo] *nm* (ZOOL) deer; (: macho) stag.

cierzo ['θjerθo] *nm* north wind.

cifra ['θifra] *nf* number, numeral; (cantidad) number, quantity; (secreta) code.

cifrar [θi'frar] *vt* to code, write in code; (resumir) to abridge.

cigala [θi'ɣala] *nf* Norway lobster.

cigarra [θi'ɣarra] *nf* cicada.

cigarrera [θiɣa'rrera] *nf* cigar case.

cigarrillo [θiɣa'rriλo] *nm* cigarette.

cigarro [θi'ɣarro] *nm* cigarette; (puro) cigar.

cigüeña [θi'ɣweɲa] *nf* stork.

cilíndrico, a [θi'lindriko, a] *a* cylindrical.

cilindro [θi'lindro] *nm* cylinder.

cima ['θima] *nf* (de montaña) top, peak; (de árbol) top; (fig) height.

címbalo ['θimbalo] *nm* cymbal.

cimbrar [θim'brar], **cimbrear** [θimbre'ar] *vt* to brandish; **~se** *vr* to sway.

cimentar [θimen'tar] *vt* to lay the foundations of; (fig: fundar) to found.

cimiento [θi'mjento] *nm* foundation.

cinc [θink] *nm* zinc.

cincel [θin'θel] *nm* chisel; **~ar** *vt* to chisel.

cinco ['θinko] *num* five.

cincuenta [θin'kwenta] *num* fifty.

cine ['θine] *nm* cinema.

cineasta [θine'asta] *nm/f* (director de cine) film director.

cinematográfico, a [θinemato-'ɣrafiko, a] *a* cine-, film *cpd*.

cínico, a ['θiniko, a] *a* cynical // *nm/f* cynic.

cinismo [θi'nismo] *nm* cynicism.

cinta ['θinta] *nf* band, strip; (de tela) ribbon; (película) reel; (de máquina de escribir) ribbon; **~ adhesiva** sticky tape; **~ magnetofónica** tape; **~ métrica** tape measure.

cinto ['θinto] *nm* belt.

cintura [θin'tura] *nf* waist.

cinturón [θintu'ron] *nm* belt; **~ de seguridad** safety belt.

ciprés [θi'pres] *nm* cypress (tree).

circo ['θirko] *nm* circus.

circuito [θir'kwito] *nm* circuit.

circulación [θirkula'θjon] *nf* circulation; (AUTO) traffic.

circular [θirku'lar] *a, nf* circular // *vi, vt* to circulate // *vi* (AUTO) to drive; **'circule por la derecha'** 'keep (to the) right'.

círculo ['θirkulo] *nm* circle.

circuncidar [θirkunθi'dar] *vt* to circumcise.

circundar [θirkun'dar] *vt* to surround.

circunferencia [θirkunfe'renθja] *nf* circumference.

circunscribir [θirkunskri'βir] *vt* to circumscribe; ~se *vr* to be limited.

circunscripción [θirkunskrip'θjon] *nf* division; (POL) constituency.

circunspecto, a [θirkuns'pekto, a] *a* circumspect, cautious.

circunstancia [θirkuns'tanθja] *nf* circumstance.

circunstante [θirkuns'tante] *nm/f* onlooker, bystander.

cirio ['θirjo] *nm* (wax) candle.

ciruela [θi'rwela] *nf* plum; ~ **pasa** prune.

cirugía [θiru'xia] *nf* surgery; ~ **estética** o **plástica** plastic surgery.

cirujano [θiru'xano] *nm* surgeon.

cisne ['θisne] *nm* swan.

cisterna [θis'terna] *nf* cistern, tank.

cita ['θita] *nf* appointment, meeting; (de novios) date; (referencia) quotation.

citación [θita'θjon] *nf* (JUR) summons *sg*.

citar [θi'tar] *vt* (gen) to make an appointment with; (JUR) to summons; (un autor, texto) to quote; ~se *vr*: **se citaron en el cine** they arranged to meet at the cinema.

cítricos ['θitrikos] *nmpl* citrus fruit(s).

ciudad [θju'ðað] *nf* town; (más grande) city; ~**anía** *nf* citizenship; ~**ano, a** *nm/f* citizen.

cívico, a ['θiβiko, a] *a* civic.

civil [θi'βil] *a* civil // *nm* (guardia) policeman.

civilización [θiβiliθa'θjon] *nf* civilization.

civilizar [θiβili'θar] *vt* to civilize.

civismo [θi'βismo] *nm* public spirit.

cizaña [θi'θaɲa] *nf* (fig) discord.

cl. *abr* (= centilitro) cl.

clamar [kla'mar] *vt* to clamour for, cry out for // *vi* to cry out, clamour.

clamor [kla'mor] *nm* (grito) cry, shout; (fig) clamour, protest.

clandestino, a [klandes'tino, a] *a* clandestine; (POL) underground.

clara ['klara] *nf* (de huevo) egg white.

claraboya [klara'βoja] *nf* skylight.

clarear [klare'ar] *vi* (el día) to dawn; (el cielo) to clear up, brighten up; ~se *vr* to be transparent.

clarete [kla'rete] *nm* rosé (wine).

claridad [klari'ðað] *nf* (del día) brightness; (de estilo) clarity.

clarificar [klarifi'kar] *vt* to clarify.

clarín [kla'rin] *nm* bugle.

clarinete [klari'nete] *nm* clarinet.

clarividencia [klariβi'ðenθja] *nf* clairvoyance; (fig) far-sightedness.

claro, a ['klaro, a] *a* clear; (luminoso) bright; (color) light; (evidente) clear, evident; (poco espeso) thin // *nm* (en bosque) clearing // *ad* clearly // *excl* of course!

clase ['klase] *nf* class; ~ **alta/media/obrera** upper/middle/working class.

clásico, a ['klasiko, a] *a* classical; (fig) classic.

clasificación [klasifika'θjon] *nf* classification; (DEPORTE) league (table).

clasificar [klasifi'kar] *vt* to classify.

claudia ['klauðja] *nf* greengage.

claudicar [klauði'kar] *vi* (fig) to back down.

claustro ['klaustro] *nm* cloister.

cláusula ['klausula] *nf* clause.

clausura [klau'sura] *nf* closing, closure; **clausurar** *vt* (congreso etc) to bring to a close.

clavar [kla'βar] *vt* (clavo) to hammer in; (cuchillo) to stick, thrust; (tablas etc) to nail (together).

clave ['klaβe] *nf* key; (MUS) clef.

clavel [kla'βel] *nm* carnation.

clavícula [kla'βikula] *nf* collar bone.

clavija [kla'βixa] *nf* peg, dowel, pin; (ELEC) plug.

clavo ['klaβo] *nm* (de metal) nail; (BOT) clove.

claxon ['klakson] (pl ~s) *nm* horn.

clemencia [kle'menθja] *nf* mercy, clemency.

cleptómano, a [klep'tomano, a] *a, nm/f* kleptomaniac.

clerical [kleri'kal] *a* clerical.

clérigo ['kleriɣo] *nm* clergyman.

clero ['klero] *nm* clergy.

cliché [kli'tʃe] *nm* cliché; (*FOTO*) negative.

cliente, a ['kljente, a] *nm/f* client, customer.

clientela [kljen'tela] *nf* clientele, customers *pl*.

clima ['klima] *nm* climate.

climatizado, a [klimati'θaðo, a] *a* air-conditioned.

clínica ['klinika] *nf* clinic; (*particular*) private hospital.

clip [klip] (*pl* ~s) *nm* paper clip.

clorhídrico, a [klo'riðriko, a] *a* hydrochloric.

club [klub] (*pl* ~s o ~es) *nm* club; ~ **de jóvenes** youth club.

cm *abr* (= *centímetro, centímetros*) cm.

C.N.T. *abr* (*Esp*) = *Confederación Nacional de Trabajo*.

coacción [koak'θjon] *nf* coercion, compulsion.

coagular [koaɣu'lar] *vt*, **coagularse** *vr* (*leche, sangre*) to clot; **coágulo** *nm* clot.

coalición [koali'θjon] *nf* coalition.

coartada [koar'taða] *nf* alibi.

coartar [koar'tar] *vt* to limit, restrict.

coba ['koβa] *nf*: **dar** ~ **a uno** to soft-soap sb.

cobarde [ko'βarðe] *a* cowardly // *nm* coward; **cobardía** *nf* cowardice.

cobaya [ko'βaja] *nf*, **cobayo** [ko'βajo] *nm* guinea pig.

cobertizo [koβer'tiθo] *nm* shelter.

cobertor [koβer'tor] *nm* bedspread.

cobertura [koβer'tura] *nf* cover.

cobija [ko'βixa] *nf* (*AM*) blanket.

cobijar [koβi'xar] *vt* (*cubrir*) to cover; (*abrigar*) to shelter; **cobijo** *nm* shelter.

cobra ['koβra] *nf* cobra.

cobrador, a [koβra'ðor, a] *nm/f* (*de autobús*) conductor/conductress; (*de impuestos, gas*) collector.

cobrar [ko'βrar] *vt* (*cheque*) to cash; (*sueldo*) to collect, draw; (*objeto*) to recover; (*precio*) to charge; (*deuda*) to collect // *vi* to draw one's pay; ~**se**

vr to recover, get well; **cóbrese al entregar** cash on delivery (COD).

cobre ['koβre] *nm* copper; ~**s** *nmpl* brass instruments.

cobro ['koβro] *nm* (*de cheque*) cashing; (*pago*) payment; **presentar al** ~ to cash.

Coca-Cola [koka'kola] *nf* ® Coca-Cola ®.

cocaína [koka'ina] *nf* cocaine.

cocción [kok'θjon] *nf* (*CULIN*) cooking; (: *el hervir*) boiling.

cocear [koθe'ar] *vi* to kick.

cocer [ko'θer] *vt*, *vi* to cook; (*en agua*) to boil; (*en horno*) to bake.

cocido [ko'θiðo] *nm* stew.

cocina [ko'θina] *nf* kitchen; (*aparato*) cooker, stove; (*acto*) cookery; ~ **eléctrica/de gas** electric/gas cooker; ~ **francesa** French cuisine; **cocinar** *vt*, *vi* to cook.

cocinero, a [koθi'nero, a] *nm/f* cook.

coco ['koko] *nm* coconut; ~**tero** *nm* coconut palm.

cocodrilo [koko'ðrilo] *nm* crocodile.

coche ['kotʃe] *nm* (*AUTO*) car (*Brit*), automobile (*US*); (*de tren, de caballos*) coach, carriage; (*para niños*) pram (*Brit*), baby carriage (*US*); ~ **celular** Black Maria, prison van; ~ **fúnebre** hearse; **coche-cama** (*pl* **coches-camas**) *nm* (*FERRO*) sleeping car, sleeper.

cochera [ko'tʃera] *nf* garage; (*de autobuses, trenes*) depot.

coche restaurante (*pl* **coches restaurante**) *nm* (*FERRO*) dining car, diner.

cochino, a [ko'tʃino, a] *a* filthy, dirty // *nm/f* pig.

codazo [ko'ðaθo] *nm*: **dar un** ~ **a uno** to nudge sb.

codear [koðe'ar] *vi* to elbow, nudge; ~**se** *vr*: ~**se con** to rub shoulders with.

codicia [ko'ðiθja] *nf* greed; (*fig*) lust; **codiciar** *vt* to covet; **codicioso, a** *a* covetous.

código ['koðiɣo] *nm* code; ~ **de barras** bar code; ~ **civil** common law.

codillo [ko'ðiʎo] nm (ZOOL) knee; (TEC) elbow (joint).

codo ['koðo] nm (ANAT, de tubo) elbow; (ZOOL) knee.

codorniz [koðor'niθ] nf quail.

coerción [koer'θjon] nf coercion.

coetáneo, a [koe'taneo, a] a, nm/f contemporary.

coexistir [koe(k)sis'tir] vi to coexist.

cofradía [kofra'ðia] nf brotherhood, fraternity.

coger [ko'xer] vt (Esp) to take (hold of); (objeto caído) to pick up; (frutas) to pick, harvest; (resfriado, ladrón, pelota) to catch // vi : **por el buen camino** to take the right road; **~se** vr (el dedo) to catch; **~se a algo** to get hold of sth.

cogollo [ko'voʎo] nm (de lechuga) heart.

cogote [ko'vote] nm back o nape of the neck.

cohabitar [koaßi'tar] vi to live together, cohabit.

cohecho [ko'etʃo] nm (acción) bribery; (soborno) bribe.

coherente [koe'rente] a coherent.

cohesión [koe'sjon] nm cohesion.

cohete [ko'ete] nm rocket.

cohibido, a [koi'ßiðo, a] a (PSICO) inhibited; (tímido) shy.

cohibir [koi'ßir] vt to restrain, restrict.

coima [ko'ima] nf (AM) bribe.

coincidencia [koinθi'ðenθja] nf coincidence.

coincidir [koinθi'ðir] vi (en idea) to coincide, agree; (en lugar) to coincide.

coito ['koito] nm intercourse, coitus.

coja etc vb ver **coger**.

cojear [koxe'ar] vi (persona) to limp, hobble; (mueble) to wobble, rock.

cojera [ko'xera] nf lameness; (andar cojo) limp.

cojín [ko'xin] nm cushion; **cojinete** nm small cushion, pad; (TEC) ball bearing.

cojo, a etc vb ver **coger** // ['koxo, a] a (que no puede andar) lame,

crippled; (mueble) wobbly // nm/f lame person, cripple.

cojón [ko'xon] nm: ¡cojones! (fam!) shit! (!); **cojonudo, a** a (fam) great, fantastic.

col [kol] nf cabbage; **~es de Bruselas** Brussels sprouts.

cola ['kola] nf tail; (de gente) queue; (lugar) end, last place; (para pegar) glue, gum; **hacer ~** to queue (up).

colaborador, a [kolaßora'ðor, a] nm/f collaborator.

colaborar [kolaßo'rar] vi to collaborate.

colada [ko'laða] nf: **hacer la ~** to do the washing.

colador [kola'ðor] nm (de té) strainer; (para verduras etc) colander.

colapso [ko'lapso] nm collapse; **~ nervioso** nervous breakdown.

colar [ko'lar] vt (líquido) to strain off; (metal) to cast // vi to ooze, seep (through); **~se** vr to jump the queue; **~se en** to get into without paying; (fiesta) to gatecrash.

colateral [kolate'ral] nm collateral.

colcha ['koltʃa] nf bedspread.

colchón [kol'tʃon] nm mattress.

colchoneta [koltʃo'neta] nf (en gimnasio) mattress.

colear [kole'ar] vi (perro) to wag its tail.

colección [kolek'θjon] nf collection; **coleccionar** vt to collect; **coleccionista** nm/f collector.

colecta [ko'lekta] nf collection.

colectivo, a [kolek'tißo, a] a collective, joint // nm (AM) (small) bus.

colector [kolek'tor] nm collector; (sumidero) sewer.

colega [ko'leva] nm/f colleague.

colegial, a [kole'xjal, a] nm/f schoolboy/girl.

colegio [ko'lexjo] nm college; (escuela) school; (de abogados etc) association.

colegir [kole'xir] vt (juntar) to collect, gather; (deducir) to infer, conclude.

cólera ['kolera] nf (ira) anger; (MED) cholera; **colérico, a** [ko'leriko, a] a angry, furious.

colesterol [koleste'rol] nm cholesterol.

coleta [ko'leta] nf pigtail.

colgante [kol'ɣante] a hanging // nm (joya) pendant.

colgar [kol'ɣar] vt to hang (up); (ropa) to hang out // vi to hang; (teléfono) to hang up.

coliflor [koli'flor] nf cauliflower.

colilla [ko'liʎa] nf cigarette end, butt.

colina [ko'lina] nf hill.

colindante [kolin'dante] a adjacent, neighbouring.

colindar [kolin'dar] vi to adjoin, be adjacent.

colisión [koli'sjon] nf collision; ~ de frente head-on crash.

colmado, a [kol'maðo, a] a full.

colmar [kol'mar] vt to fill to the brim; (fig) to fulfil, realize.

colmena [kol'mena] nf beehive.

colmillo [kol'miʎo] nm (diente) eye tooth; (de elefante) tusk; (de perro) fang.

colmo ['kolmo] nm height, summit; ¡es el ~! it's the limit!

colocación [koloka'θjon] nf (acto) placing; (empleo) job, position; (situación) place, position.

colocar [kolo'kar] vt to place, put, position; (dinero) to invest; (poner en empleo) to find a job for; ~se vr to get a job.

Colombia [ko'lombja] nf Colombia; **colombiano, a** a a, nm/f Colombian.

colonia [ko'lonja] nf colony; (de casas) housing estate; (agua de ~) cologne.

colonización [koloniθa'θjon] nf colonization; **colonizador, a** [koloniθa'ðor, a] a colonizing // nm/f colonist, settler.

colonizar [koloni'θar] vt to colonize.

coloquio [ko'lokjo] nm conversation; (congreso) conference.

color [ko'lor] nm colour.

colorado, a [kolo'raðo, a] a (rojo)

red; (chiste) rude.

colorante [kolo'rante] nm colouring.

colorar [kolo'rar] vt to colour; (teñir) to dye.

colorear [kolore'ar] vt to colour.

colorete [kolo'rete] nm blusher.

colorido [kolo'riðo] nm colouring.

columna [ko'lumna] nf column; (pilar) pillar; (apoyo) support.

columpiar [kolum'pjar] vt, **columpiarse** vr to swing; **columpio** nm swing.

collar [ko'ʎar] nm necklace; (de perro) collar.

coma ['koma] nf comma // nm (MED) coma.

comadre [ko'maðre] nf (madrina) godmother; (vecina) neighbour; (chismosa) gossip; ~ar vi to gossip.

comandancia [koman'danθja] nf command.

comandante [koman'dante] nm commandant.

comandar [koman'dar] vt to command.

comarca [ko'marka] nf region.

comba ['komba] nf (curva) curve; (cuerda) skipping rope; **saltar a la** ~ to skip.

combar [kom'bar] vt to bend, curve.

combate [kom'bate] nm fight; (fig) battle; **combatiente** nm combatant.

combatir [komba'tir] vt to fight, combat.

combinación [kombina'θjon] nf combination; (QUÍMICA) compound; (bebida) cocktail; (plan) scheme, setup; (prenda) slip.

combinar [kombi'nar] vt to combine.

combustible [kombus'tiβle] nm fuel.

combustión [kombus'tjon] nf combustion.

comedia [ko'meðja] nf comedy; (TEATRO) play, drama.

comediante [kome'ðjante] nm/f (comic) actor/actress.

comedido, a [kome'ðiðo, a] a moderate.

comedor, a [kome'ðor, a] nm/f (persona) glutton // nm (habitación) dining room; (*restaurante*) restaurant; (*cantina*) canteen.

comensal [komen'sal] *nm/f* fellow guest (o diner).

comentar [komen'tar] *vt* to comment on; (*fam*) to discuss.

comentario [komen'tarjo] *nm* comment, remark; ' (*literario*) commentary; ~s *nmpl* gossip *sg*.

comentarista [komenta'rista] *nm/f* commentator.

comenzar [komen'θar] *vt*, *vi* to begin, start, commence; ~ a hacer algo to begin *o* start doing sth.

comer [ko'mer] *vt* to eat; (*DAMAS, AJEDREZ*) to take, capture // *vi* to eat; (*almorzar*) to have lunch; ~se *vr* to eat up.

comercial [komer'θjal] *a* commercial; (*relativo al negocio*) business *cpd*.

comerciante [komer'θjante] *nm/f* trader, merchant.

comerciar [komer'θjar] *vi* to trade, do business.

comercio [ko'merθjo] *nm* commerce, trade; (*negocio*) business; (*fig*) dealings *pl*.

comestible [komes'tiβle] *a* eatable, edible; ~s *nmpl* food *sg*, foodstuffs *pl*.

cometa [ko'meta] *nm* comet // *nf* kite.

cometer [kome'ter] *vt* to commit.

cometido [kome'tiðo] *nm* (*misión*) task, assignment; (*deber*) commitment.

comezón [kome'θon] *nf* itch, itching.

comicios [ko'miθjos] *nmpl* elections.

cómico, a [ko'miko, a] *a* comic(al) // *nm/f* comedian; (*de teatro*) (comic) actor/actress.

comida [ko'miða] *nf* (*alimento*) food; (*almuerzo, cena*) meal; (*de mediodía*) lunch.

comidilla [komi'ðiʎa] *nf*: **ser la ~ de la ciudad** to be the talk of the town.

comienzo *etc vb ver* **comenzar** // [ko'mjenθo] *nm* beginning, start.

comilona [komi'lona] *nf* (*fam*)

blow-out.

comillas [ko'miʎas] *nfpl* quotation marks.

comino [ko'mino] *nm*: **(no) me importa un ~** I don't give a damn.

comisaría [komisa'ria] *nf* (*de policía*) police station; (*MIL*) commissariat.

comisario [komi'sarjo] *nm* (*MIL etc*) commissary; (*POL*) commissar.

comisión [komi'sjon] *nf* commission.

comité [komi'te] (*pl* ~s) *nm* committee.

como [ˈkomo] *ad* as; (*tal* ~) like; (*aproximadamente*) about, approximately // *conj* (*ya que*, *puesto que*) as, since; (*en cuanto*) as soon as; ¡~ no! of course!; ~ no lo haga hoy unless he does it today; ~ si as if; **es tan alto ~ ancho** it is as high as it is wide.

cómo [ˈkomo] *ad* how?, why? // *excl* what?, I beg your pardon? // *nm*: **el ~ y el porqué** the whys and wherefores.

cómoda [ˈkomoða] *nf* chest of drawers.

comodidad [komoði'ðað] *nf* comfort; **venga a su ~** come at your convenience.

comodín [komo'ðin] *nm* joker.

cómodo, a [ˈkomoðo, a] *a* comfortable; (*práctico, de fácil uso*) convenient.

compacto, a [kom'pakto, a] *a* compact.

compadecer [kompaðe'θer] *vt* to pity, be sorry for; ~se *vr*: ~se de to pity, be *o* feel sorry for.

compadre [kom'paðre] *nm* (*padrino*) godfather; (*amigo*) friend, pal.

compañero, a [kompa'ɲero, a] *nm/f* companion; (*novio*) boy/girlfriend; ~ **de clase** classmate.

compañía [kompa'ɲia] *nf* company.

comparación [kompara'θjon] *nf* comparison; **en ~ con** in comparison with.

comparar [kompa'rar] *vt* to

compare.

comparativo, a [kompara'tiƟo, a] *a* comparative.

comparecer [kompare'Ɵer] *vi* to appear (in court).

comparsa [kom'parsa] *nm/f* (*TEATRO*) extra.

compartimiento [komparti'mjento] *nm* (*FERRO*) compartment.

compartir [kompar'tir] *vt* to divide (up), share (out).

compás [kom'pas] *nm* (*MUS*) beat, rhythm; (*MAT*) compasses *pl*; (*NAUT etc*) compass.

compasión [kompa'sjon] *nf* compassion, pity.

compasivo, a [kompa'siƟo, a] *a* compassionate.

compatibilidad [kompatiƟili'ðað] *nf* compatibility.

compatible [kompa'tiƟle] *a* compatible.

compatriota [kompa'trjota] *nm/f* compatriot, fellow countryman/woman.

compendiar [kompen'djar] *vt* to summarize; (*libro*) to abridge; **compendio** *nm* summary; abridgement.

compensación [kompensa'Ɵjon] *nf* compensation.

compensar [kompen'sar] *vt* to compensate.

competencia [kompe'tenƟja] *nf* (*incumbencia*) domain, field; (*JUR, habilidad*) competence; (*rivalidad*) competition.

competente [kompe'tente] *a* (*JUR, persona*) competent; (*conveniente*) suitable.

competición [kompeti'Ɵjon] *nf* competition.

competir [kompe'tir] *vi* to compete.

compilar [kompi'lar] *vt* to compile.

complacencia [kompla'ƟenƟja] *nf* (*placer*) pleasure; (*tolerancia excesiva*) complacency.

complacer [kompla'Ɵer] *vt* to please; **~se** *vr* to be pleased.

complaciente [kompla'Ɵjente] *a* kind, obliging, helpful.

complejo, a [kom'plexo, a] *a, nm* complex.

complementario, a [komplemen'tarjo, a] *a* complementary.

completar [komple'tar] *vt* to complete.

completo, a [kom'pleto, a] *a* complete; (*perfecto*) perfect; (*lleno*) full // *nm* full complement.

complicado, a [kompli'kaðo, a] *a* complicated; **estar ~ en** to be mixed up in.

complicar [kompli'kar] *vt* to complicate.

cómplice ['kompliƟe] *nm/f* accomplice.

complot [kom'plo(t)] (*pl* ~s) *nm* plot; (*conspiración*) conspiracy.

componer [kompo'ner] *vt* to make up, put together; (*MUS, LITERATURA, IMPRENTA*) to compose; (*algo roto*) to mend, repair; (*arreglar*) to arrange; **~se** *vr*: **~se de** to consist of; **componérselas para hacer algo** to manage to do sth.

comportamiento [komporta'mjento] *nm* behaviour, conduct.

comportarse [kompor'tarse] *vr* to behave.

composición [komposi'Ɵjon] *nf* composition.

compositor, a [komposi'tor, a] *nm/f* composer.

compostura [kompos'tura] *nf* (*composición*) composition; (*reparación*) mending, repair; (*acuerdo*) agreement; (*actitud*) composure.

compra ['kompra] *nf* purchase; **~s** *nfpl* purchases, shopping *sg*; **ir de ~s** to go shopping; **comprador, a** *nm/f* buyer, purchaser.

comprar [kom'prar] *vt* to buy, purchase.

comprender [kompren'der] *vt* to understand; (*incluir*) to comprise, include.

comprensión [kompren'sjon] *nf* understanding; (*totalidad*) comprehensiveness; **comprensivo,**

a a comprehensive; (*actitud*) understanding.

compresa [kom'presa] *nf*: ~ **higiénica** sanitary towel (*Brit*) o napkin (*US*).

comprimido, a [kompri'miðo, a] *a* compressed // *nm* (*MED*) pill, tablet.

comprimir [kompri'mir] *vt* to compress; (*fig*) to control.

comprobante [kompro'βante] *nm* proof; (*COM*) voucher; ~ **de recibo** receipt.

comprobar [kompro'βar] *vt* to check; (*probar*) to prove; (*TEC*) to check, test.

comprometer [komprome'ter] *vt* to compromise; (*exponer*) to endanger; ~**se** *vr* to compromise o.s.; (*involucrarse*) to get involved.

compromiso [kompro'miso] *nm* (*obligación*) obligation; (*cometido*) commitment; (*convenio*) agreement; (*dificultad*) awkward situation.

compuesto, a [kom'pwesto, a] *a*: ~ **de** composed of, made up of // *nm* compound.

computador [komputa'ðor] *nm*, **computadora** [komputa'ðora] *nf* computer; ~ **central** mainframe computer; ~ **personal** personal computer.

cómputo ['komputo] *nm* calculation.

comulgar [komul'yar] *vi* to receive communion.

común [ko'mun] *a* common // *nm*: **el** ~ **the community.**

comunicación [komunika'θjon] *nf* communication; (*informe*) report.

comunicado [komuni'kaðo] *nm* announcement; ~ **de prensa** press release.

comunicar [komuni'kar] *vt, vi*, **comunicarse** *vr* to communicate; **está comunicando** (*TEL*) the line's engaged (*Brit*) o busy (*US*); **comunicativo, a** *a* communicative.

comunidad [komuni'ðað] *nf* community.

comunión [komu'njon] *nf* communion.

comunismo [komu'nismo] *nm* communism; **comunista** *a, nm/f* communist.

---

con [kon] ♦ *prep* **1** (*medio, compañía*) with; **comer** ~ **cuchara** to eat with a spoon; **atar algo** ~ **cuerda** to tie sth up with string; **pasear** ~ **uno** to go for a walk with sb

2 (*a pesar de*): ~ **todo, merece nuestros respetos** all the same, he deserves our respect

3 (*para* ~): **es muy bueno para** ~ **los niños** he's very good with (the) children

4 (*infin*): ~ **llegar tan tarde se quedó sin comer** by arriving so late he missed out on eating

♦ *conj*: ~ **que: será suficiente** ~ **que le escribas** it will be sufficient if you write to her.

---

conato [ko'nato] *nm* attempt; ~ **de robo** attempted robbery.

concebir [konθe'βir] *vt, vi* to conceive.

conceder [konθe'ðer] *vt* to concede.

concejal, a [konθe'xal, a] *nm/f* town councillor.

concejo [kon'θexo] *nm* council.

concentración [konθentra'θjon] *nf* concentration.

concentrar [konθen'trar] *vt*, **concentrarse** *vr* to concentrate.

concepción [konθep'θjon] *nf* conception.

concepto [kon'θepto] *nm* concept.

concertar [konθer'tar] *vt* (*MUS*) to harmonize; (*acordar: precio*) to agree; (*: tratado*) to conclude; (*trato*) to arrange, fix up; (*combinar: esfuerzos*) to coordinate; (*reconciliar: personas*) to reconcile // *vi* to harmonize, be in tune.

concesión [konθe'sjon] *nf* concession.

concesionario [konθesjo'narjo] *nm* (licensed) dealer, agent.

conciencia [kon'θjenθja] *nf* conscience; **tener/tomar ~ de** to be/become aware of; **tener la ~ limpia/tranquila** to have a clear conscience.

concienciar [konθjen'θjar] *vt* to make aware; **~se** *vr* to become aware.

concienzudo, a [konθjen'θuðo, a] *a* conscientious.

concierto *etc vb ver* **concertar** // [kon'θjerto] *nm* concert; (*obra*) concerto.

conciliar [konθi'ljar] *vt* to reconcile.

concilio [kon'θiljo] *nm* council.

conciso, a [kon'θiso, a] *a* concise.

conciudadano, a [konθjuða'ðano, a] *nm/f* fellow citizen.

concluir [konklu'ir] *vt*, *vi*, **concluirse** *vr* to conclude.

conclusión [konklu'sjon] *nf* conclusion.

concluyente [konklu'jente] *a* (*prueba, información*) conclusive.

concordar [konkor'ðar] *vt* to reconcile // *vi* to agree, tally.

concordia [kon'korðja] *nf* harmony.

concretar [konkre'tar] *vt* to make concrete, make more specific; **~se** *vr* to become more definite.

concreto, a [kon'kreto, a] *a, nm* (*AM*) concrete; **en ~** (*en resumen*) to sum up; (*específicamente*) specifically; **no hay nada en ~** there's nothing definite.

concurrencia [konku'rrenθja] *nf* turnout.

concurrido, a [konku'rriðo, a] *a* (*calle*) busy; (*local, reunión*) crowded.

concurrir [konku'rrir] *vi* (*juntarse: ríos*) to meet, come together; (: *personas*) to gather, meet.

concursante [konkur'sante] *nm/f* competitor.

concurso [kon'kurso] *nm* (*de público*) crowd; (*ESCOL, DEPORTE, competencia*) competition; (*ayuda*) help, cooperation.

concha ['kontʃa] *nf* shell.

conde ['konde] *nm* count; **condal** *a*: **la ciudad condal** Barcelona.

condecoración [kondekora'θjon] *nf* (*MIL*) medal.

condecorar [kondeko'rar] *vt* (*MIL*) to decorate.

condena [kon'dena] *nf* sentence.

condenación [kondena'θjon] *nf* condemnation; (*REL*) damnation.

condenar [konde'nar] *vt* to condemn; (*JUR*) to convict; **~se** *vr* (*JUR*) to confess (one's guilt); (*REL*) to be damned.

condensar [konden'sar] *vt* to condense.

condesa [kon'desa] *nf* countess.

condescender [kondesθen'der] *vi* to acquiesce, comply.

condición [kondi'θjon] *nf* condition; **condicional** *a* conditional.

condicionar [kondiθjo'nar] *vt* (*acondicionar*) to condition; **~ algo a** to make sth conditional on.

condimento [kondi'mento] *nm* seasoning.

condolerse [kondo'lerse] *vr* to sympathize.

condón [kon'don] *nm* condom.

conducir [kondu'θir] *vt* to take, convey; (*AUTO*) to drive // *vi* to drive; (*fig*) to lead; **~se** *vr* to behave.

conducta [kon'dukta] *nf* conduct, behaviour.

conducto [kon'dukto] *nm* pipe, tube; (*fig*) channel.

conductor, a [konduk'tor, a] *a* leading, guiding // *nm* (*FÍSICA*) conductor; (*de vehículo*) driver.

conduje *etc vb ver* **conducir**.

conduzco *etc vb ver* **conducir**.

conectado, a [konek'taðo, a] *a* (*INFORM*) on-line.

conectar [konek'tar] *vt* to connect (up); (*enchufar*) plug in.

conejo [ko'nexo] *nm* rabbit.

conexión [konek'sjon] *nf* connection.

confección [konfe(k)'θjon] *nf* preparation; (*industria*) clothing industry.

confeccionar [konfekθjo'nar] *vt*

make (up).

confederación [konfeðera'θjon] nf confederation.

conferencia [konfe'renθja] nf conference; (lección) lecture; (TEL) call.

conferir [konfe'rir] vt to award.

confesar [konfe'sar] vt to confess, admit.

confesión [konfe'sjon] nf confession.

confesionario [konfesjo'narjo] nm confessional.

confeti [kon'feti] nm confetti.

confiado, a [kon'fjaðo, a] a (crédulo) trusting; (seguro) confident; (presumido) conceited, vain.

confianza [kon'fjanθa] nf trust; (aliento, confidencia) confidence; (familiaridad) intimacy, familiarity; (pey) vanity, conceit.

confiar [kon'fjar] vt to entrust // vi to trust.

confidencia [konfi'ðenθja] nf confidence.

confidencial [konfiðen'θjal] a confidential.

confidente [konfi'ðente] nm/f confidant/e; (policial) informer.

configurar [konfiɣu'rar] vt to shape, form.

confín [kon'fin] nm limit; ~es nmpl confines, limits.

confinar [konfi'nar] vi to confine; (desterrar) to banish.

confirmar [konfir'mar] vt to confirm.

confiscar [konfis'kar] vt to confiscate.

confite [kon'fite] nm sweet (Brit), candy (US).

confitería [konfite'ria] nf confectionery; (tienda) confectioner's (shop).

confitura [konfi'tura] nf jam.

conflictivo, a [konflik'tiβo, a] a (asunto, propuesta) controversial; (país, situación) troubled.

conflicto [kon'flikto] nm conflict; (fig) clash.

confluir [konfl'wir] vi (ríos) to meet; (gente) to gather.

conformar [konfor'mar] vt to shape,

fashion // vi to agree; ~se vr to conform; (resignarse) to resign o.s.

conforme [kon'forme] a alike, similar; (de acuerdo) in agreement // ad as // excl agreed! // nm agreement // prep: ~ a in accordance with.

conformidad [konformi'ðað] nf (semejanza) similarity; (acuerdo) agreement; (resignación) resignation; **conformista** a, nm/f conformist.

confortable [konfor'taβle] a comfortable.

confortar [konfor'tar] vt to comfort.

confrontar [konfron'tar] vt to confront; (dos personas) to bring face to face; (cotejar) to compare // vi to border.

confundir [konfun'dir] vt (borrar) to blur; (equivocar) to mistake, confuse; (mezclar) to mix; (turbar) to confuse; ~se vr (hacerse borroso) to become blurred; (turbarse) to get confused; (equivocarse) to make a mistake; (mezclarse) to mix.

confusión [konfu'sjon] nf confusion.

confuso, a [kon'fuso, a] a confused.

congelado, a [konxe'laðo, a] a frozen; ~s nmpl frozen food(s); **congelador** nm, **congeladora** nf (aparato) freezer, deep freeze.

congelar [konxe'lar] vt to freeze; ~se vr (sangre, grasa) to congeal.

congeniar [konxe'njar] vi to get on (Brit) o along (US) well.

congestionar [konxestjo'nar] vt to congest; ~se vr: se le congestionó la cara his face became flushed.

congoja [kon'goxa] nf distress, grief.

congraciarse [kongra'θjarse] vr to ingratiate o.s.

congratular [kongratu'lar] vt to congratulate.

congregación [kongreɣa'θjon] nf congregation.

congregar [kongre'ɣar] vt, **congregarse** vr to gather together.

congresista [kongre'sista] nm/f delegate, congressman/woman.

congreso [kon'greso] *nm* congress.

conjetura [konxe'tura] *nf* guess; **conjeturar** *vt* to guess.

conjugar [konxu'ɣar] *vt* to combine, fit together; (*LING*) to conjugate.

conjunción [konxun'θjon] *nf* conjunction.

conjunto, a [kon'xunto, a] *a* joint, united // *nm* whole; (*MUS*) band; **en ~ as** a whole.

conjurar [konxu'rar] *vt* (*REL*) to exorcise; (*fig*) to ward off // *vi* to plot.

conmemoración [konmemora'θjon] *nf* commemoration.

conmemorar [konmemo'rar] *vt* to commemorate.

conmigo [kon'miɣo] *pron* with me.

conminar [konmi'nar] *vt* to threaten.

conmoción [konmo'θjon] *nf* shock; (*fig*) upheaval; **~ cerebral** (*MED*) concussion.

conmovedor, a [konmoβe'ðor, a] *a* touching, moving; (*emocionante*) exciting.

conmover [konmo'βer] *vt* to shake, disturb; (*fig*) to move.

conmutador [konmuta'ðor] *nm* switch; (*AM TEL: centralita*) switchboard; (: *central*) telephone exchange.

cono ['kono] *nm* cone.

conocedor, a [konoθe'ðor, a] *a* expert, knowledgeable // *nm/f* expert.

conocer [kono'θer] *vt* to know; (*por primera vez*) to meet, get to know; (*entender*) to know about; (*reconocer*) to recognize; **~se** *vr* (*una persona*) to know o.s.; (*dos personas*) to (get to) know each other.

conocido, a [kono'θiðo, a] *a* (well-)known // *nm/f* acquaintance.

conocimiento [konoθi'mjento] *nm* knowledge; (*MED*) consciousness; **~s** *nmpl* (*personas*) acquaintances; (*saber*) knowledge *sg*.

conozco *etc vb ver* **conocer**.

conque ['konke] *conj* and so, so then.

conquista [kon'kista] *nf* conquest;

conquistador, a *a* conquering // *nm* conqueror.

conquistar [konkis'tar] *vt* to conquer.

consagrar [konsa'ɣrar] *vt* (*REL*) to consecrate; (*fig*) to devote.

consciente [kons'θjente] *a* conscious.

consecución [konseku'θjon] *nf* acquisition; (*de fin*) attainment.

consecuencia [konse'kwenθja] *nf* consequence, outcome; (*firmeza*) consistency.

consecuente [konse'kwente] *a* consistent.

consecutivo, a [konseku'tiβo, a] *a* consecutive.

conseguir [konse'ɣir] *vt* to get, obtain; (*sus fines*) to attain.

consejero, a [konse'xero, a] *nm/f* adviser, consultant; (*POL*) councillor.

consejo [kon'sexo] *nm* advice; (*POL*) council.

consenso [kon'senso] *nm* consensus.

consentimiento [konsenti'mjento] *nm* consent.

consentir [konsen'tir] *vt* (*permitir, tolerar*) to consent to; (*mimar*) to pamper, spoil; (*aguantar*) to put up with // *vi* to agree, consent; **~ que uno haga algo** to allow sb to do sth.

conserje [kon'serxe] *nm* caretaker; (*portero*) porter.

conservación [konserβa'θjon] *nf* conservation; (*de alimentos, vida*) preservation.

conservador, a [konserβa'ðor, a] *a* (*POL*) conservative // *nm/f* conservative.

conservante [konser'βante] *nm* preservative.

conservar [konser'βar] *vt* to conserve, keep; (*alimentos, vida*) to preserve; **~se** *vr* to survive.

conservas [kon'serβas] *nfpl* canned food(s).

conservatorio [konserβa'torjo] *nm* (*MUS*) conservatoire.

considerable [konsiðe'raßle] *a* considerable.

consideración [konsiðera'θjon] *nf* consideration; (*estimación*) respect.

considerado, a [konsiðe'raðo, a] *a* (*atento*) considerate; (*respetado*) respected.

considerar [konsiðe'rar] *vt* to consider.

consigna [kon'sixna] *nf* (*orden*) order, instruction; (*para equipajes*) left-luggage office.

consigo *etc vb ver* **conseguir** // [kon'sixo] *pron* (*m*) with him; (*f*) with her; (*Vd.*) with you; (*reflexivo*) with o.s.

consiguiendo *etc vb ver* **conseguir.**

consiguiente [konsi'xjente] *a* consequent; **por ~** and so, therefore, consequently.

consistente [konsis'tente] *a* consistent; (*sólido*) solid, firm; (*válido*) sound.

consistir [konsis'tir] *vi:* **~ en** (*componerse de*) to consist of; (*ser resultado de*) to be due to.

consola [kon'sola] *nf* control panel.

consolación [konsola'θjon] *nf* consolation.

consolar [konso'lar] *vt* to console.

consolidar [konsoli'ðar] *vt* to consolidate.

consomé [konso'me] (*pl ~s*) *nm* consommé, clear soup.

consonante [konso'nante] *a* consonant, harmonious // *nf* consonant.

consorcio [kon'sorθjo] *nm* consortium.

conspiración [konspira'θjon] *nf* conspiracy.

conspirador, a [konspira'ðor, a] *nm/f* conspirator.

conspirar [konspi'rar] *vi* to conspire.

constancia [kons'tanθja] *nf* constancy; **dejar ~ de** to put on record.

constante [kons'tante] *a, nf* constant.

constar [kons'tar] *vi* (*evidenciarse*) to be clear *o* evident; **~ de** to consist of.

constatar [konsta'tar] *vt* (*controlar*) to check; (*observar*) to note.

consternación [konsterna'θjon] *nf* consternation.

constipado, a [konsti'paðo, a] *a:* **estar ~** to have a cold // *nm* cold.

constitución [konstitu'θjon] *nf* constitution; **constitucional** *a* constitutional.

constituir [konstitu'ir] *vt* (*formar, componer*) to constitute, make up; (*fundar, erigir, ordenar*) to constitute, establish.

constitutivo, a [konstitu'tiβo, a] *a* constitutive, constituent.

constituyente [konstitu'jente] *a* constituent.

constreñir [konstre'ɲir] *vt* (*restringir*) to restrict.

construcción [konstruk'θjon] *nf* construction, building.

constructor, a [konstruk'tor, a] *nm/f* builder.

construir [konstru'ir] *vt* to build, construct.

construyendo *etc vb ver* **construir.**

consuelo [kon'swelo] *nm* consolation, solace.

cónsul ['konsul] *nm* consul; **consulado** *nm* consulate.

consulta [kon'sulta] *nf* consultation; (*MED*): **horas de ~** surgery hours.

consultar [konsul'tar] *vt* to consult.

consultorio [konsul'torjo] *nm* (*MED*) surgery.

consumar [konsu'mar] *vt* to complete, carry out; (*crimen*) to commit; (*sentencia*) to carry out.

consumición [konsumi'θjon] *nf* consumption; (*bebida*) drink; (*comida*) food; **~ mínima** cover charge.

consumidor, a [konsumi'ðor, a] *nm/f* consumer.

consumir [konsu'mir] *vt* to consume; **~se** *vr* to be consumed; (*persona*) to waste away.

consumismo [konsu'mismo] *nm* consumerism.

consumo [kon'sumo] *nm* consumption.

contabilidad [kontaßili'ðað] nf accounting, book-keeping; (profesión) accountancy; **contable** nmf accountant.

contacto [kon'takto] nm contact; (AUTO) ignition.

contado, a [kon'taðo, a] a: ~s (escasos) numbered, scarce, few // nm: **pagar al** ~ to pay (in) cash.

contador [konta'ðor] nm (aparato) meter; (AM: contante) accountant.

contagiar [konta'xjar] vt (enfermedad) to pass on, transmit; (persona) to infect; ~se vr to become infected.

contagio [kon'taxjo] nm infection; **contagioso, a** a infectious; (fig) catching.

contaminación [kontamina'θjon] nf contamination; (polución) pollution.

contaminar [kontami'nar] vt to contaminate; (aire, agua) to pollute.

contante [kon'tante] a: **dinero** ~ (y sonante) cash.

contar [kon'tar] vt (páginas, dinero) to count; (anécdota, chiste etc) to tell // vi to count; ~ **con** to rely on, count on.

contemplación [kontempla'θjon] nf contemplation.

contemplar [kontem'plar] vt to contemplate; (mirar) to look at.

contemporáneo, a [kontempo'raneo, a] a, nm/f contemporary.

contendiente [konten'djente] nm/f contestant.

contenedor [kontene'ðor] nm container.

contener [konte'ner] vt to contain, hold; (retener) to hold back, contain; ~se vr to control o restrain o.s.

contenido, a [konte'niðo, a] a (moderado) restrained; (risa etc) suppressed // nm contents pl, content.

contentar [konten'tar] vt (satisfacer) to satisfy; (complacer) to please; ~se vr to be satisfied.

contento, a [kon'tento, a] a contented, content; (alegre) pleased;

(feliz) happy.

contestación [kontesta'θjon] nf answer, reply.

contestador [kontesta'ðor] nm: ~ **automático** answering machine.

contestar [kontes'tar] vt to answer, reply; (JUR) to corroborate, confirm.

contexto [kon'te(k)sto] nm context.

contienda [kon'tjenda] nf contest.

contigo [kon'tixo] pron with you.

contiguo, a [kon'tixwo, a] a (de al lado) next; (vecino) adjacent, adjoining.

continente [konti'nente] a, nm continent.

contingencia [kontin'xenθja] nf contingency; (riesgo) risk; **contingente** a, nm contingent.

continuación [kontinwa'θjon] nf continuation; a ~ then, next.

continuar [konti'nwar] vt to continue, go on with // vi to continue, go on; ~ **hablando** to continue talking o to talk.

continuidad [kontinwi'ðað] nf continuity.

continuo, a [kon'tinwo, a] a (sin interrupción) continuous; (acción perseverante) continual.

contorno [kon'torno] nm outline; (GEO) contour; ~s nmpl neighbourhood sg, surrounding area sg.

contorsión [kontor'sjon] nf contortion.

contra ['kontra] prep, ad against // nm inv con // nf: **la C~** (Nicaragua) the Contras pl.

contraataque [kontraa'take] nm counter-attack.

contrabajo [kontra'ßaxo] nm double bass.

contrabandista [kontraßan'dista] nm/f smuggler.

contrabando [kontra'ßando] nm (acción) smuggling; (mercancías) contraband.

contracción [kontrak'θjon] nf contraction.

contrachapado [kontratʃa'paðo] nm plywood.

contradecir [kontrade'θir] vt to contradict.

contradicción [kontraðik'θjon] nf contradiction.

contradictorio, a [kontraðik'torjo, a] a contradictory.

contraer [kontra'er] vt to contract; (limitar) to restrict; ~se vr to contract; (limitarse) to limit o.s.

contragolpe [kontra'xolpe] nm backlash.

contraluz [kontra'luθ] nf: a ~ against the light.

contramaestre [kontrama'estre] nm foreman.

contrapartida [kontrapar'tiða] nf: como ~ (de) in return (for).

contrapelo [kontra'pelo]: a ~ ad the wrong way.

contrapesar [kontrape'sar] vt to counterbalance; (fig) to offset; **contrapeso** nm counterweight.

contraproducente [kontraproðu-'θente] a counterproductive.

contrariar [kontra'rjar] vt (oponerse) to oppose; (poner obstáculo) to impede; (enfadar) to vex.

contrariedad [kontrarje'ðað] nf (oposición) opposition; (obstáculo) obstacle, setback; (disgusto) vexation, annoyance.

contrario, a [kon'trarjo, a] a contrary; (persona) opposed; (sentido, lado) opposite // nm/f enemy, adversary; (DEPORTE) opponent; al/por el ~ on the contrary; de lo ~ otherwise.

contrarrestar [kontrarres'tar] vt to counteract.

contrasentido [kontrasen'tiðo] nm: es un ~ que él ... it doesn't make sense for him to ....

contraseña [kontra'seɲa] nf (INFORM) password.

contrastar [kontras'tar] vt to resist // vi to contrast.

contraste [kon'traste] nm contrast.

contratar [kontra'tar] vt (firmar un acuerdo para) to contract for; (empleados, obreros) to hire, engage;

~se vr to sign on.

contratiempo [kontra'tjempo] nm setback.

contratista [kontra'tista] nm/f contractor.

contrato [kon'trato] nm contract.

contravenir [kontraβe'nir] vi: ~ a to contravene, violate.

contraventana [kontraβen'tana] nf shutter.

contribución [kontriβu'θjon] nf (municipal etc) tax; (ayuda) contribution.

contribuir [kontriβu'ir] vt, vi to contribute; (COM) to pay (in taxes).

contribuyente [kontriβu'jente] nm/f (COM) taxpayer; (que ayuda) contributor.

control [kon'trol] nm control; (inspección) inspection, check; ~**ador, a** nm/f controller; **controlador aéreo** air-traffic controller.

controlar [kontro'lar] vt to control; (inspeccionar) to inspect, check.

controversia [kontro'βersja] nf controversy.

contundente [kontun'dente] a (instrumento) blunt; (argumento, derrota) overwhelming.

contusión [kontu'sjon] nf bruise.

convalecencia [konβale'θenθja] nf convalescence.

convalecer [konβale'θer] vi to convalesce, get better.

convaleciente [konβale'θjente] a, nm/f convalescent.

convalidar [konβali'ðar] vt (título) to recognize.

convencer [konβen'θer] vt to convince; (persuadir) to persuade.

convencimiento [konβenθi'mjento] nm (acción) convincing; (persuasión) persuasion; (certidumbre) conviction.

convención [konβen'θjon] nf convention.

conveniencia [konβe'njenθja] nf suitability; (conformidad) agreement; (utilidad, provecho) usefulness; ~**s** nfpl conventions; (COM) property sg.

conveniente [konße'njente] a suitable; (*útil*) useful.

convenio [kon'ßenjo] nm agreement, treaty.

convenir [konße'nir] vi (*estar de acuerdo*) to agree; (*ser conveniente*) to suit, be suitable.

convento [kon'ßento] nm convent.

convenza etc vb ver **convencer**.

converger [konßer'xer], **convergir** [konßer'xir] vi to converge.

conversación [konßersa'θjon] nf conversation.

conversar [konßer'sar] vi to talk, converse.

conversión [konßer'sjon] nf conversion.

convertir [konßer'tir] vt to convert.

convicción [konßik'θjon] nf conviction.

convicto, a [kon'ßikto, a] a convicted, found guilty; (*condenado*) condemned.

convidado, a [konßi'ðaðo, a] nm/f guest.

convidar [konßi'ðar] vt to invite.

convincente [konßin'θente] a convincing.

convite [kon'ßite] nm invitation; (*banquete*) banquet.

convivencia [konßi'ßenθja] nf coexistence, living together.

convocar [konßo'kar] vt to summon, call (together).

convulsión [konßul'sjon] nf convulsion.

conyugal [konju'ɣal] a conjugal; **cónyuge** ['konjuxe] nm/f spouse.

coñac [ko'nak] (pl ~s) nm cognac, brandy.

coño ['kono] excl (*fam!: enfado*) shit! (!); (: *sorpresa*) bloody hell! (!).

cooperación [koopera'θjon] nf cooperation.

cooperar [koope'rar] vi to cooperate.

cooperativa [koopera'tißa] nf cooperative.

coordinadora [koorðina'ðora] nf (*comité*) coordinating committee.

coordinar [koorði'nar] vt to co-ordinate.

copa ['kopa] nf cup; (*vaso*) glass; (*de árbol*) top; (*de sombrero*) crown; ~s nfpl (*NAIPES*) ≈ hearts; (**tomar una**) ~ (to have a) drink.

copia ['kopja] nf copy; ~ **de respaldo** o **seguridad** (*INFORM*) back-up copy; **copiar** vt to copy.

copioso, a [ko'pjoso, a] a copious, plentiful.

copla ['kopla] nf verse; (*canción*) (popular) song.

copo ['kopo] nm: ~ **de nieve** snowflake; ~**s de maíz** cornflakes.

copropietarios [kopropje'tarjos] nmpl joint owners.

coqueta [ko'keta] a flirtatious, coquettish; **coquetear** vi to flirt.

coraje [ko'raxe] nm courage; (*ánimo*) spirit; (*ira*) anger.

coral [ko'ral] a choral // nf (*MUS*) choir // nm (*ZOOL*) coral.

coraza [ko'raθa] nf (*armadura*) armour; (*blindaje*) armour-plating.

corazón [kora'θon] nm heart.

corazonada [koraθo'naða] nf impulse; (*presentimiento*) hunch.

corbata [kor'ßata] nf tie.

corchete [kor'tfete] nm catch, clasp.

corcho [kor'tfo] nm cork; (*PESCA*) float.

cordel [kor'ðel] nm cord, line.

cordero [kor'ðero] nm lamb.

cordial [kor'ðjal] a cordial; ~**idad** nf warmth, cordiality.

cordillera [korði'ʎera] nf range (of mountains).

Córdoba ['korðoßa] n Cordova.

cordón [kor'ðon] nm (*cuerda*) cord, string; (*de zapatos*) lace; (*MIL etc*) cordon.

corneta [kor'neta] nf bugle.

coro ['koro] nm chorus; (*conjunto de cantores*) choir.

corona [ko'rona] nf crown; (*de flores*) garland; ~**ción** nf coronation; **coronar** vt to crown.

coronel [koro'nel] nm colonel.

coronilla [koro'niʎa] nf (*ANAT*)

crown (of the head).

corporación [korpora'θjon] *nf* corporation.

corporal [korpo'ral] *a* corporal, bodily.

corpulento, a [korpu'lento] a] *a* (*persona*) heavily-built.

corral [ko'rral] *nm* farmyard.

correa [ko'rrea] *nf* strap; (*cinturón*) belt; (*de perro*) lead, leash.

corrección [korrek'θjon] *nf* correction; (*represión*) rebuke; **co-reccional** *nm* reformatory.

correcto, a [ko'rrekto, a] *a* correct; (*persona*) well-mannered.

corredizo, a [korre'ðiβo, a] *a* (*puerta etc*) sliding.

corredor, a [korre'ðor, a] *a* running // *nm* (*pasillo*) corridor; (*balcón corrido*) gallery; (*COM*) agent, broker // *nm/f* (*DEPORTE*) runner.

corregir [korre'xir] *vt* (*error*) to correct; (*amonestar, reprender*) to rebuke, reprimand; ~**se** *vr* to reform.

correo [ko'rreo] *nm* post, mail; (*persona*) courier; C~**s** Post Office *sg*; ~ **aéreo** airmail.

correr [ko'rrer] *vt* to run; (*viajar*) to cover, travel; (*cortinas*) to draw; (*cerrojo*) to shoot // *vi* to run; (*líquido*) to run, flow; ~**se** *vr* to slide, move; (*colores*) to run.

correspondencia [korrespon-'denθja] *nf* correspondence; (*FERRO*) connection.

corresponder [korrespon'der] *vi* to correspond; (*convenir*) to be suitable; (*pertenecer*) to belong; (*tocar*) to concern; ~**se** *vr* (*por escrito*) to correspond; (*amarse*) to love one another.

correspondiente [korrespon'djente] *a* corresponding.

corresponsal [korrespon'sal] *nm/f* correspondent.

corrido, a [ko'rriðo, a] *a* (*avergonzado*) abashed // *nf* (*de toros*) bullfight; **3 noches corridas** 3 nights running; **un kilo** ~ **a** good

kilo.

corriente [ko'rrjente] *a* (*agua*) running; (*fig*) flowing; (*dinero etc*) current; (*común*) ordinary, normal // *nf* current // *nm* current month; ~ **eléctrica** electric current.

corrija *etc vb ver* **corregir**.

corrillo [ko'rriʎo] *nm* ring, circle (of people); (*fig*) clique.

corro ['korro] *nm* ring, circle (of people).

corroborar [korroβo'rar] *vt* to corroborate.

corroer [korro'er] *vt* to corrode; (*GEO*) to erode.

corromper [korrom'per] *vt* (*madera*) to rot; (*fig*) to corrupt.

corrosivo, a [korro'siβo, a] *a* corrosive.

corrupción [korrup'θjon] *nf* rot, decay; (*fig*) corruption.

corsé [kor'se] *nm* corset.

cortacésped [korta'θespeð] *nm* lawn mower.

cortado, a [kor'taðo, a] *a* (*gen*) cut; (*leche*) sour; (*confuso*) confused; (*desconcertado*) embarrassed // *nm* coffee (with a little milk).

cortar [kor'tar] *vt* to cut; (*suministro*) to cut off; (*un pasaje*) to cut out // *vi* to cut; ~**se** *vr* (*turbarse*) to become embarrassed; (*leche*) to turn, curdle; ~**se el pelo** to have one's hair cut.

cortauñas [korta'uɲas] *nm inv* nail clippers *pl*.

corte ['korte] *nm* cut, cutting; (*de tela*) piece, length; **las C~s** the Spanish Parliament; ~ **y confección** dressmaking; ~ **de luz** power cut.

cortedad [korte'ðað] *nf* shortness; (*fig*) bashfulness, timidity.

cortejar [korte'xar] *vt* to court.

cortejo [kor'texo] *nm* entourage; ~ **fúnebre** funeral procession.

cortés [kor'tes] *a* courteous, polite.

cortesía [korte'sia] *nf* courtesy.

corteza [kor'teθa] *nf* (*de árbol*) bark; (*de pan*) crust.

cortina [kor'tina] *nf* curtain.

corto, a ['korto, a] a (breve) short; (tímido) bashful; ~ **de luces** not very bright; ~ **de vista** short-sighted; **estar ~ de fondos** to be short of funds; ~**circuito** nm short circuit.

corvo, a ['korβo, a] a curved.

cosa ['kosa] nf thing; (asunto) affair; ~ **de** about; **eso es ~ mía** that's my business.

cosecha [ko'setʃa] nf (AGR) harvest; (de vino) vintage.

cosechar [kose'tʃar] vt to harvest, gather (in).

coser [ko'ser] vt to sew.

cosmético, a [kos'kiʎas] a, nm cosmetic.

cosquillas [kos'kiʎas] nfpl: **hacer ~** to tickle; **tener ~** to be ticklish.

costa ['kosta] nf (GEO) coast; C~ **Brava** Costa Brava; C~ **Cantábrica** Cantabrian Coast; C~ **del Sol** Costa del Sol; **a toda ~** at any price.

costado [kos'taðo] nm side.

costal [kos'tal] nm sack.

costar [kos'tar] vt (valer) to cost; (necesitar) to require, need; **me cuesta hablarle** I find it hard to talk to him.

Costa Rica nf Costa Rica; **costarricense, costarriqueño, a** a, nmf Costa Rican.

coste ['koste] nm = **costo**.

costear [koste'ar] vt to pay for.

costilla [kos'tiʎa] nf rib; (CULIN) cutlet.

costo ['kosto] nm cost, price; ~ **de la vida** cost of living; ~**so, a** a costly, expensive.

costra ['kostra] nf (corteza) crust; (MED) scab.

costumbre [kos'tumbre] nf custom, habit.

costura [kos'tura] nf sewing, needle-work; (zurcido) seam.

costurera [kostu'rera] nf dress-maker.

costurero [kostu'rero] nm sewing box o case.

cotejar [kote'xar] vt to compare.

cotidiano, a [koti'ðjano, a] a daily, day to day.

cotización [kotiθa'θjon] nf (COM) quotation, price; (de club) dues pl.

cotizar [koti'θar] vt (COM) to quote, price; ~**se** vr: ~**se a** to sell at, fetch; (BOLSA) to stand at, be quoted at.

coto ['koto] nm (terreno cercado) enclosure; (de caza) reserve.

cotorra [ko'torra] nf parrot.

COU [kou] nm abr (Esp) = Curso de Orientación Universitaria.

coyote [ko'jote] nm coyote, prairie wolf.

coyuntura [kojun'tura] nf (ANAT) joint; (fig) juncture, occasion.

coz [koθ] nf kick.

cráneo ['kraneo] nm skull, cranium.

cráter ['krater] nm crater.

creación [krea'θjon] nf creation.

creador, a [krea'ðor, a] a creative // nmf creator.

crear [kre'ar] vt to create, make.

crecer [kre'θer] vi to grow; (precio) to rise.

creces ['kreθes] : **con ~** ad amply, fully.

crecido, a [kre'θiðo, a] a (persona, planta) full-grown; (cantidad) large.

creciente [kre'θjente] a growing; (cantidad) increasing; (luna) crescent // nm crescent.

crecimiento [kreθi'mjento] nm growth; (aumento) increase.

credenciales [kreðen'θjales] nfpl credentials.

crédito ['kreðito] nm credit.

credo ['kreðo] nm creed.

crédulo, a ['kreðulo, a] a credulous.

creencia [kre'enθja] nf belief.

creer [kre'er] vt, vi to think, believe; ~**se** vr to believe o.s. (to be); ~ **en** to believe in; **¡ya lo creo!** I should think so!

creíble [kre'iβle] a credible, believable.

creído, a [kre'iðo, a] a (engreído) conceited.

crema ['krema] nf cream; (natillas)

custard.

cremallera [krema'ʎera] nf zip (fastener).

crepitar [krepi'tar] vi to crackle.

crepúsculo [kre'puskulo] nm twilight, dusk.

crespo, a ['krespo, a] a (pelo) curly.

crespón [kres'pon] nm crêpe.

cresta ['kresta] nf (GEO, ZOOL) crest.

creyendo vb ver **creer**.

creyente [kre'jente] nm/f believer.

creyó etc vb ver **creer**.

crezco etc vb ver **crecer**.

cría etc vb ver **criar** // ['kria] nf (de animales) rearing, breeding; (animal) young; ver tb **crío**.

criadero [kria'ðero] nm nursery; (ZOOL) breeding place.

criado, a [kri'aðo, a] nm servant // nf servant, maid.

criador [kria'ðor] nm breeder.

crianza [kri'anθa] nf rearing, breeding; (fig) breeding.

criar [kri'ar] vt (amamantar) to suckle, feed; (educar) to bring up; (producir) to grow, produce; (animales) to breed.

criatura [kria'tura] nf creature; (niño) baby, (small) child.

criba ['krißa] nf sieve; **cribar** vt to sieve.

crimen ['krimen] nm crime.

criminal [krimi'nal] a, nm/f criminal.

crin [krin] nf (tb: ~es nfpl) mane.

crío, a ['krio, a] nm/f (fam) kid.

crisis ['krisis] nf inv crisis; ~ **nerviosa** nervous breakdown.

crispar [kris'par] vt (músculo) to tense (up); (nervios) to set on edge.

cristal [kris'tal] nm crystal; (de ventana) glass, pane; (lente) lens; **~ino, a** a crystalline; (fig) clear // nm lens of the eye; **~izar** vt, vi to crystallize.

cristiandad [kristjan'dað] nf Christianity.

cristianismo [kristja'nismo] nm Christianity.

cristiano, a [kris'tjano, a] a, nm/f

Christian.

Cristo ['kristo] nm (Dios) Christ; (crucifijo) crucifix.

criterio [kri'terjo] nm criterion; (juicio) judgement.

criticar [kriti'kar] vt to criticize.

crítico, a ['kritiko, a] a critical // nm/f critic // nf criticism.

croar [kro'ar] vi to croak.

cromo ['kromo] nm chrome.

crónico, a ['kroniko, a] a chronic // nf chronicle, account.

cronómetro [kro'nometro] nm (DEPORTE) stopwatch.

cruce etc vb ver **cruzar** // ['kruθe] nm crossing; (de carreteras) crossroads.

crucificar [kruθifi'kar] vt to crucify.

crucifijo [kruθi'fixo] nm crucifix.

crucigrama [kruθi'vrama] nm crossword (puzzle).

crudo, a ['kruðo, a] a raw; (no maduro) unripe; (petróleo) crude; (rudo, cruel) cruel // nm crude (oil).

cruel [krwel] a cruel; **~dad** nf cruelty.

crujido [kru'xiðo] nm (de madera etc) creak.

crujiente [kru'xjente] a (galleta etc) crunchy.

crujir [kru'xir] vi (madera etc) to creak; (dedos) to crack; (dientes) to grind; (nieve, arena) to crunch.

cruz [kruθ] nf cross; (de moneda) tails sg.

cruzado, a [kru'θaðo, a] a crossed // nm crusader // nf crusade.

cruzar [kru'θar] vt to cross; **~se** vr (líneas etc) to cross; (personas) to pass each other.

Cruz Roja nf Red Cross.

cuaderno [kwa'ðerno] nm notebook; (de escuela) exercise book; (NAUT) logbook.

cuadra ['kwaðra] nf (caballeriza) stable; (AM) block.

cuadrado, a [kwa'ðraðo, a] a square // nm (MAT) square.

cuadrar [kwa'ðrar] vt to square // vi: **~ con** to square with, tally with;

~se *vr* (*soldado*) to stand to attention.

cuadrilátero [kwaðri'latero] *nm* (*DEPORTE*) boxing ring; (*GEOM*) quadrilateral.

cuadrilla [kwa'ðriʎa] *nf* party, group.

cuadro ['kwaðro] *nm* square; (*ARTE*) painting; (*TEATRO*) scene; (*diagrama*) chart; (*DEPORTE, MED*) team; (*POL*) executive; **tela a** ~**s** checked (*Brit*) o chequered (*US*) material.

cuádruplo, a ['kwaðruplo, a], **cuádruple** ['kwaðruple] *a* quadruple.

cuajar [kwa'xar] *vt* to thicken; (*leche*) to curdle; (*sangre*) to congeal; (*adornar*) to adorn; (*CULIN*) to set; ~se *vr* to curdle; to congeal; to set; (*llenarse*) to fill up.

cual [kwal] *ad* like, as // *pron*: **el** ~ *etc* which; (*persona: sujeto*) who; (: *objeto*) whom // *a* such as; **cada** ~ each one; **tal** ~ just as it is.

cuál [kwal] *pron interr* which (one).

cualesquier(a) [kwales'kjer(a)] *pl de* **cualquier(a)**.

cualidad [kwali'ðað] *nf* quality.

cualquier(a) [kwal'kjer]　　　*pl* **cualesquier(a)** *a* (*indefinido*) any; ~ **día de éstos** any day now; (*después de pron*): ~**: a**: no es un hombre ~**a** he isn't an ordinary man, he isn't just anybody; *pron*: ~**a**: **eso** ~**a lo sabe hacer** anybody can do that; **es un** ~**a** he's a nobody.

cuando ['kwando] *ad* when; (*aún si*) if, even if // *conj* (*puesto que*) since // *prep*: **yo,** ~ **niño...** when I was a child...; ~ **no sea así** even if it is not so; ~ **más** at (the) most; ~ **menos** at least; ~ **no** if not, otherwise; **de** ~ **en** ~ from time to time.

cuándo ['kwando] *ad* when; **¿desde** ~**?, ¿de** ~ **acá?** since when?

cuantioso, a [kwan'tjoso, a] *a* substantial.

cuanto, a ['kwanto, a] ◆ *a* **1** (*todo*): **tiene todo** ~ **desea** he's got everything he wants; **le daremos** ~**s ejemplares necesite** we'll give him as many copies as o all the copies he needs; ~**se hombres la ven** all the men who see her

2: **unos** ~**s: había unos** ~**s periodistas** there were (quite) a few journalists

3 (+ *más*): ~ **más vino bebes peor te sentirás** the more wine you drink the worse you'll feel

◆ *pron*: **tiene** ~ **desea** he has everything he wants; **tome** ~**/**~**s quiera** take as much/many as you want

◆ *ad*: **en** ~: **en** ~ **profesor** as a teacher; **en** ~ **a mí** as for me; *ver* **tb antes**

◆ *conj* **1**: ~ **más gana menos gasta** the more he earns the less he spends; ~ **más joven se es más se es confiado** the younger you are the more trusting you are

2: **en** ~ **llegue/llegué** as soon as I arrive/arrived

cuánto, a ['kwanto, a] *a* (*exclamación*) what a lot of; (*interr: sg*) how much?; (: *pl*) how many? // *pron*, *ad* how; (*interr: sg*) how much?; (: *pl*) how many?; ~**a gente!** what a lot of people!; ¿~ **cuesta?** how much does it cost?; ¿**a** ~ **estamos?** what's the date?; **Señor no sé** ~ Mr. So-and-So.

cuarenta [kwa'renta] *num* forty.

cuarentena [kwaren'tena] *nf* quarantine.

cuaresma [kwa'resma] *nf* Lent.

cuartear [kwarte'ar] *vt* to quarter; (*dividir*) to divide up; ~**se** *vr* to crack, split.

cuartel [kwar'tel] *nm* (*de ciudad*) quarter, district; (*MIL*) barracks *pl*; ~ **general** headquarters *pl*.

cuarteto [kwar'teto] *nm* quartet.

cuarto, a ['kwarto, a] *a* fourth // *nm* (*MAT*) quarter, fourth; (*habitación*) room // *nf* (*MAT*) quarter, fourth; (*palmo*) span; ~ **de baño** bathroom

~ **de estar** living room; ~ **de hora** quarter (of an) hour; ~ **de kilo** quarter kilo.

cuatro ['kwatro] *num* four.

cuba ['kuβa] *nf* cask, barrel.

Cuba ['kuβa] *nf* Cuba; **cubano, a** *a*, *nm/f* Cuban.

cúbico, a ['kuβiko, a] *a* cubic.

cubierto, a [ku'βjerto, a] *pp de* **cubrir** // *a* covered // *nm* cover; (*en la mesa*) place; ~**s** *nmpl* cutlery *sg* // *nf* cover, covering; (*neumático*) tyre; (*NAUT*) deck; **a** ~ **de** covered with o in.

cubil [ku'βil] *nm* den; ~**ete** *nm* (*en juegos*) cup.

cubo ['kuβo] *nm* cube; (*balde*) bucket, tub; (*TEC*) drum.

cubrecama [kuβre'kama] *nm* bedspread.

cubrir [ku'βrir] *vt* to cover; ~**se** *vr* (*cielo*) to become overcast.

cucaracha [kuka'ratʃa] *nf* cockroach.

cuco, a ['kuko, a] *a* pretty; (*astuto*) sharp // *nm* cuckoo.

cucurucho [kuku'rutʃo] *nm* cornet.

cuchara [ku'tʃara] *nf* spoon; (*TEC*) scoop; ~**da** *nf* spoonful; ~**dita** *nf* teaspoonful.

cucharita [kutʃa'rita] *nf* teaspoon.

cucharón [kutʃa'ron] *nm* ladle.

cuchichear [kutʃitʃe'ar] *vi* to whisper.

cuchilla [ku'tʃiʎa] *nf* (large) knife; (*de arma blanca*) blade; ~ **de afeitar** razor blade.

cuchillo [ku'tʃiʎo] *nm* knife.

cuchitril [kutʃi'tril] *nm* hovel; (*habitación etc*) pigsty.

cuello ['kweʎo] *nm* (*ANAT*) neck; (*de vestido, camisa*) collar.

cuenca ['kwenka] *nf* (*ANAT*) eye socket; (*GEO*) bowl, deep valley.

cuenta *etc vb ver* **contar** // ['kwenta] *nf* (*cálculo*) count, counting; (*en café, restaurante*) bill; (*COM*) account; (*de collar*) bead; (*fig*) account; **a fin de** ~**s** in the end; **caer en la** ~ to catch on; **darse** ~ to realize; **tener en** ~

to bear in mind; **echar** ~**s** to take stock; ~ **corriente/de ahorros** current/savings account; ~**kilómetros** *nm inv* = milometer; (*de velocidad*) speedometer.

cuento *etc vb ver* **contar** // ['kwento] *nm* story.

cuerda ['kwerða] *nf* rope; (*hilo*) string; (*de reloj*) spring; **dar** ~ **a un reloj** to wind up a clock.

cuerdo, a ['kwerðo, a] *a* sane; (*prudente*) wise, sensible.

cuerno ['kwerno] *nm* horn.

cuero ['kwero] *nm* (*ZOOL*) skin, hide; (*TEC*) leather; **en** ~**s** stark naked; ~ **cabelludo** scalp.

cuerpo ['kwerpo] *nm* body.

cuervo ['kwerβo] *nm* crow.

cuesta *etc vb ver* **costar** // ['kwesta] *nf* slope; (*en camino etc*) hill; ~ **arriba/abajo** uphill/downhill; **a** ~**s** on one's back.

cueste *etc vb ver* **costar**.

cueva ['kweβa] *nf* cave.

cuidado [kwi'ðaðo] *nm* care, carefulness; (*preocupación*) care, worry // *excl* careful!, look out!

cuidadoso, a [kwiða'ðoso, a] *a* careful; (*preocupado*) anxious.

cuidar [kwi'ðar] *vt* (*MED*) to care for; (*ocuparse de*) to take care of, look after // *vi*: ~ **de** to take care of, look after; ~**se** *vr* to look after o.s.; ~**se de hacer algo** to take care to do sth.

culata [ku'lata] *nf* (*de fusil*) butt.

culebra [ku'leβra] *nf* snake.

culinario, a [kuli'narjo, a] *a* culinary, cooking *cpd*.

culminación [kulmina'θjon] *nf* culmination.

culo ['kulo] *nm* bottom, backside; (*de vaso, botella*) bottom.

culpa ['kulpa] *nf* fault; (*JUR*) guilt; **por** ~ **de** because of, through; **tener la** ~ (**de**) to be to blame (for); ~**bilidad** *nf* guilt; ~**ble** *a* guilty // *nm/f* culprit.

culpar [kul'par] *vt* to blame; (*acusar*) to accuse.

cultivar [kulti'βar] *vt* to cultivate.

cultivo [kul'tiβo] *nm* (*acto*) cultivation; (*plantas*) crop.

culto, a ['kulto, a] *a* (*cultivado*) cultivated; (*que tiene cultura*) cultured, educated // *nm* (*homenaje*) worship; (*religión*) cult.

cultura [kul'tura] *nf* culture.

cumbre ['kumbre] *nf* summit, top.

cumpleaños [kumple'aɲos] *nm inv* birthday.

cumplido, a [kum'pliðo, a] *a* complete, perfect; (*abundante*) plentiful; (*cortés*) courteous // *nm* compliment; **visita de ~** courtesy call.

cumplidor, a [kumpli'ðor, a] *a* reliable.

cumplimentar [kumplimen'tar] *vt* to congratulate.

cumplimiento [kumpli'mjento] *nm* (*de un deber*) fulfilment; (*acabamiento*) completion.

cumplir [kum'plir] *vt* (*orden*) to carry out, obey; (*promesa*) to carry out, fulfil; (*condena*) to serve; (*años*) to reach, attain // *vi*: **~ con** (*deberes*) to carry out; **~se** *vr* (*plazo*) to expire; **hoy cumple dieciocho años** he is eighteen today.

cúmulo ['kumulo] *nm* heap.

cuna ['kuna] *nf* cradle, cot.

cundir [kun'dir] *vi* (*noticia, rumor, pánico*) to spread; (*rendir*) to go a long way.

cuneta [ku'neta] *nf* ditch.

cuña ['kuɲa] *nf* wedge.

cuñado, a [ku'ɲaðo, a] *nm/f* brother/sister-in-law.

cuota ['kwota] *nf* (*parte proporcional*) share; (*cotización*) fee, dues *pl*.

cupe, cupiera *etc vb ver* **caber.**

cupo *vb ver* **caber** // ['kupo] *nm* quota.

cupón [ku'pon] *nm* coupon.

cúpula ['kupula] *nf* dome.

cura ['kura] *nf* (*curación*) cure;

(*método curativo*) treatment // *nm* priest.

curación [kura'θjon] *nf* cure; (*acción*) curing.

curar [ku'rar] *vt* (*MED: herida*) to treat, dress; (*: enfermo*) to cure; (*CULIN*) to cure, salt; (*cuero*) to tan // *vi*, **~se** *vr* to get well, recover.

curiosear [kurjose'ar] *vt* to glance at, look over // *vi* to look round, wander round; (*explorar*) to poke about.

curiosidad [kurjosi'ðað] *nf* curiosity.

curioso, a [ku'rjoso, a] *a* curious // *nm/f* bystander, onlooker.

currante [ku'rrante] *nm/f* (*fam*) worker.

currar [ku'rrar], **currelar** [kurre'lar] *vi* (*fam*) to work; **curro** *nm* (*fam*) work, job.

currículo [ku'rrikolo], **currículum** [ku'rrikulum] *nm* curriculum vitae.

cursi ['kursi] *a* (*fam*) pretentious; (*: amanerado*) affected.

cursiva [kur'siβa] *nf* italics *pl*.

curso ['kurso] *nm* course; **en ~** (*año*) current; (*proceso*) going on, under way.

cursor [kur'sor] *nm* (*INFORM*) cursor.

curtido, a [kur'tiðo, a] *a* (*cara etc*) weather-beaten; (*fig: persona*) experienced.

curtir [kur'tir] *vt* (*cuero etc*) to tan.

curvo, a [ku'kurβo, a] *a* (*gen*) curved; (*torcido*) bent // *nf* (*gen*) curve, bend.

cúspide ['kuspiðe] *nf* (*GEO*) peak; (*fig*) top.

custodia [kus'toðja] *nf* safekeeping; custody; **custodiar** *vt* (*conservar*) to take care of; (*vigilar*) to guard.

custodio [kus'toðjo] *nm* guardian, keeper.

cutícula [ku'tikula] *nf* cuticle.

cutis ['kutis] *nm inv* skin, complexion.

cutre ['kutre] *a* (*fam: lugar*) grotty; (*: persona*) naff.

cuyo, a ['kujo, a] *pron* (*de quien*) whose; (*de que*) whose, of which; **en**

~ **caso** in which case.
C.V. abr (= caballos de vapor) H.P.

CH

chabacano, a [tʃaβa'kano, a] a vulgar, coarse.
chabola [tʃa'βola] nf shack; ~s nfpl shanty town sg.
chacal [tʃa'kal] nm jackal.
chacra ['tʃakra] nf (AM) smallholding.
chacha ['tʃatʃa] nf (fam) maid.
cháchara ['tʃatʃara] nf chatter; **estar de** ~ to chatter away.
chafar [tʃa'far] vt (aplastar) to crush; (arruinar) to ruin.
chal [tʃal] nm shawl.
chalado, a [tʃa'lado, a] a (fam) crazy.
chalé, chalet [tʃa'le] (pl chalés, chalets) nm villa, ~ detached house.
chaleco [tʃa'leko] nm waistcoat, vest (US); ~ **salvavidas** life jacket.
chalupa [tʃa'lupa] nf launch, boat.
champán [tʃam'pan], **champaña** [tʃam'paɲa] nm champagne.
champiñón [tʃampi'ɲon] nm mushroom.
champú [tʃam'pu] (pl **champúes**, **champús**) nm shampoo.
chamuscar [tʃamus'kar] vt to scorch, sear, singe.
chance ['tʃanθe] nm (AM) chance.
chancho, a ['tʃantʃo, a] nm/f (AM) pig.
chanchullo [tʃan'tʃuʎo] nm (fam) fiddle.
chantaje [tʃan'taxe] nm blackmail.
chapa ['tʃapa] nf (de metal) plate, sheet; (de madera) board, panel; (AM AUTO) number (Brit) o license (US) plate.
chaparrón [tʃapa'rron] nm downpour, cloudburst.
chapotear [tʃapote'ar] vt to sponge down // vi (fam) to splash about.
chapucero, a [tʃapu'θero, a] a rough, crude // nm/f bungler.

chapurrear [tʃapurre'ar] vt (idioma) to speak badly.
chapuza [tʃa'puθa] nf botched job.
chaqueta [tʃa'keta] nf jacket.
charca ['tʃarka] nf pond, pool.
charco ['tʃarko] nm pool, puddle.
charcutería [tʃarkute'ria] nf (tienda) shop selling chiefly pork meat products; (productos) cooked pork meats pl.
charla ['tʃarla] nf talk, chat; (conferencia) lecture.
charlar [tʃar'lar] vi to talk, chat.
charlatán, ana [tʃarla'tan, ana] nm/f chatterbox; (estafador) trickster.
charol [tʃa'rol] nm varnish; (cuero) patent leather.
chascarrillo [tʃaska'rriʎo] nm (fam) funny story.
chasco ['tʃasko] nm (broma) trick, joke; (desengaño) disappointment.
chasis ['tʃasis] nm inv chassis.
chasquear [tʃaske'ar] vt (látigo) to crack; (lengua) to click; **chasquido** nm (de lengua) click; (de látigo) crack.
chatarra [tʃa'tarra] nf scrap (metal).
chato, a ['tʃato, a] a flat; (nariz) snub.
chaval, a [tʃa'βal, a] nm/f kid, lad/lass.
checo(e)slovaco, a [tʃeko(e)slo'βako, a] a, nm/f Czech, Czechoslovak.
Checo(e)slovaquia [tʃeko(e)slo'βakja] nf Czechoslovakia.
cheque ['tʃeke] nm cheque (Brit), check (US); ~ **de viajero** traveller's cheque (US), traveler's check (US).
chequeo [tʃe'keo] nm (MED) checkup; (AUTO) service.
chequera [tʃe'kera] nf (AM) chequebook (Brit), checkbook (US).
chicano, a [tʃi'kano, a] a, nm/f chicano.
chicle ['tʃikle] nm chewing gum.
chico, a ['tʃiko, a] a small, little // nm/f (niño) child; (muchacho) boy/girl.
chícharo ['tʃitʃaro] nm (AM) pea.

chicharrón [tʃitʃa'rron] nm (pork) crackling.

chichón [tʃi'tʃon] nm bump, lump.

chiflado, a [tʃi'flaðo, a] a crazy.

chiflar [tʃi'flar] vt to hiss, boo.

chile ['tʃile] nm chilli pepper.

Chile ['tʃile] nm Chile; **chileno, a** a, nm/f Chilean.

chillar [tʃi'ʎar] vi (persona) to yell, scream; (animal salvaje) to howl; (cerdo) to squeal; (puerta) to creak.

chillido [tʃi'ʎiðo] nm (de persona) yell, scream; (de animal) howl; (de frenos) screech(ing).

chillón, ona [tʃi'ʎon, ona] a (niño) noisy; (color) loud, gaudy.

chimenea [tʃime'nea] nf chimney; (hogar) fireplace.

China ['tʃina] nf: (la) ~ China.

chinche ['tʃintʃe] nf (insecto) (bed)bug; (TEC) drawing pin (Brit), thumbtack (US) // nm/f nuisance, pest.

chincheta [tʃin'tʃeta] nf drawing pin (Brit), thumbtack (US).

chino, a ['tʃino, a] a, nm/f Chinese // nm (LING) Chinese.

Chipre ['tʃipre] nf Cyprus; **chipriota, chipriote** a, nm/f Cypriot.

chiquito, a [tʃi'kito, a] a very small, tiny // nm/f kid.

chiripa [tʃi'ripa] nf fluke.

chirriar [tʃi'rrjar] vi (goznes etc) to creak, squeak; (pájaros) to chirp, sing.

chirrido [tʃi'rriðo] nm creak(ing), squeak(ing); (de pájaro) chirp(ing).

chis [tʃis] excl sh!

chisme ['tʃisme] nm (habladurías) piece of gossip; (fam: objeto) thingummyjig.

chismoso, a [tʃis'moso, a] a gossiping // nm/f gossip.

chispa ['tʃispa] nf spark; (fig) sparkle; (ingenio) wit; (fam) drunkenness.

chispeante [tʃispe'ante] a sparkling.

chispear [tʃispe'ar] vi to spark; (lloviznar) to drizzle.

chisporrotear [tʃisporrote'ar] vi

(fuego) to throw out sparks; (leña) to crackle; (aceite) to hiss, splutter.

chiste ['tʃiste] nm joke, funny story.

chistoso, a [tʃis'toso, a] a (gracioso) funny, amusing; (bromista) witty.

chivo, a ['tʃiβo, a] nm/f (billy-/nanny-)goat; ~ **expiatorio** scapegoat.

chocante [tʃo'kante] a startling; (extraño) odd; (ofensivo) shocking.

chocar [tʃo'kar] vi (coches etc) to collide, crash // vt to shock; (sorprender) to startle; ~ **con** to collide with; (fig) to run into, run up against; ¡chócala! (fam) put it there!

chocolate [tʃoko'late] a, nm chocolate.

chochear [tʃotʃe'ar] vi to dodder, be senile.

chocho, a ['tʃotʃo, a] a doddering, senile; (fig) soft, doting.

chófer ['tʃofer], **chofer** [tʃo'fer] nm driver.

chollo ['tʃoʎo] nm (fam) bargain, snip.

choque etc vb ver **chocar** // ['tʃoke] nm (impacto) impact; (golpe) jolt; (AUTO) crash; (fig) conflict.

chorizo [tʃo'riθo] nm hard pork sausage, (type of) salami.

chorrear [tʃorre'ar] vi to gush (out), spout (out); (gotear) to drip, trickle.

chorro ['tʃorro] nm jet; (fig) stream.

choza ['tʃoθa] nf hut, shack.

chubasco [tʃu'βasko] nm squall.

chuleta [tʃu'leta] nf chop, cutlet.

chulo ['tʃulo] nm (pícaro) rascal; (rufián) pimp.

chupado, a [tʃu'paðo, a] a (delgado) skinny, gaunt.

chupete [tʃu'pete] nm dummy (Brit), pacifier (US).

chupar [tʃu'par] vt to suck; (absorber) to absorb; ~se vr to grow thin.

churro ['tʃurro, a] a coarse // nm (type of) fritter.

chusco, a ['tʃusko, a] a funny.

chusma ['tʃusma] nf rabble, mob.
chutar [tʃu'tar] vi (DEPORTE) to
shoot (at goal).

D

D. abr (= Don) Esq.
Da. abr = Doña.
dactilógrafo, a [dakti'loɣrafo, a]
nm/f typist.
dádiva ['daðiβa] nf (donación) donation; (regalo) gift; **dadivoso, a** a
generous.
dado, a ['daðo, a] pp de dar // nm
die; ~s nmpl dice; ~ que conj given
that.
daltónico, a [dal'toniko, a] a
colour-blind.
dama ['dama] nf (gen) lady;
(AJEDREZ) queen; ~s nfpl (juego)
draughts.
damasco [da'masko] nm damask.
damnificar [damnifi'kar] vt to harm;
(persona) to injure.
danés, esa [da'nes, esa] a Danish //
nm/f Dane.
danzar [dan'θar] vt, vi to dance.
dañar [da'nar] vt (objeto) to damage; (persona) to hurt; ~se vr
(objeto) to get damaged.
dañino, a [da'nino, a] a harmful.
daño ['dano] nm (a un objeto) damage; (a una persona) harm, injury;
~s y perjuicios (JUR) damages;
hacer ~ a to damage; (persona) to
hurt, injure; hacerse ~ to hurt o.s.

---

dar [dar] ♦ vt 1 (gen) to give; (obra
de teatro) to put on; (film) to show;
(fiesta) to hold; ~ algo a uno to
give sth to sb; ~ de beber
a uno to give sb a drink
2 (producir: intereses) to yield;
(fruta) to produce
3 (locuciones + n): da gusto escu-
charle it's a pleasure to listen to
him; ver tb paseo y otros n
4 (+ n: = perífrasis de verbo): me

da pena/asco it frightens/sickens me
5 (considerar): ~ algo por
descontado/entendido to take sth
for granted/as read; ~ algo por
concluido to consider sth finished
6 (hora): el reloj dio las 6 the
clock struck 6 (o'clock)
7: me da lo mismo it's all the
same to me; ver tb igual, más
♦ vi 1: ~ con: dimos con él dos
horas más tarde we came across
him two hours later; al final di con
la solución I eventually came up
with the answer
2: ~ en: ~ en (blanco, suelo) to hit;
el sol me da en la cara the sun is
shining (right) on my face
3: ~ de sí (zapatos etc) to stretch,
give
♦ ~se vr 1: ~se por vencido to
give up
2 (ocurrir): se han dado muchos
casos there have been a lot of cases
3: ~se a: se ha dado a la bebida
he's taken to drinking
4: se me dan bien/mal las
ciencias I'm good/bad at science
5: dárselas de: se las da de
experto he fancies himself o poses
as an expert.

---

dardo ['darðo] nm dart.
dársena ['darsena] nf dock.
datar [da'tar] vi: ~ de to date from.
dátil ['datil] nm date.
dato ['dato] nm fact, piece of information.
dcha. abr (= derecha) r.h.
d. de J.C. abr (= después de
Jesucristo) A.D.

---

de [de] prep (de + el = del) 1 (posesión) of; la casa ~ Isabel/mis padres Isabel's/my parents' house; es
~ ellos it's theirs
2 (origen, distancia, con números)
from; soy ~ Gijón I'm from Gijón;
~ 8 a 20 from 8 to 20; salir del cine
to go out of o leave the cinema; ~ ...

en ... from ... to ...; ~ **2 en 2** 2 by 2, 2 at a time

3 (*valor descriptivo*): **una copa** ~ **vino** a glass of wine; **la mesa** ~ **la cocina** the kitchen table; **un billete** ~ **1000 pesetas** a 1000 peseta note; **un niño** ~ **tres años** a three-year-old (child); **una máquina** ~ **coser** a sewing machine; **ir vestido** ~ **gris** to be dressed in grey; **la niña del vestido azul** the girl in the blue dress; **trabaja** ~ **profesora** she works as a teacher; ~ **lado** sideways; ~ **atrás/delante** rear/front

4 (*hora, tiempo*): **a las 8** ~ **la mañana** at 8 o'clock in the morning; ~ **día/noche** by day/night; ~ **hoy en ocho días** a week from now; ~ **niño era gordo** as a child he was fat

5 (*comparaciones*): **más/menos** ~ **cien personas** more/less than a hundred people; **el más caro** ~ **la tienda** the most expensive in the shop; **menos/más** ~ **lo pensado** less/more than expected

6 (*causa*): **del calor** from the heat; ~ **puro tonto** out of sheer stupidity

7 (*tema*) about; **clases** ~ **inglés** English classes; **¿sabes algo** ~ **él**? do you know anything about him?; **un libro** ~ **física** a physics book

8 (*adjetivo* + *de* + *infin*): **fácil** ~ **entender** easy to understand

9 (*oraciones pasivas*): **fue respetado** ~ **todos** he was loved by all

10 (*condicional* + *infin*) if; ~ **ser posible** if possible; ~ **no terminarlo hoy** if I *etc* don't finish it today.

dé *vb ver* **dar**.

deambular [deambu'lar] *vi* to stroll, wander.

debajo [de'βaxo] *ad* underneath; ~ **de** below, under; **por** ~ **de** beneath.

debate [de'βate] *nm* debate; **debatir** *vt* to debate.

deber [de'βer] *nm* duty / *vt* to owe / *vi*: **debe (de)** it must, it should;

~es *nmpl* (*ESCOL*) homework; **debo hacerlo** I must do it; **debe de ir** he should go; ~**se** *vr*: ~**se a** to be owing *o* due to.

debido, a [de'βiðo, a] *a* proper, just; ~ **a** due to, because of.

débil ['deβil] *a* (*persona, carácter*) weak; (*luz*) dim; **debilidad** *nf* weakness; dimness.

debilitar [deβili'tar] *vt* to weaken; ~**se** *vr* to grow weak.

debutar [deβu'tar] *vi* to make one's debut.

década ['dekaða] *nf* decade.

decadencia [deka'ðenθja] *nf* (*estado*) decadence; (*proceso*) decline, decay.

decaer [deka'er] *vi* (*declinar*) to decline; (*debilitarse*) to weaken.

decaído, a [deka'iðo, a] *a*: **estar** ~ (*abatido*) to be down.

decaimiento [dekai'mjento] *nm* (*declinación*) decline; (*desaliento*) discouragement; (*MED*: *estado débil*) weakness.

decano, a [de'kano, a] *nm/f* (*de universidad etc*) dean.

decapitar [dekapi'tar] *vt* to behead.

decena [de'θena] *nf*: **una** ~ ten (*or* so).

decencia [de'θenθja] *nf* (*modestia*) modesty; (*honestidad*) respectability.

decente [de'θente] *a* (*correcto*) seemly, proper; (*honesto*) respectable.

decepción [deθep'θjon] *nf* disappointment.

decepcionar [deθepθjo'nar] *vt* to disappoint.

decidir [deθi'ðir] *vt* (*persuadir*) to convince, persuade; (*resolver*) to decide // *vi* to decide; ~**se** *vr*: ~**se a** to make up one's mind to.

décimo, a ['deθimo, a] *a* tenth // *nm* tenth.

decir [de'θir] *vt* (*expresar*) to say; (*contar*) to tell; (*hablar*) to speak // *nm* saying; ~**se** *vr*: **se dice que** it is said that; ~ **para** *o* **entre sí** to say to o.s.; **querer** ~ to mean;

¡**digame!** (*TEL*) hello!; (*en tienda*) can I help you?

decisión [deθi'sjon] *nf* (*resolución*) decision; (*firmeza*) decisiveness.

decisivo, a [deθi'siβo, a] *a* decisive.

declamar [dekla'mar] *vt, vi* to declaim.

declaración [deklara'θjon] *nf* (*manifestación*) statement; (*explicación*) explanation.

declarar [dekla'rar] *vt* to declare, state; to explain // *vi* to declare; (*JUR*) to testify; ~**se** *vr* to propose.

declinar [dekli'nar] *vt* (*gen*) to decline; (*JUR*) to reject // *vi* (*el día*) to draw to a close.

declive [de'kliβe] *nm* (*cuesta*) slope; (*fig*) decline.

decolorarse [dekolo'rarse] *vr* to become discoloured.

decoración [dekora'θjon] *nf* decoration.

decorado [deko'raðo] *nm* (*CINE, TEATRO*) scenery, set.

decorar [deko'rar] *vt* to decorate; **decorativo, a** *a* ornamental, decorative.

decoro [de'koro] *nm* (*respeto*) respect; (*dignidad*) decency; (*recato*) propriety; ~**so,** *a* (*decente*) decent; (*modesto*) modest; (*digno*) proper.

decrecer [dekre'θer] *vi* to decrease, diminish.

decrépito, a [de'krepito, a] *a* decrepit.

decretar [dekre'tar] *vt* to decree; **decreto** *nm* decree.

dedal [de'ðal] *nm* thimble.

dedicación [deðika'θjon] *nf* dedication; **dedicar** *vt* (*libro*) to dedicate; (*tiempo, dinero*) to devote; (*palabras: decir, consagrar*) to dedicate, devote; **dedicatoria** *nf* (*de libro*) dedication.

dedo ['deðo] *nm* finger; ~ (**del pie**) toe; ~ **pulgar** thumb; ~ **índice** index finger; ~ **mayor** *o* **cordial** middle finger; ~ **anular** ring finger; ~ **meñique** little finger; **hacer** ~

(*fam*) to hitch (a lift).

deducción [deðuk'θjon] *nf* deduction.

deducir [deðu'θir] *vt* (*concluir*) to deduce, infer; (*COM*) to deduct.

defecto [de'fekto] *nm* defect, flaw; **defectuoso, a** *a* defective, faulty.

defender [defen'der] *vt* to defend.

defensa [de'fensa] *nf* defence // *nm* (*DEPORTE*) defender, back; **defensivo, a** *a* defensive // *nf*: **a la defensiva** on the defensive.

defensor, a [defen'sor, a] *a* defending // *nmf* (*abogado* ~) defending counsel; (*protector*) protector.

deficiencia [defi'θjenθja] *nf* deficiency.

deficiente [defi'θjente] *a* (*defectuoso*) defective; ~ **en** lacking *o* deficient in; **ser un** ~ **mental** to be mentally handicapped.

déficit ['defiθit] (*pl* ~s) *nm* deficit.

definir [defi'nir] *vt* (*determinar*) to determine, establish; (*decidir*) to define; (*aclarar*) to clarify; **definitivo, a** *a* definitive; **en definitiva** definitively; (*en resumen*) in short.

deformación [deforma'θjon] *nf* (*alteración*) deformation; (*RADIO etc*) distortion.

deformar [defor'mar] *vt* (*gen*) to deform; ~**se** *vr* to become deformed; **deforme** *a* (*informe*) deformed; (*feo*) ugly; (*malhecho*) misshapen.

defraudar [defrau'ðar] *vt* (*decepcionar*) to disappoint; (*estafar*) to cheat; to defraud.

defunción [defun'θjon] *nf* death, demise.

degeneración [dexenera'θjon] *nf* (*de las células*) degeneration; (*moral*) degeneracy.

degenerar [dexene'rar] *vi* to degenerate.

degollar [dexo'ʎar] *vt* to behead; (*fig*) to slaughter.

degradar [deγra'ðar] *vt* to debase, degrade; ~**se** *vr* to demean o.s.

degustación [deɣusta'θjon] nf sampling, tasting.

deificar [deifi'kar] vt (persona) to deify.

dejadez [dexa'ðeθ] nf (negligencia) neglect; (descuido) untidiness, carelessness; **dejado, a** a (negligente) careless; (indolente) lazy.

dejar [de'xar] vt to leave; (permitir) to allow, let; (abandonar) to abandon, forsake; (beneficios) to produce, yield // vi: ~ de (parar) to stop; (no hacer) to fail to; **no dejes de comprar un billete** make sure you buy a ticket; ~ **a un lado** to leave o set aside.

dejo ['dexo] nm (LING) accent.

del [del] = **de + el**, ver **de**.

delantal [delan'tal] nm apron.

delante [de'lante] ad in front, (enfrente) opposite; (adelante) ahead; ~ **de** in front of, before.

delantero, a [delan'tero, a] a front // nm (DEPORTE) forward, striker // nf (de vestido, casa etc) front part; (DEPORTE) forward line; **llevar la delantera (a uno)** to be ahead (of sb).

delatar [dela'tar] vt to inform on o against, betray; **delator, a** nm/f informer.

delegación [deleɣa'θjon] nf (acción, delegados) delegation; (COM: oficina) office, branch; ~ **de policía** police station.

delegado, a [dele'ɣaðo, a] nm/f delegate; (COM) agent.

delegar [dele'ɣar] vt to delegate.

deletrear [deletre'ar] vt to spell (out).

deleznable [deleθ'naßle] a brittle; (excusa, idea) feeble.

delfín [del'fin] nm dolphin.

delgadez [delɣa'ðeθ] nf thinness, slimness.

delgado, a [del'ɣaðo, a] a thin; (persona) slim, thin; (tierra) poor; (tela etc) light, delicate.

deliberación [deliβera'θjon] nf deliberation.

deliberar [deliβe'rar] vt to debate, discuss.

delicadeza [delika'ðeθa] nf (gen) delicacy; (refinamiento, sutileza) refinement.

delicado, a [deli'kaðo, a] a (gen) delicate; (sensible) sensitive; (quisquilloso) touchy.

delicia [de'liθja] nf delight.

delicioso, a [deli'θjoso, a] a (gracioso) delightful; (exquisito) delicious.

delincuencia [delin'kwenθja] nf delinquency; **delincuente** nm/f delinquent; (criminal) criminal.

delineante [deline'ante] nm/f draughtsman/woman.

delinear [deline'ar] vt (dibujo) to draw; (fig, contornos) to outline.

delinquir [delin'kir] vi to commit an offence.

delirante [deli'rante] a delirious.

delirar [deli'rar] vi to be delirious, rave.

delirio [de'lirjo] nm (MED) delirium; (palabras insensatas) ravings pl.

delito [de'lito] nm (gen) crime; (infracción) offence.

demacrado, a [dema'kraðo, a] a: **estar ~** to look pale and drawn, be wasted away.

demagogo, a [dema'ɣoɣo, a] nm/f demagogue.

demanda [de'manda] nf (pedido, COM) demand; (petición) request; (JUR) action, lawsuit.

demandante [deman'dante] nm/f claimant.

demandar [deman'dar] vt (gen) to demand; (JUR) to sue, file a lawsuit against.

demarcación [demarka'θjon] nf (de terreno) demarcation.

demás [de'mas] a: **los ~ niños** the other children, the remaining children // pron: **los/las ~** the others, the rest (of them); **lo ~** the rest (of it).

demasía [dema'sia] nf (exceso) excess, surplus; **comer en ~** to eat to excess.

demasiado, a [dema'sjaðo, a] *a* too, too much; ~s too many // *ad* too, too much; ¡es ~! it's too much!; ¡qué ~! (*fam*) great!

demencia [de'menθja] *nf* (*locura*) madness; **demente** *nm/f* lunatic // *a* mad, insane.

democracia [demo'kraθja] *nf* democracy.

demócrata [de'mokrata] *nm/f* democrat; **democrático, a** *a* democratic.

demoler [demo'ler] *vt* to demolish; **demolición** *nf* demolition.

demonio [de'monjo] *nm* devil, demon; ¡~s! hell!, damn!; ¿cómo ~s? how the hell?

demora [de'mora] *nf* delay; **demorar** *vt* (*retardar*) to delay, hold back; (*detener*) to hold up // *vi* to linger, stay on; ~**se** *vr* to be delayed.

demos *vb ver* **dar**.

demostración [demostra'θjon] *nf* (*de teorema*) demonstration; (*de afecto*) show, display.

demostrar [demos'trar] *vt* (*probar*) to prove; (*mostrar*) to show; (*manifestar*) to demonstrate; **demostrativo, a** *a* demonstrative.

demudado, a [demu'ðaðo, a] *a* (*rostro*) pale.

den *vb ver* **dar**.

denegar [dene'γar] *vt* (*rechazar*) to refuse; (*JUR*) to reject.

denigrar [deni'γrar] *vt* (*desacreditar, infamar*) to denigrate; (*injuriar*) to insult.

denominación [denomina'θjon] *nf* (*clase*) denomination.

denotar [deno'tar] *vt* (*indicar*) to indicate; (*significar*) to denote.

densidad [densi'ðað] *nf* (*FISICA*) density; (*fig*) thickness.

denso, a ['denso, a] *a* (*apretado*) solid; (*espeso, pastoso*) thick; (*fig*) heavy.

dentadura [denta'ðura] *nf* (*set of*) teeth *pl*; ~ **postiza** false teeth *pl*.

dentera [den'tera] *nf* (*sensación desagradable*) the shivers *pl*.

dentífrico, a [den'tifriko, a] *a* dental // *nm* toothpaste.

dentista [den'tista] *nm/f* dentist.

dentro ['dentro] *ad* inside // *prep*: ~ **de**, inside, within; **mirar por** ~ to look inside; ~ **de tres meses** within three months.

denuncia [de'nunθja] *nf* (*delación*) denunciation; (*acusación*) accusation; (*de accidente*) report; **denunciar** *vt* to report; (*delatar*) to inform on *o* against.

departamento [departa'mento] *nm* (*sección administrativa*) department, section; (*AM*: *piso*) flat (*Brit*), apartment.

departir [depar'tir] *vi* to converse.

dependencia [depen'denθja] *nf* dependence; (*POL*) dependency; (*COM*) office, section.

depender [depen'der] *vi*: ~ **de** to depend on.

dependienta [depen'djenta] *nf* saleswoman, shop assistant.

dependiente [depen'djente] *a* dependent // *nm* salesman, shop assistant.

depilar [depi'lar] *vt* (*con cera*) to wax; (*cejas*) to pluck; **depilatorio** *nm* hair remover.

deplorable [deplo'raßle] *a* deplorable.

deplorar [deplo'rar] *vt* to deplore.

deponer [depo'ner] *vt* to lay down // *vi* (*JUR*) to give evidence; (*declarar*) to make a statement.

deportar [depor'tar] *vt* to deport.

deporte [de'porte] *nm* sport; **deportista** *a* sports *cpd* // *nm/f* sportsman/woman; **deportivo, a** *a* (*club, periódico*) sports *cpd* // *nm* sports car.

depositante [deposi'tante], **depositador, a** [deposita'ðor, a] *nm/f* depositor.

depositar [deposi'tar] *vt* (*dinero*) to deposit; (*mercaderías*) to put away, store; (*persona*) to confide; ~**se** *vr* to settle; ~**io, a** *nm/f* trustee.

depósito [de'posito] *nm* (*gen*)

deposit; (de mercaderías) warehouse, store; (de agua, gasolina etc) tank.

depravar [depra'βar] vt to deprave, corrupt; ~se vr to become depraved.

depreciar [depre'θjar] vt to depreciate, reduce the value of; ~se vr to depreciate, lose value.

depredador, a [depreða'ðor, a] a (ZOOL) predatory // nm (ZOOL) predator.

depresión [depre'sjon] nf depression.

deprimido, a [depri'miðo, a] a depressed.

deprimir [depri'mir] vt to depress; ~se vr (persona) to become depressed.

deprisa [de'prisa] ad quickly, hurriedly.

depuración [depura'θjon] nf purification; (POL) purge; **depurar** vt to purify; (purgar) to purge.

derecha [de'retʃa] nf right(-hand) side; (POL) right; **a la** ~ (estar) on the right, (torcer etc) (to the) right.

derecho, a [de'retʃo, a] a right, right-hand // nm (privilegio) right; (lado) right(-hand) side; (leyes) law // ad straight, directly; ~s nmpl (de aduana) duty sg; (de autor) royalties; tener ~ a to have a right to.

deriva [de'riβa] nf: ir o estar a la ~ to drift, be adrift.

derivado [deri'βaðo] nm (COM) by-product.

derivar [deri'βar] vt to derive; (desviar) to direct // vi, ~se vr to derive, be derived; (NAUT) to drift.

derramamiento [derrama'mjento] nm (de sangre) shedding; (dispersión) spilling.

derramar [derra'mar] vt to spill; (verter) to pour out; (esparcir) to scatter; ~se vr to pour out; ~ lágrimas to weep.

derrame [de'rrame] nm (de líquido) spilling; (de sangre) shedding; (de tubo etc) overflow; (pérdida) leakage; (MED) discharge; (declive) slope.

derredor [derre'ðor] ad: **al** o **en** ~ **de** around, about.

derretido, a [derre'tiðo, a] a melted; (metal) molten.

derretir [derre'tir] vt (gen) to melt; (nieve) to thaw; (fig) to squander; ~se vr to melt.

derribar [derri'βar] vt to knock down; (construcción) to demolish; (persona, gobierno, político) to bring down.

derrocar [derro'kar] vt (gobierno) to bring down, overthrow.

derrochar [derro'tʃar] vt to squander; **derroche** nm (despilfarro) waste, squandering.

derrota [de'rrota] nf (NAUT) course; (MIL, DEPORTE etc) defeat, rout; **derrotar** vt (gen) to defeat; **derrotero** nm (rumbo) course.

derrumbar [derrum'bar] vt to throw down; ~se vr to collapse.

des vb ver **dar**.

desabotonar [desaβoto'nar] vt to unbutton, undo // vi (flores) to bloom; ~se vr to come undone.

desabrido, a [desa'βriðo, a] a (comida) insipid, tasteless; (persona) rude, surly; (respuesta) sharp; (tiempo) unpleasant.

desabrochar [desaβro'tʃar] vt (botones, broches) to undo, unfasten; ~se vr (ropa etc) to come undone.

desacato [desa'kato] nm (falta de respeto) disrespect; (JUR) contempt.

desacertado, a [desaθer'taðo, a] a (equivocado) mistaken; (inoportuno) unwise.

desacierto [desa'θjerto] nm mistake, error.

desaconsejado, a [desakonse'xaðo, a] a ill-advised.

desaconsejar [desakonse'xar] vt to advise against.

desacorde [desa'korðe] a discordant; **estar** ~ **con algo** to disagree with sth.

desacreditar [desakreði'tar] vt (desprestigiar) to discredit, bring into disrepute; (*denigrar*) to run down.

desacuerdo [desa'kwerðo] *nm* (*conflicto*) disagreement, discord; (*error*) error, blunder.

desafiar [desa'fjar] *vt* (*retar*) to challenge; (*enfrentarse a*) to defy.

desafilado, a [desafi'laðo, a] *a* blunt.

desafinado, a [desafi'naðo, a] *a*: estar ~ to be out of tune.

desafinarse [desafi'narse] *vr* to go out of tune.

desafío *etc vb ver* **desafiar** // [desa'fio] *nm* (*reto*) challenge; (*combate*) duel; (*resistencia*) defiance.

desaforado, a [desafo'raðo, a] *a* (*grito*) ear-splitting; (*comportamiento*) outrageous.

desafortunadamente [desafortunaða'mente] *ad* unfortunately.

desafortunado, a [desafortu'naðo, a] *a* (*desgraciado*) unfortunate, unlucky.

desagradable [desavra'ðaßle] *a* (*fastidioso, enojoso*) unpleasant; (*irritante*) disagreeable.

desagradar [desavra'ðar] *vi* (*disgustar*) to displease; (*molestar*) to bother.

desagradecido, a [desavraðe'θiðo, a] *a* ungrateful.

desagrado [desa'vraðo] *nm* (*disgusto*) displeasure; (*contrariedad*) dissatisfaction.

desagraviar [desavra'βjar] *vt* to make amends to; **desagravio** *nm* (*satisfacción*) amends; (*compensación*) compensation.

desagüe [des'avwe] *nm* (*de un líquido*) drainage; (*cañería*) drainpipe; (*salida*) outlet, drain.

desaguisado, a [desaxi'saðo, a] *a* illegal // *nm* outrage.

desahogado, a [desao'vaðo, a] *a* (*holgado*) comfortable; (*espacioso*) roomy, large.

desahogar [desao'var] *vt* (*aliviar*) to ease, relieve; (*ira*) to vent; ~**se** *vr* (*relajarse*) to relax; (*desfogarse*) to

let off steam.

desahogo [desa'ovo] *nm* (*alivio*) relief; (*comodidad*) comfort, ease.

desahuciar [desau'θjar] *vt* (*enfermo*) to give up hope for; (*inquilino*) to evict; **desahucio** *nm* eviction.

desairar [desai'rar] *vt* (*menospreciar*) to slight, snub; (*cosa*) to disregard.

desaire [des'aire] *nm* (*menosprecio*) slight; (*falta de garbo*) unattractiveness.

desajustar [desaxus'tar] *vt* (*desarreglar*) to disarrange; (*desconcertar*) to throw off balance; ~**se** *vr* to get out of order; (*aflojarse*) to loosen.

desajuste [desa'xuste] *nm* (*de máquina*) disorder; (*situación*) imbalance.

desalentador, a [desalenta'ðor, a] *a* disheartening.

desalentar [desalen'tar] *vt* (*desanimar*) to discourage.

desaliento *etc vb ver* **desalentar** // [desa'ljento] *nm* discouragement.

desaliño [desa'lino] *nm* (*negligencia*) slovenliness.

desalmado, a [desal'maðo, a] *a* (*cruel*) cruel, heartless.

desalojar [desalo'xar] *vt* (*expulsar, echar*) to eject; (*abandonar*) to move out of // *vi* to move out.

desamarrar [desama'rrar] *vt* to untie; (*NAUT*) to cast off.

desamor [desa'mor] *nm* (*frialdad*) indifference; (*odio*) dislike.

desamparado, a [desampa'raðo, a] *a* (*persona*) helpless; (*lugar: expuesto*) exposed; (*desierto*) deserted.

desamparar [desampa'rar] *vt* (*abandonar*) to desert, abandon; (*JUR*) to leave defenceless; (*barco*) to abandon.

desandar [desan'dar] *vt*: ~ **lo andado** *o* **el camino** to retrace one's steps.

desangrar [desan'grar] *vt* to bleed; (*fig: persona*) to bleed dry; ~**se**

to lose a lot of blood.

desanimado, a [desani'maðo, a] *a* (*persona*) downhearted; (*espectáculo, fiesta*) dull.

desanimar [desani'mar] *vt* (*desalentar*) to discourage; (*deprimir*) to depress; ~se *vr* to lose heart.

desapacible [desapa'θiβle] *a* (*gen*) unpleasant.

desaparecer [desapare'θer] *vi* (*gen*) to disappear; (*el sol, la luz*) to vanish; **desaparecido, a** *a* missing; **desaparecidos** *nmpl* (*en accidente*) people missing; **desaparición** *nf* disappearance.

desapasionado, a [desapasjo'naðo, a] *a* dispassionate, impartial.

desapego [desa'peɣo] *nm* (*frialdad*) coolness; (*distancia*) detachment.

desapercibido, a [desaperθi'βiðo, a] *a* (*desprevenido*) unprepared; **pasar** ~ to go unnoticed.

desaplicado, a [desapli'kaðo, a] *a* slack, lazy.

desaprensivo, a [desapren'siβo, a] *a* unscrupulous.

desaprobar [desapro'βar] *vt* (*reprobar*) to disapprove of; (*condenar*) to condemn; (*no consentir*) to reject.

desaprovechado, a [desaproβe-'tʃaðo, a] *a* (*oportunidad, tiempo*) wasted; (*estudiante*) slack.

desaprovechar [desaproβe'tʃar] *vt* to waste.

desarmar [desar'mar] *vt* (*MIL, fig*) to disarm; (*TEC*) to take apart, dismantle; **desarme** *nm* disarmament.

desarraigar [desarrai'ɣar] *vt* to uproot; **desarraigo** *nm* uprooting.

desarreglado, a [desarre'ɣlaðo, a] *a* (*desordenado*) disorderly, untidy.

desarreglar [desarre'ɣlar] *vt* (*desordenar*) to disarrange; (*trastocar*) to upset, disturb.

desarreglo [desa'rreɣlo] *nm* (*de casa, persona*) untidiness; (*desorden*) disorder.

desarrollar [desarro'ʎar] *vt* (*gen*) to develop; (*extender*) to unfold; ~**se**

vr to develop; (*extenderse*) to open (out); (*FOTO*) to develop; **desarrollo** *nm* development.

desarticular [desartiku'lar] *vt* (*hueso*) to dislocate; (*objeto*) to take apart; (*fig*) to break up.

desaseo [desa'seo] *nm* (*suciedad*) slovenliness; (*desarreglo*) untidiness.

desasir [desa'sir] *vt* to loosen; ~se *vr* to extricate o.s.; ~se de to let go, give up.

desasosegar [desasose'ɣar] *vt* (*inquietar*) to disturb, make uneasy; ~se *vr* to become uneasy.

desasosiego *etc vb ver* desasosegar // (*FOTO*) [desaso'sjeɣo] *nm* (*intranquilidad*) uneasiness, restlessness; (*ansiedad*) anxiety.

desastrado, a [desas'traðo, a] *a* (*desaliñado*) shabby; (*sucio*) dirty.

desastre [de'sastre] *nm* disaster; **desastroso, a** *a* disastrous.

desatado, a [desa'taðo, a] *a* (*desligado*) untied; (*violento*) violent, wild.

desatar [desa'tar] *vt* (*nudo*) to untie; (*paquete*) to undo; (*separar*) to detach; ~se *vr* (*zapatos*) to come untied; (*tormenta*) to break.

desatascar [desatas'kar] *vt* (*cañería*) to unblock, clear.

desatender [desaten'der] *vt* (*no prestar atención a*) to disregard; (*abandonar*) to neglect.

desatento, a [desa'tento, a] *a* (*distraído*) inattentive; (*descortés*) discourteous.

desatinado, a [desati'naðo, a] *a* foolish, silly; **desatino** *nm* (*idiotez*) foolishness, folly; (*error*) blunder.

desatornillar [desatorni'ʎar] *vt* to unscrew.

desautorizado, a [desautori'θaðo, a] *a* unauthorized.

desautorizar [desautori'θar] *vt* (*oficial*) to deprive of authority; (*informe*) to deny.

desavenencia [desaβe'nenθja] *nf* (*desacuerdo*) disagreement; (*discrepancia*) quarrel.

desaventajado, a [desaßenta'xaðo, a] *a* (*inferior*) inferior; (*poco ventajoso*) disadvantageous.

desayunar [desaju'nar] *vi* to have breakfast // *vt* to have for breakfast; **desayuno** *nm* breakfast.

desazón [desa'θon] *nf* (*angustia*) anxiety; (*fig*) annoyance.

desazonar [desaθo'nar] *vt* (*fig*) to annoy, upset; ~**se** *vr* (*enojarse*) to be annoyed; (*preocuparse*) to worry, be anxious.

desbandarse [desßan'darse] *vr* (*MIL*) to disband; (*fig*) to flee in disorder.

desbarajuste [desßara'xuste] *nm* confusion, disorder.

desbaratar [desßara'tar] *vt* (*deshacer, destruir*) to ruin.

desbloquear [desßloke'ar] *vt* (*negociaciones, tráfico*) to get going again; (*COM: cuenta*) to unfreeze.

desbocado, a [desßo'kaðo, a] *a* (*caballo*) runaway.

desbordar [desßor'ðar] *vt* (*sobrepasar*) to go beyond; (*exceder*) to exceed // *vi*, ~**se** *vr* (*río*) to overflow; (*entusiasmo*) to erupt.

descabalgar [deskaßal'var] *vi* to dismount.

descabellado, a [deskaße'ʎaðo, a] *a* (*disparatado*) wild, crazy.

descabellar [deskaße'ʎar] *vt* to ruffle; (*TAUR: toro*) to give the coup de grace to.

descafeinado, a [deskafei'naðo, a] *a* decaffeinated // *nm* decaffeinated coffee.

descalabro [deska'laßro] *nm* blow; (*desgracia*) misfortune.

descalificar [deskalifi'kar] *vt* to disqualify; (*desacreditar*) to discredit.

descalzar [deskal'θar] *vt* (*zapato*) to take off; **descalzo, a** *a* barefoot(ed); (*fig*) destitute.

descambiar [deskam'bjar] *vt* to exchange.

descaminado, a [deskami'naðo, a] *a* (*equivocado*) on the wrong road; (*fig*) misguided.

descampado [deskam'paðo] *nm* open space.

descansado, a [deskan'saðo, a] *a* (*gen*) rested; (*que tranquiliza*) restful.

descansar [deskan'sar] *vt* (*gen*) to rest // *vi* to rest, have a rest; (*echarse*) to lie down.

descansillo [deskan'siʎo] *nm* (*de escalera*) landing.

descanso [des'kanso] *nm* (*reposo*) rest; (*alivio*) relief; (*pausa*) break; (*DEPORTE*) interval, half time.

descapotable [deskapo'taßle] *nm* (*tb: coche* ~) convertible.

descarado, a [deska'raðo, a] *a* (*sin vergüenza*) shameless; (*insolente*) cheeky.

descarga [des'karva] *nf* (*ARQ, ELEC, MIL*) discharge; (*NAUT*) unloading.

descargar [deskar'var] *vt* to unload; (*golpe*) to let fly; ~**se** *vr* to unburden o.s.; **descargo** *nm* (*COM*) receipt; (*JUR*) evidence.

descarnado, a [deskar'naðo, a] *a* scrawny; (*fig*) bare.

descaro [des'karo] *nm* nerve.

descarriar [deska'rrjar] *vt* (*descaminar*) to misdirect; (*fig*) to lead astray; ~**se** *vr* (*perderse*) to lose one's way; (*separarse*) to stray; (*pervertirse*) to err, go astray.

descarrilamiento [deskarrila'mjento] *nm* (*de tren*) derailment.

descarrilar [deskarri'lar] *vi* to be derailed.

descartar [deskar'tar] *vt* (*rechazar*) to reject; (*eliminar*) to rule out; ~**se** *vr* (*NAIPES*) to discard; ~**se de** to shirk.

descascarillado, a [deskaskari'ʎaðo, a] *a* (*paredes*) peeling.

descendencia [desθen'denθja] *nf* (*origen*) origin, descent; (*hijos*) offspring.

descender [desθen'der] *vt* (*bajar: escalera*) to go down // *vi* to descend; (*temperatura, nivel*) to fall, drop; ~ **de** to be descended from.

descendiente [desθen'djente] *nm/f* descendant.

descenso [des'θenso] *nm* descent; *(de temperatura)* drop.

descifrar [desθi'frar] *vt* to decipher; *(mensaje)* to decode.

descolgar [deskol'var] *vt (bajar)* to take down; *(teléfono)* to pick up; ~**se** *vr* to lower o.s. down.

descolorido, a [deskolo'riðo, a] *a* faded; *(pálido)* pale.

descompaginar [deskompaxi'nar] *vt (desordenar)* to disarrange, mess up.

descompasado, a [deskompa'saðo, a] *a (sin proporción)* out of all proportion; *(excesivo)* excessive.

descomponer [deskompo'ner] *vt (desordenar)* to disarrange, disturb; *(TEC)* to put out of order; *(dividir)* to break down (into parts); *(fig)* to provoke; ~**se** *vr (corromperse)* to rot, decompose; *(el tiempo)* to change (for the worse); *(TEC)* to break down.

descomposición [deskomposi'θjon] *nf (gen)* breakdown; *(de fruta etc)* decomposition.

descompostura [deskompos'tura] *nf (TEC)* breakdown; *(desorganización)* disorganization; *(desorden)* untidiness.

descompuesto, a [deskom'pwesto, a] *a (corrompido)* decomposed; *(roto)* broken.

descomunal [deskomu'nal] *a (enorme)* huge.

desconcertado, a [deskonθer'taðo, a] *a* disconcerted, bewildered.

desconcertar [deskonθer'tar] *vt (confundir)* to baffle; *(incomodar)* to upset, put out; ~**se** *vr (turbarse)* to be upset.

desconchado, a [deskon'tʃaðo, a] *a (pintura)* peeling.

desconcierto [deskon'θjerto] *nm* ver **desconcertar** // *(gen)* disorder; *(desorientación)* uncertainty; *(inquietud)* uneasiness.

desconectar [deskonek'tar] *vt* to disconnect.

desconfianza [deskon'fjanθa] *nf* distrust.

desconfiar [deskon'fjar] *vi* to be distrustful; ~ **de** to distrust, suspect.

descongelar [deskonxe'lar] *vt* to defrost; *(COM, POL)* to unfreeze.

descongestionar [deskonxestjo'nar] *vt (cabeza, tráfico)* to clear.

desconocer [deskono'θer] *vt (ignorar)* not to know, be ignorant of; *(no aceptar)* to deny; *(repudiar)* to disown.

desconocido, a [deskono'θiðo, a] *a* unknown // *nm/f* stranger.

desconocimiento [deskonoθi'mjento] *nm (falta de conocimientos)* ignorance; *(repudio)* disregard.

desconsiderado, a [deskonsiðe'raðo, a] *a (descuidado)* inconsiderate; *(insensible)* thoughtless.

desconsolar [deskonso'lar] *vt* to distress; ~**se** *vr* to despair.

desconsuelo *etc vb* ver **desconsolar** // [deskon'swelo] *nm (tristeza)* distress; *(desesperación)* despair.

descontado, a [deskon'taðo, a] *a:* **dar por ~ (que)** to take (it) for granted (that).

descontar [deskon'tar] *vt (deducir)* to take away, deduct; *(rebajar)* to discount.

descontento, a [deskon'tento, a] *a* dissatisfied // *nm* dissatisfaction, discontent.

descorazonar [deskoraθo'nar] *vt* to discourage, dishearten.

descorchar [deskor'tʃar] *vt* to uncork.

descorrer [desko'rrer] *vt (cortinas, cerrojo)* to draw back.

descortés [deskor'tes] *a (mal educado)* discourteous; *(grosero)* rude.

descoser [desko'ser] *vt* to unstitch; ~**se** *vr* to come apart (at the seams).

descosido, a [desko'siðo, a] *a*

(*COSTURA*) unstitched; (*desordenado*) disjointed.

descrédito [des'kreðito] *nm* discredit.

descreído, a [deskre'iðo, a] *a* (*incrédulo*) incredulous; (*falto de fe*) unbelieving.

descremado, a [deskre'maðo, a] *a* skimmed.

describir [deskri'βir] *vt* to describe; **descripción** [deskrip'θjon] *nf* description.

descrito [des'krito] *pp de* **describir**.

descuartizar [deskwarti'θar] *vt* (*animal*) to cut up.

descubierto, a *pp de* **descubrir** // [desku'βjerto, a] *a* uncovered, bare; (*persona*) bareheaded // *nm* (*bancario*) overdraft; al ~ in the open.

descubrimiento [deskuβri'mjento] *nm* (*hallazgo*) discovery; (*revelación*) revelation.

descubrir [desku'βrir] *vt* to discover, find; (*inaugurar*) to unveil; (*vislumbrar*) to detect; (*revelar*) to reveal, show; (*destapar*) to uncover; ~se *vr* to reveal o.s.; (*quitarse sombrero*) to take off one's hat; (*confesar*) to confess.

descuento *etc vb ver* **descontar** // [des'kwento] *nm* discount.

descuidado, a [deskwi'ðaðo, a] *a* (*sin cuidado*) careless; (*desordenado*) untidy; (*olvidadizo*) forgetful; (*dejado*) neglected; (*desprevenido*) unprepared.

descuidar [deskwi'ðar] *vt* (*dejar*) to neglect; (*olvidar*) to overlook // *vi*, ~se *vr* (*distraerse*) to be careless; (*estar desaliñado*) to let o.s. go; (*desprevenirse*) to drop one's guard; **¡descuida!** don't worry!; **descuido** *nm* (*dejadez*) carelessness; (*olvido*) negligence.

PALABRA CLAVE

---

desde ['desðe] ◆ *prep* **1** (*lugar*) from; ~ Burgos hasta mi casa hay 30 km it's 30 kms from Burgos to my house

2 (*posición*): hablaba ~ el balcón she was speaking from the balcony

3 (*tiempo*: + *ad*, *n*): ~ **ahora** from now on; ~ **la boda** since the wedding; ~ **niño** since I *etc* was a child; ~ **3 años atrás** since 3 years ago

4 (*tiempo*: + *vb*) since; for; **nos conocemos ~ 1978/hace 20 años** we've known each other since 1978/for 20 years; **no le veo ~ 1983/hace 5 años** I haven't seen him since 1983/for 5 years

5 (*gama*): ~ los más lujosos hasta los más económicos from the most luxurious to the most reasonably priced

6: ~ **luego (que no)** of course (not) ◆ *conj*: ~ **que**: ~ **que recuerdo** for as long as o ever since I can remember; ~ **que llegó no ha salido** he hasn't been out since he arrived.

---

desdecirse [desðe'θirse] *vr* to retract; ~ de to go back on.

desdén [des'ðen] *nm* scorn.

desdeñar [desðe'ɲar] *vt* (*despreciar*) to scorn.

desdicha [des'ðitʃa] *nf* (*desgracia*) misfortune; (*infelicidad*) unhappiness; **desdichado, a** *a* (*sin suerte*) unlucky; (*infeliz*) unhappy.

desdoblar [desðo'βlar] *vt* (*extender*) to spread out; (*desplegar*) to unfold.

desear [dese'ar] *vt* to want, desire, wish for.

desecar [dese'kar] *vt*, **desecarse** *vr* to dry up.

desechar [dese'tʃar] *vt* (*basura*) to throw out o away; (*ideas*) to reject, discard; **desechos** *nmpl* rubbish *sg*, waste *sg*.

desembalar [desemba'lar] *vt* to unpack.

desembarazado, a *a* (*libre*) clear, free; (*desenvuelto*) free and easy.

desembarazar [desembara'θar] *vt* (*desocupar*) to clear; (*desenredar*) to free; ~se *vr*: ~se de to free o.s. of, get rid of.

desembarcar [desembar'kar] vt (mercancías etc) to unload // vi, ~se vr to disembark.

desembocadura [desemboka'ðura] nf (de río) mouth; (de calle) opening.

desembocar [desembo'kar] vi to flow into; (fig) to result in.

desembolso [desem'bolso] nm payment.

desembragar [desembra'var] vi to declutch.

desemejanza [deseme'xanθa] nf dissimilarity.

desempatar [desempa'tar] vi to replay, hold a play-off; **desempate** nm (FÚTBOL) replay, play-off; (TENIS) tie-break(er).

desempeñar [desempe'ɲar] vt (cargo) to hold; (papel) to perform; (lo empeñado) to redeem; ~se vr to get out of debt; ~ **un papel** (fig) to play (a role).

desempeño [desem'peɲo] nm redeeming; (de cargo) occupation.

desempleado, a [desemple'aðo, a] nm/f unemployed person; **desempleo** nm unemployment.

desempolvar [desempol'βar] vt (muebles etc) to dust; (lo olvidado) to revive.

desencadenar [desenkaðe'nar] vt to unchain; (ira) to unleash; ~se vr to break loose; (tormenta) to burst; (guerra) to break out.

desencajar [desenka'xar] vt (hueso) to put out of joint; (mandíbula) to dislocate; (mecanismo, pieza) to disconnect, disengage.

desencanto [desen'kanto] nm disillusionment.

desenchufar [desentʃu'far] vt to unplug.

desenfadado, a [desenfa'ðaðo, a] a (desenvuelto) uninhibited; (descarado) forward; **desenfado** nm (libertad) freedom; (comportamiento) ease and easy manner; (descaro) forwardness.

desenfocado, a [desenfo'kaðo, a] a

(FOTO) out of focus.

desenfrenado, a [desenfre'naðo, a] a (descontrolado) uncontrolled; (inmoderado) unbridled; **desenfreno** nm (vicio) wildness; (de las pasiones) lack of self-control.

desenganchar [desengan'tʃar] vt (gen) to unhook; (FERRO) to uncouple.

desengañar [desenga'ɲar] vt to disillusion; ~se vr to become disillusioned; **desengaño** nm disillusionment; (decepción) disappointment.

desenlace [desen'laθe] nm outcome.

desenmarañar [desenmara'ɲar] vt (fig) to unravel.

desenmascarar [desenmaska'rar] vt to unmask.

desenredar [desenre'ðar] vt (pelo) to untangle; (problema) to sort out.

desentenderse [desenten'derse] vr: ~ **de** to pretend not to know about; (apartarse) to have nothing to do with.

desenterrar [desente'rrar] vt (tesoro, fig) to exhume; (tesoro, fig) to unearth, dig up.

desentonar [desento'nar] vi (MUS) to sing (o play) out of tune; (color) to clash.

desentrañar [desentra'ɲar] vt (misterio) to unravel.

desentumecer [desentume'θer] vt (pierna) to stretch; (DEPORTE) to loosen up.

desenvoltura [desenβol'tura] nf (libertad, gracia) ease; (descaro) free and easy manner.

desenvolver [desenβol'βer] vt (paquete) to unwrap; (fig) to develop; ~se vr (desarrollarse) to unfold, develop; (arreglárselas) to cope.

deseo [de'seo] nm desire, wish; ~**so, a** a: **estar** ~**so de** to be anxious to.

desequilibrado, a [desekili'βraðo, a] a] a unbalanced.

desertar [deser'tar] vi to desert.

desértico, a [de'sertiko, a] a desert

cpd.

desesperación [desespera'θjon] *nf (impaciencia)* desperation, despair; *(irritación)* fury.

desesperar [desespe'rar] *vt* to drive to despair; *(exasperar)* to drive to distraction // *vi:* ~ **de** to despair of; ~**se** *vr* to despair, lose hope.

desestabilizar [desestaβili'θar] *vt* to destabilize.

desestimar [desesti'mar] *vt (menospreciar)* to have a low opinion of; *(rechazar)* to reject.

desfachatez [desfatʃa'teθ] *nf (insolencia)* impudence; *(descaro)* rudeness.

desfalco [des'falko] *nm* embezzlement.

desfallecer [desfaʎe'θer] *vi (perder las fuerzas)* to become weak; *(desvanecerse)* to faint.

desfasado, a [desfa'saðo, a] *a (anticuado)* old-fashioned; **desfase** *nm (diferencia)* gap.

desfavorable [desfaβo'raβle] *a* unfavourable.

desfigurar [desfiɣu'rar] *vt (cara)* to disfigure; *(cuerpo)* to deform.

desfiladero [desfila'ðero] *nm* gorge.

desfilar [desfi'lar] *vi* to parade; **desfile** *nm* procession.

desfogarse [desfo'ɣarse] *vr (fig)* to let off steam.

desgajar [desɣa'xar] *vt (arrancar)* to tear off; *(romper)* to break off; ~**se** *vr* to come off.

desgana [des'ɣana] *nf (falta de apetito)* loss of appetite; *(renuencia)* unwillingness; ~**do, a** *a:* **estar** ~ *(sin apetito)* to have no appetite; *(sin entusiasmo)* to have lost interest.

desgarrador, a [desɣarra'ðor, a] *a (fig)* heartrending.

desgarrar [desɣa'rrar] *vt* to tear (up); *(fig)* to shatter; **desgarro** *nm (en tela)* tear; *(aflicción)* grief; *(descaro)* impudence.

desgastar [desɣas'tar] *vt (deteriorar)* to wear away *o* down; *(estropear)* to spoil; ~**se** *vr* to get

worn out; **desgaste** *nm* wear (and tear).

desgracia [des'ɣraθja] *nf* misfortune; *(accidente)* accident; *(vergüenza)* disgrace; *(contratiempo)* setback; **por** ~ unfortunately.

desgraciado, a [desɣra'θjaðo, a] *a (sin suerte)* unlucky, unfortunate; *(miserable)* wretched; *(infeliz)* miserable.

desgreñado, a [desɣre'ɲaðo, a] *a* dishevelled.

deshabitado, a [desaβi'taðo, a] *a* uninhabited.

deshacer [desa'θer] *vt (casa)* to break up; *(TEC)* to take apart; *(enemigo)* to defeat; *(diluir)* to melt; *(contrato)* to break; *(intriga)* to solve; ~**se** *vr (disolverse)* to melt; *(despedazarse)* to come apart *o* undone; ~**se de** to get rid of; ~**se en lágrimas** to burst into tears.

deshecho, a [de'setʃo, a] *a* undone; *(roto)* smashed; **estar** ~ *(persona)* to be shattered.

desheredar [desere'ðar] *vt* to disinherit.

deshidratar [desiðra'tar] *vt* to dehydrate.

deshielo [des'jelo] *nm* thaw.

deshonesto, a [deso'nesto, a] *a* indecent.

deshonra [des'onra] *nf (deshonor)* dishonour; *(vergüenza)* shame; **deshonrar** *vt* to dishonour.

deshora [des'ora]: **a** ~ *ad* at the wrong time.

deshuesar [deswe'sar] *vt (carne)* to bone; *(fruta)* to stone.

desierto, a [de'sjerto, a] *a (casa, calle, negocio)* deserted // *nm* desert.

designar [desiɣ'nar] *vt (nombrar)* to designate; *(indicar)* to fix.

designio [de'siɣnjo] *nm* plan.

desigual [desi'ɣwal] *a (terreno)* uneven; *(lucha etc)* unequal.

desilusión [desilu'sjon] *nf* disillusionment; *(decepción)* disappointment; **desilusionar** *vt* to disillusion; to disappoint; **desilusionarse** *vr* to become disillusioned.

desinfectar [desinfek'tar] vt to disinfect.

desinflar [desin'flar] vt to deflate.

desintegración [desinteɣra'θjon] nf disintegration.

desinterés [desinte'res] nm (objetividad) disinterestedness; (altruismo) unselfishness.

desistir [desis'tir] vi (renunciar) to stop, desist.

desleal [desle'al] a (infiel) disloyal; (COM: competencia) unfair; **~tad** nf disloyalty.

desleír [desle'ir] vt (líquido) to dilute; (sólido) to dissolve.

deslenguado, a [deslen'gwaðo, a] a (grosero) foul-mouthed.

desligar [desli'ɣar] vt (desatar) to untie, undo; (separar) to separate; **~se** vr (de un compromiso) to extricate o.s.

desliz [des'liθ] nm (fig) lapse; **~ar** vt to slip, slide; **~arse** vr (escurrirse: persona) to slip, slide; (coche) to skid; (aguas mansas) to flow gently; (error) to creep in.

deslucido, a [deslu'θiðo, a] a dull; (torpe) awkward, graceless; (deslustrado) tarnished.

deslumbrar [deslum'brar] vt to dazzle.

desmán [des'man] nm (exceso) outrage; (abuso de poder) abuse.

desmandarse [desman'darse] vr (portarse mal) to behave badly; (excederse) to get out of hand; (caballo) to bolt.

desmantelar [desmante'lar] vt (deshacer) to dismantle; (casa) to strip.

desmaquillador [desmakiʎa'ðor] nm make-up remover.

desmayado, a [desma'jaðo, a] a (sin sentido) unconscious; (carácter) dull; (débil) faint, weak.

desmayar [desma'jar] vi to lose heart; **~se** vr (MED) to faint; **desmayo** nm (MED: acto) faint; (: estado) unconsciousness; (depresión)

dejection.

desmedido, a [desme'ðiðo, a] a excessive.

desmejorar [desmexo'rar] vt (dañar) to impair, spoil; (MED) to weaken.

desmembrar [desmem'brar] vt (MED) to dismember; (fig) to separate.

desmemoriado, a [desmemo'rjaðo, a] a forgetful.

desmentir [desmen'tir] vt (contradecir) to contradict; (refutar) to deny // vi: **~ de** to refute; **~se** vr to contradict o.s.

desmenuzar [desmenu'θar] vt (deshacer) to crumble; (carne) to chop; (examinar) to examine closely.

desmerecer [desmere'θer] vt to be unworthy of // vi (deteriorarse) to deteriorate.

desmesurado, a [desmesu'raðo, a] a disproportionate.

desmontar [desmon'tar] vt (deshacer) to dismantle; (tierra) to level // vi to dismount.

desmoralizar [desmorali'θar] vt to demoralize.

desmoronar [desmoro'nar] vt to wear away, erode; **~se** vr (edificio, dique) to fall into disrepair; (economía) to decline.

desnatado, a [desna'taðo, a] a skimmed.

desnivel [desni'βel] nm (de terreno) unevenness.

desnudar [desnu'ðar] vt (desvestir) to undress; (despojar) to strip; **~se** vr (desvestirse) to get undressed; **desnudo, a** a naked // nm/f nude; **desnudo de** devoid or bereft of.

desnutrición [desnutri'θjon] nf malnutrition; **desnutrido, a** a undernourished.

desobedecer [desoβeðe'θer] vt, vi to disobey; **desobediencia** nf disobedience.

desocupado, a [desoku'paðo, a] a at leisure; (desempleado) unemployed; (deshabitado) empty, vacant.

desocupar [desoku'par] *vt* to vacate.

desodorante [desoðo'rante] *nm* deodorant.

desolación [desola'θjon] *nf* (*lugar*) desolation; (*fig*) grief.

desolar [deso'lar] *vt* to ruin, lay waste.

desorden [des'orðen] *nm* confusion; (*politico*) disorder, unrest.

desorganizar [desorɣani'θar] *vt* (*desordenar*) to disorganize.

desorientar [desorjen'tar] *vt* (*extraviar*) to mislead; (*confundir, desconcertar*) to confuse; ~se *vr* (*perderse*) to lose one's way.

desovar [deso'ßar] *vi* (*peces*) to spawn; (*insectos*) to lay eggs.

despabilado, a [despaßi'laðo, a] *a* (*despierto*) wide-awake; (*fig*) alert, sharp.

despabilar [despaßi'lar] *vt* (*el ingenio*) to sharpen // *vi*, ~se *vr* to wake up; (*fig*) to get a move on.

despacio [des'paθjo] *ad* slowly.

despachar [despa'tʃar] *vi* (*negocio*) to do, complete; (*enviar*) to send, dispatch; (*vender*) to sell, deal in; (*billete*) to issue; (*mandar ir*) to send away.

despacho [des'patʃo] *nm* (*oficina*) office; (*de paquetes*) dispatch; (*venta*) sale; (*comunicación*) message.

desparpajo [despar'paxo] *nm* self-confidence; (*pey*) nerve.

desparramar [desparra'mar] *vt* (*esparcir*) to scatter; (*líquido*) to spill.

despavorido, a [despaßo'riðo, a] *a* terrified.

despectivo, a [despek'tißo, a] *a* (*despreciativo*) derogatory; (*LING*) pejorative.

despecho [des'petʃo] *nm* spite; a ~ de in spite of.

despedazar [despeða'θar] *vt* to tear to pieces.

despedida [despe'ðiða] *nf* (*adiós*) farewell; (*de obrero*) sacking.

despedir [despe'ðir] *vt* (*visita*) to see off, show out; (*empleado*) to dismiss; (*inquilino*) to evict; (*objeto*) to hurl; (*olor etc*) to give out o off; ~se *vr*: ~se de to say goodbye to.

despegar [despe'ɣar] *vt* to unstick // *vi* (*avión*) to take off; ~se *vr* to come loose, come unstuck; **despego** *nm* detachment.

despegue *etc vb ver* **despegar** // [des'pexe] *nm* takeoff.

despeinado, a [despei'naðo, a] *a* dishevelled, unkempt.

despejado, a [despe'xaðo, a] *a* (*lugar*) clear, free; (*cielo*) clear; (*persona*) wide-awake, bright.

despejar [despe'xar] *vt* (*gen*) to clear; (*misterio*) to clear up // *vi* (*el tiempo*) to clear; ~se *vr* (*tiempo, cielo*) to clear (up); (*misterio*) to become clearer; (*cabeza*) to clear.

despellejar [despeʎe'xar] *vt* (*animal*) to skin.

despensa [des'pensa] *nf* larder.

despeñadero [despeɲa'ðero] *nm* (*GEO*) cliff, precipice.

desperdicio [desper'ðiθjo] *nm* (*despilfarro*) squandering; ~s *nmpl* (*basura*) rubbish *sg* (*Brit*), garbage *sg* (*US*); (*residuos*) waste *sg*.

desperezarse [despere'θarse] *vr* to stretch (o.s.).

desperfecto [desper'fekto] *nm* (*deterioro*) slight damage; (*defecto*) flaw, imperfection.

despertador [desperta'ðor] *nm* alarm clock.

despertar [desper'tar] *vt* (*persona*) to wake up; (*recuerdos*) to revive; (*sentimiento*) to arouse // *vi*, ~se *vr* to awaken, wake up // *nm* awakening.

despiadado, a [despja'ðaðo, a] *a* (*ataque*) merciless; (*persona*) heartless.

despido *etc vb ver* **despedir** // [des'piðo] *nm* dismissal, sacking.

despierto, a *etc vb ver* **despertar** // [des'pjerto, a] *a* awake; (*fig*) sharp, alert.

despilfarro [despil'farro] *nm*

(derroche) squandering; *(lujo desmedido)* extravagance.

despistar [despis'tar] *vt* to throw off the track *o* scent; *(fig)* to mislead, confuse; ~**se** *vr* to take the wrong road; *(fig)* to become confused.

desplazamiento [desplaθa'mjento] *nm* displacement.

desplazar [despla'θar] *vt* to move; *(NAUT)* to displace; *(INFORM)* to scroll; *(fig)* to oust; ~**se** *vr* *(persona)* to travel.

desplegar [desple'γar] *vt* *(tela, papel)* to unfold, open out; *(bandera)* to unfurl; **despliegue** *vb etc ver* **desplegar** // [des'pljeγe] *nm* display.

desplomarse [desplo'marse] *vr* *(edificio, gobierno, persona)* to collapse.

desplumar [desplu'mar] *vt* *(ave)* to pluck; *(fam: estafar)* to fleece.

despoblado, a [despo'βlaðo, a] *a* *(sin habitantes)* uninhabited.

despojar [despo'xar] *vt* *(alguien: de sus bienes)* to divest of, deprive of; *(casa)* to strip, leave bare; *(alguien: de su cargo)* to strip of.

despojo [des'poxo] *nm* *(acto)* plundering; *(objetos)* plunder, loot; ~**s** *nmpl* *(de ave, res)* offal *sg.*

desposado, a [despo'saðo, a] *a, nm/f* newly-wed.

desposeer [despose'er] *vt*: ~ **a uno de** *(puesto, autoridad)* to strip sb of.

déspota ['despota] *nm/f* despot.

despreciar [despre'θjar] *vt* *(desdeñar)* to despise, scorn; *(afrentar)* to slight; **desprecio** *nm* scorn, contempt; slight.

desprender [despren'der] *vt* *(separar)* to separate; *(desatar)* to unfasten; *(olor)* to give off; ~**se** *vr* *(botón: caerse)* to fall off; *(: abrirse)* to unfasten; *(olor, perfume)* to be given off; ~**se de** to follow from; **se desprende que** it transpires that.

desprendimiento [desprendi'mjento] *nm* *(gen)* loosening; *(generosidad)* disinterestedness; *(indifer-*

encia) detachment; *(de gas)* leak; *(de tierra, rocas)* landslide.

despreocupado, a [despreoku'paðo, a] *a* *(sin preocupación)* unworried, nonchalant; *(negligente)* careless.

despreocuparse [despreoku'parse] *vr* to be carefree; ~ **de** to have no interest in.

desprestigiar [despresti'xjar] *vt* *(criticar)* to run down; *(desacreditar)* to discredit.

desprevenido, a [despreβe'niðo, a] *a* *(no preparado)* unprepared, unready.

desproporcionado, a [desproporθjo'naðo, a] *a* disproportionate, out of proportion.

después [des'pwes] *ad* afterwards, later; *(próximo paso)* next; ~ **de comer** after lunch; **un año** ~ a year later; ~ **se debatió el tema** next the matter was discussed; ~ **de corregido el texto** after the text had been corrected; ~ **de todo** after all.

desquite [des'kite] *nm* *(satisfacción)* satisfaction; *(venganza)* revenge.

destacar [desta'kar] *vt* to emphasize, point up; *(MIL)* to detach, detail // *vi*, ~**se** *vr* *(resaltarse)* to stand out; *(persona)* to be outstanding *o* exceptional.

destajo [des'taxo] *nm*: **trabajar a** ~ to do piecework.

destapar [desta'par] *vt* *(botella)* to open; *(cacerola)* to take the lid off; *(descubrir)* uncover; ~**se** *vr* *(revelarse)* to reveal one's true character.

destartalado, a [destarta'laðo, a] *a* *(desordenado)* untidy; *(ruinoso)* tumbledown.

destello [des'teʎo] *nm* *(de estrella)* twinkle; *(de faro)* signal light.

destemplado, a [destem'plaðo, a] *a* *(MUS)* out of tune; *(voz)* harsh; *(MED)* out of sorts; *(tiempo)* unpleasant, nasty.

desteñir [deste'ɲir] *vt* to fade // *vi*, ~**se** *vr* to fade; **esta tela no des-**

tiñe this fabric will not run.

desternillarse [desterniˈʎarse] vr: ~ **de risa** to split one's sides laughing.

desterrar [desteˈrrar] vt (exilar) to exile; (fig) to banish, dismiss.

destetar [desteˈtar] vt to wean.

destierro etc vb ver **desterrar** // [desˈtjerro] nm exile.

destilar [destiˈlar] vt to distil; **destilería** nf distillery.

destinar [destiˈnar] vt (funcionario) to appoint, assign; (fondos) to set aside (a for).

destinatario, a [destinaˈtarjo, a] nm/f addressee.

destino [desˈtino] nm (suerte) destiny; (de avión, viajero) destination.

destituir [destituˈir] vt to dismiss.

destornillador [destorniʎaˈðor] nm screwdriver.

destornillar [destorniˈʎar] vt, **destornillarse** vr (tornillo) to unscrew.

destreza [desˈtreθa] nf (habilidad) skill; (maña) dexterity.

destrozar [destroˈθar] vt (romper) to smash, break (up); (estropear) to ruin; (nervios) to shatter.

destrozo [desˈtroθo] nm (acción) destruction; (desastre) smashing; ~s nmpl (pedazos) pieces; (daños) havoc sg.

destrucción [destrukˈθjon] nf destruction.

destruir [destruˈir] vt to destroy.

desuso [desˈuso] nm disuse; **caer en** ~ to become obsolete.

desvalido, a [desβaˈliðo, a] a (desprotegido) destitute; (sin fuerzas) helpless.

desvalijar [desβaliˈxar] vt (persona) to rob; (casa, tienda) to burgle; (coche) to break into.

desván [desˈβan] nm attic.

desvanecer [desβaneˈθer] vt (disipar) to dispel; (borrar) to blur; ~se vr (humo etc) to vanish, disappear; (color) to fade; (recuerdo, sonido) to fade away; (MED) to pass out; (duda) to be dispelled.

desvanecimiento [desβaneθiˈmjento] nm (desaparición) disappearance; (de colores) fading; (evaporación) evaporation; (MED) fainting fit.

desvariar [desβaˈrjar] vi (enfermo) to be delirious; **desvarío** nm delirium.

desvelar [desβeˈlar] vt to keep awake; ~**se** vr (no poder dormir) to stay awake; (vigilar) to be vigilant o watchful.

desvencijado, a [desβenθiˈxaðo, a] a (silla) rickety; (máquina) broken-down.

desventaja [desβenˈtaxa] nf disadvantage.

desventura [desβenˈtura] nf misfortune.

desvergonzado, a [desβerɣonˈθaðo, a] a shameless.

desvergüenza [desβerˈɣwenθa] nf (descaro) shamelessness; (insolencia) impudence; (mala conducta) effrontery.

desvestir [desβesˈtir] vt, **desvestirse** vr to undress.

desviación [desβjaˈθjon] nf deviation; (AUTO) diversion, detour.

desviar [desˈβjar] vt to turn aside; (rio) to alter the course of; (navio) to divert, re-route; (conversación) to sidetrack; ~**se** vr (apartarse del camino) to turn aside; (: barco) to go off course.

desvío etc vb ver **desviar** // [desˈβio] nm (desviación) detour, diversion; (fig) indifference.

desvirtuar [desβirˈtwar] vt, **desvirtuarse** vr to spoil.

desvivirse [desβiˈβirse] vr: ~ **por** (anhelar) to long for, crave for; (hacer lo posible por) to do one's utmost for.

detallar [detaˈʎar] vt to detail.

detalle [deˈtaʎe] nm (gen); (fig) gesture, token; **al** ~ in detail; (COM) retail.

detallista [detaˈʎista] nm/f retailer.

detener [deteˈner] vt (gen) to stop;

(JUR) to arrest; (objeto) to keep; ~se vr to stop; (demorarse): ~se en to delay over, linger over.

detenidamente [deteniða'mente] ad (minuciosamente) carefully; (extensamente) at great length.

detenido, a [dete'niðo, a] a (arrestado) under arrest; (minucioso) detailed // nm/f person under arrest, prisoner.

detergente [deter'xente] nm detergent.

deteriorar [deterjo'rar] vt to spoil, damage; ~se vr to deteriorate; **deterioro** nm deterioration.

determinación [determina'θjon] nf (empeño) determination; (decisión) decision.

determinar [determi'nar] vt (plazo) to fix; (precio) to settle; ~se vr to decide.

detestar [detes'tar] vt to detest.

detonar [deto'nar] vi to detonate.

detrás [de'tras] ad behind; (atrás) at the back; ~ de behind.

detrimento [detri'mento] nm: en ~ de to the detriment of.

deuda ['deuða] nf (condición) indebtedness, debt; (cantidad) debt.

deudor, a [deu'ðor, a] nm/f debtor.

devaluación [deβalwa'θjon] nf devaluation.

devastar [deβas'tar] vt (destruir) to devastate.

devengar [deβen'gar] vt (COM) to accrue, earn.

devoción [deβo'θjon] nf devotion.

devolución [deβolu'θjon] nf (reenvío) return, sending back; (reembolso) repayment; (JUR) devolution.

devolver [deβol'βer] vt to return; (lo extraviado, lo prestado) to give back; (carta al correo) to send back; (COM) to repay, refund; (visita, la palabra) to return // vi (fam) to be sick.

devorar [deβo'rar] vt to devour.

devoto, a [de'βoto, a] a devout // nm/f admirer.

devuelto, devuelva etc vb ver devolver.

di vb ver dar; decir.

día ['dia] nm day; ¿qué ~ es? what's the date?; estar/poner al ~ to be/keep up to date; el ~ de hoy/ de mañana today/tomorrow; al ~ siguiente (on) the following day; vivir al ~ to live from hand to mouth; de ~ by day, in daylight; en pleno ~ in full daylight; en ~ festivo (Esp) or feriado (AM) holiday; ~ libre day off.

diablo ['djaβlo] nm devil; **diablura** nf prank.

diafragma [dja'fraɣma] nm diaphragm.

diagnosis [djaɣ'nosis] nf inv, **diagnóstico** [djaɣ'nostiko] nm diagnosis.

diagrama [dja'ɣrama] nm diagram; ~ de flujo flowchart.

dialecto [dja'lekto] nm dialect.

dialogar [djalo'ɣar] vi: ~ con (POL) to hold talks with.

diálogo ['djaloɣo] nm dialogue.

diamante [dja'mante] nm diamond.

diana ['djana] nf (MIL) reveille; (de blanco) centre, bull's-eye.

diapositiva [djaposi'tiβa] nf (FOTO) slide, transparency.

diario, a ['djarjo, a] a daily // nm newspaper; a ~ daily; de ~ everyday.

diarrea [dja'rrea] nf diarrhoea.

dibujar [diβu'xar] vt to draw, sketch; **dibujo** nm drawing; **dibujos animados** cartoons.

diccionario [dikθjo'narjo] nm dictionary.

dice etc vb ver decir.

diciembre [di'θjembre] nm December.

dictado [dik'taðo] nm dictation.

dictador [dikta'ðor] nm dictator; **dictadura** nf dictatorship.

dictamen [dik'tamen] nm (opinión) opinion; (juicio) judgment; (informe) report.

dictar [dik'tar] vt (carta) to dictate;

(JUR: *sentencia*) to pronounce;
(*decreto*) to issue; (AM: *clase*) to
give.

dicho, a ['ditʃo, a] *pp de* **decir** // *a*:
en ~s países in the aforementioned
countries // *nm* saying.

diecinueve [djeθi'nweβe] *num* nine-
teen.

dieciocho [djeθi'otʃo] *num* eighteen.

dieciséis [djeθi'seis] *num* sixteen.

diecisiete [djeθi'sjete] *num* seven-
teen.

diente ['djente] *nm* (ANAT, TEC)
tooth; (ZOOL) fang; (: *de elefante*)
tusk; (*de ajo*) clove; **hablar entre
~s** to mutter, mumble.

diera, dieron *etc vb ver* **dar**.

diesel ['disel] *a*: **motor ~** diesel
engine.

dieta ['djeta] *nf* diet.

diez [djeθ] *num* ten.

difamar [difa'mar] *vt* (JUR:
hablando) to slander; (: *por escrito*)
to libel.

diferencia [dife'renθja] *nf* difference;
diferenciar *vt* to differentiate
between // *vr* to differ; **diferenciarse**
vr to differ, be different;
(*distinguirse*) to distinguish o.s.

diferente [dife'rente] *a* different.

diferido [dife'riðo] *nm*: **en ~** (TV
etc) recorded.

difícil [di'fiθil] *a* difficult.

dificultad [difikul'tað] *nf* difficulty;
(*problema*) trouble; (*objeción*) objection.

dificultar [difikul'tar] *vt* (*complicar*)
to complicate, make difficult;
(*estorbar*) to obstruct.

difundir [difun'dir] *vt* (*calor, luz*) to
diffuse; (RADIO, TV) to broadcast;
~ una noticia to spread a piece of
news; **~se** *vr* to spread (out).

difunto, a [di'funto, a] *a* dead,
deceased // *nm/f* deceased (person).

diga *etc vb ver* **decir**.

digerir [dixe'rir] *vt* to digest; (*fig*) to
absorb.

digital [dixi'tal] *a* (INFORM) digital.

dignarse [diɣ'narse] *vr* to deign to.

digno, a ['diɣno, a] *a* worthy.

digo *etc vb ver* **decir**.

dije *etc vb ver* **decir**.

dilatado, a [dila'taðo, a] *a* dilated;
(*período*) long drawn-out; (*extenso*)
extensive.

dilatar [dila'tar] *vt* (*cuerpo*) to dilate;
(*prolongar*) to prolong; (*aplazar*) to
delay.

dilema [di'lema] *nm* dilemma.

diligencia [dili'xenθja] *nf* diligence;
(*ocupación*) errand, job; **~s** *nfpl*
(JUR) formalities; **diligente** *a*
diligent.

diluir [dilu'ir] *vt* to dilute.

diluvio [di'luβjo] *nm* deluge, flood.

dimensión [dimen'sjon] *nf* dimension.

diminuto, a [dimi'nuto, a] *a* tiny,
diminutive.

dimitir [dimi'tir] *vi* to resign.

dimos *vb ver* **dar**.

Dinamarca [dina'marka] *nf* Denmark; **dinamarqués, esa** *a* Danish
// *nm/f* Dane.

dinámico, a [di'namiko, a] *a* *a*
dynamic.

dinamita [dina'mita] *nf* dynamite.

dinamo ['dinamo] *nf* dynamo.

dineral [dine'ral] *nm* large sum of
money, fortune.

dinero [di'nero] *nm* money; **~
contante, ~ efectivo** cash, ready
cash.

dio *vb ver* **dar**.

dios [djos] *nm* god; **¡D~ mío!** (oh,)
my God!

diosa ['djosa] *nf* goddess.

diploma [di'ploma] *nm* diploma.

diplomacia [diplo'maθja] *nf*
diplomacy; (*fig*) tact.

diplomado, a [diplo'maðo, a] *a*
qualified.

diplomático, a [diplo'matiko, a] *a*
diplomatic // *nm/f* diplomat.

diputado, a [dipu'taðo, a] *nm/f*
delegate; (POL) ≈ member of parliament (Brit), ≈ representative (US).

dique ['dike] *nm* dyke.

diré *etc vb ver* **decir**.

dirección [direk'θjon] *nf* direction; (*señas*) address; (*AUTO*) steering; (*gerencia*) management; (*POL*) leadership; **~ única/prohibida** one-way street/no entry.

directo, a [di'rekto, a] *a* direct; (*RADIO, TV*) live; **transmitir en ~** to broadcast live.

director, a [direk'tor, a] *a* leading // *nm/f* director; (*ESCOL*) head(teacher) (*Brit*), principal (*US*); (*gerente*) manager(ess); (*PRENSA*) editor; **~ de cine** film director; **~ general** managing director.

dirigir [diri'xir] *vt* to direct; (*carta*) to address; (*obra de teatro, film*) to direct; (*MUS*) to conduct; (*comercio*) to manage; **~se a** *vr*: **~se a** to go towards, make one's way towards; (*hablar con*) to speak to.

dirija *etc vb ver* **dirigir.**

discernir [disθer'nir] *vt* (*distinguir, discriminar*) to discern.

disciplina [disθi'plina] *nf* discipline.

discípulo, a [dis'θipulo, a] *nm/f* disciple.

disco ['disko] *nm* disc; (*DEPORTE*) discus; (*TEL*) dial; (*AUTO*: *semáforo*) light; (*MUS*) record; **~ compacto/de larga duración** compact disc/long-playing record (L.P.); **~ de freno** brake disc; (*INFORM*): **~ flexible/rígido** floppy/hard disk.

disconforme [diskon'forme] *a* differing; **estar ~ (con)** to be in disagreement (with).

discordia [dis'korðja] *nf* discord.

discoteca [disko'teka] *nf* disco(theque).

discreción [diskre'θjon] *nf* discretion; (*reserva*) prudence; **comer a ~** to eat as much as one wishes; **discrecional** *a* (*facultativo*) discretionary.

discrepancia [diskre'panθja] *nf* (*diferencia*) discrepancy; (*desacuerdo*) disagreement.

discreto, a [dis'kreto, a] *a* (*diplomático*) discreet; (*sensato*)

sensible; (*reservado*) quiet; (*sobrio*) sober.

discriminación [diskrimina'θjon] *nf* discrimination.

disculpa [dis'kulpa] *nf* excuse; (*pedir perdón*) apology; **pedir ~s a/por** to apologize to/for; **disculpar** *vt* to excuse, pardon; **disculparse** *vr* to excuse o.s.; to apologize.

discurrir [disku'rrir] *vi* (*pensar, reflexionar*) to think, meditate; (*recorrer*) to roam, wander; (*el tiempo*) to pass, flow by.

discurso [dis'kurso] *nm* speech.

discutir [disku'tir] *vt* (*debatir*) to discuss; (*pelear*) to argue about; (*contradecir*) to argue against // *vi* to discuss; (*disputar*) to argue.

disecar [dise'kar] *vt* (*conservar*: *animal*) to stuff; (: *planta*) to dry.

diseminar [disemi'nar] *vt* to disseminate, spread.

diseño [di'seɲo] *nm* design; (*ARTE*) drawing.

disfraz [dis'fraθ] *nm* (*máscara*) disguise; (*excusa*) pretext; **~ar** *vt* to disguise; **~arse** *vr*: **~arse de** to disguise o.s. as.

disfrutar [disfru'tar] *vt* to enjoy // *vi* to enjoy o.s.; **~ de** to enjoy, possess.

disgustar [disɣus'tar] *vt* (*no gustar*) to displease; (*contrariar, enojar*) to annoy, upset; **~se** *vr* to be annoyed; (*dos personas*) to fall out.

disgusto [dis'ɣusto] *nm* (*repugnancia*) disgust; (*contrariedad*) annoyance; (*tristeza*) grief; (*riña*) quarrel; (*avería*) misfortune.

disidente [disi'ðente] *nm* dissident.

disimular [disimu'lar] *vt* (*ocultar*) to hide, conceal // *vi* to dissemble.

disipar [disi'par] *vt* to dispel; (*fortuna*) to squander; **~se** *vr* (*nubes*) to vanish; (*indisciplinarse*) to dissipate.

disminución [disminu'θjon] *nf* diminution.

disminuir [disminu'ir] *vt* (*acortar*) to decrease; (*achicar*) to diminish; (*estrechar*) to lessen.

disolver [disol'βer] *vt* (*gen*) to dissolve; ~**se** *vr* to dissolve; (*COM*) to go into liquidation.

disparar [dispa'rar] *vt*, *vi* to shoot, fire.

disparate [dispa'rate] *nm* (*tontería*) foolish remark; (*error*) blunder; **decir** ~**s** to talk nonsense.

disparo [dis'paro] *nm* shot.

dispensar [dispen'sar] *vt* to dispense; (*disculpar*) to excuse.

dispersar [disper'sar] *vt* to disperse; ~**se** *vr* to scatter.

disponer [dispo'ner] *vt* (*arreglar*) to arrange; (*ordenar*) to put in order; (*preparar*) to prepare, get ready // *vi*: ~ **de** to have, own; ~**se** *vr*: ~**se para** to prepare to, prepare for.

disponible [dispo'nißle] *a* available.

disposición [disposi'θjon] *nf* arrangement, disposition; (*aptitud*) aptitude; (*INFORM*) layout; **a la** ~ **de** at the disposal of.

dispositivo [disposi'tißo] *nm* device, mechanism.

dispuesto, a pp de disponer / [dis'pwesto, a] *a* (*arreglado*) arranged; (*preparado*) disposed.

disputar [dispu'tar] *vt* (*discutir*) to dispute, question; (*contender*) to contend for // *vi* to argue.

disquete [dis'kete] *nm* floppy disk, diskette.

distancia [dis'tanθja] *nf* distance.

distanciar [distan'θjar] *vt* to space out; ~**se** *vr* to become estranged.

distante [dis'tante] *a* distant.

diste, disteis *vb ver* **dar**.

distinción [distin'θjon] *nf* distinction; (*elegancia*) elegance; (*honor*) honour.

distinguido, a [distin'giðo, a] *a* distinguished.

distinguir [distin'gir] *vt* to distinguish; (*escoger*) to single out; ~**se** *vr* to be distinguished.

distinto, a [dis'tinto, a] *a* different; (*claro*) clear.

distracción [distrak'θjon] *nf* distraction; (*pasatiempo*) hobby, pastime; (*olvido*) absent-mindedness, distrac-

tion.

distraer [distra'er] *vt* (*atención*) to distract; (*divertir*) to amuse; (*fondos*) to embezzle; ~**se** *vr* (*entretenerse*) to amuse o.s.; (*perder la concentración*) to allow one's attention to wander.

distraído, a [distra'iðo, a] *a* (*gen*) absent-minded; (*entretenido*) amusing.

distribuir [distrißu'ir] *vt* to distribute.

distrito [dis'trito] *nm* (*sector, territorio*) region; (*barrio*) district.

disturbio [dis'turßjo] *nm* disturbance; (*desorden*) riot.

disuadir [diswa'ðir] *vt* to dissuade.

disuelto [di'swelto] *pp de* **disolver**.

DIU *nm abr* (= *dispositivo intrauterino*) IUD.

diurno, a ['djurno, a] *a* day *cpd*.

divagar [dißa'ɣar] *vi* (*desviarse*) to digress.

diván [di'ßan] *nm* divan.

divergencia [dißer'xenθja] *nf* divergence.

diversidad [dißersi'ðað] *nf* diversity, variety.

diversificar [dißersifi'kar] *vt* to diversify.

diversión [dißer'sjon] *nf* (*gen*) entertainment; (*actividad*) hobby, pastime.

diverso, a [di'ßerso, a] *a* diverse; ~**s** *nmpl* sundries; ~**s libros** several books.

divertido, a [dißer'tiðo, a] *a* (*chiste*) amusing; (*fiesta etc*) enjoyable.

divertir [dißer'tir] *vt* (*entretener, recrear*) to amuse; ~**se** *vr* (*pasarlo bien*) to have a good time; (*distraerse*) to amuse o.s.

dividir [dißi'ðir] *vt* (*gen*) to divide; (*separar*) to separate; (*distribuir*) to distribute, share out.

divierta *etc vb ver* **divertir**.

divino, a [di'ßino, a] *a* divine.

divirtiendo *etc vb ver* **divertir**.

divisa [di'ßisa] *nf* (*emblema, moneda*) emblem, badge; ~**s** *nfpl* foreign exchange *sg*.

divisar [diβi'sar] *vt* to make out, distinguish.

división [diβi'sjon] *nf* (*gen*) division; (*de partido*) split; (*de país*) country.

divorciar [diβor'θjar] *vt* to divorce; ~se *vr* to get divorced; **divorcio** *nm* divorce.

divulgar [diβul'γar] *vt* (*desparramar*) to spread; (*hacer circular*) to divulge, circulate; ~se *vr* to leak out.

DNI *nm abr* (*Esp*: = Documento Nacional de Identidad) national identity card.

dobladillo [doβla'ðiλo] *nm* (*de vestido*) hem; (*de pantalón*: *vuelta*) turn-up (*Brit*), cuff (*US*).

doblar [do'βlar] *vt* to double; (*papel*) to fold; (*caño*) to bend; (*la esquina*) to turn, go round; (*film*) to dub // *vi* to turn; (*campana*) to toll; ~se *vr* (*plegarse*) to fold (up), crease; (*encorvarse*) to bend.

doble ['doβle] *a* double; (*de dos aspectos*) dual; (*fig*) two-faced // *nm* double; ~s *nmpl* (*DEPORTE*) doubles *sg* // *nm/f* (*TEATRO*) double, stand-in; **con sentido ~** with a double meaning.

doblegar [doβle'γar] *vt* to fold, crease; ~se *vr* to yield.

doce ['doθe] *num* twelve; ~**na** *nf* dozen.

docente [do'θente] *a*: **centro/ personal ~** teaching establishment/ staff.

dócil ['doθil] *a* (*pasivo*) docile; (*obediente*) obedient.

doctor, a [dok'tor, a] *nm/f* doctor.

doctrina [dok'trina] *nf* doctrine, teaching.

documentación [dokumenta'θjon] *nf* documentation, papers *pl*.

documento [doku'mento] *nm* (*certificado*) document; **documental, a** *nm* documentary.

dólar ['dolar] *nm* dollar.

doler [do'ler] *vt, vi* to hurt; (*fig*) to grieve; ~se *vr* (*de su situación*) to grieve, feel sorry; (*de las desgracias*

ajenas) to sympathize; **me duele el brazo** my arm hurts.

dolor [do'lor] *nm* pain; (*fig*) grief, sorrow; ~ **de cabeza** headache; ~ **de estómago** stomachache.

domar [do'mar], **domesticar** [domesti'kar] *vt* to tame.

domiciliación [domiθilja'θjon] *nf*: ~ **de pagos** (*COM*) standing order.

domicilio [domi'θiljo] *nm* home; ~ **particular** private residence; ~ **social** (*COM*) head office; **sin ~ fijo** of no fixed abode.

dominante [domi'nante] *a* dominant; (*persona*) domineering.

dominar [domi'nar] *vt* (*gen*) to dominate; (*idiomas*) to be fluent in // *vi* to dominate, prevail; ~se *vr* to control o.s.

domingo [do'mingo] *nm* Sunday.

dominio [do'minjo] *nm* (*tierras*) domain; (*autoridad*) power, authority; (*de las pasiones*) grip, hold; (*de varios idiomas*) command.

don [don] *nm* (*talento*) gift; ~ **Juan Gómez** Mr Juan Gomez o Juan Gomez Esq.

donaire [do'naire] *nm* charm.

donar [do'nar] *vt* to donate.

doncella [don'θeλa] *nf* (*criada*) maid.

donde ['donde] *ad* where // *prep*: **el coche está allí ~ el farol** the car is over there by the lamppost o where the lamppost is; **por ~** through which; **en ~** where, in which.

dónde ['donde] *ad interr* where?; **¿a ~ vas?** where are you going (to)?; **¿de ~ vienes?** where have you come from?; **¿por ~?** where?, whereabouts?

dondequiera [donde'kjera] *ad* anywhere; **por ~** everywhere, all over the place // *conj*: ~ **que** wherever.

doña ['dona] *nf*: ~ **Alicia** Alicia; ~ **Victoria Benito** Mrs Victoria Benito.

dorado, a [do'raðo, a] *a* (*color*) golden; (*TEC*) gilt.

dormir [dor'mir] *vt*: ~ **la siesta por**

la tarde to have an afternoon nap // *vi* to sleep; **~se** *vr* to fall asleep.

dormitar [dormi'tar] *vi* to doze.

dormitorio [dormi'torjo] *nm* bedroom; **~ común** dormitory.

dorsal [dor'sal] *nm* (*DEPORTE*) number.

dos [dos] *num* two.

dosis ['dosis] *nf inv* dose, dosage.

dotado, a [do'taðo, a] *a* gifted; **~ de** endowed with.

dotar [do'tar] *vt* to endow; **dote** *nf* dowry; **dotes** *nfpl* (*talentos*) gifts.

doy *vb ver* **dar**.

drama ['drama] *nm* drama.

dramaturgo [drama'turvo] *nm* dramatist, playwright.

droga ['drova] *nf* drug.

drogadicto, a [drova'ðikto, a] *nm/f* drug addict.

droguería [drove'ria] *nf* hardware shop (*Brit*) o store (*US*).

ducha ['dutʃa] *nf* (*baño*) shower; (*MED*) douche; **ducharse** *vr* to take a shower.

duda ['duða] *nf* doubt; **dudar** *vt, vi* to doubt; **dudoso, a** [du'ðoso, a] *a* (*incierto*) hesitant; (*sospechoso*) doubtful.

duela *etc vb ver* **doler**.

duelo *vb ver* **doler** // ['dwelo] *nm* (*combate*) duel; (*luto*) mourning.

duende ['dwende] *nm* imp, goblin.

dueño, a ['dweɲo, a] *nm/f* (*propietario*) owner; (*de pensión, taberna*) landlord/lady; (*empresario*) employer.

duermo *etc vb ver* **dormir**.

dulce ['dulθe] *a* sweet // *ad* gently, softly // *nm* sweet; **~ría** *nf* (*AM*) confectioner's.

dulzura [dul'θura] *nf* sweetness; (*ternura*) gentleness.

duplicar [dupli'kar] *vt* (*hacer el doble de*) to duplicate; **~se** *vr* to double.

duque ['duke] *nm* duke; **~sa** *nf* duchess.

duración [dura'θjon] *nf* duration.

duradero, a [dura'ðero, a] *a* (*tela*)

hard-wearing; (*fe, paz*) lasting.

durante [du'rante] *ad* during.

durar [du'rar] *vi* (*permanecer*) to last; (*recuerdo*) to remain.

durazno [du'raθno] *nm* (*AM: fruta*) peach; (: *árbol*) peach tree.

durex ['dureks] *nm* (*AM: tira adhesiva*) Sellotape ® (*Brit*), Scotch tape ® (*US*).

dureza [du'reθa] *nf* (*calidad*) hardness.

durmiente [dur'mjente] *nm/f* sleeper.

duro, a ['duro, a] *a* hard; (*carácter*) tough // *ad* hard // *nm* (*moneda*) five peseta coin o piece.

E

e [e] *conj* and.

E *abr* (= *este*) E.

ebanista [eβa'nista] *nm/f* cabinet-maker.

ébano ['eβano] *nm* ebony.

ebrio, a ['eβrjo, a] *a* drunk.

ebullición [eβuʎi'θjon] *nf* boiling.

eccema [ek'θema] *nf* (*MED*) eczema.

eclesiástico, a [ekle'sjastiko, a] *a* ecclesiastical.

eclipse [e'klipse] *nm* eclipse.

eco ['eko] *nm* echo; **tener ~** to catch on.

ecología [ekolo'via] *nf* ecology.

economato [ekono'mato] *nm* co-operative store.

economía [ekono'mia] *nf* (*sistema*) economy; (*cualidad*) thrift.

económico, a [eko'nomiko, a] *a* (*barato*) cheap, economical; (*persona*) thrifty; (*COM: año etc*) financial; (: *situación*) economic.

economista [ekono'mista] *nm/f* economist.

ecuador [ekwa'ðor] *nm* equator; (**el**) E~ Ecuador.

ecuánime [e'kwanime] *a* (*carácter*) level-headed; (*estado*) calm.

ecuatoriano, a [ekwato'rjano, a] *a, nm/f* Ecuadorian.

ecuestre [e'kwestre] *a* equestrian.

echar [e'tʃar] *vt* to throw; (*agua, vino*) to pour (out); (*empleado: despedir*) to fire, sack; (*hojas*) to sprout; (*cartas*) to post; (*humo*) to emit, give out // *vi:* ~ **a correr/ llorar** to run off/burst into tears; ~**se** *vr* to lie down; ~ **llave a** to lock (up); ~ **abajo** (*gobierno*) to overthrow; (*edificio*) to demolish; ~ **mano a** to lay hands on; ~ **una mano a uno** (*ayudar*) to give sb a hand; ~ **de menos** to miss.

edad [e'ðað] *nf* age; ¿**qué** ~ **tienes?** how old are you?; **tiene ocho años de** ~ he is eight (years old); **de** ~ **mediana/avanzada** middle-aged/ advanced in years; **la E**~ **Media** the Middle Ages.

edición [eði'θjon] *nf* (*acto*) publication; (*ejemplar*) edition.

edicto [e'ðikto] *nm* edict, proclamation.

edificio [eði'fiθjo] *nm* building; (*fig*) edifice, structure.

Edimburgo [eðim'burγo] *nm* Edinburgh.

editar [eði'tar] *vt* (*publicar*) to publish; (*preparar textos*) to edit.

editor, a [eði'tor, a] *nm/f* (*que publica*) publisher; (*redactor*) editor // *a:* **casa** ~**a** publishing house, publisher; ~**ial** *a* editorial // **nm** leading article, editorial; **casa** ~**ial** publishing house, publisher.

educación [eðuka'θjon] *nf* education; (*crianza*) upbringing; (*modales*) (good) manners *pl*.

educar [eðu'kar] *vt* to educate; (*criar*) to bring up; (*voz*) to train.

EE. UU. *nmpl abr* = **Estados Unidos.**

efectista [efek'tista] *a* sensationalist.

efectivamente [efectiβa'mente] *ad* (*como respuesta*) exactly, precisely; (*verdaderamente*) really; (*de hecho*) in fact.

efectivo, a [efek'tiβo, a] *a* effective; (*real*) actual, real // *nm:* **pagar en** ~ to pay (in) cash; **hacer** ~ **un**

cheque to cash a cheque.

efecto [e'fekto] *nm* effect, result; ~**s** *nmpl* (~**s personales**) effects; (*bienes*) goods; (*COM*) assets; **en** ~ in fact; (*respuesta*) exactly, indeed.

efectuar [efek'twar] *vt* to carry out; (*viaje*) to make.

eficacia [efi'kaθja] *nf* (*de persona*) efficiency; (*de medicamento etc*) effectiveness.

eficaz [efi'kaθ] *a* (*persona*) efficient; (*acción*) effective.

efusivo, a [efu'siβo, a] *a* effusive; **mis más efusivas gracias** my warmest thanks.

EGB *nf abr* (*Esp ESCOL*) = **Educación General Básica.**

egipcio, a [e'xipθjo, a] *a, nm/f* Egyptian.

Egipto [e'xipto] *nm* Egypt.

egoísmo [eγo'ismo] *nm* egoism.

egoísta [eγo'ista] *a* egoistical, selfish // *nm/f* egoist.

egregio, a [e'γrexjo, a] *a* eminent, distinguished.

Eire ['eire] *nm* Eire.

ej. *abr* (= *ejemplo*) eg.

eje ['exe] *nm* (*GEO, MAT*) axis; (*de rueda*) axle; (*de máquina*) shaft, spindle.

ejecución [exeku'θjon] *nf* execution; (*cumplimiento*) fulfilment; (*actuación*) performance; (*JUR: embargo de deudor*) attachment.

ejecutar [exeku'tar] *vt* to execute, carry out; (*matar*) to execute; (*cumplir*) to fulfil; (*MUS*) to perform; (*JUR: embargar*) to attach, distrain (on).

ejecutivo, a [exeku'tiβo, a] *a* executive; **el** (*poder*) ~ the executive (power).

ejemplar [exem'plar] *a* exemplary // *nm* example; (*ZOOL*) specimen; (*de libro*) copy; (*de periódico*) number, issue.

ejemplo [e'xemplo] *nm* example; **por** ~ for example.

ejercer [exer'θer] *vt* to exercise; (*influencia*) to exert; (*un oficio*) to

practise // vi (practicar) to practise
(de as); (tener oficio) to hold office.
ejercicio [exer'θiθjo] nm exercise;
(período) tenure; ~ comercial
financial year.
ejército [e'xerθito] nm army; entrar
en el ~ to join the army, join up.
ejote [e'xote] nm (AM) green bean.

PALABRA CLAVE

el, la, los, los [el, la, los, las,
lo] ♦ artículo definido **1** the; el
libro/la mesa/los estudiantes the
book/table/students
2 (con n abstracto: no se traduce):
el amor/la juventud love/youth
3 (posesión: se traduce a menudo
por a posesivo): romperse el brazo
to break one's arm; levantó la
mano he put his hand up; se puso
el sombrero she put her hat on
4 (valor descriptivo): tener la boca
grande/los ojos azules to have a
big mouth/blue eyes
5 (con días) on; me iré el viernes
I'll leave on Friday; los domingos
suelo ir a nadar on Sundays I generally go swimming
6 (lo + a): lo difícil/caro what is
difficult/expensive; (= cuán): no se
da cuenta de lo pesado que es he
doesn't realise how boring he is
♦ pron demostrativo: mi libro y
el de usted my book and yours; las
de Pepe son mejores Pepe's are
better; no la(s) blanca(s) sino
la(s) gris(es) not the white one(s)
but the grey one(s)
2: lo de: lo de ayer what happened
yesterday; lo de las facturas that
business about the invoices
♦ pron relativo: lo que etc **1** (indefinido): el (los) que quiera(n)
que se vaya(n) anyone who wants
to can leave; llévese el que más le
guste take the one you like best
2 (definido): el que compré ayer
the one I bought yesterday; los que
se van those who leave
3: lo que: lo que pienso yo/más

me gusta what I think/like most
♦ con: el que: el que lo diga
the fact that he says so; el que sea tan
vago me molesta his being so lazy
bothers me
♦ excl: ¡el susto que me diste!
what a fright you gave me!
♦ pron personal **1** (persona: m)
him; (: f) her; (: pl) them; lo/las
veo I can see him/them
2 (animal, cosa: sg) it; (: pl) them;
lo (o la) veo I can see it; los (o las)
veo I can see them
3: lo (como sustición de frase): no
lo sabía I didn't know; ya lo
entiendo I understand now.

él [el] pron (persona) he; (cosa) it;
(después de prep: persona) him;
(: cosa) it.
elaborar [elaβo'rar] vt (producto) to
make, manufacture; (preparar) to
prepare; (madera, metal etc) to
work; (proyecto etc) to work on o
out.
elasticidad [elastiθi'ðað] nf
elasticity.
elástico, a [e'lastiko, a] a elastic;
(flexible) flexible // nm elastic; (un
~) elastic band.
elección [elek'θjon] nf election;
(selección) choice, selection.
electorado [elekto'raðo] nm elector-
ate, voters pl.
electricidad [elektriθi'ðað] nf electricity.
electricista [elektri'θista] nm/f electrician.
eléctrico, a [e'lektriko, a] a electric.
electrizar [elektri'θar] vt to electrify.
electro... [elektro] pref electro...;
~cución nf electrocution; **~cutar**
vt to electrocute; **electrodo** nm
electrode; **~domésticos** nmpl
(electrical) household appliances;
~imán nm electromagnet;
~magnético, a a electromagnetic.
electrónico, a [elek'troniko, a] a
electronic // nf electronics sg.
electrotecnia [elektro'teknja] nf

electrical engineering; **elec-trotécnico, a** *nm/f* electrical engineer.'

electrotermo [elektro'termo] *nm* immersion heater.

elefante [ele'fante] *nm* elephant.

elegancia [ele'γanθja] *nf* elegance, grace; (*estilo*) stylishness.

elegante [ele'γante] *a* elegant, graceful; (*estiloso*) stylish, fashionable.

elegía [ele'xia] *nf* elegy.

elegir [ele'xir] *vt* (*escoger*) to choose, select; (*optar*) to opt for; (*presidente*) to elect.

elemental [elemen'tal] *a* (*claro, obvio*) elementary; (*fundamental*) elemental, fundamental.

elemento [ele'mento] *nm* element; (*fig*) ingredient; ~s *nmpl* elements, rudiments.

elevación [eleβa'θjon] *nf* elevation; (*acto*) raising, lifting; (*de precios*) rise; (*GEO etc*) height, altitude; (*de persona*) loftiness.

elevar [ele'βar] *vt* to raise, lift (up); (*precio*) to put up; ~se *vr* (*edificio*) to rise; (*precios*) to go up; (*transportarse, enajenarse*) to get carried away.

eligiendo *etc vb ver* **elegir**.

elija *etc vb ver* **elegir**.

eliminar [elimi'nar] *vt* to eliminate, remove.

eliminatoria [elimina'torja] *nf* heat, preliminary (round).

elite [e'lite] *nf* elite.

elocuencia [elo'kwenθja] *nf* eloquence.

elogiar [elo'xjar] *vt* to praise, eulogize; **elogio** *nm* praise.

elote [e'lote] *nm* (*AM*) corn on the cob.

eludir [elu'ðir] *vt* (*evitar*) to avoid, evade; (*escapar*) to escape, elude.

ella ['eʎa] *pron* (*persona*) she; (*cosa*) it; (*después de prep: persona*) her; (: *cosa*) it.

ellas ['eʎas] *pron* (*personas y cosas*) they; (*después de prep*) them.

ello ['eʎo] *pron* it.

ellos ['eʎos] *pron* they; (*después de prep*) them.

emanar [ema'nar] *vi*: ~ de to emanate from, come from; (*derivar de*) to originate in.

emancipar [emanθi'par] *vt* to emancipate; ~se *vr* to become emancipated, free o.s.

embadurnar [embaður'nar] *vt* to smear.

embajada [emba'xaða] *nf* embassy.

embajador, a [embaxa'ðor, a] *nm/f* ambassador/ambassadress.

embalar [emba'lar] *vt* (*envolver*) to parcel, wrap (up); (*envasar*) to package // *vi* to sprint.

embalsamar [embalsa'mar] *vt* to embalm.

embalse [em'balse] *nm* (*presa*) dam; (*lago*) reservoir.

embarazada [embara'θaða] *a* pregnant // *nf* pregnant woman.

embarazar [embara'θar] *vt* to obstruct, hamper; ~se *vr* (*aturdirse*) to become embarrassed; (*confundirse*) to get into a mess.

embarazo [emba'raθo] *nm* (*de mujer*) pregnancy; (*impedimento*) obstacle, obstruction; (*timidez*) embarrassment.

embarcación [embarka'θjon] *nf* (*barco*) boat, craft; (*acto*) embarkation, boarding.

embarcadero [embarka'ðero] *nm* pier, landing stage.

embarcar [embar'kar] *vt* (*cargamento*) to ship, stow; (*persona*) to embark, put on board; ~se *vr* to embark, go on board.

embargar [embar'γar] *vt* (*JUR*) to seize, impound.

embarque *etc vb ver* **embarcar** // [em'barke] *nm* shipment, loading.

embaucar [embau'kar] *vt* to trick, fool.

embeber [embe'βer] *vt* (*absorber*) to absorb, soak up; (*empapar*) to saturate // *vi* to shrink; ~se *vr*: ~se en la lectura to be engrossed o absorbed in a book.

embellecer [embeʎeˈθer] *vt* to embellish, beautify.

embestida [embesˈtiða] *nf* attack, onslaught; (*carga*) charge; **embestir** *vt* to attack, assault; to charge, attack // *vi* to attack.

emblema [emˈblema] *nm* emblem.

embobado, a [emboˈβaðo, a] *a* (*atontado*) stunned, bewildered.

émbolo [ˈembolo] *nm* (*AUTO*) piston.

embolsar [embolˈsar] *vt* to pocket, put in one's pocket.

emborrachar [emborraˈtʃar] *vt* to make drunk, intoxicate; ~se *vr* to get drunk.

emboscada [embosˈkaða] *nf* (*celada*) ambush.

embotar [emboˈtar] *vt* to blunt, dull; ~se *vr* (*adormecerse*) to go numb.

embotellamiento [emboteʎaˈmjento] *nm* (*AUTO*) traffic jam.

embotellar [emboteˈʎar] *vt* to bottle; ~se *vr* (*circulación*) to get into a jam.

embrague [emˈbraβe] *nm* (*tb*: **pedal de ~**) clutch.

embriagar [embrjaˈvar] *vt* (*emborrachar*) to make drunk; (*alegrar*) to delight; ~se *vr* (*emborracharse*) to get drunk.

embriaguez [embrjaˈveθ] *nf* (*borrachera*) drunkenness.

embrión [emˈbrjon] *nm* embryo.

embrollar [embroˈʎar] *vt* (*el asunto*) to confuse, complicate; (*persona*) to involve, embroil; ~se *vr* (*confundirse*) to get into a muddle o mess.

embrollo [emˈbroʎo] *nm* (*enredo*) muddle, confusion; (*aprieto*) fix, jam.

embromar [embroˈmar] *vt* (*burlarse de*) to tease, make fun of.

embrujado, a [embruˈxaðo, a] *a* bewitched; **casa embrujada** haunted house.

embrutecer [embruteˈθer] *vt* (*atontar*) to stupefy; ~se *vr* to be stupefied.

embudo [emˈbuðo] *nm* funnel.

embuste [emˈbuste] *nm* trick; (*mentira*) lie; (*hum*) fib; ~**ro, a** *a* lying, deceitful // *nmf* (*tramposo*) cheat; (*mentiroso*) liar; (*hum*) fibber.

embutido [embuˈtiðo] *nm* (*CULIN*) sausage; (*TEC*) inlay.

embutir [embuˈtir] *vt* (*TEC*) to inlay; (*llenar*) to pack tight, cram.

emergencia [emerˈxenθja] *nf* emergency; (*surgimiento*) emergence.

emerger [emerˈxer] *vi* to emerge, appear.

emigración [emivraˈθjon] *nf* emigration; (*de pájaros*) migration.

emigrar [emiˈvrar] *vi* (*personas*) to emigrate; (*pájaros*) to migrate.

eminencia [emiˈnenθja] *nf* eminence; **eminente** *a* eminent, distinguished; (*elevado*) high.

emisario [emiˈsarjo] *nm* emissary.

emisión [emiˈsjon] *nf* (*acto*) emission; (*COM etc*) issue; (*RADIO, TV: acto*) broadcasting; (: *programa*) broadcast, programme (*Brit*), program (*US*).

emisora [emiˈsora] *nf* radio o broadcasting station.

emitir [emiˈtir] *vt* (*olor etc*) to emit, give off; (*moneda etc*) to issue; (*opinión*) to express; (*RADIO*) to broadcast.

emoción [emoˈθjon] *nf* emotion; (*excitación*) excitement; (*sentimiento*) feeling.

emocionante [emoθjoˈnante] *a* (*excitante*) exciting, thrilling.

emocionar [emoθjoˈnar] *vt* (*excitar*) to excite, thrill; (*conmover*) to move, touch; (*impresionar*) to impress.

emotivo, a [emoˈtiβo, a] *a* emotional.

empacar [empaˈkar] *vt* (*gen*) to pack; (*en caja*) to bale, crate.

empacho [emˈpatʃo] *nm* (*MED*) indigestion; (*fig*) embarrassment.

empadronarse [empaðroˈnarse] *vr* (*POL: como elector*) to register.

empalagoso, a [empala'ɣoso, a] *a* cloying; *(fig)* tiresome.

empalmar [empal'mar] *vt* to join, connect // *vi* (*dos caminos*) to meet, join; **empalme** *nm* joint, connection; junction; (*de trenes*) connection.

empanada [empa'naða] *nf* pie, pasty.

empantanarse [empanta'narse] *vr* to get swamped; *(fig)* to get bogged down.

empañarse [empa'ɲarse] *vr* (*nublarse*) to get misty, steam up.

empapar [empa'par] *vt* (*mojar*) to soak, saturate; (*absorber*) to soak up, absorb; **~se** *vr*: **~se de** to soak up.

empapelar [empape'lar] *vt* (*paredes*) to paper.

empaquetar [empake'tar] *vt* to pack, parcel up.

emparedado [empare'ðaðo] *nm* sandwich.

empastar [empas'tar] *vt* (*embadurnar*) to paste; (*diente*) to fill.

empaste [em'paste] *nm* (*de diente*) filling.

empatar [empa'tar] *vi* to draw, tie; **empate** *nm* draw, tie.

empecé, empecemos *vb ver* **empezar.**

empedernido, a [empeðer'niðo, a] *a* hard, heartless; *(fijado)* hardened, inveterate.

empedrado, a [empe'ðraðo, a] *a* paved // *nm* paving.

empedrar [empe'ðrar] *vt* to pave.

empeine [em'peine] *nm* (*de pie, zapato*) instep.

empeñado, a [empe'ɲaðo, a] *a* (*persona*) determined; (*objeto*) pawned.

empeñar [empe'ɲar] *vt* (*objeto*) to pawn, pledge; (*persona*) to compel; **~se** *vr* (*obligarse*) to bind o.s., pledge o.s.; (*endeudarse*) to get into debt; **~se en** to be set on, be determined to.

empeño [em'peɲo] *nm* (*determinación, insistencia*) determination, insistence; (*cosa prendada*) pledge; **casa de ~s** pawnshop.

empeorar [empeo'rar] *vt* to make worse, worsen // *vi* to get worse, deteriorate.

empequeñecer [empekeɲe'θer] *vt* to dwarf; *(fig)* to belittle.

emperador [empera'ðor] *nm* emperor.

emperatriz [empera'triθ] *nf* empress.

empezar [empe'θar] *vt, vi* to begin, start.

empiece *etc vb ver* **empezar.**

empiezo *etc vb ver* **empezar.**

empinar [empi'nar] *vt* to raise; **~se** *vr* (*persona*) to stand on tiptoe; (*animal*) to rear up; (*camino*) to climb steeply.

empírico, a [em'piriko, a] *a* empirical.

emplasto [em'plasto], **emplaste** [em'plaste] *nm* (*MED*) plaster.

emplazamiento [emplaθa'mjento] *nm* site, location; (*JUR*) summons *sg*.

emplazar [empla'θar] *vt* (*ubicar*) to site, place, locate; (*JUR*) to summons; (*convocar*) to summon.

empleado, a [emple'aðo, a] *nm/f* (*gen*) employee; (*de banco etc*) clerk.

emplear [emple'ar] *vt* (*usar*) to use, employ; (*dar trabajo a*) to employ; **~se** *vr* (*conseguir trabajo*) to be employed; (*ocuparse*) to occupy o.s.

empleo [em'pleo] *nm* (*puesto*) job; (*puestos: colectivamente*) employment; (*uso*) use, employment.

empobrecer [empoβre'θer] *vt* to impoverish; **~se** *vr* to become poor o impoverished.

empollar [empo'ʎar] *vt, vi (fam)* to swot (up); **empollón, ona** *nm/f (fam)* swot.

emporio [em'porjo] *nm* emporium, trading centre; (*AM: gran almacén*) department store.

empotrado, a [empo'traðo, a] *a*

(*armario etc*) built-in.

emprender [empren'der] *vt* (*empezar*) to begin, embark on; (*acometer*) to tackle, take on.

empresa [em'presa] *nf* (*de espíritu etc*) enterprise; (*COM*) company, firm; ~rio, a *nm/f* (*COM*) manager.

empréstito [em'prestito] *nm* (public) loan.

empujar [empu'xar] *vt* to push, shove; **empuje** *nm* thrust; (*presión*) pressure; (*fig*) vigour, drive.

empujón [empu'xon] *nm* push, shove.

empuñar [empu'nar] *vt* (*asir*) to grasp, take (firm) hold of.

emular [emu'lar] *vt* to emulate; (*rivalizar*) to rival.

PALABRA CLAVE
---

en [en] *prep* **1** (*posición*) in; (: *sobre*) on; **está ~ el cajón** it's in the drawer; ~ **Argentina/La Paz** in Argentina/La Paz; ~ **la oficina/el colegio** at the office/school; **está ~ el suelo/quinto piso** it's on the floor/the fifth floor

2 (*dirección*) into; **entró ~ el aula** she went into the classroom; **meter algo ~ el bolso** to put sth into one's bag

3 (*tiempo*) in; on; ~ **1605/3 semanas/invierno** in 1605/3 weeks/ winter; ~ (**el mes de**) **enero** in (the month of) January; ~ **aquella ocasión/aquella época** on that occasion/at that time

4 (*precio*) for; **lo vendió ~ 20 dólares** he sold it for 20 dollars

5 (*diferencia*) by; **reducir/ aumentar ~ una tercera parte/un 20 por ciento** to reduce/increase by a third/20 per cent

6 (*manera*): ~ **avión/autobús** by plane/bus; **escrito ~ inglés** written in English

7 (*después de vb que indica gastar etc*) on; **han cobrado demasiado ~ dietas** they've charged too much for expenses; **se le va la mitad del**

sueldo ~ comida he spends half his salary on food

8 (*tema, ocupación*): **experto ~ la materia** expert on the subject; **trabaja ~ la construcción** he works in the building industry

9 (*a* + ~ + *infinitivo*): **lento ~ reaccionar** slow to react.

enajenación [enaxena'θjon] *nf*, **enajenamiento** [enaxena'mjento] *nm* alienation; (*fig: distracción*) absent-mindedness; (: *embelesamiento*) rapture, trance.

enajenar [enaxe'nar] *vt* to alienate; (*fig*) to carry away.

enamorado, a [enamo'raðo, a] *a* in love // *nm/f* lover.

enamorar [enamo'rar] *vt* to win the love of; ~**se** *vr*: ~**se de alguien** to fall in love with sb.

enano, a [e'nano, a] *a* tiny // *nm/f* dwarf.

enardecer [enarðe'θer] *vt* (*pasiones*) to fire, inflame; (*persona*) to fill with enthusiasm; ~**se** *vr*: ~ **por** to get excited about; (*entusiasmarse*) to get enthusiastic about.

encabezamiento [enkaßeθa'mjento] *nm* (*de carta*) heading; (*de periódico*) headline; (*preámbulo*) foreword, preface.

encabezar [enkaße'θar] *vt* (*movimiento, revolución*) to lead, head; (*lista*) to head, be at the top of; (*carta*) to put a heading to; (*libro*) to entitle.

encadenar [enkaðe'nar] *vt* to chain (together); (*poner grilletes a*) to shackle.

encajar [enka'xar] *vt* (*ajustar*): ~ (**en**) to fit (into); (*fam: golpe*) to give, deal; (*entrometer*) to insert // *vi* to fit (well); (*fig: corresponder a*) to match; ~**se** *vr*: ~**se en un sillón** to squeeze into a chair.

encaje [en'kaxe] *nm* (*labor*) lace.

encalar [enka'lar] *vt* (*pared*) to whitewash.

encallar [enka'ʎar] *vi* (*NAUT*) to

aground.

encaminar [enkami'nar] vt to direct, send; ~se vr: ~se a to set out for.

encandilar [enkandi'lar] vt to dazzle.

encantado, a [enkan'taðo, a] a (hechizado) bewitched; (muy contento) delighted; ¡~! how do you do!, pleased to meet you.

encantador, a [enkanta'ðor, a] a charming, lovely // nm/f magician, enchanter/enchantress.

encantar [enkan'tar] vt to charm, delight; (hechizar) to bewitch, cast a spell on; **encanto** nm (magia) spell, charm; (fig) charm, delight.

encarcelar [enkarθe'lar] vt to imprison, jail.

encarecer [enkare'θer] vt to put up the price of // vi, ~se vr to get dearer.

encarecimiento [enkareθi'mjento] nm price increase.

encargado, a [enkar'gaðo, a] a in charge // nm/f agent, representative; (responsable) person in charge.

encargar [enkar'gar] vt to entrust; (recomendar) to urge, recommend; ~se vr: ~se de to look after, take charge of.

encargo [en'kargo] nm (pedido) assignment, job; (responsabilidad) responsibility; (recomendación) recommendation; (COM) order.

encariñarse [enkari'narse] vr: ~ con to grow fond of, get attached to.

encarnación [enkarna'θjon] nf incarnation, embodiment.

encarnizado, a [enkarni'θaðo, a] a (lucha) bloody, fierce.

encarrilar [enkarri'lar] vt (tren) to put back on the rails; (fig) to correct, put on the right track.

encasillar [enkasi'ʎar] vt (tb: fig) to pigeonhole; (actor) to typecast.

encauzar [enkau'θar] vt to channel.

encendedor [enθende'ðor] nm lighter.

encender [enθen'der] vt (con fuego) to light; (incendiar) to set fire to; (luz, radio) to put on, switch on;

(avivar: pasiones) to inflame; ~se vr to catch fire; (excitarse) to get excited; (de cólera) to flare up; (el rostro) to blush.

encendido [enθen'diðo] nm (AUTO) ignition.

encerado [enθe'raðo] nm (ESCOL) blackboard.

encerar [enθe'rar] vt (suelo) to wax, polish.

encerrar [enθe'rrar] vt (confinar) to shut in, shut up; (comprender, incluir) to include, contain.

encía [en'θia] nf gum.

encienda etc vb ver **encender.**

encierro etc vb ver **encerrar** // [en'θjerro] nm shutting in, shutting up; (calabozo) prison.

encima [en'θima] ad (sobre) above, over; (además) besides; ~ de (en) on, on top of; (sobre) above, over; (además de) besides, on top of; por ~ de over; ¿llevas dinero ~? have you (got) any money on you?; se me vino ~ it got on top of me.

encinta [en'θinta] a pregnant.

enclenque [en'klenke] a weak, sickly.

encoger [enko'xer] vt to shrink, contract; (fig: asustar) to scare; ~se vr to shrink, contract; (fig) to cringe; ~se de hombros to shrug one's shoulders.

encolar [enko'lar] vt (engomar) to glue, paste; (pegar) to stick down.

encolerizar [enkoleri'θar] vt to anger, provoke; ~se vr to get angry.

encomendar [enkomen'dar] vt to entrust, commend; ~se vr: ~se a to put one's trust in.

encomiar [enko'mjar] vt to praise, pay tribute to.

encomienda etc vb ver **encomendar** // [enko'mjenda] nf (encargo) charge, commission; (elogio) tribute; ~ **postal** (AM) parcel post.

encono [en'kono] nm (rencor) rancour, spite.

encontrado, a [enkon'traðo, a] a

(*contrario*) contrary, conflicting; (*hostil*) hostile.

encontrar [enkon'trar] *vt* (*hallar*) to find; (*inesperadamente*) to meet, run into; ~se *vr* to meet (each other); (*situarse*) to be (situated); (*entrar en conflicto*) to crash, collide; ~se **con** to meet; ~se **bien** (**de salud**) to feel well.

encorvar [enkor'βar] *vt* to curve; (*inclinar*) to bend (down); ~se *vr* to bend down, bend over.

encrespar [enkres'par] *vt* (*cabellos*) to curl; (*fig*) to anger, irritate; ~se *vr* (*el mar*) to get rough; (*fig*) to get cross, get irritated.

encrucijada [enkruθi'xaða] *nf* crossroads *sg*; (*empalme*) junction.

encuadernación [enkwaðerna'θjon] *nf* binding.

encuadernador, a [enkwaðerna-'ðor, a] *nm/f* bookbinder.

encuadrar [enkwa'ðrar] *vt* (*retrato*) to frame; (*ajustar*) to fit, insert; (*encerrar*) to contain.

encubrir [enku'βrir] *vt* (*ocultar*) to hide, conceal; (*criminal*) to harbour, shelter.

encuentro etc *vb ver* **encontrar** ♦ [en'kwentro] *nm* (*de personas*) meeting; (*AUTO etc*) collision, crash; (*DEPORTE*) match, game; (*MIL*) encounter.

encuesta [en'kwesta] *nf* inquiry, investigation; (*sondeo*) (*public*) opinion poll; ~ **judicial** post mortem.

encumbrado, a [enkum'braðo, a] *a* eminent, distinguished.

encumbrar [enkum'brar] *vt* (*persona*) to exalt; ~se *vr* (*fig*) to become conceited.

encharcado, a [entʃar'kaðo, a] *a* (*terreno*) flooded.

enchufar [entʃu'far] *vt* (*ELEC*) to plug in; (*TEC*) to connect, fit together; **enchufe** *nm* (*ELEC*: *clavija*) plug; (: *toma*) socket; (*de dos tubos*) joint, connection; (*fam*: *influencia*) contact, connection; (: *puesto*) cushy job.

endeble [en'deβle] *a* (*argumento, excusa, persona*) weak.

endemoniado, a [endemo'njaðo, a] *a* possessed (of the devil); (*travieso*) devilish.

enderezar [endere'θar] *vt* (*poner derecho*) to straighten (out); (: *verticalmente*) to set upright; (*fig*) to straighten *o* sort out; (*dirigir*) to direct; ~se *vr* to straighten up.

endeudarse [endeu'ðarse] *vr* to get into debt.

endiablado, a [endja'βlaðo, a] *a* devilish, diabolical; (*hum*) mischievous.

endilgar [endil'ɣar] *vt* (*fam*): ~**le algo a uno** to lumber sb with sth; ~**le un sermón a uno** to lecture sb.

endomingarse [endomin'garse] *vr* to dress up, put on one's best clothes.

endosar [endo'sar] *vt* (*cheque etc*) to endorse.

endulzar [endul'θar] *vt* to sweeten; (*suavizar*) to soften.

endurecer [endure'θer] *vt* to harden; ~se *vr* to harden, grow hard.

endurecido, a [endure'θiðo, a] *a* (*duro*) hard; (*fig*) hardy, tough; **estar ~ a algo** to be hardened *o* used to sth.

enemigo, a [ene'miɣo, a] *a* enemy, hostile ♦ *nm/f* enemy.

enemistad [enemis'tað] *nf* enmity.

enemistar [enemis'tar] *vt* to make enemies of, cause a rift between; ~se *vr* to become enemies; (*amigos*) to fall out.

energía [ener'xia] *nf* (*vigor*) energy, drive; (*empuje*) push; (*TEC, ELEC*) energy, power.

enérgico, a [e'nerxiko, a] *a* (*gen*) energetic; (*voz, modales*) forceful.

energúmeno, a [ener'yumeno, a] *nm/f* (*fig fam*) madman/woman.

enero [e'nero] *nm* January.

enfadado, a [enfa'ðaðo, a] *a* angry, annoyed.

enfadar [enfa'ðar] *vt* to anger, annoy; ~se *vr* to get angry *o* annoyed.

enfado [en'faðo] *nm* (*enojo*) anger, annoyance; (*disgusto*) trouble, bother.

énfasis ['enfasis] *nm* emphasis, stress.

enfático, a [en'fatiko, a] *a* emphatic.

enfermar [enfer'mar] *vt* to make ill // *vi* to fall ill, be taken ill.

enfermedad [enferme'ðað] *nf* illness; ~ **venérea** venereal disease.

enfermera [enfer'mera] *nf* nurse.

enfermería [enferme'ria] *nf* infirmary; (*de colegio etc*) sick bay.

enfermero [enfer'mero] *nm* male nurse.

enfermizo, a [enfer'miθo, a] *a* (*persona*) sickly, unhealthy; (*fig*) unhealthy.

enfermo, a [en'fermo, a] *a* ill, sick // *nm/f* invalid, sick person; (*en hospital*) patient.

enflaquecer [enflake'θer] *vt* (*adelgazar*) to make thin; (*debilitar*) to weaken.

enfocar [enfo'kar] *vt* (*foto etc*) to focus; (*problema etc*) to consider, look at.

enfoque *etc vb ver* **enfocar** // [en'foke] *nm* focus.

enfrentar [enfren'tar] *vt* (*peligro*) to face (up to), confront; (*oponer, carear*) to put face to face; ~**se** *vr* (*dos personas*) to face *o* confront each other; (*DEPORTE: dos equipos*) to meet; ~**se a** *o* **con** to face up to, confront.

enfrente [en'frente] *ad* opposite; **la casa de** ~ the house opposite, the house across the street; ~ **de** *prep* opposite, facing.

enfriamiento [enfria'mjento] *nm* chilling, refrigeration; (*MED*) cold, chill.

enfriar [enfri'ar] *vt* (*alimentos*) to cool, chill; (*algo caliente*) to cool down; (*habitación*) to air, freshen; ~**se** *vr* to cool down; (*MED*) to catch a chill; (*amistad*) to cool.

enfurecer [enfure'θer] *vt* to enrage, madden; ~**se** *vr* to become furious,

fly into a rage; (*mar*) to get rough.

engalanar [engala'nar] *vt* (*adornar*) to adorn; (*ciudad*) to decorate; ~**se** *vr* to get dressed up.

enganchar [engan'tʃar] *vt* to hook; (*ropa*) to hang up; (*dos vagones*) to hitch up; (*TEC*) to couple, connect; (*MIL*) to recruit; (*fam: persona*) to rope in; ~**se** *vr* (*MIL*) to enlist, join up.

enganche [en'gantʃe] *nm* hook; (*TEC*) coupling, connection; (*acto*) hooking (up); (*MIL*) recruitment, enlistment; (*AM: depósito*) deposit.

engañar [enga'nar] *vt* to deceive; (*estafar*) to cheat, swindle; ~**se** *vr* (*equivocarse*) to be wrong; (*disimular la verdad*) to deceive *o* kid o.s.

engaño [en'gano] *nm* deceit; (*estafa*) trick, swindle; (*error*) mistake, misunderstanding; (*ilusión*) delusion; ~**so, a** *a* (*tramposo*) crooked; (*mentiroso*) dishonest, deceitful; (*aspecto*) deceptive; (*consejo*) misleading.

engarzar [engar'θar] *vt* (*joya*) to set, mount; (*fig*) to link, connect.

engatusar [engatu'sar] *vt* (*fam*) to coax.

engendrar [enxen'drar] *vt* to breed; (*procrear*) to beget; (*fig*) to cause, produce; **engendro** *nm* (*BIO*) foetus; (*fig*) monstrosity; (*idea*) brainchild.

englobar [englo'βar] *vt* (*incluir*) to include, comprise.

engomar [engo'mar] *vt* to glue, stick.

engordar [engor'ðar] *vt* to fatten // *vi* to get fat, put on weight.

engorroso, a [engo'rroso, a] *a* bothersome, trying.

engranaje [engra'naxe] *nm* (*AUTO*) gear.

engrandecer [engrande'θer] *vt* to enlarge, magnify; (*alabar*) to praise, speak highly of; (*exagerar*) to exaggerate.

engrasar [engra'sar] *vt* (*TEC: poner*

grasa) to grease; (: *lubricar*) to lubricate, oil; (*manchar*) to make greasy.

engreído, a [eŋgre'iðo, a] *a* vain, conceited.

engrosar [eŋgro'sar] *vt* (*ensanchar*) to enlarge; (*aumentar*) to increase; (*hinchar*) to swell.

enhebrar [ene'βrar] *vt* to thread.

enhorabuena [enora'βwena] *nf* congratulations *pl* // *ad* well and good.

enigma [e'niɣma] *nm* enigma; (*problema*) puzzle; (*misterio*) mystery.

enjabonar [enxaβo'nar] *vt* to soap; (*fam*: *adular*) to soft-soap; (: *regañar*) to tick off.

enjambre [en'xambre] *nm* swarm.

enjaular [enxau'lar] *vt* to (put in a) cage; (*fam*) to jail, lock up.

enjuagar [enxwa'ɣar] *vt* (*ropa*) to rinse (out).

enjuague *etc vb ver* **enjuagar** // [en'xwaɣe] *nm* (*MED*) mouthwash; (*de ropa*) rinse, rinsing.

enjugar [enxu'ɣar] *vt* to wipe (off); (*lágrimas*) to dry; (*déficit*) to wipe out.

enjuiciar [enxwi'θjar] *vt* (*JUR*: *procesar*) to prosecute, try; (*fig*) to judge.

enjuto, a [en'xuto, a] *a* dry, dried up; (*fig*) lean, skinny.

enlace [en'laθe] *nm* link, connection; (*relación*) relationship; (*tb*: ~ **matrimonial**) marriage; (*de carretera, trenes*) connection; ~ **sindical** shop steward.

enlazar [enla'θar] *vt* (*unir con lazos*) to bind together; (*atar*) to tie; (*conectar*) to link, connect; (*AM*) to lasso.

enlodar [enlo'ðar] *vt* to cover in mud; (*fig*: *manchar*) to stain; (: *rebajar*) to debase.

enloquecer [enloke'θer] *vt* to drive mad // *vi*, ~**se** *vr* to go mad.

enlutado, a [enlu'taðo, a] *a* (*persona*) in mourning.

enmarañar [enmara'ɲar] *vt* (*en-*

redar) to tangle (up); entangle; (*complicar*) to complicate; (*confundir*) to confuse; ~**se** *vr* (*enredarse*) to become entangled; (*confundirse*) to get confused.

enmarcar [enmar'kar] *vt* (*cuadro*) to frame.

enmascarar [enmaska'rar] *vt* to mask; ~**se** *vr* to put on a mask.

enmendar [enmen'dar] *vt* to emend, correct; (*constitución etc*) to amend; (*comportamiento*) to reform; ~**se** *vr* to reform, mend one's ways; **enmienda** *nf* correction; amendment; reform.

enmohecerse [enmoe'θerse] *vr* (*metal*) to rust, go rusty; (*muro, plantas*) to get mouldy.

enmudecer [enmuðe'θer] *vi*, **enmudecerse** *vr* (*perder el habla*) to fall silent; (*guardar silencio*) to remain silent.

ennegrecer [enneɣre'θer] *vt* (*poner negro*) to blacken; (*oscurecer*) to darken; ~**se** *vr* to turn black; (*oscurecerse*) to get dark, darken.

ennoblecer [ennoβle'θer] *vt* to ennoble.

enojadizo, a [enoxa'ðiθo, a] *a* irritable, short-tempered.

enojar [eno'xar] *vt* (*encolerizar*) to anger; (*disgustar*) to annoy, upset; ~**se** *vr* to get angry; to get annoyed.

enojo [e'noxo] *nm* (*cólera*) anger; (*irritación*) annoyance; ~**so, a** *a* annoying.

enorgullecerse [enorɣuʎe'θerse] *vr* to be proud; ~ **de** to pride o.s. on, be proud of.

enorme [e'norme] *a* enormous, huge; (*fig*) monstrous; **enormidad** *nf* hugeness, immensity.

enraizar [enrai'θar] *vi* to take root.

enredadera [enreða'ðera] *nf* (*BOT*) creeper, climbing plant.

enredar [enre'ðar] *vt* (*cables, hilos etc*) to tangle (up), entangle; (*situación*) to complicate, confuse; (*meter cizaña*) to sow discord among o between; (*implicar*) to embroil, implicate; **~se** *vr* to get entangled, get tangled (up); (*situación*) to get complicated; (*persona*) to get embroiled; (*AM: fam*) to meddle.

enredo [en'reðo] *nm* (*maraña*) tangle; (*confusión*) mix-up, confusion; (*intriga*) intrigue.

enrevesado, a [enreβe'saðo, a] *a* (*asunto*) complicated, involved.

enriquecer [enrike'θer] *vt* to make rich, enrich; **~se** *vr* to get rich.

enrojecer [enroxe'θer] *vt* to redden // *vi*, **~se** *vr* (*persona*) to blush.

enrolar [enro'lar] *vt* (*MIL*) to enlist; (*reclutar*) to recruit; **~se** *vr* (*MIL*) to join up; (*afiliarse*) to enrol.

enrollar [enro'ʎar] *vt* to roll (up), wind (up).

enroscar [enros'kar] *vt* (*torcer, doblar*) to coil (round), wind; (*tornillo, rosca*) to screw in; **~se** *vr* to coil, wind.

ensalada [ensa'laða] *nf* salad; **ensaladilla (rusa)** *nf* Russian salad.

ensalzar [ensal'θar] *vt* (*alabar*) to praise, extol; (*exaltar*) to exalt.

ensambladura [ensambla'ðura] *nf*, **ensamblaje** [ensam'blaxe] *nm* assembly; (*TEC*) joint.

ensamblar [ensam'blar] *vt* to assemble.

ensanchar [ensan'tʃar] *vt* (*hacer más ancho*) to widen; (*agrandar*) to enlarge, expand; (*COSTURA*) to let out; **~se** *vr* to get wider, expand; (*pey*) to give o.s. airs; **ensanche** *nm* (*de calle*) widening; (*de negocio*) expansion.

ensangrentar [ensangren'tar] *vt* to stain with blood.

ensañar [ensa'ɲar] *vt* to enrage; **~se** *vr*: **~se con** to treat brutally.

ensartar [ensar'tar] *vt* (*cuentas, perlas etc*) to string (together).

ensayar [ensa'jar] *vt* to test, try (out); (*TEATRO*) to rehearse.

ensayista [ensa'jista] *nmf* essayist.

ensayo [en'sajo] *nm* test, trial; (*QUÍMICA*) experiment; (*TEATRO*) rehearsal; (*DEPORTE*) try; (*ESCOL,*

LITERATURA) essay.

ensenada [ense'naða] *nf* inlet, cove.

enseñanza [ense'naɲθa] *nf* (*educación*) education; (*acción*) teaching; (*doctrina*) teaching, doctrine.

enseñar [ense'ɲar] *vt* (*educar*) to teach; (*instruir*) to teach, instruct; (*mostrar, señalar*) to show.

enseres [en'seres] *nmpl* belongings.

ensillar [ensi'ʎar] *vt* to saddle (up).

ensimismarse [ensimis'marse] *vr* (*abstraerse*) to become lost in thought; (*estar absorto*) to be lost in thought; (*AM*) to become conceited.

ensordecer [ensorðe'θer] *vt* to deafen // *vi* to go deaf.

ensortijado, a [ensorti'xaðo, a] *a* (*pelo*) curly.

ensuciar [ensu'θjar] *vt* (*manchar*) to dirty, soil; (*fig*) to defile; **~se** *vr* (*mancharse*) to get dirty; (*fig*) to dirty o.s., wet o.s.

ensueño [en'sweɲo] *nm* (*sueño*) dream, fantasy; (*ilusión*) illusion; (*soñando despierto*) daydream.

entablado [enta'βlaðo] *nm* (*piso*) floorboards *pl*; (*armazón*) boarding.

entablar [enta'βlar] *vt* (*recubrir*) to board (up); (*AJEDREZ, DAMAS*) to set up; (*conversación*) to strike up; (*JUR*) to file // *vi* to draw.

entablillar [entaβli'ʎar] *vt* (*MED*) to put in a splint.

entallar [enta'ʎar] *vt* (*traje*) to tailor // *vi*: **el traje entalla bien** the suit fits well.

ente ['ente] *nm* (*organización*) body, organization; (*fam: persona*) odd character.

entender [enten'der] *vt* (*comprender*) to understand; (*darse cuenta*) to realize; (*querer decir*) to mean // *vi* to understand; (*creer*) think, believe; **~ de** to know all about; **~ algo de** to know a little about; **~ en** to deal with, have to do with; **~se** *vr* (*comprenderse*) to be understood; (*2 personas*) to get on together; (*ponerse de acuerdo*) to agree, reach an agreement; **~se**

mal (2 personas) to get on badly.

entendido, a [enten'diðo, a] a (comprendido) understood; (hábil) skilled; (inteligente) knowledgeable // nmf (experto) expert // excl agreed!;

entendimiento nm (comprensión) understanding; (inteligencia) mind, intellect; (juicio) judgement.

enterado, a [ente'raðo, a] a well-informed; **estar ~ de** to know about, be aware of.

enteramente [entera'mente] ad entirely, completely.

enterar [ente'rar] vt (informar) to inform, tell; **~se** vr to find out, get to know.

entereza [ente'reθa] nf (totalidad) entirety; (fig: carácter) strength of mind; (: honradez) integrity.

enternecer [enterne'θer] vt (ablandar) to soften; (apiadar) to touch, move; **~se** vr to be touched, be moved.

entero, a [en'tero, a] a (total) whole, entire; (fig: recto) honest; (: firme) firm, resolute // nm (COM: punto) point; (AM: pago) payment.

enterrador [enterra'ðor] nm gravedigger.

enterrar [ente'rrar] vt to bury.

entibiar [enti'βjar] vt (enfriar) to cool; (calentar) to warm; **~se** vr (fig) to cool.

entidad [enti'ðað] nf (empresa) firm, company; (organismo) body; (sociedad) society; (FILOSOFIA) entity.

entiendo etc vb ver **entender**.

entierro [en'tjerro] nm (acción) burial; (funeral) funeral.

entomología [entomolo'xia] nf entomology.

entonación [entona'θjon] nf (LING) intonation; (fig) conceit.

entonar [ento'nar] vt (canción) to intone; (colores) to tone; (MED) to tone up // vi to be in tune; **~se** vr (engreírse) to give o.s. airs.

entonces [en'tonθes] ad then, at that time; **desde ~** since then; **en aquel**

~ at that time; (pues) **~ and so.**

entornar [entor'nar] vt (puerta, ventana) to half close, leave ajar; (los ojos) to screw up.

entorpecer [entorpe'θer] vt (entendimiento) to dull; (impedir) to obstruct, hinder; (: tránsito) to slow down, delay.

entrada [en'traða] nf (acción) entry, access; (sitio) entrance, way in; (INFORM) input; (COM) receipts pl, takings pl; (CULIN) entrée; (DEPORTE) innings sg; (TEATRO) house, audience; (para el cine etc) ticket; (COM): **~s y salidas** income and expenditure; (TEC): **~ de aire** air intake o inlet; **de ~** from the outset.

entrado, a [en'traðo, a] a: **~ en años** elderly; **una vez ~ el verano** in the summer(time), when summer comes.

entrante [en'trante] a next, coming; **mes/año ~** next month/year.

entraña [en'traɲa] nf (fig: centro) heart, core; (raíz) root; **~s** nfpl (ANAT) entrails; (fig) heart sg; **entrañable** a close, intimate.

entrar [en'trar] vt (introducir) to bring in; (INFORM) to input // vi (meterse) to go in, come in, enter; (comenzar): **~ diciendo** to begin by saying: **no me entra** I can't get the hang of it.

entre ['entre] prep (dos) between; (más de dos) among(st).

entreabrir [entrea'βrir] vt to half-open, open halfway.

entrecejo [entre'θexo] nm: **fruncir el ~** to frown.

entrecortado, a [entrekor'taðo, a] a (respiración) difficult; (habla) faltering.

entredicho [entre'ðitʃo] nm (JUR) injunction; **poner en ~** to cast doubt on; **estar en ~** to be banned.

entrega [en'treγa] nf (de mercancías) delivery; (de novela etc) instalment.

entregar [entre'γar] vt (dar) to hand (over), deliver; **~se** vr (rendirse) to surrender, give in, submit; (*dedicarse*) to devote o.s.

entrelazar [entrela'θar] *vt* to entwine.

entremeses [entre'meses] *nmpl* hors d'œuvres.

entremeter [entreme'ter] *vt* to insert, put in; ~se *vr* to meddle, interfere; **entremetido, a** *a* meddling, interfering.

entremezclar [entremeθ'klar] *vt*, **entremezclarse** *vr* to intermingle.

entrenador, a [entrena'ðor, a] *nm/f* trainer, coach.

entrenarse [entre'narse] *vr* to train.

entrepierna [entre'pjerna] *nf* crotch.

entresacar [entresa'kar] *vt* to pick out, select.

entresuelo [entre'swelo] *nm* mezzanine, entresol.

entretanto [entre'tanto] *ad* meanwhile, meantime.

entretejer [entrete'xer] *vt* to interweave.

entretener [entrete'ner] *vt* (*divertir*) to entertain, amuse; (*detener*) to hold up, delay; (*mantener*) to maintain; ~se *vr* (*divertirse*) to amuse o.s.; (*retrasarse*) to delay, linger; **entretenido, a** *a* entertaining, amusing; **entretenimiento** *nm* entertainment, amusement; (*mantenimiento*) upkeep, maintenance.

entrever [entre'βer] *vt* to glimpse, catch a glimpse of.

entrevista [entre'βista] *nf* interview; **entrevistar** *vt* to interview; **entrevistarse** *vr* to have an interview.

entristecer [entriste'θer] *vt* to sadden, grieve; ~se *vr* to grow sad.

entrometer [entrome'ter] *vt* etc = **entremeter** etc.

entroncar [entron'kar] *vi* to be connected o related.

entumecer [entume'θer] *vt* to numb, benumb; ~se *vr* (*por el frío*) to go o become numb; **entumecido, a** *a* numb, stiff.

enturbiar [entur'βjar] *vt* (*el agua*) to

make cloudy; (*fig*) to confuse; ~se *vr* (*oscurecerse*) to become cloudy; (*fig*) to get confused, become obscure.

entusiasmar [entusjas'mar] *vt* to excite, fill with enthusiasm; (*gustar mucho*) to delight; ~se *vr*: (*gustar* o **por** o to get enthusiastic o excited about.

entusiasmo [entu'sjasmo] *nm* enthusiasm; (*excitación*) excitement.

entusiasta [entu'sjasta] *a* enthusiastic // *nm/f* enthusiast.

enumerar [enume'rar] *vt* to enumerate.

enunciación [enunθja'θjon] *nf*, **enunciado** [enun'θjaðo] *nm* enunciation; (*declaración*) declaration, statement.

envainar [enβai'nar] *vt* to sheathe.

envalentonar [enβalento'nar] *vt* to give courage to; ~se *vr* (*pey*: *jactarse*) to boast, brag.

envanecer [enβane'θer] *vt* to make conceited; ~se *vr* to grow conceited.

envasar [enβa'sar] *vt* (*empaquetar*) to pack, wrap; (*enfrascar*) to bottle; (*enlatar*) to can; (*embolsar*) to pocket.

envase [en'βase] *nm* (*en paquete*) packing, wrapping; (*en botella*) bottling; (*en lata*) canning; (*recipiente*) container; (*paquete*) package; (*botella*) bottle; (*lata*) tin (*Brit*), can.

envejecer [enβexe'θer] *vt* to make old, age // *vi*, ~se *vr* (*volverse viejo*) to grow old; (*parecer viejo*) to age.

envenenar [enβene'nar] *vt* to poison; (*fig*) to embitter.

envergadura [enβerɣa'ðura] *nf* (*fig*) scope, compass.

envés [en'βes] *nm* (*de tela*) back, wrong side.

enviar [en'βjar] *vt* to send.

envidia [en'βiðja] *nf* (*deseo ferviente*) envy; (*celos*) jealousy; **envidiar** *vt* (*desear*) to envy; (*tener celos de*) to be jealous of.

envío [en'βio] *nm* (*acción*) sending;

(de mercancías) consignment; *(de dinero)* remittance.

enviudar [enβju'ðar] *vi* to be widowed.

envoltura [enβol'tura] *nf (cobertura)* cover; *(embalaje)* wrapper, wrapping.

envolver [enβol'βer] *vt* to wrap (up); *(cubrir)* to cover; *(enemigo)* to surround; *(implicar)* to involve, implicate.

envuelto [en'βwelto] *pp de* **envolver.**

enyesar [enje'sar] *vt (pared)* to plaster; *(MED)* to put in plaster.

épico, a ['epiko, a] *a* epic // *nf* epic.

epidemia [epi'ðemja] *nf* epidemic.

epilepsia [epi'lepsja] *nf* epilepsy.

epílogo [e'piloχo] *nm* epilogue.

episodio [epi'soðjo] *nm* episode.

epístola [e'pistola] *nf* epistle.

época ['epoka] *nf* period, time; *(HISTORIA)* age, epoch; **hacer ~ to** be epoch-making.

equidad [eki'ðað] *nf* equity.

equilibrar [ekili'βrar] *vt* to balance; **equilibrio** *nm* balance, equilibrium; **equilibrista** *nmf (funámbulo)* tightrope walker; *(acróbata)* acrobat.

equipaje [eki'paxe] *nm* luggage; *(avíos)* equipment, kit; **~ de mano** hand luggage.

equipar [eki'par] *vt (proveer)* to equip.

equipararse [ekipa'rarse] *vr:* **~ con** to be on a level with.

equipo [e'kipo] *nm (conjunto de cosas)* equipment; *(DEPORTE, grupo)* team; *(: de obreros)* shift.

equis ['ekis] *nf inv* (the letter) X.

equitación [ekita'θjon] *nf (acto)* riding; *(arte)* horsemanship.

equitativo, a [ekita'tiβo, a] *a* equitable, fair.

equivalente [ekiβa'lente] *a, nm* equivalent.

equivaler [ekiβa'ler] *vi* to be equivalent *o* equal.

equivocación [ekiβoka'θjon] *nf* mistake, error.

equivocado, a [ekiβo'kaðo, a] *a* wrong, mistaken.

equivocarse [ekiβo'karse] *vr* to be wrong, make a mistake; **~ de camino** to take the wrong road.

equívoco, a [e'kiβoko, a] *a (dudoso)* suspect; *(ambiguo)* ambiguous // *nm* ambiguity; *(malentendido)* misunderstanding.

era *vb ver* **ser** // ['era] *nf* era, age.

erais *vb ver* **ser.**

éramos *vb ver* **ser.**

eran *vb ver* **ser.**

erario [e'rarjo] *nm* exchequer *(Brit)*, treasury.

eras *vb ver* **ser.**

eres *vb ver* **ser.**

erguir [er'χir] *vt* to raise, lift; *(poner derecho)* to straighten; **~se** *vr* to straighten up.

erigir [eri'χir] *vt* to erect, build; **~se** *vr:* **~se** en to set o.s. up as.

erizado, a [eri'θaðo, a] *a* bristly.

erizarse [eri'θarse] *vr (pelo: de perro)* to bristle; *(: de persona)* to stand on end.

erizo [e'riθo] *nm (ZOOL)* hedgehog; *(tb:* **~ de mar)** sea-urchin.

ermitaño, a [ermi'taɲo, a] *nm/f* hermit.

erosionar [erosjo'nar] *vt* to erode.

erótico, a [e'rotiko, a] *a* erotic; **erotismo** *nm* eroticism.

erradicar [erraði'kar] *vt* to eradicate.

errante [e'rrante] *a* wandering, errant.

errar [e'rrar] *vi (vagar)* to wander, roam; *(equivocarse)* to be mistaken // *vt:* **~ el camino** to take the wrong road; **~ el tiro** to miss.

erróneo, a [e'rroneo, a] *a (equivocado)* wrong, mistaken; *(falso)* false, untrue.

error [e'rror] *nm* error, mistake; *(INFORM)* bug; **~ de imprenta** misprint.

eructar [eruk'tar] *vt* to belch, burp.

erudito, a [eru'ðito, a] *a* erudite, learned.

erupción [erup'θjon] *nf* eruption;

(MED) rash.

es vb ver **ser**.

esa, esas a demostrativo ver **ese**.

ésa, ésas pron ver **ése**.

esbelto, a [es'βelto, a] a slim, slender.

esbozo [es'βoθo] nm sketch, outline.

escabeche [eska'βetʃe] nm brine; (de aceitunas etc) pickle; **en ~** pickled.

escabroso, a [eska'βroso, a] a (accidentado) rough, uneven; (fig) tough, difficult; (: atrevido) risqué.

escabullirse [eskaβu'ʎirse] vr to slip away, to clear out.

escafandra [eska'fandra] nf (buzo) diving suit; (~ espacial) space suit.

escala [es'kala] nf (proporción, MUS) scale; (de mano) ladder; (AVIAT) stopover; **hacer ~ en** to stop o call in at.

escalafón [eskala'fon] nm (escala de salarios) salary scale, wage scale.

escalar [eska'lar] vt to climb, scale.

escalera [eska'lera] nf stairs pl, staircase; (escala) ladder; (NAIPES) run; **~ mecánica** escalator; **~ de caracol** spiral staircase.

escalfar [eskal'far] vt (huevos) to poach.

escalinata [eskali'nata] nf staircase.

escalofrío [eskalo'frio] nm (MED) chill; **~s** nmpl (fig) shivers; **escalofriante** a chilling.

escalón [eska'lon] nm step, stair; (de escalera) rung.

escalope [eska'lope] nm (CULIN) escalope.

escama [es'kama] nf (de pez, serpiente) scale; (de jabón) flake; (fig) resentment.

escamotear [eskamote'ar] vt (fam: robar) to lift, swipe; (hacer desaparecer) to make disappear.

escampar [eskam'par] vb impersonal to stop raining.

escandalizar [eskandali'θar] vt to scandalize, shock; **~se** vr to be shocked; (ofenderse) to be offended.

escándalo [es'kandalo] nm scandal;

(alboroto, tumulto) row, uproar; **escandaloso, a** a scandalous, shocking.

escandinavo, a [eskandi'naβo, a] a, nm/f Scandinavian.

escaño [es'kaɲo] nm bench; (POL) seat.

escapar [eska'par] vi (gen) to escape, run away; (DEPORTE) to break away; **~se** vr to escape, get away; (agua, gas) to leak (out).

escaparate [eskapa'rate] nm shop window.

escape [es'kape] nm (de agua, gas) leak; (de motor) exhaust; (de persona) escape.

escarabajo [eskara'βaxo] nm beetle.

escaramuza [eskara'muθa] nf skirmish; (fig) brush.

escarbar [eskar'βar] vt (gallina) to scratch; (fig) to inquire into, investigate.

escarcha [es'kartʃa] nf frost.

escarlata [eskar'lata] a inv scarlet; **escarlatina** nf scarlet fever.

escarmentar [eskarmen'tar] vt to punish severely // vi to learn one's lesson.

escarmiento etc vb ver **escarmentar** // [eskar'mjento] nm (ejemplo) lesson; (castigo) punishment.

escarnio [es'karnjo] nm mockery; (injuria) insult.

escarola [eska'rola] nf endive.

escarpado, a [eskar'paðo, a] a (pendiente) sheer, steep; (rocas) craggy.

escasear [eskase'ar] vi to be scarce.

escasez [eska'seθ] nf (falta) shortage, scarcity; (pobreza) poverty.

escaso, a [es'kaso, a] a (poco) scarce; (raro) rare; (ralo) thin, sparse; (limitado) limited.

escatimar [eskati'mar] vt (limitar) to skimp (on), be sparing with.

escena [es'θena] nf scene.

escenario [esθe'narjo] nm (TEATRO) stage; (CINE) set; (fig) scene; **escenografía** nf set design.

escepticismo [esθepti'θismo] nm
scepticism; **escéptico, a** a sceptical
// nm/f sceptic.

esclarecer [esklare'θer] vt (iluminar)
to light up, illuminate; (misterio,
problema) to shed light on.

esclavitud [esklaβi'tuð] nf slavery.

esclavizar [esklaβi'θar] vt to enslave.

esclavo, a [es'klaβo, a] nm/f slave.

esclusa [es'klusa] nf (de canal) lock;
(compuerta) floodgate.

escoba [es'koβa] nf broom.

escocer [esko'θer] vi to burn, sting;
~se vr to chafe, get chafed.

escocés, esa [esko'θes, esa] a
Scottish // nm/f Scotsman/woman,
Scot.

Escocia [es'koθja] nf Scotland.

escoger [esko'xer] vt to choose, pick,
select; **escogido, a** a chosen,
selected; (calidad) choice, select.

escolar [esko'lar] a school cpd // nm/f
schoolboy/girl, pupil.

escolta [es'kolta] nf escort; **escoltar**
vt to escort.

escombros [es'kombros] nmpl
(basura) rubbish sg; (restos) debris
sg.

esconder [eskon'der] vt to hide, conceal; ~se vr to hide; **escondite** nm
hiding place; (juego) hide-and-seek;
escondrijo nm hiding place, hide-
out.

escopeta [esko'peta] nf shotgun.

escoria [es'korja] nf (de alto horno)
slag; (fig) scum, dregs pl.

Escorpio [es'korpjo] nm Scorpio.

escorpión [eskor'pjon] nm scorpion.

escotado, a [esko'taðo, a] a low-cut.

escote [es'kote] nm (de vestido) low
neck; **pagar a ~** to share the
expenses.

escotilla [esko'tiʎa] nf (NAUT)
hatch(way).

escozor [esko'θor] nm (dolor)
sting(ing).

escribano, a [eskri'βano, a], **es-
cribiente** [eskri'βjente] nm/f clerk.

escribir [eskri'βir] vt, vi to write; ~
a máquina to type; ¿cómo se es-

cribe? how do you spell it?

escrito, a [es'krito, a] pp de **escribir**
// nm (documento) document;
(manuscrito) text, manuscript; **por**
~ in writing.

escritor, a [eskri'tor, a] nm/f writer.

escritorio [eskri'torjo] nm desk;
(oficina) office.

escritura [eskri'tura] nf (acción) writing; (caligrafía) (hand)writing;
(JUR: documento) deed.

escrúpulo [es'krupulo] nm scruple;
(minuciosidad) scrupulousness; **escrupuloso, a** a scrupulous.

escrutar [eskru'tar] vt to scrutinize,
examine; (votos) to count.

escrutinio [eskru'tinjo] nm (examen
atento) scrutiny; (POL: recuento de
votos) count(ing).

escuadra [es'kwaðra] nf (MIL etc)
squad; (NAUT) squadron; (de coches
etc) fleet; **escuadrilla** nf (de
aviones) squadron; (AM: de obreros)
gang.

escuadrón [eskwa'ðron] nm
squadron.

escuálido, a [es'kwaliðo, a] a
skinny, scraggy; (sucio) squalid.

escuchar [esku'tʃar] vt to listen to //
vi to listen.

escudilla [esku'ðiʎa] nf bowl, basin.

escudo [es'kuðo] nm shield.

escudriñar [eskuðri'nar] vt
(examinar) to investigate, scrutinize;
(mirar de lejos) to scan.

escuela [es'kwela] nf school; ~ **de
artes y oficios** (Esp) = technical
college; ~ **normal** teacher training
college.

escueto, a [es'kweto, a] a plain;
(estilo) simple.

escuincle [es'kwinkle] nm/f (AM
fam) kid.

esculpir [eskul'pir] vt to sculpt;
(grabar) to engrave; (tallar) to
carve; **escultor, a** nm/f sculptor/
tress; **escultura** nf sculpture.

escupidera [eskupi'ðera] nf spittoon.

escupir [esku'pir] vt, vi to spit (out).

escurreplatos [eskurre'platos] nm

inv plate rack.

escurridizo, a [eskurri'ðiθo, a] *a* slippery.

escurrir [esku'rrir] *vt* (*ropa*) to wring out; (*verduras, platos*) to drain // *vi* (*los líquidos*) to drip; **~se** *vr* (*secarse*) to drain; (*resbalarse*) to slip, slide; (*escaparse*) to slip away.

ese, esa, esos, esas ['ese, 'esa, 'esos, 'esas] *a demostrativo* (*sg*) that; (*pl*) those.

ése, ésa, ésos, ésas ['ese, 'esa, 'esos, 'esas] *pron* (*sg*) that (one); (*pl*) those (ones); **~... éste...** the former... the latter...; **no me vengas con ésas** don't give me any more of that nonsense.

esencia [e'senθja] *nf* essence; **esencial** *a* essential.

esfera [es'fera] *nf* sphere; (*de reloj*) face; **esférico, a** *a* spherical.

esforzado, a [esfor'θaðo, a] *a* (*enérgico*) energetic, vigorous.

esforzarse [esfor'θarse] *vr* to exert o.s., make an effort.

esfuerzo *etc vb ver* **esforzar** // [es'fwerθo] *nm* effort.

esfumarse [esfu'marse] *vr* (*apoyo, esperanzas*) to fade away.

esgrima [es'ɣrima] *nf* fencing.

esguince [es'ɣinθe] *nm* (*MED*) sprain.

eslabón [esla'ßon] *nm* link.

esmaltar [esmal'tar] *vt* to enamel; **esmalte** *nm* enamel; **esmalte de uñas** nail varnish *o* polish.

esmerado, a [esme'raðo, a] *a* careful, neat.

esmeralda [esme'ralda] *nf* emerald.

esmerarse [esme'rarse] *vr* (*aplicarse*) to take great pains, exercise great care; (*afanarse*) to work hard.

esmero [es'mero] *nm* (great) care.

esnob [es'nob] *a inv* (*persona*) snobbish; (*coche etc*) posh // (*pl* ~s) *nm/f* snob; **~ismo** *nm* snobbery.

eso ['eso] *pron* that, that thing *o* matter; **~ de su coche** that business about his car; **~ de ir al cine** all

that about going to the cinema; **a ~ de las cinco** at about five o'clock; **en ~** thereupon, at that point; **~ es** that's it; **¡~ sí que es vida!** now that is really living!; **por ~ te lo dije** that's why I told you; **y ~ que llovía** in spite of the fact it was raining.

esos ['esos] *a demostrativo ver* **ese**.

ésos ['esos] *pron ver* **ése**.

espabilar [espaßi'lar] *vt*, **espabilarse** *vr* = **despabilar**.

espacial [espa'θjal] *a* (*del espacio*) space *cpd*.

espaciar [espa'θjar] *vt* to space (out).

espacio [es'paθjo] *nm* space; (*MUS*) interval; (*RADIO, TV*) programme (*Brit*), program (*US*); **el ~** space; **~so, a** *a* spacious, roomy.

espada [es'paða] *nf* sword; **~s** *nfpl* (*NAIPES*) spades.

espaguetis [espa'ɣetis] *nmpl* spaghetti *sg*.

espalda [es'palda] *nf* (*gen*) back; **~s** *nfpl* (*hombros*) shoulders; **a ~s de uno** behind sb's back; **tenderse de ~s** to lie (down) on one's back; **volver la ~ a alguien** to cold-shoulder sb.

espaldilla [espal'diʎa] *nf* shoulder blade.

espantadizo, a [espanta'ðiθo, a] *a* timid, easily frightened.

espantajo [espan'taxo] *nm*, **espantapájaros** [espanta'paxaros] *nm inv* scarecrow.

espantar [espan'tar] *vt* (*asustar*) to frighten, scare; (*ahuyentar*) to frighten off; (*asombrar*) to horrify, appal; **~se** *vr* to get frightened *o* scared; to be appalled.

espanto [es'panto] *nm* (*susto*) fright; (*terror*) terror; (*asombro*) astonishment; **~so, a** *a* frightening; terrifying; astonishing.

España [es'paɲa] *nf* Spain; **español, a** *a* Spanish // *nm/f* Spaniard // *nm* (*LING*) Spanish.

esparadrapo [espara'ðrapo] *nm* (sticking) plaster (*Brit*), adhesive tape (US).

esparcimiento [esparθi'mjento] nm (dispersión) spreading; (derramamiento) scattering; (fig) cheerfulness.

esparcir [espar'θir] vt to spread; (derramar) to scatter; ~**se** vr to spread (out); to scatter; (divertirse) to enjoy o.s.

espárrago [es'parraγo] nm asparagus.

espasmo [es'pasmo] nm spasm.

espátula [es'patula] nf spatula.

especia [es'peθja] nf spice.

especial [espe'θjal] a special; ~**idad** nf speciality (Brit), specialty (US).

especie [es'peθje] nf (BIO) species; (clase) kind, sort; en ~ in kind.

especificar [espeθifi'kar] vt to specify; **específico, a** specific.

espécimen [es'peθimen] (pl **especímenes**) nm specimen.

espectáculo [espek'takulo] nm (gen) spectacle; (TEATRO etc) show.

espectador, a [espekta'ðor, a] nm/f spectator.

espectro [es'pektro] nm ghost; (fig) spectre.

especular [espeku'lar] vt, vi to speculate.

espejismo [espe'xismo] nm mirage.

espejo [es'pexo] nm mirror; (fig) model; ~ **retrovisor** rear-view mirror.

espeluznante [espeluθ'nante] a horrifying, hair-raising.

espera [es'pera] nf (pausa, intervalo) wait; (JUR: plazo) respite; en ~ de waiting for; (con expectativa) expecting.

esperanza [espe'ranθa] nf (confianza) hope; (expectativa) expectation; **hay pocas ~s de que venga** there is little prospect of his coming; **esperanzar** vt to give hope to.

esperar [espe'rar] vt (aguardar) to wait for; (tener expectativa de) to expect; (desear) to hope for // vi to wait; to expect; to hope.

esperma [es'perma] nf sperm.

espesar [espe'sar] vt to thicken; ~**se** vr to thicken, get thicker.

espeso, a [es'peso, a] a thick; **espesor** nm thickness.

espía [es'pia] nm/f spy; **espiar** vt (observar) to spy on // vi: ~ **para** to spy for.

espiga [es'piγa] nf (BOT: de trigo etc) ear.

espina [es'pina] nf thorn; (de pez) bone; ~ **dorsal** (ANAT) spine.

espinaca [espi'naka] nf spinach.

espinazo [espi'naθo] nm spine, backbone.

espinilla [espi'niʎa] nf (ANAT: tibia) shin(bone); (grano) blackhead.

espino [es'pino] nm hawthorn.

espinoso, a [espi'noso, a] a (planta) thorny, prickly; (fig) difficult.

espionaje [espjo'naxe] nm spying, espionage.

espiral [espi'ral] a, nf spiral.

espirar [espi'rar] vt to breathe out, exhale.

espiritista [espiri'tista] a, nm/f spiritualist.

espíritu [es'piritu] nm spirit; **espiritual** a spiritual.

espita [es'pita] nf tap.

espléndido, a [es'plendiðo, a] a (magnífico) magnificent, splendid; (generoso) generous.

esplendor [esplen'dor] nm splendour.

espolear [espole'ar] vt to spur on.

espoleta [espo'leta] nf (de bomba) fuse.

espolvorear [espolβore'ar] vt to dust, sprinkle.

esponja [es'ponxa] nf sponge; (fig) sponger; **esponjoso, a** a spongy.

espontaneidad [espontanei'ðað] nf spontaneity; **espontáneo, a** a spontaneous.

esposa [es'posa] nf wife; ~**s** nfpl handcuffs; **esposar** vt to handcuff.

esposo [es'poso] nm husband.

espuela [es'pwela] nf spur.

espuma [es'puma] nf foam; (de cerveza) froth, head; (de jabón) lather; **espumoso, a** *a* frothy, foamy; (*vino*) sparkling.

esqueje [es'kexe] *nm* (*de planta*) cutting.

esqueleto [eske'leto] *nm* skeleton.

esquema [es'kema] *nm* (*diagrama*) diagram; (*dibujo*) plan; (*plan*) scheme; (FILOSOFÍA) schema.

esquí [es'ki] (*pl* ~s) *nm* (*objeto*) ski; (DEPORTE) skiing; ~ **acuático** water-skiing; **esquiar** *vi* to ski.

esquilar [eski'lar] *vt* to shear.

esquimal [eski'mal] *a, nm/f* Eskimo.

esquina [es'kina] *nf* corner.

esquirol [eski'rol] *nm* blackleg.

esquivar [eski'ßar] *vt* to avoid; (*evadir*) to dodge, elude.

esquivo, a [es'kißo, a] *a* (*altanero*) aloof; (*desdeñoso*) scornful, disdainful.

esta ['esta] *a demostrativo ver* **este**.

ésta ['esta] *pron ver* **éste**.

está *vb ver* **estar**.

estabilidad [estaßili'ðað] *nf* stability; **estable** *a* stable.

establecer [estaßle'θer] *vt* to establish; ~**se** *vr* to establish o.s.; (*echar raíces*) to settle (down); **establecimiento** *nm* establishment.

estaca [es'taka] *nf* stake, post; (*de tienda de campaña*) peg.

estacada [esta'kaða] *nf* (*cerca*) fence, fencing; (*palenque*) stockade.

estación [esta'θjon] *nf* station; (*del año*) season; ~ **de autobuses** bus station; ~ **balnearia** seaside resort; ~ **de servicio** service station.

estacionamiento [estaθjona'mjento] *nm* (AUTO) parking; (MIL) stationing.

estacionar [estaθjo'nar] *vt* (AUTO) to park; (MIL) to station; ~**io, a** *a* stationary; (COM: *mercado*) slack.

estadio [es'taðjo] *nm* (*fase*) stage, phase; (DEPORTE) stadium.

estadista [esta'ðista] *nm* (POL) statesman; (ESTADÍSTICA) statistician.

estadística [esta'ðistika] *nf* (*una* ~) figure, statistic; (*ciencia*) statistics

sg.

estado [es'taðo] *nm* (POL: *condición*) state; ~ **de cuenta** bank statement; ~ **civil** marital status; ~ **mayor** staff; **estar en** ~ to be pregnant; **E~s Unidos (EE.UU.)** *nmpl* United States (of America) (USA) *sg.*

estadounidense [estaðouni'ðense] *a* United States *cpd*, American // *nm/f* American.

estafa [es'tafa] *nf* swindle, trick; **estafar** *vt* to swindle, defraud.

estafeta [esta'feta] *nf* (*oficina de correos*) post office; ~ **diplomática** diplomatic bag.

estáis *vb ver* **estar**.

estallar [esta'ʎar] *vi* to burst; (*bomba*) to explode, go off; (*epidemia, guerra, rebelión*) to break out; ~ **en llanto** to burst into tears; **estallido** *nm* explosion; (*fig*) outbreak.

estampa [es'tampa] *nf* (*impresión, imprenta*) print, engraving; (*imagen, figura: de persona*) appearance.

estampado, a [estam'paðo, a] *a* printed // *nm* (*impresión: acción*) printing; (: *efecto*) print; (*marca*) stamping.

estampar [estam'par] *vt* (*imprimir*) to print; (*marcar*) to stamp; (*metal*) to engrave; (*poner sello en*) to stamp; (*fig*) to stamp, imprint.

estampida [estam'piða] *nf* stampede.

estampido [estam'piðo] *nm* bang, report.

estampilla [estam'piʎa] *nf* stamp.

están *vb ver* **estar**.

estancado, a [estan'kaðo, a] *a* stagnant.

estancar [estan'kar] *vt* (*aguas*) to hold up, hold back; (COM) to monopolize; (*fig*) to block, hold up; ~**se** *vr* to stagnate.

estancia [es'tanθja] *nf* (*permanencia*) stay; (*sala*) room; (AM) farm, ranch; **estanciero** *nm* (AM) farmer, rancher.

estanco, a [es'taŋko, a] *a* watertight // *nm* tobacconist's (shop).

estándar [es'tandar] *a, nm* standard; **estandarizar** *vt* to standardize.

estandarte [estan'darte] *nm* banner, standard.

estanque [es'taŋke] *nm* (*lago*) pool, pond; (*AGR*) reservoir.

estanquero, a [estaŋ'kero, a] *nm/f* tobacconist.

estante [es'tante] *nm* (*armario*) rack, stand; (*biblioteca*) bookcase; (*anaquel*) shelf; (*AM*) prop; **estantería** *nf* shelving, shelves *pl*.

estaño [es'taɲo] *nm* tin.

PALABRA CLAVE
---

estar [es'tar] ♦ *vi* **1** (*posición*) to be; **está en la plaza** it's in the square; **¿está Juan?** is Juan in?; **estamos a 30 km de Junín** we're 30 kms from Junín

2 (+ *adjetivo*: *estado*) to be; ~ **enfermo** to be ill; **está muy elegante** he's looking very smart; **¿cómo estás?** how are you keeping?

3 (+ *gerundio*) to be; **estoy leyendo** I'm reading

4 (*uso pasivo*): **está condenado a muerte** he's been condemned to death; **está envasado en ...** it's packed in ...

5 (*con fechas*): **¿a cuántos estamos?** what's the date today?; **estamos a 5 de mayo** it's the 5th of May

6 (*locuciones*): **¿estamos?** (*¿de acuerdo?*) okay?; (*¿listo?*) ready?; **¡ya está bien!** that's enough!

7: ~ **de**: ~ **de vacaciones/viaje** to be on holiday/away *o* on a trip; **está de camarero** he's working as a waiter

8: ~ **para**: **está para salir** he's about to leave; **no estoy para bromas** I'm not in the mood for jokes

9: ~ **por** (*propuesta etc*) to be in favour of; (*persona etc*) to support, side with; **está por limpiar** it still

has to be cleaned

10: ~ **sin**: ~ **sin dinero** to have no money; **está sin terminar** it isn't finished yet

♦ *vr*: ~**se**: **se estuvo en la cama toda la tarde** he stayed in bed all afternoon.

estas ['estas] *a ver* **este**.

éstas ['estas] *pron ver* **éste**.

estatal [esta'tal] *a* state *cpd*.

estático, a [es'tatiko, a] *a* static.

estatua [es'tatwa] *nf* statue.

estatura [esta'tura] *nf* stature, height.

estatuto [esta'tuto] *nm* (*JUR*) statute; (*de ciudad*) bye-law; (*de comité*) rule.

este ['este] *nm* east.

este, esta, estos, estas ['este, 'esta, 'estos, 'estas] *a demostrativo* (*sg*) this; (*pl*) these.

éste, ésta, éstos, éstas ['este, 'esta, 'estos, 'estas] *pron* (*sg*) this (one); (*pl*) these (ones); **ése... ~...** the former... the latter...

esté *etc vb ver* **estar**.

estela [es'tela] *nf* wake, wash; (*fig*) trail.

estén *etc vb ver* **estar**.

estenografía [estenovra'fia] *nf* shorthand.

estera [es'tera] *nf* mat(ting).

estéreo [es'tereo] *a inv, nm* stereo; **estereotipo** *nm* stereotype.

estéril [es'teril] *a* sterile, barren; (*fig*) vain, futile.

esterlina [ester'lina] *a*: **libra** ~ pound sterling.

estés *etc vb ver* **estar**.

estético, a [es'tetiko, a] *a* aesthetic // *nf* aesthetics *sg*.

estiércol [es'tjerkol] *nm* dung, manure.

estigma [es'tivma] *nm* stigma.

estilar [esti'lar] *vi*, **estilarse** *vr* (*estar de moda*) to be in fashion; (*usarse*) to be used.

estilo [es'tilo] *nm* style; (*TEC*) stylus; (*NATACIÓN*) stroke; **algo por**

el ~ something along those lines.

estima [es'tima] nf esteem, respect.

estimación [estima'θjon] nf (evaluación) estimation; (aprecio, afecto) esteem, regard.

estimar [esti'mar] vt (evaluar) to estimate; (valorar) to value; (apreciar) to esteem, respect; (pensar, considerar) to think, reckon.

estimulante [estimu'lante] a stimulating // nm stimulant.

estimular [estimu'lar] vt to stimulate; (excitar) to excite.

estímulo [es'timulo] nm stimulus; (ánimo) encouragement.

estío [es'tio] nm summer.

estipulación [estipula'θjon] nf stipulation, condition; **estipular** vt to stipulate.

estirado, a [esti'raðo, a] a (tenso) (stretched o drawn) tight; (fig: persona) stiff, pompous.

estirar [esti'rar] vt to stretch; (dinero, suma etc) to stretch out; ~se vr to stretch.

estirón [esti'ron] nm pull, tug; (crecimiento) spurt, sudden growth; **dar un ~** (niño) to shoot up.

estirpe [es'tirpe] nf stock, lineage.

estival [esti'βal] a summer cpd.

esto ['esto] pron this, this thing o matter; ~ **de la boda** this business about the wedding.

Estocolmo [esto'kolmo] nm Stockholm.

estofa [es'tofa] nf: **de baja ~** poor-quality.

estofado [esto'faðo] nm (CULIN) stew.

estofar [esto'far] vt (CULIN) to stew.

estómago [es'tomaxo] nm stomach; **tener ~** to be thick-skinned.

estorbar [estor'βar] vt to hinder, obstruct; (fig) to bother, disturb // vi to be in the way; **estorbo** [es'torβo] nm (molestia) bother, nuisance; (obstáculo) hindrance, obstacle.

estornudar [estornu'ðar] vi to sneeze.

estos ['estos] a demostrativo ver **este**.

éstos ['estos] pron ver **éste**.

estoy vb ver **estar**.

estrafalario, a [estrafa'larjo, a] a odd, eccentric; (desarreglado) slovenly, sloppy.

estrago [es'traβo] nm ruin, destruction; **hacer ~s en** to wreak havoc among.

estragón [estra'βon] nm tarragon.

estrangulador, a [estraŋgula'ðor, a] nm/f strangler // nm (TEC) throttle; (AUTO) choke.

estrangulamiento [estraŋgula-'mjento] nm (AUTO) bottleneck.

estrangular [estraŋgu'lar] vt (persona) to strangle; (MED) to strangulate.

estraperlo [estra'perlo] nm black market.

estratagema [estrata'xema] nf (MIL) stratagem; (astucia) cunning.

estrategia [estra'texja] nf strategy; **estratégico, a** a strategic.

estratificar [estratifi'kar] vt to stratify.

estrato [es'trato] nm stratum, layer.

estrechar [estre'tʃar] vt (reducir) to narrow; (COSTURA) to take in; (persona) to hug, embrace; ~se vr (reducirse) to narrow, grow narrow; (2 personas) to embrace; ~ **la mano** to shake hands.

estrechez [estre'tʃeθ] nf narrowness; (de ropa) tightness; (intimidad) intimacy; (COM) want o shortage of money; **estrecheces** nfpl financial difficulties.

estrecho, a [es'tretʃo, a] a narrow; (apretado) tight; (íntimo) close, intimate; (miserable) mean // nm strait; ~ **de miras** narrow-minded.

estrella [es'treʎa] nf star.

estrellar [estre'ʎar] vt (hacer añicos) to smash (to pieces); (huevos) to fry; ~se vr to smash; (chocarse) to crash; (fracasar) to fail.

estremecer [estreme'θer] vt to shake; ~se vr to shake, tremble; **estremecimiento** nm (temblor) trembling, shaking.

estrenar [estre'nar] vt (vestido) to wear for the first time; (casa) to move into; (película, obra de teatro) to present for the first time; **~se** vr (persona) to make one's début; **estreno** nm (primer uso) first use; (CINE etc) première.

estreñido, a [estre'niðo, a] a constipated.

estreñimiento [estreɲi'mjento] nm constipation.

estrépito [es'trepito] nm noise, racket; (fig) fuss; **estrepitoso, a** a noisy; (fiesta) rowdy.

estría [es'tria] nf groove.

estribar [estri'βar] vi: **~ en** to rest on, be supported by.

estribillo [estri'βiʎo] nm (LITERATURA) refrain; (MUS) chorus.

estribo [es'triβo] nm (de jinete) stirrup; (de coche, tren) step; (de puente) support; (GEO) spur; **perder los ~s** to fly off the handle.

estribor [estri'βor] nm (NAUT) starboard.

estricnina [estrik'nina] nf strychnine.

estricto, a [es'trikto, a] a (riguroso) strict; (severo) severe.

estropajo [estro'paxo] nm scourer.

estropear [estrope'ar] vt (arruinar) to spoil; (dañar) to damage; **~se** vr (objeto) to get damaged; (persona: la piel etc) to be ruined.

estructura [estruk'tura] nf structure.

estruendo [es'trwendo] nm (ruido) racket, din; (fig: alboroto) uproar, turmoil.

estrujar [estru'xar] vt (apretar) to squeeze; (aplastar) to crush; (fig) to drain, bleed.

estuario [es'twarjo] nm estuary.

estuche [es'tutʃe] nm box, case.

estudiante [estu'ðjante] nm/f student; **estudiantil** a student cpd.

estudiar [estu'ðjar] vt to study.

estudio [es'tuðjo] nm study; (CINE, ARTE, RADIO) studio; **~s** nmpl studies; (erudición) learning sg; **~so, a** a studious.

estufa [es'tufa] nf heater, fire.

estupefaciente [estupefa'θjente] nm drug, narcotic.

estupefacto, a [estupe'fakto, a] a speechless, thunderstruck.

estupendo, a [estu'pendo, a] a wonderful, terrific; (fam) great; **¡~!** that's great!; fantastic!

estupidez [estupi'ðeθ] nf (torpeza) stupidity; (acto) stupid thing (to do).

estúpido, a [es'tupiðo, a] a stupid, silly.

estupor [estu'por] nm stupor; (fig) astonishment, amazement.

estupro [es'tupro] nm rape.

estuve etc vb ver **estar.**

esvástica [es'βastika] nf swastika.

ETA ['eta] nf abr (Esp) ETA.

etapa [e'tapa] nf (de viaje) stage; (DEPORTE) leg; (parada) stopping place; (fig) stage, phase.

etarra [e'tarra] nm/f member of ETA.

etc. abr (= etcétera) etc.

etcétera [et'θetera] ad etcetera.

eternidad [eterni'ðað] nf eternity; **eterno, a** a eternal, everlasting.

ético, a ['etiko, a] a ethical // nf ethics pl.

etiqueta [eti'keta] nf (modales) etiquette; (rótulo) label, tag.

Eucaristía [eukaris'tia] nf Eucharist.

eufemismo [eufe'mismo] nm euphemism.

euforia [eu'forja] nf euphoria.

eunuco [eu'nuko] nm eunuch.

Europa [eu'ropa] nf Europe; **europeo, a** a, nm/f European.

éuscaro, a ['euskaro, a] a Basque // nm (LING) Basque. ·

Euskadi [eus'kaði] nm the Basque Country o Provinces pl.

euskera [eus'kera] nm (LING) Basque.

evacuación [eβakwa'θjon] nf evacuation; **evacuar** vt to evacuate.

evadir [eβa'ðir] vt to evade, avoid; **~se** vr to escape.

evaluar [eβa'lwar] vt to evaluate.

evangélico, a [eβaŋ'xeliko, a] a evangelic(al).

evangelio [eβaŋ'xeljo] nm gospel.

evaporar [eβapo'rar] *vt* to evaporate; ~**se** *vr* to vanish.

evasión [eβa'sjon] *nf* escape, flight; *(fig)* evasion.

evasivo, a [eβa'siβo, a] *a* evasive, non-committal // *nf (pretexto)* excuse.

evento [e'βento] *nm* event.

eventual [eβen'twal] *a* possible, conditional *(upon circumstances)*; *(trabajador)* casual, temporary.

evidencia [eβi'ðenθja] *nf* evidence, proof; **evidenciar** *vt (hacer evidente)* to make evident; *(probar)* to prove, show; **evidenciarse** *vr* to be evident.

evidente [eβi'ðente] *a* obvious, clear, evident.

evitar [eβi'tar] *vt (evadir)* to avoid; *(impedir)* to prevent.

evocar [eβo'kar] *vt* to evoke, call forth.

evolución [eβolu'θjon] *nf (desarrollo)* evolution, development; *(cambio)* change; *(MIL)* manoeuvre; **evolucionar** *vi* to evolve; to manoeuvre.

ex [eks] *a* ex-; **el ~ ministro** the former minister, the ex-minister.

exacerbar [eksaθer'βar] *vt* to irritate, annoy.

exactamente [eksakta'mente] *ad* exactly.

exactitud [eksakti'tuð] *nf* exactness; *(precisión)* accuracy; *(puntualidad)* punctuality; **exacto, a** *a* exact; accurate; punctual; **¡exacto!** exactly!

exageración [eksaxera'θjon] *nf* exaggeration; **exagerar** *vt, vi* to exaggerate.

exaltado, a [eksal'taðo, a] *a (apasionado)* over-excited, worked-up; *(exagerado)* extreme.

exaltar [eksal'tar] *vt* to exalt, glorify; ~**se** *vr (excitarse)* to get excited or worked-up.

examen [ek'samen] *nm* examination.

examinar [eksami'nar] *vt* to examine; ~**se** *vr* to be examined, take an examination.

exasperar [eksaspe'rar] *vt* to exasperate; ~**se** *vr* to get exasperated, lose patience.

Exca. *abr* = **Excelencia**.

excavadora [ekskaβa'ðora] *nf* excavator.

excavar [ekska'βar] *vt* to excavate.

excedente [eksθe'ðente] *a, nm* excess, surplus.

exceder [eksθe'ðer] *vt* to exceed, surpass; to go too far; *(sobrepasarse)* to excel o.s.

excelencia [eksθe'lenθja] *nf* excellence; **E~** Excellency; **excelente** *a* excellent.

excelso, a [eks'θelso, a] *a* lofty, sublime.

excentricidad [eksθentriθi'ðað] *nf* eccentricity; **excéntrico, a** *a, nm/f* eccentric.

excepción [eksθep'θjon] *nf* exception; **excepcional** *a* exceptional.

excepto [eks'θepto] *ad* excepting, except (for).

exceptuar [eksθep'twar] *vt* to except, exclude.

excesivo, a [eksθe'siβo, a] *a* excessive.

exceso [eks'θeso] *nm (gen)* excess; *(COM)* surplus; ~ **de equipaje/peso** excess luggage/weight.

excitación [eksθita'θjon] *nf (sensación)* excitement; *(acción)* excitation.

excitado, a [eksθi'taðo, a] *a* excited; *(emociones)* aroused.

excitar [eksθi'tar] *vt* to excite; *(incitar)* to urge; ~**se** *vr* to get excited.

exclamación [eksklama'θjon] *nf* exclamation; **exclamar** *vi* to exclaim.

excluir [eksklu'ir] *vt* to exclude; *(dejar fuera)* to shut out; *(descartar)* to reject; **exclusión** *nf* exclusion.

exclusiva [eksklu'siβa] *nf (PRENSA)* exclusive, scoop; *(COM)* sole right.

exclusivo, a [eksklu'siβo, a] *a* exclusive; **derecho ~** sole or exclusive right.

Excmo. *abr* = *excelentísimo*.

excomulgar [ekskomul'var] *vt (REL)* to excommunicate.

excomunión [ekskomu'njon] *nf* excommunication.

excursión [ekskur'sjon] *nf* excursion,

outing; **excursionista** *nm/f* (*turista*) sightseer.

excusa [eks'kusa] *nf* excuse; (*disculpa*) apology.

excusar [eksku'sar] *vt* to excuse; (*evitar*) to avoid, prevent; **~se** *vr* (*disculparse*) to apologize.

exento, a [ek'sento, a] *a* exempt.

exequias [ek'sekjas] *nfpl* funeral rites.

exhalar [eksa'lar] *vt* to exhale, breathe out; (*olor etc*) to give off; (*suspiro*) to breathe, heave.

exhausto, a [ek'sausto, a] *a* exhausted.

exhibición [eksiβi'θjon] *nf* exhibition, display, show.

exhibir [eksi'βir] *vt* to exhibit, display, show.

exhortación [eksorta'θjon] *nf* exhortation; **exhortar** *vt*: **exhortar a** to exhort to.

exigencia [eksi'xenθja] *nf* demand, requirement; **exigente** *a* demanding.

exigir [eksi'xir] *vt* (*gen*) to demand, require; **~ el pago** to demand payment.

exiliado, a [eksi'ljaðo, a] *a* exiled // *nm/f* exile.

exilio [ek'siljo] *nm* exile.

eximio, a [ek'simjo, a] *a* (*eminente*) distinguished, eminent.

eximir [eksi'mir] *vt* to exempt.

existencia [eksis'tenθja] *nf* existence; **~s** *nfpl* stock(s) (*pl*).

existir [eksis'tir] *vi* to exist, be.

éxito ['eksito] *nm* (*resultado*) result, outcome; (*triunfo*) success; (*MUS etc*) hit; **tener ~** to be successful.

exonerar [eksone'rar] *vt* to exonerate; **~ de una obligación** to free from an obligation.

exorcizar [eksorθi'θar] *vt* to exorcize.

exótico, a [ek'sotiko, a] *a* exotic.

expandir [ekspan'dir] *vt* to expand.

expansión [ekspan'sjon] *nf* expansion.

expatriarse [ekspa'trjarse] *vr* to emigrate; (*POL*) to go into exile.

expectativa [ekspekta'tiβa] *nf* (*espera*) expectation; (*perspectiva*) prospect.

expedición [ekspeði'θjon] *nf* (*excursión*) expedition.

expediente [ekspe'ðjente] *nm* expedient; (*JUR*: *procedimiento*) action, proceedings *pl*; (*: papeles*) dossier, file, record.

expedir [ekspe'ðir] *vt* (*despachar*) to send, forward; (*pasaporte*) to issue.

expedito, a [ekspe'ðito, a] *a* (*libre*) clear, free.

expendedor, a [ekspende'ðor, a] *nm/f* (*vendedor*) dealer; (*aparato*) (vending) machine; **~ de cigarrillos** cigarette machine.

expendeduría [ekspendedu'ria] *nf* (*estanco*) tobacconist's (shop).

expensas [eks'pensas] *nfpl*: **a ~ de** at the expense of.

experiencia [ekspe'rjenθja] *nf* experience.

experimentado, a [eksperimen'taðo, a] *a* experienced.

experimentar [eksperimen'tar] *vt* (*en laboratorio*) to experiment with; (*probar*) to test, try out; (*notar, observar*) to experience; (*deterioro, pérdida*) to suffer; **experimento** *nm* experiment.

experto, a [eks'perto, a] *a* expert, skilled // *nm/f* expert.

expiar [ekspi'ar] *vt* to atone for.

expirar [ekspi'rar] *vi* to expire.

explayarse [ekspla'jarse] *vr* (*en discurso*) to speak at length; **~ con uno** to confide in sb.

explicación [eksplika'θjon] *nf* explanation; **explicar** *vt* to explain; explicarse *vr* to explain (o.s.).

explícito, a [eks'pliθito, a] *a* explicit.

explique *etc vb ver* **explicar**.

explorador, a [eksplora'ðor, a] *nm/f* (*pionero*) explorer; (*MIL*) scout // *nm* (*MED*) probe; (*TEC*) (radar) scanner.

explorar [eksplo'rar] *vt* to explore; (*MED*) to probe; (*radar*) to scan.

explosión [eksplo'sjon] nf explosion; **explosivo, a** a explosive.

explotación [eksplota'θjon] nf exploitation; (de planta etc) running.

explotar [eksplo'tar] vt to exploit; to run, operate // vi to explode.

exponer [ekspo'ner] vt to expose; (cuadro) to display; (vida) to risk; (idea) to explain; ~se vr: ~se a (hacer) algo to run the risk of (doing) sth.

exportación [eksporta'θjon] nf (acción) export; (mercancías) exports pl; **exportar** vt to export.

exposición [eksposi'θjon] nf (gen) exposure; (de arte) show, exhibition; (explicación) explanation; (narración) account, statement.

expresar [ekspre'sar] vt to express; **expresión** nf expression.

expreso, a pp de expresar // [eks'preso, a] a (explícito) express; (claro) specific, clear; (tren) fast // nm: **mandar** ~ to send by express (delivery).

express [eks'pres] ad (AM): enviar algo ~ to send sth special delivery.

exprimidor [eksprimi'ðor] nm squeezer.

exprimir [ekspri'mir] vt (fruta) to squeeze; (zumo) to squeeze out.

expropiar [ekspro'pjar] vt to expropriate.

expuesto, a [eks'pwesto, a] a exposed; (cuadro etc) on show, on display.

expulsar [ekspul'sar] vt (echar) to eject, throw out; (alumno) to expel; (despedir) to sack, fire; (DEPORTE) to send off; **expulsión** nf expulsion; sending-off.

exquisito, a [ekski'sito, a] a exquisite; (comida) delicious.

éxtasis ['ekstasis] nm ecstasy.

extender [eksten'der] vt to extend; (los brazos) to stretch out, hold out; (mapa, tela) to spread (out), open (out); (mantequilla) to spread; (certificado) to issue; (cheque, recibo) to make out; (documento) to draw up; ~se vr (gen) to extend; (persona: en el suelo) to stretch out; (epidemia) to spread; **extendido, a** a (abierto) spread out, open; (brazos) outstretched; (prevaleciente) widespread.

extensión [eksten'sjon] nf (de terreno, mar) expanse, stretch; (de tiempo) length, duration; (TEL) extension; **en toda la ~ de la palabra** in every sense of the word.

extenso, a [eks'tenso, a] a extensive.

extenuar [ekste'nwar] vt (debilitar) to weaken.

exterior [ekste'rjor] a (de fuera) external; (afuera) outside, exterior; (apariencia) outward; (deuda, relaciones) foreign // nm (gen) exterior, outside; (aspecto) outward appearance; (DEPORTE) wing(er); (países extranjeros) abroad; **en el** ~ abroad; **al** ~ outwardly, on the surface.

exterminar [ekstermi'nar] vt to exterminate; **exterminio** nm extermination.

externo, a [eks'terno, a] a (exterior) external, outside; (superficial) outward // nm/f day pupil.

extinguir [ekstin'gir] vt (fuego) to extinguish, put out; (raza, población) to wipe out; ~se vr (fuego) to go out; (BIO) to die out, become extinct.

extinto, a [eks'tinto, a] a extinct.

extintor [ekstin'tor] nm (fire) extinguisher.

extra ['ekstra] a inv (tiempo) extra; (chocolate, vino) good-quality // nm/f extra // nm extra; (bono) bonus.

extracción [ekstrak'θjon] nf extraction; (en lotería) draw.

extracto [eks'trakto] nm extract.

extraer [ekstra'er] vt to extract, take out.

extralimitarse [ekstralimi'tarse] vr to go too far.

extranjero, a [ekstran'xero] a foreign // nm/f foreigner // nm foreign countries pl; **en el** ~ abroad.

extrañar [ekstra'ɲar] vt (sorprender) to find strange o odd; (echar de menos) to miss; ~se vr (sorprenderse) to be amazed, be surprised; (distanciarse) to become estranged, grow apart.

extrañeza [ekstra'ɲeθa] nf (rareza) strangeness, oddness; (asombro) amazement, surprise.

extraño, a [eks'traɲo, a] a (extranjero) foreign; (raro, sorprendente) strange, odd.

extraordinario, a [ekstraorði'narjo, a] a extraordinary; (edición, número) special // nm (de periódico) special edition; **horas extraordinarias** overtime sg.

extrarradio [ekstra'rraðjo] nm poor suburban area.

extravagancia [ekstraβa'ɣanθja] nf oddness; outlandishness; **extravagante** a (excéntrico) eccentric; (estrafalario) outlandish.

extraviado, a [ekstra'βjaðo, a] a lost, missing.

extraviar [ekstra'βjar] vt (persona: desorientar) to mislead, misdirect; (perder) to lose, misplace; ~se vr to lose one's way, get lost; **extravío** nm loss; (fig) deviation.

extremar [ekstre'mar] vt to carry to extremes; ~se vr to do one's utmost, make every effort.

extremaunción [ekstremaun'θjon] nf extreme unction.

extremidad [ekstremi'ðað] nf (punta) extremity; (fila) edge; ~es nfpl (ANAT) extremities.

extremo, a [eks'tremo, a] a extreme; (último) last // nm end; (límite, grado sumo) extreme; en último ~ as a last resort.

extrovertido, a [ekstroβer'tiðo, a] a, nm/f extrovert.

exuberancia [eksuβe'ranθja] nf exuberance; **exuberante** a exuberant; (fig) luxuriant, lush.

eyacular [ejaku'lar] vt, vi to ejaculate.

F

f.a.b. abr (= franco a bordo) f.o.b.

fábrica ['faβrika] nf factory; **marca de ~** trademark; **precio de ~** factory price.

fabricación [faβrika'θjon] nf (manufactura) manufacture; (producción) production; **de ~ casera** home-made; **~ en serie** mass production.

fabricante [faβri'kante] nm/f manufacturer.

fabricar [faβri'kar] vt (manufacturar) to manufacture, make; (construir) to build; (cuento) to fabricate, devise.

fábula ['faβula] nf (cuento) fable; (chisme) rumour; (mentira) fib.

facción [fak'θjon] nf (POL) faction; **facciones** nfpl (del rostro) features.

fácil ['faθil] a (simple) easy; (probable) likely.

facilidad [faθili'ðað] nf (capacidad) ease; (sencillez) simplicity; (de palabra) fluency; ~es nfpl facilities.

facilitar [faθili'tar] vt (hacer fácil) to make easy; (proporcionar) to provide.

fácilmente [faθil'mente] ad easily.

facsímil [fak'simil] nm facsimile, fax.

factible [fak'tiβle] a feasible.

factor [fak'tor] nm factor.

factura [fak'tura] nf (cuenta) bill; (hechura) manufacture; **facturar** vt (COM) to invoice, charge for; (equipaje) to register (Brit), check (US).

facultad [fakul'tað] nf (aptitud, ESCOL etc) faculty; (poder) power.

facha ['fatʃa] nf (fam: aspecto) look; (: cara) face.

fachada [fa'tʃaða] nf (ARQ) façade, front.

faena [fa'ena] nf (trabajo) work; (quehacer) task, job.

fagot [fa'ɣot] (pl ~es) [fa'ɣot] nm (MUS) bassoon.

faisán [fai'san] nm pheasant.

faja ['faxa] nf (para la cintura) sash;

(*de mujer*) corset; (*de tierra*) strip.

fajo ['faxo] *nm* (*de papeles*) bundle; (*de billetes*) wad.

Falange [fa'lanxe] *nf* (*POL*) Falange.

falda ['falda] *nf* (*prenda de vestir*) skirt.

falo ['falo] *nm* phallus.

falsedad [false'ðað] *nf* falseness; (*hipocresía*) hypocrisy; (*mentira*) falsehood.

falsificar [falsifi'kar] *vt* (*firma etc*) to forge; (*voto etc*) to rig; (*moneda*) to counterfeit.

falso, a ['falso, a] *a* false; (*erróneo*) mistaken; (*documento, moneda etc*) fake; **en ~** falsely.

falta ['falta] *nf* (*defecto*) fault, flaw; (*privación*) lack, want; (*ausencia*) absence; (*carencia*) shortage; (*equivocación*) mistake; (*DEPORTE*) foul; **echar en ~** to miss; **hacer ~ hacer algo** to be necessary to do sth; **me hace falta una pluma** I need a pen.

faltar [fal'tar] *vi* (*escasear*) to be lacking, be wanting; (*ausentarse*) to be absent, be missing; **faltan 2 horas para llegar** there are 2 hours to go till arrival; **~ el respeto a uno** to be disrespectful to sb; **¡no faltaba más!** that's the last straw!

falto, a ['falto, a] *a* (*desposeído*) deficient, lacking; (*necesitado*) poor, wretched.

falla ['faʎa] *nf* (*defecto*) fault, flaw.

fallar [fa'ʎar] *vt* (*JUR*) to pronounce sentence on // *vi* (*memoria*) to fail; (*motor*) to miss.

fallecer [faʎe'θer] *vi* to pass away, die; **fallecimiento** *nm* decease, demise.

fallido, a [fa'ʎiðo, a] *a* (*gen*) frustrated, unsuccessful.

fallo ['faʎo] *nm* (*JUR*) verdict, ruling; (*fracaso*) failure.

fama ['fama] *nf* (*renombre*) fame; (*reputación*) reputation.

famélico, a [fa'meliko, a] *a* starving.

familia [fa'milja] *nf* family.

familiar [fami'ljar] *a* (*relativo a la*

familia) family *cpd*; (*conocido, informal*) familiar // *nm* relative, relation; **~idad** *nf* (*gen*) familiarity; (*informalidad*) homeliness; **~izarse** *vr*: **~izarse con** to familiarize o.s. with.

famoso, a [fa'moso, a] *a* (*renombrado*) famous.

fanático, a [fa'natiko, a] *a* fanatical // *nm/f* fanatic; (*CINE, DEPORTE*) fan; **fanatismo** *nm* fanaticism.

fanfarrón, ona [fanfa'rron, ona] *a* boastful; (*pey*) showy.

fango ['fango] *nm* mud; **~so, a** *a* muddy.

fantasía [fanta'sia] *nf* fantasy, imagination; **joyas de ~** imitation jewellery *sg*.

fantasma [fan'tasma] *nm* (*espectro*) ghost, apparition; (*presumido*) show-off.

fantástico, a [fan'tastiko, a] *a* (*irreal, fam*) fantastic.

farmacéutico, a [farma'θeutiko, a] *a* pharmaceutical // *nm/f* chemist (*Brit*), pharmacist.

farmacia [far'maθja] *nf* chemist's (*shop*) (*Brit*), pharmacy; **~ de turno** duty chemist.

fármaco [far'mako] *nm* drug.

faro ['faro] *nm* (*NAUT: torre*) lighthouse; (*AUTO*) headlamp; (*foco*) floodlight; **~s antiniebla** fog lamps; **~s delanteros/traseros** headlights/rear lights.

farol [fa'rol] *nm* lantern, lamp.

farola [fa'rola] *nf* street lamp (*Brit*) o light (*US*).

farsa ['farsa] *nf* farce.

farsante [far'sante] *nm/f* fraud, fake.

fascículo [fas'θikulo] *nm* (*de revista*) part, instalment.

fascinar [fasθi'nar] *vt* (*gen*) to fascinate.

fascismo [fas'θismo] *nm* fascism; **fascista** *a, nm/f* fascist.

fase ['fase] *nf* phase.

fastidiar [fasti'ðjar] *vt* (*disgustar*) to annoy, bother; (*estropear*) to spoil; **~se** *vr* (*disgustarse*) to get annoyed o cross; **¡que se fastidie!** (fam) he'll just have to put up with it!

fastidio [fas'tiðjo] nm (disgusto) annoyance; **~so, a** a (molesto) annoying.

fatal [fa'tal] a (gen) fatal; (desgraciado) ill-fated; (fam: malo, pésimo) awful; **~idad** nf (destino) fate; (mala suerte) misfortune.

fatiga [fa'tixa] nf (cansancio) fatigue, weariness.

fatigar [fati'xar] vt to tire, weary; **~se** vr to get tired.

fatigoso, a [fati'xoso, a] a (cansador) tiring.

fatuo, a ['fatwo, a] a (vano) fatuous; (presuntuoso) conceited.

fauces ['fauθes] nfpl jaws, mouth sg.

favor [fa'βor] nm favour; **estar a ~ de** to be in favour of; **haga el ~ de...** would you be so good as to..., kindly...; **por ~** please; **~able** a favourable.

favorecer [faβore'θer] vt to favour; (vestido etc) to become, flatter; **este peinado le favorece** this hairstyle suits him.

favorito, a [faβo'rito, a] a, nm/f favourite.

faz [faθ] nf face; **la ~ de la tierra** the face of the earth.

fe [fe] nf (REL) faith; (confianza) belief; (documento) certificate; **prestar ~ a** to believe, credit; **actuar con buena/mala ~** to act in good/ bad faith; **dar ~ de** to bear witness to.

fealdad [feal'dað] nf ugliness.

febrero [fe'βrero] nm February.

fecundar [fekun'dar] vt (generar) to fertilize, make fertile; **fecundo, a** a (fértil) fertile; (fig) prolific; (productivo) productive.

fecha ['fetʃa] nf date; **~ de caducidad, ~ límite de venta** (de producto alimenticio) sell-by date; **en ~ próxima** soon; **hasta la ~** so far; **poner ~** to date; **fechar** vt to date.

federación [federa'θjon] nf federa-

tion.

federal [feðe'ral] a federal.

felicidad [feliθi'ðað] nf (satisfacción, contento) happiness; **~es** nfpl best wishes, congratulations.

felicitación [feliθita'θjon] nf: **¡felicitaciones!** congratulations!

felicitar [feliθi'tar] vt to congratulate.

feligrés, esa [feli'xres, esa] nm/f parishioner.

feliz [fe'liθ] a (contento) happy; (afortunado) lucky.

felpudo [fel'puðo] nm doormat.

femenino, a [feme'nino, a] a, nm feminine.

feminista [femi'nista] a, nm/f feminist.

fenómeno [fe'nomeno] nm phenomenon; (fig) freak, accident // a great // excl great!, marvellous!

feo, a ['feo, a] a (gen) ugly; (desagradable) bad, nasty.

féretro ['feretro] nm (ataúd) coffin; (sarcófago) bier.

feria ['ferja] nf (gen) fair; (descanso) holiday, rest day; (AM: mercado) village market; (: cambio) loose or small change.

fermentar [fermen'tar] vi to ferment.

ferocidad [feroθi'ðað] nf fierceness, ferocity.

feroz [fe'roθ] a (cruel) cruel; (salvaje) fierce.

férreo, a [fe'rreo, a] a iron.

ferretería [ferrete'ria] nf (tienda) ironmonger's (shop) (Brit), hardware store.

ferrocarril [ferroka'rril] nm railway.

ferroviario, a [ferro'βjarjo, a] a rail cpd.

fértil ['fertil] a (productivo) fertile; (rico) rich; **fertilidad** nf (gen) fertility; (productividad) fruitfulness.

fertilizar [fertili'θar] vt to fertilize.

fervor [fer'βor] nm fervour; **~oso, a** a fervent.

festejar [feste'xar] vt (agasajar) to wine and dine; (galantear) to court; (celebrar) to celebrate; **festejo** nm (diversión) entertainment; (galanteo) courtship; (fiesta) celebration.

festividad [festiβi'ðað] nf festivity.

festivo, a [fes'tiβo, a] a (de fiesta) festive; (fig) witty; (CINE, LITERATURA) humorous; **día** ~ holiday.

fétido, a ['fetiðo, a] a (hediondo) foul-smelling.

feto ['feto] nm foetus.

fiable ['fjaβle] a (persona) trustworthy; (máquina) reliable.

fiador, a [fia'ðor, a] nm/f (JUR) surety, guarantor; (COM) backer; **salir** ~ **por alguien** to stand bail for sb.

fiambre ['fjambre] nm cold meat.

fianza ['fjanθa] nf surety; (JUR): **libertad bajo** ~ release on bail.

fiar [fi'ar] vt (salir garante de) to guarantee; (vender a crédito) to sell on credit; (secreto) to confide (a to) // vi to trust; ~**se** vr to trust (in), rely on; ~**se de uno** to rely on sb.

fibra ['fiβra] nf fibre; ~ **óptica** optical fibre.

ficción [fik'θjon] nf fiction.

ficticio, a [fik'tiθjo, a] a (imaginario) fictitious; (falso) fabricated.

ficha ['fitʃa] nf (TEL) token; (en juegos) counter, marker; (tarjeta) (index) card; **fichar** vt (archivar) to file, index; (DEPORTE) to sign; **estar fichado** to have a record; **fichero** nm box file; (INFORM) file.

fidelidad [fiðeli'ðað] nf (lealtad) fidelity, loyalty; **alta** ~ high fidelity, hi-fi.

fideos [fi'ðeos] nmpl noodles.

fiebre ['fjeβre] nf (MED) fever; (fig) fever, excitement; ~ **amarilla/del heno** yellow/hay fever; ~ **palúdica** malaria; **tener** ~ to have a temperature.

fiel [fjel] a (leal) faithful, loyal; (fiable) reliable; (exacto) accurate, faithful // nm: **los** ~**es** the faithful.

fieltro ['fjeltro] nm felt.

fiero, a ['fjero, a] a (cruel) cruel; (feroz) fierce; (duro) harsh // nf (animal feroz) wild animal o beast; (fig) dragon // nm/f (fig) fiend.

fiesta ['fjesta] nf party; (de pueblo)

festival; (vacaciones, tb: ~s) holiday sg; (REL): ~ **de guardar** day of obligation.

figura [fi'ɣura] nf (gen) figure; (forma, imagen) shape, form; (NAIPES) face card.

figurar [fiɣu'rar] vt (representar) to represent; (fingir) to figure // vi to figure; ~**se** vr (imaginarse) to imagine; (suponer) to suppose.

fijador, a [fixa'ðor] nm (FOTO etc) fixative; (de pelo) gel.

fijar [fi'xar] vt (gen) to fix; (estampilla) to affix, stick (on); (fig) to settle (on), decide; ~**se** vr: ~**se en** to notice.

fijo, a ['fixo, a] a (gen) fixed; (firme) firm; (permanente) permanent // ad: **mirar** ~ to stare.

fila ['fila] nf row; (MIL) rank; (cadena) line; **ponerse en** ~ to line up, get into line.

filántropo, a [fi'lantropo, a] nm/f philanthropist.

filatelia [fila'telja] nf philately, stamp collecting.

filete [fi'lete] nm (carne) fillet steak; (pescado) fillet.

filial [fi'ljal] a filial // nf subsidiary.

Filipinas [fili'pinas] nfpl: **las** ~ **the** Philippines; **filipino, a**, a nm/f Philippine.

filmar [fil'mar] vt to film, shoot.

filo ['filo] nm (gen) edge; **sacar** ~ **a** to sharpen; **al** ~ **del mediodía** at about midday; **de doble** ~ double-edged.

filón [fi'lon] nm (MINERÍA) vein, lode; (fig) goldmine.

filosofía [filoso'fia] nf philosophy; **filósofo, a** nm/f philosopher.

filtrar [fil'trar] vt, vi to filter, strain; ~**se** vr to filter; (fig: dinero) to dwindle; **filtro** nm (TEC, utensilio) filter.

fin [fin] nm end; (objetivo) aim, purpose; **al** ~ **y al cabo** when all's said and done; **a** ~ **de** in order to; **por** ~ finally; **en** ~ in short; ~ **de semana** weekend.

final [fi'nal] *a* final // *nm* end, conclusion // *nf* final; **~idad** *nf* (*propósito*) purpose, intention; **~ista** *nmf* finalist; **~izar** *vt* to end, finish; (*INFORM*) to log out o off // *vi* to end, come to an end.

financiar [finan'θjar] *vt* to finance; **financiero, a** *a* financial // *nmf* financier.

finca ['finka] *nf* country estate; (*AM*) farm.

fingir [fin'xir] *vt* (*simular*) to simulate, feign; (*pretextar*) to sham, fake // *vi* (*aparentar*) to pretend; **~se** *vr* to pretend to be.

finlandés, esa [finlan'des, esa] *a* Finnish // *nmf* Finn // *nm* (*LING*) Finnish.

Finlandia [fin'landja] *nf* Finland.

fino, a ['fino, a] *a* fine; (*delgado*) slender; (*de buenas maneras*) polite, refined; (*jerez*) fino, dry.

firma ['firma] *nf* signature; (*COM*) firm, company; **firmar** *vt* to sign.

firme ['firme] *a* firm; (*estable*) stable; (*sólido*) solid; (*constante*) steady; (*decidido*) resolute // *nm* road (surface); **~mente** *ad* firmly; **~za** *nf* firmness; (*constancia*) steadiness; (*solidez*) solidity.

fiscal [fis'kal] *a* fiscal // *nmf* public prosecutor; **año ~** tax o fiscal year.

fisco ['fisko] *nm* (*hacienda*) treasury, exchequer (*Brit*).

fisgar [fis'var] *vt* to pry into.

físico, a ['fisiko, a] *a* physical // *nm* physique // *nmf* physicist // *nf* physics *sg*.

flaco, a ['flako, a] *a* (*muy delgado*) skinny, thin; (*débil*) weak, feeble.

flagrante [fla'vrante] *a* flagrant.

flamante [fla'mante] *a* (*fam*) brilliant; (: *nuevo*) brand-new.

flamenco, a [fla'menko, a] *a* (*de Flandes*) Flemish; (*baile, música*) flamenco // *nm* (*baile, música*) flamenco.

flan [flan] *nm* creme caramel.

flaqueza [fla'keθa] *nf* (*delgadez*) thinness, leanness; (*fig*) weakness.

flash [flaʃ] (*pl* ~**s** o ~**es**) *nm* (*FOTO*) flash.

flauta ['flauta] *nf* (*MUS*) flute.

fleco ['fleko] *nm* fringe.

flecha ['fletʃa] *nf* arrow.

flema ['flema] *nm* phlegm.

flequillo [fle'kiʎo] *nm* (*pelo*) fringe.

flete ['flete] *nm* (*carga*) freight; (*alquiler*) charter; (*precio*) freight-age.

flexible [flek'sißle] *a* flexible.

flipper ['fliper] *nm* pinball (machine).

flojera [flo'xera] *nf* (*AM fam*): **me da ~** I can't be bothered.

flojo, a ['floxo, a] *a* (*gen*) loose; (*sin fuerzas*) limp; (*débil*) weak.

flor [flor] *nf* flower; (*piropo*) compliment; **a ~ de** on the surface of; **~ecer** *vi* (*BOT*) to flower, bloom; (*fig*) to flourish; **~eciente** *a* (*BOT*) in flower, flowering; (*fig*) thriving; **~ero** *nm* vase; **~ista** *nmf* florist.

flota ['flota] *nf* fleet.

flotador [flota'ðor] *nm* (*gen*) float; (*para nadar*) rubber ring.

flotar [flo'tar] *vi* (*gen*) to float; **flote**: **a ~** afloat; **sacar a flote** (*fig*) to get back on one's feet.

fluctuar [fluk'twar] *vi* (*oscilar*) to fluctuate.

fluidez [flui'ðeθ] *nf* fluidity; (*fig*) fluency.

fluido, a [flu'iðo, a] *a, nm* fluid.

fluir [flu'ir] *vi* to flow.

flujo ['fluxo] *nm* flow; **~ y reflujo** ebb and flow; **~ de sangre** (*MED*) loss of blood; **~grama** *nm* flowchart.

foca ['foka] *nf* seal.

foco ['foko] *nm* focus; (*ELEC*) floodlight; (*AM*) (light) bulb.

fogón [fo'von] *nm* (*de cocina*) ring, burner.

fogoso, a [fo'voso, a] *a* spirited.

follaje [fo'ʎaxe] *nm* foliage.

folleto [fo'ʎeto] *nm* pamphlet.

follón [fo'ʎon] *nm* (*fam*: *lío*) mess; (: *conmoción*) fuss; **armar un ~** to kick up a row.

fomentar [fomen'tar] *vt* (*MED*) to

foment; **fomento** nm (promoción) promotion.

fonda ['fonda] nf inn.

fondo ['fondo] nm (de mar) bottom; (de coche, sala) back; (ARTE etc) background; (reserva) fund; ~s nmpl (COM) funds, resources; **una investigación a ~** a thorough investigation; **en el ~** at bottom, deep down.

fono ['fono] nm (AM) telephone number.

fontanería [fontane'ria] nf plumbing; **fontanero, a** nm/f plumber.

forastero, a [foras'tero, a] nm/f stranger.

forcejear [forθexe'ar] vi (luchar) to struggle.

forjar [for'xar] vt to forge.

forma ['forma] nf (figura) form, shape; (molde) mould, pattern; (MED) fitness; (método) way, means; **las ~s** the conventions; **estar en ~** to be fit.

formación [forma'θjon] nf (gen) formation; (educación) education; **~ profesional** vocational training.

formal [for'mal] a (gen) formal; (fig: persona) serious; (: de fiar) reliable; **~idad** nf formality; seriousness; **~izar** vt (JUR) to formalize; (situación) to put in order, regularize; **~izarse** vr (situación) to be put in order, be regularized.

formar [for'mar] vt (componer) to form, shape; (constituir) to make up, constitute; (ESCOL) to train, educate; **~se** vr (ESCOL) to be trained, educated; (cobrar forma) to form, take form; (desarrollarse) to develop.

formatear [formate'ar] vt to format.

formidable [formi'ðaßle] a (temible) formidable; (asombroso) tremendous.

formulario [formu'larjo] nm form.

fornido, a [for'niðo, a] a well-built.

foro ['foro] nm (gen) forum; (JUR) court.

forrar [fo'rrar] vt (abrigo) to line; (li-

bro) to cover; **forro** nm (de cuaderno) cover; (COSTURA) lining; (de sillón) upholstery.

fortalecer [fortale'θer] vt to strengthen.

fortaleza [forta'leθa] nf (MIL) fortress, stronghold; (fuerza) strength; (determinación) resolution.

fortuito, a [for'twito, a] a accidental.

fortuna [for'tuna] nf (suerte) fortune, (good) luck; (riqueza) fortune, wealth.

forzar [for'θar] vt (puerta) to force (open); (compeler) to compel.

forzoso, a [for'θoso, a] a necessary.

fosa ['fosa] nf (sepultura) grave; (en tierra) pit; (MED) cavity.

fósforo ['fosforo] nm (QUÍMICA) phosphorus; (AM) match.

foso ['foso] nm ditch; (TEATRO) pit; (AUTO): **~ de reconocimiento** inspection pit.

foto ['foto] nf photo, snap(shot); **sacar una ~** to take a photo o picture.

fotocopia [foto'kopja] nf photocopy; **~copiadora** nf photocopier; **~copiar** vt to photocopy.

fotografía [fotovra'fia] nf (ARTE) photography; (una ~) photograph; **fotografiar** vt to photograph.

fotógrafo, a [fo'tovrafo, a] nm/f photographer.

fracaso [fra'kaso] nm (desgracia, revés) failure; **fracasar** vi (gen) to fail.

fracción [frak'θjon] nf fraction; (POL) faction; **fraccionamiento** nm (AM) housing estate.

fractura [frak'tura] nf fracture, break.

fragancia [fra'vanθja] nf (olor) fragrance, perfume.

frágil ['fraxil] a (débil) fragile; (COM) breakable.

fragmento [frav'mento] nm (pedazo) fragment.

fragua ['fravwa] nf forge; **fraguar** vt to forge; (fig) to concoct // vi to harden.

fraile ['fraile] nm (REL) friar; (: monje) monk.

frambuesa [fram'bwesa] nf raspberry.

francés, esa [fran'θes, esa] a French // nm/f Frenchman/woman // nm (LING) French.

Francia ['franθja] nf France.

franco, a ['franko, a] a (cándido) frank, open; (COM: exento) free // nm (moneda) franc.

francotirador, a [frankotira'ðor, a] nm/f sniper.

franela [fra'nela] nf flannel.

franja ['franxa] nf fringe.

franquear [franke'ar] vt (camino) to clear; (carta, paquete postal) to frank, stamp; (obstáculo) to overcome.

franqueo [fran'keo] nm postage.

franqueza [fran'keθa] nf (candor) frankness.

frasco ['frasko] nm bottle, flask; ~ al vacío (vacuum) flask.

frase ['frase] nf sentence; ~ hecha set phrase.

fraude ['frauðe] nm (cualidad) dishonesty; (acto) fraud; **fraudulento, a** a fraudulent.

frazada [fra'saða] nf (AM) blanket.

frecuencia [fre'kwenθja] nf frequency; **con** ~ frequently, often.

fregadero [freɣa'ðero] nm (kitchen) sink.

fregar [fre'ɣar] vt (frotar) to scrub; (platos) to wash (up); (AM) to annoy.

fregona [fre'ɣona] nf (utensilio) mop; (pey: sirvienta) skivvy.

freír [fre'ir] vt to fry.

frenar [fre'nar] vt to brake; (fig) to check.

frenesí [frene'si] nm frenzy; **frenético, a** a frantic.

freno ['freno] nm (TEC, AUTO) brake; (de cabalgadura) bit; (fig) check.

frente ['frente] nm (ARQ, POL) front; (de objeto) front part // nf forehead, brow; ~ a in front of; (en situación opuesta a) opposite; **al** ~ **de** (fig) at the head of; **chocar de** ~ to crash head-on; **hacer** ~ **a** to face up to.

fresa ['fresa] nf (Esp) strawberry.

fresco, a ['fresko, a] a (nuevo) fresh; (frío) cool // nm (aire) fresh air; (ARTE) fresco; (AM: jugo) fruit drink // nm/f (fam) shameless person; (persona insolente) impudent person; **tomar el** ~ to get some fresh air; **frescura** nf freshness; (descaro) cheek, nerve; (calma) calmness.

frialdad [frial'dað] nf (gen) coldness; (indiferencia) indifference.

fricción [frik'θjon] nf (gen) friction; (acto) rub(bing); (MED) massage.

frigidez [frixi'ðeθ] nf frigidity.

frigorífico [friɣo'rifiko] nm refrigerator.

frijol [fri'xol] nm kidney bean.

frío, a etc vb ver **freír** // ['frio, a] a cold; (indiferente) indifferent // nm cold; indifference.

frito, a ['frito, a] a fried; **me trae ~ ese hombre** I'm sick and tired of that man.

frívolo, a ['friβolo, a] a frivolous.

frontera [fron'tera] nf frontier; **fronterizo, a** a frontier cpd; (contiguo) bordering.

frontón [fron'ton] nm (DEPORTE: cancha) pelota court; (: juego) pelota.

frotar [fro'tar] vt to rub; **~se** vr: **~se las manos** to rub one's hands.

fructífero, a [fruk'tifero, a] a fruitful.

frugal [fru'ɣal] a frugal.

fruncir [frun'θir] vt to pucker; (COSTURA) to pleat; ~ **el ceño** to knit one's brow.

frustrar [frus'trar] vt to frustrate.

fruta ['fruta] nf fruit; **frutería** nf fruit shop; **frutero, a** a fruit cpd // nm/f fruiterer // nm fruit bowl.

frutilla [fru'tiʎa] nf (AM) strawberry.

fue vb ver **ser, ir.**

fuego ['fweɣo] nm (gen) fire; a ~ lento on a low flame o gas; ¿tienes ~? have you (got) a light?

fuente ['fwente] nf fountain; (manantial, fig) spring; (origen) source; (plato) large dish.

fuera etc vb ver **ser, ir** // ['fwera] ad out(side); (en otra parte) away; (excepto, salvo) except, save // prep: ~ de outside; (fig) besides; ~ de sí beside o.s.

fuerte ['fwerte] a strong; (golpe) hard; (ruido) loud; (comida) rich; (lluvia) heavy; (dolor) intense // ad strongly; hard; loud(ly).

fuerza etc vb ver **forzar** // ['fwerθa] nf (fortaleza) strength; (TEC, ELEC) power; (coacción) force; (MIL: tb: ~s) forces pl; a ~ de by dint of; cobrar ~s to recover one's strength; tener ~s para to have the strength to; a la ~ forcibly, by force; por ~ of necessity.

fuga ['fuɣa] nf (huída) flight, escape; (de gas etc) leak.

fugarse [fu'ɣarse] vr to flee, escape.

fugaz [fu'ɣaθ] a fleeting.

fugitivo, a [fuxi'tiβo, a] a, nm/f fugitive.

fui vb ver **ser, ir.**

fulano, a [fu'lano, a] nm/f so-and-so, what's-his-name/what's-her-name.

fulgor [ful'ɣor] nm brilliance.

fumador, a [fuma'ðor, a] nm/f smoker.

fumar [fu'mar] vt, vi to smoke; ~se vr (disipar) to squander; ~ en pipa to smoke a pipe.

funámbulista [funambu'lista] nm/f tightrope walker.

función [fun'θjon] nf function; (de puesto) duties pl; (espectáculo) show; **entrar en funciones** to take up one's duties.

funcionar [funθjo'nar] vi (gen) to function; (máquina) to work; **'no funciona'** 'out of order'.

funcionario, a [funθjo'narjo, a] nm/f official; (público) civil servant.

funda ['funda] nf (gen) cover; (de almohada) pillowcase.

fundación [funda'θjon] nf foundation.

fundamental [fundamen'tal] a fundamental, basic.

fundamentar [fundamen'tar] vt (poner base) to lay the foundations of; (establecer) to found; (fig) to base; **fundamento** nm (base) foundation.

fundar [fun'dar] vt to found; ~se vr: ~se en to be founded on.

fundición [fundi'θjon] nf fusing; (fábrica) foundry.

fundir [fun'dir] vt (gen) to fuse; (metal) to smelt, melt down; (nieve etc) to melt; (COM) to merge; (estatua) to cast; ~se vr (colores etc) to merge, blend; (unirse) to fuse together; (ELEC: fusible, lámpara etc) to fuse, blow; (nieve etc) to melt.

fúnebre ['funeβre] a funeral cpd, funereal.

funeral [fune'ral] nm funeral.

furgón [fur'ɣon] nm wagon; **furgoneta** nf (AUTO, COM) (transit) van (Brit), pick-up (truck) (US).

furia ['furja] nf (ira) fury; (violencia) violence; **furibundo, a** a furious; **furioso, a** a (iracundo) furious; (violento) violent; **furor** nm (cólera) rage.

furúnculo [fu'runkulo] nm boil.

fusible [fu'siβle] nm fuse.

fusil [fu'sil] nm rifle; ~ar vt to shoot.

fusión [fu'sjon] nf (gen) melting; (unión) fusion; (COM) merger.

fusta ['fusta] nf (látigo) riding crop.

fútbol ['futβol] nm football; **futbolista** nm footballer.

fútil ['futil] a trifling; **futilidad** nf triviality.

futuro, a [fu'turo, a] a, nm future.

G

gabán [ga'βan] nm overcoat.

gabardina [gaβar'ðina] nf raincoat.

gabardine.

gabinete [gaβi'nete] nm (POL) cabinet; (estudio) study; (de abogados etc) office.

gaceta [ga'θeta] nf gazette.

gachas ['gatʃas] nfpl porridge sg.

gafar [ga'far] vt to jinx.

gafas ['gafas] nfpl glasses; ~ de sol sunglasses.

gafe ['gafe] nm jinx.

gaita ['gaita] nf bagpipes pl.

gajes ['gaxes] nmpl: los ~ del oficio occupational hazards.

gajo ['gaxo] nm (de naranja) segment.

gala ['gala] nf (traje de etiqueta) full dress; (fig: lo mejor) cream, flower; ~s nfpl finery sg; estar de ~ to be in one's best clothes; **hacer** ~ **de** to display, show off.

galán [ga'lan] nm lover; (Don Juan) ladies' man; (TEATRO): **primer** ~ leading man.

galante [ga'lante] a gallant; **galantear** vt (hacer la corte a) to court, woo; **galantería** nf (caballerosidad) gallantry; (cumplido) politeness; (comentario) compliment.

galápago [ga'lapaxo] nm (ZOOL) turtle.

galaxia [ga'laksja] nf galaxy.

galera [ga'lera] nf (nave) galley; (carro) wagon; (IMPRENTA) galley.

galería [gale'ria] nf (gen) gallery; (balcón) veranda(h); (pasillo) corridor.

Gales ['gales] nm (tb: País de ~) Wales; **galés, esa** a Welsh // nm Welshman/woman // nm (LING) Welsh.

galgo, a ['galxo, a] nm/f greyhound.

galimatías [galima'tias] nmpl (lenguaje) gibberish sg, nonsense sg.

galón [ga'lon] nm (MIL) stripe; (COSTURA) braid; (medida) gallon.

galopar [galo'par] vi to gallop.

gallardía [gaʎar'ðia] nf (galantería) dash; (valor) bravery; (elegancia) elegance.

gallego, a [ga'ʎexo, a] a, nm/f Galician.

galleta [ga'ʎeta] nf biscuit (Brit), cookie (US).

gallina [ga'ʎina] nf hen // nm/f (fam: cobarde) chicken.

gallo ['gaʎo] nm cock, rooster.

gama ['gama] nf (fig) range.

gamba ['gamba] nf prawn (Brit), shrimp (US).

gamberro, a [gam'berro, a] nm/f hooligan, lout.

gamuza [ga'muθa] nf chamois.

gana ['gana] nf (deseo) desire, wish; (apetito) appetite; (voluntad) will; (añoranza) longing; **de buena** ~ willingly; **de mala** ~ reluctantly; **me da** ~s **de** I feel like, I want to; **no me da la** ~ I don't feel like it; **tener** ~s **de** to feel like.

ganadería [ganaðe'ria] nf (ganado) livestock; (ganado vacuno) cattle pl; (cría, comercio) cattle raising.

ganado [ga'naðo] nm livestock; ~ **lanar** sheep pl; ~ **mayor** cattle pl; ~ **porcino** pigs pl.

ganador, a [gana'ðor, a] a winning // nm/f winner.

ganancia [ga'nanθja] nf (lo ganado) gain; (aumento) increase; (beneficio) profit; ~s nfpl (ingresos) earnings; (beneficios) profit sg, winnings.

ganar [ga'nar] vt (obtener) to get, obtain; (sacar ventaja) to gain; (salario etc) to earn; (DEPORTE, premio) to win; (derrotar a) to beat; (alcanzar) to reach // vi (DEPORTE) to win; ~**se** vr: ~**se la vida** to earn one's living.

gancho ['gantʃo] nm (gen) hook; (colgador) hanger.

gandul, a [gan'dul, a] a, nm/f goodfor-nothing, layabout.

ganga ['ganga] nf (cosa buena y barata) bargain; (buena situación) cushy job.

gangrena [gan'grena] nf gangrene.

gansada [gan'saða] nf (fam) stupid thing to do.

ganso, a ['ganso, a] nm/f (ZOOL) goose; (fam) idiot.

ganzúa [gan'θua] nf skeleton key.

garabatear [garaßate'ar] vi, vt (al escribir) to scribble, scrawl.

garabato [gara'ßato] nm (escritura) scrawl, scribble.

garaje [ga'raxe] nm garage.

garante [ga'rante] a responsible // nmf guarantor.

garantía [garan'tia] nf guarantee.

garantizar [garanti'θar] vt (hacerse responsable de) to vouch for; (asegurar) to guarantee.

garbanzo [gar'ßanθo] nm chickpea (Brit), garbanzo (US).

garbo ['garßo] nm grace, elegance.

garfio ['garfjo] nm grappling iron.

garganta [gar'xanta] nf (ANAT) throat; (de botella) neck; **gargantilla** nf necklace.

gárgaras ['garyaras] nfpl: **hacer ~** to gargle.

garita [ga'rita] nf cabin, hut; (MIL) sentry box.

garito [ga'rito] nm (lugar) gambling house o den.

garra ['garra] nf (de gato, TEC) claw; (de ave) talon; (fam) hand, paw.

garrafa [ga'rrafa] nf carafe, decanter.

garrapata [garra'pata] nf tick.

garrapatear [garrapate'ar] vi, vt = **garabatear**.

garrote [ga'rrote] nm (palo) stick; (porra) cudgel; (suplicio) garrotte.

garúa [ga'rua] nf (AM) drizzle.

garza ['garθa] nf heron.

gas [gas] nm gas.

gasa ['gasa] nf gauze.

gaseoso, a [gase'oso, a] a gassy, fizzy // nf lemonade, pop (Brit).

gasfitero [gasfi'tero] nm (AM) plumber.

gasoil [ga'soil], **gasóleo** [ga'soleo] nm diesel (oil).

gasolina [gaso'lina] nf petrol, gas(oline) (US); **gasolinera** nf petrol (Brit) o gas (US) station.

gastado, a [gas'taðo, a] a (rendido) spent; (raído) worn out; (usado: frase etc) trite.

gastar [gas'tar] vt (dinero, tiempo) to spend; (fuerzas) to use up;

(desperdiciar) to waste; (llevar) to wear; **~se** vr to wear out; (estropearse) to waste; **~ bromas** to crack jokes; **¿qué número gastas?** what size (shoe) do you take?

gasto ['gasto] nm (desembolso) expenditure, spending; (consumo, uso) use; **~s** nmpl (desembolsos) expenses; (cargos) charges, costs.

gatear [gate'ar] vi (andar a gatas) to go on all fours.

gatillo [ga'tiλo] nm (de arma de fuego) trigger; (de dentista) forceps.

gato, a ['gato, a] nm/f cat // nm (TEC) jack; **andar a gatas** to go on all fours.

gaveta [ga'ßeta] nf drawer.

gaviota [ga'ßjota] nf seagull.

gay [ge] a inv, nm gay, homosexual.

gazapo [ga'θapo] nm young rabbit.

gazpacho [gaθ'patʃo] nm gazpacho.

gelatina [xela'tina] nf jelly; (polvos etc) gelatine.

gema ['xema] nf gem.

gemelo, a [xe'melo, a] a, nm/f twin; **~s** nmpl (de camisa) cufflinks; **~s de campo** field glasses, binoculars.

Géminis ['xeminis] nm Gemini.

gemido [xe'miðo] nm (quejido) moan, groan; (aullido) howl.

gemir [xe'mir] vi (quejarse) to moan, groan; (aullar) to howl.

generación [xenera'θjon] nf generation.

general [xene'ral] a general // nm general; **por lo o en ~** in general; **G~itat** nf Catalan parliament; **~izar** vt to generalize; **~izarse** vr to become generalized, spread; **~mente** ad generally.

generar [xene'rar] vt to generate.

género ['xenero] nm (clase) kind, sort; (tipo) type; (BIO) genus; (LING) gender; (COM) material; **~ humano** human race.

generosidad [xenerosi'ðað] nf generosity; **generoso, a** a generous.

genial [xe'njal] a inspired; (idea) brilliant; (afable) genial.

genio ['xenjo] nm (carácter) nature,

disposition; (*humor*) temper; (*facultad creadora*) genius; **de mal ~** bad-tempered.

genitales [xeni'tales] *nmpl* genitals.

gente ['xente] *nf* (*personas*) people *pl*; (*raza*) race; (*nación*) nation; (*parientes*) relatives *pl*.

gentil [xen'til] *a* (*elegante*) graceful; (*encantador*) charming; **~eza** *nf* grace; charm; (*cortesía*) courtesy.

gentío [xen'tio] *nm* crowd, throng.

genuino [xe'nwino, a] *a* genuine.

geografía [xeovra'fia] *nf* geography.

geología [xeolo'xia] *nf* geology.

geometría [xeome'tria] *nf* geometry.

gerencia [xe'renθja] *nf* management; **gerente** *nmf* (*supervisor*) manager; (*jefe*) director.

geriatría [xeria'tria] *nf* (*MED*) geriatrics *sg*.

germen ['xermen] *nm* germ.

germinar [xermi'nar] *vi* to germinate.

gesticulación [xestikula'θjon] *nf* gesticulation; (*mueca*) grimace.

gestión [xes'tjon] *nf* management; (*diligencia, acción*) negotiation; **gestionar** *vt* (*lograr*) to try to arrange; (*llevar*) to manage.

gesto ['xesto] *nm* (*mueca*) grimace; (*ademán*) gesture.

Gibraltar [xiβral'tar] *nm* Gibraltar; **gibraltareño, a** *a*, *nmf* Gibraltarian.

gigante [xi'vante] *a*, *nmf* giant.

gilipollas [xili'poʎas] (*fam*) *a inv* daft // *nmf inv* wally.

gimnasia [xim'nasja] *nf* gymnastics *pl*; **gimnasio** *nm* gymnasium; **gimnasta** *nmf* gymnast.

gimotear [ximote'ar] *vi* to whine, whimper.

ginebra [xi'neβra] *nf* gin.

ginecólogo, a [xine'koloxo, a] *nmf* gynecologist.

gira ['xira] *nf* tour, trip.

girar [xi'rar] *vt* (*dar la vuelta*) to turn (around); (: *rápidamente*) to spin; (*COM*: *giro postal*) to draw; (*comerciar*: *letra de cambio*) to issue

// *vi* to turn (round); (*rápido*) to spin; (*COM*) to draw.

girasol [xira'sol] *nm* sunflower.

giratorio, a [xira'torjo, a] *a* (*gen*) revolving; (*puente*) swing.

giro ['xiro] *nm* (*movimiento*) turn, revolution; (*LING*) expression; (*COM*) draft; **~ bancario/postal** bank giro/postal order.

gis [xis] *nm* (*AM*) chalk.

gitano, a [xi'tano, a] *a*, *nmf* gypsy.

glacial [gla'θjal] *a* icy, freezing.

glaciar [gla'θjar] *nm* glacier.

glándula ['glandula] *nf* gland.

globo ['gloβo] *nm* (*esfera*) globe, sphere; (*aerostato, juguete*) balloon.

glóbulo ['gloβulo] *nm* globule; (*ANAT*) corpuscle.

gloria ['glorja] *nf* glory.

glorieta [glo'rjeta] *nf* (*de jardín*) bower, arbour; (*plazoleta*) roundabout (*Brit*), traffic circle (*US*).

glorificar [glorifi'kar] *vt* (*enaltecer*) to glorify, praise.

glorioso, a [glo'rjoso, a] *a* glorious.

glosa ['glosa] *nf* comment; **glosar** *vt* (*comentar*) to comment on.

glosario [glo'sarjo] *nm* glossary.

glotón, ona [glo'ton, ona] *a* gluttonous, greedy // *nmf* glutton.

gobernación [goβerna'θjon] *nf* government, governing; **G~** (*AM ADMIN*) Ministry of the Interior; **gobernador, a** *a* governing // *nmf* governor; **gobernante** *a* governing.

gobernar [goβer'nar] *vt* (*dirigir*) to guide, direct; (*POL*) to rule, govern // *vi* to govern; (*NAUT*) to steer.

gobierno *etc vb ver* **gobernar** // [go'βjerno] *nm* (*POL*) government; (*dirección*) guidance, direction; (*NAUT*) steering.

goce *etc vb ver* **gozar** // ['goθe] *nm* enjoyment.

gol [gol] *nm* goal.

golf [golf] *nm* golf.

golfo, a ['golfo, a] *nm* (*GEO*) gulf // *nmf* (*fam*: *niño*) urchin; (*gamberro*) lout // *nf* (*fam*: *mujer*) slut, whore.

golondrina [golon'drina] *nf* swallow.

golosina [golo'sina] nf titbit; (dulce) sweet; **goloso, a** a sweet-toothed.

golpe ['golpe] nm blow; (de puño) punch; (de mano) smack; (de remo) stroke; (fig: choque) 'clash; **no dar ~** to be bone idle; **de un ~** with one blow; **de ~** suddenly; **~ (de estado)** coup (d'état); **golpear** vt, vi to strike, knock; (asestar) to beat; (de puño) to punch; (golpetear) to tap.

goma ['goma] nf (caucho) rubber; (elástico) elastic; (una ~) elastic band; **~ espuma** foam rubber; **de pegar** gum, glue.

gordo, a ['gorðo, a] a (gen) fat; (persona) plump; (fam) enormous; **el (premio) ~** (en lotería) first prize; **gordura** nf fat; (corpulencia) fatness, stoutness.

gorila [go'rila] nm gorilla.

gorjear [gorxe'ar] vi to twitter, chirp.

gorra ['gorra] nf cap; (de niño) bonnet; (militar) bearskin; **entrar de ~** (fam) to gatecrash; **ir de ~** to sponge.

gorrión [go'rrjon] nm sparrow.

gorro ['gorro] nm (gen) cap; (de niño, mujer) bonnet.

gorrón, ona [go'rron, ona] nm/f scrounger.

gota ['gota] nf (gen) drop; (de sudor) bead; (MED) gout; **gotear** vi to drip; (lloviznar) to drizzle; **gotera** nf leak.

gozar [go'θar] vi to enjoy o.s.; **~ de** (disfrutar) to enjoy; (poseer) to possess.

gozne ['goθne] nm hinge.

gozo ['goθo] nm (alegría) joy; (placer) pleasure.

gr. abr (= gramo, gramos) g.

grabación [graβa'θjon] nf recording.

grabado [gra'βaðo] nm print, engraving.

grabadora [graβa'ðora] nf tape-recorder.

grabar [gra'βar] vt to engrave; (discos, cintas) to record.

gracia ['graθja] nf (encanto) grace,

gracefulness; (humor) humour, wit; **¡(muchas) ~s!** thanks (very much)!; **~s a** thanks to; **tener ~** (chiste etc) to be funny; **no me hace ~** I am not keen; **gracioso, a** a (divertido) funny, amusing; (cómico) comical // nm/f (TEATRO) comic character.

grada ['graða] nf (de escalera) step; (de anfiteatro) tier, row; **~s** nfpl (DEPORTE: de estadio) terraces.

gradación [graða'θjon] nf gradation.

gradería [graðe'ria] nf (gradas) (flight of) steps pl; (de anfiteatro) tiers pl, rows pl; (DEPORTE: de estadio) terraces pl; **~ cubierta** covered stand.

grado ['graðo] nm degree; (de aceite, vino) grade; (grada) step; (MIL) rank; **de buen ~** willingly.

graduación [graðwa'θjon] nf (del alcohol) proof, strength; (ESCOL) graduation; (MIL) rank.

gradual [gra'ðwal] a gradual.

graduar [gra'ðwar] vt (gen) to graduate; (MIL) to commission; **~se** vr to graduate; **~se la vista** to have one's eyes tested.

gráfico, a ['grafiko, a] a graphic // nm diagram // nf graph; **~s** nmpl (INFORM) graphics.

grajo ['graxo] nm rook.

Gral abr (= General) Gen.

gramática [gra'matika] nf grammar.

gramo ['gramo] nm gramme (Brit), gram (US).

gran [gran] a ver **grande**.

grana ['grana] nf (BOT) seedling; (color, tela) scarlet.

granada [gra'naða] nf pomegranate; (MIL) grenade.

Gran Bretaña [-bre'tana] nf Great Britain.

grande ['grande] a (antes de nmsg: **gran**) a (de tamaño) big, large; (alto) tall; (distinguido) great; (impresionante) grand // nm grandee; **grandeza** nf greatness.

grandioso, a [gran'djoso, a] a magnificent, grand.

granel [gra'nel]: **a ~** *ad* (COM) in bulk.

granero [gra'nero] *nm* granary, barn.

granito [gra'nito] *nm* (AGR) small grain; (roca) granite.

granizado [grani'θaðo] *nm* iced drink.

granizar [grani'θar] *vi* to hail; **granizo** *nm* hail.

granja ['granxa] *nf* (gen) farm; **granjero, a** *nm/f* farmer.

grano ['grano] *nm* grain; (semilla) seed; (baya) berry; (MED) pimple, spot; **~s** *nmpl* cereals.

granuja [gra'nuxa] *nm/f* rogue; (golfillo) urchin.

grapa ['grapa] *nf* staple; (TEC) clamp.

grasa ['grasa] *nf* (gen) grease; (de cocina) fat, lard; (sebo) suet; (mugre) filth; **grasiento, a** *a* greasy; (de aceite) oily.

gratificación [gratifika'θjon] *nf* (propina) tip; (bono) bonus; (recompensa) reward; **gratificar** *vt* to tip; to reward.

gratis ['gratis] *ad* free.

gratitud [grati'tuð] *nf* gratitude.

grato, a ['grato, a] *a* (agradable) pleasant, agreeable; (bienvenido) welcome.

gratuito, a [gra'twito, a] *a* (gratis) free; (sin razón) gratuitous.

gravamen [gra'βamen] *nm* (carga) burden; (impuesto) tax.

gravar [gra'βar] *vt* to burden; (COM) to tax.

grave ['graβe] *a* heavy; (serio) grave, serious; **~dad** *nf* gravity.

gravilla [gra'βiλa] *nf* gravel.

gravitar [graβi'tar] *vi* to gravitate; **~ sobre** to rest on.

gravoso, a [gra'βoso, a] *a* (pesado) burdensome; (costoso) costly.

graznar [graθ'nar] *vi* (cuervo) to squawk; (pato) to quack; (hablar ronco) to croak.

Grecia ['greθja] *nf* Greece.

gremio ['gremjo] *nm* (asociación)

trade, industry.

greña ['greɲa] *nf* (cabellos) shock of hair; (maraña) tangle.

gresca ['greska] *nf* uproar.

griego, a ['grjeβo, a] *a, nm/f* Greek.

grieta ['grjeta] *nf* crack.

grifo ['grifo] *nm* tap; (AM AUTO) petrol (Brit) o gas (US) station.

grilletes [gri'ʎetes] *nmpl* fetters.

grillo ['griʎo] *nm* (ZOOL) cricket; (BOT) shoot.

gripe ['gripe] *nf* flu, influenza.

gris [gris] *a* (color) grey.

gritar [gri'tar] *vt, vi* to shout, yell; **grito** *nm* shout, yell; (de horror) scream.

grosella [gro'seʎa] *nf* (red)currant; **~ negra** blackcurrant.

grosería [grose'ria] *nf* (actitud) rudeness; (comentario) vulgar comment; **grosero, a** *a* (poco cortés) rude, bad-mannered; (ordinario) vulgar, crude.

grosor [gro'sor] *nm* thickness.

grúa ['grua] *nf* (TEC) crane; (de petróleo) derrick.

grueso, a ['grweso, a] *a* thick; (persona) stout // *nm* bulk; **el ~ de** the bulk of.

grulla ['gruʎa] *nf* crane.

grumo ['grumo] *nm* clot, lump.

gruñido [gru'ɲiðo] *nm* grunt; (fig) grumble; **gruñir** *vi* (animal) to growl; (fam) to grumble.

grupa ['grupa] *nf* (ZOOL) rump.

grupo ['grupo] *nm* group; (TEC) unit, set.

gruta ['gruta] *nf* grotto.

guadaña [gwa'ðaɲa] *nf* scythe.

guagua ['gwa'ɣwa] *nf* (AM: niño) baby; (: bus) bus.

guante ['gwante] *nm* glove.

guapo, a ['gwapo, a] *a* good-looking, attractive; (hombre) handsome; (elegante) smart.

guarda ['gwarða] *nm/f* (persona) guard, keeper // *nf* (acto) guarding; (custodia) custody; **~bosques** *nm inv* gamekeeper; **~costas** *nm inv* coastguard vessel; **~dor, a** *a* protective // *nmf* guardian, protector; **~espaldas** *nmf inv* bodyguard; **~meta** *nmf* goalkeeper; **~polvo** *nm* dust cover; (*prenda de vestir*) overalls *pl*; **guardar** *vt* (*gen*) to keep; (*vigilar*) to guard, watch over; (*dinero: ahorrar*) to save; **~ cama** to stay in bed; **guardarse** *vr* (*preservarse*) to protect o.s.; (*evitar*) to avoid; **guardarropa** *nm* (*armario*) wardrobe; (*en establecimiento público*) cloakroom.

guardería [gwarðe'ria] *nf* nursery.

guardia ['gwarðja] *nf* (*MIL*) guard; (*cuidado*) care, custody // *nmf* guard; (*policía*) policeman/woman; **estar de ~** to be on guard; **montar ~** to mount guard; **G~ Civil** Civil Guard; **G~ Nacional** National Guard.

guardián, ana [gwar'ðjan, ana] *nmf* (*gen*) guardian, keeper.

guardilla [gwar'ðiʎa] *nf* attic.

guarecer [gware'θer] *vt* (*proteger*) to protect; (*abrigar*) to shelter; **~se** *vr* to take refuge.

guarida [gwa'riða] *nf* (*de animal*) den, lair; (*refugio*) refuge.

guarnecer [gwarne'θer] *vt* (*equipar*) to provide; (*adornar*) to adorn; (*TEC*) to reinforce; **guarnición** *nf* (*de vestimenta*) trimming; (*de piedra*) mount; (*CULIN*) garnish; (*arneses*) harness; (*MIL*) garrison.

guarro, a ['gwarro, a] *nm/f* pig.

guasa ['gwasa] *nf* joke; **guasón, ona** *a* witty; (*bromista*) joking // *nm/f* wit; joker.

Guatemala [gwate'mala] *nf* Guatemala.

gubernativo, a [guβerna'tiβo, a] *a* governmental.

guerra ['gerra] *nf* war; (*pelea*) struggle; **~ civil** civil war; **~ fría** cold war; **dar ~** to annoy; **guerrear** *vi* to wage war; **guerrero, a** *a* fighting; (*carácter*) warlike // *nm/f* warrior.

guerrilla [ge'rriʎa] *nf* guerrilla warfare; (*tropas*) guerrilla band *o* group.

guía *etc vb ver* **guiar** // ['gia] *nmf* (*persona*) guide // *nf* (*libro*) guidebook; **~ de ferrocarriles** railway timetable; **~ telefónica** telephone directory.

guiar [gi'ar] *vt* to guide, direct; (*AUTO*) to steer; **~se** *vr*: **~se por** to be guided by.

guijarro [gi'xarro] *nm* pebble.

guinda ['ginda] *nf* morello cherry.

guindilla [gin'diʎa] *nf* chilli pepper.

guiñapo [gi'ɲapo] *nm* (*harapo*) rag; (*persona*) reprobate, rogue.

guiñar [gi'ɲar] *vt* to wink.

guión [gi'on] *nm* (*LING*) hyphen, dash; (*CINE*) script; **guionista** *nm/f* scriptwriter.

guirnalda [gir'nalda] *nf* garland.

guisa ['gisa] *nf*: **a ~ de** as, like.

guisado [gi'saðo] *nm* stew.

guisante [gi'sante] *nm* pea.

guisar [gi'sar] *vt, vi* to cook; **guiso** *nm* cooked dish.

guitarra [gi'tarra] *nf* guitar.

gula ['gula] *nf* gluttony, greed.

gusano [gu'sano] *nm* maggot; (*lombriz*) earthworm.

gustar [gus'tar] *vt* to taste, sample // *vi* to please, be pleasing; **~ de algo** to like *o* enjoy sth; **me gustan las uvas** I like grapes; **le gusta nadar** she likes *o* enjoys swimming.

gusto ['gusto] *nm* (*sentido, sabor*) taste; (*placer*) pleasure; **tiene ~ a menta** it tastes of mint; **tener buen ~** to have good taste; **sentirse a ~** to feel at ease; **mucho ~ (en conocerle)** pleased to meet you; **el ~ es mío** the pleasure is mine; **con ~** willingly, gladly; **~so, a** *a* (*sabroso*) tasty; (*agradable*) pleasant.

gutural [gutu'ral] *a* guttural.

H

ha *vb ver* **haber**.

haba ['aβa] *nf* bean.

Habana [a'βana] *nf*: **la ~** Havana.

habano [a'βano] *nm* Havana cigar.

habéis *vb ver* **haber.**

PALABRA CLAVE
---

haber [a'ßer] ◆ *vb auxiliar* **1** (*tiempos compuestos*) to have; **he/ había comido** I have/had eaten; **antes/después de ~lo visto** before seeing/after seeing *o* having seen it
2: **¡~lo dicho antes!** you should have said so before!
3: **~ de: he de hacerlo** I have to do it; **ha de llegar mañana** it should arrive tomorrow
◆ *vb impersonal* **1** (*existencia: sg*) there is; (: *pl*) there are; **hay un hermano/dos hermanos** there is one brother/there are two brothers; **¿cuánto hay de aquí a Sucre?** how far is it from here to Sucre?
2 (*obligación*): **hay que hacer algo** something must be done; **hay que apuntarlo para acordarse** you have to write it down to remember
3: **¡hay que ver!** well I never!
4: **¡no hay de o por (AM) qué!** don't mention it!, not at all!
5: **¿qué hay?** (*¿qué pasa?*) what's up?, what's the matter?; (*¿qué tal?*) how's it going?
◆ *vr*: **habérselas con uno** to have it out with sb
◆ *vt*: **he aquí unas sugerencias** here are some suggestions; **no hay cintas blancas pero sí las hay rojas** there aren't any white ribbons but there are some red ones
◆ *nm* (*en cuenta*) credit side; **~es** assets; **¿cuánto tengo en el ~?** how much do I have in my account?; **tiene varias novelas en su ~** he has several novels to his credit.

habichuela [aßi'tʃwela] *nf* kidney bean.

hábil ['aßil] *a* (*listo*) clever, smart; (*capaz*) fit, capable; (*experto*) expert; **día ~** working day; **habilidad** *nf* (*gen*) skill, ability; (*inteligencia*) cleverness.

habilitar [aßili'tar] *vt* (*capacitar*) to enable; (*dar instrumentos*) to equip; (*financiar*) to finance.

hábilmente [aßil'mente] *ad* skilfully, expertly.

habitación [aßita'θjon] *nf* (*cuarto*) room; (*casa*) dwelling, abode; (*BIO: morada*) habitat; **~ sencilla** *o* **individual** single room; **~ doble** *o* **de matrimonio** double room.

habitante [aßi'tante] *nm/f* inhabitant.

habitar [aßi'tar] *vt* (*residir en*) to inhabit; (*ocupar*) to occupy // *vi* to live.

hábito ['aßito] *nm* habit.

habituar [aßi'twar] *vt* to accustom; **~se** *vr*: **~se a** to get used to.

habla ['aßla] *nf* (*capacidad de hablar*) speech; (*idioma*) language; (*dialecto*) dialect; **perder el ~** to become speechless; **de ~ francesa** French-speaking; **estar al ~** to be in contact; (*TEL*) to be on the line; **¡González al ~!** (*TEL*) González speaking!

hablador, a [aßla'ðor, a] *a* talkative // *nm/f* chatterbox.

habladuría [aßlaðu'ria] *nf* rumour; **~s** *nfpl* gossip *sg*.

hablante [a'ßlante] *a* speaking // *nm/ f* speaker.

hablar [a'ßlar] *vt* to speak, talk // *vi* to speak; **~se** *vr* to speak to each other; **~ con** to speak to; **~ de** to speak of *o* about; **'se habla inglés'** 'English spoken here'.

habré *etc vb ver* **haber.**

hacedor, a [aθe'ðor, a] *nm/f* maker.

hacendado [asen'daðo] *nm* (*AM*) large landowner.

hacendoso, a [aθen'doso, a] *a* industrious.

PALABRA CLAVE
---

hacer [a'θer] ◆ *vt* **1** (*fabricar, producir*) to make; (*construir*) to build; **~ una película/un ruido** to make a film/noise; **el guisado lo hice yo** I made *o* cooked the stew
2 (*ejecutar: trabajo etc*) to do; **~ la**

colada to do the washing; ~ la comida to do the cooking; ¿qué haces? what are you doing?; ~ el malo o el papel del malo (TEAT) to play the villain

3 (estudios, algunos deportes) to do; ~ español/económicas to do o study Spanish/Economics; ~ yoga/gimnasia to do yoga/go to gym

4 (transformar, incidir en): esto lo hará más difícil this will make it more difficult; salir te hará sentir mejor going out will make you feel better

5 (cálculo): 2 y 2 hacen 4 2 and 2 make 4; éste hace 100 this one makes 100

6 (+ subjun): esto hará que ganemos this will make us win; harás que no quiera venir you'll stop him wanting to come

7 (como sustituto de vb) to do; él bebió y yo hice lo mismo he drank and I did likewise

8: no hace más que criticar all he does is criticize

♦ vb semi-auxiliar: ~ + infinitivo **1** (directo): les hice venir I made o had them come; ~ trabajar a los demás to get others to work

2 (por intermedio de otros): ~ reparar algo to get sth repaired

♦ vi **1**: haz como que no lo sabes act as if you don't know

2 (ser apropiado): si os hace if it's alright with you

3: ~ de: ~ de madre para uno to be like a mother to sb; (TEATRO): ~ de Otelo to play Othello

♦ vb impersonal **1**: hace calor/frío it's hot/cold; ver tb bueno, sol, tiempo

2 (tiempo): hace 3 años 3 years ago; hace un mes que no voy I've been going/I haven't been for a month

4: ¿cómo has hecho para llegar tan rápido? how did you manage to get here so quickly?

♦ vr **1** (volverse) to become; se

hicieron amigos they became friends

2 (acostumbrarse): ~se a to get used to

3: se hace con huevos y leche it's made out of eggs and milk; eso no se hace that's not done

4 (obtener): ~se de o con algo to get hold of sth

5 (fingirse): ~se el sueco to turn a deaf ear.

hacia [ˈaθja] prep (en dirección de) towards; (cerca de) near; (actitud) towards; ~ arriba/abajo up(wards)/down(wards); ~ mediodía about noon.

hacienda [aˈθjenda] nf (propiedad) property; (finca) farm; (AM) ranch; ~ pública public finance; (Ministerio de) H~ Exchequer (Brit), Treasury Department (US).

hacha [ˈatʃa] nf axe; (antorcha) torch.

hada [ˈaða] nf fairy.

hago etc vb ver **hacer.**

Haití [aiˈti] nm Haiti.

halagar [alaˈɣar] vt (lisonjear) to flatter.

halago [aˈlaɣo] nm (adulación) flattery; **halagüeño, a** a flattering.

halcón [alˈkon] nm falcon, hawk.

hálito [ˈalito] nm breath.

halterofilia [alteroˈfilja] nf weightlifting.

hallar [aˈʎar] vt (gen) to find; (descubrir) to discover; (toparse con) to run into; ~se vr to be (situated); **hallazgo** nm discovery; (cosa) find.

hamaca [aˈmaka] nf hammock.

hambre [ˈambre] nf hunger; (carencia) famine; (fig) longing; tener ~ to be hungry; **hambriento, a** a hungry, starving.

hamburguesa [amburˈɣesa] nf hamburger.

hampón [amˈpon] nm thug.

han vb ver **haber.**

haragán, ana [araˈɣan, ana] a, nm/f good-for-nothing.

harapiento, a [ara'pjento, a] *a* tattered, in rags; **harapo** *nm* rag.

haré *etc* *vb* *ver* **hacer**.

harina [a'rina] *nf* flour.

hartar [ar'tar] *vt* to satiate, glut; *(fig)* to tire, sicken; **~se** *(de comida)* to fill o.s., gorge o.s.; *(cansarse)* to get fed up *(de with)*; **hartazgo** *nm* surfeit, glut; **harto, a** *a (lleno)* full; *(cansado)* fed up // *ad (bastante)* enough; *(muy)* very; **estar harto de** to be fed up with; **hartura** *nf (exceso)* surfeit; *(abundancia)* abundance; *(satisfacción)* satisfaction.

has *vb* *ver* **haber**.

hasta ['asta] *ad* even // *prep (alcanzando a)* as far as, up to, down to; *(de tiempo: a tal hora)* till, until; *(antes de)* before // *conj*: ~ **que** until; ~ **luego/el sábado** see you soon/ on Saturday.

hastiar [as'tjar] *vt (gen)* to weary; *(aburrir)* to bore; **~se** *vr*: **~se de** to get fed up with; **hastío** *nm* weariness; boredom.

hatillo [a'tiʎo] *nm* belongings *pl*, kit; *(montón)* bundle, heap.

hay *vb* *ver* **haber**.

Haya ['aja] *nf*: **la ~ The Hague**.

haya *etc* *vb* *ver* **haber** // ['aja] *nf* beech tree.

haz *vb* *ver* **hacer** // [aθ] *nm* bundle, bunch; *(rayo: de luz)* beam.

hazaña [a'θaɲa] *nf* feat, exploit.

hazmerreír [aθmerre'ir] *nm* *inv* laughing stock.

he *vb* *ver* **haber**.

hebilla [e'βiʎa] *nf* buckle, clasp.

hebra ['eβra] *nf* thread; *(BOT: fibra)* fibre, grain.

hebreo, a [e'βreo, a] *a*, *nm/f* Hebrew // *nm (LING)* Hebrew.

hectárea [ek'tarea] *nf* hectare.

hechizar [etʃi'θar] *vt* to cast a spell on, bewitch.

hechizo [e'tʃiθo] *nm* witchcraft, magic; *(acto de magia)* spell, charm.

hecho, a *pp* *de* **hacer** // ['etʃo, a] *a* complete; *(maduro)* mature; *(COSTURA)* ready-to-wear // *nm*

deed, act; *(dato)* fact; *(cuestión)* matter; *(suceso)* event // *excl* agreed!; done!; **¡bien ~!** well done!; **de ~** in fact, as a matter of fact.

hechura [e'tʃura] *nf* making, creation; *(producto)* product; *(forma)* form, shape; *(de persona)* build; *(TEC)* craftsmanship.

heder [e'ðer] *vi* to stink, smell; *(fig)* to be unbearable.

hediondo, a [e'ðjondo, a] *a* stinking.

hedor [e'ðor] *nm* stench.

heladera [ela'ðera] *nf (AM: refrigerador)* refrigerator.

helado, a [e'laðo, a] *a* frozen; *(glacial)* icy; *(fig)* chilly, cold // *nm* ice cream // *nf* frost.

helar [e'lar] *vt* to freeze, ice (up); *(dejar atónito)* to amaze; *(desalentar)* to discourage // *vi*, **~se** *vr* to freeze.

helecho [e'letʃo] *nm* fern.

hélice ['eliθe] *nf* spiral; *(TEC)* propeller.

helicóptero [eli'koptero] *nm* helicopter.

hembra ['embra] *nf (BOT, ZOOL)* female; *(mujer)* woman; *(TEC)* nut.

hemorroides [emo'rroiðes] *nfpl* haemorrhoids, piles.

hemos *vb* *ver* **haber**.

hendidura [endi'ðura] *nf* crack, split; *(GEO)* fissure.

heno ['eno] *nm* hay.

herbicida [erβi'θiða] *nm* weedkiller.

heredad [ere'ðað] *nf* landed property; *(granja)* farm.

heredar [ere'ðar] *vt* to inherit; **heredero, a** *nm/f* heir/heiress.

hereje [e'rexe] *nm/f* heretic.

herencia [e'renθja] *nf* inheritance.

herido, a [e'riðo, a] *a* injured, wounded // *nm/f* casualty // *nf* wound, injury.

herir [e'rir] *vt* to wound, injure; *(fig)* to offend.

hermanastro, a [erma'nastro, a] *nm/f* stepbrother/sister.

hermandad [erman'dað] *nf* brotherhood.

hermano, a [er'mano, a] *nm/f* brother/sister; ~ **gemelo** twin brother; ~ **político** brother-in-law; **hermana política** sister-in-law.

hermético, a [er'metiko, a] *a* hermetic; (*fig*) watertight.

hermoso, a [er'moso, a] *a* beautiful, lovely; (*estupendo*) splendid; (*guapo*) handsome; **hermosura** *nf* beauty.

héroe ['eroe] *nm* hero.

heroína [ero'ina] *nf* (*mujer*) heroine; (*droga*) heroin.

heroísmo [ero'ismo] *nm* heroism.

herradura [erra'ðura] *nf* horseshoe.

herramienta [erra'mjenta] *nf* tool.

herrería [erre'ria] *nf* smithy; (*TEC*) forge; **herrero** *nm* blacksmith.

herrumbre [e'rrumbre] *nf* rust.

hervidero [erβi'ðero] *nm* (*fig*) swarm; (*POL etc*) hotbed.

hervir [er'βir] *vi* to boil; (*burbujear*) to bubble; (*fig*): ~ **de** to teem with; ~ **a fuego lento** to simmer; **hervor** *nm* boiling; (*fig*) ardour, fervour.

hice *etc vb ver* **hacer**.

hidratante [iðra'tante] *a*: **crema** ~ moisturizing cream, moisturizer.

hidráulico, a [i'ðrauliko, a] *a* hydraulic // *nf* hydraulics *sg*.

hidro... [iðro] *pref* hydro..., water...; ~**eléctrico, a** *a* hydroelectric; ~**fobia** *nf* hydrophobia, rabies; **hidrógeno** *nm* hydrogen.

hiedra ['jeðra] *nf* ivy.

hiel [jel] *nf* gall, bile; (*fig*) bitterness.

hiela *etc vb ver* **helar**.

hielo ['jelo] *nm* (*gen*) ice; (*escarcha*) frost; (*fig*) coldness, reserve.

hiena ['jena] *nf* hyena.

hierba ['jerβa] *nf* (*pasto*) grass; (*CULIN, MED: planta*) herb; **mala** ~ weed; (*fig*) evil influence; ~**buena** *nf* mint.

hierro ['jerro] *nm* (*metal*) iron; (*objeto*) iron object.

hígado ['iɣaðo] *nm* liver.

higiene [i'xjene] *nf* hygiene; **higiénico, a** *a* hygienic.

higo ['iɣo] *nm* fig; **higuera** *nf* fig tree.

hijastro, a [i'xastro, a] *nm/f* stepson/daughter.

hijo, a ['ixo, a] *nm/f* son/daughter, child; ~**s** *nmpl* children, sons and daughters; ~ **de papá/mamá** daddy's/mummy's boy; ~ **de puta** (*fam!*) bastard (!), son of a bitch (!).

hilar [i'lar] *vt* to spin; ~ **fino** to split hairs.

hilera [i'lera] *nf* row, file.

hilo ['ilo] *nm* thread; (*BOT*) fibre; (*metal*) wire; (*de agua*) trickle, thin stream; (*de luz*) beam, ray.

hilvanar [ilβa'nar] *vt* (*COSTURA*) to tack (*Brit*), baste (*US*); (*fig*) to do hurriedly.

himno ['imno] *nm* hymn; ~ **nacional** national anthem.

hincapié [inka'pje] *nm*: **hacer** ~ **en** to emphasize.

hincar [in'kar] *vt* to drive (in), thrust (in); ~**se** *vr*: ~**se de rodillas** to kneel down.

hincha ['intʃa] *nm/f* (*fam*) fan.

hinchado, a [in'tʃaðo, a] *a* (*gen*) swollen; (*persona*) pompous.

hinchar [in'tʃar] *vt* (*gen*) to swell; (*inflar*) to blow up, inflate; (*fig*) to exaggerate; ~**se** *vr* (*inflarse*) to swell up; (*fam: llenarse*) to stuff o.s.; **hinchazón** *nf* (*MED*) swelling; (*altivez*) arrogance.

hinojo [i'noxo] *nm* fennel.

hipermercado [ipermer'kaðo] *nm* hypermarket, superstore.

hipnotismo [ipno'tismo] *nm* hypnotism; **hipnotizar** *vt* to hypnotize.

hipo ['ipo] *nm* hiccups *pl*.

hipocresía [ipokre'sia] *nf* hypocrisy; **hipócrita** *a* hypocritical // *nm/f* hypocrite.

hipódromo [i'poðromo] *nm* racetrack.

hipopótamo [ipo'potamo] *nm* hippopotamus.

hipoteca [ipo'teka] *nf* mortgage.

hipótesis [i'potesis] *nf inv* hypothesis.

hiriente [i'rjente] *a* offensive, wounding.

hispánico, a [is'paniko, a] *a* Hispanic.

hispano, a [is'pano, a] *a* Hispanic, Spanish, Hispano // *nm/f* Spaniard; **H~américa** *nf* Spanish *o* Latin America; **~americano, a** *a, nm/f* Spanish *o* Latin American.

histeria [is'terja] *nf* hysteria.

historia [is'torja] *nf* history; (*cuento*) story, tale; **~s** *nfpl* (*chismes*) gossip *sg*; **dejarse de ~s** to come to the point; **pasar a la ~** to go down in history; **~dor, a** *nm/f* historian.

historiar *vt* to chronicle, write the history of; **histórico, a** *a* historical; (*fig*) historic.

historieta [isto'rjeta] *nf* tale, anecdote; (*dibujos*) comic strip.

hito ['ito] *nm* (*fig*) landmark; (*objetivo*) goal, target.

hizo *vb ver* **hacer.**

Hnos *abr* (= *Hermanos*) Bros.

hocico [o'θiko] *nm* snout; (*fig*) grimace.

hockey ['xoki] *nm* hockey; **~ sobre hielo** ice hockey.

hogar [o'var] *nm* fireplace, hearth; (*casa*) home; (*vida familiar*) home life; **~eño, a** *a* home; (*persona*) home-loving.

hoguera [o'vera] *nf* (*gen*) bonfire.

hoja ['oxa] *nf* (*gen*) leaf; (*de flor*) petal; (*de papel*) sheet; (*página*) page; **~ de afeitar** razor blade.

hojalata [oxa'lata] *nf* tin(plate).

hojaldre [o'xaldre] *nm* (*CULIN*) puff pastry.

hojear [oxe'ar] *vt* to leaf through, turn the pages of.

hola ['ola] *excl* hello!

Holanda [o'landa] *nf* Holland; **holandés, esa** *a* Dutch // *nm/f* Dutchman/woman // *nm* (*LING*) Dutch.

holgado, a [ol'vaðo, a] *a* loose, baggy; (*rico*) well-to-do.

holgar [ol'var] *vi* (*descansar*) to

rest; (*sobrar*) to be superfluous; **huelga decir que** it goes without saying that.

holgazán, ana [olva'ðan, ana] *a* idle, lazy // *nm/f* loafer.

holgura [ol'vura] *nf* looseness, bagginess; (*TEC*) play, free movement; (*vida*) comfortable living, luxury.

hollín [o'ʎin] *nm* soot.

hombre ['ombre] *nm* (*gen*) man; (*raza humana*): **el ~** man(kind); (*uno*) man // *excl*: **¡sí ~!** (*claro*) of course!; (*para énfasis*) man, old boy; **~ de negocios** businessman; **~-rana** frogman; **~ de pro** honest man.

hombrera [om'brera] *nf* shoulder strap.

hombro ['ombro] *nm* shoulder.

hombruno, a [om'bruno, a] *a* mannish.

homenaje [ome'naxe] *nm* (*gen*) homage; (*tributo*) tribute.

homicida [omi'θiða] *a* homicidal // *nm/f* murderer; **homicidio** *nm* murder, homicide.

homosexual [omosek'swal] *a, nm/f* homosexual.

hondo, a ['ondo, a] *a* deep; **lo ~** the depth(s) (*pl*), the bottom; **~nada** *nf* hollow, depression; (*cañón*) ravine; (*GEO*) lowland; **hondura** *nf* depth, profundity.

Honduras [on'duras] *nf* Honduras.

hondureño, a [ondu'reno, a] *a, nm/f* Honduran.

honestidad [onesti'ðað] *nf* purity, chastity; (*decencia*) decency; **honesto, a** *a* chaste; decent, honest; (*justo*) just.

hongo ['ongo] *nm* (*BOT*: *gen*) fungus; (: *comestible*) mushroom; (: *venenoso*) toadstool.

honor [o'nor] *nm* (*gen*) honour; (*gloria*) glory; **en ~ a la verdad** to be fair; **~able** *a* honourable.

honorario, a [ono'rarjo, a] *a* honorary; **~s** *nmpl* fees.

honra ['onra] *nf* (*gen*) honour; (*renombre*) good name; **~dez** *nf* honesty; (de persona) integrity; ~do, a a honest, upright.

honrar [on'rar] vt to honour; ~se vr: ~se con algo/de hacer algo to be honoured by sth/to do sth.

honroso, a [on'roso, a] a (honrado) honourable; (respetado) respectable.

hora ['ora] nf (una ~) hour; (tiempo) time; ¿qué ~ es? what time is it?; ¿a qué ~? at what time?; media ~ half an hour; a la ~ de recreo at playtime; a primera ~ first thing (in the morning); a última ~ at the last moment; a altas ~s in the small hours; a buena ~! about time, too!; dar la ~ to strike the hour; ~s de oficina/de trabajo office/working hours; ~s de visita visiting hours; ~s extras o extraordinarias overtime sg; ~s punta rush hours.

horadar [ora'ðar] vt to drill, bore.

horario, a [o'rarjo, a] a hourly, hour cpd // nm timetable; ~ comercial business hours pl.

horca ['orka] nf gallows sg.

horcajadas [orka'xaðas]: a ~ ad astride.

horchata [or'tʃata] nf cold drink made from tiger nuts and water, tiger nut milk.

horda ['orða] nf horde.

horizontal [oriθon'tal] a horizontal.

horizonte [ori'θonte] nm horizon.

horma ['orma] nf mould.

hormiga [or'miɣa] nf ant; ~s nfpl (MED) pins and needles.

hormigón [ormi'ɣon] nm concrete; ~ armado/pretensado reinforced/prestressed concrete.

hormigueo [ormi'ɣeo] nm (comezón) itch; (fig) uneasiness.

hormona [or'mona] nf hormone.

hornada [or'naða] nf batch (of loaves etc).

hornillo [or'niʎo] nm (cocina) portable stove.

horno ['orno] nm (CULIN) oven; (TEC) furnace; alto ~ blast furnace.

horóscopo [o'roskopo] nm horoscope.

horquilla [or'kiʎa] nf hairpin; (AGR) pitchfork.

horrendo, a [o'rrendo, a] a horrendous, frightful.

horrible [o'rriβle] a horrible, dreadful.

horripilante [orripi'lante] a hairraising, horrifying.

horror [o'rror] nm horror, dread; (atrocidad) atrocity; ¡qué ~! (fam) oh, my God!; ~izar vt to horrify, frighten; ~izarse vr to be horrified; ~oso, a a horrifying, ghastly.

hortaliza [orta'liθa] nf vegetable.

hortelano, a [orte'lano, a] nm/f (market) gardener.

hosco, a ['osko, a] a dark; (persona) sullen, gloomy.

hospedar [ospe'ðar] vt to put up; ~se vr to stay, lodge.

hospital [ospi'tal] nm hospital.

hospitalario, a [ospita'larjo, a] a (acogedor) hospitable; **hospitalidad** nf hospitality.

hostal [os'tal] nm small hotel.

hostelería [ostele'ria] nf hotel business o trade.

hostelero, a [oste'lero, a] nm/f hotelkeeper, landlord/lady.

hostia ['ostja] nf (REL) host, consecrated wafer; (fam: golpe) whack, punch // excl: ¡~(s)! (fam!) damn!

hostigar [osti'ɣar] vt to whip; (fig) to harass, pester.

hostil [os'til] a hostile; ~idad nf hostility.

hotel [o'tel] nm hotel; ~ero, a a hotel cpd // nm/f hotelier.

hoy [oi] ad (este día) today; (la actualidad) now(adays) // nm present time; ~ (en) día now(adays).

hoyo ['ojo] nm hole, pit; **hoyuelo** nm dimple.

hoz [oθ] nf sickle.

hube etc vb ver **haber**.

hucha ['utʃa] nf money box.

hueco, a ['weko, a] a (vacío) hollow, empty; (resonante) booming // nm hollow, cavity.

huelga *etc vb ver* **holgar** // ['welɣa] *nf* strike; **declararse en ~** to go on strike, come out on strike; **~ de hambre** hunger strike.

huelgo *etc vb ver* **holgar**.

huelguista [wel'vista] *nm/f* striker.

huelo *etc vb ver* **oler**.

huella ['weʎa] *nf* (*acto de pisar, pisada*) tread(ing); (*marca del paso*) footprint, footstep; (: *de animal, máquina*) track; **~ digital** fingerprint.

huérfano, a ['werfano, a] *a* orphan(ed) // *nm/f* orphan.

huerta ['werta] *nf* market garden; (*en Murcia y Valencia*) irrigated region.

huerto ['werto] *nm* kitchen garden; (*de árboles frutales*) orchard.

hueso ['weso] *nm* (ANAT) bone; (*de fruta*) stone.

huésped, a ['wespeð, a] *nm/f* (*invitado*) guest; (*habitante*) resident; (*anfitrión*) host(ess).

huesudo, a [we'suðo, a] *a* bony, big-boned.

huevera [we'ßera] *nf* eggcup.

huevo ['weßo] *nm* egg; **~ duro/ escalfado/frito** (Esp) o **estrellado** (AM)/**pasado por agua** hard-boiled/ poached/fried/soft-boiled egg; **~s revueltos** scrambled eggs.

huida [u'iða] *nf* escape, flight.

huidizo, a [ui'ðiðo, a] *a* (*tímido*) shy; (*pasajero*) fleeting.

huir [u'ir] *vi* (*escapar*) to flee, escape; (*evadir*) to avoid; **~se** *vr* (*escaparse*) to escape.

hule ['ule] *nm* (*encerado*) oilskin.

humanidad [umani'ðað] *nf* (*género humano*) man(kind); (*cualidad*) humanity.

humano, a [u'mano, a] *a* (*gen*) human; (*humanitario*) humane // *nm* human; **ser ~** human being.

humareda [uma'reða] *nf* cloud of smoke.

humedad [ume'ðað] *nf* (*del clima*) humidity; (*de pared etc*) dampness; **a prueba de ~** damp-proof;

humedecer *vt* to moisten, wet; **humedecerse** *vr* to get wet.

húmedo, a ['umeðo, a] *a* (*mojado*) damp, wet; (*tiempo etc*) humid.

humildad [umil'dað] *nf* humility, humbleness; **humilde** *a* humble, modest.

humillación [umiʎa'θjon] *nf* humiliation; **humillante** *a* humiliating.

humillar [umi'ʎar] *vt* to humiliate; **~se** *vr* to humble o.s., grovel.

humo ['umo] *nm* (*de fuego*) smoke; (*gas nocivo*) fumes *pl*; (*vapor*) steam, vapour; **~s** *nmpl* (*fig*) conceit *sg*.

humor [u'mor] *nm* (*disposición*) mood, temper; (*lo que divierte*) humour; **de buen/mal ~** in a good/ bad mood; **~ismo** *nm* humour; **~ista** *nm/f* comic; **~ístico, a** *a* funny, humorous.

hundimiento [undi'mjento] *nm* (*gen*) sinking; (*colapso*) collapse.

hundir [un'dir] *vt* to sink; (*edificio, plan*) to ruin, destroy; **~se** *vr* to sink, collapse.

húngaro, a ['ungaro, a] *a, nm/f* Hungarian.

Hungría [un'gria] *nf* Hungary.

huracán [ura'kan] *nm* hurricane.

huraño, a [u'raɲo, a] *a* shy; (*antisocial*) unsociable.

hurgar [ur'var] *vt* to poke, jab; (*remover*) to stir (up); **~se** *vr*: **~ (las narices)** to pick one's nose.

hurón, ona [u'ron, ona] *nm* (ZOOL) ferret.

hurtadillas [urta'ðiʎas]: **a ~** *ad* stealthily, on the sly.

hurtar [ur'tar] *vt* to steal; **hurto** *nm* theft, stealing.

husmear [usme'ar] *vt* (*oler*) to sniff out, scent; (*fam*) to pry into // *vi* to smell bad.

huyo *etc vb ver* **huir**.

I

iba *etc vb ver* **ir.**

ibérico, a [i'βeriko, a] *a* Iberian.

iberoamericano, a [iβeroameri'kano, a] *a, nm/f* Latin American.

íbice ['iβiθe] *nm* ibex.

Ibiza [i'βiθa] *nf* Ibiza.

iceberg [iθe'βer] *nm* iceberg.

ícono ['ikono] *nm* ikon, icon.

iconoclasta [ikono'klasta] *a* iconoclastic // *nm/f* iconoclast.

ictericia [ikte'riθja] *nf* jaundice.

ida ['iða] *nf* going, departure; **~ y vuelta** round trip, return.

idea [i'ðea] *nf* idea; **no tengo la menor ~** I haven't a clue.

ideal [iðe'al] *a, nm* ideal; **~ista** *nm/f* idealist; **~izar** *vt* to idealize.

idear [iðe'ar] *vt* to think up; *(aparato)* to invent; *(viaje)* to plan.

ídem ['iðem] *pron* ditto.

idéntico, a [i'ðentiko, a] *a* identical.

identidad [iðenti'ðað] *nf* identity.

identificación [iðentifika'θjon] *nf* identification.

identificar [iðentifi'kar] *vt* to identify; **~se** *vr:* **~se con** to identify with.

ideología [iðeolo'xia] *nf* ideology.

idioma [i'ðjoma] *nm (gen)* language.

idiota [i'ðjota] *a* idiotic // *nm/f* idiot.

idiotez *nf* idiocy.

ídolo ['iðolo] *nm (tb: fig)* idol.

idóneo, a [i'ðoneo, a] *a* suitable.

iglesia [i'ɣlesja] *nf* church.

ignominia [iɣno'minja] *nf* ignominy.

ignorancia [iɣno'ranθja] *nf* ignorance; **ignorante** *a* ignorant, uninformed // *nm/f* ignoramus.

ignorar [iɣno'rar] *vt* not to know, be ignorant of; *(no hacer caso a)* to ignore.

igual [i'ɣwal] *a (gen)* equal; *(similar)* like, similar; *(mismo)* (the) same; *(constante)* constant; *(temperatura)* even // *nm/f* equal; **~ que** like, the same as; **me da o es ~** I don't

care; **son ~es** they're the same; **al ~ que** *prep, conj* like, just like.

igualada [iɣwa'laða] *nf* equaliser.

igualar [iɣwa'lar] *vt* (gen) to equalize, make equal; *(allanar, nivelar)* to level (off), even (out); **~se** *vr (platos de balanza)* to balance out.

igualdad [iɣwal'dað] *nf* equality; *(similaridad)* sameness; *(uniformidad)* uniformity.

igualmente [iɣwal'mente] *ad* equally; *(también)* also, likewise // *excl* the same to you!

ikurriña [iku'rriɲa] *nf* Basque flag.

ilegal [ile'ɣal] *a* illegal.

ilegítimo, a [ile'xitimo, a] *a* illegitimate.

ileso, a [i'leso, a] *a* unhurt.

ilícito, a [i'liθito] *a* illicit.

ilimitado, a [ilimi'taðo, a] *a* unlimited.

ilógico, a [i'loxiko, a] *a* illogical.

iluminación [ilumina'θjon] *nf* illumination; *(alumbrado)* lighting.

iluminar [ilumi'nar] *vt* to illuminate, light (up); *(fig)* to enlighten.

ilusión [ilu'sjon] *nf* illusion; *(quimera)* delusion; *(esperanza)* hope; **hacerse ilusiones** to build up one's hopes; **ilusionado, a** *a* excited.

ilusionista [ilusjo'nista] *nm/f* conjurer.

iluso, a [i'luso, a] *a* easily deceived // *nm/f* dreamer.

ilusorio, a [ilu'sorjo, a] *a (de ilusión)* illusory, deceptive; *(esperanza)* vain.

ilustración [ilustra'θjon] *nf* illustration; *(saber)* learning, erudition; **la I~** the Enlightenment; **ilustrado, a** *a* illustrated; learned.

ilustrar [ilus'trar] *vt* to illustrate; *(instruir)* to instruct; *(explicar)* to explain, make clear; **~se** *vr* to acquire knowledge.

ilustre [i'lustre] *a* famous, illustrious.

imagen [i'maxen] *nf (gen)* image; *(dibujo)* picture.

imaginación [imaxina'θjon] *nf*

imagination.

imaginar [imaxi'nar] *vt* (*gen*) to imagine; (*idear*) to think up; (*suponer*) to suppose; ~**se** *vr* to imagine; ~**io, a** *a* imaginary; **imaginativo, a** *a* imaginative.

imán [i'man] *nm* magnet.

imbécil [im'beθil] *nm/f* imbecile, idiot.

imbuir [imbu'ir] *vi* to imbue.

imitación [imita'θjon] *nf* imitation.

imitar [imi'tar] *vt* to imitate; (*parodiar, remedar*) to mimic, ape.

impaciencia [impa'θjenθja] *nf* impatience; **impaciente** *a* impatient; (*nervioso*) anxious.

impacto [im'pakto] *nm* impact.

impar [im'par] *a* odd.

imparcial [impar'θjal] *a* impartial, fair; ~**idad** *nf* impartiality, fairness.

impartir [impar'tir] *vt* to impart, give.

impasible [impa'siβle] *a* impassive.

impávido, a [im'paβiðo, a] *a* fearless, intrepid.

impecable [impe'kaβle] *a* impeccable.

impedimento [impeði'mento] *nm* impediment, obstacle.

impedir [impe'ðir] *vt* (*obstruir*) to impede, obstruct; (*estorbar*) to prevent.

impeler [impe'ler] *vt* to drive, propel; (*fig*) to impel.

impenetrable [impene'traβle] *a* impenetrable; (*fig*) incomprehensible.

imperar [impe'rar] *vi* (*reinar*) to rule, reign; (*fig*) to prevail, reign; (*precio*) to be current.

imperativo, a [impera'tiβo, a] *a* (*persona*) imperious; (*urgente, LING*) imperative.

imperceptible [imperθep'tiβle] *a* imperceptible.

imperdible [imper'ðiβle] *nm* safety pin.

imperdonable [imperðo'naβle] *a* unforgivable, inexcusable.

imperfección [imperfek'θjon] *nf* imperfection.

imperfecto, a [imper'fekto, a] *a* imperfect.

imperial [impe'rjal] *a* imperial; ~**ismo** *nm* imperialism.

imperio [im'perjo] *nm* empire; (*autoridad*) rule, authority; (*fig*) pride, haughtiness; ~**so, a** *a* imperious; (*urgente*) urgent; (*imperativo*) imperative.

impermeable [imperme'aβle] *a* (*a prueba de agua*) waterproof // *nm* raincoat.

impersonal [imperso'nal] *a* impersonal.

impertérrito, a [imper'territo, a] *a* undaunted.

impertinencia [imperti'nenθja] *nf* impertinence; **impertinente** *a* impertinent.

imperturbable [impertur'βaβle] *a* imperturbable.

ímpetu ['impetu] *nm* (*impulso*) impetus, impulse; (*impetuosidad*) impetuosity; (*violencia*) violence.

impetuoso, a [impe'twoso, a] *a* impetuous; (*río*) rushing; (*acto*) hasty.

impío, a [im'pio, a] *a* impious, ungodly.

implacable [impla'kaβle] *a* implacable.

implicar [impli'kar] *vt* to implicate, involve; (*entrañar*) to imply.

implícito, a [im'pliθito, a] *a* (*tácito*) implicit; (*sobreentendido*) implied.

implorar [implo'rar] *vt* to beg, implore.

imponente [impo'nente] *a* (*impresionante*) impressive, imposing; (*solemne*) grand.

imponer [impo'ner] *vt* (*gen*) to impose; (*exigir*) to exact, command; ~**se** *vr* to assert o.s.; (*prevalecer*) to prevail; **imponible** *a* (*COM*) taxable.

impopular [impopu'lar] *a* unpopular.

importación [importa'θjon] *nf* (*acto*) importing; (*mercancías*) imports *pl*.

importancia [impor'tanθja] *nf* importance; (valor) value, significance; (extensión) size, magnitude; **importante** a important; valuable, significant.

importar [impor'tar] vt (del extranjero) to import; (valer) to amount to, be worth // vi to be important, matter; **me importa un rábano** I don't give a damn; **no importa** it doesn't matter; **¿le importa que fume?** do you mind if I smoke?

importe [im'porte] nm (total) amount; (valor) value.

importunar [importu'nar] vt to bother, pester.

imposibilidad [imposiβili'ðað] nf impossibility; **imposibilitar** vt to make impossible, prevent.

imposible [impo'siβle] a (gen) impossible; (insoportable) unbearable, intolerable.

imposición [imposi'θjon] nf imposition; (COM: impuesto) tax; (: inversión) deposit.

impostor, a [impos'tor, a] nm/f impostor.

impotencia [impo'tenθja] nf impotence; **impotente** a impotent, powerless.

impracticable [imprakti'kaβle] a (irrealizable) impracticable; (intransitable) impassable.

imprecar [impre'kar] vi to curse.

impreciso, a [impre'θiso, a] a imprecise, vague.

impregnar [impreγ'nar] vt to impregnate; ~**se** vr to become impregnated.

imprenta [im'prenta] nf (acto) printing; (aparato) press; (casa) printer's; (letra) print.

imprescindible [impresθin'diβle] a essential, vital.

impresión [impre'sjon] nf (gen) impression; (IMPRENTA) printing; (edición) edition; (FOTO) print; (marca) imprint; ~ **digital** fingerprint.

impresionable [impresjo'naβle] a (sensible) impressionable.

impresionante [impresjo'nante] a impressive; (tremendo) tremendous; (maravilloso) great, marvellous.

impresionar [impresjo'nar] vt (conmover) to move; (afectar) to impress, strike; (película fotográfica) to expose; ~**se** vr to be impressed; (conmoverse) to be moved.

impreso, a pp de **imprimir** // [im'preso, a] a printed ~**s** nmpl; printed matter; **impresora** nf printer.

imprevisto, a [impre'βisto, a] a (gen) unforeseen; (inesperado) unexpected ~**s** nmpl; (gastos) unforeseen expenses.

imprimir [impri'mir] vt to imprint, impress, stamp; (textos) to print; (INFORM) to output, print out.

improbable [impro'βaβle] a improbable; (inverosímil) unlikely.

improcedente [improθe'ðente] a inappropriate.

improductivo, a [improduk'tiβo, a] a unproductive.

improperio [impro'perjo] nm insult.

impropiedad [impropje'ðað] nf impropriety (of language).

impropio, a [im'propjo, a] a improper.

improvisación [improβisa'θjon] nf improvisation; **improvisado, a** a improvised.

improvisar [improβi'sar] vt to improvise.

improviso, a [impro'βiso, a] a: **de** ~ unexpectedly, suddenly.

imprudencia [impru'ðenθja] nf imprudence; (indiscreción) indiscretion; (descuido) carelessness; **imprudente** a imprudent; indiscreet; (irreflexivo) unwise.

impúdico, a [im'puðiko, a] a shameless; (lujurioso) lecherous.

impudor [impu'ðor] nm shamelessness; (lujuria) lechery.

impuesto, a [im'pwesto, a] a imposed // nm tax; ~ **sobre el valor añadido (IVA)** value added tax (VAT).

impugnar [impuɣˈnar] vt to oppose, contest; (refutar) to refute, impugn.

impulsar [impulˈsar] vt = **impeler**.

impulso [imˈpulso] nm impulse; (fuerza, empuje) thrust, drive; (fig: sentimiento) urge, impulse.

impune [imˈpune] a unpunished; **impunidad** nf impunity.

impureza [impuˈreθa] nf impurity; (fig) lewdness; **impuro, a** a impure; lewd.

imputar [impuˈtar] vt (atribuir) to attribute to; (cargar) to impute to.

inacabable [inakaˈβaβle] a (infinito) endless; (interminable) interminable.

inaccesible [inakθeˈsiβle] a inaccessible.

inacción [inakˈθjon] nf (gen) inaction; (desocupación) inactivity.

inaceptable [inaθepˈtaβle] a unacceptable.

inactividad [inaktiβiˈðað] nf inactivity; (COM) dullness; **inactivo, a** a inactive.

inadaptación [inaðaptaˈθjon] nf maladjustment.

inadecuado, a [inaðeˈkwaðo, a] a (insuficiente) inadequate; (inapto) unsuitable.

inadmisible [inaðmiˈsiβle] a inadmissible.

inadvertido, a [inaðβerˈtiðo, a] a (no visto) unnoticed.

inagotable [inaɣoˈtaβle] a inexhaustible.

inaguantable [inaɣwanˈtaβle] a unbearable.

inalterable [inalteˈraβle] a immutable, unchangeable.

inanición [inaniˈθjon] nf starvation.

inanimado, a [inaniˈmaðo, a] a inanimate.

inapto, a [inˈapto] a unsuited.

inaudito, a [inauˈðito, a] a unheard-of.

inauguración [inauɣuraˈθjon] nf inauguration; (de exposición) opening; **inaugurar** vt to inaugurate; to open.

I.N.B. abr (Esp = Instituto Nacional de Bachillerato) ≈ comprehensive

school (Brit), ≈ high school (US).

inca [ˈinka] nm/f Inca; **~ico, a** a Inca cpd.

incalculable [inkalkuˈlaβle] a incalculable.

incandescente [inkandesˈθente] a incandescent.

incansable [inkanˈsaβle] a tireless, untiring.

incapacidad [inkapaθiˈðað] nf incapacity; (incompetencia) incompetence; **~ física/mental** physical/mental disability.

incapacitar [inkapaθiˈtar] vt (inhabilitar) to incapacitate, render unfit; (descalificar) to disqualify.

incapaz [inkaˈpaθ] a incapable.

incautación [inkautaˈθjon] nf confiscation.

incautarse [inkauˈtarse] vr: **~ de** to seize, confiscate.

incauto, a [inˈkauto, a] a (imprudente) incautious, unwary.

incendiar [inθenˈdjar] vt to set fire to; (fig) to inflame; **~se** vr to catch fire; **~io, a** a incendiary.

incendio [inˈθendjo] nm fire.

incentivo [inθenˈtiβo] nm incentive.

incertidumbre [inθertiˈðumbre] nf (inseguridad) uncertainty; (duda) doubt.

incesante [inθeˈsante] a incessant.

incesto [inˈθesto] nm incest.

incidencia [inθiˈðenθja] nf (MAT) incidence.

incidente [inθiˈðente] nm incident.

incidir [inθiˈðir] vi (influir) to influence; (afectar) to affect; **~ en un error** to fall into error.

incienso [inˈθjenso] nm incense.

incierto, a [inˈθjerto, a] a uncertain.

incineración [inθineraˈθjon] nf incineration; (de cadáveres) cremation.

incinerar [inθineˈrar] vt to burn; (cadáveres) to cremate.

incipiente [inθiˈpjente] a incipient.

incisión [inθiˈsjon] nf incision.

incisivo, a [inθiˈsiβo, a] a sharp, cutting; (fig) incisive.

incitar [inθi'tar] *vt* to incite, rouse.

incivil [inθi'βil] *a* rude, uncivil.

inclemencia [inkle'menθja] *nf* (*severidad*) harshness, severity; (*del tiempo*) inclemency.

inclinación [inklina'θjon] *nf* (*gen*) inclination; (*de tierras*) slope, incline; (*de cabeza*) nod, bow; (*fig*) leaning, bent.

inclinar [inkli'nar] *vt* to incline; (*cabeza*) to nod, bow; (*tierras*) to slope; ~se *vr* to bow; (*encorvarse*) to stoop; ~se a to take after, resemble; ~se ante to bow down to; me inclino a pensar que I'm inclined to think that.

incluir [inklu'ir] *vt* to include; (*incorporar*) to incorporate; (*meter*) to enclose.

inclusive [inklu'siβe] *ad* inclusive // *prep* including.

incluso, a [in'kluso, a] *a* included // *ad* inclusively; (*hasta*) even.

incógnito [in'koɣnito] *nm*: de ~ incognito.

incoherente [inkoe'rente] *a* incoherent.

incoloro, a [inko'loro, a] *a* colourless.

incólume [in'kolume] *a* (*gen*) safe; (*indemne*) unhurt, unharmed.

incomodar [inkomo'ðar] *vt* to inconvenience; (*molestar*) to bother, trouble; (*fastidiar*) to annoy; ~se *vr* to put o.s. out; (*fastidiarse*) to get annoyed.

incomodidad [inkomoði'ðað] *nf* inconvenience; (*fastidio*, *enojo*) annoyance; (*de vivienda*) discomfort.

incómodo, a [in'komoðo, a] *a* (*inconfortable*) uncomfortable; (*molesto*) annoying; (*inconveniente*) inconvenient.

incomparable [inkompa'raβle] *a* incomparable.

incompatible [inkompa'tiβle] *a* incompatible.

incompetencia [inkompe'tenθja] *nf* incompetence; **incompetente** *a* incompetent.

incompleto, a [inkom'pleto, a] *a* incomplete, unfinished.

incomprensible [inkompren'siβle] *a* incomprehensible.

incomunicado, a [inkomuni'kaðo, a] *a* (*aislado*) cut off, isolated; (*confinado*) in solitary confinement.

inconcebible [inkonθe'βiβle] *a* inconceivable.

inconcluso, a [inkon'kluso, a] *a* (*inacabado*) unfinished.

incondicional [inkondiθjo'nal] *a* unconditional; (*apoyo*) wholehearted; (*partidario*) staunch.

inconexo, a [inko'nekso, a] *a* (*gen*) unconnected; (*desunido*) disconnected.

inconfundible [inkonfun'diβle] *a* unmistakable.

incongruente [inkon'ɣruente] *a* incongruous.

inconmensurable [inkonmensu'raβle] *a* immeasurable, vast.

inconsciencia [inkons'θjenθja] *nf* unconsciousness; (*fig*) thoughtlessness; **inconsciente** *a* unconscious; thoughtless.

inconsecuente [inkonse'kwente] *a* inconsistent.

inconsiderado, a [inkonsiðe'raðo, a] *a* inconsiderate.

inconsistente [inkonsis'tente] *a* weak; (*tela*) flimsy.

inconstancia [inkon'stanθja] *nf* (*veleidad*) inconstancy; (*inestabilidad*) unsteadiness; **inconstante** *a* inconstant.

incontable [inkon'taβle] *a* countless, innumerable.

incontestable [inkontes'taβle] *a* unanswerable; (*innegable*) undeniable.

incontinencia [inkonti'nenθja] *nf* incontinence.

inconveniencia [inkombe'njenθja] *nf* unsuitability, inappropriateness; (*descortesía*) impoliteness; **inconveniente** *a* unsuitable; impolite // *nm* obstacle; (*desventaja*) disadvantage; el **inconveniente es que...** the trouble is that...

incorporación [inkorpora'θjon] nf incorporation.

incorporar [inkorpo'rar] vt to incorporate; ~se vr to sit/stand up.

incorrección [inkorrek'θjon] nf (gen) incorrectness, inaccuracy; (descortesía) bad-mannered behaviour; **incorrecto, a** a (gen) incorrect, wrong; (comportamiento) bad-mannered.

incorregible [inkorre'xiβle] a incorrigible.

incredulidad [inkreðuli'ðað] nf incredulity; (escepticismo) scepticism; **incrédulo, a** a incredulous, unbelieving; sceptical.

increíble [inkre'iβle] a incredible.

incremento [inkre'mento] nm increment; (aumento) rise, increase.

increpar [inkre'par] vt to reprimand.

incruento, a [in'krwento, a] a bloodless.

incrustar [inkrus'tar] vt to incrust; (piedras: en joya) to inlay.

incubar [inku'βar] vt to incubate; (fig) to hatch.

inculcar [inkul'kar] vt to inculcate.

inculpar [inkul'par] vt (acusar) to accuse; (achacar, atribuir) to charge, blame.

inculto, a [in'kulto, a] a (persona) uneducated; (grosero) uncouth // nm/f ignoramus.

incumplimiento [inkumpli'mjento] nm non-fulfilment; ~ **de contrato** breach of contract.

incurrir [inku'rrir] vi: ~ **en** to incur; (crimen) to commit; ~ **en un error** to fall into error.

indagación [indaɣa'θjon] nf investigation; (búsqueda) search; (JUR) inquest.

indagar [inda'ɣar] vt to investigate; to search; (averiguar) to ascertain.

indecente [inde'θente] a indecent, improper; (lascivo) obscene.

indecible [inde'θiβle] a unspeakable; (indescriptible) indescribable.

indeciso, a [inde'θiso, a] a (por decidir) undecided; (vacilante)

hesitant.

indefenso, a [inde'fenso, a] a defenceless.

indefinido, a [indefi'niðo, a] a indefinite; (vago) vague, undefined.

indeleble [inde'leβle] a indelible.

indemne [in'demne] a (objeto) undamaged; (persona) unharmed, unhurt.

indemnizar [indemni'θar] vt to indemnify; (compensar) to compensate.

independencia [indepen'denθja] nf independence.

independiente [indepen'djente] a (libre) independent; (autónomo) self-sufficient.

indeterminado, a [indetermi'naðo, a] a indefinite; (desconocido) indeterminate.

India ['indja] nf: **la** ~ India.

indicación [indika'θjon] nf indication; (señal) sign; (sugerencia) suggestion, hint.

indicador [indika'ðor] nm indicator; (TEC) gauge, meter.

indicar [indi'kar] vt (mostrar) to indicate, show; (termómetro etc) to read, register; (señalar) to point to.

índice ['indiθe] nm index; (catálogo) catalogue; (ANAT) index finger, forefinger.

indicio [in'diθjo] nm indication, sign; (pista) clue.

indiferencia [indife'renθja] nf indifference; (apatía) apathy; **indiferente** a indifferent.

indígena [in'dixena] a indigenous, native // nm/f native.

indigencia [indi'xenθja] nf poverty, need.

indigestión [indixes'tjon] nf indigestion.

indigesto, a [indi'xesto, a] a undigested; (indigestible) indigestible; (fig) turgid.

indignación [indiɣna'θjon] nf indignation.

indignar [indiɣ'nar] vt to anger, make indignant; ~se vr: ~se por to get indignant about.

indigno, a [in'divno, a] *a* (*despreciable*) low, contemptible; (*inmerecido*) unworthy.

indio, a ['indjo, a] *a, nm/f* Indian.

indirecta [indi'rekta] *nf* insinuation, innuendo; (*sugerencia*) hint.

indirecto, a [indi'rekto, a] *a* indirect.

indiscreción [indiskre'θjon] *nf* (*imprudencia*) indiscretion; (*irreflexión*) tactlessness; (*acto*) gaffe, faux pas.

indiscreto, a [indis'kreto, a] *a* indiscreet.

indiscutible [indisku'tiβle] *a* indisputable, unquestionable.

indispensable [indispen'saβle] *a* indispensable, essential.

indisponer [indispo'ner] *vt* to spoil, upset; (*salud*) to make ill; ~se to fall ill; ~se con uno to fall out with sb.

indisposición [indisposi'θjon] *nf* indisposition.

indistinto, a [indis'tinto, a] *a* indistinct; (*vago*) vague.

individual [indiβi'ðwal] *a* individual; (*habitación*) single // *nm* (*DEPORTE*) singles *sg*.

individuo, a [indi'βiðwo, a] *a* individual // *nm* individual.

índole ['indole] *nf* (*naturaleza*) nature; (*clase*) sort, kind.

indolencia [indo'lenθja] *nf* indolence, laziness.

indómito, a [in'domito, a] *a* indomitable.

inducir [indu'θir] *vt* to induce; (*inferir*) to infer; (*persuadir*) to persuade.

indudable [indu'ðaβle] *a* undoubted; (*incuestionable*) unquestionable.

indulgencia [indul'xenθja] *nf* indulgence.

indultar [indul'tar] *vt* (*perdonar*) to pardon, reprieve; (*librar de pago*) to exempt; **indulto** *nm* pardon; exemption.

industria [in'dustrja] *nf* industry; (*habilidad*) skill; **industrial** *a* in-

dustrial // *nm* industrialist.

inédito, a [in'eðito, a] *a* (*libro*) unpublished; (*fig*) new.

inefable [ine'faβle] *a* ineffable, indescribable.

ineficaz [inefi'kaθ] *a* (*inútil*) ineffective; (*ineficiente*) inefficient.

ineludible [inelu'ðiβle] *a* inescapable, unavoidable.

ineptitud [inepti'tuð] *nf* ineptitude, incompetence; **inepto, a** *a* inept, incompetent.

inequívoco, a [ine'kiβoko, a] *a* unequivocal; (*inconfundible*) unmistakable.

inercia [in'erθja] *nf* inertia; (*pasividad*) passivity.

inerme [in'erme] *a* (*sin armas*) unarmed; (*indefenso*) defenceless.

inerte [in'erte] *a* inert; (*inmóvil*) motionless.

inesperado, a [inespe'raðo, a] *a* unexpected, unforeseen.

inestable [ines'taβle] *a* unstable.

inevitable [ineβi'taβle] *a* inevitable.

inexactitud [ineksakti'tuð] *nf* inaccuracy; **inexacto, a** *a* inaccurate; (*falso*) untrue.

inexperto, a [inek'sperto, a] *a* (*novato*) inexperienced.

infalible [infa'liβle] *a* infallible; (*plan*) foolproof.

infame [in'fame] *a* infamous; (*horrible*) dreadful; **infamia** *nf* infamy; (*deshonra*) disgrace.

infancia [in'fanθja] *nf* infancy, childhood.

infante [in'fante] *nm* (*hijo del rey*) infante, prince; (*MIL*) infantryman.

infantería [infante'ria] *nf* infantry.

infantil [infan'til] *a* (*pueril, aniñado*) infantile; (*cándido*) childlike; (*literatura, ropa etc*) children's.

infarto [in'farto] *nm* (*tb*: ~ de miocardio) heart attack.

infatigable [infati'vaβle] *a* tireless, untiring.

infección [infek'θjon] *nf* infection; **infeccioso, a** *a* infectious.

infectar [infek'tar] *vt* to infect; ~se

vr to become infected.

infeliz [infe'liθ] *a* unhappy, wretched // *nm/f* wretch.

inferior [infe'rjor] *a* inferior; (*situación*) lower // *nm/f* inferior, subordinate.

inferir [infe'rir] *vt* (*deducir*) to infer, deduce; (*causar*) to cause.

infestar [infes'tar] *vt* (*apestar*) to infest; (*fig*) to harass.

infidelidad [infiðeli'ðað] *nf* (*gen*) infidelity, unfaithfulness.

infiel [in'fjel] *a* unfaithful, disloyal; (*erróneo*) inaccurate // *nm/f* infidel, unbeliever.

infierno [in'fjerno] *nm* hell.

ínfimo, a ['infimo, a] *a* (*más bajo*) lowest; (*despreciable*) vile, mean.

infinidad [infini'ðað] *nf* infinity; (*abundancia*) great quantity.

infinito, a [infi'nito, a] *a, nm* infinite.

inflación [infla'θjon] *nf* (*hinchazón*) swelling; (*monetaria*) inflation; (*fig*) conceit; **inflacionario, a** *a* inflationary.

inflamar [infla'mar] *vt* to set on fire; (*MED*) to inflame; ~**se** *vr* to catch fire; (*fig*) to become inflamed.

inflar [in'flar] *vt* (*hinchar*) to inflate, blow up; (*fig*) to exaggerate; ~**se** *vr* to swell (up); (*fig*) to get conceited.

inflexible [inflek'siβle] *a* inflexible; (*fig*) unbending.

infligir [infli'xir] *vt* to inflict.

influencia [influ'enθja] *nf* influence; **influenciar** *vt* to influence.

influir [influ'ir] *vt* to influence.

influjo [in'fluxo] *nm* influence.

influya *etc vb ver* **influir**.

influyente [influ'jente] *a* influential.

información [informa'θjon] *nf* information; (*noticias*) news *sg*; (*JUR*) inquiry; **I~** (*oficina*) Information Office; (*mostrador*) Information Desk; (*TEL*) Directory Enquiries.

informal [infor'mal] *a* (*gen*) informal.

informante [infor'mante] *nm/f* informant.

informar [infor'mar] *vt* (*gen*) to in-

form; (*revelar*) to reveal, make known // *vi* (*JUR*) to plead; (*denunciar*) to inform; (*dar cuenta de*) to report on; ~**se** *vr* to find out; ~**se de** to inquire into.

informática [infor'matika] *nf* computer science, information technology.

informe [in'forme] *a* shapeless // *nm* report.

infortunio [infor'tunjo] *nm* misfortune.

infracción [infrak'θjon] *nf* infraction, infringement.

infranqueable [infranke'aβle] *a* impassable; (*fig*) insurmountable.

infringir [infrin'xir] *vt* to infringe, contravene.

infructuoso, a [infruk'twoso, a] *a* fruitless, unsuccessful.

infundado, a [infun'daðo, a] *a* groundless, unfounded.

infundir [infun'dir] *vt* to infuse, instil.

infusión [infu'sjon] *nf* infusion; ~ **de manzanilla** camomile tea.

ingeniar [inxe'njar] *vt* to think up, devise; ~**se** *vr*: ~**se para** to manage to.

ingeniería [inxenje'ria] *nf* engineering; **ingeniero, a** *nm/f* engineer; **ingeniero de caminos/de sonido** civil engineer/sound engineer.

ingenio [in'xenjo] *nm* (*talento*) talent; (*agudeza*) wit; (*habilidad*) ingenuity, inventiveness; (*TEC*): ~ **azucarero** sugar refinery.

ingenioso, a [inxe'njoso, a] *a* ingenious, clever; (*divertido*) witty.

ingenuidad [inxenwi'ðað] *nf* ingenuousness; (*sencillez*) simplicity; **ingenuo, a** *a* ingenuous.

ingerir [inxe'rir] *vt* to ingest; (*tragar*) to swallow; (*consumir*) to consume.

Inglaterra [ingla'terra] *nf* England.

ingle ['ingle] *nf* groin.

inglés, esa [in'gles, esa] *a* English // *nm/f* Englishman/woman // *nm* (*LING*) English.

ingratitud [ingrati'tuð] nf ingratitude; **ingrato, a** a (gen) ungrateful.

ingrediente [ingre'ðjente] nm ingredient.

ingresar [ingre'sar] vt (dinero) to deposit // vi to come in; ~ **en un club** to join a club; ~ **en el hospital** to go into hospital.

ingreso [in'greso] nm (entrada) entry; (: en hospital etc) admission; ~**s** nmpl (dinero) income sg; (: COM) takings pl.

inhabitable [inaβi'taβle] a uninhabitable.

inhalar [ina'lar] vt to inhale.

inherente [ine'rente] a inherent.

inhibir [ini'βir] vt to inhibit; (REL) to restrain.

inhumano, a [inu'mano] a inhuman.

INI ['ini] nm abr (Esp = Instituto Nacional de Industria) ≈ NEB (Brit).

inicial [ini'θjal] a, nf initial.

iniciar [ini'θjar] vt (persona) to initiate; (empezar) to begin, commence; (conversación) to start up.

iniciativa [iniθja'tiβa] nf initiative; **la ~ privada** private enterprise.

inicuo, a [i'nikwo] a iniquitous.

ininterrumpido, a [ininterrum'piðo, a] a uninterrupted.

injerencia [inxe'renθja] nf interference.

injertar [inxer'tar] vt to graft; **injerto** nm graft.

injuria [in'xurja] nf (agravio, ofensa) offence; (insulto) insult; **injuriar** vt to insult; **injurioso, a** a offensive; insulting.

injusticia [inxus'tiθja] nf injustice.

injusto, a [in'xusto, a] a unjust, unfair.

inmadurez [inmaðu'reθ] nf immaturity.

inmediaciones [inmeðja'θjones] nfpl neighbourhood sg, environs.

inmediato, a [inme'ðjato, a] a immediate; (contiguo) adjoining;

(rápido) prompt; (próximo) next; **de** ~ immediately.

inmejorable [inmexo'raβle] a unsurpassable; (precio) unbeatable.

inmenso, a [in'menso, a] a immense, huge.

inmerecido, a [inmere'θiðo, a] a undeserved.

inmigración [inmixra'θjon] nf immigration.

inmiscuirse [inmisku'irse] vr to interfere, meddle.

inmobiliario, a [inmoβi'ljarjo, a] a real-estate cpd, property cpd // nf estate agency.

inmolar [inmo'lar] vt to immolate, sacrifice.

inmoral [inmo'ral] a immoral.

inmortal [inmor'tal] a immortal; **~izar** vt to immortalize.

inmóvil [in'moβil] a immobile.

inmueble [in'mweβle] a: **bienes ~s** real estate, landed property // nm property.

inmundicia [inmun'diθja] nf filth; **inmundo, a** a filthy.

inmunidad [inmuni'ðað] nf immunity.

inmutarse [inmu'tarse] vr to turn pale; **no se inmutó** he didn't turn a hair.

innato, a [in'nato, a] a innate.

innecesario, a [inneθe'sarjo, a] a unnecessary.

innoble [in'noβle] a ignoble.

innovación [innoβa'θjon] nf innovation.

innovar [inno'βar] vt to introduce.

inocencia [ino'θenθja] nf innocence.

inocentada [inoθen'taða] nf practical joke.

inocente [ino'θente] a (ingenuo) naive, innocent; (inculpable) innocent; (sin malicia) harmless // nm/f simpleton.

inodoro [ino'ðoro] nm toilet, lavatory (Brit).

inofensivo, a [inofen'siβo, a] a inoffensive, harmless.

inolvidable [inolβiˈðaβle] a unforgettable.

inoperante [inopeˈrante] a ineffective.

inopinado, a [inopiˈnaðo, a] a unexpected.

inoportuno, a [inoporˈtuno, a] a untimely; (*molesto*) inconvenient.

inoxidable [inoksiˈðaβle] a: **acero ~** stainless steel.

inquebrantable [inkeβranˈtaβle] a unbreakable.

inquietar [inkjeˈtar] vt to worry, trouble; **~se** vr to worry, get upset; **inquieto, a** a anxious, worried; **inquietud** nf anxiety, worry.

inquilino, a [inkiˈlino, a] nm/f tenant.

inquirir [inkiˈrir] vt to enquire into, investigate.

insaciable [insaˈθjaβle] a insatiable.

insalubre [insaˈluβre] a unhealthy.

inscribir [inskriˈβir] vt to inscribe; (*lista*) to list; (*censo*) to register; **~se** vr to register; (*ESCOL etc*) to enrol.

inscripción [inskripˈθjon] nf inscription; (*ESCOL etc*) enrolment; (*censo*) registration.

insecticida [insektiˈθiða] nm insecticide.

insecto [inˈsekto] nm insect.

inseguridad [inseɣuriˈðað] nf insecurity.

inseguro, a [inseˈɣuro, a] a insecure; (*inconstante*) unsteady; (*incierto*) uncertain.

insensato, a [insenˈsato, a] a foolish, stupid.

insensibilidad [insensiβiliˈðað] nf (*gen*) insensitivity; (*dureza de corazón*) callousness.

insensible [insenˈsiβle] a (*gen*) insensitive; (*movimiento*) imperceptible; (*sin sentido*) numb.

insertar [inserˈtar] vt to insert.

inservible [inserˈβiβle] a useless.

insidioso, a [insiˈðjoso, a] a insidious.

insignia [inˈsiɣnja] nf (*señal dis-*

tintiva) badge; (*estandarte*) flag.

insignificante [insiɣnifiˈkante] a insignificant.

insinuar [insiˈnwar] vt to insinuate, imply; **~se** vr: **~se con uno** to ingratiate o.s. with sb.

insípido, a [inˈsipiðo, a] a insipid.

insistencia [insisˈtenθja] nf insistence.

insistir [insisˈtir] vi to insist; **~ en algo** to insist on sth; (*enfatizar*) to stress sth.

insolación [insolaˈθjon] nf (*MED*) sunstroke.

insolencia [insoˈlenθja] nf insolence; **insolente** a insolent.

insólito, a [inˈsolito, a] a unusual.

insoluble [insoˈluβle] a insoluble.

insolvencia [insolˈβenθja] nf insolvency.

insomnio [inˈsomnjo] nm insomnia.

insondable [insonˈdaβle] a bottomless; (*fig*) impenetrable.

insonorizado, a [insonoriˈθaðo, a] a (*cuarto etc*) soundproof.

insoportable [insoporˈtaβle] a unbearable.

insospechado, a [insospeˈtʃaðo, a] a (*inesperado*) unexpected.

inspección [inspekˈθjon] nf inspection, check; **inspeccionar** vt (*examinar*) to inspect, examine; (*controlar*) to check.

inspector, a [inspekˈtor, a] nm/f inspector.

inspiración [inspiraˈθjon] nf inspiration.

inspirar [inspiˈrar] vt to inspire; (*MED*) to inhale; **~se** vr: **~se en** to be inspired by.

instalación [instalaˈθjon] nf (*equipo*) fittings pl, equipment; **~ eléctrica** wiring.

instalar [instaˈlar] vt (*establecer*) to instal; (*erguir*) to set up, erect; **~se** vr to establish o.s.; (*en una vivienda*) to move into.

instancia [insˈtanθja] nf (*JUR*) petition; (*ruego*) request; **en última ~** as a last resort.

instantáneo, a [instan'taneo, a] *a* instantaneous // *nf* snap(shot); café ~ instant coffee.

instante [ins'tante] *nm* instant, moment.

instar [ins'tar] *vt* to press, urge.

instigar [insti'ɣar] *vt* to instigate.

instinto [ins'tinto] *nm* instinct; por ~ instinctively.

institución [institu'θjon] *nf* institution, establishment.

instituir [institu'ir] *vt* to establish; *(fundar)* to found; **instituto** *nm* (gen) institute; **Instituto Nacional de Enseñanza** *(Esp)* ≈ comprehensive *(Brit)* o high *(US)* school.

institutriz [institu'triθ] *nf* governess.

instrucción [instruk'θjon] *nf* instruction.

instructivo, a [instruk'tiβo, a] *a* instructive.

instruir [instru'ir] *vt* (gen) to instruct; *(enseñar)* to teach, educate.

instrumento [instru'mento] *nm* (gen) instrument; *(herramienta)* tool, implement.

insubordinarse [insuβorði'narse] *vr* to rebel.

insuficiencia [insufi'θjenθja] *nf* (carencia) lack; *(inadecuación)* inadequacy; **insuficiente** *a* (gen) insufficient; *(ESCOL: calificación)* unsatisfactory.

insufrible [insu'friβle] *a* insufferable.

insular [insu'lar] *a* insular.

insultar [insul'tar] *vt* to insult; **insulto** *nm* insult.

insuperable [insupe'raβle] *a* (excelente) unsurpassable; *(arduo)* insurmountable.

insurgente [insur'xente] *a, nm/f* insurgent.

insurrección [insurrek'θjon] *nf* insurrection, rebellion.

intacto, a [in'takto, a] *a* intact.

intachable [inta'tʃaβle] *a* irreproachable.

integral [inte'ɣral] *a* integral; *(completo)* complete; **pan ~** whole-

meal *(Brit)* o wholewheat *(US)* bread.

integrar [inte'ɣrar] *vt* to make up, compose; *(MAT, fig)* to integrate.

integridad [inteɣri'ðað] *nf* wholeness; *(carácter)* integrity; **íntegro, a** *a* whole, entire; *(honrado)* honest.

intelectual [intelek'twal] *a, nm/f* intellectual.

inteligencia [inteli'xenθja] *nf* intelligence; *(ingenio)* ability; **inteligente** *a* intelligent.

inteligible [inteli'xiβle] *a* intelligible.

intemperie [intem'perje] *nf*: a la ~ out in the open, exposed to the elements.

intempestivo, a [intempes'tiβo, a] *a* untimely.

intención [inten'θjon] *nf* (gen) intention, purpose; **con segundas intenciones** maliciously; **con ~** deliberately.

intencionado, a [intenθjo'naðo, a] *a* deliberate; **bien/mal ~** well-meaning/ill-disposed, hostile.

intensidad [intensi'ðað] *nf* (gen) intensity; *(ELEC, TEC)* strength; **llover con ~** to rain hard.

intenso, a [in'tenso, a] *a* intense; *(sentimiento)* profound, deep.

intentar [inten'tar] *vt* (tratar) to try, attempt; **intento** *nm* (intención) intention, purpose; *(tentativa)* attempt.

intercalar [interka'lar] *vt* to insert.

intercambio [inter'kambjo] *nm* exchange, swap.

interceder [interθe'ðer] *vi* to intercede.

interceptar [interθep'tar] *vt* to intercept.

intercesión [interθe'sjon] *nf* intercession.

interés [inte'res] *nm* (gen) interest; *(parte)* share, part; *(pey)* self-interest; **intereses creados** vested interests.

interesado, a [intere'saðo, a] *a* interested; *(prejuiciado)* prejudiced; *(pey)* mercenary, self-seeking.

interesante [intere'sante] *a* interesting.

interesar [intere'sar] *vt*, *vi* to interest, be of interest to; ~**se** *vr*: ~**se en** *o* **por** to take an interest in.

interface [inter'faθe], **interfase** ['fase] *nm* (INFORM) interface.

interferir [interfe'rir] *vt* to interfere with; (TEL) to jam // *vi* to interfere.

interfono [inter'fono] *nm* intercom.

interino, a [inte'rino, a] *a* temporary // *nm/f* temporary holder of a post; (MED) locum; (ESCOL) supply teacher.

interior [inte'rjor] *a* inner, inside; (COM) domestic, internal // *nm* interior, inside; (fig) soul, mind; **Ministerio del I~** ≈ Home Office (Brit), ≈ Department of the Interior (US).

interjección [interxek'θjon] *nf* interjection.

interlocutor, a [interloku'tor, a] *nm/f* speaker.

intermediario, a [interme'ðjarjo, a] *nm/f* intermediary.

intermedio, a [inter'meðjo, a] *a* intermediate // *nm* interval.

interminable [intermi'naβle] *a* endless.

intermitente [intermi'tente] *a* intermittent // *nm* (AUTO) indicator.

internacional [internaθjo'nal] *a* international.

internado [inter'naðo] *nm* boarding school.

internar [inter'nar] *vt* to intern; (en un manicomio) to commit; ~**se** *vr* (penetrar) to penetrate.

interno, a [in'terno, a] *a* internal, interior; (POL etc) domestic // *nm/f* (alumno) boarder.

interponer [interpo'ner] *vt* to interpose, put in; ~**se** *vr* to intervene.

interpretación [interpreta'θjon] *nf* interpretation.

interpretar [interpre'tar] *vt* to interpret; (TEATRO, MUS) to perform, play; **intérprete** *nm/f* (LING) interpreter, translator; (MUS, TEATRO) performer, artist(e).

interrogación [interroγa'θjon] *nf* interrogation; (LING: *tb*: **signo de** ~) question mark.

interrogar [interro'γar] *vt* to interrogate, question.

interrumpir [interrum'pir] *vt* to interrupt.

interrupción [interrup'θjon] *nf* interruption.

interruptor [interrup'tor] *nm* (ELEC) switch.

intersección [intersek'θjon] *nf* intersection.

interurbano, a [interur'βano, a] *a*: **llamada interurbana** long-distance call.

intervalo [inter'βalo] *nm* interval; (descanso) break; **a** ~**s** at intervals, every now and then.

intervenir [interβe'nir] *vt* (controlar) to control, supervise; (MED) to operate on // *vi* (participar) to take part, participate; (mediar) to intervene.

interventor, a [interβen'tor, a] *nm/f* inspector; (COM) auditor.

interviú [inter'βju] *nf* interview.

intestino [intes'tino] *nm* intestine.

intimar [inti'mar] *vi* to become friendly.

intimidad [intimi'ðað] *nf* intimacy; (familiaridad) familiarity; (vida privada) private life; (JUR) privacy.

íntimo, a [in'timo, a] *a* intimate.

intolerable [intole'raβle] *a* intolerable, unbearable.

intranquilizarse [intrankili'θarse] *vr* to get worried *o* anxious; **intranquilo, a** *a* worried.

intransigente [intransi'xente] *a* intransigent.

intransitable [intransi'taβle] *a* impassable.

intrepidez [intrepi'ðeθ] *nf* courage, bravery; **intrépido, a** *a* intrepid.

intriga [in'triγa] *nf* intrigue; (plan) plot; **intrigar** *vt*, *vi* to intrigue.

intrincado, a [intrin'kaðo, a] *a* intricate.

intrínseco, a [in'trinseko, a] *a* intrinsic.

introducción [introðuk'θjon] *nf* introduction.

introducir [introðu'θir] *vt* (*gen*) to introduce; (*moneda etc*) to insert; (*INFORM*) to input, enter.

intromisión [intromi'sjon] *nf* interference, meddling.

introvertido, a [introβer'tiðo, a] *a, nm/f* introvert.

intruso, a [in'truso, a] *a* intrusive // *nm/f* intruder.

intuición [intwi'θjon] *nf* intuition.

inundación [inunda'θjon] *nf* flood(ing); **inundar** *vt* to flood; (*fig*) to swamp, inundate.

inusitado, a [inusi'taðo, a] *a* unusual, rare.

inútil [in'util] *a* useless; (*esfuerzo*) vain, fruitless; **inutilidad** *nf* uselessness.

inutilizar [inutili'θar] *vt* to make *o* render useless; **~se** *vr* to become useless.

invadir [inβa'ðir] *vt* to invade.

inválido, a [in'βaliðo, a] *a* invalid // *nm/f* invalid.

invariable [inβa'rjaβle] *a* invariable.

invasión [inβa'sjon] *nf* invasion.

invasor, a [inβa'sor, a] *a* invading // *nm/f* invader.

invención [inβen'θjon] *nf* invention.

inventar [inβen'tar] *vt* to invent.

inventario [inβen'tarjo] *nm* inventory.

inventiva [inβen'tiβa] *nf* inventiveness.

inventor, a [inβen'tor, a] *nm/f* inventor.

invernadero [inβerna'ðero] *nm* greenhouse.

inverosímil [inβero'simil] *a* implausible.

inversión [inβer'sjon] *nf* (*COM*) investment.

inverso, a [in'βerso, a] *a* inverse, opposite; **en el orden ~** in reverse order; **a la inversa** inversely, the other way round.

inversor, a [inβer'sor, a] *nm/f* (*COM*) investor.

invertir [inβer'tir] *vt* (*COM*) to invest; (*volcar*) to turn upside down; (*tiempo etc*) to spend.

investigación [inβestiɣa'θjon] *nf* investigation; (*ESCOL*) research; **~ de mercado** market research.

investigar [inβesti'ɣar] *vt* to investigate; (*ESCOL*) to do research into.

invicto, a [in'βikto, a] *a* unconquered.

invierno [in'βjerno] *nm* winter.

invisible [inβi'siβle] *a* invisible.

invitado, a [inβi'taðo, a] *nm/f* guest.

invitar [inβi'tar] *vt* to invite; (*incitar*) to entice; (*pagar*) to buy, pay for.

invocar [inβo'kar] *vt* to invoke, call on.

inyección [injek'θjon] *nf* injection.

inyectar [injek'tar] *vt* to inject.

PALABRA CLAVE
---

ir [ir] ◆ *vi* **1** to go; (*a pie*) to walk; (*viajar*) to travel; **~ caminando** to walk; **fui en tren** I went *o* travelled by train; **¡(ahora) voy!** (I'm just) coming!

2: **~ (a) por**: **~ (a) por el médico** to fetch the doctor

3 (*progresar*: *persona, cosa*) to go; **el trabajo va muy bien** work is going very well; **¿cómo te va?** how are things going?; **me va muy bien** I'm getting on very well; **le fue fatal** it went awfully badly for him

4 (*funcionar*): **el coche no va muy bien** the car isn't running very well

5: **te va estupendamente ese color** that colour suits you fantastically well

6 (*locuciones*): **¿vino? - ¡que va!** did he come? - of course not!; **vamos, no llores** come on, don't cry; **¡vaya coche!** what a car!, that's some car!

7: **no vaya a ser: tienes que correr, no vaya a ser que pierdas el tren** you'll have to run so as not to miss the train

8 (+ *pp*): **iba vestido muy bien** he was very well dressed

9: no me *etc* va ni me viene I *etc* don't care

◆ *vb auxiliar* **1**: ~ a: **voy/iba a hacerlo hoy** I am/was going to do it today

2 (+ *gerundio*): **iba anocheciendo** it was getting dark; **todo se me iba aclarando** everything was gradually becoming clearer to me

3 (+ *pp* = *pasivo*): **van vendidos 300 ejemplares** 300 copies have been sold so far

◆ ~se *vr* **1**: **¿por dónde se va al zoológico?** which is the way to the zoo?

2 (*marcharse*) to leave; **ya se habrán ido** they must already have left *o* gone.

ira [ˈira] *nf* anger, rage.
iracundo, a [iraˈkundo, a] *a* irascible.
Irak [iˈrak] *nm* = **Iraq**.
Irán [iˈran] *nm* Iran; **iraní** *a*, *nm/f* Iranian.
Iraq [iˈrak], **Irak** *nm* Iraq; **iraquí** [iraˈki] *a*, *nm/f* Iraqui.
iris [ˈiris] *nm* (*arco* ~) rainbow; (*ANAT*) iris.
Irlanda [irˈlanda] *nf* Ireland; **irlandés, esa** *a* Irish // *nm/f* Irishman/woman; **los irlandeses** the Irish.
ironía [iroˈnia] *nf* irony; **irónico, a** *a* ironic(al).
irreal [irreˈal] *a* unreal.
irrecuperable *a* [irrekupeˈraβle] irrecoverable, irretrievable.
irreflexión [irreflekˈsjon] *nf* thoughtlessness.
irregular [irreβuˈlar] *a* (*gen*) irregular; (*situación*) abnormal.
irremediable [irremeˈðjaβle] *a* irremediable; (*vicio*) incurable.
irresoluto, a [irresoˈluto, a] *a* irresolute, hesitant.
irrespetuoso, a [irrespeˈtwoso, a] *a* disrespectful.
irresponsable [irresponˈsaβle] *a* irresponsible.

irrigar [irriˈvar] *vt* to irrigate.
irrisorio, a [irriˈsorjo, a] *a* derisory, ridiculous.
irritar [irriˈtar] *vt* to irritate, annoy.
irrupción [irrupˈθjon] *nf* irruption; (*invasión*) invasion.
isla [ˈisla] *nf* island.
islandés, esa [islanˈdes, esa] *a* Icelandic // *nm/f* Icelander.
Islandia [isˈlandja] *nf* Iceland.
isleño, a [isˈleɲo, a] *a* island *cpd* // *nm/f* islander.
Israel [israˈel] *nm* Israel; **israelí** *a*, *nm/f* Israeli.
istmo [ˈistmo] *nm* isthmus.
Italia [iˈtalja] *nf* Italy; **italiano, a** *a*, *nm/f* Italian.
itinerario [itineˈrarjo] *nm* itinerary, route.
IVA [ˈiβa] *nm abr ver* **impuesto**.
izar [iˈθar] *vt* to hoist.
izdo, a *abr* (= *izquierdo, a*) l.
izquierda [iθˈkjerda] *nf* left; (*POL*) left (wing); **a la** ~ (*estar*) on the left; (*torcer etc*) to the left.
izquierdista [iθkjerˈðista] *nm/f* left-winger, leftist.
izquierdo, a [iθˈkjerðo, a] *a* left.

J

jabalí [xaβaˈli] *nm* wild boar.
jabalina [xaβaˈlina] *nf* javelin.
jabón [xaˈβon] *nm* soap; **jabonar** *vt* to soap.
jaca [ˈxaka] *nf* pony.
jacinto [xaˈθinto] *nm* hyacinth.
jactarse [xakˈtarse] *vr* to boast, brag.
jadear [xaðeˈar] *vi* to pant, gasp for breath; **jadeo** *nm* panting, gasping.
jaguar [xaˈxwar] *nm* jaguar.
jalbegue [xalˈβexe] *nm* (*pintura*) whitewash.
jalea [xaˈlea] *nf* jelly.
jaleo [xaˈleo] *nm* racket, uproar; **armar un** ~ to kick up a racket.
jalón [xaˈlon] *nm* (*AM*) tug.
Jamaica [xaˈmaika] *nf* Jamaica.
jamás [xaˈmas] *ad* never; (*sin nega-*

ción) ever.

jamón [xa'mon] *nm* ham; ~ **dulce,** ~ **de York** cooked ham; ~ **serrano** cured ham.

Japón [xa'pon] *nm:* **el ~** Japan; **japonés, esa** *a, nm/f* Japanese.

jaque ['xake] *nm:* ~ **mate** checkmate.

jaqueca [xa'keka] *nf* (very bad) headache, migraine.

jarabe [xa'raβe] *nm* syrup.

jarcia ['xarθja] *nf* (*NAUT*) ropes *pl*, rigging.

jardín [xar'ðin] *nm* garden; ~ **de (la) infancia** (*Esp*) o **de niños** (*AM*) nursery (school); **jardinería** *nf* gardening; **jardinero, a** *nm/f* gardener.

jarra ['xarra] *nf* jar; (*jarro*) jug.

jarro ['xarro] *nm* jug.

jaula ['xaula] *nf* cage.

jauría [xau'ria] *nf* pack of hounds.

J. C. *abr* (= *Jesucristo*) J.C.

jefa ['xefa] *nf* woman head o boss.

jefatura [xefa'tura] *nf:* ~ **de policía** police headquarters *sg.*

jefe ['xefe] *nm/f* (*gen*) chief, head; (*patrón*) boss; ~ **de camareros** head waiter; ~ **de cocina** chef; ~ **de estación** stationmaster; ~ **de estado** head of state; ~ **supremo** commander-in-chief; **ser el ~** (*fig*) to be the boss.

jengibre [xen'xiβre] *nm* ginger.

jeque ['xeke] *nm* sheik.

jerarquía [xerar'kia] *nf* (*orden*) hierarchy; (*rango*) rank; **jerárquico, a** *a* hierarchic(al).

jerez [xe'reθ] *nm* sherry.

jerga ['xerɣa] *nf* (*tela*) coarse cloth; (*lenguaje*) jargon.

jerigonza [xeri'ɣonθa] *nf* (*jerga*) jargon, slang; (*galimatías*) nonsense, gibberish.

jeringa [xe'ringa] *nf* syringe; (*AM*) annoyance, bother; ~ **de engrase** grease gun; **jeringar** *vt* (*AM*) to annoy, bother.

jeroglífico [xero'ɣlifiko] *nm* hieroglyphic.

jersé, jersey [xer'sei] (*pl* **jerseys**) *nm* jersey, pullover, jumper.

Jerusalén [xerusa'len] *n* Jerusalem.

Jesucristo [xesu'kristo] *nm* Jesus Christ.

jesuita [xe'swita] *a, nm* Jesuit.

Jesús [xe'sus] *nm* Jesus; ¡~! good heavens!; (*al estornudar*) bless you!

jet ['jet] (*pl* ~**s**) *nm* jet (plane).

jícara ['xikara] *nf* small cup.

jinete [xi'nete, a] *nm/f* horseman/woman, rider.

jipijapa [xipi'xapa] *nm* (*AM*) straw hat.

jirafa [xi'rafa] *nf* giraffe.

jirón [xi'ron] *nm* rag, shred.

jocoso, a [xo'koso, a] *a* humorous, jocular.

jofaina [xo'faina] *nf* washbasin.

jornada [xor'naða] *nf* (*viaje de un día*) day's journey; (*camino o viaje entero*) journey; (*día de trabajo*) working day.

jornal [xor'nal] *nm* (day's) wage; ~**ero** (*día*) labourer.

joroba [xo'roβa] *nf* hump, hunched back; ~**do, a** *a* hunchbacked // *nm/f* hunchback.

jota ['xota] *nf* (the letter) J; (*danza*) Aragonese dance; (*fam*) jot, iota; **no saber ni** ~ to have no idea.

joven ['xoβen] (*pl* **jóvenes**) *a* young // *nm* young man, youth // *nf* young woman, girl.

jovial [xo'βjal] *a* cheerful, jolly; ~**idad** *nf* cheerfulness, jolliness.

joya ['xoja] *nf* jewel, gem; (*fig: persona*) gem; **joyería** *nf* (*joyas*) jewellery; (*tienda*) jeweller's (shop); **joyero** (*persona*) jeweller; (*caja*) jewel case.

juanete [xwa'nete] *nm* (*del pie*) bunion.

jubilación [xuβila'θjon] *nf* (*retiro*) retirement.

jubilado, a [xuβi'laðo, a] *a* retired // *nm/f* pensioner (*Brit*), senior citizen.

jubilar [xuβi'lar] *vt* to pension off, retire; (*fam*) to discard; ~**se** *vr* to retire.

jubileo [xuβi'leo] *nm* jubilee.

júbilo ['xuβilo] *nm* joy, rejoicing; **jubiloso, a** *a* jubilant.

judía [xu'δia] *nf* Jewess; (*CULIN*) bean; ~ **verde** French bean.

judicial [xuδi'θjal] *a* judicial.

judío, a [xu'δio, a] *a* Jewish // *nm/f* Jew(ess).

judo [xuδo] *nm* judo.

juego *etc vb ver* **jugar** // ['xwexo] *nm* (*gen*) play; (*pasatiempo, partido*) game; (*en casino*) gambling; (*conjunto*) set; **fuera de** ~ (*DEPORTE: persona*) offside; (: *pelota*) out of play; **J~s Olímpicos** Olympic Games.

juerga ['xwerxa] *nf* binge; (*fiesta*) party; **ir de** ~ to go out on a binge.

jueves ['xweβes] *nm inv* Thursday.

juez [xweθ] *nm/f* judge; ~ **de línea** linesman; ~ **de salida** starter.

jugada [xu'xaδa] *nf* play; **buena** ~ good move/shot/stroke *etc*.

jugador, a [xuxa'δor, a] *nm/f* player; (*en casino*) gambler.

jugar [xu'xar] *vt, vi* to play; (*en casino*) to gamble; (*apostar*) to bet; ~ **al fútbol** to play football; ~**se** *vr* to gamble (away).

juglar [xu'xlar] *nm* minstrel.

jugo ['xuxo] *nm* (*BOT*) juice; (*fig*) essence, substance; ~ **de fruta** (*AM*) fruit juice; ~**so, a** *a* juicy; (*fig*) substantial, important.

juguete [xu'xete] *nm* toy; ~**ar** *vi* to play; ~**ría** *nf* toyshop.

juguetón, ona [xuxe'ton, ona] *a* playful.

juicio ['xwiθjo] *nm* judgement; (*razón*) sanity, reason; (*opinión*) opinion; **estar fuera de** ~ to be out of one's mind; ~**so, a** *a* wise, sensible.

julio ['xuljo] *nm* July.

junco ['xunko] *nm* rush, reed.

jungla ['xungla] *nf* jungle.

junio ['xunjo] *nm* June.

junta ['xunta] *nf ver* **junto**.

juntar [xun'tar] *vt* to join, unite; (*maquinaria*) to assemble, put

together; (*dinero*) to collect; ~**se** *vr* to join, meet; (*reunirse: personas*) to meet, assemble; (*arrimarse*) to approach, draw closer; ~**se con uno** to join sb.

junto, a ['xunto, a] *a* joined; (*unido*) united; (*anexo*) near, close; (*contiguo, próximo*) next, adjacent; ~**s** together // *ad:* **todo** ~ all at once // *nf* (*asamblea*) meeting, assembly; (*comité, consejo*) board, council, committee; (*articulación*) joint; ~ **a** near (to), next to.

jurado [xu'raδo] *nm* (*JUR: individuo*) juror; (: *grupo*) jury; (*de concurso: grupo*) panel (of judges); (: *individuo*) member of a panel.

juramento [xura'mento] *nm* oath; (*maldición*) oath, curse; **prestar** ~ to take the oath; **tomar** ~ **a** to swear in, administer the oath to.

jurar [xu'rar] *vt, vi* to swear; ~ **en falso** to commit perjury; **jurárselas a uno** to have it in for sb.

jurídico, a [xu'riδiko, a] *a* legal.

jurisdicción [xurisδik'θjon] *nf* (*poder, autoridad*) jurisdiction; (*territorio*) district.

jurisprudencia [xurispru'δenθja] *nf* jurisprudence.

jurista [xu'rista] *nm/f* jurist.

justamente [xusta'mente] *ad* justly, fairly; (*precisamente*) just, exactly.

justicia [xus'tiθja] *nf* justice; (*equidad*) fairness, justice; **justiciero, a** *a* just, righteous.

justificación [xustifika'θjon] *nf* justification; **justificar** *vt* to justify.

justo, a ['xusto, a] *a* (*equitativo*) just, fair, right; (*preciso*) exact, correct; (*ajustado*) tight // *ad* (*precisamente*) exactly, precisely; (*AM: apenas a tiempo*) just in time.

juvenil [xuβe'nil] *a* youthful.

juventud [xuβen'tuδ] *nf* (*adolescencia*) youth; (*jóvenes*) young people *pl*.

juzgado [xuθ'xaδo] *nm* tribunal; (*JUR*) court.

juzgar [xuθ'xar] *vt* to judge; **a** ~

por... to judge by..., judging by... .

K

kg abr (= kilogramo) kg.

kilo ['kilo] nm kilo // pref: **~gramo** nm kilogramme; **~metraje** nm distance in kilometres; ≈ mileage; **kilómetro** nm kilometre; **~vatio** nm kilowatt.

kiosco ['kjosko] nm = **quiosco**.

km abr (= kilómetro) km.

kv abr (= kilovatio) kw.

L

l abr (= litro) l.

la [la] artículo definido the // pron her; (Ud.) you; (cosa) it // nm (MUS) la; **~ del sombrero rojo** the girl in the red hat; tb ver **el**.

laberinto [laβe'rinto] nm labyrinth.

labia ['laβja] nf fluency; (pey) glib tongue.

labial [la'βjal] a labial.

labio ['laβjo] nm lip.

labor [la'βor] nf labour; (AGR) farm work; (tarea) job, task; (COSTURA) needlework; **~able** a (AGR) workable; **día ~able** working day; **~ar** vi to work.

laboratorio [laβora'torjo] nm laboratory.

laborioso, a [laβo'rjoso, a] a (persona) hard-working; (trabajo) tough.

laborista [laβo'rista] a: **Partido L~** Labour Party.

labrado, a [la'βraðo, a] a worked; (madera) carved; (metal) wrought // nm (AGR) cultivated field.

labrador, a [laβra'ðor, a] a farming // nm/f farmer.

labranza [la'βranθa] nf (AGR) cultivation.

labrar [la'βrar] vt (gen) to work; (madera etc) to carve; (fig) to cause, bring about.

labriego, a [la'βrjeχo, a] nm/f peasant.

laca ['laka] nf lacquer.

lacayo [la'kajo] nm lackey.

lacerar [laθe'rar] vt to lacerate.

lacio, a ['laθjo, a] a (pelo) lank, straight.

lacónico, a [la'koniko, a] a laconic.

lacrar [la'krar] vt (cerrar) to seal (with sealing wax); **lacre** nm sealing wax.

lacrimoso, a [lakri'moso, a] a tearful.

lactar [lak'tar] vt, vi to suckle.

lácteo, a ['lakteo, a] a: **productos ~s** dairy products.

ladear [laðe'ar] vt to tip, tilt // vi to tilt; **~se** vr to lean.

ladera [la'ðera] nf slope.

ladino, a [la'ðino, a] a cunning.

lado ['laðo] nm (gen) side; (fig) protection; (MIL) flank; **al ~ de** beside; **poner de ~** to put on its side; **poner a un ~** to put aside; **por todos ~s** on all sides, all round (Brit).

ladrar [la'ðrar] vi to bark; **ladrido** nm bark, barking.

ladrillo [la'ðriʎo] nm (gen) brick; (azulejo) tile.

ladrón, ona [la'ðron, ona] nm/f thief.

lagar [la'var] nm (wine/oil) press.

lagartija [lavar'tixa] nf (small) lizard.

lagarto [la'varto] nm (ZOOL) lizard.

lago ['lavo] nm lake.

lágrima ['lavrima] nf tear.

laguna [la'xuna] nf (lago) lagoon; (hueco) gap.

laico, a ['laiko, a] a lay.

lamentable [lamen'taβle] a lamentable, regrettable; (miserable) pitiful.

lamentar [lamen'tar] vt (sentir) to regret; (deplorar) to lament; **lo lamento mucho** I'm very sorry; **~se** vr to lament; **lamento** nm lament.

lamer [la'mer] vt to lick.

lámina ['lamina] nf (plancha

delgada) sheet; (para estampar, estampa) plate; **laminar** vt (en libro) to laminate.

lámpara ['lampara] nf lamp; ~ de alcohol/gas spirit/gas lamp; ~ de pie standard lamp.

lamparón [lampa'ron] nm grease spot.

lampiño [lam'piɲo] a clean-shaven.

lana ['lana] nf wool.

lance vt ver **lanzar** // ['lanθe] nm (golpe) stroke; (suceso) event, incident.

lancha ['lantʃa] nf launch; ~ de pesca fishing boat; ~ salvavidas/ torpedera lifeboat/torpedo boat.

lanero, a [la'nero, a] a woollen.

langosta [lan'gosta] nf (insecto) locust; (crustáceo) lobster; (fig) plague; **langostino** nm king prawn (Brit), crayfish (US).

lanero, a [la'nero, a] a woollen.

languidecer [langiðe'θer] vi to languish; **languidez** nf languor; **lánguido, a** a (gen) languid; (sin energía) listless.

lanilla [la'niʎa] nf nap.

lanudo, a [la'nuðo, a] a woolly.

lanza ['lanθa] nf (arma) lance, spear.

lanzadera [lanθa'ðera] nf shuttle.

lanzamiento [lanθa'mjento] nm (gen) throwing; (NAUT, COM) launch, launching; ~ de peso putting the shot.

lanzar [lan'θar] vt (gen) to throw; (DEPORTE: pelota) to bowl; (NAUT, COM) to launch; (JUR) to evict; ~se vr to throw o.s.

lapa ['lapa] nf limpet.

lapicero [lapi'θero] nm propelling (Brit) o mechanical (US) pencil; (AM: bolígrafo) Biro ®.

lápida ['lapiða] nf stone; ~ mortuoria headstone; ~ conmemorativa memorial stone; **lapidar** vt to stone; **lapidario, a** a, nm lapidary.

lápiz ['lapiθ] nm pencil; ~ de color coloured pencil; ~ de labios lipstick.

lapón, ona [la'pon, ona] nm/f Lap-

lander, Lapp.

Laponia [la'ponja] nf Lapland.

lapso ['lapso] nm (de tiempo) interval; (error) error.

lapsus ['lapsus] nm inv error, mistake.

largar [lar'var] vt (soltar) to release; (aflojar) to loosen; (lanzar) to launch; (fam) to let fly; (velas) to unfurl; (AM) to throw; ~se vr (fam) to beat it; ~se a (AM) to start to.

largo, a ['larvo, a] a (longitud) long; (tiempo) lengthy; (fig) generous // nm length; (MUS) largo // ad widely; dos años ~s two long years; tiene 9 metros de ~ it is 9 metres long; a lo ~ de along; (tiempo) all through, throughout.

laringe [la'rinxe] nf larynx; **laringitis** nf laryngitis.

larva ['larβa] nf larva.

las [las] artículo definido the // pron them; ~ que cantan the ones/ women/girls who sing; tb ver **el**.

lascivo, a [las'θiβo, a] a lewd.

láser ['laser] nm laser.

lástima ['lastima] nf (pena) pity; dar ~ to be pitiful; es una ~ que it's a pity that; ¡qué ~! what a pity!; ella está hecha una ~ she looks pitiful.

lastimar [lasti'mar] vt (herir) to wound; (ofender) to offend; ~se vr to hurt o.s.; **lastimero, a** a pitiful, pathetic.

lastre ['lastre] nm (TEC, NAUT) ballast; (fig) dead weight.

lata ['lata] nf (metal) tin (Brit), can; (caja) tin (Brit); (fam) nuisance; en ~ tinned (Brit), canned; dar (la) ~ to be a nuisance.

latente [la'tente] a latent.

lateral [late'ral] a side cpd, lateral // nm (TEATRO) wings.

latido [la'tiðo] nm (del corazón) beat.

latifundio [lati'fundjo] nm large estate; **latifundista** nm/f owner of a large estate.

latigazo [lati'yaθo] nm (golpe) lash; (sonido) crack.

látigo ['lativo] nm whip.

latín [la'tin] *nm* Latin.

latino, a [la'tino, a] *a* Latin; **~americano, a** *a, nmf* Latin-American.

latir [la'tir] *vi* (*corazón, pulso*) to beat.

latitud [lati'tuð] *nf* (*GEO*) latitude.

latón [la'ton] *nm* brass.

latoso, a [la'toso, a] *a* (*molesto*) annoying; (*aburrido*) boring.

laúd [la'uð] *nm* lute.

laureado, a [laure'aðo, a] *a* honoured // *nm* laureate.

laurel [lau'rel] *nm* (*BOT*) laurel; (*CULIN*) bay.

lava [la'βa] *nf* lava.

lavabo [la'βaβo] *nm* (*jofaina*) washbasin; (*tb:* **~s**) toilet.

lavadero [laβa'ðero] *nm* laundry.

lavado [la'βaðo] *nm* washing; (*de ropa*) laundry; (*ARTE*) wash; **~ de cerebro** brainwashing; **~ en seco** dry-cleaning.

lavadora [laβa'ðora] *nf* washing machine.

lavanda [la'βanda] *nf* lavender.

lavandería [laβande'ria] *nf* laundry; **~ automática** launderette.

lavaplatos [laβa'platos] *nm inv* dishwasher.

lavar [la'βar] *vt* to wash; (*borrar*) to wipe away; **~se** *vr* to wash o.s.; **~se las manos** to wash one's hands; **~y marcar** (*pelo*) to shampoo and set; **~ en seco** to dry-clean.

lavavajillas [laβaβa'xiλas] *nm inv* dishwasher.

laxante [lak'sante] *nm* laxative.

lazada [la'θaða] *nf* bow.

lazarillo [laθa'riλo] *nm:* **perro ~** guide dog.

lazo [la'θo] *nm* knot; (*lazada*) bow; (*para animales*) lasso; (*trampa*) snare; (*vínculo*) tie.

le [le] *pron* (*directo*) him; (*: usted*) you; (*indirecto*) to him; (*: usted*) to you.

leal [le'al] *a* loyal; **~tad** *nf* loyalty.

lebrel [le'βrel] *nm* greyhound.

lección [lek'θjon] *nf* lesson.

lector, a [lek'tor, a] *nm/f* reader.

lectura [lek'tura] *nf* reading.

leche [le'tʃe] *nf* milk; **tener mala ~** (*fam!*) to be nasty; **~ condensada/en polvo** condensed/powdered milk; **~ desnatada** skimmed milk; **~ra** *nf* (*vendedora*) milkmaid; (*recipiente*) milk churn; (*AM*) cow; **~ría** *nf* dairy; **~ro, a** *a* dairy.

lecho [le'tʃo] *nm* (*cama, de río*) bed; (*GEO*) layer.

lechón [le'tʃon] *nm* sucking (*Brit*) *o* suckling (*US*) pig.

lechoso, a [le'tʃoso, a] *a* milky.

lechuga [le'tʃuɣa] *nf* lettuce.

lechuza [le'tʃuθa] *nf* owl.

leer [le'er] *vt* to read.

legado [le'ɣaðo] *nm* (*don*) bequest; (*herencia*) legacy; (*enviado*) legate.

legajo [le'ɣaxo] *nm* file.

legal [le'ɣal] *a* (*gen*) legal; (*persona*) trustworthy; **~idad** *nf* legality; **~izar** *vt* to legalize; (*documento*) to authenticate.

legaña [le'ɣaɲa] *nf* sleep (*in eyes*).

legar [le'ɣar] *vt* to bequeath, leave.

legendario, a [lexen'darjo, a] *a* legendary.

legión [le'xjon] *nf* legion; **legionario, a** *a* legionary // *nm* legionnaire.

legislación [lexisla'θjon] *nf* legislation; **legislar** *vt* to legislate.

legitimar [lexiti'mar] *vt* to legitimize; **legítimo, a** *a* (*genuino*) authentic; (*legal*) legitimate.

lego, a [le'ɣo, a] *a* (*REL*) secular; (*ignorante*) ignorant // *nm* layman.

legua [le'ɣwa] *nf* league.

legumbres [le'ɣumbres] *nfpl* pulses.

leído, a [le'iðo, a] *a* well-read.

lejanía [lexa'nia] *nf* distance; **lejano, a** *a* far-off; (*en el tiempo*) distant; (*fig*) remote.

lejía [le'xia] *nf* bleach.

lejos [le'xos] *ad* far, far away; **a lo ~ in** the distance; **de o desde ~** from afar; **~ de** *prep* far from.

lelo, a [le'lo, a] *a* silly // *nm/f* idiot.

lema [le'ma] *nm* motto; (*POL*)

slogan.

lencería [lenθe'ria] *nf* linen, drapery.

lengua ['lengwa] *nf* tongue; (LING) language; **morderse la** ~ to hold one's tongue.

lenguado [len'gwaðo] *nm* sole.

lenguaje [len'gwaxe] *nm* language.

lengüeta [len'gweta] *nf* (ANAT) epiglottis; (zapatos, MUS) tongue.

lente ['lente] *nf* lens; (lupa) magnifying glass; ~**s** *nfpl* glasses; ~**s de contacto** contact lenses.

lenteja [len'texa] *nf* lentil; **lentejuela** *nf* sequin.

lentilla [len'tiʎa] *nf* contact lens.

lentitud [lenti'tuð] *nf* slowness; **con** ~ slowly.

lento, a ['lento, a] *a* slow.

leña ['leɲa] *nf* firewood; ~**dor, a** *nm/f* woodcutter.

leño ['leɲo] *nm* (trozo de árbol) log; (madera) timber; (fig) blockhead.

Leo ['leo] *nm* Leo.

león [le'on] *nm* lion; ~ **marino** sea lion; **leonino, a** *a* leonine.

leopardo [leo'parðo] *nm* leopard.

leotardos [leo'tarðos] *nmpl* tights.

lepra ['lepra] *nf* leprosy; **leproso, a** *nm/f* leper.

lerdo, a ['lerðo, a] *a* (lento) slow; (patoso) clumsy.

les [les] *pron* (directo) them; (: ustedes) you; (indirecto) to them; (: ustedes) to you.

lesbiana [les'ßjana] *a, nf* lesbian.

lesión [le'sjon] *nf* wound, lesion; (DEPORTE) injury; **lesionado, a** *a* injured // *nm/f* injured person.

letal [le'tal] *a* lethal.

letanía [leta'nia] *nf* litany.

letargo [le'tarvo] *nm* lethargy.

letra ['letra] *nf* letter; (escritura) handwriting; (MUS) lyrics *pl*; ~ **de cambio** bill of exchange; ~ **de imprenta** print; ~**do, a** *a* learned; (fam) pedantic // *nm* lawyer; **letrero** *nm* (cartel) sign; (etiqueta) label.

letrina [le'trina] *nf* latrine.

leucemia [leu'θemja] *nf* leukaemia.

levadizo [leßa'ðiθo] *a*: **puente** ~ drawbridge.

levadura [leßa'ðura] *nf* (para el pan) yeast; (de la cerveza) brewer's yeast.

levantamiento [leßanta'mjento] *nm* raising, lifting; (rebelión) revolt, rising; ~ **de pesos** weight-lifting.

levantar [leßan'tar] *vt* (gen) to raise; (del suelo) to pick up; (hacia arriba) to lift (up); (plan) to make, draw up; (mesa) to clear away; (campamento) to strike; (fig) to cheer up, hearten; ~**se** *vr* to get up; (enderezarse) to straighten up; (rebelarse) to rebel; ~ **el ánimo** to cheer up.

levante [le'ßante] *nm* east coast; **el L**~ region of Spain extending from Castellón to Murcia.

levar [le'ßar] *vt* to weigh anchor.

leve ['leße] *a* light; (fig) trivial; ~**dad** *nf* lightness.

levita [le'ßita] *nf* frock coat.

léxico ['leksiko] *nm* (vocabulario) vocabulary.

ley [lei] *nf* (gen) law; (metal) standard.

leyenda [le'jenda] *nf* legend.

leyó *etc vb ver* **leer.**

liar [li'ar] *vt* to tie (up); (unir) to bind; (envolver) to wrap (up); (enredar) to confuse; (cigarrillo) to roll; ~**se** *vr* (fam) to get involved; ~**se a palos** to get involved in a fight.

Líbano ['lißano] *nm*: **el** ~ the Lebanon.

libar [li'ßar] *vt* to suck.

libelo [li'ßelo] *nm* satire, lampoon; (JUR) petition.

libélula [li'ßelula] *nf* dragonfly.

liberación [lißera'ßjon] *nf* liberation; (de la cárcel) release.

liberal [liße'ral] *a, nm/f* liberal; ~**idad** *nf* liberality, generosity.

liberar [liße'rar] *vt* to liberate.

libertad [lißer'tað] *nf* liberty, freedom; ~ **de culto/de prensa/de comercio** freedom of worship/of the press/of trade; ~ **condicional** probation; ~ **bajo palabra** parole; ~

bajo fianza bail.

libertar [liβer'tar] vt (preso) to set free; (de una obligación) to release; (eximir) to exempt.

libertino, a [liβer'tino, a] a permissive // nmf permissive person.

libra ['liβra] nf pound; L~ (ASTROLOGÍA) Libra; ~ esterlina pound sterling.

librador, a [liβra'ðor, a] nmf drawer.

libramiento [liβra'mjento] nm rescue; (COM) delivery.

libranza [li'βranθa] nf (COM) draft; (letra de cambio) bill of exchange.

librar [li'βrar] vt (de peligro) to save; (batalla) to wage, fight; (de impuestos) to exempt; (cheque) to make out; (JUR) to exempt; ~se vr: ~se de to escape from, free o.s. from.

libre ['liβre] a free; (lugar) unoccupied; (asiento) vacant; (de deudas) free of debts; ~ de impuestos free of tax; tiro ~ free kick; los 100 metros ~ the 100 metres free-style (race); al aire ~ in the open air.

librería [liβre'ria] nf (tienda) bookshop; **librero, a** nmf bookseller.

libreta [li'βreta] nf notebook; ~ de ahorros savings book.

libro ['liβro] nm book; ~ de bolsillo paperback; ~ de caja cashbook; ~ de cheques chequebook (Brit), checkbook (US); ~ de texto textbook.

Lic. abr = **licenciado, a.**

licencia [li'θenθja] nf (gen) licence; (permiso) permission; ~ por enfermedad/con goce de sueldo sick leave/paid leave; ~ de caza game licence; ~do, a a licensed // nmf graduate; **licenciar** vt (empleado) to dismiss; (permitir) to permit, allow; (soldado) to discharge; (estudiante) to confer a degree upon; **licenciarse** vr: **licenciarse en letras** to graduate in arts.

licencioso, a [liθen'θjoso, a] a licentious.

liceo [li'θeo] nm (high) school.

licitar [liθi'tar] vt to bid for; (AM) to sell by auction.

lícito, a ['liθito, a] a (legal) lawful; (justo) fair, just; (permisible) permissible.

licor [li'kor] nm spirits pl (Brit), liquor (US); (de frutas etc) liqueur.

licuadora [likwa'ðora] nf blender.

licuar [li'kwar] vt to liquidize.

lid [lið] nf combat; (fig) controversy.

líder ['liðer] nmf leader; **liderato, liderazgo** nm leadership.

lidia ['liðja] nf bullfighting; (una ~) bullfight; **toros de ~** fighting bulls; **lidiar** vt, vi to fight.

liebre ['ljeβre] nf hare.

lienzo ['ljenθo] nm linen; (ARTE) canvas; (ARQ) wall.

liga ['liɣa] nf (de medias) garter, suspender; (AM: gomita) rubber band; (confederación) league.

ligadura [liɣa'ðura] nf bond, tie; (MED, MUS) ligature.

ligamento [liɣa'mento] nm (ANAT) ligament; (atadura) tie; (unión) bond.

ligar [li'ɣar] vt (atar) to tie; (unir) to join; (MED) to bind up; (MUS) to slur // vi to mix, blend; (fam) to pick up; ~se vr to commit o.s.

ligereza [lixe'reθa] nf lightness; (rapidez) swiftness; (agilidad) agility; (superficialidad) flippancy.

ligero, a [li'xero, a] a (de peso) light; (tela) thin; (rápido) swift, quick; (ágil) agile, nimble; (de importancia) slight; (de carácter) flippant, superficial // ad: **a la ligera** superficially.

liguero [li'xero] nm suspender (Brit) o garter (US) belt.

lija ['lixa] nf (ZOOL) dogfish; (papel de) ~ sandpaper.

lila ['lila] nf lilac.

lima ['lima] nf file; (BOT) lime; ~ de uñas nailfile; L~ n (GEO) Lima; **limar** vt to file.

limitación [limita'θjon] nf limitation,

limit; ~ **de velocidad** speed limit.
limitar [limi'tar] vt to limit; (reducir) to reduce, cut down // vi: ~ **con** to border on; ~**se** vr: ~**se a** to limit o.s. to.
límite ['limite] nm (gen) limit; (fin) end; (frontera) border; ~ **de velocidad** speed limit.
limítrofe [li'mitrofe] a bordering, neighbouring.
limón [li'mon] nm lemon // a: **amarillo** ~ lemon-yellow; **limonada** nf lemonade; **limonero** nm lemon tree.
limosna [li'mosna] nf alms pl; **vivir de** ~ to live on charity.
limpiabotas [limpja'βotas] nm inv bootblack (Brit), shoeshine boy/girl.
limpiaparabrisas [limpjapara'βrisas] nm inv windscreen (Brit) o windshield (US) wiper.
limpiar [lim'pjar] vt to clean; (con trapo) to wipe; (quitar) to wipe away; (zapatos) to shine, polish; (fig) to clean up.
limpieza [lim'pjeθa] nf (estado) cleanliness; (acto) cleaning; (: de las calles) cleansing; (: de zapatos) polishing; (habilidad) skill; (fig: POLICÍA) clean-up; (pureza) purity; (MIL): **operación de** ~ mopping-up operation; ~ **en seco** dry cleaning.
limpio, a ['limpjo, a] a clean; (moralmente) pure; (COM) clear, net; (fam) honest // ad: **jugar** ~ to play fair // nm: **pasar a** (Esp) o **en** (AM) ~ to make a fair copy.
linaje [li'naxe] nm lineage, family.
linaza [li'naθa] nf linseed.
lince ['linθe] nm lynx.
linchar [lin'tʃar] vt to lynch.
lindar [lin'dar] vi to adjoin; ~ **con** to border on; **linde** nm o f boundary; **lindero, a** a adjoining // nm boundary.
lindo, a ['lindo, a] a pretty, lovely // ad: **nos divertimos de lo** ~ we had a marvellous time; **canta muy** ~ (AM) he sings beautifully.
línea ['linea] nf (gen) line; **en** ~ (INFORM) on line; ~ **aérea** airline; ~

de meta goal line; (de carrera) finishing line; ~ **recta** straight line.
lingote [lin'gote] nm ingot.
lingüista [lin'gwista] nmf linguist; **lingüística** nf linguistics sg.
linimento [lini'mento] nm liniment.
lino ['lino] nm linen; (BOT) flax.
linóleo [li'noleo] nm lino, linoleum.
linterna [lin'terna] nf lantern, lamp; ~ **eléctrica** o **a pilas** torch (Brit), flashlight (US).
lío ['lio] nm bundle; (fam) fuss; (desorden) muddle, mess; **armar un** ~ to make a fuss.
liquen ['liken] nm lichen.
liquidación [likiða'θjon] nf liquidation; **venta de** ~ clearance sale.
liquidar [liki'ðar] vt (mercancías) to liquidate; (deudas) to pay off; (empresa) to wind up.
líquido, a ['likiðo, a] a liquid; (ganancia) net // nm liquid; ~ **imponible** net taxable income.
lira ['lira] nf (MUS) lyre; (moneda) lira.
lírico, a ['liriko, a] a lyrical.
lirio ['lirjo] nm (BOT) iris.
lirón [li'ron] nm (ZOOL) dormouse; (fig) sleepyhead.
Lisboa [lis'βoa] n Lisbon.
lisiado, a [li'sjaðo, a] a injured // nmf cripple.
lisiar [li'sjar] vt to maim; ~**se** vr to injure o.s.
liso, a ['liso, a] a (terreno) smooth; (cabello) straight; (superficie) even; (tela) plain.
lisonja [li'sonxa] nf flattery; **lisonjear** vt to flatter; (fig) to please; **lisonjero, a** a flattering; (agradable) gratifying, pleasing // nmf flatterer.
lista ['lista] nf list; (de alumnos) school register; (de libros) catalogue; (de platos) menu; (de precios) price list; **pasar** ~ to call the roll; ~ **de correos** poste restante; ~ **de espera** waiting list; **tela** ~**s** striped material.
listado, a [lis'taðo, a] a striped.

listo, a ['listo, a] *a* (*perspicaz*) smart, clever; (*preparado*) ready.

listón [lis'ton] *nm* (*tela*) ribbon; (*de madera, metal*) strip.

litera [li'tera] *nf* (*en barco, tren*) berth; (*en dormitorio*) bunk, bunk bed.

literal [lite'ral] *a* literal.

literario, a [lite'rarjo, a] *a* literary.

literato, a [lite'rato, a] *a* literary // *nm/f* writer.

literatura [litera'tura] *nf* literature.

litigar [liti'ɣar] *vt* to fight // *vi* (*JUR*) to go to law; (*fig*) to dispute, argue.

litigio [li'tixjo] *nm* (*JUR*) lawsuit; (*fig*): **en ~ con** in dispute with.

litografía [litoɣra'fia] *nf* lithography; (*una ~*) lithograph.

litoral [lito'ral] *a* coastal // *nm* coast, seaboard.

litro ['litro] *nm* litre.

liviano, a [li'βjano, a] *a* (*persona*) fickle; (*cosa, objeto*) trivial.

lívido, a ['liβiðo, a] *a* livid.

ll... *ver bajo la letra LL, después de L.*

lo [lo] *artículo definido neutro*; **~ bello** the beautiful, what is beautiful, that which is beautiful // *pron* (*persona*) him; (*cosa*) it; *tb ver* **el.**

loa ['loa] *nf* praise; **loable** *a* praiseworthy; **loar** *vt* to praise.

lobato [lo'βato] *nm* (*ZOOL*) wolf cub.

lobo ['loβo] *nm* wolf; **~ de mar** (*fig*) sea dog; **~ marino** seal.

lóbrego, a ['loβreɣo, a] *a* dark; (*fig*) gloomy.

lóbulo ['loβulo] *nm* lobe.

local [lo'kal] *a* local // *nm* place, site; (*oficinas*) premises *pl*; **~idad** *nf* (*barrio*) locality; (*lugar*) location; (*TEATRO*) seat, ticket; **~izar** *vt* (*ubicar*) to locate, find; (*restringir*) to localize; (*situar*) to place.

loción [lo'θjon] *nf* lotion.

loco, a ['loko, a] *a* mad // *nm/f* lunatic, mad person.

locomoción [lokomo'θjon] *nf* locomotion.

locomotora [lokomo'tora] *nf* engine, locomotive.

locuaz [lo'kwaθ] *a* loquacious.

locución [loku'θjon] *nf* expression.

locura [lo'kura] *nf* madness; (*acto*) crazy act.

locutor, a [loku'tor, a] *nm/f* (*RADIO*) announcer; (*comentarista*) commentator; (*TV*) newsreader.

locutorio [loku'torjo] *nm* (*en telefónica*) telephone booth.

lodo ['loðo] *nm* mud.

lógico, a ['loxiko, a] *a* logical // *nf* logic.

logística [lo'xistika] *nf* logistics *pl.*

lograr [lo'ɣrar] *vt* to achieve; (*obtener*) to get, obtain; **~ hacer** to manage to do; (*que uno venga*) to manage to get sb to come.

logro ['loɣro] *nm* achievement, success.

loma ['loma] *nf* hillock (*Brit*), small hill.

lombriz [lom'briθ] *nf* worm.

lomo ['lomo] *nm* (*de animal*) back; (*CULIN: de cerdo*) pork loin; (: *de vaca*) rib steak; (*de libro*) spine.

lona ['lona] *nf* canvas.

loncha ['lontʃa] *nf* = **lonja.**

lonche ['lontʃe] *nm* (*AM*) lunch; **~ría** *nf* (*AM*) snack bar, diner (*US*).

Londres ['londres] *n* London.

longaniza [longa'niθa] *nf* pork sausage.

longitud [lonxi'tuð] *nf* length; (*GEO*) longitude; **tener 3 metros de ~** to be 3 metres long; **~ de onda** wavelength.

lonja ['lonxa] *nf* slice; (*de tocino*) rasher; **~ de pescado** fish market.

loro ['loro] *nm* parrot.

los [los] *artículo definido* the // *pron* them; (*ustedes*) you; **mis libros y ~ de Ud** my books and yours; *tb ver* **el.**

losa ['losa] *nf* stone; **~ sepulcral** gravestone.

lote ['lote] *nm* portion; (*COM*) lot.

lotería [lote'ria] *nf* lottery; (*juego*) lotto.

loza [ˈloθa] *nf* crockery.

lozanía [loθaˈnia] *nf* (*lujo*) luxuriance; **lozano, a** *a* luxuriant; (*animado*) lively.

lubricante [luβriˈkante] *nm* lubricant.

lubricar [luβriˈkar] *vt* to lubricate.

lucero [luˈθero] *nm* bright star; (*fig*) brilliance.

lucidez [luθiˈðeθ] *nf* lucidity; **lúcido, a** *a* lucid.

luciérnaga [luˈθjernaɣa] *nf* glowworm.

lucimiento [luθiˈmjento] *nm* (*brillo*) brilliance; (*éxito*) success.

lucir [luˈθir] *vt* to illuminate, light (up); (*ostentar*) to show off // *vi* (*brillar*) to shine; **~se** *vr* (*irónico*) to make a fool of o.s.

lucro [ˈlukro] *nm* profit, gain.

lucha [ˈlutʃa] *nf* fight, struggle; **~ de clases** class struggle; **~ libre** wrestling; **luchar** *vi* to fight.

luego [ˈlweɣo] *ad* (*después*) next; (*mas tarde*) later, afterwards; **desde ~** of course.

lugar [luˈɣar] *nm* place; (*sitio*) spot; **en ~ de** instead of; **hacer ~** to make room; **fuera de ~** out of place; **tener ~** to take place; **~ común** commonplace.

lugareño, a [luɣaˈreɲo, a] *a* village *cpd* // *nm/f* villager.

lugarteniente [luɣarteˈnjente] *nm* deputy.

lúgubre [ˈluɣuβre] *a* mournful.

lujo [ˈluxo] *nm* luxury; (*fig*) profusion, abundance; **~so, a** *a* luxurious.

lujuria [luˈxurja] *nf* lust.

lumbre [ˈlumbre] *nf* (*gen*) light.

lumbrera [lumˈbrera] *nf* luminary.

luminoso, a [lumiˈnoso, a] *a* luminous, shining.

luna [ˈluna] *nf* moon; (*de un espejo*) glass; (*de gafas*) lens; (*fig*) crescent; **~ llena/nueva** full/new moon; **estar en la ~** to have one's head in the clouds; **~ de miel** honeymoon.

lunar [luˈnar] *a* lunar // *nm* (*ANAT*)

mole; **tela y ~es** spotted material.

lunes [ˈlunes] *nm inv* Monday.

lupa [ˈlupa] *nf* magnifying glass.

lustrar [lusˈtrar] *vt* (*mueble*) to polish; (*zapatos*) to shine; **lustre** *nm* polish; (*fig*) lustre; **dar lustre a** to polish; **lustroso, a** *a* shining.

luterano, a [luteˈrano, a] *a* Lutheran.

luto [ˈluto] *nm* mourning; (*congoja*) grief, sorrow; **llevar el o vestirse de ~** to be in mourning.

Luxemburgo [luksemˈburɣo] *nm* Luxembourg.

luz [luθ] (*pl* **luces**) *nf* light; **dar a ~ un niño** to give birth to a child; **sacar a la ~** to bring to light; (*ELEC*): **dar o encender** (*Esp*) *o* **prender** (*AM*)/**apagar la ~** to switch the light on/off; **a todas luces** by any reckoning; **hacer la ~ sobre** to shed light on; **tener pocas luces** to be dim *o* stupid; **~ roja/verde** red/green light; (*AUTO*): **~ de freno** brake light; **luces de tráfico** traffic lights; **traje de luces** bullfighter's costume.

LL

llaga [ˈʎaɣa] *nf* wound.

llama [ˈʎama] *nf* flame; (*ZOOL*) llama.

llamada [ʎaˈmaða] *nf* call; **~ al orden** call to order; **~ a pie de página** reference note.

llamamiento [ʎamaˈmjento] *nm* call.

llamar [ʎaˈmar] *vt* to call; (*atención*) to attract // *vi* (*por teléfono*) to telephone; (*a la puerta*) to knock/ring; (*por señas*) to beckon; (*MIL*) to call up; **~se** *vr* to be called, be named; **¿cómo se llama usted?** what's your name?

llamarada [ʎamaˈraða] *nf* (*llamas*) blaze; (*rubor*) flush; (*fig*) flare-up.

llamativo, a [ʎamaˈtiβo, a] *a* showy; (*color*) loud.

llamear [ʎame'ar] *vi* to blaze.

llano, a ['ʎano, a] *a* (*superficie*) flat; (*persona*) straightforward; (*estilo*) clear // *nm* plain, flat ground.

llanta ['ʎanta] *nf* (*wheel*) rim; (*AM*): ~ (**de goma**) tyre; (: *cámara*) inner (tube).

llanto ['ʎanto] *nm* weeping.

llanura [ʎa'nura] *nf* plain.

llave ['ʎaβe] *nf* key; (*del agua*) tap; (*MECÁNICA*) spanner; (*de la luz*) switch; (*MUS*) key; ~ **inglesa** monkey wrench; ~ **maestra** master key; ~ **de contacto** (*AUTO*) ignition key; ~ **de paso** stopcock; **echar** ~ **a** to lock up; ~**ro** *nm* keyring; **llavín** *nm* latchkey.

llegada [ʎe'yaða] *nf* arrival.

llegar [ʎe'yar] *vi* to arrive; (*alcanzar*) to reach; (*bastar*) to be enough; ~**se** *vr*: ~**se a** to approach; ~ **a** to manage to, succeed in; ~ **a saber** to find out; ~ **a ser** to become; ~ **a las manos de** to come into the hands of.

llenar [ʎe'nar] *vt* to fill; (*espacio*) to cover; (*formulario*) to fill in o up; (*fig*) to heap.

lleno, a ['ʎeno, a] *a* full, filled; (*repleto*) full up // *nm* (*abundancia*) abundance; (*TEATRO*) full house; **dar de** ~ **contra un muro** to hit a wall head-on.

llevadero, a [ʎeβa'ðero, a] *a* bearable, tolerable.

llevar [ʎe'βar] *vt* to take; (*ropa*) to wear; (*cargar*) to carry; (*quitar*) to take away; (*conducir a alguien*) to drive; (*transportar*) to transport; (*traer: dinero*) to carry; (*conducir*) to lead; (*MAT*) to carry; ~**se** *vr* to carry off, take away; **llevamos dos días aquí** we have been here for two days; **él me lleva 2 años** he's two years older than me; (*COM*): ~ **los libros** to keep the books; ~**se bien** to get on well (together).

llorar [ʎo'rar] *vt*, *vi* to cry, weep; ~ **de risa** to cry with laughter.

lloriquear [ʎorike'ar] *vi* to snivel, whimper.

lloro ['ʎoro] *nm* crying, weeping; **llorón, ona** *a* tearful // *nm/f* crybaby; ~**so, a** *a* (*gen*) weeping, tearful; (*triste*) sad, sorrowful.

llover [ʎo'βer] *vi* to rain.

llovizna [ʎo'βiθna] *nf* drizzle; **lloviznar** *vi* to drizzle.

llueve *etc vb ver* **llover**.

lluvia ['ʎuβja] *nf* rain; ~ **radioactiva** radioactive fallout; **lluvioso, a** *a* rainy.

M

m *abr* (= *metro*) m; (= *minuto*) m.

macarrones [maka'rrones] *nmpl* macaroni *sg*.

macedonia [maθe'ðonja] *nf*: ~ **de frutas** fruit salad.

macerar [maθe'rar] *vt* to macerate.

maceta [ma'θeta] *nf* (*de flores*) pot of flowers; (*para plantas*) flowerpot.

macizo, a [ma'θiθo, a] *a* (*grande*) massive; (*fuerte, sólido*) solid // *nm* mass, chunk.

mácula ['makula] *nf* stain, blemish.

machacar [matʃa'kar] *vt* to crush, pound // *vi* (*insistir*) to go on, keep on.

machete [ma'tʃete] *nm* (*AM*) machete, (large) knife.

machista [ma'tʃista] *a*, *nm* sexist.

macho ['matʃo] *a* male; (*fig*) virile // *nm* male; (*fig*) he-man.

machucar [matʃu'kar] *vt* to pound.

madeja [ma'ðexa] *nf* (*de lana*) skein, hank; (*de pelo*) mass, mop.

madera [ma'ðera] *nf* wood; (*fig*) nature, character; **una** ~ **a** piece of wood.

madero [ma'ðero] *nm* beam; (*fig*) ship.

madrastra [ma'ðrastra] *nf* stepmother.

madre ['maðre] *a* mother *cpd*; (*AM*) tremendous // *nf* mother; (*de vino etc*) dregs *pl*; ~ **política/soltera** mother-in-law/unmarried mother.

madreperla [maðre'perla] *nf* mother-of-pearl.

madreselva [maðre'selβa] *nf* honeysuckle.

Madrid [ma'ðrið] *n* Madrid.

madriguera [maðri'vera] *nf* burrow.

madrileño, a [maðri'leɲo, a] *a* of o from Madrid // *nm/f* native of Madrid.

madrina [ma'ðrina] *nf* godmother; (*ARQ*) prop, shore; (*TEC*) brace; ~ **de boda** bridesmaid.

madrugada [maðru'vaða] *nf* early morning; (*alba*) dawn, daybreak.

madrugador, a [maðruva'ðor, a] *a* early-rising.

madrugar [maðru'var] *vi* to get up early; (*fig*) to get ahead.

madurar [maðu'rar] *vt, vi* (*fruta*) to ripen; (*fig*) to mature; **madurez** *nf* ripeness; maturity; **maduro, a** *a* ripe; mature.

maestra [ma'estra] *nf ver* **maestro.**

maestría [maes'tria] *nf* mastery; (*habilidad*) skill, expertise.

maestro, a [ma'estro, a] *a* masterly; (*perito*) skilled, expert; (*principal*) main; (*educado*) trained // *nm/f* master/mistress; (*profesor*) teacher // *nm* (*autoridad*) authority; (*MUS*) maestro; (*AM*) skilled workman; ~ **albañil** master mason.

magia ['maxja] *nf* magic; **mágico, a** *a* magic(al) // *nm/f* magician.

magisterio [maxis'terjo] *nm* (*enseñanza*) teaching; (*profesión*) teaching profession; (*maestros*) teachers *pl*.

magistrado [maxis'traðo] *nm* magistrate.

magistral [maxis'tral] *a* magisterial; (*fig*) masterly.

magnánimo, a [mav'nanimo, a] *a* magnanimous.

magnate [mav'nate] *nm* magnate, tycoon.

magnético, a [mav'netiko, a] *a* magnetic; **magnetizar** *vt* to magnetize.

magnetofón, [mavneto'fon] **mag-netófono** [mavne'tofono] *nm* tape

recorder; **magnetofónico, a** *a*: **cinta magnetofónica** recording tape.

magnífico, a [mav'nifiko, a] *a* splendid, magnificent.

magnitud [mavni'tuð] *nf* magnitude.

mago, a ['mavo, a] *nm/f* magician; **los Reyes M~s** the Magi, the Three Wise Men.

magro, a ['mavro, a] *a* (*persona*) thin, lean; (*carne*) lean.

maguey [ma'vei] *nm* agave.

magullar [mavu'ʎar] *vt* (*amoratar*) to bruise; (*dañar*) to damage; (*fam: golpear*) to bash, beat.

mahometano, a [maome'tano, a] *a* Mohammedan.

mahonesa [mao'nesa] *nf* = mayonesa.

maíz [ma'iθ] *nm* maize (*Brit*), corn (*US*); sweet corn.

majadero, a [maxa'ðero, a] *a* silly, stupid.

majestad [maxes'tað] *nf* majesty; **majestuoso, a** *a* majestic.

majo, a ['maxo, a] *a* nice; (*guapo*) attractive, good-looking; (*elegante*) smart.

mal [mal] *ad* badly; (*equivocadamente*) wrongly; (*con dificultad*) with difficulty // *a* = **malo** // *nm* evil; (*desgracia*) misfortune; (*daño*) harm, damage; (*MED*) illness; **¡menos ~!** just as well!; ~ **que bien** rightly or wrongly.

malabarismo [malaβa'rismo] *nm* juggling; **malabarista** *nm/f* juggler.

malaconsejado, a [malakonse-'xaðo, a] *a* ill-advised.

malaria [ma'larja] *nf* malaria.

malcriado, a [mal'krjaðo, a] *a* (*consentido*) spoiled.

maldad [mal'daθ] *nf* evil, wickedness.

maldecir [malde'θir] *vt* to curse // *vi*: ~ **de** to speak ill of.

maldición [maldi'θjon] *nf* curse.

maldito, a [mal'dito, a] *a* (*condenado*) damned; (*perverso*) wicked; **¡~ sea!** damn it!

maleante [male'ante] *a* wicked // *nmf* malefactor.

malecón [male'kon] *nm* pier, jetty.

maledicencia [maleði'θenθja] *nf* slander, scandal.

maleducado, a [maleðu'kaðo. a] *a* bad-mannered, rude.

maleficio [male'fiθjo] *nm* curse, spell.

malestar [males'tar] *nm* (*gen*) discomfort; (*fig: inquietud*) uneasiness; (*POL*) unrest.

maleta [ma'leta] *nf* case, suitcase; (*AUTO*) boot (*Brit*), trunk (*US*); **maletera** *nf* (*AM AUTO*) = **maletero**; **maletero** *nm* (*AUTO*) boot (*Brit*), trunk (*US*); **maletín** *nm* small case, bag.

malévolo, a [ma'leßolo. a] *a* malicious, spiteful.

maleza [ma'leθa] *nf* (*hierbas malas*) weeds *pl*; (*arbustos*) thicket.

malgastar [malɣas'tar] *vt* (*tiempo, dinero*) to waste; (*salud*) to ruin.

malhechor, a [male'tʃor. a] *nm/f* malefactor; (*criminal*) criminal.

malhumorado, a [malumo'raðo. a] *a* bad-tempered, cross.

malicia [ma'liθja] *nf* (*maldad*) wickedness; (*astucia*) slyness, guile; (*mala intención*) malice, spite; (*carácter travieso*) mischievousness; **malicioso, a** *a* wicked, evil; sly, crafty; malicious, spiteful; mischievous.

maligno, a [ma'liɣno. a] *a* evil; (*malévolo*) malicious; (*MED*) malignant.

malo, a [ma'lo. a] *a* bad; (*falso*) false // *nm/f* villain // *nf* spell of bad luck; **estar ~** to be ill; **estar de malas** (*de mal humor*) to be in a bad mood.

malograr [malo'ɣrar] *vt* to spoil; (*plan*) to upset; (*ocasión*) to waste; **~se** *vr* (*plan etc*) to fail, come to grief; (*persona*) to die before one's time.

malparado, a [malpa'raðo. a] *a*: **salir ~** to come off badly.

malparir [malpa'rir] *vi* to have a miscarriage.

malsano, a [mal'sano. a] *a* unhealthy.

Malta [′malta] *nf* Malta.

malteada [malte'aða] *nf* (*AM*) milk shake.

maltratar [maltra'tar] *vt* to ill-treat, mistreat.

maltrecho, a [mal'tretʃo. a] *a* battered, damaged.

malvado, a [mal'βaðo. a] *a* evil, villainous.

malvavisco [malßa'ßisko] *nm* marshmallow.

malversar [malßer'sar] *vt* to embezzle, misappropriate.

Malvinas [mal'βinas]: **Islas ~** *nfpl* Falkland Islands.

malla [′maʎa] *nf* mesh; (*de baño*) swimsuit; (*de ballet, gimnasia*) leotard; **~s** *nfpl* tights; **~ de alambre** wire mesh.

Mallorca [ma'ʎorka] *nf* Majorca.

mama [′mama] *nf* (*de animal*) teat; (*de mujer*) breast.

mamá [ma'ma] (*pl* **~s**) *nf* (*fam*) mum, mummy.

mamar [ma'mar] *vt* (*pecho*) to suck; (*fig*) to absorb, assimilate // *vi* to suck.

mamarracho [mama'rratʃo] *nm* sight, mess.

mamífero [ma'mifero] *nm* mammal.

mampara [mam'para] *nf* (*entre habitaciones*) partition; (*biombo*) screen.

mampostería [mamposte'ria] *nf* masonry.

mamut [ma'mut] (*pl* **~s**) *nm* mammoth.

manada [ma'naða] *nf* (*ZOOL*) herd; (*: de leones*) pride; (*: de lobos*) pack.

Managua [ma'naɣwa] *n* Managua.

manantial [manan'tjal] *nm* spring; (*fuente*) fountain; (*fig*) source.

manar [ma'nar] *vi* to run with, flow with // *vi* to run, flow; (*abundar*) to abound.

mancilla [man'θiʎa] nf stain, blemish.

manco, a ['manko, a] a (de un brazo) one-armed; (de una mano) one-handed; (fig) defective, faulty.

mancomunar [mankomu'nar] vt to unite, bring together; (recursos) to pool; (JUR) to make jointly responsible; **mancomunidad** nf union, association; (comunidad) community; (JUR) joint responsibility.

mancha ['mantʃa] nf stain, mark; (ZOOL) patch; (boceto) sketch, outline; **manchar** vt (gen) to stain, mark; (ensuciar) to soil, dirty.

manchego, a [man'tʃevo, a] a of o from La Mancha.

mandado [man'daðo] nm (orden) order; (comisión) commission, errand.

mandamiento [manda'mjento] nm (orden) order, command; (REL) commandment; **~ judicial** warrant.

mandar [man'dar] vt (ordenar) to order; (dirigir) to lead, command; (enviar) to send; (pedir) to order, ask for // vi to be in charge; (pey) to be bossy; ¿**mande?** pardon?, excuse me?; **~ hacer un traje** to have a suit made.

mandarín [manda'rin] nm mandarin.

mandarina [manda'rina] nf (fruta) tangerine, mandarin (orange).

mandatario, a [manda'tarjo, a] nm/f (representante) agent; (AM: líder) leader.

mandato [man'dato] nm (orden) order; (INFORM) command; (POL: período) term of office; (: territorio) mandate; **~ judicial** (search) warrant.

mandíbula [man'diβula] nf jaw.

mandil [man'dil] nm (delantal) apron.

mando ['mando] nm (MIL) command; (de país) rule; (el primer lugar) lead; (POL) term of office; (TEC) control; **~ a la izquierda** left-hand drive.

mandolina [mando'lina] nf mandolin(e).

mandón, ona [man'don, ona] a bossy, domineering.

manejable [mane'xaβle] a manageable.

manejar [mane'xar] vt to manage; (máquina) to work, operate; (caballo etc) to handle; (casa) to run, manage; (AM: AUTO) to drive; **~se** vr (comportarse) to act, behave; (arreglárselas) to manage; **manejo** nm management; handling; running; driving; (facilidad de trato) ease, confidence; **manejos** nmpl intrigues.

manera [ma'nera] nf way, manner, fashion; **~s** nfpl (modales) manners; **su ~ de ser** the way he is; (aire) his manner; **de ninguna ~** no way, by no means; **de otra ~** otherwise; **de todas ~s** at any rate; **no hay ~ de persuadirle** there's no way of convincing him.

manga ['manga] nf (de camisa) sleeve; (de riego) hose.

mangana [man'gana] nf lasso.

mango ['mango] nm handle; (BOT) mango.

mangonear [mangone'ar] vi (meterse) to meddle, interfere; (ser mandón) to boss people about.

manguera [man'gera] nf (de riego) hose; (tubo) pipe.

maní [ma'ni] nm (AM) peanut.

manía [ma'nia] nf (MED) mania; (fig: moda) rage, craze; (disgusto) dislike; (malicia) spite; **maníaco, a** a maniac(al) // nm/f maniac.

maniatar [manja'tar] vt to tie the hands of.

maniático, a [ma'njatiko, a] a maniac(al) // nm/f maniac.

manicomio [mani'komjo] nm mental hospital (Brit), insane asylum (US).

manicura [mani'kura] nf manicure.

manifestación [manifesta'θjon] nf (declaración) statement, declaration; (de emoción) show, display; (POL: desfile) demonstration; (: concentración) mass meeting.

manifestar [manifes'tar] *vt* to show, manifest; (*declarar*) to state, declare; **manifiesto, a** *a* clear, manifest // *nm* manifesto.

manija [ma'nixa] *nf* handle.

maniobra [ma'njoβra] *nf* manoeuvring; (*manejo*) handling; (*fig*) manoeuvre; (*estratagema*) stratagem; **~s** *nfpl* manoeuvres; **maniobrar** *vt* to manoeuvre; (*manejar*) to handle.

manipulación [manipula'θjon] *nf* manipulation; **manipular** *vt* to manipulate; (*manejar*) to handle.

maniquí [mani'ki] *nm* dummy // *nm/f* model.

manirroto, a [mani'rroto, a] *a* lavish, extravagant // *nm/f* spendthrift.

manivela [mani'βela] *nf* crank.

manjar [man'xar] *nm* (tasty) dish.

mano ['mano] *nf* hand; (*ZOOL*) foot, paw; (*de pintura*) coat; (*serie*) lot, series; **a ~** by hand; **a ~ derecha/izquierda** on the right(-hand side)/left(-hand side); **de primera ~** (at) first hand; **de segunda ~** (at) second hand; **robo a ~ armada** armed robbery; **~ de obra** labour, manpower; **estrechar la ~ a uno** to shake sb's hand.

manojo [ma'noxo] *nm* handful, bunch; **~ de llaves** bunch of keys.

manopla [ma'nopla] *nf* (*guante*) glove; (*paño*) face cloth.

manoseado, a [manose'aðo, a] *a* well-worn; **manosear** *vt* (*tocar*) to handle, touch; (*desordenar*) to mess up, rumple; (*insistir en*) to overwork; (*AM*) to caress, fondle.

manotazo [mano'taθo] *nm* slap, smack.

mansalva [man'salβa]: **a ~** *ad* indiscriminately.

mansedumbre [manse'ðumbre] *nf* gentleness, meekness.

mansión [man'sjon] *nf* mansion.

manso, a ['manso, a] *a* gentle, mild; (*animal*) tame.

manta ['manta] *nf* blanket; (*AM: poncho*) poncho.

manteca [man'teka] *nf* fat; **~ de cacahuete/cacao** peanut/cocoa butter; **~ de cerdo** lard.

mantecado [mante'kaðo] *nm* (*AM*) ice cream.

mantel [man'tel] *nm* tablecloth.

mantendré *etc vb ver* **mantener**.

mantener [mante'ner] *vt* to support, maintain; (*alimentar*) to sustain; (*conservar*) to keep; (*TEC*) to maintain, service; **~se** *vr* (*seguir de pie*) to be still standing; (*no ceder*) to hold one's ground; (*subsistir*) to sustain o.s., keep going; **mantenimiento** *nm* maintenance; sustenance; (*sustento*) support.

mantequilla [mante'kiʎa] *nf* butter.

mantilla [man'tiʎa] *nf* mantilla; **~s** *nfpl* baby clothes.

manto ['manto] *nm* (*capa*) cloak; (*de ceremonia*) robe, gown.

mantón [man'ton] *nm* shawl.

mantuve, mantuviera *etc vb ver* **mantener**.

manual [ma'nwal] *a* manual // *nm* manual, handbook.

manufactura [manufak'tura] *nf* manufacture; (*fábrica*) factory.

manuscrito, a [manus'krito, a] *a* handwritten // *nm* manuscript.

manutención [manuten'θjon] *nf* maintenance; (*sustento*) support.

manzana [man'θana] *nf* apple; (*ARQ*) block (of houses).

manzanilla [manθa'niʎa] *nf* (*planta*) camomile; (*infusión*) camomile tea; (*vino de jerez*) manzanilla sherry.

manzano [man'θano] *nm* apple tree.

maña ['maɲa] *nf* (*gen*) skill, dexterity; (*pey*) guile; (*costumbre*) habit; (*destreza*) trick, knack.

mañana [ma'ɲana] *ad* tomorrow // *nm* future // *nf* morning; **de o por la ~** in the morning; **¡hasta ~!** see you tomorrow!; **~ por la ~** tomorrow morning; **mañanero, a** *a* early-rising.

mañoso, a [ma'ɲoso, a] *a* (*hábil*) skilful; (*astuto*) smart, clever.

mapa ['mapa] *nm* map.

maqueta [ma'keta] *nf* (scale) model.

maquillaje [maki'ʎaxe] *nm* make-up; (*acto*) making up.

maquillar [maki'ʎar] *vt* to make up; ~**se** *vr* to put on (some) make-up.

máquina ['makina] *nf* machine; (*de tren*) locomotive, engine; (*FOTO*) camera; (*fig*) machinery; (: *proyecto*) plan, project; **escrito a** ~ typewritten; ~ **de escribir** typewriter; ~ **de coser/lavar** sewing/washing machine.

maquinación [makina'θjon] *nf* machination, plot.

maquinal [maki'nal] *a* (*fig*) mechanical, automatic.

maquinaria [maki'narja] *nf* (*máquinas*) machinery; (*mecanismo*) mechanism, works *pl*.

maquinilla [maki'niʎa] *nf*: ~ **de afeitar** razor.

maquinista [maki'nista] *nm/f* (*de tren*) engine driver; (*TEC*) operator; (*NAUT*) engineer.

mar [mar] *nm o f* sea; ~ **adentro** o **afuera** out at sea; **en alta** ~ on the high seas; **la** ~ **de** (*fam*) lots of; **el M~ Negro/Báltico** the Black/Baltic Sea.

maraña [ma'raɲa] *nf* (*maleza*) thicket; (*confusión*) tangle.

maravilla [mara'βiʎa] *nf* marvel, wonder; (*BOT*) marigold; **maravillar** *vt* to astonish, amaze; **maravillarse** *vr* to be astonished, be amazed; **maravilloso, a** *a* wonderful, marvellous.

marca ['marka] *nf* (*gen*) mark; (*sello*) stamp; (*COM*) make, brand; **de** ~ excellent, outstanding; **de fábrica** trademark; ~ **registrada** registered trademark.

marcado, a [mar'kaðo, a] *a* marked, strong.

marcador [marka'ðor] *nm* (*DEPORTE*) scoreboard; (: *persona*) scorer.

marcar [mar'kar] *vt* (*gen*) to mark; (*número de teléfono*) to dial; (*gol*) to score; (*números*) to record, keep a tally of; (*pelo*) to set // *vi*

(*DEPORTE*) to score; (*TEL*) to dial.

marcial [mar'θjal] *a* martial, military.

marciano, a [mar'θjano, a] *a* Martian.

marco ['marko] *nm* frame; (*DEPORTE*) goal-posts *pl*; (*moneda*) mark; (*fig*) framework; ~ **de chimenea** mantelpiece.

marcha ['martʃa] *nf* march; (*TEC*) running, working; (*AUTO*) gear; (*velocidad*) speed; (*fig*) progress; (*dirección*) course; **poner en** ~ to put into gear; (*fig*) to set in motion, get going; **dar** ~ **atrás** to reverse, put into reverse; **estar en** ~ to be under way, be in motion.

marchar [mar'tʃar] *vi* (*ir*) to go; (*funcionar*) to work, go; ~**se** *vr* to go (away), leave.

marchitar [martʃi'tar] *vt* to wither, dry up; ~**se** *vr* (*BOT*) to wither; (*fig*) to fade away; **marchito, a** *a* withered, faded; (*fig*) in decline.

marea [ma'rea] *nf* tide; (*lloviezna*) drizzle.

marear [mare'ar] *vt* (*fig*) to annoy, upset; (*MED*): ~ **a uno** to make sb feel sick; ~**se** *vr* (*tener náuseas*) to feel sick; (*desvanecerse*) to feel faint; (*aturdirse*) to feel dizzy; (*fam: emborracharse*) to get tipsy.

maremoto [mare'moto] *nm* tidal wave.

mareo [ma'reo] *nm* (*náusea*) sick feeling; (*aturdimiento*) dizziness; (*fam: lata*) nuisance.

marfil [mar'fil] *nm* ivory.

margarina [marɣa'rina] *nf* margarine.

margarita [marɣa'rita] *nf* (*BOT*) daisy; (*rueda*) ~ daisywheel.

margen ['marxen] *nm* (*borde*) edge, border; (*fig*) margin, space // *nf* (*de río etc*) bank; **dar** ~ **para** to give an opportunity for; **mantenerse al** ~ to keep out (of things).

marica [ma'rika] *nm* (*fam*) sissy.

maricón [mari'kon] *nm* (*fam*) queer.

marido [ma'riðo] *nm* husband.

mariguana [mari'ywana], **mariuana** [mari'wana] nf marijuana, cannabis.

marimacho [mari'matʃo] nm (fam) mannish woman.

marina [ma'rina] nf navy; ~ **mercante** merchant navy.

marinero, a [mari'nero, a] a sea cpd; (barco) seaworthy // nm sailor, seaman.

marino, a [ma'rino, a] a sea cpd, marine // nm sailor.

marioneta [marjo'neta] nf puppet.

mariposa [mari'posa] nf butterfly.

mariquita [mari'kita] nf ladybird (Brit), ladybug (US).

mariscos [ma'riskos] nmpl shellfish inv, seafood(s).

marisma [ma'risma] nf marsh, swamp.

marítimo, a [ma'ritimo, a] a sea cpd, maritime.

marmita [mar'mita] nf pot.

mármol ['marmol] nm marble.

marqués, esa [mar'kes, esa] nm/f marquis/marchioness.

marrón [ma'rron] a brown.

marroquí [marro'ki] a, nm/f Moroccan // nm Morocco (leather).

Marruecos [ma'rrwekos] nm Morocco.

martes ['martes] nm inv Tuesday.

martillar [marti'ʎar] vt to hammer.

martillo [mar'tiʎo] nm hammer; ~ **neumático** pneumatic drill (Brit), jackhammer.

mártir ['martir] nm/f martyr; **martirio** [mar'tirjo] nm martyrdom; (fig) torture, torment.

marxismo [mark'sismo] nm Marxism; **marxista** a, nm/f Marxist.

marzo ['marθo] nm March.

mas [mas] conj but.

PALABRA CLAVE

más [mas] ♦ a, ad 1: ~ (que, de) (comparativo) more (than), ...+ er (than); ~ grande/inteligente bigger/more intelligent; trabaja ~ (que yo) he works more (than me); ver tb cada

2 (superlativo): el ~ the most, ...+ est; el ~ grande/inteligente (de) the biggest/most intelligent (in)

3 (negativo): no tengo ~ dinero I haven't got any more money; no viene ~ por aquí he doesn't come round here any more

4 (adicional): no le veo ~ solución que ... I see no other solution than to ...; ¿quién ~? anybody else?

5 (+ a: valor intensivo): ¡qué perro ~ sucio! what a filthy dog!; ¡es ~ tonto! he's so stupid!

6 (locuciones): o ~ menos more or less; los ~ most people; es ~ furthermore; ¡qué ~ da! what does it matter!; ver tb no

7: por ~: por ~ que te esfuerces no matter how hard you try; por ~ que quisiera ... much as I should like to ...

8: de ~: veo que aquí estoy de ~ I can see I'm not needed here; tenemos uno de ~ we've got one extra

♦ prep: 2 ~ 2 son 4 2 and o plus 2 are 4

♦ nm: este trabajo tiene sus ~ y sus menos this job's got its good points and its bad points.

---

masa ['masa] nf (mezcla) dough; (volumen) volume, mass; (FÍSICA) mass; en ~ en masse; las ~s (POL) the masses.

masacre [ma'sakre] nf massacre.

masaje [ma'saxe] nm massage.

mascar [mas'kar] vt to chew; (fig) to mumble, mutter.

máscara ['maskara] nf (gen) mask // nm/f masked person; **mascarada** nf masquerade; **mascarilla** nf (de belleza, MED) mask.

masculino, a [masku'lino, a] a masculine; (BIO) male.

mascullar [masku'kar] vt to mumble, mutter.

masilla [ma'siʎa] nf putty.

masivo, a [ma'siβo, a] a (en masa) mass, en masse.

masón [ma'son] *nm* (free)mason.

masoquista [maso'kista] *nm/f* masochist.

masticar [masti'kar] *vt* to chew; (*fig*) to ponder.

mástil ['mastil] *nm* (*de navío*) mast; (*de guitarra*) neck.

mastín [mas'tin] *nm* mastiff.

masturbación [masturβa'θjon] *nf* masturbation; **masturbarse** *vr* to masturbate.

mata ['mata] *nf* (*arbusto*) bush, shrub; (*de hierba*) tuft.

matadero [mata'ðero] *nm* slaughterhouse, abattoir.

matador, a [mata'ðor, a] *a* killing // *nm/f* killer // *nm* (*TAUR*) matador, bullfighter.

matamoscas [mata'moskas] *nm inv* (*palo*) fly swat.

matanza [ma'tanθa] *nf* (*de personas*) slaughter, killing; (*de animales*) slaughter(ing).

matar [ma'tar] *vt, vi* to kill; **~se** *vr* (*suicidarse*) to kill o.s., commit suicide; (*morir*) to be *o* get killed; **~ el hambre** to stave off hunger.

matasellos [mata'seλos] *nm inv* postmark.

mate ['mate] *a* (*sin brillo: color*) dull, matt // *nm* (*en ajedrez*) (check)mate; (*AM: hierba*) maté; (: *vasija*) gourd.

matemáticas [mate'matikas] *nfpl* mathematics; **matemático, a** *a* mathematical // *nm/f* mathematician.

materia [ma'terja] *nf* (*gen*) matter; (*TEC*) material; (*ESCOL*) subject; **en ~ de** on the subject of; **~ prima** raw material; **material** *a* material; (*dolor*) physical // *nm* material; (*TEC*) equipment; **materialismo** *nm* materialism; **materialista** *a* materialist(ic); **materialmente** *ad* materially; (*fig*) absolutely.

maternal [mater'nal] *a* motherly, maternal.

maternidad [materni'ðað] *nf* motherhood, maternity; **materno, a** *a* maternal; (*lengua*) mother *cpd*.

matinal [mati'nal] *a* morning *cpd*.

matiz [ma'tiθ] *nm* shade; **~ar** *vt* (*dar tonos de*) to tinge; tint; (*variar*) to vary; (*ARTE*) to blend.

matón [ma'ton] *nm* bully.

matorral [mato'rral] *nm* thicket.

matraca [ma'traka] *nf* rattle.

matrícula [ma'trikula] *nf* (*registro*) register; (*AUTO*) registration number; (: *placa*) number plate; **matricular** *vt* to register, enrol.

matrimonial [matrimo'njal] *a* matrimonial.

matrimonio [matri'monjo] *nm* (*pareja*) (married) couple; (*unión*) marriage.

matriz [ma'triθ] *nf* (*ANAT*) womb; (*TEC*) mould; **casa ~** (*COM*) head office.

matrona [ma'trona] *nf* (*persona de edad*) matron.

maullar [mau'λar] *vi* to mew, miaow; **maullido** [mau'λiðo] *nm* mew, miaow.

mausoleo [mauso'leo] *nm* mausoleum.

maxilar [maksi'lar] *nm* jaw(bone).

máxima ['maksima] *ver* **máximo**.

máxime ['maksime] *ad* especially.

máximo, a ['maksimo, a] *a* maximum; (*más alto*) highest; (*más grande*) greatest // *nm* maximum // *nf* maxim.

mayo ['majo] *nm* May.

mayonesa [majo'nesa] *nf* mayonnaise.

mayor [ma'jor] *a* main, chief; (*adulto*) adult; (*de edad avanzada*) elderly; (*MUS*) major; (*comparativo: de tamaño*) bigger; (*: de edad*) older; (*superlativo: de tamaño*) biggest; (: *de edad*) oldest // *nm* chief, boss; (*adulto*) adult; **al por ~** wholesale; **~ de edad** adult; **~es** *nmpl* (*antepasados*) ancestors.

mayoral [majo'ral] *nm* foreman.

mayordomo [major'ðomo] *nm* butler.

mayoría [majo'ria] *nf* majority, greater part.

mayorista [majo'rista] *nm/f* wholesaler.

mayúsculo, a [ma'juskulo, a] *a* (*fig*) big, tremendous // *nf* capital (letter).

mazapán [maθa'pan] *nm* marzipan.

mazo ['maθo] *nm* (*martillo*) mallet; (*de flores*) bunch; (*DEPORTE*) bat.

me [me] *pron* (*directo*) me; (*indirecto*) (to) me; (*reflexivo*) (to) myself; **¡dámelo!** give it to me!

mear [me'ar] *vi* (*fam*) to pee, piss.

mecánico, a [me'kaniko, a] *a* mechanical // *nm/f* mechanic // *nf* (*estudio*) mechanics *sg*; (*mecanismo*) mechanism.

mecanismo [meka'nismo] *nm* mechanism; (*marcha*) gear.

mecanografía [mekanoɣra'fia] *nf* typewriting; **mecanógrafo, a** *nm/f* typist.

mecate [me'kate] *nm* (*AM*) rope.

mecedora [meθe'ðora] *nf* rocking chair.

mecer [me'θer] *vt* (*cuna*) to rock; ~**se** *vr* to rock; (*ramo*) to sway.

mecha ['metʃa] *nf* (*de vela*) wick; (*de bomba*) fuse.

mechero [me'tʃero] *nm* (*cigarette*) lighter.

mechón [me'tʃon] *nm* (*gen*) tuft; (*manojo*) bundle; (*de pelo*) lock.

medalla [me'ðaʎa] *nf* medal.

media ['meðja] *nf ver* **medio.**

mediado, a [me'ðjaðo, a] *a* half-full; (*trabajo*) half-complete; **a** ~**s de** in the middle of, halfway through.

mediano, a [me'ðjano, a] *a* (*regular*) medium, average; (*mediocre*) mediocre.

medianoche [meðja'notʃe] *nf* midnight.

mediante [me'ðjante] *ad* by (means of), through.

mediar [me'ðjar] *vi* (*interceder*) to mediate, intervene.

medicación [meðika'θjon] *nf* medication, treatment.

medicamento [meðika'mento] *nm* medicine, drug.

medicina [meði'θina] *nf* medicine.

medición [meði'θjon] *nf* measurement.

médico, a ['meðiko, a] *a* medical // *nm/f* doctor.

medida [me'ðiða] *nf* measure; (*medición*) measurement; (*prudencia*) moderation, prudence; **en cierta/gran** ~ up to a point/to a great extent; **un traje a la** ~ made-to-measure suit; ~ **de cuello** collar size; **a** ~ **de** in proportion to; (*de acuerdo con*) in keeping with; **a** ~ **que** (*conforme*) as.

medio, a ['meðjo, a] *a* half (a); (*punto*) mid, middle; (*promedio*) average // *ad* half // *nm* (*centro*) middle, centre; (*promedio*) average; (*método*) means, way; (*ambiente*) environment // *nf* (*Esp: prenda de vestir*) stocking; (*AM: prenda de vestir*) sock; (*promedio*) average; ~**s** *nmpl* means, resources; ~ **litro** half a litre; **las tres y media** half past three; **M~ Oriente** Middle East; **a ~ terminar** half finished; **pagar a medias** to share the cost.

mediocre [me'ðjokre] *a* middling, average; (*pey*) mediocre.

mediodía [meðjo'ðia] *nm* midday, noon.

medir [me'ðir] *vt*, *vi* (*gen*) to measure.

meditar [meði'tar] *vt* to ponder, think over, meditate (on); (*planear*) to think out.

mediterráneo, a [meðite'rraneo, a] *a* Mediterranean // *nm*: **el M~** the Mediterranean.

médula ['meðula] *nf* (*ANAT*) marrow; ~ **espinal** spinal cord.

medusa [me'ðusa] *nf* (*Esp*) jellyfish.

megáfono [me'ɣafono] *nm* megaphone.

megalómano, a [meɣa'lomano, a] *nm/f* megalomaniac.

mejicano, a [mexi'kano, a] *a*, *nm/f* Mexican.

Méjico ['mexiko] *nm* Mexico.

mejilla [me'xiʎa] *nf* cheek.

mejillón [mexi'ʎon] *nm* mussel.

mejor [me'xor] *a*, *ad* (*comparativo*) better; (*superlativo*) best; **a lo** ~

probably; (*quizá*) maybe; ~ **dicho** rather; **tanto** ~ so much the better.

mejora [me'xora] *nf* improvement; **mejorar** *vt* to improve, make better // *vi*, **mejorarse** *vr* to improve, get better.

melancólico, a [melan'koliko, a] *a* (*triste*) sad, melancholy; (*soñador*) dreamy.

melena [me'lena] *nf* (*de persona*) long hair; (*ZOOL*) mane.

melocotón [meloko'ton] *nm* (*Esp*) peach.

melodía [melo'ðia] *nf* melody, tune.

melodrama [melo'ðrama] *nm* melodrama; **melodramático, a** *a* melodramatic.

melón [me'lon] *nm* melon.

meloso, a [me'loso, a] *a* honeyed, sweet.

mellizo, a [me'ʎiθo, a] *a*, *nm/f* twin; **~s** *nmpl* (*AM*) cufflinks.

membrete [mem'brete] *nm* letterhead.

membrillo [mem'briʎo] *nm* quince; **carne de** ~ quince jelly.

memorable [memo'raβle] *a* memorable.

memorándum [memo'randum] (*pl* **~s**) *nm* (*libro*) notebook; (*comunicación*) memorandum.

memoria [me'morja] *nf* (*gen*) memory; **~s** *nfpl* (*de autor*) memoirs; ~ **intermedia** (*INFORM*) buffer; **memorizar** *vt* to memorize.

menaje [me'naxe] *nm*: ~ **de cocina** kitchenware.

mencionar [menθjo'nar] *vt* to mention.

mendigar [mendi'ɣar] *vt* to beg (for).

mendigo, a [men'diɣo, a] *nm/f* beggar.

mendrugo [men'druɣo] *nm* crust.

menear [mene'ar] *vt* to move; (*fig*) to handle; **~se** *vr* to shake; (*balancearse*) to sway; (*moverse*) to move; (*fig*) to get a move on.

menester [menes'ter] *nm* (*necesidad*) necessity; **~es** *nmpl* (*de-*

beres) duties; **es** ~ it is necessary.

menestra [me'nestra] *nf*: ~ **de verduras** vegetable stew.

menguante [men'gwante] *a* decreasing, diminishing; **menguar** *vt* to lessen, diminish; (*fig*) to discredit // *vi* to diminish, decrease; (*fig*) to decline.

menopausia [meno'pausja] *nf* menopause.

menor [me'nor] *a* (*más pequeño*: *comparativo*) smaller; (: *superlativo*) smallest; (*más joven*: *comparativo*) younger; (: *superlativo*) youngest; (*MUS*) minor // *nm/f* (*joven*) young person, juvenile; **no tengo la** ~ **idea** I haven't the faintest idea; **al por** ~ retail; ~ **de edad** person under age.

Menorca [me'norka] *nf* Minorca.

menoría [meno'ria] *nf*: **a** ~ (*AM*) retail.

menos [menos] ♦ *a* 1: ~ (**que, de**) (*comparativo*: *cantidad*) less (than); (: *número*) fewer (than); **con** ~ **entusiasmo** with less enthusiasm; ~ **gente** fewer people; *ver tb* **cada**
2 (*superlativo*): **es el que** ~ **culpa tiene** he is the least to blame

♦ *ad* 1 (*comparativo*): ~ (**que, de**) less (than); **me gusta** ~ **el otro** I like it less than the other one
2 (*superlativo*): **es la** ~ **lista** (**de su clase**) she's the least bright in her class; **de todas ellas es la que** ~ **me agrada** out of all of them she's the one I like least; (**por**) **lo** ~ at (the very) least

3 (*locuciones*): **no quiero verle y** ~ **visitarle** I don't want to see him let alone visit him; **tenemos 7 de** ~ we're seven short

♦ *prep* except; (*cifras*) minus; **todos** ~ **él** everyone except (for) him; **5** ~ **2** 5 minus 2

♦ *conj*: **a** ~ **que: a** ~ **que venga mañana** unless he comes tomorrow.

menoscabar [menoska'βar] *vt*
(*estropear*) to damage, harm; (*fig*)
to discredit.

menospreciar [menospre'θjar] *vt* to
underrate, undervalue; (*despreciar*)
to scorn, despise.

mensaje [men'saxe] *nm* message;
~**ro, a** *nm/f* messenger.

menstruación [menstrua'θjon] *nf*
menstruation.

menstruar [mens'trwar] *vi* to
menstruate.

mensual [men'swal] *a* monthly; 1000
ptas ~**es** 1000 ptas a month; ~**idad**
nf (*salario*) monthly salary; (*COM*)
monthly payment, monthly instalment.

menta ['menta] *nf* mint.

mental [men'tal] *a* mental; ~**idad**
nf mentality.

mentar [men'tar] *vt* to mention,
name.

mente ['mente] *nf* mind.

mentecato, a [mente'kato, a] *a*
silly, stupid // *nm/f* fool, idiot.

mentir [men'tir] *vi* to lie.

mentira [men'tira] *nf* (*una* ~) lie;
(*acto*) lying; (*invención*) fiction;
parece ~ **que...** it seems incredible
that..., I can't believe that....

mentiroso, a [menti'roso, a] *a* lying
// *nm/f* liar.

menú [me'nu] (*pl* ~**s**) *nm* menu;
(*AM*) set meal.

menudo, a [me'nuðo, a] *a*
(*pequeño*) small, tiny; (*sin*
importancia) petty, insignificant; **¡~**
negocio! (*fam*) some deal!; **a** ~
often, frequently.

meñique [me'ɲike] *nm* little finger.

meollo [me'oʎo] *nm* (*fig*) core.

mercadería [merkaðe'ria] *nf* commodity; ~**s** *nfpl* goods, merchandise
sg.

mercado [mer'kaðo] *nm* market;
M~ Común Common Market.

mercancía [merkan'θia] *nf*
commodity; ~**s** *nfpl* goods,
merchandise *sg*.

mercantil [merkan'til] *a* mercantile,

commercial.

mercenario, a [merθe'narjo, a] *a*,
nm mercenary.

mercería [merθe'ria] *nf* haberdashery (*Brit*), notions (*US*);
(*tienda*) haberdasher's (*Brit*), notions
store (*US*); (*AM*) drapery.

mercurio [mer'kurjo] *nm* mercury.

merecer [mere'θer] *vt* to deserve,
merit // *vi* to be deserving, be
worthy; **merece la pena** it's worthwhile; **merecido, a** *a* (*well*)
deserved; **llevar su merecido** to get
one's deserts.

merendar [meren'dar] *vt* to have for
tea // *vi* to have tea; (*en el campo*)
to have a picnic.

merengue [me'renge] *nm* meringue.

meridiano [meri'ðjano] *nm* (*GEO*)
meridian.

merienda [me'rjenda] *nf* (light) tea,
afternoon snack; (*de campo*) picnic.

mérito ['merito] *nm* merit; (*valor*)
worth, value.

merluza [mer'luθa] *nf* hake.

merma ['merma] *nf* decrease;
(*pérdida*) wastage; **mermar** *vt* to
reduce, lessen // *vi* to decrease,
dwindle.

mermelada [merme'laða] *nf* jam.

mero, a ['mero, a] *a* mere; (*AM*:
fam) very.

mes [mes] *nm* month; (*salario*)
month's pay.

mesa ['mesa] *nf* table; (*de trabajo*)
desk; (*GEO*) plateau; (*ARQ*) landing; ~ **directiva** board; ~ **redonda**
(*reunión*) round table; **poner/quitar**
la ~ to lay/clear the table; **mesero,**
a *nm/f* (*AM*) waiter/waitress.

meseta [me'seta] *nf* (*GEO*) meseta,
tableland; (*ARQ*) landing.

mesilla [me'siʎa], **mesita** [me'sita]
nf: ~ (**de noche**) bedside table.

mesón [me'son] *nm* inn.

mestizo, a [mes'tiθo, a] *a* half-caste,
of mixed race; (*ZOOL*) crossbred //
nm/f half-caste.

mesura [me'sura] *nf* (*moderación*)
moderation, restraint; (*cortesía*)

courtesy.

meta ['meta] *nf* goal; (*de carrera*) finish.

metáfora [me'tafora] *nf* metaphor.

metal [me'tal] *nm* (*materia*) metal; (*MUS*) brass; **metálico, a** *a* metallic; (*de metal*) metal // *nm* (*dinero contante*) cash.

metalurgia [meta'lurxja] *nf* metallurgy.

meteoro [mete'oro] *nm* meteor.

meter [me'ter] *vt* (*colocar*) to put, place; (*introducir*) to put in, insert; (*involucrar*) to involve; (*causar*) to make, cause; ~**se** *vr*: ~**se en** to go into, enter; (*fig*) to interfere in, meddle in; ~**se a** to start; ~**se a escritor** to become a writer; ~**se con uno** to provoke sb, pick a quarrel with sb.

meticuloso, a [metiku'loso, a] *a* meticulous, thorough.

metódico, a [me'toðiko, a] *a* methodical.

metodismo [meto'ðismo] *nm* Methodism.

método [metoðo] *nm* method.

metralleta [metra'ʎeta] *nf* sub-machine-gun.

métrico, a ['metriko, a] *a* metric.

metro ['metro] *nm* metre; (*tren*) underground (*Brit*), subway (*US*).

México ['mexiko] *nm* Mexico; **Ciudad de** ~ Mexico City.

mezcla [me'θkla] *nf* mixture; **mezclar** *vt* to mix (up); **mezclarse** *vr* to mix, mingle; **mezclarse en** to get mixed up in, get involved in.

mezquino, a [meθ'kino, a] *a* (*cicatero*) mean.

mezquita [meθ'kita] *nf* mosque.

mg. *abr* (= *miligramo*) mg.

mi [mi] *adjetivo posesivo* my // *nm* (*MUS*) E.

mí [mi] *pron* me; myself.

miaja ['mjaxa] *nf* crumb.

micro ['mikro] *nm* (*AM*) minibus.

microbio [mi'kroßjo] *nm* microbe.

microbús [mikro'ßus] *nm* minibus.

micrófono [mi'krofono] *nm* micro-

phone.

microordenador [mikro(o)rðena-'ðor] *nm* microcomputer.

microscopio [mikros'kopjo] *nm* microscope.

miedo ['mjeðo] *nm* fear; (*nerviosismo*) apprehension, nervousness; **tener** ~ to be afraid; **de** ~ wonderful, marvellous; **hace un frío de** ~ (*fam*) it's terribly cold; ~**so, a** *a* fearful, timid.

miel [mjel] *nf* honey.

miembro ['mjembro] *nm* limb; (*socio*) member; ~ **viril** penis.

mientras ['mjentras] *conj* while; (*duración*) as long as // *ad* meanwhile; ~ **tanto** meanwhile; ~ **más tiene, más quiere** the more he has, the more he wants.

miércoles ['mjerkoles] *nm inv* Wednesday.

mierda [mi'jerða] *nf* (*fam!*) shit (*!*).

miga ['miva] *nf* crumb; (*fig: meollo*) essence; **hacer buenas** ~**s** (*fam*) to get on well.

migración [mivra'θjon] *nf* migration.

mil [mil] *num* thousand; **dos** ~ **libras** two thousand pounds.

milagro [mi'lavro] *nm* miracle; ~**so, a** *a* miraculous.

mili ['mili] *nf*: **hacer la** ~ (*fam*) to do one's military service.

milicia [mi'liθja] *nf* militia; (*servicio militar*) military service.

milímetro [mi'limetro] *nm* millimetre.

militante [mili'tante] *a* militant.

militar [mili'tar] *a* (*del ejército*) military // *nmf* soldier // *vi* to serve in the army; (*fig*) to be a member of a party.

milla ['miʎa] *nf* mile.

millar [mi'ʎar] *nm* thousand.

millón [mi'ʎon] *num* million; **millonario, a** *nm/f* millionaire.

mimar [mi'mar] *vt* (*gen*) to spoil, pamper.

mimbre ['mimbre] *nm* wicker.

mímica ['mimika] *nf* (*para comunicarse*) sign language; (*imitación*) mimicry.

mimo ['mimo] *nm* (*caricia*) caress; (*de niño*) spoiling; (*TEATRO*) mime; (: *actor*) mime artist.

mina ['mina] *nf* mine; **minar** *vt* to mine; (*fig*) to undermine.

mineral [mine'ral] *a* mineral // *nm* (*GEO*) mineral; (*mena*) ore.

minero, a [mi'nero, a] *a* mining *cpd* // *nm/f* miner.

miniatura [minja'tura] *a inv, nf* miniature.

minifalda [mini'falda] *nf* miniskirt.

mínimo, a ['minimo, a] *a, nm* minimum.

minino, a [mi'nino, a] *nm/f* (*fam*) puss, pussy.

ministerio [minis'terjo] *nm* Ministry; **M~ de Hacienda/del Exterior** Treasury (*Brit*), Treasury Department (*US*)/Foreign Office (*Brit*), State Department (*US*).

ministro, a [mi'nistro, a] *nm/f* minister.

minoría [mino'ria] *nf* minority.

minucioso, a [minu'θjoso, a] *a* thorough, meticulous; (*prolijo*) very detailed.

minúsculo, a [mi'nuskulo, a] *a* tiny, minute // *nf* small letter.

minusválido, a [minus'βaliðo, a] *a* (physically) handicapped // *nm/f* (physically) handicapped person.

minuta [mi'nuta] *nf* (*de comida*) menu.

minutero [minu'tero] *nm* minute hand.

minuto [mi'nuto] *nm* minute.

mío, a ['mio, a] *pron*: **el ~** mine; **un amigo ~** a friend of mine; **lo ~** what is mine.

miope [mi'ope] *a* short-sighted.

mira ['mira] *nf* (*de arma*) sight(s) (*pl*); (*fig*) aim, intention.

mirada [mi'raða] *nf* look, glance; (*expresión*) look, expression; **clavar la ~** en to stare at; **echar una ~** a to glance at.

mirado, a [mi'raðo, a] *a* (*sensato*) sensible; (*considerado*) considerate;

bien/mal ~ well/not well thought of; **bien ~** *ad* all things considered.

mirador [mira'ðor] *nm* viewpoint, vantage point.

mirar [mi'rar] *vt* to look at; (*observar*) to watch; (*considerar*) to consider, think over; (*vigilar, cuidar*) to watch, look after // *vi* to look; (*ARQ*) to face; **~se** *vr* (*dos personas*) to look at each other; **~ bien/mal** to think highly of/have a poor opinion of; **~se al espejo** to look at o.s. in the mirror.

mirilla [mi'riʎa] *nf* (*agujero*) spyhole, peephole.

mirlo ['mirlo] *nm* blackbird.

misa ['misa] *nf* mass.

miserable [mise'raβle] *a* (*avaro*) mean, stingy; (*nimio*) miserable, paltry; (*lugar*) squalid; (*fam*) vile, despicable // *nm/f* (*perverso*) rotter (*Brit*).

miseria [mi'serja] *nf* misery; (*pobreza*) poverty; (*tacañería*) meanness, stinginess; (*condiciones*) squalor; **una ~** a pittance.

misericordia [miseri'korðja] *nf* (*compasión*) compassion, pity; (*piedad*) mercy.

misil [mi'sil] *nm* missile.

misión [mi'sjon] *nf* mission; **misionero, a** *nm/f* missionary.

mismo, a ['mismo, a] *a* (*semejante*) same; (*después de pronombre*) -self; (*para énfasis*) very; **el ~ traje** the same suit; **en ese ~ momento** at that very moment; **vino el ~ Ministro** the minister himself came; **yo ~ lo vi** I saw it myself; **lo ~** the same (thing); **da lo ~** it's all the same; **quedamos en las mismas** we're no further forward // *ad*: **aquí/hoy ~** right here/this very day; **ahora ~** right now // *conj*: **lo ~ que** just like, just as; **por lo ~** for the same reason.

misterio [mis'terjo] *nm* (*gen*) mystery; (*lo secreto*) secrecy; **~so, a** *a* mysterious.

mitad [mi'tað] *nf* (*medio*) half; (*cen-*

tro) middle; **a ~ de precio** (at) half-price; **en o a ~ del camino** halfway along the road; **cortar por la ~** to cut through the middle.

mitigar [miti'ɣar] *vt* to mitigate; (*dolor*) to ease; (*sed*) to quench.

mitin ['mitin] (*pl* **mitines**) *nm* meeting.

mito ['mito] *nm* myth.

mixto, a ['miksto. a] *a* mixed.

ml. *abr* (= *mililitro*) ml.

mm. *abr* (= *milímetro*) mm.

mobiliario [moβi'ljarjo] *nm* furniture.

moción [mo'θjon] *nf* motion.

mocos ['mokos] *nmpl* mucus *sg*; (*fam*) snot *sg*.

mochila [mo't∫ila] *nf* rucksack (*Brit*), back-pack.

moda ['moða] *nf* fashion; (*estilo*) style; **a la o de ~** in fashion, fashionable; **pasado de ~** out of fashion.

modales [mo'ðales] *nmpl* manners.

modalidad [moðali'ðað] *nf* kind, variety.

modelar [moðe'lar] *vt* to model.

modelo [mo'ðelo] *a inv, nm/f* model.

moderado, a [moðe'raðo. a] *a* a moderate.

moderar [moðe'rar] *vt* to moderate; (*violencia*) to restrain, control; (*velocidad*) to reduce; **~se** *vr* to restrain o.s., control o.s.

modernizar [moðerni'θar] *vt* to modernize.

moderno, a [mo'ðerno. a] *a* modern; (*actual*) present-day.

modestia [mo'ðestja] *nf* modesty; **modesto, a** *a* modest.

módico, a ['moðiko. a] *a* moderate, reasonable.

modificar [moðifi'kar] *vt* to modify.

modista [mo'ðista] *nm/f* dressmaker.

modo ['moðo] *nm* (*manera, forma*) way, manner; (*MUS*) mode; **~s** *nmpl* manners; **de ningún ~** in no way; **de todos ~s** at any rate; **~ de empleo** directions *pl* (for use).

modorra [mo'ðorra] *nf* drowsiness.

modular [moðu'lar] *vt* to modulate.

mofa ['mofa] *nf*: **hacer ~ de** to mock; **mofarse** *vr*: **mofarse de** to mock, scoff at.

moho ['moo] *nm* (*BOT*) mould, mildew; (*en metal*) rust; **~so, a** *a* mouldy; rusty.

mojar [mo'xar] *vt* to wet; (*humedecer*) to damp(en), moisten; (*calar*) to soak; **~se** *vr* to get wet.

mojón [mo'xon] *nm* (*en un camino*) boundary stone.

molde ['molde] *nm* mould; (*COSTURA*) pattern; (*fig*) model; **~ar** *vt* to mould.

mole ['mole] *nf* mass, bulk; (*edificio*) pile.

moler [mo'ler] *vt* to grind, crush; (*cansar*) to tire out, exhaust.

molestar [moles'tar] *vt* to bother; (*fastidiar*) to annoy; (*incomodar*) to inconvenience, put out // *vi* to be a nuisance; **~se** *vr* to bother; (*incomodarse*) to go to trouble; (*ofenderse*) to take offence.

molestia [mo'lestja] *nf* bother, trouble; (*incomodidad*) inconvenience; (*MED*) discomfort; **es una ~** it's a nuisance; **molesto, a** *a* (*que fastidia*) annoying; (*incómodo*) inconvenient; (*inquieto*) uncomfortable, ill at ease; (*enfadado*) annoyed.

molinillo [moli'niʎo] *nm*: **~ de carne/café** mincer/coffee grinder.

molino [mo'lino] *nm* (*edificio*) mill; (*máquina*) grinder.

momentáneo, a [mcmen'taneo. a] *a* momentary.

momento [mo'mento] *nm* (*gen*) moment; (*TEC*) momentum; **de ~ a** the moment, for the moment.

momia ['momja] *nf* mummy.

monarca [mo'narka] *nm/f* monarch, ruler; **monarquía** *nf* monarchy; **monárquico, a** *nm/f* royalist, monarchist.

monasterio [monas'terjo] *nm* monastery.

mondadientes [monda'ðjentes] *nm inv* toothpick.

mondar [mon'dar] *vt* (*limpiar*)

clean; (*pelar*) to peel; ~**se** *vr:* ~**se de risa** (*fam*) to split one's sides laughing.

moneda [mo'neða] *nf* (*tipo de dinero*) currency, money; (*pieza*) coin; **una ~ de 5 pesetas** a 5 peseta piece; **monedero** *nm* purse; **monetario, a** *a* monetary, financial.

monja ['monxa] *nf* nun.

monje ['monxe] *nm* monk.

mono, a ['mono, a] *a* (*bonito*) lovely, pretty; (*gracioso*) nice, charming // *nmf* monkey, ape // *nm* dungarees *pl*; (*overoles*) overalls *pl*.

monopolio [mono'poljo] *nm* monopoly; **monopolizar** *vt* to monopolize.

monotonía [monoto'nia] *nf* (*sonido*) monotone; (*fig*) monotony.

monótono, a [mo'notono, a] *a* monotonous.

monstruo ['monstrwo] *nm* monster // *a inv* fantastic; ~**so, a** *a* monstrous.

monta ['monta] *nf* total, sum; **de poca ~** unimportant, of little account.

montaje [mon'taxe] *nm* assembly; (*TEATRO*) décor; (*CINE*) montage.

montaña [mon'taɲa] *nf* (*monte*) mountain; (*sierra*) mountains *pl*, mountainous area; (*AM: selva*) forest; ~ **rusa** roller coaster; **montañés, esa** *a* mountain *cpd* // *nmf* highlander.

montar [mon'tar] *vt* (*subir a*) to mount, get on; (*TEC*) to assemble, put together; (*negocio*) to set up; (*arma*) to cock; (*colocar*) to lift on to; (*CULIN*) to beat // *vi* to mount, get on; (*sobresalir*) to overlap; ~ **en cólera** to get angry; ~ **a caballo** to ride, go horseriding.

montaraz [monta'raθ] *a* mountain *cpd*, highland *cpd*; (*salvaje*) wild, untamed; (*pey*) uncivilized.

monte ['monte] *nm* (*montaña*) mountain; (*bosque*) woodland, (*tierra sin cultivar*) wild area, wild country; **M~ de Piedad** pawnshop.

Montevideo [monteβi'ðeo] *n* Mon-

tevideo.

monto ['monto] *nm* total, amount.

montón [mon'ton] *nm* heap, pile; (*fig*): **un ~ de** heaps of, lots of.

monumento [monu'mento] *nm* monument.

monzón [mon'θon] *nm* monsoon.

moño ['moɲo] *nm* bun.

mora ['mora] *nf* blackberry.

morado, a [mo'raðo, a] *a* purple, violet // *nm* bruise // *nf* (*casa*) dwelling, abode.

moral [mo'ral] *a* moral // *nf* (*ética*) ethics *pl*; (*moralidad*) morals *pl*, morality; (*ánimo*) morale.

moraleja [mora'lexa] *nf* moral.

moralizar [morali'θar] *vt* to moralize.

morboso, a [mor'βoso, a] *a* morbid.

morcilla [mor'θiʎa] *nf* blood sausage, ≈ black pudding (*Brit*).

mordaz [mor'ðaθ] *a* (*crítica*) biting, scathing.

mordaza [mor'ðaθa] *nf* (*para la boca*) gag; (*TEC*) clamp.

morder [mor'ðer] *vt* to bite; (*mordisquear*) to nibble; (*fig: consumir*) to eat away, eat into; **mordisco** *nm* bite.

moreno, a [mo'reno, a] *a* (*color*) (dark) brown; (*de tez*) dark; (*de pelo ~*) dark-haired; (*negro*) black.

moretón [more'ton] *nm* (*fam*) bruise.

morfina [mor'fina] *nf* morphine.

moribundo, a [mori'βundo, a] *a* dying.

morir [mo'rir] *vi* to die; (*fuego*) to die down; (*luz*) to go out; ~**se** *vr* to die; (*fig*) to be dying; **fue muerto en un accidente** he was killed in an accident; ~**se por algo** to be dying for sth.

moro, a ['moro, a] *a* Moorish // *nmf* Moor.

moroso, a [mo'roso, a] *nmf* (*COM*) bad debtor, defaulter.

morral [mo'rral] *nm* haversack.

morro ['morro] *nm* (*ZOOL*) snout, nose; (*AUTO, AVIAT*) nose.

morsa ['morsa] nf walrus.

mortaja [mor'taxa] nf shroud.

mortal [mor'tal] a mortal; (golpe) deadly; **~idad**, **mortandad** nf mortality.

mortero [mor'tero] nm mortar.

mortífero, a [mor'tifero, a] a deadly, lethal.

mortificar [mortifi'kar] vt to mortify.

mosca ['moska] nf fly.

Moscú [mos'ku] n Moscow.

mosquearse [moske'arse] vr (fam: enojarse) to get cross; (: ofenderse) to take offence.

mosquitero [moski'tero] nm mosquito net.

mosquito [mos'kito] nm mosquito.

mostaza [mos'taθa] nf mustard.

mostrador [mostra'ðor] nm (de tienda) counter; (de café) bar.

mostrar [mos'trar] vt to show; (exhibir) to display, exhibit; (explicar) to explain; **~se** vr: **~se amable** to be kind; to prove to be kind; **no se muestra muy inteligente** he doesn't seem (to be) very intelligent.

mota ['mota] nf speck, tiny piece; (en diseño) dot.

mote ['mote] nm (apodo) nickname.

motín [mo'tin] nm (del pueblo) revolt, rising; (del ejército) mutiny.

motivar [moti'βar] vt (causar) to cause, motivate; (explicar) to explain, justify; **motivo** nm motive, reason.

moto ['moto] (fam), **motocicleta** [motoθi'kleta] nf motorbike (Brit), motorcycle.

motor [mo'tor] nm motor, engine; **~ a chorro** o **de reacción/de explosión** jet engine/internal combustion engine.

motora [mo'tora] nf, **motorbote** [motor'βote] nm motorboat.

motosierra [moto'sjerra] nf mechanical saw.

movedizo, a [moβe'ðiθo, a] a (inseguro) unsteady; (fig) unsettled, changeable; (persona) fickle.

mover [mo'βer] vt to move; (cabeza) to shake; (accionar) to drive; (fig) to cause, provoke; **~se** vr to move; (fig) to get a move on.

móvil ['moβil] a mobile; (pieza de máquina) moving; (mueble) movable // nm motive; **movilidad** nf mobility; **movilizar** vt to mobilize.

movimiento [moβi'mjento] nm movement; (TEC) motion; (actividad) activity.

mozo, a ['moθo, a] a (joven) young // nm/f (joven) youth, young man/girl; (camarero) waiter; (camarera) waitress.

muchacho, a [mu'tʃatʃo, a] nm/f (niño) boy/girl; (criado) servant; (criada) maid.

muchedumbre [mutʃe'ðumbre] nf crowd.

mucho, a ['mutʃo, a] ◆ a **1** (cantidad) a lot of, much; (número) lots of, a lot of, many; **~ dinero** a lot of money; **hace ~ calor** it's very hot; **muchas amigas** lots o a lot of friends

2 (sg: grande): **ésta es mucha casa para él** this house is much too big for him

◆ pron: **tengo ~ que hacer** I've got a lot to do; **~s dicen que ...** a lot of people say that ...; ver tb **tener**

◆ ad **1**: **me gusta ~** I like it a lot; **lo siento ~** I'm very sorry; **come ~** he eats a lot; **¿te vas a quedar ~?** are you going to be staying long?

2 (respuesta) very; **¿estás cansado? – ¡~!** are you tired? – very!

3 (locuciones): **como ~** at (the) most; **con ~:** **el mejor con ~** by far the best; **ni ~ menos:** **no es rico ni ~ menos** he's far from being rich

4: **por ~ que:** **por ~ que le creas** no matter how o however much you believe her.

muda ['muða] *nf* change of clothes.

mudanza [mu'ðanθa] *nf* (*cambio*) change; (*de casa*) move.

mudar [mu'ðar] *vt* to change; (*ZOOL*) to shed // *vi* to change; **~se** *vr* (*la ropa*) to change; **~se de casa** to move house.

mudo, a ['muðo, a] *a* dumb; (*callado, CINE*) silent.

mueble ['mweβle] *nm* piece of furniture; **~s** *nmpl* furniture *sg*.

mueca ['mweka] *nf* face, grimace; **hacer ~s a** to make faces at.

muela ['mwela] *nf* (*diente*) tooth; (: *de atrás*) molar.

muelle ['mweʎe] *nm* spring; (*NAUT*) wharf; (*malecón*) pier.

muero *etc vb ver* **morir.**

muerte ['mwerte] *nf* death; (*homicidio*) murder; **dar ~ a** to kill.

muerto, a *pp de* morir // ['mwerto, a] *a* dead; (*color*) dull // *nm/f* dead man/woman; (*difunto*) deceased; (*cadáver*) corpse; **estar ~ de cansancio** to be dead tired.

muestra ['mwestra] *nf* (*señal*) indication, sign; (*demostración*) demonstration; (*prueba*) proof; (*estadística*) sample; (*modelo*) model, pattern; (*testimonio*) token.

muestreo [mwes'treo] *nm* sample, sampling.

muestro *etc vb ver* **mostrar.**

muevo *etc vb ver* **mover.**

mugir [mu'xir] *vi* (*vaca*) to moo.

mugre ['muxre] *nf* dirt, filth; **mugriento, a** *a* dirty, filthy.

mujer [mu'xer] *nf* woman; (*esposa*) wife; **~iego** *nm* womanizer.

mula ['mula] *nf* mule.

mulato, a [mu'lato, a] *a, nm/f* mulatto.

muleta [mu'leta] *nf* (*para andar*) crutch; (*TAUR*) stick with red cape attached.

multa ['multa] *nf* fine; **multar** *vt* to fine.

multicopista [multiko'pista] *nm* duplicator.

múltiple ['multiple] *a* multiple; (*pl*) many, numerous.

multiplicar [multipli'kar] *vt* (*MAT*) to multiply; (*fig*) to increase; **~se** *vr* (*BIO*) to multiply; (*fig*) to be everywhere at once.

multitud [multi'tuð] *nf* (*muchedumbre*) crowd; **~ de** lots of.

mullido, a [mu'ʎiðo, a] *a* (*cama*) soft; (*hierba*) soft, springy.

mundano, a [mun'dano, a] *a* worldly; (*de moda*) fashionable.

mundial [mun'djal] *a* world-wide, universal; (*guerra, récord*) world *cpd.*

mundo ['mundo] *nm* world; **todo el ~** everybody; **tener ~** to be experienced, know one's way around.

munición [muni'θjon] *nf* (*MIL*: *provisiones*) stores *pl*, supplies *pl*; (: *balas*) ammunition.

municipio [muni'θipjo] *nm* (*ayuntamiento*) town council, corporation; (*territorio administrativo*) town, municipality.

muñeca [mu'ɲeka] *nf* (*ANAT*) wrist; (*juguete*) doll.

muñeco [mu'ɲeko] *nm* (*figura*) figure; (*marioneta*) puppet; (*fig*) puppet, pawn.

mural [mu'ral] *a* mural, wall *cpd* // *nm* mural.

muralla [mu'raʎa] *nf* (*city*) wall(s) (*pl*).

murciélago [mur'θjelaxo] *nm* bat.

murmullo [mur'muʎo] *nm* murmur(ing); (*cuchicheo*) whispering; (*de arroyo*) murmur, rippling.

murmuración [murmura'θjon] *nf* gossip; **murmurar** *vi* to murmur, whisper; (*criticar*) to criticize; (*cotillear*) to gossip.

muro ['muro] *nm* wall.

muscular [musku'lar] *a* muscular.

músculo ['muskulo] *nm* muscle.

museo [mu'seo] *nm* museum.

musgo ['musxo] *nm* moss.

músico, a ['musiko, a] *a* musical // *nm/f* musician // *nf* music.

musitar [musi'tar] *vt, vi* to mutter, mumble.

muslo ['muslo] nm thigh.

mustio, a ['mustjo, a] a (persona) depressed, gloomy; (planta) faded, withered.

musulmán, ana [musul'man, ana] nm/f Moslem.

mutación [muta'θjon] nf (BIO) mutation; (: cambio) (sudden) change.

mutilar [muti'lar] vt to mutilate; (a una persona) to maim.

mutuamente [mutwa'mente] ad mutually.

mutuo, a ['mutwo, a] a mutual.

muy [mwi] ad very; (demasiado) too; M~ Señor mío Dear Sir; ~ de noche very late at night; eso es ~ de él that's just like him.

N

N abr (= norte) N.

n/ abr = **nuestro, a.**

nabo ['naβo] nm turnip.

nácar ['nakar] nm mother-of-pearl.

nacer [na'θer] vi to be born; (de huevo) to hatch; (vegetal) to sprout; (río) to rise; nací en Barcelona I was born in Barcelona; nació una sospecha en su mente a suspicion formed in her mind; **nacido, a** a born; **recién nacido** newborn; **naciente** a new, emerging; (sol) rising; **nacimiento** nm birth; (fig) birth, origin; (de Navidad) Nativity; (linaje) descent, family; (de río) source.

nación [na'θjon] nf nation; **nacional** a national; **nacionalismo** nm nationalism; **nacionalista** nm/f nationalist; **nacionalizar** vt to nationalize; **nacionalizarse** vr (persona) to become naturalized.

nada ['naða] pron nothing // ad not at all, in no way; no decir ~ to say nothing, not to say anything; de ~ don't mention it.

nadador, a [naða'ðor, a] nm/f swimmer.

nadar [na'ðar] vi to swim.

nadie ['naðje] pron nobody, no-one; ~ habló nobody spoke; no había ~ there was nobody there, there wasn't anybody there.

nado ['naðo]: **a** ~ ad: pasar a ~ to swim across.

nafta ['nafta] nf (AM) petrol (Brit), gas (US).

naipe ['naipe] nm (playing card); ~s nmpl cards.

nalgas ['nalɣas] nfpl buttocks.

nana ['nana] nf lullaby.

naranja [na'ranxa] a inv, nf orange; media ~ (fam) better half; **naranjada** nf orangeade; **naranjo** nm orange tree.

narciso [nar'θiso] nm narcissus.

narcótico, a [nar'kotiko, a] a, nm narcotic; **narcotizar** vt to drug.

nardo ['narðo] nm lily.

narigón, ona [nari'ɣon, ona] **narigudo, a** [nari'ɣuðo, a] a big-nosed.

nariz [na'riθ] nf nose; **narices** nfpl nostrils; delante de las narices de uno under one's (very) nose.

narración [narra'θjon] nf narration; **narrador, a** nm/f narrator.

narrar [na'rrar] vt to narrate, recount; **narrativa** nf narrative, story.

nata ['nata] nf cream.

natación [nata'θjon] nf swimming.

natal [na'tal] a: ciudad ~ home town; ~icio nm birthday; ~idad nf birth rate.

natillas [na'tiʎas] nfpl custard sg.

natividad [natiβi'ðað] nf nativity.

nativo, a [na'tiβo, a] a, nm/f native.

nato, a ['nato, a] a born; un músico ~ a born musician.

natural [natu'ral] a natural; (fruta etc) fresh // nm/f native // nm (disposición) nature.

naturaleza [natura'leθa] nf nature; (género) nature, kind; ~ muerta still life.

naturalidad [naturali'ðað] nf naturalness.

naturalización [naturaliθa'θjon] nf

naturalization.

naturalizarse [naturali'θarse] *vr* to become naturalized; (*aclimatarse*) to become acclimatized.

naturalmente [natural'mente] *ad* (*de modo natural*) in a natural way; ¡~! of course!

naufragar [naufra'ɣar] *vi* to sink; **naufragio** *nm* shipwreck; **náufrago, a** *nm/f* castaway, shipwrecked person.

nauseabundo, a [nausea'βundo, a] *a* nauseating, sickening.

náuseas ['nauseas] *nfpl* nausea; **me da ~ it** makes me feel sick.

náutico, a ['nautiko, a] *a* nautical.

navaja [na'βaxa] *nf* (*cortaplumas*) clasp knife (Brit), penknife; (*de barbero, peluquero*) razor.

Navarra [na'βarra] *n* Navarre.

nave ['naβe] *nf* (*barco*) ship, vessel; (ARQ) nave; **~ espacial** spaceship.

navegación [naβeɣa'θjon] *nf* navigation; (*viaje*) sea journey; **~ aérea** air traffic; **~ costera** coastal shipping; **navegante** *nm/f* navigator; **navegar** *vi* (*barco*) to sail; (*avión*) to fly // *vt* to sail; to fly; (*dirigir el rumbo*) to navigate.

navidad [naβi'ðað] *nf* Christmas; **~es** *nfpl* Christmas time; **navideño, a** *a* Christmas *cpd*.

navío [na'βio] *nm* ship.

nazca *etc vb ver* **nacer**.

nazi ['naθi] *a, nm/f* Nazi.

NE *abr* (= *nor(d)este*) NE.

neblina [ne'βlina] *nf* mist.

nebuloso, a [neβu'loso, a] *a* foggy; (*calinoso*) misty; (*indefinido*) nebulous, vague // *nf* nebula.

necedad [neθe'ðað] *nf* foolishness; (*una ~*) foolish act.

necesario, a [neθe'sarjo, a] *a* necessary.

neceser [neθe'ser] *nm* toilet bag; (*bolsa grande*) holdall.

necesidad [neθesi'ðað] *nf* need; (*lo inevitable*) necessity; (*miseria*) poverty, need; **en caso de ~** in case of need o emergency; **hacer sus**

~es to relieve o.s.

necesitado, a [neθesi'taðo, a] *a* needy, poor; **~ de** in need of.

necesitar [neθesi'tar] *vt* to need, require // *vi*: **~ de** to have need of.

necio, a ['neθjo, a] *a* foolish.

necrología [nekrolo'xia] *nf* obituary.

necrópolis [ne'kropolis] *nf inv* cemetery.

nectarina [nekta'rina] *nf* nectarine.

nefasto, a [ne'fasto, a] *a* ill-fated, unlucky.

negación [neɣa'θjon] *nf* negation; (*rechazo*) refusal, denial.

negar [ne'ɣar] *vt* (*renegar, rechazar*) to refuse; (*prohibir*) to deny; (*desmentir*) to deny; **~se** *vr*: **~se a** to refuse to.

negativo, a [neɣa'tiβo, a] *a, nm* negative // *nf* (*gen*) negative; (*rechazo*) refusal, denial.

negligencia [neɣli'xenθja] *nf* negligence; **negligente** *a* negligent.

negociable [neɣo'θjaβle] *a* (COM) negotiable.

negociado [neɣo'θjaðo] *nm* department, section.

negociante [neɣo'θjante] *nm/f* businessman/woman.

negociar [neɣo'θjar] *vt, vi* to negotiate; **~ en** to deal in, trade in.

negocio [ne'ɣoθjo] *nm* (COM) business; (*asunto*) affair, business; (*operación comercial*) deal, transaction; (AM) firm; (*lugar*) place of business; **los ~s** business *sg*; **hacer ~** to do business.

negro, a ['neɣro, a] *a* black; (*suerte*) awful // *nm* black // *nm/f* Negro/Negress, Black // *nf* (MUS) crotchet; **negrura** *nf* blackness.

nene, a ['nene, a] *nm/f* baby, small child.

nenúfar [ne'nufar] *nm* water lily.

neologismo [neolo'xismo] *nm* neologism.

neoyorquino, a [neojor'kino, a] *a* (of) New York.

nepotismo [nepo'tismo] *nm* nepotism.

nervio ['nerβjo] nm (*ANAT*) nerve; (: *tendón*) tendon; (*fig*) vigour; **nerviosismo** nm nervousness, nerves pl; **~so, a** [ner'βjoso] a nervous.

neto, a ['neto, a] a clear; (*limpio*) clean; (*COM*) net.

neumático, a [neu'matiko, a] a pneumatic // nm (*Esp*) tyre (*Brit*), tire (*US*); **~ de recambio** spare tyre.

neurastenia [neuras'tenja] nf (*MED*) neurasthenia; (*fig*) excitability.

neurólogo, a [neu'rolovo, a] nm/f neurologist.

neutral [neu'tral] a neutral; **~izar** vt to neutralize; (*contrarrestar*) to counteract.

neutro, a ['neutro, a] a (*BIO*) neuter; (*LING*) neuter.

neutrón [neu'tron] nm neutron.

nevada [ne'βaða] nf snowstorm; (*caída de nieve*) snowfall.

nevar [ne'βar] vi to snow.

nevera [ne'βera] nf (*Esp*) refrigerator (*Brit*), icebox (*US*).

nevería [neße'ria] nf (*AM*) ice-cream parlour.

nevisca [ne'βiska] nf flurry of snow.

nexo ['nekso] nm link, connection.

ni [ni] conj nor, neither; (*tb*: **~ siquiera**) not ... even; **~ que** not even if; **~ blanco ~ negro** neither white nor black.

Nicaragua [nika'raɣwa] nf Nicaragua; **nicaragüense** a, nm/f Nicaraguan.

nicotina [niko'tina] nf nicotine.

nicho ['nitʃo] nm niche.

nido ['niðo] nm nest; (*fig*) hiding place.

niebla ['njeβla] nf fog; (*neblina*) mist.

niego etc vb ver **negar**.

nieto, a ['njeto, a] nm/f grandson/daughter; **~s** nmpl grandchildren.

nieve etc vb ver **nevar** // ['njeβe] nf snow; (*AM*) icecream.

nigromancia [nivro'manθja] nf necromancy, black magic.

Nilo ['nilo] nm: **el ~ the** Nile.

nimiedad [nimje'ðað] nf smallmindedness; (*trivialidad*) triviality.

nimio, a ['nimjo, a] a trivial, insignificant.

ninfa ['ninfa] nf nymph.

ninfómana [nin'fomana] nf nymphomaniac.

ninguno, a [nin'guno, a], **ningún** [nin'gun] a no // pron (*nadie*) nobody; (*ni uno*) none, not one; (*ni uno ni otro*) neither; **de ninguna manera** by no means, not at all.

niña ['nina] nf ver **niño**.

niñera [ni'nera] nf nursemaid, nanny; **niñería** nf childish act.

niñez [ni'neθ] nf childhood; (*infancia*) infancy.

niño, a ['nino, a] a (*joven*) young; (*inmaduro*) immature // nm (*chico*) boy, child // nf (*chica*) girl, child; (*ANAT*) pupil.

nipón, ona [ni'pon, ona] a, nm/f Japanese.

níquel ['nikel] nm nickel; **niquelar** vt (*TEC*) to nickel-plate.

níspero ['nispero] nm medlar.

nitidez [niti'ðeθ] nf (*claridad*) clarity; (*de atmósfera*) brightness; (: *de imagen*) sharpness; **nítido, a** a clear; sharp.

nitrato [ni'trato] nm nitrate.

nitrógeno [ni'troxeno] nm nitrogen.

nitroglicerina [nitroɣliθe'rina] nf nitroglycerine.

nivel [ni'βel] nm (*GEO*) level; (*norma*) level, standard; (*altura*) height; **~ de aceite** oil level; **~ de aire** spirit level; **~ de vida** standard of living; **~ar** vt to level out; (*fig*) to even up; (*COM*) to balance.

NN. UU. nfpl abr (= Naciones Unidas) U.N. sg.

NO abr (= noroeste) NW.

no [no] ad no; not; (*con verbo*) not // excl no!; **~ tengo nada** I don't have anything, I have nothing; **~ es el mío** it's not mine; **ahora ~** not now; **¿~ lo sabes?** don't you know?;

mucho not much; ~ **bien termine,** lo entregaré as soon as I finish I'll hand it over; **¡a que ~ lo sabes!** I bet you don't know!; **¡cómo ~!** of course!; **los países ~ alineados** the non-aligned countries; **la ~ intervención** non-intervention.

noble ['noβle] a, nm/f noble; **~za** nf nobility.

noción [no'θjon] nf notion.

nocivo, a [no'θiβo, a] a harmful.

noctámbulo, a [nok'tambulo, a] nm/f sleepwalker.

nocturno, a [nok'turno, a] a (de la noche) nocturnal, night cpd; (de la tarde) evening cpd // nm nocturne.

noche ['notʃe] nf night, night-time; (la tarde) evening; (fig) darkness; **de ~, por la ~** at night.

nochebuena [notʃe'βwena] nf Christmas Eve.

nochevieja [notʃe'βjexa] nf New Year's Eve.

nodriza [no'ðriθa] nf wet nurse; **buque** o **nave ~** supply ship.

nogal [no'ɣal] nm walnut tree.

nómada ['nomaða] a nomadic // nm/f nomad.

nombramiento [nombra'mjento] nm naming; (a un empleo) appointment.

nombrar [nom'brar] vt (designar) to name; (mencionar) to mention; (dar puesto a) to appoint.

nombre ['nombre] nm name; (sustantivo) noun; (fama) renown; **~ y apellidos** name in full; **~ común/propio** common/proper noun; **~ de pila/de soltera** Christian/maiden name.

nomenclatura [nomenkla'tura] nf nomenclature.

nomeolvides [nomeol'βiðes] nm inv forget-me-not.

nómina ['nomina] nf (lista) list; (COM) payroll.

nominal [nomi'nal] a nominal.

nominar [nomi'nar] vt to nominate.

nominativo, a [nomina'tiβo, a] a (COM): **cheque ~ a X** cheque made

out to X.

non [non] a odd, uneven // nm odd number.

nono, a ['nono, a] a ninth.

nordeste [nor'ðeste] a north-east, north-eastern, north-easterly // nm north-east.

nórdico, a ['norðiko, a] a (del norte) northern, northerly; (escandinavo) Nordic.

noreste [no'reste] a, nm = **nordeste**.

noria ['norja] nf (AGR) waterwheel; (de carnaval) big (Brit) o Ferris (US) wheel.

normal [nor'mal] a (corriente) normal; (habitual) usual, natural; (gasolina) ~ two-star petrol; **~idad** nf normality; **restablecer la ~idad** to restore order; **~izar** vt (reglamentar) to normalize; (TEC) to standardize; **~izarse** vr to return to normal.

normando, a [nor'mando, a] a, nm/f Norman.

noroeste [noro'este] a north-west, north-western, north-westerly // nm north-west.

norte ['norte] a north, northern, northerly // nm north; (fig) guide.

norteamericano, a [norteameri-'kano, a] a, nm/f (North) American.

Noruega [no'rweɣa] nf Norway.

noruego, a [no'rweɣo, a] a, nm/f Norwegian.

nos [nos] pron (directo) us; (indirecto) us; to us; for us; (reflexivo) to ourselves; (recíproco) (to) each other; **~ levantamos a las 7** we got up at 7.

nosotros, as [no'sotros, as] pron (sujeto) we; (después de prep) us.

nostalgia [nos'talxja] nf nostalgia.

nota ['nota] nf note; (ESCOL) mark.

notable [no'taβle] a notable // nm/f notable.

notar [no'tar] vt to notice, note; **~se** vr to be obvious; **se nota que** one observes that ....

notarial [nota'rjal] a: **acta ~**

affidavit.

notario [no'tarjo] nm notary.

noticia [no'tiθja] nf (información) piece of news; las ~s the news sg; tener ~s de alguien to hear from sb.

noticiario [noti'θjarjo] nm (CINE) newsreel; (TV) news bulletin.

noticiero [noti'θjero] nm (AM) news bulletin.

notificación [notifika'θjon] nf notification; **notificar** vt to notify, inform.

notoriedad [notorje'ðað] nf fame, renown; **notorio, a** a (público) well-known; (evidente) obvious.

novato, a [no'βato, a] a inexperienced // nm/f beginner, novice.

novecientos, a [noβe'θjentos, as] a, num nine hundred.

novedad [noβe'ðað] nf (calidad de nuevo) newness; (noticia) piece of news; (cambio) change, (new) development.

novedoso, a [noβe'ðoso, a] a novel.

novel [no'βel] a new; (inexperto) inexperienced // nm/f beginner.

novela [no'βela] nf novel.

novelero, a [noβe'lero, a] a highly imaginative.

novelesco, a [noβe'lesko, a] a fictional; (romántico) romantic; (fantástico) fantastic.

noveno, a [no'βeno, a] a ninth.

noventa [no'βenta] num ninety.

novia ['noβja] nf ver **novio**.

noviazgo [no'βjaθvo] nm engagement.

novicio, a [no'βiθjo, a] nm/f novice.

noviembre [no'βjembre] nm November.

novilla [no'βiʎa] nf heifer; ~**da** nf (TAUR) bullfight with young bulls; **novillero** nm novice bullfighter; **novillo** nm young bull, bullock; **hacer novillos** (fam) to play truant.

novio, a ['noβjo, a] nm/f boyfriend/girlfriend; (prometido) fiancé/fiancée; (recién casado) bridegroom/bride; los ~s the newly-weds.

N. S. abr = Nuestro Señor.

nubarrón [nuβa'rron] nm storm cloud.

nube ['nuβe] nf cloud.

nublado, a [nu'βlaðo, a] a cloudy // nm storm cloud; **nublar** vt (oscurecer) to darken; (confundir) to cloud; **nublarse** vr to grow dark.

nuca ['nuka] nf nape of the neck.

nuclear [nukle'ar] a nuclear.

núcleo ['nukleo] nm (centro) core; (FÍSICA) nucleus.

nudillo [nu'ðiʎo] nm knuckle.

nudo ['nuðo] nm knot; (unión) bond; (de problema) crux; ~**so, a** a knotty.

nuera ['nwera] nf daughter-in-law.

nuestro, a ['nwestro, a] adjetivo posesivo our // pron ours; ~ **padre** our father; **un amigo** ~ a friend of ours; **es el** ~ it's ours.

nueva ['nweβa] af, nf ver **nuevo**.

nuevamente [nweβa'mente] ad (otra vez) again; (de nuevo) anew.

nueve ['nweβe] num nine.

nuevo, a ['nweβo, a] a (gen) new // nf piece of news; **de** ~ again; **Nueva York** n New York; **Nueva Zelandia** nf New Zealand.

nuez [nweθ] nf (fruto) nut; (del nogal) walnut; ~ **de Adán** Adam's apple; ~ **moscada** nutmeg.

nulidad [nuli'ðað] nf (incapacidad) incompetence; (abolición) nullity.

nulo, a ['nulo, a] a (inepto, torpe) useless; (inválido) (null and void); (DEPORTE) drawn, tied.

núm. abr (= número) no.

numeración [numera'θjon] nf (cifras) numbers pl; (arábiga, romana etc) numerals pl.

numeral [nume'ral] nm numeral.

numerar [nume'rar] vt to number.

numérico, a [nu'meriko, a] a numerical.

número ['numero] nm (gen) number; (tamaño: de zapato) size; (ejemplar: de diario) number, issue; **sin** ~ numberless, unnumbered; ~ **de matrícula/de teléfono**

registration/telephone number; ~
atrasado back number.
numeroso, a [nume'roso, a] *a*
numerous.
nunca ['nunka] *ad (jamás)* never; ~
lo pensé I never thought it; **no
viene** ~ he never comes; ~ **más**
never again.
nuncio ['nunθjo] *nm (REL)* nuncio.
nupcias ['nupθjas] *nfpl* wedding *sg*,
nuptials.
nutria ['nutrja] *nf* otter.
nutrición [nutri'θjon] *nf* nutrition.
nutrido, a [nu'triðo, a] *a
(alimentado)* nourished; *(fig:
grande)* large; *(abundante)*
abundant.
nutrir [nu'trir] *vt (alimentar)* to nourish; *(dar de comer)* to feed; *(fig)* to
strengthen; **nutritivo, a** *a* nourishing, nutritious.
nylon [ni'lon] *nm* nylon.

Ñ

ñato, a ['ɲato, a] *a (AM)* snubnosed.
ñoñería [ɲoɲe'ria], **ñoñez** [ɲo'neθ]
nf insipidness.
ñoño, a ['ɲoɲo, a] *a (AM: tonto)*
silly, stupid; *(soso)* insipid;
(persona) spineless.

O

o [o] *conj* or.
O *abr* (= *oeste*) W.
o/ *abr* (= *orden*) o.
oasis [o'asis] *nm inv* oasis.
obcecar [oβθe'kar] *vt* to blind.
obedecer [oβeðe'θer] *vt* to obey;
obediencia *nf* obedience;
obediente *a* obedient.
obertura [oβer'tura] *nf* overture.
obesidad [oβesi'ðað] *nf* obesity;
obeso, a *a* obese.
obispo [o'βispo] *nm* bishop.
objeción [oβxe'θjon] *nf* objection.

objetar [oβxe'tar] *vt, vi* to object.
objetivo, a [oβxe'tiβo, a] *a, nm*
objective.
objeto [oβ'xeto] *nm (cosa)* object;
(fin) aim.
objetor, a [oβxe'tor, a] *nm/f* objector.
oblicuo, a [o'βlikwo, a] *a* oblique;
(mirada) sidelong.
obligación [oβliβa'θjon] *nf* obligation; *(COM)* bond.
obligar [oβli'βar] *vt* to force; ~**se** *vr*
to bind o.s.; **obligatorio, a** *a*
compulsory, obligatory.
oboe [o'βoe] *nm* oboe.
obra ['oβra] *nf* work; *(hechura)* piece
of work; *(ARQ)* construction, building; *(TEATRO)* play; ~ **maestra**
masterpiece; o~**s públicas** public
works; **por** ~ **de** thanks to (the
efforts of); **obrar** *vt* to work; *(tener
efecto)* to have an effect on // *vi* to
act, behave; *(tener efecto)* to have
an effect; **la carta obra en su
poder** the letter is in his/her possession.
obrero, a [o'βrero, a] *a (clase)*
working; *(movimiento)* labour *cpd*;
clase obrera working class // *nm/f
(gen)* worker; *(sin oficio)* labourer.
obscenidad [oβsθeni'ðað] *nf* obscenity; **obsceno, a** *a* obscene.
obscu... = **oscu...** .
obsequiar [oβse'kjar] *vt (ofrecer)* to
present with; *(agasajar)* to make a
fuss of, lavish attention on;
obsequio *nm (regalo)* gift;
(cortesía) courtesy, attention;
obsequioso, a *a* attentive.
observación [oβserβa'θjon] *nf*
observation; *(reflexión)* remark.
observador, a [oβserβa'ðor, a] *nm/f*
observer.
observancia [oβser'βanθja] *nf*
observance.
observar [oβser'βar] *vt* to observe;
(anotar) to notice; ~**se** *vr* to keep to,
observe.
obsesión [oβse'sjon] *nf* obsession;
obsesionar *vt* to obsess.

obsesionar *vt* to obsess.

obstaculizar [oßtakuli'θar] *vt* (*dificultar*) to hinder, hamper.

obstáculo [oß'stakulo] *nm* (*gen*) obstacle; (*impedimento*) hindrance, drawback.

obstante [oß'stante]: **no ~** *ad* nevertheless // *prep* in spite of.

obstetricia [oßste'triθja] *nf* obstetrics *sg*; **obstétrico, a** *a* obstetric // *nm/f* obstetrician.

obstinado, a [oßsti'naðo, a] *a* (*gen*) obstinate, stubborn.

obstinarse [oßsti'narse] *vr* to be obstinate; **~ en** to persist in.

obstrucción [oßstruk'θjon] *nf* obstruction; **obstruir** *vt* to obstruct.

obtener [oßte'ner] *vt* (*conseguir*) to obtain; (*ganar*) to gain.

obturador [oßtura'ðor] *nm* (*FOTO*) shutter.

obtuso, a [oß'tuso, a] *a* (*filo*) blunt; (*MAT, fig*) obtuse.

obviar [oß'βjar] *vt* to obviate, remove.

obvio, a ['oßβjo, a] *a* obvious.

ocasión [oka'sjon] *nf* (*oportunidad*) opportunity, chance; (*momento*) occasion, time; (*causa*) cause; **de ~** secondhand; **ocasionar** *vt* to cause.

ocaso [o'kaso] *nm* (*fig*) decline.

occidente [okθi'ðente] *nm* west.

océano [o'θeano] *nm* ocean; **el ~ Índico** the Indian Ocean.

OCDE *nf abr* (= *Organización de Cooperación y Desarrollo Económico*) OECD.

ocio ['oθjo] *nm* (*tiempo*) leisure; (*pey*) idleness; **~sidad** *nf* idleness; **~so, a** *a* (*inactivo*) idle; (*inútil*) useless.

octanaje [okta'naxe] *nm*: **de alto ~** high octane; **octano** *nm* octane.

octavilla [okta'viʎa] *nf* leaflet, pamphlet.

octavo, a [ok'taßo, a] *a* eighth.

octogenario, a [oktoxe'narjo, a] *a* octogenarian.

octubre [ok'tußre] *nm* October.

ocular [oku'lar] *a* ocular, eye *cpd*;

testigo ~ eyewitness.

oculista [oku'lista] *nm/f* oculist.

ocultar [okul'tar] *vt* (*esconder*) to hide; (*callar*) to conceal; **oculto, a** *a* hidden; (*fig*) secret.

ocupación [okupa'θjon] *nf* occupation.

ocupado, a [oku'paðo, a] *a* (*persona*) busy; (*plaza*) occupied, taken; (*teléfono*) engaged; **ocupar** *vt* (*gen*) to occupy; **ocuparse** *vr*: **ocuparse de** *o* **en** (*gen*) to concern o.s. with; (*cuidar*) to look after.

ocurrencia [oku'rrenθja] *nf* (*suceso*) incident, event; (*idea*) bright idea.

ocurrir [oku'rrir] *vi* to happen; **~se** *vr*: **se me ocurrió que...** it occurred to me that... .

ochenta [o'tʃenta] *num* eighty.

ocho ['otʃo] *num* eight; **~ días** a week.

odiar [o'ðjar] *vt* to hate; **odio** *nm* (*gen*) hate, hatred; (*disgusto*) dislike; **odioso, a** *a* (*gen*) hateful; (*malo*) nasty.

odontólogo, a [oðon'toloxo, a] *nm/f* dentist, dental surgeon.

OEA *nf abr* (= *Organización de Estados Americanos*) OAS.

oeste [o'este] *nm* west; **una película del ~** a western.

ofender [ofen'der] *vt* (*agraviar*) to offend; (*insultar*) to insult; **~se** *vr* to take offence; **ofensa** *nf* offence; **ofensivo, a** *a* (*insultante*) insulting; (*MIL*) offensive // *nf* offensive.

oferta [o'ferta] *nf* offer; (*propuesta*) proposal; **la ~ y la demanda** supply and demand; **artículos en ~** goods on offer.

oficial [ofi'θjal] *a* official // *nm* official; (*MIL*) officer.

oficina [ofi'θina] *nf* office; **~ de correos** post office; **~ de turismo** tourist office; **oficinista** *nm/f* clerk.

oficio [o'fiθjo] *nm* (*profesión*) profession; (*puesto*) post; (*REL*) service; **ser del ~** to be an old hand; **tener mucho ~** to have a lot of experience; **~ de difuntos** funeral service; **de** ~ officially.

oficioso, a [ofi'θjoso, a] a *(pey)* officious; *(no oficial)* unofficial, informal.

ofimática [ofi'matika] nf office automation.

ofrecer [ofre'θer] vt *(dar)* to offer; *(proponer)* to propose; ~**se** vr *(persona)* to offer o.s., volunteer; *(situación)* to present itself; **¿qué se le ofrece?**, **¿se le ofrece algo?** what can I do for you?, can I get you anything?

ofrecimiento [ofreθi'mjento] nm offer, offering.

ofrendar [ofren'dar] vt to offer, contribute.

oftalmólogo, a [oftal'molovo, a] nm/f ophthalmologist.

ofuscación [ofuska'θjon] nf, **ofuscamiento** [ofuska'mjento] nm *(fig)* bewilderment.

ofuscar [ofus'kar] vt *(confundir)* to bewilder; *(enceguecer)* to dazzle, blind.

oída [o'iða] nf: **de** ~**s** by hearsay.

oído [o'iðo] nm *(ANAT)* ear; *(sentido)* hearing.

oigo etc vb ver **oir**.

oír [o'ir] vt *(gen)* to hear; *(atender a)* to listen to; **¡oiga!** listen!; ~ **misa** to attend mass.

OIT nf abr (= *Organización Internacional del Trabajo*) ILO.

ojal [o'xal] nm buttonhole.

ojalá [oxa'la] excl if only (it were so)!, some hope! // *(tb)* if only...!, would that...!; ~ **que venga hoy** I hope he comes today.

ojeada [oxe'aða] nf glance.

ojera [o'xera] nf: **tener** ~**s** to have bags under one's eyes.

ojeriza [oxe'riθa] nf ill-will.

ojeroso, a [oxe'roso, a] a haggard.

ojete [o'xete] nm eye(let).

ojo [o'xo] nm eye; *(de puente)* span; *(de cerradura)* keyhole // excl careful!; **tener** ~ **para** to have an eye for; ~ **de buey** porthole.

ola [o'la] nf wave.

olé [o'le] excl bravo!, olé!

oleada [ole'aða] nf big wave, swell; *(fig)* wave.

oleaje [ole'axe] nm swell.

óleo ['oleo] nm oil; **oleoducto** nm (oil) pipeline.

oler [o'ler] vt *(gen)* to smell; *(inquirir)* to pry into; *(fig: sospechar)* to sniff out // vi to smell; ~ **a** to smell of.

olfatear [olfate'ar] vt to smell; *(fig: sospechar)* to sniff out; *(inquirir)* to pry into; **olfato** nm sense of smell.

oligarquía [olivar'kia] nf oligarchy.

olimpíada [olim'piaða] nf: **las O**~**s** the Olympics.

oliva [o'liβa] nf *(aceituna)* olive; **aceite de** ~ olive oil; **olivo** nm olive tree.

olmo ['olmo] nm elm (tree).

olor [o'lor] nm smell; ~**oso, a** a scented.

olvidadizo, a [olβiða'ðiθo, a] a *(desmemoriado)* forgetful; *(distraído)* absent-minded.

olvidar [olβi'ðar] vt to forget; *(omitir)* to omit; ~**se** vr *(fig)* to forget o.s.; **se me olvidó** I forgot.

olvido [ol'βiðo] nm oblivion; *(despiste)* forgetfulness.

olla [o'ʎa] nf pan; *(comida)* stew; **~ a presión** o **exprés** pressure cooker; ~ **podrida** type of Spanish stew.

ombligo [om'blivo] nm navel.

ominoso, a [omi'noso, a] a ominous.

omisión [omi'sjon] nf *(abstención)* omission; *(descuido)* neglect.

omiso, a [o'miso, a] a: **hacer caso** ~ **de** to ignore, pass over.

omitir [omi'tir] vt to omit.

omnipotente [omnipo'tente] a omnipotent.

omnívoro, a [om'niβoro, a] a omnivorous.

omóplato [o'moplato] nm shoulder blade.

OMS nf abr (= *Organización Mundial de la Salud*) WHO.

once ['onθe] num eleven; ~**s** nmpl

(AM) tea break.

onda ['onda] *nf* wave; ~ **corta/larga/media** short/long/medium wave; **ondear** *vt, vi* to wave; *(agua)* to ripple; **ondearse** *vr* to swing, sway.

ondulación [ondula'θjon] *nf* undulation; **ondulado, a** *a* wavy // *nm* wave; **ondulante** *a* undulating.

ondular [ondu'lar] *vt (el pelo)* to wave // *vi*, ~**se** *vr* to undulate.

oneroso, a [one'roso, a] *a* onerous.

ONU ['onu] *nf abr* (= *Organización de las Naciones Unidas*) UNO.

opaco, a [o'pako, a] *a* opaque; *(fig)* dull.

ópalo ['opalo] *nm* opal.

opción [op'θjon] *nf (gen)* option; *(derecho)* right, option.

OPEP ['opep] *nf abr* (= *Organización de Paises Exportadores de Petróleo*) OPEC.

ópera ['opera] *nf* opera; ~ **bufa** o **cómica** comic opera.

operación [opera'θjon] *nf (gen)* operation; *(COM)* transaction, deal.

operador, a [opera'ðor, a] *nmf* operator; *(CINE: proyección)* projectionist; *(: rodaje)* cameraman.

operante [ope'rante] *a* operating.

operar [ope'rar] *vt (producir)* to produce, bring about; *(MED)* to operate on // *vi (COM)* to operate, deal; ~**se** *vr* to occur; *(MED)* to have an operation.

opereta [ope'reta] *nf* operetta.

opinar [opi'nar] *vt (estimar)* to give one's opinion // *vi (enjuiciar)* to think; **opinión** *nf (creencia)* belief; *(criterio)* opinion.

opio ['opjo] *nm* opium.

oponente [opo'nente] *nmf* opponent.

oponer [opo'ner] *vt (resistencia)* to put up, offer; *(negativa)* to raise; ~**se** *vr (objetar)* to object; *(estar frente a frente)* to be opposed; *(dos personas)* to oppose each other; ~ **a** B to set A against B; **me opongo a pensar que...** I refuse to believe o

think that... .

oportunidad [oportuni'ðað] *nf (ocasión)* opportunity; *(posibilidad)* chance.

oportunismo [oportu'nismo] *nm* opportunism; **oportunista** *nmf* opportunist.

oportuno, a [opor'tuno, a] *a (en su tiempo)* opportune, timely; *(respuesta)* suitable; **en el momento** ~ at the right moment.

oposición [oposi'θjon] *nf* opposition; **oposiciones** *nfpl* public examinations.

opositor, a [oposi'tor, a] *nmf (adversario)* opponent; *(candidato)* candidate.

opresión [opre'sjon] *nf* oppression; **opresivo, a** *a* oppressive; **opresor, a** *nmf* oppressor.

oprimir [opri'mir] *vt* to squeeze; *(fig)* to oppress.

oprobio [o'proβjo] *nm (infamia)* ignominy; *(descrédito)* shame.

optar [op'tar] *vi (elegir)* to choose; ~ **a** o **por** to opt for; **optativo, a** *a* optional.

óptico, a ['optiko, a] *a* optic(al) // *nmf* optician.

optimismo [opti'mismo] *nm* optimism; **optimista** *nmf* optimist.

óptimo, a ['optimo, a] *a (el mejor)* very best.

opuesto, a [o'pwesto, a] *a (contrario)* opposite; *(antagónico)* opposing.

opulencia [opu'lenθja] *nf* opulence; **opulento, a** *a* opulent.

oración [ora'θjon] *nf (discurso)* speech; *(REL)* prayer; *(LING)* sentence.

oráculo [o'rakulo] *nm* oracle.

orador, a [ora'ðor, a] *nmf (conferenciante)* speaker, orator.

oral [o'ral] *a* oral.

orangután [orangu'tan] *nm* orangutan.

orar [o'rar] *vi (REL)* to pray.

oratoria [ora'torja] *nf* oratory.

órbita ['orβita] *nf* orbit.

orden ['orðen] *nm (gen)* order // *nf*

(gen) order; *(INFORM)* command; ~ **del día** agenda; **de primer** ~ first-rate; **en** ~ **de prioridad** in order of priority.

ordenado, a [orðeˈnaðo, a] *a (metódico)* methodical; *(arreglado)* orderly.

ordenador [orðenaˈðor] *nm* computer; ~ **central** mainframe computer.

ordenanza [orðeˈnanθa] *nf* ordinance.

ordenar [orðeˈnar] *vt (mandar)* to order; *(poner orden)* to put in order, arrange; ~**se** *vr (REL)* to be ordained.

ordeñar [orðeˈnar] *vt* to milk.

ordinario, a [orðiˈnarjo, a] *a (común)* ordinary, usual; *(vulgar)* vulgar, common.

orégano [oˈreɣano] *nm* oregano.

oreja [oˈrexa] *nf* ear; *(MECÁNICA)* lug, flange.

orfanato [orfaˈnato] *nm* orphanage.

orfandad [orfanˈdad] *nf* orphanhood.

orfebrería [orfeβreˈria] *nf* gold/silver work.

orgánico, a [orˈɣaniko, a] *a* organic.

organigrama [orɣaniˈɣrama] *nm* flow chart.

organismo [orɣaˈnismo] *nm (BIO)* organism; *(POL)* organization.

organista [orɣaˈnista] *nm/f* organist.

organización [orɣaniθaˈθjon] *nf* organization; **organizar** *vt* to organize.

órgano [ˈorɣano] *nm* organ.

orgasmo [orˈɣasmo] *nm* orgasm.

orgía [orˈxia] *nf* orgy.

orgullo [orˈɣuʎo] *nm (altanería)* pride; *(autorespeto)* self-respect; **orgulloso, a** *a (gen)* proud; *(altanero)* haughty.

orientación [orjentaˈθjon] *nf (posición)* position; *(dirección)* direction.

orientar [orjenˈtar] *vt (situar)* to orientate; *(señalar)* to point; *(dirigir)* to direct; *(guiar)* to guide; ~**se** *vr* to get one's bearings; *(decidirse)* to decide on a course of action.

oriente [oˈrjente] *nm* east; **Cercano/Medio/Lejano O**~ Near/Middle/Far East.

origen [oˈrixen] *nm* origin; *(nacimiento)* lineage, birth.

original [orixiˈnal] *a (nuevo)* original; *(extraño)* odd, strange; ~**idad** *nf* originality.

originar [orixiˈnar] *vt* to start, cause; ~**se** *vr* to originate; ~**io, a** *a (nativo)* native; *(primordial)* original.

orilla [oˈriʎa] *nf (borde)* border; *(de río)* bank; *(de bosque, tela)* edge; *(de mar)* shore.

orín [oˈrin] *nm* rust.

orina [oˈrina] *nf* urine; **orinal** *nm* (chamber) pot; **orinar** *vi* to urinate; **orinarse** *vr* to wet o.s.; **orines** *nmpl* urine *sg*.

oriundo, a [oˈrjundo, a] *a:* ~ **de** native of.

ornamento [ornaˈmento] *nm* ornament.

ornar [orˈnar] *vt* to adorn.

ornitología [ornitoloˈxia] *nf* ornithology, bird-watching.

oro [ˈoro] *nm* gold; ~**s** *nmpl (NAIPES)* hearts.

oropel [oroˈpel] *nm* tinsel.

orquesta [orˈkesta] *nf* orchestra; ~ **de cámara/sinfónica** chamber/symphony orchestra.

orquídea [orˈkiðea] *nf* orchid.

ortiga [orˈtiɣa] *nf* nettle.

ortodoxo, a [ortoˈðokso, a] *a* orthodox.

ortografía [ortoɣraˈfia] *nf* spelling.

ortopedia [ortoˈpeðja] *nf* orthopaedics *sg*.

oruga [oˈruɣa] *nf* caterpillar.

orzuelo [orˈθwelo] *nm (MED)* stye.

os [os] *pron (gen)* you; *(a vosotros)* to you.

osa [ˈosa] *nf* (she-bear); **O**~ **Mayor/Menor** Great/Little Bear.

osadía [osaˈðia] *nf* daring.

osar [oˈsar] *vi* to dare.

oscilación [osθilaˈθjon] *nf (movimiento)* oscillation; *(fluctua-*

ción) fluctuation; (vacilación) hesitation; (columpio) swinging, movement to and fro.

oscilar [osθi'lar] vi to oscillate; to fluctuate; to hesitate.

oscurecer [oskure'θer] vt to darken // vi to grow dark; ~**se** vr to grow o get dark.

oscuridad [oskuri'ðað] nf obscurity; (tinieblas) darkness.

oscuro, a [os'kuro, a] a dark; (fig) obscure; a **oscuras** in the dark.

óseo, a ['oseo, a] a bony.

oso ['oso] nm bear; ~ **de peluche** teddy bear; ~ **hormiguero** anteater.

ostensible [osten'siβle] a obvious.

ostentación [ostenta'θjon] nf (gen) ostentation; (acto) display.

ostentar [osten'tar] vt (gen) to show; (pey) to flaunt, show off; (poseer) to have, possess; **ostentoso, a** a ostentatious, showy.

ostra ['ostra] nf oyster.

OTAN ['otan] nf abr (= Organización del Tratado del Atlántico Norte) NATO.

otear [ote'ar] vt to observe; (fig) to look into.

otitis [o'titis] nf earache.

otoñal [oto'nal] a autumnal.

otoño [o'tono] nm autumn.

otorgamiento [otorɣa'mjento] nm conferring, granting; execution.

otorgar [otor'ɣar] vt (conceder) to concede; (dar) to grant.

otorrino, a [oto'rrino, a], **otorrinolaringólogo, a** [otorrinolarin'ɣolovo, a] nm/f ear, nose and throat specialist.

PALABRA CLAVE

otro, a ['otro, a] ♦ a **1** (distinto: sg) another; (: pl) other; **con** ~**s amigos** with other o different friends **2** (adicional): **tráigame** ~ **café (más)**, **por favor** can I have another coffee please; ~**s 10 días más** another ten days

♦ pron **1**: **el** ~ the other one; (los) ~**s** (the) others; **de** ~ somebody

---

else's; **que lo haga** ~ let somebody else do it

2 (recíproco): **se odian (la) una a (la) otra** they hate one another o each other

3: ~ **tanto**: **comer** ~ **tanto** to eat the same o as much again; **recibió una decena de telegramas y otras tantas llamadas** he got about ten telegrams and as many calls.

ovación [oβa'θjon] nf ovation.

oval [o'βal], **ovalado, a** [oβa'laðo, a] a oval; óvalo nm oval.

oveja [o'βexa] nf sheep.

overol [oβe'rol] nm (AM) overalls pl.

ovillo [o'βiʎo] nm (de lana) ball of wool; **hacerse un** ~ to curl up.

OVNI ['oβni] nm abr (= objeto volante no identificado) UFO.

ovulación [oβula'θjon] nf ovulation; **óvulo** nm ovum.

oxidación [oksiða'θjon] nf rusting.

oxidar [oksi'ðar] vt to rust; ~**se** vr to go rusty.

óxido ['oksiðo] nm oxide.

oxigenado, a [oksixe'naðo, a] a (QUIMICA) oxygenated; (pelo) bleached.

oxígeno [ok'sixeno] nm oxygen.

oyente [o'jente] nm/f listener, hearer.

oyes, oyó etc vb ver **oír**.

P

P abr (= padre) Fr.

pabellón [paβe'ʎon] nm bell tent; (ARQ) pavilion; (de hospital etc) block, section; (bandera) flag.

pábilo ['paβilo] nm wick.

pacer [pa'θer] vi to graze.

paciencia [pa'θjenθja] nf patience.

paciente [pa'θjente] a, nm/f patient.

pacificación [paθifika'θjon] nf pacification.

pacificar [paθifi'kar] vt to pacify; (tranquilizar) to calm.

pacífico, a [pa'θifiko, a] a (persona)

peaceable; (*existencia*) peaceful; **el** (*océano*) **P~** the Pacific (Ocean).

pacifismo [paθi'fismo] *nm* pacifism; **pacifista** *nm/f* pacifist.

pacotilla [pako'tiʎa] *nf*: **de ~** (*actor, escritor*) third-rate; (*mueble etc*) cheap.

pactar [pak'tar] *vt* to agree to o on // *vi* to come to an agreement.

pacto ['pakto] *nm* (*tratado*) pact; (*acuerdo*) agreement.

padecer [paðe'θer] *vt* (*sufrir*) to suffer; (*soportar*) to endure, put up with; (*engaño, error*) to be a victim of; **padecimiento** *nm* suffering.

padrastro [pa'ðrastro] *nm* stepfather.

padre ['paðre] *nm* father // *a* (*fam*): **un éxito ~** a tremendous success; **~s** *nmpl* parents.

padrino [pa'ðrino] *nm* (*REL*) godfather; (*fig*: **~ de boda**) best man; (*fig*) sponsor, patron; **~s** *nmpl* godparents.

padrón [pa'ðron] *nm* (*censo*) census, roll; (*de socios*) register.

paella [pa'eʎa] *nf* paella, dish of rice with meat, shellfish etc.

pág(s). *abr* (= *página(s)*) p(p).

paga ['paxa] *nf* (*pago*) payment; (*sueldo*) pay, wages *pl*.

pagadero, a [paxa'ðero, a] *a* payable; **~ a plazos** payable in instalments.

pagano, a [pa'vano, a] *a*, *nm/f* pagan, heathen.

pagar [pa'var] *vt* to pay; (*las compras, crimen*) to pay for; (*fig*: *favor*) to repay // *vi* to pay; **~ al contado/a plazos** to pay (in) cash/in instalments.

pagaré [paxa're] *nm* I.O.U.

página ['paxina] *nf* page.

pago ['paxo] *nm* (*dinero*) payment; (*fig*) reward; **estar ~** to be quits; **~ anticipado/a cuenta/contra reembolso/en especie** advance payment/payment on account/cash on delivery/payment in kind.

pague *etc vb ver* **pagar**.

país [pa'is] *nm* (*gen*) country; (*región*) land; **los P~es Bajos** the Low Countries; **el P~ Vasco** the Basque Country.

paisaje [pai'saxe] *nm* countryside, scenery.

paisano, a [pai'sano, a] *a* of the same country // *nm/f* (*compatriota*) fellow countryman/woman; **vestir de ~** (*soldado*) to be in civvies; (*guardia*) to be in plain clothes.

paja ['paxa] *nf* straw; (*fig*) rubbish (*Brit*), trash (*US*).

pájara [paxara] *nf* hen (bird).

pajarita [paxa'rita] *nf* (*corbata*) bow tie.

pájaro ['paxaro] *nm* bird; **~ carpintero** woodpecker.

pajita [pa'xita] *nf* (drinking) straw.

pala ['pala] *nf* spade, shovel; (*raqueta etc*) bat; (: *de tenis*) racquet; (*CULIN*) slice; **~ matamoscas** fly swat.

palabra [pa'laßra] *nf* word; (*facultad*) (power of) speech; (*derecho de hablar*) right to speak; **tomar la ~** (*en mitin*) to take the floor.

palabrota [pala'brota] *nf* swearword.

palacio [pa'laθjo] *nm* palace; (*mansión*) mansion, large house; **~ de justicia** courthouse; **~ municipal** town/city hall.

paladar [pala'ðar] *nm* palate; **paladear** *vt* to taste.

palanca [pa'lanka] *nf* lever; (*fig*) pull, influence.

palangana [palan'gana] *nf* washbasin.

palco ['palko] *nm* box.

Palestina [pales'tina] *nf* Palestine; **palestino, a** *nm/f* Palestinian.

paleta [pa'leta] *nf* (*de pintor*) palette; (*de albañil*) trowel; (*de pingpong*) bat; (*AM*) ice lolly.

paliar [pa'ljar] *vt* (*mitigar*) to mitigate, alleviate; **paliativo** *nm* palliative.

palidecer [paliðe'θer] *vi* to turn pale;

palidez *nf* paleness; **pálido, a** *a* pale.

palillo [pa'liʎo] *nm* small stick; (*mondadientes*) toothpick.

paliza [pa'liθa] *nf* beating, thrashing.

palma ['palma] *nf* (*ANAT*) palm; (*árbol*) palm tree; **batir** *o* **dar** ~s to clap, applaud; ~**da** *nf* slap; ~s *nfpl* clapping *sg*, applause *sg*.

palmear [palme'ar] *vi* to clap.

palmo ['palmo] *nm* (*medida*) span; (*fig*) small amount; ~ **a** ~ inch by inch.

palmotear [palmote'ar] *vi* to clap, applaud; **palmoteo** *nm* clapping, applause.

palo ['palo] *nm* stick; (*poste*) post, pole; (*mango*) handle, shaft; (*golpe*) blow, hit; (*de golf*) club; (*de béisbol*) bat; (*NAUT*) mast; (*NAIPES*) suit.

paloma [pa'loma] *nf* dove, pigeon.

palomilla [palo'miʎa] *nf* moth; (*TEC: tuerca*) wing nut; (: *hierro*) angle iron.

palomitas [palo'mitas] *nfpl* popcorn *sg*.

palpar [pal'par] *vt* to touch, feel.

palpitación [palpita'θjon] *nf* palpitation.

palpitante [palpi'tante] *a* palpitating; (*fig*) burning.

palpitar [palpi'tar] *vi* to palpitate; (*latir*) to beat.

palta ['palta] *nf* (*AM*) avocado (pear).

palúdico, a [pa'luðiko, a] *a* marshy.

paludismo [palu'ðismo] *nm* malaria.

pampa ['pampa] *nf* (*AM*) pampa(s), prairie.

pan [pan] *nm* bread; (*una barra*) loaf; ~ **integral** wholemeal (*Brit*) *o* wholewheat (*US*) bread; ~ **rallado** breadcrumbs *pl*.

pana ['pana] *nf* corduroy.

panadería [panaðe'ria] *nf* baker's (shop); **panadero, a** *nm/f* baker.

Panamá [pana'ma] *nm* Panama; **panameño, a** *a* Panamanian.

pancarta [pan'karta] *nf* placard, banner.

panda ['panda] *nm* (*ZOOL*) panda.

pandereta [pande're ta] *nf* tambourine.

pandilla [pan'diʎa] *nf* set, group; (*de criminales*) gang; (*pey: camarilla*) clique.

panecillo [pane'θiʎo] *nm* (*bread*) roll.

panel [pa'nel] *nm* panel.

panfleto [pan'fleto] *nm* pamphlet.

pánico [pa'niko] *nm* panic.

panorama [pano'rama] *nm* panorama; (*vista*) view.

pantalón [panta'lon] *nm*, **pantalones** [panta'lones] *nmpl* trousers.

pantalla [pan'taʎa] *nf* (*de cine*) screen; (*de lámpara*) lampshade.

pantano [pan'tano] *nm* (*ciénaga*) marsh, swamp; (*depósito: de agua*) reservoir; (*fig*) jam, difficulty.

panteón [pante'on] *nm*: ~ **familiar** family tomb.

pantera [pan'tera] *nf* panther.

pantomima [panto'mima] *nf* pantomime.

pantorrilla [panto'rriʎa] *nf* calf (of the leg).

pantufla [pan'tufla] *nf* slipper.

panza ['panθa] *nf* belly, paunch; **panzón, ona, panzudo, a** *a* fat, potbellied.

pañal [pa'ɲal] *nm* nappy (*Brit*), diaper (*US*); ~**es** *nmpl* (*fig*) early stages, infancy *sg*.

pañería [paɲe'ria] *nf* drapery.

paño ['paɲo] *nm* (*tela*) cloth; (*pedazo de tela*) (piece of) cloth; (*trapo*) duster, rag; ~ **higiénico** sanitary towel; ~s **menores** underclothes.

pañuelo [pa'ɲwelo] *nm* handkerchief, hanky (*fam*); (*para la cabeza*) (head)scarf.

papa ['papa] *nf* (*AM*) potato // *nm*: el P~ the Pope.

papá [pa'pa] *nm* (*pl* ~s) *nm* (*fam*) dad(dy), pa (*US*).

papagayo [papa'ɣajo] *nm* parrot.

papanatas [papa'natas] *nm inv* (*fam*) simpleton.

paparrucha [papaˈrrutʃa] *nf* piece of nonsense.

papaya [paˈpaja] *nf* papaya.

papel [paˈpel] *nm* paper; *(hoja de ~)* sheet of paper; *(TEATRO, fig)* role; **~ de calco/carbón de cartas** tracing paper/carbon paper/stationery; **~ de envolver/pintado** wrapping paper/wallpaper; **~ de aluminio/higiénico** aluminium *(Brit)* o aluminum *(US)* foil/toilet paper; **~ de lija** sandpaper; **~ moneda** paper money; **~ secante** blotting paper.

papeleo [papeˈleo] *nm* red tape.

papelera [papeˈlera] *nf* wastepaper basket; *(escritorio)* desk.

papelería [papeleˈria] *nf* stationer's *(shop)*.

papeleta [papeˈleta] *nf* *(pedazo de papel)* slip of paper; *(POL)* ballot paper; *(ESCOL)* report.

paperas [paˈperas] *nfpl* mumps.

papilla [paˈpiʎa] *nf* *(para niños)* baby food.

paquete [paˈkete] *nm* *(de cigarrillos etc)* packet; *(CORREOS etc)* parcel; *(AM)* package tour; *(: fam)* nuisance, bore.

par [par] *a (igual)* like, equal; *(MAT)* even // *nm* equal; *(de guantes)* pair; *(de veces)* couple; *(POL)* peer; *(GOLF, COM)* par; **abrir o ~ de ~** to open wide.

para [ˈpara] *prep* for; **no es ~ comer** it's not for eating; **decir ~ sí** to say to o.s.; **¿~ qué lo quieres?** what do you want it for?; **se casaron ~ separarse otra vez** they married only to separate again; **lo tendré ~ mañana** I'll have it (for) tomorrow; **ir ~ casa** to go home, head for home; **~ profesor es muy estúpido** he's very stupid for a teacher; **¿quién es usted ~ gritar así?** who are you to shout like that?; **tengo bastante ~ vivir** I have enough to live on.

parabién [paraˈβjen] *nm* congratulations *pl*.

parábola [paˈraβola] *nf* parable;

(MAT) parabola.

parabrisas [paraˈβrisas] *nm inv* windscreen *(Brit)*, windshield *(US)*.

paracaídas [parakaˈiðas] *nm inv* parachute; **paracaidista** *nm/f* parachutist; *(MIL)* paratrooper.

parachoques [paraˈtʃokes] *nm inv* *(AUTO)* bumper; *(MECÁNICA etc)* shock absorber.

parada [paˈraða] *nf* stop; *(acto)* stopping; *(de industria)* shutdown, stoppage; *(lugar)* stopping place; **~ de autobús** bus stop.

paradero [paraˈðero] *nm* stopping-place; *(situación)* whereabouts.

parado, a [paˈraðo, a] *a (persona)* motionless, standing still; *(fábrica)* closed, at a standstill; *(coche)* stopped; *(AM)* standing (up); *(sin empleo)* unemployed, idle.

paradoja [paraˈðoxa] *nf* paradox.

parador [paraˈðor] *nm* parador, state-owned hotel.

paráfrasis [paˈrafrasis] *nf inv* paraphrase.

paraguas [paˈraɣwas] *nm inv* umbrella.

Paraguay [paraˈɣwai] *nm*: **el ~** Paraguay; **paraguayo, a** *a, nm/f* Paraguayan.

paraíso [paraˈiso] *nm* paradise, heaven.

paraje [paˈraxe] *nm* place, spot.

paralelo, a [paraˈlelo, a] *a* parallel.

parálisis [paˈralisis] *nf inv* paralysis; **paralítico, a** *a, nm/f* paralytic.

paralizar [paraliˈθar] *vt* to paralyse; **~se** *vr* to become paralysed; *(fig)* to come to a standstill.

paramilitar [paramiliˈtar] *a* paramilitary.

páramo [ˈparamo] *nm* bleak plateau.

parangón [paranˈɡon] *nm*: **sin ~** incomparable.

paranoico, a [paraˈnoiko, a] *nm/f* paranoiac.

parapléjico, a [paraˈplexiko, a] *a, nm/f* paraplegic.

parar [paˈrar] *vt* to stop; *(golpe)* to ward off // *vi* to stop; **~se** *vr* to stop;

(*AM*) to stand up; **ha parado de llover** it has stopped raining; **van a ~ en la comisaría** they're going to end up in the police station; **~se en** to pay attention to.

parásito, a [pa'rasito, a] *nm/f* parasite.

parasol [para'sol] *nm* parasol, sunshade.

parcela [par'θela] *nf* plot, piece of ground.

parcial [par'θjal] *a* (*pago*) part-; (*eclipse*) partial; (*JUR*) prejudiced, biased; (*POL*) partisan; **~idad** *nf* (*prejuicio*) prejudice, bias.

parco, a [parko, a] *a* (*moderado*) moderate.

parche [partʃe] *nm* (*gen*) patch.

parear [pare'ar] *vt* (*juntar, hacer par*) to match, put together; (*BIO*) to mate, pair.

parecer [pare'θer] *nm* (*opinión*) opinion, view; (*aspecto*) looks *pl* // *vi* (*tener apariencia*) to seem, look; (*asemejarse*) to look o seem like; (*aparecer, llegar*) to appear; **~se** *vr* to look alike, resemble each other; **~se a** to look like, resemble; **según o a lo que parece** evidently, apparently; **me parece que** I think (that), it seems to me that.

parecido, a [pare'θiðo, a] *a* similar // *nf* similarity, likeness, resemblance; **bien ~** good-looking, nice-looking.

pared [pa'reð] *nf* wall.

parejo, a [pa'rexo, a] *a* (*igual*) equal; (*liso*) smooth, even // *nf* (*par*) pair; (*dos personas*) couple; (*otro: de un par*) other one (of a pair); (*persona*) partner.

parentela [paren'tela] *nf* relations *pl*.

parentesco [paren'tesko] *nm* relationship.

paréntesis [pa'rentesis] *nm inv* parenthesis; (*digresión*) digression; (*en escrito*) bracket.

parezco *etc vb ver* **parecer**.

pariente, a [pa'rjente, a] *nm/f* relative, relation.

parir [pa'rir] *vt* to give birth to // *vi* (*mujer*) to give birth, have a baby.

París [pa'ris] *n* Paris.

parking [parkin] *nm* car park (*Brit*), parking lot (*US*).

parlamentar [parlamen'tar] *vi* (*negociar*) to parley.

parlamentario, a [parlamen'tarjo, a] *a* parliamentary // *nm/f* member of parliament.

parlamento [parla'mento] *nm* (*POL*) parliament.

parlanchín, ina [parlan'tʃin, ina] *a* indiscreet // *nm/f* chatterbox.

paro [paro] *nm* (*huelga*) stoppage (of work), strike; (*desempleo*) unemployment; **subsidio de ~** unemployment benefit; **hay ~ en la industria** work in the industry is at a standstill.

parodia [pa'roðja] *nf* parody; **parodiar** *vt* to parody.

parpadear [parpaðe'ar] *vi* (*ojos*) to blink; (*luz*) to flicker.

párpado [parpaðo] *nm* eyelid.

parque [parke] *nm* (*lugar verde*) park; **~ de atracciones/infantil/ zoológico** fairground/playground/zoo.

parquímetro [par'kimetro] *nm* parking meter.

parra [parra] *nf* (*grape*)vine.

párrafo [parrafo] *nm* paragraph; **echar un ~** (*fam*) to have a chat.

parranda [pa'rranda] *nf* (*fam*) spree, binge.

parrilla [pa'rriʎa] *nf* (*CULIN*) grill; (*de coche*) grille; (*carne a la) ~** barbecue; **~da** *nf* barbecue.

párroco [parroko] *nm* parish priest.

parroquia [pa'rrokja] *nf* parish; (*iglesia*) parish church; (*COM*) clientele, customers *pl*; **~no, a** *nm/f* parishioner; client, customer.

parte [parte] *nm* message; (*informe*) report // *nf* part; (*lado, cara*) side; (*de reparto*) share; (*JUR*) party; **en alguna ~ de Europa** somewhere in Europe; **en/por todas ~s** everywhere; **en gran ~** to a large extent; **la mayor ~ de los españoles** most

Spaniards; **de un tiempo a esta ~** for some time past; **de ~ de alguien** on sb's behalf; **¿de ~ de quién?** (TEL) who is speaking?; **por ~ de** on the part of; **yo por mí ~** I for my part; **por otra ~** on the other hand; **dar ~** to inform; **tomar ~** to take part.

partera [par'tera] *nf* midwife.

partición [parti'θjon] *nf* division, sharing-out; (POL) partition.

participación [partiθipa'θjon] *nf* (acto) participation, taking part; (parte, COM) share; (de lotería) shared prize; (aviso) notice, notification.

participante [partiθi'pante] *nm/f* participant.

participar [partiθi'par] *vt* to notify, inform // *vi* to take part, participate.

partícipe [par'tiθipe] *nm/f* participant.

particular [partiku'lar] *a* (especial) particular, special; (individual, personal) private, personal // *nm* (punto, asunto) particular, point; (individuo) individual; **tiene coche ~** he has a car of his own; **~izar** *vt* to distinguish; (especificar) to specify; (detallar) to give details about.

partida [par'tiða] *nf* (salida) departure; (COM) entry, item; (juego) game; (grupo de personas) band, group; **mala ~** dirty trick; **~ de nacimiento/matrimonio/defunción** birth/marriage/death certificate.

partidario, a [parti'ðarjo, a] *a* partisan // *nm/f* supporter, follower.

partido [par'tiðo] *nm* (POL) party; (DEPORTE: encuentro) game, match; (: equipo) team; (apoyo) support; **sacar ~ de** to profit o benefit from; **tomar ~** to take sides.

partir [par'tir] *vt* (dividir) to split, divide; (compartir, distribuir) to share (out), distribute; (romper) to break open, split open; (rebanada) to cut (off) // *vi* (ponerse en camino) to set off o out; (comenzar) to start (off

o out); **~se** *vr* to crack o split o break (in two *etc*); **a ~ de** (starting) from.

parto ['parto] *nm* birth; (fig) product, creation; **estar de ~** to be in labour.

parvulario [parβu'larjo] *nm* nursery school, kindergarten.

pasa ['pasa] *nf* raisin; **~ de Corinto/de Esmirna** currant/ sultana.

pasada [pa'saða] *af, nf ver* **pasado**.

pasadizo [pasa'ðiθo] *nm* (pasillo) passage, corridor; (callejuela) alley.

pasado, a [pa'saðo, a] *a* past; (malo: comida, fruta) bad; (muy cocido) overdone; (anticuado) out of date // *nm* past // *nf* passing, passage; **~ mañana** the day after tomorrow; **el mes ~** last month; **de pasada** in passing, incidentally; **una mala pasada** a dirty trick.

pasador [pasa'ðor] *nm* (gen) bolt; (de pelo) hair slide; (horquilla) grip.

pasaje [pa'saxe] *nm* passage; (pago de viaje) fare; (los pasajeros) passengers *pl*; (pasillo) passageway.

pasajero, a [pasa'xero, a] *a* passing // *nm/f* passenger.

pasamanos [pasa'manos] *nm* (hand)rail; (de escalera) banisters *pl*.

pasamontañas [pasamon'taɲas] *nm inv* balaclava helmet.

pasaporte [pasa'porte] *nm* passport.

pasar [pa'sar] *vt* to pass; (tiempo) to spend; (desgracias) to suffer, endure; (noticia) to give, pass on; (río) to cross; (barrera) to pass through; (falta) to overlook, tolerate; (contrincante) to surpass, do better than; (coche) to overtake; (CINE) to show; (enfermedad) to give, infect with // *vi* (gen) to pass; (terminarse) to be over; (ocurrir) to happen; **~se** *vr* (flores) to fade; (comida) to go bad o off; (fig) to overdo it, go too far; **~ de** to go beyond, exceed; **~ por** (AM) to fetch; **¡lo bien/mal** to have a good/bad time; **¡pase!** come in!; **~se al enemigo** to go over to the

enemy; se me pasó I forgot; no se
le pasa nada he misses nothing;
pase lo que pase come what may.

pasarela [pasa'rela] nf footbridge;
(en barco) gangway.

pasatiempo [pasa'tjempo] nm pastime, hobby.

Pascua ['paskwa] nf: ~ (de Resurrección) Easter; ~ de Navidad
Christmas; ~s nfpl Christmas
(time); ¡felices ~s! Merry Christmas!

pase ['pase] nm pass; (CINE)
performance, showing.

pasear [pase'ar] vt to take for a
walk; (exhibir) to parade, show off //
vi, ~se vr to walk, go for a walk; ~
en coche to go for a drive; **paseo**
nm (avenida) avenue; (distancia
corta) walk, stroll; **dar un** o **ir de**
paseo to go for a walk.

pasillo [pa'siʎo] nm passage,
corridor.

pasión [pa'sjon] nf passion.

pasivo, a [pa'siβo, a] a passive; (inactivo) inactive // nm (COM)
liabilities pl, debts pl; (LING)
passive.

pasmar [pas'mar] vt (asombrar) to
amaze, astonish; **pasmo** nm amazement, astonishment; (resfriado)
chill; (fig) wonder, marvel;
pasmoso, a a amazing, astonishing.

paso, a ['paso, a] a dried // nm step;
(modo de andar) walk; (huella)
footprint; (rapidez) speed, pace,
rate; (camino accesible) way
through, passage; (cruce) crossing;
(pasaje) passing, passage; (GEO)
pass; (estrecho) strait; ~ de
peatones pedestrian crossing; **a ese**
~ (fig) at that rate; **salir al** ~ **de** o
a to waylay; **estar de** ~ to be passing through; ~ **elevado** flyover;
prohibido el ~ no entry; **ceda el** ~
give way.

pasota [pa'sota] a, nm/f (fam) ≈
dropout; **ser un** (tipo) ~ to be a bit
of a dropout; (ser indiferente) not to
care about anything.

pasta ['pasta] nf paste; (CULIN:
masa) dough; (: de bizcochos etc)
pastry; (fam) dough; ~s nfpl
(bizcochos) biscuits, small cakes;
(fideos, espaguetis etc) pasta; ~ de
dientes o dentífrica toothpaste.

pastar [pas'tar] vt, vi to graze.

pastel [pas'tel] nm (dulce) cake; ~
de carne meat pie; (ARTE) pastel;
~**ería** nf cake shop.

pasteurizado, a [pasteuri'θaðo, a] a
pasteurized.

pastilla [pas'tiʎa] nf (de jabón,
chocolate) bar; (píldora) tablet, pill.

pasto ['pasto] nm (hierba) grass;
(lugar) pasture, field.

pastor, a [pas'tor, a] nm/f shepherd/
ess // nm (REL) clergyman, pastor.

pata ['pata] nf (pierna) leg; (pie)
foot; (de muebles) leg; ~s arriba
upside down; **meter la** ~ to put
one's foot in it; (TEC): ~ de cabra
crowbar; **tener buena/mala** ~ to be
lucky/unlucky; ~**da** nf kick; (en el
suelo) stamp.

patalear [patale'ar] vi (en el suelo)
to stamp one's feet.

patata [pa'tata] nf potato; ~s fritas
o a la española chips, French fries;
~s fritas (de bolsa) crisps.

paté [pa'te] nm pâté.

patear [pate'ar] vt (pisar) to stamp
on, trample (on); (pegar con el pie)
to kick // vi to stamp (with rage),
stamp one's feet.

patente [pa'tente] a obvious,
evident; (COM) patent // nf patent.

paternal [pater'nal] a fatherly,
paternal; **paterno, a** a paternal.

patético, a [pa'tetiko, a] a pathetic,
moving.

patillas [pa'tiʎas] nfpl sideburns.

patín [pa'tin] nm skate; (de trineo)
runner; **patinaje** nm skating;
patinar vi to skate; (resbalarse) to
skid, slip; (fam) to slip up, blunder.

patio ['patjo] nm (de casa) patio,
courtyard; ~ de recreo playground.

pato ['pato] nm duck; **pagar el** ~
(fam) to take the blame, carry the

can.

patológico, a [pato'loxiko, a] *a* pathological.

patoso, a [pa'toso, a] *a (fam)* clumsy.

patraña [pa'traɲa] *nf* story, fib.

patria ['patrja] *nf* native land, mother country.

patrimonio [patri'monjo] *nm* inheritance; *(fig)* heritage.

patriota [pa'trjota] *nm/f* patriot; **patriotismo** *nm* patriotism.

patrocinar [patroθi'nar] *vt* to sponsor; *(apoyar)* to back, support; **patrocinio** *nm* sponsorship; backing, support.

patrón, ona [pa'tron, ona] *nm/f (jefe)* boss, chief, master/mistress; *(propietario)* landlord/lady; *(REL)* patron saint // *nm (TEC, COSTURA)* pattern.

patronal [patro'nal] *a:* **la clase ~** management.

patronato [patro'nato] *nm* sponsorship; *(acto)* patronage; *(fundación benéfica)* trust, foundation.

patrulla [pa'truʎa] *nf* patrol.

pausa ['pausa] *nf* pause, break.

pausado, a [pau'saðo, a] *a* slow, deliberate.

pauta ['pauta] *nf* line, guide line.

pavimento [paβi'mento] *nm (con losas)* pavement, paving.

pavo ['paβo] *nm* turkey; **~ real** peacock.

pavor [pa'βor] *nm* dread, terror.

payaso, a [pa'jaso, a] *nm/f* clown.

payo, a [pa'jo] *nm/f (para gitanos)* non-gipsy.

paz [paθ] *nf* peace; *(tranquilidad)* peacefulness, tranquillity; **hacer las paces** to make peace; *(fig)* to make up; **La P~ n** *(GEO)* La Paz.

PC *abr = Partido Comunista.*

P.D. *abr = (posdata)* PS, ps.

peaje [pe'axe] *nm* toll.

peatón [pea'ton] *nm* pedestrian.

peca ['peka] *nf* freckle.

pecado [pe'kaðo] *nm* sin; **pecador, a** *a* sinful // *nm/f* sinner.

pecaminoso, a [pekami'noso, a] *a* sinful.

pecar [pe'kar] *vi (REL)* to sin; *(fig):* **peca de generoso** he is generous to a fault.

peculiar [peku'ljar] *a* special, peculiar; *(característico)* typical, characteristic; **~idad** *nf* peculiarity; special feature, characteristic.

pecho ['petʃo] *nm (ANAT)* chest; *(de mujer)* breast(s) *(pl)*, bosom; *(fig: corazón)* heart, breast; (: *valor)* courage, spirit; **dar el ~ a** to breast-feed; **tomar algo a ~** to take sth to heart.

pechuga [pe'tʃuɣa] *nf* breast.

pedal [pe'ðal] *nm* pedal; **~ear** *vi* to pedal.

pédalo ['peðalo] *nm* pedal boat.

pedante [pe'ðante] *a* pedantic // *nm/f* pedant; **~ría** *nf* pedantry.

pedazo [pe'ðaθo] *nm* piece, bit; **hacerse ~s** *(romperse)* to smash, shatter.

pedernal [peðer'nal] *nm* flint.

pediatra [pe'ðjatra] *nm/f* paediatrician.

pedicuro, a [peði'kuro, a] *nm/f* chiropodist.

pedido [pe'ðiðo] *nm (COM: mandado)* order; *(petición)* request.

pedir [pe'ðir] *vt* to ask for, request; *(comida, COM: mandar)* to order; *(exigir: precio)* to ask; *(necesitar)* to need, demand, require // *vi* to ask; **me pidió que cerrara la puerta** he asked me to shut the door; **¿cuánto piden por el coche?** how much are they asking for the car?

pegadizo, a [peɣa'ðiθo, a] *a (MUS)* catchy.

pegajoso, a [peɣa'xoso, a] *a* sticky, adhesive.

pegamento [peɣa'mento] *nm* gum, glue.

pegar [pe'ɣar] *vt (papel, sellos)* to stick (on); *(cartel)* to stick up; *(coser)* to sew (on); *(unir: partes)* to join, fix together; *(MED)* to give, infect with; *(dar: golpe)* to give, deal //

vi (*adherirse*) to stick, adhere; (*ir juntos*: *colores*) to match, go together; (*golpear*) to hit; (*quemar*: *el sol*) to strike hot, burn (*fig*); ~se *vr* (*gen*) to stick; (*dos personas*) to hit each other, fight; (*fam*): ~ **un grito** to let out a yell; ~ **un salto** to jump (with fright); ~ **en** to touch; ~se **un tiro** to shoot o.s.

pegatina [peɣa'tina] *nf* sticker.

peinado [pei'naðo] *nm* (*en peluquería*) hairdo; (*estilo*) hair style.

peinar [pei'nar] *vt* to comb; (*hacer estilo*) to style; ~se *vr* to comb one's hair.

peine ['peine] *nm* comb; ~**ta** *nf* ornamental comb.

p.ej. *abr* (= *por ejemplo*) eg.

Pekín [pe'kin] *n* Pekin(g).

pelado, a [pe'laðo, a] *a* (*fruta*, *patata etc*) peeled; (*cabeza*) shorn; (*campo*, *fig*) bare; (*fam*: *sin dinero*) broke.

pelaje [pe'laxe] *nm* (*ZOOL*) fur, coat; (*fig*) appearance.

pelambre [pe'lambre] *nm* (*pelo largo*) long hair, mop.

pelar [pe'lar] *vt* (*fruta*, *patatas etc*) to peel; (*cortar el pelo a*) to cut the hair of; (*quitar la piel*: *animal*) to skin; ~se *vr* (*la piel*) to peel off; **voy a** ~**me** I'm going to get my hair cut.

peldaño [pel'daɲo] *nm* step.

pelea [pe'lea] *nf* (*lucha*) fight; (*discusión*) quarrel, row.

peleado, a [pele'aðo, a] *a*: **estar** ~ (**con uno**) to have fallen out (with sb).

pelear [pele'ar] *vi* to fight; ~se *vr* to fight; (*reñirse*) to fall out, quarrel.

peletería [pelete'ria] *nf* furrier's, fur shop.

pelícano [pe'likano] *nm* pelican.

película [pe'likula] *nf* film; (*cobertura ligera*) thin covering; (*FOTO*: *rollo*) roll o reel of film.

peligro [pe'liɣro] *nm* danger; (*riesgo*) risk; **correr** ~ **de** to run the risk of; ~**so, a** *a* dangerous; risky.

pelirrojo, a [peli'rroxo, a] *a* red-haired, red-headed // *nm/f* redhead.

pelma ['pelma] *nm/f*, **pelmazo** [pel'maθo] *nm* (*fam*) pain (in the neck).

pelo [pe'lo] *nm* (*cabellos*) hair; (*de barba*, *bigote*) whisker; (*de animal*: *pellejo*) hair, fur, coat; **al** ~ just right; **venir al** ~ to be exactly what one needs; **un hombre de** ~ **en pecho** a brave man; **por los** ~**s** by the skin of one's teeth; **no tener** ~**s en la lengua** to be outspoken, not mince words; **tomar el** ~ **a uno** to pull sb's leg.

pelón, ona [pe'lon, ona] *a* hairless, bald.

pelota [pe'lota] *nf* ball; (*fam*: *cabeza*) nut; **en** ~ stark naked; **hacer la** ~ (**a uno**) (*fam*) to creep (to sb); ~ **vasca** pelota.

pelotari [pelo'tari] *nm* pelota player.

pelotón [pelo'ton] *nm* (*MIL*) squad, detachment.

peluca [pe'luka] *nf* wig.

peluche [pe'lutʃe] *nm*: **oso/muñeco de** ~ teddy bear/soft toy.

peludo, a [pe'luðo, a] *a* hairy, shaggy.

peluquería [peluke'ria] *nf* hairdresser's; (*para hombres*) barber's (shop); **peluquero, a** *nm/f* hairdresser; barber.

pelusa [pe'lusa] *nf* (*BOT*) down; (*COSTURA*) fluff.

pellejo [pe'ʎexo] *nm* (*de animal*) skin, hide.

pellizcar [peʎiθ'kar] *vt* to pinch, nip.

pena ['pena] *nf* (*congoja*) grief, sadness; (*remordimiento*) regret; (*dificultad*) trouble; (*dolor*) pain; (*JUR*) sentence; **merecer** o **valer la** ~ to be worthwhile; **a duras** ~**s** with great difficulty; ~ **de muerte** death penalty; ~ **pecuniaria** fine; **¡qué** ~! what a shame!

penal [pe'nal] *a* penal // *nm* (*cárcel*) prison.

penalidad [penali'ðað] *nf* (*problema*, *dificultad*) trouble, hardship; (*JUR*) penalty, punishment.

penalti, penalty [pe'nalti] (*pl* **penaltis, penalty(e)s, penalties**) *nm* penalty (kick).

penar [pe'nar] *vt* to penalize; (*castigar*) to punish // *vi* to suffer.

pendiente [pen'djente] *a* pending, unsettled // *nm* earring // *nf* hill, slope.

pene [']pene] *nm* penis.

penetración [penetra'θjon] *nf* (*acto*) penetration; (*agudeza*) sharpness, insight.

penetrante [pene'trante] *a* (*herida*) deep; (*persona, arma*) sharp; (*sonido*) penetrating, piercing; (*mirada*) searching; (*viento, ironía*) biting.

penetrar [pene'trar] *vt* to penetrate, pierce; (*entender*) to grasp // *vi* to penetrate, go in; (*entrar*) to enter, go in; (*líquido*) to soak in; (*fig*) to pierce.

penicilina [peniθi'lina] *nf* penicillin.

península [pe'ninsula] *nf* peninsula; **peninsular** *a* peninsular.

penique [pe'nike] *nm* penny.

penitencia [peni'tenθja] *nf* (*remordimiento*) penitence; (*castigo*) penance; **~ría** *nf* prison, penitentiary.

penoso, a [pe'noso, a] *a* (*difícil*) arduous, difficult.

pensador, a [pensa'ðor, a] *nm/f* thinker.

pensamiento [pensa'mjento] *nm* thought; (*mente*) mind; (*idea*) idea.

pensar [pen'sar] *vt* to think; (*considerar*) to think over, think out; (*proponerse*) to intend, plan; (*imaginarse*) to think up, invent // *vi* to think; **~ en** to aim at, aspire to; **pensativo, a** *a* thoughtful, pensive.

pensión [pen'sjon] *nf* (*casa*) boarding *o* guest house; (*dinero*) pension; (*cama y comida*) board and lodging; **~ completa** full board; **pensionista** *nm/f* (*jubilado*) (oldage) pensioner; (*huésped*) lodger.

penúltimo, a [pe'nultimo, a] *a*

penultimate, last but one.

penumbra [pe'numbra] *nf* half-light.

penuria [pe'nurja] *nf* shortage, want.

peña [']pena] *nf* (*roca*) rock; (*cuesta*) cliff, crag; (*grupo*) group, circle; (*AM: club*) folk club.

peñasco [pe'nasko] *nm* large rock, boulder.

peñón [pe'non] *nm* wall of rock; **el P~** the Rock (of Gibraltar).

peón [pe'on] *nm* labourer; (*AM*) farm labourer, farmhand; (*AJEDREZ*) pawn.

peonza [pe'onθa] *nf* spinning top.

peor [pe'or] *a* (*comparativo*) worse; (*superlativo*) worst // *ad* worse; worst; **de mal en ~** from bad to worse.

pepinillo [pepi'niʎo] *nm* gherkin.

pepino [pe'pino] *nm* cucumber; (**no**) **me importa un ~** I don't care one bit.

pepita [pe'pita] *nf* (*BOT*) pip; (*MINERÍA*) nugget.

pequeñez [peke'neθ] *nf* smallness, littleness; (*trivialidad*) trifle, triviality.

pequeño, a [pe'keno, a] *a* small, little.

pera [']pera] *nf* pear; **peral** *nm* pear tree.

percance [per'kanθe] *nm* setback, misfortune.

percatarse [perka'tarse] *vr*: **~ de** to notice, take note of.

percepción [perθep'θjon] *nf* (*vista*) perception; (*idea*) notion, idea.

perceptible [perθep'tiβle] *a* perceptible, noticeable; (*COM*) payable, receivable.

percibir [perθi'βir] *vt* to perceive, notice; (*COM*) to earn, get.

percusión [perku'sjon] *nf* percussion.

percha [']pertʃa] *nf* (*ganchos*) coat hooks *pl*; (*colgador*) coat hanger; (*de ave*) perch.

perdedor, a [perðe'ðor, a] *a* losing // *nm/f* loser.

perder [per'ðer] *vt* to lose; (*tiempo, palabras*) to waste; (*oportunidad*) to lose, miss; (*tren*) to miss // *vi* to lose; ~**se** *vr* (*extraviarse*) to get lost; (*desaparecer*) to disappear, be lost to view; (*arruinarse*) to be ruined; **echar** a ~ (*comida*) to spoil, ruin; (*oportunidad*) to waste.

perdición [perði'θjon] *nf* perdition, ruin.

pérdida ['perðiða] *nf* loss; (*de tiempo*) waste; ~**s** *nfpl* (COM) losses.

perdido, a [per'ðiðo, a] *a* lost.

perdiz [per'ðiθ] *nf* partridge.

perdón [per'ðon] *nm* (*disculpa*) pardon, forgiveness; (*clemencia*) mercy; ¡~! sorry!, I beg your pardon!; **perdonar** *vt* to pardon, forgive; (*la vida*) to spare; (*excusar*) to exempt, excuse; **¡perdone (usted)!** sorry!, I beg your pardon!

perdurable [perðu'raßle] *a* lasting; (*eterno*) everlasting.

perdurar [perðu'rar] *vi* (*resistir*) to last, endure; (*seguir existiendo*) to stand, still exist.

perecedero, a [pereθe'ðero, a] *a* (COM *etc*) perishable.

perecer [pere'θer] *vi* (*morir*) to perish, die; (*objeto*) to shatter.

peregrinación [perexrina'θjon] *nf* (REL) pilgrimage.

peregrino, a [pere'xrino, a] *a* (*idea*) strange, absurd // *nm/f* pilgrim.

perejil [pere'xil] *nm* parsley.

perenne [pe'renne] *a* everlasting, perennial.

perentorio, a [peren'torjo, a] *a* (*urgente*) urgent, peremptory; (*fijo*) set, fixed.

pereza [pe'reθa] *nf* laziness, idleness; **perezoso, a** *a* lazy, idle.

perfección [perfek'θjon] *nf* perfection; **perfeccionar** *vt* to perfect; (*mejorar*) to improve; (*acabar*) to complete, finish.

perfectamente [perfekta'mente] *ad* perfectly.

perfecto, a [per'fekto, a] *a* perfect; (*terminado*) complete, finished.

perfidia [per'fiðja] *nf* perfidy,

treachery.

perfil [per'fil] *nm* profile; (*contorno*) silhouette, outline; (ARQ) (cross) section; ~**es** *nmpl* features; (*fig*) social graces; ~**ado, a** *a* (*bien formado*) well-shaped; (*largo*: *cara*) long; ~**ar** *vt* (*trazar*) to outline; (*fig*) to shape, give character to.

perforación [perfora'θjon] *nf* perforation; (*con taladro*) drilling; **perforadora** *nf* punch.

perforar [perfo'rar] *vt* to perforate; (*agujero*) to drill, bore; (*papel*) to punch a hole in // *vi* to drill, bore.

perfume [per'fume] *nm* perfume, scent.

pericia [pe'riθja] *nf* skill, expertise.

periferia [peri'ferja] *nf* periphery; (*de ciudad*) outskirts *pl*.

periférico [peri'feriko] *nm* (AM) ring road (Brit), beltway (US).

perímetro [pe'rimetro] *nm* perimeter.

periódico, a [pe'rjoðiko, a] *a* periodic(al) // *nm* newspaper.

periodismo [perjo'ðismo] *nm* journalism; **periodista** *nm/f* journalist.

periodo [pe'rjoðo], **período** [pe'rioðo] *nm* period.

periquito [peri'kito] *nm* budgerigar, budgie.

perito, a [pe'rito, a] *a* (*experto*) expert; (*diestro*) skilled, skilful // *nm/f* expert; skilled worker; (*técnico*) technician.

perjudicar [perxuði'kar] *vt* (*gen*) to damage, harm; **perjudicial** *a* damaging, harmful; (*en detrimento*) detrimental; **perjuicio** *nm* damage, harm.

perjurar [perxu'rar] *vi* to commit perjury.

perla ['perla] *nf* pearl; **me viene de** ~ it suits me fine.

permanecer [permane'θer] *vi* (*quedarse*) to stay, remain; (*seguir*) to continue to be.

permanencia [perma'nenθja] *nf* permanence; (*estancia*) stay.

permanente [perma'nente] *a*

permanent, constant // nf perm.

permisible [permi'sißle] a permissible, allowable.

permiso [per'miso] nm permission; (*licencia*) permit, licence; **con ~** excuse me; **estar de ~** (*MIL*) to be on leave; **~ de conducir** driving licence (*Brit*), driver's license (*US*).

permitir [permi'tir] vt to permit, allow.

pernera [per'nera] nf trouser leg.

pernicioso, a [perni'θjoso, a] a (*maligno, MED*) pernicious; (*persona*) wicked.

pernio [per'njo] nm hinge.

perno [per'no] nm bolt.

pero ['pero] conj but; (*aún*) yet // nm (*defecto*) flaw, defect; (*reparo*) objection.

perol [pe'rol] nm, **perola** [pe'rola] nf (large metal) pan.

perpendicular [perpendiku'lar] a perpendicular.

perpetrar [perpe'trar] vt to perpetrate.

perpetuar [perpe'twar] vt to perpetuate; **perpetuo, a** a perpetual.

perplejo, a [per'plexo, a] a perplexed, bewildered.

perra ['perra] nf (*ZOOL*) bitch; (*fam: dinero*) money; **estar sin una ~** to be flat broke.

perrera [pe'rrera] nf kennel.

perro ['perro] nm dog.

persa ['persa] a, nmf Persian.

persecución [perseku'θjon] nf pursuit, chase; (*REL*) persecution.

perseguir [perse'xir] vt to pursue, hunt; (*cortejar*) to chase after; (*molestar*) to pester, annoy; (*REL, POL*) to persecute.

perseverante [perseße'rante] a persevering, persistent.

perseverar [perseße'rar] vi to persevere, persist; **~ en** to persevere in, persist with.

persiana [per'sjana] nf (Venetian) blind.

persignarse [persix'narse] vr to cross o.s.

persistente [persis'tente] a persistent.

persistir [persis'tir] vi to persist.

persona [per'sona] nf person; **~ mayor** elderly person; **10 ~s** 10 people.

personaje [perso'naxe] nm important person, celebrity; (*TEATRO etc*) character.

personal [perso'nal] a (*particular*) personal; (*para una persona*) single, for one person // nm personnel, staff; **~idad** nf personality.

personarse [perso'narse] vr to appear in person.

personificar [personifi'kar] vt to personify.

perspectiva [perspek'tißa] nf perspective; (*vista, panorama*) view, panorama; (*posibilidad futura*) outlook, prospect.

perspicacia [perspi'kaθja] nf (*fig*) discernment, perspicacity.

perspicaz [perspi'kaθ] a shrewd.

persuadir [perswa'ðir] vt (*gen*) to persuade; (*convencer*) to convince; **~se** vr to become convinced; **persuasión** nf persuasion; **persuasivo, a** a persuasive; convincing.

pertenecer [pertene'θer] vi to belong; (*fig*) to concern; **pertenencia** nf ownership; **pertenencias** nfpl possessions, property sg; **perteneciente** a: **perteneciente a** belonging to.

pertenezca etc vb ver **pertenecer**.

pértiga [per'tiva] nf: **salto de ~** pole vault.

pertinaz [perti'naθ] a (*persistente*) persistent; (*terco*) obstinate.

pertinente [perti'nente] a relevant, pertinent; (*apropiado*) appropriate; **~ a** concerning, relevant to.

perturbación [perturßa'θjon] nf (*POL*) disturbance; (*MED*) upset, disturbance.

perturbado, a [pertur'ßaðo, a] a mentally unbalanced.

perturbador, a [pertur'ßa'ðor, a] a perturbing, disturbing; (*subversivo*) subversive.

perturbar [pertur'βar] vt (el orden) to disturb; (MED) to upset, disturb; (mentalmente) to perturb.

Perú [pe'ru] nm: el ~ Peru; **peruano, a** a, nm/f Peruvian.

perversión [perβer'sjon] nf perversion; **perverso, a** a perverse; (depravado) depraved.

pervertido, a [perβer'tiðo, a] a perverted // nm/f pervert.

pervertir [perβer'tir] vt to pervert, corrupt.

pesa ['pesa] nf weight; (DEPORTE) shot.

pesadez [pesa'ðeθ] nf (peso) heaviness; (lentitud) slowness; (aburrimiento) tediousness.

pesadilla [pesa'ðiʎa] nf nightmare, bad dream.

pesado, a [pe'saðo, a] a heavy; (lento) slow; (difícil, duro) tough, hard; (aburrido) boring, tedious; (tiempo) sultry.

pesadumbre [pesa'ðumbre] nf grief, sorrow.

pésame ['pesame] nm expression of condolence, message of sympathy; dar el ~ to express one's condolences.

pesar [pe'sar] vt to weigh // vi to weigh; (ser pesado) to weigh a lot, be heavy; (fig: opinión) to carry weight; no pesa mucho it doesn't weigh much // nm (arrepentimiento) regret; (pena) grief, sorrow; a ~ de o pese a (que) in spite of, despite.

pesario [pe'sarjo] nm pessary.

pesca ['peska] nf (acto) fishing; (lo pescado) catch; ir de ~ to go fishing.

pescadería [peskaðe'ria] nf fish shop, fishmonger's (Brit).

pescado [pes'kaðo] nm fish.

pescador, a [peska'ðor, a] nm/f fisherman/woman.

pescar [pes'kar] vt (tomar) to catch; (intentar tomar) to fish for; (conseguir: trabajo) to manage to get // vi to fish, go fishing.

pescuezo [pes'kweθo] nm (ZOOL) neck.

pesebre [pe'seβre] nm manger.

peseta [pe'seta] nf peseta.

pesimista [pesi'mista] a pessimistic // nm/f pessimist.

pésimo, a ['pesimo, a] a awful, dreadful.

peso ['peso] nm weight; (balanza) scales pl; (moneda) peso; ~ bruto/neto gross/net weight; vender a ~ to sell by weight.

pesquero, a [pes'kero, a] a fishing cpd.

pesquisa [pes'kisa] nf inquiry, investigation.

pestaña [pes'taɲa] nf (ANAT) eyelash; (borde) rim; **pestañear** vi to blink.

peste ['peste] nf plague; (mal olor) stink, stench.

pesticida [pesti'θiða] nm pesticide.

pestilencia [pesti'lenθja] nf (mal olor) stink, stench.

pestillo [pes'tiʎo] nm (cerrojo) bolt; (picaporte) doorhandle.

petaca [pe'taka] nf (AM) suitcase.

pétalo ['petalo] nm petal.

petardo [pe'tarðo] nm firework, firecracker.

petición [peti'θjon] nf (pedido) request, plea; (memorial) petition; (JUR) plea.

petrificar [petrifi'kar] vt to petrify.

petróleo [pe'troleo] nm oil, petroleum; **petrolero, a** a petroleum cpd // nm (COM: persona) oil man; (buque) (oil) tanker.

peyorativo, a [pejora'tiβo, a] a pejorative.

pez [peθ] nm fish.

pezón [pe'θon] nm teat, nipple.

pezuña [pe'θuɲa] nf hoof.

piadoso, a [pja'ðoso, a] a (devoto) pious, devout; (misericordioso) kind, merciful.

pianista [pja'nista] nm/f pianist.

piano ['pjano] nm piano.

piar [pjar] vi to cheep.

pibe, a ['piβe, a] nm/f (AM) boy/girl.

picadero [pika'ðero] nm riding school.

picadillo [pika'ðiʎo] nm mince, minced meat.

picado, a [pi'kaðo, a] a pricked, punctured; (CULIN) minced, chopped; (mar) choppy; (diente) bad; (tabaco) cut; (enfadado) cross.

picador [pika'ðor] nm (TAUR) picador; (minero) faceworker.

picadura [pika'ðura] nf (pinchazo) puncture; (de abeja) sting; (de mosquito) bite; (tabaco picado) cut tobacco.

picante [pi'kante] a hot; (comentario) racy, spicy.

picaporte [pika'porte] nm (manija) doorhandle; (pestillo) latch.

picar [pi'kar] vt (agujerear, perforar) to prick, puncture; (abeja) to sting; (mosquito, serpiente) to bite; (CULIN) to mince, chop; (incitar) to incite, goad; (dañar, irritar) to annoy, bother; (quemar: lengua) to burn, sting // vi (pez) to bite, take the bait; (sol) to burn, scorch; (abeja, MED) to sting; (mosquito) to bite; ~se vr (agriarse) to turn sour, go off; (ofenderse) to take offence.

picardía [pikar'ðia] nf villainy; (astucia) slyness, craftiness; (una ~) dirty trick; (palabra) rude/bad word o expression.

pícaro, a [pi'karo, a] a (malicioso) villainous; (travieso) mischievous // nm (astuto) crafty sort; (sinvergüenza) rascal, scoundrel.

pico [piko] nm (de ave) beak; (punta) sharp point; (TEC) pick, pickaxe; (GEO) peak; summit; **y ~** and a bit.

picotear [pikote'ar] vt to peck // vi to nibble, peck.

picudo, a [pi'kuðo, a] a pointed, with a point.

pichón [pi'tʃon] nm young pigeon.

pido, pidió etc vb ver **pedir**.

pie [pje] nm (pl ~s) foot; (fig: motivo) motive, basis; (: fundamento) foothold; **ir a** ~ to go on

foot, walk; **estar de** ~ to be standing (up); **ponerse de** ~ to stand up; **de** ~**s a cabeza** from top to bottom; **al** ~ **de la letra** literally, verbatim; (copiar) exactly, word for word; **en** ~ **de guerra** on a war footing; **dar** ~ **a** to give cause for; **hacer** ~ (en el agua) to touch (the) bottom.

piedad [pje'ðað] nf (lástima) pity, compassion; (clemencia) mercy; (devoción) piety, devotion.

piedra [pje'ðra] nf stone; (roca) rock; (de mechero) flint; (METEOROLOGÍA) hailstone.

piel [pjel] nf (ANAT) skin; (ZOOL) skin, hide, fur; (cuero) leather; (BOT) skin, peel.

pienso etc vb ver **pensar**.

pierdo etc vb ver **perder**.

pierna [pjerna] nf leg.

pieza [pjeθa] nf piece; (habitación) room; ~ **de recambio** o **repuesto** spare (part).

pigmeo, a [piɣ'meo, a] a, nm/f pigmy.

pijama [pi'xama] nm pyjamas pl.

pila [pila] nf (ELEC) battery; (montón) heap, pile; (lavabo) sink.

píldora [pilðora] nf pill; **la** ~ **(anticonceptiva)** the (contraceptive) pill.

pileta [pi'leta] nf basin, bowl; (AM) swimming pool.

piloto [pi'loto] nm pilot; (de aparato) (pilot) light; (AUTO: luz) tail o rear light; (: conductor) driver.

pillaje [pi'ʎaxe] nm pillage, plunder.

pillar [pi'ʎar] vt (saquear) to pillage, plunder; (fam: coger) to catch; (: agarrar) to grasp, seize; (: entender) to grasp, catch on to; ~se vr: ~se **un dedo con la puerta** to catch one's finger in the door.

pillo, a [piʎo, a] a villainous; (astuto) sly, crafty // nm/f rascal, rogue, scoundrel.

pimentón [pimen'ton] nm paprika.

pimienta [pi'mjenta] nf pepper.

pimiento [pi'mjento] nm pepper, pimiento.

pinacoteca [pinako'teka] nf art gallery.

pinar [pi'nar] nm pine forest (Brit), pine grove (US).

pincel [pin'θel] nm paintbrush.

pinchar [pin'tʃar] vt (perforar) to prick, pierce; (neumático) to puncture; (fig) to prod.

pinchazo [pin'tʃaθo] nm (perforación) prick; (de neumático) puncture; (fig) prod.

pinchito [pin'tʃito] nm shish kebab.

pincho ['pintʃo] nm savoury (snack); ~ **moruno** shish kebab; ~ **de tortilla** small slice of omelette.

ping-pong ['pin'pon] nm table tennis.

pingüino [pin'gwino] nm penguin.

pino ['pino] nm pine (tree).

pinta ['pinta] nf spot; (de líquidos) spot, drop; (aspecto) appearance, look(s) (pl); **~do, a** a spotted; (de muchos colores) colourful.

pintar [pin'tar] vt to paint // vi to paint; (fam) to count, be important; **~se** vr to put on make-up.

pintor, a [pin'tor. a] nm/f painter.

pintoresco, a [pinto'resko. a] a picturesque.

pintura [pin'tura] nf painting; ~ **a la acuarela** watercolour; ~ **al óleo** oil painting.

pinza ['pinθa] nf (ZOOL) claw; (para colgar ropa) clothes peg; (TEC) pincers pl; **~s** nfpl (para depilar etc) tweezers pl.

piña ['pina] nf (fruto del pino) pine cone; (fruta) pineapple; (fig) group.

piñón [pi'non] nm (fruto) pine nut; (TEC) pinion.

pío, a ['pio, a] a (devoto) pious, devout; (misericordioso) merciful.

piojo ['pjoxo] nm louse.

pionero, a [pjo'nero. a] a pioneering // nm/f pioneer.

pipa ['pipa] nf pipe; (BOT) (edible) sunflower seed.

pipí [pi'pi] nm (fam): **hacer ~** to have a wee(-wee) (Brit), have to go (wee-wee) (US).

pique ['pike] nm (resentimiento) pique, resentment; (rivalidad) rivalry, competition; **irse a ~** to sink; (esperanza, familia) to be ruined.

piqueta [pi'keta] nf pick(axe).

piquete [pi'kete] nm (agujerito) small hole; (MIL) squad, party; (de obreros) picket.

piragua [pi'raxwa] nf canoe; **piragüismo** nm canoeing.

pirámide [pi'ramiðe] nf pyramid.

pirata [pi'rata] a, nm pirate.

Pirineo(s) [piri'neo(s)] nm(pl) Pyrenees pl.

piropo [pi'ropo] nm compliment, (piece of) flattery.

pirueta [pi'rweta] nf pirouette.

pisada [pi'saða] nf (paso) footstep; (huella) footprint.

pisar [pi'sar] vt (caminar sobre) to walk on, tread on; (apretar con el pie) to press; (fig) to trample on, walk all over // vi to tread, step, walk.

piscina [pis'θina] nf swimming pool.

Piscis [pis'θis] nm Pisces.

piso ['piso] nm (suelo, planta) floor; (apartamento) flat (Brit), apartment; **primer ~** (Esp) first floor; (AM) ground floor.

pisotear [pisote'ar] vt to trample (on o underfoot).

pista ['pista] nf track, trail; (indicio) clue; ~ **de aterrizaje** runway; ~ **de baile** dance floor; ~ **de tenis** tennis court; ~ **de hielo** ice rink.

pistola [pis'tola] nf pistol; (TEC) spray-gun; **pistolero, a** nm/f gunman/woman, gangster // nf holster.

pistón [pis'ton] nm (TEC) piston; (MUS) key.

pitar [pi'tar] vt (silbato) to blow; (rechiflar) to whistle at, boo // vi to whistle; (AUTO) to sound o toot one's horn; (AM) to smoke.

pitillo [pi'tiʎo] nm cigarette.

pito ['pito] nm whistle; (de coche) horn.

pitón [pi'ton] nm (ZOOL) python.

pitonisa [pito'nisa] nf fortune-teller.

pitorreo [pito'rreo] nm joke; **estar de ~** to be joking.

pizarra [pi'θarra] nf (piedra) slate; (encerado) blackboard.

pizca ['piθka] nf pinch, spot; (fig) spot, speck; **ni ~** not a bit.

placa ['plaka] nf plate; (distintivo) badge, insignia; **~ de matrícula** number plate.

placentero, a [plaθen'tero, a] a pleasant, agreeable.

placer [pla'θer] nm pleasure // vi to please.

plácido, a ['plaθiðo, a] a placid.

plaga ['plaxa] nf pest; (MED) plague; (abundancia) abundance; **plagar** vt to infest, plague; (llenar) to fill.

plagio ['plaxjo] nm plagiarism.

plan [plan] nm (esquema, proyecto) plan; (idea, intento) idea, intention; **tener ~** (fam) to have a date; **tener un ~** (fam) to have an affair; **en ~ económico** (fam) on the cheap; **vamos en ~ de turismo** we're going as tourists; **si te pones en ese ~...** if that's your attitude... .

plana ['plana] nf ver **plano**.

plancha ['plantʃa] nf (para planchar) iron; (rótulo) plate, sheet; (NAUT) gangway; **~do** nm ironing; **planchar** vt to iron // vi to do the ironing.

planeador [planea'ðor] nm glider.

planear [plane'ar] vt to plan // vi to glide.

planeta [pla'neta] nm planet.

planicie [pla'niθje] nf plain.

planificación [planifika'θjon] nf planning; **~ familiar** family planning.

plano, a ['plano, a] a flat, level, even // nm (MAT, TEC, AVIAT) plane; (FOTO) shot; (ARQ) plan; (GEO) map; (de ciudad) map, street plan // nf sheet (of paper), page; (TEC) trowel; **primer ~** close-up; **caer de ~** to fall flat; **en primera plana** on the front page; **plana mayor** nf staff.

planta ['planta] nf (BOT, TEC) plant; (ANAT) sole of the foot, foot; (piso) floor; (AM: personal) staff; **~ baja** ground floor.

plantación [planta'θjon] nf (AGR) plantation; (acto) planting.

plantar [plan'tar] vt (BOT) to plant; (levantar) to erect, set up; **~se** vr to stand firm; **~ a uno en la calle** to throw sb out; **dejar plantado a uno** (fam) to stand sb up.

plantear [plante'ar] vt (problema) to pose; (dificultad) to raise.

plantilla [plan'tiʎa] nf (de zapato) insole; (personal) personnel; **ser de ~** to be on the staff.

plantón [plan'ton] nm (MIL) guard, sentry; (fam) long wait; **dar (un) ~ a uno** to stand sb up.

plañir [pla'nir] vi to mourn.

plasmar [plas'mar] vt (dar forma) to mould, shape; (representar) to represent // vi: **~ en** to take the form of.

Plasticina ® [plasti'θina] nf Plasticine ®.

plástico, a ['plastiko, a] a plastic // nm plastic // nf (arte) of sculpture, modelling.

Plastilina ® [plasti'lina] nf (AM) Plasticine ®.

plata ['plata] nf (metal) silver; (cosas hechas de ~) silverware; (AM) cash, dough; **hablar en ~** to speak bluntly or frankly.

plataforma [plata'forma] nf platform; **~ de lanzamiento/perforación** launch(ing) pad/drilling rig.

plátano ['platano] nm (fruta) banana; (árbol) banana tree.

platea [pla'tea] nf (TEATRO) pit.

plateado, a [plate'aðo, a] a silver; (TEC) silver-plated.

plática [pla'tika] nf talk, chat; **platicar** vi to talk, chat.

platillo [pla'tiʎo] nm saucer; **~s** nmpl cymbals; **~ volador o volante** flying saucer.

platino [pla'tino] nm platinum; **~s**

nmpl (*AUTO*) contact points.

plato ['plato] *nm* plate, dish; (*parte de comida*) course; (*comida*) dish; **primer ~** first course.

playa ['plaja] *nf* beach; (*costa*) seaside; **~ de estacionamiento** (*AM*) car park.

playera [pla'jera] *nf* (*AM: camiseta*) T-shirt; **~s** *nfpl* (slip-on) canvas shoes.

plaza ['plaθa] *nf* square; (*mercado*) market(place); (*sitio*) room, space; (*en vehículo*) seat, place; (*colocación*) post, job; **~ de toros** bullring.

plazo ['plaθo] *nm* (*lapso de tiempo*) time, period; (*fecha de vencimiento*) expiry date; (*pago parcial*) instalment; **a corto/largo ~** short-/long-term; **comprar a ~s** to buy on hire purchase, pay for in instalments.

plazoleta[plaθo'leta], **plazuela** [pla'θwela] *nf* small square.

pleamar [plea'mar] *nf* high tide.

plebe ['pleβe] *nf:* **la ~** the common people *pl*, the masses (*pey*) the plebs *pl*; **~yo, a** *a* plebeian; (*pey*) coarse, common.

plebiscito [pleβis'θito] *nm* plebiscite.

plegable [ple'γaβle] *a* pliable; (*silla*) folding.

plegar [ple'γar] *vt* (*doblar*) to fold, bend; (*COSTURA*) to pleat; **~se** *vr* to yield, submit.

pleito ['pleito] *nm* (*JUR*) lawsuit, case; (*fig*) dispute, feud.

plenilunio [pleni'lunjo] *nm* full moon.

plenitud [pleni'tuð] *nf* plenitude, fullness; (*abundancia*) abundance.

pleno, a ['pleno, a] *a* full; (*completo*) complete // *nm* plenum; **en ~ día** in broad daylight; **en ~ verano** at the height of summer; **en plena cara** full in the face.

pleuresía [pleure'sia] *nf* pleurisy.

Plexiglás ® [pleksi'γlas] *nm* acrylic glass, Plexiglas (*US*).

pliego *etc vb ver* **plegar** // ['pljeγo] *nm* (*hoja*) sheet (of paper); (*carta*) sealed letter/document; **~ de**

condiciones details *pl*, specifications *pl*.

pliegue *etc vb ver* **plegar** // ['pljeγe] *nm* fold, crease; (*de vestido*) pleat.

plisado [pli'saðo] *nm* pleating.

plomero [plo'mero] *nm* (*AM*) plumber.

plomo ['plomo] *nm* (*metal*) lead; (*ELEC*) fuse.

pluma ['pluma] *nf* feather; (*para escribir*) pen.

plumero [plu'mero] *nm* (*quitapolvos*) feather duster.

plumón [plu'mon] *nm* (*AM: fino*) felt-tip pen; (*: ancho*) marker.

plural [plu'ral] *a* plural; **~idad** *nf* plurality; **una ~idad de votos** a majority of votes.

plus [plus] *nm* bonus; **~valía** *f* (*COM*) appreciation.

plutocracia [pluto'kraθja] *nf* plutocracy.

población [poβla'θjon] *nf* population; (*pueblo, ciudad*) town, city.

poblado, a [po'βlaðo, a] *a* inhabited // *nm* (*aldea*) village; (*pueblo*) (small) town; **densamente ~** densely populated.

poblador, a [poβla'ðor, a] *nm/f* settler, colonist.

poblar [po'βlar] *vt* (*colonizar*) to colonize; (*fundar*) to found; (*habitar*) to inhabit.

pobre ['poβre] *a* poor // *nm/f* poor person; **¡~!** poor thing!; **~za** *nf* poverty.

pocilga [po'θilγa] *nf* pigsty.

pocillo [po'siλo] *nm* (*AM*) coffee cup.

poción [po'θjon], **pócima** ['poθima] *nf* potion.

PALABRA CLAVE
---

poco, a ['poko, a] ♦ *a* **1** (*sg*) little, not much; **~ tiempo** little o not much time; **de ~ interés** of little interest, not very interesting; **poca cosa** not much

2 (*pl*) few, not many; **unos ~s** a few, some; **~s niños comen lo que**

les conviene few children eat what they should
◆ *ad* **1** little, not much; **cuesta ~** it doesn't cost much
2 (+ *a*: = *negativo, antónimo*): **~ amable/inteligente** not very nice/intelligent
3: por ~ me caigo I almost fell
4: a ~: a ~ de haberse casado shortly after getting married
5: ~ a ~ little by little
◆ *nm* a little, a bit; **un ~ triste/de dinero** a little sad/money.

podar [po'ðar] *vt* to prune.

PALABRA CLAVE ◆

poder [po'ðer] ◆ *vi* **1** (*capacidad*) can, be able to; **no puedo hacerlo** I can't do it, I'm unable to do it
2 (*permiso*) can, may, be allowed to; **¿se puede?** may I (o we)?; **puedes irte ahora** you may go now; **no se puede fumar en este hospital** smoking is not allowed in this hospital
3 (*posibilidad*) may, might, could; **puede llegar mañana** he may o might arrive tomorrow; **pudiste haberte hecho daño** you might o could have hurt yourself; **¡podías habérmelo dicho antes!** you might have told me before!
4: puede ser: puede ser perhaps; **puede ser que lo sepa Tomás** Tomás may o might know
5: ¡no puedo más! I've had enough!; **no pude menos que dejarlo** I couldn't help but leave it; **es tonto a más no ~** he's as stupid as they come
6: ~ con: no puedo con este crío this kid's too much for me
◆ *nm* power; **~ adquisitivo** purchasing power; **detentar** *o* **ocupar** *o* **estar en el ~** to be in power.

podrido, a [po'ðriðo, a] *a* rotten, bad; (*fig*) rotten, corrupt.

podrir [po'ðrir] = **pudrir**.
poema [po'ema] *nm* poem.
poesía [poe'sia] *nf* poetry.
poeta [po'eta] *nm* poet; **poético, a** *a* poetic(al).
poetisa [poe'tisa] *nf* (woman) poet.
póker ['poker] *nm* poker.
polaco, a [po'lako, a] *a* Polish // *nm/f* Pole.
polar [po'lar] *a* polar; **~idad** *nf* polarity; **~izarse** *vr* to polarize.
polea [po'lea] *nf* pulley.
polémica [po'lemika] *nf* polemics *sg*; (*una ~*) controversy, polemic.
polen ['polen] *nm* pollen.
policía [poli'θia] *nm/f* policeman/ woman // *nf* police; **~co, a** *a* police *cpd*; **novela policíaca** detective story; **policial** *a* police *cpd*.
polideportivo [poliðepor'tiβo] *nm* sports centre *o* complex.
polietileno [polieti'leno] *nm* polythene (*Brit*), polyethylene (*US*).
poligamia [poli'γamja] *nf* polygamy.
polilla [po'liʎa] *nf* moth.
polio ['poljo] *nf* polio.
politécnico [poli'tekniko] *nm* polytechnic.
político, a [po'litiko, a] *a* political; (*discreto*) tactful; (*de familia*) -in-law // *nm/f* politician // *nf* politics *sg*; (*económica, agraria etc*) policy; **padre ~** father-in-law; **politicastro** *nm* (*pey*) politician, político.
póliza ['poliθa] *nf* certificate, voucher; (*impuesto*) tax stamp; **~ de seguros** insurance policy.
polizón [poli'θon] *nm* (*en barco etc*) stowaway.
polo ['polo] *nm* (*GEO, ELEC*) pole; (*helado*) ice lolly; (*DEPORTE*) polo; (*suéter*) polo-neck; **~ Norte/Sur** North/South Pole.
Polonia [po'lonja] *nf* Poland.
poltrona [pol'trona] *nf* easy chair.
polución [polu'θjon] *nf* pollution.
polvera [pol'βera] *nf* powder compact.
polvo ['polβo] *nm* dust; (*QUÍMICA, CULIN, MED*) powder; **~s** *nmpl*

powder *sg*; ~ **de talco** talcum powder; **estar hecho** ~ (*fam*) to be worn out *o* exhausted.

pólvora ['polβora] *nf* gunpowder; (*fuegos artificiales*) fireworks *pl*.

polvoriento, a [polβo'rjento, a] *a* (*superficie*) dusty; (*sustancia*) powdery.

pollera [po'ʎera] *nf* (*AM*) skirt.

pollería [poʎe'ria] *nf* poulterer's (shop).

pollo ['poʎo] *nm* chicken.

pomada [po'maða] *nf* (*MED*) cream, ointment.

pomelo [po'melo] *nm* grapefruit.

pómez ['pomeθ] *nf*: **piedra** ~ pumice stone.

pompa ['pompa] *nf* (*burbuja*) bubble; (*bomba*) pump; (*esplendor*) pomp, splendour; **pomposo, a** *a* splendid, magnificent; (*pey*) pompous.

pómulo ['pomulo] *nm* cheekbone.

pon [pon] *vb ver* **poner**.

ponche ['pontʃe] *nm* punch.

poncho ['pontʃo] *nm* (*AM*) poncho, cape.

ponderar [ponde'rar] *vt* (*considerar*) to weigh up, consider; (*elogiar*) to praise highly, speak in praise of.

pondré *etc vb ver* **poner**.

poner [po'ner] ◆ *vt* 1 (*colocar*) to put; (*telegrama*) to send; (*obra de teatro*) to put on; (*película*) to show; **ponlo más fuerte** turn it up; **¿qué ponen en el Excelsior?** what's on at the Excelsior?

2 (*tienda*) to open; (*instalar: gas etc*) to put in; (*radio, TV*) to switch *o* turn on

3 (*suponer*): **pongamos que ...** let's suppose that

4 (*contribuir*): **el gobierno ha puesto otro millón** the government has contributed another million

5 (*TELEC*): **póngame con el Sr. López** can you put me through to Mr. López

6: ~ **de**: **le han puesto de director general** they've appointed him general manager

7 (+ *a*) to make; **me estás poniendo nerviosa** you're making me nervous

8 (*dar nombre*): **al hijo le pusieron Diego** they called their son Diego

◆ *vi* (*gallina*) to lay

◆ ~**se** *vr* 1 (*colocarse*): **se puso a mi lado** he came and stood beside me; **tú pónte en esa silla** you go and sit on that chair

2 (*vestido, cosméticos*) to put on; **¿por qué no te pones el vestido nuevo?** why don't you put on *o* wear your new dress?

3: (+ *a*) to turn; to get, become; **se puso muy serio** he got very serious; **después de lavarla la tela se puso azul** after washing it the material turned blue

4: ~**se a**: **se puso a llorar** he started to cry; **tienes que** ~**te a estudiar** you must get down to studying

5: ~**se a bien con uno** to make it up with sb; ~**se a mal con uno** to get on the wrong side of sb.

pongo *etc vb ver* **poner**.

poniente [po'njente] *nm* (*occidente*) west; (*viento*) west wind.

pontificado [pontifi'kaðo] *nm* papacy, pontificate; **pontífice** *nm* pope, pontiff.

pontón [pon'ton] *nm* pontoon.

ponzoña [pon'θoɲa] *nf* poison, venom.

popa ['popa] *nf* stern.

popular [popu'lar] *a* popular; (*cultura*) of the people, folk *cpd*; ~**idad** *nf* popularity; ~**izarse** *vr* to become popular.

por [por] ◆ *prep* 1 (*objetivo*) for; **luchar** ~ **la patria** to fight for one's country

2 (+ *infinitivo*): ~ **no llegar tarde**

so as not to arrive late; ~ **citar unos ejemplos** to give a few examples

3 (causa) out of, because of; ~ **escasez de fondos** through o for lack of funds

4 (tiempo): ~ **la mañana/noche** in the morning/at night; **se queda una semana** she's staying (for) a week

5 (lugar): **pasar ~ Madrid** to pass through Madrid; **ir a Guayaquil ~ Quito** to go to Guayaquil via Quito; **caminar ~ la calle** to walk along the street; ver tb **todo**

6 (cambio, precio): **te doy uno nuevo ~ el que tienes** I'll give you a new one (in return) for the one you've got

7 (valor distributivo): **550 pesetas ~ hora/cabeza** 550 pesetas an o per hour/a o per head

8 (modo, medio) by; ~ **correo/avión** by post/air; **día ~ día** day by day; **entrar ~ la entrada principal** to go in through the main entrance

9: **10 ~ 10 son 100** 10 by 10 is 100

10 (en lugar de): **vino él ~ su jefe** he came instead of his boss

11: ~ **mí que revienten** as far as I'm concerned they can drop dead.

porcelana [porθe'lana] nf porcelain; (china) china.

porcentaje [porθen'taxe] nm percentage.

porción [por'θjon] nf (parte) portion, share; (cantidad) quantity, amount.

pordiosero, a [porðjo'sero, a] nm/f beggar.

porfía [por'fia] nf persistence; (terquedad) obstinacy.

porfiado, a [por'fjaðo, a] a persistent; obstinate.

porfiar [por'fjar] vi to persist, insist; (disputar) to argue stubbornly.

pormenor [porme'nor] nm detail, particular.

pornografía [pornoɣra'fia] nf pornography.

poro ['poro] nm pore; ~**so, a** a porous.

porque ['porke] conj (a causa de) because; (ya que) since; (con el fin de) so that, in order that.

porqué [por'ke] nm reason, cause.

porquería [porke'ria] nf (suciedad) filth, dirt; (acción) dirty trick; (objeto) small thing, trifle; (fig) rubbish.

porra ['porra] nf (arma) stick, club.

porrón [po'rron] nm glass wine jar with a long spout.

portada [por'taða] nf (de revista) cover.

portador, a [porta'ðor, a] nm/f carrier, bearer; (COM) bearer, payee.

portaequipajes [portaeki'paxes] nm inv (AUTO: maletero) boot; (: baca) luggage rack.

portal [por'tal] nm (entrada) vestibule, hall; (portada) porch, doorway; (puerta de entrada) main door; (DEPORTE) goal.

portaligas [porta'liɣas] nm inv suspender belt.

portamaletas [portama'letas] nm inv (AUTO: maletero) boot; (: baca) roof rack.

portamonedas [portamo'neðas] nm inv purse.

portarse [por'tarse] vr to behave, conduct o.s.

portátil [por'tatil] a portable.

porta(a)viones [porta'(a)βjones] nm inv aircraft carrier.

portavoz [porta'βoθ] nm/f (persona) spokesman/woman.

portazo [por'taðo] nm: **dar un ~ to** slam the door.

porte ['porte] nm (COM) transport; (precio) transport charges pl.

portento [por'tento] nm marvel, wonder; ~**so, a** a marvellous, extraordinary.

porteño, a [por'teɲo, a] a of o from Buenos Aires.

portería [porte'ria] nf (oficina) porter's office; (gol) goal.

portero, a [por'tero, a] *nm/f* porter; *(conserje)* caretaker; *(ujier)* doorman; *(DEPORTE)* goalkeeper.

pórtico ['portiko] *nm (patio)* portico, porch; *(fig)* gateway; *(arcada)* arcade.

portilla [por'tiʎa] *nf*, **portillo** [por'tiʎo] *nm (cancela)* gate.

portorriqueño, a [portorri'keɲo, a] *a* Puerto Rican.

Portugal [portu'ɣal] *nm* Portugal; **portugués, esa** *a*, *nm/f* Portuguese // *nm (LING)* Portuguese.

porvenir [porβe'nir] *nm* future.

pos [pos] *prep*: **en ~ de** after, in pursuit of.

posada [po'saða] *nf (refugio)* shelter, lodging; *(mesón)* guest house; **dar ~ a** to give shelter to, take in.

posaderas [posa'ðeras] *nfpl* backside *sg*, buttocks.

posar [po'sar] *vt (en el suelo)* to lay down, put down; *(la mano)* to place, put gently // *vi* to sit, pose; **~se** *vr* to settle; *(pájaro)* to perch; *(avión)* to land, come down.

posdata [pos'ðata] *nf* postscript.

pose ['pose] *nf* pose.

poseedor, a [posee'ðor, a] *nm/f* owner, possessor; *(de récord, puesto)* holder.

poseer [pose'er] *vt* to possess, own; *(ventaja)* to enjoy; *(récord, puesto)* to hold; **poseído, a** *a* possessed.

posesión [pose'sjon] *nf* possession; **posesionarse** *vr*: **posesionarse de** to take possession of, take over.

posesivo, a [pose'siβo, a] *a* possessive.

posibilidad [posiβili'ðað] *nf* possibility; *(oportunidad)* chance; **posibilitar** *vt* to make possible; *(hacer realizable)* to make feasible.

posible [po'siβle] *a* possible; *(realizable)* feasible; **de ser ~** if possible; **en lo ~** as far as possible.

posición [posi'θjon] *nf* position; *(rango social)* status.

positivo, a [posi'tiβo, a] *a* positive // *nf (FOTO)* print.

poso ['poso] *nm* sediment; *(heces)* dregs *pl*.

posponer [pospo'ner] *vt* to put behind/below; *(aplazar)* to postpone.

posta ['posta] *nf*: **a ~ ad** deliberately, on purpose.

postal [pos'tal] *a* postal // *nf* postcard.

poste ['poste] *nm (de telégrafos etc)* post, pole; *(columna)* pillar.

póster ['poster] *(pl* **pósteres, pósters)** *nm* poster.

postergar [poster'var] *vt* to postpone, delay.

posteridad [posteri'ðað] *nf* posterity.

posterior [poste'rjor] *a* back, rear; *(siguiente)* following, subsequent; *(más tarde)* later; **~idad** *nf*: **con ~idad** later, subsequently.

postizo, a [pos'tiβo, a] *a* false, artificial // *nm* hairpiece.

postor, a [pos'tor, a] *nm/f* bidder.

postrado, a [pos'traðo, a] *a* prostrate.

postre ['postre] *nm* sweet, dessert.

postrero, a [pos'trero, a] *a (delante de nmsg)* **postrer** *(último)* last; *(que viene detrás)* rear.

postulado [postu'laðo] *nm* postulate.

póstumo, a ['postumo, a] *a* posthumous.

postura [pos'tura] *nf (del cuerpo)* posture, position; *(fig)* attitude, position.

potable [po'taβle] *a* drinkable; **agua ~** drinking water.

potaje [po'taxe] *nm* thick vegetable soup.

pote ['pote] *nm* pot, jar.

potencia [po'tenθja] *nf* power; **potenciar** *vt* to boost.

potencial [poten'θjal] *a*, *nm* potential.

potente [po'tente] *a* powerful.

potro ['potro, a] *nm/f (ZOOL)* colt/filly // *nm (de gimnasia)* vaulting horse.

pozo ['poθo] *nm* well; *(de río)* deep pool; *(de mina)* shaft.

P.P. *abr (= porte pagado)* CP.

p.p. abr (= por poder) p.p.

práctica [ˈpraktika] nf ver **práctico**.

practicable [praktiˈkaßle] a practicable; (camino) passable.

practicante [praktiˈkante] nm/f (MED: ayudante de doctor) medical assistant; (: enfermero) male nurse; (quien practica algo) practitioner // a practising.

practicar [praktiˈkar] vt to practise; (DEPORTE) to go in for (Brit) o out for (US), play; (realizar) to carry out, perform.

práctico, a [ˈpraktiko, a] a practical; (instruido: persona) skilled, expert // nm practice; (método) method; (arte, capacidad) skill; **en la práctica** in practice.

practique etc vb ver **practicar**.

pradera [praˈðera] nf meadow; (US etc) prairie.

prado [ˈpraðo] nm (campo) meadow, field; (pastizal) pasture.

Praga [ˈpraxa] n Prague.

pragmático, a [pravˈmatiko, a] a pragmatic.

preámbulo [preˈambulo] nm preamble, introduction.

precario, a [preˈkarjo, a] a precarious.

precaución [prekauˈθjon] nf (medida preventiva) preventive measure, precaution; (prudencia) caution, wariness.

precaver [prekaˈßer] vt to guard against; (impedir) to forestall; ~se vr: ~se o contra algo to be on one's guard against sth; **precavido, a** a cautious, wary.

precedencia [preθeˈðenθja] nf precedence; (prioridad) priority; (preeminencia) greater importance, superiority; **precedente** a preceding; (anterior) former // nm precedent.

preceder [preθeˈðer] vt, vi to precede, go before, come before.

precepto [preˈθepto] nm precept.

preciado, a [preˈθjaðo, a] a (estimado) esteemed, valuable.

preciar [preˈθjar] vt to esteem, value; ~se vr to boast; ~se de to pride o.s. on, boast of being.

precinto [preˈθinto] nm (tb: ~ de garantía) seal.

precio [ˈpreθjo] nm price; (costo) cost; (valor) value, worth; (de viaje) fare; ~ **al contado/de coste/de oportunidad** cash/cost/bargain price; ~ **al detalle** o **al por menor** retail price; ~ **tope** top price.

preciosidad [preθjosiˈðað] nf (valor) (high) value, (great) worth; (encanto) charm; (cosa bonita) beautiful thing; **es una** ~ it's lovely, it's really beautiful.

precioso, a [preˈθjoso, a] a precious; (de mucho valor) valuable; (fam) lovely, beautiful.

precipicio [preθiˈpiθjo] nm cliff, precipice; (fig) abyss.

precipitación [preθipitaˈθjon] nf haste; (lluvia) rainfall.

precipitado, a [preθipiˈtaðo, a] a (conducta) hasty, rash; (salida) hasty, sudden.

precipitar [preθipiˈtar] vt (arrojar) to hurl down, throw; (apresurar) to hasten; (acelerar) to speed up, accelerate; ~se vr to throw o.s.; (apresurarse) to rush; (actuar sin pensar) to act rashly.

precisamente [preθisaˈmente] ad precisely; (exactamente) precisely, exactly.

precisar [preθiˈsar] vt (necesitar) to need, require; (fijar) to determine exactly, fix; (especificar) to specify.

precisión [preθiˈsjon] nf (exactitud) precision.

preciso, a [preˈθiso, a] a (exacto) precise; (necesario) necessary, essential.

preconcebido, a [prekonθeˈßiðo, a] a preconceived.

precoz [preˈkoθ] a (persona) precocious; (calvicie etc) premature.

precursor, a [prekurˈsor, a] nm/f predecessor, forerunner.

predecir [preδe'θir] *vt* to predict, forecast.

predestinado, a [preδesti'naδo, a] *a* predestined.

predeterminar [preδetermi'nar] *vt* to predetermine.

prédica ['preδika] *nf* sermon.

predicador, a [preδika'δor, a] *nm/f* preacher.

predicar [preδi'kar] *vt, vi* to preach.

predicción [preδik'θjon] *nf* prediction.

predilecto, a [preδi'lekto, a] *a* favourite.

predisponer [preδispo'ner] *vt* to predispose; (*pey*) to prejudice; **predisposición** *nf* inclination; prejudice, bias.

predominante [preδomi'nante] *a* predominant.

predominar [preδomi'nar] *vt* to dominate // *vi* to predominate; (*prevalecer*) to prevail; **predominio** *nm* predominance; prevalence.

preescolar [pre(e)sko'lar] *a* preschool.

prefabricado, a [prefaβri'kaδo, a] *a* prefabricated.

prefacio [pre'faθjo] *nm* preface.

preferencia [prefe'renθja] *nf* preference; **de ~** preferably, for preference.

preferible [prefe'riβle] *a* preferable.

preferir [prefe'rir] *vt* to prefer.

prefiero *etc vb ver* **preferir.**

prefigurar [prefiyu'rar] *vt* to foreshadow, prefigure.

pregonar [preyo'nar] *vt* to proclaim, announce.

pregunta [pre'yunta] *nf* question; **hacer una ~** to ask *o* put (forth (US)) a question.

preguntar [preyun'tar] *vt* to ask; (*cuestionar*) to question // *vi* to ask; **~se** *vr* to wonder; **~ por alguien** to ask for sb.

preguntón, ona [preyun'ton, ona] *a* inquisitive.

prehistórico, a [preis'toriko, a] *a* prehistoric.

prejuicio [pre'xwiθjo] *nm* (*acto*) prejudgement; (*idea preconcebida*) preconception; (*parcialidad*) prejudice, bias.

preliminar [prelimi'nar] *a* preliminary.

preludio [pre'luδjo] *nm* prelude.

prematuro, a [prema'turo, a] *a* premature.

premeditación [premeδita'θjon] *nf* premeditation.

premeditar [premeδi'tar] *vt* to premeditate.

premiar [pre'mjar] *vt* to reward; (*en un concurso*) to give a prize to.

premio ['premjo] *nm* reward; prize; (*COM*) premium.

premonición [premoni'θjon] *nf* premonition.

premura [pre'mura] *nf* (*aprieto*) pressure; (*prisa*) haste, urgency.

prenatal [prena'tal] *a* antenatal, prenatal.

prenda ['prenda] *nf* (*ropa*) garment, article of clothing; (*garantía*) pledge; **~s** *nfpl* talents, gifts.

prendar [pren'dar] *vt* to captivate, enchant; **~se de uno** to fall in love with sb.

prendedor [prende'δor] *nm* brooch.

prender [pren'der] *vt* (*captar*) to catch, capture; (*detener*) to arrest; (*COSTURA*) to pin, attach; (*sujetar*) to fasten // *vi* to catch; (*arraigar*) to take root; **~se** *vr* (*encenderse*) to catch fire.

prendido, a [pren'diδo, a] *a* (*AM*: *luz etc*) on.

prensa ['prensa] *nf* press; **la P~** the press; **prensar** *vt* to press.

preñado, a [pre'ɲaδo, a] *a* (*ZOOL*) pregnant; **~ de** pregnant with, full of; **preñez** *nf* pregnancy.

preocupación [preokupa'θjon] *nf* worry, concern; (*ansiedad*) anxiety.

preocupado, a [preoku'paδo, a] *a* worried, concerned; (*ansioso*) anxious.

preocupar [preoku'par] *vt* to worry; **~se** *vr* to worry; **~se de algo**

(hacerse cargo) to take care of sth.

preparación [prepara'θjon] *nf (acto)* preparation; *(estado)* readiness; *(entrenamiento)* training.

preparado, a [prepa'raðo, a] *a (dispuesto)* prepared; *(CULIN)* ready (to serve) // *nm* preparation.

preparador, a [prepara'ðor, a] *nm/f* trainer.

preparar [prepa'rar] *vt (disponer)* to prepare, get ready; *(TEC: tratar)* to prepare, process; *(entrenar)* to teach, train; **~se** *vr:* **~se a** *o* **para** to prepare to *o* for, get ready to *o* for; **preparativo, a** *a* preparatory, preliminary; **preparativos** *nmpl* preparations; **preparatorio, a** *a* preparatory // *nf (AM)* sixth-form college *(Brit)*, senior high school *(US)*.

prerrogativa [prerroɣa'tiβa] *nf* prerogative, privilege.

presa ['presa] *nf (cosa apresada)* catch; *(víctima)* victim; *(de animal)* prey; *(de agua)* dam.

presagiar [presa'xjar] *vt* to presage, forebode.

presbítero [pres'βitero] *nm* priest.

prescindir [presθin'dir] *vi:* **~ de** *(privarse de)* to do without, go without; *(descartar)* to dispense with.

prescribir [preskri'βir] *vt* to prescribe; **prescripción** *nf* prescription.

presencia [pre'senθja] *nf* presence; **presencial** *a:* **testigo presencial** eyewitness; **presenciar** *vt* to be present at; *(asistir a)* to attend; *(ver)* to see, witness.

presentación [presenta'θjon] *nf* presentation; *(introducción)* introduction.

presentador, a [presenta'ðor, a] *nm/f* presenter, compère.

presentar [presen'tar] *vt* to present; *(ofrecer)* to offer; *(mostrar)* to show, display; *(a una persona)* to introduce; **~se** *vr (llegar inesperadamente)* to appear, turn up; *(ofrecerse como candidato)* to run, stand; *(aparecer)* to show, appear;

(solicitar empleo) to apply.

presente [pre'sente] *a* present // *nm* present; **hacer ~** to state, declare; **tener ~** to remember, bear in mind.

presentimiento [presenti'mjento] *nm* premonition, presentiment.

presentir [presen'tir] *vt* to have a premonition of.

preservación [preserβa'θjon] *nf* protection, preservation.

preservar [preser'βar] *vt* to protect, preserve; **preservativo** *nm* sheath, condom.

presidencia [presi'ðenθja] *nf* presidency; *(de comité)* chairmanship.

presidente [presi'ðente] *nm/f* president; *(de comité)* chairman/woman.

presidiario [presi'ðjarjo] *nm* convict.

presidio [pre'sidjo] *nm* prison, penitentiary.

presidir [presi'ðir] *vt (dirigir)* to preside at, preside over; *(: comité)* to take the chair at; *(dominar)* to dominate, rule // *vi* to preside; to take the chair.

presión [pre'sjon] *nf* pressure; **presionar** *vt* to press; *(fig)* to press, put pressure on // *vi:* **presionar para** to press for.

preso, a ['preso, a] *nm/f* prisoner; **tomar** *o* **llevar ~ a uno** to arrest sb, take sb prisoner.

prestado, a [pres'taðo, a] *a* on loan; **pedir ~** to borrow.

prestamista [presta'mista] *nm/f* moneylender.

préstamo ['prestamo] *nm* loan; **~ hipotecario** mortgage.

prestar [pres'tar] *vt* to lend, loan; *(atención)* to pay; *(ayuda)* to give.

presteza [pres'teθa] *nf* speed, promptness.

prestigio [pres'tixjo] *nm* prestige; **~so, a** *a (honorable)* prestigious; *(famoso, renombrado)* renowned, famous.

presto, a ['presto, a] *a (rápido)* quick, prompt; *(dispuesto)* ready // *ad* at once, right away.

presumir [presu'mir] *vt* to presume //

vi (*tener aires*) to be conceited; según cabe ~ as may be presumed, presumably; **presunción** *nf* presumption; **presunto, a** *a* (*supuesto*) supposed, presumed; (*así llamado*) so-called; **presuntuoso, a** *a* conceited, presumptuous.

presuponer [presupo'ner] *vt* to presuppose.

presupuesto *pp de* **presuponer** // [presu'pwesto] *nm* (*FINANZAS*) budget; (*estimación: de costo*) estimate.

presuroso, a [presu'roso, a] *a* (*rápido*) quick, speedy; (*que tiene prisa*) hasty.

pretencioso, a [preten'θjoso, a] *a* pretentious.

pretender [preten'der] *vt* (*intentar*) to try to, seek to; (*reivindicar*) to claim; (*buscar*) to seek, try for; (*cortejar*) to woo, court; ~ **que** to expect that; **pretendiente** *nmf* (*candidato*) candidate, applicant; (*amante*) suitor; **pretensión** *nf* (*aspiración*) aspiration; (*reivindicación*) claim; (*orgullo*) pretension.

pretexto [pre'teksto] *nm* pretext; (*excusa*) excuse.

prevalecer [preβale'θer] *vi* to prevail.

prevención [preβen'θjon] *nf* (*preparación*) preparation; (*estado*) preparedness, readiness; (*el evitar*) prevention; (*previsión*) foresight, forethought; (*precaución*) precaution.

prevenido, a [preβe'niðo, a] *a* prepared, ready; (*cauteloso*) cautious.

prevenir [preβe'nir] *vt* (*impedir*) to prevent; (*prever*) to foresee, anticipate; (*predisponer*) to prejudice, bias; (*avisar*) to warn; (*preparar*) to prepare, get ready; ~**se** *vr* to get ready, prepare; ~**se contra** to take precautions against; **preventivo, a** *a* preventive, precautionary.

prever [pre'βer] *vt* to foresee.

previo, a ['preβjo, a] *a* (*anterior*) previous; (*preliminar*) preliminary // *prep*: ~ **acuerdo de los otros** sub-

ject to the agreement of the others.

previsión [preβi'sjon] *nf* (*perspicacia*) foresight; (*predicción*) forecast.

prima ['prima] *nf ver* **primo**.

primacía [prima'θia] *nf* primacy.

primario, a [pri'marjo, a] *a* primary.

primavera [prima'βera] *nf* spring(-time).

primero, a [pri'mero, a] *a* (*delante de nmsg*: **primer**) first; (*principal*) prime // *ad* first; (*más bien*) sooner, rather // *nf* (*AUTO*) first gear; (*FERRO: tb*): **primera clase**) first class; **de primera** (*fam*) first-class, first-rate; **primera plana** front page.

primitivo, a [primi'tiβo, a] *a* primitive; (*original*) original.

primo, a [a ['primo, a] *a* prime // *nm/f* cousin; (*fam*) fool, idiot // *a* (*COM*) bonus; ~ **de seguro** insurance premium; ~ **hermano** first cousin; **materias primas** raw materials.

primogénito, a [primo'xenito, a] *a* first-born.

primordial [primor'ðjal] *a* basic, fundamental.

primoroso, a [primo'roso, a] *a* exquisite, delicate.

princesa [prin'θesa] *nf* princess.

principal [prinθi'pal] *a* principal, main // *nm* (*jefe*) chief, principal.

príncipe ['prinθipe] *nm* prince.

principiante [prinθi'pjante] *nmf* beginner.

principiar [prinθi'pjar] *vt* to begin.

principio [prin'θipjo] *nm* (*comienzo*) beginning, start; (*origen*) origin; (*primera etapa*) rudiment, basic idea; (*moral*) principle; **a** ~**s de** at the beginning of.

pringoso, a [prin'xoso, a] *a* (*grasiento*) greasy; (*pegajoso*) sticky.

pringue ['pringe] *nm* (*grasa*) grease, fat, dripping.

prioridad [priori'ðað] *nf* priority.

prisa ['prisa] *nf* (*apresuramiento*) hurry, haste; (*rapidez*) speed; (*urgencia*) (sense of) urgency; **a o**

de ~ quickly; **correr** ~ to be
urgent; **darse** ~ to hurry up; **estar
de** *o* **tener** ~ to be in a hurry.
prisión [pri'sjon] *nf* (*cárcel*) prison;
(*período de cárcel*) imprisonment;
prisionero, a *nm/f* prisoner.
prismáticos [pris'matikos] *nmpl*
binoculars.
privación [priβa'θjon] *nf* deprivation;
(*falta*) want, privation.
privado, a [pri'βaðo, a] *a* private.
privar [pri'βar] *vt* to deprive;
privativo, a *a* exclusive.
privilegiado, a [priβile'xjaðo, a] *a*
privileged; (*memoria*) very good.
privilegiar [priβile'xjar] *vt* to grant a
privilege to; (*favorecer*) to favour.
privilegio [priβi'lexjo] *nm* privilege;
(*concesión*) concession.
pro [pro] *nm o f* profit, advantage //
prep: **asociación ~ ciegos** association for the blind // *pref*: ~
soviético/americano pro-Soviet/
American; **en ~ de** on behalf of, for;
los ~s y los contras the pros and
cons.
proa ['proa] *nf* bow, prow; **de ~** bow
cpd, fore.
probabilidad [proβaβili'ðað] *nf*
probability, likelihood; (*oportunidad,
posibilidad*) chance, prospect;
probable *a* probable, likely.
probador [proβa'ðor] *nm* (*en tienda*)
fitting room.
probar [pro'βar] *vt* (*demostrar*) to
prove; (*someter a prueba*) to test,
try out; (*ropa*) to try on; (*comida*) to
taste // *vi* to try; **~se un traje** to try
on a suit.
probeta [pro'βeta] *nf* test tube.
problema [pro'βlema] *nm* problem.
procedente [proθe'ðente] *a* (*razonable*) reasonable; (*conforme a derecho*) proper, fitting; **~ de** coming
from, originating in.
proceder [proθe'ðer] *vi* (*avanzar*) to
proceed; (*actuar*) to act; (*ser
correcto*) to be right (and proper), be
fitting; **~ de** to come from, originate
in // *nm* (*comportamiento*) behaviour,

conduct; **procedimiento** *nm* procedure; (*proceso*) process; (*método*)
means *pl*, method.
procesado, a [proθe'saðo, a] *nm/f*
accused.
procesador [proθesa'ðor] *nm*: **~ de
textos** word processor.
procesar [proθe'sar] *vt* to try, put on
trial.
procesión [proθe'sjon] *nf* procession.
proceso [pro'θeso] *nm* process;
(*JUR*) trial; (*lapso*) course (of time).
proclamar [prokla'mar] *vt* to
proclaim.
procreación [prokrea'θjon] *nf*
procreation.
procrear [prokre'ar] *vt, vi* to
procreate.
procurador, a [prokura'ðor, a] *nm/f*
attorney.
procurar [proku'rar] *vt* (*intentar*) to
try, endeavour; (*conseguir*) to get,
obtain; (*asegurar*) to secure;
(*producir*) to produce.
prodigio [pro'ðixjo] *nm* prodigy;
(*milagro*) wonder, marvel; **~so, a** *a*
prodigious, marvellous.
pródigo, a ['proðixo, a] *a*: **hijo ~**
prodigal son.
producción [proðuk'θjon] *nf* (*gen*)
production; (*producto*) product; **~
en serie** mass production.
producir [proðu'θir] *vt* to produce;
(*causar*) to cause, bring about; **~se**
vr (*cambio*) to come about;
(*accidente*) to take place; (*problema
etc*) to arise; (*hacerse*) to be
produced, be made; (*estallar*) to
break out.
productividad [proðuktiβi'ðað] *nf*
productivity; **productivo, a** *a*
productive; (*provechoso*) profitable.
producto [pro'ðukto] *nm* product;
(*producción*) production.
productor, a [proðuk'tor, a] *a*
productive, producing // *nm/f*
producer.
proeza [pro'eθa] *nf* exploit, feat.
profanar [profa'nar] *vt* to desecrate,
profane; **profano, a** *a* profane //

nmf layman/woman.

profecía [profe'θia] *nf* prophecy.

proferir [profe'rir] *vt* (*palabra, sonido*) to utter; (*injuria*) to hurl, let fly.

profesar [profe'sar] *vt* (*practicar*) to practise.

profesión [profe'sjon] *nf* profession; **profesional** *a* professional.

profesor, a [profe'sor, a] *nm/f* teacher; ~**ado** *nm* teaching profession.

profeta [pro'feta] *nm/f* prophet; **profetizar** *vt, vi* to prophesy.

prófugo, a ['profuƔo, a] *nm/f* fugitive; (*MIL: desertor*) deserter.

profundidad [profundi'ðað] *nf* depth; **profundizar** *vt* (*fig*) to go deeply into; **profundo, a** *a* deep; (*misterio, pensador*) profound.

profusión [profu'sjon] *nf* (*abundancia*) profusion; (*prodigalidad*) extravagance.

progenitor [proxeni'tor] *nm* ancestor; ~**es** *nmpl* (*padres*) parents.

programa [pro'ɣrama] *nm* programme (*Brit*), program (*US*); ~**ción** *nf* programming; ~**dor, a** *nm/f* programmer; **programar** *vt* to program.

progresar [proɣre'sar] *vi* to progress, make progress; **progresista** *a, nm/f* progressive; **progresivo, a** *a* progressive; (*gradual*) gradual; (*continuo*) continuous; **progreso** *nm* progress.

prohibición [proiβi'θjon] *nf* prohibition, ban.

prohibir [proi'βir] *vt* to prohibit, ban, forbid; **se prohíbe fumar**, **prohibido fumar** no smoking.

prójimo, a ['proximo, a] *nm/f* fellow man; (*vecino*) neighbour.

proletariado [proleta'rjaðo] *nm* proletariat.

proletario, a [prole'tarjo, a] *a, nm/f* proletarian.

proliferación [prolifera'θjon] *nf* proliferation.

proliferar [prolife'rar] *vi* to proliferate; **prolífico, a** *a* prolific.

prolijo, a [pro'lixo, a] *a* long-winded, tedious.

prólogo ['proloƔo] *nm* prologue.

prolongación [prolonga'θjon] *nf* extension; **prolongado, a** *a* (*largo*) long; (*alargado*) lengthy.

prolongar [prolon'ɡar] *vt* to extend; (*reunión etc*) to prolong; (*calle, tubo*) to extend.

promedio [pro'meðjo] *nm* average; (*de distancia*) middle, mid-point.

promesa [pro'mesa] *nf* promise.

prometer [prome'ter] *vt* to promise // *vi* to show promise; ~**se** *vr* (*novios*) to get engaged; **prometido, a** *a* promised; engaged // *nm/f* fiancé/fiancée.

prominente [promi'nente] *a* prominent.

promiscuo, a [pro'miskwo, a] *a* promiscuous.

promoción [promo'θjon] *nf* promotion.

promotor [promo'tor] *nm* promoter; (*instigador*) instigator.

promover [promo'βer] *vt* to promote; (*causar*) to cause; (*instigar*) to instigate, stir up.

promulgar [promul'ɣar] *vt* to promulgate; (*fig*) to proclaim.

pronombre [pro'nombre] *nm* pronoun.

pronosticar [pronosti'kar] *vt* to predict, foretell, forecast; **pronóstico** *nm* prediction, forecast; **pronóstico del tiempo** weather forecast.

pronto, a ['pronto, a] *a* (*rápido*) prompt, quick; (*preparado*) ready // *ad* quickly, promptly; (*en seguida*) at once, right away; (*dentro de poco*) soon; (*temprano*) early // *nm*: **tener** ~**s de enojo** to be quick-tempered; **al** ~ at first; **de** ~ suddenly; **por lo** ~ meanwhile, for the present.

pronunciación [pronunθja'θjon] *nf* pronunciation.

pronunciar [pronun'θjar] *vt* to pronounce; (*discurso*) to make, deliver; ~**se** *vr* to revolt, rebel; (*declararse*) to declare o.s.

propagación [propaɣa'θjon] *nf* propagation.

propaganda [propa'vanda] *nf* (*política*) propaganda; (*comercial*) advertising.

propagar [propa'ɣar] *vt* to propagate.

propensión [propen'sjon] *nf* inclination, propensity; **propenso, a** *a* inclined to; **ser propenso a** to be inclined to, have a tendency to.

propiamente [propja'mente] *ad* properly; (*realmente*) really, exactly.

propicio, a [pro'piθjo, a] *a* favourable, propitious.

propiedad [propje'ðað] *nf* property; (*posesión*) possession, ownership; ~ **particular** private property.

propietario, a [propje'tarjo, a] *nm/f* owner, proprietor.

propina [pro'pina] *nf* tip.

propio, a ['propjo, a] *a* own, of one's own; (*característica*) characteristic, typical; (*debido*) proper; (*mismo*) selfsame, very; **el ~ ministro** the minister himself; **¿tienes casa propia?** have you a house of your own?

proponer [propo'ner] *vt* to propose, put forward; (*problema*) to pose; **~se** *vr* to propose, intend.

proporción [propor'θjon] *nf* proportion; (*MAT*) ratio; **proporciones** *nfpl* dimensions; (*fig*) size *sg*; **proporcionado, a** *a* proportionate; (*regular*) medium, middling; (*justo*) just right; **proporcionar** *vt* (*dar*) to give, supply, provide.

proposición [proposi'θjon] *nf* proposition; (*propuesta*) proposal.

propósito [pro'posito] *nm* purpose; (*intento*) aim, intention // *ad*: **a ~ by** the way, incidentally; (*a posta*) on purpose, deliberately; **a ~ de** about, with regard to.

propuesta *vb ver* **proponer** // [pro'pwesta] *nf* proposal.

propulsar [propul'sar] *vt* to drive, propel; (*fig*) to promote, encourage; **propulsión** *nf* propulsion;

propulsión a chorro *o* **por reacción** jet propulsion.

prórroga ['prorroɣa] *nf* extension; (*JUR*) stay; (*COM*) deferment; (*DEPORTE*) extra time; **prorrogar** *vt* (*período*) to extend; (*decisión*) to defer, postpone.

prorrumpir [prorrum'pir] *vi* to burst forth, break out.

prosa ['prosa] *nf* prose.

proscripción [proscrip'θjon] *nf* prohibition, ban; (*destierro*) banishment; (*de un partido*) proscription.

proscrito, a [pros'krito, a] *a* (*prohibido, desterrado*) banned.

prosecución [proseku'θjon] *nf* continuation.

proseguir [prose'ɣir] *vt* to continue, carry on // *vi* to continue, go on.

prospección [prospek'θjon] *nf* exploration; (*del oro*) prospecting.

prospecto [pros'pekto] *nm* prospectus.

prosperar [prospe'rar] *vi* to prosper, thrive, flourish; **prosperidad** *nf* prosperity; (*éxito*) success; **próspero, a** *a* prosperous, flourishing; (*que tiene éxito*) successful.

prostíbulo [pros'tiβulo] *nm* brothel (*Brit*), house of prostitution (*US*).

prostitución [prostitu'θjon] *nf* prostitution.

prostituir [prosti'twir] *vt* to prostitute; **~se** *vr* to prostitute o.s., become a prostitute.

prostituta [prosti'tuta] *nf* prostitute.

protagonista [protaɣo'nista] *nm/f* protagonist.

protagonizar [protaɣoni'θar] *vt* to take the chief role in.

protección [protek'θjon] *nf* protection.

protector, a [protek'tor, a] *a* protective, protecting // *nm/f* protector.

proteger [prote'xer] *vt* to protect; **protegido, a** *nm/f* protégé/protégée.

proteína [prote'ina] *nf* protein.

protesta [pro'testa] *nf* protest; (*declaración*) protestation.

protestante [protes'tante] *a* Protestant.

protestar [protes'tar] *vt* to protest, declare; (*fe*) to protest // *vi* to protest.

protocolo [proto'kolo] *nm* protocol.

prototipo [proto'tipo] *nm* prototype.

prov. *abr* (= *provincia*) prov.

provecho [pro'βetʃo] *nm* advantage, benefit; (FINANZAS) profit; ¡**buen ~! bon** appétit!; **en ~ de** to the benefit of; **sacar ~ de** to benefit from, profit by.

proveer [proβe'er] *vt* to provide, supply // *vi*: **~ a** to provide for.

provenir [proβe'nir] *vi*: **~ de** to come from, stem from.

proverbio [pro'βerβjo] *nm* proverb.

providencia [proβi'ðenθja] *nf* providence; (*previsión*) foresight.

provincia [pro'βinθja] *nf* province; **~no, a** *a* provincial; (*del campo*) country *cpd*.

provisión [proβi'sjon] *nf* provision; (*abastecimiento*) provision, supply; (*medida*) measure, step.

provisional [proβisjo'nal] *a* provisional.

provocación [proβoka'θjon] *nf* provocation.

provocar [proβo'kar] *vt* to provoke; (*alentar*) to tempt, invite; (*causar*) to bring about, lead to; (*promover*) to promote; (*estimular*) to rouse, stimulate; ¿**te provoca un café?** (*AM*) would you like a coffee?; **provocativo, a** *a* provocative.

próximamente [proksima'mente] *ad* shortly, soon.

proximidad [proksimi'ðað] *nf* closeness, proximity; **próximo, a** *a* near, close; (*vecino*) neighbouring; (*siguiente*) next.

proyectar [projek'tar] *vt* (*objeto*) to hurl, throw; (*luz*) to cast, shed; (*CINE*) to screen, show; (*planear*) to plan.

proyectil [projek'til] *nm* projectile, missile.

proyecto [pro'jekto] *nm* plan;

(*estimación de costo*) detailed estimate.

proyector [projek'tor] *nm* (CINE) projector.

prudencia [pru'ðenθja] *nf* (*sabiduría*) wisdom; (*cuidado*) care; **prudente** *a* sensible, wise; (*conductor*) careful.

prueba *etc* *vb* *ver* **probar** // ['prweβa] *nf* proof; (*ensayo*) test, trial; (*degustación*) tasting, sampling; (*de ropa*) fitting; **a ~** on trial; **a ~ de** proof against; **a ~ de agua/ fuego** waterproof/fireproof; **someter a ~** to put to the test.

prurito [pru'rito] *nm* itch; (*de bebé*) nappy (*Brit*) o diaper (*US*) rash.

psico... [siko] *pref* psycho...; **~análisis** *nm* *inv* psychoanalysis; **~logía** *nf* psychology; **~lógico, a** *a* psychological; **psicólogo, a** *nm/f* psychologist; **psicópata** *nm/f* psychopath; **~sis** *nf* *inv* psychosis.

psiquiatra [si'kjatra] *nm/f* psychiatrist; **psiquiátrico, a** *a* psychiatric.

psíquico, a ['sikiko, a] *a* psychic(al).

PSOE [pe'soe] *nm* *abr* = *Partido Socialista Obrero Español*.

pta(s) *abr* = **peseta(s)**.

pts *abr* = **pesetas**.

púa ['pua] *nf* sharp point; (BOT, ZOOL) prickle, spine; (*para guitarra*) plectrum (*Brit*), pick (*US*); **alambre de ~** barbed wire.

pubertad [puβer'tað] *nf* puberty.

publicación [puβlika'θjon] *nf* publication.

publicar [puβli'kar] *vt* (*editar*) to publish; (*hacer público*) to publicize; (*divulgar*) to make public, divulge.

publicidad [puβliθi'ðað] *nf* publicity; (COM: *propaganda*) advertising; **publicitario, a** *a* publicity *cpd*; advertising *cpd*.

público, a ['puβliko, a] *a* public // *nm* public; (TEATRO *etc*) audience.

puchero [pu'tʃero] *nm* (CULIN: *guiso*) stew; (: *olla*) cooking pot; **hacer ~s** to pout.

pude etc vb ver **poder**.

púdico, a [ˈpuðiko, a] a modest.

pudiente [puˈðjente] a (rico) wealthy, well-to-do.

pudiera etc vb ver **poder**.

pudor [puˈðor] nm modesty.

pudrir [puˈðrir] vt to rot; (fam) to upset, annoy; ~se vr to rot, decay.

pueblo [ˈpweβlo] nm people; (nación) nation; (aldea) village.

puedo etc vb ver **poder**.

puente [ˈpwente] nm bridge; ~ aéreo shuttle service; ~ colgante suspension bridge; hacer ~ (fam) to take an extra day off work between 2 public holidays; to take a long weekend.

puerco, a [ˈpwerko, a] nm/f pig/sow // a (sucio) dirty, filthy; (obsceno) disgusting; ~ de mar porpoise; ~ marino dolphin.

pueril [pweˈril] a childish.

puerro [ˈpwerro] nm leek.

puerta [ˈpwerta] nf door; (de jardín) gate; (portal) doorway; (fig) gateway; (portería) goal; a la ~ at the door; a ~ cerrada behind closed doors; ~ giratoria revolving door.

puertaventana [pwertaβenˈtana] nf shutter.

puerto [ˈpwerto] nm port; (paso) pass; (fig) haven, refuge.

Puerto Rico [ˈpwertoˈriko] nm Puerto Rico; **puertorriqueño, a** a, nm/f Puerto Rican.

pues [pwes] ad (entonces) then; (bueno) well, well then; (así que) so // conj (ya que) since; ¡~! (sí) yes!, certainly!

puesto, a [ˈpwesto, a] pp de **poner** // a dressed // nm (lugar, posición) place; (trabajo) post, job; (COM) stall // conj: ~ que since, as // nf (apuesta) bet, stake; puesta en marcha starting; puesta del sol sunset.

púgil [ˈpuxil] nm boxer.

pugna [ˈpuɣna] nf battle, conflict; ~cidad nf pugnacity, aggressiveness; **pugnar** vi (luchar) to struggle, fight; (pelear) to fight.

pujar [puˈxar] vi (en subasta) to bid; (esforzarse) to struggle, strain.

pulcro, a [ˈpulkro, a] a neat, tidy; (bello) exquisite.

pulga [ˈpulɣa] nf flea.

pulgada [pulˈɣaða] nf inch.

pulgar [pulˈɣar] nm thumb.

pulir [puˈlir], **pulimentar** [pulimenˈtar] vt to polish; (alisar) to smooth; (fig) to polish up, touch up.

pulmón [pulˈmon] nm lung; **pulmonía** nf pneumonia.

pulpa [ˈpulpa] nf pulp; (de fruta) flesh, soft part.

pulpería [pulpeˈria] nf (AM: tienda) small grocery store.

púlpito [ˈpulpito] nm pulpit.

pulpo [ˈpulpo] nm octopus.

pulsación [pulsaˈθjon] nf beat, pulsation; (ANAT) throb(bing).

pulsador [pulsaˈðor] nm button, push button.

pulsar [pulˈsar] vt (tecla) to touch, tap; (MUS) to play; (botón) to press, push // vi to pulsate; (latir) to beat, throb; (MED): ~ a uno to take sb's pulse.

pulsera [pulˈsera] nf bracelet.

pulso [ˈpulso] nm (ANAT) pulse; (: muñeca) wrist; (fuerza) strength; (firmeza) steadiness, steady hand; (tacto) tact, good sense.

pulverizador [pulβeriθaˈðor] nm spray, spray gun.

pulverizar [pulβeriˈθar] vt to pulverize; (líquido) to spray.

pulla [ˈpuʎa] nf cutting remark; (expresión grosera) obscene remark.

puna [ˈpuna] nf (AM MED) mountain sickness.

pungir [punˈxir] vt to puncture, pierce; (fig) to cause suffering to.

punición [puniˈθjon] nf punishment; **punitivo, a** a punitive.

punta [ˈpunta] nf point, tip; (extremidad) end; (fig) touch, trace; horas ~s peak hours, rush hours; sacar ~ a to sharpen; estar de ~ to be edgy.

puntada [pun'taða] *nf* (COSTURA) stitch.

puntal [pun'tal] *nm* prop, support.

puntapié [punta'pje] *nm* kick.

puntear [punte'ar] *vt* to tick, mark.

puntería [punte'ria] *nf* (de arma) aim, aiming; (destreza) marksmanship.

puntero, a [pun'tero, a] *a* leading // *nm* (palo) pointer.

puntiagudo, a [puntja'ɣuðo, a] *a* sharp, pointed.

puntilla [pun'tiʎa] *nf* (encaje) lace edging o trim; **(andar) de ~s** (to walk) on tiptoe.

punto ['punto] *nm* (gen) point; (señal diminuta) spot, dot; (COSTURA, MED) stitch; (lugar) spot, place; (momento) point, moment; **a ~** ready; **estar a ~** to be on the point of o about to; **en ~** on the dot; **~ muerto** dead centre; (AUTO) neutral (gear); **~ final** full stop (Brit), period (US); **~ y coma** semicolon; **~ de interrogación** question mark; **hacer ~** (tejer) to knit.

puntuación [puntwa'θjon] *nf* punctuation; (puntos: en examen) mark(s) (pl); (: DEPORTE) score.

puntual [pun'twal] *a* (a tiempo) punctual; (exacto) exact, accurate; (seguro) reliable; **~idad** *nf* punctuality; exactness, accuracy; reliability; **~izar** *vt* to fix, specify.

punzante [pun'θante] *a* (dolor) shooting, sharp; (herramienta) sharp; **punzar** *vt* to prick, pierce // *vi* to shoot, stab.

puñado [pu'naðo] *nm* handful.

puñal [pu'nal] *nm* dagger; **~ada** *nf* stab.

puñetazo [pune'taðo] *nm* punch.

puño ['puno] *nm* (ANAT) fist; (cantidad) fistful, handful; (COSTURA) cuff; (de herramienta) handle.

pupila [pu'pila] *nf* pupil.

pupitre [pu'pitre] *nm* desk.

puré [pu're] *nm* puree; (sopa) thick soup; **~ de patatas** mashed potatoes.

pureza [pu'reθa] *nf* purity.

purga ['purɣa] *nf* purge; **purgante** *a, nm* purgative; **purgar** *vt* to purge.

purgatorio [purɣa'torjo] *nm* purgatory.

purificar [purifi'kar] *vt* to purify; (refinar) to refine.

puritano, a [puri'tano, a] *a* (actitud) puritanical; (iglesia, tradición) puritan // *nm/f* puritan.

puro, a ['puro, a] *a* pure; (cielo) clear; (verdad) simple, plain // *ad*: **de ~ cansado** out of sheer tiredness // *nm* cigar.

púrpura ['purpura] *nf* purple; **purpúreo, a** *a* purple.

pus [pus] *nm* pus.

puse, pusiera *etc vb ver* **poner**.

pústula ['pustula] *nf* pimple, sore.

puta ['puta] *nf* whore, prostitute.

putrefacción [putrefak'θjon] *nf* rotting, putrefaction.

pútrido, a ['putriðo, a] *a* rotten.

PVP *abr* (Esp: = precio venta al público) RRP.

Q

q.e.p.d. *abr* (= que en paz descanse) R.I.P.

PALABRA CLAVE

que [ke] ♦ *conj* **1** (con oración subordinada): **muchas veces no se traduce**) that; **dijo ~** he said (that) he would come; **espero ~ lo encuentres** I hope (that) you find it; *ver tb* **el**

2 (en oración independiente): **¡~ entre!** send him in; **¡que se mejore tu padre!** I hope your father gets better

3 (enfático): **¿me quieres? - ¡~ sí!** do you love me? - of course!

4 (consecutivo: muchas veces no se traduce) that; **es tan grande ~ no**

lo puedo levantar it's so big (that) I can't lift it

5 (*comparaciones*) than; **yo ~ tú/él** if I were you/him; **~ tú más, menos, mismo**

6 (*valor disyuntivo*): **~ le guste o no** whether he likes it or not; **~ venga o ~ no venga** whether he comes or not

7 (*porque*): **no puedo, ~ tengo ~ quedarme en casa** I can't, I've got to stay in

♦ *pron* **1** (*cosa*) that, which; (+ *prep*) which; **el sombrero ~ te compraste** the hat (that *o* which) you bought; **la cama en ~ dormí** the bed (that *o* which) I slept in

2 (*persona*: *suj*) that, who; (: *objeto*) that, whom; **el amigo ~ me acompañó al museo** the friend that *o* who went to the museum with me; **la chica que invité** the girl (that *o* whom) I invited

qué [ke] *a* what?, which? // *pron* what?; **¡~ divertido!** how funny!; **¿~ edad tienes?** how old are you?; **¿de ~ me hablas?** what are you saying to me?; **¿~ tal?** how are you?, how are things?; **¿~ hay (de nuevo)?** what's new?

quebrada [keˈβraða] *nf ver* **quebrado**.

quebradizo, a [keβraˈðiθo, a] *a* fragile; (*persona*) frail.

quebrado, a [keˈβraðo, a] *a* (*roto*) broken // *nm/f* bankrupt // *nm* (*MAT*) fraction // *nf* ravine.

quebradura [keβraˈðura] *nf* (*fisura*) fissure; (*GEO*) gorge; (*MED*) rupture.

quebrantar [keβranˈtar] *vt* (*infringir*) to violate, transgress; **~se** *vr* (*persona*) to fail in health.

quebranto [keˈβranto] *nm* damage, harm; (*decaimiento*) exhaustion; (*dolor*) grief, pain.

quebrar [keˈβrar] *vt* to break, smash // *vi* to go bankrupt; **~se** *vr* to break, get broken; (*MED*) to be ruptured.

quedar [keˈðar] *vi* to stay, remain; (*encontrarse*: *sitio*) to be; (*restar*) to remain, be left; **~se** *vr* to remain, stay (behind); **~se (con) algo** to keep sth; **~ en** (*acordar*) to agree on/to; **~ en nada** to come to nothing; **~ por hacer** to be still to be done; **~ ciego/mudo** to be left blind/dumb; **no te queda bien ese vestido** that dress doesn't suit you; **eso queda muy lejos** that's a long way (away); **quedamos a las seis** we agreed to meet at six.

quedo, a [ˈkeðo, a] *a* still // *ad* softly, gently.

quehacer [kea'θer] *nm* task, job; **~es (domésticos)** *nmpl* household chores.

queja [ˈkexa] *nf* complaint; **quejarse** *vr* (*enfermo*) to moan, groan; (*protestar*) to complain; **quejarse de que** to complain (about the fact) that; **quejido** *nm* moan; **quejoso, a** *a* complaining.

quemado, a [keˈmaðo, a] *a* burnt.

quemadura [kemaˈðura] *nf* burn, scald.

quemar [keˈmar] *vt* to burn; (*fig*: *malgastar*) to burn up, squander // *vi* to be burning hot; **~se** *vr* (*consumirse*) to burn (up); (*del sol*) to get sunburnt.

quemarropa [kema'rropa]: **a ~** *ad* point-blank.

quemazón [kema'θon] *nf* burn; (*calor*) intense heat; (*sensación*) itch.

quepo *etc vb ver* **caber.**

querella [keˈreʎa] *nf* (*JUR*) charge; (*disputa*) dispute.

PALABRA CLAVE

querer [ke'rer] *vt* **1** (*desear*) to want; **quiero más dinero** I want more money; **quisiera o querría un té** I'd like a tea; **sin ~** unintentionally; **quiero ayudar/que vayas** I want to help/you to go

2 (*preguntas*: *para pedir algo*): **¿quiere abrir la ventana?** could you open the window?; ¿quieres **echarme una mano?** can you give me a hand?

3 (*amar*) to love; (*tener cariño a*) to be fond of; **quiere mucho a sus hijos** he's very fond of his children

4 (*requerir*): **esta planta quiere más luz** this plant needs more light

5: le pedí que me dejara ir pero no quiso I asked him to let me go but he refused.

querido, a [ke'riðo, a] *a* dear // *nm/f* darling; (*amante*) lover.

quesería [kese'ria] *nf* dairy; (*fábrica*) cheese factory.

queso ['keso] *nm* cheese; **~ crema** cream cheese.

quicio ['kiθjo] *nm* hinge; **sacar a uno de ~** to get on sb's nerves.

quiebra ['kjeβra] *nf* break, split; (*COM*) bankruptcy; (*ECON*) slump.

quiebro ['kjeβro] *nm* (*del cuerpo*) swerve.

quien [kjen] *pron* who; **hay ~ piensa que** there are those who think that; **no hay ~ lo haga** no-one will do it.

quién [kjen] *pron* who, whom; **¿~ es?** who's there?

quienquiera [kjen'kjera] (*pl* **quienesquiera**) *pron* whoever.

quiero *etc vb ver* **querer**.

quieto, a ['kjeto, a] *a* still; (*carácter*) placid; **quietud** *nf* stillness.

quijada [ki'xaða] *nf* jaw, jawbone.

quilate [ki'late] *nm* carat.

quilla ['kiʎa] *nf* keel.

quimera [ki'mera] *nf* chimera; **quimérico, a** *a* fantastic.

químico, a ['kimiko, a] *a* chemical // *nm/f* chemist // *nf* chemistry.

quincalla [kin'kaʎa] *nf* hardware, ironmongery (*Brit*).

quince ['kinθe] *num* fifteen; **~ días** a fortnight; **~añero, a** *nm/f* teenager; **~na** *nf* fortnight; (*pago*) fortnightly pay; **~nal** *a* fortnightly.

quiniela [ki'njela] *nf* football pools *pl*; **~s** *nfpl* pools coupon *sg*.

quinientos, as [ki'njentos, as] *a, num* five hundred.

quinina [ki'nina] *nf* quinine.

quinqui ['kinki] *nm* delinquent.

quinto, a ['kinto, a] *a* fifth // *nf* country house; (*MIL*) call-up, draft.

quiosco ['kjosko] *nm* (*de música*) bandstand; (*de periódicos*) news stand.

quirúrgico, a [ki'rurxiko, a] *a* surgical.

quise, quisiera *etc vb ver* **querer**.

quisquilloso, a [kiski'ʎoso, a] *a* (*susceptible*) touchy; (*meticuloso*) pernickety.

quiste ['kiste] *nm* cyst.

quitaesmalte [kitaes'malte] *nm* nail-polish remover.

quitamanchas [kita'mantʃas] *nm inv* stain remover.

quitanieves [kita'njeβes] *nm inv* snowplough (*Brit*), snowplow (*US*).

quitar [ki'tar] *vt* to remove, take away; (*ropa*) to take off; (*dolor*) to relieve; **¡quita de ahí!** get away!; **~se** *vr* to withdraw; (*ropa*) to take off; **se quitó el sombrero** he took off his hat.

quitasol [kita'sol] *nm* sunshade (*Brit*), parasol.

quite ['kite] *nm* (*esgrima*) parry; (*evasión*) dodge.

Quito ['kito] *n* Quito.

quizá(s) [ki'θa(s)] *ad* perhaps, maybe.

R

rábano ['raβano] *nm* radish; **me importa un ~** I don't give a damn.

rabia ['raβja] *nf* (*MED*) rabies *sg*; (*fig: ira*) fury, rage; **rabiar** *vi* to have rabies; to rage, be furious; **rabiar por algo** to long for sth.

rabieta [ra'βjeta] *nf* tantrum, fit of temper.

rabino [ra'βino] *nm* rabbi.

rabioso, a [ra'βjoso, a] *a* rabid; (*fig*)

furious.

rabo ['raβo] nm tail.

racial [ra'θjal] a racial, race cpd.

racimo [ra'θimo] nm bunch.

raciocinio [raθjo'θinjo] nm reason.

ración [ra'θjon] nf portion; **raciones** nfpl rations.

racional [raθjo'nal] a (razonable) reasonable; (lógico) rational; **~izar** vt to rationalize.

racionar [raθjo'nar] vt to ration (out).

racismo [ra'θismo] nm racialism, racism; **racista** a, nmf racist.

racha ['ratʃa] nf gust of wind: **buena/mala ~** (fig) spell of good/bad luck.

radar [ra'ðar] nm radar.

radiactivo, a [raðiak'tiβo, a] a = **radioactivo**.

radiador [raðja'ðor] nm radiator.

radiante [ra'ðjante] a radiant.

radical [raði'kal] a, nmf radical.

radicar [raði'kar] vi to take root; **~ en** to lie o consist in; **~se** vr to establish o.s., put down (one's) roots.

radio ['raðjo] nf radio; (aparato) radio (set) // nm (MAT) radius; (QUÍMICA) radium; **~activo, a** a radioactive; **~difusión** nf broadcasting; **~emisora** nf transmitter, radio station; **~escucha** nmf listener; **~grafía** nf X-ray; **~grafiar** vt to X-ray; **~terapia** nf radiotherapy.

raer [ra'er] vt to scrape (off).

ráfaga ['rafava] nf gust; (de luz) flash; (de tiros) burst.

raído, a [ra'iðo, a] a (ropa) threadbare.

raigambre [rai'vambre] nf (BOT) roots pl; (fig) tradition.

raíz [ra'iθ] nf root; **~ cuadrada** square root; **a ~ de** as a result of.

raja ['raxa] nf (de melón etc) slice; (grieta) crack; **rajar** vt to split; (fam) to slash; **rajarse** vr to split, crack; **rajarse** to back out of.

rajatabla [raxa'taβla]: **a ~** ad (estrictamente) strictly, to the letter.

ralo, a ['ralo, a] a thin, sparse.

rallado, a [ra'ʎaðo, a] a grated; **rallador** nm grater.

rallar [ra'ʎar] vt to grate.

RAM [ram] nf abr (= memoria de acceso aleatorio) RAM.

rama ['rama] nf branch; **~je** nm branches pl, foliage; **ramal** nm (de cuerda) strand; (FERRO) branch line (Brit); (AUTO) branch (road) (Brit).

rambla ['rambla] nf (avenida) avenue.

ramera [ra'mera] nf whore.

ramificación [ramifika'θjon] nf ramification.

ramificarse [ramifi'karse] vr to branch out.

ramillete [rami'ʎete] nm bouquet.

ramo ['ramo] nm branch; (sección) department, section.

rampa ['rampa] nf ramp.

ramplón, ona [ram'plon, ona] a uncouth, coarse.

rana ['rana] nf frog; **salto de ~** leapfrog.

rancio, a ['ranθjo, a] a (comestibles) rancid; (vino) aged, mellow; (fig) ancient.

ranchero [ran'tʃero] nm (AM) rancher; smallholder.

rancho ['rantʃo] nm grub (fam); (AM: grande) ranch; (: pequeño) small farm.

rango ['rango] nm rank, standing.

ranura [ra'nura] nf groove; (de teléfono etc) slot.

rapar [ra'par] vt to shave; (los cabellos) to crop.

rapaz [ra'paθ] a (ZOOL) predatory; nmf (f: **rapaza**) young boy/girl.

rape ['rape] nm quick shave; (pez) angler (fish); **al ~** cropped.

rapé [ra'pe] nm snuff.

rapidez [rapi'ðeθ] nf speed, rapidity; **rápido, a** a fast, quick // ad quickly // nm (FERRO) express; **rápidos** nmpl rapids.

rapiña [ra'piɲa] nm robbery; **ave de ~** bird of prey.

raptar [rap'tar] vt to kidnap; **rapto**

nm kidnapping; (*impulso*) sudden impulse; (*éxtasis*) ecstasy, rapture.

raqueta [ra'keta] *nf* racquet.

raquítico, a [ra'kitiko, a] *a* stunted; (*fig*) poor, inadequate; **raquitismo** *nm* rickets *sg*.

rareza [ra'reθa] *nf* rarity; (*fig*) eccentricity.

raro, a ['raro, a] *a* (*poco común*) rare; (*extraño*) odd, strange; (*excepcional*) remarkable.

ras [ras] *nm*: **a ~ de** level with; **a ~ de tierra** at ground level.

rasar [ra'sar] *vt* (*igualar*) to level.

rascacielos [raska'θjelos] *nm inv* skyscraper.

rascar [ras'kar] *vt* (*con las uñas etc*) to scratch; (*raspar*) to scrape; ~**se** *vr* to scratch (o.s.).

rasgar [ras'ɣar] *vt* to tear, rip (up).

rasgo ['rasɣo] *nm* (*con pluma*) stroke; ~**s** *nmpl* features, characteristics; **a grandes ~s** in outline, broadly.

rasguñar [rasɣu'ɲar] *vt* to scratch; **rasguño** *nm* scratch.

raso, a ['raso, a] *a* (*liso*) flat, level; (*a baja altura*) very low // *nm* satin; **cielo ~** clear sky.

raspadura [raspa'ðura] *nf* (*acto*) scrape, scraping; (*marca*) scratch; ~**s** *nfpl* scrapings.

raspar [ras'par] *vt* to scrape; (*arañar*) to scratch; (*limar*) to file.

rastra ['rastra] *nf* (*AGR*) rake; **a ~s** by dragging; (*fig*) unwillingly.

rastreador [rastrea'ðor] *nm* tracker; ~ **de minas** minesweeper.

rastrear [rastre'ar] *vt* (*seguir*) to track.

rastrero, a [ras'trero, a] *a* (*BOT, ZOOL*) creeping; (*fig*) despicable, mean.

rastrillar [rastri'ʎar] *vt* to rake; **rastrillo** *nm* rake.

rastro ['rastro] *nm* (*AGR*) rake; (*pista*) track, trail; (*vestigio*) trace; **el R~** the Madrid fleamarket.

rastrojo [ras'troxo] *nm* stubble.

rasurador [rasura'ðor] *nm*, **rasura-**

dora [rasura'ðora] *nf* (*AM*) electric shaver.

rasurarse [rasu'rarse] *vr* to shave.

rata ['rata] *nf* rat.

ratear [rate'ar] *vt* (*robar*) to steal.

ratería [rate'ria] *nf* petty theft.

ratero, a [ra'tero, a] *a* light-fingered // *nmf* (*carterista*) pickpocket; (*AM: de casas*) burglar.

ratificar [ratifi'kar] *vt* to ratify.

rato ['rato] *nm* while, short time; **a ~s** from time to time; **hay para ~** there's still a long way to go; **al poco ~** soon afterwards; **pasar el ~** to kill time; **pasar un buen/mal ~** to have a good/rough time.

ratón [ra'ton] *nm* mouse; **ratonera** *nf* mousetrap.

raudal [rau'ðal] *nm* torrent; **a ~es** in abundance.

raya ['raja] *nf* line; (*marca*) scratch; (*en tela*) stripe; (*de pelo*) parting; (*límite*) boundary; (*pez*) ray; (*puntuación*) hyphen; **a ~s** striped; **pasarse de la ~** to go too far; **tener a ~** to keep in check; **rayar** *vt* to line; to scratch; (*subrayar*) to underline // *vi*: **rayar en o con** to border on.

rayo ['rajo] *nm* (*del sol*) ray, beam; (*de luz*) shaft; (*en una tormenta*) (flash of) lightning; ~**s X** X-rays.

rayón [ra'jon] *nm* rayon.

raza ['raθa] *nf* race; ~ **humana** human race.

razón [ra'θon] *nf* reason; (*justicia*) right, justice; (*razonamiento*) reasoning; (*motivo*) reason, motive; (*MAT*) ratio; **a ~ de 10 cada día** at the rate of 10 a day; **'~: ...'** 'inquiries to ...'; **en ~ de** with regard to; **dar ~ a uno** to agree that sb is right; **tener ~** to be right; ~ **directa/inversa** direct/inverse proportion; ~ **de ser** raison d'être; **razonable** *a* reasonable; (*justo, moderado*) fair; **razonamiento** *nm* (*juicio*) judgement; (*argumento*) reasoning; **razonar** *vt* to reason, argue // *vi* to reason, argue.

reacción [reak'θjon] *nf* reaction; **avión a ~** jet plane; **~ en cadena** chain reaction; **reaccionar** *vi* to react; **reaccionario, a** *a* reactionary.

reacio, a [re'aθjo, a] *a* stubborn.

reactor [reak'tor] *nm* reactor.

readaptación [readapta'θjon] *nf*: **~ profesional** industrial retraining.

reajuste [rea'xuste] *nm* readjustment.

real [re'al] *a* real; (*del rey, fig*) royal.

realce [re'alθe] *nm* (*TEC*) embossing; (*lustre, fig*) splendour; (*ARTE*) highlight; **poner de ~** to emphasize.

realidad [reali'ðað] *nf* reality, fact; (*verdad*) truth.

realista [rea'lista] *nm/f* realist.

realización [realiθa'θjon] *nf* fulfilment; (*COM*) selling up (*Brit*), conversion into money (*US*).

realizador, a [realiθa'ðor, a] *nm/f* (*TV etc*) producer.

realizar [reali'θar] *vt* (*objetivo*) to achieve; (*plan*) to carry out; (*viaje*) to make, undertake; (*COM*) to sell up (*Brit*), convert into money (*US*); **~se** *vr* to come about, come true.

realmente [real'mente] *ad* really, actually.

realquilar [realki'lar] *vt* (*subarrendar*) to sublet.

realzar [real'θar] *vt* (*TEC*) to raise; (*embellecer*) to enhance; (*acentuar*) to highlight.

reanimar [reani'mar] *vt* to revive; (*alentar*) to encourage; **~se** *vr* to revive.

reanudar [reanu'ðar] *vt* (*renovar*) to renew; (*historia, viaje*) to resume.

reaparición [reapari'θjon] *nf* reappearance.

rearme [re'arme] *nm* rearmament.

rebaja [re'βaxa] *nf* (*COM*) reduction; (*menoscabo*) lessening; **~s** *nfpl* (*COM*) sale; **rebajar** *vt* (*bajar*) to lower; (*reducir*) to reduce; (*disminuir*) to lessen; (*humillar*) to humble.

rebanada [reβa'naða] *nf* slice.

rebaño [re'βaɲo] *nm* herd; (*de ovejas*) flock.

rebasar [reβa'sar] *vt* (*tb*: **~ de**) to exceed.

rebatir [reβa'tir] *vt* to refute.

rebeca [re'βeka] *nf* cardigan.

rebelarse [reβe'larse] *vr* to rebel, revolt.

rebelde [re'βelde] *a* rebellious; (*niño*) unruly // *nm/f* rebel; **rebeldía** *nf* rebelliousness; (*desobediencia*) disobedience.

rebelión [reβe'ljon] *nf* rebellion.

reblandecer [reβlande'θer] *vt* to soften.

rebosante [reβo'sante] *a* overflowing.

rebosar [reβo'sar] *vi* (*líquido, recipiente*) to overflow; (*abundar*) to abound, be plentiful.

rebotar [reβo'tar] *vt* to bounce; (*rechazar*) to repel // *vi* (*pelota*) to bounce; (*bala*) to ricochet; **rebote** *nm* rebound; **de rebote** on the rebound.

rebozado, a [reβo'θaðo, a] *a* fried in batter *o* breadcrumbs.

rebozar [reβo'θar] *vt* to wrap up; (*CULIN*) to fry in batter *o* breadcrumbs.

rebuscado, a [reβus'kaðo, a] *a* (*amanerado*) affected; (*palabra*) recherché; (*idea*) far-fetched.

rebuznar [reβuθ'nar] *vi* to bray.

recabar [reka'βar] *vt* (*obtener*) to manage to get.

recado [re'kaðo] *nm* message; **tomar un ~** (*TEL*) to take a message.

recaer [reka'er] *vi* to relapse; **~ en** to fall to *o* on; (*criminal etc*) to fall back into, relapse into; **recaída** *nf* relapse.

recalcar [rekal'kar] *vt* (*fig*) to stress, emphasize.

recalcitrante [rekalθi'trante] *a* recalcitrant.

recalentar [rekalen'tar] *vt* (*volver a calentar*) to reheat; (*calentar demasiado*) to overheat.

recámara [re'kamara] *nf* (*AM*) bedroom.

recambio [re'kambjo] *nm* spare; (*de pluma*) refill.

recapacitar [rekapaθi'tar] *vi* to reflect.

recargado, a [rekar'ɣaðo, a] *a* overloaded.

recargar [rekar'ɣar] *vt* to overload; (*batería*) to recharge; **recargo** *nm* surcharge; (*aumento*) increase.

recatado, a [reka'taðo, a] *a* (*modesto*) modest, demure; (*prudente*) cautious.

recato [re'kato] *nm* (*modestia*) modesty, demureness; (*cautela*) caution.

recaudación [rekauða'θjon] *nf* (*acción*) collection; (*cantidad*) takings *pl*; (*en deporte*) gate; **recaudador, a** *nm/f* tax collector.

recelar [reθe'lar] *vt*: ~ que (*sospechar*) to suspect that; (*temer*) to fear that // *vi*: ~ de to distrust; **recelo** *nm* distrust, suspicion; **receloso, a** *a* distrustful, suspicious.

recepción [reθep'θjon] *nf* reception; **recepcionista** *nm/f* receptionist.

receptáculo [reθep'takulo] *nm* receptacle.

receptivo, a [reθep'tiβo, a] *a* receptive.

receptor, a [reθep'tor, a] *nm/f* recipient // *nm* (TEL) receiver.

recesión [reθe'sjon] *nf* (COM) recession.

receta [re'θeta] *nf* (CULIN) recipe; (MED) prescription.

recibidor [reθiβi'ðor, a] *nm* entrance hall.

recibimiento [reθiβi'mjento] *nm* reception, welcome.

recibir [reθi'βir] *vt* to receive; (*dar la bienvenida*) to welcome // *vi* to entertain; ~**se** *vr*: ~**se de** (AM) to qualify as; **recibo** *nm* receipt.

recién [re'θjen] *ad* recently, newly; **los ~ casados** the newly-weds; **el ~ llegado** the newcomer; **el ~ nacido** the newborn child.

reciente [re'θjente] *a* recent;

(*fresco*) fresh; ~**mente** *ad* recently.

recinto [re'θinto] *nm* enclosure; (*área*) area, place.

recio, a ['reθjo, a] *a* strong, tough; (*voz*) loud // *ad* hard; loud(ly).

recipiente [reθi'pjente] *nm* receptacle.

reciprocidad [reθiproθi'ðað] *nf* reciprocity; **recíproco, a** *a* reciprocal.

recital [reθi'tal] *nm* (MUS) recital; (LITERATURA) reading.

recitar [reθi'tar] *vt* to recite.

reclamación [reklama'θjon] *nf* claim, demand; (*queja*) complaint.

reclamar [rekla'mar] *vt* to claim, demand // *vi*: ~ **contra** to complain about; ~ **a uno en justicia** to take sb to court; **reclamo** *nm* (*anuncio*) advertisement; (*tentación*) attraction.

reclinar [rekli'nar] *vt* to recline, lean; ~**se** *vr* to lean back.

recluir [reklu'ir] *vt* to intern, confine.

reclusión [reklu'sjon] *nf* (*prisión*) prison; (*refugio*) seclusion; ~ **perpetua** life imprisonment.

recluta [re'kluta] *nm/f* recruit // *nf* recruitment.

reclutamiento [rekluta'mjento] *nm* recruitment.

recobrar [reko'βrar] *vt* (*salud*) to recover; (*rescatar*) to get back; ~**se** *vr* to recover.

recodo [re'koðo] *nm* (*de río, camino*) bend.

recoger [reko'xer] *vt* to collect; (AGR) to harvest; (*levantar*) to pick up; (*juntar*) to gather; (*pasar a buscar*) to come for, get; (*dar asilo*) to give shelter to; (*faldas*) to gather up; (*pelo*) to put up; ~**se** *vr* (*retirarse*) to retire; **recogido, a** *a* (*lugar*) quiet, secluded; (*pequeño*) small // *nf* (CORREOS) collection; (AGR) harvest.

recolección [rekolek'θjon] *nf* (AGR) harvesting; (*colecta*) collection.

recomendación [rekomenda'θjon] *nf* (*sugerencia*) suggestion, recommendation; (*referencia*) reference.

recomendar [rekomen'dar] *vt* to suggest, recommend; (*confiar*) to entrust.

recompensa [rekom'pensa] *nf* reward, recompense; **recompensar** *vt* to reward, recompense.

recomponer [rekompo'ner] *vt* to mend.

reconciliación [rekonθilja'θjon] *nf* reconciliation.

reconciliar [rekonθi'ljar] *vt* to reconcile; **~se** *vr* to become reconciled.

recóndito, a [re'kondito, a] *a* (*lugar*) hidden, secret.

reconfortar [rekonfor'tar] *vt* to comfort.

reconocer [rekono'θer] *vt* to recognize; (*registrar*) to search; (*MED*) to examine; **reconocido, a** a recognized; (*agradecido*) grateful; **reconocimiento** *nm* recognition; search; examination; gratitude; (*confesión*) admission.

reconquista [rekon'kista] *nf* reconquest; **la R~** the Reconquest (of Spain).

reconstituyente [rekonstitu'jente] *nm* tonic.

reconstruir [rekonstru'ir] *vt* to reconstruct.

reconversión [rekonβer'sjon] *nf*: ~ **industrial** industrial rationalization.

recopilación [rekopila'θjon] *nf* (*resumen*) summary; (*compilación*) compilation; **recopilar** *vt* to compile.

récord ['rekorð] *a inv, nm* record.

recordar [rekor'ðar] *vt* (*acordarse de*) to remember; (*acordar a otro*) to remind // *vi* to remember.

recorrer [reko'rrer] *vt* (*país*) to cross, travel through; (*distancia*) to cover; (*registrar*) to search; (*pasar*) to look over; **recorrido** *nm* run, journey; **tren de largo recorrido** main-line train.

recortado, a [rekor'taðo, a] *a* uneven, irregular.

recortar [rekor'tar] *vt* to cut out; **recorte** *nm* (*acción, de prensa*) cutting; (*de telas, chapas*) trimming.

recostado, a [rekos'taðo, a] *a* leaning; **estar ~** to be lying down.

recostar [rekos'tar] *vt* to lean; **~se** *vr* to lie down.

recoveco [reko'βeko] *nm* (*de camino, rio etc*) bend; (*en casa*) cubby hole.

recreación [rekrea'θjon] *nf* recreation.

recrear [rekre'ar] *vt* (*entretener*) to entertain; (*volver a crear*) to recreate; **recreativo, a** a recreational; **recreo** *nm* recreation; (*ESCOL*) break, playtime.

recriminar [rekrimi'nar] *vt* to reproach // *vi* to recriminate; **~se** *vr* to reproach each other.

recrudecer [rekruðe'θer] *vt, vi*, **recrudecerse** *vr* to worsen; **recrudecimiento** [rekruðeθi'mjento] *nm* upsurge.

recta ['rekta] *nf ver* **recto**.

rectángulo, a [rek'tangulo, a] *a* rectangular // *nm* rectangle.

rectificar [rektifi'kar] *vt* to rectify; (*volverse recto*) to straighten // *vi* to correct o.s.

rectitud [rekti'tuð] *nf* straightness; (*fig*) rectitude.

recto, a ['rekto, a] *a* straight; (*persona*) honest, upright // *nm* rectum // *nf* straight line.

rector, a [rek'tor, a] *a* governing.

recua ['rekwa] *nf* mule train.

recuadro [re'kwaðro] *nm* box; (*TIPOGRAFÍA*) inset.

recuento [re'kwento] *nm* inventory; **hacer el ~** to count o reckon up.

recuerdo [re'kwerðo] *nm* souvenir; **~s** *nmpl* memories; **¡~s a tu madre!** give my regards to your mother!

recular [reku'lar] *vi* to back down.

recuperable [rekupe'raβle] *a* recoverable.

recuperación [rekupera'θjon] *nf* recovery.

recuperar [rekupe'rar] *vt* to recover; (*tiempo*) to make up; ~**se** *vr* to recuperate.

recurrir [reku'rrir] *vi* (*JUR*) to appeal; ~ **a** to resort to; (*persona*) to turn to; **recurso** *nm* resort; (*medios*) means *pl*, resources *pl*; (*JUR*) appeal.

recusar [reku'sar] *vt* to reject, refuse.

rechazar [retʃa'θar] *vt* to repel, drive back; (*idea*) to reject; (*oferta*) to turn down.

rechazo [re'tʃaθo] *nm* (*de fusil*) recoil; (*rebote*) rebound; (*negación*) rebuff.

rechifla [re'tʃifla] *nf* hissing, booing; (*fig*) derision.

rechiflar [retʃi'flar] *vt* to hiss, boo.

rechinar [retʃi'nar] *vi* to creak; (*dientes*) to grind.

rechistar [retʃis'tar] *vi*: **sin** ~ without a murmur.

rechoncho, a [re'tʃontʃo, a] *a* (*fam*) thickset (*Brit*), heavy-set (*US*).

red [reð] *nf* net, mesh; (*FERRO etc*) network; (*trampa*) trap.

redacción [reðak'θjon] *nf* (*acción*) editing; (*personal*) editorial staff; (*ESCOL*) essay, composition.

redactar [reðak'tar] *vt* to draw up, draft; (*periódico*) to edit.

redactor, a [reðak'tor, a] *nm/f* editor.

redada [re'ðaða] *nf*: ~ **policial** police raid, round-up.

rededor [reðe'ðor] *nm*: **al** *o* **en** ~ around, round about.

redención [reðen'θjon] *nf* redemption; **redentor, a** *a* redeeming.

redescubrir [reðesku'βrir] *vt* to rediscover.

redicho, a [re'ðitʃo, a] *a* affected.

redil [re'ðil] *nm* sheepfold.

redimir [reði'mir] *vt* to redeem.

rédito ['reðito] *nm* interest, yield.

redoblar [reðo'βlar] *vt* to redouble // *vi* (*tambor*) to play a roll on the drums.

redomado, a [reðo'maðo, a] *a* (*astuto*) sly, crafty; (*perfecto*) utter.

redonda [re'ðonda] *nf ver* **redondo**.

redondear [reðonde'ar] *vt* to round, round off.

redondel [reðon'del] *nm* (*círculo*) circle; (*TAUR*) bullring, arena; (*AUTO*) roundabout.

redondo, a [re'ðondo, a] *a* (*circular*) round; (*completo*) complete // *nf*: **a la redonda** around, round about.

reducción [reðuk'θjon] *nf* reduction.

reducido, a [reðu'ðiðo, a] *a* reduced; (*limitado*) limited; (*pequeño*) small.

reducir [reðu'θir] *vt* to reduce; to limit; ~**se** *vr* to diminish.

redundancia [reðun'danθja] *nf* redundancy.

reembolsar [re(e)mbol'sar] *vt* (*persona*) to reimburse; (*dinero*) to repay, pay back; (*depósito*) to refund; **reembolso** *nm* reimbursement; refund.

reemplazar [re(e)mpla'θar] *vt* to replace; **reemplazo** *nm* replacement; **de reemplazo** (*MIL*) reserve.

referencia [refe'renθja] *nf* reference; **con** ~ **a** with reference to.

referéndum [refe'rendum] (*pl* ~s) *nm* referendum.

referente [refe'rente] *a*: ~ **a** concerning, relating to.

referir [refe'rir] *vt* (*contar*) to tell, recount; (*relacionar*) to refer, relate; ~**se** *vr*: ~**se a** to refer to.

refilón [refi'lon]: **de** ~ *ad* obliquely.

refinado, a [refi'naðo, a] *a* refined.

refinamiento [refina'mjento] *nm* refinement.

refinar [refi'nar] *vt* to refine; **refinería** *nf* refinery.

reflejar [refle'xar] *vt* to reflect; **reflejo, a** *a* reflected; (*movimiento*) reflex // *nm* reflection; (*ANAT*) reflex.

reflexión [reflek'sjon] *nf* reflection; **reflexionar** *vt* to reflect on // *vi* to reflect; (*detenerse*) to pause (to think).

reflexivo, a [reflek'sißo, a] *a* thoughtful, reflective.

reflujo [re'fluxo] *nm* ebb.

reforma [re'forma] *nf* reform; (*ARQ etc*) repair; ~ **agraria** agrarian reform.

reformar [refor'mar] *vt* to reform; (*modificar*) to change, alter; (*ARQ*) to repair; **~se** *vr* to mend one's ways.

reformatorio [reforma'torjo] *nm* reformatory.

reforzar [refor'θar] *vt* to strengthen; (*ARQ*) to reinforce; (*fig*) to encourage.

refractario, a [refrak'tarjo, a] *a* (*TEC*) heat-resistant.

refrán [re'fran] *nm* proverb, saying.

refregar [refre'ɣar] *vt* to scrub.

refrenar [refre'nar] *vt* to check, restrain.

refrendar [refren'dar] *vt* (*firma*) to endorse, countersign; (*ley*) to approve.

refrescante [refres'kante] *a* refreshing, cooling.

refrescar [refres'kar] *vt* to refresh // *vi* to cool down; **~se** *vr* to get cooler; (*tomar aire fresco*) to go out for a breath of fresh air; (*beber*) to have a drink.

refresco [re'fresko] *nm* soft drink, cool drink; '~s' 'refreshments'.

refriega [re'frjeɣa] *nf* scuffle, brawl.

refrigeración [refrixera'θjon] *nf* refrigeration; (*de sala*) air-conditioning.

refrigerador [refrixera'ðor] *nm*, **refrigeradora** [-a] *nf* (*AM*) refrigerator (*Brit*), icebox (*US*).

refrigerar [refrixe'rar] *vt* to refrigerate; (*sala*) to air-condition.

refuerzo [re'fwerθo] *nm* reinforcement; (*TEC*) support.

refugiado, a [refu'xjaðo, a] *nm/f* refugee.

refugiarse [refu'xjarse] *vr* to take refuge, shelter.

refugio [re'fuxjo] *nm* refuge; (*protección*) shelter.

refulgir [reful'xir] *vi* to shine, be dazzling.

refunfuñar [refunfu'ɲar] *vi* to grunt, growl; (*quejarse*) to grumble.

refutar [refu'tar] *vt* to refute.

regadera [reɣa'ðera] *nf* watering can.

regadío [reɣa'ðio] *nm* irrigated land.

regalado, a [reɣa'laðo, a] *a* comfortable, luxurious; (*gratis*) free, for nothing.

regalar [reɣa'lar] *vt* (*dar*) to give (as a present); (*entregar*) to give away; (*mimar*) to pamper, make a fuss of.

regalía [reɣa'lia] *nf* privilege, prerogative; (*COM*) bonus; (*de autor*) royalty.

regaliz [reɣa'liθ] *nm* liquorice.

regalo [re'ɣalo] *nm* (*obsequio*) gift, present; (*gusto*) pleasure; (*comodidad*) comfort.

regalón, ona [reɣa'lon, ona] *a* spoiled, pampered.

regañadientes [reɣaɲa'ðjentes]: **a** ~ *ad* reluctantly.

regañar [reɣa'ɲar] *vt* to scold // *vi* to grumble; **regaño** *nm* scolding, telling-off; (*queja*) grumble; **regañón, ona** *a* nagging.

regar [re'ɣar] *vt* to water, irrigate; (*fig*) to scatter, sprinkle.

regatear [reɣate'ar] *vt* (*COM*) to bargain over; (*escatimar*) to be mean with // *vi* to bargain, haggle; (*DEPORTE*) to dribble; **regateo** *nm* bargaining; dribbling; (*del cuerpo*) swerve, dodge.

regazo [re'ɣaθo] *nm* lap.

regeneración [rexenera'θjon] *nf* regeneration.

regenerar [rexene'rar] *vt* to regenerate.

regentar [rexen'tar] *vt* to direct, manage; **regente** *nm* (*COM*) manager; (*POL*) regent.

régimen ['reximen] (*pl* **regímenes**) *nm* regime; (*MED*) diet.

regimiento [rexi'mjento] *nm* regiment.

regio, a ['rexjo, a] *a* royal, regal;

(fig: suntuoso) splendid; *(AM fam)* great, terrific.

región [re'xjon] *nf* region; **regionalista** *nm/f* regionalist.

regir [re'xir] *vt* to govern, rule; *(dirigir)* to manage, run // *vi* to apply, be in force.

registrador [rexistra'ðor] *nm* registrar, recorder.

registrar [rexis'trar] *vt (buscar)* to search; *(: en cajón)* to look through; *(inspeccionar)* to inspect; *(anotar)* to register, record; *(INFORM)* to log; ~**se** *vr* to register; *(ocurrir)* to happen.

registro [re'xistro] *nm (acto)* registration; *(MUS, libro)* register; *(inspección)* inspection, search; ~ **civil** registry office.

regla ['rexla] *nf (ley)* rule, regulation; *(de medir)* ruler, rule; *(MED: período)* period.

reglamentación [rexlamenta'θjon] *nf (acto)* regulation; *(lista)* rules *pl.*

reglamentar [rexlamen'tar] *vt* to regulate; **reglamentario, a** *a* statutory; **reglamento** *nm* rules *pl*, regulations *pl.*

reglar [re'xlar] *vt (acciones)* to regulate.

regocijarse [rexoθi'xarse] *vr (pasarlo bien)* to have a good time; *(alegrarse)* to rejoice; **regocijo** *nm* joy, happiness.

regodearse [rexoðe'arse] *vr* to be glad, be delighted; **regodeo** *nm* delight.

regresar [rexre'sar] *vi* to come back, go back, return; **regresivo, a** *a* backward; *(fig)* regressive; **regreso** *nm* return.

reguero [re'xero] *nm (de sangre etc)* trickle; *(de humo)* trail.

regulador [rexula'ðor] *nm* regulator; *(de radio etc)* knob, control.

regular [rexu'lar] *a* regular; *(normal)* normal, usual; *(común)* ordinary; *(organizado)* regular, orderly; *(mediano)* average; *(fam)* not bad, so-so // *ad* so-so, alright // *vt*

(controlar) to control, regulate; *(TEC)* to adjust; **por lo** ~ as a rule; ~**idad** *nf* regularity; ~**izar** *vt* to regularize.

regusto [re'xusto] *nm* aftertaste.

rehabilitación [reaβilita'θjon] *nf* rehabilitation; *(ARQ)* restoration.

rehabilitar [reaβili'tar] *vt* to rehabilitate; *(ARQ)* to restore; *(reintegrar)* to reinstate.

rehacer [rea'θer] *vt (reparar)* to mend, repair; *(volver a hacer)* to redo, repeat; ~**se** *vr (MED)* to recover.

rehén [re'en] *nm* hostage.

rehuir [reu'ir] *vt* to avoid, shun.

rehusar [reu'sar] *vt, vi* to refuse.

reina ['reina] *nf* queen; ~**do** *nm* reign.

reinante [rei'nante] *a (fig)* prevailing.

reinar [rei'nar] *vi* to reign.

reincidir [reinθi'ðir] *vi* to relapse.

reincorporarse [reinkorpo'rarse] *vr*: ~ a to rejoin.

reino ['reino] *nm* kingdom; **el R**~ **Unido** the United Kingdom.

reintegrar [reinte'xrar] *vt (reconstituir)* to reconstruct; *(persona)* to reinstate; *(dinero)* to refund, pay back; ~**se** *vr*: ~**se a** to rejoin.

reír [re'ir] *vi*, **reírse** *vr* to laugh; ~**se de** to laugh at.

reiterar [reite'rar] *vt* to reiterate.

reivindicación [reiβindika'θjon] *nf (demanda)* claim, demand; *(justificación)* vindication.

reivindicar [reiβindi'kar] *vt* to claim.

reja ['rexa] *nf (de ventana)* grille, bars *pl*; *(en la calle)* grating.

rejilla [re'xiʎa] *nf* grating, grille; *(muebles)* wickerwork; *(de ventilación)* vent; *(de coche etc)* luggage rack.

rejoneador [rexonea'ðor] *nm* mounted bullfighter.

rejuvenecer [rexuβene'θer] *vt, vi* to rejuvenate.

relación [rela'θjon] *nf* relation, relationship; *(MAT)* ratio; *(narración)* report; **relaciones públicas** public relations; **con ~ a, en ~** con in relation to; **relacionar** *vt* to relate, connect; **relacionarse** *vr* to be connected, be linked.

relajación [relaxa'θjon] *nf* relaxation.

relajado, a [rela'xaðo, a] *a* (*disoluto*) loose; (*cómodo*) relaxed; (*MED*) ruptured.

relajar [rela'xar] *vt*, **relajarse** *vr* to relax.

relamerse [rela'merse] *vr* to lick one's lips.

relamido, a [rela'miðo, a] *a* (*pulcro*) overdressed; (*afectado*) affected.

relámpago [re'lampaxo] *nm* flash of lightning; **visita/huelga ~** lightning visit/strike; **relampaguear** *vi* to flash.

relatar [rela'tar] *vt* to tell, relate.

relativo, a [rela'tiβo, a] *a* relative; **en lo ~ a** concerning.

relato [re'lato] *nm* (*narración*) story, tale.

relax [re'la(k)s] *nm*: **hacer ~** to relax.

relegar [rele'xar] *vt* to relegate.

relevante [rele'βante] *a* eminent, outstanding.

relevar [rele'βar] *vt* (*sustituir*) to relieve; **~se** *vr* to relay; **~ a uno de un cargo** to relieve sb of his post.

relevo [re'leβo] *nm* relief; **carrera de ~s** relay race.

relieve [re'ljeβe] *nm* (*ARTE, TEC*) relief; (*fig*) prominence, importance; **bajo ~** bas-relief.

religión [reli'xjon] *nf* religion; **religioso, a** *a* religious // *nm/f* monk/nun.

relinchar [relin'tʃar] *vi* to neigh; **relincho** *nm* neigh; (*acto*) neighing.

reliquia [re'likja] *nf* relic; **~ de familia** heirloom.

reloj [re'lo(x)] *nm* clock; **~ (de pulsera)** wristwatch; **~ despertador** alarm (clock); **poner el ~** to set one's watch (o the clock); **~ero, a** *nm/f* clockmaker; watchmaker.

reluciente [relu'θjente] *a* brilliant, shining.

relucir [relu'θir] *vi* to shine; (*fig*) to excel.

relumbrar [relum'brar] *vi* to dazzle, shine brilliantly.

rellano [re'ʎano] *nm* (*ARQ*) landing.

rellenar [reʎe'nar] *vt* (*llenar*) to fill up; (*CULIN*) to stuff; (*COSTURA*) to pad; **relleno, a** *a* full up; stuffed // *nm* stuffing; (*de tapicería*) padding.

remachar [rema'tʃar] *vt* to rivet; (*fig*) to hammer home, drive home; **remache** *nm* rivet.

remanente [rema'nente] *nm* remainder; (*COM*) balance; (*de producto*) surplus.

remangar [reman'gar] *vt* to roll up.

remanso [re'manso] *nm* pool.

remar [re'mar] *vi* to row.

rematado, a [rema'taðo, a] *a* complete, utter.

rematar [rema'tar] *vt* to finish off; (*COM*) to sell off cheap // *vi* to end, finish off; (*DEPORTE*) to shoot.

remate [re'mate] *nm* end, finish; (*punta*) tip; (*DEPORTE*) top; (*COM*) auction sale; **de o para ~** to crown it all (*Brit*), to top it off.

remedar [reme'ðar] *vt* to imitate.

remediar [reme'ðjar] *vt* (*subsanar*) to make good, repair; (*evitar*) to avoid.

remedio [re'meðjo] *nm* remedy; (*alivio*) relief, help; (*JUR*) recourse, remedy; **poner ~ a** to correct, stop; **no tener más ~** to have no alternative; **¡qué ~!** there's no choice!; **sin ~** hopeless.

remedo [re'meðo] *nm* imitation; (*pey*) parody.

remendar [remen'dar] *vt* to repair; (*con parche*) to patch.

remesa [re'mesa] *nf* remittance; (*COM*) shipment.

remiendo [re'mjendo] *nm* mend; (*con parche*) patch; (*cosido*) darn.

remilgado, a [remil'gaðo, a] *a* prim; (*afectado*) affected.

remilgo [re'milxo] *nm* primness;

(*afectación*) affectation.

reminiscencia [reminis'θenθja] *nf* reminiscence.

remiso, a [rɛ'miso, a] *a* slack, slow.

remitir [remi'tir] *vt* to remit, send // *vi* to slacken; (*en carta*): remite: X sender: X; **remitente** [remi'tente] *nm/f* sender.

remo ['remo] *nm* (*de barco*) oar; (*DEPORTE*) rowing.

remojar [remo'xar] *vt* to steep, soak; (*galleta etc*) to dip, dunk.

remojo [rɛ'moxo] *nm*: **dejar la ropa en ~** to leave clothes to soak.

remolacha [remo'latʃa] *nf* beet, beetroot.

remolcador [remolka'ðor] *nm* (*NAUT*) tug; (*AUTO*) breakdown lorry.

remolcar [remol'kar] *vt* to tow.

remolino [remo'lino] *nm* eddy; (*de agua*) whirlpool; (*de viento*) whirlwind; (*de gente*) crowd.

remolque [rɛ'molkɛ] *nm* tow, towing; (*cuerda*) towrope; **llevar a ~** to tow.

remontar [remon'tar] *vt* to mend; ~**se** *vr* to soar; ~**se** a (*COM*) to amount to; ~ **el vuelo** to soar.

remorder [remor'ðer] *vt* to distress, disturb; ~**le la conciencia** a uno to have a guilty conscience; **remordimiento** *nm* remorse.

remoto, a [rɛ'moto, a] *a* remote.

remover [remo'βɛr] *vt* to stir; (*tierra*) to turn over; (*objetos*) to move round.

remozar [remo'θar] *vt* (*ARQ*) to refurbish.

remuneración [remunera'θjon] *nf* remuneration.

remunerar [remune'rar] *vt* to remunerate; (*premiar*) to reward.

renacer [rena'θer] *vi* to be reborn; (*fig*) to revive; **renacimiento** *nm* rebirth; **el Renacimiento** the Renaissance.

renacuajo [rena'kwaxo] *nm* (*ZOOL*) tadpole.

renal [rɛ'nal] *a* renal, kidney *cpd*.

rencilla [rɛn'θiʎa] *nf* quarrel.

rencor [rɛn'kor] *nm* rancour, bitterness; ~**oso, a** *a* spiteful.

rendición [rendi'θjon] *nf* surrender.

rendido, a [ren'diðo, a] *a* (*sumiso*) submissive; (*cansado*) worn-out, exhausted.

rendija [ren'dixa] *nf* (*hendedura*) crack, cleft.

rendimiento [rendi'mjento] *nm* (*producción*) output; (*TEC, COM*) efficiency.

rendir [ren'dir] *vt* (*vencer*) to defeat; (*producir*) to produce; (*dar beneficio*) to yield; (*agotar*) to exhaust // *vi* to pay; ~**se** *vr* (*someterse*) to surrender; (*cansarse*) to wear o.s. out; ~ **homenaje** o **culto a** to pay homage to.

renegado, a [rene'vaðo, a] *a, nm/f* renegade.

renegar [rene'xar] *vi* (*renunciar*) to renounce; (*blasfemar*) to blaspheme; (*quejarse*) to complain.

RENFE ['renfe] *nf abr* (= Red Nacional de los Ferrocarriles Españoles) ≈ BR (*Brit*).

renglón [ren'glon] *nm* (*línea*) line; (*COM*) item, article; **a ~ seguido** immediately after.

renombrado, a [renom'braðo, a] *a* renowned.

renombre [re'nombre] *nm* renown.

renovación [renoβa'θjon] *nf* (*de contrato*) renewal; (*ARQ*) renovation.

renovar [reno'βar] *vt* to renew; (*ARQ*) to renovate.

renta ['renta] *nf* (*ingresos*) income; (*beneficio*) profit; (*alquiler*) rent; ~ **vitalicia** annuity; **rentable** *a* profitable; **rentar** *vt* to produce, yield.

rentista [ren'tista] *nm/f* (*accionista*) stockholder.

renuencia [re'nwenθja] *nf* reluctance.

renuncia [re'nunθja] *nf* resignation.

renunciar [renun'θjar] *vt* to renounce // *vi* to resign; ~ **a hacer algo** to give up doing sth.

reñido, a [re'ɲiðo, a] *a* (*batalla*) bitter, hard-fought; **estar ~ con uno**

to be on bad terms with sb.

reñir [re'nir] vt (regañar) to scold // vi (estar peleado) to quarrel, fall out; (combatir) to fight.

reo ['reo] nm/f culprit, offender; ~ **de muerte** prisoner condemned to death.

reojo [re'oxo]: **de** ~ ad out of the corner of one's eye.

reparación [repara'θjon] nf (acto) mending, repairing; (TEC) repair; (fig) amends, reparation.

reparar [repa'rar] vt to repair; (fig) to make amends for; (observar) to observe // vi: ~ **en** (darse cuenta de) to notice; (prestar atención a) to pay attention to.

reparo [re'paro] nm (advertencia) observation; (duda) doubt; (dificultad) difficulty; **poner** ~**s (a)** to raise objections (to).

repartición [reparti'θjon] nf distribution; (división) division; **repartidor, a** nm/f distributor.

repartir [repar'tir] vt to distribute, share out; (CORREOS) to deliver; **reparto** nm distribution; delivery; (TEATRO, CINE) cast; (AM: urbanización) housing estate (Brit), real estate development (US).

repasar [repa'sar] vt (ESCOL) to revise; (MECÁNICA) to check, overhaul; (COSTURA) to mend; **repaso** nm revision; overhaul; checkup; mending.

repatriar [repa'trjar] vt to repatriate.

repecho [re'petʃo] nm steep incline.

repelente [repe'lente] a repellent, repulsive.

repeler [repe'ler] vt to repel.

repensar [repen'sar] vt to reconsider.

repente [re'pente] nm: **de** ~ suddenly; ~ **de ira** fit of anger.

repentino, a [repen'tino, a] a sudden.

repercusión [reperku'sjon] nf repercussion.

repercutir [reperku'tir] vi (objeto) to rebound; (sonido) to echo; ~ **en** (fig) to have repercussions on.

repertorio [reper'torjo] nm list; (TEATRO) repertoire.

repetición [repeti'θjon] nf repetition.

repetir [repe'tir] vt to repeat; (plato) to have a second helping of // vi to repeat; (sabor) to come back; ~**se** vr (volver sobre un tema) to repeat o.s.

repicar [repi'kar] vt (campanas) to ring.

repique [re'pike] nm pealing, ringing; ~**teo** nm pealing; (de tambor) drumming.

repisa [re'pisa] nf ledge, shelf; (de ventana) windowsill; ~ **de chimenea** mantelpiece.

repito etc vb ver **repetir**.

replegarse [reple'varse] vr to fall back, retreat.

repleto, a [re'pleto, a] a replete, full up.

réplica ['replika] nf answer; (ARTE) replica.

replicar [repli'kar] vi to answer; (objetar) to argue, answer back.

repliegue [re'pljeve] nm (MIL) withdrawal.

repoblación [repoβla'θjon] nf repopulation; (de río) restocking; ~ **forestal** reafforestation.

repoblar [repo'βlar] vt to repopulate; (con árboles) to reafforest.

repollo [re'poʎo] nm cabbage.

reponer [repo'ner] vt to replace, put back; (TEATRO) to revive; ~**se** vr to recover; ~ **que** to reply that.

reportaje [repor'taxe] nm report, article.

reportero, a [repor'tero, a] nm/f reporter.

reposacabezas [reposaka'βeθas] nm inv headrest.

reposado, a [repo'saðo, a] a (descansado) restful; (tranquilo) calm.

reposar [repo'sar] vi to rest, repose.

reposición [reposi'θjon] nf replacement; (CINE) remake.

reposo [re'poso] nm rest.

repostar [repos'tar] vt to replenish; (AUTO) to fill up (with petrol (Brit) o gasoline (US)).

repostería [reposte'ria] nf confectioner's (shop); **repostero**, a nm/f confectioner.

reprender [repren'der] vt to reprimand.

represa [re'presa] nf dam; (lago artificial) lake, pool.

represalia [repre'salja] nf reprisal.

representación [representaθjon] nf representation; (TEATRO) performance; **representante** nm/f representative; performer.

representar [represen'tar] vt to represent; (TEATRO) to perform; (edad) to look; ~se vr to imagine; **representativo, a** a representative.

represión [repre'sjon] nf repression.

reprimenda [repri'menda] nf reprimand, rebuke.

reprimir [repri'mir] vt to repress.

reprobar [repro'βar] vt to censure, reprove.

réprobo, a ['reproβo, a] nm/f reprobate.

reprochar [repro'tʃar] vt to reproach; **reproche** nm reproach.

reproducción [reproðuk'θjon] nf reproduction.

reproducir [reproðu'θir] vt to reproduce; ~se vr to breed; (situación) to recur.

reproductor, a [reproðuk'tor, a] a reproductive.

reptil [rep'til] nm reptile.

república [re'puβlika] nf republic; **republicano, a** a, nm/f republican.

repudiar [repu'ðjar] vt to repudiate; (fe) to renounce; **repudio** nm repudiation.

repuesto [re'pwesto] nm (pieza de recambio) spare (part); (abastecimiento) supply; **rueda de** ~ spare wheel.

repugnancia [repux'nanθja] nf repugnance; **repugnante** a repugnant, repulsive.

repugnar [repux'nar] vt to disgust.

repujar [repu'xar] vt to emboss.

repulsa [re'pulsa] nf rebuff.

repulsión [repul'sjon] nf repulsion, aversion; **repulsivo, a** a repulsive.

reputación [reputa'θjon] nf reputation.

reputar [repu'tar] vt to consider, deem.

requemado, a [reke'maðo, a] a (quemado) scorched; (bronceado) tanned.

requerimiento [rekeri'mjento] nm request; (JUR) summons.

requerir [reke'rir] vt (pedir) to ask, request; (exigir) to require; (llamar) to send for, summon.

requesón [reke'son] nm cottage cheese.

requete... [rekete] pref extremely.

réquiem ['rekjem] (pl ~s) nm requiem.

requisa [re'kisa] nf (inspección) survey, inspection; (MIL) requisition.

requisito [reki'sito] nm requirement, requisite.

res [res] nf beast, animal.

resabido, a [resa'βiðo, a] a: **tener algo sabido y** ~ to know sth perfectly well.

resabio [re'saβjo] nm (maña) vice, bad habit; (dejo) (unpleasant) aftertaste.

resaca [re'saka] nf (en el mar) undertow, undercurrent; (fig) backlash; (fam) hangover.

resalado, a [resa'laðo, a] a (fam) lively.

resaltar [resal'tar] vi to project, stick out; (fig) to stand out.

resarcir [resar'θir] vt to compensate; ~se vr to make up for.

resbaladizo, a [resβala'ðiθo, a] a slippery.

resbalar [resβa'lar] vi, **resbalarse** vr to slip, slide; (fig) to slip (up); **resbalón** nm (acción) slip.

rescatar [reska'tar] vt (salvar) to save, rescue; (objeto) to get back, recover; (cautivos) to ransom.

rescate [res'kate] nm rescue; (objeto) recovery; **pagar un** ~ to pay a ransom.

rescindir [resθin'dir] vt to rescind.

rescisión [resθi'sjon] nf cancellation.

rescoldo [res'koldo] nm embers pl.

resecar [rese'kar] vt to dry thoroughly; (MED) to cut out, remove; ~se vr to dry up.

reseco, a [re'seko, a] a very dry; (fig) skinny.

resentido, a [resen'tiðo, a] a resentful.

resentimiento [resenti'mjento] nm resentment, bitterness.

resentirse [resen'tirse] vr (debilitarse: persona) to suffer; ~ de (consecuencias) to feel the effects of; ~ de (o por) algo to resent sth, be bitter about sth.

reseña [re'seɲa] nf (cuenta) account; (informe) report; (LITERATURA) review.

reseñar [rese'ɲar] vt to describe; (LITERATURA) to review.

reserva [re'serβa] nf reserve; (reservación) reservation; a ~ de que ... unless ...; con toda ~ in strictest confidence.

reservado, a [reser'βaðo, a] a reserved; (retraído) cold, distant // nm private room.

reservar [reser'βar] vt (guardar) to keep; (habitación, entrada) to reserve; ~se vr to save o.s.; (callar) to keep to o.s.

resfriado [resfri'aðo] nm cold; **resfriarse** vr to cool; (MED) to catch (a) cold.

resguardar [resɣwar'ðar] vt to protect, shield; ~se vr: ~se de to guard against; **resguardo** nm defence; (vale) voucher; (recibo) receipt, slip.

residencia [resi'ðenθja] nf residence; ~l nf (urbanización) housing estate.

residente [resi'ðente] a, nm/f resident.

residir [resi'ðir] vi to reside, live; ~ en to reside in, lie in.

residuo [re'siðwo] nm residue.

resignación [resiɣna'θjon] nf resignation; **resignarse** vr: **resignarse**

a o con to resign o.s. to, be resigned to.

resina [re'sina] nf resin.

resistencia [resis'tenθja] nf (dureza) endurance, strength; (oposición, ELEC) resistance; **resistente** a strong, hardy; resistant.

resistir [resis'tir] vt (soportar) to bear; (oponerse a) to resist, oppose; (aguantar) to put up with // vi to resist; (aguantar) to last, endure; ~se vr: ~se a to refuse to, resist.

resma ['resma] nf ream.

resol [re'sol] nm glare of the sun.

resolución [resolu'θjon] nf resolution; (decisión) decision; **resoluto, a** a resolute.

resolver [resol'βer] vt to resolve; (solucionar) to solve, resolve; (decidir) to decide, settle; ~se vr to make up one's mind.

resollar [reso'ʎar] vi to breathe noisily, wheeze.

resonancia [reso'nanθja] nf (del sonido) resonance; (repercusión) repercussion; **resonante** a resonant, resounding; (fig) tremendous.

resonar [reso'nar] vi to ring, echo.

resoplar [reso'plar] vi to snort; **resoplido** nm heavy breathing.

resorte [re'sorte] nm spring; (fig) lever.

respaldar [respal'dar] vt to back (up), support; ~se vr to lean back; ~se con o en (fig) to take one's stand on; **respaldo** nm (de sillón) back; (fig) support, backing.

respectivo, a [respek'tiβo, a] a respective; en lo ~ a with regard to.

respecto [res'pekto] nm: al ~ on this matter; con ~ a, ~ de with regard to, in relation to.

respetable [respe'taβle] a respectable.

respetar [respe'tar] vt to respect; **respeto** nm respect; (acatamiento) deference; **respetos** nmpl respects; **respetuoso, a** a respectful.

respingar [respin'gar] vi to shy; **respingo** nm start, jump.

respiración [respira'θjon] *nf* breathing; (MED) respiration; (ventilación) ventilation.

respirar [respi'rar] *vi* to breathe; **respiratorio, a** *a* respiratory; **respiro** *nm* breathing; (fig: descanso) respite.

resplandecer [resplande'θer] *vi* to shine; **resplandeciente** *a* resplendent, shining; **resplandor** *nm* brilliance, brightness; (de luz, fuego) blaze.

responder [respon'der] *vt* to answer // *vi* to answer; (fig) to respond; (pey) to answer back; ~ **de** *o* **por** to answer for; **respondón, ona** *a* cheeky.

responsabilidad, [responsaβili'ðað] *nf* responsibility.

responsabilizarse [responsaβili-'θarse] *vr* to make o.s. responsible, take charge.

responsable [respon'saβle] *a* responsible.

respuesta [res'pwesta] *nf* answer, reply.

resquebrajar [reskeβra'xar] *vt*, **resquebrajarse** *vr* to crack, split.

resquemor [reske'mor] *nm* resentment.

resquicio [res'kiθjo] *nm* chink; (hendedura) crack.

restablecer [restaβle'θer] *vt* to re-establish, restore; ~**se** *vr* to recover.

restallar [resta'ʎar] *vi* to crack.

restante [res'tante] *a* remaining; **lo** ~ the remainder.

restar [res'tar] *vt* (MAT) to subtract; (fig) to take away // *vi* to remain, be left.

restauración [restaura'θjon] *nf* restoration.

restaurante [restau'rante] *nm* restaurant.

restaurar [restau'rar] *vt* to restore.

restitución [restitu'θjon] *nf* return, restitution.

restituir [restitu'ir] *vt* (devolver) to return, give back; (rehabilitar) to restore.

resto ['resto] *nm* (residuo) rest, remainder; (apuesta) stake; ~**s** *nmpl* remains.

restregar [restre'ɣar] *vt* to scrub, rub.

restricción [restrik'θjon] *nf* restriction.

restrictivo, a [restrik'tiβo, a] *a* restrictive.

restringir [restrin'xir] *vt* to restrict, limit.

resucitar [resuθi'tar] *vt*, *vi* to resuscitate, revive.

resuelto, a *pp de* **resolver** // [re'swelto, a] *a* resolute, determined.

resuello [re'sweʎo] *nm* (aliento) breath; **estar sin** ~ to be breathless.

resultado [resul'taðo] *nm* result; (conclusión) outcome; **resultante** *a* resulting, resultant.

resultar [resul'tar] *vi* (ser) to be; (llegar a ser) to turn out to be; (salir bien) to turn out well; (COM) to amount to; ~ **de** to stem from; **me resulta difícil hacerlo** it's difficult for me to do it.

resumen [re'sumen] (*pl* **resúmenes**) *nm* summary, résumé; **en** ~ in short.

resumir [resu'mir] *vt* to sum up; (cortar) to abridge, cut down; (condensar) to summarize.

resurgir [resur'xir] *vi* (reaparecer) to reappear.

resurrección [resurre(k)'θjon] *nf* resurrection.

retablo [re'taβlo] *nm* altarpiece.

retaguardia [reta'ɣwarðja] *nf* rearguard.

retahíla [reta'ila] *nf* series, string.

retal [re'tal] *nm* remnant.

retar [re'tar] *vt* to challenge; (desafiar) to defy, dare.

retardar [retar'ðar] *vt* (demorar) to delay; (hacer más lento) to slow down; (retener) to hold back; **retardo** *nm* delay.

retazo [re'taθo] *nm* snippet (Brit), fragment.

rete... [rete] *pref* very, extremely.

retener [rete'ner] *vt* (*intereses*) to withhold.

retina [re'tina] *nf* retina.

retintín [retin'tin] *nm* jangle, jingle.

retirada [reti'raða] *nf* (*MIL, refugio*) retreat; (*de dinero*) withdrawal; (*de embajador*) recall; **retirado, a** *a* (*lugar*) remote; (*vida*) quiet; (*jubilado*) retired.

retirar [reti'rar] *vt* to withdraw; (*quitar*) to remove; (*jubilar*) to retire, pension off; **~se** *vr* to retreat, withdraw; to retire; (*acostarse*) to retire, go to bed; **retiro** *nm* retreat; retirement; (*pago*) pension.

reto ['reto] *nm* dare, challenge.

retocar [reto'kar] *vt* (*fotografía*) to touch up, retouch.

retoño [re'toɲo] *nm* sprout, shoot; (*fig*) offspring, child.

retoque [re'toke] *nm* retouching.

retorcer [retor'θer] *vt* to twist; (*manos, lavado*) to wring; **~se** *vr* to become twisted; (*mover el cuerpo*) to writhe.

retorcimiento [retorθi'mjento] *nm* twist, twisting.

retórica [re'torika] *nf* rhetoric; (*pey*) affectedness.

retornar [retor'nar] *vt* to return, give back // *vi* to return, go/come back; **retorno** *nm* return.

retortijón [retorti'xon] *nm* twist, twisting.

retozar [reto'θar] *vi* (*juguetear*) to frolic, romp; (*saltar*) to gambol; **retozón, ona** *a* playful.

retracción [retrak'θjon] *nf* retraction.

retractarse [retrak'tarse] *vr* to retract; **me retracto** I take that back.

retraerse [retra'erse] *vr* to withdraw; **retraído, a** *a* shy, retiring; **retraimiento** *nm* retirement; (*timidez*) shyness.

retransmisión [retransmi'sjon] *nf* repeat (broadcast).

retransmitir [retransmi'tir] *vt* (*mensaje*) to relay; (*TV etc*) to repeat, retransmit; (: *en vivo*) to broadcast live.

retrasado, a [retra'saðo, a] *a* late; (*MED*) mentally retarded; (*país etc*) backward, underdeveloped.

retrasar [retra'sar] *vt* (*demorar*) to postpone, put off; (*retardar*) to slow down // *vi*, **~se** *vr* (*atrasarse*) to be late; (*reloj*) to be slow; (*producción*) to fall (away); (*quedarse atrás*) to lag behind.

retraso [re'traso] *nm* (*demora*) delay; (*lentitud*) slowness; (*tardanza*) lateness; (*atraso*) backwardness; **~s** *nmpl* arrears; **llegar con ~** to arrive late; **~ mental** mental deficiency.

retratar [retra'tar] *vt* (*ARTE*) to paint the portrait of; (*fotografiar*) to photograph; (*fig*) to depict, describe; **~se** *vr* to have one's portrait painted; to have one's photograph taken; **retrato** *nm* portrait; (*fig*) likeness; **retrato-robot** *nm* identikit picture.

retreta [re'treta] *nf* retreat.

retrete [re'trete] *nm* toilet.

retribución [retriβu'θjon] *nf* (*recompensa*) reward; (*pago*) pay, payment.

retribuir [retri'βwir] *vt* (*recompensar*) to reward; (*pagar*) to pay.

retro... [retro] *pref* retro... .

retroactivo, a [retroak'tiβo, a] *a* retroactive, retrospective.

retroceder [retroθe'ðer] *vi* (*echarse atrás*) to move back(wards); (*fig*) to back down.

retroceso [retro'θeso] *nm* backward movement; (*MED*) relapse; (*fig*) backing down.

retrógrado, a [re'troɣraðo, a] *a* retrograde, retrogressive; (*POL*) reactionary.

retropropulsión [retropropul'sjon] *nf* jet propulsion.

retrospectivo, a [retrospek'tiβo, a] *a* retrospective.

retrovisor [retroβi'sor] *nm* rear-view mirror.

retumbar [retum'bar] *vi* to echo, resound.

reuma ['reuma], **reumatismo** [reuma'tismo] *nm* rheumatism.

reunificar [reunifi'kar] *vt* to reunify.

reunión [reu'njon] *nf* (*asamblea*) meeting; (*fiesta*) party.

reunir [reu'nir] *vt* (*juntar*) to reunite, join (together); (*recoger*) to gather (together); (*personas*) to bring together; (*cualidades*) to combine; ~se *vr* (*personas: en asamblea*) to meet, gather.

revalidar [reβali'ðar] *vt* (*ratificar*) to confirm, ratify.

revalorar [reβalo'rar], **revalorizar** [reβalori'θar] *vt* to revalue, reassess.

revancha [re'βantʃa] *nf* revenge.

revelación [reβela'θjon] *nf* revelation.

revelado [reβe'laðo] *nm* developing.

revelar [reβe'lar] *vt* to reveal; (*FOTO*) to develop.

reventar [reβen'tar] *vt* to burst, explode.

reventón [reβen'ton] *nm* (*AUTO*) blow-out (*Brit*), flat (*US*).

reverberación [reβerβera'θjon] *nf* reverberation.

reverberar [reβerβe'rar] *vi* to reverberate.

reverencia [reβe'renθja] *nf* reverence; **reverenciar** *vt* to revere.

reverendo, a [reβe'rendo, a] *a* reverend.

reverente [reβe'rente] *a* reverent.

reverso [re'βerso] *nm* back, other side; (*de moneda*) reverse.

revertir [reβer'tir] *vi* to revert.

revés [re'βes] *nm* back, wrong side; (*fig*) reverse, setback; (*DEPORTE*) backhand; **al** ~ the wrong way round; (*de arriba abajo*) upside down; (*ropa*) inside out; **volver algo al** ~ to turn sth round; (*ropa*) to turn sth inside out.

revestir [reβes'tir] *vt* (*poner*) to put on; (*cubrir*) to cover, coat; ~ **con** o **de** to invest with.

revisar [reβi'sar] *vt* (*examinar*) to check; (*texto etc*) to revise; **revisión** *nf* revision.

revisor, a [reβi'sor, a] *nm/f* inspector; (*FERRO*) ticket collector.

revista [re'βista] *nf* magazine, review; (*TEATRO*) revue; (*inspección*) inspection; **pasar** ~ a to review, inspect.

revivir [reβi'βir] *vi* to revive.

revocación [reβoka'θjon] *nf* repeal.

revocar [reβo'kar] *vt* to revoke.

revolcarse [reβol'karse] *vr* to roll about.

revolotear [reβolote'ar] *vi* to flutter.

revoltijo [reβol'tixo] *nm* mess, jumble.

revoltoso, a [reβol'toso, a] *a* (*travieso*) naughty, unruly.

revolución [reβolu'θjon] *nf* revolution; **revolucionar** *vt* to revolutionize; **revolucionario, a** *a* revolutionary.

revolver [reβol'βer] *vt* (*desordenar*) to disturb, mess up; (*mover*) to move about; (*POL*) to stir up // *vi*: ~ **en** to go through, rummage (about) in; ~se *vr* (*volver contra*) to turn on o against.

revólver [re'βolβer] *nm* revolver.

revuelo [re'βwelo] *nm* fluttering; (*fig*) commotion.

revuelto, a [re'βwelto, a] *pp de* **revolver** // *a* (*mezclado*) mixed-up, in disorder // *a* (*motín*) revolt; (*agitación*) commotion.

revulsivo [reβul'siβo] *nm* enema.

rey [rei] *nm* king; **Día de R~es** Epiphany.

reyerta [re'jerta] *nf* quarrel, brawl.

rezagado, a [reθa'ɣaðo, a] *nm/f* straggler.

rezagar [reθa'ɣar] *vt* (*dejar atrás*) to leave behind; (*retrasar*) to delay, postpone.

rezar [re'θar] *vi* to pray; ~ **con** (*fam*) to concern, have to do with; **rezo** *nm* prayer.

rezongar [reθon'gar] *vi* to grumble.

rezumar [reθu'mar] *vt* to ooze.

ría ['ria] *nf* estuary.

riada [ri'aða] *nf* flood.

ribera [ri'βera] *nf* (*de río*) bank;

(: *área*) riverside.

ribete [ri'βete] *nm* (*de vestido*) border; (*fig*) addition; **~ar** *vt* to edge, border.

ricino [ri'θino] *nm*: **aceite de ~** castor oil.

rico, a ['riko, a] *a* rich; (*adinerado*) wealthy, rich; (*lujoso*) luxurious; (*comida*) delicious; (*niño*) lovely, cute // *nm/f* rich person.

rictus ['riktus] *nm* (*mueca*) sneer, grin.

ridiculez [riðiku'leθ] *nf* absurdity.

ridiculizar [riðikuli'θar] *vt* to ridicule.

ridículo, a [ri'ðikulo, a] *a* ridiculous; **hacer el ~** to make a fool of o.s.; **poner a uno en ~** to make a fool of sb.

riego ['rjeγo] *nm* (*aspersión*) watering; (*irrigación*) irrigation.

riel [rjel] *nm* rail.

rienda ['rjenda] *nf* rein; **dar ~ suelta a** to give free rein to.

riesgo ['rjesγo] *nm* risk; **correr el ~ de** to run the risk of.

rifa ['rifa] *nf* (*lotería*) raffle; **rifar** *vt* to raffle.

rifle ['rifle] *nm* rifle.

rigidez [rixi'ðeθ] *nf* rigidity, stiffness; (*fig*) strictness; **rígido, a** *a* rigid, stiff; strict, inflexible.

rigor [ri'γor] *nm* strictness, rigour; (*inclemencia*) harshness; **de ~** de rigueur, essential; **riguroso, a** *a* rigorous; harsh; (*severo*) severe.

rimar [ri'mar] *vi* to rhyme.

rimbombante [rimbom'bante] *a* (*fig*) pompous.

rímel, rímmel ['rimel] *nm* mascara.

rincón [rin'kon] *nm* corner (*inside*).

rinoceronte [rinoθe'ronte] *nm* rhinoceros.

riña ['rina] *nf* (*disputa*) argument; (*pelea*) brawl.

riñón [ri'non] *nm* kidney; **tener riñones** to have guts.

río *etc vb ver* **reír** // ['rio] *nm* river; (*fig*) torrent, stream; **~ abajo/arriba** downstream/upstream; **~ de**

la **Plata** River Plate.

rioja [ri'oxa] *nm* (*vino*) rioja (wine).

rioplatense [riopla'tense] *a* of o from the River Plate region.

riqueza [ri'keθa] *nf* wealth, riches *pl*; (*cualidad*) richness.

risa ['risa] *nf* laughter; (*una ~*) laugh; **¡qué ~!** what a laugh!

risco ['risko] *nm* crag, cliff.

risible [ri'siβle] *a* ludicrous, laughable.

risotada [riso'taða] *nf* guffaw, loud laugh.

ristra ['ristra] *nf* string.

risueño, a [ri'sweno, a] *a* (*sonriente*) smiling; (*contento*) cheerful.

ritmo ['ritmo] *nm* rhythm; **a ~ lento** slowly; **trabajar a ~ lento** to go slow.

rito ['rito] *nm* rite.

ritual [ri'twal] *a, nm* ritual.

rival [ri'βal] *a, nm/f* rival; **~idad** *nf* rivalry; **~izar** *vi*: **~izar con** to rival, vie with.

rizado, a [ri'θaðo, a] *a* curly // *nm* curls *pl*.

rizar [ri'θar] *vt* to curl; **~se** *vr* (*pelo*) to curl; (*agua*) to ripple; **rizo** *nm* curl; ripple.

RNE *nf abr* = **Radio Nacional de España.**

robar [ro'βar] *vt* to rob; (*objeto*) to steal; (*casa etc*) to break into; (*NAIPES*) to draw.

roble ['roβle] *nm* oak; **~do, ~dal** *nm* oakwood.

robo ['roβo] *nm* robbery, theft.

robot [ro'βot] *nm* robot; **~ (de cocina)** food processor.

robustecer [roβuste'θer] *vt* to strengthen.

robusto, a [ro'βusto, a] *a* robust, strong.

roca ['roka] *nf* rock.

rocalla [ro'kaʎa] *nf* pebbles *pl*.

roce ['roθe] *nm* (*caricia*) brush; (*TEC*) friction; (*en la piel*) graze; **tener ~ con** to be in close contact with.

rociar [ro'θjar] *vt* to spray.

rocín [ro'θin] *nm* nag, hack.

rocío [ro'θio] *nm* dew.

rocoso, a [ro'koso, a] *a* rocky.

rodado, a [ro'ðaðo, a] *a* (*con ruedas*) wheeled // *nf* rut.

rodaja [ro'ðaxa] *nf* (*raja*) slice.

rodaje [ro'ðaxe] *nm* (*CINE*) shooting, filming; (*AUTO*): **en ~** running in.

rodar [ro'ðar] *vt* (*vehículo*) to roll (along); (*escalera*) to roll down; (*viajar por*) to travel (over) // *vi* to roll; (*coche*) to go, run; (*CINE*) to shoot, film.

rodear [roðe'ar] *vt* to surround // *vi* to go round; **~se** *vr*: **~se de amigos** to surround o.s. with friends.

rodeo [ro'ðeo] *nm* (*ruta indirecta*) detour; (*evasión*) evasion; (*AM*) rodeo; **hablar sin ~s** to come to the point, speak plainly.

rodilla [ro'ðiʎa] *nf* knee; **de ~s** kneeling; **ponerse de ~s** to kneel (down).

rodillo [ro'ðiʎo] *nm* roller; (*CULIN*) rolling-pin.

rododendro [roðo'ðendro] *nm* rhododendron.

roedor, a [roe'ðor, a] *a* gnawing // *nm* rodent.

roer [ro'er] *vt* (*masticar*) to gnaw; (*corroer, fig*) to corrode.

rogar [ro'γar] *vt, vi* (*pedir*) to ask for; (*suplicar*) to beg, plead; **se ruega no fumar** please do not smoke.

rojizo, a [ro'xiθo, a] *a* reddish.

rojo, a ['roxo, a] *a, nm* red; **al ~ vivo** red-hot.

rol [rol] *nm* list, roll; (*AM: papel*) role.

rollizo, a [ro'ʎiθo, a] *a* (*objeto*) cylindrical; (*persona*) plump.

rollo ['roʎo] *nm* roll; (*de cuerda*) coil; (*madera*) log; (*fam*) bore; **¡qué ~!** what a carry-on!

ROM [rom] *nf abr* (= *memoria de sólo lectura*) ROM.

Roma ['roma] *n* Rome.

romance [ro'manθe] *nm* (*idioma castellano*) Romance language; (*LITERATURA*) ballad; **hablar en ~** to speak plainly.

romanticismo [romanti'θismo] *nm* romanticism.

romántico, a [ro'mantiko, a] *a* romantic.

romería [rome'ria] *nf* (*REL*) pilgrimage; (*excursión*) trip, outing.

romero, a [ro'mero, a] *nm/f* pilgrim // *nm* rosemary.

romo, a ['romo, a] *a* blunt; (*fig*) dull.

rompecabezas [rompeka'βeθas] *nm inv* riddle, puzzle; (*juego*) jigsaw (puzzle).

rompehuelgas [rompe'welγas] *nm inv* strikebreaker, blackleg.

rompeolas [rompe'olas] *nm inv* breakwater.

romper [rom'per] *vt* to break; (*hacer pedazos*) to smash; (*papel, tela etc*) to tear, rip // *vi* (*olas*) to break; (*sol, diente*) to break through; **~ un contrato** to break a contract; **~ a** to start (suddenly) to; **~ a llorar** to burst into tears; **~ con uno** to fall out with sb.

rompimiento [rompi'mjento] *nm* (*acto*) breaking; (*fig*) break; (*quiebra*) crack.

ron [ron] *nm* rum.

roncar [ron'kar] *vi* to snore.

ronco, a ['ronko, a] *a* (*afónico*) hoarse; (*áspero*) raucous.

roncha ['rontʃa] *nf* weal; (*contusión*) bruise.

ronda ['ronda] *nf* (*gen*) round; (*patrulla*) patrol; **rondar** *vt* to patrol // *vi* to patrol; (*fig*) to prowl round.

ronquido [ron'kiðo] *nm* snore, snoring.

ronronear [ronrone'ar] *vi* to purr; **ronroneo** *nm* purr.

roña ['rona] *nf* (*VETERINARIA*) mange; (*mugre*) dirt, grime; (*óxido*) rust.

roñoso, a [ro'noso, a] *a* (*mugriento*) filthy; (*tacaño*) mean.

ropa ['ropa] *nf* clothes *pl*, clothing; **~**

blanca linen; ~ **de cama** bed linen; ~ **interior** underwear; ~ **para lavar** washing; ~**je** *nm* gown, robes *pl*; ~**vejero, a** *nm/f* second-hand clothes dealer.

ropero [ro'pero] *nm* linen cupboard; (*guardarropa*) wardrobe.

rosa ['rosa] *a inv* pink // *nf* rose; (*ANAT*) red birthmark; ~ **de los vientos** the compass.

rosado, a [ro'saðo, a] *a* pink // *nm* rosé.

rosal [ro'sal] *nm* rosebush.

rosario [ro'sarjo] *nm* (*REL*) rosary; **rezar el** ~ to say the rosary.

rosca ['roska] *nf* (*de tornillo*) thread; (*de humo*) coil, spiral; (*pan, postre*) ring-shaped roll/pastry.

rosetón [rose'ton] *nm* rosette; (*ARQ*) rose window.

rosquilla [ros'kiʎa] *nf* doughnut-shaped fritter.

rostro ['rostro] *nm* (*cara*) face.

rotación [rota'θjon] *nf* rotation; ~ **de cultivos** crop rotation.

rotativo, a [rota'tiβo, a] *a* rotary.

roto, a *pp de* **romper** // ['roto, a] *a* broken.

rótula ['rotula] *nf* kneecap; (*TEC*) ball-and-socket joint.

rotulador [rotula'ðor] *nm* felt-tip pen.

rotular [rotu'lar] *vt* (*carta, documento*) to head, entitle; (*objeto*) to label; **rótulo** *nm* heading, title; label; (*letrero*) sign.

rotundo, a [ro'tundo, a] *a* round; (*enfático*) emphatic.

rotura [ro'tura] *nf* (*rompimiento*) breaking; (*MED*) fracture.

roturar [rotu'rar] *vt* to plough.

rozadura [roθa'ðura] *nf* abrasion, graze.

rozar [ro'θar] *vt* (*frotar*) to rub; (*arañar*) to scratch; (*tocar ligeramente*) to shave, touch lightly; ~**se** *vr* to rub (together); ~**se con** (*fam*) to rub shoulders with.

r.p.m. *abr* (= *revoluciones por minuto*) rpm.

rte. *abr* (= *remite, remitente*) sender.

RTVE *nf abr* = **Radiotelevisión Española.**

rubí [ru'βi] *nm* ruby; (*de reloj*) jewel.

rubicundo, a [ruβi'kundo, a] *a* ruddy.

rubio, a ['ruβjo, a] *a* fair-haired, blond(e) // *nm/f* blond/blonde; **tabaco** ~ Virginia tobacco.

rubor [ru'βor] *nm* (*sonrojo*) blush; (*timidez*) bashfulness; ~**izarse** *vr* to blush; ~**oso, a** *a* blushing.

rúbrica ['ruβrika] *nf* (*título*) title, heading; (*de la firma*) flourish; **rubricar** *vt* (*firmar*) to sign with a flourish; (*concluir*) to sign and seal.

rudeza [ru'ðeθa] *nf* (*tosquedad*) coarseness; (*sencillez*) simplicity.

rudimento [ruði'mento] *nm* rudiment.

rudo, a ['ruðo, a] *a* (*sin pulir*) unpolished; (*grosero*) coarse; (*violento*) violent; (*sencillo*) simple.

rueda ['rweða] *nf* wheel; (*círculo*) ring, circle; (*rodaja*) slice, round; ~ **delantera/trasera/de repuesto** front/back/spare wheel; ~ **de prensa** press conference.

ruedo [rweðo] *nm* (*contorno*) edge, border; (*de vestido*) hem; (*círculo*) circle; (*TAUR*) arena, bullring.

ruego *etc vb ver* **rogar** // ['rweɣo] *nm* request.

rufián [ru'fjan] *nm* scoundrel.

rugby ['ruxβi] *nm* rugby.

rugido [ru'xiðo] *nm* roar.

rugir [ru'xir] *vi* to roar.

rugoso, a [ru'xoso, a] *a* (*arrugado*) wrinkled; (*áspero*) rough; (*desigual*) ridged.

ruibarbo [rui'βarβo] *nm* rhubarb.

ruido ['rwiðo] *nm* noise; (*sonido*) sound; (*alboroto*) racket, row; (*escándalo*) commotion, rumpus; ~**so, a** *a* noisy, loud; (*fig*) sensational.

ruin [rwin] *a* contemptible, mean.

ruina [ˈrwina] *nf* ruin; (*colapso*) collapse; (*de persona*) ruin, downfall.

ruindad [rwin'daθ] *nf* lowness, meanness; *(acto)* low o mean act.

ruinoso, a [rwi'noso, a] *a* ruinous; *(destartalado)* dilapidated, tumble-down; *(COM)* disastrous.

ruiseñor [rwise'nor] *nm* nightingale.

rula ['rula], **ruleta** [ru'leta] *nf* roulette.

rulo ['rulo] *nm (para el pelo)* curler.

rulota [ru'lota] *nf* caravan *(Brit)*, trailer *(US)*.

Rumania [ru'manja] *nf* Rumania.

rumba ['rumba] *nf* rumba.

rumbo ['rumbo] *nm (ruta)* route, direction; *(ángulo de dirección)* course, bearing; *(fig)* course of events: **ir con ~** a to be heading for.

rumboso, a [rum'boso, a] *a (generoso)* generous.

rumiante [ru'mjante] *nm* ruminant.

rumiar [ru'mjar] *vt* to chew; *(fig)* to chew over // *vi* to chew the cud.

rumor [ru'mor] *nm (ruido sordo)* low sound; *(murmuración)* murmur, buzz; **rumorearse** *vr*: **se rumorea que** it is rumoured that.

runrún [run'run] *nm (voces)* murmur, sound of voices; *(fig)* rumour.

rupestre [ru'pestre] *a* rock *cpd.*

ruptura [rup'tura] *nf* rupture.

rural [ru'ral] *a* rural.

Rusia ['rusja] *nf* Russia; **ruso, a** *a, nm/f* Russian.

rústico, a ['rustiko, a] *a* rustic; *(ordinario)* coarse, uncouth // *nm/f* yokel // *nf*: **libro en rústica** paperback.

ruta ['ruta] *nf* route.

rutina [ru'tina] *nf* routine; **~rio, a** *a* routine.

S

S *abr* (= **santo, a**) St; (= **sur**) S.

s. *abr* (= **siglo**) C.; (= **siguiente**) foll.

S.A. *abr* (= **Sociedad Anónima**) Ltd *(Brit)*, Inc *(US)*.

sábado ['saβaðo] *nm* Saturday.

---

sábana ['saβana] *nf* sheet.

sabandija [saβan'dixa] *nf* bug, insect.

sabañón [saβa'non] *nm* chilblain.

sabelotodo [saβelo'toðo] *nm/f inv* know-all.

saber [sa'βer] *vt* to know; *(llegar a conocer)* to find out, learn; *(tener capacidad de)* to know how to // *vi*: **~ a** to taste of, taste like // *nm* knowledge, learning; **a ~** namely; **¿sabes conducir/nadar?** can you drive/swim?; **¿sabes francés?** do you speak French?; **~ de memoria** to know by heart; **hacer ~ algo a uno** to inform sb of sth, let sb know sth.

sabiduría [saβiðu'ria] *nf (conocimientos)* wisdom; *(instrucción)* learning.

sabiendas [sa'βjendas]: **a ~** *ad* knowingly.

sabio, a ['saβjo,a] *a (docto)* learned; *(prudente)* wise, sensible.

sabor [sa'βor] *nm* taste, flavour; **~ear** *vt* to taste, savour; *(fig)* to relish.

sabotaje [saβo'taxe] *nm* sabotage.

saboteador, a [saβotea'ðor, a] *nm/f* saboteur.

sabotear [saβote'ar] *vt* to sabotage.

sabré *etc vb ver* **saber**.

sabroso, a [sa'βroso, a] *a (fig: fam)* racy, salty.

sacacorchos [saka'kortʃos] *nm inv* corkscrew.

sacapuntas [saka'puntas] *nm inv* pencil sharpener.

sacar [sa'kar] *vt* to take out; *(fig: extraer)* to get out; *(quitar)* to remove, get out; *(hacer salir)* to bring out; *(conclusión)* to draw; *(novela etc)* to publish, bring out; *(ropa)* to take off; *(obra)* to make; *(premio)* to receive; *(entradas)* to get; *(TENIS)* to serve; **~ adelante** *(niño)* to bring up; *(negocio)* to carry on, go on with; **~ a uno a bailar** to get sb up to dance; **~ una foto** to take a photo; **~ la lengua** to stick out one's tongue; **~ buenas/malas notas** to get good/bad marks.

sacarina [saka'rina] *nf* saccharin(e).

sacerdote [saθer'ðote] *nm* priest.

saco ['sako] *nm* bag; *(grande)* sack; *(su contenido)* bagful; *(AM)* jacket; ~ **de dormir** sleeping bag.

sacramento [sakra'mento] *nm* sacrament.

sacrificar [sakrifi'kar] *vt* to sacrifice; **sacrificio** *nm* sacrifice.

sacrilegio [sakri'lexjo] *nm* sacrilege; **sacrílego, a** *a* sacrilegious.

sacristía [sakris'tia] *nf* sacristy.

sacro, a ['sakro, a] *a* sacred.

sacudida [saku'ðiða] *nf* *(agitación)* shake, shaking; *(sacudimiento)* jolt, bump; ~ **eléctrica** electric shock.

sacudir [saku'ðir] *vt* to shake; *(golpear)* to hit.

sádico, a ['saðiko, a] *a* sadistic // *nm/f* sadist; **sadismo** *nm* sadism.

saeta [sa'eta] *nf* *(flecha)* arrow.

sagacidad [saɣaθi'ðað] *nf* shrewdness, cleverness; **sagaz** *a* shrewd, clever.

sagitario [saxi'tarjo] *nm* Sagittarius.

sagrado, a [sa'ɣraðo, a] *a* sacred, holy.

Sáhara ['saara] *nm*: **el ~ the** Sahara (desert).

sal *vb ver* **salir** // [sal] *nf* salt.

sala ['sala] *nf* *(cuarto grande)* large room; (~ **de estar**) living room; *(TEATRO)* house, auditorium; *(de hospital)* ward; ~ **de apelación** court; ~ **de espera** waiting room; ~ **de estar** living room; ~ **de fiestas** dance hall.

salado, a [sa'laðo, a] *a* salty; *(fig)* witty, amusing; **agua salada** salt water.

salar [sa'lar] *vt* to salt, add salt to.

salarial [sala'rjal] *a* *(aumento, revisión)* wage *cpd*, salary *cpd*.

salario [sa'larjo] *nm* wage, pay.

salchicha [sal'tʃitʃa] *nf* (pork) sausage; **salchichón** *nm* (salami-type) sausage.

saldar [sal'dar] *vt* to pay; *(vender)* to sell off; *(fig)* to settle, resolve; **saldo** *nm* *(pago)* settlement; *(de*

una cuenta) balance; *(lo restante)* remnant(s) *(pl)*, remainder; ~**s** *nmpl (en tienda)* sale.

saldré *etc vb ver* **salir**.

salero [sa'lero] *nm* salt cellar.

salgo *etc vb ver* **salir**.

salida [sa'liða] *nf* *(puerta etc)* exit, way out; *(acto)* leaving, going out; *(de tren, AVIAT)* departure; *(TEC)* output, production; *(fig)* way out; *(COM)* opening; *(GEO, válvula)* outlet; *(de gas)* leak; **calle sin** ~ cul-de-sac; ~ **de incendios** fire escape.

saliente [sa'ljente] *a* *(ARQ)* projecting; *(sol)* rising; *(fig)* outstanding.

salir [sa'lir] ◆ *vi* 1 *(partir: tb:* ~ **de**) to leave; **Juan ha salido Juan** is out; **salió de la cocina** he came out of the kitchen

2 *(aparecer)* to appear; *(disco, libro)* to come out; **anoche salió en la tele** she appeared *o* was on TV last night; **salió en todos los periódicos** it was in all the papers

3 *(resultar)*: **la muchacha nos salió muy trabajadora** the girl turned out to be a very hard worker; **la comida te ha salido exquisita** the food was delicious; **sale muy caro** it's very expensive

4: ~**le a uno algo**: **la entrevista que hice me salió bien/mal** the interview I did went *o* turned out well/badly

5: ~ **adelante**: **no sé como haré para** ~ **adelante** I don't know how I'll get by

◆ ~**se** *vr (líquido)* to spill; *(animal)* to escape.

saliva [sa'liβa] *nf* saliva.

salmo ['salmo] *nm* psalm.

salmón [sal'mon] *nm* salmon.

salmuera [sal'mwera] *nf* pickle, brine.

salón [sa'lon] *nm* *(de casa)* living room, lounge; *(muebles)* lounge suite; ~ **de belleza** beauty parlour;

~ **de baile** dance hall.

salpicadero [salpika'ðero] nm (AUTO) dashboard.

salpicar [salpi'kar] vt (rociar) to sprinkle, spatter; (esparcir) to scatter.

salsa ['salsa] nf sauce; (con carne asada) gravy; (fig) spice.

saltado, a [sal'taðo, a] a (botón etc) missing; (ojos) bulging.

saltamontes [salta'montes] nm inv grasshopper.

saltar [sal'tar] vt to jump (over), leap (over); (dejar de lado) to skip, miss out // vi to jump, leap; (pelota) to bounce; (al aire) to fly up; (quebrarse) to break; (al agua) to dive; (fig) to explode, blow up.

saltear [salte'ar] vt (robar) to rob (in a holdup); (asaltar) to assault, attack; (CULIN) to sauté.

saltimbanqui [saltim'banki] nm/f acrobat.

salto ['salto] nm jump, leap; (al agua) dive; ~ **de agua** waterfall; ~ **de altura** high jump.

saltón, ona [sal'ton, ona] a (ojos) bulging, popping; (dientes) protruding.

salubre [sa'lußre] a healthy, salubrious.

salud [sa'luð] nf health; ¡(a su) ~! cheers!, good health!; ~**able** a (de buena ~) healthy; (provechoso) good, beneficial.

saludar [salu'ðar] vt to greet; (MIL) to salute; **saludo** nm greeting; **saludos** (en carta) best wishes, regards.

salva ['salßa] nf: ~ **de aplausos** ovation.

salvación [salßa'θjon] nf salvation; (rescate) rescue.

salvado [sal'ßaðo] nm bran.

Salvador [salßa'ðor]: **El** ~ El Salvador; **San** ~ San Salvador; **s~eño, a** a, nm/f Salvadorian.

salvaguardar [salßaɣwar'ðar] vt to safeguard.

salvaje [sal'ßaxe] a wild; (tribu) sav-

age; **salvajismo** nm savagery.

salvar [sal'ßar] vt (rescatar) to save, rescue; (resolver) to overcome, resolve; (cubrir distancias) to cover, travel; (hacer excepción) to except, exclude; (un barco) to salvage.

salvavidas [salßa'ßiðas] a inv: bote/chaleco/cinturón ~ lifeboat/life jacket/life belt.

salvia ['salßja] nf sage.

salvo, a ['salßo, a] a safe // ad except (for), save; **a** ~ out of danger; ~ **que** unless; ~**conducto** nm safe-conduct.

san [san] a saint; ~ **Juan** St. John.

sanar [sa'nar] vt (herida) to heal; (persona) to cure // vi (persona) to get well, recover; (herida) to heal.

sanatorio [sana'torjo] nm sanatorium.

sanción [san'θjon] nf sanction; **sancionar** vt to sanction.

sandalia [san'dalja] nf sandal.

sandía [san'dia] nf watermelon.

sandwich ['sandwitʃ] (pl ~**s**, ~**es**) nm sandwich.

saneamiento [sanea'mjento] nm sanitation.

sanear [sane'ar] vt (terreno) to drain.

sangrar [san'grar] vt, vi to bleed; **sangre** nf blood.

sangría [san'gria] nf sangria, sweetened drink of red wine with fruit.

sangriento, a [san'grjento, a] a bloody.

sanguijuela [sangi'xwela] nf (ZOOL, fig) leech.

sanguinario, a [sangi'narjo, a] a bloodthirsty.

sanguíneo, a [san'gineo, a] a blood cpd.

sanidad [sani'ðað] nf sanitation; (calidad de sano) health, healthiness; ~ **pública** public health.

sanitario, a [sani'tarjo, a] a sanitary; (de la salud) health; ~**s** nmpl toilets (Brit), washroom (US).

sano, a ['sano, a] a healthy; (sin daños) sound; (comida) wholesome;

(*entero*) whole, intact; ~ **y salvo** safe and sound.

Santiago [san'tjaɣo] *nm*: ~ (**de Chile**) Santiago.

santiamén [santja'men] *nm*: **en un** ~ in no time at all.

santidad [santi'ðað] *nf* holiness, sanctity; **santificar** *vt* to sanctify, make holy.

santiguarse [santi'ɣwarse] *vr* to make the sign of the cross.

santo, a ['santo, a] *a* holy; wonderful, miraculous // *nm/f* saint // *nm* saint's day; ~ **y seña** password.

santuario [san'twarjo] *nm* sanctuary, shrine.

saña ['saɲa] *nf* rage, fury.

sapo ['sapo] *nm* toad.

saque ['sake] *nm* (*TENIS*) service, serve; (*FÚTBOL*) throw-in; ~ **de esquina** corner (kick).

saquear [sake'ar] *vt* (*MIL*) to sack; (*robar*) to loot, plunder; (*fig*) to ransack; **saqueo** *nm* sacking; looting, plundering; ransacking.

sarampión [saram'pjon] *nm* measles *sg*.

sarcasmo [sar'kasmo] *nm* sarcasm; **sarcástico, a** *a* sarcastic.

sardina [sar'ðina] *nf* sardine.

sardónico, a [sar'ðoniko, a] *a* sardonic; (*irónico*) ironical, sarcastic.

sargento [sar'xento] *nm* sergeant.

sarna ['sarna] *nf* itch; (*MED*) scabies.

sarpullido [sarpu'ʎiðo] *nm* (*MED*) rash.

sartén [sar'ten] *nf* frying pan.

sastre ['sastre] *nm* tailor; ~**ría** *nf* (*arte*) tailoring; (*tienda*) tailor's (shop).

Satanás [sata'nas] *nm* Satan.

satélite [sa'telite] *nm* satellite.

sátira ['satira] *nf* satire.

satisfacción [satisfak'θjon] *nf* satisfaction.

satisfacer [satisfa'θer] *vt* to satisfy; (*gastos*) to meet; (*pérdida*) to make good; ~**se** *vr* to satisfy o.s., be satisfied; (*vengarse*) to take revenge.

satisfecho, a *a* satisfied; (*contento*) content(ed), happy; (*de*: ~ **de sí mismo**) self-satisfied, smug.

saturar [satu'rar] *vt* to saturate.

sauce ['sauθe] *nm* willow; ~ **llorón** weeping willow.

sauna ['sauna] *nf* sauna.

savia ['saβja] *nf* sap.

saxofón [sakso'fon] *nm* saxophone.

sazonado, a [saθo'naðo, a] *a* (*fruta*) ripe; (*CULIN*) flavoured, seasoned.

sazonar [saθo'nar] *vt* to ripen; (*CULIN*) to flavour, season.

scotch [es'kotʃ] *nm* ® adhesive o sticky tape.

PALABRA CLAVE

se [se] *pron* **1** (*reflexivo*: *sg*: *m*) himself; (: *f*) herself; (: *pl*) themselves; (: *cosa*) itself; (: *de Vd*) yourself; (: *de Vds*) yourselves; ~ **está preparando** she's preparing herself; *para usos léxicos del pronombre ver el vb en cuestión, p.ej.* **arrepentirse**

2 (*con complemento indirecto*) to him; to her; to them; to it; to you; a **usted** ~ **lo dije ayer** I told you yesterday; ~ **compró un sombrero** he bought himself a hat; ~ **rompió la pierna** he broke his leg

3 (*uso recíproco*) each other, one another; ~ **miraron** (**el uno al otro**) they looked at each other o one another

4 (*en oraciones pasivas*): **se han vendido muchos libros** a lot of books have been sold

5 (*impersonal*): ~ **dice que** ... people say that, it is said that; **allí** ~ **come muy bien** the food there is very good, you can eat very well there.

SE *abr* (= *sudeste*) SE.

sé *vb ver* **saber**, **ser**.

sea *etc vb ver* **ser**.

sebo ['seβo] *nm* fat, grease.

secador [seka'ðor] *nm*: ~ **de pelo**

hair-dryer.

secadora [seka'ðora] *nf* (*ELEC*) tumble dryer.

secar [se'kar] *vt* to dry; **~se** *vr* to dry (off); (*río, planta*) to dry up.

sección [sek'θjon] *nf* section.

seco, a ['seko, a] *a* dry; (*carácter*) cold; (*respuesta*) sharp, curt; **habrá pan a secas** there will be just bread; **decir algo a secas** to say sth curtly; **parar en ~** to stop dead.

secretaría [sekreta'ria] *nf* secretariat.

secretario, a [sekre'tarjo, a] *nm/f* secretary.

secreto, a [se'kreto, a] *a* secret; (*persona*) secretive // *nm* secret; (*calidad*) secrecy.

secta ['sekta] *nf* sect; **~rio, a** *a* sectarian.

sector [sek'tor] *nm* sector.

secuela [se'kwela] *nf* consequence.

secuencia [se'kwenθja] *nf* sequence.

secuestrar [sekwes'trar] *vt* to kidnap; (*bienes*) to seize, confiscate; **secuestro** *nm* kidnapping; seizure, confiscation.

secular [seku'lar] *a* secular.

secundar [sekun'dar] *vt* to second, support.

secundario, a [sekun'darjo, a] *a* secondary.

sed [seð] *nf* thirst; **tener ~** to be thirsty.

seda ['seða] *nf* silk.

sedal [se'ðal] *nm* fishing line.

sedante [se'ðante] *nm* sedative.

sede ['seðe] *nf* (*de gobierno*) seat; (*de compañía*) headquarters *pl*; **Santa S~** Holy See.

sediento, a [se'ðjento, a] *a* thirsty.

sedimentar [seðimen'tar] *vt* to deposit; **~se** *vr* to settle; **sedimento** *nm* sediment.

sedoso, a [se'ðoso, a] *a* silky, silken.

seducción [seðuk'θjon] *nf* seduction.

seducir [seðu'θir] *vt* to seduce; (*sobornar*) to bribe; (*cautivar*) to charm, fascinate; (*atraer*) to attract;

seductor, a *a* seductive; charming, fascinating; attractive; (*engañoso*) deceptive, misleading // *nm/f* seducer.

segadora-trilladora [seɣa'ðora triʎa'ðora] *nf* combine harvester.

seglar [se'ɣlar] *a* secular, lay.

segregación [seɣreɣa'θjon] *nf* segregation. **~ racial** racial segregation.

segregar [seɣre'ɣar] *vt* to segregate, separate.

seguido, a [se'ɣiðo, a] *a* (*continuo*) continuous, unbroken; (*recto*) straight; **~s** consecutive, successive // *ad* (*directo*) straight (on); (*después*) after; (*AM: a menudo*) often // *nf*: **en seguida** at once, right away; **5 días ~s** 5 days running, 5 days in a row.

seguimiento [seɣi'mjento] *nm* chase, pursuit; (*continuación*) continuation.

seguir [se'ɣir] *vt* to follow; (*venir después*) to follow on, come after; (*proseguir*) to continue; (*perseguir*) to chase, pursue // *vi* (*gen*) to follow; (*continuar*) to continue, carry o go on; **~se** *vr* to follow; **sigo sin comprender** I still don't understand; **sigue lloviendo** it's still raining.

según [se'ɣun] *prep* according to // *ad* according to circumstances; **~ esté el tiempo** depending on the weather; **está ~ lo dejaste** it is just as you left it.

segundo, a [se'ɣundo, a] *a* second // *nm* (*gen, medida de tiempo*) second // *nf* second meaning; **segunda (clase)** second class; **segunda (marcha)** (*AUTO*) second (gear); **de segunda mano** second hand.

seguramente [seɣura'mente] *ad* surely; (*con certeza*) for sure, with certainty.

seguridad [seɣuri'ðað] *nf* safety; (*del estado, de casa etc*) security; (*certidumbre*) certainty; (*confianza*) confidence; (*estabilidad*) stability; **~ social** social security.

seguro, a [se'ɣuro, a] *a* (*cierto*)

sure, certain; (*fiel*) trustworthy; (*libre del peligro*) safe; (*bien defendido, firme*) secure // ad for sure, certainly // nm (COM) insurance; ~ **contra terceros/a todo riesgo** third party/comprehensive insurance; ~**s sociales** social security sg.

seis [seis] num six.

seísmo [se'ismo] nm tremor, earthquake.

selección [selek'θjon] nf selection; **seleccionar** vt to pick, choose, select.

selectividad [selektiβi'ðað] nf (Esp) university entrance examination.

selecto, a [se'lekto, a] a select, choice; (*escogido*) selected.

selva ['selβa] nf (*bosque*) forest, woods pl; (*jungla*) jungle.

sellar [se'Kar] vt (*documento oficial*) to seal; (*pasaporte, visado*) to stamp.

sello ['seʎo] nm stamp; (*precinto*) seal.

semáforo [se'maforo] nm (AUTO) traffic lights pl; (FERRO) signal.

semana [se'mana] nf week; **entre** ~ during the week; **S~ Santa** Holy Week; **semanal** a weekly.

semblante [sem'blante] nm face; (*fig*) look.

sembrar [sem'brar] vt to sow; (*objetos*) to sprinkle, scatter about; (*noticias etc*) to spread.

semejante [seme'xante] a (*parecido*) similar; ~**s** alike, similar // nm fellow man, fellow creature; **nunca hizo cosa** ~ he never did any such thing; **semejanza** nf similarity, resemblance.

semejar [seme'xar] vi to seem like, resemble; ~**se** vr to look alike, be similar.

semen ['semen] nm semen; ~**tal** nm stud.

semestral [semes'tral] a half-yearly, bi-annual.

semicírculo [semi'θirkulo] nm semicircle.

semiconsciente [semikons'θjente] a

semiconscious.

semifinal [semifi'nal] nf semifinal.

semilla [se'miʎa] nf seed.

seminario [semi'narjo] nm (REL) seminary; (ESCOL) seminar.

sémola ['semola] nf semolina.

sempiterno, a [sempi'terno, a] a everlasting.

Sena ['sena] nm: **el** ~ the (river) Seine.

senado [se'naðo] nm senate; **senador, a** nm/f senator.

sencillez [senθi'ʎeθ] nf simplicity; (*de persona*) naturalness; **sencillo, a** a simple; natural, unaffected.

senda ['senda] nf, **sendero** [sen'dero] nm path, track.

sendos, as ['sendos, as] apl: **les dio** ~ **golpes** he hit both of them.

senil [se'nil] a senile.

seno ['seno] nm (ANAT) bosom, bust; (*fig*) bosom; ~**s** breasts.

sensación [sensa'θjon] nf sensation; (*sentido*) sense; (*sentimiento*) feeling; **sensacional** a sensational.

sensato, a [sen'sato, a] a sensible.

sensible [sen'sible] a sensitive; (*apreciable*) perceptible, appreciable; (*pérdida*) considerable; ~**ro, a** a sentimental.

sensitivo, a [sensi'tiβo, a], **sensorial** [senso'rjal] a sense.

sensual [sen'swal] a sensual.

sentado, a [sen'taðo, a] a (*establecido*) settled; (*carácter*) sensible; **estar** ~ to sit, be sitting (down) // nf sitting; (*protesta*) sit-in; **dar por** ~ to take for granted, assume.

sentar [sen'tar] vt to sit, seat; (*fig*) to establish // vi (*vestido*) to suit; (*alimento*) ~ **bien/mal** a to agree/ disagree with; ~**se** vr (*persona*) to sit, sit down; (*el tiempo*) to settle (down); (*los depósitos*) to settle.

sentencia [sen'tenθja] nf (*máxima*) maxim, saying; (JUR) sentence; **sentenciar** vt to sentence.

sentido, a [sen'tiðo, a] a (*pérdida*) regrettable; (*carácter*) sensitive // nm sense; (*sentimiento*) feeling;

(*significado*) sense, meaning; (*dirección*) direction; **mi más ~ pésame** my deepest sympathy; **~ del humor** sense of humour; (*street*) **~ único** one-way (street); **tener ~** to make sense.

sentimental [sentimen'tal] a sentimental; **vida ~** love life.

sentimiento [senti'mjento] *nm* (*emoción*) feeling, emotion; (*sentido*) sense; (*pesar*) regret, sorrow.

sentir [sen'tir] *vt* to feel; (*percibir*) to perceive, sense; (*lamentar*) to regret, be sorry for // *vi* (*tener la sensación*) to feel; (*lamentarse*) to feel sorry // *nm* opinion, judgement; **~se bien/mal** to feel well/ill; **lo siento** I'm sorry.

seña ['sena] *nf* sign; (*MIL*) password; **~s** *nfpl* address *sg*; **~s personales** personal description *sg*.

señal [se'nal] *nf* sign; (*síntoma*) symptom; (*FERRO, TELEC*) signal; (*marca*) mark; (*COM*) deposit; **en ~ de** as a token of, as a sign of; **~ar** *vt* to mark; (*indicar*) to point out, indicate; (*fijar*) to fix, settle.

señor [se'nor] *nm* (*hombre*) man; (*caballero*) gentleman; (*dueño*) owner, master; (*trato: antes de nombre propio*) Mr; (: *hablando directamente*) sir; **muy ~ mío** Dear Sir; **el ~ alcalde/presidente** the mayor/president.

señora [se'nora] *nf* (*dama*) lady; (*trato: antes de nombre propio*) Mrs; (: *hablando directamente*) madam; (*esposa*) wife; **Nuestra S~** Our Lady.

señorita [seno'rita] *nf* (*con nombre y/o apellido*) Miss; (*mujer joven*) young lady.

señorito [seno'rito] *nm* young gentleman; (*pey*) rich kid.

señuelo [se'nwelo] *nm* decoy.

sepa *etc vb ver* **saber**.

separación [separa'θjon] *nf* separation; (*división*) division; (*distancia*) gap, distance.

separar [sepa'rar] *vt* to separate; (*dividir*) to divide; **~se** *vr* (*parte*) to

come away; (*partes*) to come apart; (*persona*) to leave, go away; (*matrimonio*) to separate; **separatismo** *nm* separatism.

sepia ['sepja] *nf* cuttlefish.

septiembre [sep'tjembre] *nm* September.

séptimo, a ['septimo, a] *a, nm* seventh.

sepultar [sepul'tar] *vt* to bury; **sepultura** *nf* (*acto*) burial; (*tumba*) grave, tomb; **sepulturero, a** *nmf* gravedigger.

sequedad [seke'ðað] *nf* dryness; (*fig*) brusqueness, curtness.

sequía [se'kia] *nf* drought.

séquito ['sekito] *nm* (*de rey etc*) retinue; (*POL*) followers *pl*.

PALABRA CLAVE

ser [ser] ◆ *vi* **1** (*descripción*) to be; **es médica/muy alta** she's a doctor/ very tall; **la familia es de Cuzco** his (*o* her *etc*) family is from Cuzco; **soy Anna** (*TELEC*) Anna speaking *o* here

2 (*propiedad*): **es de Joaquín** it's Joaquín's, it belongs to Joaquín

3 (*horas, fechas, números*): **es la una** it's one o'clock; **son las seis y media** it's half-past six; **es el 1 de junio** it's the first of June; **somos/ son seis** there are six of us/them

4 (*en oraciones pasivas*): **ha sido descubierto ya** it's already been discovered

5: **es de esperar que ...** it is to be hoped *o* I *etc* hope that ...

6 (*locuciones con subjun*): **o sea** that is to say; **sea él sea su hermana** either him or his sister

7: **a no ~ por él ...** but for him ...

8: **a no ~ que: a no ~ que tenga uno ya** unless he's got one already

◆ *nm* being; **~ humano** human being.

---

serenarse [sere'narse] *vr* to calm down.

sereno, a [se'reno, a] *a* (*persona*)

calm, unruffled; (el tiempo) fine, settled; (ambiente) calm, peaceful // nm night watchman.

serial [ser'jal] nm serial.

serie ['serje] nf series; (cadena) sequence, succession; **fuera de ~** out of order; (fig) special, out of the ordinary; **fabricación en ~** mass production.

seriedad [serje'ðað] nf seriousness; (formalidad) reliability; (de crisis) gravity, seriousness; **serio, a** a serious; reliable, dependable; grave, serious; **en serio** ad seriously.

sermón [ser'mon] nm (REL) sermon.

serpentear [serpente'ar] vi to wriggle; (camino, río) to wind, snake.

serpentina [serpen'tina] nf streamer.

serpiente [ser'pjente] nf snake; ~ **boa** boa constrictor; ~ **de cascabel** rattlesnake.

serranía [serra'nia] nf mountainous area.

serrano, a [se'rrano] a highland cpd, hill cpd // nm/f highlander.

serrar [se'rrar] vt = aserrar.

serrín [se'rrin] nm = aserrín.

serrucho [se'rrutʃo] nm saw.

servicio [ser'βiθjo] nm service; ~s nmpl toilet(s); ~ **incluido** service charge included; ~ **militar** military service.

servidor, a [serβi'ðor, a] nm/f servant.

servidumbre [serβi'ðumbre] nf (sujeción) servitude; (criados) servants pl, staff.

servil [ser'βil] a servile.

servilleta [serβi'ʎeta] nf serviette, napkin.

servir [ser'βir] vt to serve // vi to serve; (tener utilidad) to be of use, be useful; ~**se** vr to serve o help o.s.; ~**se de algo** to make use of sth, use sth; **sírvase pasar** please come in.

sesenta [se'senta] num sixty.

sesgo ['sesɣo] nm slant; (fig) slant,

twist.

sesión [se'sjon] nf (POL) session, sitting; (CINE) showing.

seso ['seso] nm brain; **sesudo, a** a sensible, wise.

seta ['seta] nf mushroom; ~ **venenosa** toadstool.

setecientos [sete'θjentos, as] a, num seven hundred.

setenta [se'tenta] num seventy.

seudo... [seuðo] pref pseudo....

seudónimo [seu'ðonimo] nm pseudonym.

severidad [seβeri'ðað] nf severity; **severo, a** a severe.

Sevilla [se'βiʎa] n Seville; **sevillano, a** a o of from Seville // nm/f native o inhabitant of Seville.

sexo ['sekso] nm sex.

sexto, a ['seksto, a] a, num sixth.

sexual [sek'swal] a sexual; **vida** ~ sex life.

si [si] conj if; **me pregunto** ~... I wonder if o whether... .

sí [si] ad yes // nm consent // pron (uso impersonal) oneself; (sg: m) himself; (: f) herself; (: de cosa) itself; (de usted) yourself; (pl) themselves; (de ustedes) yourselves; (recíproco) each other; **él no quiere pero yo** ~ he doesn't want to but I do; **ella vendrá** she will certainly come, she is sure to come; **claro que** ~ of course; **creo que** ~ I think so.

siamés, esa [sja'mes, esa] a, nm/f Siamese.

SIDA ['siða] nm abr (= Síndrome de Inmuno-deficiencia Adquirida) AIDS.

siderúrgico, a [siðe'rurxiko, a] a iron and steel cpd // nf: **la siderúrgica** the iron and steel industry.

sidra ['siðra] nf cider.

siembra ['sjembra] nf sowing.

siempre ['sjempre] ad always; (todo el tiempo) all the time; ~ **que** conj (cada vez) whenever; (dado que) provided that; **como** ~ as usual; **para** ~ for ever.

sien [sjen] *nf* temple.

siento *etc vb ver* **sentar, sentir**.

sierra ['sjerra] *nf* (*TEC*) saw; (*cadena de montañas*) mountain range.

siervo, a ['sjerβo, a] *nm/f* slave.

siesta ['sjesta] *nf* siesta, nap; **echar la ~ to** have an afternoon nap *o* a siesta.

siete ['sjete] *num* seven.

sífilis ['sifilis] *nf* syphilis.

sifón [si'fon] *nm* syphon; **whisky con ~ whisky** and soda.

sigla ['siɣla] *nf* abbreviation; acronym.

siglo ['siɣlo] *nm* century; (*fig*) age.

significación [siɣnifika'θjon] *nf* significance.

significado [siɣnifi'kaðo] *nm* significance; (*de palabra etc*) meaning.

significar [siɣnifi'kar] *vt* to mean, signify; (*notificar*) to make known, express; **significativo, a** *a* significant.

signo ['siɣno] *nm* sign; **~ de admiración** *o* **exclamación** exclamation mark; **~ de interrogación** question mark.

sigo *etc vb ver* **seguir**.

siguiente [si'ɣjente] *a* next, following.

siguió *etc vb ver* **seguir**.

sílaba ['silaβa] *nf* syllable.

silbar [sil'βar] *vt, vi* to whistle; **silbato** *nm* whistle; **silbido** *nm* whistle, whistling.

silenciador [silenθja'ðor] *nm* silencer.

silenciar [silen'θjar] *vt* (*persona*) to silence; (*escándalo*) to hush up; **silencio** *nm* silence, quiet; **silencioso, a** *a* silent, quiet.

silicio [si'liθjo] *nm* silicon.

silueta [si'lweta] *nf* silhouette; (*de edificio*) outline; (*figura*) figure.

silvestre [sil'βestre] *a* (*BOT*) wild; (*fig*) rustic, rural.

silla ['siʎa] *nf* (*asiento*) chair; (*tb: ~ de montar*) saddle; **~ de ruedas** wheelchair.

sillón [si'ʎon] *nm* armchair, easy chair.

simbólico, a [sim'boliko, a] *a* symbolic(al).

simbolizar [simboli'θar] *vt* to symbolize.

símbolo ['simbolo] *nm* symbol.

simetría [sime'tria] *nf* symmetry.

simiente [si'mjente] *nf* seed.

similar [simi'lar] *a* similar.

simio ['simjo] *nm* ape.

simpatía [simpa'tia] *nf* liking; (*afecto*) affection; (*amabilidad*) kindness; (*solidaridad*) mutual support, solidarity; **simpático, a** *a* nice, pleasant; kind.

simpatizante [simpati'θante] *nm/f* sympathizer.

simpatizar [simpati'θar] *vi*: **~ con** to get on well with.

simple ['simple] *a* simple; (*elemental*) simple, easy; (*mero*) mere; (*puro*) pure, sheer // *nm/f* simpleton; **~za** *nf* simpleness; (*necedad*) silly thing; **simplicidad** *nf* simplicity; **simplificar** *vt* to simplify.

simular [simu'lar] *vt* to simulate.

simultáneo, a [simul'taneo, a] *a* simultaneous.

sin [sin] *prep* without; **la ropa está ~ lavar** the clothes are unwashed; **~ que** *conj* without; **~ embargo** however, still.

sinagoga [sina'xoxa] *nf* synagogue.

sinceridad [sinθeri'ðað] *nf* sincerity; **sincero, a** *a* sincere.

sincronizar [sinkroni'θar] *vt* to synchronize.

sindical [sindi'kal] *a* union *cpd*, trade-union *cpd*; **~ista** *a, nm/f* trade-unionist.

sindicato [sindi'kato] *nm* (*de trabajadores*) trade(s) union; (*de negociantes*) syndicate.

sinfín [sin'fin] *nm*: **un ~ de** a great many, no end of.

sinfonía [sinfo'nia] *nf* symphony.

singular [singu'lar] *a* singular; (*fig*) outstanding, exceptional; (*pey*) peculiar, odd; **~idad** *nf* singularity, peculiarity; **~izar** *vt* to single out;

~izarse vr to distinguish o.s., stand out.

siniestro, a [si'njestro, a] a left; (fig) sinister // nm (accidente) accident.

sinnúmero [sin'numero] nm = **sinfín**.

sino ['sino] nm fate, destiny // conj (pero) but; (salvo) except, save.

sinónimo, a [si'nonimo, a] a synonymous // nm synonym.

síntesis ['sintesis] nf synthesis; **sintético, a** a synthetic.

sintetizar [sinteti'θar] vt to synthesize.

sintió vb ver **sentir**.

síntoma ['sintoma] nm symptom.

sinvergüenza [simber'ɣwenθa] nmf rogue, scoundrel; **¡es un ~!** he's got a nerve!

sionismo [sjo'nismo] nm Zionism.

siquiera [si'kjera] conj even if, even though // ad at least; **ni** ~ not even.

sirena [si'rena] nf siren.

Siria ['sirja] nf Syria; **sirio, a** a, nmf Syrian.

sirviente, a [sir'βjente, a] nmf servant.

sirvo etc vb ver **servir**.

sisear [sise'ar] vt, vi to hiss.

sismógrafo [sis'moɣrafo] nm seismograph.

sistema [sis'tema] nm system; (método) method; **sistemático, a** a systematic.

sitiar [si'tjar] vt to beseige, lay seige to.

sitio ['sitjo] nm (lugar) place; (espacio) room, space; (MIL) siege.

situación [sitwa'θjon] nf situation, position; (estatus) position, standing.

situado, a [situ'aðo] a situated, placed.

situar [si'twar] vt to place, put; (edificio) to locate, situate.

slip [slip] nm pants pl, briefs pl.

smoking ['smokin, es'mokin] (pl ~s) nm dinner jacket (Brit), tuxedo (US).

snob [es'nob] = **esnob**.

so [so] prep under.

SO abr (= suroeste) SW.

sobaco [so'βako] nm armpit.

soberanía [soβera'nia] nf sovereignty; **soberano, a** a sovereign; (fig) supreme // nmf sovereign.

soberbio, a [so'βerβjo, a] a (orgulloso) proud; (altivo) haughty, arrogant; (fig) magnificent, superb // nf pride; haughtiness, arrogance; magnificence.

sobornar [soβor'nar] vt to bribe; **soborno** nm bribe.

sobra ['soβra] nf excess, surplus; ~s nfpl left-overs, scraps; **de** ~ surplus, extra; **tengo de** ~ I've more than enough; ~**do, a** a (más que suficiente) more than enough; (superfluo) excessive // ad too, exceedingly; **sobrante** a remaining, extra // nm surplus, remainder.

sobrar [so'βrar] vt to exceed, surpass // vi (tener de más) to be more than enough; (quedar) to remain, be left (over).

sobrasada [soβra'saða] nf pork sausage spread.

sobre ['soβre] prep (gen) on; (encima) on (top of); (por encima de, arriba de) over, above; (más que) more than; (además) in addition to, besides; (alrededor de, tratando de) about // nm envelope; ~ **todo** above all.

sobrecama [soβre'kama] nf bedspread.

sobrecargar [soβrekar'var] vt (camión) to overload; (COM) to surcharge.

sobredosis [soβre'ðosis] nf inv overdose.

sobreentender [soβre(e)nten'der] vt (adivinar) to deduce, infer; ~**se** vr: **se sobreentiende que** ... it is implied that ....

sobrehumano, a [soβreu'mano, a] a superhuman.

sobrellevar [soβreʎe'βar] vt (fig) to bear, endure.

sobrenatural [soβrenatu'ral] a supernatural.

sobrepasar [soβrepa'sar] vt to exceed, surpass.

sobreponer [soβrepo'ner] vt (poner encima) to put on top; (añadir) to add; ~se vr: ~se a to win through, pull through.

sobresaliente [soβresa'ljente] a projecting; (fig) outstanding, excellent.

sobresalir [soβresa'lir] vi to project, jut out; (fig) to stand out, excel.

sobresaltar [soβresal'tar] vt (asustar) to scare, frighten; (sobrecoger) to startle; **sobresalto** [sobre'salto] nm (movimiento) start; (susto) scare; (turbación) sudden shock.

sobretodo [soβre'toðo] nm overcoat.

sobrevenir [soβreβe'nir] vi (ocurrir) to happen (unexpectedly); (resultar) to follow, ensue.

sobreviviente [soβreβi'βjente] a surviving // nm/f survivor.

sobrevivir [soβreβi'βir] vi to survive.

sobrevolar [soβreβo'lar] vt to fly over.

sobriedad [soβrje'ðað] nf sobriety, soberness; (moderación) moderation, restraint.

sobrino, a [so'βrino, a] nm/f nephew/niece.

sobrio, a ['soβrjo, a] a (moderado) moderate, restrained.

socarrón, ona [soka'rron, ona] a (sarcástico) sarcastic, ironic(al).

socavón [soka'βon] nm (hoyo) hole.

sociable [so'θjaβle] a (persona) sociable, friendly; (animal) social.

social [so'θjal] a social; (COM) company cpd.

socialdemócrata [soθjalde'mokrata] nm/f social democrat.

socialista [soθja'lista] a, nm/f socialist.

socializar [soθjali'θar] vt to socialize.

sociedad [soθje'ðað] nf society; (COM) company; ~ anónima limited company; ~ de consumo consumer society.

socio, a ['soθjo, a] nm/f (miembro) member; (COM) partner.

sociología [soθjolo'xia] nf sociology;

sociólogo, a nm/f sociologist.

socorrer [soko'rrer] vt to help; **socorrista** nm/f first aider; (en piscina, playa) lifeguard; **socorro** nm (ayuda) help, aid; (MIL) relief; ¡socorro! help!

soda ['soða] nf (sosa) soda; (bebida) soda (water).

sofá [so'fa] (pl ~s) nm sofa, settee; ~-cama nm studio couch, sofa bed.

sofisticación [sofistika'θjon] nf sophistication.

sofocar [sofo'kar] vt to suffocate; (apagar) to smother, put out; ~se vr to suffocate; (fig) to blush, feel embarrassed; **sofoco** nm suffocation; embarrassment.

soga ['soxa] nf rope.

sois vb ver **ser**.

soja ['soxa] nf soya.

sojuzgar [soxuθ'var] vt to subdue, rule despotically.

sol [sol] nm sun; (luz) sunshine, sunlight; **hace o hay ~** it is sunny.

solamente [sola'mente] ad only, just.

solapa [so'lapa] nf (de chaqueta) lapel; (de libro) jacket.

solar [so'lar] a solar, sun cpd.

solaz [so'laθ] nm recreation, relaxation; ~**ar** vt (divertir) to amuse.

soldada [sol'daða] nf pay.

soldado [sol'daðo] nm soldier; ~ **raso** private.

soldador [solda'ðor] nm soldering iron; (persona) welder.

soldar [sol'dar] vt to solder, weld; (unir) to join, unite.

soleado, a [sole'aðo, a] a sunny.

soledad [sole'ðað] nf solitude; (estado infeliz) loneliness.

solemne [so'lemne] a solemn; **solemnidad** nf solemnity.

soler [so'ler] vi to be in the habit of, be accustomed to; **suele salir a las ocho** she usually goes out at 8 o'clock.

solfeo [sol'feo] nm solfa.

solicitar [soliθi'tar] vt (permiso) to ask for, seek; (puesto) to apply for;

(*votos*) to canvass for; (*atención*) to attract; (*persona*) to pursue, chase after.

solícito, a [so'liθito, a] *a* (*diligente*) diligent; (*cuidadoso*) careful; **solicitud** *nf* (*calidad*) great care; (*petición*) request; (*a un puesto*) application.

solidaridad [soliðari'ðað] *nf* solidarity; **solidario, a** *a* (*participación*) joint, common; (*compromiso*) mutually binding.

solidez [soli'ðeθ] *nf* solidity; **sólido, a** *a* solid.

soliloquio [soli'lokjo] *nm* soliloquy.

solista [so'lista] *nm/f* soloist.

solitario, a [soli'tarjo, a] *a* (*persona*) lonely, solitary; (*lugar*) lonely, desolate // *nm/f* (*reclusa*) recluse; (*en la sociedad*) loner // *nm* solitaire.

solo, a ['solo, a] *a* (*único*) single, sole; (*sin compañía*) alone; (*solitario*) lonely; **hay una sola dificultad** there is just one difficulty; **a solas** alone, by o.s.

sólo ['solo] *ad* only, just.

solomillo [solo'miʎo] *nm* sirloin.

soltar [sol'tar] *vt* (*dejar ir*) to let go of; (*desprender*) to unfasten, loosen; (*librar*) to release, set free; (*risa etc*) to let out.

soltero, a [sol'tero, a] *a* single, unmarried // *nm/f* bachelor/single woman; **solterón, ona** *nm/f* old bachelor/spinster.

soltura [sol'tura] *nf* looseness, slackness; (*de los miembros*) agility, ease of movement; (*en el hablar*) fluency, ease.

soluble [so'luβle] *a* (*QUÍMICA*) soluble; (*problema*) solvable; ~ **en agua** soluble in water.

solución [solu'θjon] *nf* solution; **solucionar** *vt* (*problema*) to solve; (*asunto*) to settle, resolve.

solventar [solβen'tar] *vt* (*pagar*) to settle, pay; (*resolver*) to resolve.

sollozar [soʎo'θar] *vi* to sob; **sollozo** *nm* sob.

sombra ['sombra] *nf* shadow; (*como protección*) shade; ~**s** *nfpl* darkness *sg*, shadows; **tener buena/mala** ~ to be lucky/unlucky.

sombrero [som'brero] *nm* hat.

sombrilla [som'briʎa] *nf* parasol, sunshade.

sombrío, a [som'brio, a] *a* (*oscuro*) dark; (*fig*) sombre, sad; (*persona*) gloomy.

somero, a [so'mero, a] *a* superficial.

someter [some'ter] *vt* (*país*) to conquer; (*persona*) to subject to one's will; (*informe*) to present, submit; ~**se** *vr* to give in, yield, submit; ~ **a** to subject to.

somnífero [som'nifero] *nm* sleeping pill.

somos *vb ver* **ser**.

son *vb ver* **ser** // [son] *nm* sound; **en** ~ **de broma** as a joke.

sonajero [sona'xero] *nm* (baby's) rattle.

sonambulismo [sonambu'lismo] *nm* sleepwalking; **sonámbulo, a** *nm/f* sleepwalker.

sonar [so'nar] *vt* to ring // *vi* to sound; (*hacer ruido*) to make a noise; (*pronunciarse*) to be sounded, be pronounced; (*ser conocido*) to sound familiar; (*campana*) to ring; (*reloj*) to strike, chime; ~**se** *vr* (*las narices*) to blow one's nose; **me suena ese nombre** that name rings a bell.

sonda ['sonda] *nf* (*NAUT*) sounding; (*TEC*) bore, drill; (*MED*) probe.

sondear [sonde'ar] *vt* to sound; to bore (*into*), drill; to probe, sound; (*fig*) to sound out; **sondeo** *nm* sounding; boring, drilling; (*fig*) poll, enquiry.

sónico, a ['soniko, a] *a* sonic, sound *cpd*.

sonido [so'niðo] *nm* sound.

sonoro, a [so'noro, a] *a* sonorous; (*resonante*) loud, resonant.

sonreír [sonre'ir] *vi*, **sonreírse** *vr* to smile; **sonriente** *a* smiling; **sonrisa** *nf* smile.

sonrojo [son'roxo] *nm* blush.

soñador, a [soɲaˈðor, a] *nm/f* dreamer.

soñar [soˈɲar] *vt, vi* to dream; ~ **con** to dream about *o* of *o*.

soñoliento, a [soɲoˈljento, a] *a* sleepy, drowsy.

sopa [ˈsopa] *nf* soup; **sopera** *nf* soup tureen.

soplar [soˈplar] *vt* (*polvo*) to blow away, blow off; (*inflar*) to blow up; (*vela*) to blow out // *vi* to blow; **soplo** *nm* blow, puff; (*de viento*) puff, gust.

soporífero [sopoˈrifero] *nm* sleeping pill.

soportable [soporˈtaβle] *a* bearable.

soportar [soporˈtar] *vt* to bear, carry; (*fig*) to bear, put up with; **soporte** *nm* support; (*fig*) pillar, support.

soprano [soˈprano] *nf* soprano.

sorber [sorˈβer] *vt* (*chupar*) to sip; (*inhalar*) to inhale; (*tragar*) to swallow (up); (*absorber*) to soak up, absorb.

sorbete [sorˈβete] *nm* iced fruit drink.

sorbo [ˈsorβo] *nm* (*trago: grande*) gulp, swallow; (*: pequeño*) sip.

sordera [sorˈðera] *nf* deafness.

sórdido, a [ˈsorðiðo, a] *a* dirty, squalid.

sordo, a [ˈsorðo, a] *a* (*persona*) deaf // *nm/f* deaf person; ~**mudo, a** *a* deaf and dumb.

soroche [soˈrotʃe] *nm* (*AM*) mountain sickness.

sorprendente [sorprenˈdente] *a* surprising.

sorprender [sorprenˈder] *vt* to surprise; **sorpresa** *nf* surprise.

sortear [sorteˈar] *vt* to draw lots for; (*rifar*) to raffle; (*dificultad*) to avoid; **sorteo** *nm* (*en lotería*) draw; (*rifa*) raffle.

sortija [sorˈtixa] *nf* ring; (*rizo*) ringlet, curl.

sosegado, a [soseˈɣaðo, a] *a* quiet, calm.

sosegar [soseˈɣar] *vt* to quieten,

calm; (*el ánimo*) to reassure // *vi* to rest; **sosiego** *nm* quiet(ness), calm(ness).

soslayo [sosˈlajo]: **de ~** *ad* obliquely, sideways.

soso, a [ˈsoso, a] *a* (*CULIN*) tasteless; (*fig*) dull, uninteresting.

sospecha [sosˈpetʃa] *nf* suspicion; **sospechar** *vt* to suspect; **sospechoso, a** *a* suspicious; (*testimonio, opinión*) suspect // *nm/f* suspect.

sostén [sosˈten] *nm* (*apoyo*) support; (*sujetador*) bra; (*alimentación*) sustenance, food.

sostener [sosteˈner] *vt* to support; (*mantener*) to keep up, maintain; (*alimentar*) to sustain, keep going; ~**se** *vr* to support o.s.; (*seguir*) to continue, remain; **sostenido, a** *a* continuous, sustained; (*prolongado*) prolonged.

sótano [ˈsotano] *nm* basement.

soviético, a [soˈβjetiko, a] *a* Soviet; **los ~s** the Soviets.

soy *vb ver* **ser**.

Sr. *abr* (= *Señor*) Mr.

Sra. *abr* (= *Señora*) Mrs.

S.R.C. *abr* (= *se ruega contestación*) R.S.V.P.

Sres. *abr* (= *Señores*) Messrs.

Srta. *abr* (= *Señorita*) Miss.

Sta. *abr* (= *Santa*) St.

status [ˈstatus, eˈstatus] *nm inv* status.

Sto. *abr* (= *Santo*) St.

su [su] *pron* (*de él*) his; (*de ella*) her; (*de una cosa*) its; (*de ellos, ellas*) their; (*de usted, ustedes*) your.

suave [ˈswaβe] *a* gentle; (*superficie*) smooth; (*trabajo*) easy; (*música, voz*) soft, sweet; **suavidad** *nf* gentleness; smoothness, softness, sweetness; **suavizar** *vt* to soften; (*quitar la aspereza*) to smooth (out).

subalimentado, a [suβalimenˈtaðo, a] *a* undernourished.

subasta [suˈβasta] *nf* auction; **subastar** *vt* to auction (off).

subcampeón, ona [suβkampeˈon, ona] *nm/f* runner-up.

subconsciente [suβkon'sθjente] a, nm subconscious.

subdesarrollado, a [suβðesarro-'λaðo, a] a underdeveloped.

subdesarrollo [suβðesa'rroλo] nm underdevelopment.

subdirector, a [suβðirek'tor, a] nm/f assistant director.

súbdito [a ['suβðito, a] nm/f subject.

subdividir [suβðiβi'ðir] vt to subdivide.

subestimar [suβesti'mar] vt to underestimate, underrate.

subido, a [su'βiðo, a] a (color) bright, strong; (precio) high // nf (de montaña etc) ascent, climb; (de precio) rise, increase; (pendiente) slope, hill.

subir [su'βir] vt (objeto) to raise, lift up; (cuesta, calle) to go up; (colina, montaña) to climb; (precio) to raise, put up // vi to go up, come up; (a un coche) to get in; (a un autobús, tren o avión) to get on, board; (precio) to rise, go up; (río, marea) to rise; ~se vr to get up; climb.

súbito, a ['suβito, a] a (repentino) sudden; (imprevisto) unexpected.

subjetivo, a [suβxe'tiβo, a] a subjective.

sublevación [suβleβa'θjon] nf revolt, rising.

sublevar [suβle'βar] vt to rouse to revolt; ~se vr to revolt, rise.

sublime [su'βlime] a sublime.

submarino, a [suβma'rino, a] a underwater // nm submarine.

subnormal [suβnor'mal] a subnormal // nm/f subnormal person.

subordinado, a [suβorði'naðo, a] a, nm/f subordinate.

subrayar [suβra'jar] vt to underline.

subrepticio, a [suβrep'tiθjo, a] a surreptitious.

subsanar [suβsa'nar] vt (reparar) to make good; (perdonar) to excuse; (sobreponerse a) to overcome.

subscribir [suβskri'βir] vt = suscribir.

subsidiario, a [suβsi'ðjarjo, a] a subsidiary.

subsidio [suβ'siðjo] nm (ayuda) aid, financial help; (subvención) subsidy, grant; (de enfermedad, paro etc) benefit, allowance.

subsistencia [suβsis'tenθja] nf subsistence.

subsistir [suβsis'tir] vi to subsist; (vivir) to live; (sobrevivir) to survive, endure.

subterráneo, a [suβte'rraneo, a] a underground, subterranean // nm underpass, underground passage.

suburbano, a [suβur'βano, a] a suburban.

suburbio [su'βurβjo] nm (barrio) slum quarter; (afueras) suburbs pl.

subvencionar [suββenθjo'nar] vt to subsidize.

subversión [suββer'sjon] nf subversion; **subversivo, a** a subversive.

subyugar [suβju'γar] vt (país) to subjugate, subdue; (enemigo) to overpower; (voluntad) to dominate.

succión [suk'θjon] nf suction.

sucedáneo, a [suθe'ðaneo, a] a substitute // nm substitute (food).

suceder [suθe'ðer] vt, vi to happen; (seguir) to succeed, follow; **lo que sucede es que...** the fact is that...;

sucesión nf succession; (serie) sequence, series.

sucesivamente [suθesiβa'mente] ad: **y así ~** and so on.

sucesivo, a [suθe'siβo, a] a successive, following; **en lo ~** in future, from now on.

suceso [su'θeso] nm (hecho) event, happening; (incidente) incident.

suciedad [suθje'ðað] nf (estado) dirtiness; (mugre) dirt, filth.

sucinto, a [su'θinto, a] a (conciso) succinct, concise.

sucio, a ['suθjo, a] a dirty.

Sucre ['sukre] n Sucre.

suculento, a [suku'lento, a] a succulent.

sucumbir [sukum'bir] vi to succumb.

sucursal [sukur'sal] nf branch (office).

Sudáfrica [suð'afrika] *nf* South Africa.

Sudamérica [suða'merika] *nf* South America; **sudamericano** a *a*, *nm/f* South American.

sudar [su'ðar] *vt*, *vi* to sweat.

sudeste [su'ðeste] *nm* south-east.

sudoeste [suðo'este] *nm* south-west.

sudor [su'ðor] *nm* sweat; **~oso**, a *a* sweaty, sweating.

Suecia ['sweθja] *nf* Sweden; **sueco, a** *a* Swedish // *nm/f* Swede.

suegro, a ['swexro, a] *nm/f* father-/mother-in-law.

suela ['swela] *nf* sole.

sueldo ['sweldo] *nm* pay, wage(s) (pl).

suele *etc vb ver* **soler.**

suelo ['swelo] *nm* (tierra) ground; (de casa) floor.

suelto, a ['swelto, a] *a* (libre) free; (separado) detached; (ágil) quick, agile; (corriente) fluent, flowing // *nm* (loose) change, small change.

sueño *etc vb ver* **soñar** // ['sweɲo] *nm* sleep; (somnolencia) sleepiness, drowsiness; (lo soñado, fig) dream; **tener ~** to be sleepy.

suero ['swero] *nm* (MED) serum; (de leche) whey.

suerte ['swerte] *nf* (fortuna) luck; (azar) chance; (destino) fate, destiny; (condición) lot; (género) sort, kind; **tener ~** to be lucky; **de otra ~** otherwise, if not; **de ~ que** so that, in such a way that.

suéter ['sweter] *nm* sweater.

suficiente [sufi'θjente] *a* enough, sufficient // *nm* (ESCOL) pass.

sufragio [su'fraxjo] *nm* (voto) vote; (derecho de voto) suffrage.

sufrido, a [su'friðo, a] *a* (persona) tough; (paciente) long-suffering, patient.

sufrimiento [sufri'mjento] *nm* (dolor) suffering.

sufrir [su'frir] *vt* (padecer) to suffer; (soportar) to bear, put up with; (apoyar) to hold up, support // *vi* to suffer.

sugerencia [suxe'renθja] *nf* suggestion.

sugerir [suxe'rir] *vt* to suggest; (sutilmente) to hint.

sugestión [suxes'tjon] *nf* suggestion; (sutil) hint; **sugestionar** *vt* to influence.

sugestivo, a [suxes'tiβo, a] *a* stimulating; (fascinante) fascinating.

suicida [sui'θiða] *a* suicidal // *nm/f* suicidal person; (muerto) suicide, person who has committed suicide; **suicidarse** *vr* to commit suicide, kill o.s.; **suicidio** *nm* suicide.

Suiza ['swiθa] *nf* Switzerland; **suizo, a** *a*, *nm/f* Swiss.

sujeción [suxe'θjon] *nf* subjection.

sujetador [suxeta'ðor] *nm* fastener, clip; (sostén) bra.

sujetar [suxe'tar] *vt* (fijar) to fasten; (detener) to hold down; (fig) to subject, subjugate; **~se** *vr* to subject o.s.; **sujeto, a** *a* fastened, secure // *nm* subject; (individuo) individual; sujeto a subject to.

suma ['suma] *nf* (cantidad) total, sum; (de dinero) sum; (acto) adding (up), addition; **en ~** in short.

sumamente [suma'mente] *ad* extremely, exceedingly.

sumar [su'mar] *vt* to add (up); (reunir) to collect, gather // *vi* to add up.

sumario, a [su'marjo, a] *a* brief, concise // *nm* summary.

sumergir [sumer'xir] *vt* to submerge; (hundir) to sink; (bañar) to immerse, dip.

sumidero [sumi'ðero] *nm* drain, sewer; (TEC) sump.

suministrar [sumini'strar] *vt* to supply, provide; **suministro** *nm* supply; (acto) supplying, providing.

sumir [su'mir] *vt* to sink, submerge; (fig) to plunge.

sumisión [sumi'sjon] *nf* (acto) submission; (calidad) submissiveness, docility; **sumiso, a** *a* submissive, docile.

sumo, a ['sumo, a] *a* great,

extreme; *(mayor)* highest, supreme.

suntuoso, a [sun'twoso, a] *a* sumptuous, magnificent.

supe *etc vb ver* **saber.**

super... [super] *pref* super..., over...; **~bueno** great, fantastic.

súper ['super] *nm (gasolina)* threestar (petrol).

superar [supe'rar] *vt (sobreponerse a)* to overcome; *(rebasar)* to surpass, do better than; *(pasar)* to go beyond; **~se** *vr* to excel o.s.

superávit [supe'raßit] *nm inv* surplus.

superficial [superfi'θjal] *a* superficial; *(medida)* surface *cpd,* of the surface.

superficie [super'fiθje] *nf* surface; *(área)* area.

superfluo, a [su'perflwo, a] *a* superfluous.

superintendente [superinten'dente] *nm/f* supervisor, superintendent.

superior [supe'rjor] *a (piso, clase)* upper; *(temperatura, número, nivel)* higher; *(mejor: calidad, producto)* superior, better // *nm/f* superior; **~idad** *nf* superiority.

supermercado [supermer'kaðo] *nm* supermarket.

supersónico, a [super'soniko, a] *a* supersonic.

superstición [supersti'θjon] *nf* superstition; **supersticioso, a** *a* superstitious.

supervisor, a [superßi'sor, a] *nm/f* supervisor.

supervivencia [superßi'ßenθja] *nf* survival.

superviviente [superßi'ßjente] *a* surviving.

supiera *etc vb ver* **saber.**

suplantar [suplan'tar] *vt (persona)* to supplant.

suplementario, a [suplemen'tarjo, a] *a* supplementary; **suplemento** *nm* supplement.

suplente [su'plente] *a, nm/f* substitute.

supletorio, a [suple'torjo, a] *a*

supplementary // *nm* supplement; **mesa supletoria** spare table.

súplica ['suplika] *nf* request; *(JUR)* petition.

suplicar [supli'kar] *vt (cosa)* to beg (for), plead for; *(persona)* to beg, plead with.

suplicio [su'pliθjo] *nm* torture.

suplir [su'plir] *vt (compensar)* to make good, make up for; *(reemplazar)* to replace, substitute // *vi:* **~ a** to take the place of, substitute for.

supo *etc vb ver* **saber.**

suponer [supo'ner] *vt* to suppose // *vi* to have authority; **suposición** *nf* supposition.

supremacía [suprema'θia] *nf* supremacy.

supremo, a [su'premo, a] *a* supreme.

supresión [supre'sjon] *nf* suppression; *(de derecho)* abolition; *(de dificultad)* removal; *(de palabra etc)* deletion; *(de restricción)* cancellation, lifting.

suprimir [supri'mir] *vt* to suppress; *(derecho, costumbre)* to abolish; *(dificultad)* to remove; *(palabra etc)* to delete; *(restricción)* to cancel, lift.

supuesto, a *pp de* **suponer** // [su'pwesto, a] *a (hipotético)* supposed; *(falso)* false // *nm* assumption, hypothesis; **~ que** *conj* since; **por ~** of course.

sur [sur] *nm* south.

surcar [sur'kar] *vt* to plough; *(superficie)* to cut, score; **surco** *nm (en metal, disco)* groove; *(AGR)* furrow.

surgir [sur'xir] *vi* to arise, emerge; *(dificultad)* to come up, crop up.

surtido, a [sur'tiðo, a] *a* mixed, assorted // *nm (selección)* selection, assortment; *(abastecimiento)* supply, stock.

surtir [sur'tir] *vt* to supply, provide // *vi* to spout, spurt.

susceptible [susθep'tißle] *a* susceptible; *(sensible)* sensitive; **~ de** capable of.

suscitar [susθi'tar] vt to cause, provoke; (interés, sospechas) to arouse.

suscribir [suskri'βir] vt (firmar) to sign; (respaldar) to subscribe to, endorse; ~se vr to subscribe; **suscripción** nf subscription.

susodicho, a [suso'ðitʃo, a] a above-mentioned.

suspender [suspen'der] vt (objeto) to hang (up), suspend; (trabajo) to stop, suspend; (ESCOL) to fail; **suspensión** nf suspension; (fig) stoppage, suspension.

suspenso, a [sus'penso, a] a hanging, suspended; (ESCOL) failed // nm: **quedar** o **estar en** ~ to be pending.

suspicacia [suspi'kaθja] nf suspicion, mistrust; **suspicaz** a suspicious, distrustful.

suspirar [suspi'rar] vi to sigh; **suspiro** nm sigh.

sustancia [sus'tanθja] nf substance.

sustentar [susten'tar] vt (alimentar) to sustain, nourish; (objeto) to hold up, support; (idea, teoría) to maintain, uphold; (fig) to sustain, keep going; **sustento** nm support; (alimento) sustenance, food.

sustituir [sustitu'ir] vt to substitute, replace; **sustituto, a** nm/f substitute, replacement.

susto ['susto] nm fright, scare.

sustraer [sustra'er] vt to remove, take away; (MAT) to subtract.

susurrar [susu'rrar] vi to whisper; **susurro** nm whisper.

sutil [su'til] a (aroma, diferencia) subtle; (tenue) thin; (inteligencia, persona) sharp; **~eza** nf subtlety; thinness.

suyo, a ['sujo, a] a (con artículo o después del verbo ser: de él) his; (: de ella) hers; (: de ellos, ellas) theirs; (: de Ud, Uds) yours; **un amigo** ~ a friend of his o hers o theirs o yours.

T

taba ['taβa] nf (ANAT) anklebone; (juego) jacks sg.

tabacalero, a [taβaka'lero, a] nm/f (vendedor) tobacconist // nf: **T~** Spanish state tobacco monopoly.

tabaco [ta'βako] nm tobacco; (fam) cigarettes pl: **tabaquería** nf tobacconist's (Brit), cigar store (US).

taberna [ta'βerna] nf bar, pub (Brit); **tabernero, a** nm/f (encargado) publican; (camarero) barman/maid.

tabique [ta'βike] nm partition (wall).

tabla ['taβla] nf (de madera) plank; (estante) shelf; (de vestido) pleat; (ARTE) panel; **~s** nfpl: **estar** o **quedar en** ~s to draw; **~do** nm (plataforma) platform; (TEATRO) stage.

tablero [ta'βlero] nm (de madera) plank, board; (de ajedrez, damas) board; (AUTO) dashboard; ~ **de anuncios** notice (Brit) o bulletin (US) board.

tableta [ta'βleta] nf (MED) tablet; (de chocolate) bar.

tablilla [ta'βliʎa] nf small board; (MED) splint.

tablón [ta'βlon] nm (de suelo) plank; (de techo) beam; ~ **de anuncios** notice board (Brit), bulletin board (US).

tabú [ta'βu] nm taboo.

tabular [taβu'lar] vt to tabulate.

taburete [taβu'rete] nm stool.

tacaño, a [ta'kaɲo, a] a (avaro) mean.

tácito, a ['taθito, a] a tacit.

taciturno, a [taθi'turno, a] a (callado) silent; (malhumorado) sullen.

taco ['tako] nm (BILLAR) cue; (libro de billetes) book; (AM: de zapato) heel; (tarugo) peg; (palabrota) swear word.

tacón [ta'kon] nm heel; **de** ~ **alto**

high-heeled; **taconeo** nm (heel) stamping.

táctico, a ['taktiko, a] a tactical // nf tactics pl.

tacto ['takto] nm touch; (fig) tact.

tacha ['tatʃa] nf flaw; (TEC) stud; **tachar** vt (borrar) to cross out; **tachar de** to accuse of.

tafetán [tafe'tan] nm taffeta.

tafilete [tafi'lete] nm morocco leather.

tahona [ta'ona] nf (panadería) bakery.

tahur [ta'ur, a] nm/f gambler; (pey) cheat.

taimado, a [tai'maðo, a] a (astuto) sly.

taita ['taita] nm (fam) dad, daddy.

tajada [ta'xaða] nf slice.

tajante [ta'xante] a sharp.

tajar [ta'xar] vt to cut; **tajo** nm (corte) cut; (GEO) cleft.

tal [tal] a such; ~ **vez** perhaps // pron (persona) someone, such a one; (cosa) something, such a thing; ~ **como** such as; ~ **para cual** tit for tat; (dos iguales) two of a kind // ad: ~ **como** (igual) just as; ~ **cual** (como es) just as it is; ¿**qué** ~? how are things?; ¿**qué** ~ **te gusta?** how do you like it? // conj: **con** ~ **de que** provided that.

taladrar [tala'ðrar] vt to drill; **taladro** nm drill; (hoyo) drill hole.

talante [ta'lante] nm (humor) mood; (voluntad) will, willingness.

talar [ta'lar] vt to fell, cut down; (devastar) to devastate.

talco ['talko] nm (polvos) talcum powder.

talego [ta'leɣo] nm, **talega** [ta'leɣa] nf sack.

talento [ta'lento] nm talent; (capacidad) ability.

TALGO ['talɣo] nm abr (Esp = tren articulado ligero Goicoechea-Oriol) = HST (Brit).

talismán [talis'man] nm talisman.

talón [ta'lon] nm (ANAT) heel; (COM) counterfoil; (cheque) cheque

(Brit), check (US).

talonario [talo'narjo] nm (de cheques) chequebook (Brit), checkbook (US); (de billetes) book of tickets; (de recibos) receipt book.

talla ['taʎa] nf (estatura, fig, MED) height, stature; (palo) measuring rod; (ARTE) carving; (medida) size.

tallado, a [ta'ʎaðo, a] a carved // nf carving.

tallar [ta'ʎar] vt (madera) to carve; (metal etc) to engrave; (medir) to measure.

tallarines [taʎa'rines] nmpl noodles.

talle ['taʎe] nm (ANAT) waist; (fig) appearance.

taller [ta'ʎer] nm (TEC) workshop; (de artista) studio.

tallo ['taʎo] nm (de planta) stem; (de hierba) blade; (brote) shoot.

tamaño, a [ta'maɲo, a] a (tan grande) such a big; (tan pequeño) such a small // nm size; **de** ~ **natural** full-size.

tamarindo [tama'rindo] nm tamarind.

tambalearse [tambale'arse] vr (persona) to stagger; (vehículo) to sway.

también [tam'bjen] ad (igualmente) also, too, as well; (además) besides.

tambor [tam'bor] nm drum; (ANAT) eardrum; ~ **del freno** brake drum.

tamiz [ta'miθ] nm sieve; **~ar** vt to sieve.

tampoco [tam'poko] ad nor, neither; **yo** ~ **lo compré** I didn't buy it either.

tampón [tam'pon] nm tampon.

tan [tan] ad so; ~ **es así que ...** so much so that ...

tanda ['tanda] nf (gen) series; (turno) shift.

tangente [tan'xente] nf tangent.

Tánger ['tanxer] n Tangier(s).

tangible [tan'xiβle] a tangible.

tanque ['tanke] nm (cisterna, MIL) tank; (AUTO) tanker.

tantear [tante'ar] vt (calcular) to reckon (up); (medir) to take the measure of; (*probar*) to test, try out; (*tomar la medida: persona*) to take the measurements of; (*situación*) to weigh up; (*persona: opinión*) to sound out // *vi* (DEPORTE) to score; **tanteo** *nm* (*cálculo*) (rough) calculation; (*prueba*) test, trial; (DEPORTE) scoring.

tanto, a ['tanto, a] *a* (*cantidad*) so much, as many; ~s so many, as many; 20 y ~s 20-odd // *ad* (*cantidad*) so much, as much; (*tiempo*) so long, as long; ~ tú como yo both you and I; ~ como eso it's not as bad as that; ~ más ... cuanto que it's all the more ... because; ~ mejor/peor so much the better/the worse; ~ si viene como si va whether he comes or whether he goes; ~ es así que so much so that; por o por lo ~ therefore; me he vuelto ronco de o con ~ hablar I have become hoarse with so much talking // *conj*: en ~ que while; hasta ~ (que) until such time as // *nm* (*suma*) certain amount; (*proporción*) so much; (*punto*) point; (*gol*) goal; un ~ perezoso somewhat lazy // *pron*: cada uno paga ~ each one pays so much; a ~s de agosto on such and such a day in August.

tapa ['tapa] *nf* (*de caja, olla*) lid; (*de botella*) top; (*de libro*) cover; (*comida*) snack.

tapadera [tapa'ðera] *nf* lid, cover.

tapar [ta'par] *vt* (*cubrir*) to cover; (*envolver*) to wrap o cover up; (*la vista*) to obstruct; (*persona, falta*) to conceal; (AM) to fill; ~se *vr* to wrap o.s. up.

taparrabo [tapa'rraßo] *nm* loincloth.

tapete [ta'pete] *nm* table cover.

tapia ['tapja] *nf* (*garden*) wall; **tapiar** *vt* to wall in.

tapicería [tapiθe'ria] *nf* tapestry; (*para muebles*) upholstery; (*tienda*) upholsterer's (shop).

tapiz [ta'piθ] *nm* (*alfombra*) carpet; (*tela tejida*) tapestry; **~ar** *vt* (*muebles*) to upholster.

tapón [ta'pon] *nm* (*corcho*) stopper; (TEC) plug; ~ **de rosca** screw-top.

taquigrafía [takiɣra'fia] *nf* shorthand; **taquígrafo, a** *nm/f* shorthand writer, stenographer.

taquilla [ta'kiʎa] *nf* (*donde se compra*) booking office; (*suma recogida*) takings pl; **taquillero, a** *a*: **función taquillera** box office success // *nm/f* ticket clerk.

tara ['tara] *nf* (*defecto*) defect; (COM) tare.

tarántula [ta'rantula] *nf* tarantula.

tararear [tarare'ar] *vt* to hum.

tardanza [tar'ðanθa] *nf* (*demora*) delay.

tardar [tar'ðar] *vi* (*tomar tiempo*) to take a long time; (*llegar tarde*) to be late; (*demorar*) to delay; ¿**tarda mucho el tren?** does the train take (very) long?; **a más ~** at the latest; **no tardes en venir** come soon.

tarde ['tarðe] *ad* late // *nf* (*de día*) afternoon; (*al anochecer*) evening; **de ~ en ~** from time to time; **¡buenas ~s!** good afternoon!; **a o por la ~** in the afternoon; in the evening.

tardío, a [tar'ðio, a] *a* (*retrasado*) late; (*lento*) slow (to arrive).

tardo, a ['tarðo, a] *a* (*lento*) slow; (*torpe*) dull.

tarea [ta'rea] *nf* task; (ESCOL) homework.

tarifa [ta'rifa] *nf* (*lista de precios*) price list; (*precio*) tariff.

tarima [ta'rima] *nf* (*plataforma*) platform.

tarjeta [tar'xeta] *nf* card; ~ **postal/ de crédito/de Navidad** postcard/ credit card/Christmas card.

tarro ['tarro] *nm* jar, pot.

tarta ['tarta] *nf* (*pastel*) cake; (*torta*) tart.

tartamudear [tartamuðe'ar] *vi* to stammer; **tartamudo, a** *a* stammering // *nm/f* stammerer.

tártaro, a ['tartaro, a] *a*: **salsa tártara** tartare sauce.

tasa ['tasa] *nf* (*precio*) (fixed) price,

rate; (valoración) valuation; (medida, norma) measure, standard; ~ de cambio/interés exchange/interest rate; ~ción nf valuation; ~dor, a nm/f valuer.

tasar [ta'sar] vt (arreglar el precio) to fix a price for; (valorar) to value, assess.

tasca ['taska] nf (fam) pub.

tatarabuelo, a [tatara'βwelo, a] nm/f great-great-grandfather/mother.

tatuaje [ta'twaxe] nm (dibujo) tattoo; (acto) tattooing.

tatuar [ta'twar] vt to tattoo.

taurino, a [tau'rino, a] a bullfighting cpd.

Tauro ['tauro] nm Taurus.

tauromaquia [tauro'makja] nf tauromachy, (art of) bullfighting.

taxi ['taksi] nm taxi.

taxista [tak'sista] nm/f taxi driver.

taza ['taθa] nf cup; (de retrete) bowl; ~ para café coffee cup; **tazón** nm (~ grande) mug, large cup; (de fuente) basin.

te [te] pron (complemento de objeto) you; (complemento indirecto) (to) you; (reflexivo) (to) yourself; ¿~ duele mucho el brazo? does your arm hurt a lot?; ~ equivocas you're wrong; ~ cálma~! calm down!

té [te] nm tea.

tea ['tea] nf torch.

teatral [tea'tral] a theatre cpd; (fig) theatrical.

teatro [te'atro] nm theatre; (LITERATURA) plays pl, drama.

tebeo [te'βeo] nm comic.

tecla ['tekla] nf key; ~do nm keyboard; **teclear** vi to strum; (fig) to drum; **tecleo** nm (MUS: sonido) strumming; (fig) drumming.

técnico, a ['tekniko, a] a technical // nm/f technician; (experto) expert // nf (procedimientos) technique; (arte, oficio) craft.

tecnócrata [tek'nokrata] nm/f technocrat.

tecnología [teknolo'xia] nf technology; **tecnológico, a** a technolo-

logical.

techo ['tetʃo] nm (externo) roof; (interno) ceiling; ~ corredizo sunroof.

tedio ['teðjo] nm boredom, tedium; ~so, a a boring, tedious.

teja ['texa] nf (azulejo) tile; (BOT) lime (tree); ~do nm (tiled) roof.

tejanos [te'xanos] nmpl jeans.

tejemaneje [texema'nexe] nm (lío) fuss; (intriga) intrigue.

tejer [te'xer] vt to weave; (hacer punto) to knit; (fig) to fabricate; **tejido** nm (tela) material, fabric; (telaraña) web; (ANAT) tissue.

tel, teléf abr (= teléfono) tel.

tela ['tela] nf (tejido) material; (telaraña) web; (en líquido) skin; **telar** nm (máquina) loom; **telares** nmpl textile mill sg.

telaraña [tela'rapa] nf cobweb.

tele ['tele] nf (fam) telly (Brit), tube (US).

tele... [tele] pref tele...; ~**comunicación** nf telecommunication; ~**control** nm remote control; ~**diario** nm television news; ~**difusión** nf (television) broadcast; ~**dirigido, a** a remote-controlled.

telefax [tele'faks] nm inv fax; (aparato) fax (machine).

teleférico [tele'feriko] nm (tren) cable-railway; (de esquí) ski-lift.

telefonear [telefone'ar] vi to telephone.

telefónicamente [tele'fonikamente] ad by (tele)phone.

telefónico, a [tele'foniko, a] a telephone cpd.

telefonista [telefo'nista] nm/f telephonist.

teléfono [te'lefono] nm (tele)phone; estar hablando al ~ to be on the phone; llamar a uno por ~ to ring o phone sb up.

telegrafía [televra'fia] nf telegraphy.

telégrafo [te'levrafo] nm telegraph.

telegrama [tele'vrama] nm telegram.

tele: ~**impresor** nm teleprinter

(Brit), teletype (US); ~**objetivo** nm telephoto lens; ~**pático, a** a telepathic; ~**scópico, a** a telescopic; ~**scopio** nm telescope; ~**silla** nm chairlift; ~**spectador, a** nm/f viewer; ~**squí** nm ski-lift; ~**tipo** nm teletype.

televidente [teleβi'ðente] nm/f viewer.

televisar [teleβi'sar] vt to televise.

televisión [teleβi'sjon] nf television; ~ **en colores** colour television.

televisor [teleβi'sor] nm television set.

télex ['teleks] nm inv telex.

telón [te'lon] nm curtain; ~ **de acero** (POL) iron curtain; ~ **de fondo** backcloth, background.

tema ['tema] nm (asunto) subject, topic; (MUS) theme // nf (obsesión) obsession; **temático, a** a thematic.

temblar [tem'blar] vi to shake, tremble; (de frío) to shiver; **tembleque** nm shaking; **temblón, ona** a shaking; **temblor** nm trembling; (de tierra) earthquake; **tembloroso, a** a trembling.

temer [te'mer] vt to fear // vi to be afraid; **temo que llegue tarde** I am afraid he may be late.

temerario, a [teme'rarjo, a] a (descuidado) reckless; (irreflexivo) hasty; **temeridad** nf (imprudencia) rashness; (audacia) boldness.

temeroso, a [teme'roso, a] a (miedoso) fearful; (que inspira temor) frightful.

temible [te'miβle] a fearsome.

temor [te'mor] nm (miedo) fear; (duda) suspicion.

témpano ['tempano] nm: ~ **de hielo** ice-floe.

temperamento [tempera'mento] nm temperament.

temperatura [tempera'tura] nf temperature.

tempestad [tempes'tað] nf storm; **tempestuoso, a** a stormy.

templado, a [tem'plaðo, a] a (moderado) moderate; (: en el

comer) frugal; (: en el beber) abstemious; (agua) lukewarm; (clima) mild; (MUS) well-tuned; **templanza** nf moderation; abstemiousness; mildness.

templar [tem'plar] vt (moderar) to moderate; (furia) to restrain; (calor) to reduce; (afinar) to tune (up); (acero) to temper; (tuerca) to tighten up; **temple** nm (ajuste) tempering; (afinación) tuning; (clima) temperature; (pintura) tempera.

templete [tem'plete] nm bandstand.

templo ['templo] nm (iglesia) church; (pagano etc) temple.

temporada [tempo'raða] nf time, period; (estación) season.

temporal [tempo'ral] a (no permanente) temporary; (REL) temporal // nm storm.

tempranero, a [tempra'nero, a] a (BOT) early; (persona) early-rising.

temprano, a [tem'prano, a] a early; (demasiado pronto) too soon, too early.

ten vb ver **tener**.

tenaces [te'naθer] apl ver **tenaz**.

tenacidad [tenaθi'ðað] nf tenacity; (dureza) toughness; (terquedad) stubbornness.

tenacillas [tena'θiʎas] nfpl tongs; (para el pelo) curling tongs (Brit) o iron (US); (MED) forceps.

tenaz [te'naθ] a (material) tough; (persona) tenacious; (creencia, resistencia) stubborn.

tenaza(s) [te'naθa(s)] nf(pl) (MED) forceps; (TEC) pliers; (ZOOL) pincers.

tendedero [tende'ðero] nm (para ropa) drying place; (cuerda) clothes line.

tendencia [ten'denθja] nf tendency; (proceso) trend; **tener** ~ **a** to tend to, have a tendency to; **tendencioso, a** a tendentious.

tender [ten'der] vt (extender) to spread out; (colgar) to hang out; (vía férrea, cable) to lay; (estirar) to stretch // vi: ~ **a** to tend to, have a tendency towards; **~se** *vr* to lie down; **~ la cama/la mesa** (*AM*) to make the bed/lay (*Brit*) o set (*US*) the table.

tenderete [tende'rete] *nm* (*puesto*) stall; (*exposición*) display of goods.

tendero, a [ten'dero, a] *nm/f* shopkeeper.

tendido, a [ten'diðo, a] *a* (*acostado*) lying down, flat; (*colgado*) hanging // *nm* (*TAUR*) front rows of seats; **a galope ~** flat out.

tendón [ten'don] *nm* tendon.

tendré *etc vb ver* **tener.**

tenebroso, a [tene'βroso, a] *a* (*oscuro*) dark; (*fig*) gloomy; (*complot*) sinister.

tenedor [tene'ðor] *nm* (*CULIN*) fork; (*poseedor*) holder; **~ de libros** book-keeper.

teneduría [teneðu'ria] *nf* keeping; **~ de libros** book-keeping.

tenencia [te'nenθja] *nf* (*de casa*) tenancy; (*de oficio*) tenure; (*de propiedad*) possession.

PALABRA CLAVE

tener [te'ner] ♦ *vt* 1 (*poseer*, *gen*) to have; (*en la mano*) to hold; **¿tienes un boli?** have you got a pen?; **va a ~ un niño** she's going to have a baby; **¡ten** (o **tenga**)!, **¡aquí tienes!** here you are!

2 (*edad*, *medidas*) to be; **tiene 7 años** she's 7 (years old); **tiene 15 cm. de largo** it's 15 cms long; *ver* **calor, hambre** *etc*

3 (*considerar*): **lo tengo por brillante** I consider him to be brilliant; **~ en mucho a uno** to think very highly of sb

4 (+ *pp*: = *pretérito*): **tengo terminada ya la mitad del trabajo** I've done half the work already

5: **~ que hacer algo** to have to do sth; **tengo que acabar este trabajo hoy** I have to finish this job today

6: **¿qué tienes, estás enfermo?** what's the matter with you, are you

ill?

♦ **~se** *vr* 1: **~se en pie** to stand up
2: **~se por**: to think o.s.; **se tiene por muy listo** he thinks himself very clever.

tengo *etc vb ver* **tener.**

tenia ['tenja] *nf* tapeworm.

teniente [te'njente] *nm* (*rango*) lieutenant; (*ayudante*) deputy.

tenis ['tenis] *nm* tennis; **~ de mesa** table tennis; **~ta** *nm/f* tennis player.

tenor [te'nor] *nm* (*sentido*) meaning; (*MUS*) tenor; **a ~ de** on the lines of.

tensar [ten'sar] *vt* to tauten; (*arco*) to draw.

tensión [ten'sjon] *nf* tension; (*TEC*) stress; (*MED*): **~ arterial** blood pressure; **tener la ~ alta** to have high blood pressure.

tenso, a ['tenso, a] *a* tense.

tentación [tenta'θjon] *nf* temptation.

tentáculo [ten'takulo] *nm* tentacle.

tentador, a [tenta'ðor, a] *a* tempting // *nm/f* tempter/temptress.

tentar [ten'tar] *vt* (*tocar*) to touch, feel; (*seducir*) to tempt; (*atraer*) to attract; **tentativa** *nf* attempt; **tentativa de asesinato** attempted murder.

tentempié [tentem'pje] *nm* (*fam*) snack.

tenue ['tenwe] *a* (*delgado*) thin, slender; (*neblina*) light; (*lazo*, *vínculo*) slight.

teñir [te'nir] *vt* to dye; (*fig*) to tinge; **~se** *vr* to dye; **~se el pelo** to dye one's hair.

teología [teolo'xia] *nf* theology.

teorema [teo'rema] *nm* theorem.

teoría [teo'ria] *nf* theory; **en ~** in theory; **teóricamente** *ad* theoretically; **teórico, a** *a* theoretic(al) // *nm/f* theoretician, theorist; **teorizar** *vi* to theorize.

terapéutico, a [tera'peutiko, a] *a* therapeutic.

terapia [te'rapja] *nf* therapy.

tercer [ter'θer] *a ver* **tercero.**

tercermundista [terθermun'dista] *f*

Third World cpd.
tercer(o), a [ter'θer(o), a] a third // nm (JUR) third party.
terceto [ter'θeto] nm trio.
terciado, a [ter'θjaðo, a] a slanting.
terciar [ter'θjar] vt (llevar) to wear (across the shoulder) // vi (participar) to take part; (hacer de árbitro) to mediate; ~se vr to come up; ~io, a a tertiary.
tercio ['terθjo] nm·third.
terciopelo [terθjo'pelo] nm velvet.
terco, a ['terko, a] a obstinate.
tergiversar [terxißer'sar] vt to distort.
termal [ter'mal] a thermal.
termas ['termas] nfpl hot springs.
terminación [termina'θjon] nf (final) end; (conclusión) conclusion, ending.
terminal [termi'nal] a, nm, a terminal.
terminante [termi'nante] a (final) final, definitive; (tajante) categorical.
terminar [termi'nar] vt (completar) to complete, finish; (concluir) to end // vi (llegar a su fin) to end; (parar) to stop; (acabar) to finish; ~se vr to come to an end; ~ por hacer algo to end up (by) doing sth.
término ['termino] nm end, conclusion; (parada) terminus; (límite) boundary; ~ medio average; (fig) middle way; en último ~ (a fin de cuentas) in the last analysis; (como último recurso) as a last resort; en ~s de in terms of.
terminología [terminolo'xia] nf terminology.
termodinámico, a [termoði'namiko, a] a thermodynamic.
termómetro [ter'mometro] nm thermometer.
termonuclear [termonukle'ar] a thermonuclear.
termo(s) ® ['termo(s)] nm Thermos ® (flask).
termostato [termo'stato] nm thermostat.
ternero, a [ter'nero, a] nm/f (animal) calf // nf (carne) veal.

terno ['terno] nm (AM) three-piece suit.
ternura [ter'nura] nf (trato) tenderness; (palabra) endearment; (cariño) fondness.
terquedad [terke'ðað] nf obstinacy; (dureza) harshness.
terrado [te'rraðo] nm terrace.
terraplén [terra'plen] nm (AGR) terrace; (cuesta) slope.
terrateniente [terrate'njente] nm/f landowner.
terraza [te'rraθa] nf (balcón) balcony; (techo) (flat) roof; (AGR) terrace.
terremoto [terre'moto] nm earthquake.
terrenal [terre'nal] a earthly.
terreno [te'rreno] nm (tierra) land; (parcela) plot; (suelo) soil; (fig) field; un ~ a piece of land.
terrestre [te'rrestre] a terrestrial; (ruta) land cpd.
terrible [te'rrißle] a terrible, awful.
territorio [terri'torjo] nm territory.
terrón [te'rron] nm (de azúcar) lump; (de tierra) clod, lump.
terror [te'rror] nm terror; ~ífico, a a terrifying; ~ista, a, nm/f terrorist.
terroso, a [te'rroso, a] a earthy.
terruño [te'rruno] nm (parcela) plot; (fig) native soil.
terso, a ['terso, a] a (liso) smooth; (pulido) polished; **tersura** nf smoothness.
tertulia [ter'tulja] nf (reunión informal) social gathering; (grupo) group, circle.
tesis ['tesis] nf inv thesis.
tesón [te'son] nm (firmeza) firmness; (tenacidad) tenacity.
tesorero, a [teso'rero, a] nm/f treasurer.
tesoro [te'soro] nm treasure; (COM, POL) treasury.
testaferro [testa'ferro] nm figurehead.
testamentaría [testamenta'ria] nf execution of a will.
testamentario, a [testamen'tarjo,

a] *a* testamentary // *nm/f* executor/ executrix.

testamento [testa'mento] *nm* will.

testar [tes'tar] *vi* to make a will.

testarudo, a [testa'ruðo, a] *a* stubborn.

testículo [tes'tikulo] *nm* testicle.

testificar [testifi'kar] *vt* to testify; (*fig*) to attest // *vi* to give evidence.

testigo [tes'tiɣo] *nm/f* witness; ~ de cargo/descargo witness for the prosecution/defence; ~ ocular eye witness.

testimoniar [testimo'njar] *vt* to testify to; (*fig*) to show; **testimonio** *nm* testimony.

teta ['teta] *nf* (*de biberón*) teat; (*ANAT*: *pezón*) nipple; (: *fam*) breast.

tétanos ['tetanos] *nm* tetanus.

tetera [te'tera] *nf* teapot.

tetilla [te'tiʎa] *nf* (*ANAT*) nipple; (*de biberón*) teat.

tétrico, a ['tetriko, a] *a* gloomy, dismal.

textil [teks'til] *a* textile; ~es *nmpl* textiles.

texto ['teksto] *nm* text; **textual** *a* textual.

textura [teks'tura] *nf* (*de tejido*) texture.

tez [teθ] *nf* (*cutis*) complexion; (*color*) colouring.

ti [ti] *pron* you; (*reflexivo*) yourself.

tía ['tia] *nf* (*pariente*) aunt; (*fam*) chick, bird.

tibieza [ti'βjeθa] *nf* (*temperatura*) tepidness; (*fig*) coolness; **tibio, a** *a* lukewarm.

tiburón [tiβu'ron] *nm* shark.

tic [tik] *nm* (*ruido*) click; (*de reloj*) tick; (*MED*): ~ **nervioso** nervous tic.

tictac [tik'tak] *nm* (*de reloj*) tick tock.

tiempo ['tjempo] *nm* time; (*época, periodo*) age, period; (*METEOROLOGÍA*) weather; (*LING*) tense; (*DEPORTE*) half; a ~ in time; a un o al mismo ~ at the same time; al poco ~ very soon (after); se quedó poco ~ he didn't stay very long; hace poco ~ not long ago; mucho ~ a long time; de ~ en ~ from time to time; hace buen/mal ~ the weather is fine/bad; estar a ~ to be in time; hace ~ some time ago; hacer ~ to while away the time; motor de 2 ~s two-stroke engine; primer ~ first half.

tienda ['tjenda] *nf* shop, store; ~ (de campaña) tent.

tienes *etc vb ver* **tener**.

tienta *etc vb ver* **tentar** // ['tjenta] *nf*: andar a ~s to grope one's way along.

tiento *etc vb ver* **tentar** // ['tjento] *nm* (*tacto*) touch; (*precaución*) wariness.

tierno, a ['tjerno, a] *a* (*blando*) tender; (*fresco*) fresh; (*amable*) sweet.

tierra ['tjerra] *nf* earth; (*suelo*) soil; (*mundo*) earth, world; (*país*) country, land; ~ adentro inland.

tieso, a ['tjeso, a] *a* (*rígido*) rigid; (*duro*) stiff; (*fam*: *orgulloso*) conceited.

tiesto ['tjesto] *nm* flowerpot.

tifoidea [tifoi'ðea] *nf* typhoid.

tifón [ti'fon] *nm* typhoon.

tifus ['tifus] *nm* typhus.

tigre ['tiɣre] *nm* tiger.

tijera [ti'xera] *nf* scissors *pl*; (*ZOOL*) claw; ~s *nfpl* scissors; (*para plantas*) shears.

tijereta [tixe'reta] *nf* earwig.

tijeretear [tixerete'ar] *vt* to snip.

tildar [til'dar] *vt*: ~ de to brand as.

tilde ['tilde] *nf* (*TIPOGRAFÍA*) tilde.

tilín [ti'lin] *nm* tinkle.

tilo ['tilo] *nm* lime tree.

timar [ti'mar] *vt* (*robar*) to steal; (*estafar*) to swindle.

timbal [tim'bal] *nm* small drum.

timbrar [tim'brar] *vt* to stamp.

timbre ['timbre] *nm* (*sello*) stamp; (*campanilla*) bell; (*tono*) timbre; (*COM*) stamp duty.

timidez [timi'ðeθ] *nf* shyness; **tímido, a** *a* shy.

timo ['timo] *nm* swindle.

timón [ti'mon] *nm* helm, rudder; **timonel** *nm* helmsman.

tímpano ['timpano] *nm* (*ANAT*) eardrum; (*MUS*) small drum.

tina ['tina] *nf* tub; (*baño*) bath(tub); **tinaja** *nf* large jar.

tinglado [tiŋ'glaðo] *nm* (*cobertizo*) shed; (*fig: truco*) trick; (*intriga*) intrigue.

tinieblas [ti'njeβlas] *nfpl* darkness *sg*; (*sombras*) shadows.

tino ['tino] *nm* (*habilidad*) skill; (*juicio*) insight.

tinta ['tinta] *nf* ink; (*TEC*) dye; (*ARTE*) colour.

tinte ['tinte] *nm* (*acto*) dyeing.

tintero [tin'tero] *nm* inkwell.

tintinear [tintine'ar] *vt* to tinkle.

tinto, a ['tinto, a] *a* (*teñido*) dyed // *nm* red wine.

tintorería [tintore'ria] *nf* dry cleaner's.

tintura [tin'tura] *nf* (*acto*) dyeing; (*QUIMICA*) dye; (*farmacéutico*) tincture.

tío ['tio] *nm* (*pariente*) uncle; (*fam: individuo*) bloke (*Brit*), guy.

tiovivo [tio'βiβo] *nm* merry-go-round.

típico, a ['tipiko, a] *a* typical.

tiple ['tiple] *nm* soprano (*voice*) // *nf* soprano.

tipo ['tipo] *nm* (*clase*) type, kind; (*norma*) norm; (*patrón*) pattern; (*hombre*) fellow; (*ANAT: de hombre*) build; (: *de mujer*) figure; (*IMPRENTA*) type; ~ **bancario/de descuento/de interés/de cambio** bank/discount/interest/exchange rate.

tipografía [tipoγra'fia] *nf* (*tipo*) printing *cpd*; (*lugar*) printing press; **tipográfico, a** *a* printing *cpd*; **tipógrafo, a** *nm/f* printer.

tíquet ['tiket] (*pl* ~**s**) *nm* ticket; (*en tienda*) cash slip.

tiquismiquis [tikis'mikis] *nm inv* fussy person // *nmpl* (*querellas*) squabbling *sg*; (*escrúpulos*) silly scruples.

tira ['tira] *nf* strip; (*fig*) abundance;

~ **y afloja** give and take.

tirabuzón [tiraβu'θon] *nm* (*rizo*) curl.

tirachinas [tira't∫inas] *nm inv* catapult.

tiradero [tira'ðero] *nm* rubbish dump.

tirado, a [ti'raðo, a] *a* (*barato*) dirt-cheap; (*fam: fácil*) very easy // *nf* (*acto*) cast, throw; (*distancia*) distance; (*serie*) series; (*TIPOGRAFÍA*) printing, edition; **de una tirada** at one go.

tirador [tira'ðor] *nm* (*mango*) handle.

tiranía [tira'nia] *nf* tyranny; **tirano, a** *a* tyrannical // *nm/f* tyrant.

tirante [ti'rante] *a* (*cuerda etc*) tight, taut; (*relaciones*) strained // *nm* (*ARQ*) brace; (*TEC*) stay; (*correa*) shoulder strap; ~**s** *nmpl* braces (*Brit*), suspenders (*US*); **tirantez** *nf* tightness; (*fig*) tension.

tirar [ti'rar] *vt* to throw; (*dejar caer*) to drop; (*volcar*) to upset; (*derribar*) to knock down *o* over; (*jalar*) to pull; (*desechar*) to throw out *o* away; (*disipar*) to squander; (*imprimir*) to print; (*dar: golpe*) to deal // *vi* (*disparar*) to shoot; (*jalar*) to pull; (*fig*) to draw; (*fam: andar*) to go; (*tender a, buscar realizar*) to tend to; (*DEPORTE*) to shoot; ~**se** *vr* to throw o.s.; (*fig*) to cheapen o.s.; ~ **abajo** to bring down, destroy; **tira más a su padre** he takes more after his father; **ir tirando** to manage; **a todo** ~ at the most.

tirita [ti'rita] *nf* (*sticking*) plaster (*Brit*), bandaid (*US*).

tiritar [tiri'tar] *vi* to shiver.

tiro ['tiro] *nm* (*lanzamiento*) throw; (*disparo*) shot; (*disparar*) shooting; (*DEPORTE*) shot; (*GOLF, TENIS*) drive; (*alcance*) range; (*golpe*) blow; (*engaño*) hoax; ~ **al blanco** target practice; **caballo de** ~ cart-horse; **andar de** ~**s largos** to be all dressed up; **al** ~ (*AM*) at once.

tirón [ti'ron] *nm* (*sacudida*) pull, tug; **de un** ~ in one go, all at once.

tiroteo [tiro'teo] *nm* exchange of shots, shooting.

tísico, a ['tisiko, a] *a* consumptive.

tisis ['tisis] *nf inv* consumption, tuberculosis.

títere ['titere] *nm* puppet.

titilar [titi'lar] *vi* (*luz, estrella*) to twinkle; (*párpado*) to flutter.

titiritero, a [titiri'tero, a] *nm/f* puppeteer.

titubeante [tituβe'ante] *a* (*inestable*) shaky, tottering; (*farfullante*) stammering; (*dudoso*) hesitant.

titubear [tituβe'ar] *vi* to stagger; to stammer; (*fig*) to hesitate; **titubeo** *nm* staggering; stammering; hesitation.

titulado, a [titu'laðo, a] *a* (*libro*) entitled; (*persona*) titled.

titular [titu'lar] *a* titular // *nm/f* occupant // *nm* headline // *vt* to title; **~se** *vr* to be entitled; **título** *nm* title; (*de diario*) headline; (*certificado*) professional qualification; (*universitario*) (university) degree; (*fig*) right; **a título de** in the capacity of.

tiza ['tiθa] *nf* chalk.

tiznar [tiθ'nar] *vt* to blacken; (*fig*) to tarnish.

tizón [ti'θon], **tizo** [ti'θo] *nm* brand; (*fig*) stain.

toalla [to'aʎa] *nf* towel.

tobillo [to'βiʎo] *nm* ankle.

tobogán [toβo'gan] *nm* toboggan; (*montaña rusa*) roller-coaster; (*resbaladilla*) chute, slide.

toca ['toka] *nf* headdress.

tocadiscos [toka'ðiskos] *nm inv* record player.

tocado, a [to'kaðo, a] *a* (*fam*) touched // *nm* headdress.

tocador [toka'ðor] *nm* (*mueble*) dressing table; (*cuarto*) boudoir; (*fam*) ladies' toilet (*Brit*) *o* room (*US*).

tocante [to'kante]: **~ a** *prep* with regard to.

tocar [to'kar] *vt* to touch; (*MUS*) to play; (*topar con*) to run into; strike;

(*referirse a*) to allude to; (*padecer*) to suffer // *vi* (*a la puerta*) to knock (on *o* at the door); (*ser de turno*) to fall to, be the turn of; (*ser hora*) to be due; (*barco, avión*) to call at; (*atañer*) to concern; **~se** *vr* (*cubrirse la cabeza*) to cover one's head; (*tener contacto*) to touch (each other); **por lo que a mí me toca** as far as I'm concerned.

tocayo, a [to'kajo, a] *nm/f* namesake.

tocino [to'θino] *nm* bacon.

todavía [toða'βia] *ad* (*aun*) even; (*aún*) still, yet; **~ más** yet more; **~ no** not yet.

todo, a ['toðo, a] ◆ *a* **1** (*con artículo sg*) all; **toda la carne** all the meat; **toda la noche** all night, the whole night; **~ el libro** the whole book; **toda una botella** a whole bottle; **~ lo contrario** quite the opposite; **está toda sucia** she's all dirty; **por ~ el país** throughout the whole country

2 (*con artículo pl*) all; every; **~s los libros** all the books; **todas las noches** every night; **~s los que quieran salir** all those who want to leave

◆ *pron* **1** everything, all; **~s** everyone, everybody; **lo sabemos ~** we know everything; **~s querían más tiempo** everybody *o* everyone wanted more time; **nos marchamos ~s** all of us left

2: **con ~: con ~ él me sigue gustando** even so I still like him

◆ *ad* all; **vaya ~ seguido** keep straight on *o* ahead

◆ *nm*: **como un ~ as** a whole; **del ~: no me agrada del ~** I don't entirely like it.

todopoderoso, a [toðopoðe'roso, a] *a* all powerful; (*REL*) almighty.

toga ['toʝa] *nf* toga; (*ESCOL*) gown.

Tokio ['tokjo] *n* Tokyo.

toldo ['toldo] nm (para el sol) sun-shade (Brit), parasol; (tienda) marquee.

tole ['tole] nm (fam) commotion.

tolerancia [tole'ranθja] nf tolerance.

tolerar [tole'rar] vt to tolerate; (resistir) to endure.

toma ['toma] nf (acto) taking; (MED) dose; ~ **(de corriente)** socket.

tomar [to'mar] vt to take; (aspecto) to take on; (beber) to drink // vi to take; (AM) to drink; ~se vr to take; ~se por to consider o.s. to be; ~ a bien/a mal to take well/badly; ~ en serio to take seriously; ~ **el pelo a** alguien to pull sb's leg; ~**la con** uno to pick a quarrel with sb.

tomate [to'mate] nm tomato; ~**ra** nf tomato plant.

tomavistas [toma'βistas] nm inv movie camera.

tomillo [to'miʎo] nm thyme.

tomo ['tomo] nm (libro) volume.

ton [ton] abr = **tonada** // nm: **sin ~ ni son** without rhyme or reason.

tonada [to'naða] nf tune.

tonalidad [tonali'ðað] nf tune.

tonel [to'nel] nm barrel.

tonelada [tone'laða] nf ton; **tonelaje** nm tonnage.

tonelero [tone'lero] nm cooper.

tónico, a ['toniko, a] a tonic // nm (MED) tonic // nf (MUS) tonic; (fig) keynote.

tonificar [tonifi'kar] vt to tone up.

tono ['tono] nm tone; **fuera de ~** inappropriate; **darse ~** to put on airs.

tontería [tonte'ria] nf (estupidez) foolishness; (cosa) stupid thing; (acto) foolish act; ~**s** nfpl rubbish sg, nonsense sg.

tonto, a ['tonto, a] a stupid, silly // nm/f fool; (payaso) clown.

topacio [to'paθjo] nm topaz.

topar [to'par] vt (tropezar) to bump into; (encontrar) to find, come across; (ZOOL) to butt // vi: ~ **contra o en** to run into; ~ **con** to run up against.

tope ['tope] a maximum // nm (fin) end; (límite) limit; (FERRO) buffer; (AUTO) bumper; **al ~** end to end.

tópico, a ['topiko, a] a topical // nm platitude.

topo ['topo] nm (ZOOL) mole; (fig) blunderer.

topografía [topoɣra'fia] nf topography; **topógrafo, a** nm/f topographer.

toque etc vb ver **tocar** // ['toke] nm touch; (MUS) beat; (de campana) peal; (fig) crux; **dar un ~ a** to test; ~ **de queda** curfew; ~**tear** vt to handle.

toqué vb ver **tocar**.

toquilla [to'kiʎa] nf (pañuelo) head-scarf; (chal) shawl.

tórax ['toraks] nm thorax.

torbellino [torβe'ʎino] nm whirl-wind; (fig) whirl.

torcedura [torθe'ðura] nf twist; (MED) sprain.

torcer [tor'θer] vt to twist; (la esquina) to turn; (MED) to sprain // vi (desviar) to turn off; ~se vr (ladearse) to bend; (desviarse) to go astray; (fracasar) to go wrong; **torcido, a** a twisted; (fig) crooked // nm curl.

tordo, a ['torðo, a] a dappled // nm thrush.

torear [tore'ar] vt (fig: evadir) to avoid; (jugar con) to tease // vi to fight bulls; **toreo** nm bullfighting; **torero, a** nm/f bullfighter.

tormenta [tor'menta] nf storm; (fig: confusión) turmoil.

tormento [tor'mento] nm torture; (fig) anguish.

tornar [tor'nar] vt (devolver) to return, give back; (transformar) to transform // vi to go back; ~se vr (ponerse) to become.

tornasolado, a [tornaso'laðo, a] a (brillante) iridescent; (reluciente) shimmering.

torneo [tor'neo] nm tournament.

tornillo [tor'niʎo] nm screw.

torniquete [torni'kete] nm (puerta)

turnstile; (MED) tourniquet.

torno ['torno] nm (TEC) winch; (tambor) drum; **en ~ (a)** round, about.

toro ['toro] nm bull; (fam) he-man; **los ~s** bullfighting.

toronja [to'ronxa] nf grapefruit.

torpe ['torpe] a (poco hábil) clumsy, awkward; (necio) dim; (lento) slow.

torpedo [tor'peðo] nm torpedo.

torpeza [tor'peθa] nf (falta de agilidad) clumsiness; (lentitud) slowness; (error) mistake.

torre ['torre] nf tower; (de petróleo) derrick.

torrefacto, a [torre'facto, a] a roasted.

torrente [to'rrente] nm torrent.

tórrido, a ['torriðo, a] a torrid.

torrija [to'rrixa] nf French toast.

torsión [tor'sjon] nf twisting.

torso ['torso] nm torso.

torta ['torta] nf cake; (fam) slap.

tortícolis [tor'tikolis] nm inv stiff neck.

tortilla [tor'tiʎa] nf omelette; (AM) maize pancake; **~ francesa/española** plain/potato omelette.

tórtola ['tortola] nf turtledove.

tortuga [tor'tuɣa] nf tortoise.

tortuoso, a [tor'twoso, a] a winding.

tortura [tor'tura] nf torture; **torturar** vt to torture.

tos [tos] nf cough; **~ ferina** whooping cough.

tosco, a ['tosko, a] a coarse.

toser [to'ser] vi to cough.

tostado, a [tos'taðo, a] a toasted; (por el sol) dark brown; (piel) tanned.

tostador [tosta'ðor] nm toaster.

tostar [tos'tar] vt to toast; (café) to roast; (persona) to tan; **~se** vr to get brown.

total [to'tal] a total // ad in short; (al fin y al cabo) when all is said and done // nm total; **~ que** to cut (Brit) o make (US) a long story short.

totalidad [totali'ðað] nf whole.

totalitario, a [totali'tarjo, a] a

totalitarian.

tóxico, a ['toksiko, a] a toxic // poison; **toxicómano, a** nm/f drug addict.

tozudo, a [to'θuðo, a] a obstinate.

traba ['traβa] nf bond, tie; (cadena) shackle.

trabajador, a [traβaxa'ðor, a] a hard-working // nm/f worker.

trabajar [traβa'xar] vt to work; (AGR) to till; (empeñarse en) to work at; (empujar: persona) to push; (convencer) to persuade // vi to work; (esforzarse) to strive; **trabajo** nm work; (tarea) task; (POL) labour; (fig) effort; **tomarse el trabajo de** to take the trouble to; **trabajo por turno/a destajo** shift work/ piecework; **trabajoso, a** a hard.

trabalenguas [traβa'lengwas] nm inv tongue twister.

trabar [tra'βar] vt (juntar) to join, unite; (atar) to tie down, fetter; (agarrar) to seize; (amistad) to strike up; **~se** vr to become entangled; **trabársele a uno la lengua** to be tongue-tied.

tracción [trak'θjon] nf traction; **~ delantera/trasera** front-wheel/rear-wheel drive.

tractor [trak'tor] nm tractor.

tradición [traði'θjon] nf tradition; **tradicional** a traditional.

traducción [traðuk'θjon] nf translation.

traducir [traðu'θir] vt to translate; **traductor, a** nm/f translator.

traer [tra'er] vt to bring; (llevar) to carry; (ropa) to wear; (incluir) to carry; (fig) to cause; **~se** vr: **~se algo** to be up to sth.

traficar [trafi'kar] vi to trade.

tráfico ['trafiko] nm (COM) trade; (AUTO) traffic.

tragaluz [traɣa'luθ] nm skylight.

tragaperras [traɣa'perras] nm o f inv slot machine.

tragar [tra'ɣar] vt to swallow; (devorar) to devour, bolt down; **~se** vr swallow.

tragedia [tra'xeðja] nf tragedy; **trágico, a** a tragic.

trago ['traɣo] nm (líquido) drink; (bocado) gulp; (fam: de bebida) swig; (desgracia) blow.

traición [trai'θjon] nf treachery; (JUR) treason; (una ~) act of treachery; **traicionar** vt to betray.

traicionero, a [traiθjo'nero, a] a treacherous.

traidor, a [trai'ðor, a] a treacherous // nmf traitor.

traigo etc vb ver **traer**.

traje vb ver **traer** // ['traxe] nm (de hombre) suit; (de mujer) dress; (vestido típico) costume; ~ **de baño** swimsuit; ~ **de luces** bullfighter's costume.

trajera etc vb ver **traer**.

trajín [tra'xin] nm haulage; (fam: movimiento) bustle; **trajinar** vt (llevar) to carry, transport // vi (moverse) to bustle about; (viajar) to travel around.

trama ['trama] nf (intriga) plot; (de tejido) weft (Brit), woof (US); **tramar** vt to plot; (TEC) to weave.

tramitar [trami'tar] vt (asunto) to transact; (negociar) to negotiate; (manejar) to handle.

trámite ['tramite] nm (paso) step; (JUR) transaction; ~**s** nmpl (burocracia) procedure sg; (JUR) proceedings.

tramo ['tramo] nm (de tierra) plot; (de escalera) flight; (de vía) section.

tramoya [tra'moja] nf (TEATRO) piece of stage machinery; (fig) scheme; **tramoyista** nmf scene shifter; (fig) trickster.

trampa ['trampa] nf trap; (en el suelo) trapdoor; (engaño) trick; (fam) fiddle; **trampear** vt, vi to cheat.

trampolín [trampo'lin] nm trampoline; (de piscina etc) diving board.

tramposo, a [tram'poso, a] a crooked, cheating // nmf crook, cheat.

tranca ['traŋka] nf (palo) stick; (de puerta, ventana) bar; **trancar** vt to bar.

trance ['tranθe] nm (momento difícil) difficult moment o juncture; (estado hipnotizado) trance.

tranco ['traŋko] nm stride.

tranquilidad [traŋkili'ðað] nf (calma) calmness, stillness; (paz) peacefulness.

tranquilizar [traŋkili'θar] vt (calmar) to calm (down); (asegurar) to reassure; ~**se** vr to calm down; **tranquilo, a** a (calmado) calm; (apacible) peaceful; (mar) calm; (mente) untroubled.

transacción [transak'θjon] nf transaction.

transbordador [transβorða'ðor] nm ferry.

transbordar [transβor'ðar] vt to transfer; **transbordo** nm transfer; **hacer transbordo** to change (trains).

transcurrir [transku'rrir] vi (tiempo) to pass; (hecho) to turn out.

transcurso [trans'kurso] nm: ~ **del tiempo** lapse o (of time).

transeúnte [transe'unte] a transient // nmf passer-by.

transferencia [transfe'renθja] nf transference; (COM) transfer.

transferir [transfe'rir] vt to transfer.

transformador [transforma'ðor] nm (ELEC) transformer.

transformar [transfor'mar] vt to transform; (convertir) to convert.

tránsfuga ['transfuɣa] nmf (MIL) deserter; (POL) turncoat.

transfusión [transfu'sjon] nf transfusion.

transición [transi'θjon] nf transition.

transido, a [tran'siðo, a] a overcome.

transigir [transi'xir] vi to compromise, make concessions.

transistor [transis'tor] nm transistor.

transitar [transi'tar] vi to go (from place to place); **tránsito** nm transit; (AUTO) traffic; **transitorio, a** a transitory.

transmisión [transmi'sjon] *nf* (*TEC*) transmission; (*transferencia*) transfer; ~ **en directo/exterior** live/outside broadcast.

transmitir [transmi'tir] *vt* to transmit; (*RADIO, TV*) to broadcast.

transparencia [transpa'renθja] *nf* transparency; (*claridad*) clearness, clarity; (*foto*) slide.

transparentar [transparen'tar] *vt* to reveal // *vi* to be transparent; **transparente** *a* transparent; (*claro*) clear; (*ligero*) diaphanous.

transpirar [transpi'rar] *vi* to perspire; (*fig*) to transpire.

transponer [transpo'ner] *vt* to transpose; (*cambiar de sitio*) to change the place of.

transportar [transpor'tar] *vt* to transport; (*llevar*) to carry; **transporte** *nm* transport; (*COM*) haulage.

transversal [transβer'sal] *a* transverse, cross.

tranvía [tram'bia] *nm* tram.

trapecio [tra'peθjo] *nm* trapeze; **trapecista** *nmf* trapeze artist.

trapero, a [tra'pero, a] *nm/f* ragman.

trapicheo [trapi'tʃeo] *nm* (*fam*) scheme, fiddle.

trapo ['trapo] *nm* (*tela*) rag; (*de cocina*) cloth.

tráquea ['trakea] *nf* windpipe.

traqueteo [trake'teo] *nm* (*golpeteo*) rattling.

tras [tras] *prep* (*detrás*) behind; (*después de*) after; ~ **de** besides.

trascendencia [trasθen'denθja] *nf* (*importancia*) importance; (*FILOSOFIA*) transcendence.

trascendental [trasθenden'tal] *a* important; (*FILOSOFIA*) transcendental.

trascender [trasθen'der] *vi* (*noticias*) to come out; (*suceso*) to have a wide effect.

trasegar [trase'yar] *vt* (*moverse*) to move about; (*vino*) to decant.

trasero, a [tra'sero, a] *a* back, rear

// *nm* (*ANAT*) bottom.

trasfondo [tras'fondo] *nm* background.

trasgredir [trasɣre'ðir] *vt* to contravene.

trashumante [trasu'mante] *a* (*animales*) migrating.

traslado [trasla'ðar] *vt* to move; (*persona*) to transfer; (*postergar*) to postpone; (*copiar*) to copy; ~**se** *vr* (*mudarse*) to move; **traslado** *nm* move; (*mudanza*) move, removal.

traslucir [traslu'θir] *vt* to show; ~**se** *vr* to be translucent; (*fig*) to be revealed.

trasluz [tras'luθ] *nm* reflected light; **al** ~ against o up to the light.

trasnochar [trasno'tʃar] *vi* (*acostarse tarde*) to stay up late; (*no dormir*) to have a sleepless night.

traspasar [traspa'sar] *vt* (*bala etc*) to pierce, go through; (*propiedad*) to sell, transfer; (*calle*) to cross over; (*límites*) to go beyond; (*ley*) to break; **traspaso** *nm* (*venta*) transfer, sale.

traspié [tras'pje] *nm* (*tropezón*) trip; (*fig*) blunder.

trasplantar [trasplan'tar] *vt* to transplant.

traste ['traste] *nm* (*MUS*) fret; **dar al** ~ **con algo** to ruin sth.

trastienda [tras'tjenda] *nf* backshop.

trasto ['trasto] *nm* (*pey: cosa*) piece of junk; (: *persona*) dead loss.

trastornado, a [trastor'naðo, a] *a* (*loco*) mad, crazy.

trastornar [trastor'nar] *vt* to overturn, upset; (*fig: ideas*) to confuse; (: *nervios*) to shatter; (: *persona*) to drive crazy; ~**se** *vr* (*volverse loco*) to go mad o crazy; **trastorno** *nm* (*acto*) overturning; (*confusión*) confusion.

tratable [tra'taßle] *a* friendly.

tratado [tra'taðo] *nm* (*POL*) treaty; (*COM*) agreement.

tratamiento [trata'mjento] *nm* treatment.

tratar [tra'tar] *vt* (*ocuparse de*) to

treat; (*manejar, TEC*) to handle; (*MED*) to treat; (*dirigirse a: persona*) to address // *vi*: ~ **de** (*hablar sobre*) to deal with, be about; (*intentar*) to try to; ~ **con** (*COM*) to trade in; (*negociar*) to negotiate with; (*tener contactos*) to have dealings with; ~**se** *vr* to treat each other; ¿**de qué se trata?** what's it about?; **trato** *nm* dealings *pl*; (*relaciones*) relationship; (*comportamiento*) manner; (*COM*) agreement; (*título*) (form of) address.

trauma ['trauma] *nm* trauma.

través [tra'βes] *nm* (*fig*) reverse; **al ~ ad** across, crossways; **a ~ de** *prep* across; (*sobre*) over; (*por*) through.

travesaño [traβe'saɲo] *nm* (*ARQ*) crossbeam; (*DEPORTE*) crossbar.

travesía [traβe'sia] *nf* (*calle*) crossstreet; (*NAUT*) crossing.

travesura [traβe'sura] *nf* (*broma*) prank; (*ingenio*) wit; **travieso, a** *a* (*niño*) naughty // *nf* (*ARQ*) crossbeam.

trayecto [tra'jekto] *nm* (*ruta*) road, way; (*viaje*) journey; (*tramo*) stretch; (*curso*) course; ~**ria** *nf* trajectory; (*fig*) path.

traza ['traθa] *nf* (*aspecto*) looks *pl*; (*señal*) sign; ~**do, a** *a*: **bien ~do** shapely, well-formed // *nm* (*ARQ*) plan, design; (*fig*) outline.

trazar [tra'θar] *vt* (*ARQ*) to plan; (*ARTE*) to sketch; (*fig*) to trace; (*plan*) to follow; **trazo** *nm* (*línea*) line; (*bosquejo*) sketch.

trébol ['treβol] *nm* (*BOT*) clover.

trece ['treθe] *num* thirteen.

trecho ['tretʃo] *nm* (*distancia*) distance; (*de tiempo*) while; (*fam*) piece; **de ~ en ~** at intervals.

tregua ['treɣwa] *nf* (*MIL*) truce; (*fig*) lull.

treinta ['treinta] *num* thirty.

tremendo, a [tre'mendo, a] *a* (*terrible*) terrible; (*imponente: cosa*) imposing; (*fam: fabuloso*) tremendous.

trémulo, a ['tremulo, a] *a* quivering.

tren [tren] *nm* train; ~ **de aterrizaje** undercarriage.

trenza ['trenθa] *nf* (*de pelo*) plait (*Brit*), braid (*US*); **trenzar** *vt* (*pelo*) to plait; **trenzarse** *vr* (*AM*) to become involved with.

trepadora [trepa'ðora] *nf* (*BOT*) climber.

trepar [tre'par] *vt*, *vi* to climb.

trepidar [trepi'ðar] *vi* to shake, vibrate.

tres [tres] *num* three.

tresillo [tre'siʎo] *nm* three-piece suite; (*MUS*) triplet.

treta ['treta] *nf* (*COM etc*) gimmick; (*fig*) trick.

triángulo ['trjangulo] *nm* triangle.

tribu ['triβu] *nf* tribe.

tribuna [tri'βuna] *nf* (*plataforma*) platform; (*DEPORTE*) (grand)stand; (*fig*) public speaking.

tribunal [triβu'nal] *nm* (*JUR*) court; (*comisión, fig*) tribunal.

tributar [triβu'tar] *vt* (*gen*) to pay; **tributo** *nm* (*COM*) tax.

tricotar [triko'tar] *vi* to knit.

trigal [tri'ɣal] *nm* wheat field.

trigo ['triɣo] *nm* wheat.

trigueño, a [tri'ɣeɲo, a] *a* (*pelo*) corn-coloured; (*piel*) olive-skinned.

trillado, a [tri'ʎaðo, a] *a* threshed; (*fig*) trite, hackneyed; **trilladora** *nf* threshing machine.

trillar [tri'ʎar] *vt* (*AGR*) to thresh.

trimestral [trimes'tral] *a* quarterly; (*ESCOL*) termly.

trimestre [tri'mestre] *nm* (*ESCOL*) term.

trinar [tri'nar] *vi* (*pájaros*) to sing; (*rabiar*) to fume, be angry.

trincar [trin'kar] *vt* (*atar*) to tie up; (*inmovilizar*) to pinion.

trinchar [trin'tʃar] *vt* to carve.

trinchera [trin'tʃera] *nf* (*fosa*) trench.

trineo [tri'neo] *nm* sledge.

trinidad [trini'ðað] *nf* trio; (*REL*): **la T~** the Trinity.

trino ['trino] nm trill.

tripa ['tripa] nf (ANAT) intestine; (fam: tb: ~s) insides pl.

triple ['triple] a triple.

triplicado, a [tripli'kaðo, a] a: por ~ in triplicate.

tripulación [tripula'θjon] nf crew.

tripulante [tripu'lante] nm/f crewman/woman.

tripular [tripu'lar] vt (barco) to man; (AUTO) to drive.

triquiñuela [triki'nwela] nf trick.

tris [tris] nm inv crack; en un ~ in an instant.

triste ['triste] a (afligido) sad; (sombrío) melancholy, gloomy; (lamentable) sorry, miserable; **~za** nf (aflicción) sadness; (melancolía) melancholy.

triturar [tritu'rar] vt (moler) to grind; (mascar) to chew.

triunfar [trjun'far] vi (tener éxito) to triumph; (ganar) to win; **triunfo** nm triumph.

trivial [tri'βjal] a trivial; **~izar** vt to minimize, play down.

triza ['triθa] nf: hacer ~s to smash to bits; (papel) to tear to shreds.

trizar [tri'θar] vt to smash to bits; (papel) to tear to shreds.

trocar [tro'kar] vt to exchange.

trocha ['trotʃa] nf short cut.

troche ['trotʃe]: **a ~ y moche** ad helter-skelter, pell-mell.

trofeo [tro'feo] nm (premio) trophy; (éxito) success.

tromba ['tromba] nf whirlwind.

trombón [trom'bon] nm trombone.

trombosis [trom'bosis] nf inv thrombosis.

trompa ['trompa] nf horn; (trompo) humming top; (hocico) snout; (fam): **cogerse una ~** to get tight.

trompeta [trom'peta] nf trumpet; (clarín) bugle.

trompo ['trompo] nm spinning top.

trompón [trom'pon] nm bump.

tronar [tro'nar] vt (AM) to shoot // vi to thunder; (fig) to rage.

tronco ['tronko] nm (de árbol,

ANAT) trunk.

tronchar [tron'tʃar] vt (árbol) to chop down; (fig: vida) to cut short; (: esperanza) to shatter; (persona) to tire out; **~se** vr to fall down.

tronera [tro'nera] nf (MIL) loophole; (ARQ) small window.

trono ['trono] nm throne.

tropa ['tropa] nf (MIL) troop; (soldados) soldiers pl.

tropel [tro'pel] nm (muchedumbre) crowd.

tropelía [trope'lia] nm outrage.

tropezar [trope'θar] vi to trip, stumble; (fig) to slip up; **~ con** to run into; (topar con) to bump into; **tropezón** nm trip; (fig) blunder.

tropical [tropi'kal] a tropical.

trópico ['tropiko] nm tropic.

tropiezo vb ver **tropezar** // [tro'pjeθo] nm (error) slip, blunder; (desgracia) misfortune; (obstáculo) snag.

trotamundos [trota'mundos] nm inv globetrotter.

trotar [tro'tar] vi to trot; **trote** nm trot; (fam) travelling; **de mucho trote** hard-wearing.

trozo ['troθo] nm bit, piece.

truco ['truko] nm (habilidad) knack; (engaño) trick.

trucha ['trutʃa] nf trout.

trueno ['trweno] nm thunder; (estampido) bang.

trueque etc vb ver **trocar** // ['trweke] nm exchange; (COM) barter.

trufa ['trufa] nf (BOT) truffle.

truhán, ana [tru'an, ana] nm/f rogue.

truncar [trun'kar] vt (cortar) to truncate; (fig: la vida etc) to cut short; (: el desarrollo) to stunt.

tu [tu] a your.

tú [tu] pron you.

tubérculo [tu'βerkulo] nm (BOT) tuber.

tuberculosis [tuβerku'losis] nf inv tuberculosis.

tubería [tuβe'ria] nf pipes pl; (con-

ducto) pipeline.

tubo ['tuβo] *nm* tube, pipe; ~ de ensayo test tube; ~ de escape exhaust (pipe).

tuerca ['twerka] *nf* nut.

tuerto, a ['twerto, a] *a* blind in one eye // *nm/f* one-eyed person.

tuerza *etc vb ver* torcer.

tuétano ['twetano] *nm* marrow; *(BOT)* pith.

tufo ['tufo] *nm* vapour; *(fig: pey)* stench.

tugurio [tu'ɣurjo] *nm* slum.

tul [tul] *nm* tulle.

tulipán [tuli'pan] *nm* tulip.

tullido, a [tu'ʎiðo, a] *a* crippled.

tumba ['tumba] *nf (sepultura)* tomb.

tumbar [tum'bar] *vt* to knock down; ~se *vr (echarse)* to lie down; *(extenderse)* to stretch out.

tumbo ['tumbo] *nm (caída)* fall; *(de vehículo)* jolt.

tumbona [tum'bona] *nf (butaca)* easy chair; *(de playa)* deckchair *(Brit)*, beach chair *(US)*.

tumido, a [tu'miðo, a] *a* swollen.

tumor [tu'mor] *nm* tumour.

tumulto [tu'multo] *nm* turmoil.

tuna ['tuna] *nf ver* tuno.

tunante [tu'nante] *a* rascally.

tunda ['tunda] *nf (golpeo)* beating.

túnel ['tunel] *nm* tunnel.

Túnez ['tuneθ] *nm* Tunisia; *(ciudad)* Tunis.

tuno, a ['tuno, a] *nm/f (fam)* rogue // *nm* member of student music group // *nf (BOT)* prickly pear; *(MUS)* student music group.

tuntún [tun'tun]: al ~ *ad* thoughtlessly.

tupido, a [tu'piðo, a] *a (denso)* dense; *(tela)* close-woven; *(fig)* dim.

turba ['turβa] *nf* crowd.

turbación [turβa'θjon] *nf (molestia)* disturbance; *(preocupación)* worry; **turbado, a** *a (molesto)* disturbed; *(preocupado)* worried.

turbar [tur'βar] *vt (molestar)* to disturb; *(incomodar)* to upset; ~se *vr* to be disturbed.

turbina [tur'βina] *nf* turbine.

turbio, a ['turβjo, a] *a* cloudy; *(tema etc)* confused // *ad* indistinctly.

turbulencia [turβu'lenθja] *nf* turbulence; *(fig)* restlessness; **turbulento, a** *a* turbulent; *(fig: intranquilo)* restless; (: *ruidoso)* noisy.

turco, a ['turko, a] *a* Turkish // *nm/f* Turk.

turismo [tu'rismo] *nm* tourism; *(coche)* saloon car; **turista** *nm/f* tourist; **turístico, a** *a* tourist *cpd*.

turnar [tur'nar] *vi*, **turnarse** *vr* to take (it in) turns; **turno** *nm (IN-DUSTRIA)* shift; *(oportunidad, orden de prioridad)* opportunity; *(juegos etc)* turn.

turquesa [tur'kesa] *nf* turquoise.

Turquía [tur'kia] *nf* Turkey.

turrón [tur'rron] *nm (dulce)* nougat.

tutear [tute'ar] *vt* to address as familiar 'tú'; ~se *vr* to be on familiar terms.

tutela [tu'tela] *nf (legal)* guardianship; *(instrucción)* guidance; **tutelar** *a* tutelary // *vt* to protect.

tutor, a [tu'tor, a] *nm/f (legal)* guardian; *(ESCOL)* tutor.

tuve, tuviera *etc vb ver* tener.

tuyo, a ['tujo, a] *a* yours, of yours // *pron* yours; los ~s *(fam)* your relations, your family.

TV ['te'βe] *nf abr (= televisión)* TV.

TVE *nf abr = Televisión Española.*

U

u [u] *conj* or.

ubicar [uβi'kar] *vt* to place, situate; (: *fig)* to install in a post; *(AM: encontrar)* to find; ~se *vr* to lie, be located.

ubre ['uβre] *nf* udder.

UCD *nf abr = Unión del Centro Democrático.*

Ud(s) *abr = usted(es).*

ufanarse [ufa'narse] *vr* to boast; ~ de to pride o.s. on; **ufano, a** *a (arrogante)* arrogant; *(presumido)* conceited.

UGT *nf abr = Unión General de Trabajadores.*

ujier [u'xjer] *nm* usher; (*portero*) doorkeeper.

úlcera ['ulθera] *nf* ulcer.

ulcerar [ulθe'rar] *vt* to make sore; ~**se** *vr* to ulcerate.

ulterior [ulte'rjor] *a* (*más allá*) farther, further; (*subsecuente, siguiente*) subsequent.

últimamente ['ultimamente] *ad* (*recientemente*) lately, recently.

ultimar [ulti'mar] *vt* to finish; (*finalizar*) to finalize; (*AM: rematar*) to finish off.

último, a ['ultimo, a] *a* last; (*más reciente*) latest, most recent; (*más bajo*) bottom; (*más alto*) top; (*fig*) final, extreme; **en las últimas** on one's last legs; **por** ~ finally.

ultra ['ultra] *a* extreme // *nm/f* extreme right-winger.

ultrajar [ultra'xar] *vt* (*escandalizar*) to outrage; (*insultar*) to insult, abuse; **ultraje** *nm* outrage; insult.

ultramar [ultra'mar] *nm*: **de** *o* **en** ~ abroad, overseas.

ultramarinos [ultrama'rinos] *nmpl* groceries; **tienda de** ~ grocer's (shop).

ultranza [ul'tranθa]: **a** ~ *ad* (*a todo trance*) at all costs; (*completo*) outright.

ultrasónico, a [ultra'soniko, a] *a* ultrasonic.

ultratumba [ultra'tumba] *nf*: **la vida de** ~ the next life.

ulular [ulu'lar] *vi* to howl; (*búho*) to hoot.

umbral [um'bral] *nm* (*gen*) threshold.

umbroso, a [um'broso, a], **umbrío, a** [um'brio, a] *a* shady.

PALABRA CLAVE

---

un, una [un, 'una] ◆ *artículo definido a*: (*antes de vocal*) **an**; **una mujer/naranja** a woman/an orange

◆ *a*: **unos** (*o* **unas**): **hay unos**

regalos para ti there are some presents for you; **hay unas cervezas en la nevera** there are some beers in the fridge.

unánime [u'nanime] *a* unanimous; **unanimidad** *nf* unanimity.

unción [un'θjon] *nf* anointing; **extrema**~ extreme unction.

undécimo, a [un'deθimo, a] *a* eleventh.

ungir [un'xir] *vt* to rub with ointment; (*REL*) to anoint.

ungüento [un'gwento] *nm* ointment; (*fig*) salve, balm.

únicamente [u'nikamente] *ad* solely, only.

único, a ['uniko, a] *a* only, sole; (*sin par*) unique.

unidad [uni'ðað] *nf* unity; (*COM, TEC etc*) unit.

unido, a [u'niðo, a] *a* joined, linked; (*fig*) united.

unificar [unifi'kar] *vt* to unite, unify.

uniformar [unifor'mar] *vt* to make uniform, level up; (*persona*) to put into uniform.

uniforme [uni'forme] *a* uniform, equal; (*superficie*) even // *nm* uniform; **uniformidad** *nf* uniformity; (*llaneza*) levelness, evenness.

unilateral [unilate'ral] *a* unilateral.

unión [u'njon] *nf* union; (*acto*) uniting, joining; (*calidad*) unity; (*TEC*) joint; (*fig*) closeness, togetherness; **la U**~ **Soviética** the Soviet Union.

unir [u'nir] *vt* (*juntar*) to join, unite; (*atar*) to tie, fasten; (*combinar*) to combine; ~**se** *vr* to join together, unite; (*empresas*) to merge.

unísono [u'nisono] *nm*: **al** ~ in unison.

universal [uniβer'sal] *a* universal; (*mundial*) world *cpd*.

universidad [uniβersi'ðað] *nf* university.

universitario, a [uniβersi'tarjo, a] *a* university *cpd* // *nm/f* (*profesor*) lecturer; (*estudiante*) (university) student; (*graduado*) graduate.

universo [uni'ßerso] *nm* universe.

PALABRA CLAVE

uno, a ['uno, a] ◆ *a* one; **es todo** ~ it's all one and the same; **~s pocos** a few; **~s cien** about a hundred
◆ *pron* 1 one; **quiero** ~ **solo** I only want one; ~ **de ellos** one of them
2 *(alguien)* somebody, someone; **conozco a** ~ **que se te parece** I know somebody o someone who looks like you; ~ **mismo** oneself; **~s querían quedarse** some (people) wanted to stay
3: **(los) ~s ... (los) otros ...** some ... others; each other, one another; **una y otra son muy agradables** they're both very nice
◆ *nf* one; **es la una** it's one o'clock
◆ *nm* (number) one.

---

untar [un'tar] *vt* to rub; *(engrasar)* to grease, oil; *(fig)* to bribe.
uña ['uɲa] *nf (ANAT)* nail; *(garra)* claw; *(casco)* hoof; *(arrancaclavos)* claw.
uranio [u'ranjo] *nm* uranium.
urbanidad [urßani'ðað] *nf* courtesy, politeness.
urbanismo [urßa'nismo] *nm* town planning.
urbanización [urßaniθa'θjon] *nf* *(barrio, colonia)* housing estate.
urbano, a [ur'ßano, a] *a (de ciudad)* urban; *(cortés)* courteous, polite.
urbe ['urße] *nf* large city.
urdimbre [ur'ðimbre] *nf (de tejido)* warp; *(intriga)* intrigue.
urdir [ur'ðir] *vt* to warp; *(fig)* to plot, contrive.
urgencia [ur'xenθja] *nf* urgency; *(prisa)* haste, rush; *(emergencia)* emergency; **servicios de ~** emergency services; **urgente** *a* urgent.
urgir [ur'xir] *vi* to be urgent; **me urge** I'm in a hurry for it.
urinario, a [uri'narjo, a] *a* urinary // *nm* urinal.
urna ['urna] *nf* urn; *(POL)* ballot box.

urraca [u'rraka] *nf* magpie.
URSS *nf*: **la ~** the USSR.
Uruguay [uru'ɣwai] *nm*: **el ~** Uruguay; **uruguayo, a** *a, nm/f* Uruguayan.
usado, a [u'saðo, a] *a* used; *(ropa etc)* worn.
usanza [u'sanθa] *nf* custom, usage.
usar [u'sar] *vt* to use; *(ropa)* to wear; *(tener costumbre)* to be in the habit of; **~se** *vr* to be used; **uso** *nm* use; wear; *(costumbre)* usage, custom; *(moda)* fashion; **al uso** in keeping with custom; **al uso de** in the style of.
usted [us'teð] *pron (sg)* you *sg*; *(pl)* **~es** you *pl*.
usual [u'swal] *a* usual.
usuario, a [u'swarjo, a] *nm/f* user.
usufructo [usu'frukto] *nm* use.
usura [u'sura] *nf* usury; **usurero, a** *nm/f* usurer.
usurpar [usur'par] *vt* to usurp.
utensilio [uten'siljo] *nm* tool; *(CULIN)* utensil.
útero ['utero] *nm* uterus, womb.
útil ['util] *a* useful // *nm* tool; **utilidad** *nf* usefulness; *(COM)* profit; **utilizar** *vt* to use, utilize.
utopía [uto'pia] *nf* Utopia; **utópico, a** *a* Utopian.
uva ['ußa] *nf* grape.

V

v *abr* = *(voltio)* V.
va *vb ver* **ir**.
vaca ['baka] *nf (animal)* cow; **carne de ~** beef.
vacaciones [baka'θjones] *nfpl* holidays.
vacante [ba'kante] *a* vacant, empty // *nf* vacancy.
vaciar [ba'θjar] *vt* to empty out; *(ahuecar)* to hollow out; *(moldear)* to cast // *vi (río)* to flow *(en into)*; **~se** *vr* to empty.
vaciedad [baθje'ðað] *nf* emptiness.

vacilación [baθila'θjon] nf hesitation.

vacilante [baθi'lante] a unsteady; (habla) faltering; (fig) hesitant.

vacilar [baθi'lar] vi to be unsteady; (al hablar) to falter; (fig) to hesitate, waver; (memoria) to fail.

vacío, a [ba'θio, a] a empty; (puesto) vacant; (desocupado) idle; (vano) vain // nm emptiness; (FÍSICA) vacuum; (un ~) (empty) space.

vacuna [ba'kuna] nf vaccine; **vacunar** vt to vaccinate.

vacuno, a [ba'kuno, a] a cow cpd; ganado ~ cattle.

vacuo, a ['bakwo, a] a empty.

vadear [baðe'ar] vt (río) to ford; **vado** nm ford.

vagabundo, a [baɣa'ßundo, a] a wandering; (pey) vagrant // nm tramp.

vagamente [baɣa'mente] ad vaguely.

vagancia [ba'ɣanθja] nf vagrancy.

vagar [ba'ɣar] vi to wander; (no hacer nada) to idle.

vagina [ba'xina] nf vagina.

vago, a ['baɣo, a] a vague; (perezoso) lazy; (ambulante) wandering // nmf (vagabundo) tramp; (flojo) lazybones sg, idler.

vagón [ba'ɣon] nm (FERRO: de pasajeros) carriage; (: de mercancías) wagon.

vaguedad [baɣe'ðað] nf vagueness.

vaho ['bao] nm (vapor) vapour, steam; (respiración) breath.

vaina ['baina] nf sheath.

vainilla [bai'niʎa] nf vanilla.

vainita [bai'nita] nf (AM) green o French bean.

vais vb ver **ir**.

vaivén [bai'ßen] nm to-and-fro movement; (de tránsito) coming and going; **vaivenes** nmpl (fig) ups and downs.

vajilla [ba'xiʎa] nf crockery, dishes pl; lavar la ~ to do the washing-up (Brit), wash the dishes (US).

valdré etc vb ver **valer**.

vale ['bale] nm voucher; (recibo) receipt; (pagaré) IOU.

valedero, a [bale'ðero, a] a valid.

valenciano, a [balen'θjano, a] a Valencian.

valentía [balen'tia] nf courage, bravery; (acción) heroic deed; **valentón, ona** a blustering.

valer [ba'ler] vi to be worth; (costar) to cost; (ser útil) to be useful; (ser válido) to be valid; ~se vr to defend o.s.; ~se de to make use of, take advantage of; ~ la pena to be worthwhile; ¿vale? (Esp) OK?

valeroso, a [bale'roso, a] a brave, valiant.

valgo etc vb ver **valer**.

valía [ba'lia] nf worth, value.

validar [bali'ðar] vt to validate; **validez** nf validity; **válido, a** a valid.

valiente [ba'ljente] a brave, valiant // nm hero.

valija [ba'lixa] nf suitcase; ~ diplomática diplomatic bag.

valioso, a [ba'ljoso, a] a valuable; (rico) wealthy.

valor [ba'lor] nm value, worth; (precio) price; (valentía) valour, courage; (importancia) importance; ~es nmpl (COM) securities; **~ación** nf valuation; **~ar** vt to value.

vals [bals] nm inv waltz.

válvula ['balßula] nf valve.

valla ['baʎa] nf fence; (DEPORTE) hurdle; (fig) barrier; **vallar** vt to fence in.

valle ['baʎe] nm valley.

vamos vb ver **ir**.

vampiro, resa [bam'piro, 'resa] nmf vampire.

van vb ver **ir**.

vanagloriarse [banaɣlo'rjarse] vr to boast.

vándalo, a ['bandalo, a] nm/f vandal; **vandalismo** nm vandalism.

vanguardia [ban'gwardja] nf vanguard; (ARTE etc) avant-garde.

vanidad [bani'ðað] nf vanity; **vanidoso, a** a vain, conceited.

vano, a ['bano, a] a (*irreal*) unreal, vain; (*inútil*) useless; (*persona*) vain, conceited; (*frívolo*) frivolous.

vapor [ba'por] nm vapour; (*vaho*) steam; **al ~** (CULIN) steamed; **~izador** nm atomizer; **~izar** vt to vaporize; **~oso, a** a vaporous.

vaquero, a [ba'kero, a] a cattle cpd // nm cowboy; **~s** nmpl jeans.

vara ['bara] nf stick; (TEC) rod; **~ mágica** magic wand.

variable [ba'rjaßle] a, nf variable.

variación [barje'θjon] nf variation.

variar [bar'jar] vt to vary; (*modificar*) to modify; (*cambiar de posición*) to switch around // vi to vary.

varices [ba'riθes] nfpl varicose veins.

variedad [barje'ðað] nf variety.

varilla [ba'riʎa] nf stick; (BOT) twig; (TEC) rod; (*de rueda*) spoke.

vario, a ['barjo, a] a varied; **~s** various, several.

varón [ba'ron] nm male; man; **varonil** a manly, virile.

Varsovia [bar'soßja] n Warsaw.

vas vb ver **ir**.

vasco, a ['basko, a] a, nm/f Basque.

vascongado, a [baskon'gaðo, a], **vascuence** [bas'kwenθe] a Basque; **las Vascongadas** the Basque Country.

vaselina [base'lina] nf Vaseline ®.

vasija [ba'sixa] nf container, vessel.

vaso ['baso] nm glass, tumbler; (ANAT) vessel.

vástago ['bastaɣo] nm (BOT) shoot; (TEC) rod; (*fig*) offspring.

vasto, a ['basto, a] a vast, huge.

Vaticano [bati'kano] nm: **el ~** the Vatican.

vaticinio [bati'θinjo] nm prophecy.

vatio ['batjo] nm (ELEC) watt.

vaya etc vb ver **ir**.

Vd(s) abr = **usted(es)**.

ve vb ver **ir**, **ver**.

vecindad [beθin'dað] nf, **vecindario** [beθin'darjo] nm neighbourhood; (*habitantes*) residents pl.

vecino, a [be'θino, a] a neighbouring

// nm/f neighbour; (*residente*) resident.

veda ['beða] nf prohibition.

vedado [be'ðaðo] nm preserve.

vedar [be'ðar] vt (*prohibir*) to ban, prohibit; (*impedir*) to stop, prevent.

vegetación [bexeta'θjon] nf vegetation.

vegetariano, a [bexeta'rjano, a] a, nm/f vegetarian.

vegetal [bexe'tal] a, nm vegetable.

vehemencia [be(e)'menθja] nf (*insistencia*) vehemence; (*pasión*) passion; (*fervor*) fervour; (*violencia*) violence; **vehemente** a vehement; passionate; fervent.

vehículo [be'ikulo] nm vehicle; (MED) carrier.

veía etc vb ver **ver**.

veinte ['beinte] num twenty.

vejación [bexa'θjon] nf vexation; (*humillación*) humiliation.

vejar [be'xar] vt (*irritar*) to annoy, vex; (*humillar*) to humiliate.

vejez [be'xeθ] nf old age.

vejiga [be'xixa] nf (ANAT) bladder.

vela ['bela] nf (*de cera*) candle; (NAUT) sail; (*insomnio*) sleeplessness; (*vigilia*) vigil; (MIL) sentry duty; **estar a dos ~s** (*fam*) to be skint.

velado, a [be'laðo, a] a veiled; (*sonido*) muffled; (FOTO) blurred // nf soirée.

velador [bela'ðor] nm (*mesa*) pedestal table; (AM) lampshade.

velar [be'lar] vt (*vigilar*) to keep watch over // vi to stay awake; **~ por** to watch over, look after.

veleidad [belei'ðað] nf (*ligereza*) fickleness; (*capricho*) whim.

velero [be'lero] nm (NAUT) sailing ship; (AVIAT) glider.

veleta [be'leta] nf weather vane.

veliz [be'lis] nm (AM) suitcase.

velo ['belo] nm veil.

velocidad [beloθi'ðað] nf speed; (TEC, AUTO) gear.

velocímetro [belo'θimetro] nm speedometer.

veloz [be'loθ] *a* fast.

vello ['beʎo] *nm* down, fuzz; **vellón** *nm* fleece; **~so, a** *a* fuzzy; **velludo, a** *a* shaggy.

ven *vb ver* **venir**.

vena ['bena] *nf* vein.

venado [be'naðo] *nm* deer.

vencedor, a [benθe'ðor, a] *a* victorious // *nm/f* victor, winner.

vencer [ben'θer] *vt* (*dominar*) to defeat, beat; (*derrotar*) to vanquish; (*superar, controlar*) to overcome, master // *vi* (*triunfar*) to win (through), triumph; (*plazo*) to expire; **vencido, a** *a* (*derrotado*) defeated, beaten; (*COM*) due // *ad*: **pagar vencido** to pay in arrears; **vencimiento** *nm* (*COM*) maturity.

venda ['benda] *nf* bandage; **~je** *nm* bandage, dressing; **vendar** *vt* to bandage; **vendar los ojos** to blindfold.

vendaval [benda'βal] *nm* (*viento*) gale.

vendedor, a [bende'ðor, a] *nm/f* seller.

vender [ben'der] *vt* to sell; **~ al contado/al por mayor/al por menor** to sell for cash/wholesale/retail.

vendimia [ben'dimja] *nf* grape harvest.

vendré *etc vb ver* **venir**.

veneno [be'neno] *nm* poison; (*de serpiente*) venom; **~so, a** *a* poisonous; venomous.

venerable [bene'raβle] *a* venerable; **venerar** *vt* (*respetar*) to revere; (*adorar*) to worship.

venéreo, a [be'nereo, a] *a*: **enfermedad venérea** venereal disease.

venezolano, a [beneθo'lano, a] *a* Venezuelan.

Venezuela [bene'θwela] *nf* Venezuela.

venganza [ben'ganθa] *nf* vengeance, revenge; **vengar** *vt* to avenge; **vengarse** *vr* to take revenge; **vengativo, a** *a* (*persona*) vindic-

tive.

vengo *etc vb ver* **venir**.

venia ['benja] *nf* (*perdón*) pardon; (*permiso*) consent.

venial [be'njal] *a* venial.

venida [be'niða] *nf* (*llegada*) arrival; (*regreso*) return.

venidero, a [beni'ðero, a] *a* coming, future.

venir [be'nir] *vi* to come; (*llegar*) to arrive; (*ocurrir*) to happen; (*fig*): **~ de** to stem from; **~ bien/mal** to be suitable/unsuitable; **el año que viene** next year; **~se abajo** to collapse.

venta ['benta] *nf* (*COM*) sale; **~ a plazos** hire purchase; **~ al contado/al por mayor/al por menor** *o* **al detalle** cash sale/wholesale/retail; **~ con derecho a retorno** sale or return; **'en ~'** 'for sale'.

ventaja [ben'taxa] *nf* advantage; **ventajoso, a** *a* advantageous.

ventana [ben'tana] *nf* window; **~ de guillotina/salediza** sash/bay window; **ventanilla** *nf* (*de taquilla*) window (*of booking office etc*).

ventilación [bentila'θjon] *nf* ventilation; (*corriente*) draught; **ventilar** *vt* to ventilate; (*para secar*) to put out to dry; (*fig*) to air, discuss.

ventisca [ben'tiska] *nf*, **ventisquero** [bentis'kero] *nm* blizzard; (*nieve amontonada*) snowdrift.

ventoso, a [ben'toso, a] *a* windy.

ventrílocuo, a [ben'trilokwo, a] *nm/f* ventriloquist.

ventura [ben'tura] *nf* (*felicidad*) happiness; (*buena suerte*) luck; (*destino*) fortune; **a la (buena) ~** at random; **venturoso, a** *a* happy; (*afortunado*) lucky, fortunate.

veo *etc vb ver* **ver**.

ver [ber] *vt* to see; (*mirar*) to look at, watch; (*entender*) to understand; (*investigar*) to look into; // *vi* to see; to understand; **~se** *vr* (*encontrarse*) to meet; (*dejarse ~*) to be seen; (*hallarse: en un apuro*) to find o.s.-

be // *nm* looks *pl*, appearance; **a ~** let's see; **dejarse** ~ to become apparent; **no tener nada que ~** con to have nothing to do with; **a mi modo de ~** as I see it.

vera ['bera] *nf* edge, verge; *(de río)* bank.

veracidad [beraθi'ðað] *nf* truthfulness.

veranear [berane'ar] *vi* to spend the summer; **veraneo** *nm* summer holiday; **veraniego, a** *a* summer *cpd.*

verano [be'rano] *nm* summer.

veras ['beras] *nfpl* truth *sg*; **de ~** really, truly.

veraz [be'raθ] *a* truthful.

verbal [ber'βal] *a* verbal.

verbena [ber'βena] *nf* (*fiesta*) fair; (*baile*) open-air dance.

verbo [ber'βo] *nm* verb; **~so, a** *a* verbose.

verdad [ber'ðað] *nf* truth; (*fiabilidad*) reliability; **de ~** a real, proper; **a decir ~** to tell the truth; **~ero, a** *a* (*veraz*) true, truthful; (*fiable*) reliable; (*fig*) real.

verde ['berðe] *a* green; (*chiste*) blue, dirty // *nm* green; **viejo ~** dirty old man; **~ar, ~cer** *vi* to turn green; **verdor** *nm* (*lo ~*) greenness; (*BOT*) verdure.

verdugo [ber'ðuɣo] *nm* executioner.

verdulero, a [berðu'lero, a] *nm/f* greengrocer.

verduras [ber'ðuras] *nfpl* (*CULIN*) greens.

vereda [be'reða] *nf* path; (*AM*) pavement (*Brit*), sidewalk (*US*).

veredicto [bere'ðikto] *nm* verdict.

vergonzoso, a [berɣon'θoso, a] *a* shameful; (*tímido*) timid, bashful.

vergüenza [ber'ɣwenθa] *nf* shame, sense of shame; (*timidez*) bashfulness; (*pudor*) modesty; **me da ~** I'm ashamed.

verídico, a [be'riðiko, a] *a* true, truthful.

verificar [berifi'kar] *vt* to check; (*corroborar*) to verify; (*llevar a cabo*) to carry out; **~se** *vr* to occur,

happen.

verja ['berxa] *nf* grating.

vermut [ber'mut] (*pl* ~s) *nm* vermouth.

verosímil [bero'simil] *a* likely, probable; (*relato*) credible.

verruga [be'rruɣa] *nf* wart.

versado, a [ber'saðo, a] *a*: **~ en** versed in.

versátil [ber'satil] *a* versatile.

versión [ber'sjon] *nf* version.

verso ['berso] *nm* verse; **un ~** a line of poetry.

vértebra ['berteβra] *nf* vertebra.

verter [ber'ter] *vt* (*líquido: adrede*) to empty, pour (out); (: *sin querer*) to spill; (*basura*) to dump // *vi* to flow.

vertical [berti'kal] *a* vertical.

vértice ['bertiθe] *nm* vertex, apex.

vertiente [ber'tjente] *nf* slope; (*fig*) aspect.

vertiginoso, a [bertixi'noso, a] *a* giddy, dizzy.

vértigo ['bertiɣo] *nm* vertigo; (*mareo*) dizziness.

vesícula [be'sikula] *nf* blister.

vespertino, a [besper'tino, a] *a* evening *cpd.*

vestíbulo [bes'tiβulo] *nm* hall; (*de teatro*) foyer.

vestido [bes'tiðo] *pp de vestir*; **~ de azul/marinero** dressed in blue/as a sailor // *nm* (*ropa*) clothes *pl*, clothing; (*de mujer*) dress, frock.

vestigio [bes'tixjo] *nm* (*huella*) trace; **~s** *nmpl* remains.

vestimenta [besti'menta] *nf* clothing.

vestir [bes'tir] *vt* (*poner: ropa*) to put on; (*llevar: ropa*) to wear; (*proveer de ropa a*) to clothe; (*suj: sastre*) to make clothes for // *vi* to dress; (*verse bien*) to look good; **~se** *vr* to get dressed, dress o.s.

vestuario [bes'twarjo] *nm* clothes *pl*, wardrobe; (*TEATRO: cuarto*) dressing room; (*DEPORTE*) changing room.

veta ['beta] *nf* (*vena*) vein, seam; (*en*

carne) streak; *(de madera)* grain.

vetar [be'tar] *vt* to veto.

veterano, a [bete'rano, a] *a, nm* veteran.

veterinario, a [beteri'narjo, a] *nm/f* vet(erinary surgeon) // *nf* veterinary science.

veto ['beto] *nm* veto.

vetusto, a [be'tusto, a] *a* ancient.

vez [beθ] *nf* time; *(turno)* turn; **a la ~ que** at the same time as; **a su ~** in its turn; **otra ~** again; **una ~** once; **de una ~** in one go; **de una ~ para siempre** once and for all; **en ~ de** instead of; **a o algunas veces** sometimes; **una y otra ~** repeatedly; **de ~ en cuando** from time to time; **7 veces 9** 7 times 9; **hacer las veces de** to stand in for; **tal ~** perhaps.

vía ['bia] *nf* track, route; *(FERRO)* line; *(fig)* way; *(ANAT)* passage, tube // *prep* via, by way of; **por ~ judicial** by legal means; **por ~ oficial** through official channels; **en ~s de** in the process of; **~ aérea** airway; **V~ Láctea** Milky Way.

viaducto [bja'δukto] *nm* viaduct.

viajante [bja'xante] *nm* commercial traveller.

viajar [bja'xar] *vi* to travel; **viaje** *nm* journey; *(gira)* tour; *(NAUT)* voyage; **estar de viaje** to be on a journey; **viaje de ida y vuelta** round trip; **viaje de novios** honeymoon; **viajero, a** *a* travelling; *(ZOOL)* migratory // *nm/f (quien viaja)* traveller; *(pasajero)* passenger.

vial [bjal] *a* road *cpd*, traffic *cpd*.

víbora ['biβora] *nf* viper; *(AM)* poisonous snake.

vibración [biβra'θjon] *nf* vibration; **vibrador** *nm* vibrator; **vibrante** *a* vibrant.

vibrar [bi'βrar] *vt, vi* to vibrate.

vicario [bi'karjo] *nm* curate.

vicegerente [biθexe'rente] *nm* assistant manager.

vicepresidente [biθepresi'δente]

nm/f vice-president.

viceversa [biθe'βersa] *adv* vice versa.

viciado, a [bi'θjaδo, a] *a (corrompido)* corrupt; *(contaminado)* foul, contaminated; **viciar** *vt (pervertir)* to pervert; *(JUR)* to nullify; *(estropear)* to spoil; **viciarse** *vr* to become corrupted.

vicio ['biθjo] *nm* vice; *(mala costumbre)* bad habit; **~so, a** *a (muy malo)* vicious; *(corrompido)* depraved // *nm/f* depraved person.

vicisitud [biθisi'tuδ] *nf* vicissitude.

víctima ['biktima] *nf* victim.

victoria [bik'torja] *nf* victory; **victorioso, a** *a* victorious.

vicuña [bi'kuɲa] *nf* vicuna.

vid [biδ] *nf* vine.

vida ['biδa] *nf (gen)* life; *(duración)* lifetime; **de por ~** for life; **en la/mi ~** never; **estar con ~** to be still alive; **ganarse la ~** to earn one's living.

vídeo ['biδeo] *nm* video // *a inv:* **película ~** video film.

vidriero, a [bi'δrjero, a] *nm/f* glazier // *nf (ventana)* stained-glass window; *(AM: de tienda)* shop window; *(puerta)* glass door.

vidrio ['biδrjo] *nm* glass; **~so, a** *a* glassy.

vieira ['bjeira] *nf* scallop.

viejo, a ['bjexo, a] *a* old // *nm/f* old man/woman; **hacerse ~** to get old.

Viena ['bjena] *n* Vienna.

vienes *etc vb ver* **venir.**

vienés, esa [bje'nes, esa] *a* Viennese.

viento ['bjento] *nm* wind; **hacer ~** to be windy.

vientre ['bjentre] *nm* belly; *(matriz)* womb.

viernes ['bjernes] *nm inv* Friday; **V~ Santo** Good Friday.

Vietnam [bjet'nam] *nm:* **el ~** Vietnam; **vietnamita** *a* Vietnamese.

viga ['biva] *nf* beam, rafter; *(de metal)* girder.

vigencia [bi'xenθja] *nf* validity; **estar en ~** to be in force; **vigente**

a valid, in force; *(imperante)* prevailing.

vigésimo, a [bi'xesimo, a] *a* twentieth.

vigía [bi'xia] *nm* look-out // *(atalaya)* watchtower; *(acción)* watching.

vigilancia [bixi'lanθja] *nf*: **tener a uno bajo** ~ to keep watch on sb.

vigilar [bixi'lar] *vt* to watch over // *vi (gen)* to be vigilant; *(hacer guardia)* to keep watch; ~ **por** to take care of.

vigilia [vi'xilja] *nf* wakefulness, being awake; *(REL)* fast.

vigor [bi'ɣor] *nm* vigour, vitality; **en** ~ in force; **entrar/poner en** ~ to take/put into effect; ~**oso, a** a vigorous.

vil [bil] *a* vile, low; ~**eza** *nf* vileness; *(acto)* base deed.

vilipendiar [bilipen'djar] *vt* to vilify, revile.

vilo ['bilo]: **en** ~ *ad* in the air, suspended; *(fig)* on tenterhooks, in suspense.

villa ['biʎa] *nf (casa)* villa; *(pueblo)* small town; *(municipalidad)* municipality; ~ **miseria** *(AM)* shantytown.

villancico [biʎan'θiko] *nm* (Christmas) carol.

villorrio [bi'ʎorjo] *nm (AM)* shantytown.

vinagre [bi'naɣre] *nm* vinegar; ~**ras** *nfpl* cruet *sg*.

vinagreta [bina'ɣreta] *nf* vinaigrette, French dressing.

vinculación [binkula'θjon] *nf (lazo)* link, bond; *(acción)* linking.

vincular [binku'lar] *vt* to link, bind; **vínculo** *nm* link, bond.

vine *etc vb ver* **venir**.

vinicultura [binikul'tura] *nf* wine growing.

viniera *etc vb ver* **venir**.

vino *vb ver* **venir** // ['bino] *nm* wine; ~ **blanco/tinto** white/red wine.

viña ['biɲa] *nf*, **viñedo** [bi'ɲeðo] *nm* vineyard.

viola ['bjola] *nf* viola.

violación [bjola'θjon] *nf* violation; *(estupro)*; ~ **(sexual)** rape.

violar [bjo'lar] *vt* to violate; *(cometer estupro)* to rape.

violencia [bjo'lenθja] *nf (fuerza)* violence, force; *(embarazo)* embarrassment; *(acto injusto)* unjust act; **violentar** *vt* to force; *(casa)* to break into; *(agredir)* to assault; *(violar)* to violate; **violento, a** a violent; *(furioso)* furious; *(situación)* embarrassing; *(acto)* forced, unnatural.

violeta [bjo'leta] *nf* violet.

violín [bjo'lin] *nm* violin.

violón [bjo'lon] *nm* double bass.

viraje [bi'raxe] *nm* turn; *(de vehículo)* swerve; *(de carretera)* bend; *(fig)* change of direction; **virar** *vi* to change direction.

virgen [bir'xen] *a*, *nf* virgin.

Virgo ['bir'xo] *nm* Virgo.

viril [bi'ril] *a* virile; ~**idad** *nf* virility.

virtualmente [birtwal'mente] *ad* virtually.

virtud [bir'tuð] *nf* virtue; **en** ~ **de** by virtue of; **virtuoso, a** a virtuous // *nm/f* virtuoso.

viruela [bi'rwela] *nf* smallpox; ~**s** *nfpl* pockmarks.

virulento, a [biru'lento, a] *a* virulent.

virus ['birus] *nm inv* virus.

visa ['bisa] *nf (AM)*, **visado** [bi'saðo] *nm* visa.

viscoso, a [bis'koso, a] *a* viscous.

visera [bi'sera] *nf* visor.

visibilidad [bisiβili'ðað] *nf* visibility; **visible** *a* visible; *(fig)* obvious.

visillos [bi'siʎos] *nmpl* lace curtains.

visión [bi'sjon] *nf (ANAT)* vision, (eye)sight; *(fantasía)* vision, fantasy; **visionario, a** a *(que prevé)* visionary; *(alucinado)* deluded // *nm/f* visionary.

visita [bi'sita] *nf* call, visit; *(persona)* visitor; **hacer una** ~ to pay a visit.

visitar [bisi'tar] *vt* to visit, call on.

vislumbrar [bislum'brar] *vt* to

glimpse, catch a glimpse of; **vislumbre** *nf* glimpse; *(centelleo)* gleam; *(idea vaga)* glimmer.

viso ['biso] *nm (del metal)* glint, gleam; *(de tela)* sheen; *(aspecto)* appearance.

visón [bi'son] *nm* mink.

visor [bi'sor] *nm (FOTO)* viewfinder.

víspera ['bispera] *nf*: **la ~ de ...** the day before ....

vista ['bista] *nf* sight, vision; *(capacidad de ver)* eye(sight); *(mirada)* look(s) *(pl)* *(JUR)* customs officer; **a primera ~** at first glance; **hacer la ~ gorda** to turn a blind eye; **volver la ~** to look back; **está a la ~ que** it's obvious that; **en ~ de** in view of; **en ~ de que** in view of the fact that; **¡hasta la ~!** so long!, see you!; **con ~s a** with a view to; **~zo** *nm* glance; **dar o echar un ~zo a** to glance at.

visto, a *pp de* **ver** // *vb ver tb* **vestir** // ['bisto, a] *a* seen; *(considerado)* considered // *nm*: **~ bueno** approval; '**~ bueno**' approved; **por lo ~** evidently; **está ~ que** it's clear that; **está bien/mal ~** it's acceptable/unacceptable; **~ que** *conj* since, considering that.

vistoso, a [bis'toso, a] *a* colourful.

vital [bi'tal] *a* life *cpd*, living *cpd*; *(fig)* vital; *(persona)* lively, vivacious; **~icio, a** *a* for life.

vitamina [bita'mina] *nf* vitamin.

viticultor, a [bitikul'tor, a] *nm/f* wine grower; **viticultura** *nf* wine growing.

vítorear [bitore'ar] *vt* to cheer, acclaim.

vítreo, a ['bitreo, a] *a* vitreous.

vitrina [bi'trina] *nf* show case; *(AM)* shop window.

vituperio [bitu'perjo] *nm (condena)* condemnation; *(censura)* censure; *(insulto)* insult.

viudo, a ['bjuðo, a] *a* *nm/f* widower/widow; **viudez** *nf* widowhood.

vivacidad [biβaθi'ðað] *nf (vigor)* vigour; *(vida)* liveliness.

vivaracho, a [biβa'ratʃo, a] *a* jaunty, lively; *(ojos)* bright, twinkling.

vivaz [bi'βaθ] *a* lively.

víveres ['biβeres] *nmpl* provisions.

vivero [bi'βero] *nm (para plantas)* nursery; *(para peces)* fish farm; *(fig)* hotbed.

viveza [bi'βeθa] *nf* liveliness; *(agudeza: mental)* sharpness.

vivienda [bi'βjenda] *nf* housing; *(una ~)* house; *(piso)* flat *(Brit)*, apartment *(US)*.

viviente [bi'βjente] *a* living.

vivir [bi'βir] *vt, vi* to live // *nm* life, living.

vivo, a ['biβo, a] *a* living, alive; *(fig: descripción)* vivid; *(persona: astuto)* smart, clever; **en ~** *(transmisión etc)* live.

vocablo [bo'kaβlo] *nm (palabra)* word; *(término)* term.

vocabulario [bokaβu'larjo] *nm* vocabulary.

vocación [boka'θjon] *nf* vocation; **vocacional** *nf (AM)* ≈ technical college.

vocal [bo'kal] *a* vocal // *nf* vowel; **~izar** *vt* to vocalize.

vocear [boθe'ar] *vt (para vender)* to cry; *(aclamar)* to acclaim; *(fig)* to proclaim // *vi* to yell; **vocerío** *nm*, **vocería** *nf* shouting.

vocero [bo'θero] *nm/f* spokesman/woman.

voces [bo'θes] *nfpl ver* **voz**.

vociferar [boθife'rar] *vt* to shout // *vi* to yell.

vodka [bo'ðka] *nm o f* vodka.

vol *abr* = **volumen**.

volador, a [bola'ðor, a] *a* flying.

volandas [bo'landas]: **en ~** *ad* in the air; *(fig)* swiftly.

volante [bo'lante] *a* flying // *nm (de coche)* steering wheel; *(de reloj)* balance.

volar [bo'lar] *vt (edificio)* to blow up // *vi* to fly.

volátil [bo'latil] *a* volatile.

volcán [bol'kan] *nm* volcano; **~ico,**

a *a* volcanic.

volcar [bol'kar] *vt* to upset, overturn; (*tumbar, derribar*) to knock over; (*vaciar*) to empty out // *vi* to overturn; ~se *vr* to tip over.

voleibol [bolei'βol] *nm* volleyball.

volqué, volquemos *etc vb ver* **volcar.**

volquete [bol'kete] *nm* (*carro*) tipcart; (*AUTO*) dumper.

voltaje [bol'taxe] *nm* voltage.

voltear [bolte'ar] *vt* to turn over; (*volcar*) to turn upside down.

voltereta [bolte'reta] *nf* somersault.

voltio ['boltjo] *nm* volt.

voluble [bo'luβle] *a* fickle.

volumen [bo'lumen] (*pl* **volúmenes**) *nm* volume; **voluminoso, a** *a* voluminous; (*enorme*) massive.

voluntad [bolun'tað] *nf* (*resolución*) willpower; (*deseo*) desire, wish.

voluntario, a [bolun'tarjo, a] *a* voluntary // *nm/f* volunteer.

voluntarioso, a [bolunta'rjoso, a] *a* headstrong.

voluptuoso, a [bolup'twoso, a] *a* voluptuous.

volver [bol'βer] *vt* (*gen*) to turn; (*dar vuelta a*) to turn (over); (*voltear*) to turn round, turn upside down; (*poner al revés*) to turn inside out; (*devolver*) to return // *vi* to return, go back, come back; ~se *vr* to turn round; ~ **la espalda** to turn one's back; ~ **triste** *etc* **a uno** to make sb sad *etc*; ~ **a hacer** to do again; ~ **en sí** to come to; ~se **insoportable/muy caro** to get o become unbearable/very expensive; ~se **loco** to go mad.

vomitar [bomi'tar] *vt, vi* to vomit; **vómito** *nm* (*acto*) vomiting; (*resultado*) vomit.

voraz [bo'raθ] *a* voracious.

vórtice ['bortiθe] *nm* whirlpool; (*de aire*) whirlwind.

vos [bos] *pron* (*AM*) you.

vosotros, as [bo'sotros, as] *pron* you; (*reflexivo*): **entre/para** ~ among/for yourselves.

votación [bota'θjon] *nf* (*acto*) voting; (*voto*) vote.

votar [bo'tar] *vi* to vote; **voto** *nm* vote; (*promesa*) vow; **votos** (*good*) wishes.

voy *vb ver* **ir.**

voz [boθ] *nf* voice; (*grito*) shout; (*chisme*) rumour; (*LING*) voice; **dar voces** to shout, yell; **a media** ~ in a low voice; **a ~ en cuello o en grito** at the top of one's voice; **de viva** ~ verbally; **en ~ alta** aloud; ~ **de mando** command.

vuelco *vb ver* **volcar** // ['bwelko] *nm* spill, overturning.

vuelo *vb ver* **volar** // ['bwelo] *nm* flight; (*encaje*) lace, frill; **coger al** ~ to catch in flight; ~ **charter/regular** charter/regular flight.

vuelque *etc vb ver* **volcar.**

vuelta ['bwelta] *nf* (*gen*) turn; (*curva*) bend, curve; (*regreso*) return; (*revolución*) revolution; (*circuito*) lap; (*de papel, tela*) reverse; (*cambio*) change; **a la** ~ on one's return; **a** ~ **de correo** by return of post; **dar** ~ (*suj: cabeza*) to spin; **dar** ~**s a una idea** to turn over an idea in one's head; **estar de** ~ to be back; **dar una** ~ to go for a walk; (*en coche*) to go for a drive.

vuelto *pp de* **volver.**

vuelvo *etc vb ver* **volver.**

vuestro, a ['bwestro, a] *a* your; **un amigo** ~ a friend of yours // *pron*: **el** ~**/la vuestra, los** ~**s/las vuestras** yours.

vulgar [bul'ɣar] *a* (*ordinario*) vulgar; (*común*) common; ~**idad** *nf* commonness; (*acto*) vulgarity; (*expresión*) coarse expression; ~**idades** *nfpl* banalities; ~**izar** *vt* to popularize.

vulgo ['bulɣo] *nm* common people.

vulnerable [bulne'raβle] *a* vulnerable.

W

wáter ['bater] *nm* toilet.

whisky ['wiski] *nm* whisky, whiskey.

X

xenofobia [kseno'foβja] *nf* xenophobia.

xilófono [ksi'lofono] *nm* xylophone.

Y

y [i] *conj* and.

ya [ja] *ad* (*gen*) already; (*ahora*) now; (*en seguida*) at once; (*pronto*) soon // *excl* all right! // *conj* (*ahora que*) now that; ~ **lo sé** I know; ~ **que** since.

yacer [ja'θer] *vi* to lie.

yacimiento [jaθi'mjento] *nm* deposit.

yanqui ['janki] *a, nm/f* Yankee.

yate ['jate] *nm* yacht.

yazco *etc vb ver* **yacer**.

yedra ['jeðra] *nf* ivy.

yegua ['jeγwa] *nf* mare.

yema ['jema] *nf* (*del huevo*) yoke; (*BOT*) leaf bud; (*fig*) best part; ~ **del dedo** fingertip.

yergo *etc vb ver* **erguir**.

yermo, a ['jermo, a] *a* (*despoblado*) uninhabited; (*estéril, fig*) barren // *nm* wasteland.

yerno ['jerno] *nm* son-in-law.

yerro *etc vb ver* **errar**.

yerto, a ['jerto, a] *a* stiff.

yesca ['jeska] *nf* tinder.

yeso ['jeso] *nm* (*GEO*) gypsum; (*ARQ*) plaster.

yodo ['joðo] *nm* iodine.

yogur [jo'γur] *nm* yoghurt.

yugo ['juγo] *nm* yoke.

Yugoslavia [juγos'laβja] *nf* Yugoslavia.

yugular [juγu'lar] *a* jugular.

yunque ['junke] *nm* anvil.

yunta ['junta] *nf* yoke; **yuntero** *nm* ploughman.

yute ['jute] *nm* jute.

yuxtaponer [jukstapo'ner] *vt* to juxtapose; **yuxtaposición** *nf* juxtaposition.

Z

zafar [θa'far] *vt* (*soltar*) to untie; (*superficie*) to clear; ~**se** *vr* (*escaparse*) to escape; (*TEC*) to slip off.

zafio, a ['θafjo, a] *a* coarse.

zafiro [θa'firo] *nm* sapphire.

zaga ['θaγa] *nf*: **a la ~** behind, in the rear.

zagal, a [θa'γal, a] *nm/f* boy/girl; lad/lass (*Brit*).

zaguán [θa'γwan] *nm* hallway.

zaherir [θae'rir] *vt* (*criticar*) to criticize.

zahorí [θao'ri] *nm* clairvoyant.

zaino, a ['θaino, a] *a* (*color de caballo*) chestnut.

zalamería [θalame'ria] *nf* flattery; **zalamero, a** *a* flattering; (*relamido*) suave.

zamarra [θa'marra] *nf* (*piel*) sheepskin; (*chaqueta*) sheepskin jacket.

zambullirse [θambu'ʎirse] *vr* to dive; (*ocultarse*) to hide o.s.

zampar [θam'par] *vt* to gobble down // *vi* gobble (up).

zanahoria [θana'orja] *nf* carrot.

zancada [θan'kaða] *nf* stride.

zancadilla [θanka'ðiʎa] *nf* trip; (*fig*) stratagem.

zanco ['θanko] *nm* stilt.

zancudo, a [θan'kuðo, a] *a* long-legged // *nm* (*AM*) mosquito.

zángano ['θaŋgano] *nm* drone.

zanja ['θanxa] *nf* ditch; **zanjar** *vt* (*superar*) to surmount; (*resolver*) to resolve.

zapata [θa'pata] *nf* half-boot; (*MECÁNICA*) shoe.

zapatear [θapate'ar] *vi* to tap with

one's feet.

zapatería [θapate'ria] *nf* (*oficio*) shoemaking; (*tienda*) shoe shop; (*fábrica*) shoe factory; **zapatero, a** *nm/f* shoemaker.

zapatilla [θapa'tiʎa] *nf* slipper.

zapato [θa'pato] *nm* shoe.

zarandear [θaranðe'ar] *vt* (*fam*) to shake vigorously.

zarpa ['θarpa] *nf* (*garra*) claw.

zarpar [θar'par] *vi* to weigh anchor.

zarza ['θarθa] *nf* (*BOT*) bramble; **zarzal** *nm* (*matorral*) bramble patch.

zarzamora [θarθa'mora] *nf* blackberry.

zarzuela [θar'θwela] *nf* Spanish light opera.

zigzag [θiɣ'θaɣ] *nm* zigzag; **zigzaguear** *vi* to zigzag.

zinc [θiŋk] *nm* zinc.

zócalo ['θokalo] *nm* (*ARQ*) plinth, base.

zona ['θona] *nf* zone; ~ **fronteriza** border area.

zoo ['θoo] *nm* zoo.

zoología [θoolo'xia] *nf* zoology; **zoológico, a** *a* zoological // *nm* zoo; **zoólogo, a** *nm/f* zoologist.

zopenco, a [θo'penko, a] *nm/f* fool.

zopilote [θopi'lote] *nm* (*AM*) buzzard.

zoquete [θo'kete] *nm* (*madera*) block; (*fam*) blockhead.

zorro, a ['θorro, a] *a* crafty // *nm/f* fox/vixen.

zozobra [θo'θoβra] *nf* (*fig*) anxiety; **zozobrar** *vi* (*hundirse*) to capsize; (*fig*) to fail.

zueco ['θweko] *nm* clog.

zumbar [θum'bar] *vt* (*golpear*) to hit // *vi* to buzz; **zumbido** *nm* buzzing.

zumo ['θumo] *nm* juice.

zurcir [θur'θir] *vt* (*coser*) to darn.

zurdo, a ['θurðo, a] *a* (*mano*) left; (*persona*) left-handed.

zurrar [θu'rrar] *vt* (*fam*) to wallop.

zurrón [θu'rron] *nm* pouch.

zutano, a [θu'tano, a] *nm/f* so-and-so.

ENGLISH-SPANISH
INGLÉS-ESPAÑOL

A

A [eɪ] n (MUS) la m; (AUT): ~ **road** = carretera nacional.

KEYWORD

a indefinite article (before vowel or silent h: **an**) [æ, ən] **1** un(a); ~ **book** un libro; **an apple** una manzana; **she's** ~ **doctor** (ella) es médica
2 (instead of the number 'one') un(a); ~**year** **ago** hace un año; ~ **hundred/thousand** etc **pounds** cien/mil etc libras
3 (in expressing ratios, prices etc): **3** ~ **day/week** 3 al día/a la semana; **10 km an hour** 10 km por hora; **£5** ~ **person** £5 por persona; **30p** ~ **kilo** 30p el kilo.

A.A. n abbr (Brit = Automobile Association) ≈ RACE m (Sp); (= Alcoholics Anonymous) Alcohólicos Anónimos.

A.A.A. n abbr (US = American Automobile Association) ≈ RACE m (Sp).

aback [ə'bæk] ad: **to be taken** ~ quedar desconcertado.

abandon [ə'bændən] vt abandonar; (renounce) renunciar a // n abandono; (wild behaviour): **with** ~ sin reparos.

abashed [ə'bæʃt] a avergonzado.

abate [ə'beɪt] vi (noise, pain) aplacarse; (storm) amainar // vt reducir.

abattoir ['æbətwɑ:*] n (Brit) matadero.

abbey ['æbɪ] n abadía.

abbot ['æbət] n abad m.

abbreviate [ə'bri:vɪeɪt] vt abreviar; **abbreviation** [-'eɪʃən] n (short form) abreviatura; (act) abreviación f.

abdicate ['æbdɪkeɪt] vt, vi abdicar;

abdication [-'keɪʃən] n abdicación f.

abdomen ['æbdəmən] n abdomen m.

abduct [æb'dʌkt] vt raptar, secuestrar.

aberration [æbə'reɪʃən] n aberración f.

abet [ə'bet] vt see **aid**.

abeyance [ə'beɪəns] n: **in** ~ (law) en desuso; (matter) en suspenso.

abhor [əb'hɔ:*] vt aborrecer, abominar (de).

abide [ə'baɪd] vt: **I can't** ~ **it/him** no lo/le puedo ver; **to** ~ **by** vt fus atenerse a.

ability [ə'bɪlɪtɪ] n habilidad f, capacidad f; (talent) talento.

abject ['æbdʒekt] a (poverty) miserable; (apology) rastrero.

ablaze [ə'bleɪz] a en llamas, ardiendo.

able ['eɪbl] a capaz; (skilled) hábil; **to be** ~ **to do sth** poder hacer algo; ~-**bodied** a sano; **ably** ad hábilmente.

abnormal [æb'nɔːməl] a anormal.

aboard [ə'bɔːd] ad a bordo // prep a bordo de.

abode [ə'bəud] n: **of no fixed** ~ sin domicilio fijo.

abolish [ə'bɔlɪʃ] vt suprimir, abolir; **abolition** [æbəu'lɪʃən] n supresión f, abolición f.

abominable [ə'bɔmɪnəbl] a abominable.

aborigine [æbə'rɪdʒɪnɪ] n aborigen m/f.

abort [ə'bɔːt] vt abortar; ~**ion** [ə'bɔːʃən] n aborto (provocado); **to have an** ~**ion** abortarse, hacerse abortar; ~**ive** a malogrado.

abound [ə'baund] vi: **to** ~ (**in** or **with**) abundar (de or en).

about [ə'baut] ◆ ad 1 (approximately) más o menos, aproximadamente; ~ a hundred/thousand etc unos(unas) cien/mil etc; it takes ~ 10 hours se tarda unas o más o menos 10 horas; at ~ 2 o'clock sobre las dos; I've just ~ finished casi he terminado

2 (referring to place) por todas partes; to leave things lying ~ dejar las cosas (tiradas) por ahí; to run ~ correr por todas partes; to walk ~ pasearse, ir y venir

3: to be ~ to do sth estar a punto de hacer algo

◆ prep 1 (relating to) de, sobre, acerca de; a book ~ London un libro sobre o acerca de Londres; what is it ~? ¿de qué se trata?, ¿qué pasa?; we talked ~ it hablamos de eso o ello; what or how ~ doing this? ¿qué tal si hacemos esto?

2 (referring to place) por; to walk ~ the town caminar por la ciudad.

above [ə'bʌv] ad encima, por encima, arriba // prep encima de; mentioned ~ susodicho; ~ all sobre todo; ~ board a legítimo.

abrasive [ə'breɪsɪv] a abrasivo.

abreast [ə'brɛst] ad de frente; to keep ~ of mantenerse al corriente de.

abridge [ə'brɪdʒ] vt (book) abreviar.

abroad [ə'brɔːd] ad (to be) en el extranjero; (to go) al extranjero.

abrupt [ə'brʌpt] a (sudden) brusco; (gruff) áspero.

abruptly [ə'brʌptlɪ] ad (leave) repentinamente; (speak) bruscamente.

abscess ['æbsɪs] n absceso.

abscond [əb'skɒnd] vi fugarse.

absence ['æbsəns] n ausencia.

absent ['æbsənt] a ausente; ~ee [-'tiː] n ausente m/f; ~eeism [-'tiːɪzəm] n absentismo; ~-minded a distraído.

absolute ['æbsəluːt] a absoluto; ~ly [-'luːtlɪ] ad totalmente.

absolve [əb'zɒlv] vt: to ~ sb (from) absolver a alguien (de).

absorb [əb'zɔːb] vt absorber; to be ~ed in a book estar absorto en un libro; ~ent cotton n (US) algodón m hidrófilo; ~ing a absorbente.

absorption [əb'zɔːpʃən] n absorción f.

abstain [əb'steɪn] vi: to ~ (from) abstenerse (de).

abstemious [əb'stiːmɪəs] a abstemio.

abstention [əb'stɛnʃən] n abstención f.

abstinence ['æbstɪnəns] n abstinencia.

abstract ['æbstrækt] a abstracto.

abstruse [æb'struːs] a oscuro.

absurd [əb'sɜːd] a absurdo.

abundance [ə'bʌndəns] n abundancia.

abuse [ə'bjuːs] n (insults) improperios mpl, injurias fpl; (misuse) abuso // vt [ə'bjuːz] (ill-treat) maltratar; (take advantage of) abusar de; **abusive** a ofensivo.

abysmal [ə'bɪzməl] a pésimo; (ignorance) supino.

abyss [ə'bɪs] n abismo.

AC abbr (= alternating current) corriente f alterna.

academic [ækə'dɛmɪk] a académico, universitario; (pej: issue) puramente teórico // n estudioso/a; profesor/a m/f universitario/a.

academy [ə'kædəmɪ] n (learned body) academia; (school) instituto, colegio; ~ of music conservatorio.

accelerate [æk'sɛləreɪt] vt acelerar // vi acelerarse; **accelerator** n (Brit) acelerador m.

accent ['æksɛnt] n acento.

accept [ək'sɛpt] vt aceptar; (approve) aprobar; (concede) admitir; ~**able** a aceptable; admisible; ~**ance** n aceptación f; aprobación f.

access ['æksɛs] n acceso; to have ~ to tener libre acceso a; ~**ible**

[-'sɛsəblɪ] a accesible.

accessory [æk'sɛsərɪ] n accesorio; **toilet accessories** artículos mpl de tocador.

accident ['æksɪdənt] n accidente m; (*chance*) casualidad f; **by** ~ (*unintentionally*) sin querer; (*by coincidence*) por casualidad; ~**al** [-'dɛntl] a accidental, fortuito; ~**ally** [-'dɛntlɪ] ad sin querer; por casualidad; ~**-prone** a propenso a los accidentes.

acclaim [ə'kleɪm] vt aclamar, aplaudir // n aclamación f, aplausos mpl.

acclimatize [ə'klaɪmətaɪz], (US) **acclimate** [ə'klaɪmət] vt: **to become** ~**d** aclimatarse.

accolade ['ækəleɪd] n (*prize*) premio; (*praise*) alabanzas fpl.

accommodate [ə'kɒmədeɪt] vt alojar, hospedar; (*oblige, help*) complacer; **accommodating** a servicial, complaciente.

accommodation n, (US) **accommodations** npl [əkɒmə'deɪʃən(z)] alojamiento.

accompany [ə'kʌmpɪ] vt acompañar.

accomplice [ə'kʌmplɪs] n cómplice m/f.

accomplish [ə'kʌmplɪʃ] vt (*finish*) acabar; (*aim*) realizar; (*task*) llevar a cabo; ~**ed** a experto, hábil; ~**ment** n (*skill*) talento; (*feat*) hazaña; (*realization*) realización f.

accord [ə'kɔːd] n acuerdo // vt conceder; **of his own** ~ espontáneamente; ~**ance** n: **in** ~**ance with** de acuerdo con; ~**ing to** prep según; **in accordance with**) conforme a; ~**ingly** ad (*thus*) por consiguiente.

accordion [ə'kɔːdɪən] n acordeón m.

accost [ə'kɒst] vt abordar, dirigirse a.

account [ə'kaʊnt] n (*COMM*) cuenta, factura; (*report*) informe m; ~**s** npl (*COMM*) cuentas fpl; **of little** ~ de poca importancia; **on** ~ a cuenta; **on no** ~ bajo ningún concepto; **on** ~ **of** a causa de, por motivo de; **to take** **into** ~, **take** ~ **of** tener en cuenta; **to** ~ **for** vt fus (*explain*) explicar; ~**able** a responsable.

accountancy [ə'kaʊntənsɪ] n contabilidad f.

accountant [ə'kaʊntənt] n contable m/f, contador(a) m/f.

account number n (*at bank etc*) número de cuenta.

accredited [ə'krɛdɪtɪd] a (*agent etc*) autorizado.

accrue [ə'kruː] vi: ~**d interest** interés m acumulado.

accumulate [ə'kjuːmjʊleɪt] vt acumular // vi acumularse.

accuracy ['ækjʊrəsɪ] n exactitud f, precisión f.

accurate ['ækjʊrɪt] a (*number*) exacto; (*answer*) acertado; (*shot*) certero; ~**ly** ad (*count, shoot, answer*) con precisión.

accusation [ækjʊ'zeɪʃən] n acusación f.

accuse [ə'kjuːz] vt acusar; (*blame*) echar la culpa a; ~**d** n acusado/a.

accustom [ə'kʌstəm] vt acostumbrar; ~**ed** a: ~**ed to** acostumbrado a.

ace [eɪs] n as m.

acetate ['æsɪteɪt] n acetato.

ache [eɪk] n dolor m // vi doler; **my head** ~**s** me duele la cabeza.

achieve [ə'tʃiːv] vt (*reach*) alcanzar; (*realize*) realizar; (*victory, success*) lograr, conseguir; ~**ment** n (*completion*) realización f; (*success*) éxito.

acid ['æsɪd] a ácido; (*bitter*) agrio // n ácido; ~ **rain** n lluvia ácida.

acknowledge [ək'nɒlɪdʒ] vt (*letter: also:* ~ **receipt of**) acusar recibo de; (*fact*) reconocer; ~**ment** n acuse m de recibo; reconocimiento.

acne ['æknɪ] n acné m.

acorn ['eɪkɔːn] n bellota.

acoustic [ə'kuːstɪk] a acústico; ~**s** n, npl acústica sg.

acquaint [ə'kweɪnt] vt: **to** ~ **sb with sth** (*inform*) poner a uno al corriente de algo; **to be** ~**ed with**

(*person*) conocer; (*fact*) estar al corriente de; **~ance** *n* conocimiento; (*person*) conocido/a.

acquiesce [ækwɪ'ɛs] *vi*: to ~ (in) consentir (en), conformarse (con).

acquire [ə'kwaɪə*] *vt* adquirir; **acquisition** [ækwɪ'zɪʃən] *n* adquisición *f*; **acquisitive** [ə'kwɪzɪtɪv] *a* codicioso.

acquit [ə'kwɪt] *vt* absolver, exculpar; to ~ o.s. well salir con éxito; **~tal** *n* absolución *f*, exculpación *f*.

acre ['eɪkə*] *n* acre *m*.

acrid ['ækrɪd] *a* acre.

acrimonious [ækrɪ'məʊnɪəs] *a* (*remark*) mordaz; (*argument*) reñido.

acrobat ['ækrəbæt] *n* acróbata *m/f*.

acronym ['ækrənɪm] *n* siglas *fpl*.

across [ə'krɒs] *prep* (*on the other side of*) al otro lado de, del otro lado de; (*crosswise*) a través de // *ad* de un lado a otro, de una parte a otra; to ~ de través, al través; to **run/swim** ~ atravesar corriendo/nadando; ~ **from** enfrente de.

acrylic [ə'krɪlɪk] *a* acrílico.

act [ækt] *n* acto, acción *f*; (*THEATRE*) acto; (*in music hall etc*) número; (*LAW*) decreto, ley *f* // *vi* (*behave*) comportarse; (*THEATRE*) actuar; (*pretend*) fingir; (*take action*) obrar // *vt* (*part*) hacer el papel de; to ~ as actuar or hacer de; **~ing** *a* suplente // *n*: to do some **~ing** hacer algo de teatro.

action ['ækʃən] *n* acción *f*, acto; (*MIL*) acción *f*, batalla; (*LAW*) proceso, demanda; **out of** ~ (*person*) fuera de combate; (*thing*) descompuesto; to **take** ~ tomar medidas; ~ **replay** *n* (*TV*) repetición *f*.

activate ['æktɪveɪt] *vt* activar.

active ['æktɪv] *a* activo, enérgico; (*volcano*) en actividad; **~ly** *ad* (*participate*) activamente; (*discourage*, *dislike*) enérgicamente; **activist** *n* activista *m/f*; **activity** [-'tɪvɪtɪ] *n* actividad *f*.

actor ['æktə*] *n* actor *m*.

actress ['æktrɪs] *n* actriz *f*.

actual ['æktjuəl] *a* verdadero, real; **~ly** *ad* realmente, en realidad.

acumen ['ækjumən] *n* perspicacia.

acute [ə'kju:t] *a* agudo.

ad [æd] *n abbr* = **advertisement**.

A.D. *ad abbr* (= *Anno Domini*) A.C.

adamant ['ædəmənt] *a* firme, inflexible.

adapt [ə'dæpt] *vt* adaptar // *vi*: to ~ (**to**) adaptarse (a), ajustarse (a); **~able** *a* (*device*) adaptable; (*person*) que se adapta; **~er** or **~or** *n* (*ELEC*) adaptador *m*.

add [æd] *vt* añadir, agregar; (*figures*: *also*: ~ **up**) sumar // *vi*: to ~ **to** (*increase*) aumentar, acrecentar; **it doesn't** ~ **up** (*fig*) no tiene sentido.

adder ['ædə*] *n* víbora.

addict ['ædɪkt] *n* (*to drugs etc*) adicto/a; (*enthusiast*) entusiasta *m/f*; **~ed** [ə'dɪktɪd] *a*: to be **~ed to** ser adicto a; ser aficionado de; **~ion** [ə'dɪkʃən] *n* (*dependence*) hábito morboso; (*enthusiasm*) afición *f*; **~ive** [ə'dɪktɪv] *a* que causa adicción.

addition [ə'dɪʃən] *n* (*adding up*) adición *f*; (*thing added*) añadidura, añadidura; **in** ~ además, por añadidura; **in** ~ **to** además de; **~al** *a* adicional.

additive ['ædɪtɪv] *n* aditivo.

address [ə'drɛs] *n* dirección *f*, señas *fpl*; (*speech*) discurso // *vt* (*letter*) dirigir; (*speak to*) dirigir la palabra a, dirigir la palabra a.

adenoids ['ædənɔɪdz] *npl* vegetaciones *fpl* adenoideas.

adept ['ædɛpt] *a*: ~ **at** experto o hábil en.

adequate ['ædɪkwɪt] *a* (*apt*) adecuado; (*enough*) suficiente.

adhere [əd'hɪə*] *vi*: to ~ **to** pegarse a; (*fig*: *abide by*) observar.

adhesive [əd'hi:zɪv] *a*, *n* adhesivo; ~ **tape** *n* (*Brit*) cinta adhesiva; (*US*: *MED*) esparadrapo.

adjacent [ə'dʒeɪsənt] *a*: ~ **to** contiguo a, inmediato a.

adjective ['ædʒɛktɪv] *n* adjetivo.

adjoining [ə'dʒɔɪnɪŋ] *a* contiguo, vecino.

adjourn [ə'dʒɜːn] *vt* aplazar // *vi* suspenderse.

adjudicate [ə'dʒuːdɪkeɪt] *vi* sentenciar.

adjust [ə'dʒʌst] *vt* (*change*) modificar; (*machine*) ajustar // *vi*: to ~ (to) adaptarse (a); ~**able** *a* ajustable; ~**ment** *n* modificación *f*; ajuste *m*.

adjutant ['ædʒətənt] *n* ayudante *m*.

ad-lib [æd'lɪb] *vt, vi* improvisar // **ad lib** *ad* a voluntad, a discreción.

administer [əd'mɪnɪstə*] *vt* proporcionar; (*justice*) administrar; **administration** [-'treɪʃən] *n* administración *f*; (*government*) gobierno; **administrative** [-trətɪv] *a* administrativo.

admiral ['ædmərəl] *n* almirante *m*; **A~ty** *n* (*Brit*) Ministerio de Marina, Almirantazgo.

admiration [ædmə'reɪʃən] *n* admiración *f*.

admire [əd'maɪə*] *vt* admirar; ~**r** *n* admirador(a) *m/f*; (*suitor*) pretendiente *m*.

admission [əd'mɪʃən] *n* (*exhibition, nightclub*) entrada; (*enrolment*) ingreso; (*confession*) confesión *f*.

admit [əd'mɪt] *vt* dejar entrar, dar entrada a; (*permit*) admitir; (*acknowledge*) reconocer; to ~ to confesarse culpable de; ~**tance** *n* entrada; ~**tedly** *ad* de acuerdo que.

admonish [əd'mɔnɪʃ] *vt* amonestar.

ad nauseam [æd'nɔːsɪæm] *ad* hasta el cansancio.

ado [ə'duː] *n*: **without (any) more ~** sin más (ni más).

adolescence [ædəu'lɛsns] *n* adolescencia.

adolescent [ædəu'lɛsnt] *a, n* adolescente *m/f*.

adopt [ə'dɒpt] *vt* adoptar; ~**ed**, ~**ive** *a* adoptivo; ~**ion** [ə'dɒpʃən] *n* adopción *f*.

adore [ə'dɔː*] *vt* adorar.

adorn [ə'dɔːn] *vt* adornar.

Adriatic [eɪdrɪ'ætɪk] *n*: **the ~ (Sea)** el (Mar) Adriático.

adrift [ə'drɪft] *ad* a la deriva.

adult ['ædʌlt] *n* adulto/a.

adultery [ə'dʌltərɪ] *n* adulterio.

advance [əd'vɑːns] *n* adelanto, progreso; (*money*) anticipo, préstamo; (*MIL*) avance *m* // *vt* avanzar, adelantar; (*money*) anticipar // *vi* avanzar, adelantarse; **in ~** por adelantado; ~**d** *a* avanzado; (*SCOL: studies*) adelantado; ~**ment** *n* progreso; (*in rank*) ascenso.

advantage [əd'vɑːntɪdʒ] *n* (*also TENNIS*) ventaja; to take ~ of aprovecharse de; ~**ous** [ædvən'teɪdʒəs] *a* ventajoso, provechoso.

advent ['ædvənt] *n* advenimiento; **A~** Adviento.

adventure [əd'vɛntʃə*] *n* aventura; **adventurous** [-tʃərəs] *a* aventurero.

adverb ['ædvɜːb] *n* adverbio.

adversary ['ædvəsərɪ] *n* adversario/a, contrario/a.

adverse ['ædvɜːs] *a* adverso, contrario; ~ **to** adverso a.

adversity [əd'vɜːsɪtɪ] *n* infortunio.

advert ['ædvɜːt] *n abbr* (*Brit*) = **advertisement**.

advertise ['ædvətaɪz] *vi* hacer propaganda; (*in newspaper etc*) poner un anuncio; to ~ for (*staff*) buscar por medio de anuncios // *vt* anunciar; (*publicize*) dar publicidad a; ~**ment** [əd'vɜːtɪsmənt] *n* (*COMM*) anuncio; ~**r** *n* anunciante *m/f*; **advertising** *n* publicidad *f*, propaganda; anuncios *mpl*.

advice [əd'vaɪs] *n* consejo, consejos *mpl*; (*notification*) aviso; **a piece of ~** un consejo; to **take legal ~** consultar con un abogado.

advisable [əd'vaɪzəbl] *a* aconsejable, conveniente.

advise [əd'vaɪz] *vt* aconsejar; (*inform*): to ~ **sb of sth** informar a uno de algo; to ~ **sb against sth/doing sth** desaconsejar algo a uno/ aconsejar a uno que no haga algo/

~**dly** [əd'vaɪzɪdlɪ] *ad* (*deliberately*) deliberadamente; ~**r** *n* consejero/a; (*business adviser*) asesor/a *m/f*; ad**visory** *a* consultivo.

advocate ['ædvəkeɪt] *vt* (*argue for*) abogar por; (*give support to*) ser partidario de // [-kɪt] abogado/a.

Aegean [iː'dʒiːən] *n*: the ~ (Sea) el (Mar) Egeo.

aerial ['ɛərɪəl] *n* antena // *a* aéreo.

aerobics [ɛə'rəubɪks] *n* aerobic *m*.

aerodrome ['ɛərədrəum] *n* (*Brit*) aeródromo.

aeroplane ['ɛərəpleɪn] *n* (*Brit*) avión *m*.

aerosol ['ɛərəsɔl] *n* aerosol *m*.

aesthetic [iːs'θɛtɪk] *a* estético.

afar [ə'fɑː] *ad*: from ~ desde lejos.

affair [ə'fɛə] *n* asunto; (*also*: love ~) relación *f* amorosa.

affect [ə'fɛkt] *vt* afectar, influir en; (*move*) conmover; ~**ed** *a* afectado.

affection [ə'fɛkʃən] *n* afecto, cariño; ~**ate** *a* afectuoso, cariñoso.

affirmation [æfə'meɪʃən] *n* afirmación *f*.

affix [ə'fɪks] *vt* (*signature*) estampar; (*stamp*) pegar.

afflict [ə'flɪkt] *vt* afligir.

affluence ['æfluəns] *n* opulencia, riqueza.

affluent ['æfluənt] *a* acaudalado.

afford [ə'fɔːd] *vt* (*provide*) dar, proporcionar; can we ~ it/to buy it? ¿tenemos bastante dinero para comprarlo?

affront [ə'frʌnt] *n* afrenta, ofensa.

Afghanistan [æf'gænɪstæn] *n* Afganistán *m*.

afield [ə'fiːld] *ad*: far ~ muy lejos.

afloat [ə'fləut] *ad* (*floating*) a flote; (*at sea*) en el mar.

afoot [ə'fut] *ad*: there is something ~ algo se está tramando.

afraid [ə'freɪd] *a*: to be ~ of (*person*) tener miedo a; (*thing*) tener miedo de; to be ~ to tener miedo de, temer; I am ~ that me temo que.

afresh [ə'frɛʃ] *ad* de nuevo, otra vez.

Africa ['æfrɪkə] *n* África; ~**n** *a*, *n* africano/a *m/f*.

aft [ɑːft] *ad* (*to be*) en popa; (*to go*) a popa.

after ['ɑːftə] *prep* (*time*) después de; (*place*, *order*) detrás de, tras // *ad* después // *conj* después (de) que; what/who are you ~? ¿qué/a quién busca usted?; ~ having done/he left después de haber hecho/después de que se marchó; to ask ~ sb preguntar por alguien; ~ all después de todo, al fin y al cabo; ~ you! ¡pase usted!; ~**effects** *npl* consecuencias *fpl*, efectos *mpl*; ~**life** *n* vida eterna; ~**math** *n* consecuencias *fpl*, resultados *mpl*; ~**noon** *n* tarde *f*; ~**s** *n* (*col*: *dessert*) postre *m*; ~**sales service** *n* (*Brit*: for car, washing machine etc) servicio de asistencia pos-venta; ~**shave (lotion)** *n* aftershave *m*; ~**thought** *n* ocurrencia (tardía); ~**wards** *ad* después, más tarde.

again [ə'gɛn] *ad* otra vez, de nuevo; to do sth ~ volver a hacer algo; ~ and ~ una y otra vez.

against [ə'gɛnst] *prep* (*opposed*) en contra de; (*close to*) contra, junto a.

age [eɪdʒ] *n* edad *f*; (*old* ~) vejez *f*; (*period*) época // *vi* envejecer(se) // *vt* envejecer; she is 20 years of ~ tiene 20 años; to come of ~ llegar a la mayoría de edad; it's been ~s since I saw you hace siglos que no te veo; ~**d** *a*: ~d 10 de 10 años de edad; the ~**d** ['eɪdʒɪd] *npl* los ancianos; ~ **group** *n*: to be in the same ~ group tener la misma edad; ~ **limit** *n* edad *f* mínima/máxima.

agency ['eɪdʒənsɪ] *n* agencia; through *or* by the ~ of por medio de.

agenda [ə'dʒɛndə] *n* orden *m* del día.

agent ['eɪdʒənt] *n* (*gen*) agente *m/f*; (*representative*) representante *m/f*, delegado/a.

aggravate ['ægrəveɪt] *vt* agravar; (*annoy*) irritar.

aggregate [ˈægrɪgeɪt] n (whole) conjunto; (collection) agregado.

aggressive [əˈgrɛsɪv] a agresivo; (vigorous) enérgico.

aggrieved [əˈgriːvd] a ofendido, agraviado.

aghast [əˈgɑːst] a horrorizado.

agile [ˈædʒaɪl] a ágil.

agitate [ˈædʒɪteɪt] vt (shake) agitar; (trouble) inquietar; to ~ for hacer campaña pro or en favor de; **agitator** n agitador/a m/f.

ago [əˈgəʊ] ad: 2 days ~ hace 2 días; not long ~ hace poco; how long ~? ¿hace cuánto tiempo?

agog [əˈgɒg] a (anxious) ansiado; (excited) emocionado.

agonizing [ˈægənaɪzɪŋ] a (pain) atroz; (suspense) angustioso.

agony [ˈægənɪ] n (pain) dolor m agudo; (distress) angustia; to be in ~ retorcerse de dolor.

agree [əˈgriː] vt (price) acordar, quedar en // vi (statements etc) coincidir, concordar; to ~ (with) (person) estar de acuerdo (con); to ~ to do acceder a hacer; to ~ to sth consentir en algo; to ~ that (admit) estar de acuerdo en que; garlic doesn't ~ with me el ajo no me sienta bien; ~able a agradable; (person) simpático; (willing) de acuerdo, conforme; ~d a (time, place) convenido; ~ment n acuerdo; (COMM) contrato; in ~ment de acuerdo, conforme.

agricultural [ægrɪˈkʌltʃərəl] a agrícola.

agriculture [ˈægrɪkʌltʃəˈ] n agricultura.

aground [əˈgraʊnd] ad: to run ~ encallar, embarrancar.

ahead [əˈhɛd] ad delante; ~ of delante de; (fig: schedule etc) antes de; ~ of time antes de la hora; to be ~ of sth (fig) llevar la ventaja a alguien; go right or straight ~ siga adelante; they were (right) ~ of us iban (justo) delante de nosotros.

aid [eɪd] n ayuda, auxilio // vt ayudar;

auxiliar; in ~ of a beneficio de; to ~ and abet (LAW) ser cómplice de.

aide [eɪd] n (POL) ayudante m/f.

AIDS [eɪdz] n abbr (= acquired immune deficiency syndrome) SIDA m.

ailing [ˈeɪlɪŋ] a (person, economy) enfermizo.

ailment [ˈeɪlmənt] n enfermedad f, achaque m.

aim [eɪm] vt (gun, camera) apuntar; (missile, remark) dirigir; (blow) asestar // vi (also: take ~) apuntar // n puntería; (objective) propósito, meta; to ~ at (objective) aspirar a, pretender; to ~ to do tener la intención de hacer; ~less a sin propósito, sin objeto; ~lessly ad a la ventura, a la deriva.

ain't [eɪnt] (col) = am not; aren't; isn't.

air [eəˈ] n aire m; (appearance) aspecto // vt ventilar; (grievances, ideas) airear // cpd aéreo; to throw sth into the ~ (ball etc) lanzar algo al aire; by ~ (travel) en avión; to be on the ~ (RADIO, TV) estar en antena; ~ bed n (Brit) colchón m neumático; ~borne a (in the air) en el aire; (MIL) aerotransportado; ~-conditioned a climatizado; ~-conditioning n aire acondicionado; ~craft n, pl inv avión m; ~craft carrier n porta(a)viones m inv; ~field n campo de aviación; ~ force n fuerzas fpl aéreas, aviación f; ~ freshener n ambientador m; ~gun n escopeta de aire comprimido; ~ hostess (Brit) n azafata; ~ letter n (Brit) carta aérea; ~lift n puente m aéreo; ~line n línea aérea; ~liner n avión m de pasajeros; ~lock n (in pipe) esclusa de aire; ~mail n: by ~mail por avión; ~ mattress n colchón m neumático; ~plane n (US) avión m; ~port n aeropuerto; ~ raid n ataque m aéreo; ~sick a: to be ~sick marearse (en avión); ~strip n pista de aterrizaje; ~ terminal n terminal f; ~tight a hermético; ~ traffic con-

troller n controlador(a) m/f aéreo/a; **~y** a (room) bien ventilado; (manners) ligero.

aisle [aɪl] n (of church) nave f; (of theatre) pasillo.

ajar [ə'dʒɑː*] a entreabierto.

akin [ə'kɪn] a: ~ **to** parecido a.

alacrity [ə'lækrɪtɪ] n: **with** ~ con presteza.

alarm [ə'lɑːm] n alarma; (anxiety) inquietud f // vt asustar, inquietar; ~ **(clock)** n despertador m.

alas [ə'læs] ad desgraciadamente.

albeit [ɔːl'biːɪt] conj aunque.

album ['ælbəm] n álbum m; (L.P.) elepé m.

alcohol ['ælkəhɔl] n alcohol m; ~**ic** [-'hɔlɪk] a, n alcohólico/a m/f.

alcove ['ælkəʊv] n nicho, hueco.

alderman ['ɔːldəmən] n concejal m.

ale [eɪl] n cerveza.

alert [ə'lɜːt] a alerta; (sharp) despierto, despabilado // n alerta m, alarma // vt poner sobre aviso; **to be on the** ~ estar alerta or sobre aviso.

algebra ['ældʒɪbrə] n álgebra.

Algeria [æl'dʒɪərɪə] n Argelia; ~**n** a, n argelino/a m/f.

alias ['eɪlɪəs] ad alias, conocido por // n alias m.

alibi ['ælɪbaɪ] n coartada.

alien ['eɪlɪən] n (foreigner) extranjero/a m/f a: ~ **to** ajeno a; ~**ate** vt enajenar, alejar.

alight [ə'laɪt] a ardiendo // vi apearse, bajar.

align [ə'laɪn] vt alinear.

alike [ə'laɪk] a semejantes, iguales // ad igualmente, del mismo modo; **to look** ~ parecerse.

alimony ['ælɪmənɪ] n (LAW) manutención f.

alive [ə'laɪv] a (gen) vivo; (lively) activo.

KEYWORD

---

all [ɔːl] ◆ a (singular) todo/a; (plural) todos/as; ~ **day** todo el día; ~ **night** toda la noche; ~ **men** todos los hombres; ~ **five came** vinieron los cinco; ~ **the books** todos los libros; ~ **his life** toda su vida

◆ pron 1 todo; **I ate it** ~, **I ate** ~ **of it** me lo comí todo; ~ **of us went** fuimos todos; ~ **the boys went** fueron todos los chicos; **is that** ~? ¿eso es todo?, ¿algo más?; (in shop) ¿algo más?, ¿alguna cosa más?

2 (in phrases): **above** ~ sobre todo; **by all means** por encima de todo; **after** ~ después de todo; **at** ~: **not at** ~ (in answer to question) en absoluto; (in answer to thanks) ¡de nada!, ¡no hay de qué!; **I'm not at** ~ **tired** no estoy nada cansado/a; **anything at** ~ **will do** cualquier cosa viene bien; ~ **in** ~ a fin de cuentas

◆ ad: ~ **alone** completamente solo/a; **it's not as hard as** ~ **that** no es tan difícil como lo pintas; ~ **the more/the better** tanto más/mejor; ~ **but casi**; **the score is 2** ~ están empatados a 2.

allay [ə'leɪ] vt (fears) aquietar; (pain) aliviar.

all clear n (after attack etc) fin m de la alerta; (fig) luz f verde.

allegation [ælɪ'geɪʃən] n alegato.

allege [ə'ledʒ] vt pretender; ~**dly** [ə'ledʒɪdlɪ] ad supuestamente, según se afirma.

allegiance [ə'liːdʒəns] n lealtad f.

allergy ['ælədʒɪ] n alergia.

alleviate [ə'liːvɪeɪt] vt aliviar.

alley ['ælɪ] n (street) callejuela; (in garden) paseo.

alliance [ə'laɪəns] n alianza.

allied ['ælaɪd] a aliado.

alligator ['ælɪgeɪtə*] n caimán m.

all-in ['ɔːlɪn] a (Brit) (also ad: charge) todo incluido; ~ **wrestling** n lucha libre.

all-night ['ɔːl'naɪt] a (café, shop) abierto toda la noche.

allocate ['æləkeɪt] vt (share out) repartir; (devote) asignar; **allocation** [-'keɪʃən] n (of money) cuota; (distribution) reparto.

allot [ə'lɔt] vt asignar; ~**ment** n ración f; (garden) parcela.

all-out [':laut] a (effort etc) supremo; **all out** ad con todas las fuerzas.

allow [ə'lau] vt (permit) permitir, dejar; (a claim) admitir; (one's to spend etc, time estimated) dar, conceder; (concede): **to ~ that** reconocer que; **to ~ sb to do** permitir a alguien hacer; **he is ~ed to ...** se le permite ...; **to ~ for** vt fus tener en cuenta; ~**ance** n concesión f; (payment) subvención f, pensión f; (discount) descuento, rebaja; **to make ~ances for** disculpar a; tener en cuenta.

alloy ['ælɔɪ] n (mix) mezcla.

all: ~ **right** ad (feel, work) bien; (as answer) ¡conforme!, ¡está bien!; ~**round** a completo; (view) amplio; ~**time** a (record) de todos los tiempos.

allude [ə'lu:d] vi: **to ~ to** aludir a.

alluring [ə'ljuərɪŋ] a seductor(a), atractivo.

allusion [ə'lu:ʒən] n referencia, alusión f.

ally ['ælaɪ] n aliado/a.

almighty [ɔ:l'maɪtɪ] a todopoderoso.

almond ['ɑːmənd] n almendra.

almost ['ɔːlməust] ad casi.

alms [ɑːmz] npl limosna sg.

aloft [ə'lɔft] ad arriba.

alone [ə'ləun] a solo // ad sólo, solamente; **to leave ~** dejar a uno en paz; **to leave sth ~** no tocar algo, dejar algo sin tocar; **let ~ ...** sin hablar de ...

along [ə'lɔŋ] prep a lo largo de, por // ad: **is he coming ~ with us?** ¿viene con nosotros?; **he was limping ~** iba cojeando; ~ **with** junto con; **all ~** (all the time) desde el principio; ~**side** prep al lado de // ad (NAUT) de costado.

aloof [ə'lu:f] a reservado // ad: **to stand ~** mantenerse apartado.

aloud [ə'laud] ad en voz alta.

alphabet ['ælfəbet] n alfabeto; ~**ical** [-'betɪkəl] a alfabético.

alpine ['ælpaɪn] a alpino, alpestre.

Alps [ælps] npl: **the ~** los Alpes.

already [ɔːl'redɪ] ad ya.

alright [':lraɪt] ad (Brit) = **all right**.

Alsatian [æl'seɪʃən] n (Brit: dog) pastor m alemán.

also [':lsəu] ad también, además.

altar ['ɔːltə*] n altar m.

alter ['ɔːltə*] vt cambiar, modificar.

alternate [ɔl'tə:nɪt] a alterno // vi ['ɔ:ltə:neɪt]: **to ~ (with)** alternar (con); **on ~ days** un día sí y otro no; **alternating** [-'neɪtɪŋ] a (current) alterno.

alternative [ɔl'tə:nətɪv] a alternativo // n alternativa; ~**ly** ad: ~**ly one could...** por otra parte se podría... .

alternator ['ɔːltə:neɪtə*] n (AUT) alternador m.

although [ɔːl'ðəu] conj aunque; (given that) si bien.

altitude ['æltɪtjuːd] n altitud f, altura.

alto ['æltəu] n (female) contralto f; (male) alto.

altogether [ɔːltə'geðə*] ad completamente, del todo; (on the whole, in all) en total, en conjunto.

aluminium [ælju'mɪnɪəm], (US) **aluminum** [ə'lu:mɪnəm] n aluminio.

always [':lweɪz] ad siempre.

am [æm] vb see **be**.

a.m. ad abbr (= ante meridiem) de la mañana.

amalgamate [ə'mælgəmeɪt] vi amalgamarse // vt amalgamar, unir.

amass [ə'mæs] vt amontonar, acumular.

amateur ['æmətə*] n aficionado/a, amateur m/f; ~**ish** a (pej) torpe, inexperto.

amaze [ə'meɪz] vt asombrar, pasmar; **to be ~d (at)** quedar pasmado (de); ~**ment** n asombro, sorpresa; **amazing** a extraordinario, asombroso.

Amazon ['æməzən] n (GEO) Amazonas m.

ambassador [æm'bæsədə*] n embajador(a) m/f.

amber ['æmbə*] n ámbar m; **at ~ to ~** (*Brit AUT*) en el amarillo.

ambiguity [æmbɪ'gjuːtɪ] n ambigüedad f; (*of meaning*) doble sentido; **ambiguous** [-'bɪgjuəs] a ambiguo.

ambition [æm'bɪʃən] n ambición f; **ambitious** [-ʃəs] a ambicioso.

amble ['æmbl] vi (*gen*: **~ along**) deambular, andar sin prisa.

ambulance ['æmbjuləns] n ambulancia; **~man/woman** n (*Brit*) ambulanciero/a.

ambush ['æmbuʃ] n emboscada // vt tender una emboscada a.

amenable [ə'miːnəbl] a: **~ to** (*advice etc*) sensible a.

amend [ə'mɛnd] vt (*law*, *text*) enmendar; **to make ~s** enmendarlo; (*apologize*) dar cumplida satisfacción; **~ment** n enmienda.

amenities [ə'miːnɪtɪz] npl comodidades fpl.

America [ə'mɛrɪkə] n (*North ~*) América del norte; **~ na** Estados mpl Unidos; **~n** a, n norteamericano/a m/f.

amiable ['eɪmɪəbl] a (*kind*) amable, simpático.

amicable ['æmɪkəbl] a amistoso, amigable.

amid(st) [ə'mɪd(st)] prep entre, en medio de.

amiss [ə'mɪs] ad: **to take sth ~** to mar algo a mal; **there's something ~** pasa algo.

ammonia [ə'məunɪə] n amoníaco.

ammunition [æmju'nɪʃən] n municiones fpl.

amnesia [æm'niːzɪə] n amnesia.

amnesty ['æmnɪstɪ] n amnistía.

amok [ə'mɔk] ad: **to run ~** = enloquecerse, desbocarse.

among(st) [ə'mʌŋ(st)] prep entre, en medio de.

amoral [æ'mɔrəl] a amoral.

amorous ['æmərəs] a cariñoso.

amorphous [ə'mɔːfəs] a amorfo.

amount [ə'maunt] n (*gen*) cantidad f; (*of bill etc*) suma, importe m // vi:

to ~ to (*total*) sumar; (*be same as*) equivaler a, significar.

amp(ère) ['æmp(ɛə*)] n amperio.

amphibian [æm'fɪbɪən] n anfibio; **amphibious** [-bɪəs] a anfibio.

amphitheatre ['æmfɪθɪətə*] n anfiteatro.

ample ['æmpl] a (*spacious*) amplio; (*abundant*) abundante; (*enough*) bastante, suficiente.

amplifier ['æmplɪfaɪə*] n amplificador m.

amputate ['æmpjuteɪt] vt amputar.

amuck [ə'mʌk] ad = **amok**.

amuse [ə'mjuːz] vt divertir; (*distract*) distraer, entretener; **~ment** n diversión f; (*pastime*) pasatiempo; (*laughter*) risa; **~ment arcade** n mini-casino.

an [æn, ən, n] indefinite article see **a**.

anaemia [ə'niːmɪə] n (*Brit*) anemia; **anaemic** [-mɪk] a anémico; (*fig*) soso, insípido.

anaesthetic [ænɪs'θɛtɪk] n (*Brit*) anestesia; **anaesthetist** [æ'niːsθɪtɪst] n anestesista m/f.

analog(ue) ['ænələg] a (*computer*, *watch*) analógico.

analogy [ə'nælədʒɪ] n analogo.

analyse ['ænəlaɪz] vt (*Brit*) analizar; **analysis** [ə'næləsɪs], pl **-ses** [-siːz] n análisis m inv; **analyst** [-lɪst] n (*political ~*, *psycho~*) analista m/f; **analytic(al)** [-'lɪtɪk(əl)] a analítico.

analyze ['ænəlaɪz] vt (*US*) = **analyse**.

anarchist ['ænəkɪst] a, n anarquista m/f.

anarchy ['ænəkɪ] n anarquía; (*fam*) desorden m.

anathema [ə'næθɪmə] n: **that is ~ to him** eso es pecado para él.

anatomy [ə'nætəmɪ] n anatomía.

ancestor ['ænsɪstə*] n antepasado.

anchor ['æŋkə*] n ancla, áncora // vi (*also*: **to drop ~**) anclar // vt (*fig*) sujetar, afianzar; **to weigh ~** levar anclas; **~age** n ancladero.

anchovy ['æntʃəvɪ] n anchoa.

ancient ['eɪnʃənt] a antiguo.

ancillary [æn'sɪlərɪ] *a (worker, staff)* auxiliar.

and [ænd] *conj* y; *(before i-, hi- +
consonant)* e; *men ~ women* hombres y mujeres; *father ~ son* padre e hijo; *trees ~ grass* árboles y hierba; *~ so on* etcétera, y así sucesivamente; *try ~ come* procura venir; *he talked ~ talked* habló sin parar; *better ~ better* cada vez mejor.

Andalusia [ændə'luːzɪə] *n* Andalucía.

Andes ['ændiːz] *npl: the ~* los Andes.

anemia *etc* [ə'niːmɪə] *n (US) =*
anaemia *etc*.

anesthetic *etc* [ænɪs'θetɪk] *n (US) =*
anaesthetic *etc*.

anew [ə'njuː] *ad* de nuevo, otra vez.

angel ['eɪndʒəl] *n* ángel *m*.

anger ['æŋgə*] *n* cólera // *vt* enojar, enfurecer.

angina [æn'dʒaɪnə] *n* angina (del pecho).

angle ['æŋgl] *n* ángulo; *from their ~* desde su punto de vista.

angler ['æŋglə*] *n* pescador(a) *m/f* (de caña).

Anglican ['æŋglɪkən] *a, n* anglicano/a *m/f*.

angling ['æŋglɪŋ] *n* pesca con caña.

Anglo... ['æŋgləu] *pref* anglo... .

angrily ['æŋgrɪlɪ] *ad* enojado, enfadado.

angry ['æŋgrɪ] *a* enfadado, enojado; *to be ~ with sb/at sth* estar enfadado con alguien/algo por algo; *to get ~* enfadarse, enojarse.

anguish ['æŋgwɪʃ] *n (physical)* tormentos *mpl*; *(mental)* angustia.

angular ['æŋgjulə*] *a (shape)* angular; *(features)* anguloso.

animal ['ænɪməl] *n* animal *m*, bestia // *a* animal.

animate ['ænɪmeɪt] *vt (enliven)* animar; *(encourage)* estimular, alentar // *a* ['ænɪmɪt] vivo; *~d a* vivo.

animosity [ænɪ'mɒsɪtɪ] *n* animosidad *f*, rencor *m*.

aniseed ['ænɪsiːd] *n* anís *m*.

ankle ['æŋkl] *n* tobillo *m*; *~ sock n*

calcetín *m*.

annex ['æneks] *n (also: Brit:* **annexe)** *(building)* edificio anexo // *vt (territory)* anexar.

annihilate [ə'naɪəleɪt] *vt* aniquilar.

anniversary [ænɪ'vɜːsərɪ] *n* aniversario.

announce [ə'nauns] *vt (gen)* anunciar; *(inform)* comunicar; *~ment n (gen)* anuncio; *(declaration)* declaración *f*; *~r n (RADIO, TV)* locutor(a) *m/f*.

annoy [ə'nɔɪ] *vt* molestar, fastidiar; *don't get ~ed!* ¡no se enfade!; *~ance n* enojo; *(thing)* molestia; *~ing a* molesto, fastidioso; *(person)* pesado.

annual ['ænjuəl] *a* anual // *n (BOT)* anual *m*; *(book)* anuario; *~ly ad* anualmente, cada año.

annul [ə'nʌl] *vt* anular; *(law)* revocar; *~ment n* anulación *f*.

annum ['ænəm] *n see* **per**.

anomaly [ə'nɒmǝlɪ] *n* anomalía.

anonymity [ænə'nɪmɪtɪ] *n* anonimato.

anonymous [ə'nɒnɪməs] *a* anónimo.

anorak ['ænəræk] *n* anorak *m*.

anorexia [ænə'reksɪə] *n (MED)* anorexia.

another [ə'nʌðə*] *a: ~ book (one more)* otro libro; *(a different one)* un libro distinto // *pron* otro; *see also* **one**.

answer ['ɑːnsə*] *n* contestación *f*, respuesta; *(to problem)* solución *f* // *vi* contestar, responder // *vt (reply to)* contestar a, responder a; *(problem)* resolver; *to ~ the phone* contestar el teléfono; *in ~ to your letter* contestando or en contestación a su carta; *to ~ the door* acudir a la puerta; *to ~ back vi* replicar, ser respondón/ona // *to ~ for vt fus* responder de or por; *to ~ to vt fus (description)* corresponder a; *~able a: ~able to sb for sth* responsable ante uno de algo; *~ing machine n* contestador *m* automático.

ant [ænt] *n* hormiga.

antagonism [æn'tægənɪzm] n hostilidad f.

antagonize [æn'tægənaɪz] vt provocar.

Antarctic [ænt'ɑːktɪk] n: the ~ el Antártico.

antelope ['æntɪləup] n antílope m.

antenatal ['æntɪ'neɪtl] a antenatal, prenatal; ~ **clinic** n clínica prenatal.

antenna [æn'tenə], pl ~**e** [-niː] n antena.

anthem ['ænθəm] n: **national** ~ himno nacional.

anthology [æn'θɒlədʒɪ] n antología.

anthropology [ænθrə'pɒlədʒɪ] n antropología.

anti-aircraft [æntɪ'eəkrɑːft] a antiaéreo.

antibiotic [æntɪbaɪ'ɒtɪk] a, n antibiótico.

antibody ['æntɪbɒdɪ] n anticuerpo.

anticipate [æn'tɪsɪpeɪt] vt (foresee) prever; (expect) esperar, contar con; (forestall) anticiparse a, adelantarse a; **anticipation** [-'peɪʃən] n previsión f; esperanza; anticipación f.

anticlimax [æntɪ'klaɪmæks] n decepción f.

anticlockwise [æntɪ'klɒkwaɪz] ad en dirección contraria a la de las agujas del reloj.

antics ['æntɪks] npl payasadas fpl; (of child) travesuras fpl.

anticyclone [æntɪ'saɪkləun] n anticiclón m.

antidote ['æntɪdəut] n antídoto.

antifreeze ['æntɪfriːz] n anticongelante m.

antihistamine [æntɪ'hɪstəmiːn] n antihistamínico.

antipathy [æn'tɪpəθɪ] n (between people) antipatía; (to person, thing) aversión f.

antiquated ['æntɪkweɪtɪd] a anticuado.

antique [æn'tiːk] a antigüedad f // a antiguo; ~ **dealer** n anticuario/a; ~ **shop** n tienda de antigüedades.

antiquity [æn'tɪkwɪtɪ] n antigüedad f.

anti-semitism [æntɪ'semɪtɪzm] n antisemitismo.

antiseptic [æntɪ'septɪk] a, n antiséptico.

antisocial [æntɪ'səuʃəl] a antisocial.

antlers ['æntləz] npl cuernas fpl.

anus ['eɪnəs] n ano.

anvil ['ænvɪl] n yunque m.

anxiety [æŋ'zaɪətɪ] n (worry) inquietud f; (eagerness) ansia, anhelo.

anxious ['æŋkʃəs] a (worried) inquieto; (keen) deseoso.

──────────────────────
│ **KEYWORD** │
──────────────────────

any ['enɪ] ♦ a 1 (in questions etc) algún/alguna; have you ~ butter/children? ¿tienes mantequilla/hijos?; if there are ~ tickets left si quedan billetes, si queda algún billete

2 (with negative): I haven't ~ money/books no tengo dinero/libros

3 (no matter which) cualquier; excuse will do valdrá o servirá cualquier excusa; choose ~ book you like escoge el libro que quieras; ~ teacher you ask will tell you cualquier profesor al que preguntes te lo dirá

4 (in phrases): in ~ case de todas formas, en cualquier caso; ~ day now cualquier día (de estos); at ~ moment en cualquier momento, de un momento a otro; at ~ rate en todo caso; ~ time: come (at) ~ time venga cuando quieras; he might come (at) ~ time podría llegar de un momento a otro

♦ pron 1 (in questions etc): have you got ~? ¿tienes alguno/a(s)?; can ~ of you sing? ¿sabéis cantar alguno de vosotros/ustedes?

2 (with negative): I haven't ~ (of them) no tengo ninguno

3 (no matter which one(s)): take ~ of those books (you like) toma cualquier libro que quieras de ésos

♦ ad 1 (in questions etc): do you want ~ more soup/sandwiches? ¿quieres más sopa/bocadillos?; are

you feeling ~ better? ¿te sientes
algo mejor?
2 (with negative): I can't hear him
~ more ya no le oigo; don't wait ~
longer ya no esperes más.

anybody ['enɪbɔdɪ] pron cualquiera;
(in interrogative sentences) alguien;
(in negative sentences): I don't see
~ no veo a nadie; if ~ should
phone... si llama alguien...

anyhow ['enɪhau] ad (at any rate)
de todos modos, de todas formas;
(haphazard): do it ~ you like hazlo
como quieras; she leaves things
just ~ deja las cosas como quiera or
de cualquier modo; I shall go ~ de
todos modos iré.

anyone ['enɪwʌn] pron = **anybody.**

anything ['enɪθɪŋ] pron (in questions
etc) algo, alguna cosa; (with negative) nada; can you see ~? ¿ves
algo?; if ~ happens to me... si
algo me ocurre...; (no matter what):
you can say ~ you like puedes decir lo que quieras; ~ will do vale
todo or cualquier cosa; he'll eat ~
come de todo or lo que sea.

anyway ['enɪweɪ] ad (at any rate) de
todos modos, de todas formas; I
shall go ~ iré de todos modos; (besides): ~, I couldn't come even if
I wanted to además, no podría venir
aunque quisiera; why are you
phoning, ~? ¿entonces, por qué llamas?, ¿por qué llamas, pues?

anywhere ['enɪwɛə*] ad (in questions etc): can you see him ~? ¿le
ves por algún lado?; are you going
~? ¿vas a algún sitio?; (with negative): I can't see him ~ no le veo
por ninguna parte; (no matter
where): ~ in the world en cualquier
parte (del mundo); put the books
down ~ posa los libros donde quieras.

apart [ə'pɑːt] ad aparte, separadamente; 10 miles ~ separados por 10
millas; to take ~ desmontar; ~
from prep aparte de.

apartheid [ə'pɑːteɪt] n apartheid m.
apartment [ə'pɑːtmənt] n (US) piso,
departamento (LAm), apartamento;
(room) cuarto; ~ house n (US)
casa de apartamentos.

apathetic [æpə'θetɪk] a apático, indiferente.
apathy ['æpəθɪ] n apatía, indiferencia.

ape [eɪp] n mono // vt remedar.
aperitif [ə'perɪtɪf] n aperitivo.
aperture ['æpətʃuə*] n rendija, resquicio; (PHOT) abertura.
apex ['eɪpeks] n ápice m; (fig) cumbre f.
apiece [ə'piːs] ad cada uno.
aplomb [ə'plɔm] n aplomo.

apologetic [əpɔlə'dʒetɪk] a (look, remark) de disculpa.
apologize [ə'pɔlədʒaɪz] vi: to ~
(for sth to sb) disculparse (con alguien de algo).
apology [ə'pɔlədʒɪ] n disculpa, excusa.

apostle [ə'pɔsl] n apóstol m/f.
apostrophe [ə'pɔstrəfɪ] n apóstrofo
m.

appal [ə'pɔːl] vt horrorizar, espantar;
~ling a espantoso; (awful) pésimo.
apparatus [æpə'reɪtəs] n aparato;
(in gymnasium) aparatos mpl.
apparel [ə'pærəl] n (US) ropa.
apparent [ə'pærənt] a aparente; ~ly
ad por lo visto, al parecer.
appeal [ə'piːl] vi (LAW) apelar // n
(LAW) apelación f; (request) llamamiento; (plea) súplica; (charm)
atractivo, encanto; to ~ for suplicar, reclamar; to ~ to (subj: person) rogar a, suplicar a; (subj:
thing) atraer, interesar; it doesn't ~
to me no me atrae, no me llama la
atención; ~ing a (nice) atractivo;
(touching) conmovedor(a), emocionante.

appear [ə'pɪə*] vi aparecer, presentarse; (LAW) comparecer; (publication) salir (a luz), publicarse; (seem)
parecer; it would ~ that parecería
que; ~ance n aparición f; (look, as-

pect) apariencia, aspecto.

appease [ə'piːz] vt (pacify) apaciguar; (satisfy) satisfacer.

appendicitis [əpendi'saitis] n apendicitis f.

appendix [ə'pendiks], pl -dices [-disiːz] n apéndice m.

appetite ['æpitait] n apetito m; (fig) deseo, anhelo.

appetizer ['æpitaizə*] n (drink) aperitivo; (food) tapas fpl (Sp).

applaud [ə'plɔːd] vt, vi aplaudir.

applause [ə'plɔːz] n aplausos mpl.

apple ['æpl] n manzana f; ~ tree n manzano.

appliance [ə'plaiəns] n aparato m.

applicant ['æplikənt] n candidato/a; solicitante m/f.

application [æpli'keiʃən] n aplicación f; (for a job, a grant etc) solicitud f, petición f; ~ form n solicitud f.

applied [ə'plaid] a aplicado.

apply [ə'plai] vt: to ~ (to) aplicar (a); (fig) emplear (para) // vi: to ~ to (ask) dirigirse a; (be suitable for) ser aplicable a; (be relevant to) tener que ver con; to ~ for (permit, grant, job) solicitar; to ~ o.s. to aplicarse, dedicarse a.

appoint [ə'pɔint] vt (to post) nombrar; (date, place) fijar, señalar; ~ment n (engagement) cita; (date) compromiso; (act) nombramiento; (post) puesto.

appraisal [ə'preizl] n apreciación f.

appreciable [ə'priːʃəbl] a sensible.

appreciate [ə'priːʃieit] vt (like) apreciar, tener en mucho; (be grateful for) agradecer; (be aware of) comprender // vi (COMM) aumentar(se) en valor; **appreciation** [-'eiʃən] n aprecio; reconocimiento, agradecimiento; aumento en valor.

appreciative [ə'priːʃiətiv] a apreciativo, agradecido.

apprehend [æpri'hend] vt percibir; (arrest) detener.

apprehension [æpri'henʃən] n

(fear) aprensión f; **apprehensive** [-'hensiv] a aprensivo.

apprentice [ə'prentis] n aprendiz/a m/f; ~ship n aprendizaje m.

approach [ə'prəutʃ] vi acercarse // vt acercarse a; (be approximate) aproximarse a; (ask, apply to) dirigirse a // n acercamiento; aproximación f; (access) acceso; (proposal) proposición f; ~able a (person) abordable; (place) accesible.

appropriate [ə'prəupriit] a apropiado, conveniente // vt [-rieit] (take) apropiarse de; (allot): to ~ sth for destinar algo a.

approval [ə'pruːvəl] n aprobación f, visto bueno; on ~ (COMM) a prueba.

approve [ə'pruːv] vt aprobar; to ~ of vt fus aprobar; ~d school n (Brit) correccional m.

approximate [ə'prɔksimit] a aproximado; ~ly ad aproximadamente, más o menos.

apricot ['eiprikɔt] n albaricoque m (Sp), damasco (LAm).

April ['eiprəl] n abril m; ~ Fool's Day n (1 April) = día m de los Inocentes (28 December).

apron ['eiprən] n delantal m.

apt [æpt] a (to the point) acertado, oportuno; (appropriate) apropiado; (likely): to ~ to do propenso a hacer.

aqualung ['ækwəlʌŋ] n escafandra autónoma.

aquarium [ə'kweəriəm] n acuario.

Aquarius [ə'kweəriəs] n Acuario.

aquatic [ə'kwætik] a acuático.

aqueduct ['ækwidʌkt] n acueducto.

Arab ['ærəb] n árabe m/f.

Arabian [ə'reibiən] a árabe.

Arabic ['ærəbik] a (language, manuscripts) árabe // n árabe m; ~ numerals numeración f arábiga.

arable ['ærəbl] a cultivable.

Aragon ['ærəgən] n Aragón m.

arbitrary ['ɑːbitrəri] a arbitrario.

arbitration [ɑːbi'treiʃən] n arbitraje m.

arcade [ɑː'keid] n (ARCH) arcada;

(*round a square*) soportales *mpl*; (*shopping* ~) galería, pasaje *m*.

arch [ɑːtʃ] *n* arco; (*vault*) bóveda; (*of foot*) arco del pie // *vt* arquear.

archaeologist [ɑːkɪˈɔlədʒɪst] *n* arqueólogo/a.

archaeology [ɑːkɪˈɔlədʒɪ] *n* arqueología.

archaic [ɑːˈkeɪɪk] *a* arcaico.

archbishop [ɑːtʃˈbɪʃəp] *n* arzobispo.

arch-enemy [ɑːtʃˈɛnəmɪ] *n* enemigo jurado.

archeology *etc* [ɑːkɪˈɔlədʒɪ] (*US*) = **archaeology** *etc*.

archer [ˈɑːtʃə*] *n* arquero; ~**y** *n* tiro al arco.

archipelago [ɑːkɪˈpelɪgəu] *n* archipiélago.

architect [ˈɑːkɪtekt] *n* arquitecto/a; ~**ural** [ˈtektʃərəl] *a* arquitectónico; ~**ure** *n* arquitectura.

archives [ˈɑːkaɪvz] *npl* archivo *sg*.

archway [ˈɑːtʃweɪ] *n* arco, arcada.

Arctic [ˈɑːktɪk] *a* ártico // *n*: **the** ~ el Ártico.

ardent [ˈɑːdənt] *a* (*desire*) ardiente; (*supporter, lover*) apasionado.

arduous [ˈɑːdjuəs] *a* (*gen*) arduo; (*journey*) penoso.

are [ɑː*] *vb see* **be**.

area [ˈɛərɪə] *n* área; (*MATH etc*) superficie *f*, extensión *f*; (*zone*) región *f*, zona; ~ **code** *n* (*US TEL*) prefijo.

arena [əˈriːnə] *n* arena; (*of circus*) pista; (*for bullfight*) plaza, ruedo.

aren't [ɑːnt] = **are not**.

Argentina [ɑːdʒənˈtiːnə] *n* Argentina; **Argentinian** [ˈtɪnɪən] *a*, *n* argentino/a *m/f*.

arguably [ˈɑːgjuəblɪ] *ad* posiblemente.

argue [ˈɑːgjuː] *vi* (*quarrel*) discutir, pelearse; (*reason*) razonar, argumentar; **to** ~ **that** sostener que.

argument [ˈɑːgjumənt] *n* (*reasons*) argumento; (*quarrel*) discusión *f*, pelea; (*debate*) debate *m*, disputa; ~**ative** [ˈmentətɪv] *a* discutidor/a.

aria [ˈɑːrɪə] *n* (*MUS*) aria.

Aries [ˈɛərɪz] *n* Aries *m*.

arise [əˈraɪz], *pt* **arose**, *pp* **arisen** [əˈrɪzn] *vi* (*rise up*) levantarse, alzarse; (*emerge*) surgir, presentarse; **to** ~ **from** derivar de.

aristocrat [ˈærɪstəkræt] *n* aristócrata *m/f*.

arithmetic [əˈrɪθmətɪk] *n* aritmética.

ark [ɑːk] *n*: **Noah's A~** el Arca *f* de Noé.

arm [ɑːm] *n* (*ANAT*) brazo // *vt* armar; ~**s** *npl* (*weapons*) armas *fpl*; (*HERALDRY*) escudo *sg*; ~ **in** ~ cogidos del brazo; ~**s race** *n* carrera de armamentos.

armaments [ˈɑːməmənts] *npl* (*weapons*) armamentos *mpl*.

armchair [ˈɑːmtʃeə*] *n* sillón *m*.

armed [ɑːmd] *a* armado; ~ **robbery** *n* robo a mano armada.

armour, (*US*) **armor** [ˈɑːmə*] *n* armadura; ~**ed car** *n* coche *m* or carro (*LAm*) blindado; ~**y** *n* arsenal *m*.

armpit [ˈɑːmpɪt] *n* sobaco, axila.

armrest [ˈɑːmrest] *n* apoyabrazos *m inv*.

army [ˈɑːmɪ] *n* ejército.

aroma [əˈrəumə] *n* aroma *m*, fragancia.

arose [əˈrəuz] *pt of* **arise**.

around [əˈraund] *ad* alrededor; (*in the area*) a la redonda // *prep* alrededor de.

arouse [əˈrauz] *vt* despertar.

arrange [əˈreɪndʒ] *vt* arreglar, ordenar; (*programme*) organizar; **to do sth** quedar en hacer algo; ~**ment** *n* arreglo; (*agreement*) acuerdo; ~**ments** *npl* (*preparations*) preparativos *mpl*.

array [əˈreɪ] *n*: ~ **of** (*things*) serie *f* de; (*people*) conjunto de.

arrears [əˈrɪəz] *npl* atrasos *mpl*; **to be in** ~ **with one's rent** estar retrasado en el pago del alquiler.

arrest [əˈrest] *vt* detener; (*sb's attention*) llamar // *n* detención *f*; **under** ~ detenido.

arrival [əˈraɪvəl] *n* llegada; **new** ~

recién llegado/a.

arrive [əˈraɪv] n il llegar.

arrogant [ˈærəgənt] a arrogante.

arrow [ˈærəu] n flecha.

arse [aːs] n (Brit col!) culo, trasero.

arsenal [ˈaːsɪnl] n arsenal m.

arsenic [ˈaːsnɪk] n arsénico.

arson [ˈaːsn] n incendio premeditado.

art [aːt] n arte m; (skill) destreza; (technique) técnica; A~s npl (SCOL) Letras fpl.

artery [ˈaːtərɪ] n arteria.

artful [ˈaːtful] a (cunning: person, trick) mañoso.

art gallery n pinacoteca; (saleroom) galería de arte.

arthritis [aːˈθraɪtɪs] n artritis f.

artichoke [ˈaːtɪtʃəuk] n alcachofa; Jerusalem ~ aguaturma.

article [ˈaːtɪkl] n artículo, (in newspaper) artículo; (Brit LAW: training): ~s npl contrato sg de aprendizaje; ~ of clothing prenda de vestir.

articulate [aːˈtɪkjulɪt] a (speech) claro; (person) que se expresa bien // il [-leɪt] articular; ~d lorry n (Brit) trailer m.

artificial [aːtɪˈfɪʃəl] a artificial; (teeth etc) postizo.

artillery [aːˈtɪlərɪ] n artillería.

artisan [ˈaːtɪzæn] n artesano.

artist [ˈaːtɪst] n artista m/f; (MUS) intérprete m/f; ~ic [aːˈtɪstɪk] a artístico; ~ry n arte m, habilidad f (artística).

artless [ˈaːtlɪs] a (innocent) natural, sencillo; (clumsy) torpe.

art school n escuela de bellas artes.

KEYWORD

---

as [əz] conj **1** (referring to time) cuando, mientras; a medida que; ~ the years went by con el paso de los años; he came in ~ I was leaving entró cuando me marchaba; ~ from tomorrow desde or a partir de mañana

2 (in comparisons): ~ big ~ tan grande como; **twice** ~ big ~ el do-

ble de grande que; ~ much money/ many books ~ tanto dinero/tantos libros como; ~ soon ~ en cuanto

3 (since, because) como, ya que; he left early ~ he had to be home by 10 se fue temprano como tenía que estar en casa a las 10

4 (referring to manner, way): do ~ you wish haz lo que quieras; ~ she said como dijo; he gave it to me ~ a present me lo dio de regalo

5 (in the capacity of): he works ~ a barman trabaja de barman; ~ chairman of the company, he... como presidente de la compañía, ...

6 (concerning): ~ for or to that por or en lo que respecta a eso

7: ~ if or though como si: he looked~ if he was ill parecía como si estuviera enfermo, tenía aspecto de enfermo

see also **long, such, well.**

a.s.a.p. abbr (= as soon as possible) cuanto antes.

asbestos [æzˈbestəs] n asbesto, amianto.

ascend [əˈsend] vt subir; ~ancy n ascendiente m, dominio.

ascent [əˈsent] n subida; (of plane) ascenso.

ascertain [æsəˈteɪn] vt averiguar.

ascribe [əˈskraɪb] vt: to ~ sth to atribuir algo a.

ash [æʃ] n ceniza; (tree) fresno; ~can n (US) cubo or bote m (LAm) de la basura.

ashamed [əˈʃeɪmd] a avergonzado, apenado (LAm); to be ~ of avergonzarse de.

ashen [ˈæʃn] a pálido.

ashore [əˈʃɔː*] ad en tierra.

ashtray [ˈæʃtreɪ] n cenicero.

Ash Wednesday n miércoles m de Cenizas.

Asia [ˈeɪʃə] n Asia; ~tic [eɪsɪˈætɪk] a, n asiático/a m/f.

aside [əˈsaɪd] ad a un lado.

ask [aːsk] vt (question) preguntar; (demand) pedir; (invite) invitar;

~ sb sth/to do sth preguntar algo a
alguien/pedir a alguien que haga
algo; **to** ~ **sb about sth** preguntar
algo a alguien; **to** ~ **(sb) a question** hacer una pregunta (a alguien);
to ~ **sb out to dinner** invitar a cenar a uno; **to** ~ **after** *vt fus* preguntar por; **to** ~ **for** *vt fus* pedir.

askance [ə'skɑːns] *ad:* **to look** ~ **at**
sb mirar con recelo a uno.

askew [ə'skjuː] *ad* sesgado, ladeado.

asking price *n* precio inicial.

asleep [ə'sliːp] *a* dormido; **to fall** ~
dormirse, quedarse dormido.

asparagus [əs'pærəgəs] *n* espárragos
mpl.

aspect ['æspekt] *n* aspecto, apariencia; (*direction in which a building etc
faces*) orientación *f.*

aspersions [əs'pɜːʃənz] *npl:* **to cast**
~ **on** difamar a, calumniar a.

asphyxiation [æs'fɪksɪ'eɪʃən] *n* asfixia.

aspirations [æspə'reɪʃənz] *npl* anhelo *sg,* deseo *sg;* (*ambition*) ambición
fsg.

aspire [əs'paɪə*] *vi:* **to** ~ **to** aspirar
a, ambicionar.

aspirin ['æsprɪn] *n* aspirina.

ass [æs] *n* asno, burro; (*col*) imbécil
m/f; (*US col!*) culo, trasero.

assailant [ə'seɪlənt] *n* asaltador(a)
m/f, agresor(a) *m/f.*

assassin [ə'sæsɪn] *n* asesino/a; ~**ate**
vt asesinar; ~**ation** [-'neɪʃən] *n* asesinato.

assault [ə'sɔːlt] *n* (*gen: attack*) asalto // *vt* asaltar, atacar; (*sexually*)
violar.

assemble [ə'sembl] *vt* reunir, juntar; (*TECH*) montar // *vi* reunirse,
juntarse.

assembly [ə'semblɪ] *n* (*meeting*)
reunión *f,* asamblea; (*construction*)
montaje *m;* ~ **line** *n* cadena de
montaje.

assent [ə'sent] *n* asentimiento, aprobación *f* // *vi* consentir, asentir.

assert [ə'sɜːt] *vt* afirmar; (*insist on*)
hacer valer.

assess [ə'ses] *vt* valorar, calcular;
(*tax, damages*) fijar; (*property etc:
for tax*) gravar; ~**ment** *n* valora-
ción *f;* (*of man etc*) juicio *m;* ~**or** *n* ase-
sor(a) *m/f;* (*of tax*) tasador(a) *m/f.*

asset ['æset] *n* posesión *f;* (*quality*)
ventaja; ~**s** *npl* (*funds*) activo *sg,*
fondos *mpl.*

assign [ə'saɪn] *vt* (*date*) fijar; (*task*)
asignar; (*resources*) destinar; (*property*) traspasar; ~**ment** *n* asignación *f;* (*task*) tarea.

assist [ə'sɪst] *vt* ayudar; ~**ance** *n*
ayuda, auxilio; ~**ant** *n* ayudante
m/f; (*Brit: also:* **shop** ~**ant**)
dependiente/a *m/f.*

associate [ə'səʊʃɪt] *a* asociado // *n*
socio/a, colega *m/f;* (*in crime*) cómplice *m/f;* (*member*) miembro // *vb*
[-ʃɪeɪt] *vt* asociar; (*ideas*) relacionar
// *vi:* **to** ~ **with sb** tratar con alguien.

association [əsəusɪ'eɪʃən] *n* asociación *f;* (*COMM*) sociedad *f.*

assorted [ə'sɔːtɪd] *a* surtido, variado.

assortment [ə'sɔːtmənt] *n* surtido.

assume [ə'sjuːm] *vt* (*suppose*) suponer; (*responsibilities etc*) asumir;
(*attitude, name*) adoptar, tomar; ~**d
name** *n* nombre *m* falso.

assumption [ə'sʌmpʃən] *n* (*supposition*) suposición *f,* presunción *f;* (*act*)
asunción *f.*

assurance [ə'ʃuərəns] *n* garantía,
promesa; (*confidence*) confianza,
aplomo; (*insurance*) seguro.

assure [ə'ʃuə*] *vt* asegurar.

astern [ə'stɜːn] *ad* a popa.

asthma ['æsmə] *n* asma.

astonish [ə'stɒnɪʃ] *vt* asombrar, pasmar; ~**ment** *n* asombro, sorpresa.

astound [ə'staund] *vt* asombrar, pasmar.

astray [ə'streɪ] *ad:* **to go** ~ extraviarse; **to lead** ~ llevar por mal camino.

astride [ə'straɪd] *prep* a caballo or
horcajadas sobre.

astrology [əs'trɒlədʒɪ] *n* astrología.

astronaut [ˈæstrənɔːt] n astronauta
m/f.

astronomical [æstrəˈnɔmikəl] a astronómico.

astronomy [æsˈtrɒnəmɪ] n astronomía.

astute [əˈstjuːt] a astuto.

asylum [əˈsaɪləm] n (refuge) asilo; (hospital) manicomio.

KEYWORD
---

at [æt] prep **1** (referring to position) en; (direction) a; ~ **the top** en lo alto; ~ **home/school** en casa/la escuela; **to look** ~ **sth/sb** mirar algo/a uno
2 (referring to time): ~ **4 o'clock** a las 4; ~ **night** por la noche; ~ **Christmas** en Navidad; ~ **times** a veces
3 (referring to rates, speed etc): ~ **£1 a kilo** a una libra el kilo; **two** ~ **a time** de dos en dos; ~ **50 km/h** a 50 km/h
4 (referring to manner): ~ **a stroke** de un golpe; ~ **peace** en paz
5 (referring to activity): **to be** ~ **work** estar trabajando; (in the office etc) estar en el trabajo; **to play** ~ **cowboys** jugar a los vaqueros; **to be good** ~ **sth** ser bueno en algo
6 (referring to cause): **shocked/surprised/annoyed** ~ **sth** asombrado/sorprendido/fastidiado por algo; **I went** ~ **his suggestion** fui a instancias suyas.

---

ate [eɪt] pt of **eat**.

atheist [ˈeɪθɪɪst] n ateo/a.

Athens [ˈæθɪnz] n Atenas f.

athlete [ˈæθliːt] n atleta m/f.

athletic [æθˈletɪk] a atlético; ~s n atletismo.

Atlantic [ətˈlæntɪk] a atlántico // n: **the** ~ **(Ocean)** el Océano Atlántico.

atlas [ˈætləs] n atlas m.

atmosphere [ˈætməsfɪə*] n atmósfera; (fig) ambiente m.

atom [ˈætəm] n átomo; ~**ic** [əˈtɒmɪk]

a atómico; ~**(ic) bomb** n bomba atómica; ~**izer** [ˈætəmaɪzə*] n atomizador m.

atone [əˈtəʊn] vi: **to** ~ **for** expiar.

atrocious [əˈtrəʊʃəs] a atroz.

attach [əˈtætʃ] vt sujetar; (stick) pegar; (document, letter) adjuntar; **to be** ~**ed to sb/sth** (to like) tener cariño a alguien/algo.

attaché [əˈtæʃeɪ] n agregado/a; ~ **case** n (Brit) maletín m.

attachment [əˈtætʃmənt] n (tool) accesorio; (love): ~ **(to)** apego (a).

attack [əˈtæk] vt (MIL) atacar; (criminal) agredir, asaltar; (task etc) emprender // n ataque m, asalto; (on sb's life) atentado; **heart** ~ n infarto (de miocardio); ~**er** n agresor(a) m/f, asaltante m/f.

attain [əˈteɪn] vt (also: ~ **to**) alcanzar; (achieve) lograr, conseguir; ~**ments** npl (skill) talento sg.

attempt [əˈtempt] n tentativa, intento; (attack) atentado // vt intentar; ~**ed** a: ~**ed burglary** tentativa de robo.

attend [əˈtend] vt asistir a; (patient) atender; **to** ~ **to** vt fus (needs, affairs etc) ocuparse de; (speech etc) prestar atención a; (customer) atender a; ~**ance** n asistencia, presencia; (people present) concurrencia; ~**ant** n sirviente/a m/f, mozo/a; (THEATRE) acomodador/a m/f // a concomitante.

attention [əˈtenʃən] n atención f // excl (MIL) ¡firme(s)!; **for the** ~ **of...** (ADMIN) atención... .

attentive [əˈtentɪv] a atento; (polite) cortés.

attest [əˈtest] vi: **to** ~ **to** dar fe de.

attic [ˈætɪk] n desván m.

attitude [ˈætɪtjuːd] n (gen) actitud f; (disposition) disposición f.

attorney [əˈtɜːnɪ] n (lawyer) abogado/a; (having proxy) apoderado; **A~ General** n (Brit) ≈ Presidente m del Consejo del Poder Judicial (Sp); (US) ≈ ministro de justicia.

attract [ə'trækt] vt atraer; (attention) llamar; ~ion [ə'trækʃən] n (gen) encanto; (amusements) diversiones fpl; (PHYSICS) atracción f; (fig: towards sth) atractivo; ~ive a atractivo; (interesting) atrayente; (pretty) guapo, mono.

attribute ['ætribju:t] n atributo // vt [ə'tribju:t]: to ~ sth to atribuir algo a; (accuse) achacar algo a.

attrition [ə'trɪʃən] n: war of ~ guerra de agotamiento.

aubergine ['əubəʒi:n] n (Brit) berenjena.

auburn ['ɔ:bən] a color castaño rojizo.

auction ['ɔ:kʃən] n (also: sale by ~) subasta // vt subastar; ~eer [-'nɪə*] n subastador(a) m/f.

audacity [ɔ:'dæsɪti] n audacia, atrevimiento; (pej) descaro.

audience ['ɔ:dɪəns] n auditorio; (gathering) público; (interview) audiencia.

audio-typist ['ɔ:dɪəu'taɪpɪst] n mecanógrafo/a de dictáfono.

audio-visual ['ɔ:dɪəu'vɪzjuəl] a audiovisual; ~ aid n ayuda audiovisual.

audit ['ɔ:dɪt] vt revisar, intervenir.

audition [ɔ:'dɪʃən] n audición f.

auditor ['ɔ:dɪtə*] n interventor(a) m/f, censor(a) m/f de cuentas.

augment [ɔ:g'mɛnt] vt aumentar // vi aumentarse.

augur ['ɔ:gə*] vi: it ~s well es de buen agüero.

August ['ɔ:gəst] n agosto.

aunt [ɑ:nt] n tía; ~ie, ~y n diminutive of aunt.

au pair ['əu'pɛə*] n (also: ~ girl) au pair f.

aura ['ɔ:rə] n aura; (atmosphere) ambiente m.

auspices ['ɔ:spɪsɪz] npl: under the ~ of bajo los auspicios de.

auspicious [ɔ:s'pɪʃəs] a propicio, de buen augurio.

austerity [ɔs'terɪtɪ] n austeridad f.

Australia [ɔs'treɪlɪə] n Australia; ~n a, n australiano/a m/f.

Austria ['ɔstrɪə] n Austria; ~n a, n austríaco/a m/f.

authentic [ɔ:'θɛntɪk] a auténtico.

author ['ɔ:θə*] n autor(a) m/f.

authoritarian [ɔ:θɔrɪ'tɛərɪən] a autoritario.

authoritative [ɔ:'θɔrɪtətɪv] a autorizado; (manner) autoritario.

authority [ɔ:'θɔrɪtɪ] n autoridad f; the authorities npl las autoridades.

authorize ['ɔ:θəraɪz] vt autorizar.

auto ['ɔ:təu] n (US) coche m, carro (LAm), automóvil m.

autobiography [ɔ:təbaɪ'ɔgrəfɪ] n autobiografía.

autograph ['ɔ:təgrɑ:f] n autógrafo // vt firmar; (photo etc) dedicar.

automated ['ɔ:təmeɪtɪd] a automatizado.

automatic [ɔ:tə'mætɪk] a automático // n (gun) pistola automática; ~ally ad automáticamente.

automation [ɔ:tə'meɪʃən] n reconversión f.

automaton [ɔ:'tɔmətən], pl ~mata [-tə] n autómata m/f.

automobile ['ɔ:təməbi:l] n (US) coche m, carro (LAm), automóvil m.

autonomy [ɔ:'tɔnəmɪ] n autonomía.

autopsy ['ɔ:tɔpsɪ] n autopsia.

autumn ['ɔ:təm] n otoño.

auxiliary [ɔ:g'zɪlɪərɪ] a auxiliar.

Av. abbr = avenue.

avail [ə'veɪl] vt: to ~ o.s. of aprovechar(se) de, valerse de // n: to no ~ en vano, sin resultado.

available [ə'veɪləbl] a disponible.

avalanche ['ævəlɑ:nʃ] n alud m, avalancha.

avant-garde ['ævãŋ'gɑ:d] a de vanguardia.

Ave. abbr = avenue.

avenge [ə'vɛndʒ] vt vengar.

avenue ['ævənju:] n avenida; (fig) camino.

average ['ævərɪdʒ] n promedio, término medio // a (mean) medio, de término medio; (ordinary) regular, corriente // vt calcular el promedio de, prorratear; **on** ~ por regla general; **to ~ out** vi: **to ~ out** at salir en un promedio de.

averse [ə'vɜːs] a: **to be ~ to** sth/ doing sentir aversión o antipatía por algo/por hacer.

avert [ə'vɜːt] vt prevenir; (blow) desviar; (one's eyes) apartar.

aviary ['eɪvɪərɪ] n pajarera, avería.

avid ['ævɪd] a ávido, ansioso.

avocado [ævə'kɑːdəʊ] n (also: Brit: ~ **pear**) aguacate m, palta (LAm).

avoid [ə'vɔɪd] vt evitar, eludir.

avuncular [ə'vʌŋkjʊlə] a paternal.

await [ə'weɪt] vt esperar, aguardar.

awake [ə'weɪk] a despierto // (pt awoke, pp awoken or awaked) vt despertar // vi despertarse; **to be ~** estar despierto; **~ning** n el despertar.

award [ə'wɔːd] n (prize) premio; (medal) condecoración f; (LAW: fallo, sentencia; (act) concesión f // vt (prize) otorgar, conceder; (LAW: damages) adjudicar.

aware [ə'wɛə*] a consciente; (awake) despierto; (informed) enterado; **to become ~ of** darse cuenta de, enterarse de; **~ness** n conciencia, conocimiento.

awash [ə'wɒʃ] a inundado.

away [ə'weɪ] ad (gen) fuera; (far ~) lejos; **two kilometres ~** a dos kilómetros de distancia; **two hours ~ by car** a dos horas en coche; **the holiday was two weeks ~** faltaba dos semanas para las vacaciones; **~ from** lejos de, fuera de; **he's ~ for a week** estará ausente una semana; **to work/pedal ~** seguir trabajando/ pedaleando; **to fade ~** desvanecerse; (sound) apagarse; **~ game** n (SPORT) partido de fuera.

awe [ɔː] n pavor m, respeto, temor m reverencial; **~-inspiring, ~some** a imponente, pasmoso.

awful ['ɔːfʊl] a terrible, pasmoso; **~ly** ad (very) terriblemente.

awhile [ə'waɪl] ad (durante) un rato, algún tiempo.

awkward ['ɔːkwəd] a (clumsy) des-

mañado, torpe; (shape) incómodo; (problem) difícil; (embarrassing) delicado.

awning ['ɔːnɪŋ] n (of shop) toldo; (of window etc) marquesina.

awoke [ə'wəʊk], **awoken** [-kən] pt, pp of **awake**.

awry [ə'raɪ] ad: **to be ~** estar descolocado o atravesado; **to go ~** salir mal, fracasar.

axe, (US) **ax** [æks] n hacha // vt (employee) despedir; (project etc) cortar; (jobs) reducir.

axis ['æksɪs], pl **axes** [-siːz] n eje m.

axle ['æksl] n eje m, árbol m.

aye(o) [aɪ] excl (yes) sí; **the ayes** npl los que votan a favor.

B

B [biː] n (MUS) si m.

B.A. abbr = **Bachelor of Arts**.

babble ['bæbl] vi barbullar.

baby ['beɪbɪ] n bebé m/f; **~ carriage** n (US) cochecito; **~-sit** vi hacer de canguro; **~-sitter** n canguro a.

bachelor ['bætʃələ*] n soltero; **B~ of Arts/Science** (B.A./B.Sc.) licenciado/a en Filosofía y Letras/ Ciencias.

back [bæk] n (of person) espalda; (of animal) lomo; (of hand) dorso; (as opposed to front) parte f de atrás; (of room, car, etc) fondo; (of chair) respaldo; (of page) reverso; (FOOTBALL) defensa m // vt (candidate: also: ~ **up**) respaldar, apoyar; (horse: at races) apostar a; (car) dar marcha atrás a or con // vi (car etc) dar marcha atrás // a (in compounds) de atrás; **~ seats/wheels** (AUT) asientos mpl/ruedas fpl de atrás; **~ payments** pagos mpl con efecto retroactivo; **~ rent** renta atrasada // ad (not forward) (hacia) atrás; (returned) de vuelta; **he's ~** está de vuelta, ha vuelto; **he ran ~** volvió corriendo; (restitution): **throw the**

ball ~ devuelve la pelota; **can I have it** ~? can I'he devuelve?; (again): **he called** ~ llamó de nuevo; **to** ~ **down** vi echarse atrás; **to** ~ **out** vi (of promise) volverse atrás; **to** ~ **up** vt (support: person) apoyar, respaldar; (: theory) defender; (car) dar marcha atrás a; (COMPUT) hacer una copia preventiva or de reserva; ~**bencher** n (Brit) miembro del parlamento sin portafolio; ~**bone** n columna vertebral; ~**cloth** n telón de fondo; ~**date** vt (letter) poner fecha atrasada a; ~**drop** n = ~**cloth**; ~**fire** vi (AUT) petardear; (plans) fallar, salir mal; ~**ground** n fondo; (of events) antecedentes mpl; (basic knowledge) bases fpl; (experience) conocimientos mpl, educación f; **family** ~**ground** origen m, antecedentes mpl; ~**hand** n (TENNIS: also: ~**hand stroke**) revés m; ~**handed** a (fig) ambiguo, equívoco; ~**hander** n (Brit: bribe) soborno; ~**ing** n (fig) apoyo, respaldo; ~**lash** n reacción f, resaca; ~**log** n: ~**log of work** atrasos mpl; ~ **number** n (of magazine etc) número atrasado; ~**pack** n mochila; ~**pay** n pago atrasado; ~**side** n (col) trasero, culo; ~**stage** ad entre bastidores; ~**stroke** n braza de espaldas; ~**up** a (train, plane) suplementario; (COMPUT: disk, file) de reserva // n (support) apoyo; (also: ~**up file**) copia preventiva or de reserva; ~**up lights** npl (US) luces fpl de marcha atrás; ~**ward** a (movement) hacia atrás; (person, country) atrasado; (shy) tímido; ~**wards** ad (move, go) hacia atrás; (read a list) al revés; (fall) de espaldas; (fig) n atrasado or apartado; ~**water** n (fig) marasmo; ~**yard** n traspatio.

bacon ['beɪkən] n tocino, beicon m.

bad [bæd] a malo; (serious) grave; (meat, food) podrido, pasado; **his** ~ **leg** su pierna lisiada; **to go** ~ pasar-se.

bade [bæd, beɪd] pt of **bid**.

badge [bædʒ] n insignia; (metal ~) chapa, placa.

badger ['bædʒə*] n tejón m.

badly ['bædlɪ] ad (work, dress etc) mal; ~ **wounded** gravemente herido; **he needs it** ~ le hace gran falta; **to be** ~ **off** (for money) andar mal de dinero.

badminton ['bædmɪntən] n bádminton m.

bad-tempered ['bæd'tempəd] a de mal genio or carácter; (temporary) de mal humor.

baffle ['bæfl] vt desconcertar, confundir.

bag [bæg] n bolsa, saco; (handbag) bolso; (satchel) mochila; (case) maleta; (of hunter) caza // vt (col: take) coger (Sp), agarrar (LAm), pescar; ~**s of** (col: lots of) un montón de; ~**gage** n equipaje m; ~**gy** a (clothing) amplio; ~**pipes** npl gaita sg.

Bahamas [bə'hɑːməz] npl: **the** ~ las Islas Bahama.

bail [beɪl] n fianza // vt (prisoner: gen: **grant** ~ **to**) poner en libertad bajo fianza; (boat: also: ~ **out**) achicar; **on** ~ (prisoner) bajo fianza; **to** ~ **sb out** obtener la libertad de uno bajo fianza; **bail bond** n fianza; see also **bale**.

bailiff ['beɪlɪf] n alguacil m.

bait [beɪt] n cebo // vt cebar.

bake [beɪk] vt cocer (al horno) // vi (cook) cocerse; (be hot) hacer un calor terrible; ~**d beans** npl judías fpl en salsa de tomate; ~**r** n panadero; ~**ry** (or bread) panadería; (for cakes) pastelería; **baking** n (act) amasar m; (batch) hornada; **baking powder** n levadura (en polvo).

balance ['bæləns] n equilibrio; (COMM: sum) balance m; (remainder) resto; (scales) balanza // vt equilibrar; (budget) nivelar; (account) saldar; (compensate) contrapesar; ~ **of trade/payments** balanza de comercio/pagos; ~**d** a (*personality, diet*) equilibrado; ~ **sheet** n balance m.

balcony ['bælkənɪ] n (*open*) balcón m; (*closed*) galería.

bald [bɔːld] a calvo; (*tyre*) liso.

bale [beɪl] n (*AGR*) paca, fardo; to ~ **out** vi (*of a plane*) lanzarse en paracaídas.

Balearics [bælɪˈærɪks] npl: **the** ~ las Baleares.

baleful ['beɪlful] a (*look*) triste; (*sinister*) funesto, siniestro.

ball [bɔːl] n (*sphere*) bola; (*football*) balón m; (*for tennis, golf etc*) pelota; (*dance*) baile m.

ballad ['bæləd] n balada, romance m.

ballast ['bæləst] n lastre m.

ball bearings npl cojinetes mpl de bolas.

ballerina [bæləˈriːnə] n bailarina.

ballet ['bæleɪ] n ballet m; ~ **dancer** n bailarín/ina m/f.

ballistic [bəˈlɪstɪk] a balístico.

balloon [bəˈluːn] n globo.

ballot ['bælət] n votación f.

ball-point (pen) ['bɔːlpɔɪnt-] n bolígrafo.

ballroom ['bɔːlrum] n salón m de baile.

balm [bɑːm] n (*also fig*) bálsamo.

Baltic ['bɔːltɪk] a báltico // n: **the** ~ (**Sea**) el (Mar) Báltico.

balustrade [bæləstreɪd] n barandilla.

bamboo [bæmˈbuː] n bambú m.

ban [bæn] n prohibición f, proscripción f // vt prohibir, proscribir.

banal [bəˈnɑːl] a banal, vulgar.

banana [bəˈnɑːnə] n plátano, banana (*LAm*).

band [bænd] n (*group*) banda; (*gang*) pandilla; (*strip*) faja, tira; (: *circular*) anillo; (*at a dance*) orquesta; (*MIL*) banda; to ~ **together** vi juntarse, asociarse.

bandage ['bændɪdʒ] n venda, vendaje m // vt vendar.

bandaid ['bændeɪd] n ® (*US*) tirita.

bandit ['bændɪt] n bandido.

bandstand ['bændstænd] n quiosco.

bandwagon ['bændwægən] n: **to jump on the** ~ (*fig*) subirse al carro.

bandy ['bændɪ] vt (*jokes, insults*) cambiar.

bandy-legged ['bændɪˈlegd] a estevado.

bang [bæŋ] n estallido; (*of door*) portazo; (*blow*) golpe m // vt hacer estallar; (*door*) cerrar de golpe // vi estallar.

bangle ['bæŋgl] n ajorca.

bangs [bæŋz] npl (*US*) flequillo sg.

banish ['bænɪʃ] vt desterrar.

banister(s) ['bænɪstə(z)] n(pl) pasamanos m inv.

bank [bæŋk] n (*COMM*) banco; (*of river, lake*) ribera, orilla; (*of earth*) terraplén m // vi (*AVIAT*) ladearse; **to** ~ **on** vt fus contar con; ~ **account** n cuenta de banco; ~ **card** n tarjeta bancaria; ~**er** n banquero; ~**er's card** (*Brit*) = **card**; **B**~ **holiday** n (*Brit*) día m festivo; ~**ing** n banca; ~**note** n billete m de banco; ~ **rate** n tipo de interés bancario.

bankrupt ['bæŋkrʌpt] a quebrado, insolvente; **to go** ~ hacer bancarrota; **to be** ~ estar en quiebra; ~**cy** n quiebra, bancarrota.

bank statement n balance m or detalle m de cuenta.

banner ['bænə*] n bandera; (*in demonstration*) pancarta.

banns [bænz] npl amonestaciones fpl.

banquet ['bæŋkwɪt] n banquete m.

baptism ['bæptɪzəm] n bautismo.

baptize [bæpˈtaɪz] vt bautizar.

bar [bɑː*] n barra; (*on door*) tranca; (*of window, cage*) reja; (*of soap*) pastilla; (*fig: hindrance*) obstáculo; (*prohibition*) proscripción f; (*pub*) bar m; (*counter: in pub*) mostrador m; (*MUS*) barra // vt (*road*) obstruir; (*window, door*) atrancar; (*person*) excluir; (*activity*) prohibir; **behind** ~**s** entre rejas; **the B**~ (*LAW: pro-*

fession) la abogacía; (: *people*) el cuerpo de abogados; ~ **none** sin excepción.

barbaric [ba:'bærɪk] *a* bárbaro.

barbarous ['ba:bərəs] *a* bárbaro.

barbecue ['ba:bɪkju:] *n* barbacoa.

barbed wire ['ba:bd-] *n* alambre *m* de púas.

barber ['ba:bə*] *n* peluquero, barbero.

bar code *n* código de barras.

bare [beə*] *a* desnudo; (*head*) descubierto // *vt* desnudar; ~**back** *ad* sin silla; ~**faced** *a* descarado; ~**foot** *a, ad* descalzo; ~**ly** *ad* apenas.

bargain ['ba:gɪn] *n* pacto, negocio; (*good buy*) ganga // *vi* negociar; (*haggle*) regatear; **into the** ~ además, por añadidura; **to ~ for** *vt fus*: **he got more than he** ~**ed for** le resultó peor de lo que esperaba.

barge [ba:dʒ] *n* barcaza; **to ~ in** *vi* irrumpir; (*conversation*) entrometerse; **to ~ into** *vt fus* dar contra.

bark [ba:k] *n* (*of tree*) corteza; (*of dog*) ladrido // *vi* ladrar.

barley ['ba:lɪ] *n* cebada; ~ **sugar** *n* azúcar *m* cande.

barmaid ['ba:meɪd] *n* camarera.

barman ['ba:mən] *n* camarero, barman *m*.

barn [ba:n] *n* granero.

barometer [bə'rɒmɪtə*] *n* barómetro.

baron ['bærən] *n* barón *m*; ~**ess** *n* baronesa.

barracks ['bærəks] *npl* cuartel *m*.

barrage ['bæra:ʒ] *n* (*MIL*) descarga, bombardeo; (*dam*) presa; (*fig*: *of criticism etc*) lluvia, aluvión *m*.

barrel ['bærəl] *n* tonel *m*, barril *m*; (*of gun*) cañón *m*.

barren ['bærən] *a* estéril.

barricade [bærɪ'keɪd] *n* barricada // *vt* cerrar con barricadas.

barrier ['bærɪə*] *n* barrera.

barring ['ba:rɪŋ] *prep* excepto, salvo.

barrister ['bærɪstə*] *n* (*Brit*) abogado/a.

barrow ['bærəʊ] *n* (*cart*) carretilla

(de mano).

bartender ['ba:tendə*] *n* (*US*) camarero, barman *m*.

barter ['ba:tə*] *vt*: **to ~ sth for sth** trocar algo por algo.

base [beɪs] *n* base *f* // *vt*: **to ~ sth on** basar *or* fundar algo en // *a* bajo, infame.

baseball ['beɪsbɔ:l] *n* béisbol *m*.

basement ['beɪsmənt] *n* sótano.

bases ['beɪsi:z] *npl* of **basis**; ['beɪsɪz] *npl* of **base**.

bash [bæʃ] *vt* (*col*) golpear.

bashful ['bæʃful] *a* tímido, vergonzoso.

basic ['beɪsɪk] *a* básico; ~**ally** *ad* fundamentalmente, en el fondo.

basil ['bæzl] *n* albahaca.

basin ['beɪsn] *n* (*vessel*) cuenco, tazón *m*; (*GEO*) cuenca; (*also*: **wash**~) palangana, jofaina.

basis ['beɪsɪs], *pl* **bases** ['beɪsi:z] *n* base *f*.

bask [ba:sk] *vi*: **to ~ in the sun** tomar el sol.

basket ['ba:skɪt] *n* cesta, cesto; (*with handle*) canasta; ~**ball** *n* baloncesto.

Basque [bæsk] *a, n* vasco/a *m/f*; ~ **Country** *n* Euskadi *m*, País *m* Vasco.

bass [beɪs] *n* (*MUS*) contrabajo.

bassoon [bə'su:n] *n* fagot *m*.

bastard ['ba:stəd] *n* bastardo; (*col!*) hijo de puta (!).

bastion ['bæstiən] *n* baluarte *m*.

bat [bæt] *n* (*ZOOL*) murciélago; (*for ball games*) palo; (*for cricket, baseball*) bate *m*; (*Brit*: *for table tennis*) pala; **he didn't ~ an eyelid** ni pestañeó.

batch [bætʃ] *n* (*of bread*) hornada; (*of goods*) lote *m*.

bated ['beɪtɪd] *a*: **with ~ breath** sin respirar.

bath [ba:θ, *pl* ba:ðz] *n* (*action*) baño; (~**tub**) baño, bañera, tina (*LAm*); (*see also* **baths**) piscina // *vt* bañar; **to have a ~** bañarse, tomar un baño; ~**chair** *n* silla de ruedas.

bathe [beɪð] *vi* bañarse // *vt* bañar

~**r** n bañista m/f.

bathing ['beɪðɪŋ] n el bañarse; ~ **cap** n gorro de baño; ~ **costume**, (US) ~ **suit** n traje m de baño; ~ **trunks** npl bañador m.

bath: ~ **robe** n (man's) batín m; (woman's) bata; ~**room** n (cuarto de) baño.

baths [bɑːðz] npl piscina sg.

baton ['bætən] n (MUS) batuta.

battalion [bə'tælɪən] n batallón m.

batter ['bætə*] vt aplastar, azotar // n batido; ~**ed** a (hat, pan) estropeado.

battery ['bætərɪ] n batería; (of torch) pila.

battle ['bætl] n batalla; (fig) lucha // vi luchar; ~**field** n campo de batalla; ~**ship** n acorazado.

bawdy ['bɔːdɪ] a indecente; (joke) verde.

bawl [bɔːl] vi chillar, gritar.

bay [beɪ] n (GEO) bahía; (BOT) laurel m // vi aullar; **B~ of Biscay** n mar Cantábrico; **to hold sb at** ~ mantener a alguien a raya.

bay window n ventana salediza.

bazaar [bə'zɑː*] n bazar m.

b. & b., B. & B. abbr (= bed and breakfast) cama y desayuno.

BBC n abbr (= British Broadcasting Corporation) cadena de radio y televisión estatal británica.

B.C. ad abbr (= before Christ) a. de C.

---

no se veía al ladrón por ninguna parte

3 (in tag questions): **it was fun, wasn't it?** fue divertido, ¿no? or ¿verdad?; **he's good-looking, isn't he?** es guapo, ¿no te parece?; **she's back again, is she?** entonces, ¿ha vuelto?

4 (+ to + infinitive): **the house is to** ~ **sold** (necessity) hay que vender la casa; (future) van a vender la casa; **he's not to open it** no tiene que abrirlo

◆ vb + complement **1** (with noun or numeral complement, but see also 3, 4, 5 and impersonal vb below) ser; **he's a doctor** es médico; **2 and 2 are 4** 2 y 2 son 4

2 (with adjective complement: expressing permanent or inherent quality) ser; (: expressing state seen as temporary or reversible) estar; **I'm English** soy inglés/esa; **she's tall/pretty** es alta/bonita; **he's young** es joven; ~ **careful/quiet/good** ten cuidado/cállate/pórtate bien; **I'm tired** estoy cansado/a; **it's dirty** está sucio/a

3 (of health) estar; **how are you?** ¿cómo estás?; **he's very ill** está muy enfermo; **I'm better now** ya estoy mejor

4 (of age) estar; **how old are you?** ¿cuántos años tienes?; **I'm sixteen (years old)** tengo dieciséis años

5 (cost) costar; **how much was the meal?** ¿cuánto fue or costó la comida?; **that'll** ~ £5.75, **please** son £5.75, por favor; **this shirt is £17.00** esta camisa cuesta £17.00

◆ vi **1** (exist, occur etc) existir, haber; **the best singer that ever was** el mejor cantante que existió jamás; **is there a God?** ¿hay un Dios?, ¿existe Dios?; ~ **that as it may** sea como sea; **so** ~ **it** así sea

2 (referring to place) estar; **I won't** ~ **here tomorrow** no estaré aquí mañana

3 (referring to movement): **where**

KEYWORD

be [biː], pt **was, were,** pp **been** ◆ auxiliary vb **1** (with present participle: forming continuous tenses): **what are you doing?** ¿qué estás haciendo?, ¿qué haces?; **they're coming tomorrow** vienen mañana; **I've been waiting for you for hours** llevo horas esperándote

2 (with pp: forming passives) ser (but often replaced by active or reflective constructions); **to** ~ **murdered** ser asesinado; **the box had been opened** habían abierto la caja; **the thief was nowhere to** ~ **seen**

have you been? ¿dónde has estado?
♦ **impersonal** *vb* **1** (*referring to time*): **it's 5 o'clock** son las 5; **it's the 28th of April** estamos a 28 de abril
2 (*referring to distance*): **it's 10 km to the village** el pueblo está a 10 km
3 (*referring to the weather*): **it's too hot/cold** hace demasiado calor/frío; **it's windy today** hace viento hoy
4 (*emphatic*): **it's me** soy yo; **it was Maria who paid the bill** fue Maria la que pagó la cuenta.

beach [biːtʃ] *n* playa // *vt* varar.
beacon ['biːkən] *n* (*lighthouse*) faro; (*marker*) guía.
bead [biːd] *n* cuenta, abalorio; (*of sweat*) gota.
beak [biːk] *n* pico.
beaker ['biːkə*] *n* jarra.
beam [biːm] *n* (*ARCH*) viga, travesaño; (*of light*) rayo, haz *m* de luz // *vi* brillar; (*smile*) sonreír.
bean [biːn] *n* judía; **runner/broad ~** kabichuela/haba; **coffee ~** grano de café; **~sprouts** *npl* brotes *mpl* de soja.
bear [bɛə*] *n* oso // (*pt* **bore**, *pp* **borne**) *vt* (*weight etc*) llevar; (*cost*) pagar; (*responsibility*) tener; (*endure*) soportar, aguantar; (*stand up to*) resistir a; (*children*) parir // *vi*: **to ~ right/left** torcer a la derecha/izquierda; **to ~ out** *vt* (*suspicions*) corroborar, confirmar; **to ~ up** *vi* (*person: remain cheerful*) animarse.
beard [biəd] *n* barba.
bearer ['bɛərə*] *n* (*of news, cheque*) portador(a) *m/f*.
bearing ['bɛərɪŋ] *n* porte *m*, comportamiento; (*connection*) relación *f*; (*ball*) **~s** *npl* cojinetes *mpl* á bolas; **to take a ~** marcarse; **to find one's ~s** orientarse.
beast [biːst] *n* bestia; (*col*) bruto, salvaje *m*; **~ly** *a* bestial; (*awful*) horrible.
beat [biːt] *n* (*of heart*) latido; (*MUS*)

ritmo, compás *m*; (*of policeman*) ronda // *vb* (*pt* **beat**, *pp* **beaten**) *vt* (*hit*) golpear; (*eggs*) batir; (*defeat*) vencer, derrotar; (*better*) sobrepasar; (*drum*) tocar; (*rhythm*) marcar // *vi* (*heart*) latir; **off the ~ track** aislado; **to ~ it** largarse; **to ~ off** *vt* rechazar; **to ~ up** *vt* (*col: person*) dar una paliza a; **~ing** *n* golpeo.
beautiful ['bjuːtɪful] *a* hermoso, bello; **~ly** *ad* maravillosamente.
beauty ['bjuːtɪ] *n* belleza, hermosura; (*person*) belleza; **~ salon** *n* salón *m* de belleza; **~ spot** *n* lunar *m* postizo; (*Brit TOURISM*) lugar *m* pintoresco.
beaver ['biːvə*] *n* castor *m*.
became [bɪ'keɪm] *pt* of **become**.
because [bɪ'kɔz] *conj* porque; **~ of** *prep* debido a, a causa de.
beck [bɛk] *n*: **to be at the ~ and call of** estar a disposición de.
beckon ['bɛkən] *vt* (*also*: **~ to**) llamar con señas.
become [bɪ'kʌm] (*irg: like come*) *vt* (*suit*) favorecer, sentar bien a // *vi* (+ *noun*) hacerse, llegar a ser; (+ *adj*) ponerse, volverse; **to ~ fat** engordarse.
becoming [bɪ'kʌmɪŋ] *a* (*behaviour*) decoroso; (*clothes*) favorecedor(a).
bed [bɛd] *n* cama; (*of flowers*) macizo; (*of coal, clay*) capa; **to go to ~** acostarse; **~ and breakfast (b.&b.)** *n* (*place*) pensión *f*; (*terms*) cama y desayuno; **~clothes** *npl* ropa *sg* de cama; **~ding** *n* ropa de cama.
bedlam ['bɛdləm] *n* confusión *f*.
bedraggled [bɪ'drægld] *a* mojado; desastrado.
bed: **~ridden** *a* postrado (en cama); **~room** *n* dormitorio, alcoba; **~side** *n*: at sb's **~side** a la cabecera de alguien; **~sit(ter)** *n* (*Brit*) estudio, suite *m* (*LAm*); **~spread** *n* sobrecama *m*, colcha; **~time** *n* hora de acostarse.
bee [biː] *n* abeja.

beech [biːtʃ] *n* haya.

beef [biːf] *n* carne *f* de vaca; **roast** ~ rosbif *m*; **~burger** *n* hamburguesa; ~ **eater** *n* alabardero de la Torre de Londres.

bee: **~hive** *n* colmena; **~line** *n*: to make a ~line for ir derecho a.

been [biːn] *pp of* **be**.

beer [bɪə*] *n* cerveza.

beet [biːt] *n* (US) remolacha.

beetle [ˈbiːtl] *n* escarabajo.

beetroot [ˈbiːtruːt] *n* (Brit) remolacha.

before [bɪˈfɔː*] *prep* (of time) antes de; (of space) delante de // conj antes (de) que // ad (time) antes, anteriormente; (space) delante, adelante; ~ going antes de marcharse; ~ she goes antes de que se vaya; the week ~ la semana anterior; I've never seen it ~ no lo he visto nunca; **~hand** *ad* de antemano, con anticipación.

beg [beg] *vi* pedir limosna // vt pedir, rogar; (entreat) suplicar.

began [bɪˈgæn] *pt of* **begin**.

beggar [ˈbegə*] *n* mendigo/a.

begin [bɪˈgɪn], *pt* **began**, *pp* **begun** *vt, vi* empezar, comenzar; to ~ doing *or* to do sth empezar a hacer algo; **~ner** *n* principiante *m/f*; **~ning** *n* principio, comienzo.

begun [bɪˈgʌn] *pp of* **begin**.

behalf [bɪˈhɑːf] *n*: on ~ of en nombre de, por.

behave [bɪˈheɪv] *vi* (person) portarse, comportarse; (thing) funcionar; (well: also: ~ o.s.) portarse bien; **behaviour**, (US) **behavior** *n* comportamiento, conducta.

behead [bɪˈhed] *vt* decapitar.

beheld [bɪˈheld] *pt, pp of* **behold**.

behind [bɪˈhaɪnd] *prep* detrás de // ad detrás, por detrás, atrás // *n* trasero; to be ~ (schedule) ir retrasado; ~ the scenes (fig) entre bastidores.

behold [bɪˈhəʊld] *vt* (irg: like **hold**) contemplar.

beige [beɪʒ] *a* color beige.

being [ˈbiːɪŋ] *n* ser *m*; to come into ~ nacer, aparecer.

belated [bɪˈleɪtɪd] *a* atrasado, tardío.

belch [beltʃ] *vi* eructar // vt (also: ~ out: smoke etc) arrojar.

belfry [ˈbelfrɪ] *n* campanario.

Belgian [ˈbeldʒən] *a, n* belga *m/f*.

Belgium [ˈbeldʒəm] *n* Bélgica.

belie [bɪˈlaɪ] *vt* desmentir, contradecir.

belief [bɪˈliːf] *n* (opinion) opinión *f*; (trust, faith) fe *f*; (acceptance as true) creencia.

believe [bɪˈliːv] *vt, vi* creer; to ~ in creer en; **~r** *n* (in idea, activity) partidario/a; (REL) creyente *m/f*, fiel *m/f*.

belittle [bɪˈlɪtl] *vt* minimizar, despreciar.

bell [bel] *n* campana; (small) campanilla; (on door) timbre *m*; (animal's) cencerro; (on toy etc) cascabel *m*.

belligerent [bɪˈlɪdʒərənt] *a* (at war) beligerante; (fig) agresivo.

bellow [ˈbeləʊ] *vi* bramar; (person) rugir.

bellows [ˈbeləʊz] *npl* fuelle *msg*.

belly [ˈbelɪ] *n* barriga, panza.

belong [bɪˈlɒŋ] *vi*: to ~ to pertenecer a; (club etc) ser socio de; this book ~s here este libro va aquí; **~ings** *npl* pertenencias *fpl*.

beloved [bɪˈlʌvɪd] *a, n* querido/a *m/f*, amado/a *m/f*.

below [bɪˈləʊ] *prep* bajo, debajo de // ad abajo, (por) debajo; **see** ~ véase más abajo.

belt [belt] *n* cinturón *m*; (TECH) correa, cinta // vt (thrash) golpear con correa; **~way** *n* (US AUT) carretera de circunvalación.

bemused [bɪˈmjuːzd] *a* aturdido.

bench [bentʃ] *n* banco; the B~ (LAW) tribunal *m*; (people) judicatura.

bend [bend], *vb* (pt, pp bent) *vt* doblar, inclinar; (leg, arm) torcer // vi inclinarse; (road) curvarse // *n* (Brit: in road, river) recodo; (in pipe) codo; **to ~ down** *vi* inclinarse, doblarse; **to ~ over** vi inclinarse.

beneath [bɪ'niːθ] prep bajo, debajo de; (unworthy of) indigno de // ad abajo, (por) debajo.

benefactor ['bɛnɪfæktə*] n bienhechor m.

beneficial [bɛnɪ'fɪʃəl] a beneficioso.

benefit ['bɛnɪfɪt] n beneficio, provecho; (allowance of money) subsidio // vt beneficiar // vi: **he'll ~ from it** lo sacará provecho.

benevolent [bɪ'nɛvələnt] a benévolo.

benign [bɪ'naɪn] a (person, MED) benigno; (smile) afable.

bent [bɛnt] pt, pp of **bend** // n inclinación // a: **to be ~ on** estar empeñado en.

bequeath [bɪ'kwiːð] vt legar.

bequest [bɪ'kwɛst] n legado.

bereaved [bɪ'riːvd] npl: **the ~** los afligidos mpl.

beret ['bɛreɪ] n boina.

Berlin [bɜː'lɪn] n Berlín m.

berm [bɜːm] n (US AUT) arcén m.

Bermuda [bɜː'mjuːdə] n las Bermudas fpl.

berry ['bɛrɪ] n baya.

berserk [bə'sɜːk] a: **to go ~** perder los estribos.

berth [bɜːθ] n (bed) litera; (cabin) camarote m; (for ship) amarradero // vi atracar, amarrar.

beseech [bɪ'siːtʃ], pt, pp **besought** [-'sɔːt] vt suplicar.

beset [bɪ'sɛt], pt, pp **beset** vt (person) acosar.

beside [bɪ'saɪd] prep junto a, al lado de; **to be ~ o.s. with anger** estar fuera de sí; **that's ~ the point** eso no tiene nada que ver.

besides [bɪ'saɪdz] ad además // prep (as well as) además de; (except) excepto.

besiege [bɪ'siːdʒ] vt (town) sitiar; (fig) asediar.

besought [bɪ'sɔːt] pt, pp of **beseech**.

best [bɛst] a (el/la) mejor // ad (lo) mejor; **the ~ part of** (quantity) la mayor parte de; **at ~** en el mejor de

los casos; **to make the ~ of sth** sacar el mejor partido de algo; **to do one's ~** hacer todo lo posible; **to the ~ of my knowledge** que yo sepa; **to the ~ of my ability** como mejor puedo; **~ man** n padrino de boda.

bestow [bɪ'stəu] vt otorgar; (honour, praise) dispensar.

bestseller ['bɛst'sɛlə*] n éxito de librería, bestseller m.

bet [bɛt] n apuesta // vt, vi (pt, pp bet or betted) apostar (on a).

betray [bɪ'treɪ] vt traicionar; (inform on) delatar; **~al** n traición f.

better ['bɛtə*] a mejor // ad mejor // vt mejorar; (record etc) superar // n: **to get the ~ of sb** quedar por encima de alguien; **you had ~ do it** más vale que lo hagas; **he thought ~ of it** cambió de parecer; **to get ~** mejorar(se); (MED) reponerse; **~ off** a más acomodado.

betting ['bɛtɪŋ] n juego, el apostar; **~ shop** n (Brit) agencia de apuestas.

between [bɪ'twiːn] prep entre // ad (time) mientras tanto; (place) en medio.

beverage ['bɛvərɪdʒ] n bebida.

bevy ['bɛvɪ] n: **a ~ of** una bandada de.

beware [bɪ'wɛə*] vi: **to ~ (of)** tener cuidado (con) // excl ¡cuidado!

bewildered [bɪ'wɪldəd] a aturdido, perplejo.

bewitching [bɪ'wɪtʃɪŋ] a hechicero, encantador(a).

beyond [bɪ'jɔnd] prep más allá de; (exceeding) además de, fuera de; (above) superior a // ad más allá, más lejos; **~ doubt** fuera de toda duda; **~ repair** irreparable.

bias ['baɪəs] n (prejudice) prejuicio, pasión f; (preference) predisposición f; **~(s)ed** a parcial.

bib [bɪb] n babero.

Bible ['baɪbl] n Biblia.

bicarbonate of soda [baɪ'kɑːbənɪt-] n bicarbonato de soda.

bicker ['bɪkə*] vi reñir.

bicycle ['baisikl] n bicicleta.

bid [bid] n (at auction) oferta, postura; (attempt) tentativa, conato // ii (pt, pp bid) hacer una oferta // vt (at auction) ofertar, ordenar: to ~ sb good day dar a uno los buenos días; **~der** n: the highest **~der** el mejor postor; **~ding** n (at auction) ofertas fpl; (order) orden f, mandato.

bide [baid] vt: to ~ one's time esperar el momento adecuado.

bifocals [bai'fəuklz] npl gafas fpl or anteojos mpl (LAm) bifocales.

big [big] a grande.

bigamy ['bigəmi] n bigamia.

big dipper [-'dipə*] n montaña rusa.

bigheaded ['big'hedid] a engreído.

bigot ['bigət] n fanático/a, intolerante m/f; **~ed** a fanático, intolerante; **~ry** n fanatismo, intolerancia.

big top n (circus) circo; (main tent) tienda principal.

bike [baik] n bici f.

bikini [bi'ki:ni] n bikini m.

bile [bail] n bilis f.

bilingual [bai'lingwəl] a bilingüe.

bill [bil] n (account) cuenta; (invoice) factura; (POL) proyecto de ley; (US: banknote) billete m; (of bird) pico; 'post no **~s**' 'prohibido fijar carteles'; **~board** n (US) cartelera.

billet ['bilit] n alojamiento.

billfold ['bilfəuld] n (US) cartera.

billiards ['biljədz] n billar m.

billion ['biljən] n (Brit) billón m (millón de millones); (US) mil millones.

billy ['bili; n (US) porra.

bin [bin] n (gen) cubo or bote m (LAm) de la basura; **litter ~** n (Brit) papelera.

bind [baind], pt, pp **bound** vt atar, liar; (wound) vendar; (book) encuadernar; (oblige) obligar; **~ing** a (contract) obligatorio.

binge [bindʒ] n borrachera, juerga.

bingo ['bingəu] n bingo m.

binoculars [bi'nɔkjuləz] npl prismáticos mpl.

bio... [baiə] pref: **~chemistry** n

bioquímica; **~graphy** [bai'ɔgrəfi] n biografía; **~logical** a biológico; **~logy** [bai'ɔlədʒi] n biología.

birch [bə:tʃ] n abedul m; (cane) vara.

bird [bə:d] n ave f, pájaro; (Brit col: girl) chica; **~'s eye view** n vista de pájaro; **~ watcher** n ornitólogo/a.

Biro ['bairəu] n ® bolígrafo.

birth [bə:θ] n nacimiento; (MED) parto; to give ~ to parir, dar a luz; **~ certificate** n partida de nacimiento; **~ control** n control m de natalidad; (methods) métodos mpl anticonceptivos; **~day** n cumpleaños m inv; **~ rate** n (tasa de) natalidad f.

biscuit ['biskit] n (Brit) galleta, bizcocho (LAm).

bisect [bai'sεkt] vt bisecar.

bishop ['biʃəp] n obispo.

bit [bit] pt of **bite**. // n trozo, pedazo, pedacito; (COMPUT) bit m, bitio; (for horse) freno, bocado; a ~ of un poco de; a ~ mad un poco loco; ~ by ~ poco a poco.

bitch [bitʃ] n (dog) perra; (col!) zorra (!).

bite [bait] (pt bit, pp bitten) vt, vi morder; (insect etc) picar // n mordedura; (insect ~) picadura; (mouthful) bocado; to ~ one's nails comerse las uñas; let's have a ~ (to eat) comamos algo.

biting ['baitiŋ] a (wind) que traspasa los huesos; (criticism) mordaz.

bitten ['bitn] pp of **bite**.

bitter ['bitə*] a amargo; (wind, criticism) cortante, penetrante; (battle) encarnizado // n (Brit: beer) cerveza típica británica a base de lúpulos; **~ness** n (anger) rencor m.

bizarre [bi'zɑ:*] a raro, estrafalario.

blab [blæb] vi chismear, soplar.

black [blæk] a (colour) negro; (dark) oscuro // n (colour) color m negro; (person): **B~** negro/a // vt (shoes) lustrar; (Brit: INDUSTRY) boicotear; to give sb a ~ eye ponerle a uno el ojo morado; ~ **and blue** a amoratado; **to be in the ~** (*bank account*) estar en números negros; ~**berry** n zarzamora; ~**bird** n mirlo; ~**board** n pizarra; ~ **coffee** n café m solo; ~**currant** n grosella negra; ~**en** vt ennegrecer; (*fig*) denigrar; ~**head** n espinilla; ~ **ice** n hielo invisible en la carretera; ~**jack** n (*US*) veintiuna; ~**leg** n (*Brit*) esquirol m, rompehuelgas m inv; ~**list** n lista negra; ~**mail** n chantaje m // vt chantajear; ~ **market** n mercado negro; ~**out** n apagón m; (*fainting*) desmayo, pérdida de conocimiento; **the B~ Sea** n el Mar Negro; ~ **sheep** n oveja negra; ~**smith** n herrero; ~ **spot** n (*AUT*) lugar m peligroso.

bladder ['blædə*] n vejiga.

blade [bleid] n hoja; (*cutting edge*) filo; **a ~ of grass** una brizna de hierba.

blame [bleim] n culpa // vt: **to ~ sb for sth** echar a uno la culpa de algo; **to be to ~** tener la culpa de; ~**less** a (*person*) inocente.

bland [blænd] a suave; (*taste*) soso.

blank [blæŋk] a en blanco; (*shot*) sin bala; (*look*) sin expresión // n blanco, espacio en blanco; cartucho sin bala or de fogueo; ~ **cheque** n cheque m en blanco.

blanket ['blæŋkit] n manta, cobija (*LAm*).

blare [bleə*] vi resonar.

blasé ['blɑːzei] a hastiado.

blasphemy ['blæsfimi] n blasfemia.

blast [blɑːst] n (*of wind*) ráfaga, soplo; (*of whistle*) toque m; (*of explosive*) carga explosiva; (*force*) choque m // vt (*blow up*) volar; (*blow open*) abrir con carga explosiva; ~**off** n (*SPACE*) lanzamiento.

blatant ['bleitənt] a descarado.

blaze [bleiz] n (*fire*) fuego; (*flames*) llamarada; (*fig*) arranque m // vi (*fire*) arder en llamas; (*fig*) brillar // vt: **to ~ a trail** (*fig*) abrir (un) camino.

blazer ['bleizə*] n chaqueta de uni-

forme de colegial o de socio de club.

bleach [bliːtʃ] n (*also*: **household** ~) lejía // vt (*linen*) blanquear; ~**ed** a (*hair*) teñido de rubio; (*clothes*) decolorado; ~**ers** npl (*US SPORT*) gradas fpl al sol.

bleak [bliːk] a (*countryside*) desierto; (*prospect*) poco prometedor(a).

bleary-eyed ['bliəri'aid] a: **to be ~** tener ojos de cansado.

bleat [bliːt] vi balar.

bleed [bliːd], pt, pp **bled** [bled] vt, vi sangrar.

bleeper ['bliːpə*] n (*of doctor etc*) busca m.

blemish ['blemiʃ] n mancha, tacha.

blend [blend] n mezcla // vt mezclar // vi (*colours etc*) combinarse, mezclarse.

bless [bles], pt, pp **blessed** or **blest** vt bendecir; ~**ing** n bendición f; (*advantage*) beneficio, ventaja.

blew [bluː] pt of **blow**.

blight [blait] vt (*hopes etc*) frustrar, arruinar.

blimey ['blaimi] excl (*Brit col*) ¡caray!

blind [blaind] a ciego // n (*for window*) persiana // vt cegar; (*dazzle*) deslumbrar; ~ **alley** n callejón m sin salida; ~ **corner** n (*Brit*) esquina escondida; ~**ers** npl (*US*) anteojeras fpl; ~**fold** n venda // a, ad con los ojos vendados // vt vendar los ojos a; ~**ly** ad a ciegas, ciegamente; ~**ness** n ceguera; ~ **spot** n mácula.

blink [blink] vi parpadear, pestañear; (*light*) oscilar; ~**ers** npl (*esp Brit*) anteojeras fpl.

bliss [blis] n felicidad f.

blister ['blistə*] n (*on skin*) ampolla // vi (*paint*) ampollarse.

blithely ['blaiðli] ad alegremente.

blitz [blits] n bombardeo aéreo.

blizzard ['blizəd] n ventisca.

bloated ['bləutid] a hinchado.

blob [blɔb] n (*drop*) gota; (*stain, spot*) mancha.

bloc [blɔk] n (*POL*) bloque m.

block [blɔk] n bloque m; (in pipes) obstáculo; (of buildings) manzana, cuadra (LAm) // vt (gen) obstruir, cerrar; (progress) estorbar; **~ade** [-'keid] n bloqueo // vt bloquear; **~age** n estorbo, obstrucción f; **~buster** n (book) bestseller m; (film) éxito de público; **~ of flats** n (Brit) bloque m de pisos; **~ letters** npl letras fpl de molde.

bloke [bləuk] n (Brit col) tipo, tío.

blond(e) [blɔnd] a, n rubio/a m/f.

blood [blʌd] n sangre f; **~ donor** n donador(a) m/f de sangre; **~ group** n grupo sanguíneo; **~hound** n sabueso; **~ poisoning** n envenenamiento de la sangre; **~ pressure** n presión f sanguínea; **~shed** n derramamiento de sangre; **~shot** a inyectado en sangre; **~stream** n corriente f sanguínea; **~ test** n análisis m inv de sangre; **~thirsty** a sanguinario; **~ transfusion** n transfusión f de sangre; **~y** a sangriento; (Brit col!): **this ~y...** este condenado o puñetero... (!) // ad: **~y strong/good** (Brit col!) terriblemente fuerte/ bueno; **~y-minded** a (Brit col): **to be ~y-minded** ser un malasangre.

bloom [blu:m] n floración f; **in ~** en flor // vi florecer; **~ing** a (col): **this ~ing...** este condenado...

blossom ['blɔsəm] n flor f // vi (also fig) florecer; (person) realizarse.

blot [blɔt] n borrón m // vt (ink) secar; (stain) manchar; **to ~ out** vt (view) tapar; (memories) borrar.

blotchy ['blɔtʃɪ] a (complexion) lleno de manchas.

blotting paper ['blɔtɪŋ-] n papel m secante.

blouse [blauz] n blusa.

blow [bləu] n golpe m // vb (pt **blew** [blu:], pp **blown** [bləun]) vi soplar; (fuse) fundirse // vt (glass) soplar; (fuse) quemar; (instrument) tocar; **to ~ one's nose** sonarse; **to ~ away** vt llevarse, arrancar; **to ~ down** vt derribar; **to ~ off** vt

arrebatar; **to ~ out** vi apagarse; **to ~ over** vi amainar; **to ~ up** vi estallar // vt (tyre) inflar; (PHOT) ampliar; **blow-dry** n moldeado (con secador); **~lamp** n (Brit) soplete m, lámpara de soldar; **~out** n (of tyre) pinchazo; **~torch** n = **~lamp**.

blubber ['blʌbə*] n grasa de ballena // vi (pej) lloriquear.

blue [blu:] a azul; **~ film/joke** film/ chiste verde; **out of the ~** (fig) completamente inesperado; **to have the ~s** estar decaído; **~bell** n campanilla, campánula azul; **~bottle** n mosca, mosca azul; **~ jeans** npl bluejean m inv, vaqueros mpl; **~print** n (fig) anteproyecto.

bluff [blʌf] vi hacer un bluff, farolear // n bluff m, farol m; **to call sb's ~** coger a uno en un renuncio.

blunder ['blʌndə*] n patinazo, metedura de pata // vi cometer un error, meter la pata.

blunt [blʌnt] a embotado, desafilado; (person) franco, directo // vt embotar, desafilar.

blur [blə:*] n aspecto borroso // vt (vision) enturbiar; (memory) empañar.

blurb [blə:b] n comentario de sobrecubierta.

blurt [blə:t] vt: **to ~ out** (say) descolgarse con, dejar escapar.

blush [blʌʃ] vi ruborizarse, ponerse colorado // n rubor m.

blustering ['blʌstərɪŋ] a (person) fanfarrón/ona.

blustery ['blʌstərɪ] a (weather) tempestuoso, tormentoso.

boar [bɔ:*] n verraco, cerdo.

board [bɔ:d] n tabla, tablero; (on wall) tablón m; (for chess etc) tablero; (committee) junta, consejo; (in firm) mesa o junta directiva; (NAUT, AVIAT): **on ~** a bordo // vt (ship) embarcarse en; (train) subir a; **full ~** (Brit) pensión completa; **half ~** (Brit) media pensión; **to go by the ~** (fig) ser abandonado o olvidado; **to ~ up** vt (door) tapiar;

~ **and lodging** n casa y comida; ~**er** n huésped(a) m/f; (SCOL) interno/a; ~**ing card** n (Brit) tarjeta de embarque; ~**ing house** n casa de huéspedes; ~**ing pass** n (US) = ~**ing card**; ~**ing school** n internado; ~ **room** n sala de juntas.

boast [bəʊst] vi: **to** ~ (**about** or **of**) alardear (de) // vt ostentar // n alarde m, baladronada.

boat [bəʊt] n barco, buque m; (small) barca, bote m; ~**er** n (hat) canotié m; ~**swain** ['bəʊsn] n contramaestre m.

bob [bɔb] vi (boat, cork on water: also: ~ **up and down**) menearse, balancearse // n (Brit col) = **shilling**; **to** ~ **up** vi (re)aparecer de repente.

bobby ['bɔbɪ] n (Brit col) poli m.

bobsleigh ['bɔbsleɪ] n bob m.

bode [bəʊd] vi: **to** ~ **well/ill (for)** ser prometedor/poco prometedor (para).

bodily ['bɔdɪlɪ] a corpóreo, corporal // ad (move: person) en peso; (: building) de una pieza.

body ['bɔdɪ] n cuerpo; (corpse) cadáver m; (of car) caja, carrocería; (fig: organization) organismo; (fig: quantity) masa; ~**building** n culturismo; ~**guard** n guardaespaldas m inv; ~**work** n carrocería.

bog [bɔg] n pantano, ciénaga // vt: **to get** ~**ged down** (fig) empantanarse, atascarse.

boggle ['bɔgl] vi: **the mind** ~**s**! ¡no puedo creerlo!

bogus ['bəʊgəs] a falso, fraudulento; (person) fingido.

boil [bɔɪl] vt cocer; (eggs) pasar por agua // vi hervir // n (MED) furúnculo, divieso; **to come to the** (Brit) or **a** (US) ~ comenzar a hervir; **to** ~ **down to** (fig) reducirse a; **to** ~ **over** vi rebosar; (anger etc) llegar al colmo; ~**ed egg** n huevo cocido (Sp) or pasado (LAm); ~**ed potatoes** npl patatas fpl or papas fpl (LAm) hervidas; ~**er** n caldera;

~**er suit** n (Brit) mono; ~**ing point** n punto de ebullición.

boisterous ['bɔɪstərəs] a (noisy) bullicioso; (excitable) exuberante; (crowd) tumultuoso.

bold [bəʊld] a (brave) valiente, audaz; (pej) descarado; (outline) grueso; (colour) llamativo.

Bolivia [bə'lɪvɪə] n Bolivia; ~**n** a, n boliviano/a m/f.

bollard ['bɔləd] n (Brit AUT) poste m.

bolster ['bəʊlstə*] n travesero, cabezal m; **to** ~ **up** vt reforzar.

bolt [bəʊlt] n (lock) cerrojo; (with nut) perno, tornillo // ad: ~ **upright** rígido, erguido // vt (door) echar el cerrojo a; (food) engullir // vi fugarse; (horse) desbocarse.

bomb [bɔm] n bomba // vt bombardear; ~**ard** [-'bɑːd] vt bombardear; (fig) asediar; ~**ardment** [-'bɑːdmənt] n bombardeo.

bombastic [bɔm'bæstɪk] a rimbombante; (person) farolero.

bomb: ~ **disposal** n desmontaje m de explosivos; ~**er** n (AVIAT) bombardero; ~**shell** n obús m, granada; (fig) bomba.

bona fide ['bəʊnə'faɪdɪ] a genuino, auténtico.

bond [bɔnd] n (binding promise) fianza; (FINANCE) bono; (link) vínculo, lazo; (COMM): **in** ~ en depósito bajo fianza.

bondage ['bɔndɪdʒ] n esclavitud f.

bone [bəʊn] n hueso; (of fish) espina // vt deshuesar; quitar las espinas a; ~**-dry** a completamente seco; ~ **idle** a gandul.

bonfire ['bɔnfaɪə*] n hoguera, fogata.

bonnet ['bɔnɪt] n gorra; (Brit: of car) capó m.

bonus ['bəʊnəs] n sobrepaga, prima.

bony ['bəʊnɪ] a (arm, face, MED: tissue) huesudo; (meat) lleno de huesos; (fish) lleno de espinas.

boo [buː] vt abuchear, rechiflar.

booby trap ['buːbɪ-] n trampa explosiva.

book 32 bout

book [buk] n libro; (*notebook*) libreta; (*of stamps etc*) librito; (*COMM*): **~s** cuentas *fpl*, contabilidad *f* // *vt* (*ticket, seat, room*) reservar; (*driver*) fichar; **~case** n librería, estante *m* para libros; **~ing office** n (*BRIT RAIL*) despacho de billetes or boletos (*LAm*); (*THEATRE*) taquilla, boletería (*LAm*); **~keeping** n contabilidad *f*; **~let** n folleto; **~maker** n corredor *m* de apuestas; **~seller** n librero; **~shop**, **~ store** n librería.

boom [bu:m] n (*noise*) trueno, estampido; (*in prices etc*) alza rápida; (*ECON*) boom *m*, auge *m* // *vi* (*cannon*) hacer gran estruendo, retumbar; (*ECON*) estar en alza.

boon [bu:n] n favor *m*, beneficio.

boost [bu:st] n estímulo, empuje *m* // *vt* estimular, empujar; **~er** n (*MED*) reinyección *f*.

boot [bu:t] n bota; (*Brit: of car*) maleta, maletero // *vt* dar un puntapié a; (*COMPUT*) arrancar; **to ~** (*in addition*) además, por añadidura.

booth [bu:ð] n (*at fair*) barraca; (*telephone ~, voting ~*) cabina.

booty ['bu:tɪ] n botín *m*.

booze [bu:z] n (*col*) bebida, trago *m* // *vi* emborracharse.

border ['bɔ:də*] n borde *m*, margen *m*; (*of a country*) frontera // a fronterizo; the **B~s** región fronteriza entre Escocia e Inglaterra; **~ on** *vt fus* lindar con; (*fig*) rayar en; **~line** n (*fig*) frontera.

bore [bɔ:*] *pt of* **bear** // *vt* (*hole*) hacer un agujero en; (*well*) perforar; (*person*) aburrir // n (*person*) pelmazo, pesado; (*of gun*) calibre *m*; **~d** a aburrido; **~dom** n aburrimiento.

boring ['bɔ:rɪŋ] a aburrido.

born [bɔ:n] a: **to be ~** nacer; I was **~ in** 1960 nací en 1960.

borne [bɔ:n] *pp of* **bear**.

borough ['bʌrə] n municipio.

borrow ['bɔrəu] *vt*: **to ~ sth (from sb)** tomar algo prestado (a alguien).

bosom ['buzəm] n pecho; (*fig*) seno.

boss [bɔs] n jefe/a *m/f*; (*employer*)

patrón/ona *m/f*; (*political etc*) cacique *m* // *vt* (*also*: **~ about** or **around**) mangonear; **~y** a mandón/ona.

bosun ['bəusn] n contramaestre *m*.

botany ['bɔtənɪ] n botánica.

botch [bɔtʃ] *vt* (*also*: **~ up**) arruinar, estropear.

both [bəuθ] a, pron ambos/as, los/las dos; **~ of us went**, **we ~ went** fuimos los dos, ambos fuimos // ad: **~ A and B** tanto A como B.

bother ['bɔðə*] *vt* (*worry*) preocupar; (*disturb*) molestar, fastidiar // *vi* (*gen*: **~ o.s.**) molestarse // n: **what a ~!** ¡qué lata! ; **to ~ doing** tomarse la molestia de hacer.

bottle ['bɔtl] n botella; (*small*) frasco; (*baby's*) biberón *m* // *vt* embotellar; **to ~ up** *vt* suprimir; **~neck** n embotellamiento; **~opener** n abrebotellas *m inv*.

bottom ['bɔtəm] n (*of box, sea*) fondo; (*buttocks*) trasero, culo; (*of page*) pie *m*; (*of list*) final *m* // a (*lowest*) más bajo; (*last*) último; **~less** a sin fondo, insondable.

bough [bau] n rama.

bought [bɔ:t] *pt, pp of* **buy**.

boulder ['bəuldə*] n canto rodado.

bounce [bauns] *vi* (*ball*) (re)botar; (*cheque*) ser rechazado // *vt* hacer (re)botar // n (*rebound*) (re)bote *m*; **~r** n (*col*) matón/ona *m/f*.

bound [baund] *pt, pp of* **bind** // n (*leap*) salto; (*gen pl: limit*) límite *m* // *vi* (*leap*) saltar // a: **~ by** rodeado de; **to be ~ to do sth** (*obliged*) tener el deber de hacer algo; **he's ~ to come** es seguro que vendrá; **out of ~s** prohibido el paso; **~ for** con destino a.

boundary ['baundrɪ] n límite *m*.

boundless ['baundlɪs] a ilimitado.

bouquet ['bukeɪ] n (*of flowers*) ramo; (*of wine*) aroma *m*.

bourgeois ['buəʒwa:] a, n burgués/ esa *m/f*.

bout [baut] n (*of malaria etc*) ataque *m*; (*BOXING etc*) combate *m*, encuentro.

bow [bəu] n (knot) lazo; (weapon, MUS) arco // n [bau] (of the head) reverencia; (NAUT: also: ~s) proa // vi [bau] inclinarse, hacer una reverencia; (yield): **to ~ to** or **before** ceder ante, someterse a.

bowels [bauəlz] npl intestinos mpl, vientre m.

bowl [bəul] n tazón m, cuenco; (for washing) palangana, jofaina; (ball) bola // vi (CRICKET) arrojar la pelota; ~s n juego de las bochas, bolos mpl.

bow-legged [ˈbəuˈlɛgɪd] a estevado.

bowler [ˈbəulə*] n (CRICKET) lanzador m (de la pelota); (Brit: also: ~ hat) hongo, bombín m.

bowling [ˈbəulɪŋ] n (game) bochas fpl, bolos mpl; ~ **alley** n bolera; ~ **green** n pista para bochas.

bow tie [ˈbəu-] n corbata de lazo, pajarita.

box [bɔks] n (also: **cardboard** ~) caja, cajón m; (for jewels) estuche m; (for money) cofre m; (THEATRE) palco // vt encajonar // vi (SPORT) boxear; ~**er** n (person) boxeador m; (dog) boxer m; ~**ing** n (SPORT) boxeo; **B~ing Day** n (Brit) día de San Esteban, 26 de diciembre; ~**ing gloves** npl guantes mpl de boxeo; ~**ing ring** n ring m, cuadrilátero; ~ **office** n taquilla, boletería (LAm); ~ **room** n trastero.

boy [bɔɪ] n (young) niño; (older) muchacho.

boycott [ˈbɔɪkɔt] n boicot m // vt boicotear.

boyfriend [ˈbɔɪfrɛnd] n novio.

boyish [ˈbɔɪɪʃ] a muchachil.

B.R. abbr = **British Rail**.

bra [brɑː] n sostén m, sujetador m.

brace [breɪs] n refuerzo, abrazadera; (Brit: also: ~s: on teeth) corrector m; (tool) berbiquí m // vt asegurar, reforzar; ~s npl (Brit) tirantes mpl; **to ~ o.s.** (for) (fig) prepararse (para).

bracelet [ˈbreɪslɪt] n pulsera, brazale-

te m.

bracing [ˈbreɪsɪŋ] a vigorizante, tónico.

bracken [ˈbrækən] n helecho.

bracket [ˈbrækɪt] n (TECH) soporte m, puntal m; (group) clase f, categoría; (also: **brace** ~) soporte m, abrazadera; (also: **round** ~) paréntesis m inv; (gen: **square** ~) corchete m // vt (group) agrupar.

brag [bræg] vi jactarse.

braid [breɪd] n (trimming) galón m; (of hair) trenza.

brain [breɪn] n cerebro; ~s npl sesos mpl; **she's got** ~s es muy lista; ~**child** n parto del ingenio; ~**wash** vt lavar el cerebro; ~**wave** n idea luminosa; ~**y** a muy inteligente.

braise [breɪz] vt cocer a fuego lento.

brake [breɪk] n (on vehicle) freno // vt, vi frenar; ~ **fluid** n líquido de frenos; ~ **light** n luz f de frenado.

bramble [ˈbræmbl] n zarza.

bran [bræn] n salvado.

branch [brɑːntʃ] n rama; (fig) ramo; (COMM) sucursal f // vi (also: ~ **out**) ramificarse; (: fig) extenderse.

brand [brænd] n marca; (iron) hierro de marcar // vt (cattle) marcar con hierro candente.

brandish [ˈbrændɪʃ] vt blandir.

brand-new [ˈbrændˈnjuː] a flamante, completamente nuevo.

brandy [ˈbrændɪ] n coñac m, brandy m.

brash [bræʃ] a (rough) tosco; (cheeky) descarado.

brass [brɑːs] n latón m; **the** ~ (MUS) los cobres; ~ **band** n banda de metal.

brassière [ˈbræsɪə*] n sostén m, sujetador m.

brat [bræt] n (pej) mocoso/a.

bravado [brəˈvɑːdəu] n fanfarronería.

brave [breɪv] a valiente, valeroso // n guerrero indio // vt (challenge) desafiar; (resist) aguantar; ~**ry** n valor m, valentía.

brawl [brɔːl] n pendencia, reyerta //

vi pelearse.

brawn [brɔ:n] *n* fuerza muscular; (*meat*) carne *f* en gelatina.

bray [breɪ] *vi* rebuzno // *vi* rebuznar.

brazen ['breɪzn] *a* descarado, cínico // *vt*: **to ~ it out** echarle cara.

brazier ['breɪzɪə*] *n* brasero.

Brazil [brə'zɪl] *n* (el) Brasil; **~ian** *a*, *n* brasileño/a *m/f*.

breach [briːtʃ] *vt* abrir brecha en // *n* (*gap*) brecha; (*breaking*): **~ of confidence** abuso de confianza; **~ of contract** infracción *f* de contrato; **~ of the peace** perturbación *f* del orden público.

bread [bred] *n* pan *m*; **~ and butter** *n* pan con mantequilla; (*fig*) pan (de cada día) *a* común y corriente; **~bin**, (*US*) **~box** *n* panera; **~crumbs** *npl* migajas *fpl*; (*CULIN*) pan molido; **~line** *n*: **on the ~line** en la miseria.

breadth [bretθ] *n* anchura; (*fig*) amplitud *f*.

breadwinner ['bredwɪnə*] *n* sostén *m* de la familia.

break [breɪk] *vb* (*pt* **broke**, *pp* **broken**) *vt* (*gen*) romper; (*promise*) faltar a; (*fall*) amortiguar; (*journey*) interrumpir; (*law*) violar, infringir; (*record*) batir; (*news*) comunicar // *vi* romperse, quebrarse; (*storm*) estallar; (*weather*) cambiar // *n* (*gap*) abertura; (*crack*) grieta; (*fracture*) fractura; (*in relations*) ruptura; (*rest*) descanso; (*time*) intervalo; (: *at school*) (período de) recreo; (*chance*) oportunidad *f*; **to ~ down** *vt* (*figures, data*) analizar, descomponer; (*undermine*) acabar con // *vi* estropearse; (*MED*) sufrir un colapso; (*AUT*) averiarse; (*person*) romper a llorar; **to ~ even** *vi* cubrir los gastos; **to ~ free** *or* **loose** *vi* escaparse; **to ~ in** *vt* (*horse etc*) domar // *vi* (*burglar*) forzar una entrada; **to ~ into** *vt fus* (*house*) forzar; **to ~ off** *vi* (*speaker*) pararse, detenerse; (*branch*) partir; **to ~ open** *vt* (*door etc*) abrir por la fuerza, forzar;

to ~ out *vi* estallar; **to ~ out in spots** salir a unos granos; **to ~ up** *vi* (*partnership*) disolverse; (*friends*) romper // *vt* (*rocks etc*) partir; (*crowd*) disolver; **~age** *n* rotura; **~down** *n* (*AUT*) avería; (*in communications*) interrupción *f*; (*MED: also*: **nervous ~down**) colapso, crisis *f* nerviosa; **~down van** *n* (*Brit*) (camión *m*) grúa; **~er** *n* rompiente *m*.

breakfast ['brekfəst] *n* desayuno.

break: **~-in** *n* robo con allanamiento de morada; **~ing and entering** *n* (*LAW*) violación *f* de domicilio, allanamiento de morada; **~through** *n* (*fig*) avance *m*; **~water** *n* rompeolas *m inv*.

breast [brest] *n* (*of woman*) pecho, seno; (*chest*) pecho; (*of bird*) pechuga; **to ~-feed** *vt, vi* (*like feed*) amamantar, criar a los pechos; **~stroke** *n* braza de pecho.

breath [breθ] *n* aliento, respiración *f*; **out of ~** sin aliento, sofocado.

Breathalyser ['breθəlaɪzə*] *n* ® (*Brit*) alcoholímetro *m*; **~ test** *n* prueba de alcoholemia.

breathe [briːð] *vt, vi* respirar; (*noisily*) resollar; **to ~ in** *vt, vi* aspirar; **to ~ out** *vt, vi* espirar; **~r** *n* respiro; **breathing** *n* respiración *f*.

breath: **~less** *a* sin aliento, jadeante; **~taking** *a* imponente, pasmoso.

breed [briːd] *vb* (*pt, pp* **bred** [bred]) *vt* criar // *vi* reproducirse, procrear // *n* raza, casta; **~er** *n* (*person*) criador(a) *m/f*; **~ing** *n* (*of person*) educación *f*.

breeze [briːz] *n* brisa.

breezy ['briːzɪ] *a* de mucho viento, ventoso; (*person*) despreocupado.

brevity ['brevɪtɪ] *n* brevedad *f*.

brew [bruː] *vt* (*tea*) hacer; (*beer*) elaborar; (*plot*) tramar // *vi* hacerse; elaborarse; tramarse; (*storm*) amenazar; **~er** *n* cervecero; **~ery** *n* fábrica de cerveza, cervecería.

bribe [braɪb] *n* soborno // *vt* sobornar, cohechar; **~ry** *n* soborno, cohecho.

bric-a-brac ['brɪkabræk] n inv baratijas fpl.

brick [brɪk] n ladrillo; **~layer** n albañil m; **~works** n ladrillar m.

bridal ['braɪdl] a nupcial.

bride [braɪd] n novia; **~groom** n novio; **~smaid** n dama de honor.

bridge [brɪdʒ] n puente m; (NAUT) puente m de mando; (of nose) caballete m; (CARDS) bridge m // vt (river) tender un puente sobre.

bridle ['braɪdl] n brida, freno // vt poner la brida a; (fig) reprimir, refrenar; **~ path** n camino de herradura.

brief [bri:f] a breve, corto // n (LAW) escrito // vt (inform) informar; (instruct) dar instrucciones a; **~s** npl (for men) calzoncillos mpl; (for women) bragas fpl; **~case** n cartera, portafolio (LAm); **~ing** n (PRESS) informe m; **~ly** ad (smile, glance) fugazmente; (explain, say) en pocas palabras.

brigadier [brɪgə'dɪə*] n general m de brigada.

bright [braɪt] a claro; (room) luminoso; (day) de sol; (person: clever) listo, inteligente; (: lively) alegre; (colour) vivo; **~en** (also: **~en up**) vt (room) hacer más alegre // vi (weather) despejarse; (person) animarse, alegrarse.

brilliance ['brɪljəns] n brillo, brillantez f.

brilliant ['brɪljənt] a brillante.

brim [brɪm] n borde m; (of hat) ala.

brine [braɪn] n (CULIN) salmuera.

bring [brɪŋ], pt, pp **brought** (thing) traer; (person) conducir; to **~ about** vt ocasionar, producir; to **~ back** vt volver a traer; (return) devolver; to **~ down** vt bajar; (price) rebajar; to **~ forward** vt adelantar; to **~ off** vt (task, plan) lograr, conseguir; to **~ out** vt (object) sacar; to **~ round** vt (unconscious person) hacer volver en sí; (convince) convencer; to **~ up** vt (person) educar, criar; (carry up) subir; (question) sacar a colación;

(food: vomit) devolver, vomitar.

brink [brɪŋk] n borde m.

brisk [brɪsk] a enérgico, vigoroso; (speedy) rápido; (trade) activo.

brisket ['brɪskɪt] n carne f de vaca para asar.

bristle ['brɪsl] n cerda // vi erizarse.

Britain ['brɪtən] n (also: **Great ~**) Gran Bretaña.

British ['brɪtɪʃ] a británico; the **~** npl los británicos; the **~ Isles** npl las Islas Británicas; **~ Rail (B.R.)** n = RENFE f (Sp).

Briton ['brɪtən] n británico/a.

brittle ['brɪtl] a quebradizo, frágil.

broach [brəʊtʃ] vt (subject) abordar.

broad [brɔːd] a ancho, amplio; (accent) cerrado; **in ~ daylight** en pleno día; **~cast** n emisión f // vb (pt, pp **~cast**) vt (RADIO) emitir; (TV) transmitir // vi emitir; transmitir; **~casting** n radiodifusión f, difusión f; **~en** vt ensanchar // vi ensancharse; **~ly** ad en general; **~-minded** a tolerante, liberal.

broccoli ['brɒkəlɪ] n brécol m.

brochure ['brəʊʃjuə*] n folleto.

broil [brɔɪl] vt (US) asar a la parrilla.

broke [brəʊk] pt of **break** // a (col) pelado, sin blanca.

broken ['brəʊkən] pp of **break** // a: **~ leg** pierna rota; **in ~ English** en un inglés imperfecto; **~-hearted** a con el corazón partido.

broker ['brəʊkə*] n agente m/f, bolsista m/f.

brolly ['brɒlɪ] n (Brit col) paraguas m inv.

bronchitis [brɒŋ'kaɪtɪs] n bronquitis f.

bronze [brɒnz] n bronce m.

brooch [brəʊtʃ] n prendedor m.

brood [bruːd] n camada, cría; (children) progenie f // vi (hen) empollar; to **~ over** sth dejarse obsesionar por algo.

brook [brʊk] n arroyo.

broom [brʊm] n escoba; (BOT) retama; **~stick** n palo de escoba.

Bros. abbr (= Brothers) Hnos.
broth [broθ] n caldo.
brothel ['broθl] n burdel m.
brother ['brʌðə*] n hermano; **~-in-law** n cuñado.
brought [brɔːt] pt, pp of **bring**.
brow [brau] n (forehead) frente m; (of hill) cumbre f.
brown [braun] a moreno; (hair) castaño; (tanned) bronceado // n (colour) color m moreno or pardo // (tan) broncear; (CULIN) dorar; **~ bread** n pan moreno.
brownie ['brauni] n niña exploradora.
brown paper n papel m de estraza.
brown sugar n azúcar m terciado.
browse [brauz] vi (among books) hojear libros.
bruise [bruːz] n cardenal m, moretón m (LAm) // vt magullar.
brunch [brʌnʃ] n desayuno-almuerzo.
brunette [bruːˈnet] n morena.
brunt [brʌnt] n: to bear the ~ of llevar el peso de.
brush [brʌʃ] n cepillo; (large) escoba; (for painting, shaving etc) brocha; (artist's) pincel m; (BOT) maleza; (with police etc) roce m // vt (gen: ~ **past, ~ against**) rozar al pasar; **to ~ aside** vt rechazar, no hacer caso a; **to ~ up** vt (knowledge) repasar, refrescar; **~wood** n (bushes) maleza; (sticks) leña.
brusque [bruːsk] a brusco, áspero.
Brussels ['brʌslz] n Bruselas; **~ sprout** n col de Bruselas.
brutal ['bruːtl] a brutal.
brute [bruːt] n bruto; (person) bestia // a: by **~ force** a fuerza bruta.
B.Sc. abbr = **Bachelor of Science**.
bubble ['bʌbl] n burbuja; (in paint) ampolla // vi burbujear, borbotar; **~ bath** n espuma para el baño; **~ gum** n chicle m de globo.
buck [bʌk] n macho m; (US col) dólar m // vi corcovear; **to pass the ~** (to sb) echar (a uno) el muerto; **to ~ up** vi (cheer up) animarse, cobrar

ánimo.
bucket ['bʌkɪt] n cubo, balde m.
buckle ['bʌkl] n hebilla // vt abrochar con hebilla // vi combarse.
bud [bʌd] n brote m, yema; (of flower) capullo // vi brotar, echar brotes.
Buddhism ['budɪzm] n Budismo.
budding ['bʌdɪŋ] a en ciernes, en embrión.
buddy ['bʌdɪ] n (US) compañero, compinche m.
budge [bʌdʒ] vt mover; (fig) hacer ceder // vi moverse.
budgerigar ['bʌdʒərɪgaː*] n periquito.
budget ['bʌdʒɪt] n presupuesto // vi: to ~ **for** sth presupuestar algo.
budgie ['bʌdʒɪ] n = **budgerigar**.
buff [bʌf] a (colour) color de ante // n (enthusiast) entusiasta m/f.
buffalo ['bʌfələu], pl ~ or ~**es** n (Brit) búfalo; (US: bison) bisonte m.
buffer ['bʌfə*] n amortiguador m; (COMPUT) memoria intermedia.
buffet ['bufeɪ] n (Brit: bar) bar m, cafetería; (food) buffet m // vt ['bʌfɪt] (strike) abofetear; (wind etc) golpear; **~ car** n (Brit RAIL) coche-comedor m.
bug [bʌg] n (insect) chinche m; (: gen) bicho, sabandija; (germ) microbio, bacilo; (spy device) micrófono oculto // vt (fam) fastidiar; (room) poner micrófono oculto en.
bugle ['bjuːgl] n corneta, clarín m.
build [bɪld] n (of person) talle m, tipo // vt (pt, pp built) construir, edificar; **to ~ up** vt (MED) fortalecer; (stocks) acumular; **~er** n constructor(a) m/f; (contractor) contratista m/f; **~ing** n (act of) construcción f; (habitation, offices) edificio; **~ing society** n (Brit) sociedad f inmobiliaria, cooperativa de construcciones.
built [bɪlt] pt, pp of **build** // a: **~-in** (cupboard) empotrado; (device) interior, incorporado; **~-up** (area) urbanizado.
bulb [bʌlb] n (BOT) bulbo; (ELEC)

bombilla, foco (*LAm*).

Bulgaria [bʌl'geərɪə] *n* Bulgaria; ~**n** *a*, *n* búlgaro/a *m/f*.

bulge [bʌldʒ] *n* bombeo, pandeo // *vi* bombearse, pandearse; (*pocket etc*) hacer bulto.

bulk [bʌlk] *n* (*mass*) bulto, volumen *m*; (*major part*) grueso; **in** ~ (*COMM*) a granel; **the** ~ **of** la mayor parte de; ~**head** *n* mamparo; ~**y** *a* voluminoso, abultado.

bull [bul] *n* toro; ~**dog** *n* dogo.

bulldozer ['buldəuzə*] *n* aplanadora, motoniveladora.

bullet ['bulɪt] *n* bala.

bulletin ['bulɪtɪn] *n* anuncio, parte *m*; ~ **board** *n* (*US*) tablón *m* de anuncios.

bullet: ~**proof** *a* a prueba de balas; ~**wound** *n* balazo.

bullfight ['bulfaɪt] *n* corrida de toros; ~**er** *n* torero; ~**ing** *n* los toros *mpl*, el toreo; (*art of* ~*ing*) tauromaquia.

bullion ['buljən] *n* oro *or* plata en barras.

bullock ['bulək] *n* novillo.

bullring ['bulrɪŋ] *n* plaza de toros.

bull's-eye ['bulzaɪ] *n* centro del blanco.

bully ['bulɪ] *n* valentón *m*, matón *m* // *vt* intimidar, tiranizar.

bum [bʌm] *n* (*Brit*: *col*: *backside*) culo; (*tramp*) vagabundo.

bumblebee ['bʌmblbɪ:] *n* abejorro.

bump [bʌmp] *n* (*blow*) tope *m*, choque *m*; (*jolt*) sacudida; (*on road etc*) bache *m*; (*on head*) chichón *m* // *vt* (*strike*) chocar contra, topetar // *vi* dar sacudidas; **to** ~ **into** *vt fus* chocar contra, tropezar con; (*person*) topar con; ~**er** *n* (*Brit*) parachoques *m inv* // *a*: ~**er crop/harvest** cosecha abundante; ~**er cars** *npl* coches *mpl* de choque.

bumptious ['bʌmpʃəs] *a* engreído, presuntuoso.

bumpy ['bʌmpɪ] *a* (*road*) lleno de baches; (*journey*) zarandeado.

bun [bʌn] *n* (*Brit*: *cake*) pastel *m*;

(*US*: *bread*) bollo; (*of hair*) moño.

bunch [bʌntʃ] *n* (*of flowers*) ramo; (*of keys*) manojo; (*of bananas*) piña; (*of people*) grupo; (*pej*) pandilla.

bundle ['bʌndl] *n* (*gen*) bulto, fardo; (*of sticks*) haz *m*; (*of papers*) legajo // *vt* (*also*: ~ **up**) atar, envolver; **to** ~ **sth/sb into** meter algo/a alguien precipitadamente en.

bungalow ['bʌŋgələu] *n* bungalow *m*, chalé *m*.

bungle ['bʌŋgl] *vt* chapucear.

bunion ['bʌnjən] *n* juanete *m*.

bunk [bʌŋk] *n* litera; ~ **beds** *npl* literas *fpl*.

bunker ['bʌŋkə*] *n* (*coal store*) carbonera; (*MIL*) refugio; (*GOLF*) búnker *m*.

bunny ['bʌnɪ] *n* (*also*: ~ **rabbit**) conejito.

bunting ['bʌntɪŋ] *n* empavesada, banderas *fpl*.

buoy [bɔɪ] *n* boya; **to** ~ **up** *vt* mantener a flote; (*fig*) animar; ~**ancy** *n* (*of ship*) capacidad *f* para flotar; ~**ant** *a* (*carefree*) boyante, optimista.

burden ['bə:dn] *n* carga // *vt* cargar.

bureau [bjuə'rəu], *pl* ~**x** [-z] *n* (*Brit*: *writing desk*) escritorio, buró *m*; (*US*: *chest of drawers*) cómoda; (*office*) oficina, agencia.

bureaucracy [bjuə'rɔkrəsɪ] *n* burocracia; **bureaucrat** ['bjuərəkræt] *n* burócrata *m/f*.

burglar ['bə:glə*] *n* ladrón/ona *m/f*; ~ **alarm** *n* alarma de ladrones; ~**y** *n* robo con allanamiento, robo de una casa.

burial ['berɪəl] *n* entierro.

burly ['bə:lɪ] *a* fornido, membrudo.

Burma ['bə:mə] *n* Birmania.

burn [bə:n] *vb* (*pt*, *pp* **burned** *or* **burnt**) *vt* quemar; (*house*) incendiar // *vi* quemarse, arder; incendiarse; (*sting*) escocer // *n* quemadura; **to** ~ **down** *vt* incendiar; ~**er** *n* (*gas*) quemador *m*; ~**ing** *a* ardiente.

burrow ['bʌrəu] *n* madriguera // *vi* hacer una madriguera.

bursar ['bɜːsə*] n tesorero; (Brit: student) becario/a; **~y** n (Brit) beca.

burst [bɜːst] (pt, pp burst) vt (balloon, pipe) reventar; (banks etc) romper // vi reventarse; romperse; (tyre) pincharse; (bomb) estallar // n (explosion) estallido; (also: ~ pipe) reventón m; **a ~ of energy** una explosión f de energía; **to ~ into flames** estallar en llamas; **to ~ out laughing** soltar la carcajada; **to ~ into tears** deshacerse en lágrimas; **to be ~ing** with reventar por o de; **to ~ into** vt fus (room etc) irrumpir en; **to ~ open** vi abrirse de golpe.

bury ['berɪ] vt enterrar; (body) enterrar, sepultar.

bus [bʌs] n autobús m.

bush [buʃ] n arbusto; (scrub land) monte m; **to beat about the ~** andar(se) a (thick) rodeos; **~y** a (thick) espeso, poblado.

busily ['bɪzɪlɪ] ad afanosamente.

business ['bɪznɪs] n (matter) asunto; (trading) comercio, negocios mpl; (firm) empresa, casa; (occupation) oficio; (affair) asunto; **to be away on ~** estar en viaje de negocios; **it's my ~ to...** me toca o corresponde...; **it's none of my ~** yo no tengo nada que ver; **he means ~** habla en serio; **~like** a (company) serio; (person) eficiente; **~man** n hombre m de negocios; **~ trip** n viaje m de negocios; **~woman** n mujer f de negocios.

busker ['bʌskə*] n (Brit) músico/a ambulante.

bus-stop ['bʌsstɔp] n parada de autobús.

bust [bʌst] n (ANAT) pecho // a (col: broken) roto, estropeado; **to go ~** quebrarse.

bustle ['bʌsl] n bullicio, movimiento // vi menearse, apresurarse; **bustling** a (town) animado, bullicioso.

busy ['bɪzɪ] a ocupado, atareado; (shop, street) concurrido, animado // vr: **to ~ o.s. with** ocuparse en;

~body n entrometido/a; **~ signal** n (US TEL) señal f de comunicado.

but [bʌt] ♦ conj 1 pero; **he's not very bright, ~ he's hard-working** no es muy inteligente, pero es trabajador

2 (in direct contradiction) sino; **he's not English ~ French** no es inglés sino francés; **he didn't sing ~ he shouted** no cantó sino que gritó

3 (showing disagreement, surprise etc): **~ that's far too expensive!** ¡pero eso es carísimo!; **~ it does work!** ¡(pero) sí que funciona!

♦ prep (apart from, except) menos, salvo; **we've had nothing ~ trouble** no hemos tenido más que problemas; **no-one ~ him can do it** nadie más que él puede hacerlo; **who ~ a lunatic would do such a thing?** ¡sólo un loco haría una cosa así!; **~ for you/your help** si no fuera por ti/ tu ayuda; **anything ~ that** cualquier cosa menos eso

♦ ad (just, only): **she's ~ a child** no es más que una niña; **had I ~ known** si lo hubiera sabido; **I can ~ try** al menos lo puedo intentar; **it's all ~ finished** está casi acabado.

butcher ['butʃə*] n carnicero // vt hacer una carnicería con; (cattle etc for meat) matar; **~'s (shop)** n carnicería.

butler ['bʌtlə*] n mayordomo.

butt [bʌt] n (cask) tonel m; (for rain) tina; (thick end) culata, extremo; (of gun) culata; (of cigarette) colilla; (Brit fig: target) blanco // vt dar cabezadas contra, topetar; **to ~ in** vi (interrupt) interrumpir.

butter ['bʌtə*] n mantequilla // vt untar con mantequilla; **~cup** n ranúnculo.

butterfly ['bʌtəflaɪ] n mariposa; (SWIMMING: also: ~ stroke) braza de mariposa.

buttocks ['bʌtəks] npl nalgas fpl.

button ['bʌtn] n botón m // vt (also: ~ up) abotonar, abrochar // vi abrocharse.

buttress ['bʌtrɪs] n contrafuerte m; (fig) apoyo, sostén m.

buxom ['bʌksəm] a (woman) frescachona.

buy [baɪ] vt (pt, pp bought) comprar // n compra; to ~ sb sth/sth from sb comprarle algo a alguien; to ~ sb a drink invitar a alguien a tomar algo; ~er n comprador(a) m/f.

buzz [bʌz] n zumbido; (col: phone call) llamada (por teléfono) // vi zumbar.

buzzer ['bʌzə*] n timbre m.

buzz word n palabra que está de moda.

KEYWORD

by [baɪ] ◆ prep 1 (referring to cause, agent) por; de; killed ~ lightning muerto por un relámpago; a painting ~ Picasso un cuadro de Picasso 2 (referring to method, manner, means): ~ bus/car/train en autobús/coche/tren; to pay ~ cheque pagar con un cheque; ~ moonlight/candlelight a la luz de la luna/una vela; ~ saving hard, he ... ahorrando, ...

3 (via, through) por; we came ~ Dover vinimos por Dover

4 (close to, past): the house ~ the river la casa junto al río; she rushed ~ me pasó a mi lado como una exhalación; I go ~ the post office every day paso por delante de Correos todos los días

5 (time: not later than) para; (: during): ~ daylight de día; ~ 4 o'clock para las cuatro; ~ this time tomorrow para mañana a esta hora; ~ the time I got here it was too late cuando llegué ya era demasiado tarde

6 (amount): ~ the kilo/metre por kilo/metro; paid ~ the hour pagado/a por hora

7 (MATH, measure): to divide/multiply ~ 3 dividir/multiplicar por 3; a room 3 metres ~ 4 una habitación de 3 metros por 4; it's broader ~ a metre es un metro más ancho

8 (according to) según, de acuerdo con; it's 3 o'clock ~ my watch según mi reloj, son las tres; it's all right ~ me por mí, está bien

9: (all) ~ oneself etc todo solo/a; he did it (all) ~ himself lo hizo él solo; he was standing (all) ~ himself in a corner estaba de pie solo en un rincón

10: ~ the way a propósito, por cierto; this wasn't my idea ~ the way pues, no fue idea mía

◆ ad 1 see go, pass etc.

2: ~ and ~ finalmente; they'll come back ~ and ~ acabarán volviendo; ~ and large en líneas generales, en general.

---

bye(-bye) ['baɪ('baɪ)] excl adiós, hasta luego.

by(e)-law ['baɪlɔ:] n ordenanza municipal.

by-election ['baɪɪlekʃən] n (Brit) elección f parcial.

bygone ['baɪgɔn] a pasado, del pasado // n: let ~s be ~s lo pasado, pasado está.

bypass ['baɪpɑ:s] n carretera de circunvalación; (MED) (operación f de) by-pass m // vt evitar.

by-product ['baɪprɔdʌkt] n subproducto, derivado.

bystander ['baɪstændə*] n espectador(a) m/f.

byte [baɪt] n (COMPUT) byte m, octeto.

byword ['baɪwɔ:d] n: to be a ~ for ser conocidísimo por.

by-your-leave ['baɪjɔ:'li:v] n: without so much as a ~ sin decir nada, sin dar ningún tipo de explicación.

C

C [si:] n (MUS) do m.

C. abbr = **centigrade**.

C.A. abbr = **chartered accountant**.

cab [kæb] n taxi m; (of truck) cabina.

cabbage ['kæbɪdʒ] n col f, berza.

cabin ['kæbɪn] n cabaña; (on ship) camarote m.

cabinet ['kæbɪnɪt] n (POL) consejo de ministros; (furniture) armario; (also: **display** ~) vitrina; **~maker** n ebanista m.

cable ['keɪbl] n cable m // vt cablegrafiar; **~-car** n teleférico; **~ television** n televisión f por cable.

cache [kæʃ] n (of weapons, drugs etc) alijo.

cackle ['kækl] vi cacarear.

cactus ['kæktəs], pl **cacti** [-taɪ] n cacto.

cadet [kə'dɛt] n (MIL) cadete m.

cadge [kædʒ] vt gorronear.

Caesarean [si:'zɛərɪən] a: ~ (**section**) cesárea.

café ['kæfeɪ] n café m.

cafeteria [kæfɪ'tɪərɪə] n café m.

caffein(e) ['kæfiːn] n cafeína.

cage [keɪdʒ] n jaula // vt enjaular.

cagey ['keɪdʒɪ] a (col) cauteloso, reservado.

cagoule [kə'gu:l] n chubasquero.

Cairo ['kaɪərəu] n el Cairo.

cajole [kə'dʒəul] vt engatusar.

cake [keɪk] n pastel m; (of soap) pastilla; **~d** a: **~d with** cubierto de.

calculate ['kælkjuleɪt] vt calcular; **calculating** a (scheming) calculador(a); **calculation** [-'leɪʃən] n cálculo, cómputo; **calculator** n calculadora.

calendar ['kæləndə*] n calendario; ~ **month/year** n mes m/año civil.

calf [kɑ:f], pl **calves** n (of cow) ternero, becerro; (of other animals) cría; (also: **~skin**) piel f de becerro; (ANAT) pantorrilla.

calibre, (US) **caliber** ['kælɪbə*] n calibre m.

call [kɔ:l] vt (gen) llamar // vi (shout) llamar; (TEL) llamar (por teléfono), telefonear (esp LAm); (visit: also: ~ **in**, ~ **round**) hacer una visita // n (shout, TEL) llamada; (of bird) canto; (appeal) llamamiento; **to be ~ed** (person, object) llamarse; **on** ~ (nurse, doctor etc) de guardia; **to ~ back** vi (return) volver; (TEL) volver a llamar; **to ~ for** vt fus (demand) pedir, exigir; (fetch) venir por, pasar por (LAm); **to ~ off** vt suspender; (cancel) cancelar; **to ~ on** vt fus (visit) visitar; (turn to) acudir a; **to ~ out** vi gritar, dar voces; **to ~ up** vt (MIL) llamar al servicio militar; **~box** n (Brit) cabina telefónica; **~er** n visita f; (TEL) usuario/a; **~ girl** n prostituta; **~-in** n (US) (programa m) coloquio (por teléfono); **~ing** n vocación f, profesión f; **~ing card** n (US) tarjeta de visita or comercial.

callous ['kæləs] a insensible, cruel.

calm [kɑ:m] a tranquilo; (sea) liso, en calma // n calma, tranquilidad f // vt calmar, tranquilizar; **to ~ down** vi calmarse, tranquilizarse // vt calmar, tranquilizar.

Calor gas ['kælə*-] n ® butano.

calorie ['kælərɪ] n caloría.

calve [kɑ:v] vi parir.

calves [kɑ:vz] pl of **calf**.

camber ['kæmbə*] n (of road) combadura, comba.

Cambodia [kæm'bəudjə] n Camboya.

came [keɪm] pt of **come**.

camel ['kæməl] n camello.

cameo ['kæmɪəu] n camafeo.

camera ['kæmərə] n máquina fotográfica; (CINEMA, TV) cámara; **in** ~ en secreto; **~man** n cámara m.

camouflage ['kæməflɑ:ʒ] n camuflaje m // vt camuflar.

camp [kæmp] n campo, campamento // vi acampar // a afectado, afeminado.

campaign [kæm'peɪn] n (MIL, POL etc) campaña // vi hacer campaña.

camp: ~**bed** n (Brit) cama de campaña; ~**er** n campista m/f; (vehicle) caravana; ~**ing** n camping m; **to go** ~**ing** hacer camping; ~**site** n camping m.

campus ['kæmpəs] n ciudad f universitaria.

KEYWORD

can [kæn] ♦ n, vt see next headword
♦ auxiliary vb (negative **cannot**, **can't**; conditional and pt **could**) **1** (be able to) poder; **you** ~ **do it if you try** puedes hacerlo si lo intentas; **I** ~**'t see you** no te veo

2 (know how to) saber; **I** ~ **swim/play tennis/drive** sé nadar/jugar al tenis/conducir; ~ **you speak French?** ¿hablas or sabes hablar francés?

3 (may) poder; ~ **I use your phone?** ¿me dejas or puedo usar tu teléfono?

4 (expressing disbelief, puzzlement etc): **it** ~**'t be true!** ¡no puede ser (verdad)!; **what CAN he want?** ¿qué querrá?

5 (expressing possibility, suggestion etc): **he could be in the library** podría estar en la biblioteca; **she could have been delayed** pudo haberse retrasado.

---

can [kæn] auxiliary vb see previous headword // n (of oil, water) bidón m; (tin) lata, bote m // vt enlatar; (preserve) conservar en lata.

Canada ['kænədə] n el Canadá; **Canadian** [kə'neɪdɪən] a, n canadiense m/f.

canal [kə'næl] n canal m.

canary [kə'nɛərɪ] n canario; **C~ Islands** npl las (Islas) Canarias.

cancel ['kænsəl] vt cancelar; (train) suprimir; (appointment) anular; (cross out) tachar, borrar; ~**lation** [-'leɪʃən] n cancelación f; supresión f.

cancer ['kænsə*] n cáncer m; **C~**

(ASTRO) Cáncer m.

candid ['kændɪd] a franco, abierto.

candidate ['kændɪdeɪt] n candidato/a.

candle ['kændl] n vela; (in church) cirio; **by ~ light** a la luz de una vela; ~**stick** n (also: ~ **holder**) (single) candelero; (low) palmatoria; (bigger, ornate) candelabro.

candour, (US) **candor** ['kændə*] n franqueza.

candy ['kændɪ] n azúcar m cande; (US) caramelo; ~**-floss** n (Brit) algodón m (azucarado).

cane [keɪn] n (BOT) caña; (stick) vara, palmeta // vt (Brit SCOL) castigar (con palmeta).

canister ['kænɪstə*] n bote m, lata.

cannabis ['kænəbɪs] n marijuana.

canned [kænd] a en lata, de lata.

cannibal ['kænɪbəl] n caníbal m/f.

cannon ['kænən], pl ~ or ~**s** n cañón m.

cannot ['kænɔt] = **can not**.

canny ['kænɪ] a astuto.

canoe [kə'nu:] n canoa; (SPORT) piragua.

canon ['kænən] n (clergyman) canónigo; (standard) canon m.

can opener ['kænəupnə*] n abrelatas m inv.

canopy ['kænəpɪ] n dosel m; toldo.

can't [kænt] = **can not**.

cantankerous [kæn'tæŋkərəs] a arisco, malhumorado.

canteen [kæn'ti:n] n (eating place) cantina; (Brit: of cutlery) juego.

canter ['kæntə*] n medio galope // vi ir a medio galope.

canvas ['kænvəs] n (material) lona; (painting) lienzo; (NAUT) velas fpl.

canvass ['kænvəs] vt (POL) solicitar votos de; (COMM) sondear.

canyon ['kænjən] n cañón m.

cap [kæp] n (hat) gorra; (of pen) capuchón m; (of bottle) tapa, cápsula // vt (outdo) superar; (bottle etc) tapar; (tooth) poner una corona a.

capability [keɪpə'bɪlɪtɪ] n capacidad f.

capable ['keɪpəbl] *a* capaz.

capacity [kə'pæsɪtɪ] *n* capacidad *f*; (*position*) calidad *f*.

cape [keɪp] *n* capa; (*GEO*) cabo.

capital ['kæpɪtl] *n* (*also*: ~ **city**) capital *f*; (*money*) capital *m*; (*also*: ~ **letter**) mayúscula; ~ **gains tax** *n* impuesto sobre las ganancias de capital; ~**ism** *n* capitalismo; ~**ist** *a*, *n* capitalista *m/f*; ~**ize on** *vt fus* aprovechar; ~ **punishment** *n* pena de muerte.

capitulate [kə'pɪtjuleɪt] *vi* capitular, rendirse.

Capricorn ['kæprɪkɔːn] *n* Capricornio.

capsize [kæp'saɪz] *vt* volcar, hacer zozobrar // *vi* volcarse, zozobrar.

capsule ['kæpsjuːl] *n* cápsula.

captain ['kæptɪn] *n* capitán *m*.

caption ['kæpʃən] *n* (*heading*) título; (*to picture*) leyenda.

captive ['kæptɪv] *a*, *n* cautivo/a *m/f*; **captivity** [-'tɪvɪtɪ] *n* cautiverio.

capture ['kæptʃə*] *vt* prender, apresar; (*place*) tomar; (*attention*) captar, llamar // *n* apresamiento; toma; (*data* ~) formulación *f* de datos.

car [kɑː*] *n* coche *m*, carro (*LAm*), automóvil *m*; (*US RAIL*) vagón *m*.

carafe [kə'ræf] *n* garrafa.

caramel ['kærəmæl] *n* caramelo.

carat ['kærət] *n* quilate *m*.

caravan ['kærəvæn] *n* (*Brit*) caravana, ruló *f*; (*of camels*) caravana; ~ **site** *n* (*Brit*) camping *m* para caravanas.

carbohydrates [kɑːbəu'haɪdreɪts] *npl* hidratos *mpl* de carbono; (*food*) fécula *sg*.

carbon ['kɑːbən] *n* carbono; ~ **copy** *n* copia al carbón; ~ **paper** *n* papel *m* carbón.

carburettor, (*US*) **carburetor** [kɑːbju'retə*] *n* carburador *m*.

card [kɑːd] *n* (*playing* ~) carta, naipe *m*; (*visiting* ~, *post*~ *etc*) tarjeta; ~**board** *n* cartón *m*, cartulina; ~ **game** *n* juego de naipes.

cardiac ['kɑːdɪæk] *a* cardíaco.

cardigan ['kɑːdɪgən] *n* rebeca.

cardinal ['kɑːdɪnl] *a* cardinal // *n* cardenal *m*.

card index *n* fichero.

care [kɛə*] *n* cuidado; (*worry*) inquietud *f*; (*charge*) cargo, custodia // *vi*: **to** ~ **about** preocuparse por; ~ **of** en casa de, al cuidado de; **in sb's** ~ a cargo de uno; **to take** ~ to cuidarse de, tener cuidado de; **to take** ~ **of** cuidar; **I don't** ~ no me importa; **I couldn't** ~ **less** eso me trae sin cuidado; **to** ~ **for** *vt fus* cuidar a; (*like*) querer.

career [kə'rɪə*] *n* carrera // *vi* (*also*: ~ **along**) correr a toda velocidad.

carefree ['kɛəfriː] *a* despreocupado.

careful ['kɛəful] *a* cuidadoso; (*cautious*) cauteloso; (**be**) ~! ¡tenga cuidado!; ~**ly** *ad* con cuidado, cuidadosamente.

careless ['kɛəlɪs] *a* descuidado; (*heedless*) poco atento; ~**ness** *n* descuido, falta de atención.

caress [kə'rɛs] *n* caricia // *vt* acariciar.

caretaker ['kɛəteɪkə*] *n* portero, conserje *m/f*.

car-ferry ['kɑːfɛrɪ] *n* transbordador *m* para coches.

cargo ['kɑːgəu], *pl* ~**es** *n* cargamento, carga.

car hire *n* alquiler *m* de automóviles.

Caribbean [kærɪ'biːən] *n*: **the** ~ (**Sea**) el (Mar) Caribe.

caring ['kɛərɪŋ] *a* humanitario.

carnal ['kɑːnl] *a* carnal.

carnation [kɑː'neɪʃən] *n* clavel *m*.

carnival ['kɑːnɪvl] *n* carnaval *m*; (*US*) parque *m* de atracciones.

carnivorous [kɑː'nɪvrəs] *a* carnívoro.

carol ['kærəl] *n*: (**Christmas**) ~ villancico.

carp [kɑːp] *n* (*fish*) carpa; **to** ~ **at** *or* **about** *vt fus* quejarse de.

car park *n* (*Brit*) aparcamiento, parking *m*.

carpenter ['kɑːpɪntə*] *n* carpintero/a.

carpentry ['kɑːpɪntrɪ] *n* carpintería.

carpet ['kɑːpɪt] *n* alfombra // *vt* alfombrar; ~ **slippers** *npl* zapatillas *fpl*; ~ **sweeper** *n* escoba mecánica.

carriage ['kærɪdʒ] *n* coche *m*; (*Brit RAIL*) vagón *m*; (*for goods*) transporte *m*; (: *cost*) porte *m*, flete *m*; (*of typewriter*) carro; (*bearing*) porte *m*; ~ **return** *n* (*on typewriter etc*) retorno del carro; ~**way** *n* (*Brit: part of road*) calzada.

carrier ['kærɪə*] *n* trajinista *m/f*; (*company*) empresa de transportes; ~ **bag** *n* (*Brit*) bolsa de papel or plástico.

carrot ['kærət] *n* zanahoria.

carry ['kærɪ] *vt* (*subj: person*) llevar; (*transport*) transportar; (*a motion, bill*) aprobar; (*involve: responsibilities etc*) entrañar, implicar // *vi* (*sound*) oírse; **to get carried away** (*fig*) entusiasmarse; **to ~ on** *vi* (*continue*) seguir (adelante), continuar; (*fam: complain*) quejarse, protestar // *vt* proseguir, continuar; **to ~ out** *vt* (*orders*) cumplir; (*investigation*) llevar a cabo, realizar; ~**cot** *n* (*Brit*) cuna portátil; ~**-on** *n* (*col: fuss*) lío.

cart [kɑːt] *n* carro, carreta // *vt* llevar (en carro).

carton ['kɑːtən] *n* (*box*) caja (de cartón); (*of yogurt*) pote *m*.

cartoon [kɑː'tuːn] *n* (*PRESS*) caricatura; (*comic strip*) tira cómica; (*film*) dibujos *mpl* animados; ~**ist** *n* dibujante *m/f* de historietas.

cartridge ['kɑːtrɪdʒ] *n* cartucho.

carve [kɑːv] *vt* (*meat*) trinchar; (*wood, stone*) cincelar, esculpir; (*on tree*) grabar; **to ~ up** *vt* dividir, repartir; **carving** *n* (*in wood etc*) escultura, (obra de) talla; **carving knife** *n* trinchante *m*.

car wash *n* lavado de coches.

case [keɪs] *n* (*container*) caja; (*MED*) caso; (*for jewels etc*) estuche *m*; (*LAW*) causa, proceso; (*Brit: also: suit~*) maleta; **in ~ of** en caso de; **in any ~** en todo caso; **just in**

~ por si acaso; **to make a good ~** tener buenos argumentos.

cash [kæʃ] *n* dinero en efectivo, dinero contante // *vt* cobrar, hacer efectivo; **to pay (in)** ~ pagar al contado; ~ **on delivery** cóbrese al entregar; ~**book** *n* libro de caja; ~ **card** *n* tarjeta *f* dinero; ~**desk** *n* (*Brit*) caja; ~ **dispenser** *n* cajero automático.

cashew [kæ'ʃuː] *n* (*also*: ~ **nut**) anacardo.

cashier [kæ'ʃɪə*] *n* cajero/a.

cashmere ['kæʃmɪə*] *n* casimir *m*, cachemira.

cash register *n* caja.

casing ['keɪsɪŋ] *n* revestimiento.

casino [kə'siːnəu] *n* casino.

cask [kɑːsk] *n* tonel *m*, barril *m*.

casket ['kɑːskɪt] *n* cofre *m*, estuche *m*; (*US: coffin*) ataúd *m*.

casserole ['kæsərəul] *n* (*food, pot*) cazuela.

cassette [kæ'sɛt] *n* cassette *m*; ~ **player/recorder** *n* tocacassettes *m inv*.

cast [kɑːst] *vb* (*pt, pp* cast) *vt* (*throw*) echar, arrojar, lanzar; (*skin*) mudar, perder; (*metal*) fundir; (*THEATRE*): **to ~ sb as Othello** dar a alguien el papel de Otelo // *n* (*FISHING*) lanzar // *n* (*THEATRE*) reparto; (*mould*) forma, molde *m*; (*also*: **plaster** ~) vaciado; **to ~ one's vote** votar; **to ~ off** *vi* (*NAUT*) desamarrar.

castanets [kæstə'nɛts] *npl* castañuelas *fpl*.

castaway ['kɑːstəweɪ] *n* náufrago/a.

caste [kɑːst] *n* casta.

caster sugar [kɑːstə*-] *n* (*Brit*) azúcar *m* extrafino.

Castile [kæs'tiːl] *n* Castilla.

casting vote ['kɑːstɪŋ-] *n* (*Brit*) voto decisivo.

cast iron *n* hierro fundido.

castle ['kɑːsl] *n* castillo; (*CHESS*) torre *f*.

castor ['kɑːstə*] *n* (*wheel*) ruedecilla; ~ **oil** *n* aceite *m* de ricino.

castrate [kæs'treɪt] vt castrar.

casual ['kæʒjul] a (by chance) fortuito; (irregular: work etc) eventual, temporero; (unconcerned) despreocupado; (informal: clothes) de sport; **~ly** ad de manera despreocupada.

casualty ['kæʒjultɪ] n víctima, herido; (dead) muerto; (MIL) baja.

cat [kæt] n gato.

Catalan ['kætələn] a, n catalán/ana m/f.

catalogue, (US) **catalog** ['kætəlɔg] n catálogo // vt catalogar.

Catalonia [kætə'ləunɪə] n Cataluña.

catalyst ['kætəlɪst] n catalizador m.

catapult ['kætəpʌlt] n tirador m.

catarrh [kə'tɑː] n catarro.

catastrophe [kə'tæstrəfɪ] n catástrofe f.

catch [kætʃ] vb (pt, pp **caught**) vt coger (Sp), agarrar (LAm); (arrest) detener; (grasp) asir; (breath) suspender; (person: by surprise) sorprender; (attract: attention) ganar; (MED) contagiarse de, coger; (also: **~ up**) alcanzar // vi (fire) encenderse; (in branches etc) enredarse // n (fish etc) pesca; (act of catching) cogida; (trick) trampa; (of lock) pestillo, cerradura; to **~ fire** encenderse; to **~ sight of** divisar; to **~ on** vi (understand) caer en la cuenta; (grow popular) hacerse popular; to **~ up** vi (fig) ponerse al día.

catching ['kætʃɪŋ] a (MED) contagioso.

catchment area ['kætʃmənt-] n (Brit) zona de captación.

catchphrase ['kætʃfreɪz] n lema m, eslogan m.

catchy ['kætʃɪ] a (tune) pegadizo.

categorize ['kætɪgəraɪz] vt clasificar.

category ['kætɪgərɪ] n categoría, clase f.

cater ['keɪtə*] vi: to **~ for** (Brit) abastecer a; (needs) atender a; (consumers) proveer a; **~er** n abastecedor/a m/f, proveedor/a m/f; **~ing** n (trade) (ramo de la) alimentación f.

caterpillar ['kætəpɪlə*] n oruga, gusano; **~ track** n rodado de oruga.

cathedral [kə'θiːdrəl] n catedral f.

catholic ['kæθəlɪk] a católico; **C~** a, n (REL) católico/a m/f.

cat's-eye ['kætsaɪ] n (Brit AUT) catafoto.

cattle ['kætl] npl ganado sg.

catty ['kætɪ] a malicioso, rencoroso.

caucus ['kɔːkəs] n (POL: local committee) comité m local; (: US: to elect candidates) comité m electoral.

caught [kɔːt] pt, pp de **catch**.

cauliflower ['kɔlɪflauə*] n coliflor f.

cause [kɔːz] n causa, motivo, razón f // vt causar; (provoke) provocar.

caustic ['kɔːstɪk] a cáustico; (fig) mordaz.

caution ['kɔːʃən] n cautela, prudencia; (warning) advertencia, amonestación f // vt amonestar.

cautious ['kɔːʃəs] a cauteloso, prudente, precavido; **~ly** ad con cautela.

cavalier [kævə'lɪə*] a arrogante, desdeñoso.

cavalry ['kævəlrɪ] n caballería.

cave [keɪv] n cueva, caverna; to **~ in** vi (roof etc) derrumbarse, hundirse; **~man/woman** n cavernícola m/f, troglodita m/f.

cavern ['kævən] n caverna.

caviar(e) ['kævɪɑː*] n caviar m.

cavity ['kævɪtɪ] n hueco, cavidad f.

cavort [kə'vɔːt] vi dar cabrioladas.

CB n abbr (= Citizen's Band (Radio)) banda ciudadana.

CBI n abbr (= Confederation of British Industry) = C.E.O.E. f (Sp).

cc abbr (= cubic centimetres; = carbon copy).

cease [siːs] vt cesar; **~fire** n alto m el fuego; **~less** a incesante; **~lessly** ad sin cesar.

cedar ['siːdə*] n cedro.

ceiling ['siːlɪŋ] n techo; (fig) límite m.

celebrate ['selɪbreɪt] vt celebrar; (have a party) festejar // vi divertirse; **~d** a célebre; **celebration**

[-'breɪʃən] n fiesta, celebración f.
celery ['sɛlərɪ] n apio.
celibacy ['sɛlɪbəsɪ] n celibato.
cell [sɛl] n celda; (BIOL) célula; (ELEC) elemento.
cellar ['sɛlə*] n sótano; (for wine) bodega.
'cello ['tʃɛləu] n violoncelo.
cellophane ['sɛləfeɪn] n celofán m.
Celt [kɛlt, sɛlt] a, n celta m/f; **~ic** a celta.
cement [sə'mɛnt] n cemento // vt cementar; (fig) cimentar, fortalecer; **~ mixer** n hormigonera.
cemetery ['sɛmɪtrɪ] n cementerio.
censor ['sɛnsə*] n censor m // vt (cut) censurar; **~ship** n censura.
censure ['sɛnʃə*] vt censurar.
census ['sɛnsəs] n censo.
cent [sɛnt] n (US: coin) centavo, céntimo; see also per.
centenary [sɛn'tiːnərɪ] n centenario.
center ['sɛntə*] n (US) = **centre**.
centi... [sɛntɪ] pref: **~grade** a centígrado; **~litre**, (US) **~liter** n centilitro; **~metre**, (US) **~meter** n centímetro.
centipede ['sɛntɪpiːd] n ciempiés n inv.
central ['sɛntrəl] a central; (of house etc) céntrico; **C~ America** n Centroamérica; **~ heating** n calefacción f central; **~ize** vt centralizar.
centre ['sɛntə*] n centro // vt centrar; **~-forward** n (SPORT) delantero centro; **~-half** n (SPORT) medio centro.
century ['sɛntjurɪ] n siglo; **20th ~** n siglo veinte.
ceramic [sɪ'ræmɪk] a cerámico; **~s** n cerámica.
cereal ['sɪərɪəl] n cereal m.
cerebral ['sɛrɪbrəl] a cerebral; intelectual.
ceremony ['sɛrɪmənɪ] n ceremonia; **to stand on ~** hacer ceremonias, estar de cumplido.
certain ['sɜːtən] a seguro; (correct) cierto; (person) seguro; (a particular) cierto; **for ~** a ciencia cierta;

~ly ad desde luego, por supuesto; **~ty** n certeza, certidumbre f, seguridad f.
certificate [sə'tɪfɪkɪt] n certificado.
certified ['sɜːtɪfaɪd] a: **~ mail** n (US) correo certificado; **~ public accountant (C.P.A)** n (US) contable m/f diplomado/a.
certify ['sɜːtɪfaɪ] vt certificar.
cervical [sə'vaɪkl] a (of cervix: smear, cancer) cervical.
cervix ['sɜːvɪks] n cerviz f.
cessation [sə'seɪʃən] n cese m, suspensión f.
cesspit ['sɛspɪt] n pozo negro.
cf. abbr (= compare) cfr.
ch. abbr (= chapter) cap.
chafe [tʃeɪf] vt (rub) rozar; (irritate) irritar.
chaffinch ['tʃæfɪntʃ] n pinzón m (vulgar).
chagrin ['ʃægrɪn] n (annoyance) disgusto; (disappointment) desazón f.
chain [tʃeɪn] n cadena // vt (also: **~ up**) encadenar; **~-smoke** vi fumar un cigarrillo tras otro; **~ reaction** n reacción f en cadena; **~ store** n tienda de una cadena, ≈ gran almacén.
chair [tʃɛə*] n silla; (armchair) sillón m; (of university) cátedra f // vt (meeting) presidir; **~lift** n telesilla; **~man** n presidente m.
chalet ['ʃæleɪ] n chalet m.
chalk [tʃɔːk] n (GEO) creta; (for writing) tiza, gis m (LAm).
challenge ['tʃælɪndʒ] n desafío, reto // vt desafiar, retar; (statement, right) poner en duda; **to ~ sb to do sth** retar a uno a que haga algo; **challenging** a desafiante; (tone) de desafío.
chamber ['tʃeɪmbə*] n cámara, sala; **~ of commerce** cámara de comercio; **~maid** n camarera; **~ music** n música de cámara.
champagne [ʃæm'peɪn] n champaña m, champán m.
champion ['tʃæmpɪən] n campeón/ona m/f; **~ship** n campeonato.

chance [tʃɑːns] n (coincidence) casualidad f; (luck) suerte f; (fate) azar m; (opportunity) ocasión f, oportunidad f; (likelihood) posibilidad f; (risk) riesgo m // vt arriesgar, probar // a fortuito, casual; **to ~ it** arriesgarse, intentarlo; **to take a ~** arriesgarse; **by ~** por casualidad.

chancellor ['tʃɑːnsələ'] n canciller m; **C~ of the Exchequer** n (Brit) Ministro de Hacienda.

chandelier [ʃændə'lɪə'] n araña (de luces).

change [tʃeɪndʒ] vt cambiar; (replace) reemplazar; (gear) cambiar de; (clothes, house) mudarse de; (exchange) trocar; (transform) transformar // vi cambiar(se); (trains) hacer transbordo; (be transformed): **to ~ into** transformarse en // n cambio; (alteration) modificación f, transformación f; (coins) suelto, sencillo; (money returned) vuelta; **to ~ one's mind** cambiar de opinión o idea; **for a ~** para variar; **~able** a (weather) cambiable; **~ machine** n máquina de cambio; **~over** n (to new system) cambio.

changing ['tʃeɪndʒɪŋ] a cambiante; **~ room** n (Brit) vestuario.

channel ['tʃænl] n (TV) canal m; (of river) cauce m; (of sea) estrecho; (groove, fig: medium) conducto, medio // vt (river etc) encauzar; **the (English) C~** el Canal de la Mancha; **the C~ Islands** las Islas Normandas.

chant [tʃɑːnt] n canto // vt cantar.

chaos ['keɪɒs] n caos m.

chap [tʃæp] n (Brit col: man) tío, tipo.

chapel ['tʃæpl] n capilla.

chaperone ['ʃæpərəun] n carabina.

chaplain ['tʃæplɪn] n capellán m.

chapped [tʃæpt] a agrietado.

chapter ['tʃæptə'] n capítulo.

char [tʃɑː'] vt (burn) carbonizar, chamuscar // n (Brit) = **charlady**.

character ['kærɪktə'] n carácter m, naturaleza, índole f; (in novel, film)

personaje m; (role) papel m; **~istic** [-'rɪstɪk] a característico // n característica; **~ize** vt caracterizar.

charcoal ['tʃɑːkəul] n carbón m vegetal; (ART) carboncillo.

charge [tʃɑːdʒ] n carga; (LAW) cargo, acusación f; (cost) precio, coste m; (responsibility) cargo; (task) encargo // vt (LAW) acusar (with de); (gun, battery, MIL: enemy) cargar; (price) pedir; (customer) cobrar; (sb with task) encargar // vi precipitarse; (make pay) cobrar; **~s** npl: **bank ~s** comisiones fpl bancarias; **free of ~** gratis; **to reverse the ~s** (Brit TEL) revertir el cobro; **to take ~ of** hacerse cargo de, encargarse de; **to be in ~ of** estar encargado de; **how much do you ~?** ¿cuánto cobra usted?; **to ~ an expense (up) to sb's account** cargar algo a cuenta de alguien; **~ card** n tarjeta de cuenta.

charitable ['tʃærɪtəbl] a caritativo.

charity ['tʃærɪtɪ] n (gen) caridad f; (organization) sociedad f benéfica.

charlady ['tʃɑːleɪdɪ] n (Brit) mujer f de la limpieza.

charlatan ['ʃɑːlətən] n farsante m/f.

charm [tʃɑːm] n encanto, atractivo // vt encantar; **~ing** a encantador(a).

chart [tʃɑːt] n (table) cuadro; (graph) gráfica; (map) carta de navegación // vt (course) trazar.

charter ['tʃɑːtə'] vt (plane) alquilar; (ship) fletar // n (document) carta; **~ed accountant** n (Brit) contable m/f diplomado/a; **~ flight** n vuelo chárter.

charwoman ['tʃɑːwumən] n = **charlady**.

chase [tʃeɪs] vt (pursue) perseguir; (hunt) cazar // n persecución f; caza; **to ~ after** correr tras.

chasm ['kæzəm] n abismo.

chassis ['ʃæsɪ] n chasis m.

chat [tʃæt] vi (also: **have a ~**) charlar // n charla; **~ show** n (Brit) (programa m) magazine m.

chatter ['tʃætə'] vi (person) charlar; (teeth) castañetear // n (of birds) parloteo; (of people) charla, cháchara; ~**box** n parlanchín/ina m/f.

chatty ['tʃætɪ] a (style) familiar; (person) hablador(a).

chauffeur ['ʃəʊfə*] n chófer m.

chauvinist ['ʃəʊvɪnɪst] n (male ~) machista m; (nationalist) chovinista m/f.

cheap [tʃiːp] a barato; (joke) de mal gusto; (poor quality) de mala calidad // ad barato; ~**en** vt rebajar el precio, abaratar; ~**er** a más barato; ~**ly** ad barato, a bajo precio.

cheat [tʃiːt] vi hacer trampa // vt estafar, timar // n trampa; estafa; (person) tramposo/a.

check [tʃɛk] vt (examine) controlar; (facts) comprobar; (count) contar; (halt) parar, detener; (restrain) refrenar, restringir // n (inspection) control m, inspección f; (curb) freno; (bill) nota, cuenta; (US = **cheque**; (pattern: gen pl) cuadro // a (also ~**ed**: pattern, cloth) a cuadros; **to ~ in** (in hotel, airport) registrarse // vt (luggage) facturar; **to ~ out** vi (of hotel) desocupar su cuarto; **to ~ up** vi: **to ~ up on sth** comprobar algo; **to ~ up on sb** investigar a alguien; ~**ered** a (US) = **chequered**; ~**ers** n (US) juego de damas; ~**-in (desk)** n mesa de facturación; ~**ing account** n (US) cuenta corriente; ~**mate** n jaque m mate; ~**out** n caja; ~**point** n (punto de control) m; ~**room** n (US) consigna; ~**up** n (MED) reconocimiento general; (of machine) repaso.

cheek [tʃiːk] n mejilla; (impudence) descaro; ~**bone** n pómulo; ~**y** a fresco, descarado.

cheep [tʃiːp] vi piar.

cheer [tʃɪə*] vt vitorear, aplaudir; (gladden) alegrar, animar // vi aplaudir, dar vivas // n viva m; ~**s** npl aplausos mpl; ~**s!** ¡salud!; **to ~ up** vi animarse // vt alegrar, animar; ~**ful** a alegre.

cheerio [tʃɪərɪ'əʊ] excl (Brit) ¡hasta luego!

cheese [tʃiːz] n queso; ~**board** n plato de quesos.

cheetah ['tʃiːtə] n leopardo cazador.

chef [ʃɛf] n jefe/a m/f de cocina.

chemical ['kɛmɪkəl] a químico // n producto químico.

chemist ['kɛmɪst] n (Brit: pharmacist) farmacéutico/a; (scientist) químico/a; ~**ry** n química; ~**'s (shop)** n (Brit) farmacia.

cheque [tʃɛk] n (Brit) cheque m; ~**book** n libro de cheques, chequera (LAm); ~**card** n tarjeta de cheque.

chequered ['tʃɛkəd] a (fig) accidentado.

cherish ['tʃɛrɪʃ] vt (love) querer, apreciar; (protect) cuidar; (hope etc) abrigar.

cherry ['tʃɛrɪ] n cereza.

chess [tʃɛs] n ajedrez m; ~**board** n tablero de ajedrez); ~**man** n pieza, trebejo.

chest [tʃɛst] n (ANAT) pecho; (box) cofre m, cajón m; ~ **of drawers** n cómoda.

chestnut ['tʃɛsnʌt] n castaña; ~ **(tree)** n castaño.

chew [tʃuː] vt mascar, masticar; ~**ing gum** n chicle m.

chic [ʃiːk] a elegante.

chick [tʃɪk] n pollito, polluelo; (US col) chica.

chicken ['tʃɪkɪn] n gallina, pollo; (food) pollo; **to ~ out** vi (col) rajarse; ~**pox** n varicela.

chicory ['tʃɪkərɪ] n (for coffee) achicoria; (salad) escarola.

chief [tʃiːf] n jefe/a m/f // a principal; ~ **executive** n director(a) m/f general; ~**ly** ad principalmente.

chiffon ['ʃɪfɔn] n gasa.

chilblain ['tʃɪlbleɪn] n sabañón m.

child [tʃaɪld], pl ~**ren** ['tʃɪldrən] n niño/a; (offspring) hijo/a; ~**birth** n parto; ~**hood** n niñez f, infancia; ~**ish** a pueril, aniñado; ~**like** a de niño; ~**minder** n (Brit) niñera.

Chile ['tʃɪlɪ] n Chile m; ~**an** a, n chileno/a m/f.

chill [tʃɪl] n frío; (MED) resfriado // a

frío // vt enfriar; (CULIN) congelar.

chilli ['tʃɪlɪ] n (Brit) chile m, ají m (LAm).

chilly ['tʃɪlɪ] a frío.

chime [tʃaɪm] n repique m, campanada // vi repicar, sonar.

chimney ['tʃɪmnɪ] n chimenea; ~ **sweep** n deshollinador m.

chimpanzee [tʃɪmpæn'zi:] n chimpancé m.

chin [tʃɪn] n mentón m, barbilla.

china ['tʃaɪnə] n porcelana; (crockery) loza.

China ['tʃaɪnə] n China; **Chinese** [tʃaɪ'ni:z] a chino // n, pl inv chino/a; (LING) chino.

chink [tʃɪŋk] n (opening) grieta, hendedura; (noise) tintineo.

chip [tʃɪp] n (gen pl; CULIN: Brit) patata or papa (LAm) frita; (: US: also: potato ~) patata or papa frita; (of wood) astilla; (of glass, stone) lasca; (at poker) ficha; (COMPUT) chip m // vt (cup, plate) desconchar; **to ~ in** vi interrumpir; (contribute) compartir los gastos.

chiropodist [kɪ'rɔpədɪst] n (Brit) pedicuro/a.

chirp [tʃə:p] vi gorjear, piar.

chisel ['tʃɪzl] n (for wood) formón m; (for stone) cincel m.

chit [tʃɪt] n nota.

chitchat ['tʃɪttʃæt] n chismes mpl, habladurías fpl.

chivalry ['ʃɪvəlrɪ] n caballerosidad f.

chives [tʃaɪvz] npl cebollinos mpl.

chlorine ['klɔ:ri:n] n cloro.

chock [tʃɔk]: ~**-a-block**, ~**-full** a atestado.

chocolate ['tʃɔklɪt] n chocolate m.

choice [tʃɔɪs] n elección f // a escogido.

choir ['kwaɪə*] n coro; ~**boy** n corista m.

choke [tʃəuk] vi sofocarse; (on food) atragantarse // vt ahogar, sofocar; (block) obstruir // n (AUT) estárter m.

choose [tʃu:z], pt **chose**, pp **chosen** vt escoger, elegir; (team) selec-

cionar.

choosy ['tʃu:zɪ] a remilgado.

chop [tʃɔp] vt (wood) cortar, tajar; (CULIN: also: ~ **up**) picar // n golpe m cortante; (CULIN) chuleta; ~**s** npl (jaws) boca sg, labios mpl.

chopper ['tʃɔpə*] n (helicopter) helicóptero.

choppy ['tʃɔpɪ] a (sea) picado, agitado.

chopsticks ['tʃɔpstɪks] npl palillos mpl.

chord [kɔ:d] n (MUS) acorde m.

chore [tʃɔ:*] n faena, tarea; (routine task) trabajo rutinario.

chortle ['tʃɔ:tl] vi reír entre dientes.

chorus ['kɔ:rəs] n coro; (repeated part of song) estribillo.

chose [tʃəuz] pt of **choose**.

chosen ['tʃəuzn] pp of **choose**.

Christ [kraɪst] n Cristo.

christen ['krɪsn] vt bautizar.

Christian ['krɪstɪən] a, n cristiano/a m/f; ~**ity** [-'ænɪtɪ] n cristianismo; ~ **name** n nombre m de pila.

Christmas ['krɪsməs] n Navidad f; **Merry** ~! ¡Felices Pascuas!; ~ **card** n crismas m inv, tarjeta de Navidad; ~ **Day** n día m de Navidad; ~ **Eve** n Nochebuena; ~ **tree** n árbol m de Navidad.

chrome [krəum] n = **chromium plating**.

chromium ['krəumɪəm] n cromo; ~ **plating** n cromado.

chronic ['krɔnɪk] a crónico.

chronicle ['krɔnɪkl] n crónica.

chronological [krɔnə'lɔdʒɪkəl] a cronológico.

chrysanthemum [krɪ'sænθəməm] n crisantemo.

chubby ['tʃʌbɪ] a rechoncho.

chuck [tʃʌk] vt lanzar, arrojar; **to ~ out** vt echar (fuera), tirar; **to ~ (up)** vt (Brit) abandonar.

chuckle ['tʃʌkl] vi reírse entre dientes.

chug [tʃʌg] vi resoplar.

chum [tʃʌm] n compañero/a.

chunk [tʃʌŋk] n pedazo, trozo.

church [tʃəːtʃ] n iglesia; ~**yard** n campo santo.

churlish ['tʃəːlɪʃ] a grosero.

churn [tʃəːn] n (for butter) mantequera; (for milk) lechera; **to ~ out** vt producir en serie.

chute [ʃuːt] n (also: rubbish ~) vertedero; (Brit: children's slide) tobogán m.

chutney ['tʃʌtnɪ] n salsa picante.

CIA n abbr (US: = Central Intelligence Agency) CIA f.

CID n abbr (Brit: = Criminal Investigation Department) ≈ B.I.C.f (Sp).

cider ['saɪdə*] n sidra.

cigar [sɪ'gaː*] n puro.

cigarette [sɪgə'rɛt] n cigarrillo, cigarro (LAm); pitillo; ~ **case** n pitillera; ~ **end** n colilla; ~ **holder** n boquilla.

Cinderella [sɪndə'rɛlə] n Cenicienta.

cine ['sɪnɪ]: ~-**camera** n (Brit) cámara cinematográfica; ~-**film** n (Brit) película de cine.

cinema ['sɪnəmə] n cine m.

cinnamon ['sɪnəmən] n canela.

cipher ['saɪfə*] n cifra.

circle ['səːkl] n círculo; (in theatre) anfiteatro // vi dar vueltas // vt (surround) rodear, cercar; (move round) dar la vuelta a.

circuit ['səːkɪt] n circuito; (track) pista; (lap) vuelta; ~**ous** [səː'kjuɪtəs] a indirecto.

circular ['səːkjulə*] a circular // n circular f.

circulate ['səːkjuleɪt] vi circular // vt poner en circulación; **circulation** [-'leɪʃən] n circulación f; (of newspaper) tirada.

circumcise ['səːkəmsaɪz] vt circuncidar.

circumstances ['səːkəmstənsɪz] npl circunstancias fpl; (financial condition) situación f económica.

circumvent ['səːkəmvɛnt] vt burlar.

circus ['səːkəs] n circo.

cistern ['sɪstən] n tanque m, depósito; (in toilet) cisterna.

citizen ['sɪtɪzn] n (POL) ciudadano/a;

(of city) vecino/a, habitante m/f; ~**ship** n ciudadanía.

citrus fruits ['sɪtrəs-] npl agrios mpl.

city ['sɪtɪ] n ciudad f; **the C~** centro financiero de Londres.

civic ['sɪvɪk] a cívico, municipal; ~ **centre** n (Brit) centro público.

civil ['sɪvɪl] a civil; (polite) atento, cortés; (well-bred) educado; ~ **defence** n protección f civil; ~ **engineer** n ingeniero civil; ~**ian** [sɪ'vɪlɪən] a civil (no militar) // n civil m/f, paisano/a; ~**ian clothing** n ropa de paisano.

civilization [sɪvɪlaɪ'zeɪʃən] n civilización f.

civilized ['sɪvɪlaɪzd] a civilizado.

civil: ~ law n derecho civil; ~ **servant** n funcionario/a del Estado; **C~ Service** n administración f pública; ~ **war** n guerra civil.

clad [klæd] a: ~ (**in**) vestido (de).

claim [kleɪm] vt exigir, reclamar; (rights etc) reivindicar; (assert) pretender // vi (for insurance) reclamar // n reclamación f; (LAW) demanda; (pretension) pretensión f; ~**ant** n (ADMIN, LAW) demandante m/f.

clairvoyant [klɛə'vɔɪənt] n clarividente m/f.

clam [klæm] n almeja.

clamber ['klæmbə*] vi trepar.

clammy ['klæmɪ] a (cold) frío y húmedo; (sticky) pegajoso.

clamour ['klæmə*] vi: **to ~ for** clamar por, pedir a voces.

clamp [klæmp] n abrazadera, grapa // vt afianzar (con abrazadera); **to ~ down on** vt fus (subj: government, police) reforzar la lucha contra.

clan [klæn] n clan m.

clang [klæŋ] n estruendo // vi sonar, hacer estruendo.

clap [klæp] vi aplaudir; ~**ping** n aplausos mpl.

claret ['klærət] n clarete m.

clarify ['klærɪfaɪ] vt aclarar.

clarinet [klærɪ'nɛt] n clarinete m.

clarity ['klærɪtɪ] n claridad f.

clash [klæʃ] n estruendo; (fig) choque m // vi (battle) chocar; (disagree) estar en desacuerdo.

clasp [klɑːsp] n broche m; (on jewels) cierre m // vt abrochar; (hand) apretar; (embrace) abrazar.

class [klɑːs] n (gen) clase f // a clasista, de clase // vt clasificar.

classic ['klæsɪk] a, n clásico; ~al a clásico.

classified ['klæsɪfaɪd] a (information) reservado; ~ **advertisement** n anuncio por palabras.

classify ['klæsɪfaɪ] vt clasificar.

classmate n compañero/a de clase.

classroom ['klɑːsrum] n aula.

clatter ['klætə*] n ruido, estruendo; (of hooves) trápala // vi hacer ruido or estruendo.

clause [klɔːz] n cláusula; (LING) oración f.

claw [klɔː] n (of cat) uña; (of bird of prey) garra; (of lobster) pinza; (TECH) garfio; **to ~ at** vt fus arañar; (tear) desgarrar.

clay [kleɪ] n arcilla.

clean [kliːn] a limpio; (clear) neto, bien definido // vt limpiar; **to ~ out** vt limpiar; **to ~ up** vt limpiar, asear; ~**er** n (person) asistenta; ~**ing** n limpieza; ~**liness** ['klenlɪnɪs] n limpieza.

cleanse [klɛnz] vt limpiar; ~**r** n detergente; (for face) crema limpiadora; **cleansing department** n (Brit) departamento de limpieza.

clear [klɪə*] a claro; (road, way) libre // vt (space) despejar, limpiar; (LAW: suspect) absolver; (obstacle) salvar, saltar por encima de; (debt) liquidar; (cheque) pasar por un banco // vi (fog etc) despejarse // ad: ~ **of** a distancia de; **to ~ the table** recoger or levantar la mesa; **to ~ up** vt limpiar; (mystery) aclarar, resolver; ~**ance** n (removal) despeje m; (permission) acreditación f; ~**cut** a bien definido, nítido; ~**ing** n (in wood) claro; ~**ing bank** n (Brit) cámara de compensación; ~**ly** ad

claramente; ~**way** n (Brit) carretera donde no se puede aparcar.

cleaver ['kliːvə*] n cuchilla (de carnicero).

clef [klɛf] n (MUS) clave f.

cleft [klɛft] n (in rock) grieta, hendedura.

clench [klɛntʃ] vt apretar, cerrar.

clergy ['klɜːdʒɪ] n clero; ~**man** n clérigo.

clerical ['klerɪkəl] a de oficina; (REL) clerical.

clerk [klɑːk, (US) klɜːrk] n oficinista m/f; (US) dependiente/a m/f, vendedor/a m/f.

clever ['klevə*] a (mentally) inteligente, listo; (skilful) hábil; (device, arrangement) ingenioso.

click [klɪk] vt (tongue) chasquear; (heels) taconear.

client ['klaɪənt] n cliente m/f.

cliff [klɪf] n acantilado.

climate ['klaɪmɪt] n clima m.

climax ['klaɪmæks] n colmo, punto culminante; (sexual) clímax m.

climb [klaɪm] vi subir, trepar // vt (stairs) subir; (tree) trepar a; (mountain) escalar // n subida; ~**down** n vuelta atrás; ~**er** n alpinista m/f, andinista m/f (LAm); ~**ing** n alpinismo, andinismo (LAm).

clinch [klɪntʃ] vt (deal) cerrar; (argument) remachar.

cling [klɪŋ], pt, pp **clung** [klʌŋ] vi: **to ~ to** agarrarse a; (clothes) pegarse a.

clinic ['klɪnɪk] n clínica.

clink [klɪŋk] vi tintinar.

clip [klɪp] n (for hair) horquilla; (also: **paper** ~) sujetapapeles m inv, clip m; (clamp) grapa // vt (cut) cortar; (hedge) podar; (also: **to ~ together**) unir; ~**pers** npl (for gardening) tijeras fpl; (for hair) maquinilla sg; (for nails) cortaúñas m inv; ~**ping** n (newspaper) recorte m.

clique [kliːk] n camarilla.

cloak [kləuk] n capa, manto // (fig) encubrir, disimular; ~**room** n guardarropa; (Brit: WC) lavabo, aseos *mpl*, baño (*LAm*).

clock [klɔk] *n* reloj *m*; (*in taxi*) taxímetro; **to ~ in** or **on** *vi* fichar, picar; **to ~ off** or **out** *vi* fichar or picar la salida; **~wise** *ad* en el sentido de las agujas del reloj; **~work** *n* aparato de relojería // *a* (*toy*) de cuerda.

clog [klɔg] *n* zueco, chanclo // *vt* atascar // *vi* atascarse.

cloister ['klɔistə*] *n* claustro.

close *a, ad and derivatives* [kləus] *a* cercano, próximo; (*near*): **~ (to)** cerca (de); (*print, weave*) tupido, compacto; (*friend*) íntimo; (*connection*) estrecho; (*examination*) detallado, minucioso; (*weather*) bochornoso; (*atmosphere*) sofocante; (*room*) mal ventilado; **to have a ~ shave** (*fig*) escaparse por un pelo // *ad* cerca; **~ by, ~ at hand** *a, ad* muy cerca; **~ to** *prep* cerca de // *vb and derivatives* [kləuz] *vt* (*shut*) cerrar; (*end*) concluir, terminar // *vi* (*shop etc*) cerrarse; (*end*) concluirse, terminarse // *n* (*end*) fin *m*, final *m*, conclusión *f*; **to ~ down** *vi* cerrarse definitivamente; **~d** *a* (*shop etc*) cerrado; **~d shop** *n* taller *m* gremial; **~-knit** *a* (*fig*) muy unido; **~ly** *ad* (*study*) con detalle; (*listen*) con atención; (*watch*) de cerca.

closet ['klɔzit] *n* (*cupboard*) armario.

close-up ['kləusʌp] *n* primer plano.

closure ['kləuʒə*] *n* cierre *m*.

clot [klɔt] *n* (*gen*: *blood* ~) embolia; (*fam*: *idiot*) imbécil *m/f* // *vi* (*blood*) coagularse.

cloth [klɔθ] *n* (*material*) tela, paño; (*rag*) trapo.

clothe [kləuð] *vt* vestir; (*fig*) revestir; **~s** *npl* ropa *sg*; **~s brush** *n* cepillo (para la ropa); **~s line** *n* cuerda (para tender la ropa); **~s peg**, (*US*) **~s pin** *n* pinza.

clothing ['kləuðiŋ] *n* = **clothes**.

cloud [klaud] *n* nube *f*; (*storm* ~) nubarrón *m*; **~y** *a* nublado, nubloso; (*liquid*) turbio.

clout [klaut] *vt* dar un tortazo a.

clove [kləuv] *n* clavo; **~ of garlic** diente *m* de ajo.

clover ['kləuvə*] *n* trébol *m*.

clown [klaun] *n* payaso *m* // *vi* (*also*: **~ about, ~ around**) hacer el payaso.

cloying ['klɔiiŋ] *a* (*taste*) empalagoso.

club [klʌb] *n* (*society*) club *m*; (*weapon*) porra, cachiporra; (*also*: *golf* ~) palo // *vt* aporrear // *vi*: **to ~ together** (*join forces*) unir fuerzas; **~s** *npl* (*CARDS*) tréboles *mpl*; **~ car** *n* (*US RAIL*) coche *m* salón; **~house** *n* local social, sobre todo en clubs deportivos.

cluck [klʌk] *vi* cloquear.

clue [klu:] *n* pista; (*in crosswords*) indicación *f*; **I haven't a ~** no tengo ni idea.

clump [klʌmp] *n* (*of trees*) grupo.

clumsy ['klʌmzi] *a* (*person*) torpe, desmañado; (*tool*) difícil de manejar.

clung [klʌŋ] *pt, pp of* **cling**.

cluster ['klʌstə*] *n* grupo; (*BOT*) racimo // *vi* agruparse, apiñarse.

clutch [klʌtʃ] *n* (*AUT*) embrague *m*; (*pedal*) pedal *m* de embrague; **to fall into sb's ~es** caer en las garras de alguien // *vt* asir; agarrar.

clutter ['klʌtə*] *vt* atestar.

cm *abbr* (= *centimetre*) cm.

CND *n abbr* = Campaign for Nuclear Disarmament) plataforma pro desarme nuclear.

Co. *abbr* = **county**; **company**.

c/o *abbr* (= *care of*) c/a, a/c.

coach [kəutʃ] *n* (*bus*) autocar *m* (*Sp*), autobús *m*; (*horse-drawn*) coche *m*; (*of train*) vagón *m*, coche *m*; (*SPORT*) entrenador/a *m/f*, instructor(a) *m/f* // *vt* (*SPORT*) entrenar; (*student*) preparar, enseñar; **~ trip** *n* excursión *f* en autocar.

coal [kəul] *n* carbón *m*; **~ face** *n* frente *m* de carbón; **~field** *n* yacimiento de carbón.

coalition [kəuə'liʃən] *n* coalición *f*.

coal man, coal merchant *n* carbonero.

coalmine ['kəulmain] *n* mina de carbón.

coarse [kɔːs] *a* basto, burdo; (*vulgar*) grosero, ordinario.

coast [kəust] *n* costa, litoral *m* // *vi* (*AUT*) ir en punto muerto; **~al** *a* costero, costanero; **~guard** *n* guardacostas *m inv*; **~line** *n* litoral *m*.

coat [kəut] *n* (*jacket*) chaqueta; (*overcoat*) abrigo; (*of animal*) pelo, lana; (*of paint*) mano *f*, capa // *vt* cubrir, revestir; **~ of arms** *n* escudo de armas; **~ hanger** *n* percha, gancho (*LAm*); **~ing** *n* capa, baño.

coax [kəuks] *vt* engatusar.

cob [kɔb] *n* see **corn**.

cobbler ['kɔblə] *n* zapatero (remendón).

cobbles ['kɔblz], **cobblestones** ['kɔblstəunz] *npl* adoquines *mpl*.

cobweb ['kɔbweb] *n* telaraña.

cocaine [kə'keɪn] *n* cocaína.

cock [kɔk] *n* (*rooster*) gallo; (*male bird*) macho *m* // *vt* (*gun*) amartillar; **~erel** *n* gallito; **~-eyed** *a* (*fig: crooked*) torcido; (: *idea*) disparatado.

cockle ['kɔkl] *n* berberecho.

cockney ['kɔknɪ] *n* habitante *m/f* de ciertos barrios de Londres.

cockpit ['kɔkpɪt] *n* (*in aircraft*) cabina.

cockroach ['kɔkrəutʃ] *n* cucaracha.

cocktail ['kɔkteɪl] *n* coctel *m*, cóctel *m*; **~ cabinet** *n* mueble-bar *m*; **~ party** *n* coctel *m*, cóctel *m*.

cocoa ['kəukəu] *n* cacao; (*drink*) chocolate *m*.

coconut ['kəukənʌt] *n* coco.

cod [kɔd] *n* bacalao.

C.O.D. *abbr* (= *cash on delivery*) C.A.E.

code [kəud] *n* código; (*cipher*) clave *f*.

cod-liver oil ['kɔdlɪvə'-] *n* aceite *m* de hígado de bacalao.

coercion [kəu'ɔːʃən] *n* coacción *f*.

coffee ['kɔfɪ] *n* café *m*; **~ bar** *n* (*Brit*) cafetería; **~ break** *n* descanso (para tomar café); **~pot** *n* cafetera; **~ table** *n* mesita (para servir el café).

coffin ['kɔfɪn] *n* ataúd *m*.

cog [kɔg] *n* diente *m*.

cogent ['kəudʒənt] *a* convincente.

cognac ['kɔnjæk] *n* coñac *m*.

coil [kɔɪl] *n* rollo; (*rope*) adujada; (*ELEC*) bobina, carrete *m*; (*contraceptive*) espiral *f* // *vt* enrollar.

coin [kɔɪn] *n* moneda // *vt* (*word*) inventar, idear; **~age** *n* moneda; **~box** *n* (*Brit*) cabina telefónica.

coincide [kəun'saɪd] *vi* coincidir; (*agree*) estar de acuerdo; **~nce** [kəu'ɪnsɪdəns] *n* casualidad *f*.

coke [kəuk] *n* (*coal*) coque *m*.

Coke ® [kəuk] *n* Coca Cola ®.

colander ['kɔləndə*] *n* colador *m*, escurridor *m*.

cold [kəuld] *a* frío // *n* frío; (*MED*) resfriado; **it's ~** hace frío; **to be ~** tener frío; **to catch ~** resfriarse, acatarrarse; **in ~ blood** a sangre fría; **~ sore** *n* herpes *m* labial.

coleslaw ['kəulslɔː] *n* especie de ensalada de col.

colic ['kɔlɪk] *n* cólico.

collapse [kə'læps] *vi* (*gen*) hundirse, derrumbarse; (*MED*) sufrir un colapso // *n* (*gen*) hundimiento; (*MED*) colapso; **collapsible** *a* plegable.

collar ['kɔlə*] *n* (*of coat, shirt*) cuello; **~bone** *n* clavícula.

collateral [kə'lætərəl] *n* garantía colateral.

colleague ['kɔliːg] *n* colega *m/f*.

collect [kə'lekt] *vt* reunir; (*as a hobby*) coleccionar; (*Brit: call and pick up*) recoger; (*wages*) cobrar; (*debts*) recaudar; (*donations, subscriptions*) colectar // *vi* reunirse; **to call ~** (*US TEL*) llamar a cobro revertido; **~ion** [kə'lekʃən] *n* colección *f*; (*of post*) recogida.

collector [kə'lektə*] *n* coleccionista *m/f*; (*of taxes etc*) recaudador(a) *m/f*.

college ['kɔlɪdʒ] *n* colegio.

collide [kə'laɪd] *vi* chocar.

collie ['kɔlɪ] *n* perro pastor.

colliery ['kɔlɪərɪ] n (Brit) mina de carbón.

collision [kə'lɪʒən] n choque m.

colloquial [kə'loukwɪəl] a familiar, coloquial.

collusion [kə'luːʒən] n confabulación f, connivencia.

cologne [kə'loun] n = **eau de cologne**.

Colombia [kə'lɔmbɪə] n Colombia; **Colombian** a, n colombiano/a.

colon ['koulən] n (sign) dos puntos; (MED) colón m.

colonel ['kɔːnl] n coronel m.

colonial [kə'ləunɪəl] a colonial.

colony ['kɔlənɪ] n colonia.

colour, (US) **color** ['kʌlə*] n color m // vt color(e)ar; (with crayons) colorear (al pastel); (dye) teñir // vi (blush) sonrojarse; ~s npl (of party, club) colores mpl; ~ **bar** n segregación f racial; ~**blind** a daltoniano; ~**ed** a de color; (photo) en color; ~**film** n película en color; ~**ful** a lleno de color; (person) excéntrico; ~**ing** n colorido; ~**less** a incoloro, sin color; ~ **scheme** n combinación f de colores; ~ **television** n televisión f en color.

colt [koult] n potro.

column ['kɔləm] n columna; ~**ist** ['kɔləmnɪst] n columnista m/f.

coma ['koumə] n coma m.

comb [koum] n peine m; (ornamental) peineta // vt (hair) peinar; (area) registrar a fondo.

combat ['kɔmbæt] n combate m // vt combatir.

combination [kɔmbɪ'neɪʃən] n (gen) combinación f.

combine [kəm'baɪn] vt combinar; (qualities) reunir // vi combinarse // ['kɔmbaɪn] (ECON) cartel m; ~ (harvester) n cosechadora.

come [kʌm], pt **came**, pp **come** vi venir; to ~ **undone** desatarse; to ~ **loose** aflojarse; to ~ **about** vi suceder, ocurrir; to ~ **across** vt fus (person) topar con; (thing) dar con; to ~ **away** vi marcharse; despren-

derse; to ~ **back** vi volver; to ~ **by** vt fus (acquire) conseguir; to ~ **down** vi bajar; (buildings) ser derribado; (prices) bajar; to ~ **forward** vi presentarse; to ~ **from** vt fus ser de; to ~ **in** vi entrar; (train) llegar; (fashion) ponerse de moda; to ~ **in for** vt fus (criticism etc) merecer; to ~ **into** vt fus (money) heredar; to ~ **off** vi (button) soltarse, desprenderse; (succeed) salir bien; to ~ **on** vi (pupil, work, project) desarrollarse; (lights) encenderse; to ~ **on!** ¡vamos!; to ~ **out** vi salir; (book) aparecer; (be revealed) salir a luz; (strike) declararse en huelga; to ~ **out for/ against** declararse por/contra; to ~ **round** vi (after faint, operation) volver en sí; to ~ **to** vi volver en sí; (total) sumar; to ~ **up** vi subir; (sun) salir; (problem) surgir; to ~ **up against** vt fus (resistance, difficulties) tropezar con; to ~ **up with** vt fus (idea) sugerir, proponer; to ~ **upon** vt fus dar o topar con; ~**back** n: to **make a ~back** (THEATRE) volver a las tablas.

comedian [kə'miːdɪən] n cómico; **comedienne** [-'ɛn] n cómica.

comedown ['kʌmdaun] n revés m, bajón m.

comedy ['kɔmɪdɪ] n comedia.

comet ['kɔmɪt] n cometa m.

comeuppance [kʌm'ʌpəns] n: to **get one's** ~ llevar su merecido.

comfort ['kʌmfət] n comodidad f, confort m; (well-being) bienestar m; (solace) consuelo; (relief) alivio // vt consolar; ~**able** a cómodo; ~**ably** ad (sit) cómodamente; (live) holgadamente; ~**er** n (US: pacifier) chupete m; (: bed cover) colcha; ~ **station** n (US) servicios mpl.

comic ['kɔmɪk] a (also: ~**al**) cómico // n (for children) tebeo; (for adults) comic m; ~ **strip** n tira cómica.

coming ['kʌmɪŋ] n venida, llegada // a que viene; ~(**s**) **and going(s)** n(pl) ir y venir m, ajetreo.

comma ['kɒmə] n coma.

command [kə'mɑːnd] n orden f, mandato; (MIL: authority) mando; (mastery) dominio // vt (troops) mandar; (give orders to) mandar, ordenar; (be able to get) disponer de; (deserve) merecer; **~eer** [kɒmən-'dɪə*] vt requisar; **~er** n (MIL) comandante m/f, jefe/a m/f; **~ment** n (REL) mandamiento.

commando [kə'mɑːndəu] n comando.

commemorate [kə'mɛməreɪt] vt conmemorar.

commence [kə'mɛns] vt, vi comenzar, empezar.

commend [kə'mɛnd] vt (praise) elogiar, alabar; (recommend) recomendar; (entrust) encomendar.

commensurate [kə'mɛnʃərɪt] a: ~ with en proporción a, que corresponde a.

comment ['kɒmɛnt] n comentario // vi: to ~ on hacer comentarios sobre; **~ary** ['kɒməntərɪ] n comentario; **~ator** ['kɒmənteɪtə*] n comentarista m/f.

commerce ['kɒməːs] n comercio.

commercial [kə'məːʃəl] a comercial // n (TV: also: ~ **break**) anuncio.

commiserate [kə'mɪzəreɪt] vi: to ~ with compadecerse de, condolerse de.

commission [kə'mɪʃən] n (committee, fee) comisión f; (act) perpetración f // vt (MIL) nombrar; (work of art) encargar; **out of** ~ fuera de servicio; **~aire** [kəmɪʃə'nɛə*] n (Brit) portero; **~er** n comisario; (POLICE) comisario m de policía.

commit [kə'mɪt] vt (act) cometer; (to sb's care) entregar; **to ~ o.s.** (to do) comprometerse a hacer); **to ~ suicide** suicidarse; **~ment** n compromiso.

committee [kə'mɪtɪ] n comité m.

commodity [kə'mɒdɪtɪ] n mercancía.

common ['kɒmən] a (gen) común; (pej) ordinario // n campo común;

the C~s npl (Brit) (la Cámara de) los Comunes mpl; **in** ~ en común; **~er** n plebeyo; **~ law** n ley f consuetudinaria; **~ly** ad comúnmente; **C~ Market** n Mercado Común; **~place** a de lo más común; **~room** n sala común; **~ sense** n sentido común; **the C~wealth** n la Mancomunidad (Británica).

commotion [kə'məuʃən] n tumulto, confusión f.

commune ['kɒmjuːn] n (group) comuna // [kə'mjuːn]: to ~ with comulgar or conversar con.

communicate [kə'mjuːnɪkeɪt] vt // vi: to ~ (with) comunicarse (con).

communication [kəmjuːnɪ'keɪʃən] n comunicación f; **~ cord** n (Brit) timbre m de alarma.

communion [kə'mjuːnɪən] n (also: **Holy C~**) comunión f.

communiqué [kə'mjuːnɪkeɪ] n comunicado, parte m.

communism ['kɒmjunɪzəm] n comunismo; **communist** a, n comunista m/f.

community [kə'mjuːnɪtɪ] n comunidad f; (large group) colectividad f; (local) vecindario; **~ centre** n centro social; **~ chest** n (US) arca comunitaria, fondo común.

commutation ticket [kɒmju-'teɪʃən-] n (US) billete m de abono.

commute [kə'mjuːt] vi viajar a diario de la casa al trabajo // vt conmutar; **~r** n persona (que ... see vi).

compact [kəm'pækt] a compacto // n ['kɒmpækt] (pact) pacto; (also: **powder ~**) polvera; **~ disc** n compact disc m.

companion [kəm'pænɪən] n compañero/a; **~ship** n compañerismo.

company ['kʌmpənɪ] n (gen) compañía; (COMM) sociedad f, compañía; **to keep sb ~** acompañar a uno; **~ secretary** n (Brit) secretario/a de compañía.

comparative [kəm'pærətɪv] a relativo; **~ly** ad (*relatively*) relativamente.

compare [kəm'peə*] vt comparar; (*set side by side*) cotejar // vi: **to ~ (with)** compararse (con); **comparison** [-'pærisn] n comparación f; cotejo.

compartment [kəm'pɑ:tmənt] n (*also: RAIL*) departamento.

compass ['kʌmpəs] n brújula; **~es** npl compás msg.

compassion [kəm'pæʃən] n compasión f; **~ate** a compasivo.

compatible [kəm'pætibl] a compatible.

compel [kəm'pel] vt obligar; **~ling** a (*fig: argument*) convincente.

compensate ['kompənseit] vt compensar // vi: **to ~ for** compensar; **compensation** [-'seiʃən] n (*for loss*) indemnización f.

compère ['kompeə*] n presentador m.

compete [kəm'pi:t] vi (*take part*) tomar parte, concurrir; (*vie with*) competir, hacer competencia.

competence ['kompitəns] n capacidad f, aptitud f.

competent ['kompitənt] a competente, capaz.

competition [kompi'tiʃən] n (*contest*) concurso; (*ECON, rivalry*) competencia.

competitive [kəm'petitiv] a (*ECON, SPORT*) competitivo; (*spirit*) competidor(a), de competencia.

competitor [kəm'petitə*] n (*rival*) competidor(a) m/f; (*participant*) concursante m/f.

compile [kəm'pail] vt recopilar.

complacency [kəm'pleisnsi] n autosatisfacción f.

complacent [kəm'pleisənt] a autocomplaciente.

complain [kəm'plein] vi (*gen*) quejarse; (*COMM*) reclamar; **~t** n (*gen*) queja; reclamación f; (*LAW*) demanda; (*MED*) enfermedad f.

complement ['komplimənt] n complemento; (*especially of ship's crew*) dotación f // [-ment] vt (*enhance*)

complementar; **~ary** [kompli-'mentəri] a complementario.

complete [kəm'pli:t] a (*full*) completo; (*finished*) acabado // vt (*fulfil*) completar; (*finish*) acabar; (*a form*) llenar; **~ly** ad completamente; **completion** [-'pli:ʃən] n terminación f.

complex ['kompleks] a, n complejo.

complexion [kəm'plekʃən] n (*of face*) tez f, cutis m; (*fig*) aspecto.

compliance [kəm'plaiəns] n (*submission*) sumisión f; (*agreement*) conformidad f; **in ~ with** de acuerdo con.

complicate ['komplikeit] vt complicar; **~d** a complicado; **complication** [-'keiʃən] n complicación f.

complicity [kəm'plisiti] n complicidad f.

compliment n ['komplimənt] (*formal*) cumplido; (*flirtation*) piropo // vt felicitar; **~s** npl saludos mpl; **to pay sb a ~** (*formal*) hacer cumplidos a alguien; (*flirt*) piropear o echar piropos a alguien; **~ary** [-'mentəri] a lisonjero; (*free*) de favor.

comply [kəm'plai] vi: **to ~ with** cumplir con.

component [kəm'pəunənt] a componente // n (*TECH*) pieza.

compose [kəm'pəuz] vt componer; **to ~ o.s.** tranquilizarse; **~d** a sosegado; **~r** n (*MUS*) compositor(a) m/f.

composite ['kompəzit] a compuesto.

composition [kompə'ziʃən] n composición f.

compost ['kompost] n abono.

composure [kəm'pəuʒə*] n serenidad f, calma.

compound ['kompaund] n (*CHEM*) compuesto; (*LING*) palabra compuesta; (*enclosure*) recinto // a (*gen*) compuesto; (*fracture*) complicado.

comprehend [kompri'hend] vt comprender; **comprehension** [-'henʃən] n comprensión f.

comprehensive ~ [kompri'hensiv] a (*broad*) extenso; (*general*) de conjunto; (INSURANCE) contra todo riesgo; ~ (school) n centro estatal de enseñanza secundaria; ≈ Instituto Nacional de Bachillerato (Sp).

compress [kəm'pres] vt comprimir // n ['kɔmpres] (MED) compresa.

comprise [kəm'praɪz] vt (also: be ~d of) comprender, constar de.

compromise ['kɔmprəmaɪz] n (agreement) arreglo // vt comprometer // vi transigir.

compulsion [kəm'pʌlʃən] n obligación f.

compulsive [kəm'pʌlsɪv] a compulsivo.

compulsory [kəm'pʌlsərɪ] a obligatorio.

computer [kəm'pjuːtə*] n ordenador m, computador m, computadora f; ~ize vt (data) computerizar; (system) informatizar; ~ **programmer** n programador(a) m/f; ~ **programming** n programación f; ~ **science** n informática.

computing [kəm'pjuːtɪŋ] n (activity) informática.

comrade ['kɔmrɪd] n compañero/a; ~ship n camaradería, compañerismo.

con [kɔn] vt estafar // n estafa.

conceal [kən'siːl] vt ocultar; (thoughts etc) disimular.

conceit [kən'siːt] n presunción f; ~ed a presumido.

conceivable [kən'siːvəbl] a concebible.

conceive [kən'siːv] vt, vi concebir.

concentrate ['kɔnsəntreɪt] vi concentrarse // vt concentrar.

concentration [kɔnsən'treɪʃən] n concentración f; ~ **camp** n campo de concentración.

concept ['kɔnsept] n concepto.

conception [kən'sepʃən] n (idea) concepto, idea; (BIOL) concepción f.

concern [kən'sɜːn] n (matter) asunto; (COMM) empresa; (anxiety) preocupación f // vt tener que ver con; **to be ~ed** (about) interesarse (por), preocuparse (por); ~ing prep

sobre, acerca de.

concert ['kɔnsət] n concierto; ~ed [kən'sɜːtɪd] a (efforts etc) concertado; ~ **hall** n sala de conciertos.

concertina [kɔnsə'tiːnə] n concertina.

concerto [kən'tʃɜːtəu] n concierto.

concession [kən'seʃən] n concesión f; **tax** ~ privilegio fiscal.

concise [kən'saɪs] a conciso.

conclude [kən'kluːd] vt (finish) concluir; (treaty etc) firmar; (agreement) llegar a; (decide) llegar a la conclusión de; **conclusion** [-'kluːʒən] n conclusión f; **conclusive** [-'kluːsɪv] a decisivo, concluyente.

concoct [kən'kɔkt] vt (gen) confeccionar; (plot) tramar; ~ion [-'kɔkʃən] n confección f.

concourse ['kɔŋkɔːs] n (hall) vestíbulo.

concrete ['kɔŋkriːt] n hormigón m // a concreto.

concur [kən'kɜː*] vi estar de acuerdo, asentir.

concurrently [kən'kʌrntlɪ] ad al mismo tiempo.

concussion [kən'kʌʃən] n conmoción f cerebral.

condemn [kən'dem] vt condenar; ~ation [kɔndem'neɪʃən] n (gen) condena; (blame) censura.

condense [kən'dens] vi condensarse // vt condensar, abreviar; ~d **milk** n leche f condensada.

condescending [kɔndɪ'sendɪŋ] a condescendiente.

condition [kən'dɪʃən] n condición f // vt condicionar; **on** ~ **that** a condición (de) que; ~al a condicional; ~er n (for hair) acondicionador m.

condolences [kən'dəulənsɪz] npl pésame msg.

condom ['kɔndəm] n condón m.

condominium [kɔndə'mɪnɪəm] n (US) condominio.

condone [kən'dəun] vt condonar.

conducive [kən'djuːsɪv] a: ~ **to** conducente a.

conduct ['kɒndʌkt] n conducta, comportamiento // vt [kən'dʌkt] (lead) conducir; (manage) llevar, dirigir; (MUS) dirigir // vi (MUS) llevar la batuta; **to ~ o.s.** comportarse; **~ed tour** n (Brit) visita acompañada; **~or** n (of orchestra) director m; (US: on train) revisor/a m/f; (on bus) cobrador m; (ELEC) conductor m; **~ress** n (on bus) cobradora.

cone [kəun] n cono; (pine ~) piña; (for ice-cream) barquillo.

confectioner [kən'fɛkʃənə*] n (of cakes) pastelero; (of sweets) confitero/a; **~'s (shop)** n pastelería, confitería; **~y** n pasteles mpl; dulces mpl.

confer [kən'fə:*] vt: **to ~ sth on** otorgar algo a // vi conferenciar.

conference ['kɒnfərns] n (meeting) reunión f; (convention) congreso.

confess [kən'fɛs] vt confesar // vi confesarse; **~ion** [-'fɛʃən] n confesión f; **~ional** [-'fɛʃənl] n confesionario.

confetti [kən'fɛti] n confeti m.

confide [kən'faid] vi: **to ~ in** confiar en.

confidence ['kɒnfidns] n (gen, also: self ~) confianza; (secret) confidencia; **in ~** (speak, write) en confianza; **~ trick** n timo, estafa; **confident** a seguro de sí mismo; **confidential** [kɒnfi'dɛnʃəl] a confidencial; (secretary) de confianza.

confine [kən'fain] vt (limit) limitar; (shut up) encerrar; **~s** ['kɒnfainz] npl confines mpl; **~d** a (space) reducido; **~ment** n (prison) prisión f; (MED) parto.

confirm [kən'fə:m] vt confirmar; **~ation** [kɒnfə'meiʃən] n confirmación f; **~ed** a empedernido.

confiscate ['kɒnfiskeit] vt confiscar.

conflict ['kɒnflikt] n conflicto // vi [kən'flikt] (opinions) chocar; **~ing** a contradictorio.

conform [kən'fɔ:m] vi conformarse; **to ~ to** ajustarse a.

confound [kən'faund] vt confundir.

confront [kən'frʌnt] vt (problems) hacer frente a; (enemy, danger) enfrentarse con; **~ation** [kɒnfrən'teiʃən] n enfrentamiento.

confuse [kən'fju:z] vt (perplex) aturdir, desconcertar; (mix up) confundir; **~d** a confuso; (person) perplejo; **confusing** a confuso; **confusion** [-'fju:ʒən] n confusión f.

congeal [kən'dʒi:l] vi (blood) coagularse.

congenial [kən'dʒi:niəl] a agradable.

congenital [kən'dʒenitl] a congénito.

congested [kən'dʒestid] a (gen) atestado.

congestion [kən'dʒestʃən] n congestión f.

conglomerate [kən'glɒmərət] n (COMM, GEO) conglomerado.

conglomeration [kənglɒmə'reiʃən] n conglomeración f.

congratulate [kən'grætjuleit] vt: **to ~ sb (on)** felicitar a uno (por); **congratulations** [-'leiʃənz] npl felicidades fpl.

congregate ['kɒngrigeit] vi congregarse; **congregation** [-'geiʃən] n (in church) fieles mpl.

congress ['kɒngres] n congreso; **~man** n (US) miembro del Congreso.

conifer ['kɒnifə*] n conífera.

conjecture [kən'dʒektʃə*] n conjetura.

conjugal ['kɒndʒugl] a conyugal.

conjugate ['kɒndʒugeit] vt conjugar.

conjunction [kən'dʒʌŋkʃən] n conjunción f.

conjunctivitis [kəndʒʌŋkti'vaitis] n conjuntivitis f.

conjure ['kʌndʒə*] vi hacer juegos de manos; **to ~ up** vt (ghost, spirit) hacer aparecer; (memories) evocar; **~r** n ilusionista m/f.

conk out [kɒŋk-] vi (col) descomponerse.

con man ['kɒn-] n timador m.

connect [kə'nekt] vt juntar, unir; (ELEC) conectar; (fig) relacionar, asociar // vi: **to ~ with** (train) enlazar con; **to be ~ed with** (*associated*) estar relacionado con; (*related*) estar emparentado con; **~ion** [-ʃən] *n* juntura, unión *f*; (*ELEC*) conexión *f*; (*RAIL*) enlace *m*; (*TEL*) comunicación *f*; (*fig*) relación *f*.

connive [kə'naɪv] *vi*: **to ~ at** hacer la vista gorda a.

connoisseur [kɒnɪ'sə*] *n* experto/a, entendido/a.

conquer ['kɒŋkə*] *vt* (*territory*) conquistar; (*enemy, feelings*) vencer; **~or** *n* conquistador *m*.

conquest ['kɒŋkwest] *n* conquista.

cons [kɒnz] *npl see* **convenience, pro**.

conscience ['kɒnʃəns] *n* conciencia.

conscientious [kɒnʃɪ'enʃəs] *a* concienzudo; (*objection*) de conciencia.

conscious ['kɒnʃəs] *a* consciente; **~ness** *n* conciencia; (*MED*) conocimiento.

conscript ['kɒnskrɪpt] *n* recluta *m*; **~ion** [kən'skrɪpʃən] *n* servicio militar (obligatorio).

consecrate ['kɒnsɪkreɪt] *vt* consagrar.

consensus [kən'sɛnsəs] *n* consenso.

consent [kən'sɛnt] *n* consentimiento // *vi*: **to ~ (to)** consentir (en).

consequence ['kɒnsɪkwəns] *n* consecuencia.

consequently ['kɒnsɪkwəntlɪ] *ad* por consiguiente.

conservation [kɒnsə'veɪʃən] *n* conservación *f*.

conservative [kən'sə:vətɪv] *a* conservador(a); (*cautious*) cauteloso; **C~** *a*, *n* (*Brit POL*) conservador(a) *m/f*.

conservatory [kən'sə:vətrɪ] *n* (*greenhouse*) invernadero.

conserve [kən'sə:v] *vt* conservar // *n* conserva.

consider [kən'sɪdə*] *vt* considerar; (*take into account*) tomar en cuenta; (*study*) estudiar, examinar; **to ~ doing sth** pensar en (la posibilidad de) hacer algo; **~able** *a* considerable; **~ably** *ad* notablemente.

considerate [kən'sɪdərɪt] *a* considerado; **consideration** [-'reɪʃən] *n* consideración *f*; (*reward*) retribución *f*.

considering [kən'sɪdərɪŋ] *prep* teniendo en cuenta.

consign [kən'saɪn] *vt* consignar; **~ment** *n* envío.

consist [kən'sɪst] *vi*: **to ~ of** consistir en.

consistency [kən'sɪstənsɪ] *n* (*of person etc*) consecuencia; (*thickness*) consistencia.

consistent [kən'sɪstənt] *a* (*person, argument*) consecuente; (*results*) constante.

consolation [kɒnsə'leɪʃən] *n* consuelo.

console [kən'səul] *vt* consolar // *n* ['kɒnsəul] consola.

consonant ['kɒnsənənt] *n* consonante *f*.

consortium [kən'sɔ:tɪəm] *n* consorcio.

conspicuous [kən'spɪkjuəs] *a* (*visible*) visible; (*garish etc*) llamativo; (*outstanding*) notable.

conspiracy [kən'spɪrəsɪ] *n* conjura, complot *m*.

conspire [kən'spaɪə*] *vi* conspirar.

constable ['kʌnstəbl] *n* (*Brit*) policía *m/f*; **chief ~ =** jefe *m* de policía.

constabulary [kən'stæbjulərɪ] *n* = policía.

constant ['kɒnstənt] *a* (*gen*) constante; (*loyal*) leal, fiel; **~ly** *ad* constantemente.

consternation [kɒnstə'neɪʃən] *n* consternación *f*.

constipated ['kɒnstɪpeɪtəd] *a* estreñido.

constipation [kɒnstɪ'peɪʃən] *n* estreñimiento.

constituency [kən'stɪtjuənsɪ] *n* (*POL*) distrito electoral; **constituent** [-ənt] *n* (*POL*) elector/a *m/f*; (*part*) componente *m*.

constitute ['kɒnstɪtju:t] *vt* constituir.

constitution [kɒnstɪ'tju:ʃən] *n* constitución *f*; **~al** *a* constitucional.

constrain [kən'streɪn] vt obligar;
~ed a: to feel ~ed to ... sentirse
en la necesidad de ....

constraint [kən'streɪnt] n (force)
fuerza; (limit) restricción f; (restraint) reserva.

construct [kən'strʌkt] vt construir;
~ion [-ʃən] n construcción f; ~ive a
constructivo.

construe [kən'struː] vt interpretar.

consul ['kɒnsl] n cónsul m/f; ~ate
['kɒnsjulɪt] n consulado.

consult [kən'sʌlt] vt, vi consultar;
~ant n (Brit MED) especialista m/f;
(other specialist) asesor(a) m/f;
~ation [kɒnsəl'teɪʃən] n consulta;
~ing room n (Brit) consultorio.

consume [kən'sjuːm] vt (eat) comerse; (drink) beberse; (fire etc,
COMM) consumir; ~r n consumi-
dor(a) m/f; ~r goods npl bienes
mpl de consumo; ~rism n consumismo; ~r society n sociedad f de consumo.

consummate ['kɒnsʌmeɪt] vt consumar.

consumption [kən'sʌmpʃən] n consumo; (MED) tisis f.

cont. abbr = (continued) sigue.

contact ['kɒntækt] n contacto; (person) enchufe m // vt ponerse en
contacto con; ~ lenses npl lentes fpl de
contacto.

contagious [kən'teɪdʒəs] a contagioso.

contain [kən'teɪn] vt contener; to ~
o.s. contenerse; ~er n recipiente m;
(for shipping etc) contenedor m.

contaminate [kən'tæmɪneɪt] vt contaminar; **contamination** [-'neɪʃən]
n contaminación f.

cont'd abbr = (continued) sigue.

contemplate ['kɒntəmpleɪt] vt (gen)
contemplar; (reflect upon) considerar; (intend) pensar.

contemporary [kən'tempərərɪ] a, n
contemporáneo/a m/f.

contempt [kən'tempt] n desprecio;
~ of court (LAW) desacato (a los
tribunales); ~ible a despreciable;

~uous a desdeñoso.

contend [kən'tend] vt (argue) afirmar // vi (struggle) luchar; ~er n
(SPORT) contendiente m/f.

content [kən'tent] a (happy) contento; (satisfied) satisfecho // vt contentar; satisfacer // n ['kɒntent] contenido; (table of) ~s índice m de materias; ~ed a contento; satisfecho.

contention [kən'tenʃən] n discusión
f; (belief) argumento.

contentment [kən'tentmənt] n contento.

contest ['kɒntest] n contienda; (competition) concurso // vt [kən'test] (dispute) impugnar; (POL) presentarse
como candidato/a en; ~ant
[kən'testənt] n concursante m/f; (in
fight) contendiente m/f.

continent ['kɒntɪnənt] n continente
m; the C~ (Brit) el continente europeo; ~al [-'nentl] a continental; ~al
quilt n (Brit) edredón m.

contingency [kən'tɪndʒənsɪ] n contingencia.

contingent [kən'tɪndʒənt] (group)
grupo.

continual [kən'tɪnjuəl] a continuo;
~ly ad constantemente.

continuation [kəntɪnju'eɪʃən] n prolongación f; (after interruption) reanudación f.

continue [kən'tɪnjuː] vi, vt seguir,
continuar.

continuous [kən'tɪnjuəs] a continuo;
~ stationery n papel m continuo.

contort [kən'tɔːt] vt retorcer; ~ion
[-'tɔːʃən] n (movement) contorsión f.

contour ['kɒntuə*] n contorno;
(also: ~ line) curva de nivel.

contraband ['kɒntrəbænd] n contrabando.

contraception [kɒntrə'sepʃən] n
contracepción f.

contraceptive [kɒntrə'septɪv] a, n
anticonceptivo.

contract ['kɒntrækt] n contrato //
(vb: degenerate n (COMM): to ~
to do sth comprometerse por contrato a hacer algo; (become smaller)

contraerse, encogerse // vt contraer; ~on [kən'trækʃən] n contracción f; ~or n contratista m/f.

contradict [kɒntrə'dɪkt] vt (declare to be wrong) desmentir; (be contrary to) contradecir; ~ion [-ʃən] n contradicción; ~ory a (statements) contradictorio.

contraption [kən'træpʃən] n (pej) artilugio m.

contrary ['kɒntrərɪ] a (opposite, different) contrario; [kən'trɛərɪ] (perverse) terco // n: on the ~ al contrario; unless you hear to the ~ a no ser que le digan lo contrario.

contrast ['kɒntrɑːst] n contraste m // vt [kən'trɑːst] comparar; ~ing a (opinion) opuesto; (colour) que hace contraste.

contravene [kɒntrə'viːn] vt infringir.

contribute [kən'trɪbjuːt] vi contribuir // vt: to ~ to (gen) contribuir a; (newspaper) escribir para; **contribution** [kɒntrɪ'bjuːʃən] n (money) contribución f; (to debate) intervención f; (to journal) colaboración f; **contributor** n (to newspaper) colaborador(a) m/f.

contrive [kən'traɪv] vt (invent) idear // vi: to ~ to do lograr hacer.

control [kən'trəul] vt controlar; (traffic etc) dirigir; (machinery) manejar; (temper) dominar // n (command) control m; (of car) conducción f; (check) freno; ~s npl mando sg; everything is under ~ todo está bajo control; to be in ~ of tener el mando de; the car went out of ~ se perdió el control del coche; ~ **panel** n tablero de instrumentos; ~ **room** n sala de mando; ~ **tower** n (AVIAT) torre f de control.

controversial [kɒntrə'vəːʃl] a polémico.

controversy ['kɒntrəvəːsɪ] n polémica.

conurbation [kɒnəː'beɪʃən] n urbanización f.

convalesce [kɒnvə'lɛs] vi convalecer; **convalescence** n convalecen-

cia; **convalescent** a, n convaleciente m/f.

convene [kən'viːn] vt convocar // vi reunirse.

convenience [kən'viːnɪəns] n (comfort) comodidad f; (advantage) ventaja; at your ~ cuando le sea conveniente; all modern ~s, (Brit) all mod cons todo confort.

convenient [kən'viːnɪənt] a (useful) útil; (place, time) conveniente.

convent ['kɒnvənt] n convento f.

convention [kən'vɛnʃən] n convención f; (meeting) asamblea; ~al a convencional.

conversant [kən'vəːsnt] a: to be ~ with estar al tanto de.

conversation [kɒnvə'seɪʃən] n conversación f; ~al a (familiar) familiar; (talkative) locuaz.

converse ['kɒnvəːs] n inversa // vi [kən'vəːs] conversar; ~ly [-'vəːslɪ] ad a la inversa.

conversion [kən'vəːʃən] n conversión f.

convert [kən'vəːt] vt (REL, COMM) convertir; (alter) transformar // n ['kɒnvəːt] converso/a; ~ible a convertible // n descapotable m.

convex ['kɒnvɛks] a convexo.

convey [kən'veɪ] vt llevar; (thanks) comunicar; (idea) expresar; ~or **belt** n cinta transportadora.

convict [kən'vɪkt] vt (find guilty) declarar culpable a // n ['kɒnvɪkt] presidiario/a; ~ion [-ʃən] n condena; (belief) creencia, convicción f.

convince [kən'vɪns] vt convencer; ~d a: ~d of/that convencido de/de que; **convincing** a convincente.

convoluted ['kɒnvəluːtɪd] a (argument etc) enrevesado.

convoy ['kɒnvɔɪ] n convoy m.

convulse [kən'vʌls] vt convulsionar; to be ~d with laughter dislocarse de risa; **convulsion** [-'vʌlʃən] n convulsión f.

coo [kuː] vi arrullar.

cook [kuk] vt cocinar; (stew etc) guisar; (*meal*) preparar // *vi* cocer; (*person*) cocinar // *n* cocinero/a; ~ **book** *n* libro de cocina; ~**er** *n* cocina; ~**ery** *n* (*dishes*) cocina; (*art*) arte *m* culinario; ~**ery book** *n* (*Brit*) = ~ **book**; ~**ie** *n* (*US*) galleta; ~**ing** *n* cocina.

cool [kuːl] *a* fresco; (*not hot*) tibio; (*not afraid*) tranquilo; (*unfriendly*) frío // *vt* enfriar // *vi* enfriarse; ~**ness** *n* frescura; tranquilidad *f*; (*hostility*) frialdad *f*; (*indifference*) falta de entusiasmo.

coop [kuːp] *n* gallinero *m* // *vt*: **to ~ up** (*fig*) encerrar.

cooperate [kəuˈɔpəreit] *vi* cooperar, colaborar; **cooperation** [-ˈreiʃən] *n* cooperación *f*, colaboración *f*; **co-operative** [-rətiv] *a* cooperativo // *n* cooperativa.

coordinate [kəuˈɔːdineit] *vt* coordinar // *n* [kəuˈɔːdinət] (*MATH*) coordenada; ~**s** *npl* (*clothes*) coordinados *mpl*; **coordination** [-ˈneiʃən] *n* coordinación *f*.

co-ownership [kəuˈəunəʃip] *n* copropiedad *f*.

cop [kɔp] *n* (*col*) poli *m*, tira *m* (*LAm*).

cope [kəup] *vi*: **to ~ with** poder con; (*problem*) hacer frente a.

copious [ˈkəupiəs] *a* copioso, abundante.

copper [ˈkɔpə*] *n* (*metal*) cobre *m*; (*col: policeman*) poli *m*; ~**s** *npl* perras *fpl*, centavos *mpl* (*LAm*).

coppice [ˈkɔpis], **copse** [kɔps] *n* bosquecillo *m*.

copulate [ˈkɔpjuleit] *vi* copularse.

copy [ˈkɔpi] *n* copia; (*of book etc*) ejemplar *m*; (*of writing*) original *m* // *vt* copiar; ~**right** *n* derechos *mpl* de autor.

coral [ˈkɔrəl] *n* coral *m*; ~ **reef** *n* arrecife *m* (de coral).

cord [kɔːd] *n* cuerda; (*ELEC*) cable *m*; (*fabric*) pana.

cordial [ˈkɔːdiəl] *a* afectuoso // *n* cordial *m*.

cordon [ˈkɔːdn] *n* cordón *m*; **to ~**

off *vt* acordonar.

corduroy [ˈkɔːdərɔi] *n* pana.

core [kɔː*] *n* (*gen*) centro, núcleo; (*of fruit*) corazón *m* // *vt* quitar el corazón de.

coriander [kɔriˈændə*] *n* culantro.

cork [kɔːk] *n* corcho; (*tree*) alcornoque *m*; ~**screw** *n* sacacorchos *m inv*.

corn [kɔːn] *n* (*Brit: wheat*) trigo; (*US: maize*) maíz *m*; (*on foot*) callo; ~ **on the cob** (*CULIN*) maíz en la mazorca, choclo (*LAm*).

cornea [ˈkɔːniə] *n* córnea.

corned beef [ˈkɔːnd-] *n* carne *f* acecinada.

corner [ˈkɔːnə*] *n* ángulo; (*outside*) esquina; (*inside*) rincón *m*; (*in road*) curva; (*FOOTBALL*) córner *m* // *vt* (*trap*) arrinconar; (*COMM*) acaparar // *vi* (*in car*) tomar las curvas; ~**stone** *n* piedra angular.

cornet [ˈkɔːnit] *n* (*MUS*) corneta; (*Brit: of ice-cream*) barquillo.

cornflakes [ˈkɔːnfleiks] *npl* copos *mpl* de maíz, cornflakes *mpl*.

cornflour [ˈkɔːnflauə*] *n* (*Brit*) harina de maíz.

cornstarch [ˈkɔːnstɑːtʃ] *n* (*US*) = **cornflour**.

Cornwall [ˈkɔːnwəl] *n* Cornualles *m*.

corny [ˈkɔːni] *a* (*col*) gastado.

corollary [kəˈrɔləri] *n* corolario.

coronary [ˈkɔrənəri] *n*: ~ (**thrombosis**) infarto.

coronation [kɔrəˈneiʃən] *n* coronación *f*.

coroner [ˈkɔrənə*] *n* juez *m* (de instrucción).

coronet [ˈkɔrənit] *n* corona.

corporal [ˈkɔːpərl] *n* cabo // *a*: ~ **punishment** castigo corporal.

corporate [ˈkɔːpərit] *a* corporativo.

corporation [kɔːpəˈreiʃən] *n* (*of town*) ayuntamiento; (*COMM*) corporación *f*.

corps [kɔː*], *pl* **corps** [kɔːz] *n* cuerpo.

corpse [kɔːps] *n* cadáver *m*.

corpuscle [ˈkɔːpʌsl] *n* corpúsculo.

corral [kɔ'rɑːl] n corral m.

correct [kə'rekt] a (accurate) justo, exacto; (proper) correcto // vt corregir; (exam) calificar; **~ion** [-∫ən] n rectificación f; (erasure) tachadura.

correlation [kɔri'lei∫ən] n correlación f.

correspond [kɔris'pɔnd] vi (write) escribirse; (be equal to) corresponder; **~ence** n correspondencia; **~ence course** n curso por correspondencia; **~ent** n corresponsal m/f.

corridor ['kɔridɔː'] n pasillo.

corroborate [kə'rɔbəreit] vt corroborar.

corrode [kə'rəud] vt corroer // vi corroerse; **corrosion** [-'rəuʒən] n corrosión f.

corrugated ['kɔrəgeitid] a ondulado; **~ iron** n chapa ondulada.

corrupt [kə'rʌpt] a corrompido; (person) corrupto // vt corromper; (bribe) sobornar; **~ion** [-∫ən] n corrupción f.

corset ['kɔːsit] n faja.

Corsica ['kɔːsikə] n Córcega.

cortège [kɔː'teiʒ] n cortejo, desfile m.

cosh [kɔ∫] n (Brit) cachiporra.

cosmetic [kɔz'metik] n cosmético.

cosmic ['kɔzmik] a cósmico.

cosmonaut ['kɔzmənɔːt] n cosmonauta m/f.

cosmopolitan [kɔzmə'pɔlitn] a cosmopolita.

cosset ['kɔsit] vt mimar.

cost [kɔst] n (gen) coste m, costo; (price) precio; **~s** npl costas fpl // vb (pt, pp cost) vi costar, valer // vt preparar el presupuesto de; **how much does it ~?** ¿cuánto cuesta?; **at all ~s** cueste lo que cueste.

co-star ['kəustɑː'] n colega m/f de reparto.

Costa Rican ['kɔstə'riːkən] a, n costarriqueño/a m/f.

cost-effective [kɔsti'fektiv] a rentable.

costly ['kɔstli] a (expensive) costoso.

cost-of-living [kɔstəv'liviŋ] a: **~ al-**lowance plus m de carestía de vida; **~ index** n índice m del costo de vida.

cost price n (Brit) precio de coste.

costume ['kɔstjuːm] n traje m; (Brit: also: swimming ~) traje de baño; **~ jewellery** n bisutería.

cosy, (US) **cozy** ['kəuzi] a cómodo; (atmosphere) acogedor(a).

cot [kɔt] n (Brit: child's) cuna.

cottage ['kɔtidʒ] n casita de campo; (rustic) barraca; **~ cheese** n requesón m; **~ industry** n industria casera; **~ pie** n pastel m de carne cubierta de puré de patatas.

cotton ['kɔtn] n algodón m; (thread) hilo; **to ~ on to** vi fus (col) caer en la cuenta de; **~ candy** n (US) algodón m (azucarado); **~ wool** n (Brit) algodón m (hidrófilo).

couch [kaut∫] n sofá m.

couchette [kuː'∫et] n litera.

cough [kɔf] vi toser // n tos f; **~ drop** n pastilla para la tos.

could [kud] pt of **can**; **~n't** = **could not.**

council ['kaunsl] n consejo; **city** or **town ~** consejo municipal; **~ estate** n (Brit) urbanización f de viviendas municipales de alquiler; **~ house** n (Brit) vivienda municipal de alquiler; **~lor** n concejal/a m/f.

counsel ['kaunsl] n (advice) consejo; (lawyer) abogado/a // vt aconsejar; **~lor** n consejero/a; **~or** n (US) abogado/a.

count [kaunt] vt (gen) contar; (include) incluir // vi contar // n cuenta; (of votes) escrutinio; (nobleman) conde m; (sum) total m, suma; **to ~ on** vt fus contar con; **that doesn't ~!** ¡eso no vale!; **~down** n cuenta atrás.

countenance ['kauntinəns] n semblante m, rostro // vt (tolerate) aprobar, tolerar.

counter ['kauntə'] n (in shop) mostrador m; (in games) ficha // vt contrarrestar.

counterfeit ['kauntəfit] n falsifica-

ción f, simulación f // vt falsificar // a
falso, falsificado.
counterfoil ['kauntəfɔil] n (Brit) talón m.
countermand ['kauntəmɑːnd] vt revocar, cancelar.
counterpart ['kauntəpɑːt] n (of person) homólogo/a.
counter-productive [kauntəprə-
'dʌktɪv] a contraproducente.
countersign ['kauntəsain] vt refrendar.
countess ['kauntis] n condesa.
countless ['kauntlis] a innumerable.
country ['kʌntri] n país m; (native
land) patria; (as opposed to town)
campo; (region) región f, tierra; ~
dancing n (Brit) baile m regional;
~ **house** n casa de campo; ~**man**
n (national) compatriota m; (rural)
campesino, paisano; ~**side** n campo.
county ['kaunti] n condado.
coup [kuː], pl ~**s** [-z] n (also: ~
d'état) golpe m (de estado).
coupé ['kuːpei] n cupé m.
couple ['kʌpl] n (of things) par m;
(of people) pareja; (married ~) matrimonio // vt (ideas, names) unir,
juntar; (machinery) acoplar; **a ~ of**
un par de.
coupling ['kʌplɪŋ] n (RAIL) enganche m.
coupon ['kuːpɔn] n cupón m; (pools
~) boleto de quiniela.
courage ['kʌrɪdʒ] n valor m, valentía; ~**ous** [kə'reidʒəs] a valiente.
courgette [kuə'ʒet] n (Brit) calabacín m, calabacita.
courier ['kurɪə'] n mensajero/a; (diplomatic) correo; (for tourists) guía
m/f (de turismo).
course [kɔːs] n (direction) dirección
f; (of river, SCOL) curso; (of ship)
rumbo; (fig) proceder m; (GOLF)
campo; (part of meal) plato; **of ~**
ad desde luego, naturalmente; **of ~!**
¡claro!
court [kɔːt] n (royal) corte f; (LAW)
tribunal m, juzgado; (TENNIS) pista,
cancha // vt (woman) cortejar a;

(danger etc) buscar; **to take to ~**
demandar.
courteous ['kəːtiəs] a cortés.
courtesan [kɔːtɪ'zæn] n cortesana.
courtesy ['kəːtəsi] n cortesía; **by ~**
of por cortesía de.
court-house ['kɔːthaus] n (US) palacio de justicia.
courtier ['kɔːtiə'] n cortesano.
court-martial ['kɔːt'mɑːʃəl], pl
courts-martial n consejo de guerra
// vt someter a consejo de guerra.
courtroom ['kɔːtrum] n sala de justicia.
courtyard ['kɔːtjɑːd] n patio.
cousin ['kʌzn] n primo/a; **first ~**
primo/a carnal.
cove [kəuv] n cala, ensenada.
covenant ['kʌvɪnənt] n convenio.
cover ['kʌvə'] vt cubrir; (with lid)
tapar; (chairs etc) revestir; (distance) recorrer; (include) abarcar;
(protect) abrigar; (journalist) investigar; (issues) tratar // n cubierta;
(lid) tapa; (for chair etc) funda; (for
bed) cobertor m; (envelope) sobre
m; (for book) forro; (of magazine)
portada; (shelter) abrigo; (insurance) cobertura; **to take ~** (shelter)
protegerse, resguardarse; **under ~**
(indoors) bajo techo; **under ~ of**
darkness al amparo de la oscuridad;
under separate ~ (COMM) por separado; **to ~ up for sb** encubrir a
uno; ~**age** n alcance m; ~**alls** npl
(US) mono sg; ~**charge** n precio
del cubierto; ~**ing** n cubierta, envoltura; ~**ing letter**, (US) ~ **letter** n
carta de explicación; ~ **note** n (IN-
SURANCE) póliza provisional.
covert ['kʌvət] a secreto, encubier-
to.
cover-up ['kʌvərʌp] n encubrimien-
to.
covet ['kʌvɪt] vt codiciar.
cow [kau] n vaca // vt intimidar.
coward ['kauəd] n cobarde m/f;
~**ice** [-is] n cobardía; ~**ly** a cobarde.
cowboy ['kaubɔi] n vaquero.

cower ['kauə*] vi encogerse (de miedo).

coxswain ['kɔksn] n (abbr: **cox**) timonel m/f.

coy [kɔɪ] a tímido.

cozy ['kəuzɪ] a (US) = **cosy**.

CPA n abbr (US) = **certified public accountant**.

crab [kræb] n cangrejo; ~ **apple** n manzana silvestre.

crack [kræk] n grieta; (noise) crujido; (: of whip) chasquido; (joke) chiste m; **to have a** ~ **at** intentar // vt agrietar, romper; (nut) cascar; (safe) forzar; (whip etc) chasquear; (knuckles) crujir; (joke) contar // a (athlete) de primera clase; **to** ~ **down on** vt fus reprimanda fuertemente; **to** ~ **up** vi (MED) sufrir una crisis nerviosa; **~er** n (biscuit) cráker m; (Christmas cracker) petardo sorpresa.

crackle ['krækl] vi crepitar.

cradle ['kreɪdl] n cuna.

craft [krɑːft] n (skill) arte m; (trade) oficio; (cunning) astucia; (boat) barco.

craftsman ['krɑːftsmən] n artesano; **~ship** n artesanía.

crafty ['krɑːftɪ] a astuto.

crag [kræg] n peñasco.

cram [kræm] vt (fill): **to** ~ **sth with** llenar algo a (reventar) de; (put): **to** ~ **sth into** meter algo a la fuerza en // vi (for exams) empollar; **~med** a atestado.

cramp [kræmp] n (MED) calambre m; (TECH) grapa // vt (limit) poner trabas a; **~ed** a apretado, estrecho.

crampon ['kræmpən] n crampón m.

cranberry ['krænbərɪ] n arándano agrio.

crane [kreɪn] n (TECH) grúa; (bird) grulla.

crank [kræŋk] n manivela; (person) chiflado; **~shaft** n cigüeñal m.

cranny ['krænɪ] n see **nook**.

crash [kræʃ] n (noise) estrépito; (of cars etc) choque m; (of plane) accidente m de aviación; (COMM) quie-

bra // vt (plane) estrellar // vi (plane) estrellarse; (two cars) chocar; (fall noisily) caer con estrépito; ~ **course** n curso acelerado; ~ **helmet** n casco (protector); ~ **landing** n aterrizaje m forzado.

crass [kræs] a grosero, maleducado.

crate [kreɪt] n cajón m de embalaje.

crater ['kreɪtə*] n cráter m.

cravat(e) [krə'væt] n pañuelo.

crave [kreɪv] vt, vi: **to** ~ **(for)** ansiar, anhelar; **craving** n (of pregnant woman) antojo.

crawl [krɔːl] vi (drag o.s.) arrastrarse; (child) andar a gatas, gatear; (vehicle) avanzar (lentamente) // n (SWIMMING) crol m.

crayfish ['kreɪfɪʃ] n, pl inv (freshwater) cangrejo de río; (saltwater) cigala.

crayon ['kreɪɔn] n lápiz m de color.

craze [kreɪz] n manía; (fashion) moda.

crazy ['kreɪzɪ] a (person) loco; (idea) disparatado; ~ **paving** n pavimento de baldosas irregulares.

creak [kriːk] vi crujir; (hinge etc) chirriar, rechinar.

cream [kriːm] n (of milk) nata, crema; (lotion) crema; (fig) flor f y nata // a (colour) color crema; ~ **cake** n pastel m de nata; ~ **cheese** n queso crema; **~y** a cremoso.

crease [kriːs] n (fold) pliegue m; (in trousers) raya; (wrinkle) arruga // vt (fold) doblar, plegar; (wrinkle) arrugar // vi (wrinkle up) arrugarse.

create [kriˈeɪt] vt crear; **creation** [-ʃən] n creación f; **creative** a creador(a); **creator** n creador(a) m/f.

creature ['kriːtʃə*] n (animal) animal m, bicho; (living thing) criatura.

crèche, creche [krɛʃ] n (Brit) guardería (infantil).

credence ['kriːdəns] n: **to lend** or **give** ~ **to** creer en, dar crédito a.

credentials [krɪ'dɛnʃlz] npl credenciales fpl.

credible ['krɛdɪbl] a creíble.

credit ['krɛdɪt] n (gen) crédito;

(*merit*) honor *m*, mérito // *vt* (*COMM*) (*believe*) creer, prestar fe a // *a* crediticio; **~s** *npl* (*CINEMA*) fichas *fpl* técnicas; **to be in** ~ (*person*) tener saldo a favor; **to ~ sb with** (*fig*) reconocer a uno el mérito de; **~ card** *n* tarjeta de crédito; **~or** *n* acreedor(a) *m/f*.

creed [kri:d] *n* credo.

creek [kri:k] *n* cala, ensenada; (*US*) riachuelo.

creep [kri:p], *pt, pp* **crept** *vi* (*animal*) deslizarse; (*gen*) arrastrarse; (*plant*) trepar; **~er** *n* enredadera; **~y** *a* (*frightening*) horripilante.

cremate [krɪˈmeɪt] *vt* incinerar.

crematorium [krɛmǝˈtɔːrɪǝm], *pl* **-ria** [-rɪǝ] *n* crematorio.

crêpe [kreɪp] *n* (*fabric*) crespón *m*; (*also*: ~ **rubber**) crepé *m*; **~ bandage** *n* (*Brit*) venda de crepé.

crept [krɛpt] *pt, pp* of **creep**.

crescent [ˈkrɛsnt] *n* media luna; (*street*) calle *f* (*en forma de semicírculo*).

cress [krɛs] *n* berro.

crest [krɛst] *n* (*of bird*) cresta; (*of hill*) cima, cumbre *f*; (*of helmet*) cimera; (*of coat of arms*) blasón *m*; **~fallen** *a* alicaído.

crevasse [krɪˈvæs] *n* grieta.

crevice [ˈkrɛvɪs] *n* grieta, hendedura.

crew [kru:] *n* (*of ship etc*) tripulación *f*; (*gang*) banda; (*MIL*) dotación *f*; **~-cut** *n* corte *m* al rape; **~-neck** *n* cuello plano.

crib [krɪb] *n* pesebre *m* // *vt* (*col*) plagiar.

crick [krɪk] *n* (*in neck*) torticolis *m*.

cricket [ˈkrɪkɪt] *n* (*insect*) grillo; (*game*) críquet *m*.

crime [kraɪm] *n* crimen *m*; (*less serious*) delito; **criminal** [ˈkrɪmɪnl] *n* criminal *m/f*, delincuente *m/f* // *a* criminal; (*law*) penal.

crimson [ˈkrɪmzn] *a* carmesí.

cringe [krɪndʒ] *vi* agacharse, encogerse.

crinkle [ˈkrɪŋkl] *vt* arrugar.

cripple [ˈkrɪpl] *n* lisiado/a, cojo/a // *vt*

lisiar, mutilar.

crisis [ˈkraɪsɪs], *pl* **-ses** [-si:z] *n* crisis *f inv*.

crisp [krɪsp] *a* fresco; (*cooked*) tostado; (*manner*) seco; **~s** *npl* (*Brit*) patatas *fpl* or papas *fpl* fritas.

criss-cross [ˈkrɪskrɔs] *a* entrelazado.

criterion [kraɪˈtɪǝrɪǝn], *pl* **-ria** [-rɪǝ] *n* criterio.

critic [ˈkrɪtɪk] *n* (*paper*) crítico/a; **~al** *a* (*gen*) crítico; (*illness*) grave; **~ally** *ad* (*speak etc*) en tono crítico; (*ill*) gravemente; **~ism** [ˈkrɪtɪsɪzm] *n* crítica; **~ize** [ˈkrɪtɪsaɪz] *vt* criticar.

croak [krǝuk] *vi* (*frog*) croar; (*raven*) graznar.

crochet [ˈkrǝuʃeɪ] *n* ganchillo.

crockery [ˈkrɔkǝrɪ] *n* loza, vajilla.

crocodile [ˈkrɔkǝdaɪl] *n* cocodrilo.

crocus [ˈkrǝukǝs] *n* azafrán *m*.

croft [krɔft] *n* (*Brit*) granja pequeña.

crony [ˈkrǝunɪ] *n* compinche *m/f*.

crook [kruk] *n* (*fam*) ladrón/ona *m/f*; (*of shepherd*) cayado; (*of arm*) pliegue *m*; **~ed** [ˈkrukɪd] *a* torcido; (*path*) tortuoso; (*fam*) sucio.

crop [krɔp] *n* (*produce*) cultivo; (*amount produced*) cosecha; (*riding* ~) látigo de montar // *vt* cortar, recortar; **to ~ up** *vi* surgir, presentarse.

croquette [krǝˈkɛt] *n* croqueta.

cross [krɔs] *n* cruz *f* // *vt* (*street etc*) cruzar, atravesar // *a* de mal humor, enojado; **to ~ o.s.** santiguarse; **to ~ out** *vt* tachar; **to ~ over** *vi* cruzar; **~bar** *n* travesaño; **~country (race)** *n* carrera a campo traviesa, cross *m*; **to ~-examine** *vt* interrogar; **~-eyed** *a* bizco; **~fire** *n* fuego cruzado; **~ing** *n* (*road*) cruce *m*; (*rail*) paso a nivel; (*sea passage*) travesía; (*also*: **pedestrian ~ing**) paso para peatones; **~ing guard** *n* (*US*) persona encargada de ayudar a los niños a cruzar la calle; **~ purposes** *npl*: **to be at ~ purposes** malentenderse uno a otro; **~ reference** *n* contrarreferencia; **~roads** *n* cruce *m*, encrucijada; **~**

section n corte m transversal; (of population) muestra (representativa); ~**walk** n (US) paso de peatones; ~**wind** n viento de costado; ~**word** n crucigrama m.

crotch [krɔtʃ] n (of garment) entrepierna.

crotchet ['krɔtʃɪt] n (Brit MUS) negra.

crotchety ['krɔtʃɪtɪ] a (person) arisco.

crouch [krautʃ] vi agacharse, acurrucarse.

crow [krəu] n (bird) cuervo; (of cock) canto, cacareo // vi (cock) cantar; (fig) jactarse.

crowbar ['krəubɑː*] n palanca.

crowd [kraud] n muchedumbre f; (SPORT) público; (common herd) vulgo // vt (gather) amontonar; (fill) llenar // vi (gather) reunirse; (pile up) amontonarse; ~**ed** a (full) atestado; (well-attended) concurrido.

crown [kraun] n corona; (of head) coronilla; (of hat) copa; (of hill) cumbre f // vt coronar; ~ **jewels** npl joyas fpl reales; ~ **prince** n príncipe m heredero.

crow's feet npl patas fpl de gallo.

crucial ['kruːʃl] a decisivo.

crucifix ['kruːsɪfɪks] n crucifijo; ~**ion** [-'fɪkʃən] n crucifixión f.

crucify ['kruːsɪfaɪ] vt crucificar.

crude [kruːd] a (materials) bruto; (fig: basic) tosco; (: vulgar) ordinario; ~ (**oil**) n petróleo crudo.

cruel [kruəl] a cruel; ~**ty** n crueldad f.

cruet ['kruːɪt] n angarillas fpl.

cruise [kruːz] n crucero // vi (ship) hacer un crucero; (car) mantener la velocidad; ~**r** n crucero.

crumb [krʌm] n miga, migaja.

crumble ['krʌmbl] vt desmenuzar // vi (gen) desmenuzarse; (building) desmoronarse; **crumbly** a desmenuzable.

crumpet ['krʌmpɪt] n ≈ bollo para tostar.

crumple ['krʌmpl] vt (paper) estru-

jar; (material) arrugar.

crunch [krʌntʃ] vt (with teeth) ronzar; (underfoot) hacer crujir // n (fig) crisis f; ~**y** a crujiente.

crusade [kruː'seɪd] n cruzada.

crush [krʌʃ] n (crowd) aglomeración f // vt (gen) aplastar; (paper) estrujar; (cloth) arrugar; (fruit) exprimir.

crust [krʌst] n corteza.

crutch [krʌtʃ] n muleta.

crux [krʌks] n lo esencial.

cry [kraɪ] vi llorar; (shout: also: ~ **out**) gritar // n grito; **to ~ off** vi echarse atrás.

cryptic ['krɪptɪk] a enigmático, secreto.

crystal ['krɪstl] n cristal m; ~**-clear** a claro como el agua; ~**lize** vt cristalizar // vi cristalizarse.

cub [kʌb] n cachorro; (also: ~ **scout**) niño explorador.

Cuba ['kjuːbə] n Cuba; ~**n** a, n cubano/a m/f.

cubbyhole ['kʌbɪhəul] n chiribitil m.

cube [kjuːb] n cubo; (of sugar) terrón m // vt (MATH) cubicar; ~ **root** n raíz f cúbica; **cubic** a cúbico.

cubicle ['kjuːbɪkl] n (at pool) caseta; (for bed) cubículo.

cuckoo ['kuku:] n cuco; ~ **clock** n cucú m.

cucumber ['kjuːkʌmbə*] n pepino.

cuddle ['kʌdl] vt abrazar // vi abrazarse.

cue [kjuː] n (snooker ~) taco; (THEATRE etc) entrada.

cuff [kʌf] n (Brit: of shirt, coat etc) puño; (US: of trousers) vuelta; (blow) bofetada; **off the ~** ad improvisado; ~**links** npl gemelos mpl.

cuisine [kwɪ'ziːn] n cocina.

cul-de-sac ['kʌldəsæk] n callejón m sin salida.

cull [kʌl] vt (select) entresacar.

culminate ['kʌlmɪneɪt] vi: **to ~ in** terminar en; **culmination** [-'neɪʃən] n culminación f, colmo.

culottes [kuː'lɔts] npl falda fsg pantalón.

culprit ['kʌlprɪt] n culpable m/f, delincuente m/f.

cult [kʌlt] n culto.

cultivate ['kʌltɪveɪt] vt (also fig) cultivar; **~d** a culto; **cultivation** [-'veɪʃən] n cultivo; (fig) cultura.

cultural ['kʌltʃərəl] a cultural.

culture ['kʌltʃə*] n (also fig) cultura; **~d** a culto.

cumbersome ['kʌmbəsəm] a de mucho bulto, voluminoso.

cunning ['kʌnɪŋ] n astucia // a astuto.

cup [kʌp] n taza; (prize, event) copa.

cupboard ['kʌbəd] n armario; (kitchen) alacena.

cup-tie ['kʌptaɪ] n (Brit) partido de copa.

curate ['kjuərɪt] n cura m.

curator [kjuə'reɪtə*] n conservador(a) m/f.

curb [kəːb] vt refrenar // n freno; (US) bordillo.

curdle ['kəːdl] vi cuajarse.

cure [kjuə*] vt curar // n cura, curación f.

curfew ['kəːfjuː] n toque m de queda.

curio ['kjuərɪəu] n curiosidad f.

curiosity [kjuərɪ'ɔsɪtɪ] n curiosidad f.

curious ['kjuərɪəs] a curioso.

curl [kəːl] n rizo // vt (hair) rizar; (paper) arrollar; (lip) fruncir // vi rizarse; arrollarse; **to ~ up** vi arrollarse; (person) hacerse un ovillo; **~er** n bigudí m; **~y** a rizado.

currant ['kʌrnt] n pasa.

currency ['kʌrnsɪ] n moneda; **to gain ~** (fig) difundirse.

current ['kʌrnt] n corriente f // a corriente, actual; **~ account** n (Brit) cuenta corriente; **~ affairs** npl actualidades fpl; **~ly** ad actualmente.

curriculum [kə'rɪkjuləm], pl **~s** or **curricula** [-ə] n plan m de estudios; **~ vitae (CV)** n curriculum m.

curry ['kʌrɪ] n curry m // vt: **to ~ favour with** buscar favores con; **~ powder** n curry m en polvo.

curse [kəːs] vi echar pestes // vt maldecir // n maldición f; (swearword)

palabrota.

cursor ['kəːsə*] n (COMPUT) cursor m.

cursory ['kəːsərɪ] a rápido, superficial.

curt [kəːt] a corto, seco.

curtail [kəː'teɪl] vt (cut short) acortar; (restrict) restringir.

curtain ['kəːtn] n cortina; (THEATRE) telón m.

curts(e)y ['kəːtsɪ] n reverencia // vi hacer una reverencia.

curve [kəːv] n curva // vi encorvarse, torcerse; (road) hacer curva.

cushion ['kuʃən] n cojín m; (SNOOKER) banda // vt (shock) amortiguar.

custard ['kʌstəd] n (for pouring) natillas fpl.

custodian [kʌs'təudɪən] n custodio m/f.

custody ['kʌstədɪ] n custodia; **to take into ~** detener.

custom ['kʌstəm] n costumbre f; (COMM) clientela; **~ary** a acostumbrado.

customer ['kʌstəmə*] n cliente m/f.

customized ['kʌstəmaɪzd] a (car etc) hecho a encargo.

custom-made ['kʌstəm'meɪd] a hecho a la medida.

customs ['kʌstəmz] npl aduana sg; **~ duty** n derechos mpl de aduana; **~ officer** n aduanero/a.

cut [kʌt] vb (pt, pp cut) vt cortar; (price) rebajar; (record) grabar; (reduce) reducir // vi cortar; (intersect) cruzarse // n corte m; (in skin) cortadura; (with sword) tajo; (of knife) cuchillada; (in salary etc) rebaja; (slice of meat) tajada; **to ~ a tooth** echar un diente; **to ~ down** vt (tree) derribar; (reduce) reducir; **to ~ off** vt cortar; (fig) aislar; (troops) cercar; **to ~ out** vt (shape) recortar; (delete) suprimir; **to ~ up** vt cortar (en pedazos); **~back** n reducción f.

cute [kjuːt] a lindo; (shrewd) listo.

cuticle ['kjuːtɪkl] n cutícula.

cutlery ['kʌtlərɪ] n cubiertos mpl.

cutlet ['kʌtlɪt] n chuleta.

cut: ~**out** n (cardboard ~) recortable m; ~**price**, (US) ~**rate** a a precio reducido; ~**throat** n asesino/a // a feroz.

cutting ['kʌtɪŋ] a (gen) cortante; (remark) mordaz // n (Brit: from newspaper) recorte m; (: RAIL) desmonte m.

CV n abbr = **curriculum vitae.**

cwt abbr = **hundredweight(s).**

cyanide ['saɪənaɪd] n cianuro.

cycle ['saɪkl] n ciclo; (bicycle) bicicleta // vi ir en bicicleta; **cycling** n ciclismo; **cyclist** n ciclista m/f.

cyclone ['saɪkləun] n ciclón m.

cygnet ['sɪgnɪt] n pollo de cisne.

cylinder ['sɪlɪndə*] n cilindro; ~**head gasket** n junta de culata.

cymbals ['sɪmblz] npl platillos mpl.

cynic ['sɪnɪk] n cínico/a; ~**al** a cínico; ~**ism** ['sɪnɪsɪzəm] n cinismo.

cypress ['saɪprɪs] n ciprés m.

Cypriot ['sɪprɪət] a, n chipriota m/f.

Cyprus ['saɪprəs] n Chipre f.

cyst [sɪst] n quiste m; ~**itis** n cistitis f.

czar [zɑː*] n zar m.

Czech [tʃek] a, n checo/a m/f.

Czechoslovakia [tʃekəslə'vækɪə] n Checoslovaquia; ~**n** a, n checo/a m/f.

D

D [diː] n (MUS) re m.

dab [dæb] vt (eyes, wound) tocar (ligeramente); (paint, cream) mojar ligeramente // n (light stroke) toque m; (small amount) pizca.

dabble ['dæbl] vi: to ~ in ser algo aficionado a.

Dacron ['deɪkrɔn] n ® (US) terylene m.

dad [dæd], **daddy** ['dædɪ] n papá m; **daddy-long-legs** n típula.

daffodil ['dæfədɪl] n narciso.

daft [dɑːft] a chiflado.

dagger ['dægə*] n puñal m, daga.

daily ['deɪlɪ] a diario, cotidiano // n (paper) diario; (domestic help) asistenta // ad todos los días, cada día.

dainty ['deɪntɪ] a delicado; (tasteful) elegante; primoroso.

dairy ['dɛərɪ] n (shop) lechería; (on farm) vaquería // a (cow etc) lechero; ~ **farm** n granja; ~ **produce** n productos mpl lácteos.

dais ['deɪɪs] n estrado.

daisy ['deɪzɪ] n margarita; ~ **wheel** n margarita.

dale [deɪl] n valle m.

dam [dæm] n presa // vt represar.

damage ['dæmɪdʒ] n daño; (fig) perjuicio; (to machine) avería // vt dañar; perjudicar; averiar; ~**s** npl (LAW) daños mpl y perjuicios.

damn [dæm] vt condenar; (curse) maldecir // n (col): **I don't give a** ~ me importa un pito // a (col: also: ~**ed**) maldito; ~ **(it)!** ¡maldito sea!; ~**ing** a (evidence) irrecusable.

damp [dæmp] a húmedo, mojado // n humedad f // vt (also: ~**en**) (cloth, rag) mojar; (fig) desalentar; ~**ness** n humedad f.

damson ['dæmzən] n ciruela damascena.

dance [dɑːns] n baile m // vi bailar; ~ **hall** n salón m de baile; ~**r** n bailador(a) m/f; (professional) bailarín/ina m/f; **dancing** n baile m.

dandelion ['dændɪlaɪən] n diente m de león.

dandruff ['dændrəf] n caspa.

Dane [deɪn] n danés/esa m/f.

danger ['deɪndʒə*] n peligro; (risk) riesgo; ~! (on sign) ¡peligro de muerte!; **to be in** ~ of correr riesgo de; ~**ous** a peligroso; ~**ously** ad peligrosamente.

dangle ['dæŋgl] vt colgar // vi pender, estar colgado.

Danish ['deɪnɪʃ] a danés // n (LING) danés m.

dapper ['dæpə*] a pulcro, apuesto.

dare [dɛə*] vt: **to** ~ **sb to do** desafiar a uno a hacer // vi: **to** ~ **(to)**

do sth atreverse a hacer algo; **I ~ say** (*I suppose*) puede ser, a lo mejor; **~devil** n temerario/a, atrevido/a; **daring** a atrevido, osado // n atrevimiento, osadía.

dark [dɑːk] a oscuro; (*hair*, *complexion*) moreno; (*fig: cheerless*) triste, sombrío // n (*gen*) oscuridad f; (*night*) tinieblas fpl; **in the ~ about** (*fig*) en ignorancia de; **after ~** después del anochecer; **~en** vt oscurecer; (*colour*) hacer más oscuro // vi oscurecerse; (*cloud over*) anublarse; **~ glasses** npl gafas fpl negras; **~ness** n (*in room*) oscuridad f; (*night*) tinieblas fpl; **~room** n cuarto m oscuro.

darling ['dɑːlɪŋ] a, n querido/a m/f.

darn [dɑːn] vt zurcir.

dart [dɑːt] n dardo; (*in sewing*) sisa // vi precipitarse; **~ away/along** vi salir/marchar disparado; **~board** n diana; **~s** n dardos mpl.

dash [dæʃ] n (*small quantity: of liquid*) gota, chorrito; (*: of solid*) pizca; (*sign*) guión m; (*: long*) raya // vt (*break*) romper, estrellar; (*hopes*) defraudar // vi precipitarse; **to ~ away** or **off** vi marcharse apresuradamente.

dashboard ['dæʃbɔːd] n (*AUT*) tablero de instrumentos.

dashing ['dæʃɪŋ] a gallardo.

data ['deɪtə] npl datos mpl; **~base** n base f de datos; **~ processing** n proceso m de datos.

date [deɪt] n (*day*) fecha; (*with friend*) cita; (*fruit*) dátil m // vt fechar; **~ of birth** fecha de nacimiento; **to ~** ad hasta la fecha; **out of ~** pasado de moda; **up to ~** moderno; **~d** a anticuado.

daub [dɔːb] vt embadurnar.

daughter ['dɔːtə*] n hija; **~-in-law** n nuera, hija política.

daunting ['dɔːntɪŋ] a desalentador(a).

dawdle ['dɔːdl] vi (*waste time*) perder el tiempo; (*go slowly*) andar muy despacio.

dawn [dɔːn] n alba, amanecer m // vi (*day*) amanecer; (*fig*): **it ~ed on him that**... cayó en la cuenta de que...

day [deɪ] n día m; (*working ~*) jornada; **the ~ before** el día anterior; **the ~ after tomorrow** pasado mañana; **the ~ before yesterday** anteayer; **the ~ after, the following** ~ el día siguiente; **by ~** de día; **~break** n amanecer m; **~dream** vi soñar despierto; **~light** n luz f (del día); **~light saving time** n (*US*) hora de verano; **~ return** n (*Brit*) billete m de ida y vuelta (en un día); **~time** n día m; **~-to-~** a cotidiano.

daze [deɪz] vt (*stun*) aturdir // n: **in a ~** aturdido.

dazzle ['dæzl] vt deslumbrar; **dazzling** a deslumbrante.

DC abbr = **direct current** corriente f continua.

deacon ['diːkən] n diácono.

dead [dɛd] a muerto; (*limb*) dormido; (*telephone*) cortado; (*battery*) agotado // ad totalmente; **to shoot sb ~** matar a uno a tiros; **~ tired** muerto (de cansancio); **to stop ~** parar en seco; **the ~** npl los muertos; **to be a ~ loss** (*col: person*) ser un inútil; (*: thing*) ser una birria; **~en** vt (*blow, sound*) amortiguar; (*make numb*) calmar, aliviar; **~ end** n callejón m sin salida; **~ heat** n (*SPORT*) empate m; **~line** n fecha or hora tope; **~lock** n punto muerto; **~ly** a mortal, fatal; **~pan** a sin expresión.

deaf [dɛf] a sordo; **~en** vt ensordecer; **~-mute** n sordomudo/a; **~ness** n sordera.

deal [diːl] n (*agreement*) pacto, convenio; (*business*) negocio, transacción f; (*CARDS*) reparto // vt (pt, pp **dealt**) (*gen*) dar; **a great ~ (of)** bastante, mucho; **to ~ in** vt fus tratar en, comerciar en; **to ~ with** vt fus (*people*) tratar con; (*problem*) ocuparse de; (*subject*) tratar de; **~er** n comerciante m/f; (CARDS) mano f; **~ings** npl (COMM) transacciones fpl; (relations) relaciones fpl.

dean [di:n] n (REL) deán m; (SCOL) decano/a.

dear [dɪə*] a querido; (expensive) caro // n: **my ~** mi querido/a; **~ me!** ¡Dios mío!; **D~ Sir/Madam** (in letter) Muy Señor Mío, Muy Señor/Estimada Señora; **D~ Mr/Mrs X** Estimado/a Señor(a) X; **~ly** ad (love) mucho; (pay) caro.

death [deθ] n muerte f; **~ certificate** n partida de defunción; **~ duties** npl (Brit) derechos mpl de sucesión; **~ly** a mortal; (silence) profundo; **~ penalty** n pena de muerte; **~ rate** n mortalidad f.

debacle [deɪˈbɑːkl] n desastre m.

debar [dɪˈbɑːʳ] vt: **to ~ sb from doing** prohibir a uno hacer.

debase [dɪˈbeɪs] vt degradar.

debatable [dɪˈbeɪtəbl] a discutible.

debate [dɪˈbeɪt] n debate m // vt discutir.

debauchery [dɪˈbɔːtʃərɪ] n libertinaje m.

debilitating [dɪˈbɪlɪteɪtɪŋ] a (illness etc) debilitante.

debit ['debɪt] n debe m // vt: **to ~ a sum to sb** or **to sb's account** cargar una suma en cuenta a alguien.

debris ['debriː] n escombros mpl.

debt [det] n deuda; **to be in ~** tener deudas; **~or** n deudor/a m/f.

debunk [diːˈbʌŋk] vt desprestigiar, desacreditar.

début ['deɪbjuː] n presentación f.

decade [ˈdekeɪd] n decenio m.

decadence ['dekədəns] n decadencia.

decaffeinated [dɪˈkæfɪneɪtɪd] a descafeinado.

decanter [dɪˈkæntə*] n garrafa.

decay [dɪˈkeɪ] n (fig) decadencia; (of building) desmoronamiento m; (rotting) pudrición f; (of tooth) caries f inv // vi (rot) pudrirse; (fig) decaer.

deceased [dɪˈsiːst] a difunto.

deceit [dɪˈsiːt] n engaño; **~ful** a engañoso.

deceive [dɪˈsiːv] vt engañar.

December [dɪˈsembə*] n diciembre m.

decent ['diːsənt] a (proper) decente; (person) amable, bueno.

deception [dɪˈsepʃən] n engaño.

deceptive [dɪˈseptɪv] a engañoso.

decibel ['desɪbel] n decibel(io) m.

decide [dɪˈsaɪd] vt (person) decidir; (question, argument) resolver // vi: **to ~ to do/that** decidir hacer/que; **to ~ on sth** decidir por algo; **~d** a (resolute) decidido; (clear, definite) indudable; **~dly** [-dɪdlɪ] ad decididamente.

deciduous [dɪˈsɪdjuəs] a de hoja caduca.

decimal ['desɪməl] a decimal // n decimal f; **~ point** n coma decimal.

decimate ['desɪmeɪt] vt diezmar.

decipher [dɪˈsaɪfə*] vt descifrar.

decision [dɪˈsɪʒən] n decisión f.

deck [dek] n (NAUT) cubierta; (of bus) piso; (of cards) baraja; **~chair** n tumbona.

declaration [dekləˈreɪʃən] n declaración f.

declare [dɪˈkleə*] vt (gen) declarar.

decline [dɪˈklaɪn] n decaimiento, decadencia; (lessening) disminución f // vt rehusar // vi decaer; disminuir.

declutch [ˈdiːˈklʌtʃ] vi desembragar.

decode [diːˈkəud] vt descifrar.

decompose [diːkəmˈpəuz] vi descomponerse.

décor ['deɪkɔː*] n decoración f; (THEATRE) decorado.

decorate ['dekəreɪt] vt (adorn): **to ~ (with)** adornar (de), decorar (de); (paint) pintar; (paper) empapelar; **decoration** [-'reɪʃən] n adorno; (act) decoración f; (medal) condecoración f; **decorative** ['dekərətɪv] a decorativo; **decorator** n (workman) pintor m decorador.

decorum [dɪˈkɔːrəm] n decoro.

decoy ['diːkɔɪ] n señuelo.

decrease ['diːkriːs] n disminución f

(vb: [diːˈkriːs]) *vt* disminuir, reducir // *vi* reducirse.

decree [dɪˈkriː] *n* decreto; ~ **nisi** *n* sentencia provisional de divorcio.

dedicate [ˈdedɪkeɪt] *vt* dedicar; **dedication** [-ˈkeɪʃən] *n (devotion)* dedicación *f; (in book)* dedicatoria.

deduce [dɪˈdjuːs] *vt* deducir.

deduct [dɪˈdʌkt] *vt* restar; *(from wage etc)* descontar; ~**ion** [dɪˈdʌkʃən] *n (amount deducted)* descuento; *(conclusion)* deducción *f,* conclusión *f.*

deed [diːd] *n* hecho, acto; *(feat)* hazaña; *(LAW)* escritura.

deem [diːm] *vt* juzgar.

deep [diːp] *a* profundo; *(voice)* bajo; *(breath)* profundo, a pleno pulmón // *ad:* the spectators stood 20 ~ los espectadores se formaron de 20 en fondo; **to be 4 metres** ~ tener 4 metros de profundo; ~**en** *vt* ahondar, profundizar // *vi (darkness)* intensificarse; ~**-freeze** *n* congeladora; ~**fry** *vt* freír en aceite abundante; ~**ly** *ad (breathe)* a pleno pulmón; *(interested, moved, grateful)* profundamente, hondamente; ~**-sea diving** *n* buceo de altura; ~**-seated** *a (beliefs)* (profundamente) arraigado.

deer [dɪə*] *n, pl inv* ciervo.

deface [dɪˈfeɪs] *vt* desfigurar, mutilar.

defamation [defəˈmeɪʃən] *n* difamación *f.*

default [dɪˈfɔːlt] *vi* faltar al pago; *(SPORT)* dejar de presentarse // *(COMPUT)* defecto; **by** ~ *(LAW)* en rebeldía; *(SPORT)* por incomparecencia; ~**er** *n (in debt)* moroso/a.

defeat [dɪˈfiːt] *n* derrota // *vt* derrotar, vencer; *(fig: efforts)* frustrar; ~**ist** *a, n* derrotista *m/f.*

defect [ˈdiːfekt] *n* defecto // *vi* [dɪˈfekt]: **to** ~ **to the enemy** pasarse al enemigo; ~**ive** [dɪˈfektɪv] *a (gen)* defectuoso; *(person)* anormal.

defence [dɪˈfens] *n* defensa; ~**less** *a* indefenso.

defend [dɪˈfend] *vt* defender; ~**ant**

n acusado/a; *(in civil case)* demandado/a; ~**er** *n* defensor/a *m/f.*

defense [dɪˈfens] *n (US)* = **defence**.

defensive [dɪˈfensɪv] *a* defensivo; **on the** ~ a la defensiva.

defer [dɪˈfəː*] *vt (postpone)* aplazar; **to** ~ **to** diferir a ~; ~**ence** [ˈdefərəns] *n* deferencia, respeto.

defiance [dɪˈfaɪəns] *n* desafío; **in** ~ **of** en contra de.

defiant [dɪˈfaɪənt] *a (insolent)* insolente; *(challenging)* retador(a).

deficiency [dɪˈfɪʃənsɪ] *n (lack)* falta; *(defect)* defecto.

deficient [dɪˈfɪʃənt] *a (lacking)* insuficiente; *(incomplete)* incompleto; *(defective)* defectuoso; *(mentally)* anormal; ~ **in** deficiente en.

deficit [ˈdefɪsɪt] *n* déficit *m.*

defile [dɪˈfaɪl] *vt* manchar; *(violate)* violar.

define [dɪˈfaɪn] *vt* definir.

definite [ˈdefɪnɪt] *a (fixed)* determinado; *(clear, obvious)* claro; **he was** ~ **about it** no dejó lugar a dudas (sobre ello); ~**ly** *ad:* **he's** ~**ly mad** no cabe duda de que está loco.

definition [defɪˈnɪʃən] *n* definición *f.*

deflate [diːˈfleɪt] *vt (gen)* desinflar; *(person)* quitar los humos a.

deflect [dɪˈflekt] *vt* desviar.

defraud [dɪˈfrɔːd] *vt* estafar; **to** ~ **sb of sth** estafar algo a uno.

defray [dɪˈfreɪ] *vt:* **to** ~ **sb's expenses** reembolsar(le) a uno los gastos.

defrost [diːˈfrɒst] *vt (food)* deshelar; *(fridge)* descongelar; ~**er** *n (US: demister)* eliminador *m* de vaho.

deft [deft] *a* diestro, hábil.

defunct [dɪˈfʌŋkt] *a* difunto.

defuse [diːˈfjuːz] *vt* desarmar; *(situation)* calmar.

defy [dɪˈfaɪ] *vt (resist)* oponerse a; *(challenge)* desafiar; *(order)* contravenir.

degenerate [dɪˈdʒenəreɪt] *vi* degenerar // *a* [dɪˈdʒenərɪt] degenerado.

degree [dɪˈɡriː] *n* grado; *(SCOL)* título; **to have a** ~ **in maths** tener una licenciatura en matemáticas; **by** ~s (*gradually*) poco a poco, por etapas; **to some** ~ hasta cierto punto.

dehydrated [di:haɪ'dreɪtd] *a* deshidratado; (*milk*) en polvo.

de-ice [di:'aɪs] *vt* (*windscreen*) deshelar.

deign [deɪn] *vi*: **to** ~ **to do** dignarse hacer.

deity ['di:ɪtɪ] *n* deidad *f*, divinidad *f*.

dejected [dɪ'dʒɛktɪd] *a* abatido, desanimado.

delay [dɪ'leɪ] *vt* demorar, aplazar; (*person*) entretener; (*train*) retrasar // *vi* tardar // *n* demora, retraso; **without** ~ en seguida, sin tardar.

delectable [dɪ'lɛktəbl] *a* (*person*) encantador(a); (*food*) delicioso.

delegate ['dɛlɪgɪt] *n* delegado/a // *vt* ['dɛlɪgeɪt] delegar.

delete [dɪ'li:t] *vt* suprimir, tachar.

deliberate [dɪ'lɪbərɪt] *a* (*intentional*) intencionado; (*slow*) pausado, lento // *vi* [dɪ'lɪbəreɪt] deliberar; **~ly** *ad* (*on purpose*) a propósito; (*slowly*) pausadamente.

delicacy ['dɛlɪkəsɪ] *n* delicadeza; (*choice food*) golosina.

delicate ['dɛlɪkɪt] *a* (*gen*) delicado; (*fragile*) frágil.

delicatessen [dɛlɪkə'tɛsn] *n* ultramarinos *mpl* finos.

delicious [dɪ'lɪʃəs] *a* delicioso, rico.

delight [dɪ'laɪt] *n* (*feeling*) placer *m*, deleite *m*; (*object*) encanto, delicia // *vt* encantar, deleitar; **to take** ~ **in** deleitarse en; **~ed** *a*: **~ed** (**at** or **with/to do**) encantado (con/de hacer); **~ful** *a* encantador(a), delicioso.

delinquent [dɪ'lɪŋkwənt] *a*, *n* delincuente *m/f*.

delirious [dɪ'lɪrɪəs] *a*: **to be** ~ delirar, desvariar.

deliver [dɪ'lɪvə*] *vt* (*distribute*) repartir; (*hand over*) entregar; (*message*) comunicar; (*speech*) pronunciar; (*blow*) lanzar, dar; (*MED*) asistir al parto de; **~y** *n* reparto; entrega; (*of speaker*) modo de expresar-

se; (*MED*) parto, alumbramiento; **to take** ~ **of** recibir.

delude [dɪ'lu:d] *vt* engañar.

deluge ['dɛlju:dʒ] *n* diluvio // *vt* inundar.

delusion [dɪ'lu:ʒən] *n* ilusión *f*, engaño.

de luxe [də'lʌks] *a* de lujo.

delve [dɛlv] *vi*: **to** ~ **into** hurgar en.

demand [dɪ'mɑ:nd] *vt* (*gen*) exigir; (*rights*) reclamar // *n* (*gen*) exigencia; (*claim*) reclamación *f*; (*ECON*) demanda; **to be in** ~ ser muy solicitado; **on** ~ a solicitud; **~ing** *a* (*boss*) exigente; (*work*) absorbente.

demean [dɪ'mi:n] *vt*: **to** ~ **o.s.** rebajarse.

demeanour, (*US*) **demeanor** [dɪ'mi:nə*] *n* porte *m*, conducta.

demented [dɪ'mentɪd] *a* demente.

demise [dɪ'maɪz] *n* (*death*) fallecimiento.

demister [dɪ'mɪstə*] *n* (*AUT*) eliminador *m* de vaho.

demo ['dɛməu] *n abbr* (*col:* = *demonstration*) manifestación *f*.

democracy [dɪ'mɔkrəsɪ] *n* democracia; **democrat** ['dɛməkræt] *n* demócrata *m/f*; **democratic** [dɛmə'krætɪk] *a* democrático.

demolish [dɪ'mɔlɪʃ] *vt* derribar, demoler; **demolition** [dɛmə'lɪʃən] *n* derribo, demolición *f*.

demon ['di:mən] *n* (*evil spirit*) demonio.

demonstrate ['dɛmənstreɪt] *vt* demostrar // *vi* manifestarse; **demonstration** [-'streɪʃən] *n* (*POL*) manifestación *f*; (*proof*) prueba, demostración *f*; **demonstrator** *n* (*POL*) manifestante *m/f*.

demoralize [dɪ'mɔrəlaɪz] *vt* desmoralizar.

demote [dɪ'məut] *vt* degradar.

demure [dɪ'mjuə*] *a* recatado.

den [dɛn] *n* (*of animal*) guarida; (*study*) estudio.

denatured alcohol [di:'neɪtʃəd-] *n* (*US*) alcohol *m* desnaturalizado.

denial [dɪ'naɪəl] *n* (*refusal*) negativa.

(of report etc) negación f.

denim ['denɪm] n tela vaquera; ~s npl vaqueros mpl.

Denmark ['denmɑːk] n Dinamarca.

denomination [dɪnɔmɪ'neɪʃən] n valor m; (REL) confesión f.

denote [dɪ'nəut] vt indicar, significar.

denounce [dɪ'nauns] vt denunciar.

dense [dens] a (thick) espeso; (: foliage etc) tupido; (stupid) torpe; ~ly ad: ~ly populated con una alta densidad de población.

density ['densɪtɪ] n densidad f; **double-~ disk** n (COMPUT) disco de doble densidad.

dent [dent] n abolladura // vt (also: make a ~ in) abollar.

dental ['dentl] a dental; ~ **surgeon** n odontólogo.a.

dentist ['dentɪst] n dentista m/f; ~ n odontología.

dentures ['dentʃəz] npl dentadura sg (postiza).

denunciation [dɪnʌnsɪ'eɪʃən] n denuncia, denunciación f.

deny [dɪ'naɪ] vt negar; (charge) rechazar; (report) desmentir.

deodorant [diː'əudərənt] n desodorante m.

depart [dɪ'pɑːt] vi irse, marcharse; (train) salir; to ~ **from** (fig: differ from) apartarse de.

department [dɪ'pɑːtmənt] n (COMM) sección f; (SCOL) departamento; (POL) ministerio; ~ **store** n gran almacén m.

departure [dɪ'pɑːtʃə*] n partida, ida; (of train) salida; **a new ~** un nuevo rumbo; ~ **lounge** n (at airport) sala de embarque.

depend [dɪ'pend] vi: to ~ **on** depender de; (rely on) contar con; **it** ~s depende, según; ~**ing on the result** según el resultado; ~**able** a (person) formal, serio; ~**ant** n dependiente m/f; ~**ence** n dependencia; ~**ent** a: to be ~**ent on** depender de // n = ~**ant**.

depict [dɪ'pɪkt] vt (in picture) pin-

tar; (describe) representar.

depleted [dɪ'pliːtɪd] a reducido.

deplorable [dɪ'plɔːrəbl] a deplorable.

deplore [dɪ'plɔː*] vt deplorar.

deploy [dɪ'plɔɪ] vt desplegar.

depopulation ['diːpɔpju'leɪʃən] n despoblación f.

deport [dɪ'pɔːt] vt deportar.

deportment [dɪ'pɔːtmənt] n comportamiento.

depose [dɪ'pəuz] vt deponer.

deposit [dɪ'pɔzɪt] n depósito; (CHEM) sedimento; (of ore, oil) yacimiento // vt (gen) depositar; ~ **account** n (Brit) cuenta de ahorros; ~**or** n depositante m/f.

depot ['depəu] n (storehouse) depósito; (for vehicles) parque m.

depreciate [dɪ'priːʃɪeɪt] vi depreciarse, perder valor; **depreciation** [-'eɪʃən] n depreciación f.

depress [dɪ'pres] vt deprimir; (press down) apretar; ~**ed** a deprimido; ~**ing** a deprimente; ~**ion** [dɪ'preʃən] n depresión f.

deprivation [deprɪ'veɪʃən] n privación f; (loss) pérdida.

deprive [dɪ'praɪv] vt: to ~ **sb of** privar a uno de; ~**d** a necesitado.

depth [depθ] n profundidad f; **in the** ~**s of** en lo más hondo de.

deputation [depju'teɪʃən] n delegación f.

deputize ['depjutaɪz] vi: to ~ **for sb** suplir a uno.

deputy ['depjutɪ] a: ~ **head** subdirector/a m/f // n sustituto/a, suplente m/f; (POL) diputado/a; (agent) representante m/f.

derail [dɪ'reɪl] vt: to be ~**ed** descarrilarse; ~**ment** n descarrilamiento.

deranged [dɪ'reɪndʒd] a trastornado.

derby ['dɑːbɪ] n (US) hongo.

derelict ['derɪlɪkt] a abandonado.

deride [dɪ'raɪd] vt ridiculizar, mofarse de.

derisive [dɪ'raɪsɪv] a burlón/ona.

derisory [dɪ'raɪzərɪ] a (sum) irrisorio.

derivative [dɪ'rɪvətɪv] n derivado // a (work) poco original.

derive [dɪ'raɪv] vt derivar // vi: to ~ from derivarse de.

derogatory [dɪ'rɔgətərɪ] a despectivo.

derrick ['derɪk] n torre f de perforación.

derv [dəːv] n (Brit) gasoil m.

descend [dɪ'send] vt, vi descender, bajar; to ~ from descender de; ~ant n descendiente m/f.

descent [dɪ'sent] n descenso; (origin) descendencia.

describe [dɪs'kraɪb] vt describir; **description** [-'krɪpʃən] n descripción f; (sort) clase f, género.

desecrate ['desɪkreɪt] vt profanar.

desert ['dezət] n (sketch) desierto // [dɪ'zəːt] (vb: [dɪ'zəːt]) vt abandonar, desamparar // vi (MIL) desertar; ~s [dɪ'zəːts] npl: to get one's just ~s llevar su merecido; ~er n [dɪ'zəːtə] n desertor/a m/f; ~ion [dɪ'zəːʃən] n deserción f; ~ island n isla desierta.

deserve [dɪ'zəːv] vt merecer, ser digno de; **deserving** a (person) digno; (action, cause) meritorio.

design [dɪ'zaɪn] n (sketch) bosquejo; (layout, shape) diseño; (pattern) dibujo // vt (plan) diseñar; **to have ~s on sb** tener la(s) mira(s) puesta(s) en uno.

designate ['dezɪgneɪt] vt (appoint) nombrar; (destine) designar // a ['dezɪgnɪt] designado.

designer [dɪ'zaɪnə*] n diseñador/a m/f; (fashion ~) modisto/a.

desirable [dɪ'zaɪərəbl] a (proper) deseable; (attractive) atractivo.

desire [dɪ'zaɪə*] n deseo // vt desear.

desk [desk] n (in office) escritorio; (for pupil) pupitre m; (in hotel, at airport) recepción f; (Brit: in shop, restaurant) caja.

desolate ['desəlɪt] a (place) desierto; (person) afligido, **desolation** n (of place) desolación f; (of person) aflicción f.

despair [dɪs'peə*] n desesperación f // vi: **to ~ of** desesperarse de.

despatch [dɪs'pætʃ] n, vt = **dispatch**.

desperate ['despərɪt] a desesperado; (fugitive) peligroso; ~ly ad desesperadamente; (very) terriblemente, gravemente.

desperation [despə'reɪʃən] n desesperación f; **in ~** desesperado.

despicable [dɪs'pɪkəbl] a vil, despreciable.

despise [dɪs'paɪz] vt despreciar.

despite [dɪs'paɪt] prep a pesar de, pese a.

despondent [dɪs'pɔndənt] a deprimido, abatido.

dessert [dɪ'zəːt] n postre m; ~**spoon** n cuchara de (postre).

destination [destɪ'neɪʃən] n destino.

destine ['destɪn] vt destinar.

destiny ['destɪnɪ] n destino.

destitute ['destɪtjuːt] a desamparado, indigente.

destroy [dɪs'trɔɪ] vt destruir; (finish) acabar con; ~**er** n (NAUT) destructor m.

destruction [dɪs'trʌkʃən] n destrucción f; (fig) ruina.

destructive [dɪs'trʌktɪv] a destructivo, destructor(a).

detach [dɪ'tætʃ] vt separar; (unstick) despegar; ~**able** a separable; (TECH) desmontable; ~**ed** a (attitude) objetivo, imparcial; ~**ed house** n = chalé m, chalet m; ~**ment** n separación f; (MIL) destacamento; (fig) objetividad f, imparcialidad f.

detail ['diːteɪl] n detalle m // vt detallar; (MIL) destacar; **in ~** detalladamente; ~**ed** a detallado.

detain [dɪ'teɪn] vt retener; (in captivity) detener.

detect [dɪ'tekt] vt (gen) descubrir; (MED, POLICE) identificar; (MIL, RADAR, TECH) detectar; ~**ion** [dɪ'tekʃən] n descubrimiento; identificación f; ~**ive** n detective m/f; ~**ive story** n novela policíaca; ~**or** n detector m.

détente [der'ta:nt] n distensión f.

detention [dr'tenʃən] n detención f, arresto.

deter [dr'tə:*] vt (dissuade) disuadir; (prevent) impedir; **to ~ sb from doing sth** disuadir a uno de que haga algo.

detergent [dr'tə:dʒənt] n detergente m.

deteriorate [dr'tɪərɪəreɪt] vi deteriorarse; **deterioration** [-'reɪʃən] n deterioro.

determination [dɪtə:mɪ'neɪʃən] n resolución f.

determine [dr'tə:mɪn] vt determinar; **~d a: ~d to do** resuelto a hacer.

deterrent [dr'terənt] n fuerza de disuasión f.

detest [dr'test] vt aborrecer.

detonate ['detəneɪt] vi estallar // vt hacer detonar.

detour ['di:tuə*] n (gen, US AUT: diversion) desviación f // vt (US AUT) desviar.

detract [dr'trækt] vt: **to ~ from** quitar mérito a, desvirtuar.

detriment ['detrɪmənt] n: **to the ~ of** en perjuicio de; **~al** [detrɪ'mentl] a: **~ (to)** perjudicial (a).

devaluation [dɪvælju'eɪʃən] n devaluación f.

devastating ['devəsteɪtɪŋ] a devastador(a); (fig) arrollador(a).

develop [dr'veləp] vt desarrollar; (PHOT) revelar; (disease) coger; (habit) adquirir // vi desarrollarse; (advance) progresar; **~ing country** país m en (vías de) desarrollo; **~ment** n desarrollo; (advance) progreso; (of affair, case) desenvolvimiento; (of land) urbanización f.

deviate ['di:vieɪt] vi: **to ~ (from)** desviarse (de); **deviation** [-'eɪʃən] n desviación f.

device [dr'vaɪs] n (scheme) estratagema, recurso; (apparatus) aparato, mecanismo.

devil ['devl] n diablo, demonio; **~ish** a diabólico.

devious ['di:vɪəs] a intricado, enrevesado; (person) taimado.

devise [dr'vaɪz] vt idear, inventar.

devoid [dr'vɔɪd] a: **~ of** desprovisto de.

devolution [di:və'lu:ʃən] n (POL) descentralización f.

devote [dr'vəut] vt: **to ~ sth to** dedicar algo a; **~d a** (loyal) leal, fiel; **the book is ~d to politics** el libro trata de la política; **~e** [devəu'ti:] n devoto/a.

devotion [dr'vəuʃən] n dedicación f; (REL) devoción f.

devour [dr'vauə*] vt devorar.

devout [dr'vaut] a devoto.

dew [dju:] n rocío.

dexterity [deks'terɪtɪ] n destreza.

diabetes [daɪə'bi:ti:z] n diabetes f; **diabetic** [-'betɪk] a, n diabético/a m/f.

diabolical [daɪə'bɔlɪkəl] a (col: weather, behaviour) pésimo.

diagnose [daɪəg'nəuz] vt diagnosticar; **diagnosis** [-'nəusɪs], pl **-ses** [-'nəusi:z] n diagnóstico.

diagonal [daɪ'ægənl] a, n diagonal f.

diagram ['daɪəgræm] n diagrama m, esquema m.

dial ['daɪəl] n esfera, cuadrante m, cara (LAm); (of phone) disco // vt (number) marcar; **~ code** n (US) prefijo; **~ tone** n (US) señal f or tono de marcar.

dialect ['daɪəlekt] n dialecto.

dialling ['daɪəlɪŋ]: **~ code** n (Brit) prefijo; **~ tone** n (Brit) señal f or tono de marcar.

dialogue ['daɪəlɔg] n diálogo.

diameter [daɪ'æmɪtə*] n diámetro.

diamond ['daɪəmənd] n diamante m; **~s** npl (CARDS) diamantes mpl.

diaper ['daɪəpə*] n (US) pañal m.

diaphragm ['daɪəfræm] n diafragma m.

diarrhoea, (US) **diarrhea** [daɪə'ri:ə] n diarrea.

diary ['daɪərɪ] n (daily account) diario; (book) agenda.

dice [daɪs] n, pl inv dados mpl // vt

(CULIN) cortar en cuadritos.
dichotomy [dɪˈkɒtəmɪ] n dicotomía.
Dictaphone [ˈdɪktəfəun] n ® dictáfono ®.
dictate [dɪkˈteɪt] vt dictar; **~s** [ˈdɪkteɪts] npl dictados mpl; **dictation** [-ˈteɪʃən] n dictado.
dictator [dɪkˈteɪtə*] n dictador m; **~ship** n dictadura.
dictionary [ˈdɪkʃənrɪ] n diccionario.
did [dɪd] pt of **do**.
didn't [ˈdɪdənt] = **did not**.
die [daɪ] vi morir; to be dying for sth/to do sth morirse por algo/de ganas de hacer algo; **to ~ away** vi (sound, light) perderse; **to ~ down** vi (gen) apagarse; (wind) amainar; **to ~ out** vi desaparecer, extinguirse.
diehard [ˈdaɪhɑːd] n reaccionario/a.
diesel [ˈdiːzəl]: **~ engine** n motor m Diesel; **~ (oil)** n gasoil m.
diet [ˈdaɪət] n dieta; (restricted food) régimen m // vi (also: **be on a ~**) estar a dieta, hacer régimen.
differ [ˈdɪfə*] vi (be different) ser distinto, diferenciarse; (disagree) discrepar; **~ence** n diferencia; (quarrel) desacuerdo; **~ent** a diferente, distinto; **~entiate** [-ˈrɛnʃɪeɪt] vt distinguir // vi diferenciarse; **~entiate between** distinguir entre; **~ently** ad de otro modo, en forma distinta.
difficult [ˈdɪfɪkəlt] a difícil; **~y** n dificultad f.
diffident [ˈdɪfɪdənt] a tímido.
diffuse [dɪˈfjuːs] a difuso // vt [dɪˈfjuːz] difundir.
dig [dɪg] vt (pt, pp **dug**) (hole) cavar; (ground) remover // n (prod) empujón m; (archaeological) excavación f; (remark) indirecta; to **one's nails into** clavar las uñas en; **to ~ in** vi atrincherarse; **to ~ into** vt fus (savings) consumir; **to ~ out** vt (fig) sacar; **to ~ up** vt excavar; (plant) desarraigar.
digest [daɪˈdʒɛst] vt (food) digerir;

(facts) asimilar // n [ˈdaɪdʒɛst] resumen m; **~ion** [dɪˈdʒɛstʃən] n digestión f.
digit [ˈdɪdʒɪt] n (number) dígito; (finger) dedo; **~al** a digital.
dignified [ˈdɪgnɪfaɪd] a grave, solemne; (action) decoroso.
dignity [ˈdɪgnɪtɪ] n dignidad f.
digress [daɪˈgrɛs] vi: **to ~ from** apartarse de.
digs [dɪgz] npl (Brit: col) pensión fsg, alojamiento sg.
dike [daɪk] n = **dyke**.
dilapidated [dɪˈlæpɪdeɪtɪd] a desmoronado, ruinoso.
dilemma [daɪˈlɛmə] n dilema m.
diligent [ˈdɪlɪdʒənt] a diligente.
dilute [daɪˈluːt] vt diluir.
dim [dɪm] a (light) débil; (sight) turbio; (outline) indistinto; (stupid) lerdo; (room) oscuro // vt (light) bajar.
dime [daɪm] n (US) moneda de diez centavos.
dimension [dɪˈmɛnʃən] n dimensión f.
diminish [dɪˈmɪnɪʃ] vt, vi disminuir.
diminutive [dɪˈmɪnjutɪv] a diminuto // n (LING) diminutivo.
dimly [ˈdɪmlɪ] ad débilmente; (not clearly) indistintamente.
dimmer [ˈdɪmə*] n (US AUT) interruptor m.
dimple [ˈdɪmpl] n hoyuelo.
din [dɪn] n estruendo, estrépito.
dine [daɪn] vi cenar; **~r** n (person) comensal m/f; (Brit RAIL) = **dining car**; (US) restaurante m económico.
dinghy [ˈdɪŋgɪ] n bote m; (also: **rubber ~**) lancha (neumática.)
dingy [ˈdɪndʒɪ] a (room) sombrío; (dirty) sucio; (dull) deslucido.
dining [ˈdaɪnɪŋ]: **~ car** n (Brit RAIL) coche-comedor m; **~ room** n comedor m.
dinner [ˈdɪnə*] n (evening meal) cena; (lunch) comida; (public) cena, banquete m; **~'s ready!** ¡la cena está servida!; **~ jacket** n smoking m; **~ party** n cena; **~ time** n hora de cenar or comer.

dinosaur ['daɪnəsɔ:*] n dinosaurio.

dint [dɪnt] n: **by ~ of** a fuerza de.

diocese ['daɪəsɪs] n diócesis f inv.

dip [dɪp] n (slope) pendiente m; (in sea) baño // vt (in water) mojar; (ladle etc) meter; (Brit AUT): **to ~ one's lights** poner luces de cruce // vi inclinarse hacia abajo.

diphthong ['dɪfθɒŋ] n diptongo.

diploma [dɪ'pləumə] n diploma m.

diplomacy [dɪ'pləuməsɪ] n diplomacia.

diplomat ['dɪpləmæt] n diplomático/ a; **~ic** [dɪplə'mætɪk] a diplomático.

dipstick ['dɪpstɪk] n (AUT) varilla de nivel (del aceite).

dipswitch ['dɪpswɪtʃ] n (Brit AUT) interruptor m.

dire [daɪə*] a calamitoso.

direct [daɪ'rɛkt] a (gen) directo // vt dirigir; **can you ~ me to...?** ¿puede indicarme dónde está...?

direction [dɪ'rɛkʃən] n dirección f; sense of ~ sentido de la dirección; ~s npl (advice) órdenes fpl, instrucciones fpl; ~s for use modo de empleo.

directly [dɪ'rɛktlɪ] ad (in straight line) directamente; (at once) en seguida.

director [dɪ'rɛktə*] n director(a) m/f.

directory [dɪ'rɛktərɪ] n (TEL) guía (telefónica).

dirt [dɜ:t] n suciedad f; **~-cheap** a baratísimo; **~y** a sucio; (joke) verde, colorado (LAm) // vt ensuciar; (stain) manchar; **~y trick** n juego sucio.

disability [dɪsə'bɪlɪtɪ] n incapacidad f.

disabled [dɪs'eɪbld] a minusválido.

disadvantage [dɪsəd'vɑ:ntɪdʒ] n desventaja, inconveniente m.

disaffection [dɪsə'fɛkʃən] n desafecto.

disagree [dɪsə'gri:] vi (differ) discrepar; **to ~ (with)** no estar de acuerdo (con); **~able** a desagradable; **~ment** n (gen) desacuerdo; (quar-

rel) riña.

disallow ['dɪsə'lau] vt (goal) anular; (claim) rechazar.

disappear [dɪsə'pɪə*] vi desaparecer; **~ance** n desaparición f.

disappoint [dɪsə'pɔɪnt] vt decepcionar; (hopes) defraudar; **~ed** a decepcionado; **~ing** a decepcionante; **~ment** n decepción f.

disapproval [dɪsə'pru:vəl] n desaprobación f.

disapprove [dɪsə'pru:v] vi: **to ~ of** desaprobar.

disarm [dɪs'ɑ:m] vt desarmar; **~ament** n desarme m.

disarray [dɪsə'reɪ] n: **in ~** (army, organization) desorganizado; (hair, clothes) desarreglado.

disaster [dɪ'zɑ:stə*] n desastre m.

disband [dɪs'bænd] vt disolver // vi desbandarse.

disbelief [dɪsbə'li:f] n incredulidad f.

disc [dɪsk] n disco; (COMPUT) = **disk**.

discard [dɪs'kɑ:d] vt (old things) tirar; (fig) descartar.

discern [dɪ'sə:n] vt percibir, discernir; (understand) comprender; **~ing** a perspicaz.

discharge [dɪs'tʃɑ:dʒ] vt (task, duty) cumplir; (ship etc) descargar; (patient) dar de alta; (employee) despedir; (soldier) licenciar; (defendant) poner en libertad // n ['dɪstʃɑ:dʒ] (ELEC) descarga; (dismissal) despedida; (of duty) desempeño; (of debt) pago, descargo.

disciple [dɪ'saɪpl] n discípulo.

discipline ['dɪsɪplɪn] n disciplina // vt disciplinar.

disc jockey n pinchadiscos m/f inv.

disclaim [dɪs'kleɪm] vt negar.

disclose [dɪs'kləuz] vt revelar; **disclosure** [-'kləuʒə*] n revelación f.

disco ['dɪskəu] n abbr = **discothèque**.

discoloured, (US) **discolored** [dɪs'kʌləd] a descolorado.

discomfort [dɪs'kʌmfət] n incomodidad f; (unease) inquietud f; (physi-

cal) malestar *m*.

disconcert [dɪskən'səːt] *vt* desconcertar.

disconnect [dɪskə'nekt] *vt (gen)* separar; *(ELEC etc)* desconectar; *(supply)* cortar (el suministro) a.

discontent [dɪskən'tent] *n* descontento; **~ed** *a* descontento.

discontinue [dɪskən'tɪnjuː] *vt* interrumpir; *(payments)* suspender.

discord ['dɪskɔːd] *n* discordia; *(MUS)* disonancia; **~ant** [dɪs'kɔːdənt] *a* disonante.

discothèque ['dɪskəutek] *n* discoteca.

discount ['dɪskaunt] *n* descuento // *vt* [dɪs'kaunt] descontar.

discourage [dɪs'kʌrɪdʒ] *vt* desalentar; *(oppose)* oponerse a; **discouraging** *a* desalentador(a).

discover [dɪs'kʌvə*] *vt* descubrir; **~y** *n* descubrimiento.

discredit [dɪs'kredɪt] *vt* desacreditar.

discreet [dɪ'skriːt] *a (tactful)* discreto; *(careful)* circunspecto, prudente.

discrepancy [dɪ'skrepənsɪ] *n* diferencia.

discretion [dɪ'skreʃən] *n (tact)* discreción *f*; *(care)* prudencia, circunspección *f*.

discriminate [dɪ'skrɪmɪneɪt] *vi*: to **~ between** distinguir entre; to **~ against** discriminar contra; **discriminating** *a* entendido; **discrimination** [-'neɪʃən] *n (discernment)* perspicacia; *(bias)* discriminación *f*.

discuss [dɪs'kʌs] *vt (gen)* discutir; *(a theme)* tratar; **~ion** [dɪs'kʌʃən] *n* discusión *f*.

disdain [dɪs'deɪn] *n* desdén *m* // *vt* desdeñar.

disease [dɪ'ziːz] *n* enfermedad *f*.

disembark [dɪsɪm'baːk] *vt, vi* desembarcar.

disenchanted [dɪsɪn'tʃaːntɪd] *a:* ~ *(with)* desilusionado *(con)*.

disengage [dɪsɪn'geɪdʒ] *vt* soltar; to ~ **the clutch** *(AUT)* desembragar.

disentangle [dɪsɪn'tæŋgl] *vt* desenredar.

disfigure [dɪs'fɪgə*] *vt* desfigurar.

disgrace [dɪs'greɪs] *n* ignominia; *(shame)* vergüenza, escándalo // *vt* deshonrar; **~ful** *a* vergonzoso; *(behaviour)* escandaloso.

disgruntled [dɪs'grʌntld] *a* disgustado, descontento.

disguise [dɪs'gaɪz] *n* disfraz *m* // *vt* disfrazar; **in** ~ disfrazado.

disgust [dɪs'gʌst] *n* repugnancia // *vt* repugnar, dar asco a; **~ing** *a* repugnante, asqueroso.

dish [dɪʃ] *n (gen)* plato; to **do** or **wash the ~es** fregar los platos; to ~ **up** *vt* servir; to ~ **out** *vt* repartir; **~cloth** *n* paño de cocina, bayeta.

dishearten [dɪs'haːtn] *vt* desalentar.

dishevelled [dɪ'ʃevəld] *a (hair)* despeinado; *(clothes, appearance)* desarreglado.

dishonest [dɪs'ɔnɪst] *a (person)* poco honrado, tramposo; *(means)* fraudulento; **~y** *n* falta de honradez.

dishonour, *(US)* **dishonor** [dɪs'ɔnə*] *n* deshonra; **~able** *a* deshonroso.

dishtowel ['dɪʃtauəl] *n (US)* trapo de fregar.

dishwasher ['dɪʃwɔʃə*] *n* lavaplatos *m inv; (person)* friegaplatos *m/f inv*.

disillusion [dɪsɪ'luːʒən] *vt* desilusionar.

disincentive [dɪsɪn'sentɪv] *n* desincentivo.

disinfect [dɪsɪn'fekt] *vt* desinfectar; **~ant** *n* desinfectante *m*.

disintegrate [dɪs'ɪntɪgreɪt] *vi* disgregarse, desintegrarse.

disinterested [dɪs'ɪntrəstɪd] *a* desinteresado.

disjointed [dɪs'dʒɔɪntɪd] *a* inconexo.

disk [dɪsk] *n (esp US)* = **disc**; *(COMPUT)* disco, disquete *m*; **single-/double-sided** ~ disco de una cara/dos caras; ~ **drive** *n* drive *m*; **~ette** *n (US)* = **disk**.

dislike [dɪs'laɪk] *n* antipatía, aversión *f* // *vt* tener antipatía a.

dislocate ['dɪsləkeɪt] *vt* dislocar.

dislodge [dɪs'lɔdʒ] vt sacar; (enemy) desalojar.

disloyal [dɪs'lɔɪəl] a desleal.

dismal ['dɪzml] a (gloomy) deprimente, triste.

dismantle [dɪs'mæntl] vt desmontar, desarmar.

dismay [dɪs'meɪ] n consternación f.

dismiss [dɪs'mɪs] vt (worker) despedir; (official) destituir; (idea, LAW) rechazar; (possibility) descartar // vi (MIL) romper filas; **~al** n despedida; destitución f.

dismount [dɪs'maunt] vi apearse.

disobedience [dɪsə'biːdɪəns] n desobediencia.

disobedient [dɪsə'biːdɪənt] a desobediente.

disobey [dɪsə'beɪ] vt desobedecer.

disorder [dɪs'ɔːdə*] n desorden m; (rioting) disturbio; (MED) trastorno; (disease) enfermedad f; **~ly** a (untidy) desordenado; (meeting) alborotado; (conduct) escandaloso.

disorientated [dɪs'ɔːrɪenteɪtəd] a desorientado.

disown [dɪs'əun] vt desconocer.

disparaging [dɪs'pærɪdʒɪŋ] a despreciativo.

disparity [dɪs'pærɪtɪ] n disparidad f.

dispassionate [dɪs'pæʃənɪt] a (unbiased) imparcial; (unemotional) desapasionada.

dispatch [dɪs'pætʃ] vt enviar // n (sending) envío; (PRESS) informe m; (MIL) parte m.

dispel [dɪs'pel] vt disipar, dispersar.

dispensary [dɪs'pensərɪ] n dispensario, farmacia.

dispense [dɪs'pens] vt dispensar, repartir; **to ~ with** vt fus prescindir de; **~r** n (container) distribuidor m automático; **dispensing chemist** n (Brit) farmacia.

dispersal [dɪs'pɜːsl] n dispersión f.

disperse [dɪs'pɜːs] vt dispersar // vi dispersarse.

dispirited [dɪ'spɪrɪtɪd] a desanimado, desalentado.

displace [dɪs'pleɪs] vt (person) des-

plazar; (replace) reemplazar; **~d person** n desplazado/a.

display [dɪs'pleɪ] n (exhibition) exposición f; (COMPUT) visualización f; (MIL) exhibición f; (of feeling) manifestación f; (pej) aparato, pompa // vt exponer; manifestar; (ostentatiously) lucir.

displease [dɪs'pliːz] vt (offend) ofender; (annoy) fastidiar; **~d with** disgustado con; **displeasure** [-'pleʒə*] n disgusto.

disposable [dɪs'pəuzəbl] a (not reusable) desechable; (income) disponible; **~ nappy** n pañal m desechable.

disposal [dɪs'pəuzl] n (sale) venta; (of house) traspaso; (arrangement) colocación f; (of rubbish) destrucción f; **at one's ~** a su disposición.

dispose [dɪs'pəuz] vt disponer; **to ~ of** vt (time, money) disponer de; (unwanted goods) deshacerse de; (throw away) tirar; **~d a: ~d to do** dispuesto a hacer; **disposition** [-'zɪʃən] n disposición f.

disproportionate [dɪsprə'pɔːʃənət] a desproporcionado.

disprove [dɪs'pruːv] vt refutar.

dispute [dɪs'pjuːt] n (also: **industrial ~**) disputa; (verbal) discusión f; (also: **industrial ~**) conflicto (laboral) // vt (argue) disputar; (question) cuestionar.

disqualify [dɪs'kwɔlɪfaɪ] vt (SPORT) descalificar; **to ~ sb for sth/from doing sth** incapacitar a alguien para algo/hacer algo.

disquiet [dɪs'kwaɪət] n preocupación f, inquietud f.

disregard [dɪsrɪ'gɑːd] vt desatender; (ignore) no hacer caso de.

disrepair [dɪsrɪ'pɛə*] n: **to fall into ~** desmoronarse.

disreputable [dɪs'repjutəbl] a (person) de mala fama; (behaviour) vergonzoso.

disrespectful [dɪsrɪ'spektful] a irrespetuoso.

disrupt [dɪs'rʌpt] vt (plans) desbaratar, trastornar; (conversation) interrumpir; **~ion** [-'rʌpʃən] n trastorno; desbaratamiento; interrupción f.

dissatisfaction [dɪssætɪs'fækʃən] n disgusto, descontento.

dissect [dɪ'sɛkt] vt disecar.

disseminate [dɪ'sɛmɪneɪt] vt divulgar, difundir.

dissent [dɪ'sɛnt] n disensión f.

dissertation [dɪsə'teɪʃən] n tesina.

disservice [dɪs'sɜːvɪs] n: to do sb a ~ perjudicar a alguien.

dissident ['dɪsɪdnt] a, n disidente m/f.

dissimilar [dɪ'sɪmɪlə*] a distinto.

dissipate ['dɪsɪpeɪt] vt disipar; (waste) desperdiciar.

dissociate [dɪ'səʊʃɪeɪt] vt disociar.

dissolute ['dɪsəluːt] a disoluto.

dissolution [dɪsə'luːʃən] n (of organization, marriage, POL) disolución f.

dissolve [dɪ'zɒlv] vt disolver // vi disolverse.

dissuade [dɪ'sweɪd] vt: to ~ sb (from) disuadir a uno (de).

distance ['dɪstns] n distancia; **in the** ~ a lo lejos.

distant ['dɪstnt] a lejano; (manner) reservado, frío.

distaste [dɪs'teɪst] n repugnancia; **~ful** a repugnante, desagradable.

distended [dɪs'tɛndɪd] a (stomach) hinchado.

distil [dɪs'tɪl] vt destilar; **~lery** n destilería.

distinct [dɪs'tɪŋkt] a (different) distinto; (clear) claro; (unmistakeable) inequívoco; **as ~ from** a diferencia de; **~ion** [dɪs'tɪŋkʃən] n distinción f; (in exam) sobresaliente m; **~ive** a distintivo.

distinguish [dɪs'tɪŋgwɪʃ] vt distinguir; **~ed** a (eminent) distinguido; **~ing** (a feature) distintivo.

distort [dɪs'tɔːt] vt torcer, retorcer; **~ion** [dɪs'tɔːʃən] n deformación f; (of sound) distorsión f.

distract [dɪs'trækt] vt distraer; **~ed** a distraído; **~ion** [dɪs'trækʃən] n distracción f; (confusion) aturdimiento.

distraught [dɪs'trɔːt] a turbado, enloquecido.

distress [dɪs'trɛs] n (anguish) angustia; (pain) dolor m // vt afligir; (pain) doler; **~ing** a angustioso; doloroso; **~ signal** n señal f de socorro.

distribute [dɪs'trɪbjuːt] vt (gen) distribuir; (share out) repartir; **distribution** [-'bjuːʃən] n distribución f; **distributor** n (AUT) distribuidor m; (COMM) distribuidora.

district ['dɪstrɪkt] n (of country) zona, región f; (of town) barrio; (ADMIN) distrito; **~ attorney** n (US) fiscal m/f; **~ nurse** n (Brit) enfermera que atiende a pacientes a domicilio.

distrust [dɪs'trʌst] n desconfianza // vt desconfiar de.

disturb [dɪs'tɜːb] vt (person: bother, interrupt) molestar; (meeting) interrumpir; **~ance** n (political etc) disturbio; (of violence) alboroto; **~ed** a (worried, upset) preocupado, angustiado; **emotionally ~ed** trastornado; **~ing** a inquietante, perturbador(a).

disuse [dɪs'juːs] n: to fall into ~ caer en desuso.

disused [dɪs'juːzd] a abandonado.

ditch [dɪtʃ] n zanja; (irrigation ~) acequia // vt (col) deshacerse de.

dither ['dɪðə*] vi vacilar.

ditto ['dɪtəʊ] ad idem, lo mismo.

dive [daɪv] n (from board) salto; (underwater) buceo; (of submarine) sumersión f; (AVIAT) picada // vi saltar; bucear; sumergirse; picar; **~r** n (SPORT) saltador(a) m/f; (underwater) buzo.

diverge [daɪ'vɜːdʒ] vi divergir.

diverse [daɪ'vɜːs] a diversos/as, varios/as.

diversion [daɪ'vɜːʃən] n (Brit AUT) desviación f; (distraction, MIL) diversión f.

divert [daɪ'vɜːt] vt (turn aside) desviar.

divide [dɪ'vaɪd] vt dividir; (separate) separar // vi dividirse; (road) bifurcarse; **~d highway** n (US) carretera de doble calzada.

dividend ['dɪvɪdɛnd] n dividendo; (fig) beneficio.

divine [dɪ'vaɪn] a divino.

diving ['daɪvɪŋ] n (SPORT) salto; (underwater) buceo; **~ board** n trampolín m.

divinity [dɪ'vɪnɪtɪ] n divinidad f; (SCOL) teología.

division [dɪ'vɪʒən] n división f; (sharing out) repartimiento.

divorce [dɪ'vɔːs] n divorcio // vt divorciarse de; **~d** a divorciado; **~e** [-'siː] n divorciado/a.

divulge [daɪ'vʌldʒ] vt divulgar, revelar.

D.I.Y. a, n abbr (Brit) = **do-it-yourself**.

dizziness ['dɪzɪnɪs] n vértigo.

dizzy ['dɪzɪ] a (person) mareado; (height) vertiginoso; **to feel ~** marearse.

DJ n abbr = **disc jockey**.

KEYWORD

do [duː] ♦ n (col: party etc): we're having a little **~** on Saturday damos una fiestecita el sábado; it was **rather a grand ~** fue un acontecimiento a lo grande

♦ auxiliary vb (pt did, pp done) **1** (in negative constructions) not translated: **I don't understand** no entiendo

2 (to form questions) not translated: **didn't you know?** ¿no lo sabías?; **what ~ you think?** ¿qué opinas?

3 (for emphasis, in polite expressions): **people ~ make mistakes sometimes** sí que se cometen errores a veces; **she does seem rather late** a mí también me parece que se ha retrasado; **~ sit down/help yourself** siéntate/sírvete por favor; **~ take care!** ten cuidado, te pido

4 (used to avoid repeating vb): **she sings better than I ~** canta mejor que yo; **~ you agree? — yes, I ~/no, I don't** ¿estás de acuerdo? — sí

(lo estoy)/no (lo estoy); **she lives in Glasgow — so ~ I** vive en Glasgow — yo también; **he didn't like it and neither did we** no le gustó a nosotros tampoco; **who made this mess? — I did** ¿quién hizo esta chapuza? — yo; **he asked me to help him and I did** me pidió qué le ayudara y lo hice

5 (in question tags): **you like him, don't you?** te gusta, ¿verdad? or ¿no?; **I don't know him, ~ I?** creo que no le conozco

♦ vt **1** (gen, carry out, perform etc): **what are you ~ing tonight?** ¿qué haces esta noche?; **what can I ~ for you?** ¿en qué puedo servirle?; **to ~ the washing-up/cooking** fregar los platos/cocinar; **to ~ one's teeth/hair/nails** lavarse los dientes/arreglarse el pelo/arreglarse las uñas

2 (AUT etc): **the car was ~ing 100** el coche iba a 100; **we've done 200 km already** ya hemos hecho 200 km; **he can ~ 100 in that car** puede dar los 100 en ese coche

♦ vi **1** (act, behave) hacer; **~ as I ~** haz como yo

2 (get on, fare): **he's ~ing well/badly at school** va bien/mal en la escuela; **the firm is ~ing well** la empresa anda or va bien; **how ~ you ~?** mucho gusto; (less formal) ¿qué tal?

3 (suit): **will it ~?** ¿sirve?, ¿está or va bien?

4 (be sufficient) bastar; **will £10 ~?** ¿será bastante con £10?; **that'll ~** así está bien; **that'll ~!** (in annoyance) ¡ya está bien!, ¡basta ya!; **to make ~ (with)** arreglárselas (con); **to ~ away with** vt fus (kill, disease) eliminar; (abolish: law etc) abolir; (withdraw) retirar

to ~ up vt (laces) atar; (zip, dress, shirt) abrochar; (renovate: room, house) renovar

to ~ with vt fus (need): **I could ~ with a drink/some help** no me vendría mal un trago/un poco de ayuda; (*be connected*): tener que ver con; **what has it got to ~ with you?** ¿qué tiene que ver contigo? **to do without** *vi* pasar sin; **if you're late for tea then you'll ~ without** si llegas tarde para la merienda pasarás sin él ♦ *vt fus* pasar sin; **I can ~ without a car** puedo pasar sin coche.

dock [dɔk] *n* (NAUT) muelle *m*; (LAW) banquillo (de los acusados); ~**s** *npl* muelles *mpl*, puerto *sg // vi* (*enter* ~) atracar el muelle; ~**er** *n* trabajador *m* portuario, estibador *m*; ~**yard** *n* astillero.

doctor ['dɔktə*] *n* médico/a; (Ph.D. etc) doctor(a) *m/f // vt* (fig) arreglar, falsificar; (drink etc) adulterar; **D~ of Philosophy (Ph.D.)** *n* Doctor en Filosofía y Letras.

doctrine ['dɔktrɪn] *n* doctrina.

document ['dɔkjumənt] *n* documento; ~**ary** [-'mɛntərɪ] *a* documental // *n* documental *m*.

dodge [dɔdʒ] *n* (of body) regate *m*; (fig) truco *m* // vt (gen) evadir; (blow) esquivar.

dodgems ['dɔdʒəmz] *npl* (Brit) coches *mpl* de choque.

doe [dəu] *n* (deer) cierva, gama; (rabbit) coneja.

does [dʌz] *vb see* **do**; ~**n't** = **does not**.

dog [dɔg] *n* perro *m* // vt seguir los pasos de; ~ **collar** *n* collar *m* de perro; (fig) cuello del cura; ~**eared** *a* sobado.

dogged ['dɔgɪd] *a* tenaz, obstinado.

dogsbody ['dɔgzbɔdɪ] *n* (Brit) burro de carga.

doings ['duɪŋz] *npl* (events) sucesos *mpl*; (acts) hechos *mpl*.

do-it-yourself [du:ɪtjɔ:'sɛlf] *n* bricolaje *m*.

doldrums ['dɔldrəmz] *npl*: **to be in the ~** (person) estar abatido; (business) estar encalmado.

dole [dəul] *n* (Brit: payment) subsi-

dio de paro; **on the ~** parado; **to ~ out** *vt* repartir.

doleful ['dəulful] *a* triste, lúgubre.

doll [dɔl] *n* muñeca; **to ~ o.s. up** ataviarse.

dollar ['dɔlə*] *n* dólar *m*.

dolphin ['dɔlfɪn] *n* delfín *m*.

domain [də'meɪn] *n* (fig) campo, competencia; (land) dominios *mpl*.

dome [dəum] *n* (ARCH) cúpula; (shape) bóveda.

domestic [də'mɛstɪk] *a* (animal, duty) doméstico; (flight, policy) nacional; ~**ated** *a* domesticado; (home-loving) casero, hogareño.

dominant ['dɔmɪnənt] *a* dominante.

dominate ['dɔmɪneɪt] *vt* dominar.

domineering [dɔmɪ'nɪərɪŋ] *a* dominante.

dominion [də'mɪnɪən] *n* dominio.

domino ['dɔmɪnəu], *pl* ~**es** *n* ficha de dominó; ~**es** *n* (game) dominó.

don [dɔn] *n* (Brit) profesor(a) *m/f* universitario/a.

donate [də'neɪt] *vt* donar; **donation** [də'neɪʃən] *n* donativo.

done [dʌn] *pp* of **do**.

donkey ['dɔŋkɪ] *n* burro.

donor ['dəunə*] *n* donante *m/f*.

don't [dəunt] = **do not**.

doodle ['du:dl] *vi* hacer dibujos *or* garabatos.

doom [du:m] *n* (fate) suerte *f*; (death) muerte *f* // vt: **to be ~ed to failure** ser condenado al fracaso; ~**sday** *n* día *m* del juicio final.

door [dɔ:*] *n* puerta; (entry) entrada; ~**bell** *n* timbre *m*; ~**handle** *n* tirador *m*; (of car) manija; ~**man** *n* (in hotel) portero; ~**step** *n* peldaño; ~**way** *n* entrada, puerta.

dope [dəup] *n* (col: person) imbécil *m/f* // vt (horse etc) drogar.

dopey ['dəupɪ] *a* atontado.

dormant ['dɔ:mənt] *a* inactivo; (latent) latente.

dormitory ['dɔ:mɪtrɪ] *n* (Brit) dormitorio; (US) colegio mayor.

dormouse ['dɔ:maus], *pl* ~**mice**

[-maɪs] n lirón m.

DOS n abbr (= disk operating system) DOS m.

dosage ['dəʊsɪdʒ] n dosis f inv.

dose [dəʊs] n dósis f inv.

doss house ['dɒs-] n (Brit) pensión f de mala muerte.

dossier ['dɒsɪeɪ] n expediente m.

dot [dɒt] n punto; ~ted with salpicado de; **on the** ~ en punto.

dote [dəʊt]: **to** ~ **on** vt fus adorar, idolatrar.

dot matrix printer n impresora matricial (or de matriz) de puntos.

double ['dʌbl] a doble // ad (twice): **to cost** ~ costar el doble // n (gen) doble m // vt doblar; (efforts) redoblar // vi doblarse; **on the** ~, (Brit) **at the** ~ corriendo; ~**s** n (TENNIS) juego de dobles; ~ **bass** n contrabajo; ~ **bed** n cama matrimonial; ~-**breasted** a cruzado; ~**cross** vt (trick) engañar; (betray) traicionar; ~**decker** n autobús m de dos pisos; ~ **glazing** n (Brit) doble acristalamiento; ~ **room** n cuarto para dos; **doubly** ad doblemente.

doubt [daʊt] n duda // vt dudar; (suspect) dudar de; **to** ~ **that** dudar que; **there is no** ~ **that** no cabe duda de que; ~**ful** a dudoso; (person): **to be** ~**ful about** sth tener dudas sobre algo; ~**less** ad sin duda.

dough [dəʊ] n masa, pasta; ~**nut** n buñuelo.

douse [daʊs] vt (drench) mojar; (extinguish) apagar.

dove [dʌv] n paloma.

dovetail ['dʌvteɪl] vi (fig) encajar.

dowdy ['daʊdɪ] a (person) mal vestido; (clothes) pasado de moda.

down [daʊn] n (fluff) pelusa; (feathers) plumón m, flojel m // ad (~wards) abajo, hacia abajo; (on the ground) por/en tierra // prep abajo // vt (col: drink) beberse; ~ **with** X! abajo X!; ~ **under** (Australia etc) Australia, Nueva Zelanda; ~-**and-out** n vagabundo/a; ~-**at-**

heel a venido a menos; (appearance) desaliñado; ~**cast** a abatido; ~**fall** n caída, ruina; ~-**hearted** a desanimado; ~**hill** ad: **to go** ~**hill** ir cuesta abajo; ~ **payment** n entrada, pago al contado; ~**pour** n aguacero; ~**right** a (nonsense, lie) manifiesto; (refusal) terminante; ~**stairs** ad (below) (en la casa de) abajo; (~wards) escaleras abajo; ~**stream** ad aguas or río abajo; ~-**to-earth** a práctico; ~**town** ad en el centro de la ciudad; ~**ward** a, ad [-wəd], ~**wards** [-wədz] ad hacia abajo.

doz. abbr = **dozen.**

doze [dəʊz] vi dormitar; **to** ~ **off** vi quedarse medio dormido.

dozen ['dʌzn] n docena; **a** ~ **books** una docena de libros; ~**s of** cantidad de.

Dr. abbr = **doctor; drive.**

drab [dræb] a gris, monótono.

draft [drɑːft] n (first copy) borrador m; (COMM) giro; (US: call-up) quinta // vt (write roughly) hacer un borrador de; see also **draught.**

draftsman ['drɑːftsmən] n (US) = **draughtsman.**

drag [dræg] vt arrastrar; (river) dragar, rastrear // vi arrastrarse por el suelo // n (col) lata; (women's clothing): **in** ~ vestido de travesti; **to** ~ **on** vi ser interminable.

dragon ['drægən] n dragón m.

dragonfly ['drægənflaɪ] n libélula.

drain [dreɪn] n desaguadero; (in street) sumidero // vt (land, marshes) desaguar; (MED) drenar; (reservoir) desecar; (fig) agotar // vi escurrirse; **to be a** ~ **on** agotar; ~**age** n (act) desagüe m; (MED, AGR) drenaje m; (sewage) alcantarillado; ~**ing board**, (US) ~**board** n escurridera, escurridor m; ~**pipe** n tubo de desagüe.

dram [dræm] n (drink) traguito, copita.

drama ['drɑːmə] n (art) teatro;

(*play*) drama *m*; ~**tic** [drə'mætɪk] *a* dramático; ~**tist** ['dræmətɪst] *n* dramaturgo/a; ~**tize** [dræmətaɪz] *vt* (*events*) dramatizar; (*adapt: for TV, cinema*) adaptar a la televisión/al cine.

drank [dræŋk] *pt of* **drink**.

drape [dreɪp] *vt* cubrir; ~**s** *npl* (*US*) cortinas *fpl*; ~**r** *n* (*Brit*) pañero/a.

drastic ['dræstɪk] *a* (*measure, reduction*) severo; (*change*) radical.

draught, (*US*) **draft** [drɑ:ft] *n* (*of air*) corriente *f* de aire; (*drink*) trago; (*NAUT*) calado; ~**s** *n* (*Brit*) juego de damas; **on** ~ (*beer*) de barril; ~**board** (*Brit*) *n* tablero de damas.

draughtsman ['drɑ:ftsmən] *n* delineante *m*.

draw [drɔ:] *vb* (*pt* **drew**, *pp* **drawn**) *vt* (*pull*) tirar; (*take out*) sacar; (*attract*) atraer; (*picture*) dibujar; (*money*) retirar // *vi* (*SPORT*) empatar // *n* (*SPORT*) empate *m*; (*lottery*) sorteo; (*attraction*) atracción *f*; **to** ~ **near** *vi* acercarse; **to** ~ **out** *vi* (*lengthen*) alargarse; **to** ~ **up** *vi* (*stop*) pararse // *vt* (*document*) redactar; ~**back** *n* inconveniente *m*, desventaja; ~**bridge** *n* puente *m* levadizo.

drawer [drɔ:*] *n* cajón *m*; (*of cheque*) librador/a *m/f*.

drawing ['drɔ:ɪŋ] *n* dibujo; ~ **board** *n* tablero de (dibujante); ~ **pin** *n* (*Brit*) chinche *m*; ~ **room** *n* salón *m*.

drawl [drɔ:l] *n* habla lenta y cansina.

drawn [drɔ:n] *pp of* **draw**.

dread [dred] *n* pavor *m*, terror *m* // *vt* temer, tener miedo or pavor a; ~**ful** *a* espantoso.

dream [dri:m] *n* sueño // *vb*, *vi* (*pt*, *pp* **dreamed** or **dreamt** [dremt]) soñar; ~**er** *n* soñador/a *m/f*; ~**y** *a* (*distracted*) soñador/a, distraído.

dreary ['drɪərɪ] *a* monótono.

dredge [dredʒ] *vt* dragar.

dregs [dregz] *npl* heces *fpl*.

drench [drentʃ] *vt* empapar.

dress [dres] *n* vestido; (*clothing*)

ropa // *vt* vestir; (*wound*) vendar; (*CULIN*) aliñar // *vi* vestirse; **to** ~ **up** *vi* vestirse de etiqueta; (*in fancy dress*) disfrazarse; ~ **circle** *n* (*Brit*) principal *m*; ~**er** *n* (*furniture*) aparador *m*; (: *US*) cómoda con espejo (*THEAT*) camarero/a; ~**ing** *n* (*MED*) vendaje *m*; (*CULIN*) aliño; ~**ing gown** *n* (*Brit*) bata; ~**ing room** *n* (*THEATRE*) camarín *m*; (*SPORT*) vestidor *m*; ~**ing table** *n* tocador *m*; ~**maker** *n* modista, costurera; ~ **rehearsal** *n* ensayo general; ~ **shirt** *n* camisa de frac; ~**y** *a* (*col*) elegante.

drew [dru:] *pt of* **draw**.

dribble ['drɪbl] *vi* gotear, caer gota a gota; (*baby*) babear // *vt* (*ball*) regatear.

dried [draɪd] *a* (*gen*) seco; (*fruit*) paso; (*milk*) en polvo.

drier ['draɪə*] *n* = **dryer**.

drift [drɪft] *n* (*of current etc*) velocidad *f*; (*of sand*) montón *m*; (*of snow*) ventisquero; (*meaning*) significado // *vi* (*boat*) ir a la deriva; (*sand, snow*) amontonarse; ~**wood** *n* madera de deriva.

drill [drɪl] *n* taladro; (*bit*) broca; (*of dentist*) fresa; (*for mining etc*) perforadora, barrena; (*MIL*) instrucción *f* // *vt* perforar, taladrar // *vi* (*for oil*) perforar.

drink [drɪŋk] *n* bebida // *vt*, *vi* (*pt* **drank**, *pp* **drunk**) beber; **to have a** ~ tomar algo; tomar una copa or un trago; **a** ~ **of water** un trago de agua; ~**er** *n* bebedor/a *m/f*; ~**ing water** *n* agua potable.

drip [drɪp] *n* (*act*) goteo; (*one* ~) gota; (*MED*) gota a gota *m* // *vi* gotear, caer gota a gota; ~**dry** *a* (*shirt*) de lava y pon; ~**ping** *n* (*animal fat*) pringue *m*.

drive [draɪv] *n* paseo (en coche); (*journey*) viaje *m* (en coche); (*also:* ~**way**) entrada; (*energy*) energía, vigor *m*; (*PSYCH*) impulso; (*SPORT*) ataque *m*; (*COMPUT: also:* **disk** ~) drive *m* // *vb* (*pt* **drove**, *pp* **driven**) *vt* (*car*) conducir, manejar (*LAm*); (*nail*) clavar; (*push*) empujar; (*TECH: motor*) impulsar // *vi* (*AUT: at controls*) conducir; (*: travel*) pasearse en coche; **left/right-hand** ~ conducción *f* a la izquierda/derecha; **to** ~ **sb mad** volverle loco a uno.

drivel ['drɪvl] *n* (*col*) tonterías *fpl*.

driven ['drɪvn] *pp* of **drive**.

driver ['draɪvə*] *n* conductor(a) *m/f*, chofer *m* (*LAm*); (*of taxi, bus*) chofer; ~'**s license** *n* (*US*) carnet *m* de conducir.

driveway ['draɪvweɪ] *n* entrada.

driving ['draɪvɪŋ] *n* el conducir, el manejar (*LAm*); ~ **instructor** *n* instructor(a) *m/f* de conducción or manejo (*LAm*); ~ **lesson** *n* clase *f* de conducción or manejo (*LAm*); ~ **licence** *n* (*Brit*) permiso de conducir; ~ **mirror** *n* retrovisor *m*; ~ **school** *n* autoescuela; ~ **test** *n* examen *m* de conducción or manejo (*LAm*).

drizzle ['drɪzl] *n* llovizna // *vi* lloviznar.

droll [drəʊl] *a* gracioso.

drone [drəʊn] *n* (*noise*) zumbido.

drool [druːl] *vi* babear; **to** ~ **over sth** extasiarse ante algo.

droop [druːp] *vi* (*fig*) decaer, desanimarse.

drop [drɒp] *n* (*of water*) gota; (*lessening*) baja // *vt* (*allow to fall*) dejar caer; (*voice, eyes, price*) bajar; (*set down from car*) dejar; (*price, temperature*) bajar; (*wind*) amainar; ~**s** *npl* (*MED*) gotas *fpl*; **to** ~ **off** *vi* (*sleep*) dormirse // *vt* (*passenger*) bajar; **to** ~ **out** *vi* (*withdraw*) retirarse; ~**out** *n* marginado/a; ~**per** *n* cuentagotas *m inv*; ~**pings** *npl* excremento *sg*.

drought [draʊt] *n* sequía.

drove [drəʊv] *pt* of **drive**.

drown [draʊn] *vt* ahogar // *vi* ahogarse.

drowsy ['draʊzɪ] *a* soñoliento; **to be** ~ tener sueño.

drudgery ['drʌdʒərɪ] *n* trabajo mo-

nótono.

drug [drʌg] *n* medicamento; (*narcotic*) droga // *vt* drogar; ~ **addict** *n* drogadicto/a; ~**gist** *n* (*US*) farmacéutico; ~**store** *n* (*US*) farmacia.

drum [drʌm] *n* tambor *m*; (*large*) bombo; (*for oil, petrol*) bidón *m*; ~**s** *npl* batería *sg* // *vi* tocar el tambor; (*with fingers*) tamborilear; ~**mer** *n* tambor *m*.

drunk [drʌŋk] *pp* of **drink** // *a* borracho // *n* (*also*: ~**ard**) borracho/a; ~**en** *a* borracho.

dry [draɪ] *a* seco; (*day*) sin lluvia; (*climate*) árido, seco // *vt* secar; (*tears*) enjugarse // *vi* secarse; **to** ~ **up** *vi* agotarse; (*in speech*) atascarse; ~**cleaner's** *n* tintorería; ~**cleaning** *n* lavado en seco; ~**er** *n* (*for hair*) secador *m*; (*for clothes*) secadora; ~ **goods store** *n* (*US*) mercería; ~**ness** *n* sequedad *f*; ~**rot** *n* putrefacción *f* fungoide.

dual ['djuːəl] *a* doble; ~ **carriageway** *n* (*Brit*) carretera de doble calzada; ~**control** *a* de doble mando; ~ **nationality** *n* doble nacionalidad *f*; ~**purpose** *a* de doble uso.

dubbed [dʌbd] *a* (*CINEMA*) doblado.

dubious ['djuːbɪəs] *a* indeciso; (*reputation, company*) sospechoso.

duchess ['dʌtʃɪs] *n* duquesa.

duck [dʌk] *n* pato // *vi* agacharse; ~**ling** *n* patito.

duct [dʌkt] *n* conducto, canal *m*.

dud [dʌd] *n* (*shell*) obús *m* que no estalla; (*object, tool*): **it's a** ~ es una filfa // *a*: ~ **cheque** (*Brit*) cheque *m* sin fondos.

due [djuː] *a* (*proper*) debido; (*fitting*) conveniente, oportuno // *ad*: ~ **north** derecho al norte; ~**s** *npl* (*for club, union*) cuota *sg*; (*in harbour*) derechos *mpl*; **in** ~ **course** a su debido tiempo; ~ **to** debido a; **to be** ~ **to do** deberse a; **the train is** ~ **to arrive at 8.00** el tren debe llegar a las ocho.

duet [djuːˈɛt] *n* dúo.

duffel ['dʌfəl] *a*: ~ **bag** *n* bolsa de

dug [dʌg] *pt, pp of* dig.

duke [djuːk] *n* duque *m*.

dull [dʌl] *a* (*light*) apagado; (*stupid*) torpe; (*boring*) pesado; (*sound, pain*) sordo; (*weather, day*) gris // *vt* (*pain, grief*) aliviar; (*mind, senses*) entorpecer.

duly ['djuːlɪ] *ad* debidamente; (*on time*) a su debido tiempo.

dumb [dʌm] *a* mudo; (*stupid*) estúpido; **~founded** [dʌm'faundɪd] *a* pasmado.

dummy ['dʌmɪ] *n* (*tailor's model*) maniquí *m*; (*Brit: for baby*) chupete *m* // *a* falso, postizo.

dump [dʌmp] *n* (*heap*) montón *m* de basura; (*place*) basurero, vaciadero; (*col*) casucha; (*MIL*) depósito // *vt* (*put down*) dejar; (*get rid of*) deshacerse de; **~ing** *n* (*ECON*) dumping *m*; (*of rubbish*): 'no **~ing**' 'prohibido verter basura'.

dumpling ['dʌmplɪŋ] *n* bola de masa hervida.

dumpy ['dʌmpɪ] *a* regordete/a.

dunce [dʌns] *n* zopenco.

dung [dʌŋ] *n* estiércol *m*.

dungarees [dʌŋgə'riːz] *npl* mono *sg*.

dungeon ['dʌndʒən] *n* calabozo.

duo ['djuːəu] *n* (*gen, MUS*) dúo.

dupe [djuːp] *n* (*victim*) víctima // *vt* engañar.

duplex ['djuːplɛks] *n* dúplex *m*.

duplicate ['djuːplɪkət] *n* duplicado // *vt* ['djuːplɪkeɪt] duplicar; (*on machine*) multicopiar; **in ~** por duplicado.

durable ['djuərəbl] *a* duradero.

duration [djuə'reɪʃən] *n* duración *f*.

duress [djuə'rɛs] *n*: **under ~** por compulsión.

during ['djuərɪŋ] *prep* durante.

dusk [dʌsk] *n* crepúsculo, anochecer *m*.

dust [dʌst] *n* polvo // *vt* (*furniture*) desempolvar; (*cake etc*): **to ~ with** espolvorear de; **~bin** *n* (*Brit*) cubo de la basura, balde *m* (*LAm*);

~er *n* paño, trapo; (*feather ~er*) plumero; **~ jacket** *n* sobrecubierta; **~man** *n* (*Brit*) basurero; **~y** *a* polvoriento.

Dutch [dʌtʃ] *a* holandés/esa // *n* (*LING*) holandés *m*; **the ~** *npl* los holandeses; **to go ~** pagar cada uno lo suyo; **~man/woman** *n* holandés/esa *m/f*.

dutiful ['djuːtɪful] *a* obediente, sumiso.

duty ['djuːtɪ] *n* deber *m*; (*tax*) derechos *mpl* de aduana; **on ~** de servicio; (*at night etc*) de guardia; **off ~** libre (de servicio); **~-free** *a* libre de derechos de aduana.

duvet ['duːveɪ] *n* (*Brit*) edredón *m*.

dwarf [dwɔːf], *pl* **dwarves** [dwɔːvz] *n* enano/a // *vt* empequeñecer.

dwell [dwɛl], *pt, pp* **dwelt** [dwɛlt] *vi* morar; **to ~ on** *vt fus* explayarse en; **~ing** *n* vivienda.

dwindle ['dwɪndl] *vi* menguar, disminuir.

dye [daɪ] *n* tinte *m* // *vt* teñir.

dying ['daɪɪŋ] *a* moribundo, agonizante; (*moments*) final; (*words*) último.

dyke [daɪk] *n* (*Brit*) dique *m*.

dynamic [daɪ'næmɪk] *a* dinámico.

dynamite ['daɪnəmaɪt] *n* dinamita.

dynamo ['daɪnəməu] *n* dinamo *f*.

dynasty ['dɪnəstɪ] *n* dinastía *f*.

E

E [iː] *n* (*MUS*) mi *m*.

each [iːtʃ] *a* cada *inv* // *pron* cada uno; **~ other** el uno al otro; **they hate ~ other** se odian (entre ellos o mutuamente); **they have 2 books ~** tienen 2 libros por persona.

eager ['iːgə*] *a* (*gen*) impaciente; (*hopeful*) ilusionado; (*keen*) entusiasmado; **to be ~ to do sth** tener muchas ganas de hacer algo, impacientarse por hacer algo; **to be ~ for** tener muchas ganasde; (*news*) esperar ansiosamente.

eagle ['iːgl] *n* águila *f*.

ear [ɪə*] n oreja; (sense of hearing) oído; (of corn) espiga; ~**ache** n dolor m de oídos; ~**drum** n tímpano.

earl [əːl] n conde m.

early ['əːlɪ] ad (gen) temprano; (before time) con tiempo, con anticipación // a (gen) temprano; (reply) pronto; to have an ~ **night** acostarse temprano; **in the ~ or ~ in the spring/19th century** a principios de primavera/del siglo diecinueve; ~ **retirement** n jubilación f anticipada.

earmark ['ɪəmɑːk] vt: to ~ (**for**) reservar (para), destinar (a).

earn [əːn] vt (gen) ganar; (salary) percibir; (interest) devengar; (praise) merecerse.

earnest ['əːnɪst] a serio, formal; in ~ ad en serio.

earnings ['əːnɪŋz] npl (personal) sueldo sg, ingresos mpl; (company) ganancias fpl.

ear: ~**phones** npl auriculares mpl; ~**ring** n pendiente m, arete m; ~**shot** n: **within** ~**shot** al alcance del oído.

earth [əːθ] n (gen) tierra; (Brit: ELEC) cable m de toma de tierra // vt (Brit: ELEC) conectar a tierra; ~**enware** n loza (de barro); ~**quake** n terremoto; ~**y** a (fig: uncomplicated) sencillo; (: sensual) sensual.

earwig ['ɪəwɪg] n tijereta.

ease [iːz] n facilidad f; (comfort) comodidad f // vt (task) facilitar; (pain) aliviar; (loosen) soltar; (help pass): **to ~ sth in/out** meter/sacar algo con cuidado; **at ~!** (MIL) ¡descansen!; **to ~ off or up** vi (work, business) aflojar; (person) relajarse.

easel ['iːzl] n caballete m.

easily ['iːzɪlɪ] ad fácilmente; **it is ~ the best** es con mucho el/la mejor.

east [iːst] n este m, oriente m // a del este, oriental // ad al este, hacia el este; **the E~** n el Oriente.

Easter ['iːstə*] n Pascua (de Resurrección); ~ **egg** n huevo de Pas-

cua.

easterly ['iːstəlɪ] a (to the east) al este; (from the east) del este.

eastern ['iːstən] a del este, oriental.

East Germany n Alemania Oriental.

eastward(s) ['iːstwəd(z)] ad hacia el este.

easy ['iːzɪ] a fácil; (problem) sencillo; (comfortable) holgado, cómodo; (relaxed) natural, llano // ad: **to take it or things ~** (not worry) tomarlo con calma; (go slowly) ir despacio; (rest) descansar; ~ **chair** n sillón m; ~-**going** a acomodadizo.

eat [iːt], pt **ate**, pp **eaten** ['iːtn] vt comer; **to ~ into**, **to ~ away at** vt fus corroer; (wear away) desgastar.

eau de Cologne [əudəkə'ləun] n (agua de) Colonia.

eaves [iːvz] npl alero sg.

eavesdrop ['iːvzdrɔp] vi: to ~ (**on a conversation**) escuchar (una conversación) a escondidas.

ebb [eb] n reflujo // vi bajar; (fig: also: ~ **away**) decaer; ~ **tide** n marea menguante.

ebony ['ebənɪ] n ébano.

eccentric [ɪk'sɛntrɪk] a, n excéntrico/a.

echo ['ɛkəu], pl ~**es** n eco m // vt (sound) repetir // vi resonar, hacer eco.

eclipse [ɪ'klɪps] n eclipse m.

ecology [ɪ'kɔlədʒɪ] n ecología.

economic [iːkə'nɔmɪk] a económico; (business etc) rentable; ~**al** a económico; ~**s** n economía.

economize [ɪ'kɔnəmaɪz] vi economizar, ahorrar.

economy [ɪ'kɔnəmɪ] n economía.

ecstasy ['ɛkstəsɪ] n éxtasis m inv; **ecstatic** [-'tætɪk] a extático.

Ecuador ['ɛkwədɔːr] n Ecuador m; **E~ian** a, n ecuatoriano/a m/f.

eczema ['ɛksɪmə] n eczema m.

edge [edʒ] n (of knife etc) filo; (of object) borde m; (of lake etc) orilla // vt (SEWING) ribetear; **on** ~ (fig)

= **edgy**; **to ~ away from** alejarse poco a poco de; **~ways** ad: **he couldn't get a word in ~ways** no pudo meter ni baza; **edging** n (SEWING) ribete m; (of path) borde m.

edgy ['edʒɪ] a nervioso, inquieto.

edible ['edɪbl] a comestible.

edict ['iːdɪkt] n edicto.

edifice ['edɪfɪs] n edificio.

Edinburgh ['edɪnbərə] n Edimburgo.

edit ['edɪt] vt (be editor of) dirigir; (rewrite) redactar; (cut) cortar; **~ion** [ɪ'dɪʃən] n (gen) edición; (number printed) tirada; **~or** n (of newspaper) director m/f; (of book) redactor(a) m/f; **~orial** [-'tɔːrɪəl] a editorial // n editorial m.

educate ['edʒukeɪt] vt (gen) educar; (instruct) instruir.

education [edʒu'keɪʃən] n educación f; (schooling) enseñanza; (SCOL) pedagogía; **~al** (a policy etc) educacional; (teaching) docente.

EEC n abbr = European Economic Community) CEE f.

eel [iːl] n anguila.

eerie ['ɪərɪ] a (sound, experience) espeluznante.

effect [ɪ'fekt] n efecto // vt efectuar, llevar a cabo; **~s** npl efectos mpl; **to take ~** (law) entrar en vigor or vigencia; (drug) surtir efecto; **in ~** en realidad; **~ive** a (gen) eficaz; (real) efectivo; **to become ~ive** (law) entrar en vigor; **~ively** ad eficazmente; efectivamente; **~iveness** n eficacia.

effeminate [ɪ'femɪnɪt] a afeminado.

efficiency [ɪ'fɪʃənsɪ] n (gen) eficiencia; (of machine) rendimiento.

efficient [ɪ'fɪʃənt] a eficaz; (person) eficiente.

effigy ['efɪdʒɪ] n efigie f.

effort ['efət] n esfuerzo; **~less** a sin ningún esfuerzo.

effrontery [ɪ'frʌntərɪ] n descaro.

effusive [ɪ'fjuːsɪv] a efusivo.

e.g. ad abbr (= exempli gratia) p. ej.

egg [eg] n huevo; **hard-boiled/soft-**

boiled/poached ~ huevo duro/pasado por agua/escalfado; **scrambled ~s** huevos revueltos; **to ~ on** vt incitar; **~cup** n huevera; **~plant** n (esp US) berenjena; **~shell** n cáscara de huevo.

ego ['iːɡəu] n ego; **~tism** n egoísmo; **~tist** n egoísta m/f.

Egypt ['iːdʒɪpt] n Egipto; **~ian** [ɪ'dʒɪpʃən] a, n egipcio a m/f.

eiderdown ['aɪdədaun] n edredón m.

eight [eɪt] num ocho; **~een** num diez y ocho, dieciocho; **~h** a, n octavo; **~y** num ochenta.

Eire ['ɛərə] n Eire m.

either ['aɪðə*] a cualquier de los dos; (both, each) cada; **on ~ side** en ambos lados // pron: **~** (of them) cualquiera (de los dos); **I don't like ~** no me gusta ninguno de los dos // tampoco; **no, I don't ~** no, yo tampoco // conj: **~ yes or no** o sí o no.

eject [ɪ'dʒekt] vt echar; (tenant) desahuciar; **~or seat** n asiento proyectable.

eke [iːk]: **to ~ out** vt (money) hacer que alcance; (add to) suplir las deficiencias de.

elaborate [ɪ'læbərɪt] a (design) elaborado; (pattern) intrincado // vb [ɪ'læbəreɪt] vt elaborar // vi explicarse con muchos detalles.

elapse [ɪ'læps] vi transcurrir.

elastic [ɪ'læstɪk] a, n elástico; **~ band** n (Brit) gomita.

elated [ɪ'leɪtɪd] a: **to be ~** regocijarse; **elation** [ɪ'leɪʃən] n regocijo.

elbow ['elbəu] n codo.

elder ['eldə*] a mayor // n (tree) saúco; (person) mayor; (of tribe) anciano; **~ly** a de edad, mayor // npl: **the ~ly** los mayores.

eldest ['eldɪst] a, n el/la mayor.

elect [ɪ'lekt] vt elegir; **to ~ to do** optar por hacer // a: **the president ~** el presidente electo; **~ion** [ɪ'lekʃən] n elección f; **~ioneering** [ɪlekʃə'nɪərɪŋ] n campaña electoral; **~or** n elector(a) m/f; **~oral** a electoral; **~orate** n electorado.

electric [ɪ'lɛktrɪk] a eléctrico; ~**al** a eléctrico; ~ **blanket** n manta eléctrica; ~ **cooker** n cocina eléctrica; ~ **fire** n estufa eléctrica.

electrician [ɪlɛk'trɪʃən] n electricista m/f.

electricity [ɪlɛk'trɪsɪtɪ] n electricidad f.

electrify [ɪ'lɛktrɪfaɪ] vt (RAIL) electrificar; (fig: audience) electrizar.

electron [ɪ'lɛktrɔn] n electrón m.

electronic [ɪlɛk'trɔnɪk] a electrónico; ~**s** n electrónica.

elegant [ˈɛlɪgənt] a elegante.

element [ˈɛlɪmənt] n (gen) elemento; (of heater, kettle etc) resistencia; ~**ary** [-'mɛntərɪ] a elemental; (primitive) rudimentario; (school, education) primario.

elephant [ˈɛlɪfənt] n elefante m.

elevate [ˈɛlɪveɪt] vt (gen) elevar; (in rank) ascender.

elevation [ɛlɪ'veɪʃən] n elevación f; (height) altura.

elevator [ˈɛlɪveɪtə*] n (US) ascensor m.

eleven [ɪ'lɛvn] num once; ~**ses** npl (Brit) café de las once; ~**th** a undécimo.

elicit [ɪ'lɪsɪt] vt: to ~ (from) sacar (de).

eligible [ˈɛlɪdʒəbl] a elegible; to be ~ for sth llenar los requisitos para algo.

eliminate [ɪ'lɪmɪneɪt] vt eliminar; (strike out) suprimir; (suspect) descartar.

elm [ɛlm] n olmo.

elongated [ˈiːlɔŋgeɪtɪd] a alargado, estirado.

elope [ɪ'ləʊp] vi fugarse (para casarse); ~**ment** n fuga.

eloquent [ˈɛləkwənt] a elocuente.

else [ɛls] ad: something ~ otra cosa; somewhere ~ en otra parte; everywhere ~ en todas partes menos aquí; where ~? ¿dónde más?; ¿en qué otra parte?; there was little ~ to do apenas quedaba otra cosa que hacer; nobody ~ spoke no

habló nadie más; ~**where** ad (be) en otra parte; (go) a otra parte.

elucidate [ɪ'luːsɪdeɪt] vt aclarar.

elude [ɪ'luːd] vt eludir; (blow, pursuer) esquivar.

elusive [ɪ'luːsɪv] a esquivo; (answer) difícil de encontrar.

emaciated [ɪ'meɪsɪeɪtɪd] a demacrado.

emanate [ˈɛmaneɪt] vi: to ~ from (idea) surgir de; (light, smell) proceder de.

emancipate [ɪ'mænsɪpeɪt] vt emancipar.

embankment [ɪm'bæŋkmənt] n terraplén m; (riverside) dique m.

embargo [ɪm'bɑːgəu], pl ~**es** n prohibición f.

embark [ɪm'bɑːk] vi embarcarse // vi embarcar; to ~ on (fig) emprender, lanzarse a; ~**ation** [ɛmbɑː'keɪʃən] n (people) embarco; (goods) embarque m.

embarrass [ɪm'bærəs] vt avergonzar; (financially etc) poner en un aprieto; ~**ed** a azorado; ~**ing** a (situation) violento; (question) embarazoso; ~**ment** n desconcierto, azoramiento; (financial) apuros mpl.

embassy [ˈɛmbəsɪ] n embajada.

embed [ɪm'bɛd] vt (jewel) empotrar; (teeth etc) clavar.

embellish [ɪm'bɛlɪʃ] vt embellecer; (fig) adornar.

embers [ˈɛmbəz] npl rescoldo sg, ascua sg.

embezzle [ɪm'bɛzl] vt desfalcar, malversar.

embitter [ɪm'bɪtə*] vt (person) amargar; (relationship) envenenar; ~**ed** a resentido, amargado.

embody [ɪm'bɔdɪ] vt (spirit) encarnar; (ideas) expresar.

embossed [ɪm'bɔst] a realzado.

embrace [ɪm'breɪs] vt abrazar, dar un abrazo a; (include) abarcar; (adopt: idea) adherirse a // vi abrazarse // n abrazo.

embroider [ɪm'brɔɪdə*] vt bordar; (fig: story) adornar, embellecer; ~**y**

n bordado.

embryo ['embriəu] *n (also fig)* embrión *m*.

emerald ['emərəld] *n* esmeralda *f*.

emerge [ı'mə:dʒ] *vi (gen)* salir; *(arise)* surgir; **~nce** *n* salida; surgimiento.

emergency [ı'mə:dʒənsı] *n (event)* emergencia; *(crisis)* crisis *f inv*; **in an** ~ en caso de urgencia; **state of** ~ estado de emergencia; **~ cord** *n (US)* timbre *m* de alarma; **~ exit** *n* salida de emergencia; **~ landing** *n* aterrizaje *m* forzoso; **~ meeting** *n* reunión *f* extraordinaria; **the ~ services** *npl (fire, police, ambulance)* los servicios *mpl* de urgencia *or* emergencia.

emery board ['emərı-] *n* lima de uñas.

emigrant ['emigrənt] *n* emigrante *m/f*.

emigrate ['emigreit] *vi* emigrarse.

emit [ı'mıt] *vt* emitir; *(smoke)* arrojar; *(smell)* despedir; *(sound)* producir.

emotion [ı'məuʃən] *n* emoción *f*; **~al** *a (person)* sentimental; *(scene)* conmovedor(a), emocionante; **~ally** *ad* con emoción.

emotive [ı'məutıv] *a* emotivo.

emperor ['empərə*] *n* emperador *m*.

emphasis ['emfəsıs], *pl* **-ses** [-si:z] *n* énfasis *m inv*.

emphasize ['emfəsaız] *vt (word, point)* subrayar, recalcar; *(feature)* hacer resaltar.

emphatic [em'fætık] *a (reply)* categórico; *(person)* insistente; **~ally** *ad* con énfasis.

empire ['empaıə*] *n* imperio.

employ [ım'plɔı] *vt* emplear; **~ee** [-'i:] *n* empleado/a *m/f*; **~er** *n* patrón/ona *m/f*; empresario; **~ment** *n (gen)* empleo; *(work)* trabajo; **~ment agency** *n* agencia de colocaciones.

empower [ım'pauə*] *vt*: to ~ sb to do sth autorizar a uno para hacer algo.

empress ['emprıs] *n* emperatriz *f*.

emptiness ['emptınıs] *n (gen)* vacío; *(of life etc)* vaciedad *f*.

empty ['emptı] *a* vacío; *(place)* desierto; *(house)* desocupado; *(threat)* vano // *n (bottle)* envase *m* // *vt* vaciar; *(place)* dejar vacío // *vi* vaciarse; *(house)* quedar desocupado; *(place)* quedar desierto; **~-handed** *a* con las manos vacías.

emulate ['emjuleit] *vt* emular.

emulsion [ı'mʌlʃən] *n* emulsión *f*.

enable [ı'neıbl] *vt*: to ~ sb to do sth *(allow)* permitir a uno hacer algo; *(prepare)* capacitar a uno para hacer algo.

enact [ın'ækt] *vt (law)* promulgar; *(play)* representar; *(role)* hacer.

enamel [ı'næməl] *n* esmalte *m*.

enamoured [ı'næməd] *a*: to be ~ of *(person)* estar enamorado de; *(activity etc)* tener gran afición a; *(idea)* aferrarse a.

encased [ın'keıst] *a*: ~ in *(covered)* revestido de.

enchant [ın'tʃɑ:nt] *vt* encantar; **~ing** *a* encantador(a).

encircle [ın'sə:kl] *vt* rodear.

encl. *abbr* (= *enclosed*) adj.

enclose [ın'kləuz] *vt (land)* cercar; *(with letter etc)* adjuntar; *(in receptacle)*: to ~ *(with)* encerrar *(con)*; **please find ~d** le mandamos adjunto.

enclosure [ın'kləuʒə*] *n* cercado, recinto; *(COMM)* adjunto.

encompass [ın'kʌmpəs] *vt* abarcar.

encore [ɔŋ'kɔ:*] *excl* ¡otra!, ¡bis! // *n* bis *m*.

encounter [ın'kauntə*] *n* encuentro // *vt* encontrar, encontrarse con; *(difficulty)* tropezar con.

encourage [ın'kʌrıdʒ] *vt* alentar, animar; *(growth)* estimular; **~ment** *n* estímulo; *(of industry)* fomento.

encroach [ın'krəutʃ] *vi*: to ~ (up)on *(gen)* invadir; *(time)* adueñarse de.

encrusted [ın'krʌstəd] *a*: ~ with incrustado de.

encumber [ın'kʌmbə*] *vt*: to be

~d with (carry) estar cargado de; (debts) estar gravado de.

encyclop(a)edia [ensaɪkləʊ'piːdɪə] n enciclopedia.

end [ɛnd] n (gen, also aim) fin m; (of table) extremo; (of street) final m; (SPORT) lado // vt terminar, acabar; (also: **bring to an ~, put an ~ to**) acabar con // vi terminar, acabar; **in the ~** al fin; **on ~** (object) de punta, de cabeza; **to stand on ~** (hair) erizarse; **for hours on ~** hora tras hora; **to ~ up** vi to ~ up in terminar en; (place) ir a parar en.

endanger [ɪn'deɪndʒə*] vt poner en peligro.

endearing [ɪn'dɪərɪŋ] a simpático, atractivo.

endeavour, (US) **endeavor** [ɪn'dɛvə*] n esfuerzo; (attempt) tentativa // vi: **to ~ to do** esforzarse por hacer; (try) procurar hacer.

ending ['ɛndɪŋ] n fin m, conclusión f; (of book) desenlace m; (LING) terminación f.

endive ['ɛndaɪv] n endibia, escarola.

endless ['ɛndlɪs] a interminable, inacabable.

endorse [ɪn'dɔːs] vt (cheque) endosar; (approve) aprobar; ~ment n (on driving licence) nota de inhabilitación.

endow [ɪn'dau] vt (provide with money) dotar (with de); (found) fundar; **to be ~ed with** (fig) estar dotado de.

endurance [ɪn'djuərəns] n resistencia.

endure [ɪn'djuə*] vt (bear) aguantar, soportar; (resist) resistir // vi (last) durar; (resist) resistir.

enemy ['ɛnəmɪ] a, n enemigo/a m/f.

energetic [ɛnə'dʒɛtɪk] a enérgico.

energy ['ɛnədʒɪ] n energía.

enforce [ɪn'fɔːs] vt (LAW) hacer cumplir; ~d a forzoso, forzado.

engage [ɪn'geɪdʒ] vt (attention) llamar; (in conversation) abordar; (worker) contratar; (clutch) embragar // vi (TECH) engranar; **to ~ in**

dedicarse a, ocuparse en; ~d a (Brit: busy, in use) ocupado; (betrothed) prometido; **to get ~d** prometerse; **he is ~d in research** se dedica a la investigación; ~d **tone** n (Brit TEL) señal f de comunicando; ~ment n (appointment) compromiso, cita; (battle) combate m; (to marry) compromiso; (period) noviazgo; ~ment ring n alianza, anillo de prometida.

engaging [ɪn'geɪdʒɪŋ] a atractivo, simpático.

engender [ɪn'dʒɛndə*] vt engendrar.

engine ['ɛndʒɪn] n (AUT) motor m; (RAIL) locomotora; ~ **driver** n maquinista m/f.

engineer [ɛndʒɪ'nɪə*] n ingeniero; (US RAIL) maquinista m; ~**ing** n ingeniería.

England ['ɪŋglənd] n Inglaterra.

English ['ɪŋglɪʃ] a inglés/esa // n (LING) inglés m; **the ~** npl los ingleses mpl; **the ~ Channel** n (el Canal de) la Mancha; ~**man/woman** n inglés/esa m/f.

engraving [ɪn'greɪvɪŋ] n grabado.

engrossed [ɪn'grəust] a: ~ **in** absorto en.

engulf [ɪn'gʌlf] vt sumergir, hundir.

enhance [ɪn'hɑːns] vt (gen) aumentar; (beauty) realzar.

enjoy [ɪn'dʒɔɪ] vt (health, fortune) disfrutar de, gozar de; (food) comer con gusto; **I enjoy dancing** me gusta bailar; **to ~ o.s.** divertirse; ~**able** a (pleasant) agradable; (amusing) divertido; ~**ment** n (use) disfrute m; (joy) placer m.

enlarge [ɪn'lɑːdʒ] vt aumentar; (broaden) extender; (PHOT) ampliar // vi: **to ~ on** (subject) tratar con más detalles.

enlighten [ɪn'laɪtn] vt (inform) informar, ~**ed** a iluminado, (tolerant) comprensivo; **the E~ment** n (HISTORY) ≈ la Ilustración, el Siglo de las Luces.

enlist [ɪn'lɪst] vt alistar; (support) conseguir // vi alistarse.

enmity ['enmɪtɪ] *n* enemistad *f*.

enormous [ɪ'nɔːməs] *a* enorme.

enough [ɪ'nʌf] *a*: ~ **time/books** bastante tiempo/bastantes libros // *n*: **have you got** ~? ¿tiene usted bastante? // *ad*: **big** ~ bastante grande; **he has not worked** ~ no ha trabajado bastante; ~! ¡basta ya!; **that's** ~, thanks con eso basta, gracias; **I've had** ~ **of him** estoy harto de él; ...**which, funnily** ~... ...lo que, por extraño que parezca... .

enquire [ɪn'kwaɪə*] *vt, vi* = **inquire**.

enrage [ɪn'reɪdʒ] *vt* enfurecer.

enrich [ɪn'rɪtʃ] *vt* enriquecer.

enrol [ɪn'rəul] *vt* (*members*) inscribir; (*SCOL*) matricular // *vi* inscribirse; matricularse; ~**ment** *n* inscripción *f*; matriculación *f*.

en route [ɑːn'ruːt] *ad* durante el viaje.

ensign ['ensaɪn] *n* (*flag*) bandera; (*NAUT*) alférez *m*.

enslave [ɪn'sleɪv] *vt* esclavizar.

ensue [ɪn'sjuː] *vi* seguirse; (*result*) resultar.

ensure [ɪn'ʃuə*] *vt* asegurar.

entail [ɪn'teɪl] *vt* suponer.

entangle [ɪn'tæŋgl] *vt* enredar, enmarañar.

enter ['entə*] *vt* (*room*) entrar en; (*club*) hacerse socio de; (*army*) alistarse en; (*sb for a competition*) inscribir; (*write down*) anotar, apuntar; (*COMPUT*) meter // *vi* entrar; **to** ~ **for** *vt fus* presentarse para; **to** ~ **into** *vt fus* (*relations*) establecer; (*plans*) formar parte de; (*debate*) tomar parte en; (*agreement*) llegar a, firmar; **to** ~ **(up)on** *vt fus* (*career*) emprender.

enterprise ['entəpraɪz] *n* empresa; (*spirit*) iniciativa; **free** ~ la libre empresa; **private** ~ la iniciativa privada; **enterprising** *a* emprendedor(a).

entertain [entə'teɪn] *vt* (*amuse*) divertir; (*receive: guest*) recibir (en casa); (*idea*) abrigar; ~**er** *n* artista *m/f*; ~**ing** *a* divertido, entretenido;

~**ment** *n* (*amusement*) diversión *f*; (*show*) espectáculo; (*party*) fiesta.

enthralled [ɪn'θrɔːld] *a* encantado.

enthusiasm [ɪn'θuːzɪæzəm] *n* entusiasmo.

enthusiast [ɪn'θuːzɪæst] *n* entusiasta *m/f*; ~**ic** [-'æstɪk] *a* entusiasta; **to be** ~**ic about** entusiasmarse por.

entice [ɪn'taɪs] *vt* tentar; (*seduce*) seducir.

entire [ɪn'taɪə*] *a* entero; ~**ly** *ad* totalmente; ~**ty** [ɪn'taɪərətɪ] *n*: **in its** ~**ty** en su totalidad.

entitle [ɪn'taɪtl] *vt*: **to** ~ **sb to sth** dar a uno derecho a algo; ~**d** *a* (*book*) que se titula; **to be** ~**d to sth** tener derecho a hacer.

entourage [ɔntuˈrɑːʒ] *n* séquito.

entrails ['entreɪlz] *npl* entrañas *fpl*; (*US*) asadura *sg*, menudos *mpl*.

entrance ['entrəns] *n* entrada // *vt* [ɪn'trɑːns] encantar, hechizar; **to gain** ~ **to** (*university etc*) ingresar en; ~ **examination** *n* examen *m* de ingreso; ~ **fee** *n* cuota; ~ **ramp** *n* (*US AUT*) rampa de acceso.

entrant ['entrənt] *n* (*race, competition*) participante *m/f*; (*examination*) candidato/a.

entreat [ɪn'triːt] *vt* rogar, suplicar.

entrenched [ɛn'trɛntʃd] *a*: ~ **interests** intereses *mpl* creados.

entrepreneur [ɔntrəprə'nɜː] *n* empresario.

entrust [ɪn'trʌst] *vt*: **to** ~ **sth to sb** confiar algo a uno.

entry ['entrɪ] *n* entrada; (*permission to enter*) acceso; (*in register*) apunte *m*; (*in account*) partida; **no** ~ prohibido el paso; (*AUT*) dirección prohibida; ~ **phone** *n* portero automático.

enunciate [ɪ'nʌnsɪeɪt] *vt* pronunciar; (*principle etc*) enunciar.

envelop [ɪn'veləp] *vt* envolver.

envelope ['envələup] *n* sobre *m*.

envious ['envɪəs] *a* envidioso; (*look*) de envidia.

environment [ɪn'vaɪərnmənt] *n* medio ambiente; ~**al** [-'mɛntl] *a* ambiental.

envisage [ɪn'vɪzɪdʒ] *vt* (*foresee*) prever; (*imagine*) concebir.

envoy ['envɔɪ] *n* enviado.

envy ['envɪ] *n* envidia // *vt* tener envidia a; **to ~ sb sth** envidiar algo a uno.

epic ['epɪk] *n* épica // *a* épico.

epidemic [epɪ'demɪk] *n* epidemia.

epilepsy ['epɪlepsɪ] *n* epilepsia.

episode ['epɪsəud] *n* episodio.

epistle [ɪ'pɪsl] *n* epístola.

epitome [ɪ'pɪtəmɪ] *n* epítome *m*; **epitomize** *vt* epitomar, resumir.

equable ['ekwəbl] *a* (*climate*) templado; (*character*) tranquilo, afable.

equal ['iːkwl] *a* (*gen*) igual; (*treatment*) equitativo // *n* igual *m/f* // *vt* ser igual a, (*fig*) igualar; **to be ~ to** (*task*) estar a la altura de; **~ity** [iː'kwɔlɪtɪ] *n* igualdad *f*; **~ize** *vt, vi* igualar; (*SPORT*) empatar; **~izer** *n* igualada; **~ly** *ad* igualmente; (*share etc*) a partes iguales.

equanimity [ekwə'nɪmɪtɪ] *n* ecuanimidad *f*.

equate [ɪ'kweɪt] *vt*: **to ~ sth with** equiparar algo con; **equation** [ɪ'kweɪʒən] *n* (*MATH*) ecuación *f*.

equator [ɪ'kweɪtə*] *n* ecuador *m*; **~ial** [ekwə'tɔːrɪəl] *a* ecuatorial.

equilibrium [iːkwɪ'lɪbrɪəm] *n* equilibrio.

equip [ɪ'kwɪp] *vt* (*gen*) equipar; (*person*) proveer; **to be well ~ped** estar bien equipado; **~ment** *n* equipo; (*tools*) avíos *mpl*.

equitable ['ekwɪtəbl] *a* equitativo.

equities ['ekwɪtɪz] *npl* (*Brit COMM*) derechos *mpl* sobre or en el activo.

equivalent [ɪ'kwɪvələnt] *a*: **~ (to)** equivalente (a) // *n* equivalente *m*.

equivocal [ɪ'kwɪvəkl] *a* equívoco.

era ['ɪərə] *n* era, época.

eradicate [ɪ'rædɪkeɪt] *vt* erradicar, extirpar.

erase [ɪ'reɪz] *vt* borrar; **~r** *n* goma de borrar.

erect [ɪ'rekt] *a* erguido // *vt* erigir, levantar; (*assemble*) montar.

erection [ɪ'rekʃən] *n* construcción *f*; (*assembly*) montaje *m*; (*structure*) edificio; (*MED*) erección *f*.

ermine ['əːmɪn] *n* armiño.

erode [ɪ'rəud] *vt* (*GEO*) erosionar; (*metal*) corroer, desgastar.

erotic [ɪ'rɔtɪk] *a* erótico.

err [əː*] *vi* equivocarse; (*REL*) pecar.

errand ['ernd] *n* recado, mandado (*LAm*); **~ boy** *n* recadero.

erratic [ɪ'rætɪk] *a* variable; (*results etc*) desigual, poco uniforme.

erroneous [ɪ'rəunɪəs] *a* erróneo.

error ['erə*] *n* error *m*, equivocación *f*.

erupt [ɪ'rʌpt] *vi* entrar en erupción; (*MED*) hacer erupción; (*fig*) estallar; **~ion** [ɪ'rʌpʃən] *n* erupción *f*.

escalate ['eskəleɪt] *vi* extenderse, intensificarse.

escalation [eskə'leɪʃən] *n* escalamiento, intensificación *f*.

escalator ['eskəleɪtə*] *n* escalera móvil.

escapade [eskə'peɪd] *n* travesura.

escape [ɪ'skeɪp] *n* (*gen*) fuga; (*from duties*) escapatoria; (*from chase*) evasión *f* // *vi* (*gen*) escaparse; (*flee*) huir, evadirse; (*leak*) fugarse // *vt* evitar, eludir; (*consequences*) escapar a; **to ~ from** (*place*) escaparse de; (*person*) escaparse a; **escapism** *n* escapismo.

escort ['eskɔːt] *n* acompañante *m/f*; (*MIL*) escolta; (*NAUT*) convoy *m* // *vt* [ɪ'skɔːt] acompañar; (*MIL, NAUT*) escoltar.

Eskimo ['eskɪməu] *n* esquimal *m/f*.

especially [ɪ'speʃlɪ] *ad* (*gen*) especialmente; (*above all*) sobre todo; (*particularly*) en particular.

espionage ['espɪɔnɑːʒ] *n* espionaje *m*.

esplanade [esplə'neɪd] *n* (*by sea*) paseo marítimo.

espouse [ɪ'spauz] *vt* adherirse a.

Esquire [ɪ'skwaɪə*] *n* (*abbr* Esq.): J. Brown, **~** Sr. D. J. Brown.

essay ['eseɪ] *n* (*SCOL*) ensayo.

essence ['esns] *n* esencia.

essential [ɪ'sɛnʃl] a (*necessary*) imprescindible; (*basic*) esencial; ~**s** npl lo esencial sg; ~**ly** ad esencialmente.

establish [ɪ'stæblɪʃ] vt establecer; (*identity*) verificar; (*prove*) demostrar; (*relations*) entablar; ~**ment** n establecimiento; **the E~ment** la clase dirigente.

estate [ɪ'steɪt] n (*land*) finca, hacienda; (*property*) propiedad f; (*inheritance*) herencia; (POL) estado; ~ **agent** n (Brit) agente m/f inmobiliario/a; ~ **car** n (Brit) furgoneta.

esteem [ɪ'stiːm] n: **to hold sb in high** ~ estimar en mucho a uno // vt estimar.

esthetic [ɪs'θɛtɪk] a (US) = **aesthetic**.

estimate ['ɛstɪmət] n estimación f, apreciación f; (*assessment*) tasa, cálculo; (COMM) presupuesto // [-meɪt] estimar, tasar, calcular; **estimation** [-'meɪʃən] n opinión f, juicio; (*esteem*) aprecio.

estranged [ɪ'streɪndʒd] a separado.

estuary ['ɛstjuərɪ] n estuario, ria.

etc abbr (= et cetera) etc.

etching ['ɛtʃɪŋ] n aguafuerte m o f.

eternal [ɪ'tɜːnl] a eterno.

eternity [ɪ'tɜːnɪtɪ] n eternidad f.

ethical ['ɛθɪkl] a ético; (*honest*) honrado.

ethics ['ɛθɪks] n ética // npl moralidad fsg.

Ethiopia [iːθɪ'əʊpɪə] n Etiopía.

ethnic ['ɛθnɪk] a étnico.

ethos ['iːθɔs] n genio, carácter m.

etiquette ['ɛtɪkɛt] n etiqueta.

Eurocheque ['jʊərəʊtʃɛk] n Eurocheque m.

Europe ['jʊərəp] n Europa; ~**an** [-'pi:ən] a, n europeo/a m/f.

evacuate [ɪ'vækjueɪt] vt desocupar; **evacuation** [-'eɪʃən] n evacuación f.

evade [ɪ'veɪd] vt evadir, eludir.

evaluate [ɪ'væljueɪt] vt evaluar; (*value*) tasar; (*evidence*) interpretar.

evangelist [ɪ'vændʒəlɪst] n (*biblical*)

evangelista m; (*preacher*) evangelizador(a) m/f.

evaporate [ɪ'væpəreɪt] vi evaporarse; (*fig*) desvanecerse // vt evaporar; ~**d milk** n leche f evaporada.

evasion [ɪ'veɪʒən] n evasiva, evasión f.

eve [iːv] n: **on the** ~ **of** en vísperas de.

even ['iːvn] a (*level*) llano; (*smooth*) liso; (*speed, temperature*) uniforme; (*number*) par; (SPORT) igual(es) // ad hasta, incluso; ~ **if**, ~ **though** aunque + subjun; ~ **more** aun más; ~ **so** aun así; **not** ~ ni siquiera; ~ **he was there** hasta él estuvo allí; ~ **on Sundays** incluso los domingos; **to get** ~ **with sb** ajustar cuentas con uno; **to** ~ **out** vi nivelarse.

evening ['iːvnɪŋ] n tarde f; (*dusk*) atardecer m; (*night*) noche f; **in the** ~ por la tarde; ~ **class** n clase f nocturna; ~ **dress** n (*man's*) traje m de etiqueta; (*woman's*) traje m de noche.

event [ɪ'vɛnt] n suceso, acontecimiento; (SPORT) prueba; **in the** ~ **of** en caso de; ~**ful** a accidentado; (*game etc*) lleno de emoción.

eventual [ɪ'vɛntʃuəl] a final; ~**ity** [-'ælɪtɪ] n eventualidad f; ~**ly** ad (*finally*) finalmente.

ever ['ɛvə*] ad nunca, jamás; (*at all times*) siempre; **the best** ~ lo nunca visto; **have you** ~ **seen it?** ¿lo ha visto usted alguna vez?; **better than** ~ mejor que nunca; ~ **since** ad desde entonces // conj después de que; ~**green** n árbol m de hoja perenne; ~**lasting** a eterno, perpetuo.

KEYWORD

---

every ['ɛvrɪ] a **1** (*each*) cada; ~ **one of them** (*persons*) todos ellos/as; (*objects*) cada uno de ellos/as; ~ **shop in the town was closed** todas las tiendas de la ciudad estaban cerradas

2 (*all possible*) todo/a; **I gave you** ~ **assistance** te di toda la ayuda posible; **I have ~ confidence in him** tiene toda mi confianza; **we wish you ~ success** te deseamos toda suerte de éxitos

3 (*showing recurrence*) todo/a; **~ day/week** todos los días/todas las semanas; **~ other car had been broken into** habían entrado en uno de cada dos coches; **she visits me ~ other/third day** me visita cada dos/ tres días; **~ now and then** de vez en cuando.

everybody ['evribɔdi] *pron* = **everyone**.

everyone ['evriwʌn] *pron* todas/as, todo el mundo; **~ knows** that todo el mundo lo sabe; **~ has his own view** cada uno piensa de una manera.

everything ['evriθiŋ] *pron* todo; **~'s ready** está todo listo; **~ you say is true** todo lo que dices es cierto; **this shop sells ~** esta tienda vende de todo.

everywhere ['evriwɛə*] *ad*: **I've been looking for you ~** te he estado buscando por todas partes; **~ you go you meet...** en todas partes encuentras... .

evict [ı'vıkt] *vt* desahuciar; **~ion** [ı'vıkʃən] *n* desahucio.

evidence ['evidəns] *n* (*proof*) prueba; (*of witness*) testimonio; (*facts*) datos *mpl*, hechos *mpl*; **to give ~** prestar declaración, dar testimonio.

evident ['evidənt] *a* evidente, manifiesto; **~ly** *ad*: **it is ~ly difficult** por lo visto es difícil.

evil ['i:vl] *a* malo; (*influence*) funesto; (*smell*) horrible // *n* mal *m*, maldad *f*.

evocative [ı'vɔkətıv] *a* sugestivo, evocador(a.)

evoke [ı'vəuk] *vt* evocar.

evolution [i:və'lu:ʃən] *n* evolución *f*, desarrollo.

evolve [ı'vɔlv] *vt* desarrollar // *vi* evolucionar, desarrollarse.

ewe [ju:] *n* oveja.

ex- [eks] *pref* ex.

exacerbate [ıg'sæsəbeıt] *vt* (*pain, disease*) exacerbar; (*fig*) empeorar.

exact [ıg'zækt] *a* exacto // *vt*: **to ~ sth (from)** exigir algo (de); **~ing** *a* exigente; (*conditions*) arduo; **~ly** *ad* exactamente.

exaggerate [ıg'zædʒəreıt] *vt*, *vi* exagerar; **exaggeration** [-'reıʃən] *n* exageración *f*.

exalted [ıg'zɔ:ltıd] *a* (*position*) exaltado; (*elated*) excitado.

exam [ıg'zæm] *n abbr* (*SCOL*) = **examination**.

examination [ıgzæmı'neıʃən] *n* (*gen*) examen *m*; (*LAW*) interrogación *f*; (*inquiry*) investigación *f*.

examine [ıg'zæmın] *vt* (*gen*) examinar; (*inspect*) inspeccionar, escudriñar; (*SCOL, LAW: person*) interrogar; (*at customs: luggage*) registrar; **~r** *n* inspector(a) *m/f*.

example [ıg'zɑ:mpl] *n* ejemplo; **for ~** por ejemplo.

exasperate [ıg'zɑ:spəreıt] *vt* exasperar, irritar; **exasperation** [-ʃən] *n* exasperación *f*, irritación *f*.

excavate ['ekskəveıt] *vt* excavar.

exceed [ık'si:d] *vt* exceder; (*number*) pasar de; (*speed limit*) sobrepasar; (*limits*) rebasar; (*powers*) excederse en; (*hopes*) superar; **~ingly** *ad* sumamente, sobremanera.

excel [ık'sɛl] *vi* sobresalir.

excellent ['eksələnt] *a* excelente.

except [ık'sɛpt] *prep* (*also:* **~ for**, **~ing**) excepto, salvo // *vt* exceptuar, excluir; **~ if/when** excepto si/ cuando; **~ that** salvo que; **~ion** [ık'sɛpʃən] *n* excepción *f*; **to take ~ion to** ofenderse por; **~ional** [ık'sɛpʃənl] *a* excepcional.

excerpt ['eksɜ:pt] *n* extracto.

excess [ık'sɛs] *n* exceso; **~ baggage** *n* exceso de equipaje; **~ fare** *n* suplemento; **~ive** *a* excesivo.

exchange [ıks'tʃeındʒ] *n* cambio; (*of goods*) cambio *m*; (*of ideas*) intercambio; (*also:* **telephone ~**) central *f* (telefónica) // *vt*: **to ~ (for)** cambiar (por); ~ **rate** n tipo de cambio.

exchequer [ɪksˈtʃekəˣ] n: the ~ (Brit) la Hacienda del Fisco.

excise [ˈeksaɪz] n impuestos mpl sobre el comercio exterior.

excite [ɪkˈsaɪt] vt (stimulate) estimular; (anger) provocar; (move) entusiasmar; **~d** a: **to get ~d** emocionarse; **~ment** n emoción f; **exciting** a emocionante.

exclaim [ɪkˈskleɪm] vi exclamar; **exclamation** [ˌeksˈkləˈmeɪʃən] n exclamación f; **exclamation mark** n punto de admiración.

exclude [ɪkˈskluːd] vt excluir; (except) exceptuar.

exclusive [ɪkˈskluːsɪv] a exclusivo; (club, district) selecto; **~ of tax** excluyendo impuestos; **~ly** ad únicamente.

excommunicate [ˌekskəˈmjuːnɪkeɪt] vt excomulgar.

excruciating [ɪkˈskruːʃɪeɪtɪŋ] a (pain) agudísimo, atroz.

excursion [ɪkˈskəːʃən] n excursión f.

excusable [ɪkˈskjuːzəbl] a perdonable.

excuse [ɪkˈskjuːs] n disculpa, excusa; (evasion) pretexto // [ɪkˈskjuːz] disculpar, perdonar; **to ~ sb from doing sth** dispensar a uno de hacer algo; ~ **me!** ¡perdón!; **if you will** ~ **me** con su permiso.

ex-directory [ˈeksdɪˈrektərɪ] a (Brit) que no consta en la guía.

execute [ˈeksɪkjuːt] vt (plan) realizar; (order) cumplir; (person) ajusticiar, ejecutar; **execution** [-ˈkjuːʃən] n realización f; cumplimiento; ejecución f; **executioner** [-ˈkjuːʃənəˣ] n verdugo.

executive [ɪgˈzekjutɪv] n (COMM) ejecutivo; (POL) poder m ejecutivo // a ejecutivo.

executor [ɪgˈzekjutəˣ] n albacea m, testamentario.

exemplify [ɪgˈzemplɪfaɪ] vt ejemplificar.

exempt [ɪgˈzempt] a: **~ from** exento de // vt: **to ~ sb from** eximir a

uno de; **~ion** [-ʃən] n exención f; (immunity) inmunidad f.

exercise [ˈeksəsaɪz] n ejercicio // vt ejercer; (right) valerse de; (dog) llevar de paseo // vi hacer ejercicio(s); ~ **book** n cuaderno.

exert [ɪgˈzəːt] vt ejercer; **to ~ o.s.** esforzarse; **~ion** [-ʃən] n esfuerzo.

exhale [eksˈheɪl] vi despedir // vi exhalar.

exhaust [ɪgˈzɔːst] n (pipe) escape m; (fumes) gases mpl de escape // vt agotar; **~ed** a agotado; **~ion** [ɪgˈzɔːstʃən] n agotamiento; **nervous ~ion** postración f nerviosa; **~ive** a exhaustivo.

exhibit [ɪgˈzɪbɪt] n (ART) obra expuesta; (LAW) objeto expuesto // vt (show: emotions) manifestar; (:courage, skill) demostrar; (paintings) exponer; **~ion** [ˌeksɪˈbɪʃən] n exposición f.

exhilarating [ɪgˈzɪləreɪtɪŋ] a estimulante, tónico.

exile [ˈeksaɪl] n exilio; (person) exiliado/a // vt desterrar, exiliar.

exist [ɪgˈzɪst] vi existir; **~ence** n existencia; **~ing** a existente, actual.

exit [ˈeksɪt] n salida // vi (THEATRE) hacer mutis; (COMPUT) salir (al sistema); ~ **ramp** n (US AUT) vía de acceso.

exodus [ˈeksədəs] n éxodo.

exonerate [ɪgˈzɒnəreɪt] vt: **to ~ from** exculpar de.

exotic [ɪgˈzɒtɪk] a exótico.

expand [ɪkˈspænd] vt ampliar; (number) aumentar // vi (trade etc) expandirse; (gas, metal) dilatarse.

expanse [ɪkˈspæns] n extensión f.

expansion [ɪkˈspænʃən] n ampliación f; aumento; (of trade) expansión f.

expect [ɪkˈspekt] vt (gen) esperar; (count on) contar con; (suppose) suponer // vi: **to be ~ing** estar encinta; **~ancy** n (anticipation) esperanza; **life ~ancy** esperanza de vida; **~ant mother** n mujer f encinta; **~ation** [ˌekspekˈteɪʃən] n esperanza.

expectativa.

expedience [ɪkˈspiːdɪəns], **expediency** [ɪkˈspiːdɪənsɪ] n conveniencia.

expedient [ɪkˈspiːdɪənt] a conveniente, oportuno // n recurso, expediente m.

expedition [ɛkspəˈdɪʃən] n expedición f.

expel [ɪkˈspɛl] vt arrojar; (SCOL) expulsar.

expend [ɪkˈspɛnd] vt gastar; (use up) consumir; ~**able** a prescindible; ~**iture** n gastos mpl, desembolso.

expense [ɪkˈspɛns] n gasto, gastos mpl; (high cost) costa; ~**s** npl (COMM) gastos mpl; at the ~ of a costa de; ~ **account** n cuenta de gastos.

expensive [ɪkˈspɛnsɪv] a caro, costoso.

experience [ɪkˈspɪərɪəns] n experiencia // vt experimentar; (suffer) sufrir; ~**d** a experimentado.

experiment [ɪkˈspɛrɪmənt] n experimento // vi hacer experimentos; ~**al** [-ˈmɛntl] a experimental.

expert [ˈɛkspɜːt] a experto, perito // n experto/a, perito/a; (specialist) especialista m/f; ~**ise** [-ˈtiːz] n pericia.

expire [ɪkˈspaɪə*] vi (gen) caducar, vencerse; **expiry** n vencimiento.

explain [ɪkˈspleɪn] vt explicar; (mystery) aclarar; **explanation** [ɛkspləˈneɪʃən] n explicación f; aclaración f; **explanatory** [ɪkˈsplænətrɪ] a explicativo; aclaratorio.

explicit [ɪkˈsplɪsɪt] a explícito.

explode [ɪkˈspləʊd] vi estallar, explotar; (with anger) reventar // vt volar, explotar.

exploit [ˈɛksplɔɪt] n hazaña // vt [ɪkˈsplɔɪt] explotar; ~**ation** [-ˈteɪʃən] n explotación f.

exploratory [ɪkˈsplɔrətrɪ] a (fig: talks) exploratorio, preliminar.

explore [ɪkˈsplɔː*] vt explorar; (fig) examinar, sondear; ~**r** n explorador(a) m/f.

explosion [ɪkˈspləʊʒən] n explosión f.

explosive [ɪkˈspləʊsɪv] a, n explosivo.

exponent [ɪkˈspəʊnənt] n partidario/a, intérprete m/f.

export [ɛkˈspɔːt] vt exportar // n [ˈɛkspɔːt] exportación f // cpd de exportación; ~**er** n exportador m.

expose [ɪkˈspəʊz] vt exponer; (unmask) desenmascarar; ~**d** a expuesto.

exposure [ɪkˈspəʊʒə*] n exposición f; (PHOT: speed) velocidad f de obturación (: shot) fotografía; **to die from** ~ (MED) morir de frío; ~ **meter** n fotómetro.

expound [ɪkˈspaʊnd] vt exponer.

express [ɪkˈsprɛs] a (definite) expreso, explícito; (Brit: letter etc) urgente // n (train) rápido // ad (send) por correo extraordinario // vt expresar; ~**ion** [ɪkˈsprɛʃən] n expresión f; ~**ly** ad expresamente; ~**way** n (US: urban motorway) autopista.

exquisite [ɛkˈskwɪzɪt] a exquisito.

extend [ɪkˈstɛnd] vt (visit, street) prolongar; (building) ensanchar; (thanks, friendship etc) extender // vi (land) extenderse.

extension [ɪkˈstɛnʃən] n extensión f; (building) ampliación f; (TEL: line) línea derivada; (: telephone) extensión f; (of deadline) prórroga.

extensive [ɪkˈstɛnsɪv] a (gen) extenso; (damage) importante; (knowledge) amplio; ~**ly** ad: **he's travelled** ~**ly** ha viajado por muchos países.

extent [ɪkˈstɛnt] n (breadth) extensión f; (scope) alcance m; **to some** ~ hasta cierto punto; **to the** ~ **of...** hasta el punto de...; **to such an** ~ **that...** hasta tal punto que...; **to what** ~? ¿hasta qué punto?

extenuating [ɪkˈstɛnjueɪtɪŋ] a: ~ **circumstances** circunstancias fpl atenuantes.

exterior [ɛkˈstɪərɪə*] a exterior, externo // n exterior m.

exterminate [ɪkˈstəːmɪneɪt] vt exterminar; **extermination** [-ˈneɪʃən] n exterminación f.

external [ɛk'stəːnl] a externo, exterior; **~ly** ad por fuera.

extinct [ɪk'stɪŋkt] a (volcano) extinguido; (race) extinto.

extinguish [ɪk'stɪŋgwɪʃ] vt extinguir, apagar; **~er** n extintor.

extort [ɪk'stɔːt] vt: to ~ sth from sb sacar algo de uno a la fuerza; **~ion** [ɪk'stɔːʃən] n exacción f; **~ionate** [ɪk'stɔːʃnət] a excesivo, exorbitante.

extra ['ɛkstrə] a adicional // ad (in addition) de más // n (addition) extra m, suplemento; (THEATRE) extra m/f, comparsa m/f; (newspaper) edición f extraordinaria.

extra... ['ɛkstrə] pref extra... .

extract [ɪk'strækt] vt sacar; (tooth) extraer; (confession) arrancar, obtener // n ['ɛkstrækt] extracto.

extracurricular [ɛkstrəkə'rɪkjulə*] a extraescolar, extra-académico.

extradite ['ɛkstrədaɪt] vt extraditar.

extramarital [ɛkstrə'mærɪtl] a extramatrimonial.

extramural [ɛkstrə'mjuərl] a extraescolar.

extraordinary [ɪk'strɔːdnrɪ] a extraordinario; (odd) raro.

extravagance [ɪk'strævəgəns] n prodigalidad f; derroche m; (thing bought) extravagancia.

extravagant [ɪk'strævəgənt] a (lavish) pródigo; (wasteful) derrochador(a); (price) exorbitante.

extreme [ɪk'striːm] a extremo; (poverty etc) extremado; (case) excepcional // n extremo, extremidad f; **~ly** ad sumamente, extremadamente; **extremist** a, n extremista m/f.

extremity [ɪk'strɛmɪtɪ] n extremidad f, punta; (need) apuro, necesidad f.

extricate ['ɛkstrɪkeɪt] vt: to ~ o.s. from librarse de.

extrovert ['ɛkstrəvəːt] a, n extrovertido/a.

exuberant [ɪg'zjuːbərnt] a (person) eufórico; (style) exuberante.

exude [ɪg'zjuːd] vt rezumar, sudar.

exult [ɪg'zʌlt] vi regocijarse.

eye [aɪ] n ojo // vt mirar de soslayo, ojear; **to keep an ~ on** vigilar; **~ball** n globo del ojo; **~bath** n ojera; **~brow** n ceja; **~brow pencil** n lápiz m de cejas; **~drops** npl gotas fpl para los ojos; **~lash** n pestaña; **~lid** n párpado; **~liner** n lápiz m de ojos; **~-opener** n revelación f, gran sorpresa; **~shadow** n sombreador m de ojos; **~sight** n vista; **~sore** n monstruosidad f; **~witness** n testigo m/f presencial.

F

F [ɛf] n (MUS) fa m.

F. abbr = **Fahrenheit**.

fable ['feɪbl] n fábula.

fabric ['fæbrɪk] n tejido, tela.

fabrication [fæbrɪ'keɪʃən] n invención f.

fabulous ['fæbjuləs] a fabuloso.

façade [fə'saːd] n fachada.

face [feɪs] n (ANAT) cara, rostro; (of clock) esfera, cara (LAm); (side, surface) superficie f // vt (subj: person) encararse con; (: building) dar a; ~ **down** (person, card) boca abajo; **to lose** ~ desprestigiarse; **to make or pull a** ~ hacer muecas; **in the** ~ **of** (difficulties etc) ante; **on the** ~ **of it** a primera vista; ~ **to cara a cara; to** ~ **up to** vt fus hacer frente a, arrostrar; ~ **cloth** n (Brit) manopla; ~ **cream** n crema (de belleza); ~ **lift** n estirado facial; ~ **powder** n polvos mpl; **~-saving** a para salvar las apariencias.

facetious [fə'siːʃəs] a chistoso.

face value n (of stamp) valor m nominal; **to take sth at** ~ (fig) tomar algo en sentido literal.

facile ['fæsaɪl] a superficial.

facilities [fə'sɪlɪtɪz] npl facilidades fpl; **credit** ~ facilidades de crédito.

facing ['feɪsɪŋ] prep frente a // a de enfrente.

facsimile [fæk'sɪmɪlɪ] n (document) facsímil(e) m; (machine) telefax m.

fact [fækt] *n* hecho; **in ~** en realidad.

factor ['fæktə*] *n* factor *m*.

factory ['fæktərɪ] *n* fábrica.

factual ['fæktjuəl] *a* basado en los hechos.

faculty ['fækəltɪ] *n* facultad *f*; (*US*: *teaching staff*) personal *m* docente.

fad [fæd] *n* novedad *f*, moda.

fade [feɪd] *vi* desteñirse; (*sound, hope*) desvanecerse; (*light*) apagarse; (*flower*) marchitarse.

fag [fæg] *n* (*Brit*: *col*: *cigarette*) pitillo (*Sp*), cigarro; (*US*: *pej*: *homosexual*) maricón *m*.

fail [feɪl] *vt* (*candidate*) suspender; (*exam*) no aprobar (*Sp*), reprobar (*LAm*); (*subj*: *memory etc*) fallar a // *vi* suspender; (*be unsuccessful*) fracasar; (*strength, engine*) fallar; **to ~ to do sth** (*neglect*) dejar de hacer algo; (*be unable*) no poder hacer algo; **without ~** sin falta; **~ing** *n* falta, defecto // *prep* a falta de; **~ure** ['feɪljə*] *n* fracaso; (*person*) fracasado/a; (*mechanical etc*) fallo.

faint [feɪnt] *a* débil; (*recollection*) vago; (*mark*) apenas visible // *n* desmayo // *vi* desmayarse; **to feel ~** estar mareado, marearse.

fair [fɛə*] *a* justo; (*hair, person*) rubio; (*weather*) bueno; (*good enough*) regular; (*sizeable*) considerable // *ad* (*play*) limpio // *n* feria; (*Brit*: *funfair*) parque *m* de atracciones; **~ly** *ad* (*justly*) con justicia; (*equally*) equitativamente; (*quite*) bastante; **~ness** *n* justicia; (*impartiality*) imparcialidad *f*; **~ play** *n* juego limpio.

fairy ['fɛərɪ] *n* hada; **~ tale** *n* cuento de hadas.

faith [feɪθ] *n* fe *f*; (*trust*) confianza; (*sect*) religión *f*; **~ful** *a* fiel; **~fully** *ad* fielmente; **yours ~fully** (*Brit*: in letters) le saluda atentamente.

fake [feɪk] *n* (*painting etc*) falsificación *f*; (*person*) impostor/a *m/f* // *a* falso // *vt* fingir; (*painting etc*) falsificar.

falcon ['fɔːlkən] *n* halcón *m*.

fall [fɔːl] *n* caída; (*US*) otoño // *vi* (*pt fell, pp fallen* [fɔːlən]) caer(se); (*price*) bajar; **~s** *npl* (*waterfall*) cascada (*sg*, salto *sg* de agua; **to ~ flat** *vi* (*on one's face*) caerse (boca abajo); (*joke, story*) no hacer gracia; **to ~ back** *vi* retroceder; **to ~ back on** *vt fus* (*remedy etc*) recurrir a; **to ~ behind** *vi* quedarse atrás; **to ~ down** *vi* (*person*) caerse; (*building, hopes*) derrumbarse; **to ~ for** *vt fus* (*trick*) dejarse engañar por; (*person*) enamorarse de; **to ~ in** *vi* (*roof*) hundirse; (*MIL*) alinearse; **to ~ off** *vi* caerse; (*diminish*) disminuir; **to ~ out** *vi* (*friends etc*) reñir; (*MIL*) romper filas; **to ~ through** *vi* (*plan, project*) fracasar.

fallacy ['fæləsɪ] *n* error *m*.

fallen ['fɔːlən] *pp of* **fall**.

fallout ['fɔːlaut] *n* lluvia radioactiva; **~ shelter** *n* refugio antiatómico.

fallow ['fæləu] *a* en barbecho.

false [fɔːls] *a*(*en*) falso; (*hair, teeth etc*) postizo; (*disloyal*) desleal, traidor(a); **under ~ pretences** con engaños; **~ alarm** *n* falsa alarma; **~ teeth** *npl* (*Brit*) dentadura *sg* postiza.

falter ['fɔːltə*] *vi* vacilar.

fame [feɪm] *n* fama.

familiar [fə'mɪlɪə*] *a* familiar; (*well-known*) conocido; (*tone*) de confianza; **to be ~ with** (*subject*) estar enterado de; **~ity** [fəmɪlɪ'ærɪtɪ] *n* familiaridad *f*.

family ['fæmɪlɪ] *n* familia; **~ business** *n* negocio familiar; **~ doctor** *n* médico/a de cabecera.

famine ['fæmɪn] *n* hambruna.

famished ['fæmɪʃt] *a* hambriento.

famous ['feɪməs] *a* famoso, célebre; **~ly** *ad* (*get on*) estupendamente.

fan [fæn] *n* abanico; (*ELEC*) ventilador *m*; (*person*) aficionado/a *m/f* // *vt* abanicar; (*fire, quarrel*) atizar; **to ~ out** *vi* desparramarse.

fanatic [fə'nætɪk] *n* fanático/a.

fan belt *n* correa de ventilador.

fanciful ['fænsıful] a (gen) fantástico; (imaginary) fantasioso.

fancy ['fænsı] n (whim) capricho, antojo; (imagination) imaginación f // a (luxury) de lujo; (price) exorbitado // vt (feel like, want) tener ganas de; (imagine) imaginarse; **to take a** ~ **to sb** tomar cariño a uno; **he fancies her** le gusta (ella) mucho; ~ **dress** n disfraz m; ~**dress ball** n baile m de disfraces.

fanfare ['fænfɛə*] n fanfarria (de trompeta).

fang [fæŋ] n colmillo.

fantastic [fæn'tæstık] a fantástico.

fantasy ['fæntəzı] n fantasía.

far [fɑ:*] a (distant) lejano // ad lejos; ~ **away**, ~ **off** (a lo lejos) // better mucho mejor; ~ **from** lejos de; **by** ~ con mucho; **go as** ~ **as the farm** vaya hasta la granja; **as** ~ **as I know** que yo sepa; **how** ~? ¿hasta dónde?; (fig) ¿hasta qué punto?; ~**away** a remoto.

farce [fɑ:s] n farsa; **farcical** a absurdo.

fare [fɛə*] n (on trains, buses) precio (del billete); (in taxi: cost) tarifa; (: passenger) pasajero/a; (food) comida; **half/full** ~ medio pasaje/ pasaje m completo.

Far East n: **the** ~ el Extremo Oriente.

farewell [fɛə'wɛl] excl, n adiós m.

farm [fɑ:m] n granja, finca (LAm), estancia (LAm) // vt cultivar; ~**er** n granjero, estanciero (LAm); ~**hand** n peón m; ~**house** n granja, casa de hacienda (LAm); ~**ing** n (gen) agricultura; (tilling) cultivo; ~**land** n tierra de cultivo; ~ **worker** n = ~**hand**; ~**yard** n corral m.

far-reaching [fɑː'riːtʃıŋ] a (reform, effect) de gran alcance.

fart [fɑːt] (col!) n pedo(!) // vi tirarse un pedo(!)

farther ['fɑːðə*] ad más lejos, más allá // a más lejano.

farthest ['fɑːðıst] superlative of **far**.

fascinate ['fæsıneıt] vt fascinar; **fas-** cinating a fascinante; **fascination** [-'neıʃən] n fascinación f.

fascism ['fæʃızəm] n fascismo.

fashion ['fæʃən] n moda; (manner) manera // vt formar; **in** ~ a la moda; **out of** ~ pasado de moda; ~**able** a de moda; ~ **show** n desfile m de modelos.

fast [fɑːst] a rápido; (dye, colour) sólido; (clock): **to be** ~ estar adelantado // ad rápidamente, de prisa; (stuck, held) firmemente // n ayuno // vi ayunar; ~ **asleep** profundamente dormido.

fasten ['fɑːsn] vt asegurar, sujetar; (coat, belt) abrochar // vi cerrarse; ~**er**, ~**ing** n cierre m; (of door etc) cerrojo.

fast food n comida rápida, platos mpl preparados.

fastidious [fæs'tıdıəs] a (fussy) delicado; (demanding) exigente.

fat [fæt] a gordo; (meat) con mucha grasa; (greasy) grasiento // n (on animals) grasa; (on person) carnes fpl; (lard) manteca.

fatal ['feɪtl] a (mistake) fatal; (injury) mortal; (consequence) funesto; ~**ism** n fatalismo; ~**ity** [fə'tælıtı] n (road death etc) víctima f; ~**ly** ad: ~**ly injured** herido a muerte.

fate [feɪt] n destino; ~**ful** a fatídico.

father ['fɑːðə*] n padre m; ~**-in-law** n suegro; ~**ly** a paternal.

fathom ['fæðəm] n braza // vt (mystery) desentrañar; (understand) lograr comprender.

fatigue [fə'tiːg] n fatiga, cansancio.

fatten ['fætn] vt, vi engordar.

fatty ['fætı] a (food) graso // n (col) gordito/a, gordinflón/ona m/f.

fatuous ['fætjuəs] a fatuo, necio.

faucet ['fɔːsıt] n (US) grifo, llave f (LAm).

fault [fɔːlt] n (blame) culpa; (defect: in character) defecto; (in manufacture) desperfecto; (GEO) falla // vt criticar; **it's my** ~ es culpa mía; **to find** ~ **with** criticar, poner peros a; **at** ~ culpable; ~**less** a (action) in-

tachable; (person) sin defectos; ~**y**
a defectuoso.

fauna ['fɔːnə] n fauna.

faux pas ['fəu'pɑː] n plancha.

favour, (US) **favor** ['feɪvə*] n favor
m; (approval) aprobación f // vt
(proposition) estar a favor de, aprobar; (person etc) favorecer; (assist)
ser propicio a; **to ask a ~ of** pedir
un favor a; **to do sb a ~** hacer un
favor a uno; **to find ~ with** caer en
gracia de; **in ~ of** a favor de;
~**able** a favorable; ~**ite** [-rɪt] a, n
favorito, preferido; ~**itism** n favori-
tismo.

fawn [fɔːn] n cervato // a (also: ~
coloured) color de cervato, leonado
// vi: **to ~ (up)on** adular.

fax [fæks] n (document) facsímil(e)
m; (machine) telefax m // vt mandar por telefax.

FBI n abbr (US: = Federal Bureau of
Investigation) ≈ BIC f (Sp).

fear [fɪə*] n miedo, temor m // vt temer; **for ~ of** por temor a; ~**ful** a
temeroso, miedoso; (awful) terrible.

feasible ['fiːzəbl] a factible.

feast [fiːst] n banquete m; (REL:
also: ~ **day**) fiesta // vi banquetear.

feat [fiːt] n hazaña.

feather ['feðə*] n pluma.

feature ['fiːtʃə*] n (gen) característica; (ANAT) rasgo; (article) artículo
de fondo // vt (subj: film) presentar //
vi figurar; ~**s** npl (of face) facciones
fpl; ~ **film** n largometraje m.

February ['februəri] n febrero.

fed [fed] pt, pp de **feed.**

federal ['fedərəl] a federal.

fed-up ['fedʌp] a: **to be ~ (with)**
estar harto de.

fee [fiː] n (professional) derechos
mpl, honorarios mpl; (of school) matrícula; (of club) cuota.

feeble ['fiːbl] a débil.

feed [fiːd] n (gen, of baby) comida;
(of animal) pienso; (on printer) dispositivo de alimentación // vt (pt, pp
fed) (gen) alimentar; (Brit: baby:
breastfeed) dar el pecho a; (animal)

dar de comer a; (data, information):
to ~ into meter en; **to ~ on** vt fus
alimentarse de; ~**back** n reacción f,
feedback m; ~**ing bottle** n (Brit)
biberón m.

feel [fiːl] n (sensation) sensación f;
(sense of touch) tacto // vt (pt, pp
felt) tocar; (cold, pain etc) sentir;
(think, believe) creer; **to ~ hungry/
cold** tener hambre/frío; **to ~
lonely/better** sentirse solo/mejor; **I
don't ~ well** no me siento bien; **it
~s soft** es suave al tacto; **to ~ like**
(want) tener ganas de; **to ~ about
or around** vt tantear; ~**er** n (of insect) antena; **to put out ~ers** (fig)
sondear; ~**ing** n (physical) sensación f; (foreboding) presentimiento;
(emotion) sentimiento.

feet [fiːt] pl of **foot.**

feign [feɪn] vt fingir.

fell [fel] pt of **fall** // vt (tree) talar.

fellow ['feləu] n tipo, tío (Sp); (of
learned society) socio/a // cpd: ~ **stu-
dents** compañeros/as m/pl de curso;
~ **citizen** n
conciudadano/a; ~ **countryman** n
compatriota m; ~ **men** npl semejantes mpl; ~**ship** n compañerismo;
(grant) beca; ~ **student** n
compañero/a de curso.

felony ['feləni] n crimen m.

felt [felt] pt, pp of **feel** // n fieltro;
~**-tip pen** n rotulador m.

female ['fiːmeɪl] n (woman) mujer f;
(ZOOL) hembra // a femenino.

feminine ['femɪnɪn] a femenino.

feminist ['femɪnɪst] n feminista.

fence [fens] n valla, cerca // vt (also:
~ **in**) cercar // vi (SPORT) hacer esgrima; **fencing** n esgrima.

fend [fend] vi: **to ~ for o.s.** valerse
por sí mismo; **to ~ off** vt (attack)
rechazar.

fender ['fendə*] n guardafuego; (US:
AUT) parachoques m inv; (: RAIL)
trompa.

ferment [fə'ment] vi fermentar // n
['fɔːment] (fig) agitación f.

fern [fɔːn] n helecho.

ferocious [fə'rəʊʃəs] a feroz; **ferocity** [fə'rɒsɪtɪ] n ferocidad f.

ferret ['ferɪt] n hurón m // vt: **to ~ out** desentrañar.

ferry ['ferɪ] n (small) barca (de pasaje), balsa; (large: also: **~boat**) transbordador m (Sp), embarcadero (LAm) // vt transportar.

fertile ['fɜːtaɪl] a fértil; (BIOL) fecundo; **fertility** [fə'tɪlɪtɪ] n fertilidad f; fecundidad f; **fertilize** ['fɜːtɪlaɪz] vt (BIOL) fecundar; (AGR) abonar; **fertilizer** n abono.

fervent ['fɜːvənt] a (admirer) entusiasta; (hope) ferviente.

fervour ['fɜːvə*] n fervor m, ardor m.

fester ['festə*] vi ulcerarse.

festival ['festɪvəl] n (REL) fiesta; (ART, MUS) festival m.

festive ['festɪv] a festivo; the **~ season** (Brit: Christmas) las Navidades.

festivities [fes'tɪvɪtɪz] npl fiestas fpl.

festoon [fes'tuːn] vt: **to ~ with** engalanar de.

fetch [fetʃ] vt ir a buscar; (sell for) venderse por.

fetching ['fetʃɪŋ] a atractivo.

fête [feɪt] n fiesta.

fetus ['fiːtəs] n (US) = **foetus**.

feud [fjuːd] n (hostility) enemistad f; (quarrel) disputa.

feudal ['fjuːdl] a feudal.

fever ['fiːvə*] n fiebre f; **~ish** a febril.

few [fjuː] a (not many) pocos; (some) algunos, unos; **a ~** a unos pocos // pron algunos; **~er** a menos; **~est** a los/las menos.

fiancé [fɪ'ɑːnseɪ] n novio, prometido; **~e** n novia, prometida.

fib [fɪb] n mentirilla // vi decir mentirillas.

fibre, (US) **fiber** ['faɪbə*] n fibra; **~-glass** n fibra de vidrio.

fickle ['fɪkl] a inconstante.

fiction ['fɪkʃən] n (gen) ficción f; **~al** a novelesco; **fictitious** [fɪk'tɪʃəs] a ficticio.

fiddle ['fɪdl] n (MUS) violín m;

(cheating) trampa // vt (Brit: accounts) falsificar; **to ~ with** vt fus jugar con.

fidelity [fɪ'delɪtɪ] n fidelidad f.

fidget ['fɪdʒɪt] vi inquietarse.

field [fiːld] n campo; (fig) campo, esfera; (SPORT) campo, cancha (LAm); (competitors) competidores mpl; **~ marshal** n mariscal m; **~work** n trabajo de campo.

fiend [fiːnd] n demonio; **~ish** a diabólico.

fierce [fɪəs] a feroz; (wind, attack) violento; (heat) intenso; (fighting, enemy) encarnizado.

fiery ['faɪərɪ] a (burning) ardiente; (temperament) apasionado.

fifteen [fɪf'tiːn] num quince.

fifth [fɪfθ] a, n quinto.

fifty ['fɪftɪ] num cincuenta; **~-~** a: a **~-~ chance** la cincuenta por ciento de posibilidades // ad a medias, mitad por mitad.

fig [fɪg] n higo.

fight [faɪt] n (gen) pelea; (MIL) combate m; (struggle) lucha // (vb: pt, pp **fought**) vt luchar contra; (cancer, alcoholism) combatir // vi pelear, luchar; **~er** n combatiente m/f; (fig) luchador(a) m/f; (plane) caza m; **~ing** n combate m.

figment ['fɪgmənt] n: **a ~ of the imagination** una quimera.

figurative ['fɪgjʊrətɪv] a (meaning) figurado.

figure ['fɪgə*] n (DRAWING, GEOM) figura, dibujo; (number, cipher) cifra; (body, outline) talle m, tipo // vt (esp US) imaginar // vi (appear) figurar; (US: make sense) ser lógico; **to ~ out** vt (understand) comprender; **~head** n (fig) testaferro; **~ of speech** n figura retórica.

filch [fɪltʃ] vt (col: steal) hurtar, robar.

file [faɪl] n (tool) lima; (dossier) expediente m; (folder) carpeta; (COMPUT) fichero; (row) fila // vt limar; (papers) clasificar; (LAW: claim) presentar; (store) archivar; **to ~**

in/out vi entrar/salir en fila; **to ~ past** vt fus desfilar ante; **filing** n: **to do the filing** llevar los archivos; **filing cabinet** n fichero, archivo.

fill [fɪl] vt llenar // n: **to eat one's ~** llenarse; **to ~ in** vt rellenar; **to ~ up** vt llenar (hasta el borde) // vi (AUT) poner gasolina.

fillet ['fɪlɪt] n filete m; **~ steak** n filete m de ternera.

filling ['fɪlɪŋ] n (CULIN) relleno; (for tooth) empaste m; **~ station** n estación f de servicio.

film [fɪlm] n película // n (scene) filmar // vi rodar (una película); **~ star** n astro, estrella de cine; **~strip** n tira de película.

filter ['fɪltə*] n filtro // vt filtrar; **~ lane** n (Brit) carril m de selección; **~-tipped** a con filtro.

filth [fɪlθ] n suciedad f; **~y** a sucio; (language) obsceno.

fin [fɪn] n (gen) aleta.

final ['faɪnl] a (last) final, último; (definitive) definitivo, terminante // n (Brit: SPORT) final f; **~s** npl (SCOL) examen m de fin de curso; (US: SPORT) final f.

finale [fɪ'nɑːlɪ] n final m.

final: **~ist** n (SPORT) finalista m/f; **~ize** vt concluir, completar; **~ly** ad (lastly) por último, finalmente; (eventually) por fin.

finance [faɪ'næns] n (money) fondos mpl, **~s** npl finanzas fpl // vt financiar; **financial** a ['-'nænʃəl] a financiero; **financier** n financiero.

find [faɪnd] vt (pt, pp **found**) (gen) encontrar, hallar; (come upon) descubrir // n hallazgo; descubrimiento; **to ~ sb guilty** (LAW) declarar culpable a uno; **to ~ out** vt averiguar; (truth, secret) descubrir; **to ~ out about** enterarse de; **~ings** npl (LAW) veredicto sg, fallo sg; (of report) recomendaciones fpl.

fine [faɪn] a (delicate) fino; (beautiful) hermoso // ad (well) bien // n (LAW) multa // vt (LAW) multar; **the weather is ~** hace buen tiempo;

~ arts npl bellas artes fpl.

finery ['faɪnərɪ] n adornos mpl.

finesse [fɪ'nɛs] n sutileza.

finger ['fɪŋgə*] n dedo // vt (touch) manosear; (MUS) puntear; **little/ index ~** (dedo) meñique m/índice m; **~nail** n uña; **~print** n huella dactilar; **~tip** n yema del dedo.

finicky ['fɪnɪkɪ] a (fussy) delicado.

finish ['fɪnɪʃ] n (end) fin m; (SPORT) meta; (polish etc) acabado // vt, vi terminar; **to ~ doing sth** acabar de hacer algo; **to ~ third** llegar el tercero; **to ~ off** vt acabar, terminar; (kill) acabar con; **to ~ up** vt acabar, terminar // vi ir a parar, terminar; **~ing line** n línea de llegada or meta; **~ing school** n academia para señoritas.

finite ['faɪnaɪt] a finito; (verb) conjugado.

Finland ['fɪnlənd] n Finlandia.

Finn [fɪn] n finlandés/esa m/f; **~ish** a finlandés/esa // n (LING) finlandés m.

fir [fɜː*] n abeto.

fire ['faɪə*] n (gen) fuego; (accidental) incendio // vt (gun) disparar; (set fire to) incendiar; (excite) exaltar; (interest) despertar; (dismiss) despedir // vi encenderse; **on ~** ardiendo, en llamas; **~ alarm** n alarma de incendios; **~arm** n arma de fuego; **~ brigade**, (US) **~ department** n (cuerpo de) bomberos mpl; **~ engine** n coche m de bomberos; **~ escape** n escalera de incendios; **~ extinguisher** n extintor m (de fuego); **~man** n bombero; **~place** n chimenea; **~side** n: **by the ~** al lado de la chimenea; **~ station** n parque m de bomberos; **~wood** n leña; **~works** npl fuegos mpl artificiales.

firing ['faɪərɪŋ] n (MIL) disparos mpl, tiroteo; **~ squad** n pelotón m de ejecución.

firm [fɜːm] a firme // n firma, empresa; **~ly** ad firmemente; **~ness** n firmeza.

first [fɜːst] a primero // ad (before

others) primero/a; (*when listing reasons etc*) en primer lugar, primeramente // *n* (*person: in race*) primero/a; (*AUT*) primera; **at** ~ al principio; ~ **of all** ante todo; ~ **aid** *n* primera ayuda, primeros auxilios *mpl*; ~**aid kit** *n* botiquín *m*; ~**class** *a* de primera clase; ~**hand** *a* de primera mano; F~ **Lady** *n* (*esp US*) primera dama; ~**ly** en primer lugar; ~**name** *n* nombre *m* de pila; ~**rate** *a* de primera clase.

fish [fɪʃ] *n, pl inv* pez *m*; (*food*) pescado // *vt, vi* pescar; **to go ~ing** ir de pesca; ~**erman** *n* pescador *m*; ~**farm** *n* criadero de peces; ~**fingers** *npl* (*Brit*) croquetas *fpl* de pescado; ~**ing boat** *n* barca de pesca; ~**ing line** *n* sedal *m*; ~**ing rod** *n* caña (de pescar); ~**ing tackle** *n* aparejo (de pescar); ~ **market** *n* mercado de pescado; ~**monger** (*Brit*) pescadero; ~**monger's (shop)** *n* (*Brit*) pescadería; ~**sticks** *npl* (*US*) = ~ **fingers**; ~**seller** *n* (*US*) = **fishmonger**; ~**y** *a* (*fig*) sospechoso; ~**store** *n* (*US*) = **fishmonger's**.

fist [fɪst] *n* puño.

fit [fɪt] *a* (*MED, SPORT*) en (buena) forma; (*proper*) adecuado, apropiado // *vt* (*subj: clothes*) sentar bien a; (*try on: clothes*) probar; (*facts*) cuadrar or corresponder con; (*accommodate*) ajustar, adaptar // *vi* (*clothes*) entallar; (*in space, gap*) caber; (*facts*) coincidir // *n* (*MED*) ataque *m*; ~ **to** apto para; ~ **for** apropiado para; **a ~ of anger/pride** un arranque de cólera/orgullo; **this dress is a good ~** este vestido me sienta bien; **by ~s and starts** a rachas; **to ~ in** *vi* (*gen*) encajarse; (*fig: person*) llevarse bien (con todos); **to ~ out** (*Brit: also:* ~ **up**) *vt* equipar; ~**ful** *a* espasmódico, intermitente; ~**ment** *n* módulo adosable; ~**ness** *n* (*MED*) salud *f*; (*of remark*) conveniencia; ~**ted carpet** *n* moqueta; ~**ted kitchen** *n* cocina amueblada;

~**ter** *n* ajustador *m*; ~**ting** *a* apropiado // *n* (*of dress*) prueba; ~**ting room** *n* probador *m*; ~**tings** *npl* instalaciones *fpl*.

five [faɪv] *num* cinco; ~**r** *n* (*col: Brit*) billete *m* de cinco libras; (: *US*) billete *m* de cinco dólares.

fix [fɪks] *vt* (*secure*) fijar, asegurar; (*mend*) arreglar // *n*: **to be in a ~** estar en un aprieto; **to ~ up** *vt* (*meeting*) arreglar; **to ~ sb up with sth** proveer a uno de algo; ~**ed** [fɪkst] *a* (*prices etc*) fijo; ~**ture** [ˈfɪkstʃə*] (*SPORT*) encuentro; ~**tures** *npl* instalaciones *fpl* fijas.

fizz [fɪz] *vi* hacer efervescencia.

fizzle out [ˈfɪzl]: *vi* apagarse.

fizzy [ˈfɪzɪ] *a* (*drink*) gaseoso.

flabbergasted [ˈflæbəgɑːstɪd] *a* pasmado.

flabby [ˈflæbɪ] *a* flojo (*de carnes*); (*skin*) fofo.

flag [flæg] *n* bandera; (*stone*) losa // *vi* decaer; **to ~ sb down** hacer señas a uno para que se pare; ~**pole** *n* asta de bandera; ~ **stop** *n* (*US*) parada a petición.

flair [flɛə*] *n* aptitud *f* especial.

flak [flæk] *n* (*MIL*) fuego antiaéreo; (*col: criticism*) lluvia de críticas.

flake [fleɪk] *n* (*of rust, paint*) escama; (*of snow, soap powder*) copo // *vi* (*also:* ~ **off**) (*paint*) desconcharse; (*skin*) descamarse.

flamboyant [flæmˈbɔɪənt] *a* (*dress*) vistoso; (*person*) extravagante.

flame [fleɪm] *n* llama.

flamingo [fləˈmɪŋgəʊ] *n* flamenco.

flammable [ˈflæməbl] *a* inflamable.

flan [flæn] *n* (*Brit*) tarta.

flank [flæŋk] *n* flanco; (*of person*) costado // *vt* flanquear.

flannel [ˈflænl] *n* (*Brit: also:* **face ~**) manopla; (*fabric*) franela; ~**s** *npl* pantalones *mpl* de franela.

flap [flæp] *n* (*of pocket*) solapa; (*of envelope*) solapa; (*of table*) hoja (plegadiza); (*wing movement*) aleteo // *vt* (*wings*) aletear // *vi* (*sail,* *flag*) ondear.

flare |fleə*| *n* llamarada; (*MIL*) bengala; (*in skirt etc*) vuelo; **to ~ up** *vi* encenderse; (*fig: person*) encolerizarse; (: *revolt*) estallar.

flash |flæʃ| *n* relámpago; (*also: news ~*) noticias *fpl* de última hora; (*PHOT*) flash *m* // *vt* (*light, headlights*) encender y apagar; (*torch*) encender // *vi* brillar; **in a ~** en un instante; **he ~ed by** *or* **past** pasó como un rayo; **~bulb** *n* bombilla fusible; **~ cube** *n* cubo de flash; **~light** *n* linterna.

flashy |ˈflæʃɪ| *a* (*pej*) ostentoso.

flask |flɑːsk| *n* frasco; (*also:* **vacuum ~**) termo(s) *m*.

flat |flæt| *a* llano; (*smooth*) liso; (*tyre*) desinflado; (*beer*) muerto; (*MUS*) desafinado // *n* (*Brit: apartment*) piso (*Sp*), departamento (*LAm*), apartamento (*AUT*) pinchazo; (*MUS*) bemol *m*; **to work ~ out** trabajar a toda mecha; **~ly** *ad* terminantemente, de plano; **~ten** *vt* (*also:* **~ten out**) allanar; (*smooth out*) alisar.

flatter |ˈflætə*| *vt* adular, halagar; **~ing** *a* halagüeño; **~y** *n* adulación *f*.

flaunt |flɔːnt| *vt* ostentar, lucir.

flavour, (*US*) **flavor** |ˈfleɪvə*| *n* sabor *m*, gusto // *vt* sazonar, condimentar; **~ed** *a*: **strawberry ~ed** con sabor a fresa; **~ing** *n* (*in product*) aromatizante *m*.

flaw |flɔː| *n* defecto.

flax |flæks| *n* lino; **~en** *a* rubio.

flea |fliː| *n* pulga.

fleck |flɛk| *n* (*mark*) mota; (*pattern*) punto.

flee |fliː|, *pt*, *pp* **fled** |flɛd| *vt* huir de, abandonar // *vi* huir, fugarse.

fleece |fliːs| *n* vellón *m*; (*wool*) lana // *vt* (*col*) pelar.

fleet |fliːt| *n* (*of lorries etc*) escuadra.

fleeting |ˈfliːtɪŋ| *a* fugaz.

Flemish |ˈflɛmɪʃ| *a* flamenco.

flesh |flɛʃ| *n* carne *f*; (*of fruit*) pulpa; **of ~ and blood** de carne y hueso; **~ wound** *n* herida superficial.

flew |fluː| *pt* of **fly**.

flex |flɛks| *n* cordón *m* // *vt* (*muscles*) tensar; **~ibility** |-ɪˈbɪlɪtɪ| *n* flexibilidad *f*; **~ible** *a* flexible.

flick |flɪk| *n* golpecito; (*with finger*) capirotazo // *vt* dar un golpecito a; **to ~ through** *vt fus* hojear.

flicker |ˈflɪkə*| *vi* (*light*) parpadear; (*flame*) vacilar // *n* parpadeo.

flier |ˈflaɪə*| *n* aviador *a* *mf*.

flight |flaɪt| *n* vuelo; (*escape*) huida, fuga; (*also: ~ of steps*) tramo (de escaleras); **to take ~** huir, darse a la fuga; **to put to ~** ahuyentar; **~ attendant** *n* (*US*) (*male*) camarero, (*female*) azafata; **~ deck** *n* (*AVIAT*) cabina de mandos.

flimsy |ˈflɪmzɪ| *a* (*thin*) muy ligero; (*excuse*) flojo.

flinch |flɪntʃ| *vi* encogerse.

fling |flɪŋ|, *pt*, *pp* **flung** *vt* arrojar.

flint |flɪnt| *n* pedernal *m*; (*in lighter*) piedra.

flip |flɪp| *vt* dar la vuelta a; (*coin*) echar a cara o cruz.

flippant |ˈflɪpənt| *a* poco serio.

flipper |ˈflɪpə*| *n* aleta.

flirt |flɜːt| *vi* coquetear, flirtear // *n* coqueta *f*; **~ation** |-ˈteɪʃən| *n* coqueteo, flirteo.

flit |flɪt| *vi* revolotear.

float |fləut| *n* flotador *m*; (*in procession*) carroza; (*money*) reserva // *vi* flotar; (*swimmer*) hacer la plancha // *vt* (*gen*) hacer flotar; (*company*) lanzar.

flock |flɒk| *n* (*of sheep*) rebaño; (*of birds*) bandada; (*of people*) multitud *f*.

flog |flɒg| *vt* azotar; (*col*) vender.

flood |flʌd| *n* inundación *f*; (*of words, tears etc*) torrente *m* // *vt* inundar; **~ing** *n* inundación *f*; **~light** *n* foco.

floor |flɔː*| *n* suelo; (*storey*) piso; (*of sea*) fondo; (*dance ~*) pista // (*fig*) dejar sin respuesta; **ground ~**, (*US*) **first ~** planta baja; **first ~**, (*US* second ~ primer piso; **~board** n tabla; ~ **lamp** n (US) lámpara de pie; ~ **show** n cabaret m.

flop [flɔp] n fracaso.

floppy ['flɔpɪ] a flojo // n (COMPUT: also: ~ **disk**) floppy m.

flora ['flɔːrə] n flora.

florist ['flɔrɪst] n florista m/f; **~'s (shop)** n florería.

flounce [flauns] n volante m; **to ~ out** vi salir enfadado.

flounder ['flaundə*] vi tropezar // n (ZOOL) platija.

flour ['flauə*] n harina.

flourish ['flʌrɪʃ] vi florecer // n además m, movimiento (ostentoso); **~ing** a floreciente.

flout [flaut] vt burlarse de.

flow [fləu] n (movement) flujo; (direction) curso; (tide) corriente f // vi (river, traffic, blood) fluir; ~ **chart** n organigrama m.

flower ['flauə*] n flor f // vi florecer; ~ **bed** n macizo; **~pot** n tiesto; **~y** a florido.

flown [fləun] pp of **fly**.

flu [fluː] n gripe f.

fluctuate ['flʌktjueɪt] vi fluctuar.

fluent ['fluːənt] a (speech) elocuente; he speaks ~ French, he's ~ in French domina el francés; **~ly** ad con fluidez.

fluff [flʌf] n pelusa; ; **~y** a velloso.

fluid ['fluːɪd] a, n fluido, líquido.

fluke [fluːk] n (col) chiripa.

flung [flʌŋ] pt, pp of **fling**.

fluoride ['fluəraɪd] n fluoruro.

flurry ['flʌrɪ] n (of snow) temporal m; (haste) agitación f; ~ **of activity** frenesí m de actividad.

flush [flʌʃ] n (on face) rubor m; (fig: of youth, beauty) resplandor m // vt limpiar con agua // vi ruborizarse // a: ~ **with** a ras de; **to ~ the toilet** hacer funcionar el WC; **to ~ out** vt (game, birds) levantar; (fig) desalojar; **~ed** a ruborizado.

flustered ['flʌstəd] a aturdido.

flute [fluːt] n flauta.

flutter ['flʌtə*] n (of wings) revolo-

teo, aleteo // vi revolotear.

flux [flʌks] n: **to be in a state of ~** estar continuamente cambiando.

fly [flaɪ] n (insect) mosca; (on trousers: also: **flies**) bragueta // vb (pt **flew**, pp **flown**) vt (plane) pilot(e)ar; (cargo) transportar (en avión); (distances) recorrer (en avión) // vi volar; (passengers) ir en avión; (escape) evadirse; (flag) ondear; **to ~ away** or **off** vi (bird, insect) emprender el vuelo; **~ing** n (activity) (el) volar // a: **~ing visit** visita relámpago; **with ~ing colours** con lucimiento; **~ing saucer** n platillo volante; **~ing start** n: **to get off to a ~ing start** empezar con buen pie; **~over** n (Brit: bridge) paso a desnivel or superior; **~past** n desfile m aéreo; **~sheet** n (for tent) doble techo.

foal [fəul] n potro.

foam [fəum] n espuma // vi echar espuma; ~ **rubber** n espuma de caucho.

fob [fɔb] vt: **to ~ sb off with sth** despachar a uno con algo.

focus ['fəukəs], pl **~es** n foco // vt (field glasses etc) enfocar // vi: **to ~ on** enfocar a; (issue etc) centrarse en; **in/out of ~** enfocado/ desenfocado.

fodder ['fɔdə*] n pienso.

foe [fəu] n enemigo.

foetus ['fiːtəs] n feto.

fog [fɔg] n niebla; **~gy** a: **it's ~gy** hay niebla, está brumoso; ~ **lamp, (US) ~ light** n (AUT) faro de niebla.

foil [fɔɪl] vt frustrar // n hoja; (kitchen ~) papel m (de aluminio); (FENCING) florete m.

fold [fəuld] n (bend, crease) pliegue m; (AGR) redil m // vt doblar; **to ~ up** vi plegarse, doblarse; (business) quebrar // vt (map etc) plegar; **~er** n (for papers) carpeta; (brochure) folleto; **~ing** a (chair, bed) plegable.

foliage ['fəulɪɪdʒ] n follaje m.

folk [fəuk] *npl* gente *f //* a popular, folklórico; **~s** *npl* familia, parientes *mpl;* **~lore** ['fəuklɔ:*] *n* folklore *m;* **~ song** *n* canción *f* popular or folklórica.

follow ['fɔləu] *vt* seguir *// vi* seguir; (*result*) resultar; **he ~ed suit** hizo lo mismo; **to ~ up** *vt* (*letter, idea*) responder a; (*case*) investigar; **~er** *n* seguidor(a) *m/f;* (*POL*) partidario a; **~ing** *a* siguiente *// n* afición *f,* partidarios *mpl.*

folly ['fɔlɪ] *n* locura.

fond [fɔnd] *a* (*loving*) cariñoso; **to be ~ of** tener cariño a.

fondle ['fɔndl] *vt* acariciar.

fondness ['fɔndnɪs] *n* (*for things*) gusto; (*for people*) cariño.

font [fɔnt] *n* pila bautismal.

food [fu:d] *n* comida; **~ mixer** *n* batidora; **~ poisoning** *n* botulismo; **~ processor** *n* robot *m* de cocina; **~stuffs** *npl* comestibles *mpl.*

fool [fu:l] *n* tonto/a; (*CULIN*) puré *m* de frutas con nata *// vt* engañar *// vi* (*gen:* **~ around**) bromear; (*waste time*) perder el tiempo; **~hardy** *a* temerario; **~ish** *a* tonto; (*careless*) imprudente; **~proof** *a* (*plan etc*) infalible.

foot [fut], *pl* **feet** *n* pie *m;* (*measure*) pie *m* (= 304 *mms*); (*of animal*) pata *// vt* (*bill*) pagar; **on ~** a pie; **~age** *n* (*CINEMA*) imagenes *fpl;* **~ball** *n* balón *m;* (*game: Brit*) fútbol *m;* (*: US*) fútbol *m* americano; **~ball player** *n* (*Brit: also:* **~er**) *n* futbolista *m;* (*US*) jugador *m* de fútbol americano; **~brake** *n* freno de pie; **~bridge** *n* puente *m* para peatones; **~hills** *npl* estribaciones *fpl;* **~hold** *n* pie *m* firme; **~ing** *n* (*fig*) posición *f;* **to lose one's ~ing** perder el pie; **on an equal ~ing** en pie de igualdad; **~lights** *npl* candilejas *fpl;* **~man** *n* lacayo; **~note** *n* nota de pie; **~path** *n* sendero; **~print** *n* huella, pisada; **~sore** *a* con los pies doloridos; **~step** *n* paso; **~wear** *n* calzado.

for [fɔ:] ♦ *prep* **1** (*indicating destination, intention*) para; **the train ~ London** el tren con destino a or de Londres; **he left ~ Rome** marchó para Roma; **he went ~ the paper** fue por el periódico; **is this ~ me?** ¿es esto para mí?; **it's time ~ lunch** es la hora de comer

2 (*indicating purpose*) para; **what('s it) ~?** ¿para qué (es)?; **to pray ~ peace** rezar por la paz

3 (*on behalf of, representing*): **the MP ~ Hove** el diputado por Hove; **he works ~ the government/a local firm** trabaja para el gobierno/en una empresa local; **I'll ask him ~ you** se lo pediré por ti; **G ~ George** G de George

4 (*because of*) por esta razón; **~ fear of being criticized** por temor a ser criticado

5 (*with regard to*) para; **it's cold ~ July** hace frío para julio; **he has a gift ~ languages** tiene don de lenguas

6 (*in exchange for*) por; **I sold it ~ £5** lo vendí por £5; **to pay 50 pence ~ a ticket** pagar 50p por un billete

7 (*in favour of*): **are you ~ or against us?** ¿estás con nosotros o contra nosotros?; **I'm all ~ it** estoy totalmente a favor; **vote ~ X** vote (a) X

8 (*referring to distance*): **there are roadworks ~ 5 km** hay obras en 5 km; **we walked ~ miles** caminamos kilómetros y kilómetros

9 (*referring to time*): **he was away ~ 2 years** estuvo fuera (durante) dos años; **it hasn't rained ~ 3 weeks** no ha llovido durante or en 3 semanas; **I have known her ~ years** la conozco desde hace años; **can you do it ~ tomorrow?** ¿lo podrás hacer para mañana?

10 (*with infinitive clauses*): **it is not ~ me to decide** la decisión no es cosa mía; **it would be best ~ you**

to leave sería mejor que te fueras; there is still time ~ you to do it todavía te queda tiempo para hacerlo; ~ this to be possible... para que esto sea possible...

11 (in spite of) a pesar de; ~ all his complaints a pesar de sus quejas ◆ conj (since, as: rather formal) puesto que.

forage ['fɔrɪdʒ] n forraje m.

foray ['fɔreɪ] n incursión f.

forbid [fə'bɪd], pt **forbad(e)** [fə'bæd], pp **forbidden** [fə'bɪdn] vt prohibir; to ~ sb to do sth prohibir a uno hacer algo; ~ding a (landscape) inhóspito; (severe) severo.

force [fɔːs] n fuerza // vt forzar; to ~ o.s. to do hacer un esfuerzo por hacer; the F~s npl (Brit) las Fuerzas Armadas; in ~ en vigor; ~d [fɔːst] a forzado; to ~-feed vt (animal, prisoner) alimentar a la fuerza; ~ful a enérgico.

forcibly ['fɔːsəblɪ] ad a la fuerza.

ford [fɔːd] n vado // vt vadear.

fore [fɔː*] n: to the ~ en evidencia.

forearm ['fɔːraːm] n antebrazo.

foreboding [fɔː'bəudɪŋ] n presentimiento.

forecast ['fɔːkaːst] n pronóstico // vt (irg: like **cast**) pronosticar.

forecourt ['fɔːkɔːt] n (of garage) patio.

forefathers ['fɔːfɑːðəz] npl antepasados mpl.

forefinger ['fɔːfɪŋgə*] n (dedo) índice m.

forefront ['fɔːfrʌnt] n: in the ~ of en la vanguardia de.

forego vt = **forgo**.

foregone ['fɔːgɔn] a: it's a ~ conclusion es una conclusión evidente.

foreground ['fɔːgraund] n primer plano.

forehead ['fɔrɪd] n frente f.

foreign ['fɔrɪn] a extranjero; (trade) exterior; ~er n extranjero/a; ~ exchange n divisas fpl; F~ **Office** n (Brit) Ministerio de Asuntos Exterio-

res; F~ **Secretary** n (Brit) Ministro de Asuntos Exteriores.

foreleg ['fɔːleg] n pata delantera.

foreman ['fɔːmən] n capataz m; (in construction) maestro de obras.

foremost ['fɔːməust] a principal // ad: first and ~ ante todo.

forensic [fə'rensɪk] a forense.

forerunner ['fɔːrʌnə*] n precursor(a) m/f.

foresee [fɔː'siː], pt **foresaw** [fɔː'sɔː, -'sɔː, -siːn] vt prever; ~**able** a previsible.

foreshadow [fɔː'ʃædəu] vt prefigurar, anunciar.

foresight ['fɔːsaɪt] n previsión f.

forest ['fɔrɪst] n bosque m.

forestall [fɔː'stɔːl] vt prevenir.

forestry ['fɔrɪstrɪ] n silvicultura.

foretaste ['fɔːteɪst] n muestra.

foretell, pt, pp **foretold** [fɔː'tel, -'təuld] vt predecir, pronosticar.

forever [fə'revə*] ad para siempre.

foreword ['fɔːwəːd] n prefacio.

forfeit ['fɔːfɪt] n (in game) prenda // vt perder (derecho a).

forgave [fə'geɪv] pt of **forgive**.

forge [fɔːdʒ] n fragua; (smithy) herrería // vt (signature; Brit: money) falsificar; (metal) forjar; to ~ **ahead** vt avanzar constantemente; ~**r** n falsificador(a) m/f; ~**ry** n falsificación f.

forget [fə'get], pt **forgot**, pp **forgotten** vt olvidar // vi olvidarse; ~**ful** a olvidadizo; ~-**me-not** n nomeolvides f inv.

forgive [fə'gɪv], pt **forgave**, pp **forgiven** vt perdonar; to ~ sb for sth perdonar algo a uno; ~**ness** n perdón m.

forgo [fɔː'gəu], pt **forwent**, pp **forgone** vt (give up) renunciar a; (go without) privarse de.

forgot [fə'gɔt] pt of **forget**.

forgotten [fə'gɔtn] pp of **forget**.

fork [fɔːk] n (for eating) tenedor m; (for gardening) horca; (of roads) bifurcación f // (road) bifurcarse; to ~ **out** vt (col: pay) desembolsar;

~-**lift truck** n máquina elevadora.

forlorn [fə'lɔːn] a (person) triste, melancólico; (place) abandonado // a (attempt, hope) desesperado.

form [fɔːm] n forma; (Brit SCOL) clase f; (document) formulario // vt formar; **in top** ~ en plena forma.

formal ['fɔːməl] a (offer, receipt) por escrito; (person etc) correcto; (occasion, dinner) ceremonioso; (dress) de etiqueta; ~**ity** [-'mælɪtɪ] n ceremonia; ~**ly** ad oficialmente.

format ['fɔːmæt] n formato // vt (COMPUT) formatear.

formation [fɔː'meɪʃən] n formación f.

formative ['fɔːmətɪv] a (years) formativo.

former ['fɔːmə*] a anterior; (earlier) antiguo; (ex) ex; **the** ~ **... the latter** ... aquél ... éste ...; ~**ly** ad antiguamente.

formula ['fɔːmjulə] n fórmula.

forsake, pt **forsook**, pp **forsaken** [fə'seɪk, -'suk, -seɪkən] vt (gen) abandonar; (plan) renunciar a.

fort [fɔːt] n fuerte m.

forte ['fɔːtɪ] n fuerte m.

forth [fɔːθ] ad: **back and** ~ de acá para allá; **and so** ~ y así sucesivamente; ~**coming** a próximo, venidero; (character) comunicativo; ~**right** a franco; ~**with** ad en el acto.

fortify ['fɔːtɪfaɪ] vt fortalecer.

fortitude ['fɔːtɪtjuːd] n fortaleza.

fortnight ['fɔːtnaɪt] n (Brit) quincena; ~**ly** a quincenal // ad quincenalmente.

fortress ['fɔːtrɪs] n fortaleza.

fortunate ['fɔːtʃənɪt] a: **it is** ~ **that...** (es una) suerte que...; ~**ly** ad afortunadamente.

fortune ['fɔːtʃən] n suerte f; (wealth) fortuna; ~-**teller** n adivino/a.

forty ['fɔːtɪ] num cuarenta.

forum ['fɔːrəm] n foro.

forward ['fɔːwəd] a (movement, position) avanzado; (front) delantero;

(not shy) atrevido // n (SPORT) delantero // vt (letter) remitir; (career) promocionar; **to move** ~ avanzar; ~**(s)** ad (hacia) adelante.

forwent [fɔː'wɛnt] pt of **forgo**.

fossil ['fɔsl] n fósil m.

foster ['fɔstə*] vt fomentar; ~ **child** n hijo/a adoptivo/a; ~ **mother** n madre f adoptiva.

fought [fɔːt] pt, pp of **fight**.

foul [faul] a (gen) sucio, puerco; (weather, smell etc) asqueroso // n (FOOTBALL) falta // vt (dirty) ensuciar; (block) atascar; (football player) cometer una falta contra; ~ **play** n (SPORT) mala jugada; (LAW) muerte f violenta.

found [faund] pt, pp of **find** // vt (establish) fundar; ~**ation** [-'deɪʃən] n (act) fundación f; (basis) base f; (also: ~**ation cream**) crema base; ~**ations** npl (of building) cimientos mpl.

founder ['faundə*] n fundador(a) m/f // vi hundirse.

foundry ['faundrɪ] n fundición f.

fountain ['fauntɪn] n fuente f; ~ **pen** n (pluma) estilográfica, plumafuente f (LAm).

four [fɔː*] num cuatro; **on all** ~**s** a gatas; ~-**poster** (**bed**) n cama de dosel; ~**some** ['fɔːsəm] n grupo de cuatro personas; ~**teen** num catorce; ~**th** a cuarto.

fowl [faul] n ave f (de corral).

fox [fɔks] n zorro // vt confundir.

foyer ['fɔɪeɪ] n vestíbulo.

fracas ['fræːkɑː] n gresca, riña.

fraction ['frækʃən] n fracción f.

fracture ['fræktʃə*] n fractura.

fragile ['frædʒaɪl] a frágil.

fragment ['frægmənt] n fragmento.

fragrance ['freɪgrəns] n (of flowers) fragancia; (perfume) perfume m.

fragrant ['freɪgrənt] a fragante, oloroso.

frail [freɪl] a frágil; (person) débil.

frame [freɪm] n (of TECH) armazón m; (of picture, door, window) marco; (of spectacles: also: ~**s**) montura // vt encuadrar; (*reply*) formular; (*fam*) incriminar; ~ **of mind** *n* estado de ánimo; ~**work** *n* marco.

France [frɑːns] *n* Francia.

franchise ['fræntʃaɪz] *n* (POL) derecho de votar, sufragio; (COMM) licencia, concesión *f*.

frank [fræŋk] *a* franco // *vt* (Brit: *letter*) franquear; ~**ly** *ad* francamente; ~**ness** *n* franqueza.

frantic ['fræntɪk] *a* frenético.

fraternal [frə'tə:nl] *a* fraterno.

fraternity [frə'tə:nɪtɪ] *n* (*club*) fraternidad *f*; (US) club *m* de estudiantes; (*guild*) cofradía.

fraud [frɔːd] *n* fraude *m*; (*person*) impostor(a) *m/f*.

fraught [frɔːt] *a*: ~ **with** cargado de.

fray [freɪ] *n* combate *m*, lucha *f* // *vi* deshilacharse; **tempers were ~ed** el ambiente se ponía tenso.

freak [friːk] *n* (*person*) fenómeno; (*event*) suceso anormal.

freckle ['frekl] *n* peca.

free [friː] *a* (*person: at liberty*) libre; (*not fixed*) suelto; (*gratis*) gratis; (*unoccupied*) desocupado; (*liberal*) generoso // *vt* (*prisoner etc*) poner en libertad; (*jammed object*) soltar; ~ **(of charge)**, **for** ~ *ad* gratis; ~**dom** ['friːdəm] *n* libertad *f*; ~**for-all** *n* riña general; ~ **gift** *n* prima; ~**hold** *n* propiedad *f* vitalicia; ~ **kick** *n* tiro libre; ~**lance** *a*, *ad* por cuenta propia; ~**ly** *ad* libremente; generosamente; ~**mason** *n* francmasón *m*; ~**post** *n* porte pagado; ~**range** *a* (*hen, eggs*) de granja; ~ **trade** *n* libre comercio; ~**way** *n* (US) autopista; ~**wheel** *vi* ir en rueda libre; ~ **will** *n* libre albedrío *m*; **of one's own** ~ **will** por su propia voluntad.

freeze [friːz] *vb* (*pt* **froze**, *pp* **frozen**) *vi* helarse, congelarse // *vt* helar; (*prices, food, salaries*) congelar // *n* helada; congelación *f*; ~**-dried** *a* liofilizado; ~**r** *n* congelador *m* (Sp), congeladora (LAm).

freezing ['friːzɪŋ] *a* helado; ~ **point** *n* punto de congelación; **3 degrees below** ~ tres grados bajo cero.

freight [freɪt] *n* (*goods*) carga; (*money charged*) flete *m*; ~ **train** *n* (US) tren *m* de mercancías.

French [frentʃ] *a* francés/esa // *n* (LING) francés *m*; **the** ~ *npl* los franceses; ~ **bean** *n* judía verde; ~ **fried (potatoes)**, (US) ~ **fries** *npl* patatas *fpl* or papas *fpl* (LAm) fritas; ~**man/woman** *n* francés/esa *m/f*; ~ **window** *n* puertaventana.

frenzy ['frenzɪ] *n* frenesí *m*.

frequent *a* ['friːkwənt] *a* frecuente // *vt* [frɪ'kwent] frecuentar; ~**ly** [-əntlɪ] *ad* frecuentemente, a menudo.

fresh [freʃ] *a* (*gen*) fresco; (*new*) nuevo; (*water*) dulce; ~**en** *vi* (*wind, air*) soplar más recio; **to ~en up** *vi* (*person*) refrescarse; ~**er** *n* (Brit SCOL: col) estudiante *m/f* de primer año; ~**ly** *ad* (*newly*) nuevamente, (*recently*) recientemente; ~**man** *n* (US) = ~**er**; ~**ness** *n* frescura; ~**water** *a* (*fish*) de agua dulce.

fret [fret] *vi* inquietarse.

friar ['fraɪə*] *n* fraile *m*; (*before name*) fray *m*.

friction ['frɪkʃən] *n* fricción *f*.

Friday ['fraɪdɪ] *n* viernes *m inv*.

fridge [frɪdʒ] *n* (Brit) nevera, frigo, refrigeradora (LAm).

friend [frend] *n* amigo/a; ~**liness** *n* simpatía; ~**ly** *a* simpático; ~**ship** *n* amistad *f*.

frieze [friːz] *n* friso.

frigate ['frɪgɪt] *n* fragata.

fright [fraɪt] *n* susto; **to take** ~ asustarse; ~**en** *vt* asustar; ~**ened** *a* asustado; ~**ening** *a* espantoso; ~**ful** *a* espantoso, horrible; ~**fully** *ad* terriblemente.

frigid ['frɪdʒɪd] *a* (MED) frígido, frío.

frill [frɪl] *n* volante *m*.

fringe [frɪndʒ] *n* (Brit: *of hair*) flequillo; (*edge: of forest etc*) borde *m*, margen *m*; ~ **benefits** *npl* ventajas *fpl* supletorias.

frisk [frɪsk] *vt* cachear, registrar.

frisky ['frɪskɪ] a juguetón/ona.

fritter ['frɪtə*] n buñuelo; **to ~ away** vt desperdiciar.

frivolous ['frɪvələs] a frívolo.

frizzy ['frɪzɪ] a rizado.

fro [frəu] see **to**.

frock [frɔk] n vestido.

frog [frɔg] n rana; **~man** n hombre-rana m.

frolic ['frɔlɪk] vi juguetear.

KEYWORD
---

from [frɔm] prep 1 (indicating starting place) de, desde; **where do you come ~?** ¿de dónde eres?; **~ London to Glasgow** de Londres a Glasgow; **to escape ~ sth/sb** escaparse de algo/alguien

2 (indicating origin etc) de; **a letter/telephone call ~ my sister** una carta/llamada de mi hermana; **tell him ~ me that...** dígale de mi parte que...

3 (indicating time): **~ one o'clock to** or **until** or **till two de**(sde) la una a or hasta las 2; **~ January (on)** desde enero

4 (indicating distance) de; **the hotel is 1 km from the beach** el hotel está a 1 km de la playa

5 (indicating price, number etc) de; **prices range ~ £10 to £50** los precios van desde £10 a or hasta £50; **the interest rate was increased ~ 9% to 10%** el tipo de interés fue incrementado de un 9% a un 10%

6 (indicating difference) de; **he can't tell red ~ green** no sabe distinguir el rojo del verde; **to be different ~ sb/sth** ser diferente a algo/alguien

7 (because of, on the basis of): **~ what he says** por lo que dice; **weak ~ hunger** debilitado/a por el hambre.

front [frʌnt] n (foremost part) parte f delantera; (of house) fachada; (promenade: also: **sea ~**) paseo marítimo; (MIL, POL, METEOROLOGY)

frente m; (fig: appearances) apariencias fpl // a (wheel, leg) delantero; (row, line) primero; **in ~ (of)** delante (de); **~ door** n puerta principal; **~ier** ['frʌntɪə*] n frontera; **~ page** n primera plana; **~ room** n (Brit) salón m, sala; **~-wheel drive** n tracción f delantera.

frost [frɔst] n (gen) helada; (also: **hoar-**) escarcha // vt (US CULIN) escarchar; **~bite** n congelación f; **~ed** a (glass) deslustrado; **~y** a (surface) cubierto de escarcha; (welcome etc) glacial.

froth [frɔθ] n espuma.

frown [fraun] vi fruncir el ceño.

froze [frəuz] pt of **freeze**.

frozen ['frəuzn] pp of **freeze** // a (food) congelado.

fruit [fruːt] n, pl inv fruta; **~erer** n frutero/a; **~erer's (shop)** n frutería; **~ful** a provechoso; **~ion** [fruːˈɪʃən] n: **to come to ~ion** realizarse; **~ juice** n zumo or jugo (LAm) de fruta; **~ machine** n (Brit) máquina f tragaperras; **~ salad** n macedonia or ensalada (LAm) de frutas.

frustrate [frʌsˈtreɪt] vt frustrar; **~d** a frustrado/a.

fry [fraɪ], pt, pp **fried** vt freír; **small ~** gente f menuda; **~ing pan** n sartén f.

ft. abbr = **foot, feet.**

fuddy-duddy ['fʌdɪdʌdɪ] n carroza m/f.

fudge [fʌdʒ] n (CULIN) caramelo blando.

fuel [fjuəl] n (for heating) combustible m; (coal) carbón m; (wood) leña; (for engine) carburante m; **~ oil** n fuel oil m; **~ tank** n depósito (de combustible).

fugitive ['fjuːdʒɪtɪv] n fugitivo/a.

fulfil [fulˈfɪl] vt (function) cumplir con; (condition) satisfacer; (wish, desire) realizar; **~ment** n satisfacción f; realización f.

full [ful] a lleno; (fig) pleno; (complete) completo; (information) detallado // ad: ~ **well** perfectamente; **I'm** ~ (**up**) no puedo más; ~ **employment** pleno empleo; **a** ~ **two hours** dos horas completas; **at** ~ **speed** a máxima velocidad; **in** ~ (*reproduce, quote*) íntegramente; ~ **moon** n luna llena; ~**-scale** a (*attack, war*) en gran escala; (*model*) de tamaño natural; ~**-time** a (*work*) de tiempo completo // ad: **to work** ~**-time** trabajar a tiempo completo; ~**y** ad completamente; ~**y-fledged** a (*teacher, barrister*) diplomado.

fulsome ['fulsəm] a (*pej: praise, gratitude*) excesivo, exagerado.

fumble ['fʌmbl] vi: **to** ~ **for sth** buscar algo con las manos; ~ **with sth** manejar algo torpemente.

fume [fjuːm] vi humear, echar humo; ~**s** npl humo sg, gases mpl.

fun [fʌn] n (*amusement*) diversión f; (*joy*) alegría f; **to have** ~ divertirse; **for** ~ en broma; **to make** ~ **of** vt *fus* burlarse de.

function ['fʌŋkʃən] n función f // vi funcionar; ~**al** a funcional.

fund [fʌnd] n fondo; (*reserve*) reserva; ~**s** npl fondos mpl.

fundamental [fʌndə'mɛntl] a fundamental.

funeral ['fjuːnərəl] n (*burial*) entierro; (*ceremony*) funerales mpl; ~ **parlour** n (*Brit*) funeraria f; ~ **service** n misa de difuntos.

funfair ['fʌnfɛə*] n (*Brit*) parque m de atracciones.

fungus ['fʌŋgəs], pl **-gi** [-gaɪ] n hongo.

funnel ['fʌnl] n embudo; (*of ship*) chimenea.

funny ['fʌnɪ] a gracioso, divertido; (*strange*) curioso, raro.

fur [fəː*] n piel f; (*Brit: on tongue etc*) sarro; ~ **coat** n abrigo de pieles.

furious ['fjuərɪəs] a furioso; (*effort*) violento.

furlong ['fəːlɔŋ] n octava parte de una milla, = 201.17 m.

furlough ['fəːləu] n (*MIL, US*) permiso.

furnace ['fəːnɪs] n horno.

furnish ['fəːnɪʃ] vt amueblar; (*supply*) suministrar; (*information*) facilitar; ~**ings** npl muebles mpl.

furniture ['fəːnɪtʃə*] n muebles mpl; **piece of** ~ mueble m.

furrow ['fʌrəu] n surco.

furry ['fəːrɪ] a peludo.

further ['fəːðə*] a (*new*) nuevo, adicional; (*place*) más lejano // ad más lejos; (*more*) más; (*moreover*) además // vt promover, adelantar; ~ **education** n educación f superior; ~**more** [fəːðə'mɔː*] ad además.

furthest ['fəːðɪst] *superlative of* **far**.

fury ['fjuərɪ] n furia.

fuse, (*US*) **fuze** [fjuːz] n fusible m; (*for bomb etc*) mecha // vt (*metal*) fundir; (*fig*) fusionar // vi fundirse; fusionarse; (*Brit ELEC*): **to** ~ **the lights** fundir los plomos; ~ **box** n caja de fusibles.

fuss [fʌs] n (*noise*) bulla; (*dispute*) lío; (*complaining*) protesta; **to make a** ~ armar un lío or jaleo; ~**y** a (*person*) exigente.

futile ['fjuːtaɪl] a vano; **futility** ['tɪlɪtɪ] n inutilidad f.

future ['fjuːtʃə*] a (*coming*) venidero // n futuro; porvenir; **in** ~ de ahora en adelante.

fuze [fjuːz] (*US*) = **fuse**.

fuzzy ['fʌzɪ] a (*PHOT*) borroso; (*hair*) muy rizado.

G

G [dʒiː] n (*MUS*) sol m.

g. *abbr* = **gram(s)**.

gabble ['gæbl] vi hablar atropelladamente; (*gossip*) cotorrear.

gable ['geɪbl] n aguilón m.

gadget ['gædʒɪt] n aparato.

Gaelic ['geɪlɪk] a, n (*LING*) gaélico.

gaffe [gæf] n plancha.

gag [gæg] n (*on mouth*) mordaza; (*joke*) chiste m // vt amordazar.

gaiety ['geɪtɪ] n alegría.

gaily ['geɪlɪ] ad alegremente.

gain [geɪn] n ganancia // vt ganar // vi (watch) adelantarse; **to ~ by sth** sacar provecho de algo; **to ~ on sb** ganar terreno a uno; **to ~ 3 lbs** (in weight) engordar 3 libras.

gait [geɪt] n (modo de) andar m.

gal. abbr = **gallon.**

gala ['gɑːlə] n fiesta.

gale [geɪl] n (wind) vendaval m.

gallant ['gælənt] a valiente; (towards ladies) atento.

gall bladder ['gɔːl-] n vesícula biliar.

gallery ['gælərɪ] n galería; (also: art ~) pinacoteca.

galley ['gælɪ] n (ship's kitchen) cocina; (ship) galera.

gallon ['gælən] n galón m (= 8 pints; Brit = 4,546 litros, US = 3,785 litros).

gallop ['gæləp] n galope m // vi galopar.

gallows ['gæləʊz] n horca.

gallstone ['gɔːlstəʊn] n cálculo biliario.

galore [gə'lɔː*] ad en cantidad, en abundancia.

galvanize ['gælvənaɪz] vt (metal) galvanizar; (fig): **to ~ sb into action** animar a uno para que haga algo.

gambit ['gæmbɪt] n (fig): **opening ~** estrategia inicial.

gamble ['gæmbl] n (risk) riesgo; (bet) apuesta // vt: **to ~ on** apostar a; (fig) confiar en que // vi jugar; (COMM) especular; **~r** n jugador/a m/f; **gambling** n juego.

game [geɪm] n juego; (match) partido; (of cards) partida; (HUNTING) caza // a valiente; (ready): **to be ~ for anything** atreverse a todo; **big ~** caza mayor; **~keeper** n guardabosques m inv.

gammon ['gæmən] n tocino or jamón m ahumado.

gamut ['gæmət] n gama.

gang [gæŋ] n pandilla; (of workmen) brigada // vi: **to ~ up on sb** conspirar contra uno.

gangster ['gæŋstə*] n gángster m.

gangway ['gæŋweɪ] n (Brit: in theatre, bus etc) pasillo; (on ship) pasarela.

gaol [dʒeɪl] n, vt (Brit) = **jail.**

gap [gæp] n vacío, hueco (LAm); (in trees, traffic) claro; (in time) intervalo.

gape [geɪp] vi mirar boquiabierto; **gaping** a (hole) muy abierto.

garage ['gærɑːʒ] n garaje m.

garbage ['gɑːbɪdʒ] n (US) basura; **~ can** n cubo or bote m (LAm) de la basura; **~ man** n basurero.

garbled ['gɑːbld] a (distorted) falsificado, amañado.

garden ['gɑːdn] n jardín m; **~er** n jardinero/a; **~ing** n jardinería.

gargle ['gɑːgl] vi hacer gárgaras, gargarear (LAm).

gargoyle ['gɑːgɔɪl] n gárgola.

garish ['gɛərɪʃ] a chillón/ona.

garland ['gɑːlənd] n guirnalda.

garlic ['gɑːlɪk] n ajo.

garment ['gɑːmənt] n prenda (de vestir).

garnish ['gɑːnɪʃ] vt adornar; (CULIN) aderezar.

garrison ['gærɪsn] n guarnición f.

garrulous ['gærjʊləs] a charlatán/ana.

garter ['gɑːtə*] n (US) liga.

gas [gæs] n gas m; (US: gasoline) gasolina // vt asfixiar con gas; **~ cooker** n (Brit) cocina de gas; **~ cylinder** n bombona de gas; **~ fire** n estufa de gas; **~ pedal** n (US) acelerador m.

gash [gæʃ] n raja; (on face) cuchillada // vt rajar; (with knife) acuchillar.

gasket ['gæskɪt] n (AUT) junta de culata.

gas mask n careta antigás.

gas meter n contador m de gas.

gasoline ['gæsəliːn] n (US) gasolina.

gasp [gɑːsp] n grito sofocado // vi (pant) jadear; **to ~ out** vt (say) decir con voz entrecortada.

gas ring n hornillo de gas.

gas station n (US) gasolinera.

gassy ['gæsɪ] a gaseoso.

gas tap n llave f del gas.

gastric ['gæstrɪk] a gástrico.

gate [geɪt] n puerta; (RAIL) barrera; **~crash** vt (Brit) colarse en; **~way** n puerta.

gather ['gæðə*] vt (flowers, fruit) coger (Sp), recoger; (assemble) reunir; (pick up) recoger; (SEWING) fruncir; (understand) entender // vi (assemble) reunirse; **to ~ speed** ganar velocidad; **~ing** n reunión f, asamblea.

gauche [gəʊʃ] a torpe.

gaudy ['gɔːdɪ] a chillón/ona.

gauge [geɪdʒ] n calibre m; (RAIL) entrevía; (instrument) indicador m // vt medir.

gaunt [gɔːnt] a descarnado.

gauntlet ['gɔːntlɪt] n (fig): **to run the ~ of** exponerse a; **to throw down the ~** arrojar el guante.

gauze [gɔːz] n gasa.

gave [geɪv] pt of **give**.

gay [geɪ] a (person) alegre; (colour) vivo; (homosexual) gay.

gaze [geɪz] n mirada fija // vi: **to ~ at** sth mirar algo fijamente.

gazelle [gə'zɛl] n gacela.

gazetteer [gæzə'tɪə*] n diccionario geográfico.

gazumping [gə'zʌmpɪŋ] n (Brit) la subida del precio de una casa una vez que ya ha sido apalabrado.

GB abbr = **Great Britain**.

GCE n abbr (Brit) = General Certificate of Education.

GCSE n abbr (Brit: = General Certificate of Secondary Education) = Bachillerato Elemental y Superior.

gear [gɪə*] n equipo, herramientas fpl; (TECH) engranaje m; (AUT) velocidad f, marcha // vt (fig: adapt): **to ~ sth to** adaptar o ajustar algo a; **top o** (US) **high/low ~** cuarta/primera velocidad; **in ~** en marcha; **~ box** n caja de cambios; **~ lever**, (US) **~ shift** n palanca de cambio; **~ wheel** n rueda dentada.

geese [giːs] pl of **goose**.

gel [dʒel] n gel m.

gelignite ['dʒelɪgnaɪt] n gelignita.

gem [dʒem] n joya.

Gemini ['dʒemɪnaɪ] n Géminis m, Gemelos mpl.

gender ['dʒendə*] n género.

gene [dʒiːn] n gen(e) m.

general ['dʒenərl] n general m // a general; **in ~** en general; **~ delivery** n (US) lista de correos; **~ election** n elecciones fpl generales; **~ization** [-aɪ'zeɪʃən] n generalización f; **~ize** vi generalizar; **~ly** ad generalmente, en general; **~ practitioner (G.P.)** n médico general.

generate ['dʒenəreɪt] vt (ELEC) generar; (fig) producir.

generation [dʒenə'reɪʃən] n generación f.

generator ['dʒenəreɪtə*] n generador m.

generosity [dʒenə'rɔsɪtɪ] n generosidad f.

generous ['dʒenərəs] a generoso; (copious) abundante.

genetics [dʒɪ'netɪks] n genética.

Geneva [dʒɪ'niːvə] n Ginebra.

genial ['dʒiːnɪəl] a afable, simpático.

genitals ['dʒenɪtlz] npl (órganos mpl) genitales mpl.

genius ['dʒiːnɪəs] n genio.

gent [dʒent] n abbr = **gentleman**.

genteel [dʒen'tiːl] a fino, elegante.

gentle ['dʒentl] a (sweet) amable, dulce; (touch etc) ligero, suave.

gentleman ['dʒentlmən] n señor m; (well-bred man) caballero.

gentleness ['dʒentlnɪs] n dulzura; (of touch) suavidad f.

gently ['dʒentlɪ] ad suavemente.

gents [dʒents] n aseos mpl (de caballeros).

genuine ['dʒenjuɪn] a auténtico; (person) sincero.

geography [dʒɪ'ɔgrəfɪ] n geografía.

geology [dʒɪ'ɔlədʒɪ] n geología.

geometric(al) [dʒɪə'metrɪk(əl)] a geométrico.

geometry [dʒɪ'ɒmətrɪ] n geometría.

geranium [dʒɪ'reɪnɪəm] n geranio.

geriatric [dʒɛrɪ'ætrɪk] a, n geriátrico/a m/f.

germ [dʒɜːm] n (microbe) microbio, bacteria; (seed, fig) germen m.

German ['dʒɜːmən] a alemán/ana // n alemán/ana m/f; (LING) alemán m; ~ **measles** n rubéola; ~ **Shepherd Dog** n pastor m alemán.

Germany ['dʒɜːmənɪ] n Alemania.

gesture ['dʒɛstjə*] n gesto.

KEYWORD

---

get [gɛt], pt, pp **got**, pp **gotten** (US) vi 1 (become, be) ponerse, volverse; to ~ **old/tired** envejecer/cansarse; to ~ **drunk** emborracharse; to ~ **dirty** ensuciarse; to ~ **married** casarse; **when do I ~ paid?** ¿cuándo me pagan or se me paga?; it's ~**ting late** se está haciendo tarde

2 (go): to ~ **to/from** llegar a/de; to ~ **home** llegar a casa

3 (begin) empezar a; to ~ **to know sb** (llegar a) conocer a uno; I'm ~**ting to like him** me está empezando a gustar; let's ~ **going** or **started** (vamos a empezar)!

4 (modal auxiliary vb): **you've got to do it** tienes que hacerlo

♦ vt 1: to ~ **sth done** (finish) terminar algo; (have done) mandar hacer algo; to ~ **one's hair cut** cortarse el pelo; to ~ **the car going** or **to go** arrancar el coche; to ~ **sb to do sth** conseguir or hacer que alguien haga algo; to ~ **sth/sb ready** preparar algo/a alguien

2 (obtain: money, permission, results) conseguir; (find: job, flat) encontrar; (fetch: person, doctor) buscar; (object) ir a buscar, traer; to ~ **sth for sb** conseguir algo para alguien; ~ **me Mr Jones, please** (TEL) póngame or comuníqueme (LAm) con el Sr. Jones, por favor; **can I ~ you a drink?** ¿te pido algo?

3 (receive: present, letter) recibir;

(acquire: reputation) alcanzar; (: prize) ganar; **what did you ~ for your birthday?** ¿qué te regalaron por tu cumpleaños?; **how much did you ~ for the painting?** ¿cuánto sacaste por el cuadro?

4 (catch) coger (Sp), agarrar (LAm); (hit: target etc) dar en; to ~ **sb by the arm/throat** coger (Sp) or agarrar (LAm) a uno por el brazo/cuello; ~ **him!** ¡cógelo! (Sp), ¡atrápalo! (LAm); **the bullet got him in the leg** la bala le dio en una pierna

5 (take, move) llevar; to ~ **sth to sb** llevar algo a alguien; **do you think we'll ~ it through the door?** ¿crees que lo podremos meter por la puerta?

6 (catch, take: plane, bus etc) coger (Sp), tomar (LAm); **where do I ~ the train for Birmingham?** ¿dónde se coge (Sp) or se toma (LAm) el tren para Birmingham?

7 (understand) entender; (hear) oir; **I've got it!** ¡ya lo tengo!; ¡eureka!; **I don't ~ your meaning** no te entiendo; **I'm sorry, I didn't ~ your name** lo siento, no cogí su nombre

8 (have, possess): **to have got** tener.

get about vi salir mucho; (news) divulgarse

get along vi (agree) llevarse bien; (depart) marcharse; (manage) = **get by**

get at vt fus (attack) atacar; (reach) alcanzar

get away vi marcharse; (escape) escaparse

get away with vt fus hacer impunemente

get back vi (return) volver // vt recobrar

get by vi (pass) lograr pasar; (manage) arreglárselas

get down vi bajarse // vt fus bajar // vt (depress) deprimir

get down to vt fus (work) ponerse a

get in vi entrar; (train) llegar; (arrive home) volver a casa, regresar

get into vt fus entrar en; (vehicle) subir a; **to ~ into a rage** enfadarse

get off vi (from train etc) bajar; (depart: person, car) marcharse // vt (remove) quitar // vt fus (train, bus) bajar de

get on vi (at exam etc): **how are you ~ting on?** ¿cómo te va?; (agree): **to ~ on (with)** llevarse bien (con) // vt fus subir a

get out vi salir; (of vehicle) bajar // vt sacar

get out of vt fus salir de; (duty etc) escaparse de

get over vt fus (illness) recobrarse de

get round vt fus rodear; (fig: person) engatusar a

get through vi (TEL) (lograr) comunicarse

get through to vt fus (TEL) comunicar con

get together vi reunirse // vt reunir, juntar

get up vi (rise) levantarse // vt fus subir

get up to vt fus (reach) llegar a; (prank) hacer.

geyser ['gi:zə*] n (water heater) calentador m de agua; (GEO) géiser m.

Ghana ['gɑːnə] n Ghana.

ghastly ['gɑːstlɪ] a horrible.

gherkin ['gəːkɪn] n pepinillo m.

ghost [gəust] n fantasma m.

giant ['dʒaɪənt] n gigante m/f // a gigantesco, gigante.

gibberish ['dʒɪbərɪʃ] n galimatías m.

gibe [dʒaɪb] n mofa.

giblets ['dʒɪblɪts] npl menudillos mpl.

Gibraltar [dʒɪ'brɔːltə*] n Gibraltar m.

giddiness ['gɪdɪnɪs] n vértigo.

giddy ['gɪdɪ] a (height, speed) vertiginoso; **to be ~** estar mareado/a.

gift [gɪft] n regalo m; (offering) obse-

quio; (ability) talento; **~ed** a dotado; **~ token** or **voucher** n vale m canjeable por un regalo.

gigantic [dʒaɪ'gæntɪk] a gigantesco.

giggle ['gɪgl] vi reírse tontamente // n risilla.

gill [dʒɪl] n (measure) = 0.25 pints (Brit = 0.148 l, US = 0.118l).

gills [gɪlz] npl (of fish) branquias fpl, agallas fpl.

gilt [gɪlt] a, n dorado; **~-edged** a (COMM) de máxima garantía.

gimmick ['gɪmɪk] n truco.

gin [dʒɪn] n (liquor) ginebra.

ginger ['dʒɪndʒə*] n jengibre m; **~** **ale, ~ beer** n (Brit) gaseosa de jengibre; **~bread** n pan m de jengibre; **~-haired** a pelirrojo.

gingerly ['dʒɪndʒəlɪ] ad con cautela.

gipsy ['dʒɪpsɪ] n gitano/a.

giraffe [dʒɪ'rɑːf] n jirafa.

girder ['gəːdə*] n viga.

girdle ['gəːdl] n (corset) faja.

girl [gəːl] n (small) niña; (young woman) chica, joven f, muchacha; **an** **English ~** una (chica) inglesa; **~friend** n (of girl) amiga; (of boy) novia; **~ish** a de niña.

giro ['dʒaɪrəu] n (Brit: bank ~) giro bancario; (post office ~) giro postal; (state benefit) cheque quincenal del subsidio de desempleo.

girth [gəːθ] n circunferencia; (of saddle) cincha.

gist [dʒɪst] n lo esencial.

give [gɪv], pt **gave**, pp **given** vt dar; (deliver) entregar; (as gift) regalar // vi (break) romperse; (stretch: fabric) dar de sí; **to ~ sb** **sth, ~ sth to sb** dar algo a uno; **to** **~ away** vt (give free) regalar; (betray) traicionar; (disclose) revelar; **to ~ back** vt devolver; **to ~ in** vi ceder // vt entregar; **to ~ off** vt despedir; **to ~ out** vt distribuir; **to ~** **up** vi rendirse, darse por vencido // vt renunciar a; **to ~ up smoking** dejar de fumar; **to ~ o.s. up** entregarse; **to ~ way** vi ceder; (Brit AUT) ceder el paso.

glacier ['glæsɪə*] n glaciar m.

glad [glæd] a contento.

gladly ['glædlɪ] ad con mucho gusto.

glamorous ['glæmərəs] a encantador(a), atractivo.

glamour ['glæmə*] n encanto, atractivo.

glance [glɑ:ns] n ojeada, mirada // vi: to ~ at echar una ojeada a; to ~ off (bullet) rebotar; **glancing** a (blow) oblicuo.

gland [glænd] n glándula.

glare [glɛə*] n deslumbramiento, brillo // vi deslumbrar; to ~ at mirar ferozmente a; **glaring** a (mistake) manifiesto.

glass [glɑ:s] n vidrio, cristal m; (for drinking) vaso; (: with stem) copa; (also: looking ~) espejo; ~es npl gafas fpl; ~house n invernadero; ~ware n cristalería; ~y a (eyes) vidrioso.

glaze [gleɪz] vt (window) poner cristales a; (pottery) barnizar // n barniz m.

glazier ['gleɪzɪə*] n vidriero/a.

gleam [gli:m] n destello // vi brillar; ~ing a reluciente.

glean [gli:n] vt (information) recoger.

glee [gli:] n alegría, regocijo.

glen [glɛn] n cañada.

glib [glɪb] a de mucha labia.

glide [glaɪd] vi deslizarse; (AVIAT, birds) planear; ~r n (AVIAT) planeador m; **gliding** n (AVIAT) vuelo sin motor.

glimmer ['glɪmə*] n luz f tenue.

glimpse [glɪmps] n vislumbre m // vt vislumbrar, entrever.

glint [glɪnt] vi centellear.

glisten ['glɪsn] vi relucir, brillar.

glitter ['glɪtə*] vi relucir, brillar // n brillo.

gloat [gləut] vi: to ~ over (money) recrearse en; (sb's misfortune) saborear.

global ['gləubl] a mundial.

globe [gləub] n globo, esfera.

gloom [glu:m] n tinieblas fpl, oscuri-

dad f; (sadness) tristeza, melancolía; ~y a (dark) oscuro; (sad) triste; (pessimistic) pesimista.

glorious ['glɔ:rɪəs] a glorioso.

glory ['glɔ:rɪ] n gloria.

gloss [glɔs] n (shine) brillo; (paint) pintura de aceite; to ~ over vt fus encubrir.

glossary ['glɔsərɪ] n glosario.

glossy ['glɔsɪ] a lustroso.

glove [glʌv] n guante m; ~ compartment n (AUT) guantera.

glow [gləu] vi (shine) brillar // n brillo.

glower ['glauə*] vi: to ~ at mirar con ceño.

glue [glu:] n goma (de pegar), cemento (LAm) // vt pegar.

glum [glʌm] a (mood) abatido; (person, tone) melancólico.

glut [glʌt] n superabundancia.

glutton ['glʌtn] n glotón/ona m/f; a ~ for punishment masoquista m/f.

gnarled [nɑ:ld] a nudoso.

gnat [næt] n mosquito.

gnaw [nɔ:] vt roer.

gnome [nəum] n gnomo.

go [gəu] vb (pt **went**, pp **gone**) vi ir; (travel) viajar; (depart) irse, marcharse; (work) funcionar, marchar; (be sold) venderse; (time) pasar; (fit, suit): to ~ with hacer juego con; (become) ponerse; (break etc) romperse, romperse // n (pl: ~es): to have a ~ (at) probar suerte (con); to be on the ~ no parar; whose ~ is it? ¿a quién le toca?; he's going to do it va a hacerlo; to ~ for a walk ir de paseo; to ~ dancing ir a bailar; how did it ~? ¿qué tal salió or resultó?, ¿cómo ha ido?; to ~ round the back pasar por detrás; to ~ about vi (rumour) propagarse // vt fus: how do I ~ about this? ¿cómo me las arreglo para hacer esto?; to ~ ahead vi seguir adelante; to ~ along vi ir // vt fus bordear; to ~ along with (agree) estar de acuerdo con; to ~ away vi irse, marcharse; to ~

back vi volver; **to ~ back on** vt fus (promise) faltar a; **to ~ by** vi (years, time) pasar // vt fus guiarse por; **to ~ down** vi bajar; (ship) hundirse; (sun) ponerse // vt fus bajar por; **to ~ for** vt fus (fetch) ir por; (like) gustar; (attack) atacar; **to ~ in** vi entrar; **to ~ in for** vt fus (competition) presentarse a; **to ~ into** vt fus entrar en; (investigate) investigar; (embark on) dedicarse a; **to ~ off** vi irse, marcharse; (food) pasarse; (explode) estallar; (event) realizarse; **I'm going off the idea** ya no me gusta tanto ella/la idea // vt fus dejar de gustar; **to ~ on** vi (continue) seguir, continuar; (happen) pasar, ocurrir; **to ~ on doing sth** seguir haciendo algo; **to ~ out** vi salir; (fire, light) apagarse; **to ~ over** vi (ship) zozobrar // vt fus (check) revisar; **to ~ through** vt fus (town etc) atravesar; **to ~ up** vi subir; **to ~ without** vt fus pasarse sin.

goad [gəud] vt aguijonear.

go-ahead ['gəuəhɛd] a emprendedor(a) // n luz f verde.

goal [gəul] n meta; (score) gol m; **~keeper** n portero; **~-post** n poste m (de la portería).

goat [gəut] n cabra f.

gobble ['gɔbl] vt (also: ~ down, ~ up) engullirse.

go-between ['gəubitwiːn] n medianero/a, intermediario/a.

goblet ['gɔblit] n copa.

god [gɔd] n dios m; **G~** n Dios m; **~child** n ahijado/a; **~daughter** n ahijada; **~dess** n diosa; **~father** n padrino; **~forsaken** a dejado de la mano de Dios; **~mother** n madrina; **~send** n don del cielo; **~son** n ahijado.

goggles ['gɔglz] npl (AUT) anteojos mpl; (of skindiver) gafas fpl submarinas.

going ['gəuiŋ] n (conditions) estado del terreno // a: **the ~ rate** la tarifa corriente or en vigor.

gold [gəuld] n oro // a de oro; **~en** a (made of) ~ de oro; (~ in colour) dorado; **~fish** n pez m de colores; **~-plated** a chapado en oro; **~smith** n orfebre m/f.

golf [gɔlf] n golf m; **~ ball** n (for game) pelota de golf; (on typewriter) esfera; **~ club** n club m de golf; (stick) palo (de golf); **~ course** n campo de golf; **~er** n golfista m/f.

gone [gɔn] pp of **go**.

good [gud] a bueno; (kind) bueno, amable; (well-behaved) educado // a bien m, provecho; **~s** npl bienes mpl; (COMM) mercancías fpl; **~!** ¡qué bien!; **to be ~ at** tener aptitud para; **to be ~ for** servir para; **it's ~ for you** te hace bien; **would you be ~ enough to...?** ¿podría hacerme el favor de...?; ¿sería tan amable de...?; **a ~ deal (of)** mucho; **a ~ many** muchos; **to make ~** reparar; **it's no ~ complaining** no vale la pena (de) quejarse; **for ~** para siempre, definitivamente; **~ morning/afternoon** ¡buenos días/buenas tardes!; **~ evening** ¡buenas noches!; **~ night!** ¡buenas noches!; **G~ Friday** n Viernes m Santo; **~-looking** a guapo; **~-natured** a amable, simpático; (of person) bondad f; **for ~ness sake!** ¡por Dios!; **~ness gracious!** ¡Dios mío!; **~s train** n (Brit) tren m de mercancías; **~will** n buena voluntad f.

goose [guːs], pl **geese** n ganso, oca.

gooseberry ['guzbəri] n grosella espinosa.

gooseflesh ['guːsflɛʃ] n, **goose pimples** npl carne f de gallina.

gore [gɔːʳ] vt cornear // n sangre f.

gorge [gɔːdʒ] n barranco // vr: **to ~ o.s. (on)** atracarse (de).

gorgeous ['gɔːdʒəs] a magnífico, maravilloso.

gorilla [gə'rilə] n gorila m.

gorse [gɔːs] n aulaga.

gory ['gɔːri] a sangriento.

go-slow ['gəu'sləu] n (Brit) huelga

de manos caídas.

gospel ['gɒspl] *n* evangelio.

gossip ['gɒsɪp] *n* (*scandal*) chismorreo, chismes *mpl*; (*chat*) charla; (*scandalmonger*) chismoso/a; (*talker*) hablador(a) *m/f* // *vi* chismear.

got [gɒt] *pt, pp of* get; **~ten** (*US*) *pp of* **get**.

gout [gaut] *n* gota.

govern ['gʌvn] *vt* gobernar.

governess ['gʌvənɪs] *n* institutriz *f*.

government ['gʌvnmənt] *n* gobierno; **~al** ['-mentl] *a* gubernamental.

governor ['gʌvənə*] *n* gobernador(a) *m/f*; (*of jail*) director(a) *m/f*.

gown [gaun] *n* traje *m*; (*of teacher*; *Brit*: *of judge*) toga.

G.P. *n abbr = general practitioner.*

grab [græb] *vt* coger (*Sp*) *or* agarrar (*LAm*), arrebatar.

grace [greɪs] *n* gracia // *vt* (*honrar*; *adorn*) adornar; 5 **days'** ~ un plazo de 5 días; **to say** ~ bendecir la mesa; **~ful** *a* elegante, gracioso; **gracious** ['greɪʃəs] *a* amable.

grade [greɪd] *n* (*quality*) clase *f*, calidad *f*; (*in hierarchy*) grado; (*US SCOL*) curso *m* // *vt* clasificar; ~ **crossing** *n* (*US*) paso a nivel; ~ **school** *n* (*US*) escuela primaria.

gradient ['greɪdɪənt] *n* pendiente *f*.

gradual ['grædjuəl] *a* paulatino; **~ly** *ad* paulatinamente.

graduate ['grædjuɪt] *n* graduado/a, licenciado/a // *vi* ['grædjueɪt] graduarse, licenciarse; **graduation** [-'eɪʃən] *n* graduación *f*.

graffiti [grə'fiːtɪ] *n* pintadas *fpl*.

graft [grɑːft] *n* (*AGR, MED*) injerto; (*bribery*) corrupción *f* // *vt* injertar; **hard** ~ (*col*) trabajo duro.

grain [greɪn] *n* (*single particle*) grano; (*corn*) granos *mpl*, cereales *mpl*.

gram [græm] *n* (*US*) gramo.

grammar ['græmə*] *n* gramática: ~ **school** *n* (*Brit*) = instituto de segunda enseñanza, liceo (*Sp*).

grammatical [grə'mætɪkl] *a* gramatical.

gramme [græm] *n =* **gram**.

gramophone ['græməfəun] *n* (*Brit*) tocadiscos *m inv*.

granary ['grænərɪ] *n* granero, troj *f*.

grand [grænd] *a* magnífico, imponente; **~children** *npl* nietos *mpl*; **~dad** *n* yayo, abuelito; **~daughter** *n* nieta; **~eur** ['grændjə*] *n* magnificencia, lo grandioso; **~father** *n* abuelo; **~ma** *n* yaya, abuelita; **~mother** *n* abuela; **~pa** *n =* **~dad**; **~parents** *npl* abuelos *mpl*; ~ **piano** *n* piano de cola; **~son** *n* nieto; **~stand** *n* (*SPORT*) tribuna.

granite ['grænɪt] *n* granito.

granny ['grænɪ] *n* abuelita, yaya.

grant [grɑːnt] *vt* (*concede*) conceder; (*admit*) reconocer // *n* (*SCOL*) beca; **to take sth for ~ed** dar algo por sentado.

granulated ['grænjuleɪtɪd] *n*: ~ **sugar** (*Brit*) azúcar *m* blanquilla refinado.

granule ['grænjuːl] *n* gránulo.

grape [greɪp] *n* uva.

grapefruit ['greɪpfruːt] *n* pomelo, toronja (*LAm*).

graph [grɑːf] *n* gráfica; **~ic** *a* gráfico; **~ics** *n* artes *fpl* gráficas // *npl* (*COMPUT*) gráficos *mpl*.

grapple ['græpl] *vi*: **to** ~ **with** a problem enfrentar un problema.

grasp [grɑːsp] *vt* agarrar, asir; (*understand*) comprender // *n* (*grip*) asimiento; (*reach*) alcance *m*; (*understanding*) comprensión *f*; **~ing** *a* avaro.

grass [grɑːs] *n* hierba; (*lawn*) césped *m*; **~hopper** *n* saltamontes *m inv*; **~land** *n* pradera, pampa (*LAm*); **~-roots** *a* popular; ~ **snake** *n* culebra.

grate [greɪt] *n* parrilla de chimenea // *vi* chirriar // *vt* (*CULIN*) rallar.

grateful ['greɪtful] *a* agradecido.

grater ['greɪtə*] *n* rallador *m*.

gratify ['grætɪfaɪ] *vt* complacer; (*whim*) satisfacer; **~ing** *a* grato.

grating ['greɪtɪŋ] *n* (*iron bars*) rejilla // *a* (*noise*) áspero.

gratitude ['grætɪtjuːd] *n* agradecimiento.

gratuity [grə'tjuːɪtɪ] n gratificación f.

grave [greɪv] n tumba // a serio, grave.

gravel ['grævl] n grava.

gravestone ['greɪvstəun] n lápida.

graveyard ['greɪvjɑːd] n cementerio.

gravity ['grævɪtɪ] n gravedad f.

gravy ['greɪvɪ] n salsa de carne.

gray [greɪ] a = **grey**.

graze [greɪz] vi pacer // vt (touch lightly) rozar; (scrape) raspar // n (MED) abrasión f.

grease [griːs] n (fat) grasa; (lubricant) lubricante m // vt engrasar; **~proof** a a prueba de grasa; **~proof paper** n (Brit) papel m apergaminado; **greasy** a grasiento.

great [greɪt] a grande; (col) magnífico, estupendo; **G~ Britain** n Gran Bretaña; **~grandfather/ ~grandmother** n bisabuelo/a; **~ly** ad muy; (with verb) mucho; **~ness** n grandeza.

Greece [griːs] n Grecia.

greed [griːd] n (also: **~iness**) codicia, avaricia; (for food) gula; **~y** a avaro; (for food) glotón/ona.

Greek [griːk] a griego // n griego/a; (LING) griego.

green [griːn] a verde; (inexperienced) novato // n verde m; (stretch of grass) césped m; **~s** npl verduras fpl; **~ belt** n zona verde; **~card** n (AUT) carta verde; **~ery** n verdura; **~gage** n claudia; **~grocer** n (Brit) verdulero/a; **~house** n invernadero; **~ish** a verdoso.

Greenland ['griːnlənd] n Groenlandia.

greet [griːt] vt saludar; (welcome) dar la bienvenida a; **~ing** n (gen) saludo; (welcome) bienvenida; **~ing(s) card** n tarjeta de felicitaciones.

grenade [grə'neɪd] n granada.

grew [gruː] pt of **grow**.

grey [greɪ] a gris; **~-haired** a canoso; **~hound** n galgo.

grid [grɪd] n reja; (ELEC) red f.

grief [griːf] n dolor m, pena.

grievance ['griːvəns] n motivo de queja, agravio.

grieve [griːv] vi afligirse, acongojarse // vt dar pena a; **to ~ for** llorar por.

grievous a : **~ bodily harm** (LAW) daños mpl corporales graves.

grill [grɪl] n (on cooker) parrilla // vt (Brit) asar a la parrilla; (question) interrogar.

grille [grɪl] n reja.

grim [grɪm] a (place) sombrío; (person) ceñudo.

grimace [grɪ'meɪs] n mueca // vi hacer muecas.

grimy ['graɪmɪ] a mugriento.

grin [grɪn] n sonrisa abierta // vi sonreír abiertamente.

grind [graɪnd] vt (pt, pp **ground**) (coffee, pepper etc) moler; (US: meat) picar; (make sharp) afilar // n: **the daily ~** la rutina diaria; **to ~ one's teeth** hacer rechinar los dientes.

grip [grɪp] n (hold) asimiento; (of hands) apretón m; (handle) asidero; (holdall) maletín m // vt agarrar; **to get to ~s with** enfrentarse con; **~ping** a absorbente.

grisly ['grɪzlɪ] a horripilante, horrible.

gristle ['grɪsl] n cartílago.

grit [grɪt] n gravilla; (courage) valor m // vt (road) poner gravilla en; **to ~ one's teeth** apretar los dientes.

groan [grəun] n gemido; quejido // vi gemir; quejarse.

grocer ['grəusə*] n tendero de (ultramarinos); **~ies** npl comestibles mpl; **~'s (shop)** n tienda de ultramarinos or de abarrotes (LAm).

groggy ['grɔgɪ] a atontado.

groin [grɔɪn] n ingle f.

groom [gruːm] n mozo/a de cuadra; (also: **bride~**) novio // vt (horse) almohazar.

groove [gruːv] n ranura, surco.

grope [grəup] vi ir a tientas; **to ~ for** vt fus buscar a tientas.

gross [grəus] a grueso; (COMM) bruto; **~ly** ad (greatly) enormemente.

grotesque [grə'tɛsk] a grotesco.

grotto ['grɔtəu] n gruta.

ground [graund] pt, pp of **grind** // n suelo, tierra; (SPORT) campo, terreno; (reason: gen pl) causa, razón f; (US: also: **~ wire**) tierra // vt (plane) mantener en tierra; (US ELEC) conectar con tierra // vi (ship) varar, encallar; **~s** npl (of coffee etc) poso sg; (gardens etc) jardines mpl, parque m; **on the ~** en el suelo; **to the ~** al suelo; **to gain/lose** ~ ganar/ perder terreno; **~ cloth** (US) = **~sheet**; **~ing** n (in education) conocimientos mpl básicos; **~less** a infundado; **~sheet** (Brit) n tela impermeable; **~ staff** n personal m de tierra; **~work** n preparación f.

group [gru:p] n grupo; (musical) conjunto // (vb: also: **~ together**) vt agrupar // vi agruparse.

grouse [graus] n, pl inv (bird) urogallo // vi (complain) quejarse.

grove [grəuv] n arboleda.

grovel ['grɔvl] vi arrastrarse.

grow [grəu], pt **grew**, pp **grown** vi crecer; (increase) aumentarse; (expand) desarrollarse; (become) volverse; **to ~ rich/weak** enriquecerse/debilitarse // vt cultivar; (hair, beard) dejar crecer; **to ~ up** vi crecer, hacerse mayor/mujer; **~er** n cultivador(a) m/f, productor(a) m/f; **~ing** a creciente.

growl [graul] vi gruñir.

grown [grəun] pp of **grow**; **~-up** n adulto, mayor m/f.

growth [grəuθ] n crecimiento, desarrollo; (what has grown) brote m; (MED) tumor m.

grub [grʌb] n gusano; (col: food) comida.

grubby ['grʌbɪ] a sucio, mugriento.

grudge [grʌdʒ] n rencor // vt: **to ~ sb sth** dar algo a uno de mala gana; **to bear sb a ~** guardar rencor a uno; **he ~s (giving) the money** da el dinero de mala gana.

gruelling ['gruəlɪŋ] a penoso, duro.

gruesome ['gru:səm] a horrible.

gruff [grʌf] a (voice) ronco; (manner) brusco.

grumble ['grʌmbl] vi refunfuñar, quejarse.

grumpy ['grʌmpɪ] a gruñón/ona.

grunt [grʌnt] vi gruñir // n gruñido.

G-string ['dʒi:strɪŋ] n taparrabo.

guarantee [gærən'ti:] n garantía // vt garantizar.

guard [gɑ:d] n guardia; (one man) guardia m; (Brit RAIL) jefe m de tren // vt guardar; **~ed** a (fig) cauteloso; **~ian** n guardián/ana m/f; (of minor) tutor(a) m/f; **~'s van** n (Brit RAIL) furgón m.

Guatemala [gwætɪ'mɑːlə] n Guatemala; **~n** a, n guatemalteco/a m/f.

guerrilla [gə'rɪlə] n guerrillero/a; **~ warfare** n guerra de guerrillas.

guess [gɛs] vi adivinar // vt adivinar; (US) suponer // n suposición f, conjetura; **to take** or **have a ~** tratar de adivinar; **~work** n conjeturas fpl.

guest [gɛst] n invitado/a; (in hotel) huésped(a) m/f; **~-house** n casa de huéspedes, pensión f; **~ room** n cuarto de huéspedes.

guffaw [gʌ'fɔ:] n reírse a carcajadas.

guidance ['gaɪdəns] n (gen) dirección f; (advice) consejos mpl.

guide [gaɪd] n (person) guía m/f; (book, fig) guía f // vt guiar; **(girl) ~** n exploradora; **~book** n guía; **~ dog** n perro m guía; **~lines** npl (fig) directiva sg.

guild [gɪld] n gremio; **~hall** n (Brit) ayuntamiento.

guile [gaɪl] n astucia.

guillotine ['gɪləti:n] n guillotina.

guilt [gɪlt] n culpabilidad f; **~y** a culpable.

guinea pig n cobayo.

guise [gaɪz] n: **in** or **under the ~ of** bajo apariencia de

guitar [gɪ'tɑ:*] n guitarra.

gulf [gʌlf] n golfo; (abyss) abismo.

gull [gʌl] *n* gaviota.

gullet ['gʌlɪt] *n* esófago.

gullible ['gʌlɪbl] *a* crédulo.

gully ['gʌlɪ] *n* barranco.

gulp [gʌlp] *vi* tragar saliva // *vt* (*also*: ~ **down**) tragarse.

gum [gʌm] *n* (ANAT) encía; (*glue*) goma, cemento (LAm); (*sweet*) caramelo de goma; (*also*: **chewing-~**) chicle *m* // *vt* pegar con goma; **~boots** *npl* (Brit) botas *fpl* de goma.

gun [gʌn] *n* (*small*) pistola, revólver *m*; (*shotgun*) escopeta; (*rifle*) fusil *m*; (*cannon*) cañón *m*; **~boat** *n* cañonero; **~fire** *n* disparos *mpl*; **~man** *n* pistolero; **~ner** *n* artillero; **~point** *n*: **at ~point** a mano armada; **~powder** *n* pólvora; **~shot** *n* escopetazo; **~smith** *n* armero.

gurgle ['gɔːgl] *vi* gorgotear.

guru ['guːruː] *n* gurú *m*.

gush [gʌʃ] *vi* chorrear; (*fig*) deshacerse en efusiones.

gusset ['gʌsɪt] *n* escudete *m*.

gust [gʌst] *n* (*of wind*) ráfaga.

gusto ['gʌstəu] *n* entusiasmo.

gut [gʌt] *n* intestino; (MUS *etc*) cuerda de tripa; **~s** *npl* (*courage*) valor *m*.

gutter ['gʌtə*] *n* (*of roof*) canalón *m*; (*in street*) arroyo.

guy [gaɪ] *n* (*also*: **~-rope**) cuerda; (*col*: *man*) tío (Sp), tipo.

guzzle ['gʌzl] *vi* tragar // *vt* engullir.

gym [dʒɪm] *n* (*also*: **gymnasium**) gimnasio; (*also*: **gymnastics**) gimnasia; **~nast** *n* gimnasta *m/f*; **~ shoes** *npl* zapatillas *fpl* deportivas; **~ slip** *n* (Brit) túnica de colegiala.

gynaecologist, (US) **gynecologist** [gaɪnɪ'kɔlədʒɪst] *n* ginecólogo/a.

gypsy ['dʒɪpsɪ] *n* = **gipsy**.

gyrate [dʒaɪ'reɪt] *vi* girar.

H

haberdashery ['hæbə'dæʃərɪ] *n* (Brit) mercería; (US: *men's clothing*) prendas *fpl* de caballero.

habit ['hæbɪt] *n* hábito, costumbre *f*.

habitat ['hæbɪtæt] *n* hábitat *m*.

habitual [hə'bɪtjuəl] *a* acostumbrado, habitual; (*drinker, liar*) empedernido; **~ly** *ad* por costumbre.

hack [hæk] *n* (*cut*) cortar; (*slice*) tajar // *n* corte *m*; (*axe blow*) hachazo; (*pej*: *writer*) escritor(a) *m/f* a sueldo.

hackneyed ['hæknɪd] *a* trillado, gastado.

had [hæd] *pt, pp* of **have**.

haddock ['hædək], *pl* ~ *or* ~**s** *n* especie de merluza.

hadn't ['hædnt] = **had not**.

haemorrhage, (US) **hemorrhage** ['hemərɪdʒ] *n* hemorragia.

haemorrhoids, (US) **hemorrhoids** ['hemərɔɪdz] *npl* hemorroides *fpl*.

haggard ['hægəd] *a* ojeroso.

haggle ['hægl] *vi* (*argue*) discutir; (*bargain*) regatear.

Hague [heɪg] *n*: **The ~** La Haya.

hail [heɪl] *n* (*weather*) granizo // *vt* saludar; (*call*) llamar a // *vi* granizar; **~stone** *n* (piedra de) granizo.

hair [hɛə*] *n* (*gen*) pelo, cabellos *mpl*; (*one* ~) pelo, cabello; (*head of* ~) pelo, cabellera; (*on legs etc*) vello; **to do one's** ~ arreglarse el pelo; **grey** ~ canas *fpl*; **~brush** *n* cepillo (para el pelo); **~cut** *n* corte *m* (de pelo) **~do** *n* peinado; **~dresser** *n* peluquero/a; **~dresser's** *n* peluquería; **~dryer** *n* secador *m* de pelo; **~grip, ~pin** *n* horquilla; **~net** *n* redecilla; **~piece** *n* postizo; **~pin bend,** (US) **~pin curve** *n* curva de horquilla; **~raising** *a* espeluznante; **~remover** *n* depilatorio; **~ spray** *n* laca; **~style** *n* peinado; **~y** *a* peludo; velludo.

hake [heɪk] n merluza.

half [hɑːf], pl **halves** n mitad f // a medio // ad medio, a medias; ~ **an-hour** media hora; **two and a** ~ dos y media; ~ **a dozen** media docena; ~ **a pound** media libra; **to cut sth in** ~ cortar algo por la mitad; ~ **asleep** medio dormido; ~**-back** n (SPORT) medio; ~**-breed**, ~**-caste** n mestizo/a; ~**-hearted** a indiferente, poco entusiasta; ~**-hour** n media hora; ~**-mast** n: **at** ~**-mast** (flag) a media asta; ~**-price** a a mitad de precio; ~ **term** n (Brit SCOL) vacaciones de mediados del trimestre; ~**-time** n descanso; ~**way** ad a medio camino.

halibut ['hælɪbət] n, pl inv halibut m.

hall [hɔːl] n (for concerts) sala; (entrance way) entrada, vestíbulo; ~ **of residence** n (Brit) colegio mayor.

hallmark ['hɔːlmɑːk] n (mark) contraste m; (fig) sello.

hallo [hə'ləu] excl = **hello**.

Hallowe'en [hæləu'iːn] n víspera de Todos los Santos.

hallucination [həluːsɪ'neɪʃən] n alucinación f.

hallway ['hɔːlweɪ] n vestíbulo.

halo ['heɪləu] n (of saint) aureola.

halt [hɔːlt] n (stop) alto, parada; (RAIL) apeadero // vt parar // vi pararse; (process) interrumpirse.

halve [hɑːv] vt partir por la mitad.

halves [hɑːvz] pl of **half**.

ham [hæm] n jamón m (cocido).

hamburger ['hæmbɜːgə*] n hamburguesa.

hamlet ['hæmlɪt] n aldea.

hammer ['hæmə*] n martillo // vt (nail) clavar.

hammock ['hæmək] n hamaca.

hamper ['hæmpə*] vt estorbar // n cesto.

hand [hænd] n mano f; (of clock) aguja; (writing) letra; (worker) obrero // vt dar, pasar; **to give sb a** ~ echar una mano a uno, ayudar a uno; **at** ~ a la mano; **in** ~ entre manos; **on** ~ (person, services) a

mano, al alcance; **to** ~ (information etc) a mano; **on the one** ~ ..., **on the other** ~ ... por una parte ..., por otra (parte) ...; **to** ~ **in** vt entregar; **to** ~ **out** vt distribuir; **to** ~ **over** vt (deliver) entregar; (surrender) ceder; ~**bag** n bolso, cartera (LAm); ~**book** n manual m; ~**brake** n freno de mano; ~**cuffs** npl esposas fpl; ~**ful** n puñado.

handicap ['hændɪkæp] n desventaja, (SPORT) handicap m // vt estorbar; **handicapped** a: **to be mentally/ physically** ~**ped** ser deficiente m/f (mental/minusválido/a (físico/a).

handicraft ['hændɪkrɑːft] n artesanía.

handiwork ['hændɪwɜːk] n manualidad(es) f(pl); (fig) obra.

handkerchief ['hæŋkətʃɪf] n pañuelo.

handle ['hændl] n (of door etc) manija; (of cup etc) asa; (of knife etc) mango; (for winding) manivela // vt (touch) tocar; (deal with) encargarse de; (treat: people) manejar; '~ **with care**' '(manéjese) con cuidado'; **to fly off the** ~ perder los estribos; ~**bar(s)** n(pl) manillar msg.

hand: ~luggage n equipaje m de mano; ~**made** ['hændmeɪd] a hecho a mano; ~**out** ['hændaut] n (leaflet) folleto; ~**rail** ['hændreɪl] n pasamanos m inv; ~**shake** ['hændʃeɪk] n apretón m de manos.

handsome ['hænsəm] a guapo.

handwriting ['hændraɪtɪŋ] n letra.

handy ['hændɪ] a (close at hand) a la mano; (tool etc) práctico; (skilful) hábil, diestro; ~**man** n manitas m inv.

hang [hæŋ], pt, pp **hung** vt colgar; (head) bajar; (criminal: pt, pp **hanged**) ahorcar // vi colgar; **to get the** ~ **of sth** (col) lograr dominar algo; **to** ~ **about** vi haraganear; **to** ~ **on** vi (wait) esperar; **to** ~ **up** vi (TEL) colgar.

hanger ['hæŋə*] n percha.

hang-gliding ['hæŋglaɪdɪŋ] n vuelo

libre.

hangover ['hæŋəuvə*] n (after drinking) resaca.

hang-up ['hæŋʌp] n complejo.

hanker ['hæŋkə*] vi: to ~ after añorar.

hankie, hanky ['hæŋki] n abbr = **handkerchief**.

haphazard [hæp'hæzəd] a fortuito.

happen ['hæpən] vi suceder, ocurrir; (take place) tener lugar, realizarse; as it ~s da la casualidad de que; ~ing n suceso, acontecimiento.

happily ['hæpili] ad (luckily) afortunadamente; (cheerfully) alegremente.

happiness ['hæpinis] n (contentment) felicidad f; (joy) alegría.

happy ['hæpi] a feliz; (cheerful) alegre; to be ~ (with) estar contento (con); ~ birthday! ¡feliz cumpleaños!; ~-go-lucky a despreocupado.

harangue [hə'ræŋ] n arengar.

harass ['hærəs] vt acosar, hostigar; ~ment n persecución f.

harbour, (US) **harbor** ['hɑ:bə*] n puerto // vt dar abrigo a.

hard [hɑ:d] a duro; (difficult) difícil; (work) arduo; (person) severo // ad (work) mucho, duro; (think) profundamente; to look ~ at sb/sth clavar los ojos en uno/algo; to try ~ esforzarse; no ~ feelings! ¡sin rencor(es)!; to be ~ of hearing ser duro de oído; to be ~ done by ser tratado injustamente; ~back n libro de tapas duras; ~ cash n dinero contante; ~ disk n (COMPUT) disco duro or rígido; ~en vt endurecer; (fig) curtir // vi endurecerse; ~headed a poco sentimental, realista; ~ labour n trabajos mpl forzados.

hardly ['hɑ:dli] ad (scarcely) apenas; that can ~ be true eso difícilmente puede ser cierto; ~ ever casi nunca.

hardship ['hɑ:dʃip] n (troubles) penas fpl; (financial) apuro.

hard-up [hɑ:d'ʌp] a (col) sin un duro

(Sp), sin plata (LAm).

hardware ['hɑ:dwɛə*] n ferretería; (COMPUT) hardware m; ~ shop n ferretería.

hard-wearing [hɑ:d'wɛəriŋ] a resistente, duradero.

hard-working [hɑ:d'wə:kiŋ] a trabajador(a).

hardy ['hɑ:di] a fuerte; (plant) resistente.

hare [hɛə*] n liebre f; ~-brained a casquivano.

haricot (bean) ['hærikəu-] n alubia.

harm [hɑ:m] n daño, mal m // vt (person) hacer daño a; (health, interests) perjudicar; (thing) dañar; out of ~'s way a salvo; ~ful a (gen) dañino; (to reputation) perjudicial; ~less a (person) inofensivo; (drugs) inocuo.

harmonize ['hɑ:mənaiz] vt, vi armonizar.

harmony ['hɑ:məni] n armonía.

harness ['hɑ:nis] n arreos mpl // vt (horse) enjaezar; (resources) aprovechar.

harp [hɑ:p] n arpa // vi: to ~ on (about) machacar (con).

harpoon [hɑ:'pu:n] n arpón m.

harrowing ['hærəuiŋ] a angustioso.

harsh [hɑ:ʃ] a (cruel) duro, cruel; (severe) severo; (words) hosco; (colour) chillón/ona; (contrast) violento.

harvest ['hɑ:vist] n cosecha; (of grapes) vendimia // vt, vi cosechar; ~er n (machine) cosechadora.

has [hæz] vb see **have**.

hash [hæʃ] n (CULIN) picadillo; (fig: mess) lío.

hashish ['hæʃiʃ] n hachís m, hachich m.

hasn't ['hæznt] = **has not**.

hassle ['hæsl] n pelea.

haste [heist] n prisa; ~n ['heisn] vt acelerar // vi darse prisa; **hastily** ad de prisa; **hasty** a apresurado.

hat [hæt] n sombrero.

hatch [hætʃ] n (NAUT: also: ~way) escotilla // vi salir del cascarón a // vt incubar; (plot) tramar.

hatchback ['hætʃbæk] n (AUT) tres or cinco puertas m.

hatchet ['hætʃɪt] n hacha.

hate [heɪt] vt odiar, aborrecer // n odio; **~ful** a odioso; **hatred** ['heɪtrɪd] n odio.

hat trick n: to score a ~ (Brit: SPORT) marcar tres goles or tantos.

haughty ['hɔːtɪ] a altanero, arrogante.

haul [hɔːl] vt tirar; (by lorry) transportar // n (of fish) redada; (of stolen goods etc) botín m; **~age** n (Brit) transporte m; (costs) gastos mpl de transporte; **~ier**, (US) **~er** n transportista m/f.

haunch [hɔːntʃ] n anca; (of meat) pierna.

haunt [hɔːnt] vt (subj: ghost) aparecer en; (frequent) frecuentar; (obsess) obsesionar // n guarida.

---

have [hæv], pt, pp **had** ♦ auxiliary vb 1 (gen) haber; to ~ arrived/eaten haber llegado/comido; having finished or when he had finished, he left cuando terminó, se fue

2 (in tag questions): you've done it, ~n't you? lo has hecho, ¿verdad? or ¿no?

3 (in short answers and questions): I ~n't no; so I ~ pues, es verdad; we ~n't paid — yes we ~! no hemos pagado — sí que hemos pagado; I've been there before, ~ you? he estado allí antes, ¿y tú?

♦ modal auxiliary vb (be obliged): to ~ (got) to do sth tener que hacer algo; you ~n't to tell her no hay que or no debes decírselo

♦ vt 1 (possess): he has (got) blue eyes/dark hair tiene los ojos azules/el pelo negro

2 (referring to meals etc): to ~ breakfast/lunch/dinner desayunar/comer/cenar; to ~ a drink/a cigarette tomar algo/fumar un cigarrillo

3 (receive) recibir; (obtain) obtener; may I ~ your address? ¿puedes

darme tu dirección?; you can ~ it for £5 te lo puedes quedar por £5; I must ~ it by tomorrow lo necesito para mañana; to ~ a baby tener un niño or bebé

4 (maintain, allow): I won't ~ it/this nonsense! ¡no lo permitiré!/¡no permitiré estas tonterías!; we can't ~ that no podemos permitir eso

5: to ~ sth done hacer or mandar hacer algo; to ~ a hair cut cortarse el pelo; to ~ sb do sth hacer que alguien haga algo

6 (experience, suffer): to ~ a cold/flu tener un resfriado/gripe; she had her bag stolen/her arm broken le robaron el bolso/se rompió un brazo; to ~ an operation operarse

7 (+ noun): to ~ a swim/walk/bath/rest nadar/dar un paseo/darse un baño/descansar; let's ~ a look vamos a ver; to ~ a meeting/party celebrar una reunión/una fiesta; let me ~ a try déjame intentarlo;

to ~ out vt: to ~ it out with sb (settle a problem etc) dejar las cosas en claro con alguien.

---

haven ['heɪvn] n puerto; (fig) refugio.

haven't ['hævnt] = **have not**.

haversack ['hævəsæk] n mochila.

havoc ['hævək] n estragos mpl.

hawk [hɔːk] n halcón m.

hay [heɪ] n heno; **~ fever** n fiebre f del heno; **~stack** n almiar m.

haywire ['heɪwaɪə'] a (col): to go ~ (person) volverse loco; (plan) embrollarse.

hazard ['hæzəd] n riesgo; (danger) peligro // vt aventurar; **~ous** a peligroso; **~ warning lights** npl (AUT) señales fpl de emergencia.

haze [heɪz] n neblina.

hazelnut ['heɪzlnʌt] n avellana.

hazy ['heɪzɪ] a brumoso; (idea) vago.

he [hiː] pron él; **~ who...** él que..., quien... .

head [hɛd] n cabeza; (leader) jefe/a m/f // vt (list) encabezar; (group) capitanear; ~s (or tails) cara (o cruz); ~ first de cabeza; ~ over heels patas arriba; to ~ the ball cabecear (la pelota); to ~ for *vt fus* dirigirse a; ~ache *n* dolor *m* de cabeza; ~dress *n* tocado; ~ing *n* título; ~lamp *n* (*Brit*) = ~light; ~land *n* promontorio; ~light *n* faro; ~line *n* titular *m*; ~long *ad* (*fall*) de cabeza; (*rush*) precipitadamente; ~master/mistress *n* director(a) *m/f* (de escuela); ~ office *n* oficina central, central *f*; ~-on *a* (*collision*) de frente; ~phones *npl* auriculares *mpl*; ~quarters (HQ) *npl* sede *f* central; (*MIL*) cuartel *m* general; ~rest *n* reposa-cabezas *m inv*; ~room *n* (*in car*) altura interior; (*under bridge*) (límite *m* de) altura; ~scarf *n* pañuelo; ~strong *a* testarudo; ~ waiter *n* maître *m*; ~way *n*: to make ~way (*fig*) hacer progresos; ~wind *n* viento contrario; ~y *a* (*experience*, *period*) apasionante; (*wine*) cabezón.

heal [hiːl] *vt* curar // *vi* cicatrizarse.

health [hɛlθ] *n* salud *f*; ~ food *n* alimentos *mpl* orgánicos; the H~ Service *n* (*Brit*) servicio de salud pública; = Insalud *m* (*Sp*); ~y *a* (*gen*) sano.

heap [hiːp] *n* montón *m* // *vt* amontonar.

hear [hɪə*], *pt*, *pp* **heard** [həːd] *vt* oír; (*perceive*) sentir; (*listen to*) escuchar; (*lecture*) asistir a // *vi* oír; to ~ about oír hablar de; to ~ from sb tener noticias de uno; ~ing *n* (*sense*) oído; (*LAW*) vista; ~ing aid *n* audífono; ~say *n* rumores *mpl*, hablillas *fpl*.

hearse [həːs] *n* coche *m* fúnebre.

heart [haːt] *n* corazón *m*; ~s *npl* (*CARDS*) corazones *mpl*; at ~ en el fondo; by ~ (*learn*, *know*) de memoria; ~ attack *n* infarto de miocardio); ~beat *n* latido (del corazón); ~breaking *a* desgarrador(a); ~broken *a*: she was ~broken about it esto le partió el corazón;

~burn *n* acedía; ~ failure *n* fallo cardíaco; ~felt *a* (*cordial*) cordial; (*deeply felt*) más sentido.

hearth [haːθ] *n* (*gen*) hogar *m*; (*fireplace*) chimenea.

heartily ['haːtɪlɪ] *ad* sinceramente, cordialmente; (*laugh*) a carcajadas; (*eat*) con buen apetito.

heartless ['haːtlɪs] *a* cruel.

hearty ['haːtɪ] *a* cordial.

heat [hiːt] *n* (*gen*) calor *m*; (*SPORT*: *also*: qualifying ~) prueba eliminatoria // *vt* calentar; to ~ up *vi* (*gen*) calentarse; ~ed *a* caliente; (*fig*) acalorado; ~er *n* calentador *m*.

heath [hiːθ] *n* (*Brit*) brezal *m*.

heathen ['hiːðən] *a*, *n* pagano/a *m/f*.

heather ['hɛðə*] *n* brezo.

heating ['hiːtɪŋ] *n* calefacción *f*.

heatstroke ['hiːtstrəuk] *n* insolación *f*.

heatwave ['hiːtweɪv] *n* ola de calor.

heave [hiːv] *vt* (*pull*) tirar; (*push*) empujar con esfuerzo; (*lift*) levantar (con esfuerzo) // *vi* (*water*) subir y bajar // *n* tirón *m*; empujón *m*.

heaven ['hɛvn] *n* cielo; ~ly *a* celestial.

heavily ['hɛvɪlɪ] *ad* pesadamente; (*drink*, *smoke*) con exceso; (*sleep*, *sigh*) profundamente.

heavy ['hɛvɪ] *a* pesado; (*work*) duro; (*sea*, *rain*, *meal*) fuerte; (*drinker*, *smoker*) gran; ~ goods vehicle (HGV) *n* vehículo pesado; ~weight *n* (*SPORT*) peso pesado.

Hebrew ['hiːbruː] *a*, *n* (*LING*) hebreo.

Hebrides ['hɛbrɪdiːz] *npl*: the ~ las Hébridas.

heckle ['hɛkl] *vt* interrumpir.

hectic ['hɛktɪk] *a* agitado.

he'd [hiːd] = he would, he had.

hedge [hɛdʒ] *n* seto // *vt* cercar (con un seto) // *vi* contestar con evasivas; to ~ one's bets (*fig*) cubrirse.

hedgehog ['hɛdʒhɔg] *n* erizo.

heed [hiːd] *vt* (*also*: take ~ of) (*pay attention*) hacer caso de; (*bear in mind*) tener en cuenta; ~less *a* desatento.

heel [hi:l] n talón m // vt (shoe) poner tacón a.

hefty ['heftɪ] a (person) fornido; (piece) grande; (price) gordo.

heifer ['hefə*] n novilla, ternera.

height [haɪt] n (of person) talle m; (of building) altura; (high ground) cerro; (altitude) altitud f; **~en** vt elevar; (fig) aumentar.

heir [ɛə*] n heredero; **~ess** n heredera; **~loom** n reliquia de familia.

held [held] pt, pp of **hold**.

helicopter ['helɪkɔptə*] n helicóptero.

helium ['hi:lɪəm] n helio.

hell [hel] n infierno; ~! (col) ¡demonios!

he'll [hi:l] = **he will, he shall.**

hellish ['helɪʃ] a infernal.

hello [hə'ləu] excl ¡hola!; (surprise) ¡caramba!

helm [helm] n (NAUT) timón m.

helmet ['helmɪt] n casco.

help [help] n ayuda; (charwoman) criada, asistenta // vt ayudar; ~! ¡socorro!; ~ **yourself** sírvete; he can't ~ it no es culpa suya; **~er** n ayudante m/f; **~ful** a útil; (person) servicial; **~ing** n ración f; **~less** a (incapable) incapaz; (defenceless) indefenso.

hem [hem] n dobladillo // vt poner or coser el dobladillo; **to ~ in** vt cercar.

he-man ['hi:mæn] n macho.

hemorrhage ['hemərɪdʒ] n (US) = **haemorrhage.**

hemorrhoids ['hemərɔɪdz] npl (US) = **haemorrhoids.**

hen [hen] n gallina.

hence [hens] ad (therefore) por lo tanto; 2 years ~ de aquí a 2 años; **~forth** ad de hoy en adelante.

henchman ['hentʃmən] n (pej) secuaz m.

henpecked ['henpekt] a: to be ~ ser un calzonazos.

hepatitis [hepə'taɪtɪs] n hepatitis f.

her [hə:*] pron (direct) la; (indirect) le; (stressed, after prep) ella // a su; see also me, my.

herald ['herəld] n heraldo // vt anunciar.

herb [hə:b] n hierba.

herd [hə:d] n rebaño.

here [hɪə*] ad aquí; ~! (present) ¡presente!; (offering sth) ¡toma!; ~ is/are aquí está/están; ~ **she is** aquí está; **~after** ad en el futuro // n: the **~after** el más allá; **~by** ad (in letter) por la presente.

heredity [hɪ'redɪtɪ] n herencia.

heresy ['herəsɪ] n herejía.

heretic ['herətɪk] n hereje m/f.

heritage ['herɪtɪdʒ] n (gen) herencia; (fig) patrimonio.

hermetically [hə:'metɪklɪ] ad: ~ sealed cerrado herméticamente.

hermit ['hə:mɪt] n ermitaño/a.

hernia ['hə:nɪə] n hernia.

hero ['hɪərəu], pl ~**es** n héroe m; (in book, film) protagonista m; **~ic** [hɪ'rəuɪk] a heroico.

heroin ['herəuɪn] n heroína.

heroine ['herəuɪn] n heroína; (in book, film) protagonista.

heron ['herən] n garza.

herring ['herɪŋ] n arenque m.

hers [hə:z] pron (el) suyo/(la) suya etc; see also **mine.**

herself [hə:'self] pron (reflexive) se; (emphatic) ella misma; (after prep) sí (misma); see also **oneself.**

he's [hi:z] = **he is; he has.**

hesitant ['hezɪtənt] a vacilante.

hesitate ['hezɪteɪt] vi vacilar; **hesitation** [-'teɪʃən] n indecisión f.

heterosexual [hetərəu'seksjuəl] a, n heterosexual m/f.

heyday ['heɪdeɪ] n: the ~ of el apogeo de.

HGV n abbr = **heavy goods vehicle.**

hi [haɪ] excl ¡hola!

hiatus [haɪ'eɪtəs] n laguna; (LING) hiato.

hibernate ['haɪbəneɪt] vi invernar.

hiccough, hiccup ['hɪkʌp] vi hipar; **~s** npl hipo sg.

hide [haɪd] n (skin) piel f // vb (pt **hid**, pp **hidden**) vt esconder, ocultar // vi: **to ~ (from sb)** esconderse or ocultarse (de algn); **~-and-seek** n escondite m; **~away** n escondite m.

hideous ['hɪdɪəs] a horrible.

hiding ['haɪdɪŋ] n (beating) paliza; **to be in ~** (concealed) estar escondido; **~ place** n escondrijo.

hierarchy ['haɪərɑːkɪ] n jerarquía.

hi-fi ['haɪfaɪ] n estéreo, hifi m // a de alta fidelidad.

high [haɪ] a alto; (speed, number) grande; (price) elevado; (wind) fuerte; (voice) agudo // ad alto, a gran altura; **it is 20 m** ~ tiene 20 m de altura; **~ in the air** en las alturas; **~boy** n (US) cómoda alta; **~brow** a, n intelectual m/f; **~chair** n silla alta; **~er education** n educación f or enseñanza superior; **~-handed** a despótico; **~jack** = **hijack**; **~jump** n (SPORT) salto de altura; **the H~lands** npl las tierras altas de Escocia; **~light** n (fig: of event) punto culminante // vt subrayar; **~ly** ad sumamente; **~ly strung** a hipertenso; **~ness** n altura; **Her** or **His H~ness** Su Alteza; **~-pitched** a agudo; **~-rise block** n torre f de pisos; **~ school** n centro de enseñanza secundaria; ≈ Instituto Nacional de Bachillerato (Sp); **~ season** n (Brit) temporada alta; **~ street** n (Brit) calle f mayor; **~way** n carretera; **H~way Code** n (Brit) código de la circulación.

hijack ['haɪdʒæk] vt secuestrar; **~er** n secuestrador(a) m/f.

hike [haɪk] vi (go walking) ir de excursión (de pie) // n caminata; **~r** n excursionista m/f.

hilarious [hɪ'lɛərɪəs] a divertidísimo.

hill [hɪl] n colina; (high) montaña; (slope) cuesta; **~side** n ladera; **~y** a montañoso; (uneven) accidentado.

hilt [hɪlt] n (of sword) empuñadura; **to the ~** (fig: support) incondicionalmente.

him [hɪm] pron (direct) le, lo; (indi-

rect) le; (stressed, after prep) él; see also **me**; **~self** pron (reflexive) se; (emphatic) él mismo; (after prep) sí (mismo); see also **oneself**.

hind [haɪnd] a posterior // n cierva.

hinder ['hɪndə*] vt estorbar, impedir; **hindrance** ['hɪndrəns] n estorbo, obstáculo.

hindsight ['haɪndsaɪt] n: **with ~** en retrospectiva.

Hindu ['hɪnduː] n hindú m/f.

hinge [hɪndʒ] n bisagra, gozne m // vi (fig): **to ~ on** depender de.

hint [hɪnt] n indirecta; (advice) consejo // vt: **to ~ that** insinuar que // vi: **to ~ at** hacer alusión a.

hip [hɪp] n cadera.

hippopotamus [hɪpə'pɔtəməs], pl **~es** or **-mi** [-maɪ] n hipopótamo.

hire ['haɪə*] vt (Brit: car, equipment) alquilar; (worker) contratar // n alquiler m; **for ~** se alquila; (taxi) libre; **~ purchase (H.P.)** n (Brit) compra a plazos.

his [hɪz] pron (el) suyo/(la) suya etc // a su; see also **my**, **mine**.

Hispanic [hɪs'pænɪk] a hispánico.

hiss [hɪs] vi silbar.

historian [hɪ'stɔːrɪən] n historiador(a) m/f.

historic(al) [hɪ'stɔrɪk(l)] a histórico.

history ['hɪstərɪ] n historia.

hit [hɪt] vt (pt, pp hit) (strike) golpear, pegar; (reach: target) alcanzar; (collide with: car) chocar contra; (fig: affect) afectar // n golpe m; (success) éxito; **to ~ it off with sb** llevarse bien con algn; **~-and-run driver** n conductor(a) que atropella y huye.

hitch [hɪtʃ] vt (fasten) atar, amarrar; (also: **~ up**) remangar // n (difficulty) dificultad f; **to ~ a lift** hacer autostop.

hitch-hike ['hɪtʃhaɪk] vi hacer autostop; **~r** n autostopista m/f.

hi-tech ['haɪ'tɛk] a de alta tecnología.

hitherto ['hɪðə'tuː] ad hasta ahora.

hive [haɪv] n colmena; **to ~ off** vt transferir; (privatize) privatizar.

HMS abbr = His (Her) Majesty's Ship.

hoard [hɔːd] n (treasure) tesoro; (stockpile) provisión f // vi acumular; ~ing n (for posters) cartelera.

hoarfrost ['hɔːfrɔst] n escarcha.

hoarse [hɔːs] a ronco.

hoax [həuks] n trampa.

hob [hɔb] n quemador m.

hobble ['hɔbl] vi cojear.

hobby ['hɔbɪ] n pasatiempo, afición f; ~-horse n (fig) caballo de batalla.

hobo ['həubəu] n (US) vagabundo.

hockey ['hɔkɪ] n hockey m.

hoe [həu] n azadón m // vt azadonar.

hog [hɔg] n cerdo, puerco // vt (fig) acaparar; **to go the whole ~** poner toda la carne en el asador.

hoist [hɔɪst] n (crane) grúa // vt levantar, alzar.

hold [həuld] vt (pt, pp held) tener; (contain) contener; (keep back) retener; (believe) sostener; (take ~ of) coger (Sp), agarrar (LAm); (take weight) soportar; (meeting) celebrar // vi (withstand pressure) resistir; (be valid) valer; (stick) pegarse // n (grasp) asimiento; (fig) dominio; (WRESTLING) presa; (NAUT) bodega; **~ the line!** (TEL) ¡no cuelgue!; **to ~ one's own** (fig) defenderse; **to catch or get** (a) **~ of** agarrarse or asirse de; **to ~ back** vt retener; **to ~ down** vt (person) sujetar; (job) mantener; **to ~ off** vt (enemy) rechazar; **to ~ on** vi agarrarse bien; (wait) esperar; **to ~ on to** vt fus agarrarse a; (keep) guardar; **to ~ out** vt ofrecer // vi (resist) resistir; **to ~ up** vt (raise) levantar; (support) apoyar; (delay) retrasar; (rob) asaltar; **~all** n (Brit) bolsa; **~er** n (of ticket, record) poseedor(a) m/f; (of office, title etc) titular m/f; **~ing** n (share) interés m; **~up** n (robbery) atraco; (delay) retraso; (Brit: in traffic) embotellamiento.

hole [həul] n agujero // vt agujerear.

holiday ['hɔlədɪ] n vacaciones fpl; (day off) día m de fiesta, día m feriado; **on ~** de vacaciones; **~ camp** n colonia veraniega; **~-maker** n (Brit) turista m/f; **~ resort** n centro turístico.

holiness ['həulɪnɪs] n santidad f.

Holland ['hɔlənd] n Holanda.

hollow ['hɔləu] a hueco; (fig) vacío; (eyes) hundido; (sound) sordo // n (gen) hueco; (in ground) hoyo // vt: **to ~ out** ahuecar.

holly ['hɔlɪ] n acebo.

holocaust ['hɔləkɔːst] n holocausto.

holster ['həulstə*] n pistolera.

holy ['həulɪ] a (gen) santo, sagrado; (water) bendito; **H~ Ghost** or **Spirit** n Espíritu m Santo.

homage ['hɔmɪdʒ] n homenaje m.

home [həum] n casa; (country) patria; (institution) asilo // a (domestic) casero, de casa; (ECON, POL) nacional // ad (direction) a casa; **at ~** en casa; **to go/come ~** ir/volver a casa; **make yourself at ~** ¡estás en tu casa!; **~ address** n domicilio; **~ computer** n ordenador m doméstico; **~land** n tierra natal; **~less** a sin hogar, sin casa; **~ly** a (domestic) sencillo; (simple) sencillo; **~-made** a hecho en casa; **H~ Office** n (Brit) Ministerio del Interior; **~ rule** n autonomía; **H~ Secretary** n (Brit) Ministro del Interior; **~sick** a: **to be ~sick** tener morriña, sentir nostalgia; **~ town** n ciudad f natal; **~ward** ['həumwəd] a (journey) hacia casa; **~work** n deberes mpl.

homogeneous [hɔmə'dʒiːnɪəs] a homogéneo.

homicide ['hɔmɪsaɪd] n (US) homicidio.

homosexual [hɔməu'sɛksjuəl] a, n homosexual m/f.

Honduran [hɔn'djuərən] a, n hondureño/a m/f.

Honduras [hɔn'djuərəs] n Honduras f.

honest ['ɔnɪst] a honrado; (sincere) franco, sincero; **~ly** ad honradamente; francamente; ~ n honradez f.

honey [hʌnɪ] n miel f; ~**comb** n panal m; ~**moon** n luna de miel f; ~ **suckle** n madreselva.

honk [hɔŋk] vi (AUT) tocar la bocina.

honorary [ˈɔnərərɪ] a (member, president) de honor; ~ **degree** n doctorado honoris causa.

honour, (US) **honor** [ˈɔnə*] n honor m // vt honrar; ~**able** a honorable; ~**s degree** n (SCOL) título de licenciado de categoría superior.

hood [hud] n capucha; (Brit AUT) capota; (US: AUT) capó m.

hoodlum [ˈhuːdləm] n matón m.

hoodwink [ˈhudwɪŋk] vt (Brit) timar.

hoof [huːf], pl **hooves** n pezuña.

hook [huk] n gancho; (on dress) corchete m, broche m; (for fishing) anzuelo // vt enganchar.

hooligan [ˈhuːlɪgən] n gamberro.

hoop [huːp] n aro.

hoot [huːt] vi (Brit AUT) tocar la bocina; (siren) sonar la sirena // n bocinazo, toque m de sirena; to ~ with laughter morirse de risa; ~**er** n (Brit AUT) bocina; (NAUT) sirena.

hoover ® [ˈhuːvə*] (Brit) n aspiradora // vt pasar la aspiradora por.

hooves [huːvz] pl of **hoof**.

hop [hɔp] vi saltar, brincar; (on one foot) saltar con un pie.

hope [həup] vt, vi esperar // n esperanza; I ~ **so/not** espero que sí/no; ~**ful** a (person) optimista; (situation) prometedor; a; ~**fully** ad con optimismo, con esperanza; ~**less** a desesperado.

hops [hɔps] npl lúpulo sg.

horizon [həˈraɪzn] n horizonte m; ~**tal** [hɔrɪˈzɔntl] a horizontal.

hormone [ˈhɔːməun] n hormona.

horn [hɔːn] n cuerno; (MUS: also: French ~) trompa; (AUT) bocina, claxon m (LAm).

hornet [ˈhɔːnɪt] n avispón m.

horny [ˈhɔːnɪ] a (material) córneo; (hands) calloso; (col) cachondo.

horoscope [ˈhɔrəskəup] n horóscopo.

horrendous [həˈrɛndəs] a horrendo.

horrible [ˈhɔrɪbl] a horrible.

horrid [ˈhɔrɪd] a horrible, horroroso.

horrify [ˈhɔrɪfaɪ] vt horrorizar.

horror [ˈhɔrə*] n horror m; ~ **film** n película de horror.

hors d'œuvre [ɔːˈdəːvrə] n entremeses mpl.

horse [hɔːs] n caballo; **on** ~**back** a caballo; ~ **chestnut** n (tree) castaño de Indias; ~**man/woman** n jinete/a m/f; ~**power** (h.p.) n caballo (de fuerza); ~**racing** n carreras fpl de caballos; ~**radish** n rábano picante; ~**shoe** n herradura.

hose [həuz] n (also: ~**pipe**) manga.

hosiery [ˈhəuzɪərɪ] n calcetería.

hospitable [hɔsˈpɪtəbl] a hospitalario.

hospital [ˈhɔspɪtl] n hospital m.

hospitality [hɔspɪˈtælɪtɪ] n hospitalidad f.

host [həust] n anfitrión m; (of inn etc) mesonero; (REL) hostia; (large number): **a** ~ **of** multitud de.

hostage [ˈhɔstɪdʒ] n rehén m.

hostel [ˈhɔstl] n hostal m; (**youth**) ~ n albergue m juvenil.

hostess [ˈhəustɪs] n anfitriona.

hostile [ˈhɔstaɪl] a hostil; **hostility** [-ˈstɪlɪtɪ] n hostilidad f.

hot [hɔt] a caliente; (weather) caluroso, de calor; (as opposed to only warm) muy caliente; (spicy) picante; (fig) ardiente, acalorado; to be ~ (person) tener calor; (object) estar caliente; (weather) hacer calor; ~**bed** n (fig) semillero; ~ **dog** n perro caliente.

hotel [həuˈtɛl] n hotel m; ~**ier** n hotelero.

hot: ~**headed** a exaltado; ~**house** n invernadero; ~ **line** n (POL) teléfono rojo; ~**ly** ad con pasión, apasionadamente; ~**plate** n (on cooker) hornillo; ~**water bottle** n bolsa de agua caliente.

hound [haund] vt acosar // n perro de caza.

hour [′auə*] *n* hora; **~ly** *a* (de) cada hora // *ad* cada hora.

house [haus, *pl*: ′hauzɪz] *n* (*also*: *firm*) casa; (*POL*) cámara; (*THEATRE*) sala // *vt* [hauz] (*person*) alojar; **on the ~** (*fig*) la casa invita; **~boat** *n* casa flotante; **~breaking** *n* allanamiento de morada; **~coat** *n* bata; **~hold** *n* familia; **~keeper** *n* ama de llaves; **~keeping** *n* (*work*) trabajos *mpl* domésticos; **~keeping (money)** *n* dinero para gastos domésticos; **~warming party** *n* fiesta de estreno de una casa; **~wife** *n* ama de casa; **~work** *n* faenas *fpl* (de la casa).

housing [′hauzɪŋ] *n* (*act*) alojamiento; (*houses*) viviendas *fpl*; **~ development**, (*Brit*) **~ estate** *n* urbanización *f*.

hovel [′hɔvl] *n* casucha.

hover [′hɔvə*] *vi* flotar (en el aire); **~craft** *n* aerodeslizador *m*.

how [hau] *ad* (*in what way*) cómo; **~ are you?** ¿cómo estás?; **~ much milk/many people?** ¿cuánta leche/gente?; **~ much does it cost?** ¿cuánto cuesta?; **~ long have you been here?** ¿cuánto hace que estás aquí?; **~ old are you?** ¿cuántos años tienes?; **~ tall is he?** ¿cómo es de alto?; **~ is school?** ¿cómo (te) va (en) la escuela?; **~ was the film?** ¿qué tal la película?; **~ lovely/awful!** ¡qué bonito/horror!

howl [haul] *n* aullido // *vi* aullar.

H.P. *n abbr* = **hire purchase.**

h.p. *abbr* = **horse power.**

HQ *n abbr* = **headquarters.**

hub [hʌb] *n* (*of wheel*) centro.

hubbub [′hʌbʌb] *n* barahúnda, barullo.

hubcap [′hʌbkæp] *n* tapacubos *m inv.*

huddle [′hʌdl] *vi*: **to ~ together** amontonarse.

hue [hju:] *n* color *m*, matiz *m*; **~ and cry** *n* alarma.

huff [hʌf] *n*: **in a ~** enojado.

hug [hʌg] *vt* abrazar // *n* abrazo.

huge [hju:dʒ] *a* enorme.

hulk [hʌlk] *n* (*ship*) barco viejo; (*person, building etc*) mole *f*.

hull [hʌl] *n* (*of ship*) casco.

hullo [hə′lau] *excl* = **hello.**

hum [hʌm] *vt* tararear, canturrear // *vi* tararear, canturrear; (*insect*) zumbar.

human [′hju:mən] *a*, *n* humano *m/f.*

humane [hju:′meɪn] *a* humano, humanitario.

humanitarian [hju:mænɪ′tɛərɪən] *a* humanitario.

humanity [hju:′mænɪtɪ] *n* humanidad *f.*

humble [′hʌmbl] *a* humilde // *vt* humillar.

humbug [′hʌmbʌg] *n* tonterías *fpl*; (*Brit*: *sweet*) caramelo de menta.

humdrum [′hʌmdrʌm] *a* (*boring*) monótono, aburrido; (*routine*) rutinario.

humid [′hju:mɪd] *a* húmedo; **~ity** [-′mɪdɪtɪ] *n* humedad *f.*

humiliate [hju:′mɪlɪeɪt] *vt* humillar; **humiliation** [-′eɪʃən] *n* humillación *f.*

humility [hju:′mɪlɪtɪ] *n* humildad *f.*

humorous [′hju:mərəs] *a* gracioso, divertido.

humour, (*US*) **humor** [′hju:mə*] *n* humorismo, sentido del humor; (*mood*) humor *m* // *vt* (*person*) complacer.

hump [hʌmp] *n* (*in ground*) montículo; (*camel's*) giba.

hunch [hʌntʃ] *n* (*premonition*) presentimiento; **~back** *n* joroba *m/f*; **~ed** *a* jorobado.

hundred [′hʌndrəd] *num* ciento; (*before n*) cien; **~s of** centenares de; **~weight** *n* (*Brit*) = 50.8 *kg*; 112 *lb*; (*US*) = 45.3 *kg*; 100 *lb.*

hung [hʌŋ] *pt, pp* of **hang.**

Hungarian [hʌŋ′gɛərɪən] *a*, *n* húngaro/a *m/f.*

Hungary [′hʌŋgərɪ] *n* Hungría.

hunger [′hʌŋgə*] *n* hambre *f* // *vi*: **~ for** (*fig*) tener hambre de, anhelar; ~ **strike** n huelga de hambre.

hungry ['hʌŋgrɪ] a hambriento; to be ~ tener hambre.

hunk [hʌŋk] n (of bread etc) trozo, pedazo.

hunt [hʌnt] vt (seek) buscar; (SPORT) cazar // vi cazar // n caza, cacería; ~**er** n cazador(a) m/f; ~**ing** n caza.

hurdle ['hɜːdl] n (SPORT) valla; (fig) obstáculo.

hurl [hɜːl] vt lanzar, arrojar.

hurrah [hu'rɑ:], **hurray** [hu'reɪ] n ¡viva!, ¡vítor!

hurricane ['hʌrɪkən] n huracán m.

hurried ['hʌrɪd] a (fast) apresurado; (rushed) hecho de prisa; ~**ly** ad con prisa, apresuradamente.

hurry ['hʌrɪ] n prisa // vb (also: ~ up) vi apresurarse, darse prisa // vt (person) dar prisa a; (work) apresurar, hacer de prisa; to be in a ~ tener prisa.

hurt [hɜːt], pt, pp **hurt** vt hacer daño a // vi doler // a lastimado; ~**ful** a (remark etc) dañoso.

hurtle ['hɜːtl] vi: to ~ past pasar como un rayo.

husband ['hʌzbənd] n marido.

hush [hʌʃ] n silencio // vt hacer callar; (cover up) encubrir; ~! ¡chitón!, ¡cállate!

husk [hʌsk] n (of wheat) cáscara.

husky ['hʌskɪ] a ronco // n perro esquimal.

hustle ['hʌsl] vt (push) empujar; (hurry) dar prisa a // n bullicio, actividad f febril; ~ and **bustle** n vaivén m.

hut [hʌt] n cabaña; (shed) cobertizo.

hutch [hʌtʃ] n conejera.

hyacinth ['haɪəsɪnθ] n jacinto.

hydrant ['haɪdrənt] n (also: fire ~) boca de incendios.

hydraulic [haɪ'drɔːlɪk] a hidráulico.

hydroelectric [haɪdrəu'lɛktrɪk] a hidroeléctrico.

hydrofoil ['haɪdrəfɔɪl] n aerodeslizador m.

hydrogen ['haɪdrədʒən] n hidrógeno.

hyena [haɪ'iːnə] n hiena.

hygiene ['haɪdʒiːn] n higiene f; **hygienic** [-'dʒiːnɪk] a higiénico.

hymn [hɪm] n himno.

hype [haɪp] n (col) bombardeo publicitario.

hypermarket ['haɪpəmɑːkɪt] n hipermercado.

hypnotize ['hɪpnətaɪz] vt hipnotizar.

hypochondriac [haɪpəu'kɔndrɪæk] n hipocondríaco/a.

hypocrisy [hɪ'pɔkrɪsɪ] n hipocresía.

hypocrite ['hɪpəkrɪt] n hipócrita m/f; **hypocritical** [hɪpə'krɪtɪkl] a hipócrita.

hypothesis [haɪ'pɔθɪsɪs], pl -**ses** [-siːz] n hipótesis f inv.

hysteria [hɪ'stɪərɪə] n histeria; **hysterical** [-'stɛrɪkl] a histérico; **hysterics** [-'stɛrɪks] npl histeria sg, histerismo sg.

I

I [aɪ] pron yo.

ice [aɪs] n hielo // vt (cake) alcorzar // vi (also: ~ over, ~ up) helarse; ~**axe** n piqueta de alpinista); ~**berg** n iceberg m; ~**box** n (Brit) congelador m; (US) nevera, refrigeradora (LAm); ~ **cream** n helado; ~**cube** n cubito de hielo; ~ **hockey** n hockey m sobre hielo.

Iceland ['aɪslənd] n Islandia.

ice: ~ **lolly** n (Brit) polo; ~ **rink** n pista de hielo; ~ **skating** n patinaje m sobre hielo.

icicle ['aɪsɪkl] n carámbano.

icing ['aɪsɪŋ] n (CULIN) alcorza; (AVIAT etc) formación f de hielo; ~ **sugar** n (Brit) azúcar m glas(eado).

icy ['aɪsɪ] a (road) helado; (fig) glacial.

I'd [aɪd] = I would; I had.

idea [aɪ'dɪə] n idea.

ideal [aɪ'dɪəl] n ideal m // a ideal; ~**ist** n idealista m/f.

identical [aɪ'dɛntɪkl] a idéntico.

identification [aɪdentɪfɪˈkeɪʃən] n identificación f; **means of ~** documentos mpl personales.

identify [aɪˈdentɪfaɪ] vt identificar.

identikit picture [aɪˈdentɪkɪt-] n retrato-robot m.

identity [aɪˈdentɪtɪ] n identidad f; **~ card** n carnet m de identidad.

ideology [aɪdɪˈɒlədʒɪ] n ideología.

idiom [ˈɪdɪəm] n modismo; (style of speaking) lenguaje m; **~atic** [-ˈmætɪk] a idiomático.

idiosyncrasy [ɪdɪəˈsɪŋkrəsɪ] n idiosincrasia.

idiot [ˈɪdɪət] n (gen) idiota m/f; (fool) tonto/a; **~ic** [-ˈɒtɪk] a idiota; tonto.

idle [ˈaɪdl] a (lazy) holgazán/ana; (unemployed) parado, desocupado; (talk) frívolo // vi (machine) marchar en vacío // vt: **to ~ away the time** malgastar el tiempo; **~ness** n holgazanería; paro, desocupación f.

idol [ˈaɪdl] n ídolo; **~ize** vt idolatrar.

idyllic [ɪˈdɪlɪk] a idílico.

i.e. abbr (= that is) esto es.

if [ɪf] conj si; **~ necessary** si fuera necesario; **if I hiciese falta**; **~ I were you** yo en tu lugar; **~ so/not** de ser así/si no; **~ only I could!** ¡ojalá pudiera!; see also as, even.

igloo [ˈɪgluː] n iglú m.

ignite [ɪgˈnaɪt] vt (set fire to) encender // vi encenderse.

ignition [ɪgˈnɪʃən] n (AUT) encendido; **to switch on/off the ~** arrancar/apagar el motor; **~ key** n (AUT) llave f de contacto.

ignorance [ˈɪgnərəns] n ignorancia.

ignorant [ˈɪgnərənt] a ignorante; **to be ~ of** ignorar.

ignore [ɪgˈnɔː] vt (person) no hacer caso de; (fact) pasar por alto.

ill [ɪl] a enfermo, malo // n mal m // ad mal; **to take or be taken ~** caer or ponerse enfermo; **~-advised** (decision) imprudente; **he was ~-advised to go** se equivocaba al ir; **~-at-ease** a incómodo.

I'll [aɪl] = **I will, I shall.**

illegal [ɪˈliːgl] a ilegal.

illegible [ɪˈledʒɪbl] a ilegible.

illegitimate [ɪlɪˈdʒɪtɪmət] a ilegítimo.

ill-fated [ɪlˈfeɪtɪd] a malogrado.

ill feeling n rencor m.

illicit [ɪˈlɪsɪt] a ilícito.

illiterate [ɪˈlɪtərɪt] a analfabeto.

ill-mannered [ɪlˈmænəd] a mal educado.

illness [ˈɪlnɪs] n enfermedad f.

ill-treat [ɪlˈtriːt] vt maltratar.

illuminate [ɪˈluːmɪneɪt] vt (room, street) iluminar, alumbrar; (subject) aclarar; **illumination** [-ˈneɪʃən] n alumbrado; **illuminations** npl iluminaciones fpl, luces fpl.

illusion [ɪˈluːʒən] n ilusión f; **to be under the ~ that...** hacerse ilusiones de que ....

illusory [ɪˈluːsərɪ] a ilusorio.

illustrate [ˈɪləstreɪt] vt ilustrar.

illustration [ɪləˈstreɪʃən] n (example) ejemplo, ilustración f; (in book) lámina.

illustrious [ɪˈlʌstrɪəs] a ilustre.

ill will n rencor m.

I'm [aɪm] = **I am.**

image [ˈɪmɪdʒ] n imagen f; **~ry** [-ərɪ] n imágenes fpl.

imaginary [ɪˈmædʒɪnərɪ] a imaginario.

imagination [ɪmædʒɪˈneɪʃən] n imaginación f; (inventiveness) inventiva; (illusion) fantasía.

imaginative [ɪˈmædʒɪnətɪv] a imaginativo.

imagine [ɪˈmædʒɪn] vt imaginarse; (delude o.s.) hacerse la ilusión (de que).

imbalance [ɪmˈbæləns] n desequilibrio.

imbecile [ˈɪmbəsiːl] n imbécil m/f.

imitate [ˈɪmɪteɪt] vt imitar; **imitation** [-ˈteɪʃən] n imitación f; (copy) copia; (pej) remedo.

immaculate [ɪˈmækjulət] a perfectamente limpio; (REL) inmaculado.

immaterial [ɪməˈtɪərɪəl] a incorpóreo; **it is ~ whether...** no importa si... .

immature [ɪmə'tjuə*] a (person) inmaduro; (of one's youth) joven.

immediate [ɪ'miːdɪət] a inmediato; (pressing) urgente, apremiante; ~ly ad (at once) en seguida; ~ly next to muy junto a.

immense [ɪ'mens] a inmenso, enorme.

immerse [ɪ'məːs] vt (submerge) sumergir; **to be ~d in** (fig) estar absorto en.

immersion heater [ɪ'məːʃən-] n (Brit) calentador m de inmersión.

immigrant ['ɪmɪgrənt] n inmigrante m/f.

immigrate ['ɪmɪgreɪt] vi inmigrar; **immigration** [-'greɪʃən] n inmigración f.

imminent ['ɪmɪnənt] a inminente.

immobile [ɪ'məubaɪl] a inmóvil.

immoral [ɪ'mɒrl] a inmoral.

immortal [ɪ'mɔːtl] a inmortal.

immune [ɪ'mjuːn] a: ~ **(to)** inmune (contra); **immunity** n (MED, of diplomat) inmunidad f.

immunize ['ɪmjunaɪz] vt inmunizar.

imp [ɪmp] n diablillo.

impact ['ɪmpækt] n (gen) impacto.

impair [ɪm'pɛə*] vt perjudicar.

impart [ɪm'pɑːt] vt comunicar.

impartial [ɪm'pɑːʃl] a imparcial.

impassable [ɪm'pɑːsəbl] a (barrier) infranqueable; (river, road) intransitable.

impasse [æm'pɑːs] n: **to reach an ~** alcanzar un punto muerto.

impassive [ɪm'pæsɪv] a impasible.

impatience [ɪm'peɪʃəns] n impaciencia.

impatient [ɪm'peɪʃənt] a impaciente; **to get** or **grow ~** impacientarse.

impeccable [ɪm'pekəbl] a impecable.

impede [ɪm'piːd] vt estorbar.

impediment [ɪm'pedɪmənt] n obstáculo, estorbo; (also: **speech ~**) defecto (del habla).

impending [ɪm'pendɪŋ] a inminente.

impenetrable [ɪm'penɪtrəbl] a (unfathomable) inson-

dable.

imperative [ɪm'perətɪv] a (tone) imperioso; (necessary) imprescindible // n (LING) imperativo.

imperfect [ɪm'pəːfɪkt] a imperfecto; (goods etc) defectuoso; **~ion** n (blemish) desperfecto; (fault) defecto.

imperial [ɪm'pɪərɪəl] a imperial; **~ism** n imperialismo.

impersonal [ɪm'pəːsənl] a impersonal.

impersonate [ɪm'pəːsəneɪt] vt hacerse pasar por.

impertinent [ɪm'pəːtɪnənt] a impertinente, insolente.

impervious [ɪm'pəːvɪəs] a impermeable; (fig): ~ **to** insensible a.

impetuous [ɪm'petjuəs] a impetuoso.

impetus ['ɪmpətəs] n ímpetu m; (fig) impulso.

impinge [ɪm'pɪndʒ]: **to ~ on** vt fus (affect) afectar a.

implacable [ɪm'plækəbl] a implacable.

implement ['ɪmplɪmənt] n instrumento, herramienta // vt ['ɪmplɪment] hacer efectivo; (carry out) realizar.

implicate ['ɪmplɪkeɪt] vt (compromise) comprometer; (involve) enredar; **implication** [-'keɪʃən] n consecuencia.

implicit [ɪm'plɪsɪt] a (gen) implícito; (complete) absoluto.

implore [ɪm'plɔː*] vt (person) suplicar.

imply [ɪm'plaɪ] vt (involve) suponer; (hint) dar a entender.

impolite [ɪmpə'laɪt] a mal educado.

import [ɪm'pɔːt] vt importar // n ['ɪmpɔːt] (COMM) importación f; (meaning) significado, sentido.

importance [ɪm'pɔːtəns] n importancia.

important [ɪm'pɔːtənt] a importante; **it's not ~** no importa, no tiene importancia.

importer [ɪm'pɔːtə*] n importador(a) m/f.

impose [ɪm'pəuz] vt imponer // vi: to

~ **on sb** abusar de uno; **imposing**
a imponente, impresionante.

imposition [ɪmpə'zɪʃn] n (of tax
etc) imposición f; **to be an** ~ (on
person) molestar.

impossible [ɪm'pɔsɪbl] a imposible;
(person) insoportable.

impostor [ɪm'pɔstə*] n impostor(a)
m/f.

impotent ['ɪmpətənt] a impotente.

impound [ɪm'paund] vt embargar.

impoverished [ɪm'pɔvərɪʃt] a necesitado; (land) agotado.

impracticable [ɪm'præktɪkəbl] a no
factible, irrealizable.

impractical [ɪm'præktɪkl] a (person)
poco práctico.

imprecise [ɪmprɪ'saɪs] a impreciso.

impregnable [ɪm'pregnəbl] a invul-
nerable; (castle) inexpugnable.

impregnate ['ɪmpregneɪt] vt impregnar; (BIOL) fecundar.

impress [ɪm'pres] vt impresionar;
(mark) estampar // vi hacer buena
impresión; **to** ~ **sth on sb** hacer
entender algo a uno.

impression [ɪm'preʃən] n impresión
f; (footprint etc) huella; (print run)
edición f; **to be under the** ~ that
tener la impresión de que; ~**able** a
impresionable; ~**ist** n impresionista
m/f.

impressive [ɪm'presɪv] a impresionante.

imprint ['ɪmprɪnt] n (PUBLISHING)
pie m de imprenta; (fig) sello.

imprison [ɪm'prɪzn] vt encarcelar;
~**ment** n encarcelamiento; (term of
~) cárcel f.

improbable [ɪm'prɔbəbl] a improbable, inverosímil.

impromptu [ɪm'prɔmptju:] a improvisado // ad de improviso.

improper [ɪm'prɔpə*] a (incorrect)
impropio; (unseemly) indecoroso;
(indecent) indecente.

improve [ɪm'pru:v] vt mejorar; (foreign language) perfeccionar // vi mejorarse; (pupils) hacer progresos;
~**ment** n mejoramiento; perfección

f; progreso.

improvise ['ɪmprəvaɪz] vt, vi improvisar.

imprudent [ɪm'pru:dnt] a imprudente.

impudent [ɪm'pjudnt] a descarado,
insolente.

impulse ['ɪmpʌls] n impulso; **to act
on** ~ obrar sin reflexión; **impulsive**
[-'pʌlsɪv] a irreflexivo.

impunity [ɪm'pju:nɪtɪ] n: **with** ~
punemente.

impure [ɪm'pjuə*] a (adulterated)
adulterado; (morally) impuro; **impurity** n (gen) impureza.

KEYWORD

in [ɪn] ♦ prep 1 (indicating place, position, with place names) en; ~ **the
house/garden** en (la) casa/el jardín;
~ **here/there** aquí/ahí or ahí dentro;
~ **London/England** en Londres/
Inglaterra

2 (indicating time) en; ~ **spring** en
(la) primavera; ~ **the afternoon**
por la tarde; **at 4 o'clock** ~ **the
afternoon** a las 4 de la tarde; **I did
it** ~ **3 hours/days** lo hice en 3
horas/días; **I'll see you** ~ **2 weeks**
or ~ **2 weeks' time** te veré dentro
de 2 semanas

3 (indicating manner etc) en; ~ **a
loud/soft voice** en voz alta/baja; ~
pencil/ink a lápiz/bolígrafo; **the boy
** ~ **the blue shirt** el chico de la camisa azul

4 (indicating circumstances): ~ **the
sun/shade/rain** al sol/a la sombra/
bajo la lluvia; **a change** ~ **policy**
un cambio de política

5 (indicating mood, state): ~ **tears**
en lágrimas, llorando; ~ **anger/
despair** enfadado/desesperado/-a;
to live ~ **luxury** vivir lujosamente

6 (with ratios, numbers): **1** ~ **10
households, 1 household** ~ **10** una
de cada 10 familias; **20 pence** ~ **the
pound** 20 peniques por libra; **they
lined up** ~ **twos** se alinearon de dos
en dos

7 (*referring to people, works*) en; entre; **the disease is common ~ children** la enfermedad es común entre los niños; **~ (the works of) Dickens** en (las obras de) Dickens
8 (*indicating profession etc*) en; **to be ~ teaching** estar en la enseñanza
9 (*after superlative*) de; **the best pupil ~ the class** el/la mejor alumno/a de la clase
10 (*with present participle*): **~ saying this al decir esto**

◆ *ad*: **to be ~** (*person: at home*) estar en casa; (*work*) estar; (*train, ship, plane*) haber llegado; (*in fashion*) estar de moda; **she'll be ~ later today** llegará más tarde hoy; **to ask sb ~** hacer pasar a uno; **to run/limp ~** etc entrar corriendo/ cojeando *etc*

◆ *n*: **the ~s and outs** (*of proposal, situation etc*) los detalles

in., ins *abbr* = **inch**(es).
inability [ɪnə'bɪlɪtɪ] *n* incapacidad *f*.
inaccessible [ɪnæk'sɛsɪbl] *a* inaccesible.
inaccurate [ɪn'ækjurət] *a* inexacto, incorrecto.
inactivity [ɪnæk'tɪvɪtɪ] *n* inactividad *f*.
inadequate [ɪn'ædɪkwət] *a* (*insufficient*) insuficiente; (*unsuitable*) inadecuado; (*person*) incapaz.
inadvertently [ɪnəd'vɜːtɪntlɪ] *ad* por descuido.
inadvisable [ɪnəd'vaɪzəbl] *a* poco aconsejable.
inane [ɪ'neɪn] *a* necio, fatuo.
inanimate [ɪn'ænɪmət] *a* inanimado.
inappropriate [ɪnə'prəuprɪət] *a* inadecuado.
inarticulate [ɪnɑː'tɪkjulət] *a* (*person*) incapaz de expresarse; (*speech*) mal pronunciado.
inasmuch as [ɪnəz'mʌtʃæz] *conj* puesto que, ya que.
inaudible [ɪn'ɔːdɪbl] *a* inaudible.
inaugural [ɪn'ɔːgjurəl] *a* (*speech*) de apertura.

inaugurate [ɪn'ɔːgjureɪt] *vt* inaugurar; **inauguration** [-'reɪʃən] *n* ceremonia de apertura.
in-between [ɪnbɪ'twiːn] *a* intermedio.
inborn [ɪn'bɔːn] *a* (*feeling*) innato.
inbred [ɪn'brɛd] *a* innato; (*family*) engendrado por endogamia.
Inc. *abbr* (*US*) = **incorporated**.
incapable [ɪn'keɪpəbl] *a* incapaz.
incapacitate [ɪnkə'pæsɪtət] *vt*: **to ~ sb** incapacitar a uno.
incapacity [ɪnkə'pæsɪtɪ] *n* (*inability*) incapacidad *f*.
incarcerate [ɪn'kɑːsəreɪt] *vt* encarcelar.
incarnation [ɪnkɑː'neɪʃən] *n* encarnación *f*.
incendiary [ɪn'sɛndɪərɪ] *a* incendiario.
incense ['ɪnsɛns] *n* incienso // *vt* [ɪn'sɛns] (*anger*) indignar, encolerizar.
incentive [ɪn'sɛntɪv] *n* incentivo, estímulo.
incessant [ɪn'sɛsnt] *a* incesante, continuo; **~ly** *ad* constantemente.
incest ['ɪnsɛst] *n* incesto.
inch [ɪntʃ] *n* pulgada *f*; **to be within an ~ of** estar a dos dedos de; **he didn't give an ~** no dio concesión alguna; **to ~ forward** *vi* avanzar palmo a palmo.
incidence ['ɪnsɪdns] *n* (*of crime, disease*) incidencia.
incident ['ɪnsɪdnt] *n* incidente *m*; (*in book*) episodio.
incidental [ɪnsɪ'dɛntl] *a* circunstancial, accesorio; (*unplanned*) fortuito; **~ to** relacionado con; **~ music** música ambientación *f* musical; **~ly** [-'dɛntlɪ] *ad* (*by the way*) a propósito.
incinerator [ɪn'sɪnəreɪtə*] *n* incinerador *m*.
incipient [ɪn'sɪpɪənt] *a* incipiente.
incision [ɪn'sɪʒən] *n* incisión *f*.
incisive [ɪn'saɪsɪv] *a* (*mind*) penetrante; (*remark etc*) incisivo.
incite [ɪn'saɪt] *vt* provocar.
inclination [ɪnklɪ'neɪʃən] *n* (*ten-*

dency) tendencia, inclinación *f*.

incline ['ɪnklaɪn] *n* pendiente *m*, cuesta // *vb* [ɪn'klaɪn] *vt (slope)* inclinar; *(head)* poner de lado // *vi* inclinarse; **to be ~d to** *(tend)* ser propenso a; *(be willing)* estar dispuesto a.

include [ɪn'kluːd] *vt* incluir, comprender; *(in letter)* adjuntar; **including** *prep* incluso, inclusive.

inclusion [ɪn'kluːʒən] *n* inclusión *f*.

inclusive [ɪn'kluːsɪv] *a* inclusivo // *ad* inclusive; **~ of tax** incluidos los impuestos.

incognito [ɪnkɔg'niːtəu] *ad* de incógnito.

incoherent [ɪnkəu'hɪərənt] *a* incoherente.

income ['ɪŋkʌm] *n (personal)* ingresos *mpl*; *(from property etc)* renta; *(profit)* rédito; **~ tax** *n* impuesto sobre la renta; **~ tax return** *n* declaración *f* de renta.

incoming ['ɪnkʌmɪŋ] *a*: **~ flight** vuelo entrante.

incomparable [ɪn'kɔmpərəbl] *a* incomparable, sin par.

incompatible [ɪnkəm'pætɪbl] *a* incompatible.

incompetence [ɪn'kɔmpɪtəns] *n* incompetencia.

incompetent [ɪn'kɔmpɪtənt] *a* incompetente.

incomplete [ɪnkəm'pliːt] *a* incompleto; *(unfinished)* sin terminar.

incomprehensible [ɪnkɔmprɪ'hensɪbl] *a* incomprensible.

inconceivable [ɪnkən'siːvəbl] *a* inconcebible.

incongruous [ɪn'kɔŋgruəs] *a* discordante.

inconsiderate [ɪnkən'sɪdərət] *a* desconsiderado; **how ~ of him!** ¡qué falta de consideración (de su parte)!

inconsistency [ɪnkən'sɪstənsɪ] *n* inconsecuencia.

inconsistent [ɪnkən'sɪstnt] *a* inconsecuente; **~ with** (que) no concuerda con.

inconspicuous [ɪnkən'spɪkjuəs] *a*

(discreet) discreto; *(person)* que llama poca la atención.

inconvenience [ɪnkən'viːnjəns] *n (gen)* inconvenientes *mpl*; *(trouble)* molestia, incomodidad *f* // *vt* incomodar.

inconvenient [ɪnkən'viːnjənt] *a* incómodo, poco práctico; *(time, place)* inoportuno.

incorporate [ɪn'kɔːpəreɪt] *vt* incorporar; *(contain)* comprender; *(add)* agregar; **~d**: **~d company** *(US: abbr Inc.)* ≈ Sociedad *f* Anónima (S.A.).

incorrect [ɪnkə'rekt] *a* incorrecto.

incorrigible [ɪn'kɔrɪdʒəbl] *a* incorregible.

increase ['ɪnkriːs] *n* aumento // *vi* [ɪn'kriːs] aumentarse; *(grow)* crecer; *(price)* subir // *vt* aumentar; **increasing** [ɪn'kriːsɪŋ] *a* creciente, que va en aumento; **increasingly** [ɪn'kriːsɪŋlɪ] *ad* de más en más, cada vez más.

incredible [ɪn'kredɪbl] *a* increíble.

incredulous [ɪn'kredjuləs] *a* incrédulo.

increment ['ɪnkrɪmənt] *n* aumento, incremento.

incriminate [ɪn'krɪmɪneɪt] *vt* incriminar.

incubator ['ɪnkjubeɪtə*] *n* incubadora.

incumbent [ɪn'kʌmbənt] *n* titular *m/f* // *a*: **it is ~ on him to...** le incumbe...

incur [ɪn'kə:*] *vt (expenditure)* incurrir; *(loss)* sufrir.

incurable [ɪn'kjuərəbl] *a* incurable.

indebted [ɪn'detɪd] *a*: **to be ~ to sb** estar agradecido a uno.

indecent [ɪn'diːsnt] *a* indecente; **~ assault** *n (Brit)* atentado contra el pudor; **~ exposure** *n* exhibicionismo.

indecisive [ɪndɪ'saɪsɪv] *a* indeciso; *(discussion)* no resuelto, inconcluyente.

indeed [ɪn'diːd] *ad* efectivamente, en realidad; **yes ~!** ¡claro que sí!

indefinite [ɪn'defɪnɪt] a indefinido; (uncertain) incierto; ~**ly** ad (wait) indefinidamente.

indelible [ɪn'delɪbl] a imborrable.

indemnify [ɪn'demnɪfaɪ] vt indemnizar, resarcir.

indemnity [ɪn'demnɪtɪ] n (insurance) indemnidad f; (compensation) indemnización f.

independence [ɪndɪ'pendns] n independencia.

independent [ɪndɪ'pendənt] a independiente; **to become** ~ independizarse.

indestructible [ɪndɪs'trʌktəbl] a indestructible.

index ['ɪndeks] n (pl: ~es: in book) índice m; (: in library etc) catálogo; (pl: indices ['ɪndɪsiːz]: ratio, sign) exponente m; ~ **card** n ficha; ~ **finger** n índice m; ~-**linked**, (US) ~**ed** a vinculado al índice del coste de la vida.

India ['ɪndɪə] n la India; ~**n** a, n indio/a m/f; **Red** ~n piel roja m/f; **the** ~**n Ocean** n el Océano Índico.

indicate ['ɪndɪkeɪt] vt indicar; **indication** [-'keɪʃən] n indicio, señal f; **indicative** [ɪn'dɪkətɪv] a: **to be** ~ **of** indicar // a (LING) indicativo; **indicator** n (gen) indicador m.

indices ['ɪndɪsiːz] pl of **index**.

indict [ɪn'daɪt] vt acusar; ~**ment** n acusación f.

indifference [ɪn'dɪfrəns] n indiferencia.

indifferent [ɪn'dɪfrənt] a indiferente; (poor) regular.

indigenous [ɪn'dɪdʒɪnəs] a indígena.

indigestion [ɪndɪ'dʒestʃən] n indigestión f.

indignant [ɪn'dɪgnənt] a: **to be** ~ **about sth** indignarse por algo.

indignity [ɪn'dɪgnɪtɪ] n indignidad f.

indigo ['ɪndɪgəu] a de color añil // n añil m.

indirect [ɪndɪ'rekt] a indirecto; ~**ly** ad indirectamente.

indiscreet [ɪndɪ'skriːt] a indiscreto, imprudente.

indiscriminate [ɪndɪ'skrɪmɪnət] a indiscriminado.

indispensable [ɪndɪ'spensəbl] a indispensable, imprescindible.

indisposed [ɪndɪ'spəuzd] a (unwell) indispuesto.

indisputable [ɪndɪ'spjuːtəbl] a incontestable.

individual [ɪndɪ'vɪdjuəl] n individuo // a (single): (personal) personal; (for/of one only) particular; ~**ist** n individualista m/f; ~**ity** [-'ælɪtɪ] n individualidad f; ~**ly** ad individualmente; particularmente.

indoctrinate [ɪn'dɔktrɪneɪt] vt adoctrinar; **indoctrination** [-'neɪʃən] n adoctrinamiento.

indolent ['ɪndələnt] a indolente, perezoso.

Indonesia [ɪndəu'niːzɪə] n Indonesia.

indoor ['ɪndɔː*] a (swimming pool) cubierto; (plant) de interior; (sport) bajo cubierto; ~**s** [ɪn'dɔːz] ad dentro; (at home) en casa.

induce [ɪn'djuːs] vt inducir, persuadir; (bring about) producir; ~**ment** n (incentive) incentivo, aliciente m.

induction [ɪn'dʌkʃən] n (MED: of birth) inducción f; ~ **course** n (Brit) curso de inducción.

indulge [ɪn'dʌldʒ] vt (whim) satisfacer; (person) complacer; (child) mimar // vi: **to** ~ **in** darse el gusto de; ~**nce** n vicio; ~**nt** a indulgente.

industrial [ɪn'dʌstrɪəl] a industrial; ~ **action** n huelga; ~ **estate** n (Brit) polígono or zona (LAm) industrial; ~**ist** n industrial m/f; ~**ize** vt industrializar; ~ **park** n (US) = ~ **estate**.

industrious [ɪn'dʌstrɪəs] a (gen) trabajador(a); (student) aplicado.

industry ['ɪndəstrɪ] n industria; (diligence) aplicación f.

inebriated [ɪ'niːbrɪeɪtɪd] a borracho.

inedible [ɪn'edɪbl] a incomible; (plant etc) no comestible.

ineffective [ɪnɪ'fektɪv], **ineffectual** [ɪnɪ'fektʃuəl] a ineficaz, inútil.

inefficiency [ɪnɪ'fɪʃənsɪ] n ineficacia.

inefficient [ɪnɪˈfɪʃənt] a ineficaz, ineficiente.

inept [ɪˈnɛpt] a incompetente.

inequality [ɪnɪˈkwɔlɪtɪ] n desigualdad f.

inert [ɪˈnɜːt] a inerte, inactivo; *(immobile)* inmóvil; ~**ia** [ɪˈnɜːʃə] n inercia; *(laziness)* pereza.

inescapable [ɪnɪˈskeɪpəbl] a ineludible.

inevitable [ɪnˈɛvɪtəbl] a inevitable; *(necessary)* forzoso; **inevitably** ad inevitablemente.

inexcusable [ɪnɪksˈkjuːzəbl] a imperdonable.

inexhaustible [ɪnɪgˈzɔːstɪbl] a inagotable.

inexpensive [ɪnɪkˈspɛnsɪv] a económico.

inexperience [ɪnɪkˈspɪərɪəns] n falta de experiencia; ~**d** a inexperto.

inextricably [ɪnɪksˈtrɪkəblɪ] ad indisolublemente.

infallible [ɪnˈfælɪbl] a infalible.

infamous [ˈɪnfəməs] a infame.

infancy [ˈɪnfənsɪ] n infancia.

infant [ˈɪnfənt] n niño/a; ~**ile** a infantil; *(pej)* aniñado; ~ **school** n *(Brit)* escuela de párvulos.

infantry [ˈɪnfəntrɪ] n infantería.

infatuated [ɪnˈfætjueɪtɪd] a: ~ **with** *(in love)* loco por.

infatuation [ɪnfætjuˈeɪʃən] n enamoramiento.

infect [ɪnˈfɛkt] vt *(wound)* infectar; *(person)* contagiar; *(fig: pej)* corromper; ~**ed with** *(illness)* contagiado de; ~**ion** [ɪnˈfɛkʃən] n infección f; *(fig)* contagio; ~**ious** [ɪnˈfɛkʃəs] a contagioso; *(also fig)* infeccioso.

infer [ɪnˈfɜː*] vt deducir, inferir; ~**ence** [ˈɪnfərəns] n deducción f, inferencia.

inferior [ɪnˈfɪərɪə*] a, n inferior m/f; ~**ity** [-ˈrɪɔtɪ] n inferioridad f; ~**ity complex** n complejo de inferioridad.

inferno [ɪnˈfɜːnəu] n *(fire)* hoguera.

infertile [ɪnˈfɜːtaɪl] a estéril; *(person)* infecundo; **infertility** [-ˈtɪlɪtɪ] n esterilidad f; infecundidad f.

infested [ɪnˈfɛstɪd] a: ~ **with** plagado de.

in-fighting [ˈɪnfaɪtɪŋ] n *(fig)* lucha(s) f*(pl)* interna(s).

infiltrate [ˈɪnfɪltreɪt] vt *(troops etc)* infiltrar en // vi infiltrarse.

infinite [ˈɪnfɪnɪt] a infinito.

infinitive [ɪnˈfɪnɪtɪv] n infinitivo.

infinity [ɪnˈfɪnɪtɪ] n *(also MATH)* infinito; *(an ~)* infinidad f.

infirm [ɪnˈfɜːm] a enfermo, débil; ~**ary** n hospital m; ~**ity** n debilidad f; *(illness)* enfermedad f, achaque m.

inflamed [ɪnˈfleɪmd] a: to become ~ inflamarse.

inflammable [ɪnˈflæməbl] a *(Brit)* inflamable; *(situation etc)* explosivo.

inflammation [ɪnfləˈmeɪʃən] n inflamación f.

inflatable [ɪnˈfleɪtəbl] a *(ball, boat)* inflable.

inflate [ɪnˈfleɪt] vt *(tyre, balloon)* inflar; *(fig)* hinchar; **inflation** [ɪnˈfleɪʃən] n *(ECON)* inflación f.

inflict [ɪnˈflɪkt] vt: to ~ on infligir en; *(tax etc)* imponer a.

influence [ˈɪnfluəns] n influencia // vt influir en, influenciar; **under the** ~ **of alcohol** en estado de embriaguez; **influential** [-ˈɛnʃl] a influyente.

influenza [ɪnfluˈɛnzə] n gripe f.

influx [ˈɪnflʌks] n afluencia.

inform [ɪnˈfɔːm] vt: to ~ **sb of sth** informar a uno sobre or de algo; *(warn)* avisar a uno de algo; *(communicate)* comunicar algo a uno // vi: to ~ **on sb** delatar a uno.

informal [ɪnˈfɔːml] a *(manner, tone)* desenfadado; *(dress, interview, occasion)* informal; ~**ity** [-ˈmælɪtɪ] n desenfado; falta de ceremonia.

informant [ɪnˈfɔːmənt] n informante m/f.

information [ɪnfəˈmeɪʃən] n información f; *(news)* noticias fpl; *(knowledge)* conocimientos mpl; *(LAW)* delación f; **a piece of** ~ un dato; ~ **office** n información f.

informative [ɪnˈfɔːmətɪv] a informativo.

informer [in'fɔːməˀ] n delator(a) m/f; (also: police ~) soplón/ona m/f.

infra-red [infrə'red] a infrarrojo.

infrastructure ['infrəstrʌktʃəˀ] n (of system etc, ECON) infraestructura.

infringe [in'frindʒ] vt infringir, violar // vi: **to ~ on** abusar de; **~ment** n infracción f.; (of rights) usurpación f; (SPORT) falta.

infuriating [in'fjuərieitiŋ] a: **I find it ~** me saca de quicio.

infusion [in'fjuːʒən] n (tea etc) infusión f.

ingenious [in'dʒiːnjəs] a ingenioso; **ingenuity** [-dʒi'njuːiti] n ingeniosidad f.

ingenuous [in'dʒɛnjuəs] a ingenuo.

ingot ['iŋgət] n lingote m, barra.

ingrained [in'greind] a arraigado.

ingratiate [in'greiʃieit] vt: **to ~ o.s. with** congraciarse con.

ingredient [in'griːdiənt] n ingrediente m.

inhabit [in'hæbit] vt vivir en; (occupy) ocupar; **~ant** n habitante m/f.

inhale [in'heil] vt inhalar // vi (in smoking) tragar.

inherent [in'hiərənt] a: **~ in** or **to** inherente a.

inherit [in'herit] vt heredar; **~ance** n herencia; (fig) patrimonio.

inhibit [in'hibit] vt inhibir, impedir; **to ~ sb from doing sth** impedir a uno hacer algo; **~ed** a cohibido; **~ion** [-'biʃən] n cohibición f.

inhospitable [inhɔs'pitəbl] a (person) inhospitalario; (place) inhóspito.

inhuman [in'hjuːmən] a inhumano.

iniquity [i'nikwiti] n iniquidad f; (injustice) injusticia.

initial [i'niʃl] a inicial; (first) primero // n inicial f // vt firmar con las iniciales; **~s** npl iniciales fpl; (abbreviation) siglas fpl; **~ly** ad al principio.

initiate [i'niʃieit] vt (start) iniciar; **to ~ proceedings against sb** (LAW) entablar proceso contra uno; **initiation** [-'eiʃən] n (into secret etc)

iniciación f; (beginning) comienzo.

initiative [i'niʃətiv] n iniciativa.

inject [in'dʒɛkt] vt inyectar; **~ion** [in'dʒɛkʃən] n inyección f.

injunction [in'dʒʌŋkʃən] n interdicto.

injure ['indʒəˀ] vt herir; (hurt) lastimar; (fig: reputation etc) perjudicar; **~d** a (person, arm) herido; **injury** n herida, lesión f; (wrong) perjuicio, daño; **injury time** n (SPORT) descuento.

injustice [in'dʒʌstis] n injusticia.

ink [iŋk] n tinta.

inkling ['iŋkliŋ] n sospecha; (idea) idea.

inlaid ['inleid] a (wood) taraceado; (tiles) entarimado.

inland ['inlənd] a interior; (town) del interior // ad [in'lænd] tierra adentro; **I~ Revenue** n (Brit) departamento de impuestos; ≈ Hacienda (Sp).

in-laws ['inlɔːz] npl suegros mpl.

inlet ['inlet] n (GEO) ensenada, cala; (TECH) admisión f, entrada.

inmate ['inmeit] n (in prison) preso/a; presidiario/a; (in asylum) internado/a.

inn [in] n posada, mesón m.

innate [i'neit] a innato.

inner ['inəˀ] a interior, interno; **~ city** n barrios deprimidos del centro de una ciudad; **~ tube** n (of tyre) cámara or llanta (LAm).

innings ['iniŋz] n (CRICKET) entrada, turno.

innocence ['inəsns] n inocencia.

innocent ['inəsnt] a inocente.

innocuous [i'nɔkjuəs] a inocuo.

innovation [inəu'veiʃən] n novedad f.

innuendo [inju'ɛndəu], pl **~es** n indirecta.

inoculation [inɔkju'leiʃən] n inoculación f.

inopportune [in'ɔpətjuːn] a inoportuno.

inordinately [i'nɔːdinətli] ad desmesuradamente.

in-patient [ˈɪnpeɪʃənt] n paciente m/f interno/a.

input [ˈɪnput] n (ELEC) entrada; (COMPUT) entrada de datos.

inquest [ˈɪnkwɛst] n (coroner's) encuesta judicial.

inquire [ɪnˈkwaɪə*] vi preguntar // vt: to ~ whether preguntar si; to ~ about (person) preguntar por; (fact) informarse de; to ~ into vt fus investigar, indagar; **inquiry** n pregunta; (LAW) investigación f, pesquisa; (commission) comisión f investigadora; **inquiry office** n (Brit) oficina de informaciones.

inquisitive [ɪnˈkwɪzɪtɪv] a (mind) inquisitivo; (person) fisgón/ona.

inroad [ˈɪnrəud] n incursión f; (fig) invasión f.

insane [ɪnˈseɪn] a loco; (MED) demente.

insanity [ɪnˈsænɪtɪ] n demencia, locura.

insatiable [ɪnˈseɪʃəbl] a insaciable.

inscribe [ɪnˈskraɪb] vt inscribir; (book etc) to ~ (to sb) dedicar (a uno).

inscription [ɪnˈskrɪpʃən] n (gen) inscripción f; (in book) dedicatoria.

inscrutable [ɪnˈskruːtəbl] a inescrutable, insondable.

insect [ˈɪnsɛkt] n insecto; ~icide [ɪnˈsɛktɪsaɪd] n insecticida m.

insecure [ɪnsɪˈkjuə*] a inseguro.

insemination [ɪnsɛmɪˈneɪʃən] n : artificial ~ inseminación f artificial.

insensible [ɪnˈsɛnsɪbl] a inconsciente; (unconscious) sin conocimiento.

insensitive [ɪnˈsɛnsɪtɪv] a insensible.

inseparable [ɪnˈsɛprəbl] a inseparable.

insert [ɪnˈsɜːt] vt (into sth) introducir; // n [ˈɪnsɜːt] encarte m; ~ion [ɪnˈsɜːʃən] n inserción f.

in-service [ɪnˈsɜːvɪs] a (training, course) a cargo de la empresa.

inshore [ɪnˈʃɔː*] a : ~ fishing pesca f costera // ad (fish) a lo largo de la costa; (move) hacia la orilla.

inside [ɪnˈsaɪd] n interior m; (lining) forro // a interior, interno; (information) confidencial // ad (within) (por) dentro; (with movement) hacia dentro; (fam: in prison) en la cárcel // prep dentro de; (of time): ~ 10 minutes en menos de 10 minutos; ~s npl (col) tripas fpl; ~ forward n (SPORT) interior m; ~ lane n (AUT: in Britain) carril m izquierdo; ~ out ad (turn) al revés; (know) a fondo.

insidious [ɪnˈsɪdɪəs] a insidioso.

insight [ˈɪnsaɪt] n perspicacia.

insignia [ɪnˈsɪgnɪə] npl insignias fpl.

insignificant [ɪnsɪgˈnɪfɪknt] a insignificante.

insincere [ɪnsɪnˈsɪə*] a poco sincero.

insinuate [ɪnˈsɪnjueɪt] vt insinuar.

insipid [ɪnˈsɪpɪd] a soso, insulso.

insist [ɪnˈsɪst] vi insistir; to ~ on doing empeñarse en hacer; to ~ that insistir en que; (claim) exigir que; ~ence n insistencia f; (stubbornness) empeño; ~ent a insistente.

insole [ˈɪnsəul] n plantilla.

insolent [ˈɪnsələnt] a insolente, descarado.

insoluble [ɪnˈsɔljubl] a insoluble.

insomnia [ɪnˈsɔmnɪə] n insomnio.

inspect [ɪnˈspɛkt] vt inspeccionar, examinar; (troops) pasar revista a; ~ion [ɪnˈspɛkʃən] n inspección f, examen m; ~or n inspector/a m/f; (Brit: on buses, trains) revisor/a m/f.

inspiration [ɪnspəˈreɪʃən] n inspiración f; **inspire** [ɪnˈspaɪə*] vt inspirar.

instability [ɪnstəˈbɪlɪtɪ] n inestabilidad f.

install [ɪnˈstɔːl] vt instalar; ~ation [ɪnstəˈleɪʃən] n instalación f.

instalment, (US) **installment** [ɪnˈstɔːlmənt] n plazo; (of story) entrega; (of TV serial etc) capítulo; en ~s (pay, receive) a plazos; ~ **plan** n (US) compra a plazos.

instance [ˈɪnstəns] n ejemplo, caso; for ~ por ejemplo; in the first ~ en primer lugar.

instant ['ɪnstənt] n instante m, momento // a inmediato // (coffee) instantáneo.

instantly [ɪnstəntlɪ] ad en seguida.

instead [ɪn'stɛd] ad en cambio; ~ of en lugar de, en vez de.

instep ['ɪnstɛp] n empeine m.

instil [ɪn'stɪl] vt: to ~ into inculcar a.

instinct ['ɪnstɪŋkt] n instinto; ~ive [-'stɪŋktɪv] a instintivo.

institute ['ɪnstɪtjuːt] n instituto; (professional body) colegio // vt (begin) iniciar, empezar; (proceedings) entablar.

institution [ɪnstɪ'tjuːʃən] n institución f; (MED: home) asilo; (: asylum) manicomio.

instruct [ɪn'strʌkt] vt: to ~ sb in sth instruir a uno en o sobre algo; to ~ sb to do sth dar instrucciones a uno de hacer algo; ~ion [ɪn'strʌkʃən] n (teaching) instrucción f; ~ions npl órdenes fpl; ~ions (for use) modo sg de empleo; ~ive a instructivo; ~or n instructor(a) m/f.

instrument ['ɪnstrəmənt] n instrumento; ~ panel n tablero (de instrumentos); ~al [-'mɛntl] a (MUS) instrumental; to be ~al in ser (el) artífice de.

insubordinate [ɪnsə'bɔːdɪnət] a insubordinado.

insufferable [ɪn'sʌfrəbl] a insoportable.

insufficient [ɪnsə'fɪʃənt] a insuficiente.

insular ['ɪnsjuləˀ] a insular; (person) estrecho de miras.

insulate ['ɪnsjuleɪt] vt aislar; **insulating tape** n cinta aislante; **insulation** [-'leɪʃən] n aislamiento.

insulin ['ɪnsjulɪn] n insulina.

insult ['ɪnsʌlt] n insulto; (offence) ofensa // [ɪn'sʌlt] insultar; ofender; ~ing a insultante; ofensivo.

insuperable [ɪn'sjuːprəbl] a insuperable.

insurance [ɪn'ʃuərəns] n seguro; fire/life ~ seguro contra incendios/

sobre la vida; ~ agent n agente m/f de seguros; ~ policy n póliza (de seguros).

insure [ɪn'ʃuəˀ] vt asegurar.

intact [ɪn'tækt] a íntegro; (untouched) intacto.

intake ['ɪnteɪk] n (TECH) entrada, toma; (: pipe) tubo de admisión; (of food) ingestión f; (Brit SCOL): an ~ of 200 a year 200 matriculados al año.

integral ['ɪntɪgrəl] a (whole) íntegro; (part) integrante.

integrate ['ɪntɪgreɪt] vt integrar // vi integrarse.

integrity [ɪn'tɛgrɪtɪ] n honradez f, rectitud f.

intellect ['ɪntɪlɛkt] n intelecto; ~ual [-'lɛktjuəl] a, n intelectual m/f.

intelligence [ɪn'tɛlɪdʒəns] n inteligencia; I~ Service n Servicio de Inteligencia.

intelligent [ɪn'tɛlɪdʒənt] a inteligente.

intelligentsia [ɪntɛlɪ'dʒɛntsɪə] n intelectualidad f.

intelligible [ɪn'tɛlɪdʒɪbl] a inteligible, comprensible.

intend [ɪn'tɛnd] vt (gift etc): to ~ sth for destinar algo a; to ~ to do sth tener intención de o pensar hacer algo; ~ed a (effect) deseado.

intense [ɪn'tɛns] a (gen) intenso; ~ly ad intensamente; (very) sumamente.

intensify [ɪn'tɛnsɪfaɪ] vt intensificar; (increase) aumentar.

intensity [ɪn'tɛnsɪtɪ] n (gen) intensidad f.

intensive [ɪn'tɛnsɪv] a intensivo; ~ care unit n unidad de vigilancia intensiva.

intent [ɪn'tɛnt] n propósito // a (absorbed) absorto; (attentive) atento; to all ~s and purposes prácticamente; to be ~ on doing sth estar resuelto a hacer algo.

intention [ɪn'tɛnʃən] n intención f, propósito; ~al a deliberado; ~ally ad a propósito.

intently [ɪnˈtɛntlɪ] *ad* atentamente, fijamente.

interact [ɪntərˈækt] *vi* influirse mutuamente; **~ion** [-ˈækʃən] *n* interacción *f*, acción *f* recíproca.

intercede [ɪntəˈsiːd] *vi*: to ~ (with) interceder (con).

intercept [ɪntəˈsɛpt] *vt* interceptar; (*stop*) detener.

interchange [ˈɪntətʃeɪndʒ] *n* intercambio; (*on motorway*) intersección *f* // *vt* [ɪntəˈtʃeɪndʒ] intercambiar; canjear; **~able** *a* intercambiable.

intercom [ˈɪntəkɔm] *n* interfono.

intercourse [ˈɪntəkɔːs] *n* (*sexual*) relaciones *fpl* sexuales; (*social*) trato.

interest [ˈɪntrɪst] *n* (*also COMM*) interés *m* // *vt* interesar; to be ~ed in interesarse por; **~ing** *a* interesante; **~ rate** *n* tipo or tasa de interés.

interface [ˈɪntəfeɪs] *n* (*COMPUT*) junción *f*.

interfere [ɪntəˈfɪə*] *vi*: to ~ in (*quarrel, other people's business*) entrometerse en; to ~ with (*hinder*) estorbar; (*damage*) estropear; (*radio*) interferir con.

interference [ɪntəˈfɪərəns] *n* (*gen*) intromisión *f*; (*RADIO, TV*) interferencia.

interim [ˈɪntərɪm] *n*: in the ~ en el ínterin // *a* provisional.

interior [ɪnˈtɪərɪə*] *n* interior *m* // *a* interior; **~ designer** *n* interiorista *m/f*.

interlock [ɪntəˈlɔk] *vi* entrelazarse; (*wheels etc*) endentarse.

interloper [ˈɪntələʊpə*] *n* intruso/a.

interlude [ˈɪntəluːd] *n* intervalo; (*rest*) descanso; (*THEATRE*) intermedio.

intermediary [ɪntəˈmiːdɪərɪ] *n* intermediario/a.

intermediate [ɪntəˈmiːdɪət] *a* intermedio.

interminable [ɪnˈtəːmɪnəbl] *a* inacabable.

intermission [ɪntəˈmɪʃən] *n* (*THEATRE*) descanso.

intermittent [ɪntəˈmɪtnt] *a* intermi-

tente.

intern [ɪnˈtəːn] *vt* internar; (*enclose*) encerrar // *n* [ˈɪntəːn] (US) interno/a.

internal [ɪnˈtəːnl] *a* interno, interior; **~ly** *ad* interiormente; 'not to be taken ~ly' 'uso externo'; I~ Revenue Service (IRS) *n* (US) departamento de impuestos, ≈ Hacienda (*Sp*).

international [ɪntəˈnæʃnl] *a* internacional; ~ (*game*) partido internacional; ~ (*player*) jugador(a) *m/f* internacional.

interplay [ˈɪntəpleɪ] *n* interacción *f*.

interpret [ɪnˈtəːprɪt] *vt* interpretar; (*translate*) traducir; (*understand*) entender // *vi* hacer de intérprete; **~ation** [-ˈteɪʃən] *n* interpretación *f*; traducción *f*; entendimiento *f*; **~er** *n* intérprete *m/f*.

interrelated [ɪntərɪˈleɪtɪd] *a* interrelacionado.

interrogate [ɪnˈtɛrəʊgeɪt] *vt* interrogar; **interrogation** [-ˈgeɪʃən] *n* interrogatorio; **interrogative** [ɪntəˈrɔgətɪv] *a* interrogativo.

interrupt [ɪntəˈrʌpt] *vt, vi* interrumpir; **~ion** [-ˈrʌpʃən] *n* interrupción *f*.

intersect [ɪntəˈsɛkt] *vt* cruzar // *vi* (*roads*) cruzarse; **~ion** [-ˈsɛkʃən] *n* intersección *f*; (*of roads*) cruce *m*.

intersperse [ɪntəˈspəːs] *vt*: to ~ with salpicar de.

intertwine [ɪntəˈtwaɪn] *vt* entrelazar // *vi* entrelazarse.

interval [ˈɪntəvl] *n* intervalo; (*Brit: THEATRE, SPORT*) descanso; **at ~s** a ratos, de vez en cuando.

intervene [ɪntəˈviːn] *vi* intervenir; (*take part*) participar; (*occur*) sobrevenir; **intervention** [-ˈvɛnʃən] *n* intervención *f*.

interview [ˈɪntəvjuː] *n* (*RADIO, TV etc*) entrevista // *vt* entrevistarse con; **~er** *n* entrevistador(a) *m/f*.

intestine [ɪnˈtɛstɪn] *n*: **large/small ~** intestino grueso/delgado.

intimacy [ˈɪntɪməsɪ] *n* intimidad *f*; (*relations*) relaciones *fpl* íntimas.

intimate [ˈɪntɪmət] *a* íntimo;

(*friendship*) estrecho; (*knowledge*) profundo // *vt* ['ɪntɪmeɪt] (*announce*) dar a entender.

intimidate [ɪn'tɪmɪdeɪt] *vt* intimidar, amedrentar.

into ['ɪntu:] *prep* (*gen*) en; (*towards*) a; (*inside*) hacia el interior de; ~ 3 pieces/French en 3 pedazos/al francés.

intolerable [ɪn'tɔlərəbl] *a* intolerable, insoportable.

intolerance [ɪn'tɔlərəns] *n* intolerancia.

intolerant [ɪn'tɔlərənt] *a*: ~ of intolerante con o para.

intonation [ɪntəu'neɪʃən] *n* entonación *f*.

intoxicate [ɪn'tɔksɪkeɪt] *vt* embriagar; ~d *a* embriagado; **intoxication** [-'keɪʃən] *n* embriaguez *f*.

intractable [ɪn'træktəbl] *a* (*person*) intratable; (*problem*) espinoso.

intransitive [ɪn'trænsɪtɪv] *a* intransitivo.

intravenous [ɪntrə'vi:nəs] *a* intravenoso.

in-tray ['ɪntreɪ] *n* bandeja de entrada.

intricate ['ɪntrɪkət] *a* intricado; (*plot, problem*) complejo.

intrigue [ɪn'tri:g] *n* intriga // *vt* fascinar // *vi* andar en intrigas; **intriguing** *a* fascinante.

intrinsic [ɪn'trɪnsɪk] *a* intrínseco.

introduce [ɪntrə'dju:s] *vt* introducir, meter; to ~ sb (to sb) presentar uno (a otro); to ~ sb to (*pastime, technique*) introducir a uno a; **introduction** [-'dʌkʃən] *n* introducción *f*; (*of person*) presentación *f*; **introductory** [-'dʌktərɪ] *a* introductorio.

introvert ['ɪntrəvɜ:t] *a, n* introvertido/a *m/f*.

intrude [ɪn'tru:d] *vi* (*person*) entrometerse; to ~ on estorbar; ~r *n* intruso/a; **intrusion** [-ʒən] *n* invasión *f*.

intuition [ɪntju:'ɪʃən] *n* intuición *f*.

inundate ['ɪnʌndeɪt] *vt*: to ~ with inundar de.

invade [ɪn'veɪd] *vt* invadir; ~r *n* in-

vasor(a) *m/f*.

invalid ['ɪnvəlɪd] *n* minusválido/a // *a* [ɪn'vælɪd] (*not valid*) inválido, nulo.

invaluable [ɪn'væljuəbl] *a* inestimable.

invariably [ɪn'vɛərɪəblɪ] *ad* sin excepción.

invasion [ɪn'veɪʒən] *n* invasión *f*.

invent [ɪn'vent] *vt* inventar; ~**ion** [ɪn'venʃən] *n* invento; (*inventiveness*) inventiva; (*lie*) ficción *f*, mentira; ~**ive** *a* inventivo; ~**iveness** *n* ingenio, inventiva; ~**or** *n* inventor(a) *m/f*.

inventory ['ɪnvəntrɪ] *n* inventario.

invert [ɪn'vɜ:t] *vt* invertir; ~**ed commas** *npl* (*Brit*) comillas *fpl*.

invertebrate [ɪn'vɜ:tɪbrət] *n* invertebrado.

invest [ɪn'vest] *vt, vi* invertir.

investigate [ɪn'vestɪgeɪt] *vt* investigar; (*study*) estudiar, examinar; **investigation** [-'geɪʃən] *n* investigación *f*, pesquisa; examen *m*; **investigator** *n* investigador(a) *m/f*.

investment [ɪn'vestmənt] *n* inversión *f*.

investor [ɪn'vestə*] *n* inversionista *m/f*.

inveterate [ɪn'vetərət] *a* empedernido.

invidious [ɪn'vɪdɪəs] *a* odioso.

invigilate [ɪn'vɪdʒɪleɪt] *vt, vi* (*in exam*) vigilar.

invigorating [ɪn'vɪgəreɪtɪŋ] *a* vigorizante.

invincible [ɪn'vɪnsɪbl] *a* invencible.

invisible [ɪn'vɪzɪbl] *a* invisible; ~ **ink** *n* tinta simpática.

invitation [ɪnvɪ'teɪʃən] *n* invitación *f*.

invite [ɪn'vaɪt] *vt* invitar; (*opinions etc*) solicitar, pedir; (*trouble*) buscarse; **inviting** *a* atractivo; (*look*) provocativo; (*food*) apetitoso.

invoice ['ɪnvɔɪs] *n* factura // *vt* facturar.

invoke [ɪn'vəuk] *vt* invocar; (*aid*) pedir; (*law*) recurrir a.

involuntary [ɪn'vɔləntrɪ] *a* involuntario.

involve [ɪn'vɒlv] vt (entail) suponer, implicar; **to ~ sb (in)** comprometer a uno (con); **~d** a complicado; **~ment** n (gen) enredo; (obligation) compromiso; (difficulty) apuro.

inward ['ɪnwəd] a (movement) interior, interno; (thought, feeling) íntimo; **~(s)** ad hacia dentro.

I/O abbr (COMPUT = input/output) entrada/salida.

iodine ['aɪəʊdiːn] n yodo.

iota [aɪ'əʊtə] n (fig) jota, ápice m.

IOU n abbr (= I owe you) pagaré m.

IQ n abbr (= intelligence quotient) coeficiente m intelectual.

IRA n abbr (= Irish Republican Army) IRA m.

Iran [ɪ'rɑːn] n Irán m; **~ian** [ɪ'reɪnɪən] a, n iraní m/f.

Iraq [ɪ'rɑːk] n Irak; **~i** a, n iraquí m/f.

irascible [ɪ'ræsɪbl] a irascible.

irate [aɪ'reɪt] a enojado, airado.

Ireland ['aɪələnd] n Irlanda.

iris ['aɪrɪs], pl **~es** n (ANAT) iris m; (BOT) lirio.

Irish ['aɪrɪʃ] a irlandés/esa // npl: **the ~** los irlandeses; **~man/woman** n irlandés/esa m/f; **the ~ Sea** n el Mar de Irlanda.

irk [ɜːk] vt fastidiar; **~some** a fastidioso.

iron ['aɪən] n hierro; (for clothes) plancha // a de hierro // vt (clothes) planchar; **to ~ out** vt (crease) quitar; (fig) allanar; **the ~ Curtain** n el Telón de Acero.

ironic(al) [aɪ'rɒnɪk(l)] a irónico.

ironing ['aɪənɪŋ] n (act) planchado; (clothes: ironed) ropa planchada; (: to be ironed) ropa por planchar; **~ board** n tabla de planchar.

ironmonger ['aɪənmʌŋgə*] n (Brit) ferretero/a; **~'s (shop)** n ferretería, quincallería.

iron ore n mineral m de hierro.

irony ['aɪrənɪ] n ironía.

irrational [ɪ'ræʃənl] a irracional.

irreconcilable [ɪrekən'saɪləbl] a (idea) incompatible; (enemies) irreconciliable.

irregular [ɪ'regjulə*] a irregular; (surface) desigual.

irrelevant [ɪ'reləvənt] a fuera de lugar, inoportuno.

irreplaceable [ɪrɪ'pleɪsəbl] a irremplazable.

irrepressible [ɪrɪ'presəbl] a incontenible.

irresistible [ɪrɪ'zɪstɪbl] a irresistible.

irresolute [ɪ'rezəluːt] a indeciso.

irrespective [ɪrɪ'spektɪv]: **~ of** prep sin tener en cuenta, no importa.

irresponsible [ɪrɪ'spɒnsɪbl] a (act) irresponsable; (person) poco serio.

irrigate ['ɪrɪgeɪt] vt regar; **irrigation** [-'geɪʃən] n riego.

irritable ['ɪrɪtəbl] a (person: temperament) de (mal) carácter; (: mood) de mal humor.

irritate ['ɪrɪteɪt] vt fastidiar; (MED) picar; **irritating** a fastidioso; **irritation** [-'teɪʃən] n fastidio; picazón f, picor m.

IRS n abbr (US) = Internal Revenue Service.

is [ɪz] vb see be.

Islam ['ɪzlɑːm] n Islam m.

island ['aɪlənd] n isla; (also: **traffic ~**) isleta; **~er** n isleño/a.

isle [aɪl] n isla.

isn't ['ɪznt] = **is not**.

isolate ['aɪsəleɪt] vt aislar; **~d** a aislado; **isolation** [-'leɪʃən] n aislamiento.

Israel ['ɪzreɪl] n Israel m; **~i** [ɪz'reɪlɪ] a, n israelí m/f.

issue ['ɪsjuː] n cuestión f, asunto; (outcome) resultado; (of banknotes etc) emisión f; (of newspaper etc) número; (offspring) sucesión f, descendencia // vt (rations, equipment) distribuir, repartir; (orders) dar; (certificate, passport) expedir; (decree) promulgar; (magazine) publicar; (cheques) extender; (banknotes, stamps) emitir; **at ~** en cuestión; **to take ~ with sb (over)** estar en desacuerdo con uno (sobre).

isthmus ['ɪsməs] n istmo.

KEYWORD

it [ɪt] *pron* 1 (*specific: subject: not generally translated*) él/ella; (: *direct object*) lo, la; (: *indirect object*) le; (*after prep*) él/ella; (*abstract concept*) ello; ~'s **on the table** está en la mesa; **I can't find** ~ no lo (*or* la) encuentro; **give** ~ **to me** dámelo (*or* dámela); **I spoke to him about** ~ le hablé del asunto; **what did you learn from** ~? ¿qué aprendiste de él (*or* ella)?; **did you go to** ~? (*party, concert etc*) ¿fuiste?
2 (*impersonal*): ~'s **raining** llueve, está lloviendo; ~'s **6 o'clock/the 10th of August** son las 6/es el 10 de agosto; **how far is** ~? — ~'s **10 miles/2 hours on the train** ¿a qué distancia está? — a 10 millas/2 horas en tren; **who is** ~? — ~'s **me** ¿quién es? — soy yo.

Italian [ɪ'tæljən] *a* italiano // *n* italiano/a; (*LING*) italiano.
italic [ɪ'tælɪk] *a* cursivo; ~s *npl* cursiva *sg*.
Italy ['ɪtəlɪ] *n* Italia.
itch [ɪtʃ] *n* picazón *f*; (*fig*) prurito // *vi* (*person*) sentir *or* tener comezón; (*part of body*) picar; **to be** ~**ing to do sth** rabiar por hacer algo; ~**y** *a*: **to be** ~**y** = **to be** ~**ing to**.
it'd ['ɪtd] = **it would, it had.**
item ['aɪtəm] *n* artículo; (*on agenda*) asunto (*a tratar*); (*in programme*) número; (*also*: **news** ~) noticia; ~**ize** *vt* detallar.
itinerant [ɪ'tɪnərənt] *a* ambulante.
itinerary [aɪ'tɪnərərɪ] *n* itinerario.
it'll ['ɪtl] = **it will, it shall.**
its [ɪts] *a* su.
it's [ɪts] = **it is, it has.**
itself [ɪt'sɛlf] *pron* (*reflexive*) sí mismo/a; (*emphatic*) él mismo/ella misma.
ITV *n abbr* (*Brit*: = *Independent Television*) cadena de televisión comercial independiente del Estado.
I.U.D. *n abbr* (= *intra-uterine device*)

DIU *m*.
I've [aɪv] = **I have.**
ivory ['aɪvərɪ] *n* marfil *m*.
ivy ['aɪvɪ] *n* hiedra.

J

jab [dʒæb] *vt*: **to** ~ **sth into sth** clavar algo en algo // *n* (*MED*: *col*) pinchazo.
jabber ['dʒæbə*] *vi*, *vi* farfullar.
jack [dʒæk] *n* (*AUT*) gato; (*BOWLS*) boliche *m*; (*CARDS*) sota; **to** ~ **up** *vt* (*AUT*) levantar con el gato.
jackal ['dʒækɔːl] *n* (*ZOOL*) chacal *m*.
jackdaw ['dʒækdɔː] *n* grajo.
jacket ['dʒækɪt] *n* chaqueta, americana, saco (*AM*); (*of boiler etc*) camisa; (*of book*) sobrecubierta.
jack-knife ['dʒæknaɪf] *vi* colear.
jack plug *n* (*ELEC*) enchufe *m* de clavija.
jackpot ['dʒækpɔt] *n* premio gordo.
jaded ['dʒeɪdɪd] *a* (*tired*) cansado; (*fed-up*) hastiado.
jagged ['dʒægɪd] *a* dentado.
jail [dʒeɪl] *n* cárcel // *vt* encarcelar; ~**break** *n* fuga *or* evasión *f* (de la cárcel); ~**er** *n* carcelero/a.
jam [dʒæm] *n* mermelada; (*also*: **traffic** ~) embotellamiento; (*difficulty*) apuro // *vt* (*passage etc*) obstruir; (*mechanism, drawer etc*) atascar; (*RADIO*) interferir // *vi* atascarse, trabarse; **to** ~ **sth into sth** meter algo a la fuerza en algo.
Jamaica [dʒə'meɪkə] *n* Jamaica.
jangle ['dʒæŋɡl] *vi* sonar (de manera) discordante.
janitor ['dʒænɪtə*] *n* (*caretaker*) portero, conserje *m*.
January ['dʒænjuərɪ] *n* enero.
Japan [dʒə'pæn] *n* (el) Japón; ~**ese** [dʒæpə'niːz] *a* japonés/esa // *n*, *pl inv* japonés/esa *m*/*f*; (*LING*) japonés *m*.
jar [dʒɑː*] *n* (*glass: large*) jarra; (: *small*) tarro // *vi* (*sound*) chirriar; (*colours*) desentonar.
jargon ['dʒɑːɡən] *n* jerga.

jasmin(e) ['dʒæzmɪn] *n* jazmín *m*.

jaundice ['dʒɔːndɪs] *n* ictericia; ~**d** *a* (*fig*: *embittered*) amargado; (: *disillusioned*) desilusionado.

jaunt [dʒɔːnt] *n* excursión *f*; ~**y** *a* alegre.

javelin ['dʒævlɪn] *n* jabalina.

jaw [dʒɔː] *n* mandíbula.

jay [dʒeɪ] *n* (*ZOOL*) arrendajo.

jaywalker ['dʒeɪwɔːkə*] *n* peatón/ona *m/f* imprudente.

jazz [dʒæz] *n* jazz *m*; **to ~ up** *vt* (*liven up*) animar, avivar.

jealous ['dʒeləs] *a* celoso; (*envious*) envidioso; **to be ~** tener celos; tener envidia; ~**y** *n* celos *mpl*; envidia.

jeans [dʒiːnz] *npl* (*pantalones mpl*) vaqueros *mpl* o tejanos *mpl*.

jeep [dʒiːp] *n* jeep *m*.

jeer [dʒɪə*] *vi*: **to ~ (at)** (*boo*) abuchear; (*mock*) mofarse (de).

jelly ['dʒelɪ] *n* jalea, gelatina; ~**fish** *n* medusa.

jeopardize ['dʒepədaɪz] *vt* arriesgar, poner en peligro.

jeopardy ['dʒepədɪ] *n*: **to be in ~** estar en peligro.

jerk [dʒəːk] *n* (*jolt*) sacudida; (*wrench*) tirón *m* // *vt* dar una sacudida a; tirar bruscamente de // *vi* (*vehicle*) traquetear.

jerkin ['dʒəːkɪn] *n* chaleco.

jerky ['dʒəːkɪ] *a* espasmódico.

jersey ['dʒəːzɪ] *n* jersey *m*.

jest [dʒest] *n* broma.

Jesus ['dʒiːzəs] *n* Jesús *m*.

jet [dʒet] *n* (*of gas, liquid*) chorro; (*AVIAT*) avión *m* a reacción; ~**-black** *a* negro como el azabache; ~**-engine** *n* motor *m* a reacción; ~**-lag** *n* desorientación *f* después de un largo vuelo.

jettison ['dʒetɪsn] *vt* desechar.

jetty ['dʒetɪ] *n* muelle *m*, embarcadero.

Jew [dʒuː] *n* judío.

jewel ['dʒuːəl] *n* joya; (*in watch*) rubí *m*; ~**ler**, (*US*) ~**er** *n* joyero/a; ~**ler's** **(shop)**, (*US*) ~**ry store** *n* joyería; (*US*) ~**ery**, ~**lery** *n* joyas *fpl*, alha-jas *fpl*.

Jewess ['dʒuːɪs] *n* judía.

Jewish ['dʒuːɪʃ] *a* judío.

jibe [dʒaɪb] *n* mofa.

jiffy ['dʒɪfɪ] *n* (*col*): **in a ~** en un santiamén.

jig [dʒɪg] *n* jiga.

jigsaw ['dʒɪgsɔː] *n* (*also*: ~ **puzzle**) rompecabezas *m inv*.

jilt [dʒɪlt] *vt* dejar plantado a.

jingle ['dʒɪŋgl] *n* (*advert*) musiquilla // *vi* tintinear.

jinx [dʒɪŋks] *n*: **there's a ~ on it** está gafado.

jitters ['dʒɪtəz] *npl* (*col*): **to get the ~** ponerse nervioso.

job [dʒɔb] *n* trabajo; (*task*) tarea; (*duty*) deber *m*; (*post*) empleo; **it's a good ~ that...** menos mal que...; **just the ~!** ¡estupendo!; ~ **centre** *n* (*Brit*) oficina estatal de colocaciones; ~**less** *a* sin trabajo.

jockey ['dʒɔkɪ] *n* jockey *m/f* // *vi*: **to ~ for position** maniobrar para conseguir una posición.

jocular ['dʒɔkjulə*] *a* (*humorous*) gracioso; (*merry*) alegre.

jog [dʒɔg] *vt* empujar (ligeramente) // *vi* (*run*) hacer footing; ~ **along** *vi* tirando; **to ~ sb's memory** refrescar la memoria a uno; ~**ging** *n* footing *m*.

join [dʒɔɪn] *vt* (*things*) juntar, unir; (*become member of*: *club*) hacerse socio de; (*POL*: *party*) afiliarse a; (*meet*: *people*) reunirse con // *vi* (*roads*) empalmar; (*rivers*) confluir // *n* juntura; **to ~ in** *vi* tomar parte, participar // *vt fus* tomar parte en o participar en; **to ~ up** *vi* unirse; (*MIL*) alistarse.

joiner ['dʒɔɪnə*] *n* carpintero/a; ~**y** *n* carpintería.

joint [dʒɔɪnt] *n* (*TECH*) junta, unión *f*; (*ANAT*) articulación *f*; (*Brit CULIN*) pieza de carne (para asar); (*col*: *place*) garito // *a* (*common*) común; (*combined*) combinado; (*committee*) mixto; ~ **account** (*with bank etc*) cuenta común; ~**ly** *ad* en común; conjuntamente.

joist [dʒɔɪst] n viga.

joke [dʒəuk] n chiste m; (also: practical ~) broma // vi bromear; **to play a ~ on** gastar una broma a; **~r** n chistoso/a, bromista m/f; (CARDS) comodín m.

jolly [dʒɔlɪ] a (merry) alegre; (enjoyable) divertido // ad (col) muy, terriblemente.

jolt [dʒəult] n (shake) sacudida; (blow) golpe m; (shock) susto m // vt sacudir; asustar.

Jordan [dʒɔːdən] n Jordania.

jostle [dʒɔsl] vt dar empellones a, codear.

jot [dʒɔt] n: **not one ~** ni jota, ni pizca; **to ~ down** vt apuntar; **~ter** n (Brit) bloc m.

journal [dʒɔːnl] n (paper) periódico; (magazine) revista; (diary) diario; **~ism** n periodismo; **~ist** n periodista m/f, reportero/a.

journey [dʒɔːnɪ] n viaje m; (distance covered) trayecto // vi viajar.

jovial [dʒəuvɪəl] a risueño.

joy [dʒɔɪ] n alegría; **~ful, ~ous** a alegre; **~ ride** n (illegal) paseo en coche robado; **~ stick** n (AVIAT) palanca de mando; (COMPUT) palanca de control.

J.P. n abbr = **Justice of the Peace.**

Jr abbr = **junior.**

jubilant [dʒuːbɪlnt] a jubiloso.

jubilee [dʒuːbɪliː] n aniversario.

judge [dʒʌdʒ] n juez m/f // vt juzgar; (estimate) considerar; **judg(e)ment** n juicio; (punishment) sentencia, fallo.

judiciary [dʒuːdɪʃɪərɪ] n poder m judicial.

judicious [dʒuːdɪʃəs] a juicioso.

judo [dʒuːdəu] n judo.

jug [dʒʌg] n jarro.

juggernaut [dʒʌgənɔːt] n (Brit: huge truck) camionazo.

juggle [dʒʌgl] vi hacer juegos malabares; **~r** n malabarista m/f.

Jugoslav [juːgəuslɑːv] etc = **Yugoslav** etc.

juice [dʒuːs] n zumo, jugo (esp LAm); **juicy** a jugoso.

jukebox [dʒuːkbɔks] n tocadiscos m inv tragaperras.

July [dʒuːlaɪ] n julio.

jumble [dʒʌmbl] n revoltijo // vt (also: ~ **up**: mix up) revolver; (: disarrange) mezclar; **~ sale** n (Brit) venta de objetos usados con fines benéficos.

jumbo (jet) [dʒʌmbəu-] n jumbo.

jump [dʒʌmp] vi saltar, dar saltos; (start) asustarse, sobresaltarse; (increase) aumentar // vt saltar // n salto; aumento; **to ~ the queue** (Brit) colarse.

jumper [dʒʌmpə] n (Brit: pullover) suéter m, jersey m; (US: dress) mandil m; **~ cables** npl (US) = **jump leads.**

jump leads npl (Brit) cables mpl puente de batería.

jumpy [dʒʌmpɪ] a nervioso.

Jun. abbr = **junior.**

junction [dʒʌŋkʃən] n (Brit: of roads) cruce m; (RAIL) empalme m.

juncture [dʒʌŋktʃə] n: **at this ~** en este momento, en esta coyuntura.

June [dʒuːn] n junio.

jungle [dʒʌŋgl] n selva, jungla.

junior [dʒuːnɪə] a (in age) menor, más joven; (competition) juvenil; (position) subalterno // n menor m/f, joven m/f; **he's ~ to me** es menor que yo; **~ school** n (Brit) escuela primaria.

junk [dʒʌŋk] n (cheap goods) baratijas fpl; (lumber) trastos mpl viejos; (rubbish) basura; **~ food** n alimentos preparados y envasados de escaso valor nutritivo; **~ shop** n tienda de objetos usados.

Junr abbr = **junior.**

jurisdiction [dʒuərɪsdɪkʃən] n jurisdicción f.

juror [dʒuərə] n jurado.

jury [dʒuərɪ] n jurado.

just [dʒʌst] a justo // ad (exactly) exactamente; (only) sólo, solamente;

he's ~ done it/left acaba de hacerlo/irse; ~ **right** perfecto; ~ **two o'clock** las dos en punto; **she's** ~ **as clever as you** (ella) es lista como tú; ~ **as well that...** menos mal que...; ~ **as he was leaving** en el momento en que se marchaba; ~ **before/enough** justo antes/lo suficiente; ~ **here** aquí mismo; **he** ~ **missed** ha fallado por poco; ~ **listen to this** escucha esto y atento.

justice ['dʒʌstɪs] n justicia; **J~ of the Peace (J.P.)** n juez m de paz.

justifiable [dʒʌstɪ'faɪəbl] a justificable.

justify ['dʒʌstɪfaɪ] vt justificar; (text) alinear.

justly ['dʒʌstlɪ] ad (gen) justamente; (with reason) con razón.

jut [dʒʌt] vi (also: ~ **out**) sobresalir.

juvenile ['dʒuːvənaɪl] a juvenil; (court) de menores // n joven m/f, menor m de edad.

juxtapose ['dʒʌkstəpəuz] vt yuxtaponer.

K

K abbr (= one thousand) mil; (= kilobyte) kilobyte m, kilocteto.

kaleidoscope [kə'laɪdəskəup] n calidoscopio.

Kampuchea [kæmpu'tʃɪə] n Kampuchea.

kangaroo [kæŋgə'ruː] n canguro.

karate [kə'rɑːtɪ] n karate m.

kebab [kə'bæb] n pincho moruno.

keel [kiːl] n quilla; **on an even** ~ (fig) en equilibrio.

keen [kiːn] a (interest, desire) grande, vivo; (eye, intelligence) agudo; (competition) intenso; (edge) afilado; (Brit: eager) entusiasta; **to be** ~ **to do** or **on doing sth** tener muchas ganas de hacer algo; **to be** ~ **on sth/ sb** interesarse por algo/uno.

keep [kiːp] vb (pt, pp **kept**) vt (retain, preserve) guardar; (hold back)

quedarse con; (shop) ser propietario de; (feed: family etc) mantener; (promise) cumplir; (chickens, bees etc) criar // vi (food) conservarse; (remain) seguir, continuar // n (of castle) torreón m; (food etc) comida, subsistencia; (col): **for** ~**s** para siempre; **to** ~ **doing sth** seguir haciendo algo; **to** ~ **sb from doing sth** impedir a uno hacer algo; **to** ~ **sth from happening** impedir que algo ocurra; **to** ~ **sb happy** tener a uno contento; **to** ~ **a place tidy** mantener un lugar limpio; **to** ~ **sth to o.s.** guardar algo para sí mismo; **to** ~ **sth (back) from sb** ocultar algo a uno; **to** ~ **time** (clock) mantener la hora exacta; **to** ~ **on** vi seguir, continuar; **to** ~ **out** vi (stay out) permanecer fuera; '~ **out**' prohibida la entrada; **to** ~ **up** vi mantener, conservar // vi no retrasarse; **to** ~ **up with** (pace) ir a la paso de; (level) mantenerse a la altura de; ~**er** n guardián/ana m/f; ~**fit** n gimnasia (para mantenerse en forma); ~**ing** n (care) cuidado; **in** ~**ing with** de acuerdo con; ~**sake** n recuerdo.

keg [kɛg] n barrilete m, barril m.

kennel ['kɛnl] n perrera; ~**s** npl perreras fpl.

Kenya ['kɛnjə] n Kenia; ~**n** a, n keniano/a m/f.

kept [kɛpt] pt, pp of **keep**.

kerb [kɜːb] n (Brit) bordillo.

kernel ['kɜːnl] n (nut) fruta; (fig) meollo.

kerosene ['kɛrəsiːn] n keroseno.

ketchup ['kɛtʃəp] n salsa de tomate, catsup m.

kettle ['kɛtl] n hervidor m, olla; ~**drum** n (MUS) timbal m.

key [kiː] n (gen) llave f; (MUS) tono; (of piano, typewriter) tecla // vt (also: ~ **in**) teclear; ~**board** n teclado; ~**ed up** a (person) nervioso; ~**hole** n ojo de la cerradura; ~**note** n (MUS) tónica; ~**ring** n llavero.

khaki ['kɑːkɪ] n caqui.

kick [kɪk] vt (person) dar una patada a; (ball) dar un puntapié a // vi (horse) dar coces // n patada; (of rifle) culetazo; (thrill): **he does it for ~s** lo hace por pura diversión; **to ~ off** vi (SPORT) hacer el saque inicial.

kid [kɪd] n (col: child) chiquillo/a; (animal) cabrito; (leather) cabritilla // vi (col) bromear.

kidnap ['kɪdnæp] vt secuestrar; **~per** n secuestrador/a m/f; **~ping** n secuestro.

kidney ['kɪdnɪ] n riñón m.

kill [kɪl] vt matar; (murder) asesinar; (fig: story) suprimir; (rumour) acabar con; **to be ~ed (by a bullet)** ser muerto (por una bala) // n matanza; **~er** n asesino/a; **~ing** n (one) asesinato; (several) matanza; **~joy** n (Brit) aguafiestas m/f inv.

kiln [kɪln] n horno.

kilo ['kiːləu] n kilo; **~byte** n (COMPUT) kilobyte m, kilococteto; **~gram(me)** ['kɪləugræm] n kilo, kilogramo; **~metre**, (US) **~meter** ['kɪləmiːtə*] n kilómetro; **~watt** ['kɪləuwɔt] n kilovatio.

kilt [kɪlt] n falda escocesa.

kin [kɪn] n parientes mpl.

kind [kaɪnd] a (treatment) bueno, cariñoso; (person, act, word) amable, atento // n clase f, especie f; (species) género; **in ~** (COMM) en especie; **a ~ of** una especie de; **to be two of a ~** ser tal para cual.

kindergarten ['kɪndəgɑːtn] n jardín m de infantes.

kind-hearted [kaɪnd'hɑːtɪd] a bondadoso, de buen corazón.

kindle ['kɪndl] vt encender.

kindly ['kaɪndlɪ] a bondadoso; (gentle) cariñoso // ad bondadosamente, amablemente; **will you ~...** sea usted tan amable de... .

kindness ['kaɪndnɪs] n bondad f, amabilidad f.

kindred ['kɪndrɪd] a: **~ spirits** almas fpl gemelas.

kinetic [kɪ'nɛtɪk] a cinético.

king [kɪŋ] n rey m; **~dom** n reino; **~fisher** n martín m pescador; **~size** a de tamaño gigante.

kinky ['kɪŋkɪ] a (pej) perverso.

kiosk ['kiːɔsk] n quiosco; (Brit TEL) cabina.

kipper ['kɪpə*] n arenque m ahumado.

kiss [kɪs] n beso // vt besar; **to ~ (each other)** besarse.

kit [kɪt] n avíos mpl; (equipment) equipo; (set of tools etc) caja de herramientas fpl; (assembly ~) juego de armar.

kitchen ['kɪtʃɪn] n cocina; **~ sink** n fregadero.

kite [kaɪt] n (toy) cometa.

kith [kɪθ] n: **~ and kin** parientes mpl y allegados.

kitten ['kɪtn] n gatito/a.

kitty ['kɪtɪ] n (pool of money) fondo común; (CARDS) puesta.

km abbr (= kilometre) km.

knack [næk] n: **to have the ~ of doing sth** tener el don de hacer algo.

knapsack ['næpsæk] n mochila.

knead [niːd] vt amasar.

knee [niː] n rodilla; **~cap** n rótula.

kneel [niːl], pt, pp **knelt** vi (also: ~ **down**) arrodillarse.

knell [nɛl] n toque m de difuntos.

knelt [nɛlt] pt, pp of **kneel**.

knew [njuː] pt of **know**.

knickers ['nɪkəz] npl (Brit) bragas fpl.

knife [naɪf], pl **knives** n cuchillo // vt acuchillar.

knight [naɪt] n caballero; (CHESS) caballo; **~hood** n (title): **to get a ~hood** recibir el título de Sir.

knit [nɪt] vt tejer; (brows) fruncir // vi tejer, tricotar; (bones) soldarse; **to ~ together** vt (fig) unir, juntar; **~ting** n labor f de punto; **~ting machine** n máquina de tricotar; **~ting needle**, (US) **~ting needle** n aguja de tejer; **~wear** n prendas fpl de punto.

knives [naɪvz] pl of **knife**.

knob [nɔb] n (of door) tirador m; (of stick) puño; **a ~ of butter** (Brit) un pedazo de mantequilla.

knock [nɔk] vt (strike) golpear; (bump into) chocar contra; (fig: col) criticar // vi (at door etc): **to ~ at/ on** llamar a // n (blow) golpe m; (on door) llamada; **to ~ down** vt (pedestrian) atropellar; **to ~ off** vi (col: finish) salir del trabajo // vt (col: steal) birlar; **to ~ out** vt dejar sin sentido; (BOXING) poner fuera de combate, dejar K.O.; **to ~ over** vt (object) tirar; (person) atropellar; **~er** n (on door) aldaba; **~-kneed** a patizambo; **~out** n (BOXING) K.O. m, knockout m.

knot [nɔt] n (gen) nudo // vt anudar; **~ty** a (fig) complicado.

know [nəu], pt **knew**, pp **known** vt (gen) saber; (person, author, place) conocer; **to ~ how to do** saber como hacer; **to ~ how to swim** saber nadar; **to ~ about** or **of sb/sth** saber de uno/algo; **~-all** sabelotodo m/f; **~-how** n conocimientos mpl; **~-ing** a (of complicidad; **~ingly** ad (purposely) adrede; (smile, look) con complicidad.

knowledge ['nɔlidʒ] n (gen) conocimiento; (learning) saber m, conocimientos mpl; **~able** a: **~able about** enterado de.

known [nəun] pp of **know**.

knuckle ['nʌkl] n nudillo.

K.O. n abbr = **knockout**.

Koran [kɔ'rɑːn] n Corán m.

Korea [kɔ'riə] n Corea.

kosher ['kəuʃə*] a autorizado por la ley judía.

L

l. abbr = **litre**.

lab [læb] n abbr = **laboratory**.

label ['leibl] n etiqueta; (brand: of record) sello (discográfico) // vt poner etiqueta a.

laboratory [lə'bɔrətəri] n laborato-

rio.

laborious [lə'bɔːriəs] a penoso.

labour, (US) **labor** ['leibə*] n (task) trabajo; (~ force) mano f de obra; (MED) parto // vi: **to ~ (at)** trabajar (en) // vt insistir en; **in ~** (MED) de parto; **L~, the L~ party** (Brit) el partido laborista, los laboristas mpl; **~ed** a (breathing) fatigoso; (style) pesado; **~er** n peón m; (on farm) peón m; (day ~er) jornalero.

labyrinth ['læbirinθ] n laberinto.

lace [leis] n encaje m; (of shoe etc) cordón m; (of shoes: also: ~ **up**) atarse (los zapatos).

lack [læk] n (absence) falta; (scarcity) escasez f // vt faltarle a uno, carecer de; **through** or **for ~ of** por falta de; **to be ~ing** faltar, no haber.

lackadaisical [lækə'deizikl] a (careless) descuidado; (indifferent) indiferente.

lacquer ['lækə*] n laca.

lad [læd] n muchacho, chico; (in stable etc) mozo.

ladder ['lædə*] n escalera (de mano); (Brit: in tights) carrera // vt (Brit: tights) hacer una carrera en.

laden ['leidn] a: ~ **(with)** cargado (de).

ladle ['leidl] n cucharón m.

lady ['leidi] n señora; (distinguished, noble) dama; **young ~** señorita; the **ladies' (room)** los servicios de señoras; **~bird**, (US) **~bug** n mariquita; **~-in-waiting** n dama de honor; **~like** a fino; **L~ship** n: your **L~ship** su Señoría.

lag [læg] vi (also: ~ **behind**) retrasarse, quedarse atrás // vt (pipes) revestir.

lager ['lɑːgə*] n cerveza (rubia).

lagoon [lə'guːn] n laguna.

laid [leid] pt, pp of **lay**; ~ **back** a (col) relajado.

lain [lein] pp of **lie**.

lair [lɛə*] n guarida.

laity ['leiti] n laicado.

lake [leik] n lago.

lamb [læm] n cordero; (*meat*) carne f de cordero; ~ **chop** n chuleta de cordero; ~**swool** n lana de cordero.

lame [leɪm] a cojo; (*excuse*) poco convincente.

lament [ləˈmɛnt] vt lamentarse de.

laminated [ˈlæmɪneɪtɪd] a laminado.

lamp [læmp] n lámpara.

lampoon [læmˈpuːn] vt satirizar.

lamp: ~**post** n (*Brit*) (poste m de) farol m; ~**shade** n pantalla.

lance [lɑːns] n lanza // vt (*MED*) abrir con lanceta; ~ **corporal** n (*Brit*) soldado de primera clase.

land [lænd] n tierra; (*country*) país m; (*piece of* ~) terreno; (*estate*) tierras fpl, finca; (*AGR*) campo // vi (*from ship*) desembarcar; (*AVIAT*) aterrizar; (*fig: fall*) caer, terminar // vt (*obtain*) conseguir; (*passengers, goods*) desembarcar; to ~ **up** in/at ir a parar a/en; ~**ing** n desembarco; aterrizaje m; (*of staircase*) rellano; ~**ing lady** n (*of boarding house*) patrona; (*owner*) dueña; ~**lord** n propietario; (*of pub etc*) patrón m; ~**mark** n lugar m conocido; to be a ~**mark** (*fig*) hacer época; ~**owner** n terrateniente m/f.

landscape [ˈlænskeɪp] n paisaje m.

landslide [ˈlændslaɪd] n (*GEO*) corrimiento de tierras; (*fig: POL*) victoria arrolladora.

lane [leɪn] n (*in country*) camino; (*in town*) callejón m; (*AUT*) carril m; (*in race*) calle f; (*for air or sea traffic*) ruta.

language [ˈlæŋgwɪdʒ] n lenguaje m; (*national tongue*) idioma m, lengua; **bad** ~ palabrotas fpl; ~ **laboratory** n laboratorio de idiomas.

languid [ˈlæŋgwɪd] a lánguido.

languish [ˈlæŋgwɪʃ] vi languidecer.

lank [læŋk] a (*hair*) lacio.

lanky [ˈlæŋkɪ] a larguirucho.

lantern [ˈlæntn] n linterna, farol m.

lap [læp] n (*of track*) vuelta; (*of body*): **to sit on sb's** ~ sentarse en las rodillas de uno // vt (*also:* ~ **up**) lamer // vi (*waves*) chapotear.

lapel [ləˈpɛl] n solapa.

Lapland [ˈlæplænd] n Laponia.

lapse [læps] n fallo; (*moral*) desliz m // vi (*expire*) caducar; (*morally*) cometer un desliz; (*time*) pasar, transcurrir; to ~ **into bad habits** caer en malos hábitos; ~ **of time** lapso, período.

larceny [ˈlɑːsənɪ] n latrocinio.

lard [lɑːd] n manteca (de cerdo).

larder [ˈlɑːdə*] n despensa.

large [lɑːdʒ] a grande; **at** ~ (*free*) en libertad; (*generally*) en general; ~**ly** ad en gran parte; ~**scale** a (*map*) en gran escala; (*fig*) importante.

largesse [lɑːˈʒɛs] n generosidad f.

lark [lɑːk] n (*bird*) alondra; (*joke*) broma; to ~ **about** vi bromear, hacer el tonto.

larynx [ˈlærɪŋks] n laringe f.

laser [ˈleɪzə*] n láser m; ~ **printer** n impresora (por) láser.

lash [læʃ] n latigazo; (*punishment*) azote m; (*also:* **eyelash**) pestaña // vt azotar; (*tie*) atar; to ~ **out** vi (*col: spend*) gastar a la loca; to ~ **out at or against sb** lanzar invectivas contra uno.

lass [læs] n chica.

lasso [læˈsuː] n lazo.

last [lɑːst] a (*gen*) último; (*final*) último, final // ad por último // vi (*endure*) durar; (*continue*) continuar, seguir; ~ **night** anoche; ~ **week** la semana pasada; **at** ~ por fin; ~ **but one** penúltimo; ~**ditch** a (*attempt*) último, desesperado; ~**ing** a duradero; ~**ly** ad por último, finalmente; ~**minute** a de última hora.

latch [lætʃ] n picaporte m, pestillo.

late [leɪt] a (*not on time*) atrasado; (*towards end of period, life*) tardío; (*hour*) avanzado; (*dead*) fallecido // ad tarde; (*behind time, schedule*) con retraso; **of** ~ últimamente; **in ~ May** hacia fines de mayo; **the ~ Mr X** el difunto Sr X; **~comer** n recién llegado/a; **~ly** ad últimamente.

later ['leɪtə*] a (date etc) posterior; (version etc) más reciente // ad más tarde, después.

lateral ['lætərəl] a lateral.

latest ['leɪtɪst] a último; **at the ~ a** más tardar.

lathe [leɪð] n torno.

lather ['lɑːðə*] n espuma (de jabón) // vt enjabonar.

Latin ['lætɪn] n latín m // a latino; **~ America** n América latina; **~ American** a latinoamericano.

latitude ['lætɪtjuːd] n latitud f.

latrine [lə'triːn] n letrina.

latter ['lætə*] a último; (of two) segundo // n: **the ~** el último, éste; **~ly** ad últimamente.

lattice ['lætɪs] n enrejado.

laudable ['lɔːdəbl] a loable.

laugh [lɑːf] n risa; (loud) carcajada // vi reír(se); **to ~ at** vt fus reírse de; **to ~ off** vt tomar algo a risa; **~able** a ridículo; **~ing stock** n: **the ~ing stock of** el hazmerreír de; **~ter** n risa.

launch [lɔːntʃ] n (boat) lancha; see also **~ing** vt (ship, rocket, plan) lanzar; **~ing** n (of rocket etc) lanzamiento; (inauguration) estreno; **~(ing) pad** n plataforma de lanzamiento.

launder ['lɔːndə*] vt lavar.

launderette [lɔːn'drɛt], (US) **laundromat** ['lɔːdrəmæt] n lavandería (automática).

laundry ['lɔːndrɪ] n lavandería; (clothes) ropa sucia; **to do the ~** hacer la colada.

laureate ['lɔːrɪət] a see **poet.**

lavatory ['lævətərɪ] n wáter m; **lavatories** npl servicios mpl, aseos mpl, sanitarios mpl (LAm).

lavender ['lævəndə*] n lavanda.

lavish ['lævɪʃ] a abundante; (giving freely): **~ with** pródigo en // vt: **to ~ sth on sb** colmar a uno de algo.

law [lɔː] n ley f; (study) derecho; (of game) regla; **~-abiding** a respetuoso de la ley; **~ and order** n orden m público; **~ court** n tribunal m (de justicia); **~ful** a legítimo, lícito; **~fully** ad legalmente.

law school n facultad f de derecho.

lawsuit ['lɔːsuːt] n pleito.

lawyer ['lɔːjə*] n abogado/a; (for sales, wills etc) notario/a.

lax [læks] a (discipline) relajado; (person) negligente al hacer.

laxative ['læksətɪv] n laxante m.

laxity ['læksɪtɪ] n flojedad f; (moral) relajamiento; (negligence) negligencia.

lay [leɪ] pt of **lie** // a laico; (not expert) lego // vt (pt, pp **laid**) (place) colocar; (eggs, table) poner; (trap) tender; **to ~ aside** or **by** vt dejar a un lado; **to ~ down** vt (pen etc) dejar; (arms) rendir; (policy) asentar; **to ~ down the law** imponer las normas; **to ~ off** vt (workers) despedir; **to ~ on** vt (water, gas) instalar; (meal, facilities) proveer; **to ~ out** vt (plan) trazar; (display) disponer; (spend) gastar; **to ~ up** vt (store) guardar; (ship) desarmar; (subj: illness) obligar a guardar cama; **~about** n vago/a; **~-by** n (Brit AUT) área de aparcamiento.

layer ['leɪə*] n capa.

layette [leɪ'ɛt] n ajuar m (de niño).

layman ['leɪmən] n lego.

layout ['leɪaut] n (design) plan m, trazado; (disposition) disposición f; (PRESS) composición f.

laze [leɪz] vi holgazanear.

lazy ['leɪzɪ] a perezoso, vago.

laziness ['leɪzɪnɪs] n pereza.

lb. abbr = **pound** (weight).

lead [liːd] n (front position) delantera; (distance, time ahead) ventaja; (clue) pista; (ELEC) cable m; (for dog) correa; (THEATRE) papel m principal; [lɛd] (metal) plomo; (in

pencil) mina // (vb: pt, pp led) vt
conducir; (life) llevar; (be leader of)
dirigir; (SPORT) ir en cabeza de //
vi ir primero; **to be in the ~**
(SPORT) llevar la delantera; (fig) ir
a la cabeza; **to ~ astray** llevar por
mal camino; **to ~ away** vt llevar;
to ~ back vt (person, route) llevar
de vuelta; **to ~ on** vi (tease) engañar; **to ~ on to** (induce) incitar a;
to ~ to vt fus producir, provocar;
to ~ up to vt fus conducir a.

leaden ['lɛdn] a (sky, sea) plomizo;
(heavy: footsteps) pesado.

leader ['li:də*] n jefe/a m/f, líder m;
(of union etc) dirigente m/f; (guide)
guía m/f; (of newspaper) artículo de
fondo; **~ship** n dirección f.

leading ['li:dɪŋ] a (main) principal;
(outstanding) destacado; (first) primero; (front) delantero; **~ lady** n
(THEATRE) primera actriz f; **~
light** n (person) figura principal.

leaf [li:f], pl **leaves** n hoja // vi: **to ~
through** hojear; **to turn over a
new ~** reformarse.

leaflet ['li:flɪt] n folleto.

league [li:g] n sociedad f; (FOOT-
BALL) liga; **to be in ~ with** estar
de manga con.

leak [li:k] n (of liquid, gas) escape m,
fuga; (in pipe) agujero; (in roof) gotera; (in security) filtración f // vi
(shoes, ship) hacer agua; (pipe) tener (un) escape; (roof) gotear;
(also: **~ out**: liquid, gas) escaparse,
fugarse; (fig: news) divulgarse // vt
(gen) dejar escapar; (fig: information) filtrarse.

lean [li:n] a (thin) flaco; (meat) magro // (vb: pt, pp **leaned** or **leant**
[lent]) vt: **to ~ sth on** sth apoyar
algo en algo // vi (slope) inclinarse;
(rest): **to ~ against** apoyarse contra; **to ~ on** apoyarse en; (fig: rely
on) contar con (el apoyo de); **to ~
back/forward** vi inclinarse hacia
atrás/adelante; **to ~ out** vi asomar-
se; **to ~ over** vi inclinarse; **~ing**
n: **~ing (towards)** inclinación f (ha-

cia); **~-to** n cobertizo.

leap [li:p] n salto // vi (pt, pp **leaped**
or **leapt** [lept]) saltar; **~frog** n pido-
la; **~ year** n año bisiesto.

learn [lə:n], pt, pp **learned** or **learnt**
vt (gen) aprender; (come to know of)
enterarse de // vi aprender; **to ~
how to do sth** aprender a hacer
algo; **~ed** ['lə:nɪd] a erudito; **~er** n
principiante m/f; (Brit: also: **~er
driver**) aprendiz/a m/f; **~ing** n el
saber m, conocimientos mpl.

lease [li:s] n arriendo // vt arrendar.

leash [li:ʃ] n correa.

least [li:st] a (slightest) menor, más
pequeño; (smallest amount of) mínimo // ad menos // n: **the ~** lo menos;
the ~ expensive car el coche menos costoso; **at ~** por lo menos, al
menos; **not in the ~** en absoluto.

leather ['lɛðə*] n cuero.

leave [li:v], pt, pp **left** vt dejar; (go
away from) abandonar // vi irse;
(train) salir // n permiso; **to be left**
quedar, sobrar; **there's some milk
left over** sobra or queda algo de leche; **on ~** de permiso; **to ~ behind** vt (on purpose) dejar (atrás);
(accidentally) olvidar; **to take one's
~ of** despedirse de; **to ~ out** vt
omitir; **~ of absence** n permiso de
ausentarse.

leaves [li:vz] pl of **leaf**.

Lebanon ['lɛbənən] n: **the ~** el Líbano.

lecherous ['lɛtʃərəs] a lascivo.

lecture ['lɛktʃə*] n conferencia;
(SCOL) clase f // vi dar una clase //
vt (scold) sermonear; **to give a ~
on** dar una conferencia sobre; **~r** n
conferenciante m/f; (Brit : at university) profesor/a m/f.

led [lɛd] pt, pp of **lead**.

ledge [lɛdʒ] n (of window, on wall)
repisa, reborde m; (of mountain) saliente m.

ledger ['lɛdʒə*] n libro mayor.

lee [li:] n sotavento.

leech [li:tʃ] n sanguijuela.

leek [li:k] n puerro.

leer [lɪə*] vi: **to ~ at sb** mirar de manera lasciva a uno.

leeway ['li:weɪ] n (fig): **to have some ~** tener cierta libertad de acción.

left [left] pt, pp of **leave** ◊ n izquierda ◊ n izquierda ◊ ad a la izquierda; **on or to the ~** a la izquierda; **the L~** (POL) la izquierda; **~-handed** a zurdo; **the ~-hand side** n la izquierda; **~-luggage (office)** n (Brit) consigna; **~-overs** npl sobras fpl; **~-wing** a (POL) de izquierda, izquierdista.

leg [leg] n pierna; (of animal) pata; (of chair) pie m; (CULIN: of meat) pierna; (of journey) etapa; **1st/2nd ~** (SPORT) partido de ida/de vuelta.

legacy ['legəsɪ] n herencia.

legal ['li:gl] a (permitted by law) lícito; (of law) legal; (inquiry etc) jurídico; **~ holiday** n (US) fiesta oficial; **~ize** vt legalizar; **~ly** ad legalmente; **~ tender** n moneda de curso legal.

legend ['ledʒənd] n leyenda.

legislation [ledʒɪs'leɪʃən] n legislación f.

legislature ['ledʒɪslətʃə*] n cuerpo legislativo.

legitimate [lɪ'dʒɪtɪmət] a legítimo.

leg-room ['legru:m] n espacio para las piernas.

leisure ['leʒə*] n ocio, tiempo libre; **at ~** con tranquilidad; **~ centre** n centro de recreo; **~ly** a sin prisa, lento.

lemon ['lemən] n limón m; **~ade** [-'neɪd] n (fruit juice) limonada; (fizzy) gaseosa; **~ tea** n té m con limón.

lend [lend], pt, pp **lent** vt: **to ~ sth to sb** prestar algo a alguien; **~ing library** n biblioteca de préstamo.

length [leŋθ] n (size) largo, longitud f; (section: of road, pipe) tramo; (: rope etc) largo; **at ~** (at last) por fin, (lengthily) largamente; **~en** vt alargar ◊ vi alargarse; **~ways** ad a lo largo; **~y** a largo,

extenso; (meeting) prolongado.

lenient ['li:nɪənt] a indulgente.

lens [lenz] n (of spectacles) lente f; (of camera) objetivo.

Lent [lent] n Cuaresma.

lentil ['lentl] n lenteja.

Leo ['li:əu] n Leo.

leopard ['lepəd] n leopardo/a.

leotard ['li:ətɑ:d] n leotardo.

leper ['lepə*] n leproso/a.

leprosy ['leprəsɪ] n lepra.

lesbian ['lezbɪən] n lesbiana.

less [les] a (in size, degree etc) menor; (in quantity) menos ◊ pron, ad menos; **~ than half** menos de la mitad; **~ than ever** menos que nunca; **~ and ~** cada vez menos; **the ~ he works...** cuanto menos trabaja...

lessen ['lesn] vi disminuir, reducirse ◊ vt disminuir, reducir.

lesser ['lesə*] a menor; **to a ~ extent** en menor grado.

lesson ['lesn] n clase f; **a maths ~** una clase de matemáticas.

lest [lest] conj: **~ it happen** para que no pase.

let [let], pt, pp **let** vt (allow) dejar, permitir; (Brit: lease) alquilar; **to ~ sb do sth** dejar que uno haga algo; **to ~ sb know sth** comunicar algo a uno; **~'s go** ¡vamos!; **~ him come** que venga; **'to ~'** 'se alquila'; **to ~ down** vt (lower) bajar; (tyre) desinflar; (hair) soltar; (disappoint) defraudar; **to ~ go** vi soltar; (dress) dejarse ir // vt soltar; **to ~ in** vt dejar entrar; (visitor etc) hacer pasar; **to ~ off** vt dejar escapar; (firework etc) disparar; (bomb) accionar; **to ~ out** vt dejar salir; (dress) ensanchar; **to ~ up** vi amainar, disminuir.

lethal ['li:θl] a (weapon) mortífero; (poison, wound) mortal.

lethargy ['leθədʒɪ] n letargo.

letter ['letə*] n (of alphabet) letra; (correspondence) carta; **~ bomb** n carta-bomba; **~ box** n (Brit) buzón m; **~ of credit** n carta de crédito;

~**ing** n letras fpl.

lettuce ['letɪs] n lechuga.

leukaemia, (US) **leukemia** [luːˈkiːmɪə] n leucemia.

level ['levl] a (flat) llano; (flattened) nivelado; (uniform) igual // ad a nivel // n nivel m // vt nivelar; allanar; **to be** ~ **with** estar a nivel de; **'A'** ~**s** npl (Brit) ≈ Bachillerato Superior, B.U.P.; **'O'** ~**s** npl (Brit) = bachillerato elemental, octavo de básica; **on the** ~ (fig: honest) en serio; **to** ~ **off** or **out** vi (prices etc) estabilizarse; ~ **crossing** n (Brit) paso a nivel; ~**-headed** a sensato.

lever ['liːvə*] n palanca // vt: **to** ~ **up** levantar con palanca; ~**age** n (fig: influence) influencia.

levy ['levɪ] n impuesto // vt exigir, recaudar.

lewd [luːd] a lascivo; (joke) verde, colorado (LAm).

liability [laɪəˈbɪlɪtɪ] n responsabilidad f; (handicap) desventaja; **liabilities** npl obligaciones fpl; (COMM) pasivo sg.

liable ['laɪəbl] a (subject): ~ **to** sujeto a; (responsible): ~ **for** responsable de; (likely): ~ **to do** propenso a hacer.

liaise [lɪˈeɪz] vi: **to** ~ **with** enlazar con.

liaison [liːˈeɪzɒn] n (coordination) enlace m; (affair) relación f.

liar ['laɪə*] n mentiroso/a.

libel ['laɪbl] n calumnia // vt calumniar.

liberal ['lɪbərl] a (gen) liberal; (generous): ~ **with** generoso con.

liberty ['lɪbətɪ] n libertad f; **to be at** ~ **to do** estar libre para hacer.

Libra ['liːbrə] n Libra.

librarian [laɪˈbrɛərɪən] n bibliotecario/a.

library ['laɪbrərɪ] n biblioteca.

libretto [lɪˈbretəʊ] n libreto.

Libya ['lɪbɪə] n Libia; ~**n** a, n libio/a m/f.

lice [laɪs] pl of **louse**.

licence, (US) **license** ['laɪsns] n li-

cencia; (permit) permiso; (also: **driving** ~, (US) **driver's** ~) carnet m de conducir (Sp); permiso (LAm); (excessive freedom) libertad f; ~ **number** n matrícula; ~ **plate** n placa (de matrícula).

license ['laɪsns] n (US) = **licence** // vt autorizar, dar permiso a; ~**d** a (for alcohol) autorizado para vender bebidas alcohólicas.

licentious [laɪˈsenʃəs] a licencioso.

lichen ['laɪkən] n liquen m.

lick [lɪk] vt lamer // n lamedura; **a** ~ **of paint** una mano de pintura.

licorice ['lɪkərɪs] n = **liquorice**.

lid [lɪd] n (of box, case) tapa; (of pan) cobertera.

lido ['laɪdəʊ] n (Brit) piscina.

lie [laɪ] n mentira // vi mentir; (pt **lay**, pp **lain**) (rest) estar echado, estar acostado; (of object: be situated) estar, encontrarse; **to** ~ **low** (fig) mantenerse a escondidas; **to** ~ **about** vi (things) estar tirado; (Brit) (people) estar tumbado; **to have a** ~**-down** (Brit) echarse (una siesta); **to have a** ~**-in** (Brit) quedarse en la cama.

lieu [luː]: **in** ~ **of** prep en lugar de.

lieutenant [lefˈtenənt], (US) luːˈtenənt] n teniente m.

life [laɪf], pl **lives** n vida; (way of ~) modo de vivir; (of licence etc) vigencia; ~ **assurance** n (Brit) seguro de vida; ~**belt** n (Brit) cinturón m salvavidas; ~**boat** n lancha de socorro; ~**guard** n vigilante mf; ~ **insurance** n = ~ **assurance**; ~**jacket** n chaleco salvavidas; ~**less** a sin vida; (dull) soso; ~**like** a natural; ~**line** n (fig) cordón m umbilical; ~**long** a de toda la vida; ~ **preserver** n (US) = ~**belt**; ~ **saver** n socorrista m/f; ~ **sentence** n condena perpetua; ~**sized** a de tamaño natural; ~ **span** n vida; **lifestyle** n estilo de vida; ~ **support system** n (MED) sistema m de respiración asistida; ~**time** n: **in his** ~**time** durante su vida; **once in**

a ~**time** una vez en la vida.

lift [lɪft] vt levantar; (copy) plagiar // vi (fog) disparse // n (Brit: elevator) ascensor m; **to give sb a** ~ (Brit) llevar a uno en el coche; ~-**off** n despegue m.

light [laɪt] n luz f; (flame) lumbre f; (lamp) luz f, lámpara; (daylight) luz f del día; (headlight) faro; (rear ~) luz f trasera; (for cigarette etc) **have you got a** ~? ¿tienes fuego? // vt (pt, pp **lighted** or **lit**) (candle, cigarette, fire) encender (Sp), prender (LAm); (room) alumbrar // a (colour) claro; (not heavy, also fig) ligero; (room) alumbrado; **to come to** ~ salir a luz; **to** ~ **up** vi (smoke) encender un cigarrillo; (face) iluminarse // vt (illuminate) iluminar, alumbrar; ~ **bulb** n bombilla, foco (LAm); ~**en** vi (grow ~) clarear // vt (give light to) iluminar; (make lighter) aclarar; (make less heavy) aligerar; ~**er** n (also: **cigarette** ~**er**) encendedor m, mechero; ~-**headed** a (dizzy) mareado; (excited) exaltado; (by nature) casquivano; ~-**hearted** a alegre; ~**house** n faro; ~**ing** n (act) iluminación f; (system) alumbrado; ~**ly** ad ligeramente; (not seriously) con poca seriedad; **to get off** ~**ly** con castigado con poca severidad; ~**ness** n claridad f; (in weight) ligereza.

lightning [laɪtnɪŋ] n relámpago, rayo; ~ **conductor**, (US) ~ **rod** n pararrayos m inv.

light-: ~ **pen** n lápiz m óptico; ~**weight** a (suit) ligero // n (BOXING) peso ligero; ~ **year** n año luz.

like [laɪk] vt gustarle a uno // prep como // a parecido, semejante // n: **the** ~ semejante m/f; **his** ~**s** and **dislikes** sus gustos y aversiones; **I would** ~, **I'd** ~ me gustaría; (for purchase) quisiera; **would you** ~ **a coffee?** ¿te apetece un café?; **I** ~ **swimming** me gusta nadar; **she** ~**s apples** le gustan las manzanas; **to be or look** ~ sb/sth parecerse a

alguien/algo; **that's just** ~ **him** es muy de él, es característico de él; **do it** ~ **this** hazlo así; **it is nothing** ~... no tiene parecido alguno con...; ~**able** a simpático, agradable.

likelihood [laɪklɪhud] n probabilidad f.

likely [laɪklɪ] a probable; **he's** ~ **to leave** es probable que se vaya; **not** ~! ¡ni hablar!

likeness [laɪknɪs] n semejanza, parecido.

likewise [laɪkwaɪz] ad igualmente.

liking [laɪkɪŋ] n: ~ **(for)** (person) cariño (a); (thing) afición (a).

lilac [laɪlək] n lila // a (colour) de color lila.

lily [lɪlɪ] n lirio, azucena; ~ **of the valley** n lirio de los valles.

limb [lɪm] n miembro.

limber [lɪmbə*]: **to** ~ **up** vi (fig) entrenarse; (SPORT) desentumecerse.

limbo [lɪmbəu] n: **to be in** ~ (fig) quedar a la expectativa.

lime [laɪm] n (tree) limero; (fruit) lima; (GEO) cal f.

limelight [laɪmlaɪt] n: **to be in the** ~ (fig) ser el centro de atención.

limerick [lɪmərɪk] n quintilla humorística.

limestone [laɪmstəun] n piedra caliza.

limit [lɪmɪt] n límite m // vt limitar; ~**ed** a limitado; **to be** ~**ed to** limitarse a; ~**ed (liability) company (Ltd)** n (Brit) sociedad f anónima.

limousine [lɪməzɪn] n limusina.

limp [lɪmp] n: **to have a** ~ tener cojera // vi cojear // a flojo.

limpet [lɪmpɪt] n lapa.

line [laɪn] n (gen) línea; (straight ~) raya; (rope) cuerda; (for fishing) sedal m; (wire) hilo; (row, series) fila, hilera; (of writing) renglón m; (on face) arruga; (speciality) rama // vt (SEWING) forrar (with de); **to** ~ **the streets** ocupar las aceras; **in** ~ **with** de acuerdo con; **to** ~ **up** vi hacer cola // vt alinear, poner en fila.

linear [lɪnɪə*] a lineal.

lined [laɪnd] a (face) arrugado; (paper) rayado.

linen ['lɪnɪn] n ropa blanca; (cloth) lino.

liner ['laɪnə*] n vapor m de línea, transatlántico.

linesman ['laɪnzmən] n (SPORT) juez m de línea.

line-up ['laɪnʌp] n alineación f.

linger ['lɪŋgə*] vi retrasarse, tardar en marcharse; (smell, tradition) persistir.

lingerie ['lænʒəriː] n ropa interior (de mujer).

lingo ['lɪŋgəʊ], pl ~es n (pej) jerga.

linguist ['lɪŋgwɪst] n lingüista m/f; ~ic a lingüístico; ~ics n lingüística.

lining ['laɪnɪŋ] n forro.

link [lɪŋk] n (of a chain) eslabón m; (connection) conexión f; (bond) vínculo, lazo // vt vincular, unir; ~s npl (GOLF) campo sg de golf; **to ~ up** vt acoplar // vi unirse; **~-up** n (gen) unión f; (in space) acoplamiento.

lino ['laɪnəʊ], **linoleum** [lɪ'nəʊlɪəm] n linóleo.

lion ['laɪən] n león m; ~ess n leona.

lip [lɪp] n labio; (of jug) pico; (of cup etc) borde m; ~**read** vi leer los labios; ~ **salve** n crema protectora para labios; ~ **service** n: **to pay ~ service to sth** prometer algo de palabra; ~**stick** n lápiz m de labios, carmín m.

liqueur [lɪ'kjuə*] n licor m.

liquid ['lɪkwɪd] a, n líquido.

liquidize ['lɪkwɪdaɪz] vt (CULIN) licuar.

liquidizer ['lɪkwɪdaɪzə*] n licuadora.

liquor ['lɪkə*] n licor m, bebidas fpl alcohólicas.

liquorice ['lɪkərɪs] n regaliz m.

liquor store n (US) bodega, tienda de vinos y bebidas alcohólicas.

Lisbon ['lɪzbən] n Lisboa.

lisp [lɪsp] n ceceo.

list [lɪst] n lista; (of ship) inclinación f // vt (write down) hacer una lista de; (enumerate) catalogar // vi (ship) inclinarse.

listen ['lɪsn] vi escuchar, oír; (pay attention) atender; ~**er** n oyente m/f.

listless ['lɪstlɪs] a apático, indiferente.

lit [lɪt] pt, pp of **light**.

litany ['lɪtənɪ] n letanía.

liter ['liːtə*] n (US) = **litre**.

literacy ['lɪtərəsɪ] n capacidad f de leer y escribir.

literal ['lɪtərəl] a literal.

literary ['lɪtərərɪ] a literario.

literate ['lɪtərət] a que sabe leer y escribir; (fig) culto.

literature ['lɪtrɪtʃə*] n literatura; (brochures etc) folletos mpl.

lithe [laɪð] a ágil.

litigation [lɪtɪ'geɪʃən] n litigio.

litre ['liːtə*] n litro.

litter ['lɪtə*] n (rubbish) basura; (paper) papel m tirado; (young animals) camada, cría; ~ **bin** n (Brit) papelera; ~**ed** a: ~**ed with** (scattered) esparcido con; (covered with) lleno de.

little ['lɪtl] a (small) pequeño; (not much) poco; (often translated by suffix: eg ~ **house** casita) // ad poco; **a ~** un poco (de); **~ by ~** poco a poco.

live [lɪv] vi vivir // vt a (life) llevar; (experience) vivir // a [laɪv] (animal) vivo; (wire) conectado; (broadcast) en directo; (shell) cargado; **to ~ down** vt hacer olvidar; **to ~ on** vt fus (food) vivirse de, alimentarse de; **to ~ together** vi vivir juntos; **to ~ up to** vt fus (fulfil) cumplir con; (justify) justificar.

livelihood ['laɪvlɪhʊd] n sustento.

lively ['laɪvlɪ] a (gen) vivo; (talk) animado; (pace) rápido; (party, tune) alegre.

liven up ['laɪvn-] vt animar.

liver ['lɪvə*] n hígado.

livery ['lɪvərɪ] n librea.

lives [laɪvz] pl of **life**.

livestock ['laɪvstɔk] n ganado.

livid ['lɪvɪd] a lívido; (furious) furioso.

living ['lɪvɪŋ] a (*alive*) vivo // n: to earn or make a ~ ganarse la vida; ~ **conditions** npl condiciones fpl de vida; ~ **room** n sala (de estar); ~ **wage** n sueldo suficiente para vivir.

lizard ['lɪzəd] n lagartija.

load [ləud] n (*gen*) carga; (*weight*) peso // vt (*COMPUT*) cargar; (*also*: ~ **up**): to ~ (**with**) cargar (con or de); a ~ **of**, ~s **of** (*fig*) (gran) cantidad de, montones de; ~**ed** a (*dice*) cargado; (*question*) intencionado; (*col: rich*) forrado (de dinero); ~**ing bay** n área de carga.

loaf [ləuf], pl **loaves** n (barra de) pan m // vi (*also*: ~ **about**, ~ **around**) holgazanear.

loan [ləun] n préstamo; (*COMM*) empréstito // vt prestar; **on** ~ prestado.

loath [ləuθ] a: **to be** ~ **to do sth** estar poco dispuesto a hacer algo.

loathe [ləuð] vt aborrecer; (*person*) odiar; **loathing** n aversión f; odio.

loaves [ləuvz] pl of **loaf**.

lobby ['lɔbɪ] n vestíbulo, sala de espera; (*POL: pressure group*) grupo de presión // vt presionar.

lobe [ləub] n lóbulo.

lobster ['lɔbstə*] n langosta.

local ['ləukl] a local // n (*pub*) bar m; **the** ~**s** los vecinos, los del lugar; ~ **anaesthetic** n (*MED*) anestesia local; ~ **authority** n municipio, ayuntamiento (Sp); ~ **call** n (*TEL*) llamada local; ~ **government** n gobierno municipal; ~**ity** [-'kælɪtɪ] n localidad f; ~**ly** [-kəlɪ] ad en la vecindad.

locate [ləu'keɪt] vt (*find*) localizar; (*situate*) colocar.

location [ləu'keɪʃən] n situación f; **on** ~ (*CINEMA*) en exteriores.

loch [lɔx] n lago.

lock [lɔk] n (*of door, box*) cerradura; (*of canal*) esclusa; (*of hair*) mechón m // vt (*with key*) cerrar con llave; (*immobilize*) inmovilizar // vi (*door etc*) cerrarse con llave; (*wheels*) trabarse.

locker ['lɔkə*] n casillero; ~**room** n (*US SPORT*) vestuario.

locket ['lɔkɪt] n medallón m.

lockout ['lɔkaut] n paro patronal, lockout m.

locksmith ['lɔksmɪθ] n cerrajero/a.

lock-up ['lɔkʌp] n (*garage*) cochera.

locomotive [ləukə'məutɪv] n locomotora.

locum ['ləukəm] n (*MED*) (médico/a) interino/a.

locust ['ləukəst] n langosta.

lodge [lɔdʒ] n casa del guarda; (*porter's*) portería; (*FREEMASONRY*) logia // vi (*person*): to ~ (**with**) alojarse (en casa de) // vt (*complaint*) presentar; ~**r** n huésped/a m/f.

lodgings ['lɔdʒɪŋz] npl alojamiento sg; (*house*) casa sg de huéspedes.

loft [lɔft] n desván m.

lofty ['lɔftɪ] a alto; (*haughty*) orgulloso.

log [lɔg] n (*of wood*) leño, tronco; (*book*) = logbook.

logbook ['lɔgbuk] n (*NAUT*) diario de a bordo; (*AVIAT*) libro de vuelo; (*of car*) documentación f (del coche).

loggerheads ['lɔgəhedz] npl: **at** ~ (**with**) de punta (con).

logic ['lɔdʒɪk] n lógica; ~**al** a lógico.

logo ['ləugəu] n logotipo.

loin [lɔɪn] n (*CULIN*) lomo, solomillo; ~**s** npl lomos mpl.

loiter ['lɔɪtə*] vi vagar; (*pej*) merodear.

loll [lɔl] vi (*also*: ~ **about**) repantigarse.

lollipop ['lɔlɪpɔp] n pirulí m; (*iced*) polo; ~ **man/lady** n (*Brit*) persona encargada de ayudar a los niños a cruzar la calle.

London ['lʌndən] n Londres; ~**er** n londinense m/f.

lone [ləun] a solitario.

loneliness ['ləunlɪnɪs] n soledad f, aislamiento.

lonely ['ləunlɪ] a solitario, solo.

long [lɔŋ] a largo // ad mucho tiempo, largamente // vi: to ~ **for sth** anhelar algo; **in the** ~ **run** a la larga; **as** or **so as** ~ mientras, con tal que; **don't be** ~! ¡no tardes!, ¡vuelve pronto!; **how ~ is the street?** ¿cuánto tiene la calle de largo?; **how ~ is the lesson?** ¿cuánto dura la clase?; **6 metres ~** que mide 6 metros, de 6 metros de largo; **6 months ~** que dura 6 meses, de 6 meses de duración; **all night ~** toda la noche; **he no ~er comes** ya no viene; **~ before** mucho antes; **before ~** (+ *future*) dentro de poco; (+ *past*) poco tiempo después; **at ~ last** al fin, por fin; **~-distance** a (*race*) de larga distancia; (*call*) interurbano; **~-haired** a de pelo largo; **~-hand** n escritura sin abreviaturas; **~-ing** n anhelo, ansia; (*nostalgia*) nostalgia f // a endolante.

longitude ['lɒŋgitjuːd] n longitud f.

long: **~ jump** n salto de longitud; **~-lost** a desaparecido hace mucho tiempo; **~-playing record (L.P.)** n elepé m, disco de larga duración; **~-range** a de gran alcance; **~-sighted** a (*Brit*) présbita; **~-standing** a de mucho tiempo; **~-suffering** a sufrido; **~-term** a a largo plazo; **~ wave** n onda larga; **~-winded** a prolijo.

loo [luː] n (*Brit*: col) wáter m.

look [luk] vi mirar; (*seem*) parecer; (*building etc*): **to ~ south/on to the sea** dar al sur/al mar // vt mirada; (*glance*) vistazo; (*appearance*) aire m, aspecto; **~s** npl físico sg, apariencia sg; **to ~ after** vt fus cuidar; **to ~ at** vt fus mirar; (*consider*) considerar; **to ~ back** vi mirar hacia atrás; **to ~ down on** vt fus (*fig*) despreciar, mirar con desprecio; **to ~ for** vt fus buscar; **to ~ forward to** vt fus esperar con ilusión; (*in letters*): **we ~ forward to hearing from you** quedamos a la espera de sus gratas noticias; **to ~ into** vt investigar; **to ~ on** vi mirar (como espectador); **to ~ out** vi (*beware*): **to ~ out for** vt fus (*seek*) buscar; (*await*) esperar; **to ~ round** vi volver la cabeza; **to ~ up** vt fus ocu-

parse de; (*rely on*) contar con; **to ~ up** vi mirar hacia arriba; (*improve*) mejorar // vt (*word*) buscar; (*friend*) visitar; **to ~ up to** vt fus admirar; **~-out** n (*tower etc*) puesto de observación; (*person*) vigía m/f; **to be on the ~-out for sth** estar al acecho de algo.

loom [luːm] n telar m // vi (*threaten*) amenazar.

loony ['luːni] n (col) loco/a.

loop [luːp] n lazo; (*bend*) vuelta, recodo; **~hole** n escapatoria.

loose [luːs] a (*gen*) suelto; (*not tight*) flojo; (*wobbly etc*) movedizo; (*clothes*) ancho; (*morals, discipline*) relajado; **to be at a ~ end** or (*US*) **at ~ ends** no saber qué hacer; **to change ~** cambio; **~ chippings** npl (*on road*) gravilla sg suelta; **~ly** ad libremente, aproximadamente; **~n** vt (*free*) soltar; (*untie*) desatar; (*slacken*) aflojar.

loot [luːt] n botín m // vt saquear.

lop [lɒp]: **to ~ off** vt cortar; (*branches*) podar.

lop-sided ['lɒp'saidid] a desequilibrado.

lord [lɔːd] n señor m; **L~ Smith** Lord Smith; **the L~** el Señor; **the (House of) L~s** (*Brit*) la Cámara de los Lores; **~ship** n: **your L~ship** su Señoría.

lore [lɔː*] n tradiciones fpl.

lorry ['lɒri] n (*Brit*) camión m; **~ driver** n camionero/a.

lose [luːz], pt, pp **lost** vt perder // vi perder, ser vencido; **to ~ (time)** (*clock*) atrasarse; **~r** n perdedor/a m/f.

loss [lɒs] n pérdida; **heavy ~es** (*MIL*) grandes pérdidas; **to be at a ~** no saber qué hacer; **to make a ~** sufrir pérdidas.

lost [lɒst] pt, pp of **lose** // a perdido; **~ property**, (*US*) **~ and found** n objetos mpl perdidos.

lot [lɒt] n (*at auctions*) lote m; (*destiny*) suerte f; **the ~** el todo, todos; **a ~** mucho, bastante; **a ~ of**, **~s of**

mucho(s) (pl); I read a ~ leo bastante; to draw ~s (for sth) echar suertes (para decidir algo).

lotion ['ləʊʃən] n loción f.

lottery ['lɒtərɪ] n lotería.

loud [laʊd] a (voice, sound) fuerte; (laugh, shout) estrepitoso; (gaudy) chillón/ona // ad (speak etc) en alta voz; ~**hailer** n (Brit) megáfono; ~**ly** ad (noisily) fuerte; (aloud) en alta voz; ~**speaker** n altavoz m.

lounge [laʊndʒ] n salón m, sala (de estar) // vi reposar, holgazanear; ~ **suit** n (Brit) traje m de calle.

louse [laʊs], pl **lice** n piojo.

lousy ['laʊzɪ] a (fig) vil, asqueroso.

lout [laʊt] n gamberro m.

louvre, (US) **louver** ['luːvə'] a (door) de rejilla; (window) de libro.

lovable ['lʌvəbl] a amable, simpático.

love [lʌv] n amor m // vt amar, querer; to ~ to do encantarle a uno hacer; to be in ~ with estar enamorado de; to make ~ hacer el amor; for the ~ of por amor de; '15 ~' (TENNIS) 15 a cero; I ~ paella me encanta la paella; ~ **affair** n aventura sentimental; ~ **letter** n carta de amor; ~ **life** n vida sentimental.

lovely ['lʌvlɪ] a (delightful) precioso, encantador(a); (beautiful) hermoso.

lover ['lʌvə'] n amante m/f; (amateur): a ~ of un aficionado/a or un amante de.

loving ['lʌvɪŋ] a amoroso, cariñoso.

low [ləʊ] a, ad bajo // n (METEOROLOGY) área de baja presión // vi (cow) mugir; to feel ~ sentirse deprimido; to turn (down) ~ bajar; ~**-cut** a (dress) escotado.

lower ['ləʊə'] vt bajar; (reduce) reducir // vr: to ~ o.s. (fig) rebajarse a.

low: ~**-fat** a (milk, yoghurt) bajo en calorías; (diet) bajo en calorías; ~**lands** npl (GEO) tierras fpl bajas; ~**ly** a humilde; ~**-lying** a bajo.

loyal ['lɔɪəl] a leal; ~**ty** n lealtad f.

lozenge ['lɒzɪndʒ] n (MED) pastilla.

L.P. n abbr = **long-playing record.**

L-plates ['elpleɪts] npl (Brit) placas de aprendiz de conductor.

Ltd abbr (= limited company) S.A.

lubricant n lubricante m.

lubricate ['luːbrɪkeɪt] vt lubricar, engrasar.

lucid ['luːsɪd] a lúcido.

luck [lʌk] n suerte f; **bad** ~ mala suerte; **good** ~! ¡que tengas suerte!, ¡suerte!; ~**ily** ad afortunadamente; ~**y** a afortunado.

ludicrous ['luːdɪkrəs] a absurdo.

lug [lʌg] vt (drag) arrastrar.

luggage ['lʌgɪdʒ] n equipaje m; ~ **rack** n (in train) rejilla, redecilla; (on car) baca, portaequipajes m inv.

lukewarm ['luːkwɔːm] a tibio, templado.

lull [lʌl] n tregua // vt (child) acunar; (person, fear) calmar.

lullaby ['lʌləbaɪ] n nana.

lumbago [lʌm'beɪgəʊ] n lumbago.

lumber ['lʌmbə'] n (junk) trastos mpl viejos; (wood) maderos mpl; ~**jack** n maderero.

luminous ['luːmɪnəs] a luminoso.

lump [lʌmp] n terrón m; (fragment) trozo; (in sauce) grumo; (in throat) nudo; (swelling) bulto // vt (also: ~ **together**) juntar; ~ **sum** n suma global.

lunacy ['luːnəsɪ] n locura.

lunar ['luːnə'] a lunar.

lunatic ['luːnətɪk] a, n loco/a; ~ **asylum** n manicomio.

lunch [lʌntʃ] n almuerzo, comida // vi almorzar.

luncheon ['lʌntʃən] n almuerzo; ~ **meat** n tipo de fiambre; ~ **voucher** n vale m de comida.

lung [lʌŋ] n pulmón m.

lunge [lʌndʒ] vi (also: ~ **forward**) abalanzarse; to ~ at arremeter contra.

lurch [ləːtʃ] vi dar sacudidas // n sacudida; to leave sb in the ~ dejar a uno plantado.

lure [luə'] n (bait) cebo; (decoy) se-

ñuelo // vt convencer con engaños.
lurid ['luərɪd] a (colour) chillón/ona;
(account) sensacional; (detail) horripilante.
lurk [lɜːk] vi (hide) esconderse;
(wait) estar al acecho.
luscious ['lʌʃəs] a delicioso.
lush [lʌʃ] a exuberante.
lust [lʌst] n lujuria; (greed) codicia;
to ~ after vt fus codiciar.
lustre, (US) **luster** ['lʌstə*] n lustre
m, brillo.
lusty ['lʌstɪ] a robusto, fuerte.
Luxembourg ['lʌksəmbɜːg] n
Luxemburgo.
luxuriant [lʌg'zjuərɪənt] a exuberante.
luxurious [lʌg'zjuərɪəs] a lujoso.
luxury ['lʌkʃərɪ] n lujo // cpd de lujo.
lying ['laɪɪŋ] n mentiras fpl.
lyric ['lɪrɪk] a lírico; **~s** npl (of song)
letra sg; **~al** a lírico.

M

m. abbr = metre; mile; million.
M.A. abbr = Master of Arts.
mac [mæk] n (Brit) impermeable m.
macaroni [mækə'rəunɪ] n macarrones mpl.
mace [meɪs] n (weapon, ceremonial)
maza; (spice) macis f.
machine [mə'ʃiːn] n máquina // vt
(dress etc) coser a máquina; **~ gun**
n ametralladora; **~ language** n
(COMPUT) lenguaje m máquina;
~ry n maquinaria; (fig) mecanismo.
mackerel ['mækrl] n, pl inv caballa.
mackintosh ['mækɪntɔʃ] n (Brit)
impermeable m.
mad [mæd] a loco; (idea) disparatado; (angry) furioso.
madam ['mædəm] n señora.
madden ['mædn] vt volver loco.
made [meɪd] pt, pp of **make**.
Madeira [mə'dɪərə] n (GEO) Madera; (wine) vino de Madera.
made-to-measure ['meɪdtəmɛʒə*]
a (Brit) hecho a la medida.

madly ['mædlɪ] ad locamente.
madman ['mædmən] n loco.
madness ['mædnɪs] n locura.
Madrid [mə'drɪd] n Madrid.
Mafia ['mæfɪə] n Mafia.
magazine [mægə'ziːn] n revista;
(MIL: store) almacén m; (of
firearm) recámara.
maggot ['mægət] n gusano.
magic ['mædʒɪk] n magia // a mágico; **~al** a mágico; **~ian** [mə'dʒɪʃən]
n mago/a; (conjurer) prestidigita-
dor(a) m/f.
magistrate ['mædʒɪstreɪt] n juez m/f
(municipal).
magnet ['mægnɪt] n imán m; **~ic**
[-'nɛtɪk] a magnético.
magnificent [mæg'nɪfɪsnt] a magnífico.
magnify ['mægnɪfaɪ] vt aumentar;
(fig) exagerar; **~ing glass** n lupa.
magnitude ['mægnɪtjuːd] n magnitud f.
magpie ['mægpaɪ] n urraca.
mahogany [mə'hɒgənɪ] n caoba //
cpd de caoba.
maid [meɪd] n criada; **old ~** (pej)
solterona.
maiden ['meɪdn] n doncella // a (aunt
etc) soltera; (speech, voyage)
inaugural; **~ name** n nombre m de
soltera.
mail [meɪl] n correo; (letters) cartas
fpl // vt (post) echar al correo;
(send) mandar por correo; **~box** n
(US) buzón m; **~ing list** n lista de
direcciones; **~-order** n pedido
postal; (business) venta por correo.
maim [meɪm] vt mutilar, lisiar.
main [meɪn] a principal, mayor // n
(pipe) cañería maestra; (US) red f
eléctrica; **the ~s** (Brit ELEC) la red
eléctrica; **in the ~** en general;
~frame n (COMPUT) ordenador m
central; **~land** n continente m; **~ly**
ad principalmente; **~ road** n carretera; **~stay** n (fig) pilar m;
~stream n corriente f principal; **~
street** n calle f mayor.
maintain [meɪn'teɪn] vt mantener;

(affirm) sostener; **maintenance** ['meintənəns] n mantenimiento; (alimony) pensión f alimenticia.

maize [meiz] n (Brit) maíz m, choclo (LAm).

majestic [mə'dʒestik] a majestuoso.

majesty ['mædʒisti] n majestad f.

major ['meidʒə*] n (MIL) comandante m // a principal; (MUS) mayor.

Majorca [mə'jɔːkə] n Mallorca.

majority [mə'dʒɔriti] n mayoría.

make [meik] vt (pt, pp made) hacer; (manufacture) hacer, fabricar; (cause to be): to ~ sb sad hacer or poner triste a alguien; (force): to ~ sb do sth obligar a alguien a hacer algo; (equal): 2 and 2 ~ 4 2 y 2 son 4 // n marca; to ~ a fool of sb poner a alguien en ridículo; to ~ a profit/loss obtener ganancias/sufrir pérdidas; to ~ it (arrive) llegar; (achieve sth) tener éxito; what time do you ~ it? ¿qué hora tienes?; to ~ do with contentarse con; to ~ for vt fus (place) dirigirse a; to ~ out vt (decipher) descifrar; (understand) entender; (see) distinguir; (write: cheque) extender; to ~ up vt (invent) inventar; (parcel) hacer // vi reconciliarse; (with cosmetics) maquillarse; to ~ up for vt fus compensar; ~-believe n ficción f, invención f; ~r n fabricante m/f; ~shift a improvisado; ~-up n maquillaje m; ~-up remover n desmaquillador m.

making ['meikiŋ] n (fig) in the ~ en vías de formación; to have the ~s of (person) tener madera de.

malaise [mæ'leiz] n malestar m.

malaria [mə'leəriə] n malaria.

Malaya [mə'leiə] n Malaya, Malaca.

Malaysia [mə'leiziə] n Malasia.

male [meil] n (BIOL, ELEC) macho // a (sex, attitude) masculino; (child etc) varón.

malevolent [mə'levələnt] a malévolo.

malfunction [mæl'fʌŋkʃən] n mal funcionamiento.

malice ['mælis] n (ill will) malicia; (rancour) rencor m; **malicious** [mə'liʃəs] a malicioso; rencoroso.

malign [mə'lain] vt difamar, calumniar // a maligno.

malignant [mə'lignənt] a (MED) maligno.

mall [mɔːl] n (US: also: **shopping** ~) centro comercial.

malleable ['mæliəbl] a maleable.

mallet ['mælit] n mazo.

malnutrition [mælnjuː'triʃən] n desnutrición f.

malpractice [mæl'præktis] n negligencia profesional.

malt [mɔːlt] n malta.

Malta ['mɔːltə] n Malta.

maltreat [mæl'triːt] vt maltratar.

mammal ['mæml] n mamífero.

mammoth ['mæməθ] n mamut m // a gigantesco.

man [mæn], pl **men** n hombre m; (CHESS) pieza f // vt (NAUT) tripular; (MIL) guarnecer; an **old** ~ un viejo; ~ **and wife** marido y mujer.

manage ['mænidʒ] vi arreglárselas, ir tirando // vt (be in charge of) dirigir; (person etc) manejar; ~**able** a manejable; ~**ment** n dirección f, administración f; ~**r** n director m; (SPORT) entrenador m; ~**ress** n directora; (SPORT) entrenadora; ~**rial** [-ə'dʒiəriəl] a directivo; **managing director** n director(a) m/f general.

mandarin ['mændərin] n (also: ~ orange) mandarina.

mandate ['mændeit] n mandato.

mandatory ['mændətəri] a obligatorio.

mane [mein] n (of horse) crin f; (of lion) melena.

maneuver [mə'nuːvə*] (US) = **manoeuvre**.

manfully ['mænfəli] ad valientemente.

mangle ['mæŋgl] vt mutilar, destrozar // n rodillo.

mango ['mæŋgəu], pl ~**es** n mango.

mangy ['meindʒi] a roñoso; (MED) sarnoso.

manhandle ['mænhændl] vt maltratar.

manhood ['mænhud] n edad f viril; virilidad f.

man-hour ['mæn'auə*] n horahombre f.

mania ['meiniə] n manía; **~c** ['meiniæk] n maníaco/a; (fig) maniático.

manic ['mænik] a (behaviour, activity) frenético; **~-depressive** n maníaco/a depresivo/a.

manicure ['mænikjuə*] n manicura; **~ set** n estuche m de manicura.

manifest ['mænifest] vt manifestar, mostrar // a manifiesto.

manifesto [mæni'festəu] n manifiesto.

manipulate [mə'nipjuleit] vt manipular.

mankind [mæn'kaind] n humanidad f, género humano.

manly ['mænli] a varonil.

man-made ['mæn'meid] a artificial.

manner ['mænə*] n manera, modo; (behaviour) conducta, manera de ser; (type) clase f; **~s** npl modales mpl, educación fsg; **bad ~s** mala educación; **~ism** n peculiaridad f de lenguaje (or de comportamiento).

manoeuvre, (US) **maneuver** [mə'nu:və*] vt, vi maniobrar // n maniobra.

manor ['mænə*] n (also: **~ house**) casa solariega.

manpower ['mænpauə*] n mano f de obra.

mansion ['mænʃən] n palacio, casa grande.

manslaughter ['mænslɔ:tə*] n homicidio no premeditado.

mantelpiece ['mæntlpi:s] n repisa, chimenea.

manual ['mænjuəl] a manual // n manual m.

manufacture [mænju'fæktʃə*] vt fabricar // n fabricación f; **~r** n fabricante m/f.

manure [mə'njuə*] n estiércol m, abono.

manuscript ['mænjuskript] n manuscrito.

many ['meni] a muchos/as // pron muchos/as; **a great ~** muchísimos, buen número de; **~ a time** muchas veces.

map [mæp] n mapa m // vt trazar el mapa de; **to ~ out** vt proyectar.

maple ['meipl] n arce m, maple m (LAm).

mar [ma:*] vt estropear.

marathon ['mærəθən] n maratón m.

marauder [mə'rɔ:də*] n merodeador(a) m/f; intruso/a.

marble ['ma:bl] n mármol m; (toy) canica.

March [ma:tʃ] n marzo.

march [ma:tʃ] vi (MIL) marchar; (fig) caminar con resolución // n marcha; (demonstration) manifestación f; **~past** n desfile m.

mare [meə*] n yegua.

margarine [ma:dʒə'ri:n] n margarina.

margin ['ma:dʒin] n margen m; **~al** a marginal; **~al seat** n (POL) escaño electoral difícil de asegurar.

marigold ['mærigəuld] n caléndula.

marijuana [mæri'wa:nə] n marijuana.

marinate ['mærineit] vt adobar.

marine [mə'ri:n] a marino // n soldado de marina.

marital ['mæritl] a matrimonial; **~ status** estado civil.

maritime ['mæritaim] a marítimo.

marjoram ['ma:dʒərəm] n mejorana.

mark [ma:k] n marca, señal f; (imprint) huella; (stain) mancha; (Brit SCOL) nota; (currency) marco // vt marcar; manchar; (Brit SCOL) calificar, corregir; **to ~ time** marcar el paso; **to ~ out** vt trazar; **~ed** a marcado, acusado; **~er** n (sign) marcador m; (bookmark) registro.

market ['ma:kit] n mercado // vt (COMM) comercializar; **~ garden** n (Brit) huerto; **~ing** n márketing m, mercadotecnia; **~place** n mercado; **~ research** n (COMM) análisis *inv* de mercados; ~ **value** *n* valor *m* en el mercado.

marksman ['mɑːksmən] *n* tirador *m*.

marmalade ['mɑːməleɪd] *n* mermelada de naranja.

maroon [mə'ruːn] *vt* (*fig*): to be ~ed (*in or at*) quedar bloqueado (en) // *a* marrón.

marquee [mɑː'kiː] *n* entoldado.

marriage ['mærɪdʒ] *n* (*state*) matrimonio; (*wedding*) boda; (*act*) casamiento; ~ **bureau** *n* agencia matrimonial; ~ **certificate** *n* partida de casamiento.

married ['mærɪd] *a* casado; (*life, love*) conyugal.

marrow ['mærəu] *n* médula; (*vegetable*) calabacín *m*.

marry ['mærɪ] *vt* casarse con; (*subj: father, priest etc*) casar // *vi* (*also: get married*) casarse.

Mars [mɑːz] *n* Marte *m*.

marsh [mɑːʃ] *n* pantano; (*salt* ~) marisma.

marshal ['mɑːʃl] *n* (*MIL*) mariscal *m*; (*at sports meeting etc*) oficial *m*; (*US: of police, fire department*) jefe/a // *vt* (*facts*) ordenar; (*soldiers*) formar.

marshy ['mɑːʃɪ] *a* pantanoso.

martial ['mɑːʃl] *a* marcial; ~ **law** *n* ley *f* marcial.

martyr ['mɑːtə*] *n* mártir *m/f* // *vt* martirizar; ~**dom** *n* martirio.

marvel ['mɑːvl] *n* maravilla, prodigio // *vi*: to ~ (**at**) maravillarse (de); ~**lous**, (*US*) ~**ous** *a* maravilloso.

Marxist ['mɑːksɪst] *a, n* marxista *m/f*.

marzipan ['mɑːzɪpæn] *n* mazapán *m*.

mascara [mæs'kɑːrə] *n* rímel *m*.

masculine ['mæskjulɪn] *a* masculino.

mash [mæʃ] *n* (*mix*) mezcla; (*pulp*) amasijo; ~**ed potatoes** *npl* puré *m* de patatas or papas (*LAm*).

mask [mɑːsk] *n* máscara // *vt* enmascarar.

masochist ['mæsəkɪst] *n* masoquista *m/f*.

mason ['meɪsn] *n* (*also:* **stone~**) al-

bañil *m*; (*also:* **free~**) masón *m*; ~**ic** [mə'sɒnɪk] *a* masónico; ~**ry** *n* masonería; (*in building*) mampostería.

masquerade [mæskə'reɪd] *n* baile *m* de máscaras; (*fig*) mascarada // *vi*: to ~ as disfrazarse de, hacerse pasar por.

mass [mæs] *n* (*people*) muchedumbre *f*; (*PHYSICS*) masa; (*REL*) misa; (*great quantity*) montón *m* // *vi* reunirse; (*MIL*) concentrarse; **the** ~**es** las masas.

massacre ['mæsəkə*] *n* masacre *f*.

massage ['mæsɑːʒ] *n* masaje *m* // *vt* dar masaje a.

masseur [mæ'səː*] *n* masajista *m*; **masseuse** [-'səːz] *n* masajista *f*.

massive ['mæsɪv] *a* enorme; (*support, intervention*) masivo.

mass media *npl* medios *mpl* de comunicación masiva.

mass-production ['mæsprə'dʌkʃən] *n* fabricación *f* en serie.

mast [mɑːst] *n* (*NAUT*) mástil *m*; (*RADIO etc*) torre *f*.

master ['mɑːstə*] *n* maestro; (*in secondary school*) profesor *m*; (*title for boys*): **M**~ **X** Señorito X // *vt* dominar; (*learn*) aprender a fondo; **M**~ **of Arts/Science (M.A./M.Sc.)** *n* licenciatura superior en Letras/Ciencias; ~ **key** *n* llave *f* maestra; ~**ly** *a* magistral; ~**mind** *n* inteligencia superior // *vt* dirigir, planear; ~**piece** *n* obra maestra; ~**y** *n* maestría.

mat [mæt] *n* estera; (*also:* **door~**) felpudo // *a* = **matt**.

match [mætʃ] *n* cerilla, fósforo; (*game*) partido; (*fig*) igual *m/f* // *vt* emparejar; (*go well with*) hacer juego con; (*equal*) igualar // *vi* hacer juego; to be a good ~ hacer buena pareja; ~**box** *n* caja de cerillas; ~**ing** *a* que hace juego.

mate [meɪt] *n* (*work~*) colega *m/f*; (*col: friend*) amigo/a; (*animal*) macho/m/hembra *f*; (*in merchant navy*) segundo de a bordo // *vi* acoplarse, parearse // vt acoplar, parear.

material [mə'tɪərɪəl] n (substance) materia; (equipment) material m; (cloth) tela, tejido // a (important) esencial; ~s npl materiales mpl.

maternal [mə'tə:nl] a maternal.

maternity [mə'tə:nɪtɪ] n maternidad f; ~ dress n vestido premamá; ~ hospital n hospital m de maternidad.

math [mæθ] n (US) = maths.

mathematical [mæθə'mætɪkl] a matemático.

mathematician [mæθəmə'tɪʃən] n matemático/a.

mathematics [mæθə'mætɪks], **maths** [mæθs], (US) **math** [mæθ] n matemáticas fpl.

matinée ['mætɪneɪ] n función f de la tarde.

mating ['meɪtɪŋ] n aparejamiento; ~ call n llamada del macho.

matrices ['meɪtrɪsiːz] pl of matrix.

matrimonial [mætrɪ'məunɪəl] a matrimonial.

matrimony ['mætrɪmənɪ] n matrimonio.

matrix ['meɪtrɪks], pl matrices n matriz f.

matron ['meɪtrən] n (in hospital) enfermera f jefe; (in school) ama de llaves; ~ly a de matrona; (fig: figure) corpulento.

mat(t) [mæt] a mate.

matted ['mætɪd] a enmarañado.

matter ['mætə*] n cuestión f, asunto; (PHYSICS) sustancia, materia; (content) contenido; (MED: pus) pus m // vi importar; it doesn't ~ no importa; what's the ~? ¿qué pasa?; no ~ what pase lo que pase; as a ~ of course por rutina; as a ~ of fact de hecho; ~-of-fact a prosaico, práctico.

mattress ['mætrɪs] n colchón m.

mature [mə'tjuə*] a maduro // vi madurar; **maturity** n madurez f.

maul [mɔːl] vt magullar.

mauve [məuv] a de color malva or

guinda (LAm).

maxim ['mæksɪm] n máxima.

maximum ['mæksɪməm] a máximo // n (pl maxima ['mæksɪmə]) máximo.

May [meɪ] n mayo.

may [meɪ] vi (conditional: might) (indicating possibility): he ~ come puede que venga; (be allowed to): ~ I smoke? ¿puedo fumar?; (wishes): ~ God bless you! ¡que Dios te bendiga!

maybe ['meɪbɪ] ad quizá(s).

May Day n el primero de Mayo.

mayday ['meɪdeɪ] n S.O.S. m.

mayhem ['meɪhɛm] n caos m total.

mayonnaise [meɪə'neɪz] n mayonesa.

mayor [mɛə*] n alcalde m; ~ess n alcaldesa.

maze [meɪz] n laberinto.

M.D. abbr = Doctor of Medicine.

me [miː] pron (direct) me; (stressed, after pronoun) mí; can you hear ~? ¿me oyes?; he heard ME! me oyó a mí; it's ~ soy yo; give them to ~ dámelos (or dámelas); with/without ~ conmigo/sin mí.

meadow ['mɛdəu] n prado, pradera.

meagre, (US) **meager** ['miːgə*] a escaso, pobre.

meal [miːl] n comida; (flour) harina; ~time n hora de comer.

mean [miːn] vi (with money) tacaño; (unkind) mezquino, malo; (average) medio // vt (pt, pp meant) (signify) querer decir, significar; (intend): to ~ to do sth pensar or pretender hacer algo // n medio, término medio; ~s npl medio sg, manera sg; (resource) recursos mpl, medios mpl; by ~s of mediante, por medio de; by all ~s! ¡naturalmente!, ¡claro que sí!; do you ~ it? ¿lo dices en serio?; what do you ~? ¿qué quiere decir?; to be meant for sb/sth ser para uno/algo.

meander [mɪ'ændə*] vi (river) serpentear; (person) vagar.

meaning ['miːnɪŋ] n significado, sentido; ~ful a significativo; ~less sin sentido.

meanness ['mi:nnıs] n (with money) tacañería; (unkindness) maldad f, mezquindad f.

meant [ment] pt, pp of **mean**.

meantime ['mi:ntaım], **meanwhile** ['mi:nwaıl] ad (also: **in the ~**) mientras tanto.

measles ['mi:zlz] n sarampión m.

measly ['mi:zlı] a (col) miserable.

measure ['mɛʒə*] vt medir; (for clothes etc) tomar las medidas a // vi medir // n medida; (ruler) regla; **~ments** npl medidas fpl.

meat [mi:t] n carne f; **cold ~** fiambre m; **~ball** n albóndiga; **~ pie** n pastel m de carne; **~y** a carnoso; (fig) sustancioso.

Mecca ['mɛkə] n La Meca.

mechanic [mı'kænık] n mecánico/a; **~s** n mecánica // npl mecanismo sg; **~al** a mecánico.

mechanism ['mɛkənızəm] n mecanismo.

medal ['mɛdl] n medalla; **~lion** [mı'dælıən] n medallón m; **~list**, (US) **~ist** n (SPORT) medallero/a.

meddle ['mɛdl] vi: to ~ **in** entrometerse en; to ~ **with sth** manosear algo.

media ['mi:dıə] npl medios mpl de comunicación.

mediaeval [mɛdı'i:vl] a = **medieval**.

median ['mi:dıən] n (US: also: ~ **strip**) mediana.

mediate ['mi:dıeıt] vi mediar; **mediator** n intermediario/a, mediador/a m/f.

Medicaid ['mɛdıkeıd] n (US) programa de ayuda médica.

medical ['mɛdıkl] a médico // n reconocimiento médico.

Medicare ['mɛdıkɛə*] n (US) seguro médico del Estado.

medicated ['mɛdıkeıtıd] a medicinal.

medicine ['mɛdsın] n medicina; (drug) medicamento.

medieval [mɛdı'i:vl] a medieval.

mediocre [mi:dı'əukə*] a mediocre.

meditate ['mɛdıteıt] vi meditar.

Mediterranean [mɛdıtə'reınıən] a mediterráneo; the ~ **(Sea)** el (Mar) Mediterráneo.

medium ['mi:dıəm] a mediano, regular // n (pl **media**: means) medio; (pl **mediums**: person) médium m/f; **happy ~** justo medio; **~ wave** n onda media.

medley ['mɛdlı] n mezcla; (MUS) popurrí m.

meek [mi:k] a manso, sumiso.

meet [mi:t], pt, pp **met** vt encontrar; (accidentally) encontrarse con, tropezar con; (for the arrangement) reunirse con; (for the first time) conocer; (go and fetch) ir a buscar; (opponent) enfrentarse con; (obligations) cumplir // vi encontrarse; (in session) reunirse; (join: objects) unirse; (get to know) conocerse; to ~ **with** vi fus reunirse con; (difficulty) tropezar con; **~ing** n encuentro; (arranged) cita, compromiso (LAm); (session, business ~) reunión f; (POL) mitin m.

megabyte ['mɛgə'baıt] n (COMPUT) megabyte m, megaocteto.

megaphone ['mɛgəfəun] n megáfono.

melancholy ['mɛlənkəlı] n melancolía // a melancólico.

mellow ['mɛləu] a (wine) añejo; (sound, colour) suave; (fruit) maduro // vi (person) ablandar.

melody ['mɛlədı] n melodía.

melon ['mɛlən] n melón m.

melt [mɛlt] vi (metal) fundirse; (snow) derretirse; (fig) ablandarse // vt (also: ~ **down**) fundir; to ~ **away** vi desvanecerse; **~down** n (in nuclear reactor) fusión f de un reactor (nuclear); **~ing point** n punto de fusión; **~ing pot** n (fig) crisol m.

member ['mɛmbə*] n (gen) miembro; (of club) socio/a; **M~ of Parliament** (MP) (Brit) diputado/a; **M~ of the European Parliament**

(MEP) (Brit) eurodiputado/a; **~ship** n (members) número de miembros; **to seek ~ship of** pedir el ingreso a; **~ship card** carnet m de socio.

memento [mə'mentəu] n recuerdo.

memo ['meməu] n apunte m, nota.

memoirs ['memwɑːz] npl memorias fpl.

memorandum [memə'rændəm], pl **-da** [-də] n apunte m, nota; (POL) memorándum m.

memorial [mɪ'mɔːrɪəl] n monumento conmemorativo // a conmemorativo.

memorize ['meməraɪz] vt aprender de memoria.

memory ['meməri] n memoria; (recollection) recuerdo.

men [men] pl of **man**.

menace ['menəs] n amenaza // vt amenazar; **menacing** a amenazador(a).

menagerie [mɪ'nædʒərɪ] n casa de fieras.

mend [mend] vt reparar, arreglar; (darn) zurcir // vi reponerse // n (gen) remiendo; (darn) zurcido; **to be on the ~** ir mejorando; **~ing** n reparación f; (clothes) ropa por remendar.

menial ['miːnɪəl] a doméstico; (pej) bajo.

meningitis [menɪn'dʒaɪtɪs] n meningitis f.

menopause ['menəupɔːz] n menopausia.

menstruation [menstru'eɪʃən] n menstruación f.

mental ['mentl] a mental; **~ity** [-'tælɪtɪ] n mentalidad f.

mention ['menʃən] n mención f // vt mencionar; (speak of) hablar de; **don't ~ it!** ¡de nada!

mentor ['mentɔː*] n mentor m.

menu ['menjuː] n (set ~) menú m; (printed) carta; (COMPUT) menú m.

MEP n abbr = **Member of the European Parliament.**

mercenary ['məːsɪnəri] a, n mercenario.

merchandise ['məːtʃəndaɪz] n mercancías fpl.

merchant ['məːtʃənt] n comerciante m/f; **~ bank** n (Brit) banco comercial; **~ navy**, (US) **~ marine** n marina mercante.

merciful ['məːsɪful] a compasivo.

merciless ['məːsɪlɪs] a despiadado.

mercury ['məːkjurɪ] n mercurio.

mercy ['məːsɪ] n compasión f; (REL) misericordia; **at the ~ of** a la merced de.

mere [mɪə*] a simple, mero; **~ly** ad simplemente, sólo.

merge [məːdʒ] vt (join) unir; (mix) mezclar; (fuse) fundir // vi unirse; **~r** n (COMM) fusión f.

meringue [mə'ræŋ] n merengue m.

merit ['merɪt] n mérito // vt merecer.

mermaid ['məːmeɪd] n sirena.

merry ['merɪ] a alegre; **M~ Christmas!** ¡Felices Pascuas!; **~-go-round** n tiovivo.

mesh [meʃ] n malla; (TECH) engranaje m // vi (gears) engranar.

mesmerize ['mezməraɪz] vt hipnotizar.

mess [mes] n (of objects) revoltijo; (tangle) lío; (MIL) comedor m; **to ~ about** or **around** vi (col) perder el tiempo; (pass the time) entretenerse; **to ~ about** or **around with** vt fus (col: play with) divertirse con; (: handle) manosear; **to ~ up** vt (disarrange) desordenar; (spoil) estropear; (dirty) ensuciar.

message ['mesɪdʒ] n recado, mensaje m.

messenger ['mesɪndʒə*] n mensajero/a.

Messrs abbr (on letters: = Messieurs) Sres.

messy ['mesɪ] a (dirty) sucio; (untidy) desordenado.

met [met] pt, pp of **meet**.

metabolism [me'tæbəlɪzəm] n metabolismo.

metal ['metl] n metal m; **~lic** [-'tælɪk] a metálico; **~lurgy**

[-'tælədʒɪ] n metalurgia.

metaphor ['metəfə*] n metáfora.

mete [miːt]: to ~ out vt fus (punishment) imponer.

meteor ['miːtɪə*] n meteoro; ~**ite** [-aɪt] n meteorito.

meteorology [miːtɪə'rɔlədʒɪ] n meteorología.

meter ['miːtə*] n (instrument) contador m; (US: unit) = **metre** // vt (US POST) franquear.

method ['meθəd] n método; ~**ical** [mɪ'θɔdɪkl] a metódico.

Methodist ['meθədɪst] a, n metodista m/f.

meths [meθs], **methylated spirit** ['meθɪleɪtɪd-] n (Brit) alcohol m metilado or desnaturalizado.

metre, (US) **meter** ['miːtə*] n metro.

metric ['metrɪk] a métrico.

metropolis [mɪ'trɔpəlɪs] n metrópoli f.

metropolitan [metrə'pɔlɪtən] a metropolitano; the M~ **Police** n (Brit) la policía londinense.

mettle ['metl] n valor m, ánimo.

mew [mjuː] vi (cat) maullar.

mews [mjuːz] n: ~ **cottage** (Brit) casa acondicionada en antiguos establos o cocheras.

Mexican ['meksɪkən] a, n mejicano/a m/f, mexicano/a m/f (LAm).

Mexico ['meksɪkəu] n Méjico, México (LAm); ~ **City** n Ciudad f de Méjico or México (LAm).

mezzanine ['metsəniːn] n entresuelo.

miaow [miː'au] vi maullar.

mice [maɪs] pl of **mouse**.

micro... [maɪkrəu] pref micro...

microbe ['maɪkrəub] n microbio.

micro: ~**chip** n microplaqueta; ~ **(computer)** n microordenador m; ~**cosm** n microcosmo; ~**phone** n micrófono; ~**processor** n microprocesador m; ~**scope** n microscopio; ~**wave** n (also: ~**wave oven**) horno microondas.

mid [mɪd] a: in ~ May a mediados de mayo; in ~ afternoon a media

tarde; in ~ air en el aire; ~**day** n mediodía m.

middle ['mɪdl] n medio, centro; (waist) cintura // a de en medio; in the ~ of the night en plena noche; ~**aged** a de mediana edad; the M~ **Ages** npl la Edad Media; ~**class** a de clase media; the ~**class(es)** n(pl) la clase media; M~ **East** n Oriente m Medio; ~**man** n intermediario; ~ **name** n segundo nombre; ~**weight** n (BOXING) peso medio.

middling ['mɪdlɪŋ] a mediano.

midge [mɪdʒ] n mosca.

midget ['mɪdʒɪt] n enano/a.

Midlands ['mɪdləndz] npl la región central de Inglaterra.

midnight ['mɪdnaɪt] n medianoche f.

midriff ['mɪdrɪf] n diafragma m.

midst [mɪdst] n: in the ~ of en medio de.

midsummer [mɪd'sʌmə*] n: in ~ en pleno verano.

midway [mɪd'weɪ] a, ad: ~ (between) a medio camino (entre).

midweek [mɪd'wiːk] ad entre semana.

midwife ['mɪdwaɪf], pl -**wives** [-waɪvz] n comadrona, partera; ~**ry** [-wɪfərɪ] n partería.

midwinter [mɪd'wɪntə*] n: in ~ en pleno invierno.

might [maɪt] vb see **may**: he ~ be there podría estar allí, puede que esté allí; I ~ as well go lo más vale que vaya; you ~ like to try podría intentar // n fuerza, poder m; ~**y** a fuerte, poderoso.

migraine ['miːgreɪn] n jaqueca.

migrant ['maɪgrənt] n a (bird) migratorio; (worker) emigrante.

migrate [maɪ'greɪt] vi emigrar.

mike [maɪk] n abbr (= microphone) micro.

mild [maɪld] n (person) apacible; (climate) templado; (slight) ligero; (taste) suave; (illness) leve.

mildew ['mɪldjuː] n moho.

mildly ['maɪldlɪ] ad ligeramente; sua-

vemente; **to put it** ~ para no decir
más.
mile [maɪl] n milla; **~age** n número
de millas, ≈ kilometraje m; **~stone**
n mojón m.
milieu ['miːljəː] n (medio) ambiente
m.
militant ['mɪlɪtnt] a, n militante m/f.
military ['mɪlɪtərɪ] a militar.
militia [mɪ'lɪʃə] n milicia.
milk [mɪlk] n leche f // vt (cow) ordeñar; (fig) chupar; ~ **chocolate** n
chocolate m con leche; **~man** n lechero; **~ shake** n batido, malteada
(LAm); **~y** a lechoso; **M~y Way** n
Vía Láctea.
mill [mɪl] n (windmill etc) molino;
(coffee ~) molinillo; (factory) fábrica; (spinning ~) hilandería // vt moler // vi (also: ~ **about**) arremolinarse.
millennium [mɪ'lenɪəm], pl **~s** or
-ia [-nɪə] n milenio, milenario.
miller ['mɪlə*] n molinero.
millet ['mɪlɪt] n mijo.
milli... ['mɪlɪ] pref: **~gram(me)** n
miligramo; **~litre**, n (US) **~liter**
mililitro; **~metre**, (US) **~meter** n
milímetro.
milliner ['mɪlɪnə*] n sombrerero/a;
~y n sombrerería.
million ['mɪljən] n millón m; **a** ~
times un millón de veces; **~aire** n
millonario/a.
millstone ['mɪlstəun] n piedra de
molino.
milometer [maɪ'lɒmɪtə*] n (Brit) ≈
cuentakilómetros m inv.
mime [maɪm] n mímica; (actor)
mimo/a // vt remedar // vi actuar de
mimo.
mimic [mɪmɪk] n imitador(a) m/f //
a mímico // vt remedar, imitar; **~ry**
n imitación f.
min. abbr = **minute(s); minimum.**
minaret [mɪnə'rɛt] n alminar m.
mince [mɪns] vt picar // vi (in walking) andar con pasos menudos // n
(Brit CULIN) carne f picada, picadillo; **~meat** n conserva de fruta pi-

cada; ~ **pie** n empanadilla rellena
de fruta picada; **~r** n picadora de
carne.
mind [maɪnd] n (gen) espíritu // vt (attend to, look after) ocuparse de, cuidar; (be careful of) tener cuidado
con; (object to): **I don't** ~ **the
noise** no me molesta el ruido; **it is
on my** ~ me preocupa; **to my** ~ en
mi opinión; **to be out of one's** ~ estar fuera de juicio; **to bear sth in** ~
tomar o tener algo en cuenta; **to
make up one's** ~ decidirse; **I don't**
~ **me es igual; ~ you**, ... te advierto que ...; **never** ~! ¡es igual!, ¡no
importa!; (don't worry) ¡no te pre-
ocupes!; '~ **the step**' 'cuidado con
el escalón'; **~er** n guardaespaldas m
inv; **~ful** a: **~ful of** consciente de;
~less a (crime) sin motivo; (work)
de autómata.
mine [maɪn] pron el mío/la mía etc;
a friend of ~ un(a) amigo/a mío/
mía // a: **this book is** ~ este libro es
mío // n mina // vt (coal) extraer;
(ship, beach) minar; **~field** n campo de minas; **miner** n minero/a.
mineral [mɪnərəl] a mineral // n mineral m; **~s** npl (Brit: soft drinks)
aguas fpl minerales, gaseosa sg; **~
water** n agua mineral.
minesweeper ['maɪnswiːpə*] n dra-
gaminas m inv.
mingle ['mɪŋgl] vi: **to** ~ **with** mezclarse con.
miniature ['mɪnətʃə*] a (en) miniatura // n miniatura.
minibus ['mɪnɪbʌs] n microbús m.
minim ['mɪnɪm] n (Brit MUS) blanca.
minimal ['mɪnɪml] a mínimo.
minimum ['mɪnɪməm] n, pl **minima**
['mɪnɪmə] mínimo // a mínimo.
mining ['maɪnɪŋ] n explotación mi-
nera // a minero.
miniskirt ['mɪnɪskəːt] n minifalda.
minister ['mɪnɪstə*] n (Brit POL)
ministro/a (Sp), secretario/a (LAm);
(REL) pastor m // vi: **to** ~ **to** atender a; **~ial** [-'tɪərɪəl] a (Brit POL)

ministerial.

ministry ['mɪnɪstrɪ] n (Brit POL) ministerio (Sp), secretaría (LAm); (REL) sacerdocio.

mink [mɪŋk] n visón m.

minnow ['mɪnəu] n pececillo (de agua dulce).

minor ['maɪnə*] a (unimportant) secundario; (MUS) menor // n (LAW) menor m/f de edad.

Minorca [mɪ'nɔːkə] n Menorca.

minority [maɪ'nɔrɪtɪ] n minoría.

mint [mɪnt] n (plant) menta, hierbabuena; (sweet) caramelo de menta // vt (coins) acuñar; the (Royal) M~, (US) the (US) M~ la Casa de la Moneda; **in ~ condition** en perfecto estado.

minus ['maɪnəs] n (also: ~ sign) signo de menos // prep menos.

minute ['mɪnɪt] n minuto; (fig) momento; ~s npl actas fpl // a [maɪ'njuːt] diminuto; (search) minucioso; **at the last ~** a última hora.

miracle ['mɪrəkl] n milagro; **miraculous** [mɪ'rækjuləs] a milagroso.

mirage ['mɪrɑːʒ] n espejismo.

mire [maɪə*] n fango, lodo.

mirror ['mɪrə*] n espejo; (in car) retrovisor m // vt reflejar.

mirth [mɜːθ] n alegría.

misadventure [mɪsəd'vɛntʃə*] n desgracia; **death by ~** muerte f accidental.

misanthropist [mɪ'zænθrəpɪst] n misántropo/a.

misapprehension ['mɪsæprɪhɛnʃən] n equivocación f.

misbehave [mɪsbɪ'heɪv] vi portarse mal.

miscalculate [mɪs'kælkjuleɪt] vt calcular mal.

miscarriage ['mɪskærɪdʒ] n (MED) aborto; **~ of justice** error m judicial.

miscellaneous [mɪsɪ'leɪnɪəs] a varios/as, diversos/as.

mischief ['mɪstʃɪf] n (naughtiness) travesura; (harm) mal m, daño; (maliciousness) malicia; **mischie-**

vous [-ʃɪvəs] a travieso; dañoso; (playful) malicioso.

misconception ['mɪskən'sɛpʃən] n concepto erróneo; equivocación f.

misconduct [mɪs'kɔndʌkt] n mala conducta; **professional ~** falta profesional.

miscount [mɪs'kaunt] vt, vi contar mal.

misconstrue [mɪskən'struː] vt interpretar mal.

misdeed [mɪs'diːd] n delito.

misdemeanour, (US) **misdemeanor** [mɪsdɪ'miːnə*] n delito, ofensa.

miser [maɪzə*] n avaro/a.

miserable ['mɪzərəbl] a (unhappy) triste, desgraciado; (wretched) miserable.

miserly ['maɪzəlɪ] a avariento, tacaño.

misery ['mɪzərɪ] n (unhappiness) tristeza; (wretchedness) miseria, desdicha.

misfire [mɪs'faɪə*] vi fallar.

misfit ['mɪsfɪt] n (person) inadaptado/a.

misfortune [mɪs'fɔːtʃən] n desgracia.

misgiving(s) [mɪs'gɪvɪŋ(z)] n(pl) (mistrust) recelo; (apprehension) presentimiento.

misguided [mɪs'gaɪdɪd] a equivocado.

mishandle [mɪs'hændl] vt (treat roughly) maltratar; (mismanage) manejar mal.

mishap ['mɪshæp] n desgracia, contratiempo.

misinform [mɪsɪn'fɔːm] vt informar mal.

misinterpret [mɪsɪn'təːprɪt] vt interpretar mal.

misjudge [mɪs'dʒʌdʒ] vt juzgar mal.

mislay [mɪs'leɪ] (irg: like lay) vt extraviar, perder.

mislead [mɪs'liːd] (irg: like lead) vt llevar a conclusiones erróneas; **~ing** a engañoso.

mismanage [mɪs'mænɪdʒ] vt administrar mal.

misnomer [mɪs'nəumə*] *n* término inapropiado or equivocado.

misogynist [mɪ'sɔdʒɪnɪst] *n* misógino.

misplace [mɪs'pleɪs] *vt (lose)* extraviar.

misprint ['mɪsprɪnt] *n* errata, error *m* de imprenta.

Miss [mɪs] *n* Señorita.

miss [mɪs] *vt (train etc)* perder; *(fail to hit: target)* no dar en; *(regret the absence of)*: **I ~ him** (yo) le echo de menos or a faltar // *vi* fallar // *n (shot)* tiro fallido or perdido; **to ~ out** *(Brit)* omitir.

misshapen [mɪs'ʃeɪpən] *a* deforme.

missile ['mɪsaɪl] *n (AVIAT)* mísil *m*; *(object thrown)* proyectil *m*.

missing ['mɪsɪŋ] *a (pupil)* ausente; *(thing)* perdido; *(MIL)* desaparecido; **to be ~** faltar.

mission ['mɪʃən] *n* misión *f*; **~ary** *n* misionero/a.

misspent ['mɪs'spent] *a*: **his ~ youth** su juventud disipada.

mist [mɪst] *n (light)* neblina, *(heavy)* niebla; *(at sea)* bruma // *vi (also: ~ over, ~ up: weather)* nublarse; *(: Brit: windows)* empañarse.

mistake [mɪs'teɪk] *n* error *m* // *vt (irg: like* **take***)* entender mal; **by ~** por equivocación; **to make a ~** equivocarse; **to ~ A for B** confundir A con B; **~n** *a (idea etc)* equivocado; **to be ~n** equivocarse, engañarse.

mister ['mɪstə*] *n (col)* señor *m*; *see* **Mr**.

mistletoe ['mɪsltəu] *n* muérdago.

mistook [mɪs'tuk] *pt of* **mistake**.

mistress ['mɪstrɪs] *n (lover)* amante *f*; *(of house)* señora (de la casa); *(Brit: in primary school)* maestra; *(in secondary school)* profesora *f*; *see* **Mrs**.

mistrust [mɪs'trʌst] *vt* desconfiar de.

misty ['mɪstɪ] *a* nebuloso, brumoso; *(day)* de niebla; *(glasses)* empañado.

misunderstand [mɪsʌndə'stænd] *(irg: like* **understand***)* *vt, vi* enten-

der mal; **~ing** *n* malentendido.

misuse [mɪs'juːs] *n* mal uso; *(of power)* abuso // *vt* [mɪs'juːz] abusar de; *(funds)* malversar.

mitre, *(US)* **miter** ['maɪtə*] *n* mitra.

mitt(en) ['mɪt(n)] *n* manopla.

mix [mɪks] *vt (gen)* mezclar; *(combine)* unir // *vi* mezclarse; *(people)* llevarse bien // *n* mezcla; **to ~ up** *vt* mezclar; *(confuse)* confundir; **~ed** *a (assorted)* variado, surtido; *(school etc)* mixto; **~ed-up** *a (confused)* confuso, revuelto; **~er** *n (for food)* licuadora; *(person)*: **he's a good ~er** tiene don de gentes; **~ture** *n* mezcla; **~-up** *n* confusión *f*.

mm *abbr (= millimetre)* mm.

moan [məun] *n* gemido // *vi* gemir; *(col: complain)*: **to ~ (about)** quejarse (de).

moat [məut] *n* foso.

mob [mɔb] *n* multitud *f*; *(pej)*: **the ~** el populacho // *vt* acosar.

mobile ['məubaɪl] *a* móvil // *n* móvil *m*; **~ home** *n* caravana.

mock [mɔk] *vt (make ridiculous)* ridiculizar; *(laugh at)* burlarse de // *a* fingido; **~ery** *n* burla.

mod [mɔd] *a see* **convenience**.

mode [məud] *n* modo.

model ['mɔdl] *n (gen)* modelo; *(ARCH)* maqueta; *(person: for fashion, ART)* modelo *m/f* // *a* modelo // *vt* modelar // *vi* ser modelo; **~ railway** *n* ferrocarril *m* de juguete; **to ~ clothes** pasar modelos, ser modelo.

modem ['məudəm] *n* modem *m*.

moderate ['mɔdərət] *a*, *n* moderado/a *m/f* // *vb* ['mɔdəreɪt] *vi* moderarse, calmarse // *vt* moderar.

modern ['mɔdən] *a* moderno; **~ize** *vt* modernizar.

modest ['mɔdɪst] *a* modesto; **~y** *n* modestia.

modicum ['mɔdɪkəm] *n*: **a ~ of** un mínimo de.

modify ['mɔdɪfaɪ] *vt* modificar.

module ['mɔdjuːl] *n (unit, component, SPACE)* módulo.

mogul ['məugəl] n (fig) magnate m.

mohair ['məuheə*] n mohair m.

moist [mɔist] a húmedo; **~en** ['mɔisn] vt humedecer; **~ure** ['mɔistʃə*] n humedad f; **~urizer** ['mɔistʃəraizə*] n crema hidratante.

molar ['məulə*] n muela.

molasses [məu'læsiz] n melaza.

mold [məuld] n, vt (US) = **mould**.

mole [məul] n (animal) topo; (spot) lunar m.

molecule ['mɔlikjuːl] n molécula.

molest [məu'lest] vt importunar.

mollycoddle ['mɔlikɔdl] vt mimar.

molt [məult] vi (US) = **moult**.

molten ['məultən] a fundido; (lava) líquido.

mom [mɔm] n (US) = **mum**.

moment ['məumənt] n momento; at the **~** de momento, por ahora; **~ary** a momentáneo; **~ous** [-'mentəs] a trascendental, importante.

momentum [məu'mentəm] n momento; (fig) ímpetu m; to gather **~** cobrar velocidad.

mommy ['mɔmi] n (US) = **mummy**.

Monaco ['mɔnəkəu] n Mónaco.

monarch ['mɔnək] n monarca m/f; **~y** n monarquía.

monastery ['mɔnəstəri] n monasterio.

Monday ['mʌndi] n lunes m inv.

monetary ['mʌnitəri] a monetario.

money ['mʌni] n dinero; to make **~** ganar dinero; **~lender** n prestamista m/f; **~ order** n giro; **~spinner** n (col): to be a **~spinner** dar mucho dinero.

mongol ['mɔŋgəl] a, n (MED) mongólico.

mongrel ['mʌŋgrəl] n (dog) perro mestizo.

monitor ['mɔnitə*] n (SCOL) monitor m; (also: **television ~**) receptor m de control; (of computer) monitor m // vt controlar.

monk [mʌŋk] n monje m.

monkey ['mʌŋki] n mono; **~ nut** n (Brit) cacahuete m, maní (LAm) n;

wrench n llave f inglesa.

mono... [mɔnəu] pref: **~chrome** a monocromo.

monocle ['mɔnəkl] n monóculo.

monologue ['mɔnələg] n monólogo.

monopoly [mə'nɔpəli] n monopolio.

monotone ['mɔnətəun] n voz f (or tono) monocorde.

monotonous [mə'nɔtənəs] a monótono.

monotony [mə'nɔtəni] n monotonía.

monsoon [mɔn'suːn] n monzón m.

monster ['mɔnstə*] n monstruo.

monstrosity [mɔns'trɔsiti] n monstruosidad f.

monstrous ['mɔnstrəs] a (huge) enorme; (atrocious) monstruoso.

montage ['mɔntɑːʒ] n montaje m.

month [mʌnθ] n mes m; **~ly** a mensual // ad mensualmente // n (magazine) revista mensual.

monument ['mɔnjumənt] n monumento; **~al** [-'mentl] a monumental.

moo [muː] vi mugir.

mood [muːd] n humor m; to be in a good/bad **~** estar de buen/mal humor; **~y** a (changeable) de humor variable; (sullen) malhumorado.

moon [muːn] n luna; **~light** n luz f de la luna; **~lighting** n pluriempleo; **~lit** a: a **~lit** night una noche de luna.

Moor [muə*] n moro/a.

moor [muə*] n páramo // vt (ship) amarrar // vi echar las amarras.

Moorish ['muəriʃ] a moro; (architecture) árabe, morisco.

moorland ['muələnd] n páramo, brezal m.

moose [muːs] n, pl inv alce m.

mop [mɔp] n fregona; (of hair) greña, melena // vt fregar; to **~ up** vt limpiar.

mope [məup] vi estar or andar deprimido.

moped ['məuped] n ciclomotor m.

moral ['mɔrl] a moral // n moraleja; **~s** npl moralidad f, moral f.

morale [mɔ'rɑːl] n moral f.

morality [mə'ræliti] n moralidad f.

morass [mə'ræs] n pantano.

morbid ['mɔːbɪd] a (interest) morboso; (MED) mórbido.

---KEYWORD---

more [mɔː*] ◆ a 1 (greater in number etc) más; ~ **people/work than before** más gente/trabajo que antes 2 (additional) más; **do you want (some) ~ tea?** ¿quieres más té?; **is there any ~ wine?** ¿queda vino?; **it'll take a few ~ weeks** tardará unas semanas más; **it's 2 kms ~ to the house** faltan 2 kms para la casa; **~ time/letters than we expected** más tiempo del que/más cartas de las que esperábamos ◆ pron (greater amount, additional amount) más; ~ **than 10** más de 10; **it cost ~ than the other one/than we expected** costó más que el otro/más de lo que esperábamos; **is there any ~?** ¿hay más?; **many/much ~** mucho(a)/muchos(as) más ◆ ad más; ~ **dangerous/easily (than)** más peligroso/fácilmente (que); ~ **and ~ expensive** cada vez más caro; ~ **or less** más o menos; ~ **than ever** más que nunca.

moreover [mɔː'rəuvə*] ad además, por otra parte.

morgue [mɔːɡ] n depósito de cadáveres.

Mormon ['mɔːmən] n mormón/ona m/f.

morning ['mɔːnɪŋ] n (gen) mañana; (early ~) madrugada; **in the ~** por la mañana; **7 o'clock in the ~** las 7 de la mañana.

Moroccan [mə'rɔkən] a, n marroquí m/f.

Morocco [mə'rɔkəu] n Marruecos m.

moron ['mɔːrɔn] n imbécil m/f.

morose [mə'rəus] a hosco, malhumorado.

morphine ['mɔːfiːn] n morfina.

Morse [mɔːs] n (also: ~ **code**) (código) morse.

morsel ['mɔːsl] n (of food) bocado.

mortal ['mɔːtl] a, n mortal m; ~**ity** [-'tælɪtɪ] n mortalidad f.

mortar ['mɔːtə*] n argamasa; (implement) mortero.

mortgage ['mɔːɡɪdʒ] n hipoteca // vt hipotecar; ~ **company** n (US) ≈ banco hipotecario.

mortify ['mɔːtɪfaɪ] vt mortificar, humillar.

mortuary ['mɔːtjuərɪ] n depósito de cadáveres.

mosaic [məu'zeɪɪk] n mosaico.

Moscow ['mɔskəu] n Moscú m.

Moslem ['mɔzləm] a, n = **Muslim**.

mosque [mɔsk] n mezquita.

mosquito [mɔs'kiːtəu], pl ~**es** n mosquito (Sp), zancudo (LAm).

moss [mɔs] n musgo.

most [məust] a la mayor parte de, la mayoría de // pron la mayor parte, la mayoría // ad el más; (very) muy; **the ~** (also: + adjective) el más; ~ **of them** la mayor parte de ellos; **I saw the ~** yo vi el que más; **at the (very)** ~ a lo sumo, todo lo más; **to make the ~ of** aprovechar (al máximo); **a ~ interesting book** un libro interesantísimo; ~**ly** ad en su mayor parte, principalmente.

MOT n abbr (Brit = Ministry of Transport): **the ~ (test)** inspección (anual) obligatoria de coches y camiones.

motel [məu'tɛl] n motel m.

moth [mɔθ] n mariposa nocturna; (clothes ~) polilla; ~**ball** n bola de naftalina.

mother ['mʌðə*] n madre f // a materno // vt (care for) cuidar (como una madre); ~**hood** n maternidad f; ~**-in-law** n suegra; ~**ly** a maternal; ~**-of-pearl** n nácar m; ~**-to-be** n futura madre; ~** tongue** n lengua materna.

motif [məu'tiːf] n motivo; (theme) tema m.

motion ['məuʃən] n movimiento; (gesture) ademán m, señal f; (at meeting) moción f // vt, vi: **to ~ (to) sb to do sth** hacer señas a uno para que haga algo; **~less** a inmóvil; **~ picture** n película.

motivated ['məutiveitid] a motivado.

motive ['məutiv] n motivo.

motley ['mɒtli] a variado.

motor ['məutə*] n motor m; (Brit: col: vehicle) coche m, carro (LAm), automóvil m // a motor (f: motora, motriz); **~bike** n moto f; **~boat** n lancha motora; **~car** n (Brit) coche m, carro (LAm), automóvil m; **~cycle** n motocicleta; **~cycle racing** n motociclismo; **~cycling** n motociclismo m/f; **~ing** n (Brit) automovilismo; **~ist** n conductor/a m/f; **~ racing** n (Brit) carreras fpl de coches, automovilismo; **~ scooter** n moto f; **~ vehicle** n automóvil m; **~way** n (Brit) autopista.

mottled ['mɒtld] a abigarrado, multicolor.

motto ['mɒtəu], pl **~es** n lema m, (watchword) consigna.

mould, (US) **mold** [məuld] n molde m; (mildew) moho // a (fig) formar; **~er** vi (decay) decaer; **~ing** n moldura; **~y** a enmohecido.

moult, (US) **molt** [məult] vi mudar (la piel/las plumas).

mound [maund] n montón m, montículo.

mount [maunt] n monte m; (horse) montura; (for jewel etc) engarce m; (for picture) marco n // vt montar, subir a // vi (also: **~ up**) subirse, montarse.

mountain ['mauntin] n montaña // cpd de montaña; **~eer** [-'niə*] n alpinista m/f, andinista m/f (LAm); **~eering** [-'niəriŋ] n alpinismo, andinismo (LAm); **~ous** a montañoso; **~side** n ladera de la montaña.

mourn [mɔ:n] vt llorar, lamentar // vi: to **~ for** llorar la muerte de, lamentarse por; **~er** n doliente m/f; dolorido/a; **~ful** a triste, doloroso; **~ing** n luto // cpd (dress) de luto: in **~ing** de luto.

mouse [maus], pl **mice** n ratón m; (COMPUT) ratón m; **~trap** n ratonera.

mousse [mu:s] n (CULIN) crema batida; (for hair) espuma (moldeadora).

moustache [məs'tɑ:ʃ] n bigote m.

mousy ['mausi] a (person) tímido; (hair) pardusco.

mouth [mauθ], pl **~s** [-ðz] n boca; (of river) desembocadura; **~ful** n bocado; **~ organ** n armónica; **~piece** n (of musical instrument) boquilla; (spokesman) portavoz m/f; **~wash** n enjuague m; **~watering** a apetitoso.

movable ['mu:vəbl] a movible.

move [mu:v] n (movement) movimiento; (in game) jugada; (: turn to play) turno; (change of house) mudanza // vt mover; (emotionally) conmover; (POL: resolution etc) proponer // vi (gen) moverse; (traffic) circular; (also: Brit: **~ house**) trasladarse, mudarse; to **~** sb to do sth mover a uno a hacer algo; to get a **~ on** darse prisa; to **~ about** or **around** vi moverse; (travel) viajar; to **~ along** vi avanzar, adelantarse; to **~ away** vi alejarse; to **~ back** vi retroceder; to **~ forward** vi avanzar // vt adelantar; to **~ in** vi (to a house) instalarse; to **~ on** vi ponerse en camino; to **~ out** vi (of house) mudarse; to **~ over** vi apartarse; to **~ up** vi subir; (employee) ser ascendido.

movement ['mu:vmənt] n movimiento; (TECH) mecanismo.

movie ['mu:vi] n película; to go to the **~s** ir al cine; **~ camera** n cámara cinematográfica.

moving ['mu:viŋ] a (emotional) conmovedor/a; (that moves) móvil.

mow [məu], pt **mowed**, pp **mowed** or **mown** vt (grass) cortar; (corn: also: **~ down**) segar; (shoot) acribillar; **~er** n (also: **lawnmower**) cortacéspedes m inv.

MP n abbr = Member of Parliament.

m.p.h. *abbr* = miles per hour (60 m.p.h. = 96 k.p.h.).

Mr, Mr. ['mɪstə*] *n*: ~ **Smith** (el) Sr. Smith.

Mrs, Mrs. ['mɪsɪz] *n*: ~ **Smith** (la) Sra. Smith.

Ms, Ms. [mɪz] *n* (= Miss or Mrs): ~ **Smith** (la) Sr(t)a. Smith.

M.Sc. *abbr* = **Master of Science.**

much [mʌtʃ] *a* mucho // *ad, n or pron* mucho; (*before pp*) muy; **how** ~ **is it?** ¿cuánto es?, ¿cuánto cuesta?; **too** ~ demasiado; **it's not** ~ no es mucho; **as** ~ **as** tanto como; **however** ~ **he tries** por mucho que se esfuerce.

muck [mʌk] *n* (*dirt*) suciedad *f*; (*fig*) porquería *f*; **~ about** or **around** *vi* (*col*) perder el tiempo; (*enjoy o.s.*) entretenerse; **to** ~ **up** *vt* (*col: ruin*) arruinar, estropear; **~y** *a* (*dirty*) sucio.

mucus ['mjuːkəs] *n* moco.

mud [mʌd] *n* barro, lodo.

muddle ['mʌdl] *n* desorden *m*, confusión *f*; (*mix-up*) embrollo, lío // *vt* (*also*: ~ **up**) embrollar, confundir; **to** ~ **through** *vi* salir del paso.

muddy ['mʌdɪ] *a* fangoso, cubierto de lodo.

mud: **~guard** *n* guardabarros *m inv*; **~-slinging** *n* injurias *fpl*, difamación *f*.

muff [mʌf] *n* manguito *m* // *vt* (*chance*) desperdiciar; (*lines*) estropear.

muffin ['mʌfɪn] *n* mollete *m*.

muffle ['mʌfl] *vt* (*sound*) amortiguar; (*against cold*) embozar; **~r** *n* (*US AUT*) silenciador *m*.

mug [mʌg] *n* (*cup*) taza grande (*sin platillo*); (*for beer*) jarra; (*col: face*) jeta; (: *fool*) bobo // *vt* (*assault*) asaltar; **~ging** *n* asalto.

muggy ['mʌgɪ] *a* bochornoso.

mule [mjuːl] *n* mula.

mull [mʌl] **to** ~ **over** *vt* meditar sobre.

mulled [mʌld] *a*: ~ **wine** vino caliente.

multifarious [mʌltɪ'fɛərɪəs] *a* múltiple.

multi-level [mʌltɪ'lɛvl] *a* (*US*) = **multistorey.**

multiple ['mʌltɪpl] *a, n* múltiplo; **~ sclerosis** *n* esclerosis *f* múltiple; **~ store** *n* (*Brit*) (cadena de) grandes almacenes.

multiplication [mʌltɪplɪ'keɪʃən] *n* multiplicación *f*.

multiply ['mʌltɪplaɪ] *vt* multiplicar // *vi* multiplicarse.

multistorey [mʌltɪ'stɔːrɪ] *a* (*Brit: building, car park*) de muchos pisos.

multitude ['mʌltɪtjuːd] *n* multitud *f*.

mum [mʌm] *n* (*Brit*) mamá // *a*: **to keep** ~ mantener la boca cerrada.

mumble ['mʌmbl] *vt, vi* hablar entre dientes, refunfuñar.

mummy ['mʌmɪ] *n* (*Brit: mother*) mamá; (*embalmed*) momia.

mumps [mʌmps] *n* paperas *fpl*.

munch [mʌntʃ] *vt, vi* mascar.

mundane [mʌn'deɪn] *a* trivial.

municipal [mjuː'nɪsɪpl] *a* municipal; **~ity** [-'pælɪtɪ] *n* municipio.

mural ['mjuərl] *n* (*pintura*) mural *m*.

murder ['mɜːdə*] *n* asesinato; (*in law*) homicidio // *vt* asesinar; matar; **~er/~ess** *n* asesino/a; **~ous** *a* homicida.

murky ['mɜːkɪ] *a* (*water, past*) turbio; (*room*) sombrío.

murmur ['mɜːmə*] *n* murmullo // *vt, vi* murmurar.

muscle ['mʌsl] *n* músculo; **to** ~ **in** *vi* entrometerse; **muscular** ['mʌskjulə*] *a* muscular; (*person*) musculoso.

muse [mjuːz] *vi* meditar // *n* musa.

museum [mjuː'zɪəm] *n* museo.

mushroom ['mʌʃrum] *n* (*gen*) seta, hongo; (*small*) champiñón *m* // *vi* (*fig*) crecer de la noche a la mañana.

music ['mjuːzɪk] *n* música; **~al** *a* melodioso; (*person*) musical // *n* (*show*) comedia musical; **~al instrument** *n* instrumento musical; ~

hall n teatro de variedades; **~ian** [-' zıʃən] n músico/a.

Muslim ['mʌzlım] a, n musulmán/ana m/f.

muslin ['mʌzlın] n muselina.

mussel ['mʌsl] n mejillón m.

must [mʌst] auxiliary vb (obligation): **I ~ do** it debo hacerlo, tengo que hacerlo; (probability): **he ~ be** there by now ya debe (de) estar allí // n: **it's a ~** es imprescindible.

mustard ['mʌstəd] n mostaza.

muster ['mʌstə*] vt juntar, reunir.

mustn't ['mʌsnt] = must not.

musty ['mʌstı] a mohoso, que huele a humedad.

mute [mjuːt] a, n mudo/a.

muted ['mjuːtıd] a callado.

mutiny ['mjuːtını] n motín m // vi amotinarse.

mutter ['mʌtə*] vt, vi murmurar.

mutton ['mʌtn] n carne f de cordero.

mutual ['mjuːtʃuəl] a mutuo; (friend) común; **~ly** ad mutuamente.

muzzle ['mʌzl] n hocico; (protective device) bozal m; (of gun) boca // vt amordazar; (dog) poner un bozal a.

my [maı] a mi(s); **~ house/brother/sisters** mi casa/mi hermano/mis hermanas; **I've washed ~ hair/cut ~ finger** me he lavado el pelo/cortado un dedo; **is this ~ pen or yours?** ¿es este bolígrafo mío o tuyo?

myriad ['mırıəd] n (of people, things) miríada.

myself [maı'self] pron (reflexive) me; (emphatic) yo mismo; (after prep) mí (mismo); see also **oneself**.

mysterious [mıs'tıərıəs] a misterioso.

mystery ['mıstərı] n misterio.

mystify ['mıstıfaı] vt (perplex) dejar perplejo; (disconcert) desconcertar.

mystique [mıs'tiːk] n misterio (profesional etc).

myth [mıθ] n mito; **~ical** a mítico.

N

n/a abbr (= not applicable) ≈ no interesa.

nab [næb] vt (col: grab) coger (Sp), agarrar (LAm); (: catch out) pillar.

nag [næg] n (pej: horse) rocín m // vt (scold) regañar; (annoy) fastidiar; **~ging** a (doubt) persistente; (pain) continuo // n quejas fpl.

nail [neıl] n (human) uña; (metal) clavo // vt clavar; (fig: catch) coger (Sp), pillar; **to ~ sb down to doing sth** comprometer a uno a que haga algo; **~brush** n cepillo para las uñas; **~file** n lima para las uñas; **~ polish** n esmalte m or laca para las uñas; **~ polish remover** n quitaesmalte m; **~ scissors** npl tijeras fpl para las uñas; **~ varnish** n (Brit) = **~ polish**.

naïve [naı'iːv] a ingenuo.

naked ['neıkıd] a (nude) desnudo; (flame) expuesto al aire.

name [neım] n (gen) nombre m; (surname) apellido; (reputation) fama, renombre m // vt (child) poner nombre a; (appoint) nombrar; **by ~** de nombre; **in the ~ of** en nombre de; **what's your ~?** ¿cómo se llama?; **to give one's ~ and address** dar sus señas; **~less** a anónimo, sin nombre; **~ly** ad a saber; **~sake** n tocayo/a.

nanny ['nænı] n niñera.

nap [næp] n (sleep) sueñecito, siesta; **to be caught ~ping** estar desprevenido.

napalm ['neıpɑːm] n napalm m.

nape [neıp] n: **~ of the neck** nuca, cogote m.

napkin ['næpkın] n (also: **table ~**) servilleta.

nappy ['næpı] n (Brit) pañal m; **~ liner** n gasa; **~ rash** n prurito.

narcissus [nɑː'sısəs], pl **-si** [-saı] n narciso.

narcotic [nɑː'kɔtık] a, n narcótico.

narrative ['nærətɪv] n narrativa // a narrativo.

narrow ['nærəʊ] a estrecho, angosto // vi estrecharse, angostarse; (diminish) reducirse; **to have a ~ escape** escapar por los pelos; **to ~ sth down** reducir algo; **~ly** ad (miss) por poco; **~-minded** a de miras estrechas.

nasty ['nɑːstɪ] a (remark) feo; (person) antipático; (revolting: taste, smell) asqueroso; (wound, disease etc) peligroso, grave.

nation ['neɪʃən] n nación f.

national ['næʃənl] a, n nacional m/f; **~ dress** n vestido nacional; **N~ Health Service (NHS)** n (Brit) servicio nacional de salud pública; ≈ Insalud m (Sp); **N~ Insurance** n (Brit) seguro social nacional; **~ism** n nacionalismo; **~ist** a, n nacionalista m/f; **~ity** [-'nælɪtɪ] n nacionalidad f; **~ize** vt nacionalizar; **~ly** ad (nationwide) en escala nacional; (as a nation) nacionalmente, como nación.

nationwide ['neɪʃənwaɪd] a en escala or a nivel nacional.

native ['neɪtɪv] n (local inhabitant) natural m/f, nacional m/f; (in colonies) indígena m/f, nativo/a a (indigenous) indígena; (country) natal; (innate) natural, innato; **a ~ of Russia** un(a) natural m/f de Rusia; **~ language** n lengua materna; **a speaker of French** un hablante nativo de francés.

Nativity [nə'tɪvɪtɪ] n: **the ~** Navidad f.

NATO ['neɪtəʊ] n abbr (= North Atlantic Treaty Organization) OTAN f.

natural ['nætʃrəl] a natural; **~ gas** n gas m natural; **~ize** vt: **to become ~ized** (person) naturalizarse; (plant) aclimatarse; **~ly** ad (speak etc) naturalmente; (of course) desde luego, por supuesto; (instinctively) por instinto, por naturaleza.

nature ['neɪtʃə*] n naturaleza; (group, sort) género, clase f; (character) carácter m, genio; **by ~** por

naught [nɔːt] = **nought**.

naughty ['nɔːtɪ] a (child) travieso; (story, film) verde, escabroso, colorado (LAm).

nausea ['nɔːsɪə] n náusea; **~te** [-sɪeɪt] vt dar náuseas a; (fig) dar asco a.

nautical ['nɔːtɪkl] a náutico, marítimo; (mile) marino.

naval ['neɪvl] a naval, de marina; **~ officer** n oficial m/f de marina.

nave [neɪv] n nave f.

navel ['neɪvl] n ombligo.

navigate ['nævɪgeɪt] vt gobernar // vi navegar; **navigation** [-'geɪʃən] n (action) navegación f; (science) náutica; **navigator** n navegador/a m/f, navegante m/f.

navvy ['nævɪ] n (Brit) peón m caminero.

navy ['neɪvɪ] n marina de guerra; (ships) armada, flota; **~(-blue)** a azul marino.

Nazi ['nɑːtsɪ] n nazi m/f.

NB abbr (= nota bene) nótese.

near [nɪə*] a (place, relation) cercano; (time) próximo // ad cerca // prep (also: **~ to: space)** cerca de, junto a; (: time) cerca de // vt acercarse a, aproximarse a; **~by** [nɪə'baɪ] a cercano, próximo // ad cerca; **~ly** ad casi, por poco; **I ~ly fell** por poco me caigo; **~ miss** n tiro cercano; **~side** n (AUT) lado derecho; **~sighted** a miope, corto de vista.

neat [niːt] a (place) ordenado, bien cuidado; (person) pulcro; (plan) ingenioso; (spirits) puro; **~ly** ad (tidily) con esmero; (skilfully) ingeniosamente.

nebulous ['nebjʊləs] a (fig) vago, confuso.

necessarily ['nesɪsrɪlɪ] ad necesariamente.

necessary ['nesɪsrɪ] a necesario, preciso; **he did all that was ~** hizo todo lo necesario.

necessity [nɪ'sesɪtɪ] n necesidad f; **necessities** npl artículos mpl de primera necesidad.

neck [nɛk] n (ANAT) cuello; (of animal) pescuezo // vi besuquearse; ~ **and** ~ parejos.

necklace ['nɛklɪs] n collar m.

neckline ['nɛklaɪn] n escote m.

necktie ['nɛktaɪ] n (US) corbata.

née [neɪ] a: ~ Scott de soltera Scott.

need [niːd] n (lack) escasez f, falta; (necessity) necesidad f // vt (require) necesitar; **I** ~ **to do it** tengo que or debo hacerlo; **you don't** ~ **to go** no hace falta que vayas.

needle ['niːdl] n aguja // vt (fig: col) picar, fastidiar.

needless ['niːdlɪs] a innecesario, inútil; ~ **to say** huelga decir que.

needlework ['niːdlwɜːk] n (activity) costura, labor f de aguja.

needn't ['niːdnt] = **need not**.

needy ['niːdɪ] a necesitado.

negative ['nɛgətɪv] n (PHOT) negativo; (LING) negación f // a negativo.

neglect [nɪ'glɛkt] vt (one's duty) faltar a, no cumplir con; (child) descuidar, desatender // n (state) abandono; (personal) dejadez f; (of duty) incumplimiento.

negligee ['nɛglɪʒeɪ] n (nightdress) salto de cama.

negligence ['nɛglɪdʒəbl] n negligencia, descuido.

negligible ['nɛglɪdʒɪbl] a insignificante, despreciable.

negotiate [nɪ'gəʊʃɪeɪt] vt (treaty, loan) negociar; (obstacle) franquear // vi: **to** ~ (with) negociar (con); **negotiation** [-'eɪʃən] n negociación f, gestión f.

Negress ['niːgrɪs] n negra.

Negro ['niːgrəʊ] a, n negro.

neigh [neɪ] n relincho // vi relinchar.

neighbour, (US) **neighbor** ['neɪbə*] n vecino/a; ~**hood** n (place) vecindad f, barrio; (people) vecindario; ~**ing** a vecino.

neither ['naɪðə*] a ni // conj: **I didn't move and** ~ **did John** no me he movido, ni Juan tampoco // pron ninguno; ~ **is true** ninguno/a de/ las dos es cierto/a // ad: ~ **good nor bad** ni bueno ni malo.

neon ['niːɔn] n neón m; ~ **light** n lámpara de neón.

nephew ['nɛvjuː] n sobrino.

nerve [nɜːv] n (ANAT) nervio; (courage) valor m; (impudence) descaro, frescura; **a fit of** ~**s** un ataque de nervios; ~**-racking** a desquiciante.

nervous ['nɜːvəs] a (anxious, ANAT) nervioso; (timid) tímido, miedoso; ~ **breakdown** n crisis f nerviosa.

nest [nɛst] n (of bird) nido // vi anidar; ~ **egg** n (fig) ahorros mpl.

nestle ['nɛsl] vi: **to** ~ **down** acurrucarse.

net [nɛt] n (gen) red f // a (COMM) neto, líquido // vt coger (Sp) or agarrar (LAm) con red; (SPORT) marcar; ~**ball** n básquet m; ~ **curtain** n visillo.

Netherlands ['nɛðələndz] npl: **the** ~ los Países Bajos.

nett [nɛt] a = **net**.

netting ['nɛtɪŋ] n red f, redes fpl.

nettle ['nɛtl] n ortiga.

network ['nɛtwɜːk] n red f.

neurosis [njʊə'rəʊsɪs], pl **-ses** [-siːz] n neurosis f // **neurotic** [-'rɔtɪk] a, n neurótico/a m/f.

neuter ['njuːtə*] a (LING) neutro // vt castrar, capar.

neutral ['njuːtrəl] a (person) neutral; (colour etc, ELEC) neutro // n (AUT) punto muerto; ~**ize** vt neutralizar.

neutron ['njuːtrɔn] n neutrón m; ~ **bomb** n bomba de neutrones.

never ['nɛvə*] ad nunca, jamás; **I went no fui nunca;** ~ **in my life** jamás en la vida; see also **mind**; ~**-ending** a interminable, sin fin; ~**theless** [nɛvəðə'lɛs] ad sin embargo, no obstante.

new [njuː] a nuevo; (recent) reciente; ~**-born** a recién nacido; ~**comer** ['njuːkʌmə*] n recién venido/a or llegado/a; ~**-fangled** a (pej) modernísimo; ~**-found** a (friend) nuevo; (enthusiasm) recién adquirido.

~**ly** *ad* nuevamente, recién; ~**ly-weds** *npl* recién casados *mpl*; ~**moon** *n* luna nueva.

news [njuːz] *n* noticias *fpl*; **a piece of** ~ una noticia; **the** ~ (*RADIO, TV*) las noticias *fpl*, telediario; ~**agency** *n* agencia de noticias; ~**agent** *n* (*Brit*) vendedor(a) *m/f* de periódicos; ~**caster** *n* presentador(a) *m/f*, locutor(a) *m/f*; ~**dealer** *n* (*US*) = ~ **agent**; ~**flash** *n* noticia de última hora; ~**letter** *n* hoja informativa, boletín *m*; ~**paper** *n* periódico, diario; ~**print** *n* papel *m* de periódico; ~**reader** *n* = ~**caster**; ~**reel** *n* noticiario; ~**stand** *n* quiosco or puesto de periódicos.

newt [njuːt] *n* tritón *m*.

New Year *n* Año Nuevo; ~**'s Day** *n* Día *m* de Año Nuevo; ~**'s Eve** *n* Nochevieja.

New York [njuːˈjɔːk] *n* Nueva York.

New Zealand [njuːˈziːlənd] *n* Nueva Zelanda; ~**er** *n* neozelandés/esa *m/f*.

next [nekst] *a* (*house, room*) vecino; (*bus stop, meeting*) próximo; (*page*) siguiente // *ad* después; **the** ~ **day** el día siguiente; ~ **time** la próxima vez; ~ **year** el año próximo or que viene; ~ **door** *ad* en la casa de al lado // *a* vecino, de al lado; ~**-of-kin** *n* pariente *m* más cercano; ~ **to** *prep* junto a, al lado de; ~ **to nothing** casi nada.

NHS *n abbr* = **National Health Service.**

nib [nɪb] *n* plumilla.

nibble [ˈnɪbl] *vt* mordisquear, mordiscar.

Nicaragua [nɪkəˈræɡjuə] *n* Nicaragua; ~**n** *a, n* nicaragüense *m/f*.

nice [naɪs] *a* (*likeable*) simpático; (*kind*) amable; (*pleasant*) agradable; (*attractive*) bonito, mono, lindo (*LAm*); (*distinction*) fino; ~**-looking** *a* guapo; ~**ly** *ad* amablemente; bien.

niche [niːʃ] *n* nicho.

nick [nɪk] *n* (*wound*) rasguño; (*cut, indentation*) mella, muesca // *vt* (*col*)

birlar, robar; **in the** ~ **of time** justo a tiempo.

nickel [ˈnɪkl] *n* níquel *m*; (*US*) moneda de 5 centavos.

nickname [ˈnɪkneɪm] *n* apodo, mote *m* // *vt* apodar.

nicotine [ˈnɪkətiːn] *n* nicotina.

niece [niːs] *n* sobrina.

Nigeria [naɪˈdʒɪərɪə] *n* Nigeria; ~**n** *a, n* nigeriano/a *m/f*.

nigger [ˈnɪɡə*] *n* (*col!: highly offensive*) negro/a.

niggling [ˈnɪɡlɪŋ] *a* (*trifling*) nimio, insignificante; (*annoying*) molesto.

night [naɪt] *n* (*gen*) noche *f*; (*evening*) tarde *f*; **last** ~ anoche; **the** ~ **before last** antenoche; **at** ~, **by** ~ de noche, por la noche; ~**cap** *n* (*drink*) bebida que se toma antes de acostarse; ~ **club** *n* cabaret *m*; ~**dress** *n* (*Brit*) camisón *m*; ~**fall** *n* anochecer *m*; ~**gown**, ~**ie** [ˈnaɪtɪ] *n* (*Brit*) = ~**dress**.

nightingale [ˈnaɪtɪŋɡeɪl] *n* ruiseñor *m*.

nightly [ˈnaɪtlɪ] *a* de todas las noches // *ad* todas las noches, cada noche.

nightmare [ˈnaɪtmɛə*] *n* pesadilla.

night-: ~ **porter** *n* guardián *m* nocturno; ~ **school** *n* clase(s) *f(pl)* nocturna(s); ~ **shift** *n* turno nocturno or de noche; ~**time** *n* noche *f*.

nil [nɪl] *n* (*Brit SPORT*) cero, nada.

Nile [naɪl] *n*: **the** ~ el Nilo.

nimble [ˈnɪmbl] *a* (*agile*) ágil, ligero; (*skilful*) diestro.

nine [naɪn] *num* nueve; ~**teen** *num* diecinueve, diez y nueve; ~**ty** *num* noventa.

ninth [naɪnθ] *a* noveno.

nip [nɪp] *vt* (*pinch*) pellizcar; (*bite*) morder.

nipple [ˈnɪpl] *n* (*ANAT*) pezón *m*; (*of bottle*) tetilla.

nitrogen [ˈnaɪtrədʒən] *n* nitrógeno.

╔══════════════╗
║ **KEYWORD** ║
╚══════════════╝

no [nəu] ◆ *ad* (*opposite of 'yes'*) no; **are you coming?** — ~ (**I'm not**) ¿vienes? — no; **would you like**

some more? = ~ thank you ¿quieres más? no gracias
◆ a (not any): I have ~ money/time/books no tengo dinero/tiempo/libros; ~ other man would have done it ningún otro lo hubiera hecho; '~ entry' 'prohibido el paso'; '~ smoking' 'prohibido fumar'
◆ n (pl ~es) m no m.

nobility [nəʊˈbɪlɪtɪ] n nobleza.

noble [ˈnəʊbl] a noble.

nobody [ˈnəʊbədɪ] pron nadie.

nod [nɒd] vi saludar con la cabeza; (in agreement) decir que sí con la cabeza // vt: to ~ one's head inclinar la cabeza // n inclinación f de la cabeza; to ~ off vi cabecear.

noise [nɔɪz] n ruido; (din) escándalo, estrépito; **noisy** a (gen) ruidoso; (child) escandaloso.

nominal [ˈnɒmɪnl] a nominal.

nominate [ˈnɒmɪneɪt] vt (propose) proponer; (appoint) nombrar; **nomination** [-ˈneɪʃən] n propuesta; nombramiento.

nominee [nɒmɪˈniː] n candidato/a.

non... [nɒn] pref no, des..., in...; ~-**alcoholic** a no alcohólico; ~-**aligned** a no alineado.

nonchalant [ˈnɒnʃələnt] a indiferente.

non-committal [ˈnɒnkəˈmɪtl] a (reserved) reservado; (uncommitted) evasivo.

nonconformist [nɒnkənˈfɔːmɪst] a (attitude) heterodoxo; (person) inconformista m/f.

nondescript [ˈnɒndɪskrɪpt] a soso.

none [nʌn] pron ninguno/a // ad de ninguna manera; ~ **of you** ninguno de vosotros; **I've** ~ **left** no me queda ninguno/a; **he's** ~ **the worse for it** no está peor por ello.

nonentity [nɒˈnentɪtɪ] n cero a la izquierda, nulidad f.

nonetheless [nʌnðəˈles] ad sin embargo, no obstante.

non-existent [nɒnɪgˈzɪstənt] a inexistente.

non-fiction [nɒnˈfɪkʃən] n literatura no novelesca.

nonplussed [nɒnˈplʌst] a perplejo.

nonsense [ˈnɒnsəns] n tonterías fpl, disparates fpl; ~! ¡qué tonterías!

non: ~-**smoker** n no fumador(a) m/f; ~-**stick** a (pan, surface) antiadherente; ~-**stop** a continuo; (RAIL) directo // ad sin parar.

noodles [ˈnuːdlz] npl tallarines mpl.

nook [nʊk] n rincón m; ~s **and crannies** escondrijos mpl.

noon [nuːn] n mediodía m.

no-one [ˈnəʊwʌn] pron = **nobody**.

noose [nuːs] n lazo corredizo.

nor [nɔː*] conj = **neither** // ad see **neither**.

norm [nɔːm] n norma.

normal [ˈnɔːml] a normal; ~**ly** ad normalmente.

north [nɔːθ] n norte m // a del norte, norteño // ad al or hacia el norte; **N~ America** n América del Norte; ~-**east** n nor(d)este m; ~**erly** [ˈnɔːðəlɪ] a (point, direction) norteño; ~**ern** [ˈnɔːðən] a norteño, del norte; **N~ern Ireland** n Irlanda del Norte; **N~ Pole** n Polo Norte; **N~ Sea** n Mar m del Norte; ~**ward(s)** [ˈnɔːθwəd(z)] ad hacia el norte; ~-**west** n nor(d)oeste m.

Norway [ˈnɔːweɪ] n Noruega; **Norwegian** [-ˈwiːdʒən] a, n noruego/a m/f.

nose [nəʊz] n (ANAT) nariz f; (ZOOL) hocico; (sense of smell) olfato // vi: to ~ **about** curiosear; ~**bleed** n hemorragia nasal; ~-**dive** n picado vertical; ~**y** a curioso, fisgón/ona.

nostalgia [nɒsˈtældʒɪə] n nostalgia.

nostril [ˈnɒstrɪl] n ventana de la nariz.

nosy [ˈnəʊzɪ] a = **nosey**.

not [nɒt] ad no; ~ **that...** no es que...; **it's too late, isn't it?** no es demasiado tarde, ¿verdad or no?; ~ **yet/now** todavía/ahora no; **why** ~? ¿por qué no?; see also **all, only**.

notably [ˈnəʊtəblɪ] ad especialmente.

notary ['nəutərɪ] n notario/a.

notch [nɔtʃ] n muesca, corte m.

note [nəut] n (MUS, record, letter) nota; (banknote) billete m; (tone) tono // vt (observe) notar, observar; (write down) apuntar, anotar; ~**book** n libreta, cuaderno; ~**d** ['nəutɪd] a célebre, conocido; ~**pad** n bloc m; ~**paper** n papel m para cartas.

nothing ['nʌθɪŋ] n nada; (zero) cero; he does ~ no hace nada; ~ new nada nuevo; for ~ (free) gratis, sin pago; (in vain) en balde.

notice ['nəutɪs] n (announcement) anuncio; (dismissal) despido; (resignation) dimisión f // vt (observe) notar, observar; to take ~ of tomar nota de, prestar atención a; at short ~ con poca anticipación; until further ~ hasta nuevo aviso; to hand in one's ~ dimitir; ~**able** a evidente, obvio; ~ **board** n (Brit) tablón m de anuncios.

notify ['nəutɪfaɪ] vt: to ~ sb (of sth) comunicar (algo) a uno.

notion ['nəuʃən] n noción f, concepto; (opinion) opinión f; ~s n pl (US) mercería.

notorious [nəu'tɔ:rɪəs] a notorio.

notwithstanding [nɔtwɪθ'stændɪŋ] ad no obstante, sin embargo; ~ this a pesar de esto.

nougat ['nu:ga:] n turrón m.

nought [nɔ:t] n cero.

noun [naun] n nombre m, sustantivo.

nourish ['nʌrɪʃ] vt nutrir; ~**ing** a nutritivo; ~**ment** n alimento, sustento.

novel ['nɔvl] n novela // a (new) nuevo, original; (unexpected) insólito; ~**ist** n novelista m/f; ~**ty** n novedad f.

November [nəu'vɛmbə*] n noviembre m.

novice ['nɔvɪs] n principiante m/f, novato/a; (REL) novicio/a.

now [nau] ad (at the present time) ahora; (these days) actualmente, hoy día // conj: ~ (that) ya que, ahora que; right ~ ahora mismo; by ~ ya; just ~: I'll do it just ~ ahora mismo lo hago; ~ and then, ~ and again de vez en cuando; from ~ on de ahora en adelante; ~**adays** ['nauədeɪz] ad hoy (en) día, actualmente.

nowhere ['nəuwɛə*] ad (direction) a ninguna parte; (location) en ninguna parte.

nozzle ['nɔzl] n boquilla.

nuance ['nju:ɑ:ns] n matiz m.

nuclear ['nju:klɪə*] a nuclear.

nucleus ['nju:klɪəs], pl **-lei** [-lɪaɪ] n núcleo.

nude [nju:d] a, n desnudo/a m/f; in the ~ desnudo.

nudge [nʌdʒ] vt dar un codazo a.

nudist ['nju:dɪst] n nudista m/f.

nudity ['nju:dɪtɪ] n desnudez f.

nuisance ['nju:sns] n molestia, fastidio; (person) pesado, latoso; what a ~! ¡qué lata!

nuke ['nju:k] (col) n bomba atómica // vt atacar con arma nuclear.

null [nʌl] a: ~ and void nulo y sin efecto.

numb [nʌm] a entumecido; (fig) insensible // vt entumecer, entorpecer.

number ['nʌmbə*] n número; (numeral) número, cifra // vt (pages etc) numerar, poner número a; (amount to) sumar, ascender a; to be ~**ed** among figurar entre; a ~ of varios, algunos; they were ten in ~ eran diez; ~ **plate** n (Brit) matrícula, placa.

numeral ['nju:mərəl] n número, cifra.

numerate ['nju:mərɪt] a competente en la aritmética.

numerical ['nju:mɛrɪkl] a numérico.

numerous ['nju:mərəs] a numeroso, muchos.

nun [nʌn] n monja, religiosa.

nurse [nə:s] n enfermero/a; (nanny) niñera // vt (patient) cuidar, atender; (baby: Brit) mecer; (: US) criar, amamantar.

nursery ['nə:sərɪ] n (institution)

guardería infantil; (*room*) cuarto de los niños; (*for plants*) criadero, semillero; ~ **rhyme** n canción f infantil; ~ **school** n parvulario, escuela de párvulos; ~ **slope** n (*Brit SKI*) cuesta para principiantes.

nursing ['nɜːsɪŋ] n (*profession*) profesión f de enfermera; (*care*) asistencia, cuidado; ~ **home** n clínica de reposo.

nurture ['nɜːtʃə*] vt (*child, plant*) alimentar, nutrir.

nut [nʌt] n (*TECH*) tuerca; (*BOT*) nuez f; ~**crackers** npl cascanueces m inv; ~**s** a (col) loco.

nutmeg ['nʌtmeg] n nuez f moscada.

nutritious [nju:'trɪʃəs] a nutritivo, rico.

nutshell ['nʌtʃel] n cáscara de nuez; **in a** ~ en resumidas cuentas.

nylon ['naɪlɔn] n nilón m // a de nilón.

O

oak [əuk] n roble m // a de roble.

O.A.P. abbr = **old-age pensioner.**

oar [ɔː*] n remo.

oasis [əu'eɪsɪs], pl **-ses** [-siːz] n oasis m inv.

oath [əuθ] n juramento; (*swear word*) palabrota; **on** (*Brit*) or **under** ~ bajo juramento.

oatmeal ['əutmiːl] n harina de avena.

oats [əuts] n avena.

obedience [ə'biːdɪəns] n obediencia.

obedient [ə'biːdɪənt] a obediente.

obey [ə'beɪ] vt obedecer; (*instructions, regulations*) cumplir.

obituary [ə'bɪtjuərɪ] n necrología.

object ['ɔbdʒɪkt] n (*gen*) objeto; (*purpose*) objeto, propósito; (*LING*) complemento // vi [əb'dʒekt]: **to** ~ **to** (*attitude*) protestar contra; (*proposal*) oponerse a; **expense is no** ~ no importa cuánto cuesta; **I** ~ !, ¡yo protesto!; **to** ~ **that** objetar que; ~**ion** [əb'dʒekʃən] n protesta; **I**

have no ~**ion to**... no tengo inconveniente en que...; ~**ionable** a (*gen*) desagradable; (*conduct*) censurable; ~**ive**, a, n objetivo.

obligation [ɔblɪ'geɪʃən] n obligación f; (*debt*) deber m; **without** ~ sin compromiso.

oblige [ə'blaɪdʒ] vt (*do a favour for*) complacer, hacer un favor a; **to** ~ **sb to do sth** forzar or obligar a uno a hacer algo; **to be** ~**d to sb for sth** estarle agradecido a uno por algo; **obliging** a servicial, atento.

oblique [ə'bliːk] a oblicuo; (*allusion*) indirecto.

obliterate [ə'blɪtəreɪt] vt borrar.

oblivion [ə'blɪvɪən] n olvido; **oblivious** [-ɪəs] a: **oblivious of** inconsciente de.

oblong ['ɔblɔŋ] n rectángulo // a rectángulo.

obnoxious [əb'nɔkʃəs] a odioso, detestable; (*smell*) nauseabundo.

oboe ['əubəu] n oboe m.

obscene [əb'siːn] a obsceno.

obscure [əb'skjuə*] a oscuro // vt oscurecer; (*hide: sun*) esconder.

observance [əb'zɜːvns] n observancia, cumplimiento; (*ritual*) práctica.

observant [əb'zɜːvnt] a observador(a).

observation [ɔbzə'veɪʃən] n observación f; (*by police etc*) vigilancia; (*MED*) examen m.

observatory [əb'zɜːvətrɪ] n observatorio.

observe [əb'zɜːv] vt (*gen*) observar; (*rule*) cumplir; ~**r** n observador(a) m/f.

obsess [əb'ses] vt obsesionar; ~**ive** a obsesivo; obsesionante.

obsolescence [ɔbsə'lesns] n obsolescencia.

obsolete ['ɔbsəliːt] a: **to be** ~ estar en desuso.

obstacle ['ɔbstəkl] n obstáculo; (*nuisance*) estorbo; ~ **race** n carrera de obstáculos.

obstinate ['ɔbstɪnɪt] a terco, porfiado; (*determined*) tenaz.

obstruct [əb'strʌkt] vt (*block*) obstruir; (*hinder*) estorbar, obstaculizar; (*view*) impedir, obstruir; **~ion** [əb'strʌkʃən] n obstrucción f; estorbo, obstáculo.

obtain [əb'teɪn] vt (*get*) obtener; (*achieve*) conseguir; **~able** a asequible.

obtrusive [əb'truːsɪv] a (*person*) importuno, entrometido; (*building etc*) demasiado visible.

obvious ['ɒbvɪəs] a (*clear*) obvio, evidente; (*unsubtle*) poco sutil; **~ly** ad evidentemente, naturalmente.

occasion [ə'keɪʒən] n oportunidad f, ocasión f; (*event*) acontecimiento // vt ocasionar, causar; **~al** a poco frecuente, ocasional; **~ally** ad de vez en cuando.

occupant ['ɔkjupənt] n (*of house*) inquilino/a; (*of car*) ocupante mf.

occupation [ɔkju'peɪʃən] n (*of house*) tenencia; (*job*) trabajo; (*: calling*) oficio; **~al hazard** n riesgo profesional.

occupier ['ɔkjupaɪə*] n inquilino/a.

occupy ['ɔkjupaɪ] vt (*seat, area, time*) ocupar; (*house*) habitar; **to ~ o.s. with** o **by doing** (*as job*) dedicarse a hacer; (*to pass time*) pasar el tiempo haciendo.

occur [ə'kə:*] vi pasar, suceder; **to ~ to sb** ocurrírsele a uno; **~rence** [ə'kʌrəns] n acontecimiento.

ocean ['əuʃən] n océano; **~-going** a de alta mar.

ochre, (*US*) **ocher** ['əukə*] n ocre m.

OCR n abbr = **optical character recognition/reader**.

o'clock [ə'klɔk] ad: **it is 5 ~** son las 5.

octave ['ɔktɪv] n octava.

October [ɔk'təubə*] n octubre m.

octopus ['ɔktəpəs] n pulpo m.

odd [ɔd] a (*strange*) extraño, raro; (*number*) impar; (*left over*) sobrante, suelto; **60~** 60 y pico; **at ~ times** de vez en cuando; **to be the ~ one out** estar de más; **~s and**

ends npl minucias fpl; **~ity** n rareza; (*person*) excéntrico; **~jobs** npl bricolaje m; **~ly** ad curiosamente, extrañamente; **~ments** npl (*Brit COMM*) retales mpl; **~s** npl (*in betting*) puntos mpl de ventaja; **it makes no ~s** da lo mismo; **at ~s** reñidos/as.

odometer [ɔ'dɔmɪtə*] n (*US*) cuentakilómetros m inv.

odour, (*US*) **odor** ['əudə*] n olor m; (*perfume*) perfume m.

KEYWORD

of prep 1 (*gen*) de; **a friend ~ ours** un amigo nuestro; **a boy ~ 10** un chico de 10 años; **that was kind ~ you** muy amable por o de tu parte 2 (*expressing quantity, amount, dates etc*) de; **a kilo ~ flour** un kilo de harina; **there were 3 ~ them** había tres; **3 ~ us went** tres de nosotros fuimos; **the 5th ~ July** el 5 de julio 3 (*from, out of*) de; **made ~ wood** (hecho) de madera.

off [ɔf] a, ad (*engine*) desconectado; (*light*) apagado; (*tap*) cerrado; (*Brit: food: bad*) pasado, malo; (*: milk*) cortado; (*cancelled*) cancelado // prep de; **to be ~** (*to leave*) irse, marcharse; **to be ~ sick** estar enfermo o de baja; **a day ~** un día libre o sin trabajar; **to have an ~ day** tener un día malo; **he had his coat ~** se había quitado el abrigo; **10% ~** (*COMM*) (con el) 10% de descuento; **5 km ~ (the road)** a 5 km (de la carretera); **the coast is ~** the coast frente a la costa; **I'm ~ meat** (*no longer eat/like it*) paso de la carne; **on the ~ chance** por si acaso; **~ and on** de vez en cuando.

offal ['ɔfl] n (*Brit CULIN*) menudencias fpl.

off-colour ['ɔf'kʌlə*] a (*Brit: ill*) indispuesto.

offence, (*US*) **offense** [ə'fɛns] n (*crime*) delito; (*insult*) ofensa; **to take ~ at** ofenderse por.

offend [ə'fɛnd] vt (person) ofender; ~**er** n delincuente m/f; (against regulations) infractor(a) m/f.

offensive [ə'fɛnsɪv] a ofensivo; (smell etc) repugnante // n (MIL) ofensiva.

offer ['ɔfə*] n (gen) oferta, ofrecimiento; (proposal) propuesta // vt ofrecer; (opportunity) facilitar; '**on** ~' (COMM) 'en oferta'; ~**ing** n ofrenda.

offhand [ɔf'hænd] a informal // ad de improviso.

office ['ɔfɪs] n (place) oficina; (room) despacho; (position) carga, oficio; **doctor's** ~ (US) consultorio; **to take** ~ entrar en funciones; ~ **automation** n ofimática, buromática; ~ **block**, (US) ~ **building** n bloque m de oficinas; ~ **hours** npl horas fpl de oficina; (US MED) horas fpl de consulta.

officer ['ɔfɪsə*] n (MIL etc) oficial m/f; (of organization) director(a) m/f; (also: **police officer**) agente m/f de policía.

office worker n oficinista m/f.

official [ə'fɪʃl] a (authorized) oficial, autorizado // n funcionario, oficial m; ~**dom** n burocracia.

offing ['ɔfɪŋ] n: **in the** ~ (fig) en perspectiva.

off: ~**licence** n (Brit: shop) bodega, tienda de vinos y bebidas alcohólicas; ~**line**, a, ad (COMPUT) fuera de línea; ~**peak** a (holiday) de temporada baja; (electricity) de banda económica; ~**putting** a (Brit) asqueroso; desalentador(a); ~**season** a, ad fuera de temporada.

offset ['ɔfsɛt] (irg: like set) vt (counteract) contrarrestar, compensar.

offshoot ['ɔfʃuːt] n (fig) ramificación f.

offshore [ɔf'ʃɔː*] a (breeze, island) costera; (fishing) de bajura.

offside ['ɔf'saɪd] a (SPORT) fuera de juego; (AUT) del lado izquierdo.

offspring ['ɔfsprɪŋ] n descendencia.

off: ~**stage** ad entre bastidores; ~**the-peg**, (US) ~**the-rack** ad confeccionado; ~**white** a blanco grisáceo.

often ['ɔfn] ad a menudo, con frecuencia; **how** ~ **do you go?** ¿cada cuánto vas?

ogle ['əʊgl] vt comerse con los ojos

oh [əʊ] excl ¡ah!

oil [ɔɪl] n aceite m; (petroleum) petróleo // vt (machine) engrasar; ~**can** n lata de aceite; ~**field** n campo petrolífero; ~ **filter** n (AUT) filtro de aceite; ~**fired** a que quema aceite combustible; ~ **painting** n pintura al óleo; ~ **rig** n torre f de perforación; ~**skins** npl impermeables mpl de hule, chubasquero sg; ~ **tanker** n petrolero; ~ **well** n pozo (de petróleo); ~**y** a aceitoso; (food) grasiento.

ointment ['ɔɪntmənt] n ungüento.

O.K., okay ['əʊ'keɪ] excl O.K., ¡está bien!, ¡vale! // a bien // vt dar el visto bueno a.

old [əʊld] a (gen) viejo; (former) antiguo; **how** ~ **are you?** ¿cuántos años tienes?, ¿qué edad tienes?; **he's 10 years** ~ tiene 10 años; ~**er brother** hermano mayor; ~ **age** n vejez f; ~**age pensioner (O.A.P.)** n (Brit) jubilado/a; ~**fashioned** a anticuado, pasado de moda.

olive ['ɔlɪv] n (fruit) aceituna; (tree) olivo // a (also: ~**green**) verde oliva; ~ **oil** n aceite m de oliva.

Olympic [əʊ'lɪmpɪk] a olímpico; the ~ **Games**, the ~**s** npl las Olimpíadas fpl.

omelet(te) ['ɔmlɪt] n tortilla, tortilla de huevo (LAm).

omen ['əʊmən] n presagio.

ominous ['ɔmɪnəs] a de mal agüero, amenazador(a).

omit [əʊ'mɪt] vt omitir.

KEYWORD

---

on [ɔn] ♦ prep **1** (indicating position) en; sobre; ~ **the wall** en la pared;

once

it's ~ **the table** está sobre *or* en la mesa; ~ **the left** a la izquierda
2 (*indicating means, method, condition etc*): ~ **foot** a pie; ~ **the train/plane** (*go*) en tren/avión; (*be*) en el tren/el avión; ~ **the radio/television/telephone** por *or* en la radio/televisión/al teléfono; **to be** ~ **drugs** drogarse; (*MED*) estar a tratamiento; **to be** ~ **holiday/business** estar de vacaciones/en viaje de negocios
3 (*referring to time*): ~ **Friday** el viernes; ~ **Fridays** los viernes; ~ **June 20th** el 20 de junio; **a week** ~ **Friday** del viernes en una semana; ~ **arrival** al llegar; ~ **seeing this** al ver esto
4 (*about, concerning*) sobre, acerca de; **a book** ~ **physics** un libro de *or* sobre física
♦ *ad* **1** (*referring to dress*): **to have one's coat** ~ tener *or* llevar el abrigo puesto; **she put her gloves** ~ se puso los guantes
2 (*referring to covering*): **'screw the lid** ~ **tightly'** 'cerrar bien la tapa'
3 (*further, continuously*): **to walk** *etc* ~ seguir caminando *etc*
♦ *a* **1** (*functioning, in operation*): *machine, radio, TV, light* encendido/a, prendido/a (*LAm*); (: *tap*) abierto/a; (: *brakes*) echado/a, puesto/a; **is the meeting still** ~? (*in progress*; *not cancelled*) ¿todavía continúa la reunión?; **there's a good film** ~ **at the cinema** ponen una buena película en el cine
2: **that's not** ~! (*col : not possible*) ¡eso ni hablar!, ¡eso no está bien!; (: *not acceptable*) ¡eso no se hace!

once [wʌns] *ad* una vez; (*formerly*) antiguamente // *conj* una vez que; ~ **he had left/it was done** una vez que se había marchado/se hizo; **at** ~ en seguida, inmediatamente; (*simultaneously*) a la vez; ~ **a week** una vez por semana; ~ **more** otra vez; ~

and for all de una vez por todas; ~ **upon a time** érase una vez.

oncoming ['ɔnkʌmɪŋ] *a* (*traffic*) que viene de frente.

KEYWORD

one [wʌn] ♦ *num* un(o)/una; ~ **hundred and fifty** ciento cincuenta; ~ **by** ~ uno a uno
♦ *a* **1** (*sole*) único; **the** ~ **book which** el único libro que; **the** ~ **man who** el único que
2 (*same*) mismo/a; **they came in the** ~ **car** vinieron en un solo coche
♦ *pron* **1**: **this** ~ éste/ésta; **that** ~ ése/ésa; (*more remote*) aquél/aquella; **I've already got a (red)** ~ ya tengo una/o (roja/o); ~ **by** ~ uno/a por uno/a
2: ~ **another** os (*Sp*), se (+ *el uno al otro, unos a otros etc*); **do you two ever see** ~ **another?** ¿vosotros dos os veis alguna vez? (*Sp*), ¿se ven ustedes dos alguna vez?; **the boys didn't dare look at** ~ **another** los chicos no se atrevieron a mirarse (el uno al otro); **they all kissed** ~ **another** se besaron unos a otros
3 (*impersonal*): ~ **never knows** nunca se sabe; **to cut** ~**'s finger** cortarse el dedo; ~ **needs to eat** hay que comer.

one: ~**-armed bandit** *n* máquina tragaperras; ~**-day excursion** *n* (*US*) billete *m* de ida y vuelta en un día; ~**-man** *a* (*business*) individual; ~**-man band** *n* hombre-orquesta *m*; ~**-off** *n* (*Brit col: event*) acontecimiento único.

oneself [wʌn'sɛlf] *pron* (*reflexive*) se; (*after prep*) sí; (*emphatic*) uno/a mismo/a; **to hurt** ~ hacerse daño; **to keep sth for** ~ guardarse algo; **to talk to** ~ hablar solo.

one: ~**-sided** *a* (*argument*) parcial; ~**-to-**~ *a* (*relationship*) de dos; ~**upmanship** *n* arte *m* de aventajar a los demás.

ongoing ['ɔngəʊɪŋ] *a* continuo.

onion ['ʌnjən] n cebolla.

on-line ['ɔnlaɪn] a, ad (COMPUT) en línea.

onlooker ['ɔnlukə'] n espectador/a m/f.

only ['əunlɪ] ad solamente, sólo // a único, solo // conj solamente que, pero; **an ~ child** un hijo único; **not ~ ... but also...** no sólo ... sino también...

onset ['ɔnset] n comienzo.

onshore ['ɔnʃɔː'] a (wind) que sopla del mar hacia la tierra.

onslaught ['ɔnslɔːt] n ataque m, embestida.

onto ['ɔntu] prep = **on to**.

onus ['əunəs] n responsabilidad f.

onward(s) ['ɔnwəd(z)] ad (move) (hacia) adelante.

ooze [uːz] vi rezumar.

opaque [əu'peɪk] a opaco.

OPEC ['əupek] n abbr (= Organization of Petroleum-Exporting Countries) OPEP f.

open ['əupn] a abierto; (car) descubierto; (road, view) despejado; (meeting) público; (admiration) manifiesto // vt abrir // vi (flower, eyes, door, debate) abrirse; (book etc: commence) comenzar; **in the ~ (air)** al aire libre; **to ~ on to** vt fus (subj: room, door) dar a; **to ~ up** vt abrir; (blocked road) despejar // vi abrirse, empezar; **~ing** n abertura, comienzo; (opportunity) oportunidad f; (job) puesto vacante, vacante f; **~ly** ad abiertamente; **~-minded** a imparcial; **~-plan** a: **~-plan office** gran oficina sin particiones.

opera ['ɔpərə] n ópera; **~ house** n teatro de la ópera.

operate ['ɔpəreɪt] vt (machine) hacer funcionar; (company) dirigir // vi funcionar; (drug) hacer efecto; **to ~ on sb** (MED) operar a uno.

operatic [ɔpə'rætɪk] a de ópera.

operating ['ɔpəreɪtɪŋ] a: **~ table/theatre** mesa/sala de operaciones.

operation [ɔpə'reɪʃən] n (gen) operación f; (of machine) funcionamiento; **to be in ~** estar funcionando or en funcionamiento; **to have an ~** (MED) ser operado; **~al** a operacional, en buen estado.

operative ['ɔpərətɪv] a (measure) en vigor.

operator ['ɔpəreɪtə'] n (of machine) maquinista m/f, operario/a; (TEL) operador(a) m/f, telefonista m/f.

ophthalmic [ɔf'θælmɪk] a oftálmico.

opinion [ə'pɪnɪən] n (gen) opinión f; **in my ~** en mi opinión, a mi juicio; **~ated** a testarudo; **~ poll** n encuesta, sondeo.

opponent [ə'pəunənt] n adversario/a, contrincante m/f.

opportunist [ɔpə'tjuːnɪst] n oportunista m/f.

opportunity [ɔpə'tjuːnɪtɪ] n oportunidad f; **to take the ~ of doing** aprovechar la ocasión para hacer.

oppose [ə'pəuz] vt oponerse a; **to be ~d to sth** oponerse a algo; **as ~d to** a diferencia de; **opposing** a (side) opuesto, contrario.

opposite ['ɔpəzɪt] a opuesto, contrario a; (house etc) de enfrente // ad en frente // prep en frente de, frente a // n lo contrario.

opposition [ɔpə'zɪʃən] n oposición f.

oppress [ə'pres] vt oprimir.

opt [ɔpt] vi: **to ~ for** optar por; **to ~ to do** optar por hacer; **to ~ out of** optar por no hacer.

optical ['ɔptɪkl] a óptico; **~ character recognition/reader (OCR)** n reconocimiento/lector m óptico de caracteres.

optician [ɔp'tɪʃən] n óptico m/f.

optimist ['ɔptɪmɪst] n optimista m/f; **~ic** [-'mɪstɪk] a optimista.

optimum ['ɔptɪməm] a óptimo.

option ['ɔpʃən] n opción f; **to keep one's ~s open** (fig) mantener las opciones abiertas; **~al** a facultativo, discrecional.

or [ɔː'] conj o; (before o, ho) u; (with negative): **he hasn't seen ~ heard anything** no ha visto ni oído nada; **~**

else si no.

oracle ['ɒrəkl] n oráculo.

oral ['ɔːrəl] a oral // n examen m oral.

orange ['ɒrɪndʒ] n (fruit) naranja // a color naranja.

orator ['ɒrətə*] n orador(a) m/f.

orbit ['ɔːbɪt] n órbita // vt, vi orbitar.

orchard ['ɔːtʃəd] n huerto.

orchestra ['ɔːkɪstrə] n orquesta; (US: seating) platea; **~l** [-'kestrəl] a de orquesta.

orchid ['ɔːkɪd] n orquídea.

ordain [ɔː'deɪn] vt (REL) ordenar, decretar; (decide) mandar.

ordeal [ɔː'diːl] n experiencia horrorosa.

order ['ɔːdə*] n orden m; (command) orden f; (type, kind) clase f; (state) estado; (COMM) pedido, encargo // vt (also: put in ~) arreglar, poner en orden; (COMM) encargar, pedir; (command) mandar, ordenar; **in ~** (gen) en orden; (of document) en regla; **in ~ (working)** en funcionamiento; **in ~ to do** para hacer algo; **on ~** (COMM) pedido; **to ~ sb to do sth** mandar a uno hacer algo; **~form** n hoja de pedido; **~ly** n (MIL) ordenanza m; (MED) enfermero/a (auxiliar) // a ordenado.

ordinary ['ɔːdnrɪ] a corriente, normal, (pej) común y corriente; **out of the ~** fuera de lo común.

ordnance ['ɔːdnəns] n (MIL: unit) artillería.

ore [ɔː*] n mineral m.

organ ['ɔːgən] n órgano; **~ic** [ɔː'gænɪk] a orgánico.

organization [ɔːgənaɪ'zeɪʃən] n organización f.

organize ['ɔːgənaɪz] vt organizar; **~r** n organizador(a) m/f.

orgasm ['ɔːgæzəm] n orgasmo.

orgy ['ɔːdʒɪ] n orgía.

Orient ['ɔːrɪənt] n Oriente m; **oriental** [-'entl] a oriental.

origin ['ɒrɪdʒɪn] n origen m; (point of departure) procedencia.

original [ə'rɪdʒɪnl] a original; (first) primero; (earlier) primitivo // n ori-

ginal m; **~ity** [-'nælɪtɪ] n originalidad f; **~ly** ad (at first) al principio; (with originality) con originalidad.

originate [ə'rɪdʒɪneɪt] vi: **to ~ from, to ~ in** surgir de, tener su origen en.

Orkneys ['ɔːknɪz] npl: **the ~** (also: **the Orkney Islands**) las Orcadas.

ornament ['ɔːnəmənt] n adorno; (trinket) chuchería; **~al** [-'mentl] a decorativo, de adorno.

ornate [ɔː'neɪt] a muy ornado, vistoso.

orphan ['ɔːfn] n huérfano/a // vt: **to be ~ed** quedar huérfano/a; **~age** n orfanato.

orthodox ['ɔːθədɒks] a ortodoxo; **~y** n ortodoxia.

orthopaedic, (US) **orthopedic** [ɔːθə'piːdɪk] a ortopédico.

oscillate ['ɒsɪleɪt] vi oscilar; (person) vacilar.

ostensibly [ɒs'tensɪblɪ] ad aparentemente.

ostentatious [ɒsten'teɪʃəs] a ostentoso.

osteopath ['ɒstɪəpæθ] n osteópata m/f.

ostracize ['ɒstrəsaɪz] vt hacer el vacío a.

ostrich ['ɒstrɪtʃ] n avestruz m.

other ['ʌðə*] a otro // pron: **the ~ (one)** el/la otro/a; **~s** (~ people) otros; **~ than** (apart from) aparte de; **~wise** ad, conj de otra manera; (if not) si no.

otter ['ɒtə*] n nutria.

ouch [autʃ] excl ¡ay!

ought [ɔːt], pt **ought** auxiliary vb: **I ~ to do it** debería hacerlo; **this ~ to have been corrected** esto debiera de haberse corregido; **he ~ to win** (probability) debe or debería ganar.

ounce [auns] n onza (28.35g).

our ['auə*] a nuestro; see also **my**; **~s** pron (el) nuestro/(la) nuestra etc; see also **mine**; **~selves** pron (reflexive, after prep) nosotros; (emphatic) nosotros mismos; see also oneself vt.

oust [aust] vt desalojar.

out [aut] ad fuera, afuera; (not at home) fuera (de casa); (light, fire) apagado; ~ there allí (fuera); he's ~ (absent) no está, ha salido; to be ~ in one's calculations equivocarse (en sus cálculos); to run ~ salir corriendo; ~ loud en alta voz; ~ of (outside) fuera de; (because of: anger etc) por; ~ of petrol sin gasolina; '~ of order' 'no funciona'; ~ -and-~ a (liar, thief etc) redomado, empedernido.

outback ['autbæk] n interior m.

outboard ['autbɔːd] a: ~ motor (motor m) fuera borda m.

outbreak ['autbreɪk] n (of war) comienzo, (of disease) epidemia, (of violence etc) ola.

outburst ['autbɜːst] n explosión f, arranque m.

outcast ['autkɑːst] n paria m/f.

outcome ['autkʌm] n resultado.

outcrop ['autkrɔp] n (of rock) afloramiento.

outcry ['autkraɪ] n protestas fpl.

outdated [aut'deɪtɪd] a anticuado, fuera de moda.

outdo [aut'duː] (irg: like do) vt superar.

outdoor [aut'dɔː'] a, ~s ad al aire libre.

outer ['autə'] a exterior, externo; ~ space n espacio exterior.

outfit ['autfɪt] n equipo; (clothes) traje m; ~ter's n (Brit) sastrería.

outgoing ['autgəuɪŋ] a (character) extrovertido; ~s npl (Brit) gastos mpl.

outgrow [aut'grəu] (irg: like grow) vt: he has ~n his clothes su ropa le queda pequeña ya.

outhouse ['authaus] n dependencia.

outing ['autɪŋ] n excursión f, paseo.

outlandish [aut'lændɪʃ] a estrafalario.

outlaw ['autlɔː] n proscrito.

outlay ['autleɪ] n inversión f.

outlet ['autlet] n salida; (of pipe)

desagüe m; (US ELEC) toma de corriente; (for emotion) desahogo; (also: retail ~) punto de venta.

outline ['autlaɪn] n (shape) contorno, perfil m; in ~ (fig) a grandes rasgos.

outlive [aut'lɪv] vt sobrevivir a.

outlook ['autluk] n perspectiva; (opinion) punto de vista.

outlying ['autlaɪŋ] a remoto, aislado.

outmoded [aut'məudɪd] a anticuado, pasado de moda.

outnumber [aut'nʌmbə'] vt exceder en número.

out-of-date [autəv'deɪt] a (passport) caducado; (clothes) pasado de moda.

out-of-the-way [autəvðə'weɪ] a (place) apartado.

outpatient ['autpeɪʃənt] n paciente m/f externo/a.

outpost ['autpəust] n puesto avanzado.

output ['autput] n (volumen m de) producción f, rendimiento; (COMPUT) salida.

outrage ['autreɪdʒ] n (scandal) escándalo; (atrocity) atrocidad f // vt ultrajar; ~ous [-'reɪdʒəs] a monstruoso.

outright [aut'raɪt] ad (win) de manera absoluta; (be killed) en el acto; (completely) completamente // a ['autraɪt] completo.

outset ['autset] n principio.

outside [aut'saɪd] n exterior m // a exterior, externo // ad fuera // prep fuera de; (beyond) más allá de; at the ~ (fig) a lo sumo; ~ lane n (AUT: in Britain) carril m de la derecha; ~-left/right n (FOOTBALL) extremo izquierdo/derecho; ~ line n (TEL) línea (exterior); ~r n (stranger) extraño, forastero.

outsize ['autsaɪz] a (clothes) de talla grande.

outskirts ['autskɜːts] npl alrededores mpl, afueras fpl.

outspoken [aut'spəukən] a muy franco.

outstanding [aut'stændıŋ] a excepcional, destacado; (*unfinished*) pendiente.

outstay [aut'steı] vt: **to ~ one's welcome** quedarse más de la cuenta.

outstretched [aut'stretʃt] a (*hand*) extendido.

outstrip [aut'strıp] vt (*competitors, demand*) dejar atrás, aventajar.

out-tray [auttreı] n bandeja de salida.

outward ['autwəd] a (*sign, appearances*) externo; (*journey*) de ida; **~ly** ad por fuera.

outweigh [aut'weı] vt pesar más que.

outwit [aut'wıt] vt ser más listo que.

oval ['əuvl] a ovalado // n óvalo.

ovary ['əuvəri] n ovario.

oven ['ʌvn] n horno; **~proof** a resistente al horno.

over ['əuvə*] ad encima, por encima // a (*or ad*) (*finished*) terminado; (*surplus*) de sobra // prep (por) encima de; (*above*) sobre; (*on the other side of*) al otro lado de; (*more than*) más de; (*during*) durante; **~ here** (por) aquí; **~ there** (por) allí or allá; **~ and ~** (*everywhere*) por todas partes; **~ and ~** (*again*) una y otra vez; **~ and above** además de; **to ask sb ~** invitar a uno a casa; **to bend ~** inclinarse.

overall ['əuvərɔːl] a (*length*) total; (*study*) de conjunto // ad [əuvər'ɔːl] en conjunto // n (Brit) guardapolvo; **~s** npl mono sg, overol msg (LAm).

overawe [əuvər'ɔː] vt: **to be ~d (by)** quedar impresionado (con).

overbalance [əuvə'bæləns] vi perder el equilibrio.

overbearing [əuvə'beərıŋ] a autoritario, imperioso.

overboard ['əuvəbɔːd] ad (NAUT) por la borda.

overbook [əuvə'buk] vt sobrereservar.

overcast ['əuvəkɑːst] a encapotado.

overcharge [əuvə'tʃɑːdʒ] vt: **to ~ sb** cobrar un precio excesivo a uno.

overcoat ['əuvəkəut] n abrigo, sobretodo.

overcome [əuvə'kʌm] (*irg: like come*) vt (*gen*) vencer; (*difficulty*) superar.

overcrowded [əuvə'kraudıd] a atestado de gente; (*city, country*) superpoblado.

overdo [əuvə'duː] (*irg: like do*) vt exagerar; (*overcook*) cocer demasiado.

overdose ['əuvədəus] n sobredosis f inv.

overdraft ['əuvədrɑːft] n saldo deudor.

overdrawn [əuvə'drɔːn] a (*account*) en descubierto.

overdue [əuvə'djuː] a retrasado; (*recognition*) tardío.

overestimate [əuvər'estımeıt] vt sobreestimar.

overflow [əuvə'fləu] vi desbordarse // n ['əuvəfləu] (*excess*) exceso; (*of river*) desbordamiento; (*also: ~ pipe*) (cañería de) desagüe m.

overgrown [əuvə'grəun] a (*garden*) invadido por la vegetación.

overhaul [əuvə'hɔːl] vt revisar, repasar // n ['əuvəhɔːl] revisión f.

overhead [əuvə'hed] ad por arriba or encima // a ['əuvəhed] (*cable*) aéreo; (*railway*) elevado, aéreo // n (US) = **~s**; **~s** npl gastos mpl generales.

overhear [əuvə'hıə*] vt (*irg: like hear*) vt oír por casualidad.

overheat [əuvə'hiːt] vi (*engine*) recalentarse.

overjoyed [əuvə'dʒɔıd] a encantado, lleno de alegría.

overkill ['əuvəkıl] n: **that would be ~** eso sería sobrepasarse.

overland ['əuvəlænd] a, ad por tierra.

overlap [əuvə'læp] vi traslaparse.

overleaf [əuvə'liːf] ad al dorso.

overload [əuvə'ləud] vt sobrecargar.

overlook [əuvə'luk] vt (*have view of*) dar a, tener vistas a; (*miss*) pasar por alto; (*forgive*) hacer la vista gorda a.

overnight [əuvə'naɪt] ad durante la noche; (fig) de la noche a la mañana // a de noche; **to stay** ~ pasar la noche.

overpass ['əuvəpɑːs] n (US) paso superior.

overpower [əuvə'pauə*] vt dominar; (fig) embargar; ~**ing** a (heat) agobiante; (smell) penetrante.

overrate [əuvə'reɪt] vt sobreestimar.

override [əuvə'raɪd] (irg: like ride) vt (order, objection) no hacer caso de; **overriding** a predominante.

overrule [əuvə'ruːl] vt (decision) anular; (claim) denegar.

overrun [əuvə'rʌn] (irg: like run) vt (country) invadir; (time limit) rebasar, exceder.

overseas [əuvə'siːz] ad en ultramar; (abroad) en el extranjero // a (trade) exterior; (visitor) extranjero.

overseer ['əuvəsiə*] n (in factory) superintendente m/f; (foreman) capataz m.

overshadow [əuvə'ʃædəu] vt (fig) eclipsar.

overshoot [əuvə'ʃuːt] (irg: like shoot) vt excederse.

oversight ['əuvəsaɪt] n descuido.

oversleep [əuvə'sliːp] (irg: like sleep) vi quedarse dormido.

overspill ['əuvəspɪl] n exceso de población.

overstep [əuvə'stɛp] vt: **to** ~ **the mark** pasarse de la raya.

overt [əu'vɜːt] a abierto.

overtake [əuvə'teɪk] (irg: like take) vt sobrepasar; (Brit AUT) adelantar.

overthrow [əuvə'θrəu] (irg: like throw) vt (government) derrocar.

overtime ['əuvətaɪm] n horas fpl extraordinarias.

overtone ['əuvətəun] n (fig) tono.

overture ['əuvətʃuə*] n (MUS) obertura; (fig) preludio.

overturn [əuvə'tɜːn] vt, vi volcar.

overweight [əuvə'weɪt] a demasiado gordo or pesado.

overwhelm [əuvə'wɛlm] vt aplas-

tar; ~**ing** a (victory, defeat) arrollador(a); (desire) irresistible.

overwork [əuvə'wɜːk] n trabajo excesivo // vi trabajar demasiado.

overwrought [əuvə'rɔːt] a sobreexcitado.

owe [əu] vt deber; **to** ~ **sb sth, to** ~ **sth to sb** deber algo a uno; **owing to** prep debido a, por causa de.

owl [aul] n búho, lechuza.

own [əun] vt tener, poseer // a propio; **a room of my** ~ una habitación propia mía; **to get one's** ~ **back** tomar revancha; **on one's** ~ solo, a solas; **to** ~ **up** vi confesar; ~**er** n dueño/a; ~**ership** n posesión f.

ox [ɔks], pl ~**en** ['ɔksn] n buey m.

oxtail ['ɔksteɪl] n: ~ **soup** sopa de rabo de buey.

oxygen ['ɔksɪdʒən] n oxígeno; ~ **mask/tent** n máscara/tienda de oxígeno.

oyster ['ɔɪstə*] n ostra.

oz. abbr = **ounce(s)**.

ozone ['əuzəun] n: ~ **layer** capa de ozono or ozónica.

P

p [piː] abbr = **penny, pence**.

P.A. n abbr = **personal assistant; public address system**.

p.a. abbr = **per annum**.

pa [pɑː] n (col) papá m.

pace [peɪs] n paso; (rhythm) ritmo // vi: **to** ~ **up and down** pasearse de un lado a otro; **to keep** ~ **with** llevar el mismo paso que; (events) mantenerse a la altura de or al corriente de; ~**maker** n (MED) regulador m cardíaco, marcapasos m inv.

pacific [pə'sɪfɪk] a pacífico // n: **the P~ (Ocean)** el Océano m Pacífico.

pacify ['pæsɪfaɪ] vt (soothe) apaciguar; (country) pacificar.

pack [pæk] n (packet) paquete m; (of hounds) jauría; (of thieves etc) manada, bando; (of cards) baraja;

(bundle) fardo; *(US: of cigarettes)* paquete *m* // *vt (wrap)* empaquetar; *(fill)* llenar; *(in suitcase etc)* meter, poner; *(cram)* llenar, atestar; *(fig: meeting etc)* llenar de partidarios; **to ~ one's bags)** hacerse la maleta; **to ~ sb off** despachar a uno; **~ it in!** *(col)* ¡déjalo!

package ['pækɪdʒ] *n* paquete *m*; *(bulky)* bulto; *(also: ~ deal)* acuerdo global; **~ tour** *n* viaje *m* organizado.

packed lunch *n* almuerzo frío.

packet ['pækɪt] *n* paquete *m*.

packing ['pækɪŋ] *n* embalaje *m*; **~ case** *n* cajón *m* de embalaje.

pact [pækt] *n* pacto.

pad [pæd] *n (of paper)* bloc *m*; *(cushion)* cojinete *m*; *(launching ~)* plataforma *f* de lanzamiento; *(col: flat)* casa // *vt* rellenar; **~ding** *n* relleno; *(fig)* paja.

paddle ['pædl] *n (oar)* canalete *m*; *(US: for table tennis)* raqueta // *vt* impulsar con canalete // *vi (with feet)* chapotear; **~ steamer** *n* vapor *m* de ruedas; **paddling pool** *n (Brit)* estanque *m* de juegos.

paddock ['pædək] *n* corral *m*.

paddy field ['pædɪ-] *n* arrozal *m*.

padlock ['pædlɔk] *n* candado.

paediatrics [piːdɪ'ætrɪks] *n* pediatría.

pagan ['peɪgən] *a*, *n* pagano/a *m/f*.

page [peɪdʒ] *n (of book)* página; *(of newspaper)* plana; *(also: ~ boy)* paje *m* // *vt (in hotel etc)* llamar por altavoz a.

pageant ['pædʒənt] *n (procession)* desfile *m*; *(show)* espectáculo; **~ry** *n* pompa.

paid [peɪd] *pt, pp* of **pay** // *a (work)* remunerado; *(official)* asalariado; **to put ~ to** *(Brit)* acabar con.

pail [peɪl] *n* cubo, balde *m*.

pain [peɪn] *n* dolor *m*; **to be in ~** sufrir; **to take ~s over/to do sth** hacerse grandes molestias con/en hacer algo; **~ed** *a (expression)* afligido; **~ful** *a* doloroso; *(difficult)* peno-

so; *(disagreeable)* desagradable; **~fully** *ad (fig: very)* terriblemente; **~killer** *n* analgésico; **~less** *a* que no causa dolor; **~staking** ['peɪnzteɪkɪŋ] *a (person)* concienzudo, esmerado.

paint [peɪnt] *n* pintura // *vt* pintar; **to ~ the door blue** pintar la puerta de azul; **~brush** *n (artist's)* pincel *m*; *(decorator's)* brocha; **~er** *n* pintor(a) *m/f*; **~ing** *n* pintura; **~work** *n* pintura.

pair [peə*] *n (of shoes, gloves etc)* par *m*; *(of people)* pareja; **a ~ of scissors** unas tijeras; **a ~ of trousers** unos pantalones, un pantalón.

pajamas [pɪ'dʒɑːməz] *npl (US)* pijama *msg*.

Pakistan [pɑːkɪ'stɑːn] *n* Paquistán // *a*, *n* paquistaní *m/f*.

pal [pæl] *n (col)* compinche *m/f*, compañero/a.

palace ['pæləs] *n* palacio.

palatable ['pælɪtəbl] *a* sabroso; *(acceptable)* aceptable.

palate ['pælɪt] *n* paladar *m*.

palatial [pə'leɪʃəl] *a (surroundings, residence)* suntuoso, espléndido.

palaver [pə'lɑːvə*] *n (fuss)* lío.

pale [peɪl] *a (gen)* pálido; *(colour)* claro // *n*: **to be beyond the ~** pasarse de la raya; **to grow ~** palidecer.

Palestine ['pælɪstaɪn] *n* Palestina; **Palestinian** [-'tɪnɪən] *a*, *n* palestino/a *m/f*.

palette ['pælɪt] *n* paleta.

paling ['peɪlɪŋ] *n (stake)* estaca; *(fence)* valla.

pall [pɔːl] *n (of smoke)* capa (de humo) // *vi* perder el sabor.

pallet ['pælɪt] *n (for goods)* pallet *m*.

pallor ['pælə*] *n* palidez *f*.

pallid ['pælɪd] *a* pálido.

palm [pɑːm] *n (ANAT)* palma; *(also: ~ tree)* palmera, palma // *vt*: **to ~ sth off on sb** *(Brit col)* encajar algo a uno; **P~ Sunday** *n* Domingo de Ramos.

palpable ['pælpəbl] *a* palpable.

palpitation [pælpɪ'teɪʃən] n palpitación f; **to have ~s** tener vahídos.

paltry ['pɔːltrɪ] a (quantity) irrisorio; (person) despreciable.

pamper ['pæmpə*] vt mimar.

pamphlet ['pæmflət] n folleto.

pan [pæn] n (also: sauce~) cacerola, cazuela, olla; (also: frying ~) sartén m; (of lavatory) taza // vi (CINEMA) tomar panorámicas.

panache [pə'næʃ] n: **with ~** con estilo.

Panama ['pænəmɑː] n Panamá m; **the ~ Canal** el Canal de Panamá.

pancake ['pænkeɪk] n crepe f.

panda ['pændə] n panda m; **~ car** n (Brit) coche m Z.

pandemonium [pændɪ'məunɪəm] n: **there was ~** se armó un tremendo jaleo.

pander ['pændə*] vi: **to ~** to complacer a.

pane [peɪn] n cristal m.

panel ['pænl] n (of wood) panel m; (of cloth) paño; (RADIO, TV) panel m de invitados; **~ling,** (US) **~ing** n paneles mpl.

pang [pæŋ] n: **~s of conscience** remordimiento sg; **~s of hunger** dolores mpl del hambre.

panic ['pænɪk] n (terror m) pánico // vi dejarse llevar por el pánico; **~ky** a (person) asustadizo; **~-stricken** a preso de pánico.

pansy ['pænzɪ] n (BOT) pensamiento; (col: pej) maricón m.

pant [pænt] vi jadear.

panther ['pænθə*] n pantera.

panties ['pæntɪz] npl bragas fpl, pantis mpl.

pantihose ['pæntɪhəuz] n (US) pantimedias fpl.

pantomime ['pæntəmaɪm] n (Brit) revista musical representada en Navidad, basada en cuentos de hadas.

pantry ['pæntrɪ] n despensa.

pants [pænts] n (Brit: underwear: woman's) bragas fpl; (: man's) calzoncillos mpl; (US: trousers) pantalones mpl.

papal ['peɪpəl] a papal.

paper ['peɪpə*] n papel m; (also: news~) periódico, diario; (study, article) artículo; (exam) examen m // a de papel // vt empapelar, tapizar (LAm); (identity) **~s** npl papeles mpl, documentos mpl; **~back** n libro de bolsillo; **~ bag** n bolsa de papel; **~ clip** n clip m; **~ hankie** n pañuelo de papel; **~weight** n pisapapeles m inv; **~work** n trabajo administrativo; (pej) papeleo.

papier-mâché ['pæpɪeɪ'mæʃeɪ] n cartón m piedra.

paprika ['pæprɪkə] n pimienta húngara or roja.

par [pɑː*] n par f; (GOLF) par m; **to be on a ~ with** estar a la par con.

parable ['pærəbl] n parábola.

parachute ['pærəʃuːt] n paracaídas m inv // vi lanzarse en paracaídas.

parade [pə'reɪd] n desfile m // vt (gen) recorrer, desfilar por; (show off) hacer alarde de // vi desfilar; (MIL) pasar revista.

paradise ['pærədaɪs] n paraíso.

paradox ['pærədɔks] n paradoja; **~ically** [-'dɔksɪklɪ] ad paradójicamente.

paraffin ['pærəfɪn] n (Brit): **~ (oil)** parafina.

paragon ['pærəgən] n modelo.

paragraph ['pærəgrɑːf] n párrafo.

Paraguay ['pærəgwaɪ] n Paraguay m.

parallel ['pærəlɛl] a en paralelo; (fig) semejante // n (line) paralela; (fig, GEO) paralelo.

paralysis [pə'rælɪsɪs] n parálisis f inv.

paralyze ['pærəlaɪz] vt paralizar.

paramedic [pærəmedɪk] n (US) ambulanciero/a.

paramount ['pærəmaunt] a: **of ~ importance** de suma importancia.

paranoid ['pærənɔɪd] a (person, feeling) paranoico.

paraphernalia [pærəfə'neɪlɪə] n (gear) avíos mpl.

parasite ['pærəsaɪt] n parásito/a.

parasol ['pærəsɒl] n sombrilla, quitasol m.

paratrooper ['pærətruːpə*] n paracaidista m/f.

parcel ['pɑːsl] n paquete m // vt (also: ~ up) empaquetar, embalar.

parch [pɑːtʃ] vt secar, resecar; ~ed a (person) muerto de sed.

parchment ['pɑːtʃmənt] n pergamino.

pardon ['pɑːdn] n perdón m; (LAW) indulto // vt perdonar; indultar; ~ me!, I beg your ~! ¡perdone usted!; (I beg your) ~?, (US) ~ me? ¿cómo?

parent ['pɛərənt] n: ~s npl padres mpl; ~al [pə'rɛntl] a paternal/maternal.

parenthesis [pə'rɛnθɪsɪs], pl -theses [-θɪsiːz] n paréntesis m inv.

Paris ['pærɪs] n Paris m.

parish ['pærɪʃ] n parroquia.

parity ['pærɪtɪ] n paridad f, igualdad f.

park [pɑːk] n parque m // vt aparcar, estacionar // vi aparcar, estacionarse.

parking ['pɑːkɪŋ] n aparcamiento, estacionamiento; 'no ~' 'prohibido estacionarse'; ~ lot n (US) parking m; ~ meter n parquímetro; ~ ticket n multa de aparcamiento.

parlance ['pɑːləns] n lenguaje m.

parliament ['pɑːləmənt] n parlamento; (Spanish) Cortes fpl; ~ary [-'mɛntrɪ] a parlamentario.

parlour, (US) **parlor** ['pɑːlə*] n sala de recibo, salón m, living (LAm).

parochial [pə'rəukɪəl] a parroquial; (pej) de miras estrechas.

parody ['pærədɪ] n parodia.

parole [pə'rəul] n: on ~ libre bajo palabra.

parquet ['pɑːkeɪ] n: ~ floor(ing) parquet m.

parrot ['pærət] n loro, papagayo.

parry ['pærɪ] vt parar.

parsimonious [pɑːsɪ'məunɪəs] a tacaño.

parsley ['pɑːslɪ] n perejil m.

parsnip ['pɑːsnɪp] n chirivía.

parson ['pɑːsn] n cura m.

part [pɑːt] n (gen, MUS) parte f; (bit) trozo; (of machine) pieza; (THEATRE etc) papel m; (of serial) entrega; (US: in hair) raya // ad = **partly** // vt separar; (break) partir // vi (people) separarse; (roads) bifurcarse; (crowd) apartarse; (break) romperse; **to take ~ in** participar or tomar parte en; **to take sth in good ~** tomar algo en buena parte; **to take sb's ~** defender a uno; **for my ~** por mi parte; **for the most ~** en su mayor parte; (people) en su mayoría; **to ~ with** vt fus ceder, entregar; (money) pagar; (get rid of) deshacerse de; ~ **exchange** n (Brit): **in ~ exchange** como parte del pago.

partial ['pɑːʃl] a parcial; **to be ~ to** ser aficionado a.

participant [pɑː'tɪsɪpənt] n (in competition) concursante m/f.

participate [pɑː'tɪsɪpeɪt] vi: **to ~ in** participar en; **participation** [-'peɪʃən] n participación f.

participle ['pɑːtɪsɪpl] n participio.

particle ['pɑːtɪkl] n partícula; (of dust) grano; (fig) pizca.

particular [pə'tɪkjulə*] a (special) particular; (concrete) concreto; (given) determinado; (detailed) detallado, minucioso; (fussy) quisquilloso, exigente; ~s npl (information) datos mpl, detalles mpl; (details) pormenores mpl; **in ~** en particular; ~**ly** ad especialmente, en particular.

parting ['pɑːtɪŋ] n (act of) separación f; (farewell) despedida; (Brit: in hair) raya // a de despedida.

partisan [pɑːtɪ'zæn] a, n partidario/a.

partition [pɑː'tɪʃən] n (POL) división f; (wall) tabique m.

partly ['pɑːtlɪ] ad en parte.

partner ['pɑːtnə*] n (COMM) socio/a; (SPORT, at dance) pareja; (spouse) cónyuge m/f; (friend etc) compañero/a // vt acompañar; ~**ship** n (gen) asociación f; (COMM) sociedad f.

partridge [ˈpɑːtrɪdʒ] n perdiz f.

part-time [ˈpɑːtˈtaɪm] a, ad a tiempo parcial.

party [ˈpɑːtɪ] n (POL) partido; (celebration) fiesta; (group) grupo; (LAW) parte f, interesado // a (POL) de partido; (dress etc) de fiesta, de gala; ~ **line** n (TEL) línea compartida.

pass [pɑːs] vt (time, object) pasar; (place) pasar por; (exam) aprobar; (overtake, surpass) rebasar; (approve) aprobar // vi pasar; (SCOL) aprobar, ser aprobado // n (permit) permiso; (membership card) carnet m; (in mountains) puerto, desfiladero; (SPORT) pase m; (SCOL: also: ~ **mark**): **to get a** ~ **in** aprobar en; **to** ~ **sth** hacer pasar algo por algo; **to make a** ~ **at sb** (col) hacer proposiciones a uno; **to** ~ **away** vi fallecer; **to** ~ **by** vi pasar // vt (ignore) pasar por alto; **to** ~ **for** pasar por; **to** ~ **on** vt transmitir; **to** ~ **out** vi desmayarse; **to** ~ **up** vt (opportunity) renunciar a; ~**able** a (road) transitable; (tolerable) pasable.

passage [ˈpæsɪdʒ] n (also: ~**way**) pasillo; (act of passing) tránsito; (fare, in book) pasaje m; (by boat) travesía.

passbook [ˈpɑːsbuk] n libreta de banco.

passenger [ˈpæsɪndʒə*] n pasajero/a, viajero/a.

passer-by [ˈpɑːsəˈbaɪ] n transeúnte m/f.

passing [ˈpɑːsɪŋ] a (fleeting) pasajero; **in** ~ de paso; ~ **place** n (AUT) apartadero.

passion [ˈpæʃən] n pasión f; ~**ate** a apasionado.

passive [ˈpæsɪv] a (also LING) pasivo.

Passover [ˈpɑːsəuvə*] n Pascua (de los judíos).

passport [ˈpɑːspɔːt] n pasaporte m; ~ **control** n control m de pasaporte.

password [ˈpɑːswɜːd] n contraseña.

past [pɑːst] prep (further than) más allá de; (later than) después de // a pasado; (president etc) antiguo // n (time) el pasado; (of person) antecedentes mpl; **he's** ~ **forty** tiene más de cuarenta años; **for the** ~ **few/3 days** durante los últimos días/últimos 3 días; **to run** ~ **sb** pasar a uno corriendo.

pasta [ˈpæstə] n pasta.

paste [peɪst] n (gen) pasta; (glue) engrudo // vt (stick) pegar; (glue) engomar.

pasteurized [ˈpæstəraɪzd] a pasteurizado.

pastille [ˈpæstl] n pastilla.

pastime [ˈpɑːstaɪm] n pasatiempo.

pastor [ˈpɑːstə*] n pastor m.

pastry [ˈpeɪstrɪ] n (dough) pasta; (cake) pastel m.

pasture [ˈpɑːstʃə*] n (grass) pasto.

pasty n [ˈpæstɪ] n empanada // a [ˈpeɪstɪ] pastoso; (complexion) pálido.

pat [pæt] vt dar una palmadita a; (dog etc) acariciar.

patch [pætʃ] n (of material) parche m; (mended part) remiendo; (of land) terreno // vt (clothes) remendar; **(to go through) a bad** ~ (pasar por) una mala racha; **to** ~ **up** vt (mend temporarily) reparar; (quarrel) hacer las paces en; ~**work** n labor m de retazos; ~**y** a desigual.

pâté [ˈpæteɪ] n paté m.

patent [ˈpeɪtnt] n patente f // vt patentar // a patente, evidente; ~ **leather** n charol m.

paternal [pəˈtɜːnl] a paternal; (relation) paterno.

paternity [pəˈtɜːnɪtɪ] n paternidad f.

path [pɑːθ] n camino, sendero; (trail, track) pista; (of missile) trayectoria.

pathetic [pəˈθetɪk] a (pitiful) patético, lastimoso; (very bad) malísimo; (moving) conmovedor(a).

pathological [pæθəˈlɒdʒɪkəl] a patológico.

pathology [pəˈθɒlədʒɪ] n patología.

pathos [ˈpeɪθɒs] n patetismo.

pathway ['pɑːθweɪ] *n* sendero, vereda.

patience ['peɪʃns] *n* paciencia; (*Brit CARDS*) solitario.

patient ['peɪʃt] *n* paciente *m/f // a* a paciente, sufrido.

patio ['pætɪəʊ] *n* patio.

patriotic [pætrɪ'ɒtɪk] *a* patriótico.

patrol [pə'trəʊl] *n* patrulla *// vt* patrullar por; ~ **car** *n* coche *m* patrulla; ~**man** *n* (*US*) policía *m*.

patron ['peɪtrən] *n* (*in shop*) cliente *m/f*; (*of charity*) patrocinador/a *m/f*; ~ **of the arts** mecenas *m*; ~**ize** ['pætrənaɪz] *vt* (*shop*) ser cliente de; (*look down on*) condescender con.

patter ['pætə*] *n* golpeteo; (*sales talk*) labia *// vi* (*rain*) tamborilear.

pattern ['pætən] *n* (*SEWING*) patrón *m*; (*design*) dibujo.

paunch [pɔːntʃ] *n* panza, barriga.

pauper ['pɔːpə*] *n* pobre *m/f*.

pause [pɔːz] *n* pausa; (*interval*) intérvalo *// vi* hacer una pausa.

pave [peɪv] *vt* pavimentar; **to ~ the way for** preparar el terreno para.

pavement ['peɪvmənt] *n* (*Brit*) acera, vereda (*LAm*).

pavilion [pə'vɪlɪən] *n* pabellón *m*; (*SPORT*) caseta.

paving ['peɪvɪŋ] *n* pavimento, enlosado; ~ **stone** *n* losa.

paw [pɔː] *n* pata; (*claw*) garra.

pawn [pɔːn] *n* (*CHESS*) peón *m*; (*fig*) instrumento *// vt* empeñar; ~**broker** *n* prestamista *m/f*; ~**shop** *n* monte *m* de piedad.

pay [peɪ] *n* paga; (*wage etc*) sueldo, salario *// (vb: pt, pp paid) vt* pagar *// vi* pagar; (*be profitable*) rendir; **to ~ attention (to)** prestar atención (a); **to ~ back** *vt* (*money*) reembolsar; (*person*) pagar; **to ~ for** *vt* pagar; **to ~ in** *vt* ingresar; **to ~ off** *vt* liquidar *// vi* (*scheme, decision*) dar resultado; **to ~ up** *vt* pagar (de mala gana); ~**able** *a* pagadero; ~**day** *n* día *m* de paga; ~**ee** *n* portador(a) *m/f*; ~ **envelope** *n* (*US*) =

~ **packet**; ~**ment** *n* pago; advance ~**ment** mensualidad *f*; ~ **packet** *n* (*Brit*) sobre *m* de (paga); ~**-phone** *n* teléfono público; ~**roll** *n* nómina; ~ **slip** *n* recibo de sueldo.

PC *n abbr* = **personal computer**.

p.c. *abbr* = **per cent**.

pea [piː] *n* guisante *m*, chícharo (*LAm*), arveja (*LAm*).

peace [piːs] *n* paz *f*; (*calm*) paz *f*, tranquilidad *f*; ~**able** *a* pacífico; ~**ful** *a* (*gentle*) pacífico; (*calm*) tranquilo, sosegado.

peach [piːtʃ] *n* melocotón *m*, durazno (*LAm*).

peacock ['piːkɔk] *n* pavo real.

peak [piːk] *n* (*of mountain: top*) cumbre *f*, cima; (: *point*) pico; (*of cap*) visera; (*fig*) cumbre *f*; ~ **hours** *npl*, ~ **period** *n* horas *fpl* punta.

peal [piːl] *n* (*of bells*) repique *m*; ~ **of laughter** carcajada.

peanut ['piːnʌt] *n* cacahuete *m*, maní *m* (*LAm*).

pear [peə*] *n* pera.

pearl [pɜːl] *n* perla.

peasant ['peznt] *n* campesino/a.

peat [piːt] *n* turba.

pebble ['pebl] *n* guijarro.

peck [pek] *vt* (*also*: ~ **at**) picotear; (*food*) comer sin ganas *// n* picotazo; (*kiss*) besito; ~**ing order** *n* orden *m* de jerarquía; ~**ish** *a* (*Brit col*): **I feel ~ish** tengo ganas de picar algo.

peculiar [pɪ'kjuːlɪə*] *a* (*odd*) extraño, raro; (*typical*) propio, característico; ~ **to** propio de; ~**ity** [pɪkjuːlɪ'ærɪtɪ] *n* peculiaridad *f*, característica.

pedal ['pedl] *n* pedal *m // vi* pedalear.

pedantic [pɪ'dæntɪk] *a* pedante.

peddler ['pedlə*] *n* vendedor/a *m/f* ambulante.

pedestal ['pedəstl] *n* pedestal *m*.

pedestrian [pɪ'destrɪən] *n* peatón/ona *m/f // a* a pedestre; ~ **crossing** *n* (*Brit*) paso de peatones.

pediatrics [piːdɪ'ætrɪks] *n* (*US*) = **paediatrics**.

pedigree ['pedɪgriː] n genealogía; (of animal) raza // (of animal) raza // cpd (animal) de raza, de casta.

pedlar ['pedlə*] n = **peddler**.

pee [piː] vi (col) mear.

peek [piːk] vi mirar a hurtadillas.

peel [piːl] n piel f; (of orange, lemon) cáscara; (: removed) peladuras fpl // vt pelar // vi (paint etc) desconcharse; (wallpaper) despegarse, desprenderse.

peep [piːp] n (Brit: look) mirada furtiva; (sound) pío // vi (Brit) piar; to ~ out vi asomar la cabeza; ~hole n mirilla.

peer [pɪə*] vi: to ~ at escudriñar // n (noble) par m; (equal) igual m; ~age n nobleza.

peeved [piːvd] a enojado.

peevish ['piːvɪʃ] a malhumorado.

peg [peg] n clavija; (for coat etc) gancho, colgadero; (Brit: also: clothes ~) pinza; (tent ~) estaca // vt (prices) fijar.

Peking [piː'kɪŋ] n Pekín.

pekinese [piːkɪ'niːz] n pequinés/esa m/f.

pelican ['pelɪkən] n pelícano; ~ crossing n (Brit AUT) paso de peatones señalizado.

pellet ['pelɪt] n bolita; (bullet) perdigón m.

pelmet ['pelmɪt] n galería.

pelt [pelt] vt: to ~ sb with sth arrojarle algo a uno // vi (rain) llover a cántaros // n pellejo.

pen [pen] n pluma; (for sheep) redil m.

penal ['piːnl] a penal; ~ize vt (punish: SPORT) castigar.

penalty ['penltɪ] n (gen) pena; (fine) multa; (SPORT) castigo; ~ (kick) n (FOOTBALL) penalty m.

penance ['penəns] n penitencia.

pence [pens] pl of **penny**.

pencil ['pensl] n lápiz m, lapicero (LAm); ~ case n estuche m; ~ sharpener n sacapuntas m inv.

pendant ['pendnt] n pendiente m.

pending ['pendɪŋ] prep antes de // a

pendiente; ~ the arrival of ... hasta que llegue ...

pendulum ['pendjuləm] n péndulo.

penetrate ['penɪtreɪt] vt penetrar.

penfriend ['penfrend] n (Brit) amigo/a por carta.

penguin ['peŋgwɪn] n pingüino.

penicillin [penɪ'sɪlɪn] n penicilina.

peninsula [pə'nɪnsjulə] n península.

penis ['piːnɪs] n pene m.

penitent ['penɪtnt] a arrepentido; (REL) penitente.

penitentiary [penɪ'tenʃərɪ] n (US) cárcel f, presidio.

penknife ['pennaɪf] n navaja.

pen name n seudónimo.

penniless ['penɪlɪs] a sin dinero.

penny ['penɪ], pl **pennies** ['penɪz] or (Brit) **pence** [pens] n penique m; (US) centavo.

penpal ['penpæl] n amigo/a por carta.

pension ['penʃən] n (allowance, state payment) pensión f; (old-age) jubilación f; ~er n (Brit) jubilado/a.

pensive ['pensɪv] a pensativo; (withdrawn) preocupado.

pentagon ['pentəgən] n: the P~ (US POL) el Pentágono.

Pentecost ['pentɪkɔst] n Pentecostés m.

penthouse ['penthaus] n ático de lujo.

pent-up ['pentʌp] a (feelings) reprimido.

people ['piːpl] npl gente f; (citizens) pueblo sg, ciudadanos mpl // n (nation, race) pueblo, nación f // vt poblar; several ~ came vinieron varias personas; ~ say that... dice la gente que... .

pep [pep] n (col) energía; to ~ up vt animar.

pepper ['pepə*] n (spice) pimienta; (vegetable) pimiento // vt (fig) salpicar; ~mint n menta; (sweet) pastilla de menta.

peptalk ['peptɔːk] n: to give sb a ~ darle a uno una inyección de ánimo.

per [pɜː*] prep por; ~ day/person

por día/persona; ~ **annum** ad al año; ~ **capita** a, ad per cápita.

perceive [pə'siːv] vt percibir; (*realize*) darse cuenta de.

per cent n por ciento.

percentage [pə'sɛntɪdʒ] n porcentaje m.

perception [pə'sɛpʃən] n percepción f; (*insight*) perspicacia; **perceptive** [-'sɛptɪv] a perspicaz.

perch [pɔːtʃ] n (*fish*) perca; (*for bird*) percha // vi posarse.

percolator ['pɔːkəleɪtə*] n cafetera de filtro.

perennial [pə'rɛnɪəl] a perenne.

perfect ['pɔːfɪkt] a perfecto // n (*also*: ~ **tense**) perfecto // vt [pə'fɛkt] perfeccionar; **~ly** ad perfectamente.

perforate ['pɔːfəreɪt] vt perforar; **perforation** [-'reɪʃən] n perforación f.

perform [pə'fɔːm] vt (*carry out*) realizar, llevar a cabo; (*THEATRE*) representar; (*piece of music*) interpretar // vi (*THEATRE*) actuar; (*TECH*) funcionar; **~ance** n (*of task*) realización f; (*of a play*) representación f; (*of player etc*) actuación f; (*of car, engine*) rendimiento f; (*of function*) desempeño; **~er** n (*actor*) actor m, actriz f; (*MUS*) intérprete m/f; **~ing** a (*animal*) amaestrado.

perfume ['pɔːfjuːm] n perfume m.

perfunctory [pə'fʌŋktərɪ] a superficial.

perhaps [pə'hæps] ad quizá(s), tal vez.

peril ['pɛrɪl] n peligro, riesgo.

perimeter [pə'rɪmɪtə*] n perímetro.

period ['pɪərɪəd] n periodo; (*HISTORY*) época; (*SCOL*) clase f; (*full stop*) punto; (*MED*) regla // (*costume, furniture*) de época; **~ic** [-'ɔdɪk] a periódico; **~ical** [-'ɔdɪkl] n periódico; **~ically** [-'ɔdɪklɪ] ad de vez en cuando, cada cierto tiempo.

peripheral [pə'rɪfərəl] a periférico // n (*COMPUT*) periférico, unidad f periférica.

perish ['pɛrɪʃ] vi perecer; (*decay*) echarse a perder; **~able** a perecedero.

perjury ['pɔːdʒərɪ] n (*LAW*) perjurio.

perk [pɔːk] n extra m; **to ~ up** vi (*cheer up*) animarse; **~y** a alegre, despabilado.

perm [pɔːm] n permanente f.

permanent ['pɔːmənənt] a permanente.

permeate ['pɔːmɪeɪt] vi penetrar, trascender // vt penetrar, trascender a.

permissible [pə'mɪsɪbl] a permisible, lícito.

permission [pə'mɪʃən] n permiso.

permissive [pə'mɪsɪv] a permisivo.

permit ['pɔːmɪt] n permiso, licencia // vt [pə'mɪt] permitir; (*accept*) tolerar.

pernicious [pə'nɪʃəs] a nocivo; (*MED*) pernicioso.

perpetrate ['pɔːpɪtreɪt] vt cometer.

perpetual [pə'pɛtjuəl] a perpetuo.

perplex [pə'plɛks] vt dejar perplejo.

persecute ['pɔːsɪkjuːt] vt (*pursue*) perseguir; (*harass*) acosar.

perseverance [pɔːsɪ'vɪərəns] n perseverancia.

persevere [pɔːsɪ'vɪə*] vi persistir.

Persian ['pɔːʃən] a, n persa m/f; **the** (~) **Gulf** el Golfo Pérsico.

persist [pə'sɪst] vi: **to ~** (**in doing sth**) persistir (en hacer algo); **~ence** n empeño; **~ent** a persistente; (*determined*) porfiado; (*continuing*) constante.

person ['pɔːsn] n persona; **in ~** en persona; **~able** a atractivo; (*at a personal; individual; (visit)* en persona; **~al** a personal, individual; (*visit*) en persona; **~al assistant** (**P.A.**) n ayudante m/f personal; **~al column** n anuncios mpl personales; **~al computer** (**PC**) n computador m personal; **~ality** [-'nælɪtɪ] n personalidad f; **~ally** ad personalmente; **~ify** [-'sɔnɪfaɪ] vt encarnar.

personnel [pɔːsə'nɛl] n personal m.

perspective [pə'spɛktɪv] n perspectiva.

Perspex ['pɜːspeks] n ® plexiglás m.

perspiration [pɜːspɪ'reɪʃən] n transpiración f.

persuade [pə'sweɪd] vt: **to ~ sb to do sth** persuadir a uno para que haga algo.

pert [pɜːt] a impertinente, fresco.

pertaining [pɜː'teɪnɪŋ]: **~ to** prep relacionado con.

pertinent ['pɜːtɪnənt] a pertinente, a propósito.

Peru [pə'ruː] n el Perú.

peruse [pə'ruːz] vt leer con detención, examinar.

Peruvian [pə'ruːvɪən] a, n peruano/a m/f.

pervade [pə'veɪd] vt impregnar, infundirse en.

perverse [pə'vɜːs] a perverso; (stubborn) terco; (wayward) travieso.

pervert ['pɜːvɜːt] n pervertido/a // vt [pə'vɜːt] pervertir.

pessimist ['pesɪmɪst] n pesimista m/f; **~ic** [-'mɪstɪk] a pesimista.

pest [pest] n (insect) insecto nocivo; (fig) lata, molestia.

pester ['pestə*] vt molestar, acosar.

pet [pet] n animal m doméstico; (favourite) favorito/a // a acariciar // vi (col) besuquearse.

petal ['petl] n pétalo.

peter ['piːtə*]: **to ~ out** vi agotarse, acabarse.

petite [pə'tiːt] a chiquito.

petition [pə'tɪʃən] n petición f.

petrified ['petrɪfaɪd] a horrorizado.

petrol ['petrəl] (Brit) n gasolina; (for lighter) bencina; **two/four-star ~** gasolina normal/súper; **~ can** n bidón m de gasolina.

petroleum [pə'trəʊlɪəm] n petróleo.

petrol: ~ pump n (Brit) (in car) bomba de gasolina; (in garage) surtidor m de gasolina; **~ station** n (Brit) gasolinera; **~ tank** n (Brit) depósito de gasolina.

petticoat ['petɪkəʊt] n enaguas fpl.

petty ['petɪ] a (mean) mezquino; (unimportant) insignificante; **~ cash** n dinero para gastos menores; **~**

officer n contramaestre m.

petulant ['petjulənt] a malhumorado.

pew [pjuː] n banco.

pewter ['pjuːtə*] n peltre m.

phantom ['fæntəm] n fantasma m.

pharmacist ['faːməsɪst] n farmacéutico/a.

pharmacy ['faːməsɪ] n farmacia.

phase [feɪz] n fase f // vt: **to ~ sth in/out** introducir/retirar algo por etapas.

Ph.D. abbr = Doctor of Philosophy.

pheasant ['feznt] n faisán m.

phenomenon [fə'nɒmɪnən], pl **phenomena** [-nə] n fenómeno.

phial ['faɪəl] n ampolla.

philately [fɪ'lætəlɪ] n filatelia.

Philippines ['fɪlɪpiːnz]: **the ~** las Filipinas.

philosopher [fɪ'lɒsəfə*] n filósofo/a.

philosophy [fɪ'lɒsəfɪ] n filosofía.

phlegm [flem] n flema; **~atic** [fleg'mætɪk] a flemático.

phobia ['fəʊbjə] n fobia.

phone [fəʊn] n teléfono // vt telefonear, llamar por teléfono; **to be on the ~** tener teléfono; (be calling) estar hablando por teléfono; **to ~ back**, vi, vt volver a llamar; **to ~ up** vt, vi llamar por teléfono; **~ book** n guía telefónica; **~ box** or **booth** cabina telefónica; **~ call** n llamada (telefónica); **~-in** n (Brit RADIO, TV) programa m de participación (telefónica).

phonetics [fə'netɪks] n fonética.

phoney ['fəʊnɪ] a falso // n (person) farsante m/f.

phonograph ['fəʊnəgræf] n (US) fonógrafo, tocadiscos m inv.

phosphate ['fɒsfeɪt] n fosfato.

photo ['fəʊtəu] n foto f.

photo... ['fəʊtəu] pref: **~copier** n fotocopiadora; **~copy** n fotocopia // vt fotocopiar; **~graph** n fotografía // vt fotografiar; **~grapher** [fə'tɒgrəfə*] n fotógrafo; **~graphy** [fə'tɒgrəfɪ] n fotografía.

phrase [freɪz] n frase f // vt expresar; ~ **book** n libro de frases.

physical ['fɪzɪkl] a físico; ~ **education** n educación f física; ~**ly** ad físicamente.

physician [fɪ'zɪʃən] n médico/a.

physicist ['fɪzɪsɪst] n físico/a.

physics ['fɪzɪks] n física.

physiotherapy [fɪzɪəʊ'θerəpɪ] n fisioterapia.

physique [fɪ'ziːk] n físico.

pianist ['piːənɪst] n pianista m/f.

piano [pɪ'ænəʊ] n piano.

piccolo ['pɪkələʊ] n (MUS) flautín m.

pick [pɪk] n (tool: also: ~-axe) pica, piqueta // vt (select) elegir, escoger; (gather) coger (Sp), recoger (LAm); (lock) abrir con ganzúa; **take your** ~ escoja lo que quiera; **the** ~ **of** lo mejor de; **to** ~ **one's nose/teeth** hurgarse las narices/limpiarse los dientes; **to** ~ **pockets** ratear ser carterista; **to** ~ **off** vt (kill) matar uno a uno; **to** ~ **on** vt fus (person) meterse con; **to** ~ **out** vt escoger; (distinguish) identificar; **to** ~ **up** vi (improve: sales) ir mejor; (: patient) reponerse; (: FINANCE) recobrarse // vt (from floor) recoger; (buy) comprar; (find) encontrar; (learn) aprender; **to** ~ **up speed** acelerarse; **to** ~ **o.s. up** levantarse.

picket ['pɪkɪt] n (in strike) piquete m // vt piquetear; ~ **line** n piquete m.

pickle ['pɪkl] n (also: ~s: as condiment) escabeche m; (fig: mess) apuro // vt encurtir; (in vinegar) envinagrar.

pickpocket ['pɪkpɒkɪt] n carterista m/f.

pickup ['pɪkʌp] n (Brit: on record player) pickup m; (small truck) furgoneta.

picnic ['pɪknɪk] n merienda // vi ir de merienda.

pictorial [pɪk'tɔːrɪəl] a pictórico; (magazine etc) ilustrado.

picture ['pɪktʃə*] n cuadro; (painting) pintura; (photograph) fotografía; (film) película // vt pintar; **the** ~**s** (Brit) el cine; ~ **book** n libro de

dibujos.

picturesque [pɪktʃə'resk] a pintoresco.

pie [paɪ] n pastel m; (open) tarta; (small: of meat) empanada.

piece [piːs] n pedazo, trozo; (of cake) trozo; (item): **a** ~ **of furniture/advice** un mueble/un consejo // vt: **to** ~ **together** juntar; (TECH) armar; **to take to** ~**s** desmontar; ~**meal** ad poco a poco; ~**work** n trabajo a destajo.

pie chart n gráfico de sectores or tarta.

pier [pɪə*] n muelle m, embarcadero.

pierce [pɪəs] vt penetrar en; perforar.

piercing ['pɪəsɪŋ] a (cry) penetrante.

piety ['paɪətɪ] n piedad f.

pig [pɪg] n cerdo, puerco; (fig) cochino.

pigeon ['pɪdʒən] n paloma; (as food) pichón m; ~**hole** n casilla.

piggy bank ['pɪgɪbæŋk] n hucha (en forma de cerdito).

pigheaded ['pɪg'hedɪd] a terco, testarudo.

pigskin ['pɪgskɪn] n piel f de cerdo.

pigsty ['pɪgstaɪ] n pocilga.

pigtail ['pɪgteɪl] n (girl's) trenza; (Chinese, TAUR) coleta.

pike [paɪk] n (spear) pica; (fish) lucio.

pilchard ['pɪltʃəd] n sardina.

pile [paɪl] n (heap) montón m; (of carpet) pelo // vb: also: ~ **up**) amontonar; (fig) acumular // vi amontonarse; **to** ~ **into** (car) meterse en.

piles [paɪlz] npl (MED) almorranas fpl, hemorroides mpl.

pile-up ['paɪlʌp] n (AUT) accidente m múltiple.

pilfering ['pɪlfərɪŋ] n ratería.

pilgrim ['pɪlgrɪm] n peregrino/a; ~**age** n peregrinación f, romería.

pill [pɪl] n píldora; **the** ~ la píldora.

pillage ['pɪlɪdʒ] vt pillar, saquear.

pillar ['pɪlə*] n (gen) pilar m; (concrete) columna; ~ **box** n (Brit) buzón m.

pillion ['pɪljən] n (of motorcycle) asiento trasero.

pillow ['pɪləʊ] n almohada; ~**case** n funda.

pilot ['paɪlət] n piloto // a (scheme etc) piloto // vt pilotar; (fig) guiar, conducir; ~ **light** n piloto.

pimp [pɪmp] n chulo, cafiche m (LAm).

pimple ['pɪmpl] n grano.

pin [pɪn] n alfiler m; (TECH) perno; (: wooden) clavija // vt prender (con alfiler); sujetar con perno; ~**s and needles** npl hormigueo sg; **to ~ sb down** (fig) hacer que uno concrete; **to ~ sth on sb** (fig) colgarle a uno el sambenito de algo.

pinafore ['pɪnəfɔ:*] n delantal m; ~ **dress** n (Brit) mandil m.

pinball ['pɪnbɔ:l] n flíper m.

pincers ['pɪnsəz] npl pinzas fpl, tenazas fpl.

pinch [pɪntʃ] n pellizco; (of salt etc) pizca // vt pellizcar; (col: steal) birlar // vi (shoe) apretar; **at a ~** en caso de apuro.

pincushion ['pɪnkʊʃən] n acerico.

pine [paɪn] n (also: ~ **tree**) pino // vi: **to ~ for** suspirar por; **to ~ away** vi morirse de pena.

pineapple ['paɪnæpl] n piña, ananás m.

ping [pɪŋ] n (noise) sonido agudo; ~**pong** ® n pingpong m ®.

pink [pɪŋk] n rosado, (color de) rosa // a (colour) rosa; (BOT) clavel m, clavellina f.

pinnacle ['pɪnəkl] n cumbre f.

pinpoint ['pɪnpɔɪnt] vt precisar.

pint [paɪnt] n pinta (Brit = 0.57 l, US = 0.47 l.); (Brit col: of beer) pinta de cerveza, ≈ jarra (Sp).

pioneer [paɪə'nɪə*] n pionero/a.

pious ['paɪəs] a piadoso, devoto.

pip [pɪp] n (seed) pepita; the ~**s** (Brit TEL) la señal.

pipe [paɪp] n tubo, caño; (for smoking) pipa // vt conducir en cañerías; ~**s** npl (gen) cañería sg; (also:

bag~**s**) gaita sg; **to ~ down** vi (col) callarse; ~ **cleaner** n limpiapipas m inv; ~ **dream** n sueño imposible; ~**line** n tubería, cañería; (for oil) oleoducto; (for gas) gasoducto; ~**r** n (gen) flautista m/f; (with bagpipes) gaitero/a.

piping ['paɪpɪŋ] ad: **to be ~ hot** estar que quema.

piquant ['pi:kənt] a picante.

pique [pi:k] n pique m, resentimiento.

pirate ['paɪərət] n pirata m/f; ~ **radio** n (Brit) emisora pirata.

pirouette [pɪru'ɛt] n pirueta // vi piruetear.

Pisces ['paɪsi:z] n Piscis m.

piss [pɪs] vi (col) mear; ~**ed** a (col: drunk) borracho.

pistol ['pɪstl] n pistola.

piston ['pɪstən] n pistón m, émbolo.

pit [pɪt] n hoyo; (also: coal ~) mina; (in garage) foso de inspección; (also: **orchestra ~**) platea // vt: **to ~ A against B** oponer A a B; ~**s** npl (AUT) box msg.

pitch [pɪtʃ] n (throw) lanzamiento; (MUS) tono; (Brit SPORT) campo, terreno; (tar) brea; (in market etc) puesto // vt (throw) arrojar, lanzar // vi (fall) caer(se); (NAUT) cabecear; **to ~ a tent** montar una tienda (de campaña); ~**black** a negro como boca de lobo; ~**ed battle** n batalla campal.

pitcher ['pɪtʃə*] n cántaro, jarro.

pitchfork ['pɪtʃfɔ:k] n horca.

piteous ['pɪtɪəs] a lastimoso.

pitfall ['pɪtfɔ:l] n riesgo.

pith [pɪθ] n (of orange) médula; (fig) meollo.

pithy ['pɪθɪ] a jugoso.

pitiful ['pɪtɪful] a (touching) lastimoso, conmovedor(a); (contemptible) lamentable, miserable.

pitiless ['pɪtɪlɪs] a despiadado.

pittance ['pɪtns] n miseria.

pity ['pɪtɪ] n compasión f, piedad f // vt compadecer(se de); **what a ~**! ¡qué pena!

pivot ['pɪvət] n eje m.

pizza ['piːtsə] n pizza.

placard ['plækɑːd] n (in march etc) pancarta.

placate [plə'keɪt] vt apaciguar.

place [pleɪs] n lugar m, sitio; (rank) rango; (seat) plaza, asiento; (post) puesto; (home): at/to his ~ en/a su casa // vt (object) poner, colocar; (identify) reconocer; (find a post for) dar un puesto a; colocar; **to take** ~ tener lugar; **to be** ~**d** (in race, exam) colocarse; **out of** ~ (not suitable) fuera de lugar; **in the first** ~ (first of all) en primer lugar; **to change** ~**s with sb** cambiarse de sitio con alguien.

placid ['plæsɪd] a apacible.

plague [pleɪg] n plaga; (MED) peste f // (fig) acosar, atormentar.

plaice [pleɪs] n, pl inv platija.

plaid [plæd] n (material) tartán m.

plain [pleɪn] a (clear) claro, evidente; (simple) sencillo; (frank) franco, abierto; (not handsome) poco atractivo; (pure) natural, puro // ad claramente // n llano, llanura; **in ~ clothes** (police) vestido de paisano; ~**ly** ad claramente, evidentemente; (frankly) francamente.

plaintiff ['pleɪntɪf] n demandante m/f.

plait [plæt] n trenza // vt trenzar.

plan [plæn] n (drawing) plano; (scheme) plan m, proyecto // vt (think) pensar; (prepare, programme) planificar // vi hacer proyectos; **to ~ to do** pensar hacer.

plane [pleɪn] n (AVIAT) avión m; (tree) plátano; (tool) cepillo; (MATH) plano.

planet ['plænɪt] n planeta m.

plank [plæŋk] n tabla.

planner ['plænə*] n planificador(a) m/f.

planning n planificación f; **family ~** planificación familiar; ~ **permission** n permiso para realizar obras.

plant [plɑːnt] n planta; (machinery) maquinaria; (factory) fábrica // vt

plantar; (field) sembrar; (bomb) colocar.

plaque [plæk] n placa.

plaster ['plɑːstə*] n (for walls) yeso; (also: ~ **of Paris**) yeso mate; (Brit: also: **sticking** ~) tirita, esparadrapo, curita (LAm) // vt enyesar; (cover): **to ~ with** llenar o cubrir de; ~**ed** a (col) borracho; ~**er** n yesero.

plastic ['plæstɪk] n plástico // a de plástico; ~ **bag** n bolsa de plástico.

plasticine ['plæstɪsiːn] n (Brit) ® plastilina f.

plastic surgery n cirujía plástica.

plate [pleɪt] n (dish) plato; (metal, in book) lámina; (PHOT) placa.

plateau ['plætəu], pl ~**s** or ~**x** [-z] n meseta, altiplanicie f.

plate glass n vidrio cilindrado.

platform ['plætfɔːm] n (RAIL) andén m; (stage) plataforma; (at meeting) tribuna; (POL) programa m (electoral); ~ **ticket** n (Brit) billete m de andén.

platinum ['plætɪnəm] n platino.

platitude ['plætɪtjuːd] n lugar m común, tópico.

platoon [plə'tuːn] n pelotón m.

platter ['plætə*] n fuente f.

plausible ['plɔːzɪbl] a verosímil, (person) convincente.

play [pleɪ] n (gen) juego; (THEATRE) obra, comedia // vt (game) jugar; (instrument) tocar; (THEATRE) representar; (: part) hacer el papel de; (fig) desempeñar // vi jugar; (frolic) juguetear; **to ~ safe** ir a lo seguro; **to ~ down** vt quitar importancia a; **to ~ up** vi (cause trouble) dar guerra; ~**boy** n playboy m; ~**er** n jugador(a) m/f; (THEATRE) actor m/actriz f; (MUS) músico/a; ~**ful** a juguetón/ona; ~**ground** n (in school) patio de recreo; ~**group** n jardín m de niños; ~**ing card** n naipe m, carta; ~**ing field** n campo de deportes; ~**mate** n compañero/a de juego; ~**off** n (SPORT) (partido de) desempate m;

~**pen** n corral m; ~**school** n = ~ **group**; ~**thing** n juguete m; ~**wright** n dramaturgo/a.

plc abbr (= *public limited company*) S.A.

plea [pli:] n (*request*) súplica, petición f; (*excuse*) pretexto, disculpa; (*LAW*) alegato, defensa.

plead [pli:d] vt (*LAW*): **to ~** sb's case defender a uno; (*give as excuse*) poner como pretexto // vi (*LAW*) declararse; (*beg*): **to ~ with** sb suplicar or rogar a uno.

pleasant ['plɛznt] a agradable; ~**ries** npl (*polite remarks*) cortesías fpl.

please [pli:z] vt (*give pleasure to*) dar gusto a, agradar // vi (*think fit*): **do as you ~** haz lo que quieras; ~! ¡por favor!; ~ **yourself!** ¡haz lo que quieras!, ¡como quieras!; ~**d** a (*happy*) alegre, contento; ~**d** (**with**) satisfecho (de); ~**d to meet you** ¡encantado!, ¡tanto gusto!; **pleasing** a agradable, grato.

pleasure ['plɛʒə*] n placer m, gusto; (*will*) voluntad f; **'it's a ~'** el gusto es mío.

pleat [pli:t] n pliegue m.

pledge [plɛdʒ] n (*object*) prenda; (*promise*) promesa, voto // vt empeñar; prometer.

plentiful ['plɛntiful] a copioso, abundante.

plenty ['plɛnti] n abundancia; ~ **of** mucho(s)/a(s).

pliable ['plaiəbl] a flexible.

pliers ['plaiəz] npl alicates mpl, tenazas fpl.

plight [plait] n situación f difícil.

plimsolls ['plimsəlz] npl (*Brit*) zapatos mpl de tenis.

plinth [plinθ] n plinto.

plod [plɔd] vi caminar con paso pesado; (*fig*) trabajar laboriosamente; ~**der** n trabajador(a) m/f diligente pero lento/a.

plonk [plɔŋk] (*col*) n (*Brit: wine*) vino peleón // vt: **to ~ sth down** de-

jar caer algo.

plot [plɔt] n (*scheme*) complot m, conjura; (*of story, play*) argumento; (*of land*) terreno, lote m // vt (*mark out*) trazar; (*conspire*) tramar, urdir // vi conspirar; ~**ter** n (*instrument*) trazador m de gráficos.

plough, (*US*) **plow** [plau] n arado // vt (*earth*) arar; **to ~ back** vt (*COMM*) reinvertir; **to ~ through** vt fus (*crowd*) abrirse paso por la fuerza por; (*book, work*) roer.

ploy [plɔi] n truco, estratagema.

pluck [plʌk] vt (*fruit*) coger (Sp), recoger (LAm); (*musical instrument*) puntear; (*bird*) desplumar // n valor m, ánimo; **to ~ up courage** hacer de tripas corazón; ~**y** a valiente.

plug [plʌg] n tapón m; (*ELEC*) enchufe m, clavija; (*AUT: also*: **spark(ing) ~**) bujía // vt (*hole*) tapar; (*col: advertise*) dar publicidad a; **to ~ in** vt (*ELEC*) enchufar.

plum [plʌm] n (*fruit*) ciruela // a: ~ **job** (*col*) puesto (de trabajo) muy codiciado.

plumb [plʌm] a vertical // n plomo // ad (*exactly*) exactamente, en punto // vt sondar; (*fig*) sondear.

plumber ['plʌmə*] n fontanero/a, plomero/a.

plumbing ['plʌmiŋ] n (*trade*) fontanería; (*piping*) cañería.

plume [plu:m] n pluma.

plummet ['plʌmit] vi: **to ~ (down)** caer a plomo.

plump [plʌmp] a rechoncho, rollizo // vt: **to ~ sth (down) on** dejar caer algo en; **to ~ for** vt fus (*col: choose*) optar por.

plunder ['plʌndə*] n pillaje m; (*loot*) botín m // vt pillar, saquear.

plunge [plʌndʒ] n zambullida // vt sumergir, hundir // vi (*fall*) caer; (*dive*) saltar; (*person*) arrojarse; (*sink*) hundirse; **to take the ~** lanzarse; ~**r** n émbolo; (*for drain*) desatascador m.

pluperfect [plu:'pə:fikt] n pluscuamperfecto.

plural ['pluərl] n plural m.

plus [plʌs] n (also: ~ **sign**) signo más // prep más, y, además de; **ten/ twenty** ~ más de diez/veinte.

plush [plʌʃ] a de felpa.

plutonium [pluː'təunɪəm] n plutonio.

ply [plaɪ] vt (a trade) ejercer // vi (ship) ir y venir; (for hire) ofrecerse (para alquilar); **to** ~ **sb with drink** insistir en ofrecer a alguien muchas copas; **~wood** n madera contrachapada.

P.M. abbr = Prime Minister.

p.m. ad abbr (= post meridiem) de la tarde or noche.

pneumatic [njuː'mætɪk] a neumático; ~ **drill** n martillo neumático.

pneumonia [njuː'məunɪə] n pulmonía.

poach [pəutʃ] vt (cook) escalfar; (steal) cazar/pescar en vedado // vi cazar/pescar en vedado; **~ed** a (egg) escalfado; **~er** n cazador/a m/f furtivo/a; **~ing** n caza/pesca furtiva.

P.O. Box n abbr = Post Office Box.

pocket ['pɒkɪt] n bolsillo; (of air, GEO, fig) bolsa; (BILLIARDS) tronera // vt meter en el bolsillo; (steal) embolsar; (BILLIARDS) entronerar; **to be out of** ~ salir perdiendo; **~book** n (US: wallet) cartera; **~knife** n navaja; **~ money** n asignación f.

pod [pɒd] n vaina.

podgy ['pɒdʒɪ] a gordinflón/ona.

pediatrist [pɔ'diːətrɪst] n (US) pedi_curo/a.

poem ['pəuɪm] n poema m.

poet ['pəuɪt] n poeta m/f; **~ic** [-'ɛtɪk] a poético; ~ **laureate** n poeta m laureado; **~ry** n poesía.

poignant ['pɔɪnjənt] a conmovedor(a).

point [pɔɪnt] n punto; (tip) punta; (purpose) fin m, propósito; (use) utilidad f; (significant part) lo significativo; (also: **decimal** ~): **2** ~ **3** (2.3) dos coma tres (2,3) // vt (gun etc) **to**

~ **sth at sb** apuntar algo a uno // vi señalar con el dedo; **~s** npl (AUT) contactos mpl; (RAIL) agujas fpl; **to be on the** ~ **of doing sth** estar a punto de hacer algo; **to make a** ~ **of** poner empeño en; **to get the** ~ comprender; **to come to the** ~ ir al meollo; **there's no** ~ **(in doing)** no tiene sentido (hacer); **to** ~ **out** vt señalar; **to** ~ **to** vt fus indicar con el dedo; (fig) indicar, señalar; **~blank** ad (also: at **~blank range**) a quemarropa; **~ed** a (shape) puntiagudo, afilado; (remark) intencionado; **~edly** ad intencionadamente; **~er** n (stick) puntero; (needle) aguja, indicador m; **~less** a sin sentido; **~ of view** n punto de vista.

poise [pɔɪz] n (of head, body) porte m; (calmness) aplomo, elegancia.

poison ['pɔɪzn] n veneno // vt envenenar; **~ing** n envenenamiento; **~ous** a venenoso; (fumes etc) tóxico; (fig) pernicioso.

poke [pəuk] vt (fire) hurgar, atizar; (jab with finger, stick etc) empujar; (put): **to** ~ **sth in(to)** introducir algo en; **to** ~ **about** vi fisgonear.

poker ['pəukə*] n atizador m; (CARDS) póker m; **~-faced** a de cara impasible.

Poland ['pəulənd] n Polonia.

polar ['pəulə*] a polar.

Pole [pəul] n polaco/a.

pole [pəul] n palo; (GEO) polo; (TEL) poste m; (flag) ~ asta; (tent) ~ mástil m; ~ **bean** n (US) judía trepadora; ~ **vault** n salto con pértiga.

police [pə'liːs] n policía // vt vigilar; ~ **car** n coche-patrulla m; **~man** n policía m, guardia m; ~ **state** n estado policial; ~ **station** n comisaría; **~woman** n mujer f policía.

policy ['pɒlɪsɪ] n política; (also: **insurance** ~) póliza.

polio ['pəulɪəu] n polio f.

Polish ['pəulɪʃ] a polaco // n (LING) polaco.

polish ['polɪʃ] n (for shoes) betún m; (for floor) cera (de lustrar); (for nails) esmalte m; (shine) brillo, lustre m; (fig: refinement) educación f // vt (shoes) limpiar; (make shiny) pulir, sacar brillo a; (fig: improve) perfeccionar; **to ~ off** vt (work) terminar; (food) despachar; **~ed** a (fig: person) elegante.

polite [pə'laɪt] a cortés, atento; (formal) correcto; **~ness** n cortesía.

politic ['polɪtɪk] a prudente; **~al** [pə'lɪtɪkl] a político; **~ian** [-'tɪʃən] n político/a; **~s** n política.

polka ['polkə] n polca; **~ dot** n lunar m.

poll [pəul] n (votes) votación f, votos mpl; (also: opinion ~) sondeo, encuesta // vt (votes) obtener.

pollen ['polən] n polen m.

polling ['pəulɪŋ] (Brit): **~ booth** n cabina de votar; **~ day** n día m de elecciones; **~ station** n centro electoral.

pollution [pə'luːʃən] n polución f, contaminación f del medio ambiente.

polo ['pəuləu] n (sport) polo; **~-neck** a de cuello vuelto.

polyester [polɪ'estə*] n poliéster m.

polyethylene [polɪ'eθɪliːn] n (US) polietino.

Polynesia [polɪ'niːzɪə] n Polinesia.

polystyrene [polɪ'staɪriːn] n poliestireno.

polytechnic [polɪ'teknɪk] n ≈ escuela de formación profesional.

polythene ['polɪθiːn] n (Brit) polietino.

pomegranate ['pomɪgrænɪt] n granada.

pomp [pomp] n pompa.

pompom ['pompom], **pompon** ['pompən] n borla.

pompous ['pompəs] a pomposo.

pond [pond] n (natural) charca; (artificial) estanque m.

ponder ['pondə*] vt meditar; **~ous** a pesado.

pong [poŋ] n (Brit col) hedor m.

pontoon [pon'tuːn] n pontón m;

(Brit: card game) veintiuna.

pony ['pəunɪ] n poney m, jaca, potro (LAm); **~tail** n cola de caballo; **~ trekking** n (Brit) excursión f a caballo.

poodle ['puːdl] n caniche m.

pool [puːl] n (natural) charca; (pond) estanque m; (also: swimming ~) piscina, alberca (LAm); (billiards) chapolín // vt juntar; (football) **~s** npl quinielas fpl.

poor [puə*] a pobre; (bad) de mala calidad // npl: **the ~** los pobres; **~ly** a mal, enfermo.

pop [pop] n (sound) ruido seco; (MUS) (música) pop m; (US: col: father) papá m; (lemonade) gaseosa // vt (burst) hacer reventar // vi reventar; (cork) saltar; **to ~ in/out** vi entrar/salir un momento; **to ~ up** vi aparecer inesperadamente; **~ concert** n concierto pop; **~corn** n palomitas fpl.

pope [pəup] n papa m.

poplar ['poplə*] n álamo.

poppy ['popɪ] n amapola.

popsicle ['popsɪkl] n (US) polo.

populace ['popjuləs] n pueblo, plebe f.

popular ['popjulə*] a popular; **~ize** vt popularizar; (disseminate) vulgarizar.

population [popju'leɪʃən] n población f.

porcelain ['poːslɪn] n porcelana.

porch [poːtʃ] n pórtico, entrada.

porcupine ['poːkjupaɪn] n puerco m espín.

pore [poː*] n poro // vi: **to ~ over** engolfarse en.

pork [poːk] n carne f de cerdo or chancho (LAm).

pornography [poː'nogrəfɪ] n pornografía.

porous ['poːrəs] a poroso.

porpoise ['poːpəs] n marsopa.

porridge ['porɪdʒ] n gachas fpl de avena.

port [poːt] n (harbour) puerto;

(*NAUT: left side*) babor *m*; (*wine*) vino de Oporto; **~ of call** puerto de escala.

portable ['pɔːtəbl] *a* portátil.

portent ['pɔːtent] *n* presagio, augurio.

porter ['pɔːtə*] *n* (*for luggage*) maletero; (*doorkeeper*) portero/a, conserje *m/f*.

portfolio [pɔːt'fəuliəu] *n* (*case, of artist*) cartera, carpeta; (*POL, FINANCE*) cartera.

porthole ['pɔːthəul] *n* portilla.

portion ['pɔːʃən] *n* porción *f*; (*helping*) ración *f*.

portly ['pɔːtlɪ] *a* corpulento.

portrait ['pɔːtreɪt] *n* retrato.

portray [pɔː'treɪ] *vt* retratar; (*in writing*) describir.

Portugal ['pɔːtjugl] *n* Portugal *m*.

Portuguese [pɔːtju'giːz] *a* portugués/esa // *n, pl inv* portugués/esa *m/f*; (*LING*) portugués *m*.

pose [pəuz] *n* postura, actitud *f*; (*pej*) afectación *f*, pose *f* // *vi* posar; (*pretend*): **to ~ as** hacerse pasar por // *vt* (*question*) plantear.

posh [pɔʃ] *a* (*col*) elegante, de lujo.

position [pə'zɪʃən] *n* posición *f*; (*job*) puesto // *vt* colocar.

positive ['pɔzɪtɪv] *a* positivo; (*certain*) seguro; (*definite*) definitivo.

posse ['pɔsɪ] *n* (*US*) pelotón *m*.

possess [pə'zes] *vt* poseer; **~ion** [pə'zeʃən] *n* posesión *f*.

possibility [pɔsɪ'bɪlɪtɪ] *n* posibilidad *f*.

possible ['pɔsɪbl] *a* posible; **as big as ~** lo más grande posible; **possibly** *ad* (*perhaps*) tal vez; **I cannot possibly come** me es imposible venir.

post [pəust] *n* (*Brit: letters, delivery*) correo; (*pole, situation*) puesto; (*pole*) poste *m* // *vt* (*Brit: send by post*) echar al correo; (*MIL*) apostar; (*bills*) fijar, pegar; (*Brit: appoint*): **to ~** to enviar a; **~age** *n* porte *m*, franqueo; **~al** *a* postal, de correos; **~al order** *n* giro postal; **~box** *n*

(*Brit*) buzón *m*; **~card** *n* tarjeta postal; **~code** *n* (*Brit*) código postal.

postdate [pəust'deɪt] *vt* (*cheque*) poner fecha adelantada a.

poster ['pəustə*] *n* cartel *m*.

poste restante [pəust'restɔ̃nt] *n* (*Brit*) lista de correos.

posterior [pɔs'tɪərɪə*] *n* (*col*) culo, trasero.

postgraduate ['pəust'grædjuət] *n* posgraduado/a.

posthumous ['pɔstjuməs] *a* póstumo.

post: **~man** *n* cartero; **~mark** *n* matasellos *m inv*; **~master** *n* administrador *m* de correos.

post-mortem [pəust'mɔːtəm] *n* autopsia.

post office *n* (*building*) (oficina de) correos *m*; (*organization*): **the P-O~** Administración *f* General de Correos; **P~ O~ Box** (**P.O. Box**) *n* apartado postal, casilla de correos (*LAm*).

postpone [pəs'pəun] *vt* aplazar.

postscript ['pəustskrɪpt] *n* posdata.

posture ['pɔstʃə*] *n* postura, actitud *f*.

postwar [pəust'wɔː*] *a* de la posguerra.

posy ['pəuzɪ] *n* ramillete *m* (de flores).

pot [pɔt] *n* (*for cooking*) olla; (*for flowers*) maceta; (*for jam*) tarro, pote *m*; (*col: marijuana*) costo // *vt* (*plant*) poner en tiesto; (*conserve*) conservar; **to go to ~** (*col: work, performance*) irse al traste.

potato [pə'teɪtəu], *pl* **~es** *n* patata, papa (*LAm*); **~ peeler** *n* pelapatatas *m inv*.

potent ['pəutnt] *a* potente, poderoso; (*drink*) fuerte.

potential [pə'tɛnʃl] *a* potencial, posible // *n* potencial *m*; **~ly** *ad* en potencia.

pothole ['pɔthəul] *n* (*in road*) bache *m*; (*Brit: underground*) gruta; **potholing** *n* (*Brit*): **to go potho-**

ing dedicarse a la espeleología.

potion ['pəʊʃən] n poción f, pócima.

potluck [pɒt'lʌk] n: **to take ~** tomar lo que haya.

potshot ['pɒtʃɒt] n: **to take a ~ at** sth tirar a algo sin apuntar.

potted ['pɒtɪd] a (food) en conserva; (plant) en tiesto or maceta.

potter ['pɒtə*] n alfarero/a // vi: to **~ around**, **~ about** hacer trabajitos; **~y** n cerámica; alfarería.

potty ['pɒtɪ] a (col: mad) chiflado // n orinal m de niño.

pouch [paʊtʃ] n (ZOOL) bolsa; (for tobacco) petaca.

poultry ['pəʊltrɪ] n aves fpl de corral; (dead) pollos mpl.

pounce [paʊns] vi: **to ~ on** precipitarse sobre.

pound [paʊnd] n libra (weight = 453g, 16oz; money = 100 pence); (for dogs) corral m; (for cars) depósito // vt (beat) golpear; (crush) machacar // vi (beat) dar golpes.

pour [pɔ:*] vt echar; (tea) servir // vi correr, fluir; (rain) llover a cántaros; **to ~ away** or **off** vt vaciar, verter; **to ~ in/out** vi (people) entrar/salir en tropel // vt (drink) echar, servir; **~ing** a: **~ing rain** lluvia torrencial.

pout [paʊt] vi hacer pucheros.

poverty ['pɒvətɪ] n pobreza, miseria; **~-stricken** a necesitado.

powder ['paʊdə*] n polvo; (face ~) polvos mpl; (gun ~) pólvora // vt polvorear; **to ~ one's face** ponerse polvos; **~ compact** n polvera; **~ed milk** n leche f en polvo; **~ puff** n borla; **~ room** n aseos mpl.

power ['paʊə*] n poder m; (strength) fuerza; (nation, TECH) potencia; (drive) empuje m; (ELEC) fuerza, energía // vt impulsar; **to be in ~** (POL) estar en el poder; **~ cut** n (Brit) apagón m; **~ed a: ~ed by** impulsado por; **~ failure** n = **~ cut**; **~ful** a poderoso; (engine) potente; **~less** a impotente, ineficaz; **~ point** n (Brit) enchufe m; **~ sta-**

tion n central f eléctrica.

p.p. abbr (= per procurationem): **J. Smith p.p.** (por poder de) J. Smith.

PR n abbr = **public relations**.

practicable ['præktɪkəbl] a (scheme) factible.

practical ['præktɪkl] a práctico; **~ity** [-'kælɪtɪ] n (of situation etc) factibilidad f; **~ joke** n broma pesada; **~ly** ad (almost) casi.

practice ['præktɪs] n (habit) costumbre f; (exercise) práctica, ejercicio; (training) adiestramiento; (MED) clientela // vt, vi (US) = **practise**; **in ~** (in reality) en la práctica; **out of ~** desentrenado.

practise, (US) **practice** ['præktɪs] vt (carry out) practicar; (profession) ejercer; (train at) practicar // vi ejercer; (train) practicar; **practising** a (Christian etc) practicante; (lawyer) que ejerce.

practitioner [præk'tɪʃənə*] n practicante m/f; (MED) médico/a.

prairie ['prɛərɪ] n (in N. America) pampa.

praise [preɪz] n alabanza(s) f(pl), elogio(s) m(pl); // vt alabar, elogiar; **~worthy** a loable.

pram [præm] n (Brit) cochecito de niño.

prance [prɑ:ns] vi (horse) hacer cabriolas.

prank [præŋk] n travesura.

prawn [prɔ:n] n gamba.

pray [preɪ] vi rezar.

prayer [prɛə*] n oración f, rezo; (entreaty) ruego, súplica; **~ book** n devocionario, misal m.

preach [pri:tʃ] vi predicar.

precaution [prɪ'kɔ:ʃən] n precaución f.

precede [prɪ'si:d] vt, vi preceder.

precedence ['presɪdəns] n precedencia; (priority) prioridad f.

precedent ['presɪdənt] n precedente m.

precinct ['pri:sɪŋkt] n recinto; **~s** npl contornos mpl; **pedestrian ~** (Brit) zona peatonal; **shopping**

(*Brit*) centro comercial.

precious ['prɛʃəs] a precioso.

precipice ['prɛsɪpɪs] n precipicio.

precipitate [prɪ'sɪpɪtɪt] a (*hasty*) precipitado // vt [prɪ'sɪpɪteɪt] precipitar.

precise [prɪ'saɪs] a preciso, exacto; ~**ly** ad exactamente, precisamente.

preclude [prɪ'kluːd] vt excluir.

precocious [prɪ'kəʊʃəs] a precoz.

precondition [priːkən'dɪʃən] n condición f previa.

predator ['prɛdətə*] n animal m de rapiña.

predecessor ['priːdɪsɛsə*] n antecesor(a) m/f.

predicament [prɪ'dɪkəmənt] n apuro.

predict [prɪ'dɪkt] vt pronosticar; ~**able** a previsible.

predominantly [prɪ'dɔmɪnəntlɪ] ad en su mayoría.

preen [priːn] vt: **to ~ itself** (*bird*) limpiarse (las plumas); **to ~ o.s.** pavonearse.

prefab ['priːfæb] n casa prefabricada.

preface ['prɛfəs] n prefacio.

prefect ['priːfɛkt] n (*Brit: in school*) monitor(a) m/f.

prefer [prɪ'fəː*] vt preferir; ~**able** ['prɛfrəbl] a preferible; ~**ably** ['prɛfrəblɪ] ad de preferencia; ~**ence** ['prɛfrəns] n preferencia; (*priority*) prioridad f; ~**ential** [prɛfə'rɛnʃəl] a preferente.

prefix ['priːfɪks] n prefijo.

pregnancy ['prɛgnənsɪ] n embarazo.

pregnant ['prɛgnənt] a embarazada.

prehistoric ['priːhɪs'tɔrɪk] a prehistórico.

prejudice ['prɛdʒudɪs] n (*bias*) prejuicio; (*harm*) perjuicio // vt (*bias*) predisponer; (*harm*) perjudicar; ~**d** a (*person*) predispuesto; (*view*) parcial, interesado.

prelude ['prɛljuːd] n preludio.

premarital ['priː'mærɪtl] a premarital.

premature ['prɛmətʃuə*] a prematuro.

premier ['prɛmɪə*] a primero, principal // n (*POL*) primer(a) ministro/a.

première ['prɛmɪə*] n estreno.

premise ['prɛmɪs] n premisa; ~**s** npl local msg; **on the ~s** en el lugar mismo.

premium ['priːmɪəm] n premio; (*COMM*) prima; **to be at a ~** ser muy solicitado; ~ **bond** n (*Brit*) bono del estado que participa en una lotería nacional.

premonition [prɛmə'nɪʃən] n presentimiento.

preoccupied [priː'ɔkjupaɪd] a (*worried*) preocupado; (*absorbed*) ensimismado.

prep [prɛp] n (*SCOL: study*) deberes mpl; ~ **school** n = **preparatory school**.

prepaid [priː'peɪd] a porte pagado.

preparation [prɛpə'reɪʃən] n preparación f; ~**s** npl preparativos mpl.

preparatory [prɪ'pærətərɪ] a preparatorio, preliminar; ~ **school** n escuela preparatoria.

prepare [prɪ'pɛə*] vt preparar, disponer // vi: **to ~ for** prepararse or disponerse para; (*make preparations*) hacer preparativos para; ~**d** **to** dispuesto a.

preposition [prɛpə'zɪʃən] n preposición f.

preposterous [prɪ'pɔstərəs] a absurdo, ridículo.

prerequisite [priː'rɛkwɪzɪt] n requisito.

prerogative [prɪ'rɔgətɪv] n prerrogativa.

preschool ['priː'skuːl] a preescolar.

prescribe [prɪ'skraɪb] vt prescribir; (*MED*) recetar.

prescription [prɪ'skrɪpʃən] n (*MED*) receta.

presence ['prɛzns] n presencia; (*attendance*) asistencia; ~ **of mind** aplomo.

present ['prɛznt] a (*in attendance*) presente; (*current*) actual // n (*gift*) regalo; (*actuality*) actualidad f, presente m // vt [prɪ'zɛnt] (*introduce*) presentar; (*expound*) exponer; (*give*) presentar, dar, ofrecer; (*THEATRE*) representar; **to give sb a** ~ regalar algo a uno; **at** ~ actualmente; ~**able** [prɪˈzɛntəbl] *a*: **to make o.s.** ~**able** arreglarse; ~**ation** [-ˈteɪʃən] *n* presentación *f*; (*gift*) obsequio, (*of case*) exposición *f*, (*THEATRE*) representación *f*; ~**day** *a* actual; ~**er** [prɪˈzɛntə*] *n* (*RADIO*, *TV*) locutor/a *m/f*; ~**ly** *ad* (*soon*) dentro de poco.

preservation [prɛzəˈveɪʃən] *n* conservación *f*.

preservative [prɪˈzəːvətɪv] *n* conservante *m*.

preserve [prɪˈzəːv] *vt* (*keep safe*) preservar, proteger; (*maintain*) mantener; (*food*) conservar; (*in salt*) salar // *n* (*for game*) coto, vedado; (*often pl: jam*) conserva, confitura.

president [ˈprɛzɪdənt] *n* presidente *m/f*; ~**ial** [-ˈdɛnʃl] *a* presidencial.

press [prɛs] *n* (*tool, machine, newspapers*) prensa; (*printer's*) imprenta; (*of hand*) apretón *m* // *vt* (*push*) empujar; (*squeeze*) apretar; (*grapes*) pisar; (*clothes: iron*) planchar; (*pressure*) presionar; (*insist*): **to** ~ **sth on sb** insistir en que uno acepte algo // *vi* (*squeeze*) apretar; (*pressurize*) ejercer presión; **we are** ~**ed for time** tenemos poco tiempo; **to** ~ **on** *vi* avanzar; (*hurry*) apretar el paso; ~ **agency** *n* agencia de prensa; ~ **conference** *n* rueda de prensa; ~**ing** *a* apremiante; ~ **stud** *n* (*Brit*) botón *m* de presión; ~**up** *n* (*Brit*) plancha.

pressure [ˈprɛʃə*] *n* presión *f*; ~ **cooker** *n* olla a presión; ~ **gauge** *n* manómetro; ~ **group** *n* grupo de presión; **pressurized** *a* (*container*) a presión.

prestige [prɛsˈtiːʒ] *n* prestigio.

presumably [prɪˈzjuːməblɪ] *ad* es de suponer que, cabe presumir que.

presume [prɪˈzjuːm] *vt* presumir, suponer; **to** ~ **to do** (*dare*) atreverse a hacer.

presumption [prɪˈzʌmpʃən] *n* supo-

sición *f*; (*pretension*) presunción *f*.

presumptuous [prɪˈzʌmptjuəs] *a* presumido.

pretence, (*US*) **pretense** [prɪˈtɛns] *n* (*claim*) pretensión *f*; (*pretext*) pretexto; (*make-believe*) fingimiento; **on the** ~ **of** bajo pretexto de.

pretend [prɪˈtɛnd] *vt* (*feign*) fingir // *vi* (*feign*) fingir; (*claim*): **to** ~ **to** sth pretender a algo.

pretense [prɪˈtɛns] *n* (*US*) = **pretence**.

pretension [prɪˈtɛnʃən] *n* (*claim*) pretensión *f*.

pretentious [prɪˈtɛnʃəs] *a* presumido; (*ostentatious*) ostentoso, aparatoso.

pretext [ˈpriːtɛkst] *n* pretexto.

pretty [ˈprɪtɪ] *a* (*gen*) bonito, lindo (*LAm*) // *ad* bastante.

prevail [prɪˈveɪl] *vi* (*gain mastery*) prevalecer; (*be current*) predominar; (*persuade*): **to** ~ **(up)on sb to do** sth persuadir a uno para que haga algo; ~**ing** *a* (*dominant*) predominante.

prevalent [ˈprɛvələnt] *a* (*dominant*) dominante; (*widespread*) extendido; (*fashionable*) de moda.

prevent [prɪˈvɛnt] *vt*: **to** ~ **(sb from doing sth)** impedir (a uno hacer algo); ~**ive** *a* preventivo.

preview [ˈpriːvjuː] *n* (*of film*) preestreno.

previous [ˈpriːvɪəs] *a* previo, anterior; ~**ly** *ad* antes.

prewar [priːˈwɔː*] *a* de antes de la guerra.

prey [preɪ] *n* presa *f* // *vi*: **to** ~ **on** vivir a costa de; (*feed on*) alimentarse de.

price [praɪs] *n* precio // *vt* (*goods*) fijar el precio de; ~**less** *a* que no tiene precio; ~ **list** *n* tarifa.

prick [prɪk] *n* (*sensation*) picor *m*; (*BOT*) espina; (*ZOOL*) púa; **prickly** *a* espinoso; (*fig: person*) enojadizo;

prick [prɪk] *n* pinchazo; (*sting*) picadura // *vt* pinchar; picar; **to** ~ **up** one's ears aguzar el oído.

prickle [ˈprɪkl] *n* (*sensation*) picor *m*; (*BOT*) espina; (*ZOOL*) púa; **prickly** *a* espinoso; (*fig: person*) enojadizo;

prickly heat n sarpullido causado por exceso de calor.

pride [praɪd] n orgullo; (pej) soberbia // vt: **to ~ o.s. on** enorgullecerse de.

priest [priːst] n sacerdote m; **~ess** n sacerdotisa; **~hood** n (practice) sacerdocio; (priests) clero.

prig [prɪg] n gazmoño/a.

prim [prɪm] a (demure) remilgado; (prudish) gazmoño/a.

primarily ['praɪmərɪlɪ] ad (above all) ante todo.

primary ['praɪmərɪ] a primario; (first in importance) principal; **~ school** n (Brit) escuela primaria.

primate ['praɪmɪt] n (REL) primado // n ['praɪmeɪt] (ZOOL) primate m.

prime [praɪm] a primero, principal; (basic) fundamental; (excellent) selecto, de primera clase // n: **in the ~ of life** en la flor de la vida // vt (gun, pump) cebar; (fig) preparar; **P~ Minister (P.M.)** n primer/a ministro/a.

primer ['praɪmə*] n (book) texto elemental; (paint) imprimación f.

primeval [praɪˈmiːvəl] a primitivo.

primitive ['prɪmɪtɪv] a primitivo; (crude) rudimentario.

primrose ['prɪmrəʊz] n primavera, prímula.

primus (stove) ['praɪməs-] n ® (Brit) hornillo de camping.

prince [prɪns] n príncipe m.

princess [prɪnˈsɛs] n princesa.

principal ['prɪnsɪpl] a principal, mayor // n director/a m/f.

principle ['prɪnsɪpl] n principio; **in ~** en principio; **on ~** por principio.

print [prɪnt] n (impression) marca, impresión f, huella; (letters) letra de molde; (fabric) estampado; (ART) grabado; (PHOT) impresión f // vt (gen) imprimir; (on mind) grabar; (write in capitals) escribir en letras de molde; **out of ~** agotado; **~ed matter** n impresos mpl; **~er** n (person) impresor/a m/f; (machine) impresora; **~ing** n (art) imprenta;

(act) impresión f; (quantity) tirada; **~out** n (COMPUT) impresión f.

prior ['praɪə*] a anterior, previo // n prior m; **~ to doing** antes de hacer.

priority [praɪˈɔrɪtɪ] n prioridad f.

prise [praɪz] vt: **to ~ open** abrir con palanca.

prison ['prɪzn] n cárcel f, prisión f // cpd carcelario; **~er** n (in prison) preso/a; (under arrest) detenido/a; (in dock) acusado/a.

privacy ['prɪvəsɪ] n (seclusion) soledad f; (intimacy) intimidad f.

private ['praɪvɪt] a (personal) particular; (confidential) secreto, confidencial; (sitting etc) a puertas cerradas // n soldado raso; '**~**' (on envelope) 'confidencial'; (on door) 'prohibido el paso'; **in ~** en privado; **~ enterprise** n la empresa privada; **~ eye** n detective m/f privado/a; **~ly** ad en privado; (in o.s.) personalmente; **~ property** n propiedad f privada; **~ school** n colegio particular.

privet ['prɪvɪt] n alheña.

privilege ['prɪvɪlɪdʒ] n privilegio; (prerogative) prerrogativa.

privy ['prɪvɪ] a: **to be ~ to** estar enterado de; **P~ Council** n Consejo del Estado.

prize [praɪz] n premio // a (first class) de primera clase // vt apreciar, estimar; **~-giving** n distribución f de premios; **~winner** n premiado/a.

pro [prəʊ] n (SPORT) profesional m/f; **the ~s and cons** los pros y los contras.

probability [prɒbəˈbɪlɪtɪ] n probabilidad f.

probable ['prɒbəbl] a probable.

probably ['prɒbəblɪ] ad probablemente.

probation [prəˈbeɪʃən] n: **on ~** (employee) a prueba; (LAW) en libertad condicional.

probe [prəʊb] n (MED, SPACE) sonda; (enquiry) encuesta, investigación f // vt sondar; (investigate) investigar.

problem ['prɒbləm] n problema m.

procedure [prə'siːdʒə*] n procedimiento; (bureaucratic) trámites mpl.

proceed [prə'siːd] vi proceder; (continue): to ~ (with) continuar or seguir (con); ~s ['prəusiːdz] npl ganancias fpl, ingresos mpl; ~**ings** npl acto sg, actos mpl; (LAW) proceso sg; (meeting) función fsg; (records) actas fpl.

process ['prəuses] n proceso; (method) método, sistema m // vt tratar, elaborar; **in** ~ en curso; ~**ing** n tratamiento, elaboración f.

procession [prə'sɛʃən] n desfile m; funeral ~ cortejo fúnebre.

proclaim [prə'kleɪm] vt proclamar; (announce) anunciar; **proclamation** [prɒklə'meɪʃən] n proclamación f; (written) proclama.

procrastinate [prəu'kræstɪneɪt] vi demorarse.

procure [prə'kjuə*] vt conseguir

prod [prɒd] vt empujar.

prodigal ['prɒdɪgl] a pródigo.

prodigy ['prɒdɪdʒɪ] n prodigio.

produce ['prɒdjuːs] n (AGR) productos mpl agrícolas // vt [prə'djuːs] producir; (yield) rendir; (show) presentar, mostrar; (THEATRE) presentar, poner en escena; (offspring) dar a luz; ~ **dealer** n (US) verdulero/a; ~**r** n (THEATRE) director/a m/f; (AGR, CINEMA) productor/a m/f.

product ['prɒdʌkt] n producto; (result) fruto, producto.

production [prə'dʌkʃən] n (act) producción f; (THEATRE) presentación f; ~ **line** n línea de producción.

productive [prə'dʌktɪv] a productivo; **productivity** [prɒdʌk'tɪvɪtɪ] n productividad f.

profane [prə'feɪn] a profano.

profession [prə'fɛʃən] n profesión f; ~**al** n profesional m/f // a profesional; (by profession) de profesión.

professor [prə'fɛsə*] n (Brit) catedrático/a; (US) profesor/a m/f.

proficiency [prə'fɪʃənsɪ] n capacidad, habilidad f.

proficient [prə'fɪʃənt] a experto, há-

bil.

profile ['prəufaɪl] n perfil m.

profit ['prɒfɪt] n (COMM) ganancia; (fig) provecho; **to make a** ~ obtener beneficios // vi: **to** ~ **by** or **from** aprovechar or sacar provecho de; ~**ability** [-ə'bɪlɪtɪ] n rentabilidad f; ~**able** a (ECON) rentable; (beneficial) provechoso; ~**eering** [-'tɪərɪŋ] n (pej) explotación f.

profound [prə'faund] a profundo.

profusely [prə'fjuːslɪ] ad profusamente; **profusion** [-'fjuːʒən] n profusión f, abundancia.

progeny ['prɒdʒɪnɪ] n progenie f.

programme, (US) **program** ['prəugræm] n programa m // vt programar; ~**r**, (US) **programer** n programador/a m/f; **programming**, (US) **programing** n programación f.

progress ['prəugres] n progreso; (development) desarrollo // vi [prə'gres] progresar, avanzar; desarrollarse; **in** ~ en curso; ~**ive** [-'gresɪv] a progresivo; (person) progresista.

prohibit [prə'hɪbɪt] vt prohibir; **to** ~ **sb from doing sth** prohibir a uno hacer algo.

project ['prɒdʒekt] n proyecto // (vb: [prə'dʒekt]) vt proyectar // vi (stick out) salir, sobresalir.

projectile [prə'dʒektaɪl] n proyectil m.

projection [prə'dʒekʃən] n proyección f; (overhang) saliente m.

projector [prə'dʒektə*] n proyector m.

proletariat [prəulɪ'tɛərɪət] n proletariado.

prologue ['prəulɒg] n prólogo.

prolong [prə'lɒŋ] vt prolongar, extender.

prom [prɒm] n abbr = **promenade**; (US: ball) baile m de gala.

promenade [prɒmə'nɑːd] n (by sea) paseo marítimo; ~ **concert** n concierto (en que parte del público permanece de pie).

prominence ['prɒmɪnəns] n (fig) importancia.

prominent ['prɔmɪnənt] a (standing out) saliente; (important) eminente, importante.

promiscuous [prə'mɪskjuəs] a (sexually) promiscuo.

promise ['prɔmɪs] n promesa // vt, vi prometer; **promising** a prometedor(a).

promontory ['prɔmɔntrɪ] n promontorio.

promote [prə'məut] vt promover; (new product) hacer propaganda por; (MIL) ascender; ~r n (of sporting event) promotor(a) m/f; **promotion** [-'məuʃən] n (advertising) promoción f; (in rank) ascenso.

prompt [prɔmpt] a (punctual) puntual; (quick) rápido // ad: at 6 o'clock ~ a las seis en punto // n (COMPUT) aviso // vt (urge) mover, incitar; (THEATRE) apuntar; to ~ sb to do sth instar a uno a hacer algo; ~ly ad puntualmente; rápidamente.

prone [prəun] a (lying) postrado; ~ to propenso a.

prong [prɔŋ] n diente m, punta.

pronoun ['prəunaun] n pronombre m.

pronounce [prə'nauns] vt pronunciar // vi: to ~ (up)on pronunciarse sobre; ~d a (marked) marcado; ~ment n declaración f.

pronunciation [prənʌnsɪ'eɪʃən] n pronunciación f.

proof [pruːf] n prueba; **70°** ~ graduación f del 70 por 100 // a: ~ against a prueba de.

prop [prɔp] n apoyo // (fig) sostén m // vt (also: ~ up) apoyar; (lean): to ~ sth against apoyar algo contra.

propaganda [prɔpə'gændə] n propaganda.

propel [prə'pɛl] vt impulsar, propulsar; ~ler n hélice f; ~ling pencil n (Brit) lapicero.

propensity [prə'pɛnsɪtɪ] n propensión f.

proper ['prɔpə*] a (suited, right)

propio; (exact) justo; (apt) apropiado, conveniente; (timely) oportuno; (seemly) correcto, decente; (authentic) verdadero; (col: real) auténtico; ~ly ad (adequately) correctamente; (decently) decentemente; ~ noun n nombre m propio.

property ['prɔpətɪ] n propiedad f; (personal) bienes mpl muebles; (estate) finca; ~ owner n dueño/a de propiedades.

prophecy ['prɔfɪsɪ] n profecía.

prophesy ['prɔfɪsaɪ] vt profetizar; (fig) predecir.

prophet ['prɔfɪt] n profeta m.

proportion [prə'pɔːʃən] n proporción f; (share) parte f; ~al a proporcional; ~ate a proporcionada.

proposal [prə'pəuzl] n propuesta; (offer of marriage) oferta de matrimonio; (plan) proyecto.

propose [prə'pəuz] vt proponer // vi declararse; to ~ to do sth tener intención de hacer algo.

proposition [prɔpə'zɪʃən] n propuesta.

proprietor [prə'praɪətə*] n propietario/a, dueño/a.

propriety [prə'praɪətɪ] n decoro.

pro rata [prəu'rɑːtə] ad a prorrateo.

prose [prəuz] n prosa; (SCOL) traducción f inversa.

prosecute ['prɔsɪkjuːt] vt (LAW) procesar; **prosecution** [-'kjuːʃən] n proceso, causa; (accusing side) acusación f; **prosecutor** n acusador(a) m/f; (also: **public prosecutor**) fiscal m/f.

prospect ['prɔspɛkt] n (view) vista; (outlook) perspectiva; (hope) esperanza // vb [prə'spɛkt] vt explorar // vi buscar; ~s npl (for work etc) perspectivas fpl; ~ing n prospección f; ~ive [prə'spɛktɪv] a (possible) probable, eventual; (certain) futuro; ~or [prə'spɛktə*] n explorador/a m/f.

prospectus [prə'spɛktəs] n prospecto.

prosper ['prɔspə*] vi prosperar; ~ity [-'spɛrɪtɪ] n prosperidad f;

~ous *a* próspero.

prostitute ['prɔstɪtjuːt] *n* prostituta.

prostrate ['prɔstreɪt] *a* postrado.

protagonist [prə'tægənɪst] *n* protagonista *m/f*.

protect [prə'tɛkt] *vt* proteger; ~ion [-'tɛkʃən] *n* protección *f*; ~ive *a* protector(a).

protégé ['prəʊteʒeɪ] *n* protegido/a.

protein ['prəʊtiːn] *n* proteína.

protest ['prəʊtɛst] *n* protesta // *vb*: [prə'tɛst] *vi* protestar // *vt* (*affirm*) afirmar, declarar.

Protestant ['prɔtɪstənt] *a, n* protestante *m/f*.

protester [prə'tɛstə*] *n* manifestante *m/f*.

protracted [prə'træktɪd] *a* prolongado.

protrude [prə'truːd] *vi* salir, sobresalir.

proud [praʊd] *a* orgulloso; (*pej*) soberbio, altanero.

prove [pruːv] *vt* probar; (*verify*) comprobar; (*show*) demostrar // *vi*: to ~ correct resultar correcto; to ~ o.s. probar su valía.

proverb ['prɔvɜːb] *n* refrán *m*.

provide [prə'vaɪd] *vt* proporcionar, dar; to ~ sb with sth proveer a uno de algo; ~d (that) *conj* con tal de que, a condición de que; to ~ for *vt fus* (*person*) mantener a; (*problem etc*) tener en cuenta.

providing [prə'vaɪdɪŋ] *conj* a condición de que, con tal de que.

province ['prɔvɪns] *n* provincia; (*fig*) esfera; **provincial** [prə'vɪnʃəl] *a* provincial; (*pej*) provinciano.

provision [prə'vɪʒən] *n* provisión *f*; (*supply*) suministro, abastecimiento; ~s *npl* (*food*) comestibles *mpl*; ~al *a* provisional; (*temporary*) interino.

proviso [prə'vaɪzəʊ] *n* condición *f*, estipulación *f*.

provocative [prə'vɔkətɪv] *a* provocativo.

provoke [prə'vəʊk] *vt* (*arouse*) provocar, incitar; (*anger*) enojar.

prow [praʊ] *n* proa.

prowess ['praʊɪs] *n* destreza.

prowl [praʊl] *vi* (*also*: ~ about, ~ around) merodear // *n*: on the ~ de merodeo; ~er *n* merodeador(a) *m/f*.

proxy ['prɔksɪ] *n* poder *m*; (*person*) apoderado/a; by ~ por poderes.

prudence ['pruːdns] *n* prudencia.

prudent ['pruːdənt] *a* prudente.

prudish ['pruːdɪʃ] *a* gazmoño.

prune [pruːn] *n* ciruela pasa // *vt* podar.

pry [praɪ] *vi*: to ~ into entrometerse en.

PS *n abbr* (= *postscript*) P.D.

psalm [sɑːm] *n* salmo.

pseudo- [sjuːdəʊ] *pref* seudo-; **pseudonym** *n* seudónimo.

psyche ['saɪkɪ] *n* psique *f*.

psychiatric [saɪkɪ'ætrɪk] *a* psiquiátrico.

psychiatrist [saɪ'kaɪətrɪst] *n* psiquiatra *m/f*.

psychiatry [saɪ'kaɪətrɪ] *n* psiquiatría.

psychic ['saɪkɪk] *a* (*also*: ~al) psíquico.

psychoanalysis [saɪkəʊə'nælɪsɪs] *n* psicoanálisis *m inv*; **psychoanalyst** [-'ænəlɪst] *n* psicoanalista *m/f*.

psychological [saɪkə'lɔdʒɪkl] *a* psicológico.

psychologist [saɪ'kɔlədʒɪst] *n* psicólogo/a.

psychology [saɪ'kɔlədʒɪ] *n* psicología.

PTO *abbr* (= *please turn over*) sigue.

pub [pʌb] *n abbr* (= *public house*) pub *m*, taberna.

puberty ['pjuːbətɪ] *n* pubertad *f*.

pubic ['pjuːbɪk] *a* púbico.

public ['pʌblɪk] *a, n* público; in ~ en público; ~ address system (P.A.) *n* megafonía.

publican ['pʌblɪkən] *n* tabernero/a.

publication [pʌblɪ'keɪʃən] *n* publicación *f*.

public: ~ company *n* sociedad *f* anónima; ~ convenience *n* (*Brit*) aseos *mpl* públicos, sanitarios *mpl* (*LAm*); ~ holiday *n* día de fiesta, (día) feriado (*LAm*); ~ house *n*

(*Brit*) bar *m*, pub *m*.

publicity [pʌb'lɪsɪtɪ] *n* publicidad *f*.

publicize ['pʌblɪsaɪz] *vt* publicitar; (*advertise*) hacer propaganda de.

publicly ['pʌblɪklɪ] *ad* públicamente, en público.

public: ~ **opinion** *n* opinión *f* pública; ~ **relations** (PR) *n* relaciones *fpl* públicas; ~ **school** *n* (*Brit*) escuela privada; (*US*) instituto; ~-**spirited** *a* que tiene sentido del deber ciudadano; ~ **transport** *n* transporte *m* público.

publish ['pʌblɪʃ] *vt* publicar; ~**er** *n* (*person*) editor(a) *m/f*; (*firm*) editorial *f*; ~**ing** *n* (*industry*) industria del libro.

puce [pjuːs] *a* de color pardo rojizo.

pucker ['pʌkə*'] *vt* (*pleat*) arrugar; (*brow etc*) fruncir.

pudding ['pudɪŋ] *n* pudín *m*; (*Brit: sweet*) postre *m*; **black** ~ morcilla.

puddle ['pʌdl] *n* charco *m*.

puff [pʌf] *n* soplo *m*; (*of smoke*) bocanada; (*of breathing, engine*) resoplido // *vt*: **to** ~ **one's pipe** chupar la pipa // *vi* (*gen*) soplar; (*pant*) jadear; **to** ~ **out smoke** echar humo; ~**ed** (*col: out of breath*) sin aliento.

puff pastry *n* hojaldre *m*.

puffy ['pʌfɪ] *a* hinchado.

pull [pul] *n* (*tug*): **to give sth a** ~ dar un tirón a algo; (*influence*) influencia // *vt* tirar de; (*muscle*) agarrotarse; (*haul*) tirar, arrastrar // *vi* tirar; **to** ~ **to pieces** hacer pedazos; **to** ~ **one's punches** (*fig*) no andarse con bromas; **to** ~ **one's weight** hacer su parte; **to** ~ **o.s.** **together** tranquilizarse; **to** ~ **sb's leg** tomar el pelo a uno; **to** ~ **apart** *vt* (*take apart*) desmontar; **to** ~ **down** *vt* (*house*) derribar; **to** ~ **in** *vi* (AUT: *at the kerb*) parar (junto a la acera); (RAIL) llegar a la estación; **to** ~ **off** *vt* (*deal etc*) cerrar; **to** ~ **out** *vi* irse, marcharse; (AUT: *from kerb*) salir // *vt* sacar, arrancar; **to** ~ **over** *vi* (AUT) hacerse a un lado;

to ~ **through** *vi* salir adelante; (MED) recobrar la salud; **to** ~ **up** *vi* (*stop*) parar // *vt* (*uproot*) arrancar, desarraigar; (*stop*) parar.

pulley ['pulɪ] *n* polea.

pullover ['puləʊvə*'] *n* jersey *m*, suéter *m*.

pulp [pʌlp] *n* (*of fruit*) pulpa; (*for paper*) pasta.

pulpit ['pulpɪt] *n* púlpito.

pulsate [pʌl'seɪt] *vi* pulsar, latir.

pulse [pʌls] *n* (ANAT) pulso; (*of music, engine*) pulsación *f*; (BOT) legumbre *f*.

pummel ['pʌml] *vt* aporrear.

pump [pʌmp] *n* bomba; (*shoe*) zapatilla // *vt* sacar con una bomba; (*fig: col*) sonsacar; **to** ~ **up** *vt* inflar.

pumpkin ['pʌmpkɪn] *n* calabaza.

pun [pʌn] *n* juego de palabras.

punch [pʌntʃ] *n* (*blow*) golpe *m*, puñetazo; (*tool*) punzón *m*; (*for paper*) perforadora; (*for tickets*) taladro; (*drink*) ponche *m* // *vt* (*hit*): **to** ~ **sb/sth** dar un puñetazo or golpear a uno/algo; (*make a hole in*) punzar; perforar; ~**line** *n* palabras que rematan un chiste; ~-**up** *n* (Brit *col*) riña.

punctual ['pʌŋktjuəl] *a* puntual.

punctuation [pʌŋktju'eɪʃən] *n* puntuación *f*.

puncture ['pʌŋktʃə*'] (*Brit*) *n* pinchazo // *vt* pinchar.

pundit ['pʌndɪt] *n* experto/a.

pungent ['pʌndʒənt] *a* acre.

punish ['pʌnɪʃ] *vt* castigar; ~**ment** *n* castigo.

punk [pʌŋk] *n* (*also:* ~ **rocker**) punki *m/f*; (*also:* ~ **rock**) música punk; (US *col: hoodlum*) rufián *m*.

punt [pʌnt] *n* (*boat*) batea.

punter ['pʌntə*'] *n* (Brit: *gambler*) jugador/a *m/f*.

puny ['pjuːnɪ] *a* débil.

pup [pʌp] *n* cachorro.

pupil ['pjuːpl] *n* alumno/a.

puppet ['pʌpɪt] *n* títere *m*.

puppy ['pʌpɪ] *n* cachorro, perrito.

purchase ['pəːtʃɪs] *n* compra // *vt*

comprar; **~r** *n* comprador(a) *m/f*.

pure [pjuə'] *a* puro.

purée ['pjuəreɪ] *n* puré *m*.

purely ['pjuəlɪ] *ad* puramente.

purge [pəːdʒ] *n* (*MED, POL*) purga *f*
// *vt* purgar.

purify ['pjuərɪfaɪ] *vt* purificar, depurar.

puritan ['pjuərɪtən] *n* puritano/a.

purity ['pjuərɪtɪ] *n* pureza.

purl [pəːl] *n* punto del revés.

purple ['pəːpl] *a* purpúreo; morado.

purport [pəː'pɔːt] *vi*: **to ~ to be/do**
dar a entender que es/hace.

purpose ['pəːpəs] *n* propósito; **on ~**
a propósito, adrede; **~ful** *a* resuelto,
determinado.

purr [pəː'] *vi* ronronear.

purse [pəːs] *n* monedero; (*US*) bolsa,
cartera (*LAm*) // *vt* fruncir.

purser ['pəːsə'] *n* (*NAUT*)
comisario/a.

pursue [pə'sjuː] *vt* seguir; **~r** *n* perseguidor(a) *m/f*.

pursuit [pə'sjuːt] *n* (*chase*) caza;
(*occupation*) actividad *f*.

purveyor [pə'veɪə'] *n* proveedor(a)
m/f.

push [puʃ] *n* empuje *m*, empujón *m*;
(*MIL*) ataque *m*; (*drive*) empuje *m* //
vt empujar; (*button*) apretar; (*promote*) promover; (*thrust*): **to ~ sth
(into)** meter algo a la fuerza (en) //
vi empujar; (*fig*) hacer esfuerzos; **to
~ aside** *vt* apartar con la mano; **to
~ off** *vi* (*col*) largarse; **to ~ on** *vi*
(*continue*) seguir adelante; **to ~
through** *vt* (*measure*) despachar; **to
~ up** *vt* (*total, prices*) hacer subir; **~chair** *n* (*Brit*) sillita de ruedas; **~er** *n* (*drug ~er*) traficante *m/f*
de drogas; **~over** *n* (*col*): **it's a
~over** está tirado; **~-up** *n* (*US*)
plancha; **~y** *a* (*pej*) agresivo.

puss [pus], **pussy(-cat)** ['pusɪ(kæt)]
n minino.

put [put], *pt, pp* **put** *vt* (*place*) poner, colocar; (*say*) meter; (*say*)
expresar; (*a question*) hacer; **to ~
about** *vi* (*NAUT*) virar // *vt* (*ru-*
mour) diseminar; **to ~ across** *vt*
(*ideas etc*) comunicar; **to ~ away**
vt (*store*) guardar; **to ~ back** *vt*
(*replace*) devolver a su lugar; (*postpone*) aplazar; **to ~ by** *vt* (*money*)
guardar; **to ~ down** *vt* (*on
ground*) poner en el suelo; (*animal*)
sacrificar; (*in writing*) apuntar;
(*suppress: revolt etc*) sofocar; (*attribute*) atribuir; **to ~ forward** *vt*
(*ideas*) presentar, proponer; (*date*)
adelantar; **to ~ in** *vt* (*application,
complaint*) presentar; **to ~ off** *vt*
(*postpone*) aplazar; (*discourage*) desanimar; **to ~ on** *vt* (*clothes, lipstick etc*) ponerse; (*light etc*) encender; (*play etc*) presentar; (*weight*)
ganar; (*brake*) echar; **to ~ out** *vt*
(*fire, light*) apagar; (*one's hand*)
alargar; (*news, rumour*) hacer circular; (*tongue etc*) sacar; (*person: inconvenience*) molestar, fastidiar; **to
~ up** *vt* (*raise*) levantar, alzar;
(*hang*) colgar; (*build*) construir; (*increase*) aumentar; (*accommodate*)
alojar; **to ~ up with** *vt fus* aguantar.

putrid ['pjuːtrɪd] *a* podrido.

putt [pʌt] *vt* hacer un putt // *n* putt
m, golpe *m* corto; **~ing green** *n*
green *m*; minigolf *m*.

putty ['pʌtɪ] *n* masilla.

puzzle ['pʌzl] *n* (*riddle*) acertijo;
(*jigsaw*) rompecabezas *m inv*; (*also:
crossword ~*) crucigrama *m*;
(*mystery*) misterio // *vt* dejar perplejo, confundir // *vi*: **to ~ about** quebrar la cabeza por; **puzzling** *a* misterioso, extraño.

pyjamas [pɪ'dʒɑːməz] *npl* (*Brit*) pijama *m*.

pylon ['paɪlən] *n* torre *f* de conducción eléctrica.

pyramid ['pɪrəmɪd] *n* pirámide *f*.

Pyrenees [pɪrə'niːz] *npl*: **the ~** los
Pirineos.

python ['paɪθən] *n* pitón *m*.

Q

quack [kwæk] *n* (*of duck*) graznido; (*pej: doctor*) curandero/a.

quad [kwɔd] *n abbr* = **quadrangle**; **quadruplet**.

quadrangle ['kwɔdræŋgl] *n* (*Brit: courtyard: abbr:* **quad**) patio.

quadruple [kwɔ'drupl] *vt, vi* cuadruplicar.

quadruplet [kwɔ'dru:plɪt] *n* cuatrillizo/a.

quagmire ['kwægmaɪə*] *n* lodazal *m*, cenegal *m*.

quail [kweɪl] *n* (*bird*) codorniz *f* // *vi* amedrentarse.

quaint [kweɪnt] *a* extraño; (*picturesque*) pintoresco.

quake [kweɪk] *vi* temblar // *n abbr* = **earthquake**.

Quaker ['kweɪkə*] *n* cuáquero/a.

qualification [kwɔlɪfɪ'keɪʃən] *n* (*ability*) capacidad *f*; (*requirement*) requisito; (*diploma etc*) título.

qualified ['kwɔlɪfaɪd] *a* (*trained, fit*) capacitado; (*professionally*) titulado; (*limited*) limitado.

qualify ['kwɔlɪfaɪ] *vt* (*LING*) calificar a; (*capacitate*) capacitar; (*modify*) modificar // *vi* (*SPORT*) clasificarse; **to ~ (as)** calificarse (de), graduarse (en); **to ~ (for)** reunir los requisitos (para).

quality ['kwɔlɪtɪ] *n* calidad *f*; (*moral*) cualidad *f*.

qualm [kwɑ:m] *n* escrúpulo.

quandary ['kwɔndrɪ] *n*: **to be in a ~** tener dudas.

quantity ['kwɔntɪtɪ] *n* cantidad *f*; **~ surveyor** *n* aparejador(a) *m/f*.

quarantine ['kwɔrnti:n] *n* cuarentena.

quarrel ['kwɔrl] *n* riña, pelea // *vi* reñir, pelearse; **~some** *a* pendenciero.

quarry ['kwɔrɪ] *n* (*for stone*) cantera; (*animal*) presa.

quart [kwɔ:t] *n* cuarto de galón =

1.136 *l*.

quarter ['kwɔ:tə*] *n* cuarto, cuarta parte *f*; (*of year*) trimestre *m*; (*district*) barrio // *vt* dividir en cuartos; (*MIL: lodge*) alojar; **~s** *npl* (*barracks*) cuartel *m*; (*living ~s*) alojamiento *sg*; **a ~ of an hour** un cuarto de hora; **~ final** *n* cuarto de final; **~ly** *a* trimestral // *ad* cada 3 meses, trimestralmente; **~master** *n* (*MIL*) comisario, intendente *m* militar.

quartet(te) [kwɔ:'tet] *n* cuarteto.

quartz [kwɔ:ts] *n* cuarzo.

quash [kwɔʃ] *vt* (*verdict*) anular.

quasi- ['kweɪzaɪ] *pref* cuasi.

quaver ['kweɪvə*] *n* (*Brit MUS*) corchea // *vi* temblar.

quay [ki:] *n* (*also: ~side*) muelle *m*.

queasy ['kwi:zɪ] *a*: **to feel ~** tener náuseas.

queen [kwi:n] *n* reina; (*CARDS*) dama; **~ mother** *n* reina madre.

queer [kwɪə*] *a* (*odd*) raro, extraño // *n* (*pej: col*) maricón *m*.

quell [kwel] *vt* (*feeling*) calmar; (*rebellion etc*) sofocar.

quench [kwentʃ] *vt* (*flames*) apagar; **to ~ one's thirst** apagar la sed.

querulous ['kwerʊləs] *a* (*person, voice*) quejumbroso.

query ['kwɪərɪ] *n* (*question*) pregunta; (*doubt*) duda // *vt* dudar de.

quest [kwest] *n* busca, búsqueda.

question ['kwestʃən] *n* pregunta; (*matter*) asunto, cuestión *f* // *vt* (*doubt*) dudar de; (*interrogate*) interrogar, hacer preguntas a; **beyond ~** fuera de toda duda; **it's out of the ~** imposible, ni hablar; **~able** *a* discutible; (*doubtful*) dudoso; **~ mark** *n* punto de interrogación; **~naire** [-'nɛə*] *n* cuestionario.

queue [kju:] *n* (*Brit*) cola // *vi* hacer cola.

quibble ['kwɪbl] *vi* sutilizar.

quick [kwɪk] *a* rápido; (*temper*) vivo; (*mind*) listo; (*eye*) agudo // *n*: **cut to the ~** (*fig*) herido en lo vivo; **be ~!** ¡date prisa!; **~en** *vt* apresurar // vi apresurarse, darse prisa; **~ly** ad rápidamente, de prisa; **~sand** n arenas fpl movedizas; **~witted** a perspicaz.

quid [kwɪd] n, pl inv (Brit col) libra.

quiet ['kwaɪət] a tranquilo; (person) callado; (discreet) discreto // n silencio, tranquilidad f // vt, vi (US) = **~en; keep ~!** ¡cállate!; ¡silencio!; **~en** (also: **~en down**) vi (grow calm) calmarse; (grow silent) callarse // vt calmar; hacer callar; **~ly** ad tranquilamente; (silently) silenciosamente; **~ness** n (silence) silencio; (calm) tranquilidad f.

quilt [kwɪlt] n (Brit) edredón m.

quin [kwɪn] n abbr = **quintuplet**.

quinine [kwɪ'niːn] n quinina.

quintet(te) [kwɪn'tet] n quinteto.

quintuplet [kwɪn'tjuːplɪt] n quintillizo/a

quip [kwɪp] n pulla.

quirk [kwɜːk] n peculiaridad f.

quit [kwɪt], pt, pp **quit** or **quitted** vt dejar, abandonar; (premises) desocupar // vi (give up) renunciar; (go away) irse; (resign) dimitir.

quite [kwaɪt] ad (rather) bastante; (entirely) completamente; **~ a few of them** un buen número de ellos; **(so)!** ¡así es!, ¡exactamente!

quits [kwɪts] a: **~ (with)** en paz (con); **let's call it ~** dejémoslo en tablas.

quiver ['kwɪvə*] vi estremecerse

quiz [kwɪz] n (game) concurso; (: TV, RADIO) programa-concurso // vt interrogar; **~zical** a burlón(ona).

quota ['kwəʊtə] n cuota.

quotation [kwəʊ'teɪʃən] n cita; (estimate) presupuesto; **~ marks** npl comillas fpl.

quote [kwəʊt] n cita // vt (sentence) citar; (price) cotizar // vi: **to ~ from** citar de.

quotient ['kwəʊʃənt] n cociente m.

R

rabbi ['ræbaɪ] n rabino.

rabbit ['ræbɪt] n conejo; **~ hutch** n conejera.

rabble ['ræbl] n (pej) chusma, populacho.

rabies ['reɪbɪːz] n rabia.

RAC n abbr (Brit) = Royal Automobile Club.

race [reɪs] n carrera; (species) raza // vt (horse) hacer correr; (person) competir contra; (engine) acelerar // vi (compete) competir; (run) correr; (pulse) latir a ritmo acelerado; **~ car** n (US) = **racing car**; **~ car driver** n (US) = **racing driver**; **~course** n hipódromo; **~horse** n caballo de carreras; **~track** n hipódromo; (for cars) autódromo.

racial ['reɪʃl] a racial; **~ist** a, n racista m/f.

racing ['reɪsɪŋ] n carreras fpl; **~ car** n (Brit) coche m de carreras; **~ driver** n (Brit) corredor(a) m/f de coches.

racism ['reɪsɪzm] n racismo; **racist** [-sɪst] a, n racista m/f.

rack [ræk] n (also: **luggage ~**) rejilla; (shelf) estante m; (also: **roof ~**) baca, portaequipajes m inv; (clothes **~**) percha // vt (cause pain to) atormentar; **to ~ one's brains** devanarse los sesos.

racket ['rækɪt] n (for tennis) raqueta; (noise) ruido, estrépito; (swindle) estafa, timo.

racquet ['rækɪt] n raqueta.

racy ['reɪsɪ] a picante, salado.

radar ['reɪdɑː*] n radar m.

radiance ['reɪdɪəns] n brillantez f, resplandor m.

radiant ['reɪdɪənt] a brillante, resplandeciente.

radiate ['reɪdɪeɪt] vt (heat) radiar, irradiar // vi (lines) extenderse.

radiation [reɪdɪ'eɪʃən] n radiación f.

radiator ['reɪdɪeɪtə*] n radiador m.

radical ['rædɪkl] a radical.

radii ['reɪdɪaɪ] npl of **radius**.

radio ['reɪdɪəʊ] n radio f; **on the ~** por radio.

radio... ['reɪdɪəʊ] pref: **~active** a radioactivo.

radio-controlled [reɪdɪəʊkən'trəʊld] a teledirigido.

radiography [reɪdɪ'ɒgrəfɪ] n radiografía.

radiology [reɪdɪ'ɒlədʒɪ] n radiología.

radio station n emisora.

radiotherapy ['reɪdɪəʊθerəpɪ] n radioterapia.

radish ['rædɪʃ] n rábano.

radius ['reɪdɪəs], pl **radii** [-ɪaɪ] n radio.

RAF n abbr = **Royal Air Force**.

raffle ['ræfl] n rifa, sorteo // vt rifar.

raft [rɑːft] n (craft) baba; (also: **life ~**) balsa salvavidas.

rafter ['rɑːftə*] n viga.

rag [ræg] n (piece of cloth) trapo; (torn cloth) harapo; (pej: newspaper) periodicucho; (for charity) actividades estudiantiles benéficas // n (Brit) tomar el pelo a; **~s** npl harapos mpl; **~-and-bone man** n (Brit) = **~man**; **~ doll** n muñeca de trapo.

rage [reɪdʒ] n (fury) rabia, furor m // vi (person) rabiar, estar furioso; (storm) bramar; **it's all the ~** es lo último.

ragged ['rægɪd] a (edge) desigual, mellado; (cuff) roto; (appearance) andrajoso, harapiento.

ragman ['rægmæn] n trapero.

raid [reɪd] n (MIL) incursión f; (criminal) asalto; (by police) redada // vt invadir, atacar; asaltar; **~er** n invasor(a) m/f.

rail [reɪl] n (on stair) barandilla, pasamanos m inv; (on bridge, balcony) pretil m; (of ship) barandilla; (for train) riel m, carril m; **~s** npl vía sg; **by ~** por ferrocarril m; **~ing(s)** n(pl) verja sg, enrejado sg; **~road** n (US) = **~way**; **~way** n (Brit) ferrocarril m, vía férrea; **~way line**

n (Brit) línea (de ferrocarril); **~wayman** n (Brit) ferroviario; **~way station** n (Brit) estación f de ferrocarril.

rain [reɪn] n lluvia // vi llover; **in the ~** bajo la lluvia; **it's ~ing** llueve, está lloviendo; **~bow** n arco iris; **~coat** n impermeable m; **~drop** n gota de lluvia; **~fall** n lluvia; **~y** a lluvioso.

raise [reɪz] n aumento // vt (lift) levantar; (build) erigir, edificar; (increase) aumentar; (doubts) suscitar; (a question) plantear; (cattle, family) criar; (crop) cultivar; (army) reclutar; (funds) reunir; (loan) obtener; **to ~ one's voice** alzar la voz.

raisin ['reɪzn] n pasa de Corinto.

rake [reɪk] n (tool) rastrillo; (person) libertino // vt (garden) rastrillar; (fire) hurgar; (with machine gun) barrer.

rally ['rælɪ] n (POL etc) reunión f, mitin m; (AUT) rallye m; (TENNIS) peloteo // vt reunir // vi reunirse; (sick person, Stock Exchange) recuperarse; **to ~ round** vt fus (fig) dar apoyo a.

RAM [ræm] n abbr (= random access memory) RAM f.

ram [ræm] n carnero; (TECH) pisón m // vt (crash into) dar contra, chocar con; (tread down) apisonar.

ramble ['ræmbl] n caminata, excursión f en el campo // vi (pej: also: **~ on**) divagar; **~r** n excursionista m/f; (BOT) trepadora; **rambling** a (speech) inconexo; (BOT) trepador(a).

ramp [ræmp] n rampa; **on/off ~** n (US AUT) vía de acceso/salida.

rampage [ræm'peɪdʒ] n: **to be on the ~** desmandarse.

rampant ['ræmpənt] a (disease etc): **to be ~** estar extendiéndose mucho.

rampart ['ræmpɑːt] n terraplén m; (wall) muralla.

ramshackle ['ræmʃækl] a destartalado.

ran [ræn] pt of **run**.

ranch [rɑːntʃ] *n* (US) hacienda, estancia; **~er** *n* ganadero.

rancid [ˈrænsɪd] *a* rancio.

rancour, (US) **rancor** [ˈræŋkəʳ] *n* rencor *m*.

random [ˈrændəm] *a* fortuito, sin orden; (COMPUT, MATH) aleatorio // *n*: **at** ~ al azar.

randy [ˈrændɪ] *a* (Brit col) cachondo.

rang [ræŋ] *pt of* **ring**.

range [reɪndʒ] *n* (of mountains) cadena de montañas, cordillera; (of missile) alcance *m*; (of voice) registro; (series) serie *f*; (of products) surtido; (MIL: also: **shooting** ~) campo de tiro; (also: **kitchen** ~) fogón *m* // *vt* (place) colocar; (arrange) arreglar // *vi*: **to** ~ **over** (wander) recorrer; (extend) extenderse por; **to** ~ **from** ... **to**... oscilar entre ... y...

ranger [ˈreɪndʒəʳ] *n* guardabosques *m inv*.

rank [ræŋk] *n* (row) fila; (MIL) rango; (status) categoría; (Brit: also: **taxi** ~) parada // *vi*: **to** ~ **among** figurar entre // *a* (stinking) fétido, rancio; **the** ~ **and file** (fig) la base.

rankle [ˈræŋkl] *vi* (insult) doler.

ransack [ˈrænsæk] *vt* (search) registrar; (plunder) saquear.

ransom [ˈrænsəm] *n* rescate *m*; **to hold sb to** ~ (fig) hacer chantaje a uno.

rant [rænt] *vi* divagar, desvariar.

rap [ræp] *vt* golpear, dar un golpecito en.

rape [reɪp] *n* violación *f*; (BOT) colza *f* // *vt* violar; ~ (**seed**) **oil** *n* aceite *m* de colza.

rapid [ˈræpɪd] *a* rápido; ~**s** *npl* (GEO) rápidos *mpl*; ~**ity** [rəˈpɪdɪtɪ] *n* rapidez *f*; ~**ly** *ad* rápidamente.

rapist [ˈreɪpɪst] *n* violador *m*.

rapport [ræˈpɔːʳ] *n* simpatía.

rapture [ˈræptʃəʳ] *n* éxtasis *m*.

rare [rɛəʳ] *a* raro, poco común; (CULIN: steak) poco hecho.

rarely [ˈrɛəlɪ] *ad* pocas veces.

raring [ˈrɛərɪŋ] *a*: **to be** ~ **to go** (col) tener muchas ganas de empezar.

rarity [ˈrɛərɪtɪ] *n* rareza.

rascal [ˈrɑːskl] *n* pillo, pícaro.

rash [ræʃ] *a* imprudente, precipitado // *n* (MED) salpullido, erupción *f* (cutánea).

rasher [ˈræʃəʳ] *n* lonja.

raspberry [ˈrɑːzbərɪ] *n* frambuesa.

rasping [ˈrɑːspɪŋ] *a*: **a** ~ **noise** un ruido áspero.

rat [ræt] *n* rata.

rate [reɪt] *n* (ratio) razón *f*; (percentage) tanto por ciento; (price) precio; (: of hotel) tasa; (of interest) tipo; (speed) velocidad *f* // *vt* (value) tasar; (estimate) estimar; **to** ~ **as** ser considerado como; ~**s** *npl* (Brit) impuesto *sg* municipal; (fees) tarifa *sg*; ~**able value** *n* (Brit) valor *m* impuesto; ~**payer** *n* (Brit) contribuyente *m/f*.

rather [ˈrɑːðəʳ] *ad*: **it's** ~ **expensive** es algo caro; (too much) es demasiado caro; **there's** ~ **a lot** hay bastante; **I would** or **I'd** ~ **go** preferiría ir; or ~ mejor dicho.

ratify [ˈrætɪfaɪ] *vt* ratificar.

rating [ˈreɪtɪŋ] *n* (valuation) tasación *f*; (standing) posición *f*; (Brit NAUT: sailor) marinero.

ratio [ˈreɪʃɪəʊ] *n* razón *f*; **in the** ~ **of 100 to 1** a razón de 100 a 1.

ration [ˈræʃən] *n* ración *f*; ~**s** *npl* víveres *mpl* // *vt* racionar.

rational [ˈræʃənl] *a* racional; (solution, reasoning) lógico, razonable; (person) cuerdo, sensato; ~**e** [ræʃəˈnɑːl] *n* razón *f* fundamental; ~**ize** *vt* (industry) reconvertir; (behaviour) justificar.

rationing [ˈræʃnɪŋ] *n* racionamiento.

rat race *n* lucha incesante por la supervivencia.

rattle [ˈrætl] *n* golpeteo; (of train etc) traqueteo; (object: of baby) sonaja, sonajero; (: of sports fan) matraca *f* // *vi* sonar, golpear; traquetear; (small objects) castañetear // *vt* hacer sonar agitando; ~**snake** *n* serpiente *f* de cascabel.

raucous [ˈrɔːkəs] *a* estridente, ronco.

ravage ['rævidʒ] vt hacer estragos en, destrozar; ~s npl estragos mpl.

rave [reiv] vi (in anger) encolerizarse; (with enthusiasm) entusiasmarse; (MED) delirar, desvariar.

raven ['reivən] n cuervo.

ravenous ['rævənəs] a hambriento.

ravine [rə'viːn] n barranco.

raving ['reiviŋ] a: ~ **lunatic** loco de atar.

ravishing ['ræviʃiŋ] a encantador(a).

raw [rɔː] a (uncooked) crudo; (not processed) bruto; (sore) vivo; (inexperienced) novato, inexperto; ~ **deal** n injusticia; ~ **material** n materia prima.

ray [rei] n rayo; ~ **of hope** (rayo de) esperanza.

rayon ['reiɔn] n rayón m.

raze [reiz] vt arrasar.

razor ['reizə*] n (open) navaja; (safety ~) máquina de afeitar; ~ **blade** n hoja de afeitar.

Rd abbr = **road**.

re [riː] prep con referencia a.

reach [riːtʃ] n alcance m; (BOXING) envergadura; (of river etc) extensión f entre dos recodos // vt alcanzar, llegar a; (achieve) lograr // vi extenderse; **within** ~ al alcance (de la mano); **out of** ~ fuera del alcance; **to** ~ **out for sth** alargar o tender la mano para tomar algo.

react [riː'ækt] vi reaccionar; ~**ion** [-'ækʃən] n reacción f.

reactor [riː'æktə*] n reactor m.

read [riːd], pt, pp **read** [rɛd] vi leer // vt leer; (understand) entender; (study) estudiar; **to** ~ **out** vt leer en alta voz; ~**able** a (writing) legible; (book) leíble; ~**er** n lector(a) m/f; (book) libro de lecturas; (Brit: at university) profesor-a m/f adjunto/a; ~**ership** n (of paper etc) (número de) lectores mpl.

readily ['rɛdili] ad (willingly) de buena gana; (easily) fácilmente; (quickly) en seguida.

readiness ['rɛdinis] n buena voluntad; (preparedness) preparación f;

in ~ (prepared) listo, preparado.

reading ['riːdiŋ] n lectura; (understanding) comprensión f; (on instrument) indicación f.

readjust [riːə'dʒʌst] vt reajustar // vi (person): **to** ~ **to** reajustarse a.

ready ['rɛdi] a listo, preparado; (willing) dispuesto; (available) disponible // ad: ~**-cooked** listo para comer // n: **at the** ~ (MIL) listo para tirar; **to get** ~ vi prepararse // vt preparar; ~**-made** a confeccionado; ~**-money** n dinero contante; ~**-reckoner** n libro de cálculos hechos; ~**-to-wear** a confeccionado.

real [riəl] a verdadero, auténtico; **in** ~ **terms** en términos reales; ~ **estate** n bienes mpl raíces; ~**istic** [-'listik] a realista.

reality [riː'æliti] n realidad f.

realization [riəlai'zeiʃən] n comprensión f; realización f.

realize ['riəlaiz] vt (understand) darse cuenta de; (a project; COMM: asset) realizar.

really ['riəli] ad realmente; ~? ¿de veras?

realm [rɛlm] n reino; (fig) esfera.

realtor ['riəltɔː*] n (US) corredor a m/f de bienes raíces.

reap [riːp] vt segar; (fig) cosechar, recoger.

reappear [riːə'piə*] vi reaparecer.

rear [riə*] a trasero // n parte f trasera // vt (cattle, family) criar // vi (also: ~ **up**) (animal) encabritarse; ~**guard** n retaguardia.

rearmament [riː'ɑːməmənt] n rearme m.

rearrange [riːə'reindʒ] vt ordenar o arreglar de nuevo.

rear-view ['riəvjuː]: ~ **mirror** n (AUT) (espejo) retrovisor m.

reason ['riːzn] n razón f // vi: **to** ~ **with sb** tratar de que uno entre en razón, it **stands to** ~ **that** es lógico que; ~**able** a razonable; (sensible) sensato; ~**ably** ad razonablemente; ~**ed** a (argument) razonado; ~**ing** n razonamiento, argumentos mpl.

reassurance [riːəˈʃuərəns] n consuelo.

reassure [riːəˈʃuə*] vt tranquilizar, alentar; to ~ sb that tranquilizar a uno asegurando que; **reassuring** a alentador(a).

rebate [ˈriːbeɪt] n (on product) rebaja; (on tax etc) descuento; (repayment) reembolso.

rebel [ˈrɛbl] n rebelde m/f // [rɪˈbɛl] vi rebelarse, sublevarse; **~lion** [rɪˈbeljən] n rebelión f, sublevación f; **~lious** [rɪˈbeljəs] a rebelde; (child) revoltoso.

rebound [rɪˈbaund] vi (ball) rebotar // n [ˈriːbaund] rebote m.

rebuff [rɪˈbʌf] n desaire m, rechazo.

rebuild [riːˈbɪld] vt (irg: like build) vt reconstruir.

rebuke [rɪˈbjuːk] vt reprender.

rebut [rɪˈbʌt] vt rebatir.

recalcitrant [rɪˈkælsɪtrənt] a reacio.

recall [rɪˈkɔːl] vt (remember) recordar; (ambassador etc) retirar // n recuerdo.

recant [rɪˈkænt] vi retractarse.

recap [ˈriːkæp] vt, vi recapitular.

recapitulate [riːkəˈpɪtjuleɪt] vt, vi = recap.

rec'd abbr (= received) rbdo.

recede [rɪˈsiːd] vi retroceder; **receding** a (forehead, chin) huidizo; receding hairline entradas fpl.

receipt [rɪˈsiːt] n (document) recibo; (for parcel etc) acuse m de recibo; (act of receiving) recepción f; **~s** npl (COMM) ingresos mpl.

receive [rɪˈsiːv] vt recibir; (guest) acoger; (wound) sufrir; **~r** n (TEL) auricular m; (RADIO) receptor m; (of stolen goods) perista m/f; (LAW) administrador m jurídico.

recent [ˈriːsnt] a reciente; **~ly** ad recientemente; **~ly arrived** recién llegado.

receptacle [rɪˈsɛptɪkl] n receptáculo.

reception [rɪˈsɛpʃən] n (gen) recepción f; (welcome) acogida; **~ desk** n recepción f; **~ist** n recepcionista m/f.

recess [rɪˈsɛs] n (in room) hueco; (for bed) nicho; (secret place) escondrijo; (POL etc: holiday) clausura; **~ion** [-ˈsɛʃən] n recesión f.

recharge [riːˈtʃɑːdʒ] vt (battery) recargar.

recipe [ˈrɛsɪpɪ] n receta.

recipient [rɪˈsɪpɪənt] n recibidor(a) m/f; (of letter) destinatario/a.

recital [rɪˈsaɪtl] n recital m.

recite [rɪˈsaɪt] vt (poem) recitar; (complaints etc) enumerar.

reckless [ˈrɛkləs] a temerario, imprudente; (speed) peligroso; **~ly** ad imprudentemente; de modo peligroso.

reckon [ˈrɛkən] vt (count) contar; (consider) considerar; I ~ that... me parece que...; **to ~ on** vt fus contar con; **~ing** n (calculation) cálculo.

reclaim [rɪˈkleɪm] vt (land) recuperar; (: from sea) rescatar; (demand back) reclamar.

recline [rɪˈklaɪn] vi reclinarse; **reclining** a (seat) reclinable.

recluse [rɪˈkluːs] n recluso/a.

recognition [rɛkəgˈnɪʃən] n reconocimiento; **transformed beyond ~** irreconocible.

recognizable [ˈrɛkəgnaɪzəbl] a: **~ (by)** reconocible (por).

recognize [ˈrɛkəgnaɪz] vt: **to ~ (by/as)** reconocer (por/como).

recoil [rɪˈkɔɪl] vi (person): **to ~ from doing sth** retraerse de hacer algo // n (of gun) retroceso.

recollect [rɛkəˈlɛkt] vt recordar, acordarse de; **~ion** [-ˈlɛkʃən] n recuerdo.

recommend [rɛkəˈmɛnd] vt recomendar.

recompense [ˈrɛkəmpɛns] vt recompensar // n recompensa.

reconcile [ˈrɛkənsaɪl] vt (two people) reconciliar; (two facts) compaginar; **to ~ o.s. to sth** conformarse a algo.

recondition [riːkənˈdɪʃən] vt (machine) reacondicionar.

reconnaissance [rɪˈkɔnɪsns] n (MIL) reconocimiento.

reconnoitre, (US) **reconnoiter** [rekə'nɔɪtə*] vt, vi (MIL) reconocer.

reconsider [ri:kən'sɪdə*] vt repensar.

reconstruct [ri:kən'strʌkt] vt reconstruir.

record ['rekɔːd] n (MUS) disco; (of meeting etc) relación f; (register) registro, partida; (file) archivo; (also: police ~) antecedentes mpl, (written) expediente m; (SPORT) récord m // vt ['rikɔːd] (set down) registrar; (relate) hacer constar; (MUS: song etc) grabar; **in ~ time** en un tiempo récord; **off the ~** a no oficial // ad confidencialmente; **~ card** n (in file) ficha; **~ed delivery** n (Brit POST) entrega con acuse de recibo; **~er** n (MUS) flauta de pico; (TECH) contador m; **~ holder** n (SPORT) actual poseedor(a) m/f del récord; **~ing** n (MUS) grabación f; **~ player** n tocadiscos m inv.

recount [rɪ'kaʊnt] vt contar.

re-count ['riːkaʊnt] n (POL: of votes) segundo escrutinio // vt [riː'kaʊnt] volver a contar.

recoup [rɪ'kuːp] vt: **to ~ one's losses** recuperar las pérdidas.

recourse [rɪ'kɔːs] n recurso.

recover [rɪ'kʌvə*] vt recuperar; (rescue) rescatar // vi (from illness, shock) recuperarse; (country) recuperar; **~y** n recuperación f; rescate m; (MED): **to make a ~y** restablecerse.

recreation [rekrɪ'eɪʃən] n (amusement, SCOL) recreo; **~al** a de recreo.

recruit [rɪ'kruːt] n recluta m/f // vt reclutar; (staff) contratar (personal); **~ment** n reclutamiento.

rectangle ['rektæŋgl] n rectángulo; **rectangular** [-'tæŋgjulə*] a rectangular.

rectify ['rektɪfaɪ] vt rectificar.

rector ['rektə*] n (REL) párroco; **~y** n casa del párroco.

recuperate [rɪ'kuːpəreɪt] vi reponerse, restablecerse.

recur [rɪ'kɜː*] vi repetirse; (pain, illness) producirse de nuevo; **~rence** [rɪ'kʌrəns] n repetición f; **~rent** [rɪ'kʌrənt] a repetido.

red [red] n rojo // a rojo; **to be in the ~** (account) estar en números rojos; (business) tener un saldo negativo; **to give sb the ~ carpet treatment** recibir a uno con todos los honores; **R~ Cross** n Cruz f Roja; **~currant** n grosella roja; **~den** vt enrojecer // vi enrojecerse; **~dish** a (hair) rojizo.

redeem [rɪ'diːm] vt (sth in pawn) desempeñar; (fig, also REL) rescatar; **~ing** a: **~ing feature** rasgo bueno or favorable.

redeploy [riːdɪ'plɔɪ] vt (resources) reorganizar.

red: **~-haired** a pelirrojo; **~-handed** a: **to be caught ~-handed** cogerse (Sp) or pillarse (LAm) con las manos en la masa; **~head** n pelirrojo/a; **~ herring** n (fig) pista falsa; **~-hot** a candente.

redirect [riːdaɪ'rekt] vt (mail) reexpedir.

red light n: **to go through a ~** (AUT) pasar la luz roja; **red-light district** n barrio chino.

redo [riː'duː] vt (irg: like do) rehacer.

redolent ['redələnt] a: **~ of** (smell) con fragancia a; **to be ~ of** (fig) recordar.

redouble [riː'dʌbl] vt: **to ~ one's efforts** intensificar los esfuerzos.

redress [rɪ'dres] n reparación f // vt reparar.

Red Sea n: **the ~** el mar Rojo.

redskin ['redskɪn] n piel roja m/f.

red tape n (fig) trámites mpl.

reduce [rɪ'djuːs] vt reducir; (lower) rebajar; **'~ speed now'** (AUT) 'reduzca la velocidad'; **at a ~d price** (of goods) (a precio) rebajado; **reduction** [rɪ'dʌkʃən] n reducción f; (of price) rebaja; (discount) descuento.

redundancy [rɪ'dʌndənsɪ] n desempleo.

redundant [rɪ'dʌndnt] a (Brit) (worker) parado, sin trabajo; (detail, object) superfluo; **to be made ~** quedar(se) sin trabajo.

reed [riːd] n (BOT) junco, caña.

reef [riːf] n (at sea) arrecife m.

reek [riːk] vi: **to ~ (of)** apestar a.

reel [riːl] n carrete m, bobina; (of film) rollo // vt (TECH) devanar; (also: ~ in) sacar // vi (sway) tambalear(se).

ref [rɛf] n abbr (col) = **referee**.

refectory [rɪ'fɛktərɪ] n comedor m.

refer [rɪ'fəː*] vt (send) remitir; (ascribe) referir a, relacionar con // vi: **to ~ to** (allude to) referirse a, aludir a; (apply to) relacionarse con; (consult) consultar.

referee [rɛfə'riː] n árbitro; (Brit: for job application) valedor m; **to be a ~** (for job application) proporcionar referencias // vt (match) arbitrar en.

reference ['rɛfrəns] n (mention) referencia; (for job application: letter) carta de recomendación; **with ~ to** con referencia a; (COMM: in letter) me remito a; **~ book** n libro de consulta; **~ number** n número de referencia.

refill [riː'fɪl] vt rellenar // n ['riːfɪl] repuesto, recambio.

refine [rɪ'faɪn] vt (sugar, oil) refinar; **~d** a (person, taste) fino; **~ment** n (of person) cultura, educación f.

reflect [rɪ'flɛkt] vt (light, image) reflejar // vi (think) reflexionar, pensar; **it ~s badly/well on him** le perjudica/le hace honor; **~ion** [-'flɛkʃən] n (act) reflexión f; (image) reflejo; (discredit) crítica; come in pensándolo bien; **~or** n (AUT) captafaros m inv; (telescope) reflector m.

reflex ['riːflɛks] a, n reflejo; **~ive** [rɪ'flɛksɪv] a (LING) reflexivo.

reform [rɪ'fɔːm] n reforma // vt reformar; **the R~ation** [rɛfə'meɪʃən] n la Reforma; **~atory** n (US) reformatorio; **~er** n reformador(a) m/f.

refrain [rɪ'freɪn] vi: **to ~ from doing** abstenerse de hacer // n estribillo.

refresh [rɪ'frɛʃ] vt refrescar; **~er course** n (Brit) curso de repaso; **~ing** a (drink) refrescante; (change etc) estimulante; **~ments** npl (drinks) refrescos mpl.

refrigerator [rɪ'frɪdʒəreɪtə*] n nevera, refrigeradora (LAm).

refuel [riː'fjuəl] vi repostar (combustible).

refuge ['rɛfjuːdʒ] n refugio, asilo; **to take ~ in** refugiarse en.

refugee [rɛfju'dʒiː] n refugiado/a.

refund [rɪ'fʌnd] n reembolso // vt [rɪ'fʌnd] devolver, reembolsar.

refurbish [riː'fəːbɪʃ] vt restaurar, renovar.

refusal [rɪ'fjuːzəl] n negativa; **to have first ~ on** tener la primera opción a.

refuse ['rɛfjuːs] n basura // vb [rɪ'fjuːz] vt rechazar // vi negarse; (horse) rehusar; **~ collection** recolección f de basuras.

regain [rɪ'geɪn] vt recobrar, recuperar.

regal ['riːgəl] a regio, real.

regalia [rɪ'geɪlɪə] n insignias fpl.

regard [rɪ'gɑːd] n (esteem) respeto, consideración f // vt (consider) considerar; **to give one's ~s to** saludar de su parte a; **'with kindest ~s'** 'con muchos recuerdos'; **~ing, as ~s, with ~ to** prep con respecto a, en cuanto a; **~less** ad a pesar de todo; **~less of** sin reparar en.

régime [reɪ'ʒiːm] n régimen m.

regiment ['rɛdʒɪmənt] n regimiento // vt reglamentar; **~al** [-'mɛntl] a militar.

region ['riːdʒən] n región f; **in the ~ of** (fig) alrededor de; **~al** a regional.

register ['rɛdʒɪstə*] n registro // vt registrar; (birth) declarar; (letter) certificar; (subj: instrument) marcar, indicar // vi (at hotel) registrarse; (sign on) inscribirse; (make impression) producir impresión; **~ed** a (*design*) registrado; (*Brit: letter*) certificado; **~ed trademark** n marca registrada.

registrar ['redʒɪstrɑː*] n secretario/a (del registro civil).

registration [redʒɪs'treɪʃən] n (*act*) declaración f; (*AUT: also*: ~ **number**) matrícula.

registry ['redʒɪstrɪ] n registro, ~ **office** n (*Brit*) registro civil; **to get married in a** ~ **office** casarse por lo civil.

regret [rɪ'gret] n sentimiento, pesar m; (*remorse*) remordimiento m // vt sentir, lamentar; (*repent of*) arrepentirse de; **~fully** ad con pesar; **~table** a lamentable; (*loss*) sensible.

regroup [riː'gruːp] vt reagrupar // vi reagruparse.

regular ['regjulə*] a regular; (*soldier*) profesional; (*col: intensive*) verdadero // n (*client etc*) cliente/a m/f habitual; **~ity** [-'lærɪtɪ] n regularidad f; **~ly** ad con regularidad.

regulate ['regjuleɪt] vt (*gen*) controlar; **regulation** [-'leɪʃən] n (*rule*) regla, reglamento; (*adjustment*) regulación f.

rehearsal [rɪ'həːsəl] n ensayo.

rehearse [rɪ'həːs] vt ensayar.

reign [reɪn] n reinado; (*fig*) predominio // vi reinar; (*fig*) imperar.

reimburse [riːɪm'bəːs] vt reembolsar.

rein [reɪn] n (*for horse*) rienda.

reindeer ['reɪndɪə*] n, pl inv reno.

reinforce [riːɪn'fɔːs] vt reforzar; **~d concrete** n hormigón m armado; **~ment** n (*action*) refuerzo; **~ments** npl (*MIL*) refuerzos mpl.

reinstate [riːɪn'steɪt] vt (*worker*) reintegrar (a su puesto).

reiterate [riː'ɪtəreɪt] vt reiterar, repetir.

reject [rɪ'dʒekt] n (*thing*) desecho // vt [rɪ'dʒekt] rechazar; (*suggestion*) descartar; **~ion** [rɪ'dʒekʃən] n rechazo.

rejoice [rɪ'dʒɔɪs] vi: **to** ~ **at** or **over** regocijarse or alegrarse de.

rejuvenate [rɪ'dʒuːvəneɪt] vt rejuvenecer.

relapse [rɪ'læps] n (*MED*) recaída.

relate [rɪ'leɪt] vt (*tell*) contar, relatar; (*connect*) relacionar // vi relacionarse; **~d to** a afín; (*person*) emparentado; **~d to** (*subject*) relacionado con; **relating to** prep referente a.

relation [rɪ'leɪʃən] n (*person*) pariente/a m/f; (*link*) relación f; **~ship** n relación f; (*personal*) relaciones fpl; (*also*: **family ~ship**) parentesco.

relative [rɪ'lətɪv] n pariente/a m/f, familiar m/f a / a relativo; **~ly** ad (*comparatively*) relativamente.

relax [rɪ'læks] vi descansar; (*unwind*) relajarse // vt relajar; (*mind, person*) descansar; **~ation** [riːlæk'seɪʃən] n (*rest*) descanso; (*entertainment*) diversión f; **~ed** a relajado; (*tranquil*) tranquilo; **~ing** a relajante.

relay ['riːleɪ] n (*race*) carrera de relevos // vt (*RADIO, TV, pass on*) retransmitir.

release [rɪ'liːs] n (*liberation*) liberación f; (*discharge*) puesta en libertad f; (*of gas etc*) escape m; (*of film etc*) estreno // vt (*prisoner*) poner en libertad; (*film*) estrenar; (*book*) publicar; (*piece of news*) difundir; (*gas etc*) despedir, arrojar; (*free: from wreckage etc*) soltar; (*TECH: catch, spring etc*) desenganchar; (*let go*) soltar, aflojar.

relegate ['relɪgeɪt] vt relegar; (*SPORT*): **to be ~d** to bajar a.

relent [rɪ'lent] vi ablandarse; **~less** a implacable.

relevant ['relɪvənt] a (*fact*) pertinente; **relevant to** relacionado con.

reliability [rɪlaɪə'bɪlɪtɪ] n fiabilidad f; seguridad f; veracidad f.

reliable [rɪ'laɪəbl] a (*person, firm*) de confianza, de fiar; (*method, machine*) seguro; (*source*) fidedigno; **reliably** ad: **to be reliably informed that...** saber de fuente fidedigna que...

reliance [rɪ'laɪəns] n: ~ (**on**) dependencia (de).

relic ['rɛlɪk] n (REL) reliquia; (of the past) vestigio.

relief [rɪ'liːf] n (from pain, anxiety) alivio; (help, supplies) socorro, ayuda; (ART, GEO) relieve m.

relieve [rɪ'liːv] vt (pain, patient) aliviar; (bring help to) ayudar, socorrer; (burden) aligerar; (take over from: gen) sustituir; (: guard) relevar; to ~ sb of sth quitar algo a uno; to ~ o.s. hacer sus necesidades.

religion [rɪ'lɪdʒən] n religión f; **religious** a religioso.

relinquish [rɪ'lɪŋkwɪʃ] vt abandonar; (plan, habit) renunciar a.

relish ['rɛlɪʃ] n (CULIN) salsa; (enjoyment) entusiasmo // vt (food etc) saborear; to ~ doing gustar mucho de hacer.

relocate [riːləu'keɪt] vt cambiar de lugar, mudar // vi mudarse.

reluctance [rɪ'lʌktəns] n renuencia; **reluctant** a renuente; **reluctantly** ad de mala gana.

rely [rɪ'laɪ]: to ~ on vt fus confiar en, fiarse de; (be dependent on) depender de.

remain [rɪ'meɪn] vi (survive) quedar; (be left) sobrar; (continue) quedar(se), permanecer; ~**der** n resto; ~**ing** a sobrante; ~**s** npl restos mpl.

remand [rɪ'mɑːnd]: on ~ detenido (bajo custodia) // vt: to ~ in custody mantener bajo custodia; ~ **home** n (Brit) reformatorio.

remark [rɪ'mɑːk] n comentario // vt comentar; ~**able** a notable; (outstanding) extraordinario.

remarry [rɪ'mærɪ] vi volver a casarse.

remedial [rɪ'miːdɪəl] a: ~ **education** educación f de los niños atrasados.

remedy ['rɛmədɪ] n remedio // vt remediar, curar.

remember [rɪ'mɛmbə*] vt recordar, acordarse de; (bear in mind) tener presente; **remembrance** n: in remembrance of en conmemoración de.

remind [rɪ'maɪnd] vt: to ~ sb to do sth recordar a uno que haga algo; to ~ sb of sth recordar algo a uno; she ~**s me of her mother** me recuerda a su madre; ~**er** n notificación f; (memento) recuerdo.

reminisce [rɛmɪ'nɪs] vi recordar (viejas historias); ~**nt** a: to be ~**nt** of sth recordar algo a.

remiss [rɪ'mɪs] a descuidado; it was ~ **of him** fue un descuido de su parte.

remission [rɪ'mɪʃən] n remisión f; (of sentence) disminución f de pena.

remit [rɪ'mɪt] vt (send: money) remitir, enviar; ~**tance** n remesa, envío.

remnant ['rɛmnənt] n resto; (of cloth) retazo; ~**s** npl (COMM) restos mpl de serie.

remorse [rɪ'mɔːs] n remordimientos mpl; ~**ful** a arrepentido; ~**less** a (fig) implacable; inexorable.

remote [rɪ'məut] a (distant) lejano; (person) distante; ~ **control** n telecontrol m; ~**ly** ad remotamente; (slightly) levemente.

remould [rɪ'məuld] n (Brit: tyre) neumático or llanta (LAm) recauchutado/a.

removable [rɪ'muːvəbl] a (detachable) separable.

removal [rɪ'muːvəl] n (taking away) el quitar; (Brit: from house) mudanza; (from office: dismissal) destitución f; (MED) extirpación f; ~ **van** n (Brit) camión m de mudanzas.

remove [rɪ'muːv] vt quitar; (employee) destituir; (name: from list) tachar, borrar; (doubt) disipar; (abuse) suprimir, acabar con; (TECH) retirar, separar; (MED) extirpar; ~**rs** npl (Brit: company) agencia de mudanzas.

Renaissance [rɪ'neɪsɒns] n: the ~ el Renacimiento.

render ['rɛndə*] vt (thanks) dar; (aid) proporcionar, prestar; (honour) dar, conceder; (assistance) dar, prestar; to ~ **sth** ~ a volver algo a; ~**ing** n (MUS etc) interpretación f.

rendez-vous ['rɔndɪvuː] n cita.

renegade ['renɪgeɪd] n renegado/a.

renew [rɪ'njuː] vt renovar; (resume) reanudar; (extend date) prorrogar; ~**al** n renovación f; reanudación f; prórroga.

renounce [rɪ'nauns] vt renunciar a; (right, inheritance) renunciar.

renovate ['renəveɪt] vt renovar.

renown [rɪ'naun] n renombre m; ~**ed** a renombrado.

rent [rent] n alquiler m; (for house) arriendo, renta // vt alquilar; ~**al** n (for television, car) alquiler m.

renunciation [rɪnʌnsɪ'eɪʃən] n renuncia.

rep [rep] n abbr = **representative**; **repertory**.

repair [rɪ'pɛə*] n reparación f, compostura // vt reparar, componer; (shoes) remendar; **in good/bad** ~ en buen/mal estado; ~ **kit** n caja de herramientas.

repartee [repɑː'tiː] n réplicas fpl agudas.

repatriate [riː'pætrɪeɪt] vt repatriar.

repay [riː'peɪ] (irg: like **pay**) vt (money) devolver, reembolsar; (person) pagar; (debt) liquidar; (sb's efforts) devolver, corresponder a; ~**ment** n reembolso, devolución f; (sum of money) recompensa.

repeal [rɪ'piːl] n revocación f // vt revocar.

repeat [rɪ'piːt] n (RADIO, TV) reposición f // vt repetir // vi repetirse; ~**edly** ad repetidas veces.

repel [rɪ'pel] vt (fig) repugnar; ~**lent** a repugnante // n: **insect** ~**lent** crema/loción f insecticida.

repent [rɪ'pent] vi: **to** ~ (**of**) arrepentirse (de); ~**ance** n arrepentimiento.

repercussion [riːpə'kʌʃən] n (consequence) repercusión f; **to have** ~**s** repercutir.

repertoire ['repətwɑː*] n repertorio.

repertory ['repətərɪ] n (also: ~ **theatre**) teatro de repertorio.

repetition [repɪ'tɪʃən] n repetición f.

repetitive [rɪ'petɪtɪv] a repetitivo.

replace [rɪ'pleɪs] vt (put back) devolver a su sitio; (take the place of) reemplazar, sustituir; ~**ment** n (act) reposición f; (thing) recambio; (person) suplente m/f.

replay ['riːpleɪ] n (SPORT) desempate m; (of tape, film) repetición f.

replenish [rɪ'plenɪʃ] vt (tank etc) rellenar; (stock etc) reponer.

replete [rɪ'pliːt] a repleto, lleno.

replica ['replɪkə] n copia, reproducción f (exacta).

reply [rɪ'plaɪ] n respuesta, contestación f // vi contestar, responder; ~ **coupon** n cupón-respuesta m.

report [rɪ'pɔːt] n informe m; (PRESS etc) reportaje m; (Brit: also: **school** ~) boletín m escolar; (of gun) estallido f // vt informar de; (PRESS etc) hacer un reportaje sobre; (notify: accident, culprit) denunciar // vi (make a report) presentar un informe; (present o.s.): **to** ~ (**to sb**) presentarse (ante uno); ~ **card** n (US, Scottish) cartilla escolar; ~**edly** ad según se dice; ~**er** n periodista m/f.

repose [rɪ'pəuz] n: **in** ~ (face, mouth) en reposo.

reprehensible [reprɪ'hensɪbl] a reprensible, censurable.

represent [reprɪ'zent] vt representar; (COMM) ser agente de; ~**ation** [-'teɪʃən] n representación f; ~**ations** npl (protest) quejas fpl; ~**ative** n (gen) representante m/f; (US POL) diputado/a // a representativo.

repress [rɪ'pres] vt reprimir; ~**ion** [-'preʃən] n represión f.

reprieve [rɪ'priːv] n (LAW) indulto; (fig) alivio.

reprimand ['reprɪmɑːnd] n reprimenda // vt reprender.

reprisal [rɪ'praɪzl] n represalia.

reproach [rɪ'prəutʃ] n reproche m // vt: **to** ~ **sb with sth** reprochar algo a uno; ~**ful** a de reproche, de acusación.

reproduce [riːprə'djuːs] vt reprodu-

cir // vi reproducirse; **reproduction**
[-'dʌkʃən] n reproducción f.

reproof [rɪ'pruːf] n reproche m.

reprove [rɪ'pruːv] vt: to ~ sb for
sth reprochar algo a uno.

reptile ['reptaɪl] n reptil m.

republic [rɪ'pʌblɪk] n república;
~**an** a, n republicano/a m/f.

repudiate [rɪ'pjuːdɪeɪt] vt (accusation) rechazar; (obligation) desconocer.

repulse [rɪ'pʌls] vt rechazar; **repulsive** a repulsivo.

reputable ['repjutəbl] a (make etc)
de renombre.

reputation [repju'teɪʃən] n reputación f.

repute [rɪ'pjuːt] n reputación f,
fama; ~**dly** ad se-
gún dicen or se dice.

request [rɪ'kwest] n solicitud f; petición // vt: to ~ sth of or from sb
solicitar algo a uno; ~ **stop** n (Brit)
parada discrecional.

require [rɪ'kwaɪə*] vt (need: subj:
person) necesitar, tener necesidad
de; (: thing, situation) exigir; (want)
pedir; (demand) insistir en que;
~**ment** n requisito; (need) necesidad f.

requisite ['rekwɪzɪt] n requisito // a
necesario.

requisition [rekwɪ'zɪʃən] n: ~ (for)
solicitud f (de) // vt (MIL) requisar.

rescind [rɪ'sɪnd] vt (LAW) abrogar;
(contract, order etc) anular.

rescue ['reskjuː] n rescate m // vt
rescatar; to ~ from librar de; ~
party n expedición f de salvamento;
~**r** n salvador/a m/f.

research [rɪ'səːtʃ] n investigaciones
fpl // vi investigar; ~**er** n investiga-
dor/a m/f.

resemblance [rɪ'zembləns] n parecido.

resemble [rɪ'zembl] vt parecerse a.

resent [rɪ'zent] vt tomar a mal; ~**ful**
a resentido; ~**ment** n resentimiento.

reservation [rezə'veɪʃən] n (area of
land, doubt) reserva; (booking) re-

servación f; (Brit: also: **central** ~)
mediana.

reserve [rɪ'zəːv] n reserva; (SPORT)
suplente m/f // (seats etc) reservar; ~**s** npl (MIL) reserva sg; **in** ~
de reserva; ~ **d** a reservado.

reservoir ['rezəvwɑː*] n (for irrigation, etc) embalse m; (tank etc) depósito.

reshape [riː'ʃeɪp] vt (policy) reformar, rehacer.

reshuffle [riː'ʃʌfl] n: **cabinet** ~
(POL) remodelación f del gabinete.

reside [rɪ'zaɪd] vi residir, vivir.

residence ['rezɪdəns] n residencia;
(formal: home) domicilio; (length of
stay) permanencia; ~ **permit** n
(Brit) permiso de permanencia.

resident ['rezɪdənt] n (of area)
vecino/a; (in hotel) huésped(a) m/f //
a (population) permanente; ~**ial**
[-'denʃəl] a residencial.

residue ['rezɪdjuː] n resto (CHEM,
PHYSICS) residuo.

resign [rɪ'zaɪn] vt (gen) renunciar a
// vi dimitir; to ~ **o.s. to** (endure)
resignarse a; ~**ation** [rezɪg'neɪʃən]
n dimisión f; (state of mind) resignación f; ~**ed** a resignado.

resilience [rɪ'zɪlɪəns] n (of material)
elasticidad f; (of person) resistencia.

resilient [rɪ'zɪlɪənt] a (person) resistente.

resin ['rezɪn] n resina.

resist [rɪ'zɪst] vt resistir, oponerse a;
~**ance** n resistencia.

resolute ['rezəluːt] a resuelto.

resolution [rezə'luːʃən] n (gen) resolución f.

resolve [rɪ'zɒlv] n resolución f // vt
resolver // vi resolverse; **to ~ to do**
resolver hacer; ~**d** a resuelto.

resort [rɪ'zɔːt] n (town) centro turístico; (recourse) recurso // vi: **to ~**
recurrir a; **in the last** ~ como último recurso.

resound [rɪ'zaund] vi: **to ~ (with)**
resonar (con); ~**ing** a sonoro; (fig)
clamoroso.

resource [rɪ'sɔːs] n recurso; ~**s** npl

recursos *mpl*; ~**ful** *a* despabilado, ingenioso.

respect [rɪs'pɛkt] *n* (*consideration*) respeto; ~**s** *npl* recuerdos *mpl*, saludos *mpl* // *vt* respetar; **with** ~ **to** con respecto a; **in this** ~ en cuanto a eso; ~**able** *a* respetable; (*large*) apreciable; (*passable*) tolerable; ~**ful** *a* respetuoso.

respective [rɪs'pɛktɪv] *a* respectivo; ~**ly** *ad* respectivamente.

respite ['rɛspaɪt] *n* respiro; (*LAW*) prórroga.

resplendent [rɪs'plɛndənt] *a* resplandeciente.

respond [rɪs'pɔnd] *vi* responder; (*react*) reaccionar; **response** [-'pɔns] *n* respuesta; reacción *f*.

responsibility [rɪspɔnsɪ'bɪlɪtɪ] *n* responsabilidad *f*.

responsible [rɪs'pɔnsɪbl] *a* (*character*) serio, formal; (*job*) de confianza; (*liable*): ~ (**for**) responsable (de).

responsive [rɪs'pɔnsɪv] *a* sensible.

rest [rɛst] *n* descanso, reposo; (*MUS*) pausa, silencio; (*support*) apoyo; (*remainder*) resto // *vi* descansar; (*be supported*): **to** ~ **on** descansar sobre // *vt* (*lean*): **to** ~ **sth on/against** apoyar algo en or sobre/contra; **the** ~ **of them** (*people, objects*) los demás; **it** '**s with him** depende de él.

restaurant ['rɛstərɔŋ] *n* restorán *m*, restaurante *m*; ~ **car** *n* (*Brit RAIL*) coche-comedor *m*.

restful ['rɛstful] *a* descansado, tranquilo.

rest home *n* residencia para jubilados.

restitution [rɛstɪ'tjuːʃən] *n*: **to make** ~ **to sb for sth** indemnizar a uno por algo.

restive ['rɛstɪv] *a* inquieto; (*horse*) rebelón(ona).

restless ['rɛstlɪs] *a* inquieto.

restoration [rɛstə'reɪʃən] *n* restauración *f*; devolución *f*.

restore [rɪs'tɔː*] *vt* (*building*) restaurar; (*sth stolen*) devolver; (*health*)

restablecer.

restrain [rɪs'treɪn] *vt* (*feeling*) contener, refrenar; (*person*): **to** ~ (**from doing**) disuadir (de hacer); ~**ed** *a* (*style*) reservado; ~**t** *n* (*restriction*) restricción *f*; (*of manner*) reserva.

restrict [rɪs'trɪkt] *vt* restringir, limitar; ~**ion** [-kʃən] *n* restricción *f*, limitación *f*; ~**ive** *a* restrictivo.

rest room *n* (*US*) aseos *mpl*.

result [rɪ'zʌlt] *n* resultado // *vi*: **to** ~ **in** terminar en, tener por resultado; **as a** ~ **of** a consecuencia de.

resume [rɪ'zjuːm] *vt* (*work, journey*) reanudar // *vi* (*meeting*) continuar.

résumé ['reɪzjuːmeɪ] *n* resumen *m*.

resumption [rɪ'zʌmpʃən] *n* reanudación *f*.

resurgence [rɪ'sɜːdʒəns] *n* resurgimiento.

resurrection [rɛzə'rɛkʃən] *n* resurrección *f*.

resuscitate [rɪ'sʌsɪteɪt] *vt* (*MED*) resucitar.

retail ['riːteɪl] *n* venta al por menor // *cpd* al por menor // *vt* vender al por menor; ~**er** *n* detallista *m/f* ~ **price** *n* precio de venta al público.

retain [rɪ'teɪn] *vt* (*keep*) retener, conservar; (*employ*) contratar; ~**er** *n* (*servant*) criado; (*fee*) anticipo.

retaliate [rɪ'tælɪeɪt] *vi*: **to** ~ (**against**) tomar represalias (contra); **retaliation** [-'eɪʃən] *n* represalias *fpl*.

retarded [rɪ'tɑːdɪd] *a* retrasado.

retch [rɛtʃ] *vi* dársele a uno arcadas.

retentive [rɪ'tɛntɪv] *a* (*memory*) retentivo.

reticent ['rɛtɪsnt] *a* reservado.

retina ['rɛtɪnə] *n* retina.

retinue ['rɛtɪnjuː] *n* séquito, comitiva.

retire [rɪ'taɪə*] *vi* (*give up work*) jubilarse; (*withdraw*) retirarse; (*go to bed*) acostarse; ~**d** *a* (*person*) jubilado; ~**ment** *n* (*state*) retiro; (*act*) jubilación *f*; **retiring** *a* (*leaving*) saliente; (*shy*) retraído.

retort [rɪ'tɔːt] *n* (*reply*) réplica // *vi*

contestar.

retrace [riːˈtreɪs] *vt:* to ~ one's steps volver sobre sus pasos, desandar lo andado.

retract [riːˈtrækt] *vt (statement)* retirar; *(claws)* retraer; *(undercarriage, aerial)* replegar // *vi* retractarse.

retrain [riːˈtreɪn] *vt* reciclar; ~**ing** *n* readaptación *f* profesional.

retread [ˈriːtred] *n* neumático *or* llanta *(LAm)* recauchutado/a.

retreat [riːˈtriːt] *n (place)* retiro; *(MIL)* retirada // *vi* retirarse; *(flood)* bajar.

retribution [retrɪˈbjuːʃən] *n* desquite *m*.

retrieval [riːˈtriːvəl] *n* recuperación *f*; **information** ~ recuperación *f* de datos.

retrieve [riːˈtriːv] *vt* recobrar; *(situation, honour)* salvar; *(COMPUT)* recuperar; *(error)* reparar; ~**r** *n* perro cobrador.

retrograde [ˈretrəgreɪd] *a* retrógrado.

retrospect [ˈretrəspekt] *n:* in ~ retrospectivamente; ~**ive** [-ˈspektɪv] *a* restrospectivo; *(law)* retroactivo.

return [riːˈtəːn] *n (going or coming back)* vuelta, regreso; *(of sth stolen etc)* devolución *f*; *(recompense)* recompensa; *(FINANCE: from land, shares)* ganancia, ingresos *mpl* // *cpd (journey)* de regreso; *(Brit: ticket)* de ida y vuelta; *(match)* de desquite // *vi (person etc: come or go back)* volver, regresar; *(symptoms etc)* reaparecer // *vt* devolver; *(favour, love etc)* corresponder a; *(verdict)* pronunciar; *(POL: candidate)* elegir; ~**s** *npl (COMM)* ingresos *mpl*; in ~ (for) en cambio (de); by ~ of post a vuelta de correo; **many happy** ~**s** (of the day)! ¡feliz cumpleaños!

reunion [riːˈjuːnɪən] *n* reunión *f*.

reunite [riːjuːˈnaɪt] *vt* reunir; *(reconcile)* reconciliar.

rev [rev] *(AUT) n abbr* (= *revolution*) revolución *f* // *(vb: also:* ~ **up**) *vt* girar // *vi (engine)* girarse; *(driver)* gi-

rar el motor.

revamp [riːˈvæmp] *vt (company, organization)* reorganizar.

reveal [riːˈviːl] *vt (make known)* revelar; ~**ing** *a* revelador(a).

reveille [riːˈvælɪ] *n (MIL)* diana.

revel [ˈrevl] *vi:* to ~ in sth/in doing sth gozar de algo/con hacer algo.

revelry [ˈrevlrɪ] *n* jarana, juerga.

revenge [riːˈvendʒ] *n* venganza; *(in sport)* revancha; **to take** ~ **on** vengarse de.

revenue [ˈrevənjuː] *n* ingresos *mpl*, rentas *fpl*.

reverberate [riːˈvəːbəreɪt] *vi (sound)* resonar, retumbar; **reverberation** [-ˈreɪʃən] *n* retumbo, eco.

revere [riːˈvɪə*] *vt* venerar; ~**nce** [ˈrevərəns] *n* reverencia.

Reverend [ˈrevərənd] *a (in titles):* **the** ~ **John Smith** *(Anglican)* el Reverendo John Smith; *(Catholic)* el Padre John Smith; *(Protestant)* el Pastor John Smith.

reverie [ˈrevərɪ] *n* ensueño.

reversal [riːˈvəːsl] *n (of order)* inversión *f*; *(of policy)* cambio; *(of decision)* revocación *f*.

reverse [riːˈvəːs] *n (opposite)* contrario; *(back: of cloth)* revés *m*; *(: of coin)* reverso, *(: of paper)* dorso; *(AUT: also:* ~ **gear**) marcha atrás // *a (order)* inverso; *(direction)* contrario // *vt (decision, AUT)* dar marcha atrás a; *(position, function)* invertir // *vi (Brit AUT)* dar marcha atrás; ~-**charge call** *n (Brit)* llamada a cobro revertido; **reversing lights** *npl (Brit AUT)* luces *fpl* de marcha atrás.

revert [riːˈvəːt] *vi:* to ~ to volver a.

review [riːˈvjuː] *n (magazine, MIL)* revista; *(of book, film)* reseña; *(US: examination)* repaso, examen *m* // *vt* repasar, examinar; *(MIL)* pasar revista a; *(book, film)* reseñar; ~**er** *n* crítico/a.

revile [riːˈvaɪl] *vt* injuriar, vilipendiar.

revise [riːˈvaɪz] *vt (manuscript)* corregir; *(opinion)* modificar; *(Brit:*

study: subject) repasar; *(look over)* revisar; **revision** [rɪˈvɪʒən] *n* corrección *f;* modificación *f;* repaso; revisión *f.*

revitalize [riːˈvaɪtəlaɪz] *vt* revivificar.

revival [rɪˈvaɪvəl] *n (recovery)* reanimación *f;* (POL) resurgimiento; *(of interest)* renacimiento; (THEATRE) reestreno; *(of faith)* despertar *m.*

revive [rɪˈvaɪv] *vt* resucitar; *(custom)* restablecer; *(hope, interest)* despertar; *(play)* reestrenar // *vi (person)* volver en sí; *(from tiredness)* reponerse; *(business)* reactivarse.

revolt [rɪˈvəʊlt] *n* rebelión *f* // *vi* rebelarse, sublevarse // *vt* dar asco a, repugnar; **~ing** *a* asqueroso, repugnante.

revolution [revəˈluːʃən] *n* revolución *f;* **~ary** *a, n* revolucionario/a *m/f.*

revolve [rɪˈvɒlv] *vi* dar vueltas, girar.

revolver [rɪˈvɒlvə*] *n* revólver *m.*

revolving [rɪˈvɒlvɪŋ] *a (chair, door etc)* giratorio.

revue [rɪˈvjuː] *n* (THEATRE) revista.

revulsion [rɪˈvʌlʃən] *n* asco, repugnancia.

reward [rɪˈwɔːd] *n* premio, recompensa *f* // *vt:* **to ~ (for)** recompensar *or* premiar (por); **~ing** *a (fig)* valioso.

rewire [riːˈwaɪə*] *vt (house)* renovar la instalación eléctrica de.

reword [riːˈwɜːd] *vt* expresar en otras palabras.

rewrite [riːˈraɪt] *(irg: like* **write)** *vt* reescribir.

rhapsody [ˈræpsədɪ] *n* (MUS) rapsodia.

rhetoric [ˈretərɪk] *n* retórica; **~al** [rɪˈtɒrɪkl] *a* retórico.

rheumatism [ˈruːmətɪzəm] *n* reumatismo, reúma *m.*

Rhine [raɪn] *n:* **the ~** el *(río)* Rin.

rhinoceros [raɪˈnɒsərəs] *n* rinoceronte *m.*

rhododendron [rəʊdəˈdendrn] *n* rododendro.

Rhone [rəʊn] *n:* **the ~** el *(río)* Ródano.

rhubarb [ˈruːbɑːb] *n* ruibarbo.

rhyme [raɪm] *n* rima; *(verse)* poesía.

rhythm [ˈrɪðm] *n* ritmo.

rib [rɪb] *n* (ANAT) costilla // *vt (mock)* tomar el pelo a.

ribald [ˈrɪbəld] *a* escabroso.

ribbon [ˈrɪbən] *n* cinta; **in ~s** *(torn)* hecho trizas.

rice [raɪs] *n* arroz *m;* **~ pudding** *n* arroz *m* con leche.

rich [rɪtʃ] *a* rico; *(soil)* fértil; *(food)* pesado; (: *sweet)* empalagoso; **the ~** *npl* los ricos; **~es** *npl* riqueza *sg;* **~ly** *ad* ricamente; **~ness** *n* riqueza; fertilidad *f.*

rickets [ˈrɪkɪts] *n* raquitismo.

rickety [ˈrɪkɪtɪ] *a (old)* desvencijado; *(shaky)* tambaleante.

rickshaw [ˈrɪkʃɔː] *n* carro de culi.

ricochet [ˈrɪkəʃeɪ] *n* rebote *m* // *vi* rebotar.

rid [rɪd], *pt, pp* **rid** *vt:* **to ~ sb of sth** librar a uno de algo; **to get ~ of** deshacerse *or* desembarazarse de.

ridden [ˈrɪdn] *pp of* **ride.**

riddle [ˈrɪdl] *n (puzzle)* acertijo; *(mystery)* enigma *m,* misterio // *vt:* **to be ~d with** ser lleno *or* plagado de.

ride [raɪd] *n* paseo; *(distance covered)* viaje *m,* recorrido // *(vb: pt* **rode,** *pp* **ridden)** *vi (horse: as sport)* montar; *(go somewhere: on horse, bicycle)* dar un paseo, pasearse; *(journey: on bicycle, motor cycle, bus)* viajar // *vt (a horse)* montar a; *(distance)* recorrer; **to ~ a bicycle** andar en bicicleta; **to ~ at anchor** (NAUT) estar fondeado; **to take sb for a ~** *(fig)* engañar a uno; **~r** *n (on horse)* jinete/a *m/f;* *(on bicycle)* ciclista *m/f;* *(on motorcycle)* motociclista *m/f.*

ridge [rɪdʒ] *n (of hill)* cresta; *(of roof)* caballete *m.*

ridicule [ˈrɪdɪkjuːl] *n* irrisión *f,* burla // *vt* poner en ridículo, burlarse de; **ridiculous** [-ˈdɪkjuləs] *a* ridículo.

riding ['raɪdɪŋ] n equitación f; I like ~ me gusta montar a caballo; ~ school n escuela de equitación.

rife [raɪf] a: to be ~ ser muy común; to be ~ with abundar en.

riffraff ['rɪfræf] n gentuza.

rifle ['raɪfl] n rifle m, fusil m // vt saquear; ~ **range** n campo de tiro; (at fair) tiro al blanco.

rift [rɪft] n (fig: between friends) desavenencia; (: in party) ruptura f.

rig [rɪg] n (also: oil ~: on land) torre f de perforación; (: at sea) plataforma petrolera // vt (election etc) amañar; to ~ out vt (Brit) ataviar; to ~ up vt improvisar; ~ging n (NAUT) aparejo.

right [raɪt] a (true, correct) correcto, exacto; (suitable) indicado, debido; (proper) apropiado; (just) justo; (morally good) bueno; (not left) derecho // n (title, claim) derecho; (not left) derecha // ad (correctly) bien, correctamente; (straight) derecho, directamente; (not left) a la derecha; (to the ~) hacia la derecha // vt enderezar // excl ¡bueno!; ¡está bien!; to be ~ (person) tener razón; by ~s en justicia; on the ~ a la derecha; to be in the ~ tener razón; ~ now ahora mismo; ~ in the middle exactamente en el centro; ~ away en seguida; ~ angle n ángulo recto; ~eous ['raɪtʃəs] a justado, honrado; (anger) justificado; ~ful a (heir) legítimo; ~-handed a (person) que usa la mano derecha; ~- hand man n brazo derecho; the ~-hand side n la derecha; ~ly ad correctamente, debidamente; (with reason) con razón; ~ of way n (on path etc) derecho de paso; (AUT) prioridad f; ~-wing a (POL) derechista.

rigid ['rɪdʒɪd] a rígido; (person, ideas) inflexible; ~ity [rɪ'dʒɪdɪtɪ] n rigidez f; inflexibilidad f.

rigmarole ['rɪgmərəʊl] n galimatías m inv.

rigorous ['rɪgərəs] a riguroso.

rigour, (US) **rigor** ['rɪgə*] n rigor m, severidad f.

rile [raɪl] vt irritar.

rim [rɪm] n borde m; (of spectacles) aro; (of wheel) llanta.

rind [raɪnd] n (of bacon) corteza; (of lemon etc) cáscara; (of cheese) costra.

ring [rɪŋ] n (of metal) aro; (on finger) anillo; (also: wedding ~) alianza; (of people) corro; (of objects) círculo; (gang) banda; (for boxing) cuadrilátero; (of circus) pista; (bull ~) ruedo, plaza; (sound of bell) toque m; (telephone call) llamada // vb (pt rang, pp rung) vi (on telephone) llamar por teléfono; (large bell) repicar; (also: ~ out: voice, words) sonar; (ears) zumbar // vt (Brit TEL: also: ~ up) llamar, telefonear (esp LAm); (bell etc) hacer sonar; (doorbell) tocar; to ~ back vt, vi (Brit TEL) devolver la llamada; to ~ off vi (Brit TEL) colgar, cortar la comunicación; ~ing n (of large bell) repique m; (in ears) zumbido; ~ing tone n (TEL) tono de llamada; ~leader n (of gang) cabecilla m.

ringlets ['rɪŋlɪts] npl rizos mpl, bucles mpl.

ring road n (Brit) carretera periférica or de circunvalación.

rink [rɪŋk] n (also: ice ~) pista de hielo.

rinse [rɪns] vt (dishes) enjuagar; (clothes) aclarar; (hair) dar reflejos a.

riot ['raɪət] n motín m, disturbio // vi amotinarse; to run ~ desmandarse; ~er n amotinado; ~ous a alborotado; (party) bullicioso; (uncontrolled) desenfrenado.

rip [rɪp] n rasgón m, rasgadura // vt rasgar, desgarrar // vi rasgarse, desgarrarse; ~cord n cabo de desgarre.

ripe [raɪp] a (fruit) maduro; ~n vt madurar // vi madurarse.

rip-off ['rɪpɒf] n (col): it's a ~! ¡es una estafa!

ripple ['rɪpl] n onda, rizo; (sound) murmullo m // vi rizarse // vt rizar.

rise [raɪz] n (slope) cuesta, pendiente f; (hill) altura; (increase: in wages: Brit) aumento; (: in prices, temperature) subida; (fig: to power etc) ascenso // vi (pt **rose**, pp **risen** ['rɪzn]) (gen) elevarse; (prices) subir; (waters) crecer; (river) nacer; (sun) salir; (person: from bed etc) levantarse; (also: ~ **up**: rebel) sublevarse; (in rank) ascender; **to give** ~ **to** dar lugar or origen a; **to** ~ **to the occasion** ponerse a la altura de las circunstancias; **rising** a (increasing: number) creciente; (: prices) en aumento or alza; (tide) creciente; (sun, moon) naciente // n (uprising) sublevación f.

risk [rɪsk] n riesgo, peligro // vt arriesgar; (run the ~ of) exponerse a; **to take** or **run the** ~ **of doing** correr el riesgo de hacer; **at** ~ en peligro; **at one's own** ~ bajo su propia responsabilidad; ~**y** a arriesgado, peligroso.

risqué ['ri:skeɪ] a (joke) subido de color.

rissole ['rɪsəʊl] n croqueta.

rite [raɪt] n rito; **last** ~**s** exequias fpl.

ritual ['rɪtjʊəl] a ritual // n ritual m, rito.

rival ['raɪvl] n rival m/f; (in business) competidor(a) m/f // a rival, opuesto // vt competir con; ~**ry** n rivalidad f, competencia.

river ['rɪvə*] n río m // cpd (port, fish) de río; (traffic) fluvial; **up/down** ~ río arriba/abajo; ~**bank** n orilla (del río); ~**bed** n lecho, cauce m.

rivet ['rɪvɪt] n roblón m, remache m // vt remachar; (fig) captar.

Riviera [rɪvɪ'eərə] n: **the** (French) ~ la Costa Azul (francesa); **the Italian** ~ la Riviera italiana.

road [rəʊd] n (gen) camino; (motorway etc) carretera; (in town) calle f; **major/minor** ~ carretera principal/secundaria; ~**block** n barricada; ~**hog** n loco/a del volante; ~ **map**

n mapa m de carreteras; ~ **safety** n seguridad f vial; ~**side** n borde m (del camino) // cpd al lado de la carretera; ~**sign** n señal f de tráfico; ~ **user** n usuario/a de la vía pública; ~**way** n calzada; ~**works** fpl obras fpl; ~**worthy** a (car) en buen estado para circular.

roam [rəʊm] vi vagar // vt vagar por.

roar [rɔ:*] n (of animal) rugido, bramido; (of crowd) rugido; (of vehicle, storm) estruendo; (of laughter) carcajada // vi rugir; bramar; hacer estruendo; **to** ~ **with laughter** reírse a carcajadas; **to do a** ~**ing trade** hacer buen negocio.

roast [rəʊst] n carne f asada, asado // vt (meat) asar; (coffee) tostar; ~ **beef** n rosbif m.

rob [rɒb] vt robar; **to** ~ **sb of sth** robar algo a uno; (fig: deprive) quitar algo a uno; ~**ber** n ladrón/ona m/f; ~**bery** n robo.

robe [rəʊb] n (for ceremony etc) toga; (also: **bath** ~) bata.

robin ['rɒbɪn] n petirrojo.

robot ['rəʊbɒt] n robot m.

robust [rəʊ'bʌst] a robusto, fuerte.

rock [rɒk] n (gen) roca; (boulder) peña, peñasco; (Brit: sweet) = piruli // vt (swing gently: cradle) balancear, mecer; (: child) arrullar; (shake) sacudir // vi mecerse, balancearse; sacudirse; **on the** ~**s** (drink) con hielo; (marriage etc) en ruinas; ~ **and roll** n rocanrol m; ~**-bottom** n (fig) punto más bajo // a: **at** ~-**bottom prices** a precios regalados; ~**ery** n cuadro alpino.

rocket ['rɒkɪt] n cohete m.

rocking ['rɒkɪŋ]: ~ **chair** n mecedora; ~ **horse** n caballo de balancín.

rocky ['rɒkɪ] a (gen) rocoso; (unsteady: table) inestable.

rod [rɒd] n vara, varilla; (TECH) barra; (also: **fishing** ~) caña.

rode [rəʊd] pt of **ride**.

rodent ['rəʊdnt] n roedor m.

roe [rəʊ] n (species: also: ~ **deer**) corzo; (of fish): **hard/soft** ~ hueva/

lecha.

rogue [rəug] n pícaro, pillo.

role [rəul] n papel m, rol m.

roll [rəul] n rollo; (of bank notes) fajo; (also: **bread** ~) panecillo; (register) lista, nómina; (sound: of drums etc) redoble m; (movement: of ship) balanceo // vt hacer rodar; (also: ~ **up**: string) enrollar; (: sleeves) arremangar; (cigarettes) liar; (also: ~ **out**: pastry) aplanar // vi (gen) rodar; (drum) redoblar; (in walking) bambolearse; (ship) balancearse; **to** ~ **about** or **around** vi (person) revolcarse; **to** ~ **by** vi (time) pasar; **to** ~ **in** vi (mail, cash) entrar a raudales; **to** ~ **over** vi dar una vuelta; **to** ~ **up** vi (col: arrive) aparecer // vt (carpet) arrollar; ~ **call** n: **to take a** ~ **call** pasar lista; ~**er** n rodillo; (wheel) rueda; ~**er coaster** n montaña rusa; ~**er skates** npl patines mpl de rueda.

rolling [ˈrəuliŋ] a (landscape) ondulado; ~ **pin** n rodillo (de cocina); ~ **stock** n (RAIL) material m rodante.

ROM [rɔm] n abbr (= read only memory) ROM f.

Roman [ˈrəumən] a, n romano/a m/f; ~ **Catholic** a, n católico/a m/f (romano/a).

romance [rəˈmæns] n (love affair) amor m; (charm) lo romántico; (novel) novela de amor.

Romania [ruːˈmeiniə] n = **Rumania**.

Roman numeral n número romano.

romantic [rəˈmæntik] a romántico.

Rome [rəum] n Roma.

romp [rɔmp] n retozo, juego // vi (also: ~ **about**) jugar, brincar.

rompers [ˈrɔmpəz] npl pelele m.

roof [ruːf], pl ~**s** n (gen) techo; (of house) techo, tejado; (of car) baca // vt techar, poner techo a; **the** ~ **of the mouth** n el paladar; ~**ing** n techumbre f; ~ **rack** n (AUT) baca, portaequipajes m inv.

rook [ruk] n (bird) graja; (CHESS) torre f.

room [ruːm] n (in house) cuarto, habitación f, pieza (LAm); (also: **bed**~) dormitorio; (in school etc) sala; (space) sitio, cabida; ~**s** npl (lodging) alojamiento sg; '~**s to let**', (US) '~**s for rent**' 'se alquilan pisos or cuartos'; **single/double** ~ habitación individual/doble or para dos personas; ~**ing house** n (US) pensión f; ~**mate** n compañero de cuarto; ~ **service** n servicio de habitaciones; ~**y** a espacioso.

roost [ruːst] n percha // vi pasar la noche.

rooster [ˈruːstə*] n gallo.

root [ruːt] n (BOT, MATH) raíz f // vi (plant, belief) arraigarse; **to** ~ **about** vi (fig) buscar y rebuscar; **to** ~ **for** vt fus apoyar a; **to** ~ **out** vt desarraigar.

rope [rəup] n cuerda; (NAUT) cable m // vt (box) atar or amarrar con (una) cuerda; (climbers: also: ~ **together**) encordarse; **to** ~ **sb in** (fig) persuadir a uno a tomar parte; **to know the** ~**s** (fig) conocer los trucos (del oficio); ~ **ladder** n escala de cuerda.

rosary [ˈrəuzəri] n rosario.

rose [rəuz] pt of **rise** // n rosa; (also: ~**bush**) rosal m; (on watering can) roseta // a color de rosa.

rosé [ˈrəuzei] n vino rosado.

rose: ~**bud** n capullo de rosa; ~**bush** n rosal m.

rosemary [ˈrəuzməri] n romero.

rosette [rəuˈzet] n escarapela.

roster [ˈrɔstə*] n: **duty** ~ lista de deberes.

rostrum [ˈrɔstrəm] n tribuna.

rosy [ˈrəuzi] a rosado, sonrosado; **the future looks** ~ el futuro parece prometedor.

rot [rɔt] n (fig: pej) tonterías fpl // vt, vi pudrirse; **it has** ~ está podrido.

rota [ˈrəutə] n lista (de tandas).

rotary [ˈrəutəri] a rotativo.

rotate [rəuˈteit] vt (revolve) hacer

girar, dar vueltas a; (*change round: crops*) cultivar en rotación; (: *jobs*) alternar // *vi* (*revolve*) girar, dar vueltas; **rotating** *a* (*movement*) rotativo.

rote [rəʊt] *n*: **by ~** maquinalmente, de memoria.

rotten [ˈrɔtn] *a* (*decayed*) podrido; (*dishonest*) corrompido; (*col: bad*) pésimo; **to feel ~** (*ill*) sentirse muy mal.

rouge [ruːʒ] *n* colorete *m*.

rough [rʌf] *a* (*skin, surface*) áspero; (*terrain*) quebrado; (*road*) desigual; (*voice*) bronco; (*person, manner: coarse*) tosco, grosero; (*weather*) borrascoso; (*treatment*) brutal; (*sea*) bravo; (*cloth*) basto; (*plan*) preliminar; (*guess*) aproximado; (*violent*) violento // *n* (GOLF): **in the ~** en las hierbas altas; **to ~ it** vivir sin comodidades; **to sleep ~** (*Brit*) pasar la noche al raso; **~age** *n* fibra(s) *f(pl)*; **~-and-ready** *a* improvisado; **~cast** *n* mezcla gruesa; **~ copy**, **~ draft** *n* borrador *m*; **~en** *vt* (*a surface*) poner áspero; **~ly** *ad* (*handle*) torpemente; (*make*) toscamente; (*approximately*) aproximadamente.

roulette [ruːˈlet] *n* ruleta.

Roumania [ruːˈmeɪnɪə] *n* = **Rumania**.

round [raʊnd] *a* redondo // *n* círculo; (*Brit: of toast*) rodaja; (*of policeman*) ronda; (*of milkman*) recorrido; (*of doctor*) visitas *fpl*; (*game: of cards, in competition*) partida; (*of ammunition*) cartucho; (BOXING) asalto; (*of talks*) ronda // *vt* (*corner*) doblar // *prep* alrededor de // *ad*: **all ~** por todos lados; **the long way ~** por el camino menos directo; **all the year ~** durante todo el año; **it's just ~ the corner** (*fig*) está a la vuelta de la esquina; **the clock** *ad* las 24 horas; **to go ~** to sb's (*house*) ir a casa de uno; **to go ~ the back** pasar por atrás; **to go ~ a house** visitar una casa; **enough to go ~** bastante (para todos); **to go the ~s**

(*story*) circular; **a ~ of applause** una salva de aplausos; **a ~ of drinks/sandwiches** una ronda de bebidas/bocadillos; **to ~ off** *vt* (*speech etc*) acabar, poner término a; **to ~ up** *vt* (*cattle*) acorralar; (*people*) reunir; (*prices*) redondear; **~about** *n* (*Brit:* AUT) isleta; (: *at fair*) tiovivo // *a* (*route, means*) indirecto; **~ers** *n* (*Brit: game*) juego similar al béisbol; **~ly** *ad* (*fig*) rotundamente; **~-shouldered** *a* cargado de espaldas; **~ trip** *n* viaje *m* de ida y vuelta; **~up** *n* rodeo; (*of criminals*) redada.

rouse [raʊz] *vt* (*wake up*) despertar; (*stir up*) suscitar; **rousing** *a* (*applause*) caluroso; (*speech*) conmovedor(a).

rout [raʊt] *n* (MIL) derrota.

route [ruːt] *n* ruta, camino; (*of bus*) recorrido; (*of shipping*) derrota; **~ map** *n* (*Brit: for journey*) mapa *m* de carreteras.

routine [ruːˈtiːn] *a* (*work*) rutinario // *n* rutina; (THEATRE) número.

roving [ˈrəʊvɪŋ] *a* (*wandering*) errante; (*salesman*) ambulante.

row [rəʊ] *n* (*line*) fila, hilera; (KNITTING) pasada; [raʊ] (*noise*) escándalo; (*dispute*) bronca, pelea; (*fuss*) jaleo; (*scolding*) regaño // *vi* (*in boat*) remar; [raʊ] reñir(se) // *vt* (*boat*) conducir remando; **4 days in a ~** 4 días seguidos; **~boat** *n* (US) bote *m* de remos.

rowdy [ˈraʊdɪ] *a* (*person: noisy*) ruidoso; (: *quarrelsome*) pendenciero; (*occasion*) alborotado // *n* pendenciero.

row houses (US) casas *fpl* adosadas.

rowing [ˈrəʊɪŋ] *n* remo; **~ boat** *n* (*Brit*) bote *m* de remos.

royal [ˈrɔɪəl] *a* real; **R~ Air Force** (RAF) *n* Fuerzas Aéreas Británicas *fpl*; **~ty** *n* (~ *persons*) familia real; (*payment to author*) derechos *mpl* de autor.

rpm *abbr* = *revs per minute*) r.p.m.

R.S.V.P. abbr (= *répondez s'il vous plaît*) SRC.

Rt.Hon. abbr (Brit: = *Right Honourable*) título honorífico de diputado.

rub [rʌb] vt (gen) frotar; (hard) restregar // n (gen) frotamiento; (touch) roce m; **to ~ sb up** or (US) ~ **sb the wrong way** entrarle uno por mal ojo; **to ~ off** vi borrarse; **to ~ off on** vt fus influir en; **to ~ out** vt borrar.

rubber ['rʌbə*] n caucho, goma; (Brit: *eraser*) goma de borrar; ~ **band** n goma, gomita; ~ **plant** n ficus m; **~y** a elástico.

rubbish ['rʌbɪʃ] n (Brit) (from household) basura; (waste) desperdicios mpl; (fig: pej) tonterías fpl; (trash) pacotilla; ~ **bin** n cubo or bote m (LAm) de la basura; ~ **dump** n (in town) vertedero, basurero.

rubble ['rʌbl] n escombros mpl.

ruby ['ru:bɪ] n rubí m.

rucksack ['rʌksæk] n mochila.

ructions ['rʌkʃənz] npl lío sg.

rudder ['rʌdə*] n timón m.

ruddy ['rʌdɪ] a (face) rubicundo; (col: *damned*) condenado.

rude [ru:d] a (impolite: person) mal educado; (: word, manners) grosero; (indecent) indecente.

rueful ['ru:ful] a arrepentido.

ruffian ['rʌfɪən] n matón m, criminal m.

ruffle ['rʌfl] vt (hair) despeinar; (clothes) arrugar; **to get ~d** (fig: person) alterarse.

rug [rʌg] n alfombra; (Brit: for knees) manta.

rugby ['rʌgbɪ] n (also: ~ **football**) rugby m.

rugged ['rʌgɪd] a (landscape) accidentado; (features) robusto.

rugger ['rʌgə*] n (Brit col) rugby m.

ruin ['ru:ɪn] n ruina // vt arruinar; (spoil) estropear; **~s** npl ruinas fpl, restos mpl.

rule [ru:l] n (norm) norma, costumbre f; (regulation) regla; (govern-

ment) dominio // vt (country, person) gobernar; (decide) disponer // vi gobernar; (LAW) fallar; **as a** ~ por regla general; **to ~ out** vt excluir; **~d** a (paper) rayado; **~r** n (sovereign) soberano; (for measuring) regla; **ruling** a (party) gobernante; (class) dirigente // n (LAW) fallo, decisión f.

rum [rʌm] n ron m.

Rumania [ruːˈmeɪnɪə] n Rumania; **~n** a, n rumano/a m/f.

rumble ['rʌmbl] vi retumbar, hacer un ruido sordo; (stomach, pipe) sonar.

rummage ['rʌmɪdʒ] vi: **to ~** (in or among) revolver (en).

rumour, (US) **rumor** ['ruːmə*] n rumor m // vt: **it is ~ed that...** se rumorea que... .

rump [rʌmp] n (of animal) ancas fpl, grupa; ~ **steak** n filete m de lomo.

rumpus ['rʌmpəs] n (col) lío, jaleo; (quarrel) pelea, riña.

run [rʌn] n (SPORT) carrera; (outing) paseo, excursión f; (distance travelled) trayecto; (series) serie f; (THEATRE) temporada; (SKI) pista; (in tights, stockings) carrera; // vb (pt **ran**, pp **run**) vt (operate: business) dirigir; (: competition, course) organizar; (: hotel, house) administrar, llevar; (COMPUT) procesar; (to pass: hand) pasar; (bath): **to ~ a bath** llenar la bañera // vi (gen) correr; (work: machine) funcionar, marchar; (bus, train: operate) circular, ir; (: travel) ir; (: continue: play) seguir; (: contract) ser válido; (flow: river, bath) fluir; (colours, washing) desteñirse; (in election) ser candidato; **there was a ~ on** (meat, tickets) hubo mucha demanda de; **in the long ~** a la larga; **on the ~** en fuga; **I'll ~ you to the station** te llevaré a la estación en coche; **to ~ a risk** correr un riesgo; **to ~ about** or **around** vi (children) correr por todos lados; **to ~ across** vt fus (find) dar or topar con; **to ~**

away *vi* huir; **to ~ down** *vi* (*clock*) parar // *vt* (*production*) ir reduciendo; (*factory*) ir restringiendo la producción en; (*AUT*) atropellar; (*criticize*) criticar; **to be ~ down** (*person: tired*) estar debilitado; **to ~ in** *vt* (*Brit: car*) rodar; **to ~ into** *vt fus* (*meet: person, trouble*) tropezar con; (*collide with*) chocar con; **to ~ off** *vt* (*water*) dejar correr // *vi* huir corriendo; **to ~ out** *vi* (*person*) salir corriendo; (*liquid*) irse; (*lease*) caducar, vencer; (*money*) acabarse; **to ~ out of** *vt fus* quedar sin; **to ~ over** *vt* (*AUT*) atropellar // *vt fus* (*revise*) repasar; **to ~ through** *vt fus* (*instructions*) repasar; **to ~ up** *vt* (*debt*) contraer; **to ~ up against** (*difficulties*) tropezar con; **~away** (*a horse*) desbocado; (*truck*) sin frenos; (*inflation*) galopante.

rung [rʌŋ] *pp of* **ring** // (*of ladder*) escalón *m*, peldaño.

runner [ˈrʌnə*] *n* (*in race: person*) corredor(a) *m/f*; (: *horse*) caballo; (*on sledge*) patín *m*; (*wheel*) ruedecilla; **~ bean** *n* (*Brit*) judía escarlata; **~up** *n* subcampeón/ona *m/f*.

running [ˈrʌnɪŋ] *n* (*sport*) atletismo *m*; (*race*) carrera // *a* (*water, costs*) corriente; (*commentary*) continuo; **to be in/out of the ~ for sth** tener/no tener posibilidades de ganar algo; **6 days ~** 6 días seguidos.

runny [ˈrʌnɪ] *a* derretido.

run-of-the-mill [ˈrʌnəvðəˈmɪl] *a* común y corriente.

runt [rʌnt] *n* (*also pej*) redrojo, enano.

run-up [ˈrʌnʌp] *n*: **~ to** (*election etc*) periodo previo a.

runway [ˈrʌnweɪ] *n* (*AVIAT*) pista de aterrizaje.

rupee [ruːˈpiː] *n* rupia.

rupture [ˈrʌptʃə*] *n* (*MED*) hernia // *vt*: **to ~ o.s.** causarse una hernia.

rural [ˈruərl] *a* rural.

ruse [ruːz] *n* ardid *m*.

rush [rʌʃ] *n* ímpetu *m*; (*hurry*) prisa; (*COMM*) demanda repentina; (*BOT*) junco; (*current*) corriente *f* fuerte, ráfaga // *vt* apresurar; (*work*) hacer de prisa; (*attack: town etc*) asaltar // *vi* correr, precipitarse; **~ hour** *n* horas *fpl* punta.

rusk [rʌsk] *n* bizcocho tostado.

Russia [ˈrʌʃə] *n* Rusia; **~n** *a, n* ruso/a *m/f*.

rust [rʌst] *n* herrumbre *f*, moho // *vi* oxidarse.

rustic [ˈrʌstɪk] *a* rústico.

rustle [ˈrʌsl] *vi* susurrar // *vt* (*paper*) hacer crujir; (*US: cattle*) hurtar, robar.

rustproof [ˈrʌstpruːf] *a* inoxidable.

rusty [ˈrʌstɪ] *a* oxidado.

rut [rʌt] *n* surco; (*ZOOL*) celo; **to be in a ~** ser esclavo de la rutina.

ruthless [ˈruːθlɪs] *a* despiadado.

rye [raɪ] *n* centeno; **~ bread** *n* pan de centeno.

S

sabbath [ˈsæbəθ] *n* domingo; (*Jewish*) sábado.

sabotage [ˈsæbətɑːʒ] *n* sabotaje *m* // *vt* sabotear.

saccharin(e) [ˈsækərɪn] *n* sacarina.

sachet [ˈsæʃeɪ] *n* sobrecito.

sack [sæk] *n* (*bag*) saco, costal *m* // *vt* (*dismiss*) despedir; (*plunder*) saquear; **to get the ~** ser despedido; **~ing** *n* (*material*) arpillera.

sacred [ˈseɪkrɪd] *a* sagrado, santo.

sacrifice [ˈsækrɪfaɪs] *n* sacrificio // *vt* sacrificar.

sacrilege [ˈsækrɪlɪdʒ] *n* sacrilegio.

sacrosanct [ˈsækrəʊsæŋkt] *a* sacrosanto.

sad [sæd] *a* (*unhappy*) triste; (*deplorable*) lamentable.

saddle [ˈsædl] *n* silla (de montar); (*of cycle*) sillín *m* // *vt* (*horse*) ensillar; **to be ~d with sth** (*col*) quedar cargado con algo; **~bag** *n* alforja.

sadistic [səˈdɪstɪk] *a* sádico.

sadness [ˈsædnɪs] *n* tristeza.

s.a.e. *abbr* (= *stamped addressed envelope*) sobre con las propias señas de uno y con sello.

safari [sə'fɑ:rɪ] *n* safari *m*.

safe [seɪf] *a* (*out of danger*) fuera de peligro; (*not dangerous, sure*) seguro; (*unharmed*) ileso; (*trustworthy*) digno de confianza // *n* caja de caudales, caja fuerte; ~ **and sound** sano y salvo; (**just**) **to be on the** ~ **side** para mayor seguridad; ~ **conduct** *n* salvoconducto; ~ **deposit** *n* (*vault*) cámara acorazada; (*box*) caja de seguridad; ~**guard** *n* protección *f*, garantía // *vt* proteger, defender; ~**keeping** *n* custodia; ~**ly** *ad* seguramente, con seguridad; **to arrive** ~**ly** llegar bien.

safety ['seɪftɪ] *n* seguridad *f* // *a* de seguridad; ~ **first!** ¡precaución!; ~ **belt** *n* cinturón *m* (de seguridad); ~ **pin** *n* imperdible *m*, seguro *m* (*LAm*).

saffron ['sæfrən] *n* azafrán *m*.

sag [sæg] *vi* aflojarse.

sage [seɪdʒ] *n* (*herb*) salvia; (*man*) sabio.

Sagittarius [sædʒɪ'tɛərɪəs] *n* Sagitario.

Sahara [sə'hɑ:rə] *n*: **the** ~ (*Desert*) el (desierto del) Sáhara.

said [sed] *pt, pp* of **say**.

sail [seɪl] *n* (*on boat*) vela // *vt* (*boat*) gobernar // *vi* (*travel: ship*) navegar; (: *passenger*) pasear en barco; (*set off*) zarpar; **to go for a** ~ dar un paseo en barco; **they** ~**ed into Copenhagen** arribaron a Copenhagen; **to** ~ **through** *vt fus* (*exam*) no tener problemas para aprobar; ~**boat** *n* (*US*) velero, barco de vela; ~**ing** *n* (*SPORT*) balandrismo; **to go** ~**ing** salir en balandro; ~**ing ship** *n* barco de vela; ~**or** *n* marinero, marino.

saint [seɪnt] *n* santo; ~**ly** *a* santo.

sake [seɪk] *n*: **for the** ~ **of** por.

salad ['sæləd] *n* ensalada; ~ **bowl** *n* ensaladera; ~ **cream** *n* (*Brit*) (especie de) mayonesa; ~ **dressing** *n* aliño.

salary ['sælərɪ] *n* sueldo.

sale [seɪl] *n* venta; (*at reduced prices*) liquidación *f*, saldo; '**for** ~' 'se vende'; **on** ~ en venta; **on** ~ **or return** (*goods*) venta por reposición; ~**room** *n* sala de subastas; ~**s assistant**, (*US*) ~**s clerk** *n* dependiente/a *m/f*; ~**sman/woman** *n* vendedor(a) *m/f*; (*in shop*) dependiente/a *m/f*; (*representative*) viajante *m/f*.

salient ['seɪlɪənt] *a* sobresaliente.

saliva [sə'laɪvə] *n* saliva.

sallow ['sæləu] *a* cetrino.

salmon ['sæmən] *n, pl inv* salmón *m*.

salon ['sælɒn] *n* salón *m*.

saloon [sə'lu:n] *n* (*US*) bar *m*, taberna; (*Brit AUT*) (coche *m* de) turismo; (*ship's lounge*) cámara, salón *m*.

salt [sɔlt] *n* sal *f* // *vt* salar; (*put on*) poner sal en; **to** ~ **away** *vt* (*col: money*) ahorrar; ~ **cellar** *n* salero; ~**water** *a* de agua salada; ~**y** *a* salado.

salutary ['sæljutərɪ] *a* saludable.

salute [sə'lu:t] *n* saludo; (*of guns*) salva // *vt* saludar.

salvage ['sælvɪdʒ] *n* (*saving*) salvamento, recuperación *f*; (*things saved*) objetos *mpl* salvados // *vt* salvar.

salvation [sæl'veɪʃən] *n* salvación *f*; **S~ Army** *n* Ejército de Salvación.

same [seɪm] *a* mismo // *pron*: **the** ~ el/la mismo/a, los/las mismos/as; **the** ~ **book** as el mismo libro que; **at the** ~ **time** (*at the* ~ *moment*) al mismo tiempo; (*yet*) sin embargo; **all or just the** ~ sin embargo, aun así; **to do the** ~ (**as sb**) hacer lo mismo (que uno); **the** ~ **to you!** ¡igualmente!

sample ['sɑ:mpl] *n* muestra // *vt* (*food, wine*) probar.

sanatorium [sænə'tɔ:rɪəm], *pl* -**ria** [-rɪə] *n* (*Brit*) sanatorio.

sanction ['sæŋkʃən] *n* sanción *f* // *vt* sancionar.

sanctity ['sæŋktɪtɪ] *n* (*gen*) santidad *f*; (*inviolability*) inviolabilidad *f*.

sanctuary ['sæŋktjuəri] n santuario; (refuge) asilo, refugio; (for wild life) reserva.

sand [sænd] n arena // vt (also: ~ down) lijar.

sandal ['sændl] n sandalia; ~**wood** n sándalo.

sand: ~**box** n (US) = ~**pit**; ~**castle** n castillo de arena; ~ **dune** n duna; ~**paper** n papel de lija; ~**pit** n (for children) cajón m de arena; ~**stone** n piedra arenisca.

sandwich ['sændwɪtʃ] n bocadillo (Sp), sandwich m (LAm) // vt (also: ~ in) intercalar; ~**ed between** apretujado entre; **cheese/ham** ~ sandwich de queso/jamón; ~ **board** n cartelón m; ~ **course** n (Brit) curso de medio tiempo.

sandy ['sændɪ] a arenoso; (colour) rojizo.

sane [seɪn] a cuerdo, sensato.

sang [sæŋ] pt of **sing**.

sanitarium [sænɪ'teərɪəm] n (US) = **sanatorium**.

sanitary ['sænɪtərɪ] a (system, arrangements) sanitario; (clean) higiénico; ~ **towel**, (US) ~ **napkin** n paño higiénico, compresa f.

sanitation [sænɪ'teɪʃən] n (in house) servicios mpl higiénicos; (in town) servicio de desinfección; ~ **department** n (US) departamento de limpieza y recogida de basuras.

sanity ['sænɪtɪ] n cordura; (of judgment) sensatez f.

sank [sæŋk] pt of **sink**.

Santa Claus [sæntə'klɔːz] n San Nicolás, Papá Noel.

sap [sæp] n (of plants) savia // vt (strength) minar, agotar.

sapling ['sæplɪŋ] n árbol nuevo or joven.

sapphire ['sæfaɪə*] n zafiro.

sarcasm ['sɑːkæzm] n sarcasmo.

sardine [sɑː'diːn] n sardina.

Sardinia [sɑː'dɪnɪə] n Cerdeña.

sash [sæʃ] n faja.

sat [sæt] pt, pp of **sit**.

Satan ['seɪtn] n Satanás m.

satchel ['sætʃl] n (child's) cartera, mochila (LAm).

sated ['seɪtɪd] a (appetite, person) saciado.

satellite ['sætəlaɪt] n satélite m.

satin ['sætɪn] n raso // a de raso.

satire ['sætaɪə*] n sátira.

satisfaction [sætɪs'fækʃən] n satisfacción f.

satisfactory [sætɪs'fæktərɪ] a satisfactorio.

satisfy ['sætɪsfaɪ] vt satisfacer; (convince) convencer; ~**ing** a satisfactorio.

saturate ['sætʃəreɪt] vt: to ~ (with) empapar or saturar (de).

Saturday ['sætədɪ] n sábado.

sauce [sɔːs] n salsa; (sweet) crema; ~**pan** n cacerola, olla.

saucer ['sɔːsə*] n platillo.

saucy ['sɔːsɪ] a fresco, descarado.

Saudi ['saʊdɪ]: ~ **Arabia** n Arabia Saudí or Saudita; ~ **(Arabian)** a, n saudí m/f, saudita m/f.

sauna ['sɔːnə] n sauna.

saunter ['sɔːntə*] vi: to ~ **in/out** entrar/salir sin prisa.

sausage ['sɔsɪdʒ] n salchicha; ~ **roll** n empanadita de salchicha.

sautéed ['səʊteɪd] a salteado.

savage ['sævɪdʒ] a (cruel, fierce) feroz, furioso; (primitive) salvaje // n salvaje m/f // vt (attack) embestir.

save [seɪv] vt (rescue) salvar, rescatar; (money, time) ahorrar; (put by) guardar; (COMPUT) salvar y guardar; (avoid: trouble) evitar // vi (also: ~ up) ahorrar // n (SPORT) parada // prep salvo, excepto.

saving ['seɪvɪŋ] n (on price etc) economía // a: the ~ **grace** of el único mérito de; ~**s** npl ahorros mpl; ~**s account** n cuenta de ahorros; ~**s bank** n caja de ahorros.

saviour, (US) **savior** ['seɪvjə*] n salvador(a) m/f.

savour, (US) **savor** ['seɪvə*] n sabor m, gusto // vt saborear; ~**y** a sabroso; (dish: not sweet) salado.

saw [sɔː] pt of **see** // n (tool) sierra //

vt (*pt* sawed, *pp* sawed *or* sawn) serrar; ~**dust** *n* (a)serrín *m*; ~**mill** *n* aserradero; ~**n-off shotgun** *n* escopeta de cañones recortados.

saxophone ['sæksəfəʊn] *n* saxófono.

say [seɪ] *n*: to have one's ~ expresar su opinión; to have a *or* some ~ in sth tener voz *or* tener que ver en algo // *vt* (*pt*, *pp* said) decir; to ~ yes/no decir que sí/no; that is to ~ es decir; that goes without ~ing ni que decir tiene; ~**ing** *n* dicho, refrán *m*.

scab [skæb] *n* costra; (*pej*) esquirol *m*.

scaffold ['skæfəʊld] *n* (*for execution*) cadalso; ~**ing** *n* andamio, andamiaje *m*.

scald [skɔːld] *n* escaldadura // *vt* escaldar.

scale [skeɪl] *n* (*gen*, *MUS*) escala; (*of fish*) escama; (*of salaries, fees etc*) escalafón *m* // *vt* (*mountain*) escalar; (*tree*) trepar; ~**s** *npl* (*small*) balanza *sg*; (*large*) báscula *sg*; on a large ~ en gran escala; ~ **of charges** tarifa, lista de precios; to ~ **down** *vt* reducir a escala; ~**model** *n* modelo a escala.

scallop ['skɔləp] *n* (*ZOOL*) venera; (*SEWING*) festón *m*.

scalp [skælp] *n* cabellera // *vt* escalpar.

scalpel ['skælpl] *n* bisturí *m*.

scamper ['skæmpə*] *vi*: to ~ **away**, ~ **off** irse corriendo.

scampi ['skæmpɪ] *npl* gambas *fpl*.

scan [skæn] *vt* (*examine*) escudriñar; (*glance at quickly*) dar un vistazo a; (*TV, RADAR*) explorar, registrar.

scandal ['skændl] *n* escándalo; (*gossip*) chismes *mpl*.

Scandinavia [skændɪ'neɪvɪə] *n* Escandinavia; ~**n** *a*, *n* escandinavo/a *m/f*.

scant [skænt] *a* escaso; ~**y** *a* (*meal*) insuficiente; (*clothes*) ligero.

scapegoat ['skeɪpgəʊt] *n* cabeza de turco, chivo expiatorio.

scar [skɑː] *n* cicatriz *f*.

scarce [skɛəs] *a* escaso; ~**ly** *ad* apenas; **scarcity** *n* escasez *f*.

scare [skɛə*] *n* susto, sobresalto; (*panic*) pánico *m*; *vt* asustar, espantar; to ~ **sb stiff** dar a uno un susto de muerte; **bomb ~** amenaza de bomba; ~**crow** *n* espantapájaros *m inv*; ~**d** *a*: to be ~**d** to be ~**d** estar asustado.

scarf [skɑːf], *pl* **scarves** [skɑːvz] *n* (*long*) bufanda; (*square*) pañuelo.

scarlet ['skɑːlɪt] *a* escarlata; ~ **fever** *n* escarlatina.

scarves [skɑːvz] *pl of* **scarf**.

scathing ['skeɪðɪŋ] *a* mordaz.

scatter ['skætə*] *vt* (*spread*) esparcir, desparramar; (*put to flight*) dispersar // *vi* desparramarse; dispersarse; ~**brained** *a* ligero de cascos.

scavenger ['skævəndʒə*] *n* (*person*) basurero/a; (*ZOOL*: *animal*) animal *m* de carroña; (: *bird*) ave *f* de carroña.

scenario [sɪ'nɑːrɪəʊ] *n* (*THEATRE*) argumento; (*CINEMA*) guión *m*; (*fig*) escenario.

scene [siːn] *n* (*THEATRE*, *fig etc*) escena; (*of crime, accident*) escenario; (*sight, view*) panorama *m*; (*fuss*) escándalo; ~**ry** *n* (*THEATRE*) decorado; (*landscape*) paisaje *m*; **scenic** *a* (*picturesque*) pintoresco.

scent [sɛnt] *n* perfume *m*, olor *m*; (*fig*: *track*) rastro, pista; (*sense of smell*) olfato.

sceptic, (*US*) **skeptic** ['skɛptɪk] *n* escéptico/a; ~**al** *a* escéptico; ~**ism** ['skɛptɪsɪzm] *n* escepticismo.

sceptre, (*US*) **scepter** ['sɛptə*] *n* cetro.

schedule ['ʃɛdjuːl] *n* (*of trains*) horario; (*of events*) programa *m*; (*list*) lista // *vt* (*visit*) fijar la hora de; **to arrive on ~** llegar a la hora debida; **to be ahead of/behind ~** estar adelantado/en retraso; ~**d flight** *n* vuelo regular.

schematic [skɪ'mætɪk] *a* (*diagram etc*) esquemático.

scheme [skiːm] *n* (*plan*) plan *m*, proyecto; (*method*) esquema *m*; (*plot*) intriga; (*trick*) ardid *m*; (*arrangement*) disposición *f*; (*pension* ~ etc) sistema *m* // *vt* proyectar // *vi* (*plan*) hacer proyectos; (*intrigue*) intrigar; **scheming** *a* intrigante.

schism ['skɪzəm] *n* cisma *m*.

scholar ['skɔlə*] *n* (*learned person*) sabio/a, erudito/a; ~**ly** *a* erudito; ~**ship** *n* erudición *f*; (*grant*) beca.

school [sku:l] *n* (*gen*) escuela, colegio; (*in university*) facultad *f* // *vt* (*animal*) amaestrar; ~ **age** *n* edad *f* escolar; ~**book** *n* libro de texto; ~**boy** *n* alumno; ~ **children** *npl* alumnos *mpl*; ~**days** *npl* años *mpl* del colegio; ~**girl** *n* alumna; ~**ing** *n* enseñanza; ~**master/mistress** *n* (*primary*) maestro/a; (*secondary*) profesor/a *m/f*; ~**teacher** *n* (*primary*) maestro/a; (*secondary*) profesor(a) *mf*.

schooner ['sku:nə*] *n* (*ship*) goleta.

sciatica [saɪ'ætɪkə] *n* ciática.

science ['saɪəns] *n* ciencia; ~ **fiction** *n* ciencia-ficción *f*; **scientific** [-'tɪfɪk] *a* científico; **scientist** *n* científico/a.

scintillating ['sɪntɪleɪtɪŋ] *a* brillante, ingenioso.

scissors ['sɪzəz] *npl* tijeras *fpl*; **a pair of** ~ unas tijeras.

scoff [skɔf] *n* (*Brit col: eat*) engullir // *vi*: **to** ~ (**at**) (*mock*) mofarse (de).

scold [skəuld] *vt* regañar.

scone [skɔn] *n* pastel de pan.

scoop [sku:p] *n* cucharón *m*; (*for flour etc*) pala; (*PRESS*) exclusiva; **to** ~ **out** *vt* excavar; **to** ~ **up** *vt* recoger.

scooter ['sku:tə*] *n* (*motor cycle*) moto *f*; (*toy*) patinete *m*.

scope [skəup] *n* (*of plan, undertaking*) ámbito; (*reach*) alcance *m*; (*of person*) competencia; (*opportunity*) libertad *f* (de acción).

scorch [skɔ:tʃ] *vt* (*clothes*) chamuscar; (*earth, grass*) quemar, secar; ~**ing** *a* abrasador(a).

score [skɔ:*] *n* (*points etc*) puntua-

ción *f*; (*MUS*) partitura; (*reckoning*) cuenta; (*twenty*) veintena *f* // *vt* (*goal, point*) ganar; (*mark*) rayar // *vi* marcar un tanto; (*FOOTBALL*) marcar (un) gol; (*keep score*) llevar el tanteo; **on that** ~ en lo que se refiere a eso; **to** ~ **6 out of 10** obtener una puntuación de 6 sobre 10; **to** ~ **out** *vt* tachar; ~**board** *n* marcador *m*; ~**r** *n* marcador *m*; (*keeping score*) tanteador/a *mf*.

scorn [skɔ:n] *n* desprecio // *vt* despreciar; ~**ful** *a* desdeñoso, despreciativo.

Scorpio ['skɔ:pɪəu] *n* Escorpión *m*.

scorpion ['skɔ:pɪən] *n* alacrán *m*.

Scot [skɔt] *n* escocés/esa *mf*.

scotch [skɔtʃ] *vt* (*rumour*) desmentir; (*plan*) abandonar; **S**~ *n* whisky *m* escocés; **S**~ **tape** *n* ® (*US*) cinta adhesiva, celo, scotch *m* (*LAm*).

scot-free [skɔt'fri:] *ad*: **to get off** ~ (*unpunished*) salir impune.

Scotland ['skɔtlənd] *n* Escocia.

Scots [skɔts] *a* escocés/esa; ~**man/woman** *n* escocés/esa *mf*; **Scottish** ['skɔtɪʃ] *a* escocés/esa.

scoundrel ['skaundrəl] *n* canalla *mf*, sinvergüenza *mf*.

scour ['skauə*] *vt* (*clean*) fregar, estregar; (*search*) recorrer, registrar.

scourge [skə:dʒ] *n* azote *m*.

scout [skaut] *n* (*MIL, also: boy* ~) explorador *m*; **to** ~ **around** *vi* reconocer el terreno.

scowl [skaul] *vi* fruncir el ceño; **to** ~ **at sb** mirar con ceño a uno.

scrabble ['skræbl] *vi* (*claw*); **to** ~ (**at**) arañar; (*also:* ~ **around**: *search*) revolver todo buscando // *n*: **S**~ ® Scrabble *m* ®.

scraggy ['skrægɪ] *a* flaco, descarnado.

scram [skræm] *vi* (*col*) largarse.

scramble ['skræmbl] *n* (*climb*) subida (difícil); (*struggle*) pelea // *vi*: **to** ~ **out/through** salir/abrirse paso con dificultad; **to** ~ **for** pelear por; ~**d eggs** *npl* huevos *mpl* revueltos.

scrap [skræp] *n* (*bit*) pedacito; (*fig*)

pizca; *(fight)* riña, bronca; *(also:* ~ **iron)** chatarra, hierro viejo // *vt (discard)* desechar, descartar // *vi* reñir, armar (una) bronca; ~s *npl (waste)* sobras *fpl*, desperdicios *mpl*; ~**book** *n* álbum *m* de recortes; ~ **dealer** *n* chatarrero/a.

scrape [skreɪp] *n*: **to get into a** ~ meterse en un lio // *vt* raspar; *(skin etc)* rasguñar; *(~ against)* rozar // *vi*: **to** ~ **through** *(exam)* aprobar por los pelos; ~**r** *n* raspador *m*.

scrap: ~ **heap** *n (fig)*: **to be on the** ~ **heap** estar acabado; ~ **merchant** *n (Brit)* chatarrero/a; ~ **paper** *n* pedazos *mpl* de papel.

scratch [skrætʃ] *n* rasguño; *(from claw)* arañazo // *a*: ~ **team** equipo improvisado // *vt (record)* rayar; *(with claw, nail)* rasguñar, arañar // *vi* rascarse; **to start from** ~ partir de cero; **to be up to** ~ cumplir con los requisitos.

scrawl [skrɔːl] *n* garabatos *mpl* // *vi* hacer garabatos.

scrawny [ˈskrɔːnɪ] *a (person, neck)* flaco.

scream [skriːm] *n* chillido // *vi* chillar.

scree [skriː] *n* cono de desmoronamiento.

screech [skriːtʃ] *vi* chirriar.

screen [skriːn] *n (CINEMA, TV)* pantalla; *(movable)* biombo; *(wall)* tabique *m*; *(also:* **wind**~) parabrisas *m inv* // *vt (conceal)* tapar; *(from the wind etc)* proteger; *(film)* proyectar; *(candidates etc)* investigar a; ~**ing** *n (MED)* investigación *f* médica; ~**play** *n* guión *m*.

screw [skruː] *n* tornillo; *(propeller)* hélice *f* // *vt* atornillar; **to** ~ **up** *vt (paper etc)* arrugar; *(col: ruin)* fastidiar; **to** ~ **up one's eyes** arrugar el entrecejo; ~**driver** *n* destornillador *m*.

scribble [ˈskrɪbl] *n* garabatos *mpl* // *vt* escribir con prisa.

script [skrɪpt] *n (CINEMA etc)* guión *m*; *(writing)* escritura, letra.

Scripture [ˈskrɪptʃə*] *n* Sagrada Escritura.

scroll [skrəʊl] *n* rollo.

scrounge [skraʊndʒ] *vt (col)*: **to** ~ **sth off or from sb** obtener algo de uno de gorra // *vi*: **to** ~ **on sb** vivir a costa de uno; ~**r** *n* gorrón/ona *m/f*.

scrub [skrʌb] *n (clean)* fregado; *(land)* maleza // *vt* fregar, restregar; *(reject)* cancelar, anular.

scruff [skrʌf] *n*: **by the** ~ **of the neck** por el pescuezo.

scruffy [ˈskrʌfɪ] *a* desaliñado, piojoso.

scrum(mage) [ˈskrʌm(mɪdʒ)] *n (RUGBY)* melée *f*.

scruple [ˈskruːpl] *n* escrúpulo.

scrutinize [ˈskruːtɪnaɪz] *vt* escudriñar; *(votes)* escrutar.

scrutiny [ˈskruːtɪnɪ] *n* escrutinio, examen *m*.

scuff [skʌf] *vt (shoes, floor)* rayar.

scuffle [ˈskʌfl] *n* refriega.

scullery [ˈskʌlərɪ] *n* trascocina.

sculptor [ˈskʌlptə*] *n* escultor(a) *m/f*.

sculpture [ˈskʌlptʃə*] *n* escultura.

scum [skʌm] *n (on liquid)* espuma; *(pej: person)* canalla *m*.

scupper [ˈskʌpə*] *vt (plans)* dar al traste con.

scurrilous [ˈskʌrɪləs] *a* difamatorio, calumnioso.

scurry [ˈskʌrɪ] *vi*: **to** ~ **off** escabullirse.

scuttle [ˈskʌtl] *n (also:* **coal** ~) cubo, carbonera // *vt (ship)* barrenar // *vi (scamper)*: **to** ~ **away,** ~ **off** escabullirse.

scythe [saɪð] *n* guadaña.

SDP *n abbr (Brit)* = Social Democratic Party.

sea [siː] *n* mar *m* // *cpd* de mar, marítimo; **by** ~ *(travel)* en barco; **on the** ~ *(boat)* en el mar; *(town)* junto al mar; **to be all at** ~ *(fig)* estar despistado; **out to** *or* **at** ~ en alta mar; ~**board** *n* litoral *m*; ~ **breeze** *n* brisa de mar; ~**food** *n* mariscos *mpl*; ~ **front** *n* paseo marítimo; ~**gull** *n* gaviota.

seal [si:l] n (animal) foca; (stamp) sello // vt (close) cerrar; (: with ~) sellar; **to ~ off** vt (area) acordonar.

sea level n nivel m del mar.

seam [si:m] n costura; (of metal) juntura; (of coal) veta, filón m.

seaman ['si:mən] n marinero.

seamy ['si:mi] a sórdido.

seance ['seɪɒns] n sesión f de espiritismo.

sea plane ['si:pleɪn] n hidroavión m.

seaport ['si:pɔ:t] n puerto de mar.

search [sɔːtʃ] n (for person, thing) busca, búsqueda; (of drawer, pockets) registro; (inspection) reconocimiento // vt (look in) buscar en; (examine) examinar; (person, place) registrar // vi: **to ~ for** buscar; **in ~ of** en busca de; **to ~ through** vt fus registrar; **~ing** a penetrante; **~light** n reflector m; **~ party** n pelotón m de salvamento; **~ warrant** n mandamiento (judicial).

sea: ~shore n playa, orilla del mar; **~sick** a mareado; **~side** n playa, orilla del mar; **~side resort** n playa.

season ['si:zn] n (of year) estación f; (sporting etc) temporada; (gen) época, período // vt (food) sazonar; **~al** a estacional; **~ed** a (fig) experimentado; **~ing** n condimento, aderezo; **~ ticket** n abono.

seat [si:t] n (in bus, train: place) asiento; (chair) silla; (PARLIAMENT) escaño; (buttocks) culo, trasero; (of government) sede f // vt sentar; (have room for) tener cabida para; **to be ~ed** sentarse; **~ belt** n cinturón m de seguridad.

sea: ~ water n agua del mar; **~weed** n alga marina; **~worthy** a en condiciones de navegar.

sec. abbr = **second(s)**.

secluded [sɪ'klu:dɪd] a retirado.

second ['sekənd] a segundo // ad (in race etc) en segundo lugar // n (gen) segundo; (AUT: also: **~ gear**) segunda; (COMM) artículo con algún

desperfecto // vt (motion) apoyar; **~ary** a secundario; **~ary school** n escuela secundaria; **~class** a de segunda clase // ad (RAIL) en segunda; **~hand** a de segunda mano, usado; **~ hand** n (on clock) segundero; **~ly** ad en segundo lugar; **~ment** [sɪ'kɔndmənt] n (Brit) traslado temporal; **~rate** a de segunda categoría; **~ thoughts** npl: **to have ~ thoughts** cambiar de opinión; **on ~ thoughts** or (US) **thought** pensándolo bien.

secrecy ['si:krəsi] n secreto.

secret ['si:krɪt] a, n secreto; **in ~** ad en secreto.

secretarial [sekrɪ'teərɪəl] a de secretario.

secretariat [sekrɪ'teərɪət] n secretaría.

secretary ['sekrətərɪ] n secretario/a; **S~ of State (for)** (Brit POL) Ministro (de).

secretion [sɪ'kri:ʃən] n secreción f.

secretive ['si:krətɪv] a reservado, sigiloso.

secretly ['si:krɪtlɪ] ad en secreto.

sect [sekt] n secta; **~arian** [-'teərɪən] a sectario.

section ['sekʃən] n sección f; (part) parte f; (of document) artículo; (of opinion) sector m.

sector ['sektə'] n sector m.

secular ['sekjulə'] a secular, seglar.

secure [sɪ'kjuə'] a (free from anxiety) seguro; (firmly fixed) firme, fijo // vt (fix) asegurar, afianzar; (get) conseguir.

security [sɪ'kjuərɪtɪ] n seguridad f; (for loan) fianza; (: object) prenda.

sedan [sɪ'dæn] n (US AUT) sedán m.

sedate [sɪ'deɪt] a tranquilo // vt tratar con sedantes.

sedation [sɪ'deɪʃən] n (MED) sedación f.

sedative ['sedɪtɪv] n sedante m, sedativo.

seduce [sɪ'dju:s] vt (gen) seducir; **seduction** [-'dʌkʃən] n seducción f; **seductive** [-'dʌktɪv] a seductor(a).

see [si:] (pt **saw**, pp **seen**) vt ver; (understand) ver, comprender //

vi ver // *n* (*arz*)obispado; **to ~ sb to the door** acompañar a uno hasta la puerta; **to ~ that** (*ensure*) asegurar que; **~ you soon!** ¡hasta pronto!; **to ~ about** *vt fus* atender a, encargarse de; **to ~ off** *vt* despedir; **to ~ through** *vt fus* calar // *vt* (*plan*) llevar a cabo; **to ~ to** *vt fus* atender a, encargarse de.

seed [siːd] *n* semilla; (*in fruit*) pepita; (*fig*) germen *m*; (*TENNIS*) preseleccionado/a; **to go to ~** (*plant*) granar; (*fig*) descuidarse; **~ling** *n* planta de semillero; **~y** *a* (*shabby*) desaseado, raído.

seeing [ˈsiːɪŋ] *conj*: **~ (that)** visto que, en vista de que.

seek [siːk], *pt, pp* **sought** *vt* (*gen*) buscar; (*post*) solicitar.

seem [siːm] *vi* parecer; **there seems to be...** parece que hay; **~ingly** *ad* aparentemente, según parece.

seen [siːn] *pp* of **see**.

seep [siːp] *vi* filtrarse.

seesaw [ˈsiːsɔː] *n* balancín *m*, columpio.

seethe [siːð] *vi* hervir; **to ~ with anger** estar furioso.

see-through [ˈsiːθruː] *a* transparente.

segregate [ˈsɛɡrɪɡeɪt] *vt* segregar.

seize [siːz] *vt* (*grasp*) agarrar, asir; (*take possession of*) secuestrar; (: *territory*) apoderarse de; (*opportunity*) aprovecharse de; **to ~ (up)on** *vt fus* aprovechar; **to ~ up** *vi* (*TECH*) agarrotarse.

seizure [ˈsiːʒəˌ] *n* (*MED*) ataque *m*; (*LAW*) incautación *f*.

seldom [ˈsɛldəm] *ad* rara vez.

select [sɪˈlɛkt] *a* selecto, escogido // *vt* escoger, elegir; (*SPORT*) seleccionar; **~ion** [-ˈlɛkʃən] *n* selección *f*, elección *f*; (*COMM*) surtido.

self [sɛlf] *n* (*pl* **selves**) uno mismo; **the ~** el yo // *pref* auto...; **~-assured** *a* seguro de sí mismo; **~-catering** *a* (*Brit*) con cocina; **~-centred**, (*US*) **~-centered** *a* egocéntrico; **~-coloured**, (*US*)

~-colored *a* de color natural; (*of one colour*) de un color; **~-confidence** *n* confianza en sí mismo; **~-conscious** *a* cohibido; **~-contained** *a* (*gen*) autónomo; (*Brit: flat*) con entrada particular; **~-control** *n* autodominio; **~-defence**, (*US*) **~-defense** *n* defensa propia; **~-discipline** *n* autodisciplina; **~-employed** *a* que trabaja por cuenta propia; **~-evident** *a* patente; **~-governing** *a* autónomo; **~-indulgent** *a* autocomplaciente; **~-interest** *n* egoísmo; **~-ish** *a* egoísta; **~-ishness** *n* egoísmo; **~-less** *a* desinteresado; **~-made** *a*: **~-made man** hombre *m* que se ha hecho a sí mismo; **~-pity** *n* lástima de sí mismo; **~-portrait** *n* autorretrato; **~-possessed** *a* sereno, dueño de sí mismo; **~-preservation** *n* propia conservación *f*; **~-reliant** *a* independiente, autosuficiente; **~-respect** *n* amor *m* propio; **~-righteous** *a* santurrón/ona; **~-sacrifice** *n* abnegación *f*; **~-satisfied** *a* satisfecho de sí mismo; **~-sufficient** *a* autosuficiente; **~-taught** *a* autodidacta.

sell [sɛl], *pt, pp* **sold** *vt* vender // *vi* venderse; **to ~ at** or **for £10** venderse a 10 libros; **to ~ off** *vt* liquidar; **to ~ out** *vi* transigir, transar (*LAm*); **~-by date** *n* fecha de caducidad; **~er** *n* vendedor(a) *m/f*; **~ing price** *n* precio de venta.

sellotape [ˈsɛləʊteɪp] *n* ® (*Brit*) cinta adhesiva, celo, scotch *m* (*LAm*).

sellout [ˈsɛlaʊt] *n* traición *f*; **it was a ~** (*THEATRE etc*) fue un éxito de taquilla.

selves [sɛlvz] *pl* of **self**.

semaphore [ˈsɛməfɔːˌ] *n* semáforo.

semblance [ˈsɛmbləns] *n* apariencia.

semen [ˈsiːmən] *n* semen *m*.

semester [sɪˈmɛstəˌ] *n* (*US*) semestre *m*.

semi... [ˈsɛmɪ] *pref* semi..., medio...; **~circle** *n* semicírculo; **~colon** *n* punto y coma; **~conductor** *n* semiconductor *m*; ~**detached** (**house**) *n* (*casa*) semiseparada; ~**final** *n* semi-final *m*.

seminar ['semɪnɑ:*] *n* seminario.

seminary ['semɪnərɪ] *n* (*REL*) seminario.

semiskilled ['semɪskɪld] *a* (*work, worker*) semi-cualificado.

senate ['senɪt] *n* senado; **senator** *n* senador(a) *m/f*.

send [send], *pt, pp* **sent** *vt* mandar, enviar; **to ~ away** *vt* (*letter, goods*) despachar; **to ~ away for** *vt fus* pedir; **to ~ back** *vt* devolver; **to ~ for** *vt fus* mandar traer; **to ~ off** *vt* (*goods*) despachar; (*Brit SPORT: player*) expulsar; **to ~ out** *vt* (*invitation*) mandar; (*signal*) emitir; **to ~ up** *vt* (*person, price*) hacer subir; (*Brit: parody*) parodiar; ~**er** *n* remitente *m/f*; ~**off** *n*: a good ~**off** una buena despedida.

senior ['si:nɪə*] *a* (*older*) mayor, más viejo; (*: on staff*) de más antigüedad; (*of higher rank*) superior // *n* mayor *m*; ~ **citizen** *n* persona de la tercera edad; ~**ity** [-'ɔrɪtɪ] *n* antigüedad *f*.

sensation [sɛn'seɪʃən] *n* sensación *f*; ~**al** *a* sensacional.

sense [sens] *n* (*faculty, meaning*) sentido; (*feeling*) sensación *f*; (*good ~*) sentido común, juicio // *vt* sentir, percibir; ~ **of humour** sentido del humor; **it makes ~** tiene sentido; ~**less** *a* estúpido, insensato; (*unconscious*) sin conocimiento.

sensibility [sensɪ'bɪlɪtɪ] *n* sensibilidad *f*; **sensibilities** *npl* susceptibilidades *fpl*.

sensible ['sensɪbl] *a* sensato; (*reasonable*) razonable, lógico.

sensitive ['sensɪtɪv] *a* sensible; (*touchy*) susceptible.

sensual ['sensjuəl] *a* sensual.

sensuous ['sensjuəs] *a* sensual.

sent [sent] *pt, pp of* **send**.

sentence ['sentns] *n* (*LING*) oración *f*; (*LAW*) sentencia, fallo // *vt*: **to ~ sb to death/to 5 years** condenar a

uno a muerte/a 5 años de cárcel.

sentiment ['sentɪmənt] *n* sentimiento; (*opinion*) opinión *f*; ~**al** [-'mentl] *a* sentimental.

sentry ['sentrɪ] *n* centinela *m*.

separate ['seprɪt] *a* separado; (*distinct*) distinto // *vb* ['sepəreɪt] *vt* separar; (*part*) dividir // *vi* separarse; ~**s** *npl* (*clothes*) coordinados *mpl*; ~**ly** *ad* por separado; **separation** [-'reɪʃən] *n* separación *f*.

September [sep'tembə*] *n* se(p)tiembre *m*.

septic ['septɪk] *a* séptico; ~ **tank** *n* fosa séptica.

sequel ['si:kwl] *n* consecuencia, resultado; (*of story*) continuación *f*.

sequence ['si:kwəns] *n* sucesión *f*, serie *f*; (*CINEMA*) secuencia.

serene [sɪ'ri:n] *a* sereno, tranquilo.

sergeant ['sɑ:dʒənt] *n* sargento.

serial ['sɪərɪəl] *n* (*TV*) telenovela, serie *f* televisiva; ~ **number** *n* número de serie.

series ['sɪərɪz] *n, pl inv* serie *f*.

serious ['sɪərɪəs] *a* serio; (*grave*) grave; ~**ly** *ad* en serio; (*ill, wounded etc*) gravemente; ~**ness** *n* seriedad *f*; gravedad *f*.

sermon ['sə:mən] *n* sermón *m*.

serrated [sɪ'reɪtɪd] *a* serrado, dentellado.

serum ['sɪərəm] *n* suero.

servant ['sə:vənt] *n* (*gen*) servidor(a) *m/f*; (*house*) criado/a.

serve [sə:v] *vt* servir; (*customer*) atender; (*subj: train*) pasar por; (*apprenticeship*) hacer; (*prison term*) cumplir // *vi* (*also TENNIS*) sacar; **to ~ as/for/to do** servir de/para/hacer // *n* (*TENNIS*) saque *m*; **it ~s him right** se lo merece, se lo tiene merecido; **to ~ out, ~ up** *vt* (*food*) servir.

service ['sə:vɪs] *n* (*gen*) servicio; (*REL*) misa; (*AUT*) mantenimiento; (*of dishes*) juego *m* // *vt* (*car, washing machine*) mantener; (*: repair*) reparar; **the S~s** las fuerzas armadas; **to be of ~ to sb** ser útil a uno;

~**able** a servible, utilizable; ~ **area** n (on motorway) servicios mpl; ~ **charge** n (Brit) servicio; ~**man** n militar m; ~ **station** n estación f de servicio.

serviette [sə:vɪ'et] n (Brit) servilleta.

session ['seʃən] n (sitting) sesión f; **to be in** ~ estar en sesión.

set [set] n juego; (RADIO) aparato; (TV) televisor m; (of utensils) batería; (of cutlery) cubierto; (of books) colección f; (TENNIS) set m; (group of people) grupo; (CINEMA) plató m; (THEATRE) decorado; (HAIRDRESSING) marcado // a (fixed) fijo; (ready) listo; (resolved) resuelto, decidido // vb (pt, pp set) vt (place) poner, colocar; (fix) fijar; (adjust) ajustar, arreglar; (decide: rules etc) establecer, decidir // vi (sun) ponerse; (jam, jelly) cuajarse; (concrete) fraguar; **to** ~ **on doing sth** estar empeñado en hacer algo; **to** ~ **to music** poner música a; **to** ~ **on fire** incendiar, poner fuego a; **to** ~ **free** poner en libertad; **to** ~ **sth going** poner algo en marcha; **to** ~ **sail** zarpar, hacerse a la vela; **to** ~ **about** vt fus: **to** ~ **about doing sth** ponerse a hacer algo; **to** ~ **aside** vt poner aparte, dejar de lado; **to** ~ **back** vt: **to** ~ **back** (by) retrasar (por); **to** ~ **off** vi partir // vt (bomb) hacer estallar; (cause to start) poner en marcha; (show up well) hacer resaltar; **to** ~ **out** vi: **to** ~ **out to do sth** proponerse hacer algo // vt (arrange) disponer; (state) exponer; **to** ~ **up** vt (organization) establecer; ~**back** n (hitch) revés m, contratiempo; ~ **menu** n menú m.

settee [se'ti:] n sofá m.

setting ['setɪŋ] n (scenery) marco; (of jewel) engaste m, montadura.

settle ['setl] vt (argument, matter) resolver; (accounts) ajustar, liquidar; (land) colonizar; (MED: calm) calmar, sosegar // vi (dust etc) depo-

sitarse; (weather) serenarse; (also: ~ **down**) instalarse; tranquilizarse; **to** ~ **for sth** convenir en aceptar algo; **to** ~ **on sth** decidirse por algo; **to** ~ **up with sb** ajustar cuentas con uno; **to** ~ **in** vi instalarse; ~**ment** n (payment) liquidación f; (agreement) acuerdo, convenio; (village etc) pueblo; ~**r** n colono/a, colonizador(a) m/f.

setup ['setʌp] n sistema m.

seven ['sevn] num siete; ~**teen** num diez y siete, diecisiete; ~**th** a séptimo; ~**ty** num setenta.

sever ['sevə*] vt cortar; (relations) romper.

several ['sevərl] a, pron varios/as m/fpl, algunos/as m/fpl; ~ **of us** varios de nosotros.

severance ['sevərəns] n (of relations) ruptura; ~ **pay** n pago de despedida.

severe [sɪ'vɪə*] a severo; (serious) grave; (hard) duro; (pain) intenso; **severity** [sɪ'verɪtɪ] n severidad f; gravedad f; intensidad f.

sew [səu], pt **sewed**, pp **sewn** vt, vi coser; **to** ~ **up** vt coser, zurcir.

sewage ['su:ɪdʒ] n aguas fpl residuales.

sewer ['su:ə*] n alcantarilla, cloaca.

sewing ['səuɪŋ] n costura; ~ **machine** n máquina de coser.

sewn [səun] pp of **sew**.

sex [seks] n sexo; **to have** ~ **with sb** tener relaciones (sexuales) con uno; ~**ist** a, n sexista m/f.

sexual ['seksjuəl] a sexual.

sexy ['seksɪ] a sexy.

shabby ['ʃæbɪ] a (person) desharrapado; (clothes) raído, gastado.

shack [ʃæk] n choza, chabola.

shackles ['ʃæklz] npl grillos mpl, grilletes mpl.

shade [ʃeɪd] n sombra; (for lamp) pantalla; (for eyes) visera; (of colour) matiz m, tonalidad f // vt dar sombra a; **in the** ~ en la sombra; **a** ~ **of** un poquito de; **a** ~ **smaller** un poquito menor.

shadow ['ʃædəu] *n* sombra // *vt* (*follow*) seguir y vigilar; ~ **cabinet** *n* (*Brit* POL) gabinete paralelo formado por el partido de oposición; ~**y** *a* oscuro; (*dim*) indistinto.

shady ['ʃeɪdɪ] *a* sombreado; (*fig: dishonest*) sospechoso; (: *deal*) turbio.

shaft [ʃɑːft] *n* (*of arrow, spear*) astil *m*; (AUT, TECH) eje *m*, árbol *m*; (*of mine*) pozo; (*of lift*) hueco, caja; (*of light*) rayo.

shaggy ['ʃægɪ] *a* peludo.

shake [ʃeɪk] *vb* (*pt* **shook**, *pp* **shaken**) *vt* sacudir; (*building*) hacer temblar; (*bottle, cocktail*) agitar // *vi* (*tremble*) temblar // *n* (*movement*) sacudida; to ~ **one's head** (*in refusal*) negar con la cabeza; (*in dismay*) mover or menear la cabeza, increíblo; to ~ **hands with sb** estrechar la mano a uno; to ~ **off** *vt* sacudirse; (*fig*) deshacerse de; to ~ **up** *vt* agitar; **shaky** *a* (*hand, voice*) trémulo; (*building*) inestable.

shall [ʃæl] *auxiliary vb*: I ~ **go** iré; ~ I **help you?** ¿quieres que te ayude?; I'll **buy three,** ~ I? compro tres, ¿no te parece?

shallow ['ʃæləu] *a* poco profundo; (*fig*) superficial.

sham [ʃæm] *n* fraude *m*, engaño // *a* falso, fingido // *vt* fingir, simular.

shambles ['ʃæmblz] *n* confusión *f*.

shame [ʃeɪm] *n* vergüenza; (*pity*) lástima // *vt* avergonzar; it **is a** ~ **that/to do** es una lástima que/hacer; **what a** ~! ¡qué lástima!; ~**faced** *a* avergonzado; ~**ful** *a* vergonzoso; ~**less** *a* descarado.

shampoo [ʃæm'puː] *n* champú *m* // *vt* lavar con champú; ~ **and set** *n* lavado y marcado.

shamrock ['ʃæmrɔk] *n* trébol *m* (*emblema nacional irlandés*).

shandy ['ʃændɪ], (*US*) **shandygaff** ['ʃændɪgæf] *n* mezcla de cerveza con gaseosa.

shan't [ʃɑːnt] = **shall not.**

shanty town ['ʃæntɪ-] *n* barrio de chabolas.

shape [ʃeɪp] *n* forma // *vt* formar, dar forma a; (*sb's ideas*) formar; (*sb's life*) determinar // *vi* (*also:* ~ **up**) (*events*) desarrollarse; (*person*) formarse; **to take** ~ tomar forma; ~**d** *suffix*: **heart**~**d** en forma de corazón; ~**less** *a* informe, sin forma definida; ~**ly** *a* bien formado or proporcionado.

share [ʃeə*] *n* (*part*) parte *f*, porción *f*; (*contribution*) cuota; (COMM) acción *f* // *vt* dividir; (*have in common*) compartir; **to** ~ **out** (*among* or *between*) repartir (*entre*); ~**holder** *n* (*Brit*) accionista *m/f*.

shark [ʃɑːk] *n* tiburón *m*.

sharp [ʃɑːp] *a* (*razor, knife*) afilado; (*point*) puntiagudo; (*outline*) definido; (*pain*) intenso; (MUS) desafinado; (*contrast*) marcado; (*voice*) agudo; (*person: quick-witted*) astuto; (: *dishonest*) poco escrupuloso // *n* (MUS) sostenido // *ad*: **at 2 o'clock** ~ a las 2 en punto; ~**en** *vt* afilar; (*pencil*) sacar punta a; (*fig*) agudizar; ~**ener** *n* (*also:* **pencil** ~**ener**) sacapuntas *m inv*; ~**-eyed** *a* de vista aguda; ~**ly** *ad* (*turn, stop*) bruscamente; (*stand out, contrast*) claramente; (*criticize, retort*) severamente.

shatter ['ʃætə*] *vt* hacer añicos or pedazos; (*fig: ruin*) destruir, acabar con // *vi* hacerse añicos.

shave [ʃeɪv] *vb* (*pt* **shaved**, *pp* **shaved** or **shaven**) *vt* afeitar, rasurar // *vi* afeitarse // *n*: **to have a** ~ afeitarse; ~**r** *n* (*also:* **electric** ~**r**) máquina de afeitar (*eléctrica*).

shaving ['ʃeɪvɪŋ] *n* (*action*) el afeitarse, rasurado; ~**s** *npl* (*of wood etc*) virutas *fpl*; ~ **brush** *n* brocha (de afeitar); ~ **cream** *n* crema (de afeitar).

shawl [ʃɔːl] *n* chal *m*.

she [ʃiː] *pron* ella; ~**-cat** *n* gata; NB: *for ships, countries follow the gender of your translation.*

sheaf [ʃiːf], *pl* **sheaves** [ʃiːvz] *n* (*of*

corn) gavilla; (*of arrows*) haz *m*; (*of papers*) fajo.

shear [ʃɪə*] *vb* (*pt* **sheared**, *pp* **sheared** *or* **shorn**) *vt* (*sheep*) esquilar, trasquilar; **~s** *npl* (*for hedge*) tijeras *fpl* de jardín; **to ~ off** *vi* romperse.

sheath [ʃi:θ] *n* vaina; (*contraceptive*) preservativo.

sheaves [ʃi:vz] *pl of* **sheaf.**

shed [ʃɛd] *n* cobertizo // *vt* (*pt*, *pp* **shed**) (*skin*) mudar; (*tears*) derramar.

she'd [ʃi:d] = **she had; she would.**

sheen [ʃi:n] *n* brillo, lustre *m.*

sheep [ʃi:p] *n*, *pl inv* oveja; **~dog** *n* perro pastor; **~ish** *a* tímido, vergonzoso; **~skin** *n* piel *f* de carnero.

sheer [ʃɪə*] *a* (*utter*) puro, completo; (*steep*) escarpado; (*material*) diáfano // *ad* verticalmente.

sheet [ʃi:t] *n* (*on bed*) sábana; (*of paper*) hoja; (*of glass, metal*) lámina.

sheik(h) [ʃeɪk] *n* jeque *m.*

shelf [ʃelf], *pl* **shelves** *n* estante *m.*

shell [ʃɛl] *n* (*on beach*) concha; (*of egg, nut etc*) cáscara; (*explosive*) proyectil *m*, obús *m*; (*of building*) armazón *f* // *vt* (*peas*) desenvainar; (*MIL*) bombardear.

she'll [ʃi:l] = **she will; she shall.**

shellfish [ʃelfɪʃ] *n*, *pl inv* crustáceo; (*pl: as food*) mariscos *mpl.*

shelter [ʃeltə*] *n* abrigo, refugio // *vt* (*aid*) amparar, proteger; (*give lodging to*) abrigar; (*hide*) esconder // *vi* abrigarse, refugiarse; **~ed** *a* (*life*) protegido; (*spot*) abrigado.

shelve [ʃelv] *vt* (*fig*) aplazar; **~s** *pl of* **shelf.**

shepherd [ʃepəd] *n* pastor *m* // *vt* (*guide*) guiar, conducir; **~'s pie** *n* pastel de carne y patatas.

sherry [ʃerɪ] *n* jerez *m.*

she's [ʃi:z] = **she is; she has.**

Shetland [ʃetlənd] *n* (*also*: **the ~s**, **the ~ Isles**) las Islas *fpl* de Zetlandia.

shield [ʃi:ld] *n* escudo; (*TECH*) blindaje *m* // *vt*: **to ~ (from)** proteger (de).

shift [ʃɪft] *n* (*change*) cambio; (*at work*) turno // *vt* trasladar; (*remove*) quitar // *vi* moverse; (*change place*) cambiar de sitio; **~less** *a* (*person*) perezoso; **~ work** *n* (*Brit*) trabajo por turno; **~y** *a* tramposo; (*eyes*) furtivo.

shilling [ʃɪlɪŋ] *n* (*Brit*) chelín *m.*

shilly-shally [ʃɪlɪʃælɪ] *vi* titubear, vacilar.

shimmer [ʃɪmə*] *n* reflejo trémulo // *vi* relucir.

shin [ʃɪn] *n* espinilla.

shine [ʃaɪn] *n* brillo, lustre *m* // (*vb*: *pt*, *pp* **shone**) *vi* brillar, relucir // *vt* (*shoes*) lustrar, sacar brillo a; **to ~ a torch on sth** dirigir una linterna hacia algo.

shingle [ʃɪŋgl] *n* (*on beach*) guijarras *fpl*; **~s** *n* (*MED*) herpes *mpl* or *fpl.*

shiny [ʃaɪnɪ] *a* brillante, lustroso.

ship [ʃɪp] *n* buque *m*, barco // *vt* (*goods*) embarcar; (*oars*) desarmar; (*send*) transportar o enviar por vía marítima; **~building** *n* construcción *f* de buques; **~ment** *n* (*act*) embarque *m*; (*goods*) envío; **~per** *n* exportador(a) *m/f*; **~ping** *n* (*act*) embarque *m*; (*traffic*) buques *mpl*; **~shape** *a* en buen orden; **~wreck** *n* naufragio // *vt*: **to be ~wrecked** naufragar; **~yard** *n* astillero.

shire [ʃaɪə*] *n* (*Brit*) condado.

shirk [ʃə:k] *vt* eludir, esquivar; (*obligations*) faltar a.

shirt [ʃə:t] *n* camisa; **in ~ sleeves** en mangas de camisa.

shit [ʃɪt] *excl* (*col!*) ¡mierda! (*col!*)

shiver [ʃɪvə*] *vi* temblar, estremecerse; (*with cold*) tiritar.

shoal [ʃəul] *n* (*of fish*) banco.

shock [ʃɔk] *n* (*impact*) choque *m*; (*ELEC*) descarga (eléctrica); (*emotional*) conmoción *f*; (*start*) sobresalto, susto; (*MED*) postración *f* nerviosa // *vt* dar un susto a; (*offend*) escandalizar; ~ **absorber** n amortiguador m; ~**ing** a (awful) espantoso; (improper) escandaloso.

shod [ʃɔd] pt, pp of **shoe**.

shoddy ['ʃɔdi] a de pacotilla.

shoe [ʃuː] n zapato m, (for horse) herradura; (brake ~) zapata // vt (pt, pp shod) (horse) herrar; ~**brush** n cepillo para zapatos; ~**horn** n calzador m; ~**lace** n cordón m; ~**polish** n betún m; ~**shop** n zapatería; ~**string** n (fig): on a ~**string** con muy poco dinero.

shone [ʃɔn] pt, pp of **shine**.

shoo [ʃuː] excl ¡fuera!

shook [ʃuk] pt of **shake**.

shoot [ʃuːt] n (on branch, seedling) retoño, vástago // vt (pt, pp shot) vt disparar; (kill) matar a tiros (ejecute) fusilar; (film) rodar, filmar // vi (FOOTBALL) chutar; to ~ (at) tirar (a); to ~ **down** vt (plane) derribar; to ~ **in/out** vi entrar corriendo/salir disparado; to ~ **up** vi (prices) dispararse; ~**ing** n (shots) tiros mpl; (HUNTING) caza con escopeta; ~**ing star** n estrella fugaz.

shop [ʃɔp] n (tienda, (workshop) taller m // vi (also: go ~**ping**) ir de compras; ~ **assistant** n (Brit) dependiente/a m/f; ~ **floor** n (Brit fig) taller m, fábrica; ~**keeper** n (Brit) tendero/a; ~**lifting** n mechería; ~**per** n comprador/a m/f; ~**ping** n (goods) compras fpl; ~**ping bag** n bolsa (de compras); ~**ping centre**, (US) ~**ping center** n centro comercial; ~**soiled** a (Brit) usado; ~ **steward** n (Brit INDUSTRY) enlace m sindical; ~**window** n escaparate m, vidriera (LAm); ~**worn** a (US) usado.

shore [ʃɔː] n (of sea, lake) orilla // vt: to ~ (up) reforzar.

shorn [ʃɔːn] pp of **shear**.

short [ʃɔːt] a (not long) corto; (in time) breve, de corta duración; (person) bajo; (curt) brusco, seco // n (also: ~ film) cortometraje m; (a

pair of) ~s (unos) pantalones mpl cortos; to be ~ of sth estar falto de algo; in ~ en pocas palabras; ~ of doing... fuera de hacer...; everything ~ of... todo menos...; it is ~ for es la forma abreviada de; to cut ~ (speech, visit) interrumpir, terminar inesperadamente; to fall ~ of no alcanzar; to stop ~ parar en seco; to stop ~ of detenerse antes de; ~**age** n escasez f, falta; ~**bread** n especie de mantecada; ~**change** vt no dar el cambio completo a; ~**circuit** n cortocircuito // vt poner en cortocircuito // vi ponerse en cortocircuito; ~**coming** n defecto, deficiencia; ~(**crust**) **pastry** n (Brit) pasta quebradiza; ~**cut** n atajo; ~**en** vt acortar; (visit) interrumpir; ~**fall** n déficit m; ~**hand** n (Brit) taquigrafía; ~**hand typist** n (Brit) taquimecanógrafo/a; ~ **list** n (Brit: for job) lista de candidatos escogidos; ~**ly** ad en breve, dentro de poco; ~**sighted** a (Brit) corto de vista, miope; (fig) imprudente; ~**staffed** a falto de personal; ~**story** n cuento; ~**tempered** a enojadizo; ~**term** a (effect) a corto plazo; ~**wave** n (RADIO) onda corta.

shot [ʃɔt] pt, pp of **shoot** // n (sound) tiro, disparo; (person) tirador/a m/f; (try) tentativa; (injection) inyección f; (PHOT) toma, fotografía; like a ~ (without any delay) como un rayo; ~**gun** n escopeta.

should [ʃud] auxiliary vb: I ~ go now debo irme ahora; he ~ be there now debe de haber llegado (ya); I ~ go if I were you yo en tu lugar me iría; I ~ like to me gustaría.

shoulder ['ʃəuldə*] n hombro; (Brit: of road): hard ~ andén m // vt (fig) cargar con; ~ **blade** n omóplato; ~ **strap** n tirante m.

shouldn't ['ʃudnt] = should not.

shout [ʃaut] n grito // vt gritar // vi gritar, dar voces; to ~ **down** vt hundir a gritos; ~**ing** n griterío.

shove [ʃʌv] n empujón m // vt empujar; (col: put): **to ~ sth in** meter algo a empellones; **to ~ off** vi (NAUT) alejarse del muelle; (fig: col) largarse.

shovel ['ʃʌvl] n pala; (mechanical) excavadora // vt mover con pala.

show [ʃəu] n (of emotion) demostración f; (semblance) apariencia; (exhibition) exposición f; (THEATRE) función f, espectáculo f // vb (pt showed, pp shown) vt mostrar, enseñar; (courage etc) mostrar, manifestar; (exhibit) exponer; (film) proyectar // vi mostrarse; (appear) aparecer; **on ~** (exhibits etc) expuesto; **to ~ in** vt (person) hacer pasar; **to ~ off** vi (pej) presumir // vt (display) (pej) hacer gala de; **to ~ out** vt: **to ~ sb out** acompañar a uno a la puerta; (col: turn up) aparecer // vt descubrir; (unmask) desenmascarar; **~ business** n el mundo del espectáculo; **~down** n enfrentamiento (final).

shower ['ʃauə*] n (rain) chaparrón m, chubasco; (of stones etc) lluvia; (also: **~bath**) ducha, regadera (LAm) // vi llover // vt: **to ~ sb with** sth colmar a uno de algo; **~proof** a impermeable.

showing ['ʃəuɪŋ] n (of film) proyección f.

show jumping n hipismo.

shown [ʃəun] pp of **show**.

show: **~-off** n (col: person) presumido/a; **~piece** n (of exhibition etc) objeto cumbre; **~room** n sala de muestras.

shrank [ʃræŋk] pt of **shrink**.

shrapnel ['ʃræpnl] n metralla.

shred [ʃred] n (gen pl) triza, jirón m // vt hacer trizas; (CULIN) desmenuzar; **~der** n (vegetable ~der) picadora; (document ~der) trituradora (de papel).

shrewd [ʃruːd] a astuto.

shriek [ʃriːk] n chillido // vt, vi chillar.

shrill [ʃrɪl] a agudo, estridente.

shrimp [ʃrɪmp] n camarón m.

shrine [ʃraɪn] n santuario, sepulcro.

shrink [ʃrɪŋk], pt **shrank**, pp **shrunk** vi encogerse; (be reduced) reducirse // vt encoger; **to ~ from doing sth** no atreverse a hacer algo; **~age** n encogimiento; reducción f; **~wrap** vt empaquetar al vacío.

shrivel ['ʃrɪvl] (also: **~ up**) vt secar; (crease) arrugar // vi secarse; arrugarse.

shroud [ʃraud] n sudario // vt: **~ed in mystery** envuelto en el misterio.

Shrove Tuesday ['ʃrəuv-] n martes m de carnaval.

shrub [ʃrʌb] n arbusto; **~bery** n arbustos mpl.

shrug [ʃrʌg] n encogimiento de hombros // vt, vi: **to ~ (one's shoulders)** encogerse de hombros; **to ~ off** vt negar importancia a.

shrunk [ʃrʌŋk] pp of **shrink**.

shudder ['ʃʌdə*] n estremecimiento, escalofrío // vi estremecerse.

shuffle ['ʃʌfl] vt (cards) barajar; **to ~ (one's feet)** arrastrar los pies.

shun [ʃʌn] vt rehuir, esquivar.

shunt [ʃʌnt] vt (RAIL) maniobrar.

shut [ʃʌt], pt, pp **shut** vt cerrar // vi cerrarse; **to ~ down** vt, vi cerrar; **to ~ off** vt (supply etc) interrumpir, cortar; **to ~ up** vi (col: keep quiet) callarse // vt (close) cerrar; (silence) callar; **~ter** n contraventana; (PHOT) obturador m.

shuttle ['ʃʌtl] n lanzadera; (also: **~ service**: AVIAT) puente m aéreo.

shuttlecock ['ʃʌtlkɔk] n volante m.

shy [ʃaɪ] a tímido; **~ness** n timidez f.

sibling ['sɪblɪŋ] n hermano/a.

Sicily ['sɪsɪlɪ] n Sicilia.

sick [sɪk] a (ill) enfermo; (nauseated) mareado; (humour) negro; **to be ~** (Brit) vomitar; **to feel ~** tener náuseas; **to be ~ of** (fig) estar harto de; **~ bay** n enfermería; **~en** vt dar asco a // vi enfermar; **~ening** a (fig) asqueroso.

sickle ['sɪkl] n hoz f.

sick: ~ **leave** n baja por enfermedad; ~**ly** a enfermizo; (taste) empalagoso; ~**ness** n enfermedad f, mal m; (vomiting) náuseas fpl; ~ **pay** n subsidio de enfermedad.

side [saɪd] n (gen) lado; (of body) costado; (of lake) orilla; (team) equipo; (of hill) ladera // cpd (door, entrance) lateral // vi: **to** ~ **with sb** tomar el partido de uno; **by the** ~ **of** al lado de; ~ **by** ~ juntos/as; **from all** ~**s** de todos lados; **to take** ~**s (with)** tomar partido (con); ~**board** n aparador m; ~**boards** (Brit), ~**burns** npl patillas fpl; ~ **effect** n efecto secundario; ~**light** n (AUT) luz f lateral; ~**line** n (SPORT) línea lateral; (fig) empleo suplementario; ~**long** a de soslayo; ~**saddle** ad a mujeriegas, a la inglesa; ~ **show** n (stall) caseta; ~**step** vt (fig) evitar // vi; ~**street** n calle f lateral; ~**track** vt (fig) desviar (de su propósito); ~**walk** n (US) acera; ~**ways** ad de lado.

siding ['saɪdɪŋ] n (RAIL) apartadero, vía muerta.

sidle ['saɪdl] vi: **to** ~ **up (to)** acercarse furtivamente (a).

siege [siːdʒ] n cerco, sitio.

sieve [sɪv] n colador m // vt cribar.

sift [sɪft] vt cribar; (fig: information) escudriñar.

sigh [saɪ] n suspiro // vi suspirar.

sight [saɪt] n (faculty) vista; (spectacle) espectáculo; (on gun) mira, alza // vt divisar; **in** ~ a la vista; **out of** ~ fuera de (la) vista; ~**seeing** n excursionismo, turismo; **to go** ~**seeing** hacer turismo.

sign [saɪn] n (with hand) señal f, seña; (trace) huella, rastro; (notice) letrero; (written) signo // vt firmar; **to** ~ **sth over to sb** firmar el traspaso de algo a uno; **to** ~ **on** vi (MIL) alistarse; (as unemployed) registrarse como desempleado // vt (MIL) alistar; (employee) contratar; **to** ~ **up** vi (MIL) alistarse // vt

(contract) contratar.

signal ['sɪɡnl] n señal f // vi (AUT) hacer señales // vt (person) hacer señas a; (message) comunicar por señales; ~**man** n (RAIL) guardavía m.

signature ['sɪɡnətʃə*] n firma; ~ **tune** n sintonía de apertura de un programa.

signet ring ['sɪɡnət-] n anillo de sello.

significance [sɪɡ'nɪfɪkəns] n significado; (importance) trascendencia.

significant [sɪɡ'nɪfɪkənt] a significativo; trascendente.

signify ['sɪɡnɪfaɪ] vt significar.

signpost ['saɪnpəust] n indicador m.

silence ['saɪlns] n silencio // vt hacer callar; (guns) reducir al silencio; ~**r** n (on gun, Brit AUT) silenciador m.

silent ['saɪlnt] a (gen) silencioso; (not speaking) callado; (film) mudo; **to remain** ~ guardar silencio; ~ **partner** n (COMM) socio/a comanditario/a.

silhouette [sɪluː'et] n silueta.

silicon chip ['sɪlɪkən-] n plaqueta de silicio.

silk [sɪlk] n seda // cpd de seda; ~**y** a sedoso.

silly ['sɪlɪ] a (person) tonto; (idea) absurdo.

silo ['saɪləu] n silo.

silt [sɪlt] n sedimento.

silver ['sɪlvə*] n plata; (money) moneda suelta // cpd de plata; ~ **paper** n (Brit) papel m de plata; ~**-plated** a plateado; ~**smith** n platero/a; ~**ware** n plata; ~**y** a plateado.

similar ['sɪmɪlə*] a: ~ **to** parecido o semejante a; ~**ly** ad del mismo modo.

simile ['sɪmɪlɪ] n símil m.

simmer ['sɪmə*] vi hervir a fuego lento.

simpering ['sɪmpərɪŋ] a afectado; (foolish) bobo.

simple ['sɪmpl] a (easy) sencillo; (foolish, COMM: interest) simple; **simplicity** [-'plɪsɪtɪ] n sencillez f;

simplify ['sɪmplɪfaɪ] vt simplificar.

simply ['sɪmplɪ] ad (live, talk) sencillamente; (just, merely) sólo.

simultaneous [sɪmɔl'teɪnɪəs] a simultáneo; **~ly** ad simultáneamente.

sin [sɪn] n pecado // vi pecar.

since [sɪns] ad desde entonces, después // prep desde // conj (time) desde que; (because) ya que, puesto que; **~ then** desde entonces.

sincere [sɪn'sɪə*] a sincero; **~ly** ad: **yours ~ly**, (US) **~ly yours** (in letters) le saluda atentamente; **sincerity** [-'sɛrɪtɪ] n sinceridad f.

sinew ['sɪnju:] n tendón m.

sinful ['sɪnful] a (thought) pecaminoso; (person) pecador(a).

sing [sɪŋ], pt **sang**, pp **sung** vt cantar // vi cantar.

Singapore [sɪŋə'pɔ:*] n Singapur m.

singe [sɪndʒ] vt chamuscar.

singer ['sɪŋə*] n cantante m/f.

singing ['sɪŋɪŋ] n (gen) canto; (songs) canciones fpl.

single ['sɪŋgl] a único, solo; (unmarried) soltero; (not double) simple, sencillo // n (Brit: also: **~ ticket**) billete m sencillo; (record) sencillo, single m; **~s** npl (TENNIS) individual msg; **to ~ out** vt (choose) escoger; **~ bed** n cama individual; **~-breasted** a (jacket, suit) recto; **single-file** n: **in ~** file en fila de uno; **~-handed** ad sin ayuda; **~-minded** a resuelto, firme; **~ room** n cuarto individual.

singlet ['sɪŋglɪt] n camiseta.

singly ['sɪŋglɪ] ad uno por uno.

singular ['sɪŋgjulə*] a (odd) raro, extraño; (LING) singular // n (LING) singular m.

sinister ['sɪnɪstə*] a siniestro.

sink [sɪŋk] n fregadero // vb (pt **sank**, pp **sunk**) vt (ship) hundir, echar a pique; (foundations) excavar; (piles etc): **to ~ sth into** hundir algo en // vi (gen) hundirse; **to ~ in** vi (fig) penetrar, calar.

sinner ['sɪnə*] n pecador(a) m/f.

sinus ['saɪnəs] n (ANAT) seno.

sip [sɪp] n sorbo // vt sorber, beber a sorbitos.

siphon ['saɪfən] n sifón m; **to ~ off** vt desviar.

sir [sə*] n señor m; S~ John Smith Sir John Smith; **yes ~** sí, señor.

siren ['saɪərən] n sirena.

sirloin ['sə:lɔɪn] n solomillo.

sissy ['sɪsɪ] n (col) marica m.

sister ['sɪstə*] n hermana; (Brit: nurse) enfermera jefe; **~-in-law** n cuñada.

sit [sɪt], pt, pp **sat** vi sentarse; (be sitting) estar sentado; (assembly) reunirse // vt (exam) presentarse a; **to ~ down** vi sentarse; **to ~ in on** vt fus asistir a; **to ~ up** vi incorporarse; (not go to bed) velar.

sitcom ['sɪtkɔm] n abbr (= situation comedy) comedia de situación.

site [saɪt] n sitio; (also: **building ~**) solar m // vt situar.

sit-in ['sɪtɪn] n (demonstration) ocupación f.

sitting ['sɪtɪŋ] n (of assembly etc) sesión f; (in canteen) turno; **~ room** n sala de estar.

situated ['sɪtjueɪtɪd] a situado.

situation [sɪtju'eɪʃən] n situación f; '**~s vacant**' (Brit) 'ofrecen trabajo'.

six [sɪks] num seis; **~teen** num diez y seis, dieciséis; **~th** a sexto; **~ty** num sesenta.

size [saɪz] n (gen) tamaño; (extent) extensión f; (of clothing) talla; (of shoes) número; **to ~ up** vt formarse una idea de; **~able** a importante, considerable.

sizzle ['sɪzl] vi crepitar.

skate [skeɪt] n patín m; (fish: pl inv) raya // vi patinar; **~board** n monopatín m; **~r** n patinador(a) m/f; **skating** n patinaje m; **skating rink** n pista de patinaje.

skeleton ['skɛlɪtn] n esqueleto; (TECH) armazón f; (outline) esquema m; **~ key** n llave f maestra; **~ staff** n personal m reducido.

skeptic ['skɛptɪk] etc (US) = **sceptic**.

sketch [skɛtʃ] *n* (*drawing*) dibujo; (*outline*) esbozo, bosquejo; (*THEATRE*) sketch *m* // *vt* dibujar; esbozar; ~ **book** *n* libro de dibujos; ~**y** *a* incompleto.

skewer ['skjuːə*] *n* broqueta.

ski [skiː] *n* esquí *m* // *vi* esquiar; ~ **boot** *n* bota de esquí.

skid [skɪd] *n* patinazo // *vi* patinar.

ski: ~**er** *n* esquiador(a) *m/f*; ~**ing** *n* esquí *m*; ~ **jump** *n* salto con esquís.

skilful ['skɪlful] *a* diestro, experto.

ski lift *n* telesilla *m*, telesquí *m*.

skill [skɪl] *n* destreza, pericia; ~**ed** *a* hábil, diestro; (*worker*) cualificado.

skim [skɪm] *vt* (*milk*) desnatar; (*glide over*) rozar, rasar // *vi*: to ~ **through** (*book*) hojear; ~**med milk** *n* leche *f* descremada.

skimp [skɪmp] *vt* (*work*) chapucear; (*cloth etc*) escatimar; ~**y** *a* (*meagre*) escaso; (*skirt*) muy corto.

skin [skɪn] *n* (*gen*) piel *f*; (*complexion*) cutis *m* // *vt* (*fruit etc*) pelar; (*animal*) despellejar; ~**deep** *a* superficial; ~ **diving** *n* buceo; ~**ny** *a* flaco; ~**tight** *a* (*dress etc*) muy ajustado.

skip [skɪp] *n* brinco, salto; (*container*) cuba // *vi* brincar; (*with rope*) saltar a la comba // *vt* (*pass over*) omitir, saltar.

ski pants *npl* pantalones *mpl* de esquí.

ski pole *n* bastón *m* de esquiar.

skipper ['skɪpə*] *n* (*NAUT, SPORT*) capitán *m*.

skipping rope ['skɪpɪŋ-] *n* (*Brit*) cuerda (de saltar).

skirmish ['skəːmɪʃ] *n* escaramuza.

skirt [skəːt] *n* falda, pollera (*LAm*) // *vt* (*surround*) ceñir, rodear; (*go round*) ladear.

ski suit *n* traje *m* de esquiar.

skit [skɪt] *n* sátira, parodia.

skittle ['skɪtl] *n* bolo; ~**s** *n* (*game*) boliche *m*.

skive [skaɪv] *vi* (*Brit col*) gandulear.

skulk [skʌlk] *vi* esconderse.

skull [skʌl] *n* calavera; (*ANAT*) cráneo.

skunk [skʌŋk] *n* mofeta.

sky [skaɪ] *n* cielo; ~**light** *n* tragaluz *m*, claraboya; ~**scraper** *n* rascacielos *m inv*.

slab [slæb] *n* (*stone*) bloque *m*; (*flat*) losa; (*of cake*) trozo.

slack [slæk] *a* (*loose*) flojo; (*slow* de poca actividad; (*careless*) descuidado; ~**s** *npl* pantalones *mpl*; ~**en** (*also*: ~**en off**) *vi* aflojarse // *vt* aflojar; (*speed*) disminuir.

slag [slæg] *n* escoria, escombros *mpl*; ~ **heap** *n* escorial *m*, escombrera.

slain [sleɪn] *pp* of **slay**.

slam [slæm] *vt* (*throw*) arrojar (violentamente); **to ~ the door** dar un portazo // *vi* cerrarse de golpe.

slander ['slɑːndə*] *n* calumnia, difamación *f* // *vt* calumniar, difamar.

slang [slæŋ] *n* argot *m*; (*jargon*) jerga.

slant [slɑːnt] *n* sesgo, inclinación *f*; (*fig*) interpretación *f*; ~**ed** *a* parcial; ~**ing** *a* inclinado.

slap [slæp] *n* palmada; (*in face*) bofetada // *vt* dar una palmada/bofetada a // *ad* (*directly*) exactamente, directamente; ~**dash** *a* descuidado; ~**stick** *n*: ~**stick comedy** comedia de golpe y porrazo; ~**up** *a*: a ~**up meal** (*Brit*) un banquetazo, una comilona.

slash [slæʃ] *vt* acuchillar; (*fig: prices*) quemar.

slat [slæt] *n* tablilla, listón *m*.

slate [sleɪt] *n* pizarra // *vt* (*Brit: fig: criticise*) criticar duramente.

slaughter ['slɔːtə*] *n* (*of animals*) matanza; (*of people*) carnicería // *vt* matar; ~**house** *n* matadero.

Slav [slɑːv] *a* eslavo.

slave [sleɪv] *n* esclavo/a // *vi* (*also*: ~ **away**) sudar tinta; ~**ry** *n* esclavitud *f*.

slay [sleɪ], *pt* **slew**, *pp* **slain** *vt* matar.

SLD *n abbr* = **Social and Liberal Democrats**.

sleazy ['sliːzɪ] *a* de mala fama.

sled [sled] *n* (*US*) trineo.

sledge [sledʒ] *n* (*Brit*) trineo; **~hammer** *n* mazo.

sleek [sliːk] *a* (*shiny*) lustroso.

sleep [sliːp] *n* sueño // *vi* (*pt, pp* slept) dormir; **to go to ~** quedarse dormido; **to ~ in** *vi* (*oversleep*) quedarse dormido; **~er** *n* (*person*) durmiente *m/f*; (*Brit RAIL: on track*) traviesa; (: *train*) coche-cama *m*; **~ing bag** *n* saco de dormir; **~ing car** *n* coche-cama *m*; **~ing pill** *n* somnífero; **~less** *a*: **a ~less night** una noche en blanco; **~walker** *n* sonámbulo/a; **~y** *a* soñoliento.

sleet [sliːt] *n* nevisca.

sleeve [sliːv] *n* manga; (*TECH*) manguito.

sleigh [sleɪ] *n* trineo.

sleight [slaɪt] *n*: **~ of hand** escamoteo.

slender ['slendə*] *a* delgado; (*means*) escaso.

slept [slept] *pt, pp of* **sleep**.

slew [sluː] *vi* (*veer*) torcerse // *pt of* **slay**.

slice [slaɪs] *n* (*of meat*) tajada; (*of bread*) rebanada; (*of lemon*) rodaja; (*utensil*) pala // *vt* cortar (en tajos); rebanar.

slick [slɪk] *a* (*skilful*) hábil, diestro // *n* (*also*: **oil ~**) marea negra.

slide [slaɪd] *n* (*in playground*) tobogán *m*; (*PHOT*) diapositiva; (*Brit: also*: **hair ~**) pasador *m* // *vb* (*pt, pp* slid) *vt* correr, deslizar // *vi* (*slip*) resbalarse; (*glide*) deslizarse; **~ rule** *n* regla de cálculo; **sliding** *a* (*door*) corredizo; **sliding scale** *n* escala móvil.

slight [slaɪt] *a* (*slim*) delgado; (*frail*) delicado; (*pain etc*) leve; (*trivial*) insignificante; (*small*) pequeño // *n* desaire *m* // *vt* (*offend*) ofender, desairar; **not in the ~est** in absoluto; **~ly** *ad* ligeramente, un poco.

slim [slɪm] *a* delgado, esbelto // *vi* adelgazar.

slime [slaɪm] *n* limo, cieno.

slimming ['slɪmɪŋ] *n* adelgazamiento.

sling [slɪŋ] *n* (*MED*) cabestrillo; (*weapon*) honda // *vt* (*pt, pp* slung) tirar, arrojar.

slip [slɪp] *n* (*slide*) resbalón *m*; (*mistake*) descuido; (*underskirt*) combinación *f*; (*of paper*) papelito // *vt* (*slide*) deslizar // *vi* (*slide*) deslizarse; (*stumble*) resbalar(se); (*decline*) decaer; (*move smoothly*): **to ~ into/out of** (*room etc*) introducirse en/salirse de; **to give sb the ~** eludir a uno; **a ~ of the tongue** un lapsus; **to ~ sth on/off** ponerse/quitarse algo; **to ~ away** *vi* escabullirse; **to ~ in** *vt* meter // *vi* meterse; **to ~ out** *vi* (*go out*) salir (un momento); **~ped disc** *n* vértebra dislocada.

slipper ['slɪpə*] *n* zapatilla, pantufla.

slippery ['slɪpərɪ] *a* resbaladizo.

slip: ~ road *n* (*Brit*) carretera de acceso; **~shod** *a* descuidado; **~up** *n* (*error*) descuido *m*; **~way** *n* grada, gradas *fpl*.

slit [slɪt] *n* raja; (*cut*) corte *m* // *vt* (*pt, pp* slit) rajar, cortar.

slither ['slɪðə*] *vi* deslizarse.

sliver ['slɪvə*] *n* (*of glass, wood*) astilla; (*of cheese etc*) raja.

slob [slɒb] *n* (*col*) patán/ana *m/f*.

slog [slɒg] (*Brit*) *vi* sudar tinta; **it was a ~** costó trabajo (hacerlo).

slogan ['sləʊgən] *n* eslogan *m*, lema *m*.

slop [slɒp] *vi* (*also*: **~ over**) derramarse, desbordarse // *vt* derramar, verter.

slope [sləʊp] *n* (*up*) cuesta, pendiente *f*; (*down*) declive *m*; (*side of mountain*) falda, vertiente *m* // *vi*: **to ~ down** estar en declive; **to ~ up** inclinarse; **sloping** *a* en pendiente; en declive.

sloppy ['slɒpɪ] *a* (*work*) descuidado; (*appearance*) desaliñado.

slot [slɒt] *n* ranura // *vt*: **to ~ into** encajar en.

sloth [sləʊθ] *n* (*laziness*) pereza.

slot machine *n* (*Brit*: *vending machine*) aparato vendedor, distribuidor *m* automático; (*for gambling*) máquina tragaperras.

slouch [slautʃ] *vi*: to ~ about (*laze*) gandulear.

slovenly ['slʌvənlɪ] *a* (*dirty*) desaliñado, desaseado; (*careless*) descuidado.

slow [sləu] *a* lento; (*watch*): to be ~ atrasarse // *ad* lentamente, despacio // *vt, vi* (*also*: ~ down, ~ up) retardar; '~' (*road sign*) 'disminuir velocidad'; ~ down *n* (*US*) huelga de manos caídas; ~**ly** *ad* lentamente, despacio; **slow motion** *n*: in ~ motion a cámara lenta.

sludge [slʌdʒ] *n* lodo, fango.

slug [slʌg] *n* babosa; (*bullet*) posta; ~**gish** *a* (*slow*) lento; (*lazy*) perezoso.

sluice [slu:s] *n* (*gate*) esclusa; (*channel*) canal *m*.

slum [slʌm] *n* casucha.

slumber ['slʌmbə*] *n* sueño.

slump [slʌmp] *n* (*economic*) depresión *f* // *vi* hundirse.

slung [slʌŋ] *pt, pp* de **sling**.

slur [slə:*] *n* calumnia // *vt* calumniar, difamar; (*word*) pronunciar mal.

slush [slʌʃ] *n* nieve *f* a medio derretir; ~ **fund** *n* caja negra (*fondos para sobornar*).

slut [slʌt] *n* (*sloppy*) marrana.

sly [slaɪ] *a* astuto.

smack [smæk] *n* (*slap*) manotada; (*blow*) golpe *m* // *vt* dar una manotada a; golpear con la mano // *vi*: to ~ of saber a, oler a.

small [smɔ:l] *a* pequeño; ~ **ads** *npl* (*Brit*) anuncios *mpl* por palabras; ~ **change** *n* suelto, cambio; ~**holder** *n* (*Brit*) granjero/a, parcelero/a; ~ **hours** *npl*: in the ~ hours en las altas horas (de la noche); ~**pox** *n* viruela; ~ **talk** *n* cháchara.

smart [smɑ:t] *a* elegante; (*clever*) listo, inteligente; (*quick*) rápido, vivo // *vi* escocer, picar; to ~ **en up** *vi* arreglarse // *vt* arreglar.

smash [smæʃ] *n* (*also*: ~-up) choque

m // *vt* (*break*) hacer pedazos; (*car etc*) estrellar; (*SPORT: record*) batir // *vi* hacerse pedazos; (*against wall etc*) estrellarse; ~**ing** *a* (*col*) cojonudo.

smattering ['smætərɪŋ] *n*: a ~ of Spanish algo de español.

smear [smɪə*] *n* mancha; (*MED*) frotis *m inv* // *vt* untar; (*fig*) calumniar, difamar.

smell [smel] *n* olor *m*; (*sense*) olfato // (*pt, pp* **smelt** *or* **smelled**) *vt, vi* oler; it ~**s good**/of garlic huele bien/a ajo; ~**y** *a* maloliente.

smile [smaɪl] *n* sonrisa // *vi* sonreír; **smiling** *a* sonriente.

smirk [smə:k] *n* sonrisa falsa *or* afectada.

smith [smɪθ] *n* herrero; ~**y** ['smɪðɪ] *n* herrería.

smock [smɔk] *n* blusa; (*children's*) delantal *m*; (*US: overall*) guardapolvo.

smog [smɔg] *n* esmog *m*.

smoke [sməuk] *n* humo // *vi* fumar; (*chimney*) echar humo // *vt* (*cigarettes*) fumar; ~**d** *a* (*bacon, glass*) ahumado; ~**r** *n* (*person*) fumador/a *m/f*; (*RAIL*) coche *m* fumador; ~ **screen** *n* cortina de humo; ~ **shop** *n* (*US*) estanco, tabaquería (*LAm*); **smoking** *n*: 'no smoking' 'prohibido fumar'; **smoky** *a* (*room*) lleno de humo.

smolder ['sməuldə*] *vi* (*US*) = **smoulder**.

smooth [smu:ð] *a* liso; (*sea*) tranquilo; (*flavour, movement*) suave; (*person: pej*) meloso // *vt* alisar; (*also*: ~ **out**: *creases, difficulties*) allanar.

smother ['smʌðə*] *vt* sofocar; (*repress*) contener.

smoulder, (*US*) **smolder** ['sməuldə*] *vi* arder sin llama.

smudge [smʌdʒ] *n* mancha // *vt* manchar.

smug [smʌg] *a* presumido.

smuggle ['smʌgl] *vt* pasar de contrabando; ~**r** *n* contrabandista *m/f*;

smuggling n contrabando.

smutty ['smʌtɪ] a (fig) verde, obsceno.

snack [snæk] n bocado; ~ **bar** n cafetería.

snag [snæg] n problema m.

snail [sneɪl] n caracol m.

snake [sneɪk] n (gen) serpiente f; (harmless) culebra; (poisonous) víbora.

snap [snæp] n (sound) chasquido; golpe m seco; (photograph) foto f // a (decision) instantáneo // vt (fingers etc) castañetear; (break) quebrar; (photograph) tomar una foto de // vi (break) quebrarse; (fig: person) contestar bruscamente; to ~ **shut** cerrarse de golpe; to ~ **at** vt fus (subj: dog) intentar morder; to ~ **off** vi (break) partirse; to ~ **up** vt agarrar; ~ **fastener** n (US) botón m de presión; ~**py** a (col: answer) instantáneo; (slogan) conciso; **make it** ~**py!** (hurry up) ¡date prisa!; ~**shot** n foto f (instantánea).

snare [snɛə*] n trampa // vt cazar con trampa; (fig) engañar.

snarl [snɑːl] n gruñido // vi gruñir.

snatch [snætʃ] n (fig) robo; ~**es** of trocitos mpl de // vt (~ away) arrebatar; (grasp) agarrar (Sp), agarrar.

sneak [sniːk] vi: to ~ **in/out** entrar/salir a hurtadillas // n (col) soplón/ona m/f; ~**ers** npl (US) zapatos mpl de lona; ~**y** a furtivo.

sneer [snɪə*] n sonreír con desprecio.

sneeze [sniːz] vi estornudar.

sniff [snɪf] vi sorber (por la nariz) // vt husmear, oler.

snigger ['snɪɡə*] vi reírse con disimulo.

snip [snɪp] n (piece) recorte m; (bargain) ganga // vt tijeretear.

sniper ['snaɪpə*] n francotirador(a) m/f.

snippet ['snɪpɪt] n retazo.

snivelling ['snɪvlɪŋ] a llorón/ona.

snob [snɔb] n (e)snob m/f; ~**bery** n (e)snobismo; ~**bish** a (e)snob.

snooker ['snuːkə*] n especie de billar.

snoop [snuːp] vi: to ~ **about** fisgonear.

snooty ['snuːtɪ] a (e)snob.

snooze [snuːz] n siesta // vi echar una siesta.

snore [snɔː*] vi roncar; **snoring** n ronquidos mpl.

snorkel ['snɔːkl] n (tubo) respirador m.

snort [snɔːt] n bufido // vi bufar.

snout [snaʊt] n hocico, morro.

snow [snəʊ] n nieve f // vi nevar; ~**ball** n bola de nieve; ~**bound** a bloqueado por la nieve; ~**drift** n ventisquero; ~**drop** n campanilla; ~**fall** n nevada; ~**flake** n copo de nieve; ~**man** n figura de nieve; ~**plough**, (US) ~**plow** n quitanieves m inv; ~**shoe** n raqueta de nieve; ~**storm** n nevada, nevasca.

snub [snʌb] vt: to ~ **sb** desairar a alguien // n desaire m, repulsa; ~-**nosed** a chato.

snuff [snʌf] n rapé m.

snug [snʌɡ] a (cosy) cómodo; (fitted) ajustado.

snuggle ['snʌɡl] vi: to ~ **up to sb** arrimarse a uno.

KEYWORD

so [səʊ] ♦ ad 1 (thus, likewise) así, de este modo; **if** ~ de ser así; **I like swimming** — **do I** a mí me gusta nadar — a mí también; **I've got work to do** — **has Paul** tengo trabajo que hacer — Paul también; **it's 5 o'clock** — **it is!** son las cinco — ¡pues es verdad!; **I hope/think** ~ espero/creo que sí; **far** hasta ahora; (in past) hasta este momento
2 (in comparisons etc; to such a degree) tan; ~ **quickly (that)** tan rápido (que); ~ **big (that)** tan grande (que); **she's not** ~ **clever as her brother** no es tan lista como su hermano; **we were** ~ **worried** estábamos preocupadísimos
3: ~ **much** a tanto/a // ad tanto;

many tantos/as

4 (*phrases*): **10 or** ~ unos 10, 10 o así; ~ **long!** (*col: goodbye*) ¡hasta luego!

◆ *conj* **1** (*expressing purpose*): ~ **as** to do para hacer; ~ (**that**) para que + *subjun*

2 (*expressing result*) así que; ~ **you see, I could have gone** así que ya ves, (yo) podría haber ido.

soak [səuk] *vt* (*drench*) empapar; (*put in water*) remojar // *vi* remojarse, estar a remojo; **to ~ in** *vi* penetrar; **to ~ up** *vt* absorber.

so-and-so [ˈsəuənsəu] *n* (*somebody*) fulano/a tal.

soap [səup] *n* jabón *m*; **~flakes** *npl* escamas *fpl* de jabón; **~opera** *n* telenovela; **~ powder** *n* jabón *m* en polvo; **~y** *a* jabonoso.

soar [sɔː*] *vi* (*on wings*) remontarse; (*building etc*) elevarse.

sob [sɔb] *n* sollozo // *vi* sollozar.

sober [ˈsəubə*] *a* (*moderate*) moderado; (*not drunk*) sobrio; (*colour, style*) discreto; **to ~ up** *vt* pasársele a uno la borrachera.

so-called [ˈsəuˈkɔːld] *a* así llamado.

soccer [ˈsɔkə*] *n* fútbol *m*.

social [ˈsəuʃl] *a* social // *n* velada, fiesta; ~ **club** *n* club *m*; **~ism** *n* socialismo; **~ist** *a, n* socialista *m/f*; **~ize** *vi*: **to ~ize (with)** alternar (con); **~ly** *ad* socialmente; ~ **security** *n* seguridad *f* social; ~ **work** *n* asistencia social; ~ **worker** *n* asistente/a *m/f*.

society [səˈsaiəti] *n* sociedad *f*; (*club*) asociación *f*; (*also*: **high** ~) buena sociedad.

sociologist [səusiˈɔlədʒist] *n* sociólogo/a.

sociology [səusiˈɔlədʒi] *n* sociología.

sock [sɔk] *n* calcetín *m*, media (*LAm*).

socket [ˈsɔkit] *n* (*ELEC*) enchufe *m*.

sod [sɔd] *n* (*of earth*) césped *m*; (*col!*) cabrón/ona *m/f* (!).

soda [ˈsəudə] *n* (*CHEM*) sosa; (*also:*

~ **water**) soda; (*US: also:* ~ **pop**) gaseosa.

sodden [ˈsɔdn] *a* empapado.

sodium [ˈsəudiəm] *n* sodio.

sofa [ˈsəufə] *n* sofá *m*.

soft [sɔft] *a* (*not hard, lenient*) blando; (*gentle, not loud*) suave; (*stupid*) bobo; ~ **drink** *n* bebida no alcohólica; **~en** [ˈsɔfn] *vt* ablandar; suavizar // *vi* ablandarse; suavizarse; **~ly** *ad* suavemente; (*gently*) delicadamente, con delicadeza; **~ness** *n* blandura; suavidad *f*; **~ware** *n* (*COMPUT*) software *m*.

soggy [ˈsɔgi] *a* empapado.

soil [sɔil] *n* (*earth*) tierra, suelo // *vt* ensuciar; **~ed** *a* sucio.

solace [ˈsɔlis] *n* consuelo.

sold [səuld] *pt, pp* *of* **sell**; ~ **out** *a* (*COMM*) agotado.

solder [ˈsəuldə*] *vt* soldar // *n* soldadura.

soldier [ˈsəuldʒə*] *n* (*gen*) soldado; (*army man*) militar *m*.

sole [səul] *n* (*of foot*) planta; (*of shoe*) suela; (*fish: pl inv*) lenguado // *a* único.

solemn [ˈsɔləm] *a* solemne.

solicit [səˈlisit] *vt* (*request*) solicitar // *vi* (*prostitute*) importunar.

solicitor [səˈlisitə*] *n* (*Brit: for wills etc*) ~ notario/a; (: *in court*) ~ abogado/a.

solid [ˈsɔlid] *a* sólido; (*gold etc*) macizo // *n* sólido.

solidarity [sɔliˈdæriti] *n* solidaridad *f*.

solitaire [sɔliˈtɛə*] *n* (*game, gem*) solitario.

solitary [ˈsɔlitəri] *a* solitario, solo; ~ **confinement** *n* incomunicación *f*.

solitude [ˈsɔlitjuːd] *n* soledad *f*.

solo [ˈsəuləu] *n* solo; **~ist** *n* solista *m/f*.

solution [səˈluːʃən] *n* solución *f*.

solve [sɔlv] *vt* resolver, solucionar.

solvent [ˈsɔlvənt] *a* (*COMM*) solvente // *n* (*CHEM*) solvente *m*.

sombre, (*US*) **somber** [ˈsɔmbə*] *a* sombrío.

some [sʌm] ◆ a **1** (*a certain amount or number of*): ~ tea/water/biscuits té/agua/(unas) galletas; there's ~ milk in the fridge hay leche en el frigo; there were ~ people outside había algunas personas fuera; I've got ~ money, but not much tengo algo de dinero, pero no mucho **2** (*certain: in contrasts*) algunos/as; ~ people say that ... hay quien dice que ...; ~ films were excellent, but most were mediocre hubo películas excelentes, pero la mayoría fueron mediocres **3** (*unspecified*): ~ woman was asking for you una mujer estuvo preguntando por ti; he was asking for ~ book (or other) pedía un libro; ~ day algún día; ~ day next week un día de la semana que viene
◆ pron **1** (*a certain number*): I've got ~ (*books etc*) tengo algunos/as **2** (*a certain amount*) algo; I've got ~ (*money, milk*) tengo algo; could I have ~ of that cheese? ¿me puede dar un poco de ese queso?; I've read ~ of the book he leído parte del libro
◆ ad: ~ **10 people** unas 10 personas, una decena de personas

somebody ['sʌmbədi] pron = **someone.**
somehow ['sʌmhau] ad de alguna manera; (*for some reason*) por una u otra razón.
someone ['sʌmwʌn] pron alguien.
someplace ['sʌmpleis] ad (US) = **somewhere.**
somersault ['sʌməsɔːlt] n (*deliberate*) salto mortal; (*accidental*) vuelco // vi dar un salto mortal; dar vuelcos.
something ['sʌmθiŋ] pron algo; would you like ~ to eat/drink? ¿te gustaría cenar/tomar algo?
sometime ['sʌmtaim] ad (*in future*) algún día, en algún momento; ~ last

month durante el mes pasado.
sometimes ['sʌmtaimz] ad a veces.
somewhat ['sʌmwɔt] ad algo.
somewhere ['sʌmwɛə*] ad (*be*) en alguna parte; (*go*) a alguna parte; ~ else (*be*) en otra parte; (*go*) a otra parte.
son [sʌn] n hijo.
song [sɔŋ] n canción f.
sonic ['sɔnik] a (*boom*) sónico.
son-in-law ['sʌninlɔː] n yerno.
sonnet ['sɔnit] n soneto.
sonny ['sʌni] n (col) hijo.
soon [suːn] ad pronto, dentro de poco; ~ **afterwards** poco después; see also **as**; ~**er** ad (*time*) antes, más temprano; I would ~**er** do that preferiría hacer eso; ~**er or later** tarde o temprano.
soot [sut] n hollín m.
soothe [suːð] vt tranquilizar; (*pain*) aliviar.
sophisticated [sə'fistikeitid] a sofisticado.
sophomore ['sɔfəmɔː*] n (US) estudiante m/f de segundo año.
soporific [sɔpə'rifik] a soporífero.
sopping ['sɔpiŋ] a: ~ (*wet*) empapado.
soppy ['sɔpi] a (pej) bobo, tonto.
soprano [sə'prɑːnəu] n soprano f.
sorcerer ['sɔːsərə*] n hechicero.
sore [sɔː*] a (*painful*) doloroso, que duele; (*offended*) resentido // n llaga; ~**ly** ad: I am ~**ly** tempted to estoy muy tentado a.
sorrow ['sɔrəu] n pena, dolor m.
sorry ['sɔri] a (*regretful*) arrepentido; (*condition, excuse*) lastimoso; ~! ¡perdón!, ¡perdone!; to feel ~ for sb tener lástima a uno; I feel ~ for him me da lástima.
sort [sɔːt] n clase f, género, tipo // vt (*also*: ~ **out**: *papers*) clasificar; (: *problems*) arreglar, solucionar; ~**ing office** n sala de batalla.
SOS n abbr (= *save our souls*) SOS m.
so-so ['səusəu] ad regular, así así.
soufflé ['suːflei] n suflé m.

sought [sɔ:t] *pt, pp of* **seek**.

soul [səul] *n* alma *f*; ~**destroying** *a* (*work*) deprimente; ~**ful** *a* lleno de sentimiento.

sound [saund] *a* (*healthy*) sano; (*safe, not damaged*) en buen estado; (*reliable: person*) digno de confianza; (*sensible*) sensato, razonable // *ad*: ~ **asleep** profundamente dormido // *n* (*noise*) sonido, ruido; (*GEO*) estrecho // *vt* (*alarm*) sonar; (*also*: ~ **out**: *opinions*) consultar, sondear // *vi* sonar, resonar; (*fig: seem*) parecer; **to** ~ **like** sonar a; ~ **barrier** *n* barrera del sonido; ~ **effects** *npl* efectos *mpl* sonoros; ~**ing** *n* (*NAUT etc*) sondeo; ~**ly** *ad* (*sleep*) profundamente; (*beat*) completamente; ~**proof** *a* insonorizado; ~**track** *n* (*of film*) banda sonora.

soup [su:p] *n* (*thick*) sopa; (*thin*) caldo; **in the** ~ (*fig*) en apuros; ~**plate** *n* plato sopero; ~**spoon** *n* cuchara sopera.

sour ['sauə*] *a* agrio; (*milk*) cortado; **it's just** ~ **grapes!** (*fig*) ¡están verdes!

source [sɔ:s] *n* fuente *f*.

south [sauθ] *n* sur *m* // *a* del sur // *ad* al sur, hacia el sur; **S~ Africa** *n* África del Sur; **S~ African** *a, n* sudafricano/a; **S~ America** *n* América del Sur, Sudamérica; **S~ American** *a, n* sudamericano/a *m/f*; ~**east** *n* sudeste *m*; ~**erly** ['sʌðəlɪ] *a* sur; (*from the* ~) del sur; ~**ern** ['sʌðən] *a* del sur, meridional; **S~ Pole** *n* Polo Sur; ~**ward(s)** *ad* hacia el sur; ~**west** *n* suroeste *m*.

souvenir [su:və'nɪə*] *n* recuerdo.

sovereign ['sɔvrɪn] *a, n* soberano/a *m/f*.

soviet ['səuvɪət] *a* soviético; **the S~ Union** la Unión Soviética.

sow [sau] *n* cerda, puerca // *vt* ([sou], *pt* **sowed**, *pp* **sown** [səun]) (*gen*) sembrar.

soya ['sɔɪə], (*US*) **soy** [sɔɪ] *n* soja.

spa [spa:] *n* balneario.

space [speɪs] *n* espacio; (*room*) sitio // *vt* (*also*: ~ **out**) espaciar; ~**craft** *n* nave *f* espacial; ~**man/woman** *n* astronauta *m/f*, cosmonauta *m/f*; ~**ship** *n* = ~**craft**; **spacing** *n* espaciamiento.

spacious ['speɪʃəs] *a* amplio.

spade [speɪd] *n* (*tool*) pala, laya; ~**s** *npl* (*CARDS*: *British*) picos *mpl*; (: *Spanish*) espadas *fpl*.

spaghetti [spə'getɪ] *n* espaguetis *mpl*, fideos *mpl*.

Spain [speɪn] *n* España.

span [spæn] *n* (*of bird, plane*) envergadura; (*of hand*) palmo; (*of arch*) luz *f*; (*in time*) lapso // *vt* extenderse sobre, cruzar; (*fig*) abarcar.

Spaniard ['spænjəd] *n* español(a) *m/f*.

spaniel ['spænjəl] *n* perro de aguas.

Spanish ['spænɪʃ] *a* español(a) // *n* (*LING*) español *m*, castellano; **the** ~ *npl* los españoles.

spank [spæŋk] *vt* zurrar.

spanner ['spænə*] *n* (*Brit*) llave *f* (inglesa).

spar [spa:*] *n* palo, verga // *vi* (*BOXING*) entrenarse.

spare [spεə*] *a* de reserva; (*surplus*) sobrante, de más // *n* (*part*) pieza de repuesto // *vt* (*do without*) pasarse sin; (*afford to give*) tener de sobra; (*refrain from hurting*) perdonar; (*details etc*) ahorrar; **to** ~ (*surplus*) sobrante, de sobra; ~ **part** *n* pieza de repuesto; ~ **time** *n* tiempo libre; ~ **wheel** *n* (*AUT*) rueda de recambio.

sparing ['spεərɪŋ] *a*: **to be** ~ **with** ser parco en *f*; ~**ly** *ad* poco; con moderación.

spark [spa:k] *n* chispa; ~ **plug**, (*Brit*) ~**ing plug** *n* bujía.

sparkle ['spa:kl] *n* centelleo, destello // *vi* centellear; (*shine*) relucir, brillar; **sparkling** *a* centelleante; (*wine*) espumoso.

sparrow ['spærəu] *n* gorrión *m*.

sparse [spa:s] *a* esparcido, escaso.

spartan ['spa:tən] *a* (*fig*) espartano.

spasm ['spæzəm] *n* (*MED*) espasmo; (*fig*) arranque *m*, ataque *m*.

spastic ['spæstɪk] n espástico/a.

spat [spæt] pt, pp of **spit**.

spate [speɪt] n (fig): ~ of torrente m de; **in** ~ (river) crecido.

spatter ['spætə*] vt: **to** ~ **with** salpicar de.

spawn [spɔːn] vi desovar, frezar // n huevas fpl.

speak [spiːk], pt **spoke**, pp **spoken** vt (language) hablar; (truth) decir // vi hablar; (make a speech) intervenir; **to** ~ **to sb/of** or **about sth** hablar con uno/de or sobre algo; ~ **up!** ¡habla fuerte!; ~**er** n (in public) orador(a) m/f; (also: **loud**~**er**) altavoz m; (for stereo etc) bafle m; (POL): **the S**~**er** (Brit) el Presidente de la Cámara de los Comunes; (US) el Presidente del Congreso.

spear [spɪə*] n lanza; (for fishing) arpón m // vt alancear; arponear; ~**head** vt (attack etc) encabezar.

spec [spek] n (col): **on** ~ como especulación.

special ['spɛʃl] a especial; (edition etc) extraordinario; (delivery) urgente; ~**ist** n especialista m/f; ~**ity** [spɛʃɪˈælɪtɪ] n (Brit) especialidad f; ~**ize** vi: **to** ~**ize** (**in**) especializarse en; ~**ly** ad sobre todo, en particular; ~**ty** n (US) = ~**ity**.

species ['spiːʃiːz] n especie f.

specific [spəˈsɪfɪk] a específico; ~**ally** ad específicamente.

specify ['spɛsɪfaɪ] vt, vi especificar, precisar.

specimen ['spɛsɪmən] n ejemplar m; (MED: of urine) espécimen m (: of blood) muestra.

speck [spɛk] n grano, mota.

speckled ['spɛkld] n a moteado.

specs [spɛks] npl (col) gafas fpl (Sp), anteojos mpl.

spectacle ['spɛktəkl] n espectáculo; ~**s** npl (Brit) gafas fpl (Sp), anteojos mpl; **spectacular** [-ˈtækjulə*] a espectacular; (success) impresionante.

spectator [spɛkˈteɪtə*] n espectador(a) m/f.

spectre, (US) **specter** ['spɛktə*] n

espectro, fantasma m.

spectrum ['spɛktrəm], pl **-tra** [-trə] n espectro.

speculation [spɛkjuˈleɪʃən] n especulación f.

speech [spiːtʃ] n (faculty) habla; (formal talk) discurso; (words) palabras fpl; (manner of speaking) forma de hablar; lenguaje m; ~**less** a mudo, estupefacto.

speed [spiːd] n velocidad f; (haste) prisa; (promptness) rapidez f; **at full** or **top** ~ a máxima velocidad; **to** ~ **up** vi acelerarse // vt acelerar; ~**boat** n lancha motora; ~**ily** ad rápido, rápidamente; ~**ing** n (AUT) exceso de velocidad; ~**limit** n límite m de velocidad, velocidad f máxima; ~**ometer** [spɪˈdɒmɪtə*] n velocímetro; ~**way** n (SPORT) pista de carrera; ~**y** a (fast) veloz, rápido; (prompt) pronto.

spell [spɛl] n (also: **magic** ~) encanto, hechizo; (period of time) rato, período; (turn) turno // vt (pt, pp **spelt** (Brit) or **spelled** (also: ~ **out**) deletrear; (fig) anunciar, presagiar; **to cast a** ~ **on sb** hechizar a uno; **he can't** ~ no sabe escribir bien, sabe poco de ortografía; ~**bound** a embelesado, hechizado; ~**ing** n ortografía.

spend [spɛnd], pt, pp **spent** [spɛnt] vt (money) gastar; (time) pasar; (life) dedicar; ~**thrift** n derrochador(a) m/f, pródigo/a.

sperm [spɜːm] n esperma.

spew [spjuː] vt vomitar, arrojar.

sphere [sfɪə*] n esfera.

spice [spaɪs] n especia.

spick-and-span ['spɪkən'spæn] a aseado, (bien) arreglado.

spider ['spaɪdə*] n araña.

spike [spaɪk] n (point) punta; (ZOOL) pincho, púa; (BOT) espiga.

spill [spɪl], pt, pp **spilt** or **spilled** vt derramar, verter // vi derramarse; **to** ~ **over** desbordarse.

spin [spɪn] n (revolution of wheel) vuelta, revolución f; (AVIAT) barre-

na; *(trip in car)* paseo (en coche) //
vb (pt, pp **spun**) *vt* (wool etc) hilar;
(wheel) girar // *vi* girar, dar vueltas;
to ~ out *vt* alargar, prolongar.

spinach ['spɪnɪtʃ] *n* espinaca; *(as
food)* espinacas *fpl*.

spinal ['spaɪnl] *a* espinal; **~ cord** *n*
columna vertebral.

spindly ['spɪndlɪ] *a* (leg) zanquivano.

spin-dryer [spɪn'draɪə*] *n* (Brit) secador *m* centrifugo.

spine [spaɪn] *n* espinazo, columna
vertebral; *(thorn)* espina.

spinning ['spɪnɪŋ] *n* (of thread) hila-
do; *(art)* hilandería; **~ top** *n* peonza; **~ wheel** *n* rueca, torno de hilar.

spin-off ['spɪnɔf] *n* derivado, producto secundario.

spinster ['spɪnstə*] *n* soltera.

spiral ['spaɪərl] *n* espiral // *a* en espiral; **~ staircase** *n* escalera de caracol.

spire ['spaɪə*] *n* aguja, chapitel *m*.

spirit ['spɪrɪt] *n* (soul) alma *f*;
(ghost) fantasma *m*; *(attitude)* espíritu *m*; *(courage)* valor *m*, ánimo;
~s *npl* (drink) alcohol *msg*, bebidas
fpl alcohólicas; **in good ~s** alegre,
de buen ánimo; **~ed** *a* enérgico, vigoroso; **~ level** *n* nivel *m* de aire.

spiritual ['spɪrɪtjuəl] *a* espiritual.

spit [spɪt] *n* (for roasting) asador *m*,
espetón *m* // *vi* (pt, pp **spat**) escupir;
(sound) chisporrotear.

spite [spaɪt] *n* rencor *m*, ojeriza //
vt causar pena, mortificar; **in ~ of** a
pesar de, pese a; **~ful** *a* rencoroso,
malévolo.

spittle ['spɪtl] *n* saliva, baba.

splash [splæʃ] *n* (sound) chapoteo;
(of colour) mancha // *vt* salpicar de //
vi (also: **~ about**) chapotear.

spleen [spliːn] *n* (ANAT) bazo.

splendid ['splendɪd] *a* espléndido.

splint [splɪnt] *n* tablilla.

splinter ['splɪntə*] *n* (of wood) astilla; *(in finger)* espigón *m* // *vi* asti-
llarse, hacer astillas.

split [splɪt] *n* hendedura, raja; *(fig)*
división *f*; *(POL)* escisión *f* // *vb* (pt,

pp **split**) *vt* partir, rajar; *(party)* dividir; *(work, profits)* repartir // *vi*
(divide) dividirse, escindirse; **to ~
up** *vi* (couple) separarse; *(meeting)*
acabarse.

splutter ['splʌtə*] *vi* chisporrotear;
(person) balbucear.

spoil [spɔɪl], pt, pp **spoilt** or **spoiled**
vt (damage) dañar; (ruin) estropear,
echar a perder; (child) mimar, consentir; **~s** *npl* despojo *sg*, botín *msg*;
~ed *a* (US: food: bad) pasado,
malo; (: child) cortado; **~sport** *n*
aguafiestas *m inv*.

spoke [spəʊk] pt of **speak** // *n* rayo,
radio.

spoken ['spəʊkn] pp of **speak**.

spokesman ['spəʊksmən] *n*,
spokeswoman [-wʊmən] *n* vocero
m/f, portavoz *m/f*.

sponge [spʌndʒ] *n* esponja // *vt*
(wash) lavar con esponja // *vi*: **to ~
off** or **on sb** vivir a costa de uno; **~
bag** *n* (Brit) esponjera; **~ cake** *n*
bizcocho.

sponsor ['spɒnsə*] *n* (RADIO, TV)
patrocinador(a) *m/f*; *(for membership)* padrino/madrina; *(COMM)* fia-
dor(a) *m/f* // *vt* patrocinar; apadrinar; *(idea etc)* presentar, promover;
~ship *n* patrocinio.

spontaneous [spɒn'teɪnɪəs] *a* espontáneo.

spooky ['spuːkɪ] *a* espeluznante, horripilante.

spool [spuːl] *n* carrete *m*; *(of sewing
machine)* canilla.

spoon [spuːn] *n* cuchara; **~-feed** *vt*
dar de comer con cuchara; *(fig)*
tratar como un niño a; **~ful** *n* cucharada.

sport [spɔːt] *n* deporte *m*; *(person)*:
to be a good ~ ser muy majo;
~ing *a* deportivo; **to give sb a
~ing chance** darle a uno una (buena) oportunidad; **~s car** *n* coche *m*
sport; **~s jacket**, (US) **~ jacket** *n*
chaqueta deportiva; **~sman** *n* deportista *m*; **~smanship** *n* deportivi-
dad *f*; **~swear** *n* trajes *mpl* de de-

porte *or* sport; **~swoman** *n* deportista; **~y** *a* deportivo.

spot [spɔt] *n* sitio, lugar *m*; *(dot: on pattern)* punto, mancha; *(pimple)* grano; *(small amount):* **a ~** of un poquito de // *vt (notice)* notar, observar; **on the ~** en el sitio, acto seguido; **~ check** *n* reconocimiento rápido; **~less** *a* perfectamente limpio; **~light** *n* foco, reflector *m*; *(AUT)* faro auxiliar; **~ted** *a (pattern)* de puntos; **~ty** *a (face)* con granos.

spouse [spauz] *n* cónyuge *m/f*.

spout [spaut] *n (of jug)* pico; *(pipe)* caño // *vi* chorrear.

sprain [sprein] *n* torcedura // *vt:* to **~ one's ankle** torcerse el tobillo.

sprang [spræŋ] *pt of* **spring.**

sprawl [sprɔːl] *vi* tumbarse.

spray [sprei] *n* rociada; *(of sea)* espuma; *(container)* atomizador *m*; *(of paint)* pistola rociadora; *(of flowers)* ramita // *vt* rociar; *(crops)* regar.

spread [spred] *n* extensión *f*; *(of idea)* diseminación *f*; *(food)* pasta para untar // *vb (pt, pp spread) vt* extender; *(butter)* untar; *(wings, sails)* desplegar; *(scatter)* esparcir // *vi* diseminarse; diseminarse; untarse; desplegarse; esparcirse; **~-eagled** *a* a pata tendida; **~sheet** *n (COMPUT)* hoja electrónica *or* de cálculo.

spree [spriː] *n*: **to go on a ~** ir de juerga.

sprightly [ˈspraitli] *a* vivo, enérgico.

spring [spriŋ] *n (season)* primavera; *(leap)* salto, brinco; *(coiled metal)* resorte *m*; *(of water)* fuente *f*, manantial *m* // *vi (pt* **sprang**, *pp* **sprung)** *(arise)* brotar, nacer; *(leap)* saltar, brincar; **to ~ up** *vi (problem)* surgir; **~board** *n* trampolín *m*; **~-clean** *n (also: ~cleaning)* limpieza general; **~time** *n* primavera; **~y** *a* elástico; *(grass)* muelle.

sprinkle [ˈsprinkl] *vt (pour)* rociar; **to ~ water etc on,** **~ with water etc** rociar *or* salpicar de agua *etc*; **~r** *n (for lawn)* rociadera; *(to put*

out fire) aparato de rociadura automática.

sprint [sprint] *n* esprint *m* // *vi* esprintar.

sprout [spraut] *vi* brotar, retoñar; **(Brussels) ~s** *npl* coles *fpl* de Bruselas.

spruce [spruːs] *n (BOT)* picea // *a* aseado, pulcro.

sprung [sprʌŋ] *pp of* **spring.**

spry [sprai] *a* ágil, activo.

spun [spʌn] *pt, pp of* **spin.**

spur [spəː] *n* espuela; *(fig)* estímulo, aguijón *m* // *vt (also:* **~ on)** estimular, incitar; **on the ~ of the moment** de improviso.

spurious [ˈspjuəriəs] *a* falso.

spurn [spəːn] *vt* desdeñar, rechazar.

spurt [spəːt] *n* chorro; *(of energy)* arrebato // *vi* chorrear.

spy [spai] *n* espía *m/f* // *vi*: **to ~ on** espiar // *vt (see)* divisar, lograr ver; **~ing** *n* espionaje *m*.

sq. *abbr* = **square.**

squabble [ˈskwɔbl] *vi* reñir, pelear.

squad [skwɔd] *n (MIL)* pelotón *m*; *(POLICE)* brigada; *(SPORT)* equipo.

squadron [ˈskwɔdrən] *n (MIL)* escuadrón *m*; *(AVIAT, NAUT)* escuadra.

squalid [ˈskwɔlid] *a* vil, miserable.

squall [skwɔːl] *n (storm)* chubasco; *(wind)* ráfaga.

squalor [ˈskwɔlə*] *n* miseria.

squander [ˈskwɔndə*] *vt (money)* derrochar, despilfarrar; *(chances)* desperdiciar.

square [skwɛə*] *n* cuadro; *(in town)* plaza // *a* cuadrado; *(col: ideas, tastes)* trasnochado // *a (arrange)* arreglar; *(MATH)* cuadrar // *vi* cuadrar, conformarse; **a ~** igual(es); **to have a ~ meal** comer caliente; **2 metres ~** 2 metros en cuadro; **~ly** *ad (fully)* de lleno.

squash [skwɔʃ] *n (Brit: drink):* lemon/orange **~** zumo *(Sp)* or jugo *(LAm)* de limón/naranja; *(SPORT)* squash *m*, frontenis *m* // *vt* aplastar.

squat [skwɔt] *a* achaparrado // *vi*

agacharse, sentarse en cuclillas; ~**ter** n persona que ocupa ilegalmente una casa.

squawk [skwɔːk] vi graznar.

squeak [skwiːk] vi (hinge, wheel) chirriar, rechinar; (shoe, wood) crujir.

squeal [skwiːl] vi chillar, dar gritos agudos.

squeamish ['skwiːmɪʃ] a delicado, remilgado.

squeeze [skwiːz] n presión f; (of hand) apretón m; (COMM) restricción f // vt (lemon etc) exprimir; (hand, arm) apretar; **to ~ out** vt exprimir; (fig) excluir.

squelch [skweltʃ] vi chapotear.

squid [skwɪd] n calamar m.

squiggle ['skwɪgl] n garabato.

squint [skwɪnt] vi bizquear, ser bizco // n (MED) estrabismo; **to ~ at** sth mirar algo de soslayo.

squire ['skwaɪə*] n (Brit) terrateniente m.

squirm [skwɜːm] vi retorcerse, revolverse.

squirrel ['skwɪrəl] n ardilla.

squirt [skwɜːt] vi salir a chorros.

Sr abbr = **senior**.

St abbr = **saint; street**.

stab [stæb] n (of pain) pinchazo; **to have a ~ at** (doing) sth (col) intentar (hacer) algo // vt apuñalar.

stable ['steɪbl] a estable // n cuadra, caballeriza.

stack [stæk] n montón m, pila // vt amontonar, apilar.

stadium ['steɪdɪəm] n estadio.

staff [stɑːf] n (work force) personal m, plantilla; (Brit SCOL) cuerpo docente; (stick) bastón m // vt proveer de personal.

stag [stæg] n ciervo, venado.

stage [steɪdʒ] n escena; (point) etapa; (platform) plataforma; **the ~** el escenario, el teatro // vt (play) poner en escena, representar; (organize) montar, organizar; (fig: perform: recovery etc) efectuar; **in ~s** por etapas; **~coach** n diligencia; **~ door**

n entrada de artistas; **~ manager** n director(a) m/f de escena.

stagger ['stægə*] vi tambalear // vt (amaze) asombrar; (hours, holidays) escalonar.

stagnant ['stægnənt] a estancado.

stagnate [stæg'neɪt] vi estancarse.

stag night, stag party n despedida de soltero.

staid [steɪd] a (clothes) serio, formal.

stain [steɪn] n mancha; (colouring) tintura // vt manchar; (wood) teñir; **~ed glass window** n vidriera de colores; **~less** a (steel) inoxidable; **~ remover** n quitamanchas m inv.

stair [stɛə*] n (step) peldaño, escalón m; **~s** npl escaleras fpl; **~case, ~way** n escalera.

stake [steɪk] n estaca, poste m; (BETTING) apuesta // vt apostar; **to be at ~** estar en juego.

stale [steɪl] a (bread) duro; (food) pasado.

stalemate ['steɪlmeɪt] n tablas fpl (por ahogado); n tablas ~ (fig) estancarse.

stalk [stɔːk] n tallo, caña // vt acechar, cazar al acecho; **to ~ off** irse airado.

stall [stɔːl] n (in market) puesto; (in stable) casilla (de establo) // n (AUT) parar // vi (AUT) pararse; (fig) buscar evasivas; **~s** npl (Brit: in cinema, theatre) butacas fpl.

stallion ['stælɪən] n semental m.

stalwart ['stɔːlwət] n partidario/a incondicional.

stamina ['stæmɪnə] n resistencia.

stammer ['stæmə*] n tartamudeo // vi tartamudear.

stamp [stæmp] n sello, estampilla (LAm); (mark, also fig) marca, huella; (on document) timbre m // vi (also: **~ one's foot**) patear, golpear con el pie; (letter) poner con sello; (with rubber ~) marcar con sello; **~ album** n álbum m para sellos; **~ collecting** n filatelia.

stampede [stæm'piːd] n estampida.

stance [stæns] n postura.

stand [stænd] n (attitude) posición f, postura; (for taxis) parada; (SPORT) tribuna; (at exhibition) stand m // vb (pt, pp stood) vi (be) estar, encontrarse; (be on foot) estar de pie; (rise) levantarse; (remain) quedar en pie // vt (place) poner, colocar; (tolerate, withstand) aguantar, soportar; to make a ~ resistir; (fig) mantener una postura firme; to ~ for parliament (Brit) presentarse (como candidato) a las elecciones; to ~ by vi (be ready) estar listo // vt fus (opinion) aferrarse a; to ~ down vi (withdraw) ceder el puesto; to ~ for vt fus (signify) significar; (tolerate) aguantar, permitir; to ~ in for vt fus suplir a; to ~ out vi (be prominent) destacarse; to ~ up vi (rise) levantarse, ponerse de pie; to ~ up for vt fus defender; to ~ up to vt fus hacer frente a.

standard ['stændəd] n patrón m, norma; (flag) estandarte m // a (size etc) normal, corriente, estándar; ~s npl (morals) valores mpl morales; ~ lamp n (Brit) lámpara de pie; ~ of living n nivel m de vida.

stand-by ['stændbaɪ] n (alert) alerta, aviso; to be on ~ estar sobre aviso; ~ ticket n (AVIAT) (billete m) standby m.

stand-in ['stændɪn] n suplente m/f; (CINEMA) doble m/f.

standing ['stændɪŋ] a (upright) derecho; (on foot) de pie, en pie // n reputación f; (of many years' ~ que lleva muchos años; ~ order n (Brit: at bank) orden f de pago permanente; ~ orders npl (MIL) reglamento sg general; ~ room n sitio para estar de pie.

stand: ~-offish a reservado, poco afable; ~ point n punto de vista; ~still n: at a ~still (industry, traffic) paralizado; (car) parado; to come to a ~still quedar paralizado; pararse.

stank [stæŋk] pt of **stink**.

staple ['steɪpl] n (for papers) grapa // a (food etc) básico // vt engrapar; ~r n grapadora.

star [stɑ:*] n estrella; (celebrity) estrella, astro // vi: to ~ in ser la estrella o el astro de.

starboard ['stɑ:bəd] n estribor m.

starch [stɑ:tʃ] n almidón m.

stardom ['stɑ:dəm] n estrellato.

stare [stɛə*] n mirada fija // vi: to ~ at mirar fijo.

starfish ['stɑ:fɪʃ] n estrella de mar.

stark [stɑ:k] a (bleak) severo, escueto // ad: ~ naked en cueros.

starling ['stɑ:lɪŋ] n estornino.

starry ['stɑ:rɪ] a estrellado; ~-eyed a (innocent) inocentón/ona, ingenuo.

start [stɑ:t] n (beginning) principio, comienzo; (of race) salida; (sudden movement) salto, sobresalto // vt empezar, comenzar; (cause) causar; (found) fundar; (engine) poner en marcha // vi (begin) comenzar, empezar; (with fright) asustarse, sobresaltarse; (train etc) salir; to ~ doing or to do sth empezar a hacer algo; to ~ off vi empezar, comenzar; (leave) salir, ponerse en camino; to ~ up vi comenzar; (car) ponerse en marcha // vt comenzar; (car) poner en marcha; ~er n (AUT) botón m de arranque; (SPORT: official) juez m/f de salida; (: runner) corredor(a) m/f; (Brit CULIN) entrada; ~ing point n punto de partida.

startle ['stɑ:tl] vt asustar, sobrecoger; **startling** a alarmante.

starvation [stɑ:'veɪʃən] n hambre f.

starve [stɑ:v] vi pasar hambre; to ~ to death morir de hambre // vt hacer pasar hambre; (fig) privar de; I'm starving estoy muerto de hambre.

state [steɪt] n estado // vt (say, declare) afirmar; (a case) presentar, exponer; to be in a ~ estar agitado; the S~s los Estados Unidos; ~ly a majestuoso, imponente; ~ment n afirmación f; (LAW) declaración f; ~sman n estadista m.

static ['stætɪk] n (RADIO) parásitos mpl // a estático; ~ **electricity** n estática.

station ['steɪʃən] n (gen) estación f; (RADIO) emisora; (rank) posición f social // vt colocar, situar; (MIL) apostar.

stationary ['steɪʃnərɪ] a estacionario, fijo.

stationer ['steɪʃənə*] n papelero/a; ~'**s (shop)** n (Brit) papelería; ~**y** [-nərɪ] n papel m de escribir, artículos mpl de escritorio.

station master n (RAIL) jefe m de estación.

station wagon n (US) furgoneta.

statistic [stə'tɪstɪk] n estadística; ~**s** n (science) estadística; ~**al** a estadístico.

statue ['stætjuː] n estatua.

status ['steɪtəs] n estado; (reputation) estatus m; ~ **symbol** n símbolo de prestigio.

statute ['stætjuːt] n estatuto, ley f; **statutory** a estatutario.

staunch [stɔːntʃ] a leal, incondicional.

stave [steɪv] vt: **to ~ off** (attack) rechazar; (threat) evitar.

stay [steɪ] n (period of time) estancia // vi (remain) quedar(se); (as guest) hospedarse; **to ~ put** seguir en el mismo sitio; **to ~ the night/5 days** pasar la noche/estar 5 días; **to ~ behind** vi quedar atrás; **to ~ in** vi (at home) quedarse en casa; **to ~ on** vi quedarse; **to ~ out** vi (of house) no volver a casa; **to ~ up** vi (at night) no acostarse; ~**ing power** n aguante m.

stead [sted] n: **in sb's ~** en lugar de uno; **to stand sb in good ~** ser muy útil a uno.

steadfast ['stedfɑːst] a firme, resuelto.

steadily ['stedɪlɪ] ad (improve, grow) constantemente; (work) sin parar; (gaze) fijamente.

steady ['stedɪ] a (fixed) firme, fijo; (regular) regular; (person, charac-

ter) sensato, juicioso // vt (hold) mantener firme; (stabilize) estabilizar; (nerves) calmar; **to ~ o.s. on** or **against sth** afirmarse en algo.

steak [steɪk] n (gen) filete m; (beef) bistec m.

steal [stiːl], pt **stole**, pp **stolen** vt, vi robar.

stealth [stelθ] n: **by ~** a escondidas, sigilosamente; ~**y** a cauteloso, sigiloso.

steam [stiːm] n vapor m; (mist) vaho, humo // vt (CULIN) cocer al vapor // vi echar vapor; (ship): **to ~ along** avanzar, ir avanzando; **to ~ up** vt empañar; ~ **engine** n máquina de vapor; ~**er** n (buque m de vapor m; ~**roller** n apisonadora; ~**ship** n = ~**er**; ~**y** a (room) lleno de vapor; (window) empañado.

steel [stiːl] n acero // cpd de acero; ~**works** n acería.

steep [stiːp] a escarpado, abrupto; (stair) empinado; (price) exorbitante, excesivo // vt empapar, remojar.

steeple ['stiːpl] n aguja.

steer [stɪə*] vt (car) conducir (Sp), manejar (LAm); (person) dirigir // vi conducir; ~**ing** n (AUT) dirección f; ~**ing wheel** n volante m.

stem [stem] n (of plant) tallo; (of glass) pie m; (of pipe) cañón m // vt detener; (blood) restañar; **to ~ from** vt fus ser consecuencia de.

stench [stentʃ] n hedor m.

stencil ['stensl] n (typed) cliché m, clisé m; (lettering) plantilla // vt hacer un cliché de.

stenographer [ste'nɔgrəfə*] n (US) taquígrafo/a.

step [step] n paso; (sound) paso, pisada; (on stair) peldaño, escalón m // vi: **to ~ forward** dar un paso adelante; ~**s** npl (Brit) = **ladder**; **to be in/out of ~ with** estar acorde con/estar en disonancia con; **to ~ down** vi (fig) retirarse; **to ~ off** vt fus bajar de; **to ~ up** vt (increase) aumentar; ~**brother** n hermanastro; ~**daughter** n hijastra;

~**father** n padrastro; ~**ladder** n escalera doble or de tijera; ~**mother** n madrastra; ~**ping stone** n pasadera; (fig) trampolín m; ~**sister** n hermanastra; ~**son** n hijastro.

stereo ['stɛrɪəu] n estéreo // a (also: ~**phonic**) estéreo, estereofónico.

sterile ['stɛraɪl] a estéril; **sterilize** ['stɛrɪlaɪz] vt esterilizar.

sterling ['stɜ:lɪŋ] a (silver) de ley // n (ECON) (libras fpl) esterlinas fpl; a **pound** ~ una libra esterlina.

stern [stə:n] a severo, austero // n (NAUT) popa.

stethoscope ['stɛθəskəup] n estetoscopio.

stew [stju:] n cocido, estofado, guisado (LAm) // vt estofar, guisar; (fruit) cocer.

steward ['stju:əd] n (Brit: AVIAT, NAUT, RAIL) camarero; ~**ess** n azafata.

stick [stɪk] n palo; (as weapon) porra; (walking ~) bastón m // vb (pt, pp **stuck**) vt (glue) pegar; (col: put) meter; (: tolerate) aguantar, soportar // vi pegarse; (come to a stop) quedarse parado; **to** ~ **sth into** clavar or hincar algo en; **to** ~ **out**, ~ **up** vi sobresalir; **to** ~ **up for** vt fus defender; ~**er** n (label) etiqueta engomada; (with slogan) pegatina; ~**ing plaster** n (Brit) esparadrapo.

stickler ['stɪklə*] n: **to be a** ~ **for** insistir mucho en.

stick-up ['stɪkʌp] n asalto, atraco.

sticky ['stɪkɪ] a pegajoso; (label) engomado; (fig) difícil.

stiff [stɪf] a rígido, tieso; (hard) duro; (difficult) difícil; (person) inflexible; (price) exhorbitante; ~**en** vt hacer más rígido; (limb) entumecer // vi endurecerse; (grow stronger) fortalecerse; ~ **neck** n torticolis m inv; ~**ness** n rigidez f, tiesura.

stifle ['staɪfl] vt ahogar, sofocar; **stifling** a (heat) sofocante, bochornoso.

stigma ['stɪgmə], pl (BOT, MED, REL) ~**ta** [-tə], (fig) ~**s** n estigma

m.

stile [staɪl] n escalera (para pasar una cerca).

stiletto [stɪ'lɛtəu] n (Brit: also: ~ **heel**) tacón m de aguja.

still [stɪl] a inmóvil, quieto // ad (up to this time) todavía; (even) aun; (nonetheless) sin embargo, aun así; ~**born** a nacido muerto; ~ **life** n naturaleza muerta.

stilt [stɪlt] n zanco; (pile) pilar m, soporte m.

stilted ['stɪltɪd] a afectado.

stimulate ['stɪmjuleɪt] vt estimular.

stimulus ['stɪmjuləs], pl -**li** [-laɪ] n estímulo, incentivo.

sting [stɪŋ] n (wound) picadura; (pain) escozor m, picazón f; (organ) aguijón m // vb (pt, pp **stung**) vt picar // vi picar, escocer.

stingy ['stɪndʒɪ] a tacaño.

stink [stɪŋk] n hedor m, tufo // vi (pt **stank**, pp **stunk**) heder, apestar; ~**ing** a hediondo, fétido; (fig: col) horrible.

stint [stɪnt] n tarea, destajo // vi: **to** ~ **on** escatimar; **to do one's** ~ hacer su parte.

stir [stə:*] n (fig: agitation) conmoción f // vt (tea etc) remover; (move) agitar; (fig: emotions) provocar // vi moverse; **to** ~ **up** vt excitar; (trouble) fomentar.

stirrup ['stɪrəp] n estribo.

stitch [stɪtʃ] n (SEWING) puntada; (KNITTING) punto; (MED) punto (de sutura); (pain) punzada // vt coser; (MED) suturar.

stoat [stəut] n armiño.

stock [stɔk] n (COMM: reserves) existencias fpl, stock m; (: selection) surtido; (AGR) ganado, ganadería; (CULIN) caldo; (FINANCE) capital m; (: shares) acciones fpl // a (fig: reply etc) clásico // vt (have in ~) tener existencias de; (supply) proveer, abastecer; ~**s** npl cepo sg; **in** ~ en existencia or almacén; **out of** ~ agotado; **to take** ~ **of** (fig) asesorar, examinar; ~**s and shares** acciones y valores; **to ~ up with** vt fus abastecerse de.

stockbroker ['stɔkbrəʊkə*] n agente m/f o corredor(a) m/f de bolsa.

stock cube n pastilla de caldo.

stock exchange n bolsa.

stocking ['stɔkɪŋ] n media.

stock: ~**holder** n (US) accionista m/f; ~**ist** n (Brit) distribuidor(a) m/f; ~ **market** n bolsa (de valores); ~ **phrase** n cliché m; ~**pile** n reserva // vt acumular, almacenar; ~**taking** n (Brit COMM) inventario.

stocky ['stɔkɪ] a (strong) robusto; (short) achaparrado.

stodgy ['stɔdʒɪ] a indigesto, pesado.

stoke [stəʊk] vt atizar.

stole [stəʊl] pt of **steal** // n estola.

stolen ['stəʊln] pp of **steal**.

stolid ['stɔlɪd] a (person) imperturbable, impasible.

stomach ['stʌmək] n (ANAT) estómago; (abdomen) vientre m // vt tragar, aguantar; ~ **ache** n dolor m de estómago.

stone [stəʊn] n piedra; (in fruit) hueso; (Brit: weight) = 6.348kg; 14 pounds // cpd de piedra // vt apedrear; ~**cold** a helado; ~**deaf** a sordo como una tapia; ~**work** n (art) cantería.

stood [stud] pt, pp of **stand**.

stool [stu:l] n taburete m.

stoop [stu:p] vi (also: **have a ~**) ser cargado de espaldas.

stop [stɔp] n parada, alto; (in punctuation) punto // vt parar, detener; (break off) suspender; (block) tapar, cerrar; (also: **put a ~ to**) poner término a // vi pararse, detenerse; (end) acabarse; **to ~ doing sth** dejar de hacer algo; **to ~ dead** pararse en seco; **to ~ off** vi interrumpir el viaje; **to ~ up** vt (hole) tapar; ~**gap** n (person) interino/a; ~**lights** npl (AUT) luces fpl de parada; ~**over** n parada; (AVIAT) rescala.

stoppage ['stɔpɪdʒ] n (strike) paro; (temporary stop) interrupción f; (of pay) suspensión f; (blockage) obstrucción f.

stopper ['stɔpə*] n tapón m.

stop press n noticias fpl de última hora.

stopwatch ['stɔpwɔtʃ] n cronómetro.

storage ['stɔ:rɪdʒ] n almacenaje m; (COMPUT) almacenamiento; ~ **heater** n acumulador m.

store [stɔ:*] n (stock) provisión f; (depot; Brit: large shop) almacén m; (US) tienda; (reserve) reserva, repuesto // vt almacenar; (keep) guardar; ~**s** npl víveres mpl; **to ~ up** vt acumular; ~**keeper** n (US) tendero/a; ~**room** n despensa.

storey, (US) **story** ['stɔ:rɪ] n piso.

stork [stɔ:k] n cigüeña.

storm [stɔ:m] n tormenta; (wind) vendaval m // vi rabiar // vt tomar por asalto; ~**y** a tempestuoso.

story ['stɔ:rɪ] n historia; (joke) cuento, chiste m; (US) = **storey;** ~**book** n libro de cuentos; ~**teller** n cuentista m/f.

stout [staʊt] a (strong) sólido; (fat) gordo, corpulento // n cerveza negra.

stove [stəʊv] n (for cooking) cocina; (for heating) estufa.

stow [stəʊ] vt meter, poner; (NAUT) estibar; ~**away** n polizón/ona m/f.

straddle ['strædl] vt montar a horcajadas.

straggle ['strægl] vi (lag behind) rezagarse; ~**r** n rezagado.

straight [streɪt] a recto, derecho; (frank) franco, directo // ad derecho, directamente; (drink) sin mezcla; **to put** o **get sth ~** dejar algo en claro; ~ **away,** ~ **off** (at once) en seguida; ~**en** vt (also: ~**en out**) enderezar, poner derecho; ~**faced** a serio; ~**forward** a (simple) sencillo; (honest) honrado, franco.

strain [streɪn] n (gen) tensión f; (MED) torcedura // vt (back etc) torcerse; (tire) cansar; (stretch) estirar; (filter) filtrar // vi esforzarse; ~**s** npl (MUS) son m; ~**ed** a (muscle) torcido; (laugh) forzado; (relations) tenso; ~**er** n colador m.

strait [streɪt] n (GEO) estrecho; ~-**jacket** n camisa de fuerza; ~-**laced** a mojigato, gazmoño.

strand [strænd] n (of thread) hebra; (of hair) trenza; ~**ed** a (person: without money) desamparado/a; (: transport) colgado.

strange [streɪndʒ] a (not known) desconocido; (odd) extraño, raro; ~**r** n desconocido/a; (from another area) forastero/a.

strangle ['stræŋgl] vt estrangular; ~**hold** n (fig): to have a ~**hold** on sth dominar algo completamente.

strap [stræp] n correa; (of slip, dress) tirante m // vt atar con correa.

strapping ['stræpɪŋ] a robusto, fornido.

stratagem ['strætɪdʒəm] n estratagema.

strategic [strə'tiːdʒɪk] a estratégico.

strategy ['strætɪdʒɪ] n estrategia.

straw [strɔː] n paja; (drinking ~) caña, pajita; **that's the last ~!** ¡eso es el colmo!

strawberry ['strɔːbərɪ] n fresa, frutilla (LAm).

stray [streɪ] a (animal) extraviado; (bullet) perdido // vi extraviarse, perderse.

streak [striːk] n raya; (fig: of madness etc) vena // vt rayar // vi: to ~ past pasar como un rayo.

stream [striːm] n riachuelo, arroyo; (jet) chorro; (flow) corriente f; (of people) oleada // vt (SCOL) dividir en grupos por habilidad // vi correr, fluir; to ~ in/out (people) entrar/salir en tropel.

streamer ['striːmə*] n serpentina.

streamlined ['striːmlaɪnd] a aerodinámico; (fig) racionalizado.

street [striːt] n calle f // cpd callejero; ~**car** n (US) tranvía m; ~ **lamp** n farol m; ~ **plan** n plano; ~**wise** a (col) que tiene mucha calle.

strength [streŋθ] n fuerza; (of girder, knot etc) resistencia; ~**en** vt fortalecer, reforzar.

strenuous ['strenjuəs] a (tough) arduo; (energetic) enérgico.

stress [stres] n (force, pressure) presión f; (mental strain) estrés m; (accent) acento; (TECH) tensión f, carga // vt subrayar, recalcar.

stretch [stretʃ] n (of sand etc) trecho; (of road) tramo // vi estirarse // vt extender, estirar; (make demands of) exigir el máximo esfuerzo a; to ~ to or as far as extenderse hasta; to ~ out vi tenderse // vt (arm etc) extender; (spread) estirar.

stretcher ['stretʃə*] n camilla.

strewn [struːn] a: ~ **with** cubierto or sembrado de.

stricken ['strɪkən] a (person) herido; (city, industry etc) condenado; ~ **with** (disease) afligido por.

strict [strɪkt] a estricto; ~**ly** ad estrictamente; (totally) terminantemente.

stride [straɪd] n zancada, tranco // vi (pt **strode**, pp **stridden** ['strɪdn]) dar zancadas, andar a trancos.

strident ['straɪdnt] a estridente; (colour) chillón/ona.

strife [straɪf] n lucha.

strike [straɪk] n huelga; (of oil etc) descubrimiento; (attack) ataque m; (SPORT) golpe m // vb (pt, pp **struck**) vt golpear, pegar; (oil etc) descubrir; (obstacle) topar con // vi declarar la huelga; (attack) atacar; (clock) dar la hora; on ~ (workers) en huelga; to ~ **a match** encender un fósforo; to ~ **down** vt derribar; to ~ **out** vt borrar, tachar; to ~ **up** vt (MUS) empezar a tocar; (conversation) entablar; (friendship) trabar; ~**r** n huelguista m/f; (SPORT) delantero; **striking** a llamativo; (obvious: resemblance) notorio.

string [strɪŋ] n (gen) cuerda; (row) hilera // vt (pt, pp **strung**) to ~ together ensartar; to ~ **out** extenderse; the ~**s** npl (MUS) los instrumentos de cuerda; to **pull** ~**s** (fig) mover palancas; ~ **bean** n judía verde, habichuela; ~(**ed**) **instrument** n

(*MUS*) instrumento de cuerda.

stringent ['strɪndʒənt] *a* riguroso, severo.

strip [strɪp] *n* tira; (*of land*) franja; (*of metal*) cinta, lámina // *vt* desnudar; (*also: ~ down: machine*) desmontar // *vi* desnudarse; **~ cartoon** *n* tira cómica, historieta (*LAm*).

stripe [straɪp] *n* raya; (*MIL*) galón *m*; **~d** *a* a rayas, rayado.

strip lighting *n* alumbrado fluorescente.

stripper ['strɪpə*] *n* artista *m/f* de striptease.

strive [straɪv], *pt* **strove**, *pp* **striven** ['strɪvn] *vi*: **~ to do** sth esforzarse or luchar por hacer algo.

strode [strəud] *pt of* **stride**.

stroke [strəuk] *n* (*blow*) golpe *m*; (*MED*) apoplejía; (*caress*) caricia // *vt* acariciar; **at a ~** de un solo golpe.

stroll [strəul] *n* paseo, vuelta // *vi* dar un paseo *or* una vuelta; **~er** *n* (*US: for child*) sillita de ruedas.

strong [strɔŋ] *a* fuerte; **they are 50 ~** son 50; **~hold** *n* fortaleza; (*fig*) baluarte *m*; **~ly** *ad* fuertemente, con fuerza; (*believe*) firmemente; **~room** *n* cámara acorazada.

strove [strəuv] *pt of* **strive**.

struck [strʌk] *pt*, *pp of* **strike**.

structure ['strʌktʃə*] *n* estructura; (*building*) construcción *f*.

struggle ['strʌgl] *n* lucha // *vi* luchar.

strum [strʌm] *vt* (*guitar*) rasguear.

strung [strʌŋ] *pt*, *pp of* **string**.

strut [strʌt] *n* puntal *m* // *vi* pavonearse.

stub [stʌb] *n* (*of ticket etc*) talón *m*; (*of cigarette*) colilla; **to ~ one's toe** dar con el dedo (del pie) contra algo; **to ~ out** *vt* apagar.

stubble ['stʌbl] *n* rastrojo; (*on chin*) barba (incipiente).

stubborn ['stʌbən] *a* terco, testarudo.

stucco ['stʌkəu] *n* estuco.

stuck [stʌk] *pt*, *pp of* **stick** // *a* (*jam-*

med) atascado; **~-up** *a* engreído, presumido.

stud [stʌd] *n* (*shirt ~*) corchete *m*; (*of boot*) taco; (*of horses*) caballeriza; (*also: ~ horse*) caballo semental // *vt* (*fig*): **~ded with** salpicado de.

student ['stju:dənt] *n* estudiante *m/f* // *cpd* estudiantil; **~ driver** *n* (*US AUT*) aprendiz/a *m/f*.

studio ['stju:dɪəu] *n* estudio; (*artist's*) taller *m*; **~ flat**, (*US*) **~ apartment** *n* estudio.

studious ['stju:dɪəs] *a* estudioso; (*studied*) calculado; **~ly** *ad* (*carefully*) con esmero.

study ['stʌdɪ] *n* estudio // *vt* estudiar; (*examine*) examinar, investigar // *vi* estudiar.

stuff [stʌf] *n* materia; (*cloth*) tela; (*substance*) material *m*, sustancia; (*things, belongings*) cosas *fpl* // *vt* llenar; (*CULIN*) rellenar; (*animals*) disecar; **~ing** *n* relleno; **~y** *a* (*room*) mal ventilado; (*person*) de miras estrechas.

stumble ['stʌmbl] *vi* tropezar, dar un traspié; **to ~ across** (*fig*) tropezar con; **stumbling block** *n* tropiezo, obstáculo.

stump [stʌmp] *n* (*of tree*) tocón *m*; (*of limb*) muñón *m* // *vt*: **to be ~ed for an answer** no saber qué contestar.

stun [stʌn] *vt* dejar sin sentido.

stung [stʌŋ] *pt*, *pp of* **sting**.

stunk [stʌŋk] *pp of* **stink**.

stunning ['stʌnɪŋ] *a* (*news*) pasmoso; (*fabulous*) sensacional.

stunt [stʌnt] *n* (*AVIAT*) vuelo acrobático; (*publicity*) truco publicitario; **~ed** *a* enano, achaparrado; **~man** *n* especialista *m*.

stupefy ['stju:pɪfaɪ] *vt* dejar estupefacto.

stupendous [stju:'pendəs] *a* estupendo, asombroso.

stupid ['stju:pɪd] *a* estúpido, tonto; **~ity** [-'pɪdɪtɪ] *n* estupidez *f*.

sturdy ['stə:dɪ] *a* robusto, fuerte.

stutter ['stʌtə*] *vi* tartamudear.

sty [staɪ] n (for pigs) pocilga.

stye [staɪ] n (MED) orzuelo.

style [staɪl] n estilo; (fashion) moda; **stylish** a elegante, a la moda; **stylist** n (hair stylist) peluquero/a.

stylus ['staɪləs] n (of record player) aguja.

suave [swɑːv] a cortés; (pej) zalamero.

sub... [sʌb] pref sub...; **~conscious** a subconsciente // n subconsciente m; **~contract** vt subcontratar; **~divide** vt subdividir.

subdue [səb'djuː] vt sojuzgar; (passions) dominar; **~d** a (light) tenue; (person) sumiso, manso.

subject ['sʌbdʒɪkt] n súbdito; (SCOL) tema m, materia // vt [səb'dʒɛkt]: **to ~ to** sb to sth someter a uno a algo; **to be ~ to** (law) estar sujeto a; (subj: person) ser propenso a; **~ive** [-'dʒɛktɪv] a subjetivo; **~ matter** n materia; (content) contenido.

subjunctive [səb'dʒʌŋktɪv] a, n subjuntivo.

sublet [sʌb'lɛt] vt subarrendar.

submachine gun ['sʌbmə'ʃiːn-] n metralleta.

submarine [sʌbmə'riːn] n submarino.

submerge [səb'məːdʒ] vt sumergir; (flood) inundar // vi sumergirse.

submissive [səb'mɪsɪv] a sumiso.

submit [səb'mɪt] vt someter // vi someterse.

subnormal [sʌb'nɔːməl] a subnormal.

subordinate [sə'bɔːdɪnət] a, n subordinado/a m/f.

subpoena [səb'piːnə] n (LAW) citación f // vt citar.

subscribe [səb'skraɪb] vi suscribir; **to ~ to** (opinion, fund) suscribir, aprobar; (newspaper) suscribirse a; **~r** (to periodical, telephone) abonado/a.

subscription [səb'skrɪpʃən] n (to club) abono; (to magazine) suscripción f.

subsequent ['sʌbsɪkwənt] a subsiguiente, posterior; **~ly** ad posteriormente, más tarde.

subside [səb'saɪd] vi hundirse; (flood) bajar; (wind) amainar; **~nce** [-'saɪdns] n hundimiento; (in road) socavón m.

subsidiary [səb'sɪdɪərɪ] n sucursal f, filial f.

subsidize ['sʌbsɪdaɪz] vt subvencionar.

subsidy ['sʌbsɪdɪ] n subvención f.

substance ['sʌbstəns] n sustancia; (fig) esencia.

substantial [səb'stænʃl] a sustancial, sustancioso; (fig) importante.

substantiate [səb'stænʃɪeɪt] vt comprobar.

substitute ['sʌbstɪtjuːt] n (person) suplente m/f; (thing) sustituto // vt: **to ~ A for B** sustituir B por A, reemplazar A por B.

subtitle ['sʌbtaɪtl] n subtítulo.

subtle ['sʌtl] a sutil; **~ty** n sutileza.

subtract [səb'trækt] vt restar; sustraer; **~ion** [-'trækʃən] n resta; sustracción f.

suburb ['sʌbəːb] n suburbio; **the ~s** las afueras (de la ciudad); **~an** [sə'bəːbən] a suburbano; (train etc) de cercanías; **~ia** [sə'bəːbɪə] n barrios mpl residenciales.

subway ['sʌbweɪ] n (Brit) paso subterráneo or inferior; (US) metro.

succeed [sək'siːd] vi (person) tener éxito; (plan) salir bien // vt suceder a; **to ~ in doing** lograr hacer; **~ing** a (following) sucesivo.

success [sək'sɛs] n éxito; **~ful** a (venture, person) exitoso; (business) próspero; **to be ~ful (in doing)** lograr (hacer); **~fully** ad con éxito.

succession [sək'sɛʃən] n sucesión f, serie f.

successive [sək'sɛsɪv] a sucesivo, consecutivo.

succinct [sək'sɪŋkt] a sucinto.

such [sʌtʃ] a tal, semejante; (of that kind): **~ a book** tal libro; (so much): **~ courage** tanto valor // ad tan; ~ **a long trip** un viaje tan largo; ~ **a lot of** tanto(s)/a(s); ~ **as** (like) tal como; **a noise** ~ **as** to un ruido tal que; **as** ~ **ad** como tal; ~ **and**~ tal o cual.

suck [sʌk] vt chupar; (bottle) sorber; (breast) mamar; ~**er** n (BOT) serpollo; (ZOOL) ventosa; (col) bobo, primo.

suction ['sʌkʃən] n succión f.

Sudan [su'dæn] n Sudán m.

sudden ['sʌdn] a (rapid) repentino, súbito; (unexpected) imprevisto; **all of a** ~ ad de repente; ~**ly** ad de repente.

suds [sʌdz] npl espuma sg de jabón.

sue [su:] vt demandar.

suede [sweɪd] n ante m, gamuza (LAm).

suet ['suɪt] n sebo.

Suez ['su:ɪz] n: **the** ~ **Canal** el Canal de Suez.

suffer ['sʌfə*] vt sufrir, padecer; (tolerate) aguantar, soportar // vi sufrir; ~**er** n víctima, f; (MED) enfermo/a; ~**ing** n sufrimiento; (pain) dolor m.

suffice [sə'faɪs] vi bastar, ser suficiente.

sufficient [sə'fɪʃənt] a suficiente, bastante; ~**ly** ad suficientemente, bastante.

suffocate ['sʌfəkeɪt] vi ahogarse, asfixiarse.

suffrage ['sʌfrɪdʒ] n sufragio.

suffused [sə'fju:zd] a: ~ **with** bañado de.

sugar ['ʃugə*] n azúcar m // vt echar azúcar a, azucarar; ~ **beet** n remolacha; ~ **cane** n caña de azúcar; ~**y** a azucarado.

suggest [sə'dʒɛst] vt sugerir; (recommend) aconsejar; ~**ion** [-'dʒɛstʃən] n sugerencia.

suicide ['suɪsaɪd] n suicidio; (person) suicida m/f.

suit [su:t] n (man's) traje m; (woman's) conjunto; (LAW) pleito; (CARDS) palo // vt convenir; (clothes) sentar a, ir bien a; (adapt)

to ~ **sth to** adaptar or ajustar algo a; **well** ~**ed** (well matched: couple) hechos el uno para el otro; ~**able** a conveniente; (apt) indicado; ~**ably** ad convenientemente; en forma debida.

suitcase ['su:tkeɪs] n maleta, valija (LAm).

suite [swi:t] n (of rooms, MUS) suite f; (furniture): **bedroom/dining room** ~ (juego de) dormitorio/comedor m.

suitor ['su:tə*] n pretendiente m.

sulfur ['sʌlfə*] n (US) = **sulphur**.

sulk [sʌlk] vi estar de mal humor; ~**y** a malhumorado.

sullen ['sʌlən] a hosco, malhumorado.

sulphur, (US) **sulfur** ['sʌlfə*] n azufre m.

sultana [sʌl'tɑ:nə] n (fruit) pasa de Esmirna.

sultry ['sʌltrɪ] a (weather) bochornoso.

sum [sʌm] n suma; (total) total m; **to** ~ **up** vt resumir // vi hacer un resumen.

summarize ['sʌməraɪz] vt resumir.

summary ['sʌmərɪ] n resumen m // a (justice) sumario.

summer ['sʌmə*] n verano // cpd de verano, ~**house** n (in garden) cenador m, glorieta; ~**time** n (season) verano; ~ **time** n (Brit: by clock) hora de verano.

summit ['sʌmɪt] n cima, cumbre f; ~ **(conference)** n (conferencia) cumbre f.

summon ['sʌmən] vt (person) llamar; (meeting) convocar; (LAW) citar; **to** ~ **up** vt (courage) armarse de; ~**s** n llamamiento, llamada // vt citar, emplazar.

sump [sʌmp] n (Brit AUT) cárter m.

sumptuous ['sʌmptjuəs] a suntuoso.

sun [sʌn] n sol m.

sunbathe ['sʌnbeɪð] vi tomar el sol.

sunburn ['sʌnbə:n] n (painful) quemadura; (tan) bronceado.

Sunday ['sʌndɪ] n domingo; ~

school n catequesis f dominical.

sundial ['sʌndaɪəl] n reloj m de sol.

sundown ['sʌndaun] n anochecer m.

sundry ['sʌndrɪ] a varios/as, diversos/as; **all and ~** todos sin excepción; **sundries** npl géneros mpl diversos.

sunflower ['sʌnflauə*] n girasol m.

sung [sʌŋ] pp of **sing**.

sunglasses ['sʌnglɑ:sɪz] npl gafas fpl or anteojos mpl (LAm) de sol.

sunk [sʌŋk] pp of **sink**.

sun: **~light** n luz f del sol; **~lit** a iluminado por el sol; **~ny** a soleado; (day) de sol; (fig) alegre; **~rise** n salida del sol; **~roof** n (AUT) techo corredizo; **~set** n puesta del sol; **~shade** n (over table) sombrilla; **~shine** n sol m; **~stroke** n insolación f; **~tan** n bronceado; **~tan oil** n aceite m bronceador.

super ['su:pə*] a (col) bárbaro.

superannuation [su:pərænju'eɪʃən] n cuota de jubilación.

superb [su:'pə:b] a magnífico, espléndido.

supercilious [su:pə'sɪlɪəs] a altanero.

superfluous [su'pə:fluəs] a superfluo, de sobra.

superhuman [su:pə'hju:mən] a sobrehumano.

superimpose ['su:pərɪm'pəuz] vt superponer.

superintendent [su:pərɪn'tɛndənt] n director(a) m/f; (police ~) subjefe/a m/f.

superior [su'pɪərɪə*] a superior; (smug) desdeñoso // n superior m; **~ity** [-'ɔrɪtɪ] n superioridad f; desdén m.

superlative [su'pə:lətɪv] a, n superlativo.

superman ['su:pəmæn] n superhombre m.

supermarket ['su:pəmɑ:kɪt] n supermercado.

supernatural [su:pə'nætʃərəl] a sobrenatural.

superpower ['su:pəpauə*] n (POL) superpotencia.

supersede [su:pə'si:d] vt suplantar.

supersonic ['su:pə'sɔnɪk] a supersónico.

superstitious [su:pə'stɪʃəs] a supersticioso.

supertanker ['su:pətæŋkə*] n superpetrolero.

supervise ['su:pəvaɪz] vt supervisar; **supervision** [-'vɪʒən] n supervisión f; **supervisor** n supervisor(a) m/f.

supper ['sʌpə*] n cena; **to have ~** cenar.

supplant [sə'plɑ:nt] vt suplantar.

supple ['sʌpl] a flexible.

supplement ['sʌplɪmənt] n suplemento // a [sʌplɪ'mɛnt] suplir; **~ary** [-'mɛntərɪ] a suplementario.

supplier [sə'plaɪə*] n suministrador(a) m/f; (COMM) distribuidor(a) m/f.

supply [sə'plaɪ] vt (provide) suministrar; (information) facilitar; (equip): **to ~ (with)** proveer (de) // n provisión f; (gas, water etc) suministro // cpd (Brit: teacher etc) suplente; **supplies** npl (food) víveres mpl; (MIL) pertrechos mpl.

support [sə'pɔ:t] n (moral, financial etc) apoyo; (TECH) soporte m // vt apoyar; (financially) mantener; (uphold) sostener; **~er** n (POL etc) partidario/a; (SPORT) aficionado/a.

suppose [sə'pəuz] vt, vi suponer; (imagine) imaginar; **to be ~d to do sth** deber hacer algo; **~dly** [sə'pəuzɪdlɪ] ad según cabe suponer.

supposing conj en caso de que.

suppress [sə'prɛs] vt suprimir; (yawn) ahogar.

supreme [su'pri:m] a supremo.

surcharge ['sə:tʃɑ:dʒ] n sobretasa, recargo.

sure [ʃuə*] a (definite, convinced) cierto; **to make ~ of sth/ that** asegurarse de algo/asegurar que; **~!** (of course) ¡claro!, ¡por supuesto!; **~ enough** efectivamente; **~ly** ad (certainly) seguramente.

surety ['ʃuərətɪ] n fianza; (person)

fiador(a) *m/f*.

surf ['sɜːf] *n* olas *fpl*.

surface ['sɜːfɪs] *n* superficie *f* // *vt* (*road*) revestir // *vi* salir a la superficie; **~ mail** *n* vía terrestre.

surfboard ['sɜːfbɔːd] *n* plancha (de surf).

surfeit ['sɜːfɪt] *n*: **a ~ of** un exceso de.

surfing ['sɜːfɪŋ] *n* surf *m*.

surge [sɜːdʒ] *n* oleada, oleaje *m* // *vi* avanzar a tropel.

surgeon ['sɜːdʒən] *n* cirujano/a.

surgery ['sɜːdʒərɪ] *n* cirugía; (*Brit: room*) consultorio; **to undergo ~** operarse; **~ hours** *npl* (*Brit*) horas *fpl* de consulta.

surgical ['sɜːdʒɪkl] *a* quirúrgico; **~ spirit** *n* (*Brit*) alcohol *m* de 90°.

surly ['sɜːlɪ] *a* hosco, malhumorado.

surmount [sɜː'maunt] *vt* superar, vencer.

surname ['sɜːneɪm] *n* apellido.

surpass [sɜː'pɑːs] *vt* superar, exceder.

surplus ['sɜːpləs] *n* excedente *m*; (*COMM*) superávit *m* // *a* excedente, sobrante.

surprise [sə'praɪz] *n* sorpresa // *vt* sorprender; **surprising** *a* sorprendente; **surprisingly** *ad* (*easy, helpful*) de modo sorprendente.

surrender [sə'rendə*] *n* rendición *f*, entrega // *vi* rendirse, entregarse.

surreptitious [sʌrəp'tɪʃəs] *a* subrepticio.

surrogate ['sʌrəgɪt] *n* sucedáneo; **~ mother** *n* madre *f* portadora.

surround [sə'raund] *vt* rodear, circundar; (*MIL etc*) cercar; **~ing** *a* circundante; **~ings** *npl* alrededores *mpl*, cercanías *fpl*.

surveillance [sɜː'veɪləns] *n* vigilancia.

survey ['sɜːveɪ] *n* inspección *f*, reconocimiento; (*inquiry*) encuesta // *vt* [sɜː'veɪ] examinar, inspeccionar; (*look at*) mirar, contemplar; (*make inquiries about*) hacer una encuesta de; **~or** *n* (*Brit*) agrimensor/a *m/f*.

survival [sə'vaɪvl] *n* supervivencia.

survive [sə'vaɪv] *vi* sobrevivir; (*custom etc*) perdurar // *vt* sobrevivir a; **survivor** *n* superviviente *m/f*.

susceptible [sə'septəbl] *a*: **~ (to)** (*disease*) susceptible (a); (*flattery*) sensible (a).

suspect ['sʌspekt] *a*, *n* sospechoso/a *m/f* // *vt* [səs'pekt] sospechar.

suspend [səs'pend] *vt* suspender; **~ed sentence** *n* (*LAW*) libertad *f* condicional; **~er belt** *n* portaligas *m inv*; **~ers** *npl* (*Brit*) ligas *fpl*; (*US*) tirantes *mpl*.

suspense [səs'pens] *n* incertidumbre *f*, duda; (*in film etc*) suspense *m*.

suspension [səs'penʃən] *n* (*gen, AUT*) suspensión *f*; (*of driving licence*) privación *f*; **~ bridge** *n* puente *m* colgante.

suspicion [səs'pɪʃən] *n* sospecha; (*distrust*) recelo; (*trace*) traza; **suspicious** [-ʃəs] *a* (*suspecting*) receloso; (*causing ~*) sospechoso.

sustain [səs'teɪn] *vt* sostener, apoyar; (*suffer*) sufrir, padecer; **~ed** *a* (*effort*) sostenido.

sustenance ['sʌstɪnəns] *n* sustento.

swab [swɔb] *n* (*MED*) algodón *n*; (*for specimen*) frotis *m inv*.

swagger ['swægə*] *vi* pavonearse.

swallow ['swɔləu] *n* (*bird*) golondrina // *vt* tragar; **to ~ up** *vt* (*savings etc*) consumir.

swam [swæm] *pt* of **swim**.

swamp [swɔmp] *n* pantano, ciénaga // *vt*: **to ~ (with)** abrumar (de), agobiar (de); **~y** *a* pantanoso.

swan [swɔn] *n* cisne *m*.

swap [swɔp] *vt*: **to ~ (for)** canjear (por).

swarm [swɔːm] *n* (*of bees*) enjambre *m*; (*fig*) multitud *f* // *vi*: **to ~ (with)** pulular (de).

swarthy ['swɔːðɪ] *a* moreno.

swastika ['swɔstɪkə] *n* esvástika, cruz *f* gamada.

swat [swɔt] *vt* aplastar.

sway [sweɪ] *vi* mecerse, balancearse // *vt* (*influence*) mover, influir en.

swear [swɛə*], pt **swore**, pp **sworn** vi jurar; **to ~ to** sth declarar algo bajo juramento; **~word** n taco, palabrota.

sweat [swɛt] n sudor m // vi sudar.

sweater ['swɛtə*], **sweatshirt** ['swɛtʃəːt] n suéter m.

sweaty ['swɛtɪ] a sudoroso.

Swede [swiːd] n sueco/a.

swede [swiːd] n (Brit) nabo.

Sweden ['swiːdn] n Suecia.

Swedish ['swiːdɪʃ] a sueco // n (LING) sueco.

sweep [swiːp] n (act) barrido; (of arm) manotazo; (curve) curva, alcance m; (also: **chimney ~**) deshollinador(a) m/f // vb (pt, pp **swept**) vt, vi barrer; **to ~ away** vt barrer; (rub out) borrar; **to ~ past** vi pasar majestuosamente; **to ~ up** vi barrer; **~ing** n (gesture) dramático; (generalized) generalizado.

sweet [swiːt] n (candy) dulce m, caramelo; (Brit: pudding) postre m // a dulce; (sugary) azucarado; (fig) dulce, amable; **~corn** n maíz m; **~en** vt (person) endulzar; (add sugar to) poner azúcar a; **~heart** n novio/a; **~ness** n (gen) dulzura; **~ pea** n guisante m de olor.

swell [swɛl] n (of sea) marejada, oleaje m // a (US: col: excellent) estupendo, fenomenal // vb (pt **swelled**, pp **swollen** or **swelled**) vt hinchar, inflar // vi hincharse, inflarse; **~ing** n (MED) hinchazón f.

sweltering ['swɛltərɪŋ] a sofocante, de mucho calor.

swept [swɛpt] pt, pp of **sweep**.

swerve [swəːv] vi desviarse bruscamente.

swift [swɪft] n (bird) vencejo // a rápido, veloz; **~ly** ad rápidamente.

swig [swɪg] n (col: drink) trago.

swill [swɪl] n bazofia // vt (also: **~ out**, **~ down**) lavar, limpiar con agua.

swim [swɪm] n: **to go for a ~** ir a nadar or a bañarse // vb (pt **swam**, pp **swum**) vi nadar; (head, room)

dar vueltas // vt pasar or cruzar a nado; **~mer** n nadador(a) m/f; **~ming** n natación f; **~ming cap** n gorro de baño; **~ming costume** n bañador m, traje m de baño; **~ming pool** n piscina, alberca (LAm); **~suit** n = **~ming costume**.

swindle ['swɪndl] n estafa // vt estafar.

swine [swaɪn] n, pl inv cerdos mpl, puercos mpl; (col!) canalla sg(!).

swing [swɪŋ] n (in playground) columpio; (movement) balanceo, vaivén m; (change of direction) viraje m; (rhythm) ritmo // vb (pt, pp **swung**) vt balancear; (on a ~) columpiar; (also: **~ round**) voltear, girar // vi balancearse, columpiarse; (also: **~ round**) dar media vuelta; **to be in full ~** estar en plena marcha; **~ bridge** n puente m giratorio; **~ door**, (US) **~ing door** n puerta giratoria.

swingeing ['swɪndʒɪŋ] a (Brit) abrumador(a).

swipe [swaɪp] vt (hit) golpear fuerte; (col: steal) guindar.

swirl [swəːl] vi arremolinarse.

swish [swɪʃ] a (col: smart) elegante // vi chasquear.

Swiss [swɪs] a, n, pl inv suizo/a m/f.

switch [swɪtʃ] n (for light, radio etc) interruptor m; (change) cambio // vt (change) cambiar de; **to ~ off** vt apagar; (engine) parar; **to ~ on** vt encender, prender (LAm); (engine, machine) arrancar; **~board** n (TEL) centralita (de teléfonos), conmutador m (LAm).

Switzerland ['swɪtsələnd] n Suiza.

swivel ['swɪvl] vi (also: **~ round**) girar.

swollen ['swəulən] pp of **swell**.

swoon [swuːn] vi desmayarse.

swoop [swuːp] n (by police etc) redada // vi (also: **~ down**) calarse.

swop [swɔp] = **swap**.

sword [sɔːd] n espada; **~fish** n pez m espada.

swore [swɔː*] pt of **swear**.

sworn [swɔːn] *pp* of **swear**.

swot [swɔt] (*Brit*) *vt*, *vi* empollar.

swum [swʌm] *pp* of **swim**.

swung [swʌŋ] *pt*, *pp* of **swing**.

sycamore ['sɪkəmɔː*] *n* sicómoro.

syllable ['sɪləbl] *n* sílaba.

syllabus ['sɪləbəs] *n* programa *m* de estudios.

symbol ['sɪmbl] *n* símbolo.

symmetry ['sɪmɪtrɪ] *n* simetría.

sympathetic [sɪmpə'θetɪk] *a* compasivo; (*understanding*) comprensivo.

sympathize ['sɪmpəθaɪz] *vi*: to ~ with sb compadecerse de uno; ~r *n* (*POL*) simpatizante *m/f*.

sympathy ['sɪmpəθɪ] *n* (*pity*) compasión *f*; (*understanding*) comprensión *f*; with our deepest ~ nuestro más sentido pésame.

symphony ['sɪmfənɪ] *n* sinfonía.

symposium [sɪm'pəuzɪəm] *n* simposio.

symptom ['sɪmptəm] *n* síntoma *m*, indicio.

synagogue ['sɪnəgɔg] *n* sinagoga.

syndicate ['sɪndɪkɪt] *n* (*gen*) sindicato; (*of newspapers*) agencia (de noticias).

syndrome ['sɪndrəum] *n* síndrome *m*.

synonym ['sɪnənɪm] *n* sinónimo.

synopsis [sɪ'nɔpsɪs], *pl* **-ses** [-siːz] *n* sinopsis *f inv*.

syntax ['sɪntæks] *n* sintaxis *f inv*.

synthesis ['sɪnθəsɪs], *pl* **-ses** [-siːz] *n* síntesis *f inv*.

synthetic [sɪn'θetɪk] *a* sintético.

syphilis ['sɪfɪlɪs] *n* sífilis *f*.

syphon ['saɪfən] = **siphon**.

Syria ['sɪrɪə] *n* Siria; ~n *a*, *n* sirio/a *m/f*.

syringe [sɪ'rɪndʒ] *n* jeringa.

syrup ['sɪrəp] *n* jarabe *m*, almíbar *m*.

system ['sɪstəm] *n* sistema *m*; (*ANAT*) organismo; ~**atic** [-'mætɪk] *a* sistemático; metódico; ~ **disk** *n* (*COMPUT*) disco del sistema; ~**s analyst** *n* analista *m/f* de sistemas.

T

ta [tɑː] *excl* (*Brit col*) ¡gracias!

tab [tæb] *n* lengüeta; (*label*) etiqueta; to keep ~s on (*fig*) vigilar.

tabby ['tæbɪ] *n* (*also:* ~ **cat**) gato atigrado.

table ['teɪbl] *n* mesa; (*of statistics etc*) cuadro, tabla // *vt* (*Brit: motion etc*) presentar; to lay or set the ~ poner la mesa; ~**cloth** *n* mantel *m*; ~ **of contents** *n* índice *m* de materias; ~ **d'hôte** [tɑːbl'dəut] *n* menú *m*; ~ **lamp** *n* lámpara de mesa; ~**mat** *n* salvamantel *m*; ~**spoon** *n* cuchara grande; (*also:* ~**spoonful**: *as measurement*) cucharada.

tablet ['tæblɪt] *n* (*MED*) pastilla, comprimido; (*for writing*) bloc *m*; (*of stone*) lápida.

table tennis *n* ping-pong *m*, tenis *m* de mesa.

table wine *n* vino de mesa.

tabloid ['tæblɔɪd] *n* periódico popular sensacionalista; the ~s la prensa amarilla.

tabulate ['tæbjuleɪt] *vt* disponer en tablas.

tacit ['tæsɪt] *a* tácito.

tack [tæk] *n* (*nail*) tachuela; (*stitch*) hilván *m*; (*NAUT*) bordada // *vt* (*nail*) clavar con tachuelas; (*stitch*) hilvanar // *vi* virar.

tackle ['tækl] *n* (*gear*) equipo; (*fishing* ~, *for lifting*) aparejo; (*RUGBY*) placaje *m* // *vt* (*difficulty*) enfrentar; (*grapple with*) agarrar; (*RUGBY*) placar.

tacky ['tækɪ] *a* pegajoso.

tact [tækt] *n* tacto, discreción *f*; ~**ful** *a* discreto, diplomático.

tactical ['tæktɪkl] *a* táctico.

tactics ['tæktɪks] *n*, *npl* táctica *sg*.

tactless ['tæktlɪs] *a* indiscreto.

tadpole ['tædpəul] *n* renacuajo.

taffy ['tæfɪ] *n* (*US*) melcocha.

tag [tæg] *n* (*label*) etiqueta; to ~ along with sb acompañar a uno.

tail [teɪl] n cola; (of shirt, coat) faldón m // vt (follow) vigilar la; to ~ away, ~ off vi (in size, quality etc) ir disminuyendo; ~**back** n (Brit AUT) cola; ~ **coat** n frac m; ~ **end** n cola, parte f final; ~**gate** n (AUT) puerta trasera.

tailor ['teɪlə*] n sastre m; ~**ing** n (cut) corte m; ~**made** a (also fig) hecho a la medida.

tailwind ['teɪlwɪnd] n viento de cola.

tainted ['teɪntɪd] a (water, air) contaminado; (fig) manchado.

take [teɪk], pt **took**, pp **taken** vt tomar; (grab) coger (Sp), agarrar (LAm); (gain: prize) ganar; (require: effort, courage) exigir; (support weight of) aguantar; (hold: passengers etc) tener cabida para; (accompany, bring, carry) llevar; (exam) presentarse a; to ~ sth from (drawer etc) sacar algo de; (person) coger (Sp) or tomar (LAm) algo a; I ~ it that... supongo que...; to ~ after vt fus parecerse a; to ~ apart vt desmontar; to ~ away vt (remove) quitar; (carry off) llevar; to ~ back vt (return) devolver; (one's words) retractar; to ~ down vt (building) derribar; (letter etc) apuntar; to ~ in vt (Brit: deceive) engañar; (understand) entender; (include) abarcar; (lodger) acoger, recibir; to ~ off vi (AVIAT) despegar // vt (remove) quitar; (imitate) imitar; to ~ on vt (work) aceptar; (employee) contratar; (opponent) desafiar; to ~ out vt sacar; (remove) quitar; to ~ over vt (business) tomar posesión de // vi: to ~ over from sb reemplazar a uno; to ~ to vt fus (person) coger cariño a (Sp), encariñarse con (LAm); (activity) aficionarse a; to ~ up vt (a dress) acortar; (occupy: time, space) ocupar; (engage in: hobby etc) dedicarse a; ~**away** n (Brit: food) para llevar; ~**home pay** n sueldo neto; ~**off** n (AVIAT) despegue m; ~**over** n (COMM) absorción f.

takings ['teɪkɪŋz] npl (COMM) ingresos mpl.

talc [tælk] n (also: ~**um powder**) talco.

tale [teɪl] n (story) cuento m; (account) relación f; to **tell** ~s (fig) chismear.

talent ['tælnt] n talento; ~**ed** a talentoso.

talk [tɔːk] n charla; (gossip) habladurías fpl, (conversation) conversación f // vi (speak) hablar; (chatter) charlar; ~s npl (POL etc) conversaciones fpl; to ~ **about** hablar de; to ~ **sb into doing sth** convencer a uno para que haga algo; to ~ **sb out of doing sth** disuadir a uno de que haga algo; to ~ **shop** hablar del trabajo; to ~ **over** vt discutir; ~**ative** a hablador(a); ~ **show** n programa m magazine.

tall [tɔːl] a alto; (tree) grande; to **be** 6 **feet** ~ ≈ medir 1 metro 80, tener 1 metro 80 de alto; ~**boy** n (Brit) cómoda alta; ~ **story** n cuento chino.

tally ['tælɪ] n cuenta // vi: to ~ (**with**) corresponder (con).

talon ['tælən] n garra.

tambourine [tæmbə'riːn] n pandereta.

tame [teɪm] a (mild) manso; (tamed) domesticado; (fig: story, style) mediocre.

tamper ['tæmpə*] vi: to ~ **with** tocar, andar con.

tampon ['tæmpən] n tampón m.

tan [tæn] n (also: **sun**~) bronceado // vt broncear // vi ponerse moreno // a (colour) marrón.

tang [tæŋ] n sabor m fuerte.

tangent ['tændʒənt] n (MATH) tangente f; to **go off at a** ~ (fig) salirse por la tangente.

tangerine [tændʒə'riːn] n mandarina.

tangle ['tæŋgl] n enredo; to **get in(to) a** ~ enredarse.

tank [tæŋk] n (water ~) depósito, tanque m; (for fish) acuario; (MIL) tanque m.

tanker ['tæŋkə*] n (ship) buque m cisterna; (truck) camión m cisterna.

tanned [tænd] a (skin) moreno, bronceado.

tantalizing ['tæntəlaızıŋ] a tentador(a).

tantamount ['tæntəmaunt] a: ~ to equivalente a.

tantrum ['tæntrəm] n rabieta.

tap [tæp] n (Brit: on sink etc) grifo, canilla (LAm); (gentle blow) golpecito; (gas ~) llave f // vt (table etc) tamborilear; (shoulder etc) palmear; (resources) utilizar, explotar; (telephone) intervenir; **on** ~ (fig: resources) a mano; ~**-dancing** n zapateado.

tape [teɪp] n cinta; (also: magnetic ~) cinta magnética; (sticky ~) cinta adhesiva // vt (record) grabar (en cinta); ~ **measure** n cinta métrica, metro.

taper ['teɪpə*] n cirio // vi afilarse.

tape recorder n grabadora.

tapestry ['tæpıstrı] n (object) tapiz m; (art) tapicería.

tar [tɑ:] n alquitrán m, brea.

target ['tɑ:gɪt] n (gen) blanco; ~ **practice** n tiro al blanco.

tariff ['tærɪf] n tarifa.

tarmac ['tɑ:mæk] n (Brit: on road) alquitranado; (AVIAT) pista (de aterrizaje).

tarnish ['tɑ:nıʃ] vt deslustrar.

tarpaulin [tɑ:'pɔ:lɪn] n alquitranado.

tart [tɑ:t] n (CULIN) tarta; (Brit col: pej: woman) puta // a (flavour) agrio, ácido; **to** ~ **up** vt (room, building) dar tono a.

tartan ['tɑ:tn] n tartán m, escocés m // a de tartán.

tartar ['tɑ:tə*] n (on teeth) sarro; ~(**e**) **sauce** n salsa tártara.

task [tɑ:sk] n tarea; **to take to** ~ reprender; ~ **force** n (MIL, POLICE) grupo de operaciones.

tassel ['tæsl] n borla.

taste [teɪst] n sabor m, gusto; (also: after~) dejo; (sip) sorbo; (fig: glimpse, idea) muestra, idea // vt

probar // vi: **to** ~ **of** or **like** (fish etc) saber a; **you can** ~ **the garlic (in it)** se nota el sabor a ajo; **can I have a** ~ **of this wine?** ¿puedo probar este vino?; **to have a** ~ **for sth** ser aficionado a algo; **in good/bad** ~ de buen/mal gusto; ~**ful** a de buen gusto; ~**less** a (food) soso; (remark) de mal gusto; **tasty** a sabroso, rico.

tatters ['tætəz] npl: **in** ~ (also: tattered) hecho jirones.

tattoo [tə'tu:] n tatuaje m; (spectacle) espectáculo militar // vt tatuar.

tatty ['tætɪ] a (Brit col) raído.

taught [tɔːt] pt, pp **of** teach.

taunt [tɔ:nt] n burla // vt burlarse de.

Taurus ['tɔ:rəs] n Tauro.

taut [tɔ:t] a tirante, tenso.

tawdry ['tɔ:drı] a de mal gusto.

tax [tæks] n impuesto // vt gravar (con un impuesto); (fig: test) poner a prueba (: patience) agotar; ~**able** a (income) imponible; ~**ation** [-'seɪʃən] n impuestos mpl; ~**avoidance** n evasión f de impuestos; ~ **collector** n recaudador(a) m/f; ~ **disc** n (Brit AUT) pegatina del impuesto de circulación; ~ **evasion** n evasión f fiscal; ~**-free** a libre de impuestos.

taxi ['tæksı] n taxi m // vi (AVIAT) rodar por la pista; ~ **driver** n taxista m/f; (Brit) ~ **rank**, ~ **stand** n parada de taxis.

tax: ~ **payer** n contribuyente m/f; ~ **relief** n desgravación f fiscal; ~ **return** n declaración f de ingresos.

TB n abbr = **tuberculosis**.

tea [ti:] n té m; (Brit: snack) merienda; **high** ~ (Brit) merienda-cena; ~ **bag** n bolsita de té; ~ **break** n (Brit) descanso para el té.

teach [ti:tʃ], pt, pp **taught** vt: **to** ~ **sb sth,** ~ **sth to sb** enseñar algo a uno // vi enseñar; (be a teacher) ser profesor(a); ~**er** n (in secondary school) profesor(a) m/f; (in primary school) maestro/a; ~**ing** n enseñanza.

tea cosy n cubretetera m.

teacup ['tiːkʌp] n taza para el té.

teak [tiːk] n (madera de) teca.

team [tiːm] n equipo; (of animals) pareja; ~**work** n trabajo en equipo.

teapot ['tiːpɔt] n tetera.

tear [tɛəˀ] n rasgón m, desgarrón m // n [tɪəˀ] lágrima f // vb (pt tore, pp torn) vt romper, rasgar // vi rasgarse; **in** ~**s** llorando; **to** ~ **along** vi (rush) precipitarse; **to** ~ **up** vt (sheet of paper etc) romper; ~**ful** a lloroso; ~ **gas** n gas m lacrimógeno.

tearoom ['tiːruːm] n salón m de té, cafetería.

tease [tiːz] n bromista m/f // vt tomar el pelo a.

tea: ~ **set** n servicio de té; ~**spoon** n cucharita; (also: ~**spoonful**: as measurement) cucharadita.

teat [tiːt] n (of bottle) tetina.

teatime ['tiːtaɪm] n hora del té.

tea towel n (Brit) paño de cocina.

technical ['tɛknɪk] a técnico; ~**ity** [-'kælɪtɪ] n detalle m técnico.

technician [tɛk'nɪʃn] n técnico/a.

technique [tɛk'niːk] n técnica.

technological [tɛknə'lɔdʒɪkl] a tecnológico.

technology [tɛk'nɔlədʒɪ] n tecnología.

teddy (bear) ['tɛdɪ-] n osito de felpa.

tedious ['tiːdɪəs] a pesado, aburrido.

tee [tiː] n (GOLF) tee m.

teem [tiːm] vi: **to** ~ **with** rebosar de; **it is** ~**ing (with rain)** llueve a mares.

teenage ['tiːneɪdʒ] a (fashions etc) juvenil; ~**r** n adolescente m/f.

teens [tiːnz] npl: **to be in one's** ~ ser adolescente.

tee-shirt ['tiːʃəːt] n = T-shirt.

teeter ['tiːtəˀ] vi balancearse.

teeth [tiːθ] npl of tooth.

teethe [tiːð] vi echar los dientes.

teething ['tiːðɪŋ]: ~ **ring** n mordedor m; ~ **troubles** npl (fig) dificultades fpl iniciales.

teetotal ['tiː'təutl] a (person) abstemio.

telegram ['tɛlɪgræm] n telegrama m.

telegraph ['tɛlɪgrɑːf] n telégrafo.

telepathy [tə'lɛpəθɪ] n telepatía.

telephone ['tɛlɪfəun] n teléfono // llamar por teléfono, telefonear; ~ **booth**, (Brit) ~ **box** n cabina telefónica; ~ **call** n llamada (telefónica); ~ **directory** n guía (telefónica); ~ **number** n número de teléfono; **telephonist** [tə'lɛfənɪst] n (Brit) telefonista m/f.

telephoto ['tɛlɪ'fəutəu] a: ~ **lens** n teleobjetivo.

telescope ['tɛlɪskəup] n telescopio.

televise ['tɛlɪvaɪz] vt televisar.

television ['tɛlɪvɪʒən] n televisión f; ~ **set** n televisor m.

telex ['tɛlɛks] n télex m // vt, vi enviar un télex (a).

tell [tɛl], pt, pp **told** vt decir; (relate: story) contar; (distinguish): **to** ~ **sth from** distinguir algo de // vi (talk): **to** ~ **(of)** contar; (have effect) tener efecto; **to** ~ **sb to do sth** mandar a uno hacer algo; **to** ~ **off** vt: **to** ~ **sb off** regañar a uno; ~**er** n (in bank) cajero/a; ~**ing** a (remark, detail) revelador(a); ~**tale** a (sign) indicador/a.

telly ['tɛlɪ] n (Brit col) tele f.

temp [tɛmp] n abbr (Brit: = temporary) temporero/a // vi trabajar de interino/a.

temper ['tɛmpəˀ] n (mood) humor m; (bad) ~ (mal) genio; (fit of anger) ira; (of child) rabieta f // vt (moderate) moderar; **to be in a** ~ estar furioso; **to lose one's** ~ enfadarse, enojarse (LAm).

temperament ['tɛmprəmənt] n (nature) temperamento.

temperate ['tɛmprət] a moderado; (climate) templado.

temperature ['tɛmprətʃəˀ] n temperatura; **to have** or **run a** ~ tener fiebre.

tempest ['tɛmpɪst] n tempestad f.

template ['tɛmplɪt] n plantilla.

temple ['templ] n (building) templo; (ANAT) sien f.

temporarily ['tempərərɪlɪ] ad temporalmente.

temporary ['tempərərɪ] a provisional, temporal; (passing) transitorio; (worker) temporero.

tempt [tempt] vt tentar; to ~ sb into doing sth tentar or inducir a uno a hacer algo; ~ation [temp'teɪʃən] n tentación f; ~ing a tentador(a).

ten [ten] num diez.

tenable ['tenəbl] a sostenible.

tenacity [tə'næsɪtɪ] n tenacidad f.

tenancy ['tenənsɪ] n alquiler m; (of house) inquilinato.

tenant ['tenənt] n (rent-payer) inquilino/a; (occupant) habitante m/f.

tend [tend] vt cuidar // vi: to ~ to do sth tener tendencia a hacer algo.

tendency ['tendənsɪ] n tendencia.

tender ['tendə*] a (meat) tierno; (sore) sensible; (affectionate) tierno, cariñoso // n (COMM: offer) oferta; (money): legal ~ moneda de curso legal // vt ofrecer; ~ness n ternura; (of meat) blandura.

tenement ['tenəmənt] n casa de pisos or vecinos (Sp).

tenet ['tenət] n principio.

tennis ['tenɪs] n tenis m; ~ ball n pelota de tenis; ~ court n cancha de tenis; ~ player n tenista m/f; ~ racket n raqueta de tenis; ~ shoes npl zapatillas fpl de tenis.

tenor ['tenə*] n (MUS) tenor m.

tense [tens] a (moment, atmosphere) tenso; (stretched) tirante; (stiff) rígido, tieso; (person) nervioso // n (LING) tiempo.

tension ['tenʃən] n tensión f.

tent [tent] n tienda (de campaña), carpa (LAm).

tentacle ['tentəkl] n tentáculo.

tenterhooks ['tentəhuks] npl: on ~ sobre ascuas.

tenth [tenθ] a décimo.

tent peg n clavija, estaca.

tent pole n mástil m.

tenuous ['tenjuəs] a tenue.

tenure ['tenjuə*] n (of land) tenencia; (of job: period) ejercicio.

tepid ['tepɪd] a tibio.

term [tə:m] n (COMM: time limit) plazo; (word) término; (period) período; (SCOL) trimestre m // vt llamar; ~s npl (conditions) condiciones fpl; in the short/long ~ a corto/largo plazo; to be on good ~s with sb llevarse bien con uno; to come to ~s with (problem) adaptarse a.

terminal ['tə:mɪnl] a (disease) mortal // n (ELEC) borne m; (COMPUT) terminal m; (also: air ~) terminal f; (Brit: also: coach ~) (estación f) terminal f.

terminate ['tə:mɪneɪt] vt terminar // vi: to ~ in acabar por.

terminus ['tə:mɪnəs], pl -mini [-mɪnaɪ] n término, (estación f) terminal f.

terrace ['terəs] n terraza; (Brit: row of houses) hilera de casas adosadas; the ~s (Brit SPORT) las gradas fpl; ~d a (garden) colgante; (house) adosado.

terrain [te'reɪn] n terreno.

terrible ['terɪbl] a terrible, horrible; (fam) atroz; **terribly** ad terriblemente; (very badly) malísimamente.

terrier ['terɪə*] n terrier m.

terrific [tə'rɪfɪk] a fantástico, fenomenal; (wonderful) maravilloso.

terrify ['terɪfaɪ] vt aterrorizar.

territory ['terɪtərɪ] n territorio.

terror ['terə*] n terror m; ~ism n terrorismo; ~ist n terrorista m/f; ~ize vt aterrorizar.

terse [tə:s] a (style) conciso; (reply) brusco.

Terylene ['terɪli:n] n ® (Brit) terylene m ®.

test [test] n (trial, check) prueba, ensayo; (: of goods in factory) control m; (of courage etc, CHEM) prueba; (MED) examen m; (exam) examen m, test m; (also: driving ~) examen m de conducir // vt probar, poner a prueba; (MED) examinar.

testament ['testəmənt] n testamento; **the Old/New T~** el Antiguo/ Nuevo Testamento.

testicle ['testɪkl] n testículo.

testify ['testɪfaɪ] vi (LAW) prestar declaración; **to ~ to sth** atestiguar algo.

testimony ['testɪmənɪ] n (LAW) testimonio, declaración f.

test: **~ match** n (CRICKET, RUGBY) partido internacional; **~ pilot** n piloto/mujer piloto m/f de pruebas; **~ tube** n probeta; **~ tube baby** n niño/a probeta.

tetanus ['tetənəs] n tétano.

tether ['tɛðə*] vt atar (con una cuerda) // n: **to be at the end of one's ~** no aguantar más.

text [tɛkst] n texto; **~book** n libro de texto.

textiles ['tɛkstaɪlz] npl textiles mpl, tejidos mpl.

texture ['tɛkstʃə*] n textura.

Thai [taɪ] a, n tailandés/esa m/f; **~land** n Tailandia.

Thames [tɛmz] n: **the ~** el (río) Támesis.

than [ðæn] conj (in comparisons): **more ~ 10/once** más de 10/una vez; **I have more/less ~ you/Paul** tengo más/menos que tú/Paul; **she is older ~ you think** es mayor de lo que piensas.

thank [θæŋk] vt dar las gracias a, agradecer; **~ you (very much)** muchas gracias; **~s** npl gracias fpl // excl ¡gracias!; **~s to** prep gracias a; **~ful for (for)** agradecido (por); **~less** a ingrato; **T~sgiving (Day)** n día m de Acción de Gracias.

that [ðæt] ♦ a (demonstrative: pl those) ese/a, pl esos/as; (more remote) aquel/aquella, pl aquellos/as; **leave those books on the table** deja esos libros sobre la mesa; **~ one** ése/ésa; (more remote) aquél/aquélla; **~ one over there** ése/ésa de ahí; aquél/aquélla de allí

♦ pron 1 (demonstrative: pl

those) ése/a, pl ésos/as; (neuter) eso; (more remote) aquél/aquélla, pl aquéllos/as; (neuter) aquello; **what's ~?** ¿qué es eso (or aquello)?; **who's ~?** ¿quién es ése/a (or aquél/ aquélla)?; **is ~ you?** ¿eres tú?; **will you eat all ~?** ¿vas a comer todo eso?; **~'s my house** ésa es mi casa; **~'s what he said** eso es lo que dijo; **~ is** (to say) es decir

2 (relative: subject, object) que; (with preposition) (el/la) que etc, el/ la cual etc; **the book (~) I read** el libro que leí; **the books ~ are in the library** los libros que están en la biblioteca; **all (~) I have** todo lo que tengo; **the box (~) I put it in** la caja en la que or donde lo puse; **the people (~) I spoke to** la gente con la que hablé

3 (relative: of time) que; **the day (~) he came** el día (en) que vino

♦ conj que; **he thought ~ I was ill** creyó que estaba enfermo

♦ ad (demonstrative): **I can't work ~ much** no puedo trabajar tanto; **I didn't realise it was ~ bad** no creí que fuera tan malo; **~ high** así de alto.

thatched [θætʃt] a (roof) de paja; **~ cottage** casita con tejado de paja.

thaw [θɔ:] n deshielo // vi (ice) derretirse; (food) descongelarse // vt (food) descongelar.

the [ði:, ðə] definite article 1 (gen) el, f la, pl los, fpl las (NB = immediately before f noun beginning with stressed (h)a; a + el = al; de + el = del); **~ boy/girl** el chico/la chica; **~ books/flowers** los libros/las flores; **to ~ postman/from ~ drawer** al cartero/del cajón; **I haven't ~ time/money** no tengo tiempo/dinero

2 (+ adjective to form noun) **~ rich and ~ poor** los ricos y los pobres; **to attempt ~ impossible** intentar lo imposible

3 (in titles): **Elizabeth ~ First** Isabel primera; **Peter ~ Great** Pedro el Grande

4 (in comparisons): **~ more he works ~ more he earns** cuanto más trabaja más gana.

theatre, (US) **theater** ['θɪətə*] n teatro; **~-goer** n aficionado/a al teatro.

theatrical [θɪ'ætrɪkl] a teatral.

theft [θɛft] n robo.

their [ðɛə*] a su; **~s** pron (el) suyo/ (la) suya etc; see also **my**, **mine**.

them [ðɛm, ðəm] pron (direct) los/ las; (indirect) les; (stressed, after prep) ellos/ellas; see also **me**.

theme [θiːm] n tema m; **~ song** n tema m (musical).

themselves [ðəm'sɛlvz] pl pron (subject) ellos mismos/ellas mismas; (complement) se; (after prep) sí (mismos/as); see also **oneself**.

then [ðɛn] ad (at that time) entonces; (next) pues; (later) luego, después; (and also) además // conj (therefore) en ese caso, entonces // a: **the ~ president** el entonces presidente; **from ~ on** desde entonces.

theology [θɪ'ɔlədʒɪ] n teología.

theoretical [θɪə'rɛtɪkl] a teórico.

theory ['θɪərɪ] n teoría.

therapist ['θɛrəpɪst] n terapeuta m/f.

therapy [θɛrəpɪ] n terapia.

KEYWORD

there ['ðɛə*] ad 1: **~ is**, **~ are** hay; **~ is no-one here/no bread left** no hay nadie aquí/no queda pan; **~ has been an accident** ha habido un accidente

2 (referring to place) ahí; (distant) allí; **it's ~** está ahí; **put it in/on/up/down ~** ponlo ahí dentro/encima/ arriba/abajo; **I want that book ~** quiero ese libro de ahí; **~ he is!** ¡ahí está!

3: **~, ~** (esp to child) ea, ea.

there: ~abouts ad por ahí; **~after** ad después; **~by** ad así, de ese modo; **~fore** ad por lo tanto; **~'s = ~ is**; **~ has**.

thermal ['θəːml] a termal; (paper) térmico; **~ printer** n termoimpresora.

thermometer [θə'mɔmɪtə*] n mómetro.

Thermos ['θəːməs] n ® (also: **~ flask**) termo.

thermostat ['θəːməustæt] n termostato.

thesaurus [θɪ'sɔːrəs] n tesoro.

these [ðiːz] pl a estos/as // pl pron éstos/as.

thesis ['θiːsɪs], pl **-ses** [-siːz] n tesis f inv.

they [ðeɪ] pl pron ellos/ellas; (stressed) ellos (mismos)/ellas mismas); **~ say that...** (it is said that) se dice que...; **~'d = they had**, **they would**; **~'ll = they shall**, **they will**; **~'re = they are**; **~'ve = they have**.

thick [θɪk] a (liquid, smoke) espeso; (wall, slice) grueso; (vegetation, beard) tupido; (stupid) torpe // n: **in the ~ of the battle** en lo más reñido de la batalla; **it's 20 cm ~** tiene 20 cm de espesor; **~en** vi espesarse // vt (sauce etc) espesar; **~ness** n espesor m, grueso; **~set** a fornido; **~-skinned** a (fig) insensible.

thief [θiːf], pl **thieves** [θiːvz] n ladrón/ona m/f.

thigh [θaɪ] n muslo.

thimble ['θɪmbl] n dedal m.

thin [θɪn] a (person, animal) flaco; (material) delgado; (liquid) poco denso; (soup) aguado; (fog) ligero; (crowd) escaso // vt: to **~ (down)** (sauce, paint) diluir.

thing [θɪŋ] n cosa; (object) objeto, artículo; (contraption) chisme m; **~s** npl (belongings) efectos mpl (personales); **the best ~ would be to...** lo mejor sería...; **how are ~s?** ¿qué tal?

think [θɪŋk], pt, pp **thought** vi pensar // vt pensar, creer; **what did you ~ of them?** ¿qué te parecieron?; **to ~ about sth/sb** pensar en algo/uno; **I'll ~ about it** lo pensaré; **to ~ of doing sth** pensar en hacer algo; **I ~ so/not** creo que sí/no; **to ~ well of** sb tener buen concepto de uno; **to ~ over** vt reflexionar sobre, meditar; **to ~ up** vt imaginar; **~ tank** n gabinete m de estrategia.

third [θəːd] a tercer(a) // n tercero/a; (fraction) tercio; (Brit SCOL: degree) de tercera clase; **~ly** ad en tercer lugar; **~ party insurance** n (Brit) seguro contra terceros; **~rate** a (de calidad) mediocre; **the T~ World** el Tercer Mundo.

thirst [θəːst] n sed f; **~y** a: **to be ~y** tener sed.

thirteen ['θəː'tiːn] num trece.

thirty ['θəːtɪ] num treinta.

─────────────────────
| **KEYWORD** |
─────────────────────

this [ðɪs] ♦ a (demonstrative: pl these) este/a; pl estos/as; (neuter) esto; **~ man/woman** este hombre/ esta mujer; **these children/flowers** estos chicos/estas flores; **~ one** (here) éste/a, esto (de aquí)
♦ pron (demonstrative: pl these) éste/a; pl estos/as; (neuter) esto; **who is ~?** ¿quién es éste/ésta?; **what is ~?** ¿qué es esto?; **~ is where I live** aquí vivo; **~ is what he said** esto es lo que dijo; **~ is Mr Brown** (in introductions) le presento al Sr. Brown; (photo) éste es el Sr. Brown; (on telephone) habla el Sr. Brown
♦ ad (demonstrative): **~ high/long** etc así de alto/largo etc; **~ far** hasta aquí.

─────────────────────

thistle ['θɪsl] n cardo.

thong [θɒŋ] n correa.

thorn [θɔːn] n espina.

thorough ['θʌrə] a (search) minucioso; (knowledge, research) profundo; **~bred** a (horse) de pura sangre; **~fare** n calle f; **'no ~fare'**

'prohibido el paso'; **~ly** ad minuciosamente; profundamente, a fondo.

those [ðəuz] pl pron ésos/ésas; (more remote) aquéllos/as // pl a esos/esas; aquellos/as.

though [ðəu] conj aunque // ad sin embargo.

thought [θɔːt] pt, pp of **think** // n pensamiento; (opinion) opinión f; (intention) intención f; **~ful** a pensativo; (considerate) atento; **~less** a desconsiderado.

thousand ['θauzənd] num mil; **two ~ dos** mil; **~s of** miles de; **~th** a milésimo.

thrash [θræʃ] vt apalear; (defeat) derrotar; **to ~ about** vi revolcarse; **to ~ out** vi discutir a fondo.

thread [θred] n hilo; (of screw) rosca // vt (needle) enhebrar; **~bare** a raído.

threat [θret] n amenaza; **~en** vi amenazar // vt: **to ~en sb with sth/ to do** amenazar a uno con algo/con hacer.

three [θriː] num tres; **~-dimensional** a tridimensional; **~-piece suit** n traje m de tres piezas; **~-piece suite** n tresillo; **~-ply** a (wool) triple; **~-wheeler** n (car) coche m cabina.

thresh [θreʃ] vt (AGR) trillar.

threshold ['θreʃhəuld] n umbral m.

threw [θruː] pt of **throw**.

thrifty ['θrɪftɪ] a económico.

thrill [θrɪl] n (excitement) emoción f // vt emocionar; **to be ~ed** (with gift etc) estar encantado; **~er** n película/novela de suspense.

thrilling ['θrɪlɪŋ] a emocionante.

thrive [θraɪv], pt **thrived** or **throve** [θrəuv], pp **thrived** or **thriven** ['θrɪvn] vi (grow) crecer; (do well) prosperar; **thriving** a próspero.

throat [θrəut] n garganta; **to have a sore ~** tener dolor de garganta.

throb [θrɒb] vi (heart) latir; (engine) vibrar; (with pain) dar punzadas.

throes [θrəuz] npl: **in the ~ of** en medio de.

throne [θrəʊn] *n* trono.

throng [θrɒŋ] *n* multitud *f*, muchedumbre *f* // *vt* agolparse en.

throttle [ˈθrɒtl] *n* (AUT) acelerador *m* // *vt* estrangular.

through [θruː] *prep* por, a través de; (time) durante; (by means of) por medio de, mediante; (thanks to) gracias a // *a* (ticket, train) directo // *ad* completamente, de parte a parte; de principio a fin; **to put sb ~ to sb** (TEL) poner or pasar a uno con uno; **to be ~** (TEL) tener comunicación; (have finished) haber terminado; **'no ~ road'** (Brit) 'calle sin salida'; **~out** *prep* (place) por todas partes de, por todo; (time) durante todo // *ad* por or en todas partes.

throve [θrəʊv] *pt of* **thrive**.

throw [θrəʊ] *n* tiro, (SPORT) lanzamiento // *vt* (pt **threw**, pp **thrown**) tirar, echar; (SPORT) lanzar; (rider) derribar; (fig) desconcertar; **to ~ a party** dar una fiesta; **to ~ away** *vt* tirar; **to ~ off** *vt* deshacerse de; **to ~ out** *vt* tirar; **to ~ up** *vi* vomitar; **~away** *a* para tirar, desechable; **~-in** *n* (SPORT) saque *m*.

thru [θruː] (US) = **through**.

thrush [θrʌʃ] *n* zorzal *m*, tordo.

thrust [θrʌst] *n* (TECH) empuje *m* // *vt* (pt, pp **thrust**) empujar; (push in) introducir.

thud [θʌd] *n* golpe *m* sordo.

thug [θʌg] *n* gamberro/a.

thumb [θʌm] *n* (ANAT) pulgar *m* // *vt*: **to ~ a lift** hacer autostop; **to ~ through** *vt fus* (book) hojear; **~tack** *n* (US) chincheta, chinche *f* (LAm).

thump [θʌmp] *n* golpe *m*; (sound) ruido seco or sordo // *vt*, *vi* golpear.

thunder [ˈθʌndə*] *n* trueno; (of applause etc) estruendo // *vi* tronar; (train etc): **to ~ past** pasar como un trueno; **~bolt** *n* rayo; **~clap** *n* trueno; **~storm** *n* tormenta; **~y** *a* tormentoso.

Thursday [ˈθəːzdɪ] *n* jueves *m inv*.

thus [ðʌs] *ad* así, de este modo.

thwart [θwɔːt] *vt* frustrar.

thyme [taɪm] *n* tomillo.

thyroid [ˈθaɪrɔɪd] *n* tiroides *m inv*.

tiara [tɪˈɑːrə] *n* tiara, diadema.

tic [tɪk] *n* tic *m*.

tick [tɪk] *n* (sound: of clock) tictac *m*; (mark) palomita; (ZOOL) garrapata; (Brit col): **in a ~** en un instante // *vi* hacer tictac // *vt* marcar; **to ~ off** *vt* marcar; (person) reñir; **to ~ over** *vi* (engine) girar en marcha lenta; (fig) ir tirando.

ticket [ˈtɪkɪt] *n* billete *m*, tiquet *m* boleto (LAm); (for cinema etc) entrada, boleto (LAm); (in shop: on goods) etiqueta; (for library) tarjeta; **~ collector** *n* revisor(a) *m/f*; **~ office** *n* (THEATRE) taquilla, boletería (LAm); (RAIL) despacho de billetes or boletos (LAm).

tickle [ˈtɪkl] *n* // *vt* hacer cosquillas a uno // *vt* hacer cosquillas a; **ticklish** *a* (person) cosquilloso.

tidal [ˈtaɪdl] *a* de marea; **~ wave** *n* maremoto.

tidbit [ˈtɪdbɪt] (US) = **titbit**.

tiddlywinks [ˈtɪdlɪwɪŋks] *n* juego infantil de habilidad con fichas de plástico.

tide [taɪd] *n* marea; (fig: of events) curso, marcha; **high/low ~** marea alta/baja.

tidy [ˈtaɪdɪ] *a* (room) ordenado; (drawing, work) limpio; (person) (bien) arreglado // *vt* (also: **~ up**) poner en orden.

tie [taɪ] *n* (string etc) atadura; (Brit: neck~) corbata; (fig: link) vínculo, lazo; (SPORT: draw) empate *m* // *vt* atar // *vi* (SPORT) empatar; **to ~ in a bow** atar con un lazo; **to ~ a knot in sth** hacer un nudo en algo; **to ~ down** *vt* atar; (fig): **to ~ sb down** to obligar a uno a; **to ~ up** *vt* (parcel) envolver; (dog) atar; (boat) amarrar; (arrangements) concluir; **to be ~d up** (busy) estar ocupado.

tier [tɪə*] *n* grada; (of cake) piso.

tiger [ˈtaɪgə*] *n* tigre *m*.

tight [taɪt] *a* (rope) tirante; (clothes,

budget) ajustado; (*programme*) apretado; (*bend*) cerrado; (*col: drunk*) borracho // *ad* (*squeeze*) muy fuerte; (*shut*) herméticamente; ~s *npl* (*Brit*) pantimedias *fpl*; ~en *vt* (*rope*) estirar; (*screw*) apretar // *vi* apretarse; estirarse; ~-fisted *a* tacaño; ~ly *ad* (*grasp*) muy fuerte; ~rope *n* cuerda floja.

tile [taɪl] *n* (*on roof*) teja; (*on floor*) baldosa; (*on wall*) azulejo; ~d *a* embaldosado.

till [tɪl] *n* caja (registradora) // *vt* (*land*) cultivar // *prep, conj* = **until**.

tiller [ˈtɪlə*] *n* (*NAUT*) caña del timón.

tilt [tɪlt] *vt* inclinar // *vi* inclinarse.

timber [ˈtɪmbə*] *n* (*material*) madera; (*trees*) árboles *mpl*.

time [taɪm] *n* tiempo; (*epoch: often pl*) época; (*by clock*) hora; (*moment*) momento; (*occasion*) vez *f*; (*MUS*) compás *m* // *vt* calcular o medir el tiempo de; (*race*) cronometrar; (*remark etc*) elegir el momento para; **a long** ~ mucho tiempo; **4** *at* **a** ~ 4 a la vez; **for the** ~ **being** de momento, por ahora; **from** ~ **to** ~ de vez en cuando; **in** ~ (*soon enough*) a tiempo; (*after some time*) con el tiempo; (*MUS*) al compás; **in a week's** ~ dentro de una semana; **in no** ~ en un abrir y cerrar de ojos; **any** ~ cuando sea; **on** ~ a la hora; **5** ~**s 5** por **5**; **what** ~ **is it?** ¿qué hora es?; **to have a good** ~ pasarlo bien, divertirse; ~ **bomb** *n* bomba de efecto retardado; ~ **lag** *n* desfase *m*; ~**less** *a* eterno; ~**ly** *a* oportuno; ~ **off** *n* tiempo libre; ~r *n* (~ *switch*) interruptor *m*; (*in kitchen etc*) programador *m* horario; ~ **scale** *n* escala de tiempo; ~ **switch** *n* (*Brit*) interruptor *m* (horario); ~**table** *n* horario; ~ **zone** *n* huso horario.

timid [ˈtɪmɪd] *a* tímido.

timing [ˈtaɪmɪŋ] *n* (*SPORT*) cronometraje *m*; **the** ~ **of his resignation** el momento que eligió para dimitir.

timpani [ˈtɪmpənɪ] *npl* tímpanos *mpl*.

tin [tɪn] *n* estaño; (*also*: ~ **plate**) hojalata; (*Brit: can*) lata; ~**foil** *n* papel *m* de estaño.

tinge [tɪndʒ] *n* matiz *m* // *vt*: ~d **with** teñido de.

tingle [ˈtɪŋgl] *vi* sentir hormigueo.

tinker [ˈtɪŋkə*] *n* calderero/a; (*gipsy*) gitano/a; **to** ~ **with** *vt fus* jugar con, tocar.

tinkle [ˈtɪŋkl] *vi* tintinear.

tinned [tɪnd] *a* (*Brit: food*) en lata, en conserva.

tin opener [-əupnə*] *n* (*Brit*) abrelatas *m inv*.

tinsel [ˈtɪnsl] *n* oropel *m*.

tint [tɪnt] *n* matiz *m*; (*for hair*) tinte *m*; ~**ed** *a* (*hair*) teñido; (*glass, spectacles*) ahumado.

tiny [ˈtaɪnɪ] *a* minúsculo, pequeñito.

tip [tɪp] *n* (*end*) punta; (*gratuity*) propina; (*Brit: for rubbish*) vertedero; (*advice*) consejo // *vt* (*waiter*) dar una propina a; (*tilt*) inclinar; (*empty: also* ~ *out*) vaciar, echar; **to** ~ **over** *vi* volcar // *vi* volcarse; ~-**off** *n* (*hint*) advertencia; ~**ped** *a* (*Brit: cigarette*) con filtro.

tipsy [ˈtɪpsɪ] *a* alegre, mareado.

tiptoe [ˈtɪptəu] *n* (*Brit*): **on** ~ de puntillas.

tiptop [ˈtɪptɔp] *a*: **in** ~ **condition** en perfectas condiciones.

tire [ˈtaɪə*] *n* (*US*) = **tyre** // *vt* cansar // *vi* (*also*: ~ **out**) cansarse; (*become bored*) aburrirse; ~**d** *a* cansado; **to be** ~**d of sth** estar harto de algo; ~**less** *a* incansable; ~**some** *a* aburrido; **tiring** *a* cansado.

tissue [ˈtɪʃu:] *n* tejido; (*paper handkerchief*) pañuelo de papel, kleenex *m* ®; ~ **paper** *n* papel *m* de seda.

tit [tɪt] *n* (*bird*) herrerillo común; **to give** ~ **for tat** dar ojo por ojo.

titbit [ˈtɪtbɪt], (*US*) **tidbit** *n* (*food*) golosina; (*news*) pedazo.

titillate [ˈtɪtɪleɪt] *vt* estimular, excitar.

titivate [ˈtɪtɪveɪt] *vt* emperejilar.

title [ˈtaɪtl] *n* título; ~ **deed** *n*

(*LAW*) título de propiedad; ~ **role** *n* papel *m* principal.

titter ['tɪtə*] *vi* reírse entre dientes.

titular ['tɪtjʊlə*] *a* (*in name only*) nominal.

TM *abbr* (= *trademark*) marca de fábrica.

KEYWORD

to [tuː, tə] ◆ *prep* **1** (*direction*) a; to go ~ **France/London/school/the station** ir a Francia/Londres/al colegio/a la estación; **to go** ~ **Claude's/the doctor's** ir a casa de Claude/al médico; **the road** ~ **Edinburgh** la carretera de Edimburgo

2 (*as far as*) hasta, a; **from here** ~ **London** de aquí a or hasta Londres; **to count** ~ **10** contar hasta 10; **from 40** ~ **50 people** entre 40 y 50 personas

3 (*with expressions of time*): **a quarter/twenty** ~ **5** las 5 menos cuarto/veinte

4 (*for, of*); **the key** ~ **the front door** la llave de la puerta principal; **she is secretary** ~ **the director** es la secretaria del director; **a letter** ~ **his wife** una carta a or para su mujer

5 (*expressing indirect object*); **to give sth** ~ **sb** darle algo a alguien; **to talk** ~ **sb** hablar con alguien; **to be a danger** ~ **sb** ser un peligro para alguien; **to carry out repairs** ~ **sth** hacer reparaciones en algo

6 (*in relation to*): **3 goals** ~ **2** 3 goles a 2; **30 miles** ~ **the gallon** ~ 9,4 litros a los cien (kms)

7 (*purpose, result*): **to come** ~ **sb's aid** venir en auxilio or ayuda de alguien; **to sentence sb** ~ **death** condenar a uno a muerte; ~ **my great surprise** con gran sorpresa mía

◆ *with vb* **1** (*simple infinitive*): ~ **go/eat** ir/comer

2 (*following another vb*): **to want/try/start** ~ **do** querer/intentar/empezar a hacer; *see also relevant verb*

3 (*with vb omitted*): **I don't want** ~ no quiero

4 (*purpose, result*) para; **I did it** ~ **help you** lo hice para ayudarte; **he came** ~ **see you** vino a verte

5 (*equivalent to relative clause*): **I have things** ~ **do** tengo cosas que hacer; **the main thing is** ~ **try** lo principal es intentarlo

6 (*after adjective etc*): **ready** ~ **go** listo para irse; **too old** ~ ... demasiado viejo (como) para ...

◆ *ad*: **pull/push the door** ~ tirar de/empujar la puerta

---

toad [təʊd] *n* sapo; ~**stool** *n* hongo venenoso.

toast [təʊst] *n* (*CULIN: also*: **piece of** ~) tostada; (*drink, speech*) brindis *m* // *vt* (*CULIN*) tostar; (*drink to*) brindar; ~**er** *n* tostador *m*.

tobacco [tə'bækəʊ] *n* tabaco; ~**nist** *n* estanquero/a, tabaquero/a (*LAm*); ~**nist's (shop)** *n* (*Brit*) estanco, tabaquería (*LAm*); ~ **shop** (*US*) = ~**nist's (shop)**.

toboggan [tə'bɔgən] *n* tobogán *m*.

today [tə'deɪ] *ad, n* (*also: fig*) hoy *m*.

toddler ['tɒdlə*] *n* niño/a (que empieza a andar).

toddy ['tɒdɪ] *n* ponche *m*.

to-do [tə'duː] *n* (*fuss*) lío.

toe [təʊ] *n* dedo (del pie); (*of shoe*) punta; **to** ~ **the line** (*fig*) conformarse; ~**nail** *n* uña del pie.

toffee ['tɒfɪ] *n* caramelo.

together [tə'gɛðə*] *ad* juntos; (*at same time*) al mismo tiempo, a la vez; ~ **with** *prep* junto con.

toil [tɔɪl] *n* trabajo duro, labor *f*.

toilet ['tɔɪlət] *n* (*Brit: lavatory*) servicios *mpl*, water *m*, sanitario (*LAm*) // *cpd* (*soap etc*) de aseo; ~ **bag** *n* esponjera; ~ **bowl** *n* taza (de retrete); ~ **paper** *n* papel *m* higiénico; ~**ries** *npl* artículos *mpl* de aseo; (*make-up etc*) artículos *mpl* de tocador; ~ **roll** *n* rollo de papel higiénico; ~ **water** *n* (agua de) colonia.

token ['təʊkən] *n* (*sign*) señal *f*,

muestra; (*souvenir*) recuerdo; (*voucher*) vale *m*; (*disc*) ficha; book/record ~ (*Brit*) vale *m* para comprar libros/discos.

Tokyo ['təukjəu] *n* Tokio, Tokio.

told [təuld] *pt, pp of* **tell**.

tolerable ['tɔlərəbl] *a* (*bearable*) soportable; (*fairly good*) pasable.

tolerance ['tɔlərns] *n* (*also: TECH*) tolerancia.

tolerant ['tɔlərnt] *a*: ~ **of** tolerante con.

tolerate ['tɔləreɪt] *vt* tolerar.

toll [təul] *n* (*of casualties*) número de víctimas; (*tax, charge*) peaje *m* // *vi* (*bell*) doblar.

tomato [tə'mɑːtəu], *pl* ~**es** *n* tomate *m*.

tomb [tuːm] *n* tumba.

tomboy ['tɔmbɔɪ] *n* marimacho.

tombstone ['tuːmstəun] *n* lápida.

tomcat ['tɔmkæt] *n* gato.

tomorrow [tə'mɔrəu] *ad, n* (*also: fig*) mañana; **the day after** ~ pasado mañana; ~ **morning** mañana por la mañana; **a week** ~ de mañana en ocho (días).

ton [tʌn] *n* tonelada (*Brit* = 1016 *kg*; *US* = 907 *kg*); (*metric* ~) tonelada métrica; ~**s** *pl* (*col*) montones de.

tone [təun] *n* tono // *vi* armonizar; to ~ **down** *vt* (*criticism*) suavizar; (*colour*) atenuar; to ~ **up** *vt* (*muscles*) tonificar; ~**-deaf** *a* que no tiene oído musical.

tongs [tɔŋz] *npl* (*for coal*) tenazas *fpl*; (*for hair*) tenacillas *fpl*.

tongue [tʌŋ] *n* lengua; ~ **in cheek** *ad* irónicamente; ~**-tied** *a* (*fig*) mudo; ~**-twister** *n* trabalenguas *m inv*.

tonic ['tɔnɪk] *n* (*MED*) tónico; (*MUS*) tónica; (*also*: ~ **water**) (agua) tónica.

tonight [tə'naɪt] *ad, n* esta noche.

tonnage ['tʌnɪdʒ] *n* (*NAUT*) tonelaje *m*.

tonsil ['tɔnsl] *n* amígdala; ~**litis** [-'laɪtɪs] *n* amigdalitis *f*.

too [tuː] *ad* (*excessively*) demasiado; (*also*) también; ~ **much** *ad, a* demasiado; ~ **many** *a* demasiados/as; ~ **bad!** ¡mala suerte!

took [tuk] *pt of* **take**.

tool [tuːl] *n* herramienta; ~ **box** *n* caja de herramientas.

toot [tuːt] *vi* (*with car horn*) tocar la bocina.

tooth [tuːθ], *pl* **teeth** *n* (*ANAT, TECH*) diente *m*; (*molar*) muela; ~**ache** *n* dolor *m* de muelas; ~**brush** *n* cepillo de dientes; ~**paste** *n* pasta de dientes; ~**pick** *n* palillo.

top [tɔp] *n* (*of mountain*) cumbre *f*, cima; (*of head*) coronilla; (*of ladder*) lo alto; (*of cupboard, table*) superficie *f*; (*lid: of box, jar*) tapa; (: *of bottle*) tapón *m*; (*of list etc*) cabeza; (*toy*) peonza // ... (*at the*) de arriba; (*in rank*) principal, primero; (*best*) mejor // *vt* (*exceed*) exceder; (*be first in*) encabezar; **on** ~ **of** sobre, encima de; **from** ~ **to bottom** de pies a cabeza; to ~ **up**, (*US*) to ~ **off** *vt* llenar; ~ **floor** *n* último piso; ~ **hat** *n* sombrero de copa; ~**-heavy** *a* (*object*) descompensado en la parte superior.

topic ['tɔpɪk] *n* tema *m*; ~**al** *a* actual.

top: ~**less** *a* (*bather etc*) topless; ~**-level** *a* (*talks*) al más alto nivel; ~**-most** *a* más alto.

topple ['tɔpl] *vt* volcar, derribar // *vi* caerse.

top-secret ['tɔp'siːkrɪt] *a* de alto secreto.

topsy-turvy ['tɔpsɪ'təːvɪ] *a, ad* patas arriba.

torch [tɔːtʃ] *n* antorcha; (*Brit: electric*) linterna.

tore [tɔː*] *pt of* **tear**.

torment ['tɔːmɛnt] *n* tormento // *vt* [tɔː'mɛnt] atormentar; (*fig: annoy*) fastidiar.

torn [tɔːn] *pp of* **tear**.

torrent ['tɔrnt] *n* torrente *m*.

torrid ['tɔrɪd] *a* (*fig*) apasionado.

tortoise ['tɔːtəs] *n* tortuga; ~**shell**

['tɔːtəfcl] a de carey.

torture ['tɔːtʃə*] n tortura // vt torturar; (fig) atormentar.

Tory ['tɔːri] a, n (Brit POL) conservador/a m/f.

toss [tɔs] vt tirar, echar; (head) sacudir; **to ~ a coin** echar a cara o cruz; **to ~ up for sth** jugar a cara o cruz algo; **to ~ and turn** (in bed) dar vueltas.

tot [tɔt] n (Brit: drink) copita; (child) nene/a m/f.

total ['təutl] a total, entero // n total m, suma // vt (add up) sumar; (amount to) ascender a.

totalitarian [təutælɪ'tɛərɪən] a totalitario.

totally ['təutəlɪ] ad totalmente.

totter ['tɔtə*] vi tambalearse.

touch [tʌtʃ] n tacto; (contact) contacto; (FOOTBALL): **to be in ~** estar fuera de juego // vt tocar; (emotionally) conmover; **a ~ of** (fig) una pizca or un poquito de; **to get in ~ with sb** ponerse en contacto con uno; **to lose ~** (friends) perder contacto; **to ~ on** vt fus (topic) aludir (brevemente) a; **to ~ up** vt (paint) retocar; **~-and-go** a arriesgado; **~down** n aterrizaje m; (on sea) amerizaje m; (US FOOTBALL) ensayo; **~ed** a conmovido; (col) chiflado; **~ing** a conmovedor(a); **~line** n (SPORT) línea de banda; **~y** a (person) quisquilloso.

tough [tʌf] a (meat) duro; (difficult) difícil; (resistant) resistente; (person) fuerte // n (gangster etc) gorila m; **~en** vt endurecer.

toupée ['tuːpeɪ] n peluca.

tour ['tuə*] n viaje m, vuelta; (also: package ~) viaje m todo comprendido; (of town, museum) visita // vi viajar por; **~ing** n viajes mpl turísticos, turismo.

tourism ['tuərɪzm] n turismo.

tourist ['tuərɪst] n turista m/f // cpd turístico; **~ office** n oficina de turismo.

tournament ['tuənəmənt] n torneo.

tousled ['tauzld] a (hair) despeinado.

tout [taut] vi: **to ~ for business** solicitar clientes // n (also: ticket ~) revendedor/a m/f.

tow [təu] vt remolcar; **'on** or (US) **in ~'** (AUT) 'a remolque'.

toward(s) [tə'wɔːd(z)] prep hacia; (of attitude) respecto a, con; (of purpose) para.

towel ['tauəl] n toalla; **~ling** n (fabric) felpa; **~ rail**, (US) **~ rack** n toallero.

tower ['tauə*] n torre f; **~ block** n (Brit) torre f (de pisos); **~ing** a muy alto, imponente.

town [taun] n ciudad f; **to go to ~** ir a la ciudad; (fig) echar los botes por; **~ centre** n centro de la ciudad; **~ clerk** n secretario/a del ayuntamiento; **~ council** n ayuntamiento, consejo municipal; **~ hall** n ayuntamiento; **~ plan** n plano de la ciudad; **~ planning** n urbanismo.

towrope ['təurəup] n cable m de remolque.

tow truck n (US) camión m grúa.

toy [tɔɪ] n juguete m; **to ~ with** vt fus jugar con; (idea) acariciar; **~shop** n juguetería.

trace [treɪs] n rastro // vt (draw) trazar, delinear; (locate) encontrar; **tracing paper** n papel m de calco.

track [træk] n (mark) huella, pista; (path: gen) camino, senda; (: of bullet etc) trayectoria; (: of suspect, animal) pista, rastro; (RAIL) vía; (SPORT) pista; (on record) canción f // vt seguir la pista de; **to keep ~ of** mantenerse al tanto de, seguir; **to ~ down** vt (person) localizar; (sth lost) encontrar; **~suit** n chandal m.

tract [trækt] n (GEO) región f; (pamphlet) folleto.

traction ['trækʃən] n (AUT, power) tracción f; **in ~** (MED) en tracción.

tractor ['træktə*] n tractor m.

trade [treɪd] n comercio; (skill, job) oficio // vi negociar, comerciar; **to ~ in sth** comerciar en algo; **to ~ in** vt (old car etc) ofrecer como parte del pago; ~ **fair** n feria comercial; ~**in price** n valor de un objeto usado que se descuenta del precio de otro nuevo; ~**mark** n marca de fábrica; ~ **name** n marca registrada; ~**r** n comerciante m/f; ~**sman** n (shopkeeper) tendero; ~ **union** n sindicato; ~**unionist** n sindicalista m/f; **trading** n comercio; **trading estate** n (Brit) zona comercial.

tradition [trə'dɪʃən] n tradición f; ~**al** a tradicional.

traffic ['træfɪk] n (gen, AUT) tráfico, circulación f, tránsito (LAm); **air** ~ tránsito aéreo // vi: **to** ~ **in** (pej: liquor, drugs) traficar en; ~ **circle** n (US) glorieta de tráfico; ~ **jam** n embotellamiento; ~ **lights** npl semáforo sg; ~ **warden** n guardia m/f de tráfico.

tragedy ['trædʒədɪ] n tragedia.

tragic ['trædʒɪk] a trágico.

trail [treɪl] n (tracks) rastro, pista; (path) camino, sendero; (dust, smoke) estela // vt (drag) arrastrar; (follow) seguir la pista de; (follow closely) vigilar // vi arrastrarse; **to** ~ **behind** vi quedar a la zaga; ~**er** n (AUT) remolque m; (caravan) caravana; (CINEMA) trailer m, avance m; ~ **truck** n (US) trailer m.

train [treɪn] n tren m; (of dress) cola; (series) serie f // vt (teach skills to) adiestrar; (sportsman) entrenar; (dog) amaestrar; (point: gun etc) to ~ **on** apuntar a // vi (SPORT) entrenarse; (be educated) formarse; **one's** ~ **of thought** razonamiento de uno; ~**ed** a (worker) cualificado; (animal) amaestrado; ~**ee** [treɪ'niː] n aprendiz(a) m/f; ~**er** n (SPORT) entrenador(a) m/f; (of animals) domador(a) m/f; ~**ing** n formación f; entrenamiento; **to be in** ~**ing** (SPORT) estar entrenando; (: fit) estar en forma; ~**ing college** n (gen) colegio de formación profesional; (for teachers) escuela normal; ~**ing shoes** npl zapatillas fpl (de deporte).

traipse [treɪps] vi andar penosamente.

trait [treɪt] n rasgo.

traitor ['treɪtə*] n traidor(a) m/f.

tram [træm] n (Brit: also: ~**car**) tranvía m.

tramp [træmp] n (person) vagabundo/a; (col: offensive: woman) puta // vi andar con pasos pesados.

trample ['træmpl] vt: **to** ~ (**underfoot**) pisotear.

trampoline ['træmpəlɪn] n trampolín m.

tranquil ['træŋkwɪl] a tranquilo; ~**lizer** n (MED) tranquilizante m.

transact [træn'zækt] vt (business) tramitar; ~**ion** [-'zækʃən] n transacción f, operación f.

transcend [træn'send] vt rebasar.

transcript ['trænskrɪpt] n copia; ~**ion** [-'skrɪpʃən] n transcripción f.

transfer ['trænsfə*] n transferencia; (SPORT) traspaso; (picture, design) calcomanía // vt [træns'fə:*] trasladar, pasar; **to** ~ **the charges** (Brit TEL) llamar a cobro revertido.

transform [træns'fɔ:m] vt transformar.

transfusion [træns'fju:ʒən] n transfusión f.

transient ['trænzɪənt] a transitorio.

transistor [træn'zɪstə*] n (ELEC) transistor m; ~ **radio** n transistor m.

transit ['trænzɪt] n: **in** ~ en tránsito.

transitive ['trænzɪtɪv] a (LING) transitivo.

translate [trænz'leɪt] vt traducir; **translation** [-'leɪʃən] n traducción f; **translator** n traductor(a) m/f.

transmission [trænz'mɪʃən] n transmisión f.

transmit [trænz'mɪt] vt transmitir; ~**ter** n transmisor m; (station) emisora.

transparency [træns'pɛərnsɪ] n (Brit PHOT) diapositiva.

transparent [træns'pærnt] a transparente.

transpire [træns'paɪə*] vi (turn out) resultar; (happen) ocurrir, suceder; it ~d that ... se supo que ...

transplant [træns'plɑːnt] vt transplantar // n ['trænsplɑːnt] (MED) transplante m.

transport [træns'pɔːt] n transporte m // vt [-'pɔːt] transportar; ~ation [-'teɪʃən] n transporte m; (of prisoners) deportación f; ~ café n (Brit) bar-restaurant m de carretera.

trap [træp] n (snare, trick) trampa; (carriage) cabriolé m // vt coger (Sp) or agarrar (LAm) en una trampa; (immobilize) bloquear; (jam) atascar; ~ door n escotilla.

trapeze [trə'piːz] n trapecio.

trappings ['træpɪŋz] mpl adornos mpl.

trash [træʃ] n (pej: goods) pacotilla; (: nonsense) tonterías fpl; ~ can n (US) cubo or balde m (LAm) de la basura.

travel ['trævl] n viaje m // vi viajar // vt (distance) recorrer; ~ agency n agencia de viajes; ~ agent n agente m/f de viajes; ~ler, (US) ~er n viajero/a; ~ler's cheque, (US) ~er's check n cheque m de viajero; ~ling, (US) ~ing n los viajes mpl, el viajar; ~ sickness n mareo.

travesty ['trævəstɪ] n parodia.

trawler ['trɔːlə*] n pesquero de arrastre.

tray [treɪ] n (for carrying) bandeja; (on desk) cajón m.

treachery ['tretʃərɪ] n traición f.

treacle ['triːkl] n (Brit) melaza.

tread [tred] n (step) paso, pisada; (sound) ruido de pasos; (of tyre) banda de rodadura // vi (pt trod, pp trodden) pisar; to ~ on vt fus pisar.

treason ['triːzn] n traición f.

treasure ['treʒə*] n tesoro // vt (value) apreciar, valorar.

treasurer ['treʒərə*] n tesorero/a.

treasury ['treʒərɪ] n: the T~, (US) the T~ Department el Ministerio de Hacienda.

treat [triːt] n (present) regalo; (pleasure) placer m // vt tratar; to ~ sb to sth invitar a uno a algo.

treatise ['triːtɪz] n tratado.

treatment ['triːtmənt] n tratamiento.

treaty ['triːtɪ] n tratado.

treble ['trebl] a triple // vt triplicar // vi triplicarse; ~ clef n (MUS) clave f de sol.

tree [triː] n árbol m.

trek [trek] n (long journey) expedición f; (tiring walk) caminata.

trellis ['trelɪs] n enrejado.

tremble ['trembl] vi temblar.

tremendous [trɪ'mendəs] a tremendo; (enormous) enorme; (excellent) estupendo.

tremor ['tremə*] n temblor m; (also: earth ~) temblor m de tierra.

trench [trentʃ] n zanja; (MIL) trinchera.

trend [trend] n (tendency) tendencia; (of events) curso; (fashion) moda; ~y a de moda.

trepidation [trepɪ'deɪʃən] n inquietud f.

trespass ['trespəs] vi: to ~ on entrar sin permiso en; 'no ~ing' 'prohibido el paso'.

tress [tres] n trenza.

trestle ['tresl] n caballete m; ~ table n mesa de caballete.

trial ['traɪəl] n (LAW) juicio, proceso; (test: of machine etc) prueba; (hardship) desgracia; by ~ and error a fuerza de probar.

triangle ['traɪæŋgl] n (MATH, MUS) triángulo.

tribe [traɪb] n tribu f.

tribunal [traɪ'bjuːnl] n tribunal m.

tributary ['trɪbjuːtərɪ] n (river) afluente m.

tribute ['trɪbjuːt] n homenaje m, tributo; to pay ~ to rendir homenaje a.

trice [traɪs] n: in a ~ en un santiamén.

trick [trɪk] n (skill) trampa; (conjuring ~, deceit) truco; (joke) broma; (CARDS) baza // vt engañar; to play a ~ on sb gastar una broma a uno; that should do the ~ a ver si funciona así; **~ery** n engaño.

trickle ['trɪkl] n (of water etc) chorrito // vi gotear.

tricky ['trɪkɪ] a difícil; delicado.

tricycle ['traɪsɪkl] n triciclo.

trifle ['traɪfl] n bagatela; (CULIN) dulce de bizcocho borracho, gelatina, fruta y natillas // ad: **a ~ long** un poquito largo; **trifling** a insignificante.

trigger ['trɪgə*] n (of gun) gatillo; **to ~ off** vt desencadenar.

trill [trɪl] n (of bird) gorjeo.

trim [trɪm] a (elegant) aseado; (house, garden) en buen estado; (figure) de talle esbelto // n (haircut etc) recorte m // vt (neaten) arreglar; (cut) recortar; (decorate) adornar; (NAUT: a sail) orientar; **~mings** npl (extras) accesorios mpl; (cuttings) recortes mpl.

trinket ['trɪŋkɪt] n chuchería, baratija.

trip [trɪp] n viaje m; (excursion) excursión f; (stumble) traspié m // vi (stumble) tropezar; (go lightly) andar a paso ligero; **on a ~** de viaje; **to ~ up** vi tropezar, caerse // vt hacer tropezar or caer.

tripe [traɪp] n (CULIN) callos mpl; (pej: rubbish) bobadas fpl.

triple ['trɪpl] a triple.

triplets ['trɪplɪts] npl trillizos/as m/fpl.

triplicate ['trɪplɪkət] n: **in ~** por triplicado.

tripod ['traɪpɔd] n trípode m.

trite [traɪt] a trillado.

triumph ['traɪʌmf] n triunfo // vi: **to ~ (over)** vencer.

trivia ['trɪvɪə] npl trivialidades fpl.

trivial ['trɪvɪəl] a insignificante, trivial.

trod [trɔd], **trodden** ['trɔdn] pt, pp of **tread**.

trolley ['trɔlɪ] n carrito.

trombone [trɔm'bəun] n trombón m.

troop [tru:p] n grupo, banda; **~s** npl

(MIL) tropas fpl; **to ~ in/out** vi entrar/salir en tropel; **~er** n (MIL) soldado (de caballería); **~ing the colour** n (ceremony) presentación f de la bandera.

trophy ['trəufɪ] n trofeo.

tropic ['trɔpɪk] n trópico; **~al** a tropical.

trot [trɔt] n trote m // vi trotar; **on the ~** (Brit fig) seguidos/as.

trouble ['trʌbl] n problema m, dificultad f; (worry) preocupación f; (bother, effort) molestia, esfuerzo; (unrest) inquietud f; (MED): **stomach ~** problemas mpl gástricos // vt molestar; (worry) preocupar, inquietar // vi: **to ~ to do sth** molestarse en hacer algo; **~s** npl (POL etc) conflictos mpl; **to be in ~** estar en un apuro; **to go to the ~ of doing sth** tomarse la molestia de hacer algo; **what's the ~?** ¿qué pasa?; **~d** a (person) preocupado; (epoch, life) agitado; **~maker** n agitador(a) m/f; **~shooter** n (in conflict) conciliador(a) m/f; **~some** a molesto, inoportuno.

trough [trɔf] n (also: **drinking ~**) abrevadero; (also: **feeding ~**) comedero; (channel) canal m.

troupe [tru:p] n grupo.

trousers ['trauzəz] npl pantalones mpl; **short ~** pantalones mpl cortos.

trousseau ['tru:səu], pl **~x** or **~s** [-z] n ajuar m.

trout [traut] n, pl inv trucha.

trowel ['trauəl] n paleta.

truant ['truənt] n: **to play ~** (Brit) hacer novillos.

truce [tru:s] n tregua.

truck [trʌk] n (US) camión m; (RAIL) vagón m; **~ driver** n camionero; **~ farm** n (US) huerto de hortalizas.

truculent ['trʌkjulənt] a agresivo.

trudge [trʌdʒ] vi caminar penosamente.

true [tru:] a verdadero; (accurate) exacto; (genuine) auténtico; (faithful) fiel.

truffle ['trʌfl] n trufa.

truly ['truːlɪ] ad (genuinely, emphatic: very) realmente; (faithfully) fielmente.

trump [trʌmp] n triunfo; **~ed-up** a inventado.

trumpet ['trʌmpɪt] n trompeta.

truncheon ['trʌntʃən] n (Brit) porra.

trundle ['trʌndl] vt, vi: **to ~ along** rodar haciendo ruido.

trunk [trʌŋk] n (of tree, person) tronco; (of elephant) trompa; (case) baúl m; (US AUT) maletero; **~s** npl (also: **swimming ~s**) bañador m; **~ call** n (Brit TEL) llamada interurbana.

truss [trʌs] n (MED) braguero; **to ~ (up)** vt atar; (CULIN) espetar.

trust [trʌst] n confianza; (COMM) trust m; (LAW) fideicomiso // vt (rely on) tener confianza en; (entrust): **to ~ sth to sb** confiar algo a uno; **~ed** a de confianza; **~ee** [trʌs'tiː] n (LAW) fideicomisario; **~ful, ~ing** a confiado; **~worthy** a digno de confianza.

truth [truːθ] n, pl **~s** [truːðz] n verdad f; **~ful** a (person) veraz.

try [traɪ] n tentativa, intento; (RUGBY) ensayo // vt (LAW) juzgar, procesar; (test: sth new) probar, someter a prueba; (attempt) intentar; (strain: patience) hacer perder // vi probar; **to ~ to do sth** intentar hacer algo; **to ~ on** vt (clothes) probarse; **to ~ out** vt probar, poner a prueba; **~ing** a cansado; (person) pesado.

T-shirt ['tiːʃəːt] n camiseta.

T-square ['tiːskwɛəʳ] n regla en T.

tub [tʌb] n cubo (Sp), balde m (LAm); (bath) tina, bañera.

tuba ['tjuːbə] n tuba.

tubby ['tʌbɪ] a regordete.

tube [tjuːb] n tubo; (Brit: underground) metro.

tuberculosis [tjubəːkjuˈləʊsɪs] n tuberculosis f inv.

tubing ['tjuːbɪŋ] n tubería (Sp), cañería; **a piece of ~** un trozo de tubo.

tubular ['tjuːbjʊləʳ] a tubular.

TUC n abbr (Brit: = Trades Union Congress) federación nacional de sindicatos.

tuck [tʌk] n (SEWING) pliegue m // vt (put) poner; **to ~ away** vt esconder; **to ~ in** vt meter dentro; (child) arropar // vi (eat) comer con apetito; **to ~ up** vt (child) arropar; **~ shop** n (SCOL) tienda de golosinas.

Tuesday ['tjuːzdɪ] n martes m inv.

tuft [tʌft] n mechón m; (of grass etc) manojo.

tug [tʌɡ] n (ship) remolcador m // vt remolcar; **~-of-war** n lucha de tiro de cuerda.

tuition [tjuːˈɪʃən] n (Brit) enseñanza; (: private ~) clases fpl particulares; (US: school fees) matrícula.

tulip ['tjuːlɪp] n tulipán m.

tumble ['tʌmbl] n (fall) caída // vi caerse, tropezar; **to ~ to sth** (col) caer en la cuenta de algo; **~down** a destartalado; **~ dryer** n (Brit) secadora.

tumbler ['tʌmbləʳ] n vaso.

tummy ['tʌmɪ] n (col) barriga, vientre m.

tumour, (US) **tumor** ['tjuːməʳ] n tumor m.

tuna ['tjuːnə] n, pl inv (also: **~ fish**) atún m.

tune [tjuːn] n (melody) melodía // vt (MUS) afinar; (RADIO, TV, AUT) sintonizar; **to be in/out of ~** (instrument) estar afinado/desafinado; (singer) cantar afinadamente/desafinar; **to ~ in (to)** vi (RADIO, TV) sintonizar (con); **to ~ up** vi (musician) afinar (su instrumento); **~ful** a melodioso; **~r** n (radio set) sintonizador m; **piano ~r** n afinador(a) m/f de pianos.

tunic ['tjuːnɪk] n túnica.

tuning ['tjuːnɪŋ] n sintonización f; (MUS) afinación f; **~ fork** n diapasón m.

Tunisia [tjuːˈnɪzɪə] n Túnez m.

tunnel ['tʌnl] n túnel m; (in mine) galería // vi construir un túnel/una galería.

turban ['tə:bən] n turbante m.

turbine ['tə:bain] n turbina.

turbulence ['tə:bjuləns] n (AVIAT) turbulencia.

tureen [tə'ri:n] n sopera.

turf [tə:f] n césped m; (clod) tepe m // vi cubrir con césped; **to ~ out** vt (col) echar a la calle.

turgid ['tə:dʒid] a (prose) pesado.

Turk [tə:k] n turco/a.

Turkey ['tə:ki] n Turquía.

turkey ['tə:ki] n pavo.

Turkish ['tə:kiʃ] a turco.

turmoil ['tə:mɔil] n desorden m, alboroto.

turn [tə:n] n turno; (in road) curva; (THEATRE) número; (MED) ataque m // vt girar, volver; (collar, steak) dar la vuelta a; (change): **to ~ sth into** convertir algo en // vi volver; (person: look back) volverse; (reverse direction) dar la vuelta; (milk) cortarse; (change) cambiar; (become) convertirse en; **a good** ~ un favor; **it gave me quite a** ~ me dio un susto; **'no left** ~' (AUT) 'prohibido girar a la izquierda'; **it's your** ~ te toca a ti; **in** ~ por turnos; **to take** ~s turnarse; **to ~ away** vi apartar la vista; **to ~ back** vi volverse atrás; **to ~ down** vt (refuse) rechazar; (reduce) bajar; (fold) doblar; **to ~ in** vi (col: go to bed) acostarse // vt (fold) doblar hacia dentro; **to ~ off** vi (from road) desviarse // vt (light, radio etc) apagar; (engine) parar; **to ~ on** vt (light, radio etc) encender, prender (LAm); (engine) poner en marcha; **to ~ out** vt (light, gas) apagar // vi: **to ~ out to be...** resultar ser...; **to ~ over** vi (person) volverse // vt (object) dar la vuelta a; (page) volver; **to ~ round** vi volverse; (rotate) girar; **to ~ up** vi (person) llegar, presentarse; (lost object) aparecer // vt (gen) subir; **~ing** n (in road)

vuelta; **~ing point** n (fig) momento decisivo.

turnip ['tə:nip] n nabo.

turnout ['tə:naut] n concurrencia.

turnover ['tə:nəuvə*] n (COMM: amount of money) facturación f; (: of goods) movimiento.

turnpike ['tə:npaik] n (US) autopista de peaje.

turnstile ['tə:nstail] n torniquete m.

turntable ['tə:nteibl] n plato.

turn-up ['tə:nʌp] n (Brit: on trousers) vuelta.

turpentine ['tə:pəntain] n (also: turps) trementina.

turquoise ['tə:kwɔiz] n (stone) turquesa // a color turquesa.

turret ['tʌrit] n torreón m.

turtle ['tə:tl] n galápago; **~neck (sweater)** n (jersey m de) cuello cisne.

tusk [tʌsk] n colmillo.

tussle ['tʌsl] n lucha, pelea.

tutor ['tju:tə*] n profesor(a) m/f; **~ial** [-'tɔ:riəl] n (SCOL) seminario.

tuxedo [tʌk'si:dəu] n (US) smóking m, esmoquin m.

TV [ti:'vi:] n abbr (= television) tele f.

twang [twæŋ] n (of instrument) punteado; (of voice) timbre m nasal.

tweezers ['twi:zəz] npl pinzas fpl (de depilar).

twelfth [twelfθ] a duodécimo.

twelve [twelv] num doce; **at** ~ **o'clock** (midday) a mediodía; (midnight) a medianoche.

twentieth ['twentiθ] a vigésimo.

twenty ['twenti] num veinte.

twice [twais] ad dos veces; ~ **as much** dos veces más.

twiddle ['twidl] vt, vi: **to ~ (with)** sth dar vueltas a algo; **to ~ one's thumbs** (fig) estar mano sobre mano.

twig [twig] n ramita // vi (col) caer en la cuenta.

twilight ['twailait] n crepúsculo.

twin [twin] a, n gemelo/a m/f // vt hermanar; **~-bedded room** n habitación f con camas gemelas.

twine [twaɪn] n bramante m // vi (plant) enroscarse.

twinge [twɪndʒ] n (of pain) punzada; (of conscience) remordimiento.

twinkle ['twɪŋkl] vi centellear; (eyes) parpadear.

twirl [twəːl] n giro // vt dar vueltas a // vi piruetear.

twist [twɪst] n (action) torsión f; (in road, coil) vuelta; (in wire, flex) doblez f; (in story) giro // vt torcer, retorcer; (roll around) enrollar; (fig) deformar // vi serpentear.

twit [twɪt] n (col) tonto.

twitch [twɪtʃ] vi moverse nerviosamente.

two [tuː] num dos; **to put ~ and ~ together** (fig) atar cabos; **~-door** a (AUT) de dos puertas; **~-faced** a (pej: person) falso; **~fold** ad: **to increase ~fold** doblarse; **~-piece (suit)** n traje m de dos piezas; **~-piece (swimsuit)** n dos piezas m inv, bikini m; **~-seater plane/car** n avión m/coche m de dos plazas; **~some** n (people) pareja; **~-way** a: **~-way traffic** circulación f de dos sentidos.

tycoon [taɪˈkuːn] n: **(business) ~** magnate m/f.

type [taɪp] n (category) tipo, género; (model) modelo; (TYP) tipo, letra // vt (letter etc) escribir a máquina; **~-cast** n (actor) encasillado; **~-face** n tipo; **~-script** n texto mecanografiado; **~-writer** n máquina de escribir; **~-written** a mecanografiado.

typhoid ['taɪfɔɪd] n tifoidea.

typical ['tɪpɪkl] a típico.

typing ['taɪpɪŋ] n mecanografía.

typist ['taɪpɪst] n mecanógrafo/a.

tyranny ['tɪrənɪ] n tiranía.

tyrant ['taɪərnt] n tirano.

tyre, (US) **tire** ['taɪəʳ] n neumático, llanta (LAm); **~ pressure** n presión f de los neumáticos.

U

U-bend ['juːˈbend] n (AUT, in pipe) recodo.

udder ['ʌdəʳ] n ubre f.

UFO ['juːfəu] n abbr = (unidentified flying object) OVNI m.

ugh [əːh] excl ¡uf!

ugly ['ʌglɪ] a feo; (dangerous) peligroso.

UK n abbr = United Kingdom.

ulcer ['ʌlsəʳ] n úlcera.

Ulster ['ʌlstəʳ] n Ulster m.

ulterior [ʌlˈtɪərɪəʳ] a ulterior; **~ motive** segundas intenciones fpl.

ultimate ['ʌltɪmət] a último, final; (authority) más alto; **~ly** ad (in the end) por último, al final; (fundamentally) a or en fin de cuentas.

ultrasound [ʌltrəˈsaund] n (MED) ultrasonido.

umbilical cord [ʌmˈbɪlɪkl-] n cordón m umbilical.

umbrella [ʌmˈbrelə] n paraguas m inv.

umpire ['ʌmpaɪəʳ] n árbitro.

umpteen [ʌmpˈtiːn] a enésimos/as; **for the ~th time** por enésima vez.

UN n abbr = United Nations (Organization).

unable [ʌnˈeɪbl] a: **to be ~ to do** sth no poder hacer algo.

unaccompanied [ʌnəˈkʌmpənɪd] a no acompañado.

unaccountably [ʌnəˈkauntəblɪ] ad inexplicablemente.

unaccustomed [ʌnəˈkʌstəmd] a: **to be ~ to** no estar acostumbrado a.

unanimous [juːˈnænɪməs] a unánime; **~ly** ad unánimemente.

unarmed [ʌnˈɑːmd] a desarmado.

unassuming [ʌnəˈsjuːmɪŋ] a modesto, sin pretensiones.

unattached [ʌnəˈtætʃt] a (person) sin pareja; (part etc) suelto.

unattended [ʌnəˈtendɪd] a (car, luggage) sin atender.

unauthorized [ʌnˈɔːθəraɪzd] a no

autorizado.

unavoidable [ʌnəˈvɔidəbl] a inevitable.

unaware [ʌnəˈweəˢ] a: **to be ~ of** ignorar; **~s** ad de improviso.

unbalanced [ʌnˈbælənst] a desequilibrado; (*mentally*) trastornado.

unbearable [ʌnˈbeərəbl] a insoportable.

unbeknown(st) [ʌnbɪˈnəun(st)] ad: **~ to me** sin saberlo yo.

unbelievable [ʌnbɪˈliːvəbl] a increíble.

unbend [ʌnˈbend] (*irg: like* bend) vi (*fig: person*) relajarse // vt (*wire*) enderezar.

unbiased [ʌnˈbaɪəst] a imparcial.

unborn [ʌnˈbɔːn] a que va a nacer.

unbreakable [ʌnˈbreɪkəbl] a irrompible.

unbroken [ʌnˈbrəukən] a (*seal*) intacto; (*series*) continuo; (*record*) no batido; (*spirit*) indómito.

unbutton [ʌnˈbʌtn] vt desabrochar.

uncalled-for [ʌnˈkɔːldfɔːˢ] a gratuito, inmerecido.

uncanny [ʌnˈkænɪ] a extraño, extraordinario.

unceasing [ʌnˈsiːsɪŋ] a incesante.

unceremonious [ˈʌnserɪˈməunɪəs] a (*abrupt, rude*) brusco, hosco.

uncertain [ʌnˈsəːtn] a incierto; (*indecisive*) indeciso; **~ty** n incertidumbre f.

unchecked [ʌnˈtʃekt] a desenfrenado.

uncivilized [ʌnˈsɪvɪlaɪzd] a (*gen*) inculto; (*fig: behaviour etc*) bárbaro.

uncle [ˈʌŋkl] n tío.

uncomfortable [ʌnˈkʌmfətəbl] a incómodo; (*uneasy*) inquieto.

uncommon [ʌnˈkəmən] a poco común, raro.

uncompromising [ʌnˈkɒmprəmaɪzɪŋ] a intransigente.

unconcerned [ʌnkənˈsəːnd] a indiferente, despreocupado.

unconditional [ʌnkənˈdɪʃənl] a incondicional.

unconscious [ʌnˈkɒnʃəs] a sin senti-

do; (*unaware*) inconsciente // n: **the ~** el inconsciente; **~ly** ad inconscientemente.

uncontrollable [ʌnkənˈtrəuləbl] a (*temper*) indomable; (*laughter*) incontenible.

unconventional [ʌnkənˈvenʃənl] a poco convencional.

uncouth [ʌnˈkuːθ] a grosero, inculto.

uncover [ʌnˈkʌvəˢ] vt (*gen*) descubrir; (*take lid off*) destapar.

undecided [ʌndɪˈsaɪdɪd] a (*character*) indeciso; (*question*) no resuelto, pendiente.

under [ˈʌndəˢ] prep debajo de; (*less than*) menos de; (*according to*) según, de acuerdo con // ad debajo, abajo; **~ there** allí abajo; **~ construction** bajo construcción.

under... [ˈʌndəˢ] pref sub; **~age** a menor de edad; **~carriage** n (*Brit AVIAT*) tren m de aterrizaje; **~charge** vt cobrar menos de la cuenta; **~clothes** npl ropa sg interior o íntima (*LAm*); **~coat** n (*paint*) primera mano; **~cover** a clandestino; **~current** n corriente f submarina; (*fig*) tendencia oculta; **~cut** vt irg vender más barato que; **~developed** a subdesarrollado; **~dog** n desvalido/a; **~done** a (*CULIN*) poco hecho; **~estimate** vt subestimar; **~exposed** a (*PHOT*) subexpuesto; **~fed** a subalimentado; **~foot** ad: it's wet **~foot** el suelo está mojado; **~go** vt irg sufrir; (*treatment*) recibir; **~graduate** n estudiante m/f; **~ground** n (*Brit: railway*) metro; (*POL*) movimiento clandestino // a subterráneo; **~growth** n maleza; **~hand(ed)** a (*fig*) socarrón; **~lie** vt irg (*fig*) ser la razón fundamental de; **~line** vt subrayar; **~ling** [ˈʌndəlɪŋ] n (*pej*) subalterno/a; **~mine** vt socavar, minar; **~neath** [ʌndəˈniːθ] ad // prep debajo de, bajo; **~paid** a mal pagado; **~pants** npl calzoncillos mpl; **~pass** n (*Brit*) paso subterráneo; **~privileged** a desvalido;

~**rate** vt menospreciar, subestimar; ~**shirt** n (US) camiseta; ~**shorts** npl (US) calzoncillos mpl; ~**side** n parte f femenina, revés m; ~**skirt** n (Brit) enaguas fpl.

understand [ˌʌndəˈstænd] (irg: like **stand**) vt, vi entender, comprender; (assume) tener entendido; ~**able** a comprensible; ~**ing** a comprensivo // n comprensión f, entendimiento m; (agreement) acuerdo.

understatement [ˌʌndəˈsteɪtmənt] n subestimación f; (modesty) modestia (excesiva).

understood [ˌʌndəˈstud] pt, pp of **understand** // a entendido; (implied): **it is** ~ **that** se sobreentiende que.

understudy [ˈʌndəˌstʌdɪ] n suplente m/f.

undertake [ˌʌndəˈteɪk] (irg: like **take**) vt emprender; **to** ~ **to do sth** comprometerse a hacer algo.

undertaker [ˈʌndəˌteɪkəʳ] n director(a) m/f de pompas fúnebres.

undertaking [ˌʌndəˈteɪkɪŋ] n empresa; (promise) promesa.

undertone [ˈʌndətəʊn] n: **in an** ~ en voz baja.

underwater [ˌʌndəˈwɔːtəʳ] ad bajo el agua // a submarino.

underwear [ˈʌndəwɛəʳ] n ropa interior or íntima (LAm).

underworld [ˈʌndəwɜːld] n (of crime) hampa, inframundo.

underwriter [ˈʌndəraɪtəʳ] n (INSURANCE) asegurador/a mf.

undies [ˈʌndɪz] npl (col) ropa interior or íntima (LAm).

undo [ʌnˈduː] (irg: like **do**) vt deshacer; ~**ing** n ruina, perdición f.

undoubted [ʌnˈdautɪd] a indudable; ~**ly** ad indudablemente, sin duda.

undress [ʌnˈdrɛs] vi desnudarse.

undue [ʌnˈdjuː] a indebido, excesivo.

undulating [ˈʌndjuleɪtɪŋ] a ondulante.

unduly [ʌnˈdjuːlɪ] ad excesivamente, demasiado.

unearth [ʌnˈɜːθ] vt desenterrar.

~**rate** vt menospreciar, subestimar;

unearthly [ʌnˈɜːθlɪ] a (hour) inverosímil.

uneasy [ʌnˈiːzɪ] a intranquilo; (worried) preocupado.

uneducated [ʌnˈɛdjukeɪtɪd] a ignorante, inculto.

unemployed [ʌnɪmˈplɔɪd] a parado, sin trabajo // n: **the** ~ los parados.

unemployment [ʌnɪmˈplɔɪmənt] n paro, desempleo.

unending [ʌnˈɛndɪŋ] a interminable.

unerring [ʌnˈɜːrɪŋ] a infalible.

uneven [ʌnˈiːvn] a desigual; (road etc) quebrado.

unexpected [ʌnɪkˈspɛktɪd] a inesperado; ~**ly** ad inesperadamente.

unfailing [ʌnˈfeɪlɪŋ] a (support) indefectible; (energy) inagotable.

unfair [ʌnˈfɛəʳ] a: ~ **(to sb)** injusto (con uno).

unfaithful [ʌnˈfeɪθful] a infiel.

unfamiliar [ʌnfəˈmɪlɪəʳ] a extraño, desconocido.

unfashionable [ʌnˈfæʃnəbl] a pasado or fuera de moda.

unfasten [ʌnˈfɑːsn] vt desatar.

unfavourable, (US) **unfavorable** [ʌnˈfeɪvərəbl] a desfavorable.

unfeeling [ʌnˈfiːlɪŋ] a insensible.

unfinished [ʌnˈfɪnɪʃt] a inacabado, sin terminar.

unfit [ʌnˈfɪt] a indispuesto, enfermo; (incompetent) incapaz; ~ **for work** no apto para trabajar.

unfold [ʌnˈfəʊld] vt desdoblar; (fig) revelar // vi abrirse; revelarse.

unforeseen [ˈʌnfɔːˈsiːn] a imprevisto.

unforgettable [ʌnfəˈgɛtəbl] a inolvidable.

unforgivable [ʌnfəˈgɪvəbl] a imperdonable.

unfortunate [ʌnˈfɔːtʃnət] a desgraciado; (event, remark) inoportuno; ~**ly** ad desgraciadamente.

unfounded [ʌnˈfaundɪd] a infundado.

unfriendly [ʌnˈfrɛndlɪ] a antipático.

ungainly [ʌnˈgeɪnlɪ] a (walk) desgarbado.

ungodly [ʌnˈgɔdlɪ] *a*: at an ~ hour a una hora inverosímil.

ungrateful [ʌnˈgreɪtful] *a* ingrato.

unhappiness [ʌnˈhæpɪnəs] *n* tristeza.

unhappy [ʌnˈhæpɪ] *a* (*sad*) triste; (*unfortunate*) desgraciado; (*childhood*) infeliz; ~ **with** (*arrangements etc*) poco contento con, descontento de.

unharmed [ʌnˈhɑːmd] *a* (*person*) ileso.

unhealthy [ʌnˈhelθɪ] *a* (*gen*) malsano; (*person*) enfermizo.

unheard-of [ʌnˈhɜːdɔv] *a* inaudito, sin precedente.

unhook [ʌnˈhuk] *vt* desenganchar; (*from wall*) descolgar; (*undo*) desabrochar.

unhurt [ʌnˈhɜːt] *a* ileso.

uniform [ˈjuːnɪfɔːm] *n* uniforme *m* // *a* uniforme; **~ity** [-ˈfɔːmɪtɪ] *n* uniformidad *f*.

unify [ˈjuːnɪfaɪ] *vt* unificar, unir.

uninhabited [ʌnɪnˈhæbɪtɪd] *a* desierto.

unintentional [ʌnɪnˈtɛnʃənəl] *a* involuntario.

union [ˈjuːnjən] *n* unión *f*; (*also*: **trade ~**) sindicato // *cpd* sindical; **U~ Jack** *n* bandera del Reino Unido.

unique [juːˈniːk] *a* único.

unison [ˈjuːnɪsn] *n*: **in ~** (*speak, reply*) al unísono; **in ~ with** junto con.

unit [ˈjuːnɪt] *n* unidad *f*; (*team, squad*) grupo; **kitchen ~** módulo de cocina.

unite [juːˈnaɪt] *vt* unir // *vi* unirse; **~d** *a* unido; **U~d Kingdom (UK)** *n* Reino Unido; **U~d Nations (Organization) (UN, UNO)** *n* Naciones *fpl* Unidas (ONU *f*); **U~d States (of America) (US, USA)** *n* Estados *mpl* Unidos (EE.UU.).

unit trust *n* (*Brit*) bono fiduciario.

unity [ˈjuːnɪtɪ] *n* unidad *f*.

universal [juːnɪˈvɜːsl] *a* universal.

universe [ˈjuːnɪvɜːs] *n* universo.

university [juːnɪˈvɜːsɪtɪ] *n* universidad *f*.

unjust [ʌnˈdʒʌst] *a* injusto.

unkempt [ʌnˈkempt] *a* descuidado; (*hair*) despeinado.

unkind [ʌnˈkaɪnd] *a* poco amable; (*comment etc*) cruel.

unknown [ʌnˈnəun] *a* desconocido.

unlawful [ʌnˈlɔːful] *a* ilegal, ilícito.

unleash [ʌnˈliːʃ] *vt* desatar.

unless [ʌnˈles] *conj* a menos que; ~ **he comes** a menos que venga; ~ **otherwise stated** salvo indicación contraria.

unlike [ʌnˈlaɪk] *a* distinto // *prep* a diferencia de.

unlikely [ʌnˈlaɪklɪ] *a* improbable.

unlisted [ʌnˈlɪstɪd] *a* (*US TEL*) que no consta en la guía.

unload [ʌnˈləud] *vt* descargar.

unlock [ʌnˈlɔk] *vt* abrir (con llave).

unlucky [ʌnˈlʌkɪ] *a* desgraciado; (*object, number*) que da mala suerte; **to be ~** tener mala suerte.

unmarried [ʌnˈmærɪd] *a* soltero.

unmistakable [ʌnmɪsˈteɪkəbl] *a* inconfundible.

unmitigated [ʌnˈmɪtɪgeɪtɪd] *a* rematado, absoluto.

unnatural [ʌnˈnætʃrəl] *a* (*gen*) antinatural; (*manner*) afectado; (*habit*) perverso.

unnecessary [ʌnˈnesəsərɪ] *a* innecesario, inútil.

unnoticed [ʌnˈnəutɪst] *a*: **to go ~** pasar desapercibido.

UNO [ˈjuːnəu] *n abbr* = **United Nations Organization**.

unobtainable [ʌnəbˈteɪnəbl] *a* inconseguible; (*TEL*) inexistente.

unobtrusive [ʌnəbˈtruːsɪv] *a* discreto.

unofficial [ʌnəˈfɪʃl] *a* no oficial.

unpack [ʌnˈpæk] *vi* deshacer las maletas, desempacar (*LAm*).

unpalatable [ʌnˈpælətəbl] *a* (*truth*) desagradable.

unparalleled [ʌnˈpærəleld] *a* (*unequalled*) sin par; (*unique*) sin precedentes.

unpleasant [ʌn'plɛznt] a (disagreeable) desagradable; (person, manner) antipático.

unplug [ʌn'plʌg] vt desenchufar, desconectar.

unpopular [ʌn'pɔpjulə*] a poco popular.

unprecedented [ʌn'prɛsidəntid] a sin precedentes.

unpredictable [ʌnprɪ'dɪktəbl] a imprevisible.

unprofessional [ʌnprə'fɛʃənl] a: ~ conduct negligencia.

unqualified [ʌn'kwɔlifaid] a sin título, no cualificado; (success) total, incondicional.

unquestionably [ʌn'kwɛstʃənəbli] ad indiscutiblemente.

unravel [ʌn'rævl] vt desenmarañar.

unreal [ʌn'rɪəl] a irreal.

unrealistic [ʌnrɪə'lɪstɪk] a poco realista.

unreasonable [ʌn'ri:znəbl] a irrazonable; (demand) excesivo.

unrelated [ʌnrɪ'leitid] a sin relación; (family) no emparentado.

unreliable [ʌnrɪ'laiəbl] a (person) informal; (machine) poco fiable.

unremitting [ʌnrɪ'mitiŋ] a constante.

unreservedly [ʌnrɪ'zə:vidli] ad sin reserva.

unrest [ʌn'rɛst] n inquietud f, malestar m; (POL) disturbios mpl.

unroll [ʌn'rəul] vt desenrollar.

unruly [ʌn'ru:li] a indisciplinado.

unsafe [ʌn'seif] a peligroso.

unsaid [ʌn'sɛd] a: to leave sth ~ dejar algo sin decir.

unsatisfactory ['ʌnsætis'fæktəri] a poco satisfactorio.

unsavoury, (US) **unsavory** [ʌn'seivəri] a (fig) repugnante.

unscathed [ʌn'skeiðd] a ileso.

unscrew [ʌn'skru:] vt destornillar.

unscrupulous [ʌn'skru:pjuləs] a sin escrúpulos.

unsettled [ʌn'sɛtld] a inquieto, (situation) inestable; (weather) variable.

unshaven [ʌn'ʃeivn] a sin afeitar.

unsightly [ʌn'saitli] a feo.

unskilled [ʌn'skild] a: ~ workers mano fsg de obra no cualificada.

unspeakable [ʌn'spi:kəbl] a indecible; (awful) incalificable.

unstable [ʌn'steibl] a inestable.

unsteady [ʌn'stɛdi] a inestable.

unstuck [ʌn'stʌk] a: to come ~ despegarse; (fig) fracasar.

unsuccessful [ʌnsək'sɛsful] a (attempt) infructuoso; (writer, proposal) sin éxito; to be ~ (in attempting sth) no tener éxito, fracasar; ~ly ad en vano, sin éxito.

unsuitable [ʌn'su:təbl] a inapropiado; (time) inoportuno.

unsure [ʌn'ʃuə*] a inseguro, poco seguro.

unsympathetic [ʌnsimpə'θɛtik] a poco comprensivo.

untapped [ʌn'tæpt] a (resources) sin explotar.

unthinkable [ʌn'θiŋkəbl] a inconcebible, impensable.

untidy [ʌn'taidi] a (room) desordenado, en desorden; (appearance) desaliñado.

untie [ʌn'tai] vt desatar.

until [ən'til] prep hasta // conj hasta que; ~ he comes hasta que venga; ~ now hasta ahora; ~ then hasta entonces.

untimely [ʌn'taimli] a inoportuno; (death) prematuro.

untold [ʌn'təuld] a (story) nunca contado; (suffering) indecible; (wealth) incalculable.

untoward [ʌntə'wɔ:d] a (behaviour) impropio; (event) adverso.

unused [ʌn'ju:zd] a sin usar.

unusual [ʌn'ju:ʒuəl] a insólito, poco común.

unveil [ʌn'veil] vt (statue) descubrir.

unwavering [ʌn'weivəriŋ] a inquebrantable.

unwelcome [ʌn'wɛlkəm] a (at a bad time) inoportuno.

unwell [ʌn'wɛl] a: to feel ~ estar indispuesto.

unwieldy [ʌn'wi:ldi] a difícil de manejar.

unwilling [ʌn'wɪlɪŋ] a: to be ~ to do sth estar poco dispuesto a hacer algo; **~ly** ad de mala gana.

unwind [ʌn'waɪnd] (irg: like wind) vt desenvolver // vi (relax) relajarse.

unwise [ʌn'waɪz] a imprudente.

unwitting [ʌn'wɪtɪŋ] a inconsciente.

unworkable [ʌn'wɜːkəbl] a (plan) impráctico.

unworthy [ʌn'wɜːðɪ] a indigno.

unwrap [ʌn'ræp] vt deshacer.

unwritten [ʌn'rɪtn] a (agreement) tácito; (rules, law) no escrito.

KEYWORD

up [ʌp] ♦ prep: to go/be ~ sth subir/estar subido en algo; he went ~ the stairs/the hill subió las escaleras/la colina; we walked/climbed ~ the hill subimos la colina; they live further ~ the street viven más arriba en la calle; go ~ that road and turn left sigue por esa calle y gira a la izquierda
♦ ad 1 (upwards, higher) más arriba; ~ in the mountains en lo alto (de la montaña); put it a bit higher ~ ponlo un poco más arriba or alto; ~ there ahí or allí arriba; ~ above en lo alto, por encima, arriba
2: to be ~ (out of bed) estar levantado; (prices, level) haber subido
3: ~ to (as far as) hasta; ~ to now hasta ahora or la fecha
4: to be ~ to (depending on): it's ~ to you depende de ti; he's not ~ to it (job, task etc) no es capaz de hacerlo; his work is not ~ to the required standard su trabajo no da la talla; (col: be doing): what is he ~ to? ¿que estará tramando?
♦ n: ~s and downs altibajos mpl.

up-and-coming [ʌpənd'kʌmɪŋ] a prometedor(a).

upbringing ['ʌpbrɪŋɪŋ] n educación f.

update [ʌp'deɪt] vt poner al día.

upheaval [ʌp'hiːvl] n trastornos

mpl; (POL) agitación f.

uphill [ʌp'hɪl] a cuesta arriba; (fig: task) penoso, difícil // ad: to go ~ ir cuesta arriba.

uphold [ʌp'həuld] (irg: like hold) vt sostener.

upholstery [ʌp'həulstərɪ] n tapicería.

upkeep ['ʌpkiːp] n mantenimiento.

upon [ə'pɔn] prep sobre.

upper ['ʌpə] a superior, de arriba // n (of shoe: also: ~s) pala; **~-class** a de clase alta; **~ hand** n: to have the ~ hand tener la sartén por el mango; **~most** a el más alto; what was ~most in my mind lo que me preocupaba más.

upright ['ʌpraɪt] a vertical; (fig) honrado.

uprising ['ʌpraɪzɪŋ] n sublevación f.

uproar ['ʌprɔː'] n tumulto, escándalo.

uproot [ʌp'ruːt] vt desarraigar.

upset ['ʌpset] n (to plan etc) revés m, contratiempo; (MED) trastorno // vt (ʌp'set) (irg: like set) (glass etc) volcar; (spill) derramar; (plan) alterar; (person) molestar, perturbar // a [ʌp'set] molesto, perturbado; (stomach) revuelto.

upshot ['ʌpʃɔt] n resultado.

upside-down ['ʌpsaɪd'daun] ad al revés.

upstairs [ʌp'stɛəz] ad arriba // a (room) de arriba // n piso superior.

upstart ['ʌpstɑːt] n advenedizo/a.

upstream [ʌp'striːm] ad río arriba.

uptake ['ʌpteɪk] n: he is quick/slow on the ~ es muy listo/torpe.

uptight [ʌp'taɪt] a tenso, nervioso.

up-to-date ['ʌptə'deɪt] a moderno, actual.

upturn ['ʌptəːn] n (in luck) mejora; (COMM: in market) resurgimiento económico.

upward ['ʌpwəd] a ascendente; **~(s)** ad hacia arriba.

urban ['əːbən] a urbano.

urbane [əː'beɪn] a cortés, urbano.

urchin ['əːtʃɪn] n pilluelo, golfillo.

urge [ɔ:dʒ] n (force) impulso; (desire) deseo // vt: to ~ sb to do sth animar a uno a hacer algo.

urgency [ɔ:dʒənsɪ] n urgencia.

urgent [ɔ:dʒənt] a urgente.

urinate [juərɪneɪt] vi orinar.

urine [juərɪn] n orina, orines mpl.

urn [ɔ:n] n urna; (also: **tea** ~) cacharro metálico grande para hacer té.

Uruguay [juerəgwaɪ] n el Uruguay; ~an a, n uruguayo/a m/f.

us [ʌs] pron nos; (also: after prep) nosotros/as; see also me.

US, USA n abbr = **United States (of America)**.

usage [ju:zɪdʒ] n (LING) uso; (utilization) utilización f.

use [ju:s] n uso, empleo; (usefulness) utilidad f // vt [ju:z] usar, emplear; she ~d to do it (ella) solía or acostumbraba hacerlo; in ~ en uso; out of ~ en desuso; to be of ~ servir; it's no ~ (pointless) es inútil; (not useful) no sirve; to be ~d to estar acostumbrado a, acostumbrar; to ~ up vt agotar; (a car) usar; ~ful a útil; ~fulness n utilidad; ~less a inútil; ~r n usuario/a; ~-friendly a (computer) amistoso.

usher [ʌʃə*] n (at wedding) ujier m; (in cinema etc) acomodador m; ~ette [-'rɛt] n (in cinema) acomodadora.

USSR n abbr: the ~ la URSS.

usual [ju:ʒuəl] a normal, corriente; as ~ como de costumbre; ~ly ad normalmente.

utensil [ju:tɛnsl] n utensilio; kitchen ~s batería sg de cocina.

uterus [ju:tərəs] n útero.

utilitarian [ju:tɪlɪˈtɛərɪən] a utilitario.

utility [ju:ˈtɪlɪtɪ] n utilidad f; ~ room n trascocina.

utilize [ju:tɪlaɪz] vt utilizar.

utmost [ʌtməust] a mayor // n: to do one's ~ hacer todo lo posible.

utter [ʌtə*] a total, completo // vt pronunciar, proferir; ~ance n palabras fpl, declaración f; ~ly ad com-

pletamente, totalmente.

U-turn [ju:tə:n] n viraje m en U.

V

v. abbr = **verse; versus; volt**; (= vide) véase.

vacancy [veɪkənsɪ] n (Brit: job) vacante f; (room) cuarto libre.

vacant [veɪkənt] a desocupado, libre; (expression) distraído; ~ **lot** n (US) solar m.

vacate [vəˈkeɪt] vt (house, room) desocupar; (job) dejar (vacante).

vacation [vəˈkeɪʃən] n vacaciones fpl; ~ **er** n (US) turista m/f.

vaccinate [væksɪneɪt] vt vacunar.

vaccine [væksi:n] n vacuna.

vacuum [vækjum] n vacío; ~ **bottle** n (US) = ~ **flask**; ~ **cleaner** n aspiradora; ~ **flask** (Brit) n termo; ~-**packed** a empaquetado al vacío.

vagina [vəˈdʒaɪnə] n vagina.

vagrant [veɪɡrənt] n vagabundo/a.

vague [veɪɡ] a vago; (blurred: memory) borroso; (ambiguous) impreciso; (person) distraído; ~**ly** ad vagamente.

vain [veɪn] a (conceited) presumido; (useless) vano, inútil; **in** ~ en vano.

valentine [vælntaɪn] n (also: ~ **card**) tarjeta del Día de los Enamorados.

valet [væleɪ] n ayuda m de cámara.

valiant [vælɪənt] a valiente.

valid [vælɪd] a válido, -a; (ticket) valedero; (law) vigente.

valley [vælɪ] n valle m.

valour, (US) **valor** [vælə*] n valor m, valentía.

valuable [væljuəbl] a (jewel) de valor; (time) valioso; ~**s** npl objetos mpl de valor.

valuation [væljuˈeɪʃən] n tasación f, valuación f.

value [vælju:] n valor m; (importance) importancia // vt (fix price of) tasar, valorar; (esteem) apreciar; ~ **added tax (VAT)** n (Brit) impuesto

sobre el valor añadido (IVA *m*); **~d**
a (*appreciated*) apreciado.

valve [vælv] *n* (ANAT, TECH) válvula.

van [væn] *n* (AUT) furgoneta, camioneta (*LAm*); (*Brit* RAIL) furgón *m*
(de equipajes).

vandal ['vændl] *n* vándalo/a; **~ism** *n*
vandalismo; **~ize** *vt* dañar, destruir.

vanilla [və'nɪlə] *n* vainilla.

vanish ['vænɪʃ] *vi* desaparecer, esfumarse.

vanity ['vænɪtɪ] *n* vanidad *f*; **~ case**
n neceser *m*.

vantage point ['vɑːntɪdʒ-] *n* (*for
views*) punto panorámico.

vapour, (*US*) **vapor** ['veɪpə*] *n* vapor *m*; (*on breath, window*) vaho.

variable ['vɛərɪəbl] *a* variable; (*person*) voluble.

variance ['vɛərɪəns] *n*: **to be at ~**
(**with**) estar en desacuerdo (con).

variation [vɛərɪ'eɪʃən] *n* variación *f*.

varicose ['værɪkəus] *a*: **~ veins** varices *fpl*.

varied ['vɛərɪd] *a* variado.

variety [və'raɪətɪ] *n* variedad *f*; **~
show** *n* espectáculo de variedades.

various ['vɛərɪəs] *a* varios/as,
diversos/as.

varnish ['vɑːnɪʃ] *n* barniz *m* // *vt* barnizar; (*nails*) pintar (con esmalte).

vary ['vɛərɪ] *vt* variar; (*change*)
cambiar // *vi* variar.

vase [vɑːz] *n* florero.

Vaseline ['væsɪliːn] *n* ® Vaselina ®.

vast [vɑːst] *a* enorme; (*success*)
abrumador/a.

VAT [væt] *n* (*Brit*) *abbr* = **value
added tax.**

vat [væt] *n* tina, tinaja.

Vatican ['vætɪkən] *n*: **the ~ el** Vaticano.

vault [vɔːlt] *n* (*of roof*) bóveda;
(*tomb*) panteón *m*; (*in bank*) cámara
acorazada // *vt* (*also*: **~ over**) saltar
(por encima de).

vaunted ['vɔːntɪd] *a*: **much ~** cacareado, alardeado.

VCR *n abbr* = **video cassette re-**

corder.

VD *n abbr* = **venereal disease.**

VDU *n abbr* = **visual display unit.**

veal [viːl] *n* ternera.

veer [vɪə*] *vi* (*ship*) virar.

vegetable ['vedʒtəbl] *n* (BOT) vegetal *m*; (*edible plant*) legumbre *f*, hortaliza // *a* vegetal; **~s** *npl* (*cooked*)
verduras *fpl*.

vegetarian [vedʒɪ'tɛərɪən] *a*, *n*
vegetariano/a *m/f*.

vehement ['viːɪmənt] *a* vehemente,
apasionado.

vehicle ['viːɪkl] *n* vehículo.

veil [veɪl] *n* velo // *vt* velar.

vein [veɪn] *n* vena; (*of ore etc*) veta.

velocity [vɪ'lɒsɪtɪ] *n* velocidad *f*.

velvet ['velvɪt] *n* terciopelo.

vending machine ['vendɪŋ-] *n* distribuidor *m* automático.

vendor ['vendə*] *n* vendedor(a) *m/f*.

veneer [və'nɪə*] *n* chapa, enchapado;
(*fig*) barniz *m*.

venereal [vɪ'nɪərɪəl] *a*: **~ disease**
(**VD**) enfermedad *f* venérea.

Venetian blind [vɪ'niːʃən-] *n* persiana.

Venezuela [venɪ'zweɪlə] *n* Venezuela; **~n** *a, n* venezolano/a *m/f*.

vengeance ['vendʒəns] *n* venganza;
with a ~ (*fig*) con creces.

venison ['venɪsn] *n* carne *f* de venado.

venom ['venəm] *n* veneno.

vent [vent] *n* (*opening*) abertura;
(*air-hole*) respiradero; (*in wall*) rejilla (de ventilación) // *vt* (*fig: feelings*) desahogar.

ventilate ['ventɪleɪt] *vt* ventilar;
ventilator *n* ventilador *m*.

ventriloquist [ven'trɪləkwɪst] *n*
ventrílocuo/a.

venture ['ventʃə*] *n* empresa // *vt*
arriesgar; (*opinion*) aventurar // *vi*
arriesgarse, lanzarse.

venue ['venjuː] *n* lugar *m* de reunión.

veranda(h) [və'rændə] *n* terraza;
(*with glass*) galería.

verb [vəːb] *n* verbo; **~al** *a* verbal.

verbatim [vəː'beɪtɪm] *a, ad* palabra

por palabra.

verbose ['vəːbəus] *a* prolijo.

verdict ['vəːdɪkt] *n* veredicto, fallo; (*fig*) opinión *f*, juicio.

verge [vəːdʒ] *n* (*Brit*) borde *m*; **to be on the ~ of** doing sth estar a punto de hacer algo; **to ~ on** *vt fus* rayar en.

verify ['verɪfaɪ] *vt* comprobar, verificar.

veritable ['verɪtəbl] *a* verdadero, auténtico.

vermin ['vəːmɪn] *npl* (*animals*) bichos *mpl*; (*insects*, *fig*) sabandijas *fpl*.

vermouth ['vəːməθ] *n* vermut *m*.

versatile ['vəːsətaɪl] *a* (*person*) polifacético; (*machine*, *tool etc*) versátil.

verse [vəːs] *n* versos *mpl*, poesía; (*stanza*) estrofa; (*in bible*) versículo.

versed [vəːst] *a*: (**well-**)**~** versado en.

version ['vəːʃən] *n* versión *f*.

versus ['vəːsəs] *prep* contra.

vertebra ['vəːtɪbrə], *pl* **~e** [-briː] *n* vértebra.

vertical ['vəːtɪkl] *a* vertical.

vertigo ['vəːtɪgəu] *n* vértigo.

verve [vəːv] *n* brío.

very ['verɪ] *ad* muy // *a*: **the ~** book which el mismo libro que; **the ~** last el último de todos; **at the ~** least al menos; **~ much** muchísimo.

vessel ['vesl] *n* (*ANAT*) vaso; (*ship*) barco; (*container*) vasija.

vest [vest] *n* (*Brit*) camiseta; (*US*: *waistcoat*) chaleco; **~ed interests** *npl* (*COMM*) intereses *mpl* creados.

vestibule ['vestɪbjuːl] *n* vestíbulo.

vestige ['vestɪdʒ] *n* vestigio, rastro.

vestry ['vestrɪ] *n* sacristía.

vet [vet] *n abbr* = **veterinary surgeon** // *vt* repasar, revisar.

veteran ['vetərn] *n* veterano.

veterinary ['vetrɪnərɪ] *a* veterinario; **~ surgeon**, (*US*) **veterinarian** *n* veterinario/a *m/f*.

veto ['viːtəu], *pl* **~es** *n* veto // *vt* prohibir, vedar.

vex [veks] *vt* fastidiar; **~ed** *a* (*ques-*

tion) controvertido.

VHF *abbr* (= *very high frequency*) muy alta frecuencia.

via ['vaɪə] *prep* por, por vía de.

vibrate [vaɪ'breɪt] *vi* vibrar.

vicar ['vɪkə*] *n* párroco (de la Iglesia Anglicana); **~age** *n* parroquia.

vicarious [vɪ'kɛərɪəs] *a* indirecto.

vice [vaɪs] *n* (*evil*) vicio; (*TECH*) torno de banco.

vice- [vaɪs] *pref* vice-; **~-chairman** *n* vicepresidente *m*.

vice versa ['vaɪsɪ'vəːsə] *ad* viceversa.

vicinity [vɪ'sɪnɪtɪ] *n* vecindad *f*; **in the ~ (of)** cercano a.

vicious ['vɪʃəs] *a* (*remark*) malicioso; (*blow*) fuerte; **~ circle** *n* círculo vicioso.

victim ['vɪktɪm] *n* víctima; **~ize** *vt* (*strikers etc*) tomar represalias contra.

victor ['vɪktə*] *n* vencedor(a) *m/f*.

victory ['vɪktərɪ] *n* victoria.

video ['vɪdɪəu] *cpd* vídeo // *n* (**~ film**) vídeofilm *m*; (*also*: **~ cassette**) videocassette *f*; (*also*: **~ cassette recorder**) videograbadora; **~ tape** *n* cinta de vídeo.

vie [vaɪ] *vi*: **to ~ with** competir con.

Vienna [vɪ'enə] *n* Viena.

Vietnam [vjet'næm] *n* Vietnam *m*.

view [vjuː] *n* vista, perspectiva; (*landscape*) paisaje *m*; (*opinion*) opinión *f*, criterio // *vt* (*look at*) mirar; (*examine*) examinar; **on ~** (*in museum etc*) expuesto; **in full ~ (of)** en plena vista (de); **in ~ of the fact that** en vista del hecho de que; **~er** *n* (*small projector*) visionadora; (*TV*) televidente *m/f*; **~finder** *n* visor *m* de imagen; **~point** *n* punto de vista.

vigil ['vɪdʒɪl] *n* vigilia.

vigorous ['vɪgərəs] *a* enérgico, vigoroso.

vigour, (*US*) **vigor** ['vɪgə*] *n* energía, vigor *m*.

vile [vaɪl] *a* (*action*) vil, infame; (*smell*) asqueroso.

vilify ['vɪlɪfaɪ] *vt* vilipendiar.

villa ['vɪlə] n (country house) casa de campo; (suburban house) chalet m.

village ['vɪlɪdʒ] n aldea; ~**r** n aldeano/a.

villain ['vɪlən] n (scoundrel) malvado/a; (criminal) maleante m/f.

vindicate ['vɪndɪkeɪt] vt vindicar, justificar.

vindictive [vɪn'dɪktɪv] a vengativo.

vine [vaɪn] n vid f.

vinegar ['vɪnɪgə*] n vinagre m.

vineyard ['vɪnjɑːd] n viña, viñedo.

vintage ['vɪntɪdʒ] n (year) vendimia, cosecha; ~ **wine** n vino añejo.

vinyl ['vaɪnl] n vinilo.

viola [vɪ'əulə] n (MUS) viola.

violate ['vaɪəleɪt] vt violar.

violence ['vaɪələns] n violencia.

violent ['vaɪələnt] a (gen) violento; (pain) intenso.

violet ['vaɪələt] a violado, violeta // n (plant) violeta.

violin [vaɪə'lɪn] n violín m; ~**ist** n violinista m/f.

VIP n abbr (= very important person) VIP m.

viper ['vaɪpə*] n víbora.

virgin ['vɜːdʒɪn] n virgen f // a virgen.

Virgo ['vɜːgəu] n Virgo.

virile ['vɪraɪl] a viril.

virtually ['vɜːtjuəlɪ] ad prácticamente.

virtue ['vɜːtjuː] n virtud f; **by** ~ **of** en virtud de.

virtuous ['vɜːtjuəs] a virtuoso.

virus ['vaɪərəs] n virus m.

visa ['viːzə] n visado, visa (LAm).

vis-à-vis [viːzə'viː] prep con respecto a.

visibility [vɪzɪ'bɪlɪtɪ] n visibilidad f.

visible ['vɪzəbl] a visible.

vision ['vɪʒən] n (sight) vista; (foresight, in dream) visión f.

visit ['vɪzɪt] n visita // vt (person) visitar, hacer una visita a; (place) ir a, (ir a) conocer; ~**ing hours** npl (in hospital etc) horas de visita; ~**or** n (in museum) visitante m/f; (tourist) turista m/f; **to have** ~**ors** (at

home) tener visita; ~**ors' book** n libro de visitas.

visor ['vaɪzə*] n visera.

vista ['vɪstə] n vista, panorama.

visual ['vɪzjuəl] a visual; ~ **aid** n medio visual; ~ **display unit (VDU)** n unidad f de presentación visual (UPV); ~**ize** vt imaginarse; (foresee) prever.

vital ['vaɪtl] a (essential) esencial, imprescindible; (dynamic) dinámico ~**ly** ad: ~**ly important** de primera importancia; ~ **statistics** npl (fig) medidas fpl vitales.

vitamin ['vɪtəmɪn] n vitamina.

vivacious [vɪ'veɪʃəs] a vivaz, alegre.

vivid ['vɪvɪd] a (account) gráfico; (light) intenso; (imagination) vivo; ~**ly** ad (describe) como si fuera hoy; (remember) con claridad.

V-neck ['viːnek] n cuello de pico.

vocabulary [vəu'kæbjulərɪ] n vocabulario.

vocal ['vəukl] a vocal; (articulate) elocuente; ~ **chords** npl cuerdas fpl vocales.

vocation [vəu'keɪʃən] n vocación f; ~**al** a profesional.

vociferous [vəu'sɪfərəs] a vociferante.

vodka ['vɔdkə] n vodka m.

vogue [vəug] n boga, moda.

voice [vɔɪs] n voz f // vt (opinion) expresar.

void [vɔɪd] n vacío; (hole) hueco // a (invalid) nulo, inválido; (empty): ~ **of** carente o desprovisto de.

volatile ['vɔlətaɪl] a volátil.

volcano [vɔl'keɪnəu], pl -**es** n volcán m.

volition [və'lɪʃən] n: **of one's own** ~ de su propia voluntad.

volley ['vɔlɪ] n (of gunfire) descarga; (of stones etc) lluvia; (TENNIS etc) volea; ~**ball** n vol(e)ibol m.

volt [vəult] n voltio; ~**age** n voltaje m.

voluble ['vɔljubl] a locuaz, hablador(a).

volume ['vɔljuːm] n (gen) volumen m; (book) tomo.

voluntarily ['vɒləntrɪlɪ] *ad* libremente, voluntariamente.

voluntary ['vɒləntərɪ] *a* voluntario; (*statement*) espontáneo.

volunteer [vɒlən'tɪə*] *n* voluntario/a // *vi* ofrecerse (de voluntario); **to ~ to do** ofrecerse a hacer.

vomit ['vɒmɪt] *n* vómito // *vt, vi* vomitar.

vote [vəut] *n* voto; (*votes cast*) votación *f*; (*right to ~*) derecho de votar; (*franchise*) sufragio // *vi* elegir // *vi* votar, ir a votar; **~ of thanks** voto de gracias; **~r** *n* votante *m/f*; **voting** *n* votación *f*.

vouch [vautʃ]: **to ~ for** *vt fus* garantizar, responder de.

voucher ['vautʃə*] *n* (*for meal, petrol*) vale *m*.

vow [vau] *n* voto // *vi* jurar.

vowel ['vauəl] *n* vocal *f*.

voyage ['vɔɪɪdʒ] *n* (*journey*) viaje *m*; (*crossing*) travesía.

vulgar ['vʌlgə*] *a* (*rude*) ordinario, grosero; (*in bad taste*) de mal gusto; **~ity** [-'gærɪtɪ] *n* grosería; mal gusto.

vulnerable ['vʌlnərəbl] *a* vulnerable.

vulture ['vʌltʃə*] *n* buitre *m*.

W

wad [wɒd] *n* (*of cotton wool, paper*) bolita; (*of banknotes etc*) fajo.

waddle ['wɒdl] *vi* anadear.

wade [weɪd] *vi*: **to ~ through** (*water*) caminar por; (*fig: a book*) leer con dificultad; **wading pool** *n* (*US*) piscina para niños.

wafer ['weɪfə*] *n* (*biscuit*) galleta, barquillo; (*COMPUT, REL*) oblea.

waffle ['wɒfl] *n* (*CULIN*) gofre *m* // *vi* dar el rollo.

waft [wɒft] *vt* llevar por el aire // *vi* flotar.

wag [wæg] *vt* menear, agitar // *vi* moverse, menearse.

wage [weɪdʒ] *n* (*also: ~s*) sueldo, salario // *vt*: **to ~ war** hacer la guerra; **~ earner** *n* asalariado/a; **~**

packet *n* sobre *m* de paga.

wager ['weɪdʒə*] *n* apuesta // *vt* apostar.

waggle ['wægl] *vt, vi* menear, mover.

wag(g)on ['wægən] *n* (*horse-drawn*) carro; (*Brit RAIL*) vagón *m*.

wail [weɪl] *n* gemido // *vi* gemir.

waist [weɪst] *n* cintura, talle *m*; **~coat** *n* (*Brit*) chaleco; **~line** *n* talle *m*.

wait [weɪt] *n* espera; (*interval*) pausa // *vi* esperar; **to lie in ~ for** acechar a; **I can't ~ to** (*fig*) estoy deseando; **to ~ for** esperar (a); **to ~ behind** *vi* quedarse; **to ~ on** *vt fus* servir a; **~er** *n* camarero; **~ing** *n*: **'no ~ing'** (*Brit AUT*) 'prohibido estacionarse'; **~ing list** *n* lista de espera; **~ing room** *n* sala de espera; **~ress** *n* camarera.

waive [weɪv] *vt* suspender.

wake [weɪk] *vb* (*pt* **woke** *or* **waked**, *pp* **woken** *or* **waked**) *vt* (*also: ~* **up**) despertar // *vi* (*also: ~* **up**) despertarse // *n* (*for dead person*) vela, velatorio; (*NAUT*) estela; **~n** *vt, vi* **= wake**.

Wales [weɪlz] *n* País *m* de Gales.

walk [wɔːk] *n* (*walk*) paseo; (*hike*) excursión *f* a pie, caminata; (*gait*) paso, andar *m*; (*in park etc*) paseo, alameda // *vi* andar, caminar; (*for pleasure, exercise*) pasearse // *vt* (*distance*) recorrer a pie, andar; (*dog*) pasear; **10 minutes' ~ from here** a 10 minutos de aquí andando; **people from all ~s of life** gente de todas las esferas; **to walk out on** *vt fus* (*col*) abandonar; **~er** *n* (*person*) paseante *m/f*, caminante *m/f*; **~ie-talkie** ['wɔːki'tɔːki] *n* walkie-talkie *m*; **~ing** *n* el andar; **~ing shoes** *npl* zapatos *mpl* para andar; **~ing stick** *n* bastón *m*; **~out** *n* (*of workers*) huelga; **~over** *n* (*col*) pan *m* comido; **~way** *n* paseo.

wall [wɔːl] *n* pared *f*; (*exterior*) muro; (*city ~ etc*) muralla; **~ed** *a* (*city*) amurallado; (*garden*) tapia.

wallet ['wɔlɪt] n cartera, billetera (LAm).

wallflower ['wɔ:lflauə*] n alhelí m; **to be a ~** (fig) comer pavo.

wallop ['wɔləp] vt (col) zurrar.

wallow ['wɔləu] vi revolcarse.

wallpaper ['wɔ:lpeɪpə*] n papel m pintado.

wally ['wɔlɪ] n (Brit: col) palurdo/a.

walnut ['wɔ:lnʌt] n nuez f; (tree) nogal m.

walrus ['wɔ:lrəs], pl ~ or ~es n morsa.

waltz [wɔ:lts] n vals m // vi bailar el vals.

wan [wɔn] a pálido.

wand [wɔnd] n (also: **magic ~**) varita (mágica).

wander ['wɔndə*] vi (person) vagar; deambular; (thoughts) divagar; (get lost) extraviarse // vt recorrer, vagar por.

wane [weɪn] vi menguar.

wangle ['wæŋgl] vt (Brit col): **to ~ sth** agenciarse algo.

want [wɔnt] vt (wish for) querer, desear; (need) necesitar; (lack) carecer de // n: **for ~** of por falta de; **~s** npl (needs) necesidades fpl; **to do sth** querer hacer; **to ~ sb to do sth** querer que uno haga algo; **~ing: to be found ~ing** no estar a la altura de las circunstancias.

wanton ['wɔntn] a (playful) juguetón/ona; (licentious) lascivo.

war [wɔ:*] n guerra; **to make ~** hacer la guerra.

ward [wɔ:d] n (in hospital) sala; (POL) distrito electoral; (LAW: child) pupilo/a; **to ~ off** vt (blow) desviar, parar; (attack) rechazar.

warden ['wɔ:dn] n (Brit: of institution) director/a m/f; (of park, game reserve) guardián/ana m/f; (Brit: also: **traffic ~**) guardia m/f.

warder ['wɔ:də*] n (Brit) guardián/ana m/f, carcelero/a.

wardrobe ['wɔ:drəub] n armario, guardarropa, ropero (esp LAm).

warehouse ['wɛəhaus] n almacén

m, depósito.

wares [wɛəz] npl mercancías fpl.

warfare ['wɔ:fɛə*] n guerra.

warhead ['wɔ:hɛd] n cabeza armada.

warily ['wɛərɪlɪ] ad con cautela, cautelosamente.

warm [wɔ:m] a caliente; (thanks) efusivo; (clothes etc) abrigado; (welcome, day) caluroso; **it's ~** hace calor; **I'm ~** tengo calor; **to ~ up** vi (room) calentarse; (person) entrar en calor; (athlete) hacer ejercicios de calentamiento // vt calentar; **~-hearted** a afectuoso; **~ly** ad afectuosamente; **~th** n calor m.

warn [wɔ:n] vt avisar, advertir; **~ing** n aviso, advertencia; **~ing light** n luz f de advertencia; **~ing triangle** n (AUT) triángulo señalizador.

warp [wɔ:p] n (wood) combarse // vt combar; (mind) pervertir.

warrant ['wɔrnt] n (LAW: to arrest) orden f de detención; (: to search) mandamiento de registro.

warranty ['wɔrəntɪ] n garantía.

warren ['wɔrən] n (of rabbits) madriguera; (fig) laberinto.

warrior ['wɔrɪə*] n guerrero/a.

Warsaw ['wɔ:sɔ:] n Varsovia.

warship ['wɔ:ʃɪp] n buque m o barco de guerra.

wart [wɔ:t] n verruga.

wartime ['wɔ:taɪm] n: **in ~** en tiempos de guerra, en la guerra.

wary ['wɛərɪ] a cauteloso.

was [wɔz] pt of **be**.

wash [wɔʃ] vt lavar // vi lavarse // n (clothes etc) lavado; (bath) baño; (of ship) estela; **to have a ~** lavarse; **to ~ away** vt (stain) quitar lavando; (subj: river etc) llevarse; (fig) limpiar; **to ~ off** vt quitar lavando; **to ~ up** vi (Brit) fregar los platos; (US) lavarse; **~able** a lavable; **~basin**, (US) **~bowl** n lavabo; **~cloth** n (US) manopla; **~er** n (TECH) arandela; **~ing** n (dirty) ropa sucia; (clean) colada; ~ing machine n lavadora; ~ing powder n (Brit) detergente m (en polvo); ~ing-up n fregado, platos mpl (para fregar); ~ing-up liquid n liquido lavavajillas; ~-out n (col) fracaso; ~room n servicios mpl.

wasn't ['wɒznt] = was not.

wasp [wɒsp] n avispa.

wastage ['weistidʒ] n desgaste m; (loss) pérdida; natural ~ desgaste natural.

waste [weist] n derroche m, despilfarro; (misuse) desgaste m; (of time) pérdida; (food) sobras fpl; (rubbish) basura, desperdicios mpl // a (material) de desecho; (left over) sobrante // vt (squander) malgastar, derrochar; (time) perder; (opportunity) desperdiciar; ~s npl (area of land) tierras fpl baldías; to lay ~ devastar, arrasar; to ~ away vi consumirse; ~ disposal unit n (Brit) triturador m de basura; ~ful a derrochador(a); (process) antieconómico; ~ ground n (Brit) terreno baldío; ~paper basket n papelera; ~ pipe n tubo de desagüe.

watch [wɒtʃ] n reloj m; (MIL: guard) centinela m; (: spell of duty) guardia // vt (look at) mirar, observar; (: match, programme) ver; (spy on, guard) vigilar; (be careful of) cuidarse de, tener cuidado de // vi ver, mirar; (keep guard) montar guardia; to keep ~ on sb mantener a uno bajo vigilancia; to ~ out vi cuidarse, tener cuidado; ~dog n perro guardián; ~ful a vigilante, sobre aviso; ~maker n relojero/a; ~man n guardián m; (also: night ~man) sereno, vigilante m (LAm); (in factory) vigilante nocturno; ~ strap n pulsera (de reloj).

water ['wɔːtə*] n agua // vt (plant) regar // vi (eyes) hacerse agua; in British ~s en aguas británicas; to ~ down vt (milk etc) aguar; ~ closet n wáter m; ~colour n acua-

rela; ~cress n berro; ~fall n cascada, salto de agua; ~heater n calentador m de agua; ~ing can n regadera; ~level n nivel m del agua; ~ lily n nenúfar m; ~line n (NAUT) línea de flotación; ~logged a (boat) anegado; (ground) inundado; ~ main n cañería del agua; ~mark n (on paper) filigrana; ~melon n sandía; ~ polo n polo acuático; ~proof a impermeable; ~shed n (GEO) cuenca; (fig) momento crítico; ~-skiing n esquí m acuático; ~ tank n depósito de agua; ~tight a hermético; ~way n vía fluvial or navegable; ~works npl central f depuradora; ~y a (colour) desvaído; (coffee) aguado; (eyes) lloroso.

watt [wɒt] n vatio.

wave [weiv] n ola; (of hand) señal f con la mano; (RADIO, in hair) onda; (fig) oleada // vi agitar la mano; (flag) ondear // vt (handkerchief, gun) agitar; ~length n longitud f de onda.

waver ['weivə*] vi (flame etc) oscilar; (confidence) disminuir; (faith) flaquear.

wavy ['weivi] a ondulado.

wax [wæks] n cera // vt encerar // vi (moon) crecer; ~ paper n (US) papel apergaminado; ~works npl museo sg de cera.

way [wei] n camino; (distance) trayecto, recorrido; (direction) dirección f, sentido; (manner) modo, manera; (habit) costumbre f; which ~? — this — ¿por dónde?, ¿en qué dirección? — por aquí; on the ~ (en route) en (el) camino; to be on one's ~ estar en camino; to be in the ~ bloquear el camino; (fig) estorbar; to go out of one's ~ to do sth desvivirse por hacer algo; to lose one's ~ extraviarse; in a ~ en cierto modo or sentido; by the ~ a propósito; '~ in' (Brit) 'entrada'; '~ out' (Brit) 'salida'; the ~ back el camino de vuelta; 'give ~' (Brit

AUT) 'ceda el paso'; **no** ~! *(col)* ¡ni pensarlo!

waylay [wer'leɪ] *(irg: like lay) vt*: **I was waylaid (by)** me entretuve (con).

wayward ['weɪwəd] *a* díscolo; caprichoso.

W.C. [*ˈdʌblju:ˈsi:*] *n (Brit)* wáter *m*.

we [wi:] *pl pron* nosotros/as.

weak [wi:k] *a* débil, flojo; *(tea)* claro; ~**en** *vi* debilitarse; *(give way)* ceder // *vt* debilitar; ~**ling** *n* debilucho/a; ~**ness** *n* debilidad *f*; *(fault)* punto débil.

wealth [welθ] *n (money, resources)* riqueza; *(of details)* abundancia; ~**y** *a* rico.

wean [wi:n] *vt* destetar.

weapon ['wepən] *n* arma.

wear [wεə*] *n (use)* uso; *(deterioration through use)* desgaste *m*; *(clothing)*: **sports/baby**~ ropa de deportes/de niños // *vb (pt* **wore***, pp* **worn)** *vt (clothes)* llevar; *(shoes)* calzar; *(damage: through use)* gastar, usar // *vi (last)* durar; *(rub through etc)* desgastarse; **evening** ~ *(man's)* traje *m* de etiqueta; *(woman's)* traje *m* de noche; **to** ~ **away** *vt* gastar // *vi* desgastarse; **to** ~ **down** *vt* gastar; *(strength)* agotar; **to** ~ **off** *vi (pain etc)* pasar, desaparecer; **to** ~ **out** *vt* desgastar; *(person, strength)* agotar; ~ **and tear** *n* desgaste *m*.

weary ['wɪərɪ] *a (tired)* cansado; *(dispirited)* abatido.

weasel ['wi:zl] *n (ZOOL)* comadreja.

weather ['weðə*] *n* tiempo // *vt (storm, crisis)* hacer frente a; **under the** ~ *(fig: ill)* indispuesto, pachucho; ~**beaten** *a* curtido; ~**cock** *n* veleta; ~**forecast** *n* boletín *m* meteorológico; ~ **vane** *n* = ~**cock**.

weave [wi:v] *, pt* **wove***, pp* **woven** *vt (cloth)* tejer; *(fig)* entretejer; ~**r** *n* tejedor/a *m/f*.

web [web] *n (of spider)* telaraña; *(on foot)* membrana; *(network)* red *f*.

wed [wed] *, pt, pp* **wedded** *vt* casar

// *vi* casarse.

we'd [wi:d] = **we had; we would.**

wedding ['wedɪŋ] *n* boda, casamiento; **silver/golden** ~ **anniversary** bodas *fpl* de plata/de oro; ~ **day** *n* día *m* de la boda; ~ **dress** *n* traje *m* de novia; ~ **present** *n* regalo de boda; ~ **ring** *n* alianza.

wedge [wedʒ] *n (of wood etc)* cuña; *(of cake)* trozo // *vt* acuñar; *(push)* apretar.

wedlock ['wedlɔk] *n* matrimonio.

Wednesday ['wednzdɪ] *n* miércoles *m inv.*

wee [wi:] *a (Scottish)* pequeñito.

weed [wi:d] *n* mala hierba, maleza // *vt* escardar, desherbar; ~**killer** *n* herbicida *m*; ~**y** *a (person)* debilucho.

week [wi:k] *n* semana; **a** ~ **today/on Friday** de hoy/del viernes en ocho días; ~**day** *n* día *m* laborable; ~**end** *n* fin *m* de semana; ~**ly** *ad* semanalmente, cada semana // *a* semanal // *n* semanario.

weep [wi:p] *, pt, pp* **wept** *vi, vt* llorar; ~**ing willow** *n* sauce *m* llorón.

weigh [weɪ] *vt, vi* pesar; **to** ~ **anchor** levar anclas; **to** ~ **down** *vt* sobrecargar; *(fig: with worry)* agobiar; **to** ~ **up** *vt* pesar.

weight [weɪt] *n* peso; *(metal* ~*)* pesa; **to lose/put on** ~ adelgazar/engordar; ~**ing** *n (allowance)*: **(London)** ~**ing** dietas *fpl (por residir en Londres)*; ~ **lifter** *n* levantador/a *m/f* de pesas; ~**y** *a* pesado.

weir [wɪə*] *n* presa.

weird [wɪəd] *a* raro, extraño.

welcome ['welkəm] *a* bienvenido // *n* bienvenida // *vt* dar la bienvenida a; *(be glad of)* alegrarse de; **thank you** — **you're** — gracias — de nada.

weld [weld] *n* soldadura // *vt* soldar.

welfare ['welfεə*] *n* bienestar *m*; *(social aid)* asistencia social; **W**~ **n** *(US)* subsidio de paro; ~ **state** *n* estado del bienestar; ~ **work** *n* asistencia social.

well [wel] *n* fuente *f*, pozo // *ad* bien;

a: to be ~ estar bien (de salud) // *excl* ¡vaya!, ¡bueno!; **as ~** también; **as ~ as** además de; **~ done!** ¡bien hecho!; **get ~ soon!** ¡que te mejores pronto!; **to do ~** (*business*) ir bien; (*in exam*) salir bien; **to ~ up** *vi* brotar.

we'll [wi:l] = **we will**; **we shall**.

well: **~-behaved** *a* modoso; **~-being** *n* bienestar *m*; **~-built** *a* (*person*) fornido; **~-deserved** *a* merecido; **~-dressed** *a* bien vestido; **~-heeled** *a* (*col: wealthy*) rico.

wellingtons ['welɪŋtənz] *npl* (*also: wellington boots*) botas *fpl* de goma.

well: **~-known** *a* (*person*) conocido; **~-mannered** *a* educado; **~-meaning** *a* bienintencionado; **~-off** *a* acomodado; **~-read** *a* leído; **~-to-do** *a* acomodado; **~-wisher** *n* admirador(a) *m/f*.

Welsh [welʃ] *a* galés/esa // *n* (*LING*) galés *m*; **the ~** *npl* los galeses; **~man/woman** *n* galés/esa *m/f*; **~ rarebit** *n* pan *m* con queso tostado.

went [went] *pt* of **go**.

wept [wept] *pt, pp* of **weep**.

were [wəː*] *pt* of **be**.

we're [wɪə*] = **we are**.

weren't [wəːnt] = **were not**.

west [west] *n* oeste *m* // *a* occidental, del oeste // *ad* al o hacia el oeste; **the W~** *n* el Oeste, el Occidente; **the W~ Country** *n* (*Brit*) el suroeste de Inglaterra; **~erly** *a* (*wind*) del oeste; **~ern** *a* occidental // *n* (*CINEMA*) película del oeste; **W~ Germany** *n* Alemania Occidental; **W~ Indian** *a, n* antillano/a *m/f*; **W~ Indies** *npl* Antillas *fpl*; **~ward(s)** *ad* hacia el oeste.

wet [wet] *a* (*damp*) húmedo; (~ *through*) mojado; (*rainy*) lluvioso; **to get ~** mojarse; **'~ paint'** 'recién pintado'; **~ blanket** *n*: **to be a ~ blanket** (*fig*) ser una aguafiestas; **~ suit** *n* traje *m* de buzo.

we've [wiːv] = **we have**.

whack [wæk] *vt* dar un buen golpe a.

whale [weɪl] *n* (*ZOOL*) ballena.

wharf [wɔːf], *pl* **wharves** [wɔːvz] *n* muelle *m*.

KEYWORD

what [wɔt] ◆ *a* **1** (*in direct/indirect questions*) qué; ~ **size is he?** ¿qué talla usa?; ~ **colour/shape is it?** ¿de qué color/forma es?

2 (*in exclamations*): ~ **a mess!** ¡qué desastre!; ~ **a fool I am!** ¡qué tonto soy!

◆ *pron* **1** (*interrogative*) qué; ~ **are you doing?** ¿qué haces *or* estás haciendo?; ~ **is happening?** ¿qué pasa *or* está pasando?; ~ **is it called?** ¿cómo se llama?; ~ **about me?** ¿y yo qué?; ~ **about doing ...?** ¿qué tal si hacemos ...?

2 (*relative*) lo que; **I saw ~ you did/was on the table** vi lo que hiciste/había en la mesa

◆ *excl* (*disbelieving*) ¡cómo!; ~, **no coffee!** ¡que no hay café!

whatever [wɔt'ɛvə*] *a*: ~ **book you choose** cualquier libro que elijas ◆ *pron*: **do ~ is necessary** haga lo que sea necesario; **no reason ~** *or* **whatsoever** ninguna razón sea la que sea; **nothing ~** nada en absoluto.

wheat [wiːt] *n* trigo.

wheedle ['wiːdl] *vt*: **to ~ sb into doing sth** engatusar a uno para que haga algo; **to ~ sth out of sb** sonsacar algo a uno.

wheel [wiːl] *n* rueda; (*AUT: also: steering ~*) volante *m*; (*NAUT*) timón *m* // *vt* (*pram etc*) empujar // *vi* (*also: ~ round*) dar la vuelta, girar; **~barrow** *n* carretilla; **~chair** *n* silla de ruedas; **~ clamp** *n* (*AUT*) cepo.

wheeze [wiːz] *vi* resollar.

KEYWORD

when [wen] ◆ *ad* cuando; ~ **did it happen?** ¿cuándo ocurrió?; **I know ~ it happened** sé cuándo ocurrió

◆ conj 1 (at, during, after the time that) cuando; **be careful ~ you cross the road** ten cuidado al cruzar la calle; **that was ~ I needed you** fue entonces que te necesité
2 (on, at which): **on the day ~ I met him** el día en qué le conocí
3 (whereas) cuando.

whenever [wɛn'ɛvə*] conj cuando; (every time) cada vez que.

where [wɛə*] ad dónde // conj donde; **this is ~** aquí es donde; **~abouts** ad dónde // n: **nobody knows his ~abouts** nadie conoce su paradero; **~as** conj visto que, mientras; **~by** pron por lo cual; **~upon** conj con lo cual, después de lo cual; **~ver** [-'ɛvə*] ad dondequiera que; (interrogative) dónde; **~withal** n recursos mpl.

whet [wɛt] vt estimular.

whether ['wɛðə*] conj si; **I don't know ~** to accept or not no sé si aceptar o no; **~ you go or not** vayas o no vayas.

KEYWORD

---

which [wɪtʃ] ◆ a 1 (interrogative: direct, indirect) qué; **~ picture(s) do you want?** ¿qué cuadro(s) quieres?; **~ one?** ¿cuál?
2: **in ~ case** en cuyo caso; **we got there at 8 pm, by ~ time the cinema was full** llegamos allí a las 8, cuando el cine estaba lleno
◆ pron 1 (interrogative) cual; **I don't mind ~** el/la que sea
2 (relative: replacing noun) que; (: replacing clause) lo que; (: after preposition) (el/la) que etc, el/la cual etc; **the apple ~ you ate/~** is on the table la manzana que comiste/que está en la mesa; **the chair on ~ you are sitting** la silla en la que estás sentado; **he said he knew, ~ is true/I feared** dijo que lo sabía, lo cual or lo que es cierto/me temía.

whichever [wɪtʃ'ɛvə*] a: **take ~**

book you prefer coja el libro que prefiera; **~ book you take** cualquier libro que coja.

whiff [wɪf] n bocanada.

while [waɪl] n rato, momento // conj durante; (whereas) mientras; (although) aunque; **for a ~** durante algún tiempo; **to ~ away the time** pasar el rato.

whim [wɪm] n capricho.

whimper ['wɪmpə*] vi (weep) lloriquear; (moan) quejarse.

whimsical ['wɪmzɪkl] a (person) caprichoso.

whine [waɪn] vi (with pain) gemir; (engine) zumbar.

whip [wɪp] n látigo; (POL: person) encargado/a de la disciplina partidaria en el parlamento // vt azotar; (snatch) arrebatar; (US: CULIN) batir; **~ped cream** n nata or crema montada; **~-round** n (Brit) colecta.

whirl [wəːl] vt hacer girar, dar vueltas a // vi girar, dar vueltas; (leaves, water etc) arremolinarse; **~pool** n remolino; **~wind** n torbellino.

whirr [wəː*] vi zumbar.

whisk [wɪsk] n (Brit: CULIN) batidor m // vt (Brit: CULIN) batir; **to ~ sb away or off** llevar volando a uno.

whisker ['wɪskə*] n: **~s** (of animal) bigotes mpl; (of man: side ~s) patillas fpl.

whisky, (US, Ireland) **whiskey** ['wɪskɪ] n whisky m.

whisper ['wɪspə*] vi cuchichear, hablar bajo // vt decir en voz muy baja.

whistle ['wɪsl] n (sound) silbido; (object) silbato // vi silbar.

white [waɪt] a blanco; (pale) pálido // n blanco; (of egg) clara; **~ coffee** n (Brit) café m con leche; **~-collar worker** n oficinista m/f; **~ elephant** n (fig) maula; **~ lie** n mentirilla; **~ness** n blancura; **~ noise** n sonido blanco; **~ paper** n (POL) libro rojo; **~wash** n (paint) jalbegue m, cal f // vt (also fig) encubrir.

whiting ['waɪtɪŋ] n, pl inv (fish) pescadilla.

Whitsun ['wɪtsn] n (Brit) pentecostés m.

whittle ['wɪtl] vt: to ~ away, ~ down ir reduciendo.

whizz [wɪz] vi: to ~ past or by pasar a toda velocidad; ~ **kid** n (col) prodigio.

KEYWORD

who [huː] pron **1** (interrogative) quién; ~ is it?, ~'s there? ¿quién es?; ~ **are you looking for?** ¿a quién buscas?; **I told her** ~ **I was** le dije quién era yo

2 (relative) que; **the man/woman** ~ **spoke to me** el hombre/la mujer que habló conmigo; **those** ~ **can swim** los que saben or sepan nadar.

whodun(n)it [huːˈdʌnɪt] n (col) novela policíaca.

whoever [huːˈɛvəʳ] pron: ~ **finds it** cualquiera or quienquiera que lo encuentre; **ask** ~ **you like** pregunta a quien quieras; ~ **he marries** no importa con quién se case.

whole [həʊl] a (not broken) intacto; (all): **the** ~ **of the town** toda la ciudad, la ciudad entera // n (total) total m; (sum) conjunto; **on the** ~, **as a** ~ en general; ~**hearted** a sincero, cordial; ~**meal** a integral; ~**sale** n venta al por mayor // a al por mayor; (destruction) sistemático; ~**saler** n mayorista m/f; ~**some** a sano; ~**wheat** a = ~**meal**; **wholly** ad totalmente, enteramente.

KEYWORD

whom [huːm] pron **1** (interrogative): ~ **did you see?** ¿a quién viste?; **to** ~ **did you give it?** ¿a quién se lo diste?; **tell me from** ~ **you received it** dígame de quién lo recibió

2 (relative): direct object) que; **to** ~ a quien(es); **of** ~ de quien(es), del/de la que etc; **the man** ~ **I saw/to** ~ **I wrote** el hombre que vi/a quien escribí; **the lady about/with** ~ **I**

was talking la señora de/con quien or (la) que hablaba.

whooping cough ['huːpɪŋ-] n tos f ferina.

whore [hɔːʳ] n (col: pej) puta.

KEYWORD

whose [huːz] ♦ a **1** (possessive: interrogative): ~ **book is this?** ¿de quién es este libro?; ~ **pencil have you taken?** ¿de quién es el lápiz que has cogido?; ~ **daughter are you?** ¿de quién eres hija?

2 (possessive: relative) cuyo/a, pl cuyos/as; **the man** ~ **son you rescued** el hombre cuyo hijo rescataste; **those** ~ **passports I have** aquellas personas cuyos pasaportes tengo; **the woman** ~ **car was stolen** la mujer a quien le robaron el coche

♦ pron de quién; ~ **is this?** ¿de quién es esto?; **I know** ~ **it is** sé de quién es.

KEYWORD

why [waɪ] ♦ ad por qué; ~ **not?** ¿por qué no?; ~ **not do it now?** ¿por qué no lo haces (or hacemos etc) ahora?

♦ conj: **I wonder** ~ **he said that** me pregunto por qué dijo eso; **that's not** ~ **I'm here** no es por eso (por lo) que estoy aquí; **the reason** ~ la razón por la que

♦ excl (expressing surprise, shock, annoyance) ¡hombre!, ¡vaya! (explaining): ~, **it's you!** ¡hombre, eres tú!; ~, **that's impossible** ¡pero si eso es imposible!

wick [wɪk] n mecha.

wicked ['wɪkɪd] a malvado, cruel.

wicker ['wɪkəʳ] n (also: ~**work**) artículos mpl de mimbre // cpd de mimbre.

wicket ['wɪkɪt] n (CRICKET) palos mpl.

wide [waɪd] a ancho; (area, knowledge) vasto, grande; (choice) grande // ad: **to open ~** abrir de par en par; **to shoot ~** errar el tiro; **~-angle lens** n objetivo granangular; **~-awake** a bien despierto; **~ly** ad (differing) muy; **it is ~ly believed that...** hay una convicción general de que...; **~n** vt ensanchar; **~ open** a abierto de par en par; **~spread** a (belief etc) extendido, general.

widow ['wɪdəu] n viuda; **~ed** a viudo; **~er** n viudo.

width [wɪdθ] n anchura; (of cloth) ancho.

wield [wiːld] vt (sword) manejar; (power) ejercer.

wife [waɪf], pl **wives** [waɪvz] n mujer f, esposa.

wig [wɪg] n peluca.

wiggle ['wɪgl] vt menear // vi menearse.

wild [waɪld] a (animal) salvaje; (plant) silvestre; (rough) furioso, violento; (idea) descabellado; **~s** npl regiones fpl salvajes, tierras fpl vírgenes; **~erness** ['wɪldənɪs] n desierto; **~-goose chase** n (fig) búsqueda inútil; **~life** n fauna; **~ly** ad (roughly) violentamente; (foolishly) locamente; (rashly) descabelladamente.

wilful ['wɪlful] a (action) deliberado; (obstinate) testarudo.

<hr>

KEYWORD

<hr>

will [wɪl] ♦ auxiliary vb **1** (forming future tense): **I ~ finish it tomorrow** lo terminaré or voy a terminar mañana; **I ~ have finished it by tomorrow** mañana lo habré terminado para mañana; **~ you do it? — yes I ~ / no I won't** ¿lo harás? — sí/no
2 (in conjectures, predictions): **he ~ or he'll be there by now** ya habrá or debe (de) haber llegado; **that ~ be the postman** será or debe ser el cartero
3 (in commands, requests, offers): **~ you be quiet!** ¡quieres callarte?;

you help me? ¿quieres ayudarme?; **~ you have a cup of tea?** ¿te apetece un té?; **I won't put up with it!** ¡no lo soporto!
♦ vt (pt, pp **willed**): **to ~ sb to do sth** desear que alguien haga algo; **he ~ed himself to go on** con gran fuerza de voluntad, continuó
♦ n voluntad f; (testament) testamento.

willing ['wɪlɪŋ] a (with goodwill) de buena voluntad; complaciente; **he's ~ to do it** está dispuesto a hacerlo; **~ly** ad con mucho gusto; **~ness** n buena voluntad.

willow ['wɪləu] n sauce m.

will power n fuerza de voluntad.

willy-nilly [wɪlɪ'nɪlɪ] ad quiérase o no.

wilt [wɪlt] vi marchitarse.

wily ['waɪlɪ] a astuto.

win [wɪn] n (in sports etc) victoria, triunfo // vb (pt, pp **won**) vt ganar; (obtain) conseguir, lograr // vi ganar; **to ~ over**, (Brit) **~ round** vt convencer a.

wince [wɪns] vi encogerse.

winch [wɪntʃ] n torno.

wind [wɪnd] n viento; (MED) gases mpl // vb [waɪnd] (pt, pp **wound**) vt (wrap) enrollar; (wrap) envolver; (clock, toy) dar cuerda a // vi (road, river) serpentear // vt [waɪnd] (take breath away from) dejar sin aliento a; **to ~ up** vt (clock) dar cuerda a; (debate) concluir, terminar; **~fall** n golpe m de suerte; **~ing** a (road) tortuoso; **~ instrument** n (MUS) instrumento de viento; **~mill** n molino de viento.

window ['wɪndəu] n ventana; (in car, train) ventanilla; (in shop etc) escaparate m, vitrina (LAm), vidriera (LAm); **~ box** n jardinera de ventana; **~ cleaner** n (person) limpiacristales m inv; **~ ledge** n alféizar m, repisa (LAm); **~ pane** n cristal m; **~sill** n alféizar m, repisa (LAm).

windpipe ['wɪndpaɪp] n tráquea.

windscreen ['wɪndskriːn], (*US*) **windshield** ['wɪndʃiːld] *n* parabrisas *m inv*; ~ **washer** *n* lavaparabrisas *m inv*; ~ **wiper** *n* limpiaparabrisas *m inv*.

windswept ['wɪndswept] *a* azotado por el viento.

windy [wɪn] *a* de mucho viento; it's ~ hace viento.

wine [waɪn] *n* vino; ~ **cellar** *n* bodega; ~ **glass** *n* copa (para vino); ~ **list** *n* lista de vinos; ~ **merchant** *n* vinatero; ~ **tasting** *n* degustación *f* de vinos; ~ **waiter** *n* escanciador *m*.

wing [wɪŋ] *n* ala; (*Brit AUT*) aleta; ~s *npl* (*THEATRE*) bastidores *mpl*; ~**er** *n* (*SPORT*) extremo.

wink [wɪŋk] *n* guiño, pestañeo // *vi* guiñar, pestañear; (*light etc*) parpadear.

winner ['wɪnə*] *n* ganador(a) *m/f*.

winning ['wɪnɪŋ] *a* (*team*) ganador(a); (*goal*) decisivo; ~**s** *npl* ganancias *fpl*; ~ **post** *n* meta.

winter ['wɪntə*] *n* invierno // *vi* invernar; ~ **sports** *npl* deportes *mpl* de invierno.

wintry ['wɪntrɪ] *a* invernal.

wipe [waɪp] *n*: to give sth a ~ pasar un trapo sobre algo // *vt* limpiar; to ~ **off** *vt* limpiar con un trapo; to ~ **out** *vt* (*debt*) liquidar; (*memory*) borrar; (*destroy*) destruir; to ~ **up** *vt* limpiar.

wire [waɪə*] *n* alambre *m*; (*ELEC*) cable *m* (eléctrico); (*TEL*) telegrama *m* // *vt* (*house*) instalar el alambrado en; (*also*: ~ **up**) conectar.

wireless ['waɪəlɪs] *n* (*Brit*) radio *f*.

wiring ['waɪərɪŋ] *n* alambrado.

wiry ['waɪərɪ] *a* enjuto y fuerte.

wisdom ['wɪzdəm] *n* sabiduría, saber *m*; (*good sense*) cordura; ~ **tooth** *n* muela del juicio.

wise [waɪz] *a* sabio; (*sensible*) juicioso.

...wise [waɪz] *suffix*: time~ en cuanto a *o* respecto al tiempo.

wisecrack ['waɪzkræk] *n* broma.

wish [wɪʃ] *n* (*desire*) deseo // *vt* desear; (*want*) querer; best ~es (*on birthday etc*) felicidades *fpl*; with best ~es (*in letter*) saludos *mpl*, recuerdos *mpl*; to ~ **sb** goodbye despedirse de uno; he ~ed me well me deseó mucha suerte; to ~ to do/sb to do sth querer hacer/que alguien haga algo; to ~ **for** desear; ~**ful** *n*: it's ~**ful** thinking eso sería soñar

wishy-washy ['wɪʃɪwɒʃɪ] *a* (col: *colour, ideas*) desvaído.

wisp [wɪsp] *n* mechón *m*; (*of smoke*) voluta.

wistful ['wɪstful] *a* pensativo.

wit [wɪt] *n* (*wittiness*) ingenio, gracia; (*intelligence*: *also*: ~**s**) inteligencia; (*person*) chistoso/a.

witch [wɪtʃ] *n* bruja.

KEYWORD

with [wɪð, wɪθ] *prep* 1 (*accompanying, in the company of*) con (con ~ *mí*, *ti*, *si* = conmigo, contigo, consigo); I was ~ him estaba con él; we stayed ~ friends nos hospedamos en casa de unos amigos; I'm (not) ~ you (*understand*) (no) te entiendo; to be ~ it (*col*: *person*: *up-to-date*) estar al tanto; (: *alert*) ser despabilado

2 (*descriptive, indicating manner etc*) con; de; a room ~ a view una habitación con vistas; the man ~ the grey hair/blue eyes el hombre del sombrero gris/de los ojos azules; red ~ anger rojo/a de ira; to shake ~ fear temblar de miedo; to fill sth ~ water llenar algo de agua.

---

withdraw [wɪθ'drɔː] (*irg*: *like draw*) *vt* retirar, sacar // *vi* retirarse; (*go back on promise*) retractarse; to ~ **money** (**from the bank**) retirar fondos (del banco); ~**al** *n* retirada; ~**n** *a* (*person*) reservado, introvertido.

wither ['wɪðə*] *vi* marchitarse.

withhold [wɪθ'həuld] (*irg*: *like hold*) *vt* (*money*) retener; (*decision*) aplazar; (*permission*) negar; (*informa-tion*) ocultar.

within [wɪð'ɪn] *prep* dentro de // al dentro; ~ **reach** al alcance de la mano; ~ **sight** of a la vista de; ~ the week antes de acabar la semana.

without [wɪð'aut] *prep* sin.

withstand [wɪθ'stænd] (*irg: like stand*) *vt* resistir a.

witness ['wɪtnɪs] *n* (*person*) testigo m/f; (*evidence*) testimonio m // *vt* (*event*) presenciar; (*document*) atestiguar la veracidad de; ~ **box**, (*US*) ~ **stand** *n* tribuna de los testigos.

witticism ['wɪtɪsɪzm] *n* ocurrencia.

witty ['wɪtɪ] *a* ingenioso.

wives [waɪvz] *npl of* **wife**.

wizard ['wɪzəd] *n* hechicero.

wk *abbr* = **week**.

wobble ['wɒbl] *vi* tambalearse; (*chair*) ser poco firme.

woe [wəu] *n* desgracia.

woke [wəuk], **woken** ['wəukən] *pt, pp of* **wake**.

wolf [wulf], *pl* **wolves** [wulvz] *n* lobo.

woman ['wumən], *pl* **women** ['wɪmɪn] *n* mujer *f*; ~ **doctor** *n* médica; **women's lib** *n* (*pej*) la liberación de la mujer; ~**ly** *a* femenino.

womb [wu:m] *n* (*ANAT*) matriz *f*, útero.

women ['wɪmɪn] *npl of* **woman**.

won [wʌn] *pt, pp of* **win**.

wonder ['wʌndə*] *n* maravilla, prodigio; (*feeling*) asombro // *vi*: to ~ whether preguntarse si; to ~ at asombrarse de; to ~ about pensar sobre *or* en; it's no ~ that no es de extrañarse que + *subjun*; ~**ful** *a* maravilloso; ~**fully** *ad* maravillosamente, estupendamente.

won't [wəunt] = **will not**.

woo [wu:] *vt* (*woman*) cortejar.

wood [wud] *n* (*timber*) madera; (*forest*) bosque *m*; ~ **alcohol** *n* (*US*) alcohol *m* desnaturalizado; ~ **carving** *n* tallado en madera; ~**ed** *a* arbolado; ~**en** *a* de madera; (*fig*)

inexpresivo; ~**pecker** *n* pájaro carpintero; ~**wind** *n* (*MUS*) instrumentos *mpl* de viento de madera; ~**work** *n* carpintería; ~**worm** *n* carcoma.

wool [wul] *n* lana; to pull the ~ over sb's eyes (*fig*) dar a uno gato por liebre; ~**len**, (*US*) ~**en** *a* de lana; ~**lens** *npl* géneros *mpl* de lana; ~**ly**, (*US*) ~**y** *a* lanudo, de lana; (*fig: ideas*) confuso.

word [wə:d] *n* palabra; (*news*) noticia; (*promise*) palabra (de honor) // *vt* redactar; in other words palabras; to break/keep one's ~ faltar a la palabra/cumplir la promesa; ~**ing** *n* redacción *f*; ~ **processing** *n* proceso de textos; ~ **processor** *n* procesador de palabras.

wore [wɔ:*] *pt of* **wear**.

work [wə:k] *n* trabajo; (*job*) empleo, trabajo; (*ART, LITERATURE*) obra // *vi* trabajar; (*mechanism*) funcionar, marchar; (*medicine*) ser eficaz, surtir efecto // *vt* (*shape*) trabajar; (*stone etc*) tallar; (*mine etc*) explotar; (*machine*) manejar, hacer funcionar; to be out of ~ estar parado, no tener trabajo; ~**s** *n* (*Brit: factory*) fábrica // *npl* (*of clock, machine*) mecanismo *sg*; to ~ loose *vi* (*part*) desprenderse; (*knot*) aflojarse; to ~ **on** *vi fus* trabajar en, dedicarse a; (*principle*) basarse en; to ~ **out** *vi* (*plans etc*) salir bien, funcionar // *vt* (*problem*) resolver; (*plan*) elaborar; it ~s out at £100 suma 100 libras; to ~ **up** *vt*: to get ~ed up excitarse; ~**able** *a* (*solution*) práctico, factible; ~**aholic** *n* trabajador(a) obsesivo/a m/f; ~**er** *n* trabajador(a) m/f, obrero/a; ~**force** *n* mano *f* de obra; ~**ing class** *n* clase *f* obrera; ~**ing-class** *a* obrero; ~**ing order** *n*: in ~ing order en funcionamiento; ~**man** *n* obrero; ~**manship** *n* (*art*) hechura, arte *m*; (*skill*) habilidad *f*, trabajo; ~**mate** *n* compañero/a de trabajo; ~**sheet** *n* hoja de trabajo; ~**shop** *n* taller m; ~ **station** n puesto or estación f de trabajo; ~**to-rule** n (Brit) huelga de brazos caídos.

world [wɔːld] n mundo // cpd (champion) del mundo; (power, war) mundial; to think the ~ of sb (fig) tener un concepto muy alto de uno; ~**ly** a mundano; ~**-wide** a mundial, universal.

worm [wɔːm] n gusano; (earth ~) lombriz f.

worn [wɔːn] pp of **wear** // a usado; ~**-out** a (object) gastado; (person) rendido, agotado.

worried [ˈwʌrɪd] a preocupado.

worry [ˈwʌrɪ] n preocupación f // vt preocupar, inquietar // vi preocuparse; ~**ing** a inquietante.

worse [wɔːs] a, ad peor // n lo peor; **a change for the** ~ un empeoramiento; ~**n** vt, vi empeorar; ~**off** a (fig): **you'll be** ~ **off** this way de esta forma estarás peor que nunca.

worship [ˈwɔːʃɪp] n (organized ~) culto; (act) adoración f // vt adorar; **Your W~** (Brit: to mayor) señor alcalde; (: to judge) señor juez.

worst [wɔːst] a el/la peor // ad peor // n lo peor; **at** ~ en lo peor de los casos.

worsted [ˈwʊstɪd] n: (wool) ~ estambre m.

worth [wɔːθ] n valor m // a: **to be** ~ valer; **it's** ~ **it** vale or merece la pena; **to be** ~ **one's while** (to do) merecer la pena (hacer); ~**less** a sin valor; (useless) inútil; ~**while** a (activity) que vale la pena; (cause) loable.

worthy [ˈwɔːðɪ] a (person) respetable; (motive) honesto; ~ **of** digno de.

KEYWORD

would [wʊd] auxiliary vb **1** (conditional tense): **if you asked him he** ~ **do it** si se lo pidieras, lo haría; **if you had asked him he** ~ **have done it** si se lo hubieras pedido, lo habría or hubiera hecho

2 (in offers, invitations, requests): ~ **you like a biscuit?** ¿quiere(s) una galleta?; (formal) ¿querría una galleta?; ~ **you ask him to come in?** ¿quiere(s) hacerle pasar?; ~ **you open the window please?** ¿quiere or podría abrir la ventana, por favor?

3 (in indirect speech): **I said I** ~ **do it** dije que lo haría

4 (emphatic): **it WOULD have to snow today!** ¡tenía que nevar precisamente hoy!

5 (insistence): **she** ~**n't behave** no quiso comportarse bien

6 (conjecture): **it** ~ **have been midnight** sería medianoche; **it** ~ **seem so** parece ser que sí

7 (indicating habit): **he** ~ **go there on Mondays** iba allí los lunes.

would-be [ˈwʊdbiː] a (pej) presunto.

wouldn't [ˈwʊdnt] = **would not**.

wound [waʊnd] pt, pp of **wind** // [wuːnd] herida // vt herir.

wove [wəʊv], **woven** [ˈwəʊvən] pt, pp of **weave**.

wrangle [ˈræŋgl] n riña // vi reñir.

wrap [ræp] n (stole) chal m // vt (also: ~ **up**) envolver; ~**per** n (Brit: of book) sobrecubierta; ~**ping paper** n papel m de envolver.

wrath [rɔθ] n cólera.

wreak [riːk] vt: **to** ~ **havoc (on)** hacer estragos (en); **to** ~ **vengeance (on)** vengarse (de).

wreath [riːθ], pl ~**s** [riːðz] n (funeral ~) corona; (of flowers) guirnalda.

wreck [rɛk] n (ship: destruction) naufragio; (: remains) restos mpl del barco; (pej: person) ruina // vt (ship) hundir; (fig) arruinar; ~**age** n (remains) restos mpl; (of building) escombros mpl.

wren [rɛn] n (ZOOL) reyezuelo.

wrench [rɛntʃ] n (TECH) llave f inglesa; (tug) tirón m // vt arrancar; **to** ~ **sth from sb** arrebatar algo violentamente a uno.

wrestle [ˈrɛsl] vi: **to** ~ **(with sb)** lu-

char (con or contra uno); ~**r** n luchador(a) m/f (de lucha libre);
wrestling n lucha libre.
wretched ['rɛtʃɪd] a miserable.
wriggle ['rɪgl] vi serpentear.
wring [rɪŋ], pt, pp **wrung** vt torcer, retorcer; (wet clothes) escurrir; (fig): **to ~ sth out of sb** sacar algo por la fuerza a uno.
wrinkle ['rɪŋkl] n arruga // vt arrugar // vi arrugarse.
wrist [rɪst] n muñeca; ~ **watch** n reloj m de pulsera.
writ [rɪt] n mandato judicial.
write [raɪt], pt **wrote**, pp **written** vt, vi escribir; **to ~ down** vt escribir; (note) apuntar; **to ~ off** vt (debt) borrar (como incobrable); (fig) desechar por inútil; **to ~ out** vt escribir; **to ~ up** vt redactar; ~**off** n pérdida total; **the car is a ~off** el coche quedó para chatarra; ~**r** n escritor(a) m/f.
writhe [raɪð] vi retorcerse.
writing ['raɪtɪŋ] n escritura; (hand-~) letra; (of author) obras fpl; **in ~** por escrito; ~ **paper** n papel m de escribir.
written ['rɪtn] pp of **write**.
wrong [rɒŋ] a (wicked) malo; (unfair) injusto; (incorrect) equivocado, incorrecto; (not suitable) inoportuno, inconveniente // ad mal; equivocadamente // n mal m; (injustice) injusticia // vt ser injusto con; (hurt) agraviar; **you are ~ to do it** haces mal en hacerlo; **you are ~ about that, you've got it ~** en eso estás equivocado; **to be in the ~** no tener razón, tener la culpa; **what's ~?** ¿qué pasa?; **to go ~** (person) equivocarse; (plan) salir mal; (machine) estropearse; ~**ful** a injusto; ~**ly** ad injustamente.
wrote [raut] pt of **write**.
wrought [rɔːt] a: ~ **iron** hierro forjado.
wrung [rʌŋ] pt, pp of **wring**.
wry [raɪ] a irónico.
wt. abbr = **weight**.

X

Xmas ['ɛksməs] n abbr = **Christmas**.
X-ray [ɛks'reɪ] n radiografía; ~**s** npl rayos mpl X.
xylophone ['zaɪləfəun] n xilófono.

Y

yacht [jɒt] n yate m; ~**ing** n (sport) balandrismo; ~**sman/woman** n balandrista m/f.
Yank [jæŋk], **Yankee** ['jæŋkɪ] n (pej) yanqui m/f.
yap [jæp] vi (dog) aullar.
yard [jɑːd] n patio; (measure) yarda; ~**stick** n (fig) criterio, norma.
yarn [jɑːn] n hilo; (tale) cuento, historia.
yawn [jɔːn] n bostezo // vi bostezar; ~**ing** a (gap) muy abierto.
yd(s). abbr = **yard(s)**.
yeah [jɛə] ad (col) sí.
year [jɪə*] n año; **to be 8 ~s old** tener 8 años; **an eight-~-old child** un niño de ocho años (de edad); ~**ly** a anual // ad anualmente, cada año.
yearn [jɔːn] vi: **to ~ for sth** añorar algo, suspirar por algo; ~**ing** n ansia, añoranza.
yeast [jiːst] n levadura.
yell [jɛl] n grito, alarido // vi gritar.
yellow ['jɛləu] a, n amarillo.
yelp [jɛlp] n aullido // vi aullar.
yeoman ['jəumən] n: **Y~ of the Guard** alabardero de la Casa Real.
yes [jɛs] ad, n sí m; **to say/answer ~** decir/contestar que sí.
yesterday ['jɛstədɪ] ad, n ayer m; ~ **morning/evening** ayer por la mañana/tarde; **all day ~** todo el día de ayer.
yet [jɛt] ad todavía // conj sin embargo, a pesar de todo; **it is not finished** ~ todavía no está acabado; **the best ~** el/la mejor hasta ahora;

as ~ hasta ahora, todavía.

yew [juː] n tejo.

yield [jiːld] n producción f; (AGR) cosecha; (COMM) rendimiento // vt producir, dar; (profit) rendir // vi rendirse, ceder; (US AUT) ceder el paso.

YMCA n abbr (= Young Men's Christian Association) Asociación f de Jóvenes Cristianos.

yoga ['jəʊgə] n yoga m.

yog(h)ourt, yog(h)urt ['jəʊgət] n yogur m.

yoke [jəʊk] n yugo.

yolk [jəʊk] n yema (de huevo).

yonder ['jɒndə*] ad allá (a lo lejos).

KEYWORD

you [juː] pron 1 (subject: familiar) tú, pl vosotros/as (Sp), ustedes (LAm); (polite) usted, pl ustedes; ~ are very kind eres/es etc muy amable; ~ French enjoy your food a vosotros (or ustedes) los franceses os (or les) gusta la comida; ~ and I will go iremos tú y yo
2 (object: direct: familiar: te, pl os (Sp), les (LAm); (polite) le, pl les, f la, pl las; I know ~ te/le etc conozco
3 (object: indirect: familiar: te, pl os (Sp), les (LAm); (polite) le, pl les; I gave the letter to ~ yesterday te/os etc di la carta ayer
4 (stressed): I told YOU to do it te dije a ti que lo hicieras, es a ti a quien dije que lo hicieras; see also 3, 5
5 (after prep: NB: con + ti = contigo: familiar) ti, pl vosotros/as (Sp), ustedes (LAm); (polite) usted, pl ustedes; it's for ~ es para ti/ vosotros etc
6 (comparisons: familiar) tú, pl vosotros/as (Sp), ustedes (LAm); (: polite) usted, pl ustedes; she's younger than ~ es más joven que tú/ vosotros etc
7 (impersonal: one): fresh air does ~ good el aire puro (te) hace bien; ~ never know nunca se sabe; ~

---

can't do that! ¡eso no se hace!

you'd [juːd] = you had, you would.

you'll [juːl] = you will, you shall.

young [jʌŋ] a joven // npl (of animal) cría sg; (people): the ~ los jóvenes, la juventud sg; ~er a (brother etc) menor; ~ster n joven m/f.

your [jɔː*] a tu; (pl) vuestro; (formal) su; see also my.

you're [juə*] = you are.

yours [jɔːz] pron tuyo; (: pl) vuestro; (formal) suyo; see also faithfully, mine, sincerely.

yourself [jɔː'sɛlf] pron (reflexive) tú mismo; (complement) te; (after prep) ti (mismo); (formal) usted mismo; (: complement) se; (after prep) sí (mismo); **yourselves** pl pron vosotros mismos; (after prep) vosotros (mismos); (formal) ustedes (mismos); (: complement) se; (: after prep) sí mismos; see also oneself.

youth [juːθ] n juventud f; (young man: pl ~s [juːðz]) joven m; ~ club n club m juvenil; ~ful a juvenil; ~ hostel n albergue m de juventud.

you've [juːv] = you have.

YTS n abbr (Brit: = Youth Training Scheme) plan de inserción profesional juvenil.

Yugoslav ['juːgəʊslɑːv] a, n yugo(e)slavo/a m/f.

Yugoslavia [juːgəʊ'slɑːvɪə] n Yugoslavia.

yuppie ['jʌpɪ] (col) a, n yuppie m/f.

YWCA n abbr (= Young Women's Christian Association) Asociación f de Jóvenes Cristianas.

Z

zany ['zeɪnɪ] *a* estrafalario.

zap [zæp] *vt* (*COMPUT*) borrar.

zeal [ziːl] *n* celo, entusiasmo.

zebra ['ziːbrə] *n* cebra; ~ **crossing** *n* (*Brit*) paso de peatones.

zenith ['zenɪθ] *n* cénit *m*.

zero ['zɪərəu] *n* cero.

zest [zest] *n* ánimo, vivacidad *f*.

zigzag ['zɪgzæg] *n* zigzag *m*.

zinc [zɪŋk] *n* cinc *m*, zinc *m*.

zip [zɪp] *n* (*also*: ~ **fastener**, (*US*) ~**per**) cremallera, cierre *m* (*LAm*) // *vt* (*also*: ~ **up**) cerrar la cremallera de; ~ **code** *n* (*US*) código postal.

zodiac ['zəudɪæk] *n* zodiaco.

zone [zəun] *n* zona.

zoo [zuː] *n* (jardín *m*) zoológico.

zoologist [zuː'ɔlədʒɪst] *n* zoólogo/a.

zoology [zuː'ɔlədʒɪ] *n* zoología.

zoom [zuːm] *vi*: **to ~ past** pasar zumbando; ~ **lens** *n* zoom *m*.

zucchini [zuː'kiːnɪ] *n(pl)* (*US*) calabacín(ines) *m(pl)*.

SPANISH VERB TABLES

1 Gerund. *2* Imperative. *3* Present. *4* Preterite. *5* Future. *6* Present subjunctive. *7* Imperfect subjunctive. *8* Past participle. *9* Imperfect. *Etc* indicates that the irregular root is used for all persons of the tense, e.g. **oír**: *6* oiga, oigas, oigamos, oigáis, oigan.

acertar *2* acierta *3* acierto, aciertas, acierta, aciertan *6* acierte, aciertes, acierte, acierten

acordar *2* acuerda *3* acuerdo, acuerdas, acuerda, acuerdan *6* acuerde, acuerdes, acuerde, acuerden

advertir *1* advirtiendo *2* advierte *3* advierto, adviertes, advierte, advierten *4* advirtió, advirtieron *6* advierta, adviertas, advierta, advirtamos, advirtáis, adviertan *7* advirtiera *etc*

agradecer *3* agradezco *6* agradezca *etc*

aparecer *3* aparezco *6* aparezca *etc*

aprobar *2* aprueba *3* apruebo, apruebas, aprueba, aprueban *6* apruebe, apruebes, apruebe, aprueben

atravesar *2* atraviesa *3* atravieso, atraviesas, atraviesa, atraviesan *6* atraviese, atravieses, atraviese, atraviesen

caber *3* quepo *4* cupe, cupiste, cupo, cupimos, cupisteis, cupieron *5* cabré *etc* *6* quepa *etc* *7* cupiera *etc*

caer *1* cayendo *3* caigo *4* cayó, cayeron *6* caiga *etc* *7* cayera *etc*

calentar *2* calienta *3* caliento, calientas, calienta, calientan

6 caliente, calientes, caliente, calienten

cerrar *2* cierra *3* cierro, cierras, cierra, cierran *6* cierre, cierres, cierre, cierren

COMER *1* comiendo *2* come, comed *3* como, comes, come comemos, coméis, comen *4* comí, comiste, comió, comimos, comisteis, comieron *5* comeré, comerás, comerá, comeremos, comeréis, comerán *6* coma, comas, coma, comamos, comáis, coman *7* comiera, comieras, comiera, comiéramos, comierais, comieran *8* comido *9* comía, comías, comía, comíamos, comíais, comían

conocer *3* conozco *6* conozca *etc*

contar *2* cuenta *3* cuento, cuentas, cuenta, cuentan *6* cuente, cuentes, cuente, cuenten

costar *2* cuesta *3* cuesto, cuestas, cuesta, cuestan *6* cueste, cuestes, cueste, cuesten

dar *3* doy *4* di, diste, dio, dimos, disteis, dieron *7* diera *etc*

decir *2* di *3* digo *4* dije, dijiste, dijo, dijimos, dijisteis, dijeron *5* diré *etc* *6* diga *etc* *7* dijera *etc* *8* dicho

despertar *2* despierta *3* despierto, despiertas, despierta, despiertan *6* despierte, despiertes, despierten

divirtir *1* divirtiendo *2* divierte *3* divierto, diviertes, divierte, divierten *4* divirtió, divirtieren *6* divierta, diviertas, divierta, divirtamos, divirtáis, diviertan *7* divirtiera *etc*

dormir *1* durmiendo *2* duerme *3* duermo, duermes, duerme, duermen *4* durmió, durmieron *6* duerma, duermas, duerma, durmamos, durmáis, duerman *7* durmiera *etc*

empezar *2* empieza *3* empiezo, empiezas, empieza, empiezan *4* empecé *6* empiece, empieces, empecemos, empecéis, empiecen

entender *2* entiende *3* entiendo, entiendes, entiende, entienden *6* entienda, entiendas, entienda, entiendan

ESTAR *2* está *3* estoy, estás, está, están *4* estuve, estuviste, estuvo, estuvimos, estuvisteis, estuvieron *6* esté, estés, esté, estén *7* estuviera *etc*

HABER *3* he, has, ha, hemos, han *4* hube, hubiste, hubo, hubimos, hubisteis, hubieron *5* habré *etc* *6* haya *etc* *7* hubiera *etc*

HABLAR *1* hablando *2* habla, hablad *3* hablo, hablas, habla, hablamos, habláis, hablan *4* hablé, hablaste, habló, hablamos, hablasteis, hablaron *5* hablaré, hablarás, hablará, hablaremos, hablaréis, hablarán *6* hable, hables, hable, hablemos, habléis, hablen *7* hablara, hablaras, hablara, habláramos, hablarais, hablaran *8* hablado *9* hablaba, hablabas, hablaba, hablábamos, hablabais, hablaban

hacer *2* haz *3* hago *4* hice, hiciste, hizo, hicimos, hicisteis, hicieron *5* haré *etc* *6* haga *etc* *7* hiciera *etc* *8* hecho

instruir *1* instruyendo *2* instruye *3* instruyo, instruyes, instruye, instruyen *4* instruyó, instruyeron *6* instruya *etc* *7* instruyera *etc*

ir *1* yendo *2* ve *3* voy, vas, va, vamos, vais, van *4* fui, fuiste, fue, fuimos, fuisteis, fueron *6* vaya, vayas, vaya, vayamos, vayáis, vayan *7* fuera *etc* *8* iba, ibas, iba, íbamos, ibais, iban

jugar *2* juega *3* juego, juegas, juega, juegan *4* jugué *6* juegue *etc*

leer *1* leyendo *4* leyó, leyeron *7* leyera *etc*

morir *1* muriendo *2* muere *3* muero, mueres, muere, mueren *4* murió, murieron *6* muera, mueras, muera, muramos, muráis, mueran *7* muriera *etc* *8* muerto

mostrar *2* muestra *3* muestro, muestras, muestra, muestran *6* muestre, muestres, muestre, muestren

mover *2* mueve *3* muevo, mueves, mueve, mueven *6* mueva, muevas, mueva, muevan

negar *2* niega *3* niego, niegas, niega, niegan *4* negué *6* niegue, niegues, niegue, neguemos, neguéis, nieguen

ofrecer *3* ofrezco *6* ofrezca *etc*

oír *1* oyendo *2* oye *3* oigo, oyes, oye, oyen *4* oyó, oyeron *6* oiga *etc* *7* oyera *etc*

oler *2* huele *3* huelo, hueles, huele, huelen *6* huela, huelas, huela, huelan

318

parecer *3* parezco *6* parezca *etc*

pedir *1* pidiendo *2* pide *3* pido, pides, pide, piden *4* pidió, pidieron *6* pida *etc* *7* pidiera *etc*

pensar *2* piensa *3* pienso, piensas, piensa, piensan *6* piense, pienses, piense, piensen

perder *2* pierde *3* pierdo, pierdes, pierde, pierden *6* pierda, pierdas, pierda, pierdan

poder *1* pudiendo *2* puede *3* puedo, puedes, puede, pueden *4* pude, pudiste, pudo, pudimos, pudisteis, pudieron *5* podré *etc* *6* pueda, puedas, pueda, puedan *7* pudiera *etc*

poner *2* pon *3* pongo *4* puse, pusiste, puso, pusimos, pusisteis, pusieron *5* pondré *etc* *6* ponga *etc* *7* pusiera *etc* *8* puesto

preferir *1* prefiriendo *2* prefiere *3* prefiero, prefieres, prefiere, prefieren *4* prefirió, prefirieron *6* prefiera, prefieras, prefiera, prefiramos, prefiráis, prefieran *7* prefiriera *etc*

querer *2* quiere *3* quiero, quieres, quiere, quieren *4* quise, quisiste, quiso, quisimos, quisisteis, quisieron *5* querré *etc* *6* quiera, quieras, quiera, quieran *7* quisiera *etc*

reír *2* ríe *3* río, ríes, ríe, ríen *4* rio, rieron *6* ría, rías, ría, riamos, riáis, rían *7* riera *etc*

repetir *1* repitiendo *2* repite *3* repito, repites, repite, repiten *4* repitió, repitieron *6* repita *etc* *7* repitiera *etc*

rogar *2* ruega *3* ruego, ruegas, ruega, ruegan *4* rogué *6* ruegue, ruegues, ruegue, roguemos, roguéis, rueguen

saber *3* sé *4* supe, supiste, supo, supimos, supisteis, supieron *5* sabré *etc* *6* sepa *etc* *7* supiera *etc*

salir *2* sal *3* salgo *5* saldré *etc* *6* salga *etc*

seguir *1* siguiendo *2* sigue *3* sigo, sigues, sigue, siguen *4* siguió, siguieron *6* siga *etc* *7* siguiera *etc*

sentar *2* sienta *3* siento, sientas, sienta, sientan *6* siente, sientes, siente, sienten

sentir *1* sintiendo *2* siente *3* siento, sientes, siente, sienten *4* sintió, sintieron *6* sienta, sientas, sienta, sintamos, sintáis, sientan *7* sintiera *etc*

SER *2* sé *3* soy, eres, es, somos, sois, son *4* fui, fuiste, fue, fuimos, fuisteis, fueron *6* sea *etc* *7* fuera *etc* *9* era, eras, era, éramos, erais, eran

servir *1* sirviendo *2* sirve *3* sirvo, sirves, sirve, sirven *4* sirvió, sirvieron *6* sirva *etc* *7* sirviera *etc*

soñar *2* sueña *3* sueño, sueñas, sueña, sueñan *6* sueñe, sueñes, sueñe, sueñen

tener *2* ten *3* tengo, tienes, tiene, tienen *4* tuve, tuviste, tuvo, tuvimos, tuvisteis, tuvieron *5* tendré *etc* *6* tenga *etc* *7* tuviera *etc*

traer *1* trayendo *3* traigo *4* traje, trajiste, trajo, trajimos, trajisteis, trajeron *6* traiga *etc* *7* trajera *etc*

valer *2* val *3* valgo *5* valdré *etc* *6* valga *etc*

venir *2* ven *3* vengo, vienes, viene, vienen *4* vine, viniste, vino, vinimos, vinisteis, vinieron *5* vendré *etc* *6* venga *etc* *7* viniera *etc*

ver *3* veo *6* vea *etc* *8* visto *9* veía *etc*

vestir *1* vistiendo *2* viste *3* visto, vistes, viste, visten *4* vistió, vistieron *6* vista *etc* *7* vistiera *etc*

VIVIR *1* viviendo *2* vive, vivid *3* vivo, vives, vive, vivimos, vivís, viven *4* viví, viviste, vivió, vivimos, vivisteis, vivieron *5* viviré, vivirás, vivirá, viviremos, viviréis, vivirán *6* viva, vivas, viva, vivamos, viváis, vivan *7* viviera, vivieras, viviera, viviéramos, vivierais, vivieran *8* vivido *9* vivía, vivías, vivía, vivíamos, vivías, vivian

volver *2* vuelve *3* vuelvo, vuelves, vuelve, vuelven *6* vuelva, vuelvas, vuelva, vuelvan *8* vuelto

VERBOS IRREGULARES EN INGLÉS

present	pt	pp	present	pt	pp
arise	arose	arisen	dig	dug	dug
awake	awoke	awaked	do (3rd	did	done
be (am, is,	was,	been	person;		
are;	were		he/she/it/		
being)			does)		
bear	bore	born(e)	draw	drew	drawn
beat	beat	beaten	dream	dreamed,	dreamed,
become	became	become		dreamt	dreamt
begin	began	begun	drink	drank	drunk
behold	beheld	beheld	drive	drove	driven
bend	bent	bent	dwell	dwelt	dwelt
beset	beset	beset	eat	ate	eaten
bet	bet,	bet,	fall	fell	fallen
	betted	betted	feed	fed	fed
bid	bid,	bid,	feel	felt	felt
	bade	bidden	fight	fought	fought
bind	bound	bound	find	found	found
bite	bit	bitten	flee	fled	fled
bleed	bled	bled	fling	flung	flung
blow	blew	blown	fly (flies)	flew	flown
break	broke	broken	forbid	forbade	forbidden
breed	bred	bred	forecast	forecast	forecast
bring	brought	brought	forget	forgot	forgotten
build	built	built	forgive	forgave	forgiven
burn	burnt,	burnt,	forsake	forsook	forsaken
	burned	burned	freeze	froze	frozen
burst	burst	burst	get	got	got, (US)
buy	bought	bought			gotten
can	could	(been	give	gave	given
		able)	go (goes)	went	gone
cast	cast	cast	grind	ground	ground
catch	caught	caught	grow	grew	grown
choose	chose	chosen	hang	hung,	hung,
cling	clung	clung		hanged	hanged
come	came	come	have (has;	had	had
cost	cost	cost	having)		
creep	crept	crept	hear	heard	heard
cut	cut	cut	hide	hid	hidden
deal	dealt	dealt	hit	hit	hit

321

present	pt	pp	present	pt	pp
hold	held	held	sell	sold	sold
hurt	hurt	hurt	send	sent	sent
keep	kept	kept	set	set	set
kneel	knelt,	knelt,	shake	shook	shaken
	kneeled	kneeled	shall	should	—
know	knew	known	shear	sheared	shorn,
lay	laid	laid			sheared
lead	led	led	shed	shed	shed
lean	leant,	leant,	shine	shone	shone
	leaned	leaned	shoot	shot	shot
leap	leapt,	leapt,	show	showed	shown
	leaped	leaped	shrink	shrank	shrunk
learn	learnt,	learnt,	shut	shut	shut
	learned	learned	sing	sang	sung
leave	left	left	sink	sank	sunk
lend	lent	lent	sit	sat	sat
let	let	let	slay	slew	slain
lie (lying)	lay	lain	sleep	slept	slept
light	lit,	lit,	slide	slid	slid
	lighted	lighted	sling	slung	slung
lose	lost	lost	slit	slit	slit
make	made	made	smell	smelt,	smelt,
may	might	—			smelled smelled
mean	meant	meant	sow	sowed	sown,
meet	met	met			sowed
mistake	mistook	mistaken	speak	spoke	spoken
mow	mowed	mown,	speed	sped,	sped,
		mowed		speeded	speeded
must	(had to)	(had to)	spell	spelt,	spelt,
pay	paid	paid		spelled	spelled
put	put	put	spend	spent	spent
quit	quit,	quit,	spill	spilt,	spilt,
	quitted	quitted		spilled	spilled
read	read	read	spin	spun	spun
rid	rid	rid	spit	spat	spat
ride	rode	ridden	split	split	split
ring	rang	rung	spoil	spoiled,	spoiled,
rise	rose	risen		spoilt	spoilt
run	ran	run	spread	spread	spread
saw	sawed	sawn	spring	sprang	sprung
say	said	said	stand	stood	stood
see	saw	seen	steal	stole	stolen
seek	sought	sought	stick	stuck	stuck

present	pt	pp	present	pt	pp
sting	stung	stung	**think**	thought	thought
stink	stank	stunk	**throw**	threw	thrown
stride	strode	stridden	**thrust**	thrust	thrust
strike	struck	struck, stricken	**tread**	trod	trodden
			wake	woke, waked	woken, waked
strive	strove	striven			
swear	swore	sworn	**wear**	wore	worn
sweep	swept	swept	**weave**	wove, weaved	woven, weaved
swell	swelled	swollen, swelled	**wed**	wedded, wed	wedded, wed
swim	swam	swum			
swing	swung	swung	**weep**	wept	wept
take	took	taken	**win**	won	won
teach	taught	taught	**wind**	wound	wound
tear	tore	torn	**wring**	wrung	wrung
tell	told	told	**write**	wrote	written

LOS NÚMEROS

NUMBERS

un, uno(a)	1	one
dos	2	two
tres	3	three
cuatro	4	four
cinco	5	five
seis	6	six
siete	7	seven
ocho	8	eight
nueve	9	nine
diez	10	ten
once	11	eleven
doce	12	twelve
trece	13	thirteen
catorce	14	fourteen
quince	15	fifteen
dieciséis	16	sixteen
diecisiete	17	seventeen
dieciocho	18	eighteen
diecinueve	19	nineteen
veinte	20	twenty
veintiuno	21	twenty-one
veintidós	22	twenty-two
treinta	30	thirty
treinta y uno(a)	31	thirty-one
treinta y dos	32	thirty-two
cuarenta	40	forty
cuarenta y uno(a)	41	forty-one
cincuenta	50	fifty
sesenta	60	sixty
setenta	70	seventy
ochenta	80	eighty
noventa	90	ninety
cien, ciento	100	a hundred, one hundred
ciento uno(a)	101	a hundred and one
doscientos(as)	200	two hundred
doscientos(as) uno(a)	201	two hundred and one
trescientos(as)	300	three hundred
trescientos(as) uno(a)	301	three hundred and one
cuatrocientos(as)	400	four hundred
quiniento(as)	500	five hundred
seiscientos(as)	600	six hundred

LOS NÚMEROS

NUMBERS

setecientos(as)	700	seven hundred
ochocientos(as)	800	eight hundred
novecientos(as)	900	nine hundred
mil	1 000	a thousand
mil dos	1 002	a thousand and two
cinco mil	5 000	five thousand
un millón	1 000 000	a million

primer, primero(a), 1º, 1er (1ª, 1era)	first, 1st
segundo(a) 2º (2ª)	second, 2nd
tercer, tercero(a), 3º (3ª)	third, 3rd
cuarto(a), 4º (4ª)	fourth, 4th
quinto(a), 5º (5ª)	fifth, 5th
sexto(a), 6º (6ª)	sixth, 6th
séptimo(a)	seventh
octavo(a)	eighth
noveno(a)	ninth
décimo(a)	tenth
undécimo(a)	eleventh
duodécimo(a)	twelfth
decimotercio(a)	thirteenth
decimocuarto(a)	fourteenth
decimoquinto(a)	fifteenth
decimosexto(a)	sixteenth
decimoséptimo(a)	seventeenth
decimoctavo(a)	eighteenth
decimonoveno(a)	nineteenth
vigésimo(a)	twentieth
vigésimo(a) primero(a)	twenty-first
vigésimo(a) segundo(a)	twenty-second
trigésimo(a)	thirtieth
centésimo(a)	hundredth
centésimo(a) primero(a)	hundred-and-first
milésimo(a)	thousandth

LOS NÚMEROS

NUMBERS

Números Quebrados etc

Fractions etc

un medio	a half
un tercio	a third
dos tercios	two thirds
un cuarto	a quarter
un quinto	a fifth
cero coma cinco, 0,5	(nought) point five, 0.5
tres coma cuatro, 3,4	three point four, 3.4
diez por cien(to)	ten per cent
cien por cien	a hundred per cent

Ejemplos

Examples

va a llegar el 7 (de mayo)

he's arriving on the 7th (of May)

vive en el número 7

he lives at number 7

el capítulo/la página 7

chapter/page 7

llegó séptimo

he came in 7th

N.B. In Spanish the ordinal numbers from 1 to 10 are commonly used; from 11 to 20 rather less; above 21 they are rarely written and almost never heard in speech. The custom is to replace the forms for 21 and above by the cardinal number.

LA HORA	THE TIME
¿qué hora es?	*what time is it?*
es/son	*it's o it is*
medianoche, las doce (de la noche)	midnight, twelve p.m.
la una (de la madrugada)	one o'clock (in the morning), one (a.m.)
la una y cinco	five past one
la una y diez	ten past one
la una y cuarto *or* quince	a quarter past one, one fifteen
la una y veinticinco	twenty-five past one, one twenty-five
la una y media *or* treinta	half-past one, one thirty
las dos menos veinticinco, la una treinta y cinco	twenty-five to two, one thirty-five
las dos menos veinte, la una cuarenta	twenty to two, one forty
las dos menos cuarto, la una cuarenta y cinco	a quarter to two, one forty-five
las dos menos diez, la una cincuenta	ten to two, one fifty
mediodía, las doce (de la tarde)	twelve o'clock, midday, noon
la una (de la tarde)	one o'clock (in the afternoon), one (p.m.)
las siete (de la tarde)	seven o'clock (in the evening), seven (p.m.)
¿a qué hora?	*(at) what time?*
a medianoche	at midnight
a las siete	at seven o'clock
en veinte minutos	in twenty minutes
hace quince minutos	fifteen minutes ago